THE ROUGH GUIDE TO

Central America

ON A BUDGET

written and researched by

Alasdair Baverstock, Dawn Curtis, Keith Drew, Steven
Horak, Sara Humphreys, Stephen Keeling, Shafik
Meghji, AnneLise Sorensen, Iain Stewart and Greg Ward

ROUGH
GUIDES

roughguides.com

Contents

Introduction to
Central America

From Maya kings and Spanish conquistadors to runaway slaves and thrill-seeking surfers, Central America has tantalized adventurers for centuries. Today, with its exotic blend of volcano-studded landscapes, dazzling colonial towns, jungle-smothered relics and bone-white beaches, the region makes a tempting target for budget travellers; prices remain low and the sheer diversity of activities is hard to match. In the space of a day you could be snorkelling off a Caribbean reef or jaguar-spotting in lush tropical forest, before spending your evening sampling local rum and dancing the night away in some laidback surf town. Another day could be spent whitewater rafting, volcano hiking, and soothing your aches and pains in hot springs, followed by a home-cooked dinner of stuffed tacos, rice and beans.

While the nations of Central America – with the notable exception of Belize – share a common **Spanish** heritage, their indigenous roots go far deeper. Some of the greatest **Mesoamerican ruins** – Tikal, Caracol and Copán – are here, not in Mexico, and you'll find **traditions** that can be traced back to the pre-Columbian era remain vibrant throughout the region, from the rich Maya culture of Guatemala to the Lenca of Honduras and Guna of Panama. Indeed, it's the clash of cultures – primarily indigenous, **culinary tradition** that stretches from Caribbean creole to Maya-influenced Spanish-style cooking, while gorgeous **colonial cities** such as Antigua, León and Granada testify to the intriguing Spanish-American culture that developed here from the sixteenth century onwards. Similarly, the region's **fiestas** and **religious beliefs** mix various traditions – in Guatemala, the Maya folk saint Maximón is every bit as venerated as are his Catholic counterparts at pilgrimage sites such as Esquipulas, where the Black Christ is represented by a miraculous crucifix carved by the celebrated artist Quirio Cataño in 1594.

ABOVE CAYOS COCHINOS, HONDURAS (P.429); **OPPOSITE** MONDAY MARKET, ANTIGUA GUATEMALA (P.288)

What often surprises travellers the most, however, is the region's **natural beauty**. It may look insignificant on the map – at its narrowest point the isthmus squeezes to a mere 65km across – but Central America's unique topography ensures there's enough here to fill months of exploration. Crammed into this small area, coral-fringed Caribbean **beaches** give way to dense **jungle** that, in turn, yield to brooding **volcanic highlands**. Pounding Pacific **surf** lies within a short ride of tranquil national parks containing multicoloured parrots, howler monkeys and tapirs.

Now is a good time to visit. Central America was known for much of the twentieth century for its bitter civil wars, poverty and crime. Though crime in some areas remains high, today the whole region is free of war, and rapidly developing economies are slowly reducing levels of poverty. Infrastructure, communications and life in general are improving as never before.

While towering Maya ruins find their modern-day counterpart in the skyscraper-stacked skylines of **metropolises** such as Panama City, San Salvador and Guatemala City, costs, even in the cities, remain affordable, with plenty of budget accommodation options, cheap eats and attractions that charge minimal entrance fees. Though Guatemala has the largest GDP, Costa Rica and Panama are generally more expensive, with Nicaragua and Honduras the cheapest destinations.

Travelling from place to place in Central America remains easy and won't break the bank, either: a combination of the infamous "chicken buses" (repurposed US school buses), border-crossing international coaches and *lanchas* will get you wherever the fancy takes you.

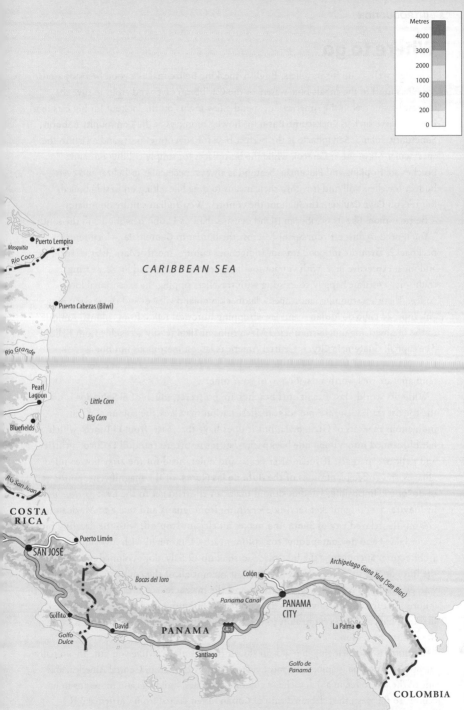

Metres
4000
3000
2000
1000
500
200
0

Mosquitia • Puerto Lempira
Río Coco

CARIBBEAN SEA

• Puerto Cabezas (Bilwi)

Río Grande

Pearl
Lagoon   *Little Corn*

Big Corn

Bluefields •

Río San Juan

COSTA
RICA

• Puerto Limón

● SAN JOSÉ

Bocas del Toro   Colón •   Archipelago Guna Yala (San Blas)

Panama Canal   PANAMA
CITY

Golfito •   ● David   PANAMA   • La Palma

*Golfo
Dulce*   ● Santiago

*Golfo de
Panamá*

COLOMBIA

Where to go

Relatively well set up for travellers, English-speaking **Belize** makes a good first stop; most travellers head to the cobalt-blue waters of the Caribbean cayes and atolls to dive the longest barrier reef in the Americas, or spend a few nights on the lookout for big cats in a jaguar reserve such as **Cockscomb Basin**, or howler monkeys at the **Community Baboon Sanctuary**. Inland, **San Ignacio** is the perfect base for adventure sports and a visit to the spectacular Maya site at **Caracol**, while the best places for simply chilling on sandy beaches are **Hopkins** and **Placencia**. Seafood is always spectacular in Belize: and even budget travellers will find it within their means to dine like a king on freshly boiled lobsters on **Caye Caulker**. Throughout the country, West Indian culture dominates – Belize is more like its Caribbean island cousins than its Latino neighbours to the south.

You'll need to dust off your Spanish across the border in **Guatemala**, which remains a backpacker favourite for good reason. Indigenous culture, mostly Maya, is at its strongest and most expressive here, with vibrant markets, arts and crafts, and locals wearing traditional costume happily co-existing with travellers sipping the exceptional local coffee. There are stunning landscapes – laidback highland villages and the sky-scraping volcanoes of **Lago de Atitlán** – and jaw-dropping historical relics, from colonial **Antigua** to the mesmerizing jungle-smothered Maya ruins of **Tikal** (easily accessible from Belize). The capital, **Guatemala City**, is Central America's largest metropolis but not as intimidating as the hype suggests; its museums, restaurants and cache of colonial remnants are well worth a day or two of your time.

While its world-class Pacific surf beaches are no secret, much of **El Salvador** is off the tourist trail: Central America's smallest nation may lack the colour and the indigenous markets of Guatemala, but it does have the coast, from **El Tunco**, which has blossomed into a bona fide backpacker/surfer resort, to tranquil **El Cuco**, a turtle and pelican sanctuary. If you're after peace and quiet, head for the artsy flower-filled villages and coffee plantations of the **Ruta de las Flores**, or the magnificent rainforest of **Bosque El Imposible**. Foodies should make an effort to get to the *feria gastronómica* in **Juayúa**, a weekly market serving everything from iguana and snake to Mexican ice cream. The relaxed city of **Santa Ana** makes an elegant stop-off, with the dazzling blue crater lake, **Lago de Coatepeque**, to explore nearby. Crammed with low-slung Spanish architecture, **Suchitoto** is the best place to soak up El Salvador's colonial past, while the **Ruta de Paz** in the east leads to poignant memorials of the country's bitter civil war, especially in bomb-ravaged **Perquín** and the massacre site at **El Mozote**. And don't ignore the capital, **San Salvador** – its economy is booming, and it offers lively markets, bars and cafés more akin to the Latino culture in Miami or Puerto Rico than the rest of the region.

Honduras is also changing, but at a far slower pace – enjoy it while you can. The initially chaotic **Tegucigalpa** is among the most visitor-friendly capitals in Central America, and one of the few to retain a rich cache of colonial churches, buildings and museums in its centre. To the west, the celebrated ruin of **Copán** (often visited from Guatemala) is

TOP TEN BEACH RESORTS

Only in Central America can you jump between Atlantic, Caribbean and Pacific beaches so quickly (in Panama the oceans are separated by just 65km), and the region has some fabulous beach resorts where you can while away long lazy days. Here are ten of the best:

Bocas del Toro, Panama Explore the nine main islands, beaches and coral reefs of this sparkling archipelago, home to the Parque Nacional Marino Isla Bastimentos. See p.583

The Corn Islands, Nicaragua Sugary beaches, idyllic desert islands and a dose of languid Caribbean culture. See p.509

El Cuco, El Salvador Tranquil beaches, cheap lodgings, decent surfing and a chance to see turtles and pelicans sauntering across the sands. See p.226

Nicoya Peninsula, Costa Rica Surf Tamarindo or just swim and lounge on the golden sands at Nosara and Sámara. See p.157

Placencia, Belize Pristine white-sand Caribbean beaches, shaded by palms, where you can enjoy kayaking, snorkelling, diving, saltwater fly-fishing or whale-shark watching. See p.94

Playa El Tunco, El Salvador Laidback backpacker and surf resort, with gnarly waves and banging nightlife. See p.220

Puerto Viejo de Talamanca, Costa Rica Tackle the challenging waves and high-octane party scene at Costa Rica's premier surf resort. See p.139

Roatán and Utila, Bay Islands, Honduras Dazzling strips of pure white sand and some of the best diving and snorkelling in the region. See p.435

San Juan del Sur, Nicaragua This congenial backpacker surf resort offers dark-sand beaches, fresh seafood and waterfront bars. See p.491

Tortuguero, Costa Rica Palm-fringed sandbar that's the best place in the region to witness turtles laying eggs – a magical experience. See p.133

ABOVE PLACENCIA, BELIZE (P.94) **OPPOSITE** GRANADA, NICARAGUA (P.484)

another enchanting Maya site, rich in carvings. Even so, the **Bay Islands** are the main attraction in Honduras: the archetypal Caribbean dream of swaying palms and powdery white sand, they also provide plenty of opportunities for watersports on a budget. At the other end of the tourism scale, the largely uninhabited **Mosquitia** offers an enormous variety of wildlife, mysterious ruins and the possibility of trips to remote Garífuna villages.

The up-and-coming travel destination of the Americas, **Nicaragua** makes up for its intimidating capital, **Managua**, with the beguiling Spanish colonial cities of **León** and **Granada**, both loaded with fine art, gorgeous architecture and a dynamic local and foreign student population. Nestled on the banks of vast **Lago de Nicaragua**, Granada is especially attractive and traveller-friendly, making the ideal base from which to explore the lake – serene **Isla de Ometepe** is the highlight of any excursion, its two gorgeous volcanoes separated by lush tropical forest. Indeed, Nicaragua is richly endowed with volcano-strewn landscapes, though sun-seekers should make for its very own idyllic, low-key Caribbean island, **Little Corn**. Surfers can head to **San Juan del Sur**, now a major backpacker destination, while in the far south you can spy sloths, monkeys, caimans and parrots as you drift down the **Río San Juan**, a fantastic trip that takes you past the historic fortress of **El Castillo**.

Costa Rica is the region's most established destination. Travelling is easy, if no longer as cheap as it used to be, and its million-year-old rainforests and pristine beaches are exceptionally beautiful. You can learn to surf at **Talamanca** or **Playa Sámara**, admire macaws in **Parque Nacional Corcovado**, or watch turtles lay their eggs on the Caribbean coast at **Tortuguero**. The hectic capital, **San José**, offers a decent array of restaurants and museums, while provincial **Liberia** is a cowboy town with fiestas, rodeos and even bull-running.

With its historic ties to Colombia and the US, **Panama** offers a subtle but definite contrast to the rest of the region. Costs may be a little higher here, but the range of tropical landscapes, wildlife viewing and adventure sports is overwhelming. The country is perhaps best known for its history-altering **canal**, a triumph of engineering that's well worth seeing up close. Buzzing **Panama City** is the most exciting city in Central America, with colonial history, skyscrapers and dazzling nightlife. There are simpler pleasures here, too: few travellers will want to leave without trying Panama's tasty national dish – *sancocho* – at restaurants such as *El Rincón Tableño*. The laidback **Bocas del Toro** archipelago is celebrated for its unmissable diving and chilled-out surf scene, or you could explore the highlands around **Boquete**, home to hiking trails, hot springs and what many regard to be the world's finest coffee. Finally, the wild and unspoiled forests of **Parque Nacional Darién** and the **Guna Yala** region on the north coast, home to the Guna people, are literally the ends of the road. Many travellers are disappointed to find that there is no road link between Panama (Central America) and Colombia (South America). As it is forbidden to cross the dangerous jungle of the **Darién Gap** by land, you can only continue south by plane or boat.

When to go

Subtropical Central America is brimming with verdant landscapes, nourished by the semiannual rhythms of the wet and dry seasons. Tourism is at its peak during the **dry season** – or "summer" (*verano*) – that runs from roughly December to April. The **rainy season**, often called "winter" (*invierno*), lasts from May until November. The different seasons are more distinctly felt on the Pacific side of the isthmus than they are on the Caribbean, and the major determining factor of climate is altitude. Coming from sea level or the lowland plains to the interior highlands can grant welcome relief from high heat and humidity. Average **temperatures** here are a good 10°C (15–20°F) cooler than in low-lying areas, where humidity levels can be uncomfortable and temperatures hover in the mid-thirties (95°F) for much of the year. See the "When to visit" information at the start of each chapter for a country-specific overview.

Coming to Central America to escape the dreary winter days of chillier climes is always welcome, but it's worth considering a trip during the wet season, also known as the "green season", when tourism lulls and cut-price deals are to be found. Take extra care when planning a trip at this time of year, however, as **road conditions** can deteriorate significantly with heavy rains, making travel more difficult. However, more often than not the rain showers you'll experience will be short-lived afternoon downpours, and there's a good chance that changes in the weather will hardly interfere with your trip at all.

Author picks

Climbing ash-strewn volcanoes, surfing monstrous waves and traversing some of the region's most bone-shaking roads, our hard-travelling authors have visited Central America's every corner. Here are some of their personal favourite moments:

Local feasts Relish Guatemala's Huehuetenango highland coffee (p.325) and Belize's top artisanal chocolate producers (see box, p.99), or get adventurous with lizard, jungle-rat and snake at Juayúa's *feria gastronómica* in El Salvador (p.251).

Volcanic adventures In El Salvador, you can take a dip in an active crater, complete with volcanic mud facepacks, in Alegría (p.231); it's also possible to climb up, and then board down, the active Cerro Negro volcano in Nicaragua (see p.470).

Wonderful wildlife In Costa Rica you'll encounter an amazing range of wildlife, including big cats if you're lucky, in Corcovado (p.188), while Panama's San San Pond Sak Wetlands offer magical opportunities to see manatees (p.585).

Best hikes The ascent of Cerro Chirripó is tough but spectacular, following a steep trail through cloudforest with amazing views (p.180). Other phenomenal hikes lead to the sulphurous crater atop Volcán Santa Ana in El Salvador (p.258), and along Panama's Sendero los Quetzales (p.580), where you may glimpse iridescent quetzals.

Taking to the water For rafting and kayaking head for Río Cangrejal's rapids in Honduras (p.427), or kayak along Guatemala's incomparable Río Dulce gorge (p.342). Winding in a motorized dugout along Panama's serpentine Río Sambú, deep in the Darién, is a real adventure (p.557).

Indiana Jones moments Swim through the Maya caves of Actun Tunichil Muknal in Belize (p.82) for a torchlight tête-à-tête with skeletal sacrificial remains. Or hike on Costa Rica's Isla del Caño (p.186), to encounter the mysterious stone spheres left here by the vanished Diquí people.

Diving It's hard to imagine a more idyllic spot to dive or snorkel than off Nicaragua's Corn Islands (p.509), while the Honduran island of Utila (p.436) is among the least expensive places in the world to learn to dive – and has a great backpacker scene.

> Our author recommendations don't end here. We've flagged up our favourite places – a perfectly sited hotel, an atmospheric café, a special restaurant – throughout the Guide, highlighted with the ★ symbol.

FROM TOP ACTUN TUNICHIL MUKNAL; COFFEE BERRIES, HUEHUETENANGO; MANATEE, SAN SAN POND SAK WETLANDS

Festivals and events

Architectural splendour

1 ANTIGUA, GUATEMALA
Page 288
Gorgeous, traveller-friendly colonial town, ringed by towering volcanoes.

2 CASCO VIEJO, PANAMA CITY
Page 527
The grandest Spanish colonial enclave in the region, studded with elegant *palacios*, churches and museums.

3 LEÓN, NICARAGUA
Page 467
The energetic old capital is home to a dazzling array of colonial buildings, churches and monuments to national poet Rubén Darío.

TIKAL, GUATEMALA
4 Page 364
The greatest Maya ruins in Mesoamerica boast six awe-inspiring pyramids towering above the rainforest.

CARACOL, BELIZE
5 Page 88
Vast Maya city in the jungle, the largest ancient site in Belize and home to the awe-inspiring Caana, the 42m-high "Sky Palace".

6 PARQUE ARQUEOLÓGICO DE COPÁN, HONDURAS
Page 412
Magnificent Maya site, especially lauded for its ensemble of exquisite carvings and statues.

The great outdoors

1 **SURFING, EL SALVADOR**
Page 226
The Pacific coast boasts some of Central America's best surfing beaches. Las Flores, with its jungle setting and black sand, is one of the best.

2 **VOLCANO-HOPPING, COSTA RICA**
Page 174
Zipline, hike, horseride, cycle, abseil or raft across this picture-perfect volcanic landscape.

3 **RAFTING, PANAMA**
Page 578
Panama's Río Chiriquí Viejo offers amazing and exhilarating whitewater adventures.

4 **DIVING IN THE BAY ISLANDS, HONDURAS**
Page 435
Abundant marine life, clear waters and a stunning coral reef.

5 **JAGUAR-SPOTTING, BELIZE**
Page 93
Explore the stunning Belizean rainforest in search of these beautiful creatures.

6 **VOLCANO-BOARDING, NICARAGUA**
Page 470
Hike up the ashy black slopes of Cerro Negro then surf all the way down.

Indigenous cultures

Itineraries

You can't expect to fit everything Central America has to offer into one trip, and we don't suggest you try. On the following pages is a selection of itineraries that guide you through the different countries, picking out a few of the best experiences and major attractions along the way.

THE GRAND TOUR

❶ Belizean cayes and atolls Snorkel, scuba dive or fish off the hundreds of cayes which form part of Belize's spectacular Barrier Reef. **See p.61**

❷ The Maya Mountain Caves, Belize Well-preserved jungle caves, once used in Maya rituals, offer up-close encounters with ancient history. Those at Actun Tunichil Muknal (ATM) provide one of the most spectacular archeological experiences in Central America. **See p.82**

❸ Tikal, Guatemala Arguably the most impressive Maya ruin in Central America, this ancient city is dominated by six temples and surrounded by thousands of other structures, all engulfed by jungle. **See p.364**

❹ Guatemala Highlands One of Guatemala's most beautiful areas, complete with volcanoes, mountain ranges, lakes and valleys. **See p.309**

❺ Bay Islands, Honduras To catch a glimpse of the elusive whale shark, head here in October or November – or simply spend days sailing or fishing on a remote island. **See p.435**

❻ San Salvador, El Salvador At the foot of a volcano, El Salvador's buzzing capital is a heady mix of galleries, museums and nightclubs. **See p.203**

❼ Granada, Nicaragua With its elegant colonial buildings, Granada is Nicaragua's architectural gem, an ideal base for exploring nearby lakes and volcanoes. **See p.484**

❽ Isla de Ometepe, Nicaragua This magical island, formed by two volcanoes, sits in the middle of a freshwater lake. There's jungle rainforest teeming with monkeys as well as beaches and mountains to explore. **See p.495**

❾ Monteverde and Santa Elena, Costa Rica The flora in these nature reserves is known as cloudforest because of the high altitude. Take a canopy tour to see lush vegetation and hundreds of wildlife species. **See p.143**

❿ Parque Nacional Corcovado, Costa Rica Most people come to the park in search of rare animals like ocelot and tapir, and it also holds deserted beaches, waterfalls and rainforests to explore. **See p.188**

⓫ Bocas del Toro archipelago, Panama Famed for surfing and snorkelling, this diverse archipelago has it all: tropical rainforests, beaches and mangroves, contrasting cultures, and the chance to dance on the sand until dawn. **See p.583**

⓬ Guna Yala archipelago, Panama Strung out along the Caribbean coast, the vast majority of these islands are uninhabited. Come here to get away from it all. **See p.558**

MAYA RUINS

❶ Caracol, Belize Belize's largest Maya site, an impressive jungle city that once defeated nearby Tikal, counts among its well-restored ruins a temple that is still today the tallest man-made structure in the country. **See p.86**

ABOVE SAN JUAN DEL SUR, NICARAGUA

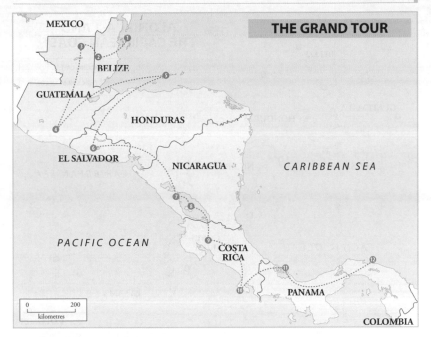

THE GRAND TOUR

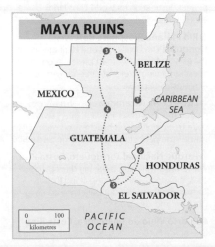

MAYA RUINS

❷ Tikal, Guatemala Tikal is the superstar Maya attraction, a couple of hours east of the Belize border. **See p.364**

❸ El Mirador, Guatemala Remote and mysterious Preclassic Maya city, much of it still enveloped in jungle. Getting here requires time and stamina – it's best reached by foot and mule, and most opt for a five-day trip from Flores, including up to eight hours' jungle

trekking a day – but the reward is spectacular. **See p.371**

❹ Cancuén, Guatemala This affluent Maya trading town is a little-visited but worthwhile site. The road from Flores to Cobán passes near several other Maya sites too. **See p.355**

❺ Tazumal, El Salvador Smaller than its Guatemalan counterparts, but with a certain charm, the site features both Maya and Pipil constructions. **See p.257**

❻ Copán, Honduras One of the country's main tourist destinations, Copán is smaller than Tikal but features exquisite carvings and sculpture. **See p.412**

ALONG CA-1

From Guatemala to Panama, Central America Highway 1 runs for more than 1000km past beaches, cities and jungles. The following sites are all en – or just off – route.

❶ Quetzaltenango, Guatemala This beautifully sited city, a popular spot for learning Spanish or volunteering, is ideally placed for a leisurely tour of the highlands. **See p.317**

❷ San Salvador, El Salvador El Salvador's buzzing capital is seldom peaceful. But with its

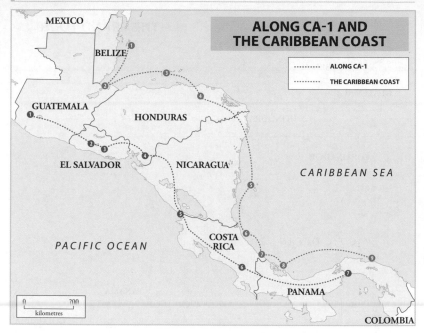

ALONG CA-1 AND
THE CARIBBEAN COAST

·········· ALONG CA-1
·········· THE CARIBBEAN COAST

MEXICO
BELIZE
GUATEMALA
HONDURAS
EL SALVADOR
NICARAGUA
CARIBBEAN SEA
PACIFIC OCEAN
COSTA RICA
PANAMA
COLOMBIA

Centro Histórico, green outskirts and politicized museums, it repays a visit. **See p.203**

❸ **San Vicente, El Salvador** Climb El Salvador's second-highest volcano, eye the famous clock tower and relish the stunning drive to this relaxed city. **See p.230**

❹ **Choluteca, Honduras** Steamy, substantial city containing one of Honduras's finest old colonial quarters. **See p.396**

❺ **San Juan del Sur, Nicaragua** Just off the highway in a gorgeous bay washed with rolling Pacific waves, this gringo-friendly beach town offers surfing, turtle-watching, fishing and plenty of nightlife. **See p.491**

❻ **Parque Nacional Chirripó, Costa Rica** Hike up Mount Chirripó, Costa Rica's highest mountain, from the tiny village of San Gerardo de Rivas, or simply explore the lush countryside surroundings. **See p.180**

❼ **Panama City, Panama** Both a base for visiting the nearby wildlife and famous canal and a sparkling, cosmopolitan city, this is one of the region's must-visits. **See p.526**

THE CARIBBEAN COAST

❶ **Caye Caulker, Belize** It may lack postcard-perfect beaches, but this laidback spot pulls in a

younger crowd for its island-style nightlife and brilliant watersports – including snorkelling, diving, kayaking and kiteboarding. **See p.62**

❷ **Lívingston, Guatemala** Carib cuisine, punta rock and reggae make Lívingston a great place to party, and an intriguing contrast to Guatemala's latino interior. **See p.340**

❸ **Bay Islands, Honduras** This 125km chain of islands off Honduras's Caribbean coast is a perfect destination for world-class (and affordable) diving, sailing and fishing. **See p.435**

❹ **Río Plátano Biosphere Reserve, Honduras** This UNESCO World Heritage Site on the remote Mosquito Coast preserves one of the finest remaining stretches of Central American rainforest. **See p.434**

❺ **Little Corn, Nicaragua** Once a haven for pirates, this tiny, unspoilt island offers swaying palm trees, white-sand beaches and warm, clear water – the perfect place to recharge. **See p.509**

❻ **Parque Nacional Tortuguero, Costa Rica** While turtle-watching is the big draw at this coastal national park, the trip along the Tortuguero Canal in a dugout canoe comes a close second. **See p.134**

❼ **Puerto Viejo de Talamanca, Costa Rica** One of the liveliest backpacker towns in Central

America, Puerto Viejo also boasts one of the best surf breaks on the Caribbean. **See p.139**

❽ Bocas del Toro archipelago, Panama This once-isolated region offers opportunities to explore reefs and rainforests, sample diverse cultures and sip cocktails at sunset. **See p.583**

❾ Guna Yala archipelago, Panama Part of the autonomous Guna region, these idyllic offshore islands offer a fabulous beach holiday and the chance to sample a unique culture. **See p.558**

WILDLIFE

❶ Belize's Barrier Reef Running the length of Belize's coastline, this network of coral and cayes – the second largest in the world – is home to a dazzling array of marine life. **See p.61**

❷ Cockscomb Basin Wildlife Sanctuary, Belize An excellent trail network provides exhilarating glimpses of tapirs, anteaters and, for the lucky few, jaguars. **See p.93**

❸ Biotopo del Quetzal, Guatemala Spend dawn or dusk scouring the forest for this most beautiful of birds, venerated by the Maya, and now Guatemala's national symbol. **See p.347**

❹ Bay Islands, Honduras This string of idyllic white-sand islands is one of the few places on Earth where you can swim with whale sharks. **See p.435**

❺ Lago de Yojoa, Honduras Take an early-morning paddle in this picturesque lake, surrounded by mountains and home to over four hundred bird species. **See p.400**

❻ Reserva Biológica Indio Maíz, Nicaragua Downstream from El Castillo, the Río Bartola branches off from the Río San Juan at the start of the Indio Maíz Reserve. This vast rainforest is home to tapirs, poison-dart frogs, scarlet macaws, toucans and hundreds of other species. **See p.503**

❼ Parque Nacional Tortuguero, Costa Rica The fantastic journey here – drifting through verdant jungle, past wooden houses on stilts – is only a sideshow to the main event: the *desove*, where hundreds of green, hawksbill and leatherback turtles haul themselves ashore each night to lay their eggs. **See p.134**

❽ Parque Nacional Corcovado, Costa Rica The most biologically diverse area in Central America harbours everything from tapirs to tayras; stumble across them on one of the park's jungle treks. **See p.188**

❾ Isla Coiba, Panama Central America's largest island boasts extraordinary biodiversity, both in its rainforests and marine surroundings, providing superlative wildlife viewing and world-class diving. **See p.572**

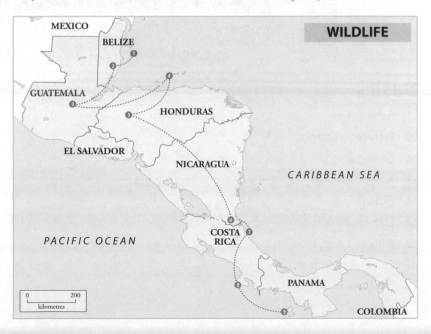

CHICKEN BUS, ANTIGUA, GUATEMALA

Basics

Getting there

While you can travel to Central America overland from Mexico or by sea from Colombia, your most likely point of entry is through one of the region's international airports. Of these, the most popular gateways are Guatemala City, San José (Costa Rica) and Panama City.

Prices for flights to the region with established carriers vary hugely. For the best fares on scheduled flights, book well in advance of travel, as airlines only have a fixed number of seats at their lowest prices. Be sure to check conditions before you book, however, as these cheap fares are almost always heavily restricted, especially with regards to the length of your trip. Generally the cheapest prices allow a maximum stay of one to three months; rates rise significantly for a six-month duration, and even higher for a year's validity. It is not always cheapest to book direct with the airline; some **travel agents** (see p.29) can negotiate discounted fares, in particular for students or those under 26. It may be worth considering a **one-way ticket** if you are planning a long trip, although if you don't have an onward ticket you may experience difficulties passing through immigration (see p.29).

Another option is to look into routes operated by **charter airlines** to package-holiday destinations. From the US, these tend to be available to Belize, Costa Rica and Panama, while from the UK it's also possible to reach Cancún in Mexico's Yucatán Peninsula. Charter flights allow limited flexibility, usually for a fixed period of one or two weeks, but can be picked up last-minute at very reasonable prices.

If you're planning a substantial amount of overland travel in Central America, consider buying an **open-jaw ticket** (for example, arriving in Guatemala City and returning from Panama City). Prices for open-jaw tickets are usually comparable to a straightforward return. Alternatively, **round-the-world (RTW)** itineraries can incorporate Central American destinations if you travel via the US and onward to Auckland, Sydney, etc (see box, p.29).

From the UK and Ireland

There are **no direct flights** from the UK or Ireland to Central America. Most routes are offered by US carriers – American, United and Delta and involve connections in the States (see p.28). Onward flights from the US to Central America may also be operated by regional airlines such as Copa (W copaair.com) and Avianca (W avianca.com). A few European airlines also offer flights through their hub cities to Guatemala City, San José or Panama City – these include Iberia (via Madrid; W iberia.com) and KLM (via Amsterdam; W klm.com). As clearing US immigration and customs can be a lengthy process, these European flights can frequently be faster. Alternatively – and less expensively – a wide network of carriers flies from Europe direct to Mexico, from where you can travel to Central America (see p.28).

Journey times from the UK and Ireland vary according to connection times, but it is possible to get door-to-door in a day. Return **fares** from London to Central American capitals start at around £550 in winter, and rise substantially in summer.

From the US and Canada

US carriers operate **direct flights** to all Central American capitals. The main US hubs, offering good connections with other North American cities, are Houston (United; W united.com), Fort Lauderdale (Spirit Airlines; W spiritair.com), Dallas (American; W aa.com), Miami (both Spirit and American), and Atlanta (Delta; W delta.com), but there are also direct routes from New York and Los Angeles to Guatemala City, San Salvador, San José and Panama City. Flights are frequent and can take as little as two hours (Miami to Belize City, for example). Low-cost carrier Jet Blue (W jetblue.com) also flies to San José (Costa Rica) from Fort Lauderdale and Orlando, and to Liberia (Costa Rica) from New York and Boston. Prices vary – advance return fares start from as little as US$350 (including taxes), though a more realistic estimate would be in the region of US$400–600.

A BETTER KIND OF TRAVEL

At Rough Guides we are passionately committed to travel. We believe it helps us understand the world we live in and the people we share it with – and of course tourism is vital to many developing economies. But the scale of modern tourism has also damaged some places irreparably, and climate change is accelerated by most forms of transport, especially flying. All Rough Guides' flights are carbon-offset, and every year we donate money to a variety of environmental charities.

TRAVEL VIA THE US: ESTA CLEARANCE

The US government requires those travellers coming to or through the US on the Visa Waiver Program to apply online for clearance via **ESTA** (Electronic System for Travel Authorization) – if you arrive at the airport without having done so, the airline won't allow you to check in. To **apply for clearance** visit ⓦesta.cbp.dhs.gov at least three days before you travel; you'll need your passport details, and the admin fee at the time of publication is US$14. Clearance remains valid for two years. Ignore any companies that advertise assistance with ESTA clearance; no officially recognized bodies provide this service.

Note that Visa Waiver Program qualifiers who enter the US overland (via Mexico or Canada) do not need to have ESTA authorization – you just fill in the green I-94W form at the border instead (make sure you hand in the form when you leave).

From **Canada** you can fly direct with Air Canada (ⓦaircanada.com) from Toronto to Costa Rica (San José; 7hr). There are also seasonal direct flights from Toronto and Montréal to Costa Rica, Honduras and Panama with Air Transat (ⓦairtransat.com), and from Toronto to Liberia (Costa Rica) with WestJet (ⓦwestjet.com). Return trips between Canada and Central America start at about Can$650, although several travel companies offer seasonal packages with flights from Can$600. Alternatively, you can connect to all Central American capitals via the US.

From Australia, New Zealand and South Africa

There are **no direct flights** from Australasia or South Africa to Central America, so you'll have to connect with flights in the US or Europe. From **Australia** and **New Zealand**, the quickest route is through Los Angeles and then Dallas or Houston (approximately 20hr; from Aus$1700/NZ$2000). From **South Africa** (Johannesburg) the options include BA (ⓦba.com) or American via London and New York, Iberia via Madrid and Delta via Dakar and Atlanta (from ZAR12,000). Connections are not great: the journey takes at least 24 hours.

From Mexico

Travelling overland **by bus** from Mexico to Guatemala or Belize is fairly straightforward. Several companies offer services with varying degrees of comfort (worth taking into consideration, given the length of most trips – Palenque to Flores is eight hours, Tulum to Belize City is nine). Popular **routes** include: Cancún/Tulum (via Chetumal/Corozal) to Belize City; Palenque (via Frontera Corozal/Bethel) to Flores, Guatemala; San Cristóbal de Las Casas (via Ciudad Cuauhtémoc/La Mesilla) to Huehuetenango, Guatemala; and the Mexican Pacific coast (via Ciudad Hidalgo/Ciudad Tecún Umán) to Quetzaltenango, Guatemala.

Unfortunately, many travellers – particularly those crossing into Guatemala – experience the annoyance of being asked to pay unofficial **"fees"** at immigration, usually by some third party rather than immigration officials. It's often easier to go with local services than with a long-distance carrier – travelling with a busload of gringos can prove expensive. It is worth changing pesos at the border with moneychangers, as an opportunity may not arise later. Be sure to do your sums before you agree to any transaction, and check what you're given before you hand over your cash.

It's possible, too, to **fly** from many of Mexico's airports to Central America's main cities with airlines such as Aeroméxico (ⓦaeromexico.com), Avianca and Copa. One-way fares for Interjet's Mexico City to Guatemala City flight, for example, start at around US$130 (ⓦinterjet.com.mx).

From South America

Thanks to the lack of infrastructure, and the continuing guerrilla presence in the Darién jungle bordering Colombia and Panama, there is currently **no overland passage** between Central and South America. Intercontinental travellers can therefore only cross this break in the Carretera Panamericana (called "Carretera Interamericana" in Panama, and usually translated as "Panamerican Highway"), known as the "Darién Gap", **by air** or **by sea**.

Unless you're using an airpass or RTW ticket, it's generally cheaper to buy **flights** from South to Central America in the country of departure, where agents have access to discounted fares. As always, booking at the last minute can mean settling for the highest prices, so ideally you should plan at least a few weeks in advance. One-way fares from Quito/Bogotá to Panama are in the region of US$500 (considerably less with a student card).

There's a steady flow of **sea traffic** between Panama and Colombia via the Caribbean. A new ferry

ROUND-THE-WORLD (RTW) FLIGHTS

Round-the-world flights connect Sydney, Perth, Auckland and Johannesburg to Mexico City, Guatemala City, San José and Panama City, usually via Los Angeles or London using American Airlines or code-share partners. It is also possible to reach Australasia from both Santiago (Chile) and Buenos Aires (Argentina) as part of the same RTW tickets with BA/Qantas's Oneworld (Ⓦqantas.com). British Airways/Qantas and United/Air New Zealand (Ⓦairnz.co.nz) Star Alliance fares from London start at around £1500, and allow multiple stops in several continents within a certain mileage.

service, Ferry Express (Ⓦferryxpress.com), connects Cartagena in Colombia with the cruise ship terminal in Colón, Panama, while private sailboats often offer passage as crew on the same route (see box, p.550).

AGENTS AND OPERATORS

Ceiba International US ☎ 1 800 217 1060, Ⓦceibainternational .com. Adventure trips, including rafting, kayaking, caving and archeological tours throughout the Maya region.

Coco Tours Honduras ☎ 504 3335 4599, Ⓦcocotours.org. Small, locally based tour company leading various Central American tours, including cultural Garífuna visits, with a portion of profits supporting Garífuna projects.

Dragoman UK ☎ 01728 861133, Ⓦdragoman.com. Overland adventure specialists with offices all over the world. Their 28-day trip runs from Guatemala to Panama City, and the 160-day trip continues south to Lima.

eXito US ☎ 1800 655 4053, Ⓦexitotravel.com. North America's top specialist for travel to Latin America.

Exodus UK ☎ 0845 287 3573, Ⓦexodus.co.uk. A huge range of adventure travel packages, from 14-day camping trips around Belize to 16-day cycling tours of Costa Rica, Nicaragua and Panama.

Geckos Adventures Australia ☎ 1300 854 444, Ⓦgeckos adventures.com. Australian-based agency, offering tours led by local guides within Latin America that range from 17 to 58 days.

Hosteltrail Ⓦhosteltrail.com. Online network of backpacker hostels and tour operators throughout Central America.

Intrepid Travel UK ☎ 0800 781 1660, US ☎ 1800 970 7299, Australia ☎ 1300 797010, New Zealand ☎ 0800 600 610, Ⓦintrepidtravel.com. Specializing in small-group, off-the-beaten-path tours through Central America, from 9 to 58 days.

Journey Latin America UK ☎ 020 3432 1503, Ⓦjourneylatin america.co.uk. Well-established tour operator offering tailor-made itineraries as well as sound advice on travel in the region.

Keka's Travel Agency ☎ 1 800 593 5352, Ⓦkekastravel.com. Miami-based operators specializing in Latin American travel, offering low airfares and budget packages.

North South Travel UK ☎ 01245 608 291, Ⓦnorthsouthtravel .co.uk. Friendly, competitive travel agency, offering discounted fares worldwide. Profits are used to support projects in the developing world, especially the promotion of sustainable tourism.

Quetzaltrekkers Guatemala ☎ 502 7765 5895, Ⓦquetzaltrekkers.com. Nonprofit organization providing trekking tours in Guatemala, with profits directly funding children's educational and recreational projects.

REI Adventures US ☎ 1800 622 2236, Ⓦrei.com/adventures. Outdoor adventure experts offering kayaking, jungle and multisport trips to Belize, and Arenal Volcano, jungle and sea adventures to Costa Rica.

Saddle Skedaddle Ⓦskedaddle.co.uk. A choice of three separate 12-day guided cycle tours in Costa Rica.

STA Travel UK ☎ 0333 321 0099, US ☎ 1 800 781 4040, Australia ☎ 134 782, New Zealand ☎ 0800 474 400, South Africa ☎ 0861 781 781, Ⓦstatravel.com. Worldwide specialists in independent travel; also student IDs, travel insurance, car rental, rail passes, and more. Good discounts for students and under-26s.

Trailfinders UK ☎ 0207 7368 1200, Republic of Ireland ☎ 01 677 7888, Australia ☎ 1300 780 212, Ⓦtrailfinders.com. One of the best informed and most efficient agents for independent travellers.

Tucan Travel UK ☎ 0800 804 8435, Australia ☎ 0293 266 633, Ⓦtucantravel.com. An independently owned agency offering a variety of worldwide tours, including comprehensive budget expeditions.

Wilderness Travel US ☎ 1800 368 2794, Ⓦwildernesstravel .com. Off-the-beaten-path adventure tours, safaris and treks in Belize, Costa Rica, Guatemala, Honduras and Panama.

Yampu Tours UK ☎ 0800 011 2424, Australia ☎ 1800 224 201, US ☎ 1 888 926 7801, Ⓦyampu.com. Small indie outfit, offering a large number of tours within Latin America.

Entry requirements

Nationals of the UK, Ireland, Canada, the US, Australia and New Zealand do not need visas to visit any of the seven Central American countries. Visitors are eligible for stays of either thirty days (Belize, Panama) or, in the case of Costa Rica and the CA-4 countries, ninety days (see box, p.30).

You should be able to **extend** this period by leaving the country and re-entering, or you can pay for a thirty- or ninety-day visa extension at immigration offices. You should have a valid **passport** with at least six months remaining and, officially, an onward ticket (these are seldom checked but may be a sticking point at border crossings or customs, especially entering Costa Rica).

All countries charge **entry fees** (sometimes referred to as a "tourist card") to certain nationalities, depending on relations between the countries. Investigate your destination's entry requirements before travelling, and arrive prepared with cash. For more information about specific countries and border crossings in Central America, see the relevant chapters, and always check with your embassy before travelling.

CENTRAL AMERICAN EMBASSIES ABROAD

Belize UK: Belize High Commission, 3/F, 45 Crawford Place, London W1H 4LP (☎ 020 7723 3603, ⓦ belizehighcommission .com); US: 2535 Massachusetts Ave NW, Washington DC 20008 (☎ 202 332 9636, ⓦ embassyofbelize.org).

Costa Rica Canada: 350 Sparks St, Suite 701, Ontario, ON K1R 7S8 (☎ 613 562 2855, ⓦ costaricaembassy.com); UK: Flat 1, 14 Lancaster Gate, London W2 3LH (☎ 020 7706 8844, ⓦ costaricanembassy.co.uk); US: 2114 S St NW, Washington DC 20008 (☎ 202 499 2991, ⓦ costarica-embassy.org).

El Salvador Canada: 209 Kent St, Ottawa, ON K2P 1Z8 (☎ 613 238 2939); UK: 8 Dorset Square, London NW1 6PU (☎ 020 7224 9800, ⓔ embajadalondres@rree.gob.sv); US: 1400 16th St NW, Suite 100, Washington DC 20036 (☎ 202 595 7500, ⓦ www .elsalvador.org).

Guatemala Canada: 130 Albert St, Suite 1010, Ottawa, ON K1P 5G4 (☎ 613 233 7237, ⓦ canada.minex.gob.gt); UK: 13A Fawcett St, London SW10 9HN (☎ 020 7351 3042, ⓦ www.minex.gob.gt); US: 2220 R St NW, Washington DC 20008 (☎ 202 745 4953, ⓦ guatemalaembassyusa.org).

Honduras Canada: 151 Slater St, Suite 805-A, Ottawa, ON K1P 5H3 (☎ 1 613 233 8900, ⓦ embassyhondurasca.moonfruit.com); UK: 115 Gloucester Place, London W1U 6JT (☎ 020 7486 4880); US: 1014 M St NW, Washington DC 20001 (☎ 202 506 4995, ⓦ hondurasemb.org).

Nicaragua UK: Vicarage House, Suite 31, 58–60 Kensington Church St, London W8 4DB (☎ 020 7938 2373, ⓔ emb.ofnicaragua @virgin.net); US: 1627 New Hampshire Ave NW, Washington DC 20009 (☎ 202 966 7702).

Panama Canada: 130 Albert St, Suite 300, Ottawa, ON K1P 5G4 (☎ 613 236 7177, ⓦ embassyofpanama.ca); UK: Panama House, 40 Hertford St, London W1Y 7TG (☎ 020 7409 2255, ⓦ panamaconsul.co.uk); US: 2862 McGill Terrace NW, Washington DC 20008 (☎ 202 483 1407, ⓦ embassyofpanama.org).

Getting around

If you're not in a hurry and are willing to travel on public transport, you can get around most of Central America on US$1–2 per hour (probably slightly more in Belize, Costa Rica and Panama). While public transport systems are sometimes slow, and almost always crowded and sweaty, they can also be extremely efficient: in most places you won't have to wait long for onward transport. Along major roads, especially, buses run with high frequency and can offer a great insight into the day-to-day life of the country. Flights are relatively expensive but shuttle long-distance between major cities and can help access remote areas, such as the region's many wonderful islands.

The following is a general guide to Central American transport. More specific information can be found in the "Getting around" section of each country's "Basics" section.

CENTRAL AMERICA BORDER CONTROL AGREEMENT

Guatemala, El Salvador, Honduras and Nicaragua are party to the **Central America Border Control Agreement (CA-4)**. Under the terms of this agreement, tourists may travel within any of these four countries for a period of up to ninety days without completing entry and exit formalities at border and immigration checkpoints (though officers will still check your passport), aside from paying entry fees. The ninety-day period begins at the first point of entry to any of the CA-4 countries. Fines are applied if you exceed the ninety-day limit (at least US$115), although a request for an extension can be made for up to ninety additional days by paying a fee (around US$15–20), before the limit expires, in one of the countries themselves (to do this in El Salvador you must be sponsored by a CA-4 national). Note that you can only extend your visa once – you must leave the CA-4 area after the second ninety days expires. You can avoid the extension process by travelling to a country outside the CA-4, and then re-entering (usually after a minimum of 24 hours) – you'll then get a fresh ninety-day visa.

As this book went to press, the governments of Honduras and Guatemala had recently announced the creation of a bilateral customs union between their two countries, effective from December 2015. In principle, this should mean that travellers with an entry stamp for one country can pass freely into the other, without any queuing or bureaucracy – whether it works out like that in practice, only time will tell.

BORDER CROSSINGS

Most travellers in Central America take advantage of the close proximity of the region's many distinct nations, crossing international borders regularly. While this is usually straightforward, "border days" can also be some of the most exhausting of your trip – follow the tips below to ease the strain.

- Always check specific entry requirements before heading for the border.
- Ensure that your passport is stamped on both entry and exit.
- Try to cross in the morning, when public transport links are more frequent and queues lighter.
- Research current exchange rates online at ⓦ oanda.com or ⓦ xe.com, and be savvy when dealing with moneychangers.
- If asked for "processing fees" request a receipt (such as the stamp given by Panama). Without one, these fees are not legal. Be sure to carry a small amount of US dollars for any unexpected fees.
- Do not discuss your business with strangers. Borders are notorious hangouts for petty criminals and con men. If you are confused about how to proceed, ask a uniformed official.
- At popular crossings avoid group transport, which will slow your progress considerably. Chicken buses operate these routes as frequently as any other (although not at night).
- If you're given a stamped entry document, do not lose it – you will require it later for departure.

By bus

Travelling **by bus** is by far the most convenient, cheap and comprehensive way to get around Central America. The **cost** of travel depends mainly on the quality of the transport – you can look forward to paying anywhere from approximately US$1 per hour for one of the region's infamous "chicken buses" to US$6 per hour for a guaranteed seat on a more comfortable "Pullman"-style coach.

Chicken buses (see box, p.32) generally serve as second-class, or local, services. They stop on demand, wherever passengers ask to get off or people flag down passing services. Sometimes it can seem like you're stopping every few metres, but these buses are handy for impromptu itineraries and each country's extensive network of routes allows you to get off the beaten path with relative ease. In most places chicken buses tend to run **on demand** rather than to schedules, departing when full. In Costa Rica, Nicaragua and Panama, however, schedules are more regular, so be sure to check for current timetable information at bus terminals before you travel. You usually buy **tickets** on board, once the journey is under way, either from the conductor or from his assistant – check the price before you board, to avoid being ripped off. **Luggage** usually goes on the roof; always keep valuables on your person and

an eye on your stuff as best you can, as theft on buses is unfortunately all too common – interior overhead luggage racks are particularly risky.

Pullman buses generally cover long-distance routes and operate to a schedule, making much quicker progress and so remaining economical when you wish to cover ground more rapidly. Seats should be reserved at the appropriate ticket office in advance. Several bus companies run services from one country to another as well as within individual countries.

In addition to the sites listed below, ⓦ thebus schedule.com provides a useful English-language rundown of bus **schedules** in Central America.

REGIONAL BUS CONTACTS

Hedman Alas ⓦ hedmanalas.com. Connections between major cities in Honduras and Guatemala.

Platinum/King Quality ⓦ platinumcentroamerica.com. Comfortable bus connections between Guatemala, Honduras, El Salvador and Nicaragua.

Pullmantur ⓦ pullmantur.com. Luxury buses from San Salvador (El Salvador) to Tegucigalpa (Honduras) and Guatemala City.

Tica Bus ⓦ ticabus.com. Tica Bus covers the most ground, spanning the region from Panama City through to Chiapas, Mexico, and stopping at most major cities.

Transnica ⓦ transnica.com. Routes from Managua (Nicaragua) to San José (Costa Rica) and Tegucigalpa (Honduras).

Transportes Galgos ⓦ transgalgosinter.com.gt. For travel between Tapachula in Mexico, El Salvador and Quetzaltenango and Guatemala City in Guatemala.

NAVIGATING CENTRAL AMERICAN CITIES

Most Central American cities are laid out on a **grid system**, making navigation fairly straightforward: usually numbered calles (streets) run east–west and numbered avenidas (avenues) run north–south, with a *parque* or plaza as the point zero. For more information on navigating specific cities, see the relevant chapters.

CHICKEN BUSES

Central America's "**chicken buses**" are legendary. These are old school buses from North America, with a few important modifications to get them ready for the rigours of travel: most likely some Jesus stickers, elongated seats for extra bums and a speaker system for the reggaetón soundtrack. Once you find the bus you need, get on and wait for it to fill up around you; luggage (livestock, bicycles, chickens, the kitchen sink, your backpack) goes wherever it will fit. Just when you think the bus couldn't possibly get any fuller, twenty snack vendors will jump aboard, screaming at you to buy full-fat goodies. Journeys are never dull. But besides entertainment, all the madness does provide one of the best opportunities to chat to local people. Even if your Spanish is shaky, a smile and a simple "Buenas" goes a long way. Once the ice is broken, your fellow passengers will undoubtedly help you to reach your destination with ease.

By plane

Central America has a good **international flight network**, connecting the region's key points of interest with its capital cities. However, unless you are severely pushed for time, few flights are worth the money – distances are usually short and accessible by bus, and prices aren't particularly cheap (around US$400/US$200 standard/student one-way for Guatemala City–San José).

Regional carriers Avianca/TACA (Ⓦavianca.com) and Copa (Ⓦcopaair.com) both offer youth fares; to be eligible you need to have an ISIC card (see box, p.41). If you do plan to do a bit of flying, consider buying an **airpass**, which will allow short hops within Central America, as well as routes to Mexico, the US and some South American destinations. Passes can be bought in conjunction with your international ticket in your country of origin. However, these usually force you to specify your route in advance and rarely allow for trips to your preferred destinations (most travellers are not necessarily interested in visiting the region's chaotic capital cities).

Of greater interest to budget travellers are the **domestic flights** that connect the region's more populous areas to isolated tourist destinations – such as Nicaragua's Corn Islands, Panama's Bocas del Toro and Honduras's Bay Islands, all of which are more than a day's travel by bus from their respective capital cities. Internal flights can be reasonably priced, especially if bought in advance, but as a rule you have to purchase them locally.

By boat

You're likely to travel **by boat** at some point if you spend any time in Central America – in some places watercraft are the only way to get around, in others they can provide a welcome break from the monotony of bumpy bus rides. Vessels range from the canoe-like *lanchas* with outboard motor to chugging ferries and speedy catamarans. Watery journeys of note include: Punta Gorda (Belize) to Lívingston (Guatemala) and onward to the Río Dulce area (see p.340); across Lago de Nicaragua to Isla de Ometepe (see p.496); down the Río San Juan to the Caribbean (see p.502). There are also some budget-friendly options through the Panama Canal (see p.543).

By car

Considering the prevalence of public transport and the relative expense of **car rental**, renting a vehicle is unlikely to hold much appeal. If, however, you want to reach isolated spots, and can find a trusted group to share the costs and/or risks, renting a car (or 4WD) does give you some flexibility. **Prices** vary throughout the region (US$25–40/day, depending on your location, for the cheapest vehicles, with insurance extra). Always familiarize yourself with the rental conditions before you sign a contract, and be aware that in the event of an accident, insurance excess levels are usually huge, sometimes up to US$1000 – so you'll have to pay for fairly common damages (such as dented bumpers and burst tyres), costing several hundred dollars (the excess can sometimes be reduced by paying a higher daily insurance premium). With no insurance you'll be liable for the cost of a new car in the event of accident or theft.

If you do decide to rent a vehicle you will need a full driving licence, credit card and passport. Some agencies do not rent to under-25s, although others may have an age limit of 21. Always park securely, preferably in a car park with attendant, especially in cities. No breakdown services are available, but petrol stations are plentiful; the price of fuel is slightly higher than in the US but considerably cheaper than in Europe.

Taxis

Travelling by **taxi** in Central America is something of a gamble, but a necessary one: drivers are either some of the friendliest, most helpful folk you'll encounter or some of the biggest swindlers, but at night, especially in large cities, they provide the only safe mode of transport. Always settle a **price** before getting in (even if there is a meter, try to get an estimate), clarifying that the price is for the journey, regardless of the number of passengers or amount of luggage; throughout the region most short journeys will cost a minimum US$2–5.

For reasons of safety, you should always use registered taxis. Costa Rica and Nicaragua in particular have been prone to taxi-jackings; as many taxis are **colectivos**, picking up random passengers en route, drivers have been known to pick up armed passengers who forcibly ask you to hand over your cash (if you are lucky), or drive you around to drain your bank accounts with ATM withdrawals. Ask at tourist information offices and local hotels for recommended drivers, and be alert. It also pays to keep an eye on the map as your journey progresses – a possible deterrent to drivers quite literally taking you for a ride. Note that the colectivo taxi is unknown in Guatemala, where, as in Honduras and El Salvador, the three-wheeled tuk-tuk, or **moto-taxi**, is becoming more common.

By bike

Though many locals travel by bicycle, **bike rental** is not widely available in Central America. However, some countries, like Belize, are seeing increased bicycle tourism, and a number of travellers also tour the region with their own bikes. Notwithstanding the dangers of Central America's anarchic road customs, cycling is facilitated by the mostly flat terrain, relatively short distances between settlements and ease of transporting bicycles aboard buses.

Accommodation

Budget accommodation in Central America is plentiful, and often of excellent quality. The best places to stay are truly memorable for their warm atmosphere, great facilities and stunning location – they are also invariably the best places to get up-to-date travel information. Others, however, have little to offer beyond cockroaches, poor sanitation and noisy neighbours. It's always worth shopping around, and inspecting rooms before paying.

Do not be afraid to walk away and look at alternatives – this may even precipitate a drop in prices. **Booking ahead** is generally not necessary, except during holiday periods in busy tourist centres – plan to arrive early, or call well in advance.

Hotels and guesthouses

The mainstays of travellers' accommodation in Central America are **hotels** and **guesthouses** (and their regional equivalents: posadas, pensiones, cabinas, cabañas and hospedajes). Cabinas and cabañas, where accommodation is in individual structures, detached from other guests, are usually found at the beach or in the jungle.

The room rates given throughout this guide are for the **cheapest double room in high season**. A basic double room (around US$20) will have a bed, a light and probably a fan (ventilador). Most places offer the choice of private or shared **bathroom**; a private bath (baño privado) will cost a few dollars more than a shared one (baño compartido). **Hot water** is a rarity unless you're splurging on a swankier room; keep an eye out for gas-fired hot water systems – the standard (and decidedly dodgy) electrical

---

TOP 5 JUNGLE LODGES

Throughout Central America, you'll come across rural **jungle lodges** in truly magical locations. While many charge high prices, not all are beyond the means of budget travellers, and splurging some money and/or detouring out of your way to stay at a lodge may provide one of the true highlights of your trip. Be warned, though, that because lodges tend to be isolated, you're liable to end up spending all your cash in one place – not least because their canny owners lay on all sorts of tempting treats.

Grand River Lodge Sábalos, Nicaragua (see p.504)
Hotel Los Quetzales Ecolodge & Spa Guadalupe, Panama (see p.582)
Nabitunich San José Succotz, Belize (see p.87)

Rainbow Valley Lodge Santa Elena, Costa Rica (see p.148)
Round House Río Dulce gorge, Guatemala (see p.344)

TOP 5 HOSTELS

Any budget traveller exploring Central America is likely to depend on **hostels** for affordable accommodation. Some are simply functional places to sleep; some are convenient and convivial; and some are truly exceptional. Here's a list of five favourite hostels that count as destinations in their own right, and deserve to be incorporated into any itinerary:

Bello Horizonte Jungle Hostel Puerto Jiménez, Costa Rica (see p.185)

Casa Verde Santa Ana, El Salvador (see p.260)

Tropicana Hostel Antigua, Guatemala (see p.294)

Sea Side Utila Hostel Utila, Honduras (see p.439)

Hostel Eco-Venao Playa Venao, Panama (see p.569)

---

showerheads tend to produce tepid water at best and can also deliver electric shocks. Some hotels will provide you with towels and soap and most with toilet paper. By paying a few extra dollars you can also find rooms that come with cable TV, fridge, a/c, mosquito nets and/or balcony. Double rooms are often equivalent in price to two dorm beds (good news for couples and something for friends to consider). Private **single rooms**, on the other hand, are often only marginally discounted (if at all) from the standard price for a double. **Internet**, especially wi-fi, is increasingly available throughout the region, and is often provided free to hotel guests.

Hostels

Hostels, often run by foreigners with a keen eye for backpackers' needs, are becoming increasingly common in Central America. These establishments offer some of the most sociable and comfortable lodgings in the region. A dorm bed should cost around US$7–12, but in capital cities (especially San José and Panama City) expect to pay around US$15. Most hostels have a few private rooms as well as dorms.

The best hostels may provide **facilities** such as a kitchen, internet and/or wi-fi access, lockers, bar and restaurant areas, TV and movies, as well as tours and activities. The lockers are a definite plus – theft does occur, so do not leave valuables lying around, and, ideally bring your own padlock. Some hostels will even offer free board and lodging if you want to stay put and **work** for a period (see p.38).

Hostelling International cards are of little or no use in Central America.

Camping

Organized **campsites** are rare in Central America. However, some **national parks** do allow camping and have limited facilities such as drinking water, toilets and campfire provisions. Expect to pay around US$3–5 per person to pitch a tent (though Costa Rica can be pricier). Camping doesn't hold much appeal for locals, so don't expect to find gear on sale or for rent – you will have to carry what you need. It is also possible to pay to hang a **hammock** (your own or hired) in some areas. This may seem more appealing than an airless room, but the **mosquitoes** can be fierce – make sure you have a net.

Health

There's always a risk of illness in a country with a different climate, food and bacteria – still more so in a poor country with lower standards of sanitation than you might be used to. Most visitors who observe basic precautions about hygiene, untreated water and insect bites, however, get through Central America without experiencing anything more serious than an upset stomach.

Above all, it's important to get the best **advice** you can before you depart: visit your doctor or a travel clinic. You should also invest in **health insurance** (see p.42).

General precautions

While there's no need to go overboard, it's worth carrying a **travel medical kit** with you. Components to consider include: painkillers and anti-inflammatory drugs, antiseptic cream, plasters (Band-Aids) and gauze bandages, surgical tape, antidiarrhoeal medicine (Imodium or Lomotil) and rehydration salts, stomach remedies (Pepto Bismol or similar), insect repellent, sun block, antifungal cream, and sterile scissors and tweezers.

Once in Central America, basic hygiene will go a long way towards keeping you healthy. **Bathe** frequently, **wash your hands** before eating and avoid sharing water bottles or utensils. Make sure to eat a **balanced diet**. Eating peeled fresh fruit helps keep up your vitamin and mineral intake, while malnutrition can lower your resistance to germs and bacteria. Hepatitis B, HIV and AIDS – all transmitted through blood or sexual contact – are common in Central America. You should take all the usual, well-publicized precautions to avoid them.

Two other causes of problems in the region are **altitude** and the **sun**. The answer in both cases is to take it easy; allow yourself time to acclimatize and build up exposure to the sun gradually. Avoid dehydration by drinking enough – water or fruit juice rather than beer or coffee, though you should take care with water (see p.35). Overheating can cause heatstroke, which is potentially fatal. Lowering body temperature (by taking a tepid shower, for example) is the first step in treatment.

Inoculations

If possible, sort out all **inoculations** at your local health clinic, at least ten weeks before departure. The only obligatory jab that may be required to enter Central America is a **yellow fever** vaccination; however, this is only needed if you're arriving from a "high-risk" area – northern South America and much of central Africa – in which case you need to carry your vaccination certificate. A yellow fever shot is also highly recommended for anyone travelling in Panama east of the canal. Long-term travellers should consider the combined hepatitis A and B and the rabies vaccines, and all travellers should check that they are up to date with the usual polio, diphtheria, tetanus, typhoid and hepatitis A jabs.

Food and water

People differ in their sensitivity to **food**. If you are worried or prone to digestive upsets then there are a few simple things to keep in mind. Steer clear of raw shellfish and seafood when inland; only eat raw fruit and vegetables if they can be peeled; and avoid salads unless rinsed in purified water.

Contaminated water is a major cause of sickness in Central America. Even if it looks clean, drinking water should be regarded with caution, even when cleaning teeth and showering. That said, however, it's also essential to increase fluid intake to prevent dehydration. **Bottled and bagged water** is widely available, but always check that the seal is intact, since refilling empties with tap water for resale is not unknown. Many restaurants use purified water (*agua purificada*), but always ask.

There are various methods of **treating water** while you are travelling: boiling for a minimum of five minutes is the most effective method of sterilization, but it is not always practical, and will not remove unpleasant tastes. Water filters remove visible impurities and larger pathogenic organisms (most bacteria and parasites). To be really sure your filtered water is also purified, however, chemical sterilization – using either chlorine or iodine tablets, or a tincture of iodine liquid – is advisable; iodine is more effective in destroying amoebic cysts. Both chlorine and iodine unfortunately leave a nasty aftertaste (which can be masked with lime juice). Pregnant women or people with thyroid problems should consult their doctor before using iodine tablets or purifiers. Inexpensive iodine-removal filters are recommended if treated water is being used continuously for more than a month. Any good outdoor equipment shop will stock water treatment products.

Intestinal troubles

Diarrhoea is the stomach ailment you're most likely to encounter. Its main cause is simply the change in your diet; the food in Central America contains a whole new set of bacteria, as well as perhaps rather more of them than you're used to. Don't try anything too exotic in the first few days, but do try to find some local natural yoghurt, which is a good way to introduce friendly bacteria to your system. Powdered milk, however, can be troublesome, due to being an unfamiliar form of lactose.

If you're afflicted with a bout of diarrhoea, the best cure is the simplest one: take it easy for a day or two and make sure you rehydrate. It's a good idea to carry sachets of rehydration salts, although you can make up your own solution by dissolving five teaspoons of sugar or honey and half a teaspoon of salt in a litre of water. Reintroduce only bland foods at first (rice, dry toast, etc) – papaya and coconut are also good. Diarrhoea remedies like Imodium and Lomotil should be saved for emergencies, for example if you need to travel immediately. Only if the symptoms last more than four or five days do you need to worry. If you can't get to a doctor for an exact diagnosis, a last resort would be a course of Ciproxin (ciprofloxacin) – you may want to consider asking your doctor for a prescription and carrying some in your medical kit.

Cholera, an acute bacterial infection, is recognizable by watery diarrhoea and vomiting, though many victims may have only mild or even no symptoms. However, the risk of infection is very low: Central America was recently declared a cholera-free zone by the Pan American Health Organization.

If you're spending any time in rural areas you also run the risk of picking up various **parasitic infections**: protozoa – amoeba and giardia – and intestinal worms. These sound hideous, but they're easily treated once detected. If you suspect you have an infestation, take a stool sample to a good pathology lab and go to a doctor or pharmacist (see p.37) with the test results. More serious is amoebic dysentery, which is endemic in many parts of the region. The symptoms are more or less the same as a bad case of diarrhoea, but include bleeding. On the whole, a course of Flagyl (metronidazole or tinidozole) will cure it; if you plan to visit the isolated rural reaches of Central America then it's worth carrying these, just in case. If possible, get some, together with advice on their usage, from a doctor before you go. To avoid contracting such parasites think carefully before swimming in rivers and lakes during or just after the rainy season, when waste washes down hillsides into the water.

Malaria and dengue fever

Malaria, caused by the transmission of a parasite in the saliva of an infected anopheles mosquito (active at night), is endemic in many parts of Central America, especially in the rural Caribbean lowlands. Several different antimalarial **prophylactics** are available, all of which must be started in advance of travel, so make sure you leave plenty of time to visit your doctor. The recommended prophylactic for all of Central America, except for the area east of the Panama Canal, is Chloroquine; east of the canal, including the San Blas Islands, it's Malarone, causing minimal side effects. Consult your doctor as to which drug will be best for you. It's extremely important to finish your course of antimalarials, as there is a time lag between bite and infection. If you do become ill after you return home, let your doctor know that you've been in a malarial risk area – **symptoms** usually occur ten days to four weeks after infection, though they can appear as early as eight days or as long as a year after infection.

In addition to malaria, mosquitoes can also transmit **dengue fever**, a viral infection that is prevalent – and on the increase – throughout Central America (usually occurring in epidemic outbreaks). Thankfully, the more deadly strain of hemorrhagic dengue is less prevalent in Central America. Unlike malaria, the mosquitoes that pass dengue fever are active during the day, and there's no preventative vaccine or specific treatment, so you need to pay attention to avoiding bites (see below).

Other bites and stings

It's essential to take steps to avoid being bitten by insects, particularly **mosquitoes**. In general, you should sleep in screened rooms or under nets, burn mosquito coils containing permethrin (available everywhere), cover up arms and legs (though note that mosquitoes are attracted to dark-coloured clothing), especially around dawn and dusk when mosquitoes are most active, and use insect repellent containing more than 35 percent DEET.

Sandflies, often present on beaches, are tiny and very difficult to see, and hence to avoid – you will become aware of their presence only when they bite, by which time it can be too late. The bites, usually found around the ankles, itch like hell and last for days. Don't give in to the temptation to scratch, as this causes the bites to get worse and last longer. Sandflies can spread cutaneous leishmaniasis, an extremely unpleasant disease characterized by skin lesions that can take months and even years to heal if left untreated.

Scorpions are common: mostly nocturnal, they hide during the heat of the day under rocks and in crevices. Their sting is painful (occasionally fatal) and can become infected, so you should seek medical treatment. You're less likely to be bitten by a spider, but the advice is the same as for scorpions and venomous insects – seek medical treatment if the pain persists or increases.

You're unlikely to see **snakes**, but wearing boots and long trousers will go a long way towards preventing a bite in the event that you do – walk heavily and they will usually slither away. Most snakes are harmless – exceptions are the fer-de-lance (which lives in both wet and dry environments, in both forest and open country, but rarely emerges during the day), and the bushmaster (found in places with heavy rainfall, or near streams and rivers), both of which can be aggressive, and whose venom can be fatal. If you do get bitten, remember what the snake looked like (kill it if it's safe to do so), and wrap a lightly restrictive bandage above and below the bite area, but don't apply enough pressure to restrict blood flow and never use a tourniquet. Disinfect the bite area and apply hard pressure with a gauze pad, taped in place; then immobilize the bitten limb as far as possible. Seek medical help immediately.

Swimming and snorkelling might bring you into contact with potentially dangerous **sea**

creatures. You're extremely unlikely to fall victim to a shark attack, but jellyfish are common and all corals will sting. Some jellyfish, like the Portuguese man-o'-war, with its distinctive purple, bag-like sail, have very long tentacles with stinging cells, and an encounter will result in raw, red welts. Equally painful is a brush against fire coral: in each case clean the wound with vinegar or iodine and seek medical help if the pain persists or infection develops.

Rabies does exist in Central America. You'll see stray dogs everywhere; the best advice is to give them a wide berth. Bats can also carry the rabies virus; keep an eye out for them when entering caves. If you are bitten or scratched, wash the wound immediately with soap and running water for five minutes and apply alcohol or iodine. Seek treatment immediately – rabies is fatal once symptoms appear. If you're going to be working with animals or planning a long stay, especially in rural areas far from medical help, you may well want to consider a pre-exposure vaccination, despite the hefty cost. Although this won't give you complete immunity, it will give you a window of 24–48 hours to seek treatment and reduce the amount of post-exposure vaccine you'll need if bitten.

Getting medical help

For minor medical problems, head for the local **pharmacy** (*farmacia*) – look for a green cross. Pharmacists are knowledgeable and helpful, and many speak some English. They can also sell drugs over the counter (if necessary) that are only available by prescription at home. Most large cities have doctors and dentists, many trained in the US, who are experienced in treating visitors and speak good English. Your embassy will have a list of recommended doctors and hospitals, and we've included some in this guide, in the "Directory" sections of the main town accounts. Medical insurance (see p.42) is essential.

If you suspect something is amiss with your insides, it might be worth heading straight for a **pathology lab** (*laboratorio médico*), found in all main towns, before you see a doctor, as the doctor will probably send you there anyway. Many rural communities have a **health centre** (*centro de salud* or *puesto de salud*), where healthcare is free, although there may be only a nurse or health-worker available and you can't rely on finding an English speaker. Should you need an injection or transfusion, make sure that the equipment is sterile and that any blood you receive is screened.

Medical resources for travellers

Travellers should check the latest health advice before travelling to Central America, and if suffering any symptoms after returning home.

UK AND IRELAND

Fit for Travel ⓦ fitfortravel.nhs.uk.
Hospital for Tropical Diseases ⓦ www.thehtd.org.
MASTA (Medical Advisory Service for Travellers Abroad)
ⓦ masta-travel-health.com.
Tropical Medical Bureau ⓦ tmb.ie.

US AND CANADA

Canadian Society for International Health ⓦ csih.org.
CDC ⓦ wwwnc.cdc.gov/travel.
International Society of Travel Medicine ⓦ istm.org.
Travel Health Online ⓦ tripprep.com.

AUSTRALIA, NEW ZEALAND AND SOUTH AFRICA

Travel Doctor ⓦ traveldoctor.com.au.

Culture and etiquette

Forget those stereotypes of a scantily clad world of steamy salsa: the reality in Central America is much more conservative. Throughout the region the Church (both Catholic and Evangelical Protestant) retains a powerful influence on everyday life.

Traditional **family values** are dominant throughout Central America: children are considered to be a blessing – a sign of virility and in many cases an economic asset – and consequently families are often large. **Homosexual** relationships are publicly frowned upon if not actively condemned; gay and lesbian travellers should be discreet.

While undeniably friendly and fun-loving (especially in the cities), local people may seem shy and unsure about the gringos squeezed into their chicken bus. You will seldom experience hostility, but it pays to greet fellow passengers with a simple "Buenas" and a smile to break the ice. **Politeness** is valued highly, so even if your Spanish is poor, take the trouble to learn key pleasantries and they'll serve you well.

Information about social customs specific to each country is given in the relevant chapter.

Dress

Most locals **dress modestly** but smartly, and visitors not wishing to draw unwelcome attention should do the same. You will make a better impression if you do – especially worthwhile when you come into contact with officials. Flashy exhibitions of wealth are not recommended (jewellery should be left at home). Shorts (for men and women) are not generally worn away from beaches, but low-cut tops for women are becoming more usual, especially among the young. In the cities, men wearing T-shirts or untucked shirts will be considered a bit scruffy in formal settings, and even in clubs and posher bars. If visiting places of worship, especially, dress modestly – skimpy shorts and flesh-revealing tops are not appropriate. Women will probably also want something to cover their heads.

Money matters

Travellers to Central America, especially Westerners, are likely to experience the uncomfortable assumption by locals that you are in fact a multimillionaire (even if you are poorly dressed). Although you may be on a strict budget, the very fact that you have been able to travel abroad, coupled with your potential earning power back home, means you have an economic freedom unobtainable to many you will encounter. As a rule, however, you will ultimately be judged on your conduct and not your wealth: it isn't helpful, therefore, to be too liberal or too mean with your cash. Instead, show appreciation for good service by **tipping** (take tips into account when working out your budget), and paying what will satisfy both parties when haggling. **Haggling** is accepted in markets (both tourist and local) and when setting taxi fares. Prices for tours and hotel rooms tend to be fixed, though you can usually get lower accommodation rates for stays of one week or longer. Prices in shops are generally fixed as well, although it's usually worth asking if there are discounts if you buy more than one item.

Women travellers

Machismo is an ingrained part of Central American culture – **female travellers** will frequently experience whistling, tssking and even blatant catcalls, though probably not anything more sinister than guys showing off to their friends. Ignoring such attention is the easiest way to deal with these situations, as retorts or put-downs are often seen as encouragement. No matter how modestly you behave, though, you will probably not counteract the view that foreign women are not only desirable, but also easily attainable. Conversely, women travelling as part of a straight couple should be prepared to be invisible in many social interactions. Even if the woman is the only one to speak Spanish, for example, locals (especially men) will often automatically address their reply to the man, for fear of causing offence.

Despite this, most female travellers report positive experiences in the region. There are, however, still **precautions** to be taken. At night, try to move in groups, and remember it's always possible simply to ask for help if you feel uncomfortable.

Work and study

High unemployment and innumerable bureaucratic hurdles make the possibility of finding paid work in Central America very unlikely, although there are limited opportunities to teach English, especially in wealthier countries like Costa Rica. It's far easier to work as a volunteer – many NGOs operate in the region, relying mainly on volunteer staff. Opportunities to study Spanish are plentiful and often fairly cheap, with a number of congenial Central American locations drawing students from all over the world.

Teaching English

If you want to **teach English** in Central America, you have two options: find work before you go, or simply wing it and see what you come up with after arriving. The latter is slightly less risky if you already have a degree and/or teaching experience. You can get a **CELTA** (Certificate in English Language Teaching to Adults), a **TEFL** (Teaching English as a Foreign Language) or a **TESOL** (Teaching English to Speakers of Other Languages) qualification before you leave home or even while you're abroad. Courses are not cheap (about £1350/US$2150/Aus$1550 for one month's full-time tuition) and you are unlikely to recoup this investment at all quickly on Central American wages. Once you have the necessary qualifications, check the **British Council**'s website (Ⓦ britishcouncil.org) and the **TEFL** website (Ⓦ tefl.com) for a list of English-teaching vacancies.

Places like Guatemala City and San José in Costa Rica are your best bet for teaching in Central

America, although colonial, tourist-oriented towns like Antigua in Guatemala and Granada in Nicaragua are also likely spots.

Volunteering

Volunteer positions available in Central America include everything from conservation in Costa Rica to human-rights work in Guatemala. If you have a useful skill or specialization, you might have your room and board paid for and perhaps even earn a little pocket money, but more often than not you'll have to fund yourself. If you don't have any particular skills you'll almost definitely have to pay for the privilege of volunteering, and in many cases – particularly in conservation work – this doesn't come cheap. While many positions are organized prior to arrival, it's also possible to arrange something on the ground through word of mouth. Noticeboards in the more popular backpacker hostels are good sources of information.

Studying Spanish

Some people travel to Central America solely to learn Spanish, and many cities and towns hold highly respected schools. Antigua and Quetzaltenango in Guatemala, San José in Costa Rica and, to a lesser extent, Granada and San Juan del Sur in Nicaragua are all noted centres for language instruction. **Prices** vary, but you can expect to pay around US$200 per week; this includes room and board with a local family, a standard feature of many Spanish courses and great for full cultural immersion. Some schools will also include activities, allowing you to take your learning out of the classroom and providing an insight into the local area. Courses usually run from Monday to Friday, but should include seven nights' homestay to take in the weekend as well. Cheaper courses are available – lessons without lodging or activities – but your learning curve is unlikely to be as steep.

Useful contacts

Though it is possible to arrange Spanish lessons last minute, you'll need to book several weeks or months ahead if planning to volunteer or teach English.

UK AND IRELAND

British Council ☎ 020 7930 8466, Ⓦ britishcouncil.org. Opportunities for language courses, study programmes, and TEFL postings worldwide.

I to I Volunteering ☎ 01273 647210, Ⓦ i-to-i.com/volunteer. Runs a range of volunteer projects in Costa Rica, from sea turtle preservation and teaching English to working with children and building homes for underprivileged families.

Volunteer Service Overseas ☎ 020 8780 7500, Ⓦ vso.org.uk. UK-based charity organization, offering volunteer opportunities across the globe.

US AND CANADA

AFS Intercultural Programs US ☎ 212 807 8686, Canada ☎ 1 800 361 7248 or ☎ 514 288 3282; US Ⓦ afs.org, Canada Ⓦ afscanada.org. Cultural immersion programmes in Costa Rica, Guatemala, Honduras and Panama.

American Institute for Foreign Study ☎ 1 866 906 2437, Ⓦ aifs.com. Language study and cultural immersion in Costa Rica.

AmeriSpan ☎ 1 800 511 0179, Ⓦ amerispan.com. Language programmes, volunteer/internship placements (English teaching, healthcare, environment, social work, etc) and academic study-abroad courses throughout Central America.

Amigos de las Américas ☎ 1 800 231 7796 or ☎ 713 782 5290, Ⓦ amigoslink.org. Veteran nonprofit organization placing high-school and college-age students in child health promotion and other community projects in Central America.

Peace Corps ☎ 855 855 1961, Ⓦ peacecorps.gov. US institution that recruits volunteers of all ages (minimum 18) and from all walks of professional life for two-year postings throughout Central America. All applicants must be US citizens.

World Learning ☎ 202 408 5530, Ⓦ worldlearning.org. Accredited college semesters abroad; the large Latin American studies programme includes a tropical ecology course in Panama and a politics-themed course in Nicaragua.

AUSTRALIA, NEW ZEALAND AND SOUTH AFRICA

AFS Australia ☎ 1300 131 736, Ⓦ afs.org.au; NZ ☎ 04 494 6029, Ⓦ afs.org.nz; South Africa ☎ 11 431 0113, Ⓦ afs.org.za. Cultural immersion programmes.

WORLDWIDE

Cactus Language Ⓦ cactuslanguage.com. Language-holiday specialist with a wide range of courses in Costa Rica, Guatemala and Panama. Prices are often lower than if applying directly to the schools.

Council on International Educational Exchange (CIEE) US ☎ 207 533 4000, Ⓦ ciee.org. Leading NGO offering study programmes and volunteer projects around the world.

Earthwatch Institute Ⓦ earthwatch.org. International nonprofit organization dedicated to environmental sustainability. Voluntary positions assisting archeologists, biologists and even ethnomusicologists in Costa Rica, Nicaragua and Belize.

Gapyear.com Ⓦ gapyear.com. Comprehensive resource with search engine providing links to volunteer and language teaching/learning options worldwide.

Global Volunteer Network Ⓦ globalvolunteernetwork.org. Voluntary placements on community projects in Costa Rica, Guatemala and Panama.

Global Vision International Australia ☎ 1300 795 013, Ⓦ gvi australia.com.au; US ☎ 1 888 653 6028, Ⓦ gviusa.com; UK ☎ 017 2725 0250, Ⓦ gvi.co.uk. Worldwide placements, many in Central America, including marine conservation and teaching work.

Idealist Ⓦ idealist.org. A comprehensive portal of global volunteering positions, connecting applicants with jobs and volunteer placements within the nonprofit sector.

Peace Brigades International Ⓦ peacebrigades.org. NGO dedicated to protecting human rights, with placements accompanying human-rights workers in Guatemala. Costs (including a small monthly stipend) are covered, although fundraising is encouraged. Applicants need to be 25 or older and fluent in Spanish.

Projects Abroad Australia ☎ 1300 132 831, Ⓦ projects-abroad .com.au; Canada ☎ 1 877 921 9666, Ⓦ projects-abroad.ca; South Africa ☎ 21671 7008, Ⓦ projects-abroad.org.za; UK ☎ 1903 441121, Ⓦ projects-abroad.co.uk; US ☎ 1 888 839 3535, Ⓦ projects-abroad.org. The leading global organizer of overseas volunteer work, ranging from teaching and conservation to healthcare and sports.

Raleigh International ☎ 020 7183 1270, Ⓦ raleighinternational .org. Long-established youth-development charity working on community and environmental projects worldwide. Opportunities for both young volunteers (17–25) and older skilled staff (over 25). Central American projects in Costa Rica and Nicaragua.

Crime and personal safety

While political violence has decreased over recent years, crime rates in Central America remain high, and tourists make handy targets. Though the majority of crime is opportunistic theft – bag-snatching or pickpocketing – some criminals do operate in gangs and are prepared to use extreme violence. It is commonly accepted that Guatemala tops the list for crimes committed against tourists, but it is possible to be the victim of crime anywhere in the region, especially if you let your guard down.

General precautions

When you're packing, keep the sentimental value of what you take with you to a minimum. Do not wear **jewellery**, and carry only a small amount of **cash** in your wallet. Larger volumes of cash and credit cards should be kept close to your body – in a money belt, hidden pocket or even in your shoes. Scan any important **documents** (passport, insurance, etc) and email them to yourself, so you can access them even if you lose everything. It's worth carrying a paper copy too, so that you can leave the originals in a hotel safe. There is always a dilemma about whether to carry **electronic devices** (such as a camera, tablet or MP3 player) on your person or leave them in your hotel. If you choose to leave them, make sure they're not accessible – consider packing a small padlock and short length of chain (or cable lock), so that you can create a DIY safe in a wardrobe or under a bed.

It's very important in Central America to **keep an eye on your belongings** at all times. Never put anything down or let your possessions out of your sight unless you're confident they are in a safe place. The highest-risk areas for opportunistic theft are large urban centres, bus stations, at ATMs and at border crossings. **Buses** are also a focus for petty thievery. When travelling by bus you'll often be separated from your main bag – it will usually end up on the roof. This is generally safe enough (and you'll probably have little option in any case). Theft of the bag itself is unlikely, but opportunist thieves may dip into zips and outer pockets, so don't leave anything you'd miss accessible. Some travellers choose to put their pack into a sack to disguise it, prevent pilfering and also keep it clean and dry – not a bad idea. If you carry a day-pack, fill it wisely and keep it on your person (preferably strapped to you). Do not use overhead racks on buses. Needless to say, there is a greater risk of crime after dark, so try to arrive in new towns in daylight so that you're not wandering unlit streets with all your gear. Bear in mind, too, that there's also the possibility of petty crime from unscrupulous fellow travellers.

Violent crime does occur in Central America. Muggings at knifepoint, armed robbery and rape are all dangers to be aware of. If threatened with a weapon, do not resist. You can reduce your chances of falling victim to such crimes by staying in populated areas or around other travellers. However, it should be noted that tourist shuttles are actually more likely to be a target for hijackers, especially at night.

Armed **hold-ups of cars** are rare but do happen (typically small groups of masked men with guns will try to block the road). You're especially vulnerable if you drive alone – avoid isolated roads and try to travel with a group. These *banditos* are unlikely to take your car – they want your cash. Most locals advise that you should simply drive on without stopping (especially if you are already going fast), as they're unlikely to shoot. It's a tough call, but if you do stop, do not resist and just pay up.

Drugs

Drugs of all kinds are available everywhere, but we strongly advise against buying or using – quite apart from the risks inherent in the substances themselves, doing so may bring you into contact with some very dangerous people. **Drug gangs** are a major problem, especially in Honduras, Guatemala and El Salvador, and are largely responsible for the region's high crime rates. In addition, penalties if you are arrested with drugs are very strict; your embassy will probably send someone to visit you, and maybe find an English-speaking lawyer, but otherwise you're on your own. Practically every capital city has foreigners incarcerated for drug offences who'd never do it again now they know what the punishment is like.

Reporting a crime

If you are unfortunate enough to suffer a crime, report the incident immediately to the **police** – if there is a tourist police force, try them first – if only to get a copy of the report (*denuncia*), which you'll need for insurance purposes. The police in Central America are poorly paid and, in the case of petty crime, you can't expect them to do much more than make out the report. If you can, also report the crime to your embassy – it helps the consular staff to build up a higher-level case for the better protection of tourists.

Travel essentials

Costs

Your **daily expenses** are likely to include accommodation, food and drink, and transport. You may wish to budget separately for activities, as one-off costs (for example, a day's snorkelling or diving) can be high and would blow a daily budget. In general, the cheapest countries in the region are

Honduras, Nicaragua, Guatemala and El Salvador, while Belize, Costa Rica and Panama are more expensive. However, even in these countries it is still possible to travel on a budget of around US$35 per day, with the most significant difference being the cost of public transport and accommodation.

Generally speaking, the price quoted in restaurants and hotels is the price you pay. However, in some more upmarket establishments an additional **tax** will appear on your bill; it's worth checking whether tax is included from the outset. Service is almost never included, and, while not expected, **tipping** for good service can make a huge impact on the basic wage. Prices for accommodation (as well as some airfares and organized tours) can be considerably cheaper in **low season** (generally Sept–Dec), when it's always worth negotiating to obtain the best price. Note that the hotel prices given in this guide are based on high-season rates.

Tiered pricing (charging foreigners more than nationals) is becoming more common, in particular for entrance fees. This is based on the premise that tourists can afford to pay considerably more to visit attractions than those on local salaries.

BUDGET TIPS

• Slow down. Racing from place to place eats into your budget, as you'll be forking out for transport and tours every day.

• Eat and drink as the locals do. Local staples can be half the price of even the most reasonable tourist menu. Set lunches in traditional *comedores* are great value.

• Cut down your beer bill. When buying booze it's cheapest to get it from small *tiendas* (shops) and take back the bottles to claim the deposit. Litre bottles are more economical than the 330ml ones.

• Refill your water bottle. Many hostels/hotels offer water refills for free or a small fee. Alternatively, in some countries you can buy 500ml bags (*bolsitas*) of water. If you're not moving around, invest in larger gallon bottles.

• Use local transport. Tourist shuttles should be the exception, not the norm.

• Let your money work for you. Try to get a bank account that allows free withdrawals at foreign ATMs. This also allows you to carry small amounts of cash, as ATMs are plentiful.

• Share costs with other travellers. The price of a private room for two is often cheaper than two dorm beds; a triple is even better value.

• Walk as much as possible, during the day at least. Taxis are often very expensive (though often the only safe option at night, when you should take them).

• Shop in markets, bakeries and supermarkets. Self-catering is worthwhile if you're staying in one place and can eat your leftovers for breakfast.

• Learn to haggle – bargaining can be fun. Don't be afraid to confront taxi drivers or chancers who you suspect are trying to rip you off. However, don't be too aggressive – a traveller from a comparatively rich country arguing over a few cents is not cool.

Electricity

All countries in the region use sockets that accept the flat two-pronged plug common to the majority of the Americas. Standard **voltage** is 110–120v. Be wary of **electric shower-heads**, often with protruding wires, in budget accommodation. If it isn't working (more than likely), do not touch the fitting. You may want to consider using a towel to turn off the conductive taps, too.

Gay and lesbian travellers

Apart from in Belize – where homosexual acts are illegal, and which officially bans gay foreigners from entering the country (though these laws have never yet been enforced) – consensual homosexual acts are **legal** throughout Central America (and in Mexico, which is far more liberal). In reality, however, homosexuality is barely tolerated by conservative Central American society, and harassment does exist in certain areas. Gay and lesbian travellers are unlikely to experience problems, however, if they remain discreet. Not surprisingly, there is little in the way of an open gay community or scene. In the more cosmopolitan capital cities a few gay clubs exist, although these are almost entirely geared towards men.

Insurance

It's essential to take out a **travel insurance policy** to cover against theft, loss, illness or injury. Before paying for a new policy, however, check whether you are already covered on any existing home or medical insurance policies that you may hold. A typical travel insurance policy usually provides cover for the loss of baggage, tickets and – up to a certain limit – cash or cheques, as well as cancellation or curtailment of your journey. Most of them exclude so-called dangerous sports unless an extra premium is paid: in Central America this can mean scuba diving, whitewater rafting, surfing and trekking. It is also useful to have a policy providing a 24-hour medical emergency number.

When securing baggage cover, make sure that the per-article limit – typically under £500/US$1000 – will cover your most valuable possession. If you need to **make a claim**, you should keep receipts for medicines and medical treatment as well as any high-value items that are being insured. In the event that you have anything stolen, you must obtain a *denuncia* from the police.

Several companies now offer tailored "backpacker" insurance, which provides low-cost coverage for extended durations (beyond the standard thirty-day holiday policies). These include Rough Guides' own recommended insurance (see box opposite).

Internet

Central America is **well connected** to the internet and you should have little difficulty getting online. Even smaller towns usually have at least one internet café, often populated by noisy gaming schoolkids, and many hostels, restaurants and hotels offer free wi-fi. Internet cafés are usually well equipped with webcams and headphones as well as the facility to download digital photos onto CD.

Mail

Stamps are rarely available anywhere other than the post office (*correo*), although it can be worth asking if you are buying a postcard, for example, as occasionally souvenir shops and stationers do stock them. Sending mail from the main post office in any capital city is probably the best way to ensure speedy and efficient delivery. The cost and speed of mailing items varies from country to country, but is by far cheapest and quickest from Panama. To receive mail by **poste restante** you should address it to yourself at "Lista de Correos" at the "Correo Central" in the capital city of the appropriate country.

Maps

The best **overall map** of Central America, covering the region at a scale of 1:100,000, is produced by Canada's International Travel Maps and Books (Ⓦitmb.com). They also publish individual country maps at various scales. Maps are generally hard to find once you get to Central America, so it's wise to bring them with you when possible.

Money

Cash payments are the norm in Central America, with the most convenient way to access money being via an **ATM** (*cajero automático*). Most machines accept Visa and MasterCard credit cards, as well as Visa debit cards, and are increasingly widespread throughout the region. However, be sure to check the Directory sections of specific destinations in this guide before you go there, to confirm whether smaller settlements have an ATM – not all do. If you are relying on ATMs, it's worth having a back-up card in case the first is lost or stolen. If you plan to travel for a significant period, it is worth thoroughly researching your bank's terms for cash withdrawals abroad – some charge substantial amounts for each transaction, while others make no charge at all, allowing you to make frequent withdrawals and carry only small amounts of cash around urban areas. As a possible alternative some banks will give **cash advances** over the counter (sometimes for a small fee). Try to hoard notes of small denominations; you will constantly encounter problems obtaining change from local businesses, often stalling transactions as no one has anything smaller than a US$1 bill (or its equivalent). In general, budget-friendly hotels and restaurants do not take **credit cards**, though a few mid-range establishments and tourist handicraft shops may accept them. **Travellers' cheques** are increasingly difficult to change for the same reason, but are good to carry as a backup. Note that most Central American ATMs do not accept five-digit PINs; contact your bank at home in advance if you have one.

Belize, Guatemala, Honduras, Nicaragua and Costa Rica each have their own **national currency**, while El Salvador and Panama both use the US dollar (in Panama the dollar is divided into 100 balboas – although US cents are also legal tender). However, **US dollars** are accepted throughout Central America, and in many places prices for tourist services (language school fees, plane tickets, tour fees) are quoted exclusively in them. Indeed, some ATMs (particularly those in Nicaragua) will actually dispense dollars on request. Local currency is always accepted at the current exchange rate, so there is no need to carry huge amounts of dollars in cash, though it's certainly useful to carry some to exchange at border

ROUGH GUIDES TRAVEL INSURANCE

Rough Guides has teamed up with Ⓦworldnomads.com to offer great **travel insurance** deals. Policies are available to residents of more than 150 countries, with cover for a wide range of **adventure sports**, 24hr emergency assistance, high levels of medical and evacuation cover and a stream of **travel safety information**. Ⓦroughguides.com users can take advantage of their policies online 24/7, from anywhere in the world – even if you're already travelling. And since plans often change when you're on the road, you can extend your policy and even claim online. In addition, buying travel insurance with Ⓦworldnomads.com can also leave a positive footprint and donate to a community development project. For more information go to **Ⓦroughguides.com/travel-insurance**.

crossings. Generally speaking, you should also get rid of any remaining unwanted local currency at border crossings, as it will be more difficult to exchange the further away from the border you are. Try to research the current exchange rates before dealing with moneychangers (Ⓦoanda.com or Ⓦxe.com).

Phones

It's easy enough to phone home from most cities and towns in Central America. Each country has a national telecommunications company with offices throughout the country. It's also worth keeping an eye out for internet cafés that offer **Skype**, for excellent-value international calls. **Mobile phones** are as abundant as they are in the developed world; despite living in relative poverty, the rural population can often be spotted checking their text messages. You may find that taking your own phone comes in useful in emergencies, but on the other hand, it does become one more item to keep secure. Also remember that rates to receive calls and messages while abroad are often extortionate. Alternatively, you may consider buying a phone locally, as packages that include call-time are reasonable. However, practically speaking, if you only anticipate making the odd call, forget the mobile and simply use local **payphones**, which are usually easy to come by (except in El Salvador, where they have largely been replaced by mobiles).

Shopping

When it comes to shopping you'll find that what's on offer is either significantly cheaper or significantly different to what's available back home – from places like the Guatemalan highlands, where indigenous **craft markets** abound, to Panama City, where glitzy **shopping malls** offer cut-price designer clothing and shoes. Throughout the region you can also buy locally sourced **coffee**, thereby supporting local farmers.

In markets **haggling** is standard. Try not to get cornered by stallholders, who will try to pressure you into buying on the spot. It is always wise to compare various sellers' best prices before agreeing to a sale. If you're looking for crafts, it's also worth scouting out official **tourist shops** (where prices are fixed) to get a ballpark figure to try and beat in markets. If you plan to buy several items you will get the best prices if you buy in bulk from the same seller. Haggling is not commonplace in shops. However, if you are unsure about whether or not prices are fixed, simply ask if discounts apply: "*Hay descuentos?*"

Time

Panama is GMT –5, and all the other countries are GMT –6, in the **Central Time Zone** (same as Central Standard Time in the US). In recent years, Central American governments have gone back and forth on the issue of whether or not to apply daylight savings as an energy-saving measure, and will no doubt continue to do so in the future.

Tourist information

Official sources of tourist information in Central America are spotty at best; for budget travellers, often the best way to obtain the latest advice is to talk to other backpackers. Popular **hostels** usually offer noticeboards, and the best have clued-up staff with local knowledge. All Central American countries have their own official **tourist offices**, which we have detailed in each country's "Basics" section, but you won't often come across offices on the ground. See the "… Online" boxes in the "Basics" sections for more suggestions.

USEFUL WEBSITES

Ⓦ **2backpackers.com** Blog from a well-travelled couple who have journeyed extensively in Central America (and most other places).

Ⓦ **centralamericanpolitics.blogspot.com** Blog that follows Central American politics by associate professor of political science at the University of Scranton (US).

Ⓦ **lanic.utexas.edu/country/central/** Latin American Network Information Center.

Ⓦ **latinnews.com** Real-time news feed with major stories from all over Latin America in English.

Ⓦ **onlinenewspapers.com** One page of news per country, with links to Spanish and English papers.

Ⓦ **thebusschedule.com** Useful online bus schedules for Central (and South) America.

Travellers with disabilities

Central America is not the most accessible part of the world for travellers with disabilities. On the whole, it's the top-end hotels and services that may offer equipped facilities – out of the price range for most budget travellers. However, for the most part, Central American society is community-oriented, and strangers take pleasure in helping and facilitating the passage of others. **Costa Rica** (where tourist facilities are well developed) and **Panama** (where there is a large expat community) have the best infrastructure. Specialist websites advising travellers with disabilities include Ⓦable2travel.com, Ⓦmiusa.org and Ⓦdisabledtraveladvice.co.uk.

BLUE HOLE

Belize

HIGHLIGHTS

❶ Caye Caulker A watersports haven with a relaxed island nightlife. **See p.62**

❷ Blue Hole Dive the inky waters of this coral-encrusted cavern. **See p.70**

❸ San Ignacio Excellent base for Maya ruins and adventure trips. **See p.79**

❹ Caracol Explore Belize's greatest and most extensive Maya site. **See p.86**

❺ Cockscomb Basin Wildlife Sanctuary Hike deserted jungle trails in this jaguar reserve. See **p.93**

❻ Placencia Chill out on Belize's most beautiful white-sand beaches. **See p.94**

HIGHLIGHTS ARE MARKED ON THE MAP ON P.47

ROUGH COSTS

Daily budget Basic US$35/occasional treat US$70

Drink Beer US$2

Food Jerk chicken US$5

Hostel/budget hotel US$15/US$30

Travel Belize City–San Ignacio (120km) by bus: 2hr 30min, US$4

FACT FILE

Population 340,000

Languages English (official), Kriol (unofficial)

Currency Belize dollar (Bz$)

Capital Belmopan (population: 20,000)

International phone code ☎ 501

Time zone GMT -6hr

1

Introduction

With far less of a language barrier to overcome than elsewhere in Central America, Belize, perched on the isthmus's northeast corner, is the ideal first stop on a tour of the region. And, although it is among the most expensive countries in Central America, its reliable public transport, numerous hotels and restaurants and small size make it an ideal place to travel independently.

Belize offers some of the most **breathtaking scenery** anywhere in the region: thick tropical forests envelop much of the country's southern and western regions, stretching up towards the misty heights of the sparsely populated Maya Mountains, while just offshore radiant turquoise shallows and cobalt depths surround the **Mesoamerican Barrier Reef**, the longest such reef in the western hemisphere. Here too are the jewels in Belize's natural crown: three of the four **coral atolls** in the Caribbean.

Scattered along the barrier reef, a chain of islands – known as **cayes** – protect the mainland from the ocean swell, and make wonderful bases for **snorkelling and diving**; the cayes are most travellers' top destination in the country. **Ambergris Caye** and **Caye Caulker** are the best known, though many of the less developed islands, including the picture-perfect **Glover's Atoll**, are gaining in popularity. The **interior** has remained relatively untouched, thanks to a national emphasis on conservation: in the west, the dramatic landscape – especially the tropical forests and cave systems – of the **Cayo District** provides numerous

opportunities for adventure-seekers and culture vultures. Inexpensive **San Ignacio**, the region's transport hub, gives access to the heights of the **Mountain Pine Ridge Forest Reserve** and the rapids of the **Macal** and **Mopan rivers**, as well as the impressive Maya sites including **Caracol**, **Xunantunich** and **Actun Tunichil Muknal**. **Dangriga**, the main town of the south-central region, serves as a jumping-off point for heavenly **Tobacco Caye** and the **Cockscomb Basin Wildlife Sanctuary**; to the south, the small fishing village of **Hopkins** and more developed **Placencia peninsula** have some of the country's best **beaches**. Belize's most isolated region – the far south – is dominated by the **Maya Mountains**, which rise to more than 1100m and shelter some of the world's finest **cacao** farms.

CHRONOLOGY

200–800 AD Classic period: Maya culture flourishes throughout Belize.

800–900 AD Maya cities across central and southern Belize decline, though Lamanai and other northern cities continue to thrive throughout the Postclassic period (900–1540 AD).

1530s The Spanish, led by Francisco de Montejo, engage in the first of numerous unsuccessful attempts to conquer the Maya of Belize.

1544 Gaspar Pacheco subdues Maya resistance and founds a town on Lake Balcar.

1570 Spanish mission is established at Lamanai.

1630–70 British buccaneers, later known as Baymen, plunder Spanish treasure ships along the Belizean coast, then begin to settle the coastline and harvest logwood, used for textile dyes in Europe. They rely heavily on slave labour from Africa.

1638 The Maya rebel, forcing the Spanish to abandon the areas they have settled.

1700s Spain and Britain clash over control of Belize. In 1763, Spain officially grants British settlers logging rights,

WHEN TO VISIT

The country's **climate** is subtropical, with temperatures warm throughout the year, generally 20–27ºC from January to May (the dry season) and 22–32ºC from June to December (the wet season). The best time to visit is usually between January and March, when it's not (quite) as hot or humid. That said, these months are also Belize's peak tourist season, and prices tend to be higher.

but does not abandon territorial claims on the region.

1798 The British defeat the Spanish in the Battle of St George's Caye, gaining control of the region.

1838 Slavery is abolished.

1839 Citing Spanish territorial claims, newly independent Guatemala asserts sovereign authority over Belize.

1847 Mexican refugees fleeing the Caste Wars in the Yucatán arrive in Belize.

1859 Britain and Guatemala sign a treaty that acknowledges British sovereignty over Belize.

1862 Belize officially becomes a British colony, and part of the Commonwealth, called British Honduras.

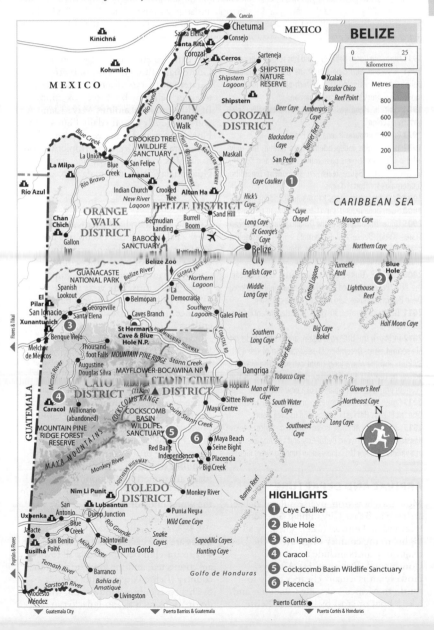

HIGHLIGHTS

1 Caye Caulker

2 Blue Hole

3 San Ignacio

4 Caracol

5 Cockscomb Basin Wildlife Sanctuary

6 Placencia

1

BELIZE'S ETHNIC GROUPS

For a tiny nation, Belize is home to several strongly identified **ethnic groups** – including the Maya and Garinagu (or Garífuna) cultures. **Creoles** – descendants of the slaves and slave owners who arrived during the area's logging boom in the 1800s – make up about a fifth of the country's population, with both the language and food widespread throughout the country. Belizean Kriol, with roots in English and various African languages, is spoken by around 70 percent of the population – although the language is not formally acknowledged, it is unanimously recognized as a glue that unites most of Belize's multicultural population.

1931 Hurricane floods Belize City and kills several thousand.

1961 A second hurricane (Hurricane Hattie) devastates Belize City and kills 262, after which plans are made to move the country's capital to Belmopan.

1964 British Honduras becomes an internally self-governing colony.

1973 British Honduras is renamed Belize.

1981 Belize gains independence from Britain, but only after a UN Resolution is passed in its favour, and Britain, Guatemala and Belize reach an agreement regarding Guatemala's territorial claims.

1992 Guatemala recognizes Belize's independent status.

2000 Guatemala reasserts its claim to Belizean territory.

2005 Under the auspices of the Organization of American States (OAS), Belize and Guatemala agree to establish peaceful negotiations concerning the border dispute, though the issue remains unresolved.

2008 The UDP (United Democratic Party) easily defeats the PUP (People's United Party) in the national elections; Dean Barrow replaces Said Musa as prime minister.

2011 Belize celebrates 30 years of independence from Britain.

2012 In March the UDP wins again, and Barrow kicks off his second term. December 21 sees the end of the 13th B'Aktun and the Maya long-count calendar. The Maya of Belize, in contrast to doomsday theorists, honoured the event in prayer as the beginning of a new era.

2013 Cruise industry continues to grow; Norwegian Cruise Line (NCL) buys Harvest Caye to build its own resort.

2015 American Airlines begin offering twice-weekly nonstop service between Belize City and Los Angeles, one of a variety of major U.S. airlines now running direct flights.

ARRIVAL AND DEPARTURE

Most travellers from overseas **fly** to Belize, arriving at Belize City's **Philip Goldson International Airport (BZE)**. Virtually all flights to the country originate in the US; major operators include American, Continental, Delta and US Airways. However, it is usually cheaper to fly to southern Mexico – usually Cancún – and take a **boat** or cross by land into Belize.

You can also enter Belize by land from Guatemala, though from southern Guatemala or Honduras it's often easier to enter Belize by **boat** (see box opposite). In addition, **local airlines** Maya Island Air and Tropic Air operate daily flights from Flores, Guatemala, and San Pedro Sula, Honduras, to Belize City. Tropic Air also has flights to Cancún, Mexico, and Guatemala City, Guatemala.

VISAS

Citizens of Australia, Canada, the EU, New Zealand and the US do not need **visas** for stays in Belize of up to **thirty days**. Citizens of most other countries – with the exception of cruise-ship passengers – must buy visas (from US$50; valid for up to ninety days) in advance from a Belizean consulate or embassy (see p.61).

Leaving Belize, you'll have to pay a Bz$37.50/US$18.75 **exit tax**.

GETTING AROUND

Belize has just three major highways (the Northern, now called the Philip Goldson Highway; the Western, now the George Price Highway; and the Southern), but the majority of the country is well served by **public transport**. The unpaved side roads are sometimes in poor repair, though they are usually passable except in the worst rainstorms.

BY BUS

Buses are the cheapest, and most efficient, way to travel in Belize – nearly all towns are connected, and the longest trip in the country (Belize City to Punta Gorda; 5–7hr) costs only around Bz$28, while destinations such as San Ignacio can be reached from Belize City (2–3hr) for Bz$7. You buy **tickets** from the conductor. The main towns are served by frequent daily buses, while villages off the main highways rely on **local services**, often with just one bus a day running Monday to Saturday only. These brightly painted, recycled North American school buses, known to travellers as "chicken buses" (see box, p.32), will pick up and drop off anywhere along the roadside. The most frequent services operate along the Western (George Price) and Northern (Philip Goldson) highways, usually from very early in the morning to mid-evening. The Hummingbird and Southern highways, to Dangriga, Placencia and Punta Gorda, are not quite so well provided for, though services are improving.

BY TAXI

All official **taxis** in Belize are licensed, and can be identified by their green plates. They operate from special ranks in the centre of all mainland towns. There are no meters, so establish your fare in advance; within towns a Bz$6–10 **fixed rate** should apply. It is also possible to negotiate official taxi rides between cities, though this option can be quite expensive: usually at least US$75–100 per person for a three-hour ride.

BY CAR

In the most remote parts of Belize bus services will probably only operate once a day, if at all, and unless you have your own transport – which is expensive – you will need time and patience to cope with the inconvenient schedules. If **car rental**, which starts at about US$65 per day

(without insurance), is beyond your budget, you may be able to ask around and find a local **"cab"** – a resident with a car – to drive you. This kind of "ride" should cost the price of the fuel plus a small tip; agree on a rate beforehand. Otherwise, hitching may be your only option, but if you go for this you should be extremely cautious – there are always risks involved, especially for female travellers.

BY BIKE

Cycling can be a great way to reach Belize's more isolated ruins and towns. **Bikes** are increasingly available for rent – usually around Bz$15–25 per day – especially in San Ignacio and Hopkins. Though biking along major highways is certainly possible, it is uncommon, and drivers will not be watching for cyclists; it is therefore important to remain exceptionally alert during the day and to avoid cycling at night. You'll find repair shops in all towns. One thing to note, however, is that Belizean buses don't have roof racks; if there's room, the driver might let you take your bike onto the bus.

BY BOAT

If you plan on visiting the cayes, you'll have to travel by **boat**, which will likely be a fast **skiff**, or partially covered speedboat. **Tickets**, usually Bz$25–45, can be bought in advance for domestic routes, but it's generally worth showing up half an hour before departure time to ensure your seat. Numerous boats make multiple daily runs between Belize City, Caye Caulker and Ambergris Caye, and one connects Ambergris Caye with Corozal (see p.76).

LAND AND SEA ROUTES TO BELIZE

There are **two land border crossings** into Belize: one from Chetumal, **Mexico**, to Santa Elena (see box, p.77), and one from Melchor de Menchos, **Guatemala**, to Benque Viejo del Carmen (see box, p.361).

There are numerous **sea routes** to Belize from **Mexico**, **Guatemala** and **Honduras**. One ferry shuttles travellers between Chetumal and San Pedro (see p.68), while another runs from Puerto Cortés, Honduras, via Dangriga (see box, p.420) to Belize City. Connections to Guatemala include daily skiffs between Punta Gorda and Puerto Barrios, and services between Punta Gorda and Lívingston (see p.99), while a weekly boat moves tourists between Placencia and Puerto Cortés, Honduras (see p.96).

The exit fee at any border is Bz$37.50 (around US$19).

1

BY PLANE

Though it is quite expensive, some budget travellers do choose to travel by **air**, as flights are not only much faster than buses, but also connect destinations unreachable by road. Maya Island Air (☎223 1140, ⓦmayaislandair.com) and Tropic Air (☎226 2012, ⓦtropicair.com) each operate numerous daily flights from both the municipal and international airports in Belize City to San Pedro, Caye Caulker, Dangriga, San Ignacio, Placencia and Punta Gorda. Flights also run from San Pedro to Corozal. Prices start at around Bz$70–90.

ACCOMMODATION

While Belizean **accommodation** is generally expensive by Central American standards, there are budget hotels in all the towns, and the most popular backpacker destinations – Caye Caulker, San Ignacio, Hopkins and Punta Gorda – have a great deal of choice and are often less expensive than the rest of the country. **Finding a room** is usually no problem, though at Christmas, New Year and Easter, booking ahead is advisable.

Hostels are still quite thin on the ground in much of Belize, though some dormitory accommodation (usually US$10–15) is available in Caye Caulker, Dangriga, Hopkins and San Ignacio. In other cities and towns most budget travellers rely on **budget hotels**, which usually charge from US$25 for a double, depending on the city. For this price you should get a private bathroom, TV and a fan; a/c will add at least US$10 more to the cost per night. Check out Belize Explorer (ⓦbelizeexplorer.com), which lists most of the country's accommodation for under US$70, for ideas. The Belize Hotel Association (ⓦbelizehotels.org) is a local trade organization that features vetted member accommodation throughout the country, with updated information, deals and offers.

There are also a few proper **campsites** in Belize, most of which charge US$5–10 for pitching a tent, and some mid-priced hotels in smaller villages and on the coast will allow you to camp on their grounds for about the same rate. In order to camp in any protected area (fees around US$10/tent) you'll have to get permission from park authorities – in person, at the ranger's office, or through an organized tour.

In smaller communities, such as Sarteneja, Community Baboon Sanctuary, and in the Toledo district, **homestays** – usually under US$30 and including meals – are an alternative solution to hotels. Ask at regional offices of the Belize Tourist Board, or see individual listings of the areas mentioned above for contact information.

The accommodation prices quoted throughout this chapter are **inclusive of tax**.

FOOD AND DRINK

Belizean food is a mix of Latin American and Caribbean, with Creole flavours dominating the scene in local restaurants, but with a number of international options as well – numerous Chinese restaurants and the odd Indian curry house can be found across the nation. The basis of any Creole main meal is **rice and beans**, and this features heavily in smaller restaurants, where most meals cost around Bz$8–12. The white rice and red beans are cooked together in coconut oil and usually served with stewed chicken or beef, or fried fish; there's always a bottle of hot sauce on the table for extra spice. **Seafood** is almost always excellent. Red snapper and grouper are the most commonly seen on restaurant menus, but you might also try a barracuda steak, conch fritters or a plate of fresh shrimp. In San Pedro, Caye Caulker, San Ignacio and Placencia the food can be exceptional, and the only concern is that you might get bored with **lobster**, which is served in a vast array of dishes. Note that the **closed season** for lobster fishing is from mid-February to mid-June; if you do order some during this period, it will either be illegal or frozen.

Breakfast (Bz$6–10) is usually served from 7am to 10am and generally includes eggs and flour tortillas, or fry jacks, a deep-fried dough often stuffed with meat/veg fillings. The **lunch hour** (noon–1pm) is observed with almost religious devotion – you will not be able

KRIOL SLANG

Belizean **Kriol**, derived mainly from English, is the native language of the majority of the country's inhabitants. Some 70 percent of the population speak it, and it's not unusual to hear English and Kriol being used interchangeably in conversation.

Aarait Fine
Dah how yuh di du? How are you?
Fu chroo? For real?
Gud maanin Good morning
Hall yuh rass! Get the hell out!
Humoch dis kaas? How much does this cost?
I gwen I'm going

Ih noh mata It doesn't matter
Mee noh andastan I don't understand
Mee noh know I don't know
Mi naym dah ... My name is ...
Weh di go'ahn? What's up?
Weh I deh? Where am I?
Weh taim yuh gat? What time is it?
Weh yuh naym? What's your name?

to get anything else done at that time. **Dinner** is usually eaten quite early, between 6 and 8pm; few restaurants stay open much later.

Vegetables are scarce in Creole food, but there's often a side dish of potato or coleslaw. There are a few specifically **vegetarian** restaurants, but in touristy areas many places offer a couple of vegetarian dishes and the ubiquitous Chinese restaurants always have a few veggie dishes on offer.

DRINK

Tap water, in the towns at least, is safe but highly chlorinated, and most villages (though not Caye Caulker) also have drinkable water. Many travellers nonetheless choose to buy filtered bottled water, which is sold everywhere for around Bz$2 per bottle. **Fruit juices** are widely available, with fresh orange, lime, watermelon and pineapple being the most popular options. **Coffee**, except in the best establishments, will almost certainly be instant, though decent **tea** is quite prevalent. Belikin, Belize's (only) national **beer**, comes in several varieties: regular, a lager-type bottled and draught beer; bottled stout; Lighthouse and Premium lagers; and seasonal brews. The Belikin factory offers tours and sampling sessions. Home-made **wines** of varying strengths, including cashew nut and blackberry, are bottled and sold throughout the country, and you can also get hold of imported wine, though it's not cheap. Local **rum**, in numerous dark and clear varieties, is inexpensive. The legal drinking age in Belize is 18.

One last drink that deserves a mention is **seaweed**, a milkshake-style blend of seaweed, milk, cinnamon, sugar and cream. You'll find it at local restaurants and cafés in seaside towns and cities along the coast.

CULTURE AND ETIQUETTE

Belizeans are generally welcoming and accustomed to tourists, though it's important to remember that the country is, on the whole, quite conservative. Dress, except among professionals, is usually casual, though tourists – especially women – who wear revealing clothing will probably be looked down upon, particularly in Belize's many churches.

The country's laidback attitude usually carries over into conversation; when approaching Belizeans, it's best to be friendly, relaxed and patient. **Women travellers** may receive advances from local men. Ignoring such attentions completely will sometimes only be met by greater persistence; walking away while flashing a quick smile and wave usually gets the message across, while remaining polite.

Belizeans are not particularly accepting of **homosexuality** and rarely open about sexual orientation; some may find the community in San Pedro more tolerant than elsewhere. Though it is unlikely that locals will express disapproval, it is a good idea for gay travellers to avoid public displays of affection. Those wishing to visit gay-friendly venues should visit ⓦgaytravel belize.com for current information.

One of the more egregious holdovers from colonial times is Belize's anti-sodomy

1

laws, which punish gay sex with up to ten years in prison and prohibit foreign homosexuals from entering Belize (though this ban has yet to actually be applied). It's high time for change: these archaic laws are now being vociferously challenged by **LGBT activists** and others in Belize, the UK, the US and beyond.

Belizeans rarely **tip**, though foreigners are usually expected to give around ten percent in taxis and in restaurants. **Haggling** is also uncommon and will usually be considered rude, except at street markets.

SPORTS AND OUTDOOR ACTIVITIES

Football (soccer) and **basketball** are very popular in Belize, though the country's size and resources limit teams to the semiprofessional level, and visitors will find few spectator events.

However, Belize is a haven for a wide range of **outdoor activities**. Many travellers will participate in some form of **watersports**, including snorkelling, diving, windsurfing, kayaking and sailing. Companies in San Pedro, Caye Caulker and Placencia offer **diving courses** and lead multiday kayaking and sailing trips to the cayes. In the Cayo region, operators organize **hiking** trips through the local jungle and Mountain Pine Ridge Forest, as well as **horseriding** excursions to Maya ruins and other sights. Stunning cave systems dot the south and west and **caving tours** are becoming more widespread and popular. There are a number of operators in San Ignacio (see box, p.81).

COMMUNICATIONS

Though most towns have post offices, and the service is more efficient (and expensive) than in the rest of Central America, Belizean **postal services** can still be unreliable. Sending letters, cards and parcels home is straightforward; prices start at Bz$0.75 for a letter and Bz$0.40 for a postcard.

Belize has a modern phone system, with **payphones** plentiful throughout the country. These can only be used with **phonecards**, which are widely available

from BTL (Belize Telecommunications Limited) offices, as well as hotels, shops and stations. Phonecards can be used for both local and international calls. There are **no area codes** in Belize, so you need to dial all seven digits. Making a reverse charge (collect) call home is easy using the Home Country Direct service, available at BTL offices, most payphones and larger hotels – dial the access code (printed on some payphones and in the phone book) to connect with an operator in your home country. **Mobile phones** are common in Belize, and almost all of the country receives excellent service. North Americans can usually connect to local systems with their regular service, albeit at very high roaming charges. Alternatively, BTL sells SIM cards to visitors with compatible international phones. **Web access** is readily available in all the main towns and for guests at many hotels, though it can be expensive in tourist areas – up to Bz$12 per hour.

CRIME AND SAFETY

Though Belize does have a relatively high **crime** rate, general crime against tourists is rare, especially in comparison to other Central American countries, and **violent crime** against tourists is seldom experienced, even in Belize City (see box, p.55).

The last decade saw several attacks on tourist groups near the Benque/Melchor border with Guatemala, but tour operators now take precautions to prevent this; solo trekkers should be on alert, however, and it is not recommended to hike alone in this region. Elsewhere in the country, theft does occur, the majority of cases involving **break-ins** at hotels. Bear this in mind when you're searching for a room; doors should have good locks and it's even better if the room has a safe – valuables should never be left lying around, in any case.

STREET CRIME

Out and about there's always a slight danger of **pickpockets**, but with a bit of common sense you've nothing to fear. The vast majority of this harassment is

1

EMERGENCY NUMBERS

Ambulance ☎ 223 3292 (B.E.R.T.; Belize
Emergency Response Team)
Ambulance and fire (Belize City) ☎ 90
Police ☎ 90 or ☎ 911
Tourism police (Belize City) ☎ 227 6082

harmless, though the situation can be more
threatening for **women travelling alone** (see
p.51). If you need to **report a crime**, your
first stop should be the tourism police,
ubiquitous in Belize City and becoming
more common in many tourist hotspots,
including San Ignacio, Caye Caulker,
Ambergris Caye and Placencia.

Many of the country's violent crimes are
related to the **drug trade**, as Belize is an
important link in the chain between
South and North America. Marijuana,
cocaine and crack are all readily available,
and whether you like it or not you'll
receive regular offers. All such substances
are **illegal**, and despite the fact that dope
is often smoked openly in the streets, the
police do arrest people for possession
– they particularly enjoy catching tourists.
If you are arrested you'll probably spend a
couple of days in jail and pay a fine of
several hundred US dollars; expect no
sympathy from your embassy.

HEALTH

Health standards in Belize are quite high
for the region, and Belize City has
hospitals as well as a number of **private
physicians** (see p.61). All other large
towns have well-stocked **pharmacies and
clinics**, which are usually free, though
many will expect a donation for their
services.

INFORMATION AND MAPS

Information on travelling in Belize is
abundant, though often only available
online, as even some major towns (except
Belize City, Punta Gorda, Placencia and
San Pedro) don't have a local tourist
office. The office of the country's official
source of tourist information, the **Belize
Tourism Board** (BTB; ⓦ travelbelize.org),
in Belize City, has plenty of helpful
information, and their website is also
top-notch (see p.59). The **Belize Tourism
Industry Association** (BTIA; ⓦ btia.org),
which regulates many of the country's
tourism businesses, has knowledgeable
representatives in touristed areas; they can
put you in touch with local businesses
and tour operators.

Local **maps** can be difficult to find and
are often nonexistent in smaller towns and
villages (where most streets don't have
names), though the better hotels will
usually be able to provide them to guests.

MONEY AND BANKS

The national currency is the **Belize dollar**,
which is divided into 100 cents and fixed
at two to one with the US dollar (US$1 =
Bz$2); US dollars are also widely accepted,
either in cash or travellers' cheques, and it
can be cheaper to pay this way (see p.54).
On account of this dual-currency system,
always check whether the price you are
quoted is in Belizean or US dollars; we
have noted prices in local currency unless
an operation has specifically quoted their
fees in US dollars.

Credit and debit cards are widely used in
Belize. Visa is the best option, though
many establishments also accept
MasterCard. Before you pay, check with

BELIZE ONLINE

ⓦ **belize.gov.bz** The government's own website is worth a look for an overview on current
politics and tourism trends.
ⓦ **belizeaudubon.org** The latest information on Belize's growing number of reserves,
national parks and associated visitor centres.
ⓦ **belizebus.wordpress.com** Excellent guide to transport routes and timetables.
ⓦ **belizefirst.com** Online magazine dedicated to Belize, featuring accurate reviews and
articles about hotels, restaurants and destinations.
ⓦ **travelbelize.org** Belize's official tourism website offers excellent advice on travelling in
Belize and can even help book accommodation and tours.

1

the establishment if there's a charge for using plastic, as you might have to pay an extra five or seven percent for the privilege. Any bank can give you a Visa/MasterCard **cash advance**, and most of them have **ATMs** that accept foreign-issued cards, although your own bank is likely to charge a fee for use abroad.

Taxes in Belize are quite high: sales tax is 12.5 percent and hotel tax is 9 percent. The hotel prices we quote throughout this chapter include tax.

You'll find at least one **bank** in every town. Although the exchange rate is fixed, banks in Belize will give slightly less than Bz$2 for US$1 for both cash and travellers' cheques, so it can be a good idea simply to **pay in US dollars** if they are accepted and if you have them. Other than banks, only licensed casas de cambio, which can be difficult to find, are allowed to **exchange currency**, though there's usually a shop where locals go. To buy US dollars, you'll have to show an onward ticket.

OPENING HOURS AND HOLIDAYS

It's difficult to be specific about **opening hours** in Belize, but in general **shops** are open from 8am to noon and 1pm to 5pm. The **lunch hour** (noon–1pm) is almost universally observed. Some shops and businesses work a half-day on Saturday, and everything is liable to close early on Friday. **Banks** (generally Mon–Thurs 8am–2pm, Fri 8am–4pm) and government offices are only open Monday to Friday. **Post offices** are usually open Monday to Friday 8am to noon, and 1pm to 4pm. Watch out for **Sundays**, when shops and restaurants outside tourist areas are likely to be closed, and fewer bus services and internal flights operate. **Archeological sites**, however, are open every day. Virtually everything will be closed on the main **public holidays**, but note that if the holiday falls midweek, it is observed on the following Monday.

FESTIVALS

Belize's calendar is full of **festivals**, ranging from the local to the national. The calendar here includes a few

> ### PUBLIC HOLIDAYS
>
> **Jan 1** New Year's Day
> **March 9** Baron Bliss Day
> **March/April (variable)** Good Friday, Holy Saturday, Easter Monday
> **May 1** Labour Day
> **May 24** Commonwealth Day
> **Sept 10** St George's Caye Day/National Day
> **Sept 21** Independence Day
> **Oct 12** Columbus Day (Pan America Day)
> **Nov 19** Garífuna Settlement Day
> **Dec 25** Christmas Day
> **Dec 26** Boxing Day

highlights – but you'll find plenty of entertainment whenever you come.

February Carnaval is celebrated in the week before Lent with a week of dancing, parades, costumes and drinking.
March Celebrations throughout the country in honour of Baron Bliss Day – March 9 (see box above); La Ruta Maya River Challenge in San Ignacio.
May Cashew Festival in Crooked Tree; Toledo Cacao-Fest in Punta Gorda; Coconut Festival in Caye Caulker.
June Caye Caulker Lobster Festival; three-day Día de San Pedro festival in San Pedro; Placencia Lobster Festival.
July Belize international film festival in Belize City.
August Week-long Deer Dance Festival in San Antonio; Costa Maya festival in San Pedro.
September Celebrations commemorating St George's Caye Day (Sept 10) and Independence Day (Sept 21).
November 19 Garífuna Settlement Day.

Belize City

Even to the most hardened cosmopolite **BELIZE CITY** – the country's largest city, though not the capital – can be a daunting place. Dilapidated wooden buildings stand right on the edge of the road, offering pedestrians little refuge from the incessant traffic, and local attention ranges from simple curiosity and good-natured joking to outright heckling. Still, travellers who approach the city with an open mind may actually enjoy themselves. The streets, which certainly are chaotic, buzz with an energy that arises from the diversity of the city's sixty thousand or so citizens. And Belize City is, without a doubt, an experience;

those who manage to feel comfortable here should have no problems anywhere else in the country.

WHAT TO SEE AND DO

Belize City is divided into northern and southern halves by **Haulover Creek**, a branch of the Belize River. The few sights are within **walking** distance of one another, and can all be visited within an afternoon. The pivotal (literally) point of the city centre is the Liverpool-made **Swing Bridge**, the only manually operated swing bridge left in the Americas. Formerly opened twice a day, it is now only operated on request due to the decrease in river traffic. **East** of the bridge is the most touristy part of town, with a scenic stretch of seafront, breezy parks and the majority of the city's decent hotels and restaurants. Immediately **south** of the Swing Bridge is Albert Street and the commercial zone, home to the city's banks, shops and a couple of supermarkets. This commercial centre sits on the fringes of a rougher area of the city (see box below), so be wary of straying from the recommended sights.

Image Factory

The **Image Factory**, north of the Swing Bridge at 91 N Front St (Mon–Fri 9am–5pm, or by appointment; donations welcome; ☎610 5072, ⊚imagefactorybz .com), hosts displays by Belize's hottest contemporary artists. The gallery holds outstanding, frequently provocative exhibitions, and you often get a chance to chat with the artists themselves. The factory is also home to a good **bookshop** (see p.61).

Tourism Village

If you continue east along North Front Street from the Image Factory, you'll encounter an advance guard of trinket sellers, street musicians, hustlers and hair-braiders, announcing you're near **Tourism Village**, Belize's **cruise-ship terminal**. The Village itself can usually only be accessed by ship passengers; across the street, the **Fort Street Plaza** serves as an extension of the Village and includes a restaurant, bar and additional shops. On ship days, a number of vendors line the streets in this area, though the items tend to be overpriced; be prepared to haggle here.

The seafront

Beyond the Tourism Village, the road follows the north shore of the river-mouth, reaching the **Fort George Lighthouse**, which marks the tomb of **Baron Bliss**, Belize's greatest benefactor (see box, p.58). On the seafront itself, **Memorial Park** honours the Belizean dead of the world wars, and in the streets around the park you'll find several colonial mansions, many of which now house upmarket hotels. At the corner of Hutson Street and Gabourel Lane a block from the sea is the former **US Embassy**: a superb "colonial" building actually constructed in New England in the nineteenth century, then dismantled and shipped to Belize.

Museum of Belize

At the north end of Queen Street, in front of the Central Bank building, the city's former colonial prison, built in

---

SAFETY IN BELIZE CITY

Due to increasing gang activity, walking in the city's south side is not recommended at any time, but walking in the touristy areas of Belize City in **daylight** is perfectly safe if you use common sense: be civil, don't provoke trouble by arguing too forcefully and never show large sums of money on the street. Women should dress conservatively: female travellers, especially those wearing short shorts or skirts, are likely to attract mild verbal harassment from local men (see p.51). However, the presence of specially trained **tourism police** (☎227 6082), who wear Tourist Unit badges on their sleeves, generally prevents serious crime.

The chances of being mugged do increase **after dark**, but you'll find that you can walk around the main streets in relative safety (it's best to stay in a group if possible); you'll certainly encounter tourism police in this area. If you're venturing further afield, or if you've just arrived by bus at night, travel by taxi.

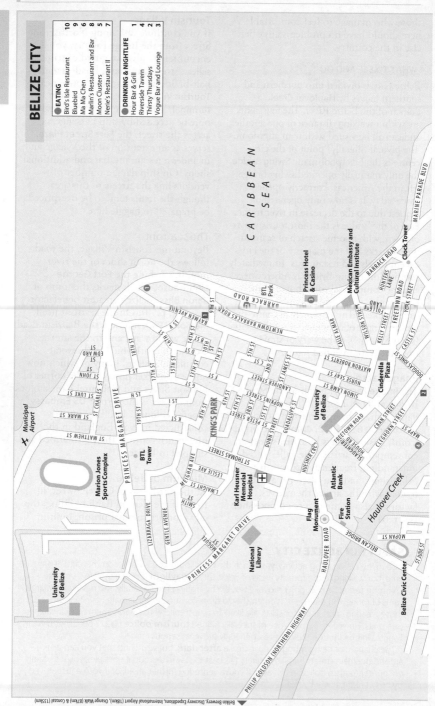

BELIZE CITY

● EATING

Bird's Isle Restaurant	10
Bluebird	9
Ma Ma Chen	6
Marlin's Restaurant and Bar	8
Moon Clusters	5
Nerie's Restaurant II	7

● DRINKING & NIGHTLIFE

Hour Bar & Grill	1
Riverside Tavern	4
Thirsty Thursdays	2
Vogue Bar and Lounge	3

1

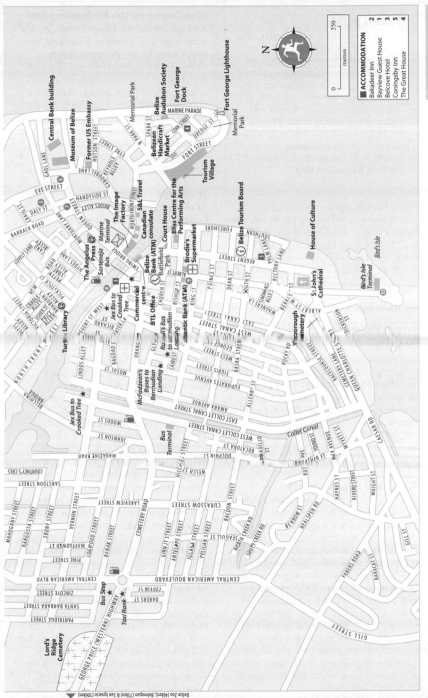

■ ACCOMMODATION	
Bakadeer Inn	2
Bayview Guest House	1
Belcove Hotel	3
Coningsby Inn	5
The Great House	4

Belize Zoo (46km), **Belmopan** (75km) & **San Ignacio** (106km)

▲ Belize Zoo (46km), Belmopan (75km) & San Ignacio (106km)

1

1857, has undergone a remarkable transformation to become the **Museum of Belize** (Mon–Fri 8.30am–5pm; Bz$10; ☎223 4524, ⓦnichbelize.org). The lower floor, with exposed brickwork and barred windows, includes a reconstruction of a cell as well as a small exhibition on the jail's former occupants. The majority of the floor, however, is devoted to photographs and artefacts chronicling the city's history. Though these are quite interesting, the star attractions are upstairs, in the Maya Masterpieces gallery: a first-class collection of the best of Belize's **Maya artefacts**, including some of the finest painted Maya ceramics anywhere, like the famed *Buenavista Vase* from Cayo. Visitors can also peruse a comprehensive collection of Belizean stamps and an excellent selection of the country's insects.

Albert and Regent streets

South of the Swing Bridge, **Albert Street** is Belize City's main commercial thoroughfare, lined with banks and clothing and souvenir shops. On the parallel **Regent Street** are several former colonial administration and court buildings, collectively known as the **Court House**. Completed in 1926, these well-preserved examples of colonial architecture, with columns and fine wrought-iron, overlook **Battlefield Park** (named to commemorate the noisy political meetings that took place here before independence), really just a patch of grass and trees with a dry ornamental fountain in the centre.

Bliss Centre for the Performing Arts

A block behind the Court House, on the waterfront at 2 Southern Foreshore, the **Bliss Centre for the Performing Arts** (Mon–Fri 8am–5pm; free; ☎227 2110, ⓦnichbelize.org) not only hosts an eclectic mix of plays and concerts in its 600-seat auditorium, but also holds the country's national art collection, puts on temporary exhibitions and has a café/bar. Performances showcase local talent, including children's groups, solo acts and Garífuna dancers and drummers.

St John's Cathedral

At the end of Albert Street is **St John's Cathedral** (daily 6am–6pm; free), the oldest Anglican cathedral in Central America – begun in 1812 – and one of the oldest remaining buildings in Belize. Its red bricks were brought over as ballast in British ships – and it does look more like a large English parish church than most of the other buildings here.

House of Culture

East of the cathedral, on the seafront, the renovated former Government House, now renamed the House of Culture (daily 9am–4pm; Bz$10; ☎227 3050, ⓦnichbelize.org), is one of the most beautiful spots in Belize City, with its manicured lawns and sea views. Built in 1814, the structure served as the British governor's residence until Belizean independence in 1981. The main room downstairs exhibits the possessions of former governors as well as colonial silverware, glasses and furniture; temporary historical and cultural exhibitions are also on this floor. Upstairs are rooms for painting, dance and drumming workshops, art exhibitions and musical performances.

Travellers One Barrel

Rich and dark, with a hint of molasses and tropical fruit, Travellers One Barrel is the finest rum in Belize. History has a lot to do with it: Travellers is Belize's oldest rum distillery, originally launched as a bar in 1953 by Jaime Omario Perdomo Sr and given the name "Travellers" because its customers were always en route to somewhere else. Since the 1970s, it's been run by Don Omario's sons and continues to flourish; for an overview of the rum's history (and, more importantly, a tasting), head to the distillery (Mile 2.5 Philip Goldson Hwy; Mon–Fri 9am–5pm; Bz$2; ☎223 2855, ⓦonebarrelrum.com), where you can peruse displays of old photos, vintage rum bottles and storytelling dioramas, as well as views of the bottling factory. The tour includes tastings of the famous One Barrel rum, along with white and flavoured rums.

ARRIVAL AND DEPARTURE

BY PLANE
Philip Goldson International Airport International flights (see p.48) land here, 17km northwest of the city. Taxis are the only way to get into town; they cost Bz$50. There's a branch of the Belize Bank (with ATM) in the terminal.

Municipal airport Domestic flights (see p.48) to and from San Pedro, San Ignacio, Placencia, Dangriga, Caye Caulker and Punta Gorda come and go from the municipal airport, a few kilometres north of town on the edge of the sea; taxis from here to the city centre charge Bz$10.

BY BUS
Terminals Most buses depart from the central bus terminal at 19 West Collet Canal St (☎227 2255), which is in a fairly run-down area on the western side of the city. It's only 1km or so from the centre, so you can walk to any of the recommended hotels, but take a taxi at night. Other smaller companies leave from different points in the city (see box, p.60).

Schedules Most services operate daily, though departure times may be erratic on Sundays and/or holidays. Enquire about schedules at the central bus terminal or the Marine Terminal, which generally has reliable information on bus (and boat) schedules.

Destinations Belmopan (NTSL, JA, BBOC; hourly 5am–9pm [express]; 1hr 15min); Benque Viejo del Carmen, for the Guatemalan border (NTSL, BBOC; hourly 5am–9pm [express]; 3hr 30min); Bermudian Landing, for the Community Baboon Sanctuary (MF, RU; Mon–Sat noon, 4pm & 5pm; 1hr 15min); Chetumal, Mexico (NTSL; hourly 5am–7pm [express]; 3hr 30min); Corozal (NTSL, BBOC; hourly 5am–7pm [express]; 2hr 30min); Crooked Tree (JX; Mon–Sat 10.55am & 4.30pm; 1hr 30min); Dangriga (JA; 11 daily 6am–5pm [express]; 3hr 30min via Belmopan); Orange Walk (NTSL, BBOC; hourly 5am–7pm [express]; 1hr 30min); Placencia (JA; 4 daily, via Belmopan and Dangriga; 5–7hr); Punta Gorda (JA; 12 daily, all via Belmopan and Dangriga [express]; 5–8hr); San Ignacio (NTSL, BBOC; hourly 5am–9pm, via Belmopan; 2hr 30min); Sarteneja (SC; Mon–Fri 4 daily [10.30am, noon, 4pm, 5pm]; 3 on Sat [10.30am, noon, 4pm]).

BY BOAT
Caye Caulker Water Taxi Association Skiffs to Caye Caulker (45min) and Ambergris Caye (1hr 15min) depart from the Marine Terminal on the north side of the Swing Bridge (daily 8am–4.30pm, at least every 1hr 30min; ☎223 5752, ⓦcayecaulkerwatertaxi.com).

San Pedro Water Jets Express Several daily runs to the cayes from a terminal at Bird's Isle (☎226 2194, ⓦsanpedrowatertaxi.com).

Information and schedules The shop inside the Marine Terminal has boat schedules.

GETTING AROUND

On foot The best way to get around Belize City's compact centre is on foot; even going from one side to the other should only take around 20min. Increasing gang violence on the city's south side makes much of the rest of the city highly undesirable for walking, so ask your hotel for advice on areas to avoid and use taxis after dark.

By taxi Identified by green numberplates, taxis charge Bz$7–10 for one or two passengers within the city limits.

INFORMATION AND TOURS

Belize Tourism Board 64 Regent St (Mon–Thurs 8am–5pm, Fri 8am–4pm; ☎227 2420, ⓦtravelbelize.org). The office hands out city maps, hotel guides and brochures; they can also recommend tour guides for nearby sights.

Tour operators A number of operators organize daytrips from Belize City, the most popular going to the Maya ruins at Altun Ha (US$45–60). Reliable options include the excellent S & L Travel, 91 N Front St (☎227 7593, ⓦsltravelbelize.com), and Discovery Expeditions, 5916 Manatee Drive (☎223 0748, ⓦdiscoverybelize.com).

ACCOMMODATION

Accommodation in Belize City is more expensive than elsewhere in the country, so prices for even budget rooms can come as quite a shock. There's usually no need to book in advance unless you're eager to stay in a particular hotel – you'll always be able to get something in the price range you're looking for. Keep in mind, however, that the further south and west you go, the more dangerous the area becomes; if you are travelling alone you may want to stay north of the river near Queen Street, the city's most populated area.

NORTH OF THE RIVER
Bakadeer Inn 63 Cleghorn St ☎223 0659, ⓦbakadeerinn. Safe and clean, with accommodating staff and comfortable, if dim, rooms with private bath. **US$50**
Bayview Guest House 58 Baymen Ave ☎223 4179, ⓦbelize-guesthouse-hotel.com. Well located for sampling the city's nightlife, the *Bayview* offers worn but clean rooms with private bath, and shared kitchen facilities. **US$40**

1

BUS COMPANIES AND STOPS

Belize's main bus company is National Transport Services Limited (NTSL). Note that the company's original name – Novelo's – still appears on some signs. Other, smaller companies also serve specific destinations, leaving from a variety of stops. The following are the main operators.

BBOC A co-operative of bus companies running services along the Philip Goldson (Northern) Highway and George Price (Western) Highway.

James Bus (JA; ☎ 722 2049) Buses for Dangriga and Punta Gorda (via Belmopan), leaving from the terminal.

Jex Bus (JX; ☎ 225 7017) Departs for Crooked Tree from Regent St West (Mon–Sat 10.55am) and Pound Yard, Collet Canal (Mon–Fri 4.30pm & 5.15pm).

McFadzean's Bus (MF) Departs for Bermudian

Landing (via Burrell Boom) from Euphrates Ave, off Orange St, near the main bus depot.

NTSL (☎ 227 6372) Serving all major destinations from the terminal.

Russell's Bus (RU) Departs for Bermudian Landing from Cairo St, near the corner of Cemetery Rd and Euphrates Ave.

Sarteneja Bus Company (SC) Buses to Sarteneja via Orange Walk, from the south side of the Swing Bridge.

SOUTH OF THE RIVER

Belcove Hotel 9 Regent St West ☎ 227 3054, ⓦ belcove .com. Basic, very clean rooms, some with a/c and private bath. Although it's on the edge of the dangerous part of the town, the hotel itself is quite safe and enjoys great views of Swing Bridge from the balcony. US$33

Coningsby Inn 76 Regent St ☎ 227 1566. Decent rooms with tiled floors, a/c and private bath in a relatively quiet part of the city centre. US$50

EATING

Belize City's selection of restaurants is quite varied, though simple Creole food (rice and beans) still predominates at the lower end of the price scale. Note that many restaurants close early in the evening and on Sundays.

NORTH OF THE RIVER

Ma Ma Chen 7 Eve St ☎ 223 4568. Simple vegetarian restaurant, with adjoining guesthouse, serving tasty Taiwanese food, including spring rolls for Bz$8 and rice dishes for Bz$10. Daily 8am–7pm.

Moon Clusters 36 Daly St. One of the only true coffee shops in Belize City; another branch on Albert St serves an identical menu of coffees and cakes in a less inviting space. Relax in the bright and quirky interior with an excellent cup for Bz$7. Mon–Sat 7.30am–5pm.

Nerie's Restaurant II Queen St, at Daly St ☎ 223 4028. Great Belizean food at reasonable prices: main dishes run from Bz$8 for rice and beans to Bz$12 for fish. Daily 8am–7pm.

SOUTH OF THE RIVER

Bird's Isle Restaurant 90 Albert St ☎ 207 2179. Relax under a thatched roof by the sea and enjoy nicely priced Belizean fare (Bz$15–25), like grilled conch, stewed chicken, plantains and, on Saturday, a boil-up – a one-pot stew of root vegetables and chicken or beef. A friendly, community-oriented place, with kids encouraged to use

the adjoining basketball court. There's karaoke on Thursday. Mon–Sat 11am–2.30pm & 5–10pm.

Bluebird 35 Albert St. The best ice-cream bar in the city with a variety of exotic flavours, including ginger and soursop, at Bz$2 a scoop. Mon–Sat 7am–6pm.

Marlin's Restaurant and Bar 11 Regent St W ☎ 227 6995. Tasty, large portions of inexpensive Belizean and Mexican-influenced dishes – *escabeche*, stewed chicken, grilled catch of the day – served indoors or on the veranda overlooking the creek. Filling breakfasts. Mon–Sat 7am–9pm.

DRINKING AND NIGHTLIFE

Belize City's nightlife really comes into its own on Fridays and Saturdays; any other night of the week, you're likely to find the city deserted after 9pm, with only a few hard-drinking (and often rowdy) locals frequenting the bars that are open. On weekends, however, there are plenty of venues to choose from, playing everything from techno to Latin grooves to reggae. A relatively safe area of town with a variety of bars and clubs is the strip of Barrack Road around the *Princess Hotel & Casino*.

Hour Bar & Grill 1 Princess Margaret Drive ☎ 223 3737. Enjoy cocktails with spot-on views of the Caribbean Sea at this breezy waterfront bar and grill. In between drinks, fill up on juicy burgers, pulled pork and nachos. They also host

---

★ TREAT YOURSELF

The Great House 13 Cork St, Fort George ☎ 223 3400, ⓦ greathousebelize.com. From the setting to the staff to the rum cocktails at the on-site *Smoky Mermaid*, this is one of the best places to stay in Belize City. The modernized, four-storey wooden building – painted a gleaming white – lies just 100yd from the sea, and the spacious a/c rooms all have private bath, TV and hardwood floors. US$150

fun events, including sports nights, all-you-can-eat Taco Sundays and more. Daily noon–midnight; kitchen usually closed on Sun.

Riverside Tavern 2 Mapp St. Owned by the Belikin brewery, this is one of the classier spots in town. Popular with locals and tourists alike, it has a spacious outdoor patio and decent cocktail menu, as well as draught beer on tap. Mon–Wed 11am–10pm, Thurs 11am–midnight, Fri 11am–2am, Sat noon–2am.

Thirsty Thursdays 164 Newtown Barracks Rd ☎ 223 1677. A buzzing bar set on a large balcony, where you'll find polished young Belizeans bouncing to electro-pop and hip-hop, and sipping drinks from the long cocktail list (from Bz$6) – be prepared to pay a cover charge (from Bz$15, with "ladies" half-price). Thurs–Sat 5pm–2am.

Vogue Bar and Lounge In the *Princess Hotel & Casino*, Barrack Rd ☎ 223 2670, ⓦ princessbelize.com. A lively local favourite. DJs play a variety of music and the dancefloor is packed late on Fri and Sat nights. Hours vary, but generally Thurs–Sat 5pm–3am.

ENTERTAINMENT

Cinema At the *Princess Hotel & Casino*, on Barrack Rd. The only cinema in the city, with one showing nightly of a recent Hollywood blockbuster.

Performing arts The cultural centre of Belize is the Bliss Centre for the Performing Arts (see p.58), which stages a variety of events – from plays to concerts – in its large auditorium. The House of Culture (see p.58) also hosts exhibitions and events, including classical concerts, in its intimate upstairs rooms. Both venues are affordable (from free to Bz$30), but shows can be sporadic. Check ⓦ nichbelize.com for schedules.

SHOPPING

The Angelus Press 10 Queen St ☎ 223 5777. Good bookshop with a wide range of Belize-related books and maps. Mon–Fri 7.30am–5.30pm, Sat 8am–noon.

Belizean Handicraft Market Place Memorial Park ☎ 223 3627. For authentic souvenirs, stop by this market, which is filled with Belizean hardwood crafts, including bowls, picture frames and chopping boards, as well as Maya basketry and hot sauces and spices. Hours vary, but generally Mon–Sat 9am–5pm.

The Image Factory 91 N Front St ☎ 223 4093, ⓦ imagefactorybelize.com. This superb gallery (see p.55) also has a well-stocked bookshop, with a good selection of Belizean literature, travel guides and current pop fiction novels. Mon–Fri 9am–5pm.

Supermarket Albert St, south of the Swing Bridge, is the city's central commercial district. A number of supermarkets line the street, including the city's largest, Brodie's, which is quite expensive, as most of the selection is imported.

DIRECTORY

Banks and exchange The main banks have branches on Albert St (usually Mon–Thurs 8am–2pm, Fri 8am–4.30pm); most have ATMs that accept foreign-issued cards.

Consulates Current addresses and phone numbers can be found under "Diplomatic Listings" in the green pages of the telephone directory. Canada ☎ 223 1060; Guatemala ☎ 223 3150; Honduras ☎ 224 5889; Mexico ☎ 223 0193. Most are normally open in the mornings from Monday to Friday. The US embassy (☎ 822 4011) and British High Commission (☎ 822 2146) are in Belmopan (see p.79).

Health Karl Heusner Memorial Hospital, Princess Margaret Drive, near the junction with the Philip Goldson (Northern) Highway (☎ 223 1548). There are a number of pharmacies on Albert St.

Immigration In the Government Complex on Mahogany St, near the junction with Central American Blvd and the George Price (Western) Highway (Mon–Thurs 8.30am–4pm, Fri 8.30am–3.30pm; ☎ 222 4620). Thirty-day extensions of stay (the maximum allowed) cost US$30.

Internet The Angelus Press, 10 Queen St (Bz$4/hr), and Turton Library, N Front St (☎ 227 3401; Bz$2.50/hr), are central options. Many hotels offer internet access to guests.

Police The main police station is on Queen St, a block north of the Swing Bridge (☎ 227 1118). Alternatively, contact the Tourism Police (see box, p.55).

Post office North Front St, opposite the Marine Terminal (Mon–Fri 8am–noon & 1–4pm).

Telephones There are payphones (operated using pre-paid cards) dotting the whole city. The main BTL office, 1 Church St (Mon–Fri 8am–6pm), also has fax and email services.

The cayes and atolls

Belize's spectacular **Barrier Reef**, with its dazzling variety of underwater life, string of exquisite **cayes** (pronounced "keys") and extensive opportunities for all kinds of watersports, is the country's main attraction for most first-time visitors. The longest barrier reef in the western hemisphere, it runs the entire length of the coastline, usually 15 to 40km from the mainland, with most of the cayes lying in shallow water behind the shelter of the reef. **Caye Caulker** is the most popular destination for budget travellers. The town of **San Pedro** on **Ambergris**

1

Caye, meanwhile, has transformed from a predominantly fishing community to one dominated by tourism. There are still some beautiful spots though, notably the protected sections of reef at either end of the caye: **Bacalar Chico National Park** and **Hol Chan Marine Reserve**.

Beyond the barrier reef are two of Belize's three **atolls** (the third being Glover's Reef, see p.93), the **Turneffe Atoll** and **Lighthouse Reef**, regularly visited on day-trips from San Pedro and Caye Caulker. Lighthouse Reef has two spectacular diving and snorkelling sites – Half Moon – **Half Moon Caye Natural Monument** and the **Great Blue Hole**, an enormous collapsed cave.

CAYE CAULKER

A firm favourite on the backpacker trail, **CAYE CAULKER**, 35km northeast of Belize

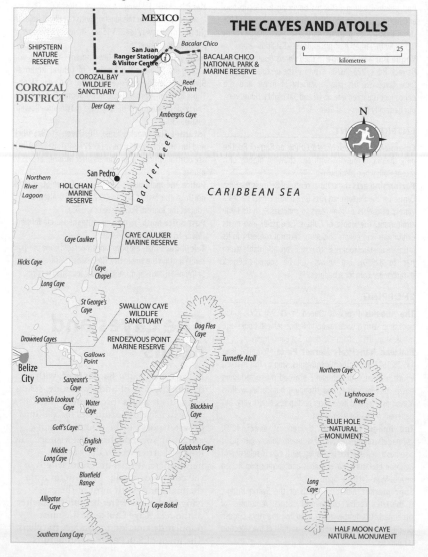

THE CAYES AND ATOLLS

MEXICO

SHIPSTERN NATURE RESERVE

San Juan Ranger Station & Visitor Centre

Bacalar Chico

BACALAR CHICO NATIONAL PARK & MARINE RESERVE

COROZAL DISTRICT

COROZAL BAY WILDLIFE SANCTUARY

Reef Point

Deer Caye

Ambergris Caye

0 — 25
kilometres

N

Northern River Lagoon

San Pedro

HOL CHAN MARINE RESERVE

Barrier Reef

CARIBBEAN SEA

Caye Caulker

CAYE CAULKER MARINE RESERVE

Hicks Caye

Caye Chapel

Long Caye

St George's Caye

SWALLOW CAYE WILDLIFE SANCTUARY

Dog Flea Caye

Drowned Cayes

Gallows Point

RENDEZVOUS POINT MARINE RESERVE

Turneffe Atoll

Northern Caye

Lighthouse Reef

Belize City

Sargeant's Caye

Spanish Lookout Caye

Water Caye

Goff's Caye

Blackbird Caye

BLUE HOLE NATURAL MONUMENT

English Caye

Middle Long Caye

Calabash Caye

Bluefield Range

Long Caye

Alligator Caye

Caye Bokel

Southern Long Caye

HALF MOON CAYE NATURAL MONUMENT

SAFEGUARDING THE CORAL REEF

Coral reefs are among the most **fragile ecosystems** on earth. Colonies grow less than 5cm a year; once damaged, the coral is far more susceptible to bacterial infection, which can quickly lead to large-scale irreversible deterioration. All licensed **tour guides** in Belize are trained in reef ecology, and should brief you on reef precautions. If exploring independently, keep the following points in mind:
• Never anchor boats on the reef – use the permanently secured buoys.
• Never touch or stand on the reef.
• Don't remove shells, sponges or other creatures, or buy reef products from souvenir shops.
• Avoid disturbing the seabed around corals – clouds of sand smother coral colonies.
• If you're a beginner or out-of-practice diver, practise away from the reef first.
• Don't use suntan lotion in reef areas – the oils remain on the water's surface; instead, wear a T-shirt to guard against sunburn.
• Don't feed or interfere with fish or marine life; this can harm not only sea creatures, but snorkellers and divers too – large fish may attack, trying to get their share.

City, is relaxed, easy-going and more than merits its "Go Slow" motto. The **reef**, 1.5km offshore, is a **marine reserve**, offering unbelievable opportunities for any imaginable watersport. Though the number of expensive places is increasing, in general the island is affordable, with an abundance of inexpensive accommodation and tour operators. Though it's hard to imagine today, up until about fifteen years ago tourism existed almost as a sideline to the island's main source of income, **lobster fishing**. The money might be coming from tourists these days but there are still plenty of the spiny creatures around, most notably at the annual **Lobster Fest**, normally held in the third weekend of June to celebrate the start of the season.

WHAT TO SEE AND DO

Caye Caulker is a little over 8km long. The settlement is at the southern end, which curves west like a hook; the northern tip, meanwhile, forms the **Caye Caulker Forest Reserve**, designated to protect the caye's littoral forest, one of the rarest habitats in Belize. Although there's a reasonable beach along the front of the caye (created by pumping sand from the back of the island), the waterfront is heavily developed, and the sea nearby is full of sea grass. If you want to go for a dip you'd do best to head for "**the Split**" at the northern end of the village – a narrow (but widening) channel cut by Hurricane Hattie in 1961; it's a popular place to relax and swim.

Snorkelling

Snorkelling the reef is an experience not to be missed; its coral canyons are home to an astonishing range of fish, including eagle rays and perhaps even the odd shark (almost certainly harmless nurse sharks). Because of the reef's fragility, visits to the marine reserves and the reef itself must be accompanied by a licensed guide (see p.65). Trips are easily arranged at the island's snorkel and dive shops – expect to pay from US$40 per person for a half-day and from US$75 for a full day. Most day-trips stop at the reef as well as **Hol Chan Marine Reserve** (see p.68) and **Shark-Ray Alley**.

Sea-kayaks (see p.65) are useful for independent snorkelling closer to the island, where some coral is visible.

Diving

Diving here is also excellent, and instruction and trips are usually cheaper than in San Pedro: open-water certification starts at US$300, two-tank dives at US$70, trips to the **Blue Hole** (see p.70) at US$280 and trips to the **Turneffe Atoll** (see p.70) at US$200. Most places in town offer enthusiastic, knowledgeable local guides, regular fast boat trips and a wide range of diving courses.

Sailing and other activities

One romantic way to enjoy the sea and the reef is to spend the day on a **sailboat**, which costs around US$60–70 per person, and usually includes several

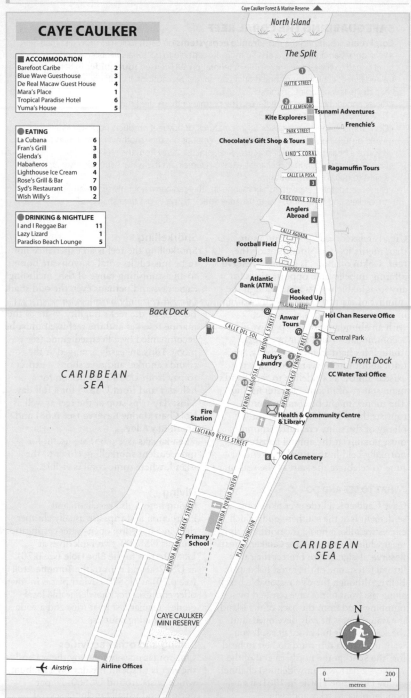

CAYE CAULKER

Caye Caulker Forest & Marine Reserve

North Island

The Split

ACCOMMODATION

Barefoot Caribe	2
Blue Wave Guesthouse	3
De Real Macaw Guest House	4
Mara's Place	1
Tropical Paradise Hotel	6
Yuma's House	5

EATING

La Cubana	6
Fran's Grill	3
Glenda's	8
Habañeros	9
Lighthouse Ice Cream	4
Rose's Grill & Bar	7
Syd's Restaurant	10
Wish Willy's	2

DRINKING & NIGHTLIFE

I and I Reggae Bar	11
Lazy Lizard	1
Paradiso Beach Lounge	5

HATTIE STREET

CALLE ALMENDRO

Tsunami Adventures

Kite Explorers

Frenchie's

PARK STREET

Chocolate's Gift Shop & Tours

LIND'S CORAL

Ragamuffin Tours

CALLE LA POSA

CROCODILE STREET

Anglers Abroad

CALLE AGUADA

Football Field

Belize Diving Services

CHAPOOSE STREET

Atlantic Bank (ATM)

Get Hooked Up

TIBEAU STREET

Back Dock

Anwar Tours

Hol Chan Reserve Office

CALLE DEL SOL

Central Park

Front Dock

Ruby's Laundry

CC Water Taxi Office

Fire Station

Health & Community Centre & Library

LUCIANO REYES STREET

Old Cemetery

AVENIDA MANGLE (BACK STREET)

AVENIDA LANGOSTA

AVENIDA HICACO (FRONT STREET)

AVENIDA PUEBLO NUEVO

PLAYA ASUNCIÓN

Primary School

CARIBBEAN SEA

CARIBBEAN SEA

CAYE CAULKER MINI RESERVE

N

Airstrip

Airline Offices

0   200
metres

snorkelling stops and lunch, arriving back
as the sun goes down.

    Kayaking is another good option for
those wishing to snorkel without a guide.
Some hotels lend kayaks to guests for
free, and a number of establishments
along Front Street rent them, including
Tsunami Adventures (see below), from
around US$50 per hour.

ARRIVAL AND INFORMATION

By plane The airstrip is about 1km (a 15min walk) south
of the town centre. Alternatively, you can take one of the
island's numerous golf carts (Bz$8–10), which usually
wait to meet flights.

By boat Boats pull into the front dock, which is in the
middle of the island's eastern edge and within easy
walking distance of all of the hotels listed below. Boats
operated by the Caye Caulker Water Taxi Association
(☎ 226 0992, Ⓦ ccwatertaxi.com) arrive and depart for
Belize City (45min; Bz$20), with 5–8 daily departures
(8am–6pm) and for San Pedro (30min; Bz$20), with
2–4 daily departures (8am–6pm). San Pedro Water
Jets Express (☎ 226 2194, Ⓦ sanpedrowatertaxi.com)
also provides several daily runs between Belize City and
San Pedro.

Tourist information There's no official tourist office, but
the town's websites (Ⓦ gocayecaulker.com and
Ⓦ cayecaulkerbelize.net) are helpful.

TOURS AND ACTIVITIES

DIVING

Belize Diving Services Back St (☎ 226 0143,
Ⓦ belizedivingservices.net).

Frenchie's Towards the northern end of the village
(☎ 226 0234, Ⓦ frenchiesdivingbelize.com).

Red Mangrove Offers educational and eco-aware small-
group tours, specializing in local sites and Turneffe. Eco
Adventures Beachfront, near village centre (☎ 226 0069,
Ⓦ mangrovebelize.com).

FISHING

Anglers Abroad Hattie St, near the Split. Fishing trips
(including overnight), from fly-fishing to deep-sea fishing
to night fishing (☎ 226 0602, Ⓦ anglersabroad.com).

Get Hooked Up Cnr Avda Langosta & Pasero St. Fishing
trips and rents gear; also rents bicycles for US$12/day
(☎ 226 0270).

SNORKELLING AND WATERSPORTS

Anwar Tours North of the front dock (☎ 226 0327,
Ⓦ anwartours.page.tl).

Raggamuffin Tours Near the north end of Front
St. Options include sunset cruises for US$25/person
(8 minimum) with rum cocktails and chips with salsa
included (☎ 226 0348, Ⓦ raggamuffintours.com).

Reef Watersports Front St. For an adrenaline rush, zip
across the Caribbean on a jet ski. You can also try flyboarding
and waterskiing (☎ 635 7219, Ⓦ reefwatersports.com).

Tsunami Adventures Near the Split (☎ 226 0462,
Ⓦ tsunamiadventures.com).

ACCOMMODATION

Caye Caulker has a range of accommodation, from simply
furnished, inexpensive rooms in brightly painted clapboard
guesthouses to mid-range B&Bs and sleek resorts with
swimming pools. Book in advance, especially at Christmas
and New Year.

Barefoot Caribe North end of Front St ☎ 226 0161,
Ⓦ barefootcaribe.com. Run by a friendly family, this
welcoming spot has comfortable rooms, either with sea or
courtyard views, with a/c and private bath. **US$40**

Blue Wave Guesthouse North end of Front St ☎ 206
0114, Ⓦ bluewaveguesthouse.com. Pleasant family-run
place just paces from the shoreline, with well-maintained
a/c rooms with showers and cable TV. Option of en-suite or
shared bathroom facilities. Shared-bath rooms **US$15**, en
suites **US$70**

De Real Macaw Guest House Front St, south of the
Split ☎ 226 0459, Ⓦ derealmacaw.biz. Cosy, good-value
rooms and thatched cabañas facing the sea. Variety of
accommodation, including beachfront rooms with fan or
a/c and cabañas with ceiling fan. Doubles **US$25**, cabañas
US$50

Mara's Place Near the Split ☎ 600 0080, ✉ maras
_place@hotmail.com. Comfortable, clean, quiet cabins
with private bath, TV and porch. There's also a communal
kitchen and private sundeck. **US$45**

★ **Tropical Paradise Hotel** At the southern end of Front
St ☎ 226 0124. A wide range of rooms, all with hot showers,
private baths and fans, and some with a/c, in a series of
brightly painted wooden buildings. The adjoining outdoor
restaurant, with views over the leafy cemetery and sea,
serves excellent local food – try the lobster omelette for
breakfast and the chicken with rice and beans. **US$50**

1

Yuma's House 75m north of Front Dock, along the beach ☎ 206 0019, ⓦ yumashousebelize.com. Dorm beds and small, shared-bath rooms in an atmospheric wooden beach house with communal kitchen. Downstairs offers plenty of chill-out hammocks and chairs in a pretty sand garden. Reservations necessary. Dorms US$14, doubles US$29

EATING

Reasonable prices and local cuisine characterize many of the island's restaurants, several of which are sprinkled along Front Street. Lobster (in season) and seafood are generally good value. Beachfront grill stands line the sand on the island's east side, where BBQ plates go for Bz$8–20, while "walking bakeries" sell home-made banana bread, coconut cakes and other goodies from carts on the street. You can also self-cater, stocking up at several shops and supermarkets. Note that the tap water is unfit to drink; rainwater and bottled water are widely available. Aim to eat in the early to mid-evening, as many places close by 9–10pm.

La Cubana Front St, across from San Pedro Express Water Taxi. Most days of the week, a pig is roasted on a skewer in front of this welcoming joint, where you can fill up on everything from roast pork sandwiches (Bz$14) and grilled shrimp (Bz$15) to the all-you-can-eat buffet (Bz$20–28), which changes daily, but may include roast pork, rice and beans, potato salad and more. Daily 6am–9pm.

Fran's Grill Just north of the Front Dock, on the beach. Look for this green-painted beach hut for excellent lobster and other fresh seafood, grilled to order, which you can enjoy at picnic tables, with your toes in the sand. Mains Bz$15–30. Hours vary, but usually daily noon–9pm.

Glenda's Back St. Busy brunch spot, known for cinnamon rolls and breakfast sandwiches (Bz$4–10). Daily breakfast and lunch.

Lighthouse Ice Cream Front St. Cool off with tasty home-made ice cream – try local flavours like soursop or coconut. Daily 9am–7pm.

Rose's Grill & Bar C del Sol at Front St. One of the best places in town to eat lobster; the good (seasonal) selection starts at Bz$30 a plate. Daily 11am–11pm.

Syd's Restaurant Middle St ☎ 206 0294. This long-established favourite has been serving Belizean comfort dishes at great prices for over thirty years. As well as its legendary fried chicken dinner (includes two side dishes;

> ### ★ TREAT YOURSELF
>
> **Habañeros** Front St ☎ 226 0487. The island's poshest restaurant: attentive staff serve up superb seafood and creative, Latin-inspired dishes (Bz$30–50), accompanied by fine wines on a romantic, open-air veranda. Reservations recommended. Closed Thurs.

Bz$9), you can fill up on lobster burritos, chicken and rice and beans, home-made tortillas and more. Mains Bz$9–16. Hours vary, but usually Mon–Sat 10am–3pm & 6–9pm.

Wish Willy's At north end of the island ☎ 660 7194, ⓦ wish-willy.com. A true Caye Caulker experience: friendly, relaxed restaurant in a ramshackle building at the back of the island, where Belizean chef Maurice Moore creates tasty seafood dishes, like whole grilled fish with coconut and lime. Mains Bz$20–40. Daily 5pm–midnight; occasionally open for breakfast or lunch.

DRINKING AND NIGHTLIFE

Many bars offer a happy hour from 3–7pm, with local spirits being the least expensive option.

I and I Reggae Bar Luciano Reyes St. A favourite among tourists and locals, with strong cocktails, a sweaty dancefloor and a breezy rooftop space to cool off. Daily 4pm–1am.

Lazy Lizard On the Split. A typical night out on the island begins with a sunset drink at the Split's *Lazy Lizard* beach bar, the main social gathering spot on the island. Daily 10am–midnight.

Paradiso Beach Lounge North of Front Dock, on the beach. They host a popular "movies under the stars" event here in the high season (Bz$10). Mon, Wed & Fri nights.

DIRECTORY

Bank Atlantic Bank, just north of the centre, has a 24hr ATM.

Internet Cayeboard Connection (daily 8am–9pm) on Front St also has a book exchange; they charge around Bz$12/hr to connect.

Laundry Drop-off services at Ruby's, C del Sol, roughly from 9am–5pm (closes for lunch).

Post office Front St.

AMBERGRIS CAYE AND SAN PEDRO

AMBERGRIS CAYE is the most northerly and, at almost 40km long, by far the largest of the cayes. The island's main attraction is the former fishing village of **SAN PEDRO**, facing the reef just a few kilometres from the caye's southern tip. Though not a large town – you're never more than a shell's throw from the sea – its population of over five thousand is the highest in all the cayes. San Pedro is the main destination for more than half of all visitors to Belize. Some of the country's most exclusive hotels and restaurants are here, though the island is also packed with mid-range and budget places, particularly in the "original"

1

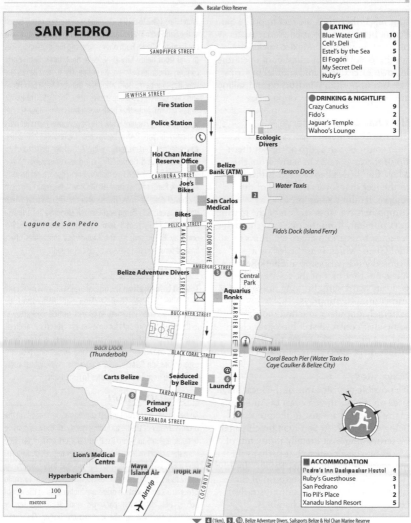

SAN PEDRO

● EATING	
Blue Water Grill	10
Celi's Deli	6
Estel's by the Sea	5
El Fogón	8
My Secret Deli	1
Ruby's	7

● DRINKING & NIGHTLIFE	
Crazy Canucks	9
Fido's	2
Jaguar's Temple	4
Wahoo's Lounge	3

■ ACCOMMODATION	
Pedro's Inn Backpacker Hostel	4
Ruby's Guesthouse	3
San Pedrano	1
Tio Pil's Place	2
Xanadu Island Resort	5

▼ 4 (1km), 5, 10, Belize Adventure Divers, Sailsports Belize & Hol Chan Marine Reserve

(pre-tourism expansion) village of San Pedro, which is also where most of the action takes place.

WHAT TO SEE AND DO

San Pedro's main streets are only half a dozen blocks long and the town does not boast any particular sights. Activity focuses on the **sea** and the **reef**, with everything from simple sunbathing to windsurfing, sailing, fishing, diving, snorkelling and glass-bottomed-boat rides on offer. **Beaches** on the caye are narrow

and the sea immediately offshore is shallow, with a lot of sea grass, so in town you'll usually need to walk to the end of a dock if you want to **swim**. Be careful, though: there have been accidents in San Pedro in which speeding boats have hit people swimming from the docks. A line of buoys indicates the "safe area", but speedboat drivers can be a bit macho, so do take care and watch where you swim.

Diving, snorkelling and watersports
The most central snorkelling and diving

1

spot on Ambergris is the **reef** opposite San Pedro, but it's heavily used. You're better off heading north, to **Mexico Rocks**, or south, to **Hol Chan**. A number of operators in town offer diving and snorkelling trips (see box opposite). **Windsurfing** and **sailing** are also popular (see box opposite).

Hol Chan Marine Reserve

The **Hol Chan Marine Reserve** (Bz$20), 8km south of San Pedro at the southern tip of the caye, takes its name from the Maya for "little channel" – it is this break in the reef that forms the focus of the reserve. Its three zones preserve a comprehensive cross-section of the marine environment, from the open sea through sea grass beds and mangroves. Tours to Hol Chan, which must be led by a licensed guide, also stop at **Shark-Ray Alley**, another part of the reserve, where you can swim with 3m-long **nurse sharks** and enormous **stingrays**. This is an extremely popular attraction, but it's also somewhat controversial: biologists claim that the practice of feeding the fish to attract them alters their natural behaviour.

Maya sites

It's possible to visit some of the local **Maya sites** on the northwest coast of Ambergris, many of which are just in the process of being excavated. At **San Juan** beach you'll be scrunching over literally thousands of pieces of Maya pottery, but perhaps the most appealing site is **Chac Balam**, slightly further north on the western tip of the island, a ceremonial and administrative centre with deep burial chambers.

ARRIVAL AND DEPARTURE

By plane The airport is just south of the city centre, within easy walking distance of any of the recommended hotels, though golf buggies and taxis also line up to give you a ride for around Bz$8–10.

By boat Boats from Belize City and/or Caye Caulker dock at the Coral Beach pier on the front (reef) side of the island at the eastern end of Black Coral St. From this central dock, you're pretty much within walking distance of most of the hotels listed below.

Destinations From Belize City, boats to Ambergris Caye are operated by the Caye Caulker Water Taxi Association (☎ 226 0992, ⓦ ccwatertaxi.com), which depart from the Marine Terminal near the Swing Bridge, and the San Pedro Express

Water Taxi (☎ 226 2194, ⓦ sanpedrowatertaxi.com), based at the San Pedro Water Taxi Terminal, on North Front St near the Tourism Village. Both offer similar trip duration and prices to and from Belize City (5–8 daily departures, 8am–6pm, confirm schedules online or via phone; 1hr 30 min; Bz$25 one way, Bz$45 return). Both also offer trips between San Pedro and Caye Caulker (2–4 departures daily; 1hr; Bz$20 one way, Bz$35 return). Note that both water taxis often have special seasonal deals; enquire when booking. Another smaller boat company is San Pedro Water Jets Express (☎ 226 2194, ⓦ sanpedrowatertaxi.com), with 2–3 daily departures to Caye Caulker and Belize City (at prices comparable to the other water taxis), and two daily morning departures (usually at 7am & 8am) to Chetumal (Bz$45 one way), returning from Chetumal daily at 3pm. There's also the *Thunderbolt*, which runs between San Pedro and Corozal, stopping at Sarteneja on request (daily 7am & 3pm; 1hr 30min; starting at Bz$45 one way, Bz$90 return). The *Thunderbolt* sometimes offers limited service in the off season, so call ahead.

INFORMATION

Tourist information The official tourist office is on Barrier Reef Drive at Black Coral St (Mon–Sat 10am–1pm). Be careful with other "information booths" dotted around town, as they are usually fronts for timeshares or resorts. Ambergris Caye has a good website (ⓦ ambergriscaye.com) with links to most of the businesses on the island. For listings, pick up a copy of *The San Pedro Sun* or *Ambergris Today*, which cover everything from new boat routes to restaurants.

ACCOMMODATION

Ambergris Caye has the highest concentration of hotels in the country. Many of these, including nearly all the inexpensive options, are in San Pedro itself, just a short walk or taxi ride from the airport or from where the water taxis dock. Resorts, which range from rustic-chic to five-star luxe, stretch for many miles along the beaches north and south of town. In general, accommodation prices are higher than in the rest of Belize, but discounts, packages and deals are readily available, especially in the low season. During Christmas, New Year and Easter, it's important to book ahead.

★ TREAT YOURSELF

Xanadu Island Resort On the beach, 1.5 miles south of town ☎ 226 2814, ⓦ xanaduislandresort.com. *Xanadu* more than lives up to its name, with lovely condominum suites, all built in environmentally friendly monolithic domes that are grouped around a palm-shaded pool, with the beach just a few lazy paces away. They also run Carts Belize (see p.70), with a top fleet of carts to rent.

TOURS AND ACTIVITIES

In addition to the specialist activities detailed below, several operators also offer inland tours to Maya ruins, manatee tours and fishing trips.

Diving For qualified divers, a two-tank local dive from Ambergris Caye costs around US$100, while more involved dive trips start at US$200. Open-water certification courses are around US$435, while a more basic, single-dive resort course costs from US$150; both include equipment. For diving trips and courses try Belize Diving Adventures (☏ 226 3082, ⓦ belizedivingadventures.net), Ecologic Divers (☏ 226 4118, ⓦ ecologicdivers.com), Seaduced by Belize (☏ 226 2254, ⓦ seaducedbybelize.com) or Amigos del Mar (☏ 226 2706, ⓦ amigosdive.com).

Snorkelling All the dive shops in San Pedro also offer snorkelling trips, costing around US$25–35 for 2–3hr and US$40–55 for 4–5hr, and many will rent snorkelling supplies; trips to the Blue Hole (see p.70) cost around US$250 and trips to the Turneffe Atoll (see p.70) US$185.

Windsurfing and sailing The best rental and instruction for both is offered by SailSports Belize (☏ 226 4488, ⓦ sailsportsbelize.com), on the beach at *Caribbean Villas*. Sailboard rentals cost US$22/hr and catamaran rentals from US$38/hr, with discounts for multiple hours. They also offer kitesurfing and sailing lessons.

Pedro's Inn Backpacker Hostel Coconut Drive, 1km south of town ☏ 226 3825, ⓦ sanpedroshotel.com. A bit of a walk from town, and the rooms are very basic (single beds, lockers and shared showers), but they're clean and among the cheapest on the island. There are two pools, a lively bar, bike rental and wi-fi, and the knowledgeable staff can organize a range of tours. Per person US$10

Ruby's Guesthouse Barrier Reef Drive, just north of the airstrip ☏ 226 2063, ⓦ ambergriscaye.com/rubys. Family-run hotel on the seafront; rooms with a/c, with private baths and on the higher floors cost more, but all are good value, especially those in the annexe on the lagoon. US$40

San Pedrano Cnr Barrier Reef Drive & Caribeña St ☏ 226 2054, ⓔ sanpedrano@btl.net. Family-run hotel in a wooden building set back slightly from the sea, with comfortable rooms with bath (some with a/c and all with TV) and breezy verandas. US$35

Tio Pil's Place On the beach near Caribeña St ☏ 206 2059, ⓦ tiopilshotel.com. Formerly Lily's, this family-owned beachfront wooden-and-concrete structure has rooms with fridge, a/c and TV; some have sea views. US$45

EATING

San Pedro features some of the best restaurants in the country, and an island highlight is, naturally, seafood, including excellent lobster and conch. Prices are generally higher than elsewhere in Belize, but you can also find plenty of local places, usually in the town centre, that offer excellent value, especially at lunchtime.

Celi's Deli Opposite the *Hotel Holiday* on Barrier Reef Drive. Home-made tortillas, Johnny cakes – a cornmeal flatbread – and meat pies make *Celi's* a local favourite, as well as cheap tacos, burritos and sarnies for Bz$2–10. Daily 5am–5pm.

Estel's by the Sea On the beach just south of the park ☏ 226 2019, ⓦ ambergriscaye.com/estels. This locally owned, laidback restaurant serves breakfast all day and Belizean food at lunch for Bz$7–30. Fri–Wed 6am–5pm.

El Fogón Off Tarpon St, just north of the airstrip ☏ 206 2121. This casual, thatched-roof restaurant is one of the few on the caye where traditional Belizean cuisine is cooked over an actual "fire hearth" (in Kriol, "fyah haat"). Try any number of local delicacies, including gibnut (a type of nocturnal rodent – much better than it sounds) and cow foot soup. Mains Bz$10–20. Mon–Sat 11.30am–3pm & 6.30–9pm.

My Secret Deli Caribeña St opposite Joe's Bikes ☏ 226 3223. The best budget restaurant and busiest lunchtime spot on Ambergris, serving large plates of Belizean food for Bz$5–12; the conch soup is a local speciality. Mon–Sat 7am–3pm & 6–9pm, Sun 11.30am–3pm.

Ruby's Barrier Reef Drive, next to *Ruby's Guesthouse*. Delicious home-made cakes, pies and sandwiches, and freshly brewed coffee. Popular with locals. Daily 5am–5pm.

DRINKING AND NIGHTLIFE

San Pedro, with a lively tourist/expat crowd, is the tourist entertainment capital of Belize, and if you check locally, you'll find live music on somewhere every night of the week. Most of the hotels have bars, several of which offer happy hours.

Crazy Canucks South of town, at *Exotic Caye Beach Resort* ☏ 206 2031, ⓦ belizeisfun.com. One of the more popular bars on the island, with potent tropical cocktails like the Dirty Howler Monkey, made with Kahlua, dark rum and banana. Come by on "Sunday Funday", with jam sessions starting at 3pm. Daily 11am–midnight.

Fido's Barrier Reef Drive. An American comfort food restaurant by day, by night *Fido's* becomes one of the most popular evening spots in San Pedro, frequently hosting live bands and karaoke nights till midnight.

1

★ **TREAT YOURSELF**

Blue Water Grill At the *Sunbreeze Hotel*
☎ 226 3347, ⓦ bluewatergrillbelize.com.
Wonderfully imaginative dishes match the
breezy setting, on a low-key stretch of
beach. While rooted in Belize, the menu
spans the world, and includes spiced
calamari with pickled ginger (Bz$21), grilled
lobster tail with cilantro-whipped mashed
potatoes (Bz$55) and seared snapper with
jalapeño chicken sausage (Bz$52). Plus,
there's a quality wine list. Daily 7–10.30am,
11.30am–2.30pm & 6–9.30pm.

Jaguar's Temple Barrier Reef Drive, opposite the park. This large, colourfully painted club has a heaving dancefloor and is open late. Thurs–Sat 9pm–4am.
Wahoo's Lounge At the *Spindrift Hotel* ☎ 226 2002. Formerly Pier Lounge, this relaxed bar gets packed every Wednesday evening (6pm) for the caye's famous "chicken drop". It also hosts lively karaoke on Sunday nights. Daily noon–midnight (or until last person leaves).

DIRECTORY

Banks Belize Bank near Central Park on Barrier Reef Drive has an ATM, and the other banks will give cash advances, but US dollars are accepted – even preferred – everywhere.
Bicycles Joe's Bikes, on Caribeña St, rents bikes for Bz$5/hr or Bz$20/day.
Golf carts ☎ 226 4084, ⓦ cartsbelize.com. Rent carts from various locations, including one block north of the airstrip and at *Xanadu Island Resort* (see box, p.68).
Books Aquarius Books on Pescador Drive has a selection of used paperbacks, mainly thrillers and romantic novels, for less than Bz$5 (Mon–Sat 9am–4pm).
Internet Caribbean Connection, on Barrier Reef Drive, offers access for Bz$10/hr (daily 7am–10pm).
Laundry Nellie's Laundromat, Pescador Drive, charges about $6 a load (Mon–Sat 7am–9pm, Sun 8am–2pm).
Post office Pescador Drive.

TURNEFFE ATOLL

Although Caye Caulker and San Pedro are the only villages on the reef, there are a couple of dozen other inhabited islands, as well as some excellent diving spots. The virtually uninhabited **TURNEFFE ATOLL**, 40km from Belize City and south of cayes Caulker and Ambergris, comprises an oval archipelago of low-lying mangrove islands around a shallow lagoon 60km long. These are enclosed by a beautiful coral reef, which offers some of the best **diving** and snorkelling in Belize. The island boasts several resorts, all of which are out of the reach of the typical budget traveller, but you can still visit this incredible spot on a day-trip from San Pedro (see p.66) and Caye Caulker (see p.62).

LIGHTHOUSE REEF

About 80km east of Belize City is Belize's outermost atoll, **LIGHTHOUSE REEF**, home to the popular underwater attractions of the **Blue Hole** and **Half Moon Caye Natural Monument**.

The Blue Hole

The **Blue Hole**, technically a karst-eroded sinkhole, is more than 300m in diameter and 135m deep, dropping through the bottom of the lagoon and opening out into a complex network of caves and crevices; its depth gives it an astonishing deep-blue colour that is, unfortunately, best appreciated from the air. Though visibility is generally limited, many divers still find the trip worthwhile for the drop-offs and underwater caves, which include stalactites and stalagmites. Unfortunately for budget travellers, trips to the Blue Hole – which must be led by a licensed guide or company – usually cost at least US$200.

Half Moon Caye Natural Monument

The **Half Moon Caye Natural Monument**, the first marine conservation area in Belize, was declared a national park in 1982 and became one of Belize's first World Heritage Sites in 1996. The 180,000-square-metre caye is divided into two distinct ecosystems. In the west, guano from sea birds fertilizes the soil, enabling the growth of dense vegetation, while the eastern half has mostly coconut palms. A total of 98 bird species has been recorded here, including frigate birds, ospreys and a resident population of four thousand red-footed boobies, one of only two such nesting colonies in the Caribbean. Upon arrival (most people come as part of a tour), visitors must pay the Bz$20 entrance fee at the visitors' centre.

The north

The level expanses of northern Belize are a mixture of farmland and rainforest, dotted with swamps, savanna and lagoons. Most visitors come to the region for its **Maya ruins** and **wildlife reserves**. The largest Maya site, **Lamanai**, served by regular boat tours along the New River Lagoon, features some of the most impressive pyramids and beautiful scenery in the country. The site of **Altun Ha**, meanwhile, is usually visited on a day-trip from Belize City. The northern reserves also host an astonishingly diverse array of wildlife. At the **Community Baboon Sanctuary**, a group of farmers have combined agriculture with conservation to the benefit of the black howler monkey, and at the stunning **Crooked Tree Wildlife Sanctuary**, rivers and lagoons offer protection to a range of migratory birds.

Many of the original residents in this region were refugees from the nineteenth-century Caste Wars in Yucatan, and some of the northernmost towns are mainly **Spanish-speaking**. The largest settlement today is **Orange Walk**, the country's main centre for sugar production. Further north, near the border with Mexico, **Corozal** is a small Caribbean town, strongly influenced by Maya and mestizo culture.

COMMUNITY BABOON SANCTUARY

A 45-minute drive north of Belize City, the **COMMUNITY BABOON SANCTUARY** (ⓦhowlermonkeys.org), to the west off the Philip Goldson (Northern) Highway, is one of the most interesting conservation projects in Belize. It was established in 1985 by Dr Rob Horwich and a group of local farmers (with help from the World Wide Fund for Nature), who developed a code of conduct of sustainable living and farming practices. A mixture of farmland and broad-leaved forest along the banks of the Belize River, the sanctuary coordinates seven villages, of which **Bermudian Landing** is the most conveniently accessed, and more than a hundred landowners, in a project of conservation, education and tourism.

The main focus of attention is the **black howler monkey** (known locally as a "baboon"). These primates generally live in groups of between four and eight, and spend the day wandering through the canopy, feasting on leaves, flowers and fruits. At dawn and dusk they let rip with their famous howl: a deep and rasping roar that carries for many kilometres. The sanctuary is also home to more than two hundred bird species, as well as iguanas, peccaries and coatis. You can find exhibits and information on the riverside habitats and animals you are likely to see in the tiny **natural history museum** at the visitors' centre in Bermudian Landing.

ARRIVAL AND INFORMATION

By bus Four to five daily buses connect Belize City (Mon–Sat; 1hr 15min; from Bz$4) and the village of Bermudian Landing. The central stop is at the sanctuary's visitors' centre.

Tourist information The reserve's visitors' centre (daily 8am–5pm; ☏ 220 2181) is at the west end of Bermudian Landing. The Bz$14 entrance fee includes a guided nature walk and a tour of the small museum. The reserve also organizes a range of inexpensive activities including horseriding, canoeing and night hikes.

ACCOMMODATION AND EATING

There are limited accommodation and food options in the area; the easiest way to visit is via a tour company (like the excellent S & L Travel; see p.59) from Belize City.
Camping If you have your own tent, you can camp at the visitors' centre. Per person U̲S̲$̲5̲

★TREAT YOURSELF

Black Orchid Resort 2 Dawson Lane, Burrell Boom ☏ 225 9158, ⓦblackorchid resort.com. This lovely resort maximizes its perch on the river, with leafy grounds that gently roll down to the water. The restaurant and patio bar have riverfront views, and serve a menu of excellent Belizean specialities. A kidney-shaped pool presides over the centre of the resort and a rooftop jacuzzi and spa invites soaking and pampering. Spacious rooms are outfitted in native hardwoods and have well-appointed bathrooms. Transfer to and from the airport is included. U̲S̲$̲1̲2̲5̲

1

Homestays Ask at the visitors' centre, or email centre staff (✉ cbsbelize@gmail.com) about homestays with local families. Rates include three meals a day. Per person from US$40

ALTUN HA

Some 55km north of Belize City and just 9km from the sea, the remarkable Maya site of **ALTUN HA** (daily 8am–5pm; Bz$10) was occupied for twelve hundred years until it was abandoned around 900 AD. Its position near the Caribbean suggests that it was sustained as much by trade as by agriculture – a theory upheld by the discovery here of obsidian and jade, neither of which occurs naturally in Belize.

Altun Ha clusters around two Classic-period plazas. Entering from the road, you come first to **Plaza A**, enclosed by large temples on all sides. A magnificent tomb was discovered beneath Temple A-1, the **Temple of the Green Tomb**. Dating from 550 AD, this yielded jades, jewellery, stingray spines, skin, flints and the remains of a Maya book. The adjacent **Plaza B** is dominated by the site's largest temple, the **Temple of the Masonry Altars**. Several tombs have been uncovered within the main structure; in one, archeologists discovered a carved jade head of Kinich Ahau, the Maya sun god. Just under 15cm high, it is the largest carved jade found in the Maya world; a replica is on display in the Museum of Belize (see p.55).

ARRIVAL AND INFORMATION

By bus Altun Ha is difficult to reach independently. In theory there are buses from the Belize City terminal to the village of Maskall, passing the turn-off to the site at the village of Lucky Strike, but service is erratic.

Tours Travel agents such as Experience Belize (ⓦ experiencebelizetours.com) and S & L Travel (see p.59) can arrange the trip (from US$45/person), and tourists also visit on day-trips from San Pedro and Caye Caulker (from US$95/person).

CROOKED TREE WILDLIFE SANCTUARY

Midway between Belize City and Orange Walk, a branch road heads west to **CROOKED TREE WILDLIFE SANCTUARY** (daily 8am–4.30pm; Bz$8), a reserve that encompasses swamps, wetlands and four separate lagoons. Designated Belize's first Ramsar site (to protect wetlands of international importance), the sanctuary provides a resting place for thousands of migrating and resident birds, such as snail kites, tiger herons, snowy egrets, ospreys and black-collared hawks. The reserve's most famous visitor is the **jabiru stork**, the largest flying bird in Latin America, with a wingspan of 2.5m. The **best months** for birdwatching are late February to June, when the lagoons shrink to a string of pools, forcing wildlife to congregate for food and water.

In the middle of the reserve, straggling around the shores of a lagoon, is the village of **Crooked Tree**, which is linked to the mainland by a **causeway**. One of the oldest inland villages in the country, Crooked Tree is also one of Belize's loveliest, with well-kept houses and lawns dotted along tree-lined lanes. Though guided tours to the lagoon are quite expensive (at least US$50–80), numerous trails, signposted from the roads, wind around the island and along the shoreline, where you'll see plenty of birds and wildlife even without a guide.

ARRIVAL AND INFORMATION

By bus Buses from Belize City (Mon–Fri 3 daily, 1 on Sat; 1hr 30min; from Bz$4) make a loop around the village of Crooked Tree before heading to the causeway. Alternatively, frequent buses run between Belize City and Orange Walk from the junction with the Philip Goldson (Northern) Highway.

Tourist information The wildlife sanctuary visitors' centre (8am–4.30pm) is at the end of the causeway in Crooked Tree. Pay the reserve's Bz$8 entrance fee here.

ACCOMMODATION AND EATING

Most of the accommodation in Crooked Tree is in mid-priced hotels, though some of these also have camping space.

Crooked Tree Lodge Crooked Tree Village ☎ 626 3820, ⓦ crookedtreelodgebelize.com. Gaze out at the lagoon from your comfortable cabaña at this relaxed lodge. They also offer camping on their eleven-acre property, and can arrange top-notch birding tours. Enjoy homecooked meals on the breezy deck. Camping/tent US$10, cabañas US$75

Tillet's Village Lodge In the centre of the village along the bus route ☎ 245 7016, ⓦ tilletvillage.com. Good-value hotel set amid lovely gardens. Rustic cabins have private baths, hot water and fans; comfortable rooms – with fan

Bird's Eye View Lodge On the lakeshore, clearly signposted through the village ☎ 225 7027, ⓦ birdseyeviewbelize.com. Worth the splurge for its idyllic, isolated location right on the lagoon. Comfortable rooms, some with balconies, have private baths and a/c, or you can pitch a tent in the grounds. The restaurant serves good meals around the clock. Safari tours of the sanctuary, as well as trips to nearby Maya sites, can be arranged. Camping/person **US$10**, doubles **US$80**

or a/c – share a balcony. There's a small shop, a restaurant serving three daily meals, and tours can be arranged. Doubles **US$35**, cabins **US$50**

ORANGE WALK

Like many of Belize's northern cities, **ORANGE WALK**, the largest town in the region, was founded by mestizo refugees fleeing the Caste Wars in the Yucatán. Long before their arrival, however, the area around Orange Walk had been worked as some of the most productive arable farmland in Belize – aerial surveys have revealed evidence of raised fields and a network of irrigation canals dating from ancient Maya times. Today, Orange Walk is a thriving community by Belizean standards, and though there aren't any sights in town as such, it's a pleasant, low-key base for those looking to explore one of the region's highlights: the nearby ruins at Lamanai.

WHAT TO SEE AND DO

At the centre of town, on the distinctly Mexican-style formal plaza, the town hall is referred to as the Palacio Municipal, reinforcing the town's strong historical links to Mexico. The only formal attraction is the **Banquitas House of Culture** (Mon–Fri 8.30am–5pm; free; ☎ 322 0517, ⓦ nichbelize.org), on the riverbank near the bridge, which houses a permanent exhibition charting the history of Orange Walk District from Maya times to the present, as well as travelling exhibitions from NICH (the National Institute of Culture and History).

ARRIVAL AND TOURS

By bus Hourly buses from Belize City and Corozal pull up on the main road in the centre of town, officially Queen Victoria Ave but always referred to as the Belize–Corozal Rd. Services to and from Sarteneja stop opposite *St Christopher's Hotel* on Main St. Local buses to the surrounding villages leave from the market area, behind the town hall and fire station.

Destinations Belize City (hourly; 1hr 30min); Chetumal (hourly; 2hr); Corozal (hourly; 1hr); Sarteneja (3 daily Mon–Sat; 2hr).

Tour operators The easiest (and most interesting) way to visit Lamanai is via the river. Numerous operators in Orange Walk organize day-trips starting from Bz$150/person, departing around 9am; the price will usually include a picnic lunch at the site. Note that nearly all hotels have an arrangement with various tour companies, so you can book trips directly at the hotel. Among the tour companies are Lamanai Eco Adventures (☎ 610 2020, ⓦ lamanaiecoadventures.com), Errol Cadle's Lamanai Eco Tours (☎ 610 1753, ✉ errolcadle1@yahoo.com) and Jungle River Tours (☎ 302 2293; call to confirm, as tours may be intermittent). Also, numerous tour companies offer Lamanai trips from elsewhere in Belize, among them Seaduced by Belize (see p.69) in San Pedro and Dave's Eco Tours (☎ 205 5597, ⓦ davesecotours.com) in Belize City.

ACCOMMODATION

★**Hotel de la Fuente** 14 Main St ☎ 322 2290, ⓦ hoteldelafuente.com. Bright rooms in this great-value hotel include private baths, mini-fridges, coffee-makers, wi-fi and a/c. All local tours can be arranged with the front desk. **US$35**

Lamanai Riverside Retreat Lamanai Alley, on the bank of the New River ☎ 302 3955. Some camping space, and basic riverside cabins, with private bath, sleeping up to four. There's an excellent restaurant, too (see beow). Camping/tent **US$10**, cabins **US$40**

St Christopher's Hotel 10 Main St ☎ 302 1064. Very clean, attractive rooms with TVs, private baths, wi-fi and balconies overlooking a riverside garden. Laundry services and tour bookings are also available. **US$35**

EATING

Orange Walk has a variety of restaurants offering Creole, Mexican-influenced and Chinese food. The street near the market, behind the town hall, has a line of cafés and vendors offering cheap eats for Bz$2–8.

Lamanai Riverside Retreat Lamanai Alley, on the bank of the New River ☎ 302 3955. Enjoy breakfast, dinner or just a beer on an outdoor patio right on the riverbank where you might just spot one of the local river crocodiles. The restaurant offers a wide variety of Mexican-influenced and traditional Creole dishes as well as burgers and fries

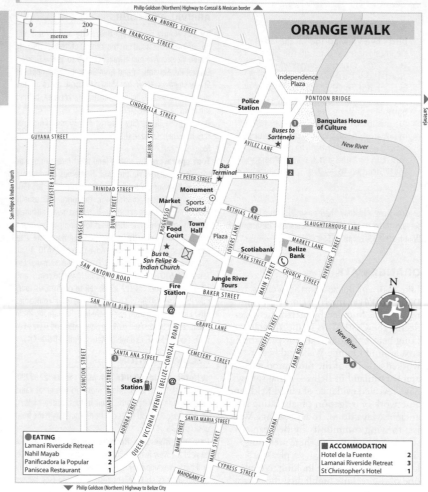

ORANGE WALK

EATING
Lamani Riverside Retreat	4
Nahil Mayab	3
Panificadora la Popular	2
Paniscea Restaurant	1

ACCOMMODATION
Hotel de la Fuente	2
Lamanai Riverside Retreat	3
St Christopher's Hotel	1

for Bz$10–25. One of the few places in town open on Sun. Daily 7.30am–10pm.

★**Nahil Mayab** Guadelupe St & Santa Ana St ☎322 0831. "Maya-inspired" plates and American food for Bz$10–30; brave the insects on the pretty garden patio if the a/c is too cool to handle. Mon 10am–3pm, Tues–Thurs 10am–11pm, Fri & Sat 10am–11.30pm.

Panificadora la Popular Bethias Lane. An excellent bakery that's been around for decades, serving fresh bread and cakes (Bz$2–10). Daily 6.30am–7pm.

Paniscea Restaurant Main St, at Las Banquitas House of Culture ☎623 7200. Take in riverside views at this outdoor restaurant with an international menu, including smoked pork chops, seafood and a good array of vegetarian dishes. Mains Bz$10–20. 11am–midnight; closed Tues.

DIRECTORY

Internet Access is cheap and plentiful; K & N Printshop, on the Belize–Corozal Rd two blocks south of the post office, is open daily (7am–noon & 2–5.30pm) and charges Bz$4/hr.
Post office Right in the centre of town, on Queen Victoria Ave.

LAMANAI

Extensive restoration, a spacious museum and a stunning jungle setting make **LAMANAI** (daily 8am–5pm; Bz$20) the most impressive Maya site in northern Belize. It is also one of the few sites whose original Maya name – *Lama'an ayin*

("Submerged Crocodile") – is known, which also explains the numerous representations of crocodiles on stucco carvings and artefacts found here. *Lamanai*, however, is a seventeenth-century mis-transliteration, which actually means "Drowned Insect". The site was continually occupied from around 1500 BC up until the sixteenth century, when Spanish missionaries built a church alongside to lure the Indians from their "heathen" ways.

Today the site is perched on a bank of the New River Lagoon inside a 950-acre archeological reserve, where the jungle surroundings give the site a feeling of tranquillity. Before heading to the ruins, visit the spacious new **archeological museum**, which houses an impressive collection of artefacts, eccentric flints and original steles. Within the site itself, the most remarkable structure is the N10-43 (informally the "High Temple"), a massive **Late Preclassic temple** that is more than 37m tall and the largest from the period in the Maya region. The view across the surrounding forest and along the lagoon from the top of the temple is magnificent, and well worth the daunting climb.

ARRIVAL AND TOURS

By river tour The easiest, most pleasant way to get to Lamanai is by river, and the cheapest and most informative way to do this is as part of an organized tour. Various operators in Orange Walk (see p.73) offer day-trips departing around 9am; the price (US$40–50) will usually include lunch.

SARTENEJA AND SHIPSTERN NATURE RESERVE

Across Chetumal Bay from Corozal, the largely uninhabited **Sarteneja peninsula** is covered with dense forests and swamps that support an amazing array of wildlife. **SARTENEJA**, the peninsula's only settlement, is a peaceful, Spanish-speaking, lobster-fishing community.

All buses to Sarteneja pass the entrance to **SHIPSTERN NATURE RESERVE** (daily 8am–5pm, but call ahead to confirm; from Bz$10; wcsfi.bz), 5km before the village, though you can also get here by

renting a bike from *Fernando's* or *Backpackers Paradise* in Sarteneja (see below). The reserve encompasses an area of eighty square kilometres, including large areas of tropical moist forest, some wide belts of savanna, and most of the shallow Shipstern Lagoon, dotted with mangrove islands. The **visitors' centre** offers a variety of guided walks, though even if you choose the shortest, you'll encounter more named plant species here than on any other trail in Belize. Shipstern is also a birdwatcher's paradise: the lagoon system supports blue-winged teal, American coot and huge flocks of lesser scaup, while the forest is home to keel-billed toucans and at least five species of parrot. Other wildlife in the reserve includes crocodiles, jaguars, peccaries and an abundance of wonderful butterflies.

ARRIVAL AND TOURS

By boat The *Thunderbolt* skiff runs (☎ 422 0226 or ☎ 601 4475) between Corozal and Ambergris Caye and will call at Sarteneja if there's sufficient demand, pulling into the main dock on North Front St.

By bus Buses from Belize City travel regularly to Sarteneja via Orange Walk (see p.73). The buses drop off in the centre of town.

Destinations Belize City (several daily Mon–Sat 4–6.30am, 1 on Sun 6am; 3hr 30min); Chetumal (daily, usually 6am; 3hr 30min). All buses to and from Sarteneja pass through Orange Walk.

Tour operators All the accommodation options can arrange local trips and tours.

ACCOMMODATION AND EATING

Backpackers Paradise La Bandera Rd ☎ 423 2016, w backpackers.bluegreenbelize.com. Cheap cabañas and camping just a 5min drive out of town; ask the bus driver to drop you off at the Sarteneja Monument, or arrange a pier pick-up in advance. Bike rental (Bz$10/day), horseriding tours (Bz$18/hr) and free wi-fi are also available. Owner/Chef Nathalie's excellent on-site restaurant serves local, vegetarian and French dishes throughout the day for Bz$8–20. Camping/tent U̲S̲$̲4̲, cabañas from U̲S̲$̲1̲4̲

Fernando's Guesthouse North Front St, 100m along the shoreline from the main dock ☎ 423 2085, w fernandosseaside.com. Large, tiled rooms, with fan or a/c and private baths, share a veranda overlooking the sea. Snorkelling and nature tours can be arranged, and bike rentals are available. U̲S̲$̲4̲5̲

1

COROZAL

COROZAL, near the mouth of the New River, is Belize's most northerly town, just twenty minutes from the Mexican border. The **ancient Maya** prospered here by controlling river- and seaborne trade, and the impressive site of **Cerros** is nearby, if complicated to reach. Present-day Corozal was founded in 1849 by refugees from Mexico's Caste Wars, although today's grid-pattern town, a neat mix of Mexican and Caribbean, is largely a result of reconstruction in the wake of Hurricane Janet in 1955.

WHAT TO SEE AND DO

Though Corozal has few big sights, it's a relaxing spot to spend a day or two and perhaps use as a base for day-trips throughout northern Belize. The breezy shoreline **park** is good for a stroll, while on the tree-shaded main plaza, the **town hall** is worth a look inside for a mural by Manuel Villamar Reyes, which vividly describes local history. The **Corozal House of Culture** (Mon–Fri 8am–5pm; free), a historical waterfront building, has a small museum and gallery space. In the block west of the plaza you can see the remains of **Fort Barlee**, built to ward off Maya attacks in the 1870s.

Santa Rita

The small Maya site of **Santa Rita** (daily 24hr; free) is within walking distance of the centre, about fifteen minutes northwest of town; follow the main road towards the border, bear right at the fork and turn left at the Super Santa Rita store. Though it is an interesting enough spot if

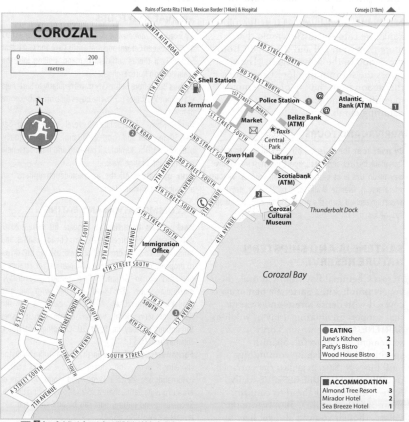

▲ Ruins of Santa Rita (1km), Mexican Border (14km) & Hospital   Consejo (11km) ▲

COROZAL

0 _____ 200
metres

N

SANTA RITA ROAD
11TH AVENUE
10TH AVENUE
3RD STREET NORTH
2ND STREET NORTH
1ST STREET NORTH

Shell Station
Bus Terminal
1ST STREET
Police Station
@
Atlantic Bank (ATM)
1ST STREET NORTH

COTTAGE ROAD

Market
Belize Bank (ATM)
★ *Taxis*
Central Park

2ND STREET SOUTH
Town Hall
Library
7TH AVENUE
3RD STREET SOUTH
4TH STREET SOUTH
5TH AVENUE
Scotiabank (ATM)
1ST AVENUE

5TH STREET SOUTH
5TH AVENUE
2
Corozal Cultural Museum
Thunderbolt Dock

G STREET SOUTH
9TH AVENUE
7TH AVENUE
Immigration Office
6TH STREET SOUTH
4TH AVENUE

Corozal Bay

9TH STREET SOUTH
G STREET SOUTH
C STREET SOUTH
B STREET SOUTH
5TH AVENUE
7TH ST SOUTH
3
1ST AVENUE
8TH ST SOUTH

SOUTH STREET
A STREET SOUTH
7TH AVENUE

● **EATING**
June's Kitchen 2
Patty's Bistro 1
Wood House Bistro ... 3

■ **ACCOMMODATION**
Almond Tree Resort ... 3
Mirador Hotel 2
Sea Breeze Hotel 1

▼ 3 , Copper Bank, Airstrip, Sarteneja, Orange Walk (48km) & Belize City (135km)

INTO MEXICO: SANTA ELENA

It's less than 4hr by bus along the Philip Goldson (Northern) Highway from Belize City to **Chetumal**, Mexico, via the border crossing at **Santa Elena**.

Entering Belize, you'll find Mexican immigration and customs posts on the northern bank of the Río Hondo, 12km from Chetumal; when you're finished there, the bus will pick you up again to take you to Belizean immigration.

When you **leave Belize** via a land border, you'll have to pay an exit tax of Bz$37.50, payable in Belize or US dollars. Upon entering Mexico, you'll get a maximum of thirty days in the country by filling out the Belize immigration form. **Moneychangers** wait on the Belize side of the border; make sure to get rid of your Belize dollars before crossing into Mexico.

you have time to kill, the site is no longer maintained and does not justify extending your stay in Corozal. Founded around 1500 BC, Santa Rita was in all probability the powerful Maya city later known as Chactemal. The main remaining building is a small pyramid, and excavations here have uncovered the burial sites of an elaborately bejewelled elderly woman and a Classic-period warlord.

ARRIVAL AND INFORMATION

By plane Both Tropic Air and Maya Island Air operate daily flights between Corozal and San Pedro (25 min). El Ranchito Airport is a few miles south of town; taxis generally meet all flights, and charge Bz$8–10 for a trip to the centre.

By boat The *Thunderbolt* skiff (☎422 0226 or ☎601 4475, Bz$45; erratic low-season service; 2hr) arriving from San Pedro pulls into the main dock on 1st Ave, just two blocks southeast of the town centre.

By bus The Northern Transport depot is near the northern edge of town, opposite the Shell station. In addition to local services between Belize City and Corozal, express buses pass through Corozal en route to Chetumal, Mexico, roughly hourly in each direction. Buses for surrounding villages (including Copper Bank) leave from the market area.

Destinations Belize City (hourly 4am–6pm; 2hr 30min); Chetumal (hourly 6am–9pm; 1hr); Orange Walk (hourly; 1hr).

INFORMATION AND TOURS

Tour operators All hotels have information on local tours or offer trips themselves. The reliable Belize Transfer and Tours (☎422 2725, ⊚belizetransfers.com) has a variety of tours to Maya sites in the area, cave tubing and more.

Tourist information Corozal has no tourist office, but the city's website (⊚corozal.com) is useful.

ACCOMMODATION

Almond Tree Resort 425 Bayshore Drive ☎628 9224, ⊚almondtreeresort.com. Airy waterfront resort with bright, elegant rooms and leafy, landscaped grounds with

a pool. Plus, they serve fresh, home-made seafood meals, like tangy shrimp *ceviche*. **US$45**

Mirador Hotel 4th Ave at 2nd St South, near the seafront ☎422 0189, ⊚mirador.bz. Large, well-maintained hotel with rooftop views both across the bay and over Corozal, best enjoyed from the hammocks. Rooms (of varying sizes) come equipped with cable TV, and some have a/c and bay views. **US$35**

Sea Breeze Hotel 23 1st Ave ☎422 3051, ⊚theseabreezehotel.com. One of the best budget choices in Belize, with friendly staff, a low key bar, clean, secure accommodation and free use of bicycles. Rooms include private baths, fans and cable TV; some have a/c. Guests can charter the owner's speedboat for trips to Cerros (see below) for US$30/person. **US$25**

EATING

June's Kitchen 3rd St South ☎422 2559. Feast on a range of local dishes, from rice and beans with roast pork to conch soup (from Bz$10) served by Miss June herself. Breakfast is also tops, with fat omelettes, hash browns (Bz$10) and fresh orange juice. Open breakfast and lunch.

Patty's Bistro 7 2nd St North ☎402 0174. Good Belizean, Mexican and American food – from cheeseburgers to fish soups – for Bz$7–25. Daily noon–9.30pm.

Wood House Bistro 1st St. One of the best Asian restaurants in Belize, with an extensive Chinese-oriented menu (Bz$8–20), funky decor and open-air seating with pleasant ocean views. Mon & Wed–Sun 11am–10pm.

DIRECTORY

Bank Belize Bank (with 24hr ATM), on the north side of the plaza.

Immigration The office is on 5th Ave.

Internet Easy to find; look for signs along 4th and 5th aves (from Bz$4/hr).

Post office On the west side of the plaza.

CERROS

Built in a strategic position at the mouth of the New River, the late Preclassic

1

centre of **CERROS** (daily 8am–5pm; Bz$20) was one of the first places in the Maya world to adopt the rule of kings. Despite this initial success, however, Cerros was abandoned by the Classic period. The ruins of the site now include three large acropolis structures, ball courts and plazas flanked by pyramids. The largest building is a 22m-high temple, whose intricate stucco masks represent the rising and setting sun.

Mosquitoes around the Cerros site are particularly pesky – prepare accordingly.

ARRIVAL AND DEPARTURE

By boat The most comfortable and reliable way to reach the ruins is by boat. Hotels in Corozal can advise on charters, which operate either with a guided tour (from US$75/person) or without (from US$30/person).

ACCOMMODATION AND EATING

Cerros Beach Resort ☏ 623 9763, ⓦ cerrosbeachresort .com. If you want to stay in the atmospheric surroundings of the ruins for a night or two, try these charming cabañas with private bath, TV and wi-fi. There's also a bar/ restaurant serving local and international cuisine at Bz$8– 25 to guests and day-trippers. US$60

The west

Heading west from Belize City towards the Guatemalan border, you'll traverse varied landscapes, from open grassland to dense tropical forest. A fast, paved road, the **George Price Highway** – still often referred to as the **Western Highway** – runs the entire way, leading from the heat and humidity of the coast to the cooler, lush foothills of the Maya Mountains.

Before reaching Belize's tiny capital, **Belmopan**, the road passes the excellent **Belize Zoo**. West of Belmopan, it follows the Belize River valley, skirting the **Maya Mountains**, into **Cayo District**, the largest and arguably the most beautiful of Belize's six districts. South of the highway, the **Mountain Pine Ridge** is a pleasantly cool region of hills and pine woods. **San Ignacio**, on the Macal River, makes an ideal base for exploring the forests, rivers and ruins of western Belize, including **Caracol**, the country's largest

Maya site, and several dramatic **caves** that hold Maya artefacts.

BELIZE ZOO

The **BELIZE ZOO**, at Mile 29 on the George Price (Western) Highway (daily 8.30am–5pm; Bz$30; ☏ 822 8000, ⓦ belizezoo.org), is easily visited on a half-day trip from Belize City or as a stop on the way west. Long recognized as a phenomenal conservation achievement, the zoo opened in 1983. Organized around the theme of "a walk through Belize", the zoo offers the chance to see the country's native animals at close quarters. Residents include tapirs, a wide variety of birds – including a harpy eagle – and all the Belizean cats. These animals, many of which have been rescued and cannot be released into the wild, enjoy spacious and natural enclosures – the most authentic slice of natural habitat that such animals are ever likely to occupy.

ARRIVAL AND DEPARTURE

By bus Take any bus between Belize City and Belmopan and ask the driver to drop you at the signed turn-off, a 200m walk from the entrance; you can leave your luggage at the visitors' centre.

ACCOMMODATION

Belize Zoo Jungle Lodge Across the highway from the zoo, 300m back towards Belize City ☏ 832 2004, ⓦ belizezoo .org. If you'd like to stay overnight in the area, try this well-appointed facility with wooden dorms (shared bath and hot showers) set on 84 acres of pine savanna. Also on offer are pricier private cabins. Guests can take a night-time tour of the zoo for Bz$30pp. Dorms US$35, cabins US$70

GUANACASTE NATIONAL PARK

Just off the highway at the turn-off towards Belmopan, tiny **GUANACASTE NATIONAL PARK** (daily 8am–4.30pm; Bz$5; ⓦ belizeaudubon.org) is a 52-acre area of beautiful tropical forest. While not a must-see attraction for anyone planning to spend time in Belize's other forested areas, it provides an excellent introduction to the country's flora and fauna and is exceptionally accessible. Several short loop trails leave from the visitors' centre, winding through the forest and passing the Belize and Roaring rivers; there's even a spot for swimming.

BELMOPAN

At Guanacaste, the Hummingbird Highway (see p.87) splits from the George Price (Western) Highway and heads south. Immediately south of the junction, the national capital, **BELMOPAN**, was founded in 1970, after Hurricane Hattie swept much of Belize City into the sea. The government decided both to seize the opportunity to move to higher ground and to focus development on the interior, and chose a site at the geographical heart of the country. Its name combines "Belize" with "Mopan", the language spoken by the Maya of Cayo, while the layout of the main government buildings, grouped around a central plaza, is modelled loosely on a Maya city.

Belmopan was intended to symbolize a new era, with tree-lined avenues, banks, embassies and communications worthy of a world centre. Few Belizeans other than government officials (who had no option) have moved here, however, so the population stands at around twelve thousand, and Belmopan remains one of the smallest capital cities in the world. There's little reason to stay any longer than it takes your bus to leave.

ARRIVAL AND DEPARTURE

By bus All buses from Belize City to San Ignacio, Benque Viejo, Dangriga and Punta Gorda stop in Belmopan, so there's at least one service in either direction every hour. The terminal is in the town centre, where Constitution Drive meets Bliss Parade, within walking distance of most hotels. Destinations Belize City (at least hourly, 6.30am–9.30pm; 1hr 15min); Benque Viejo del Carmen, for the Guatemalan border (at least hourly, 5.30am–11pm; 1hr 30min); Dangriga (hourly, 6.15am–7.30pm; 1hr 45min); Independence, for Placencia (hourly, 6.15am–5pm; 2hr 45min); Punta Gorda (hourly, 6.15am–5pm; 4hr 15min); San Ignacio (at least hourly, 5.30am–11pm; 1hr).

ACCOMMODATION AND EATING

Belmopan's accommodation is for the most part expensive and aimed at government officials and professionals. On Sundays, when many restaurants are closed, snacks from the bus terminal may be the only option for travellers passing through.

Caladium Beside the bus terminal. Good Belizean food, with a Bz$12 daily special, in a/c surroundings. Mon–Fri 7.30am–8pm, Sat 7.30am–7pm.

Corkers Hibiscus Plaza. Good pastas, salads and pub grub served indoors or on the outside patio. Mon–Wed 11am–8pm, Thurs–Sat 11am–10pm.

Hibiscus Hotel Melhado Parade, off Constitution Drive ☏ 822 0400, ⓦ hibiscusbelize.com. Very central, British-owned hotel with simple a/c motel-style rooms. Profits support bird conservation. **US$60**

El Rey Hotel 23 Moho St ☏ 822 3438, ⓦ elreyhotel.com. Unassuming "budget boutique" hotel, with helpful English owners, a 20min walk from the bus terminal. All rooms are en suite; the cheapest have ceiling fans, fancier options have vivid murals and a/c. All meals available; try the home-made cheesecake. **US$45**

DIRECTORY

Banks Banks (with ATMs) are close to the bus terminal.
Immigration The office is in the main government building by the fire station.

SAN IGNACIO

The friendly, relaxed town of **SAN IGNACIO**, on the west bank of the Macal River 35km west of Belmopan, draws together much of the best of inland Belize. The heart of Cayo District and the focal point of tourism in western Belize, it offers good food, inexpensive hotels and restaurants, and frequent buses. Undoubtedly its best feature is its riverside location, amid beautiful countryside and surrounded by hills, streams, archeological sites, caves and forests.

Many locals refer to the town as **Cayo**, the same word that the Spanish used to describe the offshore islands – an apt reflection of its setting, on a peninsula between two converging rivers. The early Spanish Conquest in 1544 made little impact here, and this was a centre of rebellion in the following decades. **Spanish friars** arrived in 1618, but the population continued to practise "idolatry", and in 1641 Maya priests threw out some Spanish clerics. Tipu, the region's capital, retained a measure of independence until 1707, when the population was forcibly removed to Guatemala.

1

WHAT TO SEE AND DO

Aside from a visit to the ruins at **Cahal Pech**, or the **Iguana Conservation Project**, there's little to do in San Ignacio proper, though you can spend many pleasant days here; it's a relaxed and inexpensive base for exploring nearby sights. Most hotels, along with numerous independent operators (see box opposite) offer superb guided trips to attractions including Actun Tunichil Muknal (see p.82), Caracol (see p.86), and Tikal in Guatemala (see p.364).

Cahal Pech

The hilltop Maya site of **Cahal Pech** (daily 6am–6pm; Bz$20), twenty minutes' walk

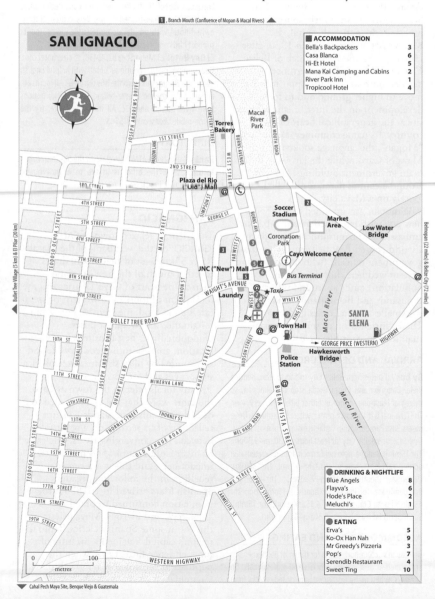

1 , Branch Mouth (Confluence of Mopan & Macal Rivers)

SAN IGNACIO

N

■ ACCOMMODATION
Bella's Backpackers	3
Casa Blanca	6
Hi-Et Hotel	5
Mana Kai Camping and Cabins	2
River Park Inn	1
Tropicool Hotel	4

JOSEPH ANDREWS DRIVE

CEMETERY STREET

Torres Bakery

Macal River Park

BRANCH MOUTH ROAD

1ST STREET

PASLOW LANE

BURNS AVENUE

WEST STREET

2ND STREET

Plaza del Rio ("Old") Mall

1BD STREET

4TH STREET

SIMPSON ST

GEORGE ST

Soccer Stadium

Market Area

Low Water Bridge

5TH STREET

BURNS AVE

Coronation Park

Belmopan (22 miles) & Belize City (72 miles)

TEODOSO OCHOA STREET

6TH STREET

MAYA STREET

FARVEY ST

Cayo Welcome Center

7TH STREET

8TH STREET

LEBANON ST

JNC ("New") Mall

Bus Terminal

9TH STREET

WAIGHT'S AVENUE

Laundry

Taxis

WYATT ST

Macal River

SANTA ELENA

Bullet Tree Village (5.1km) & El Pilar (20 km)

BULLET TREE ROAD

WEST ST

KING ST

Rx

10TH ST

GUADALUPE ST

JOSEPH ANDREWS DRIVE

HUDSON STREET

Town Hall

GEORGE PRICE (WESTERN) HIGHWAY

Hawkesworth Bridge

11TH STREET

QUARRY HILL RD

CHURCH STREET

Police Station

BUENA VISTA STREET

Macal River

12TH STREET

MINERVA LANE

13TH ST

THORNLY ST

THORNLY STREET

14TH STREET

VACA RD

15TH STREET

OLD BENQUE ROAD

MEL HADO ROAD

TEODOSO OCHOA STREET

16TH STREET

17TH STREET

AWE STREET

APOLLO STREET

CARMELITA ST

● DRINKING & NIGHTLIFE
Blue Angels	8
Flayva's	6
Hode's Place	2
Meluchi's	1

18TH STREET

19TH STREET

WESTERN HIGHWAY

0   100
metres

● EATING
Erva's	5
Ko-Ox Han Nah	9
Mr Greedy's Pizzeria	3
Pop's	7
Serendib Restaurant	4
Sweet Ting	10

▼ Cahal Pech Maya Site, Benque Viejo & Guatemala

southwest of San Ignacio centre, on the uphill road towards Benque Viejo, is well worth a visit. There's a good chance you'll have the forested ruins all to yourself, and although the structures are not particularly tall, the maze of restored corridors, stairways, plazas and temples is enchanting.

Cahal Pech was the royal acropolis-palace of an elite Maya family during the Classic period, and there's evidence of monumental construction from at least as early as 400 BC, though most of the remaining structures date from the eighth century AD. The **visitors' centre and museum** has a scale model, excellent displays and a variety of artefacts. Entering the site itself, via **Plaza B**, your gaze is drawn to Structure 1, the **Audiencia**, the highest building at Cahal Pech. From the top, the ruins of Xunantunich (see p.86) are clearly visible to the southwest. Behind Structure 1, in **Plaza A**, is a restored three-storey temple, as well as other sacred buildings.

Iguana Conservation Project

The **Iguana Conservation Project** (daily 8am–4pm; Bz$18), housed within the *San Ignacio Resort Hotel* grounds, works to breed and raise endangered green iguanas which have yet to reach their full adult length (up to 6ft), before releasing them into the wild. Large groups of tourists and students join the hourly tours, during which you can handle the dragon-like reptiles and pose for photographs.

ARRIVAL AND INFORMATION

By plane San Ignacio's airport, a 15min drive west of town towards Benque, is served by daily flights from Belize City on Tropic Air. Ideally, arrange transport to town in advance through your accommodation, though taxis often wait to shuttle visitors in (from Bz$10). For domestic and international air tickets head to Exodus Travel, 2 Burns Ave (☎ 824 4400, ⓦ aquallos.com/exodustravel).

By bus Services to and from Belize City stop in the centre, just south of Coronation Park, an easy walking distance from

all recommended hotels. A useful shuttle service also connects Belize International Airport with San Ignacio (from US$35pp; ☎ 631 1749, ⓦ belizeshuttlesandtransfers.com).

Destinations Belize City via Belmopan (every 30min 4am–6pm; 3hr); Benque Viejo del Carmen, for the Guatemalan border (every 30min; 15min).

By taxi Getting to or from the Guatemalan border is most comfortable by shared taxi. The Savannah Taxi Coop (☎ 824 2155) will carry up to four passengers for Bz$25.

Tourist information The modern Cayo Welcome Center is in Coronation Park near the bus stop (daily 9am–5pm; ☎ 824 2939, ⓦ travelbelize.org).

Cayo Adventure Tours 29 Burns Ave ☎ 824 3246, ⓦ cayoadventure.com. Customized trips to caves and ruins, plus birding and nature tours.

K'Atun Ahaw Tours 10 Burns Ave ☎ 824 2661, ⓦ belizeculturetours.com. Specializing in day-trips to Tikal, Elias Cambranes also leads trips to the caves and ruins at Xunantunich and Caracol (US$75–115).

Maximum Adventures 27 Burns Ave ☎ 623 4880, ⓦ sanignaciobelizetours.com. Max's family-run operation offers tours to all the local sights at excellent prices; trips to Actun Tunichil Muknal and Barton Creek Cave and zipline go for US$85–95/person.

MayaWalk Tours 19 Burns Ave ☎ 824 3070, ⓦ mayawalk.com. Extremely popular tours to all the major sights, with a/c minibus shuttles and experienced guides. Trips cost about US$20 more per person than other local operations, but you're paying for speed and comfort. Prices include entry fees, equipment, lunch and snacks.

★**Pacz Tours** 30 Burns Ave ☎ 824 0536, ⓦ pacz tours.net. Informative tours, including to Actun Tunichil Muknal and Caracol (US$110), with the most experienced local operator.

River Rat Expeditions Benque del Viejo town, beyond Xunantunich towards the border ☎ 628 6033, ⓦ riverratexpeditions.com. Informative guides with off-road transport, especially to archeological sites and ruins.

ACCOMMODATION

San Ignacio has some of the best-value budget accommodation in the country, and you'll almost always find space.

Bella's Backpackers 4 Galves St ☎ 824 2248, ⓦ bellasin belize.com. San Ignacio's only true hostel offers bunk beds in dorms and a few private rooms, plus a communal kitchen and several common areas. Dorms US$10, doubles US$23

TOURS AND ACTIVITIES AROUND SAN IGNACIO

Tour and activity operators based in and around San Ignacio offer all sorts of guided tours in the Cayo District and beyond. Local hotels and lodges also offer very similar tours, but the independent operators tend to be a little cheaper, and because so many have offices on San Ignacio's central Burns Avenue, it's easy to shop around.

1

Casa Blanca 10 Burns Ave ☎824 2080, ⓦcasablanca guesthouse.com. Very popular, central hotel with immaculate en-suite rooms, all with cable TV and some with a/c, plus a comfortable sitting area with fridge, coffee and tea. The all-but-identical *Mallorca Hotel* next door is run by the same family. US$30

★ **Hi-Et Hotel** 12 West St ☎824 2828, ⓦaguallos.com /hietguesthouse. Deservedly popular budget hotel offering shared-bath rooms in a charming wooden colonial-era building – those upstairs come with a tiny balcony – and larger en-suite rooms with private bath in a concrete annexe. Book ahead. US$13

Mana Kai Camping and Cabins Branch Mouth Rd ☎624 6538, ⓦmanakaibz.weebly.com. Central campground, close to the Macal River, that offers tent camping with hammocks, showers and outdoor cooking, and screened rustic cabins, each with bathroom and veranda, and sleeping up to four. Camping/person US$7.50, cabins US$20

River Park Inn 1km along the Branch Mouth Rd ☎824 2116, ⓦriverparkinnbelize.com. This ever-expanding budget resort offers campers showers, flush toilets and a kitchen, plus simple rooms, suites and cabins, some en suite and most sharing hot-water showers. Camping/ person US$7.50, cabins US$50

Tropicool Hotel 30 Burns Ave ☎804 3052, ⓔtropicool gift@gmail.com. Bright, clean rooms with shared hot-water baths, and wooden cabins (sleeping up to four) with private showers and cable TV. Doubles US$25, cabins US$60

EATING

San Ignacio has lots of good, inexpensive restaurants, and a Saturday market that's the best in Belize, with local farmers bringing in fresh produce.

★ **Erva's** 4 Far West St, under *Pacz Hotel*. Traditional Belizean dishes such as the delicious "black dinner" for less than Bz$20, popular with both budget travellers and locals. Mon–Sat 8am–3pm & 6–10pm.

★ **Ko-Ox Han Nah** 5 Burns Ave ☎824 3014. Small, hugely popular restaurant that serves unusual Belizean cuisine, including Bz$8 weekday lunch specials, plus Indian-style curries for Bz$20–30 and more ordinary international dishes like spaghetti and meatballs. Arrive early or you may well have to wait. Mon–Sat 6am–9pm.

Mr Greedy's Pizzeria 34 Burns Ave. A central location, free wi-fi, game nights, and decent thick-crust pies from US$9 – not to mention happy-hour drinks specials and a late-opening bar. Daily 6am–midnight.

Pop's Far West St ☎824 3366. Small, much-loved local restaurant, serving huge Bz$10 breakfasts until 2pm, with bottomless cups of coffee, plus inexpensive Belizean dishes. Daily 6.30am–2pm & 6.30–9pm.

Serendib Restaurant 27 Burns Ave. Good curries and Sri Lankan-style cuisine for Bz$14–22. Mon–Sat 11am–2pm & 5–10pm.

Sweet Ting 96 Benque Viejo Rd. Brilliant little café on the western edge of town that serves espresso coffees, hot chocolate, and fabulous cakes and pastries. Daily noon–9pm.

DRINKING AND NIGHTLIFE

Attracting weekending Belizeans as well as international visitors, San Ignacio holds plenty of **bars**, some of which get quite rowdy later at night. It's easy to find live music and dancing at the weekend.

Blue Angels Hudson St. This dark upstairs club has the only real dancefloor in town, usually filled with sweaty bodies. Locals head here to grind and wind to dancehall; it's quite rough around the edges, offering an authentic taste of Belizean nightlife.

Flayva's 22 Burns Ave. A laidback restaurant by day – offering decent grub, free wi-fi, and an on-site tour operation – which becomes a mellow reggae bar at night, with live music in the garden courtyard.

Hode's Place Savannah Rd. A great spot for an evening drink, this large garden-set bar/restaurant, near the river north of the centre, also serves a full international menu ranging from Bz$6 burgers upwards.

★ **Meluchi's** Joseph Andrew Drive, overlooking the cemetery. Good happy-hour specials, decent bar snacks and frequent events – from live music to late-night karaoke – ensure a steady stream of locals and visitors.

DIRECTORY

Banks and exchange Belize, Scotia and Atlantic banks on Burns Ave have 24hr ATMs. Moneychangers approach anyone heading west to exchange Guatemalan quetzals, and board Benque-bound buses before departure.

Internet Tradewinds, above the post office (Mon–Sat 7am–10pm, Sun 10am–10pm; Bz$4/hr).

Laundry Drop-off laundry at *Martha's Guest House*, 10 Far West St.

Post office Next to Courts furniture store on Hudson St in the town centre.

AROUND SAN IGNACIO

San Ignacio makes a great base from which to explore the **Cayo District**'s impressive **Maya ruins** and stunning scenery. Several local highlights can only be visited in the company of a local guide, but that's often a good idea anyway, to get the best experience (see box, p.81).

Actun Tunichil Muknal

The ancient Maya site known as Actun Tunichil Muknal or "ATM" is one of the most amazing places you're ever

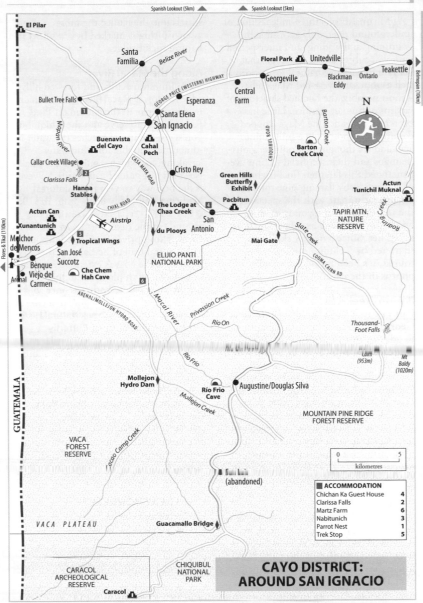

**CAYO DISTRICT:
AROUND SAN IGNACIO**

■ ACCOMMODATION	
Chichan Ka Guest House	4
Clarissa Falls	2
Martz Farm	6
Nabitunich	3
Parrot Nest	1
Trek Stop	5

likely to see. Discovered in 1986, the "cave of the stone sepulchre" lies 26km southwest of Belmopan or 40km southeast of San Ignacio, but don't try to visit on your own – you can only enter it on strenuous organized tours that combine adrenaline-filled adventure with astonishing archeological remains (tours from US$110, including lunch and transport to and from San Ignacio or local hotels). It's one of the priciest excursions in Belize, but it's not an experience to miss if at all possible.

1

ATM consists of a three-mile section of underground river, only accessible by swimming and wading, and interspersed with vast subterranean chambers that contain remarkable natural formations as well as thousand-year-old Maya relics – most notably, the calcified skeletons of victims of human sacrifice. Little has been touched since the Maya stopped coming here more than a millennium ago, and it's thought that only religious shamans and their sacrificial victims ever penetrated this far, their final frightful procession lit by flaming pine torches.

Tours culminate with the spectacle of the full skeleton of a young woman lying near the stone axe that may have killed her. Since a nearby skull was shattered by a clumsy camera-toting tourist, it's been forbidden to take photos in the cave.

Barton Creek Cave

Barton Creek Cave, 8 miles southeast of George Price Hwy along the Chiquibul Road, can only be accessed by river, in guided canoe trips. Like ATM (see p.82), it holds stunning formations as well as ancient artefacts and sacrificial skeletons. San Ignacio-based operators including David's Adventure Tours (☎804 3674, ⓦdavidsadventuretours.net) charge from US$45 per person, or you can make your own way here – via very rough dirt roads – and arrange a tour via the on-site operator, Mike's Place (US$160 for 1 or 2 people; ☎670 0441, ⓦbartoncreekcave .com), which also offers horserides and ziplines.

Framed by jungle, the cave's entrance is at the far side of a jade-green pool, where you board your canoe. Visitors follow the river underground, crouching in places where the cave roof dips low, to emerge after 1600m into a gallery blocked by a huge rockfall. Following rain, a subterranean waterfall cascades over the rocks – an unforgettable sight. Beyond lie many more miles of passageways, accessible only on a fully equipped expedition. The clear, slow-moving river fills most of the width of the cave, though in places the roof soars 100m overhead. Maya burial sites surrounded by pottery vessels line the banks; the most awe-inspiring is marked by a skull set in a natural rock bridge.

Along the Macal River

Steep limestone cliffs and forested hills edge the lower **Macal River**, whose main tributaries rise in the Mountain Pine Ridge Forest Reserve and the Chiquibul Forest. In the upper reaches the water is sometimes suitable for whitewater kayaking, for which a guide is essential (see p.81). A guided canoe trip, however, is the best way to visit the **Rainforest Medicine Trail** (daily 8am–5pm; Bz$10; ☎824 2037, ⓦchaacreek.com), in the grounds of the luxurious *Lodge at Chaa Creek*, 5km upriver from San Ignacio. This natural trail of herbal remedies highlights the Maya's extensive medical knowledge, with plants including the negrito tree, whose bark was once sold in Europe for its weight in gold as a cure for dysentery. The **Chaa Creek Natural History Centre and Blue Morpho Butterfly Breeding Centre**, just uphill (daily 8am–5pm; Bz$10), offers a marvellous introduction to Cayo's history, geography and wildlife.

At *du Plooy's* resort, a few kilometres upstream, the ambitious **Belize Botanic Gardens** (daily 7am–5pm; Bz$15; ☎824 3101, ⓦbelizebotanic.org) aim to conserve Belize's native plant species in small areas representative of their habitats.

★ TREAT YOURSELF

Martz Farm Mile 8.5 Arenal/Mollejon Hydro Rd ☎614 6462 or ☎663 3849, ⓦmartzfarm.com. An ideal budget river resort for anyone crossing to/from Guatemala, 13km southwest of Benque Viejo via dirt road; the Martínez family will pick up from the border or San Ignacio. Accommodation is in shared-bath options that include a treehouse, three-bed garden rooms, a bunkhouse perched above a rushing, crystal-clear creek, or en-suite cabins. Rates include breakfast; lunch and dinner cost US$25 extra. Bunkhouse <u>US$44</u>, treehouse <u>US$71</u>, rooms or cabins <u>US$82</u>

MOUNTAIN PINE RIDGE FOREST RESERVE

Southeast of San Ignacio, the **MOUNTAIN PINE RIDGE FOREST RESERVE** comprises a spectacular range of rolling hills, jagged peaks and gorges interspersed with grassland and pine forest. In the warm river valleys the vegetation is gallery forest, giving way to rainforest south of the Guacamallo Bridge, which crosses the upper Macal River. One of the most scenic of the many small rivers in the Pine Ridge is the **Río On**, rushing over cataracts and into a gorge. On the northern side of the ridge the **Thousand-Foot Falls** are the highest in Central America. The reserve also includes limestone areas riddled with caves, the most accessible being the **Río Frio**. The area is virtually uninhabited apart from a few tourist lodges and one small settlement, **Augustine/Douglas Silva**, site of the reserve headquarters.

WHAT TO SEE AND DO

With few roads, it's very difficult to get around the reserve. The whole area is perfect for **hiking** and **mountain biking**; hitching is another option.

San Antonio

The southernmost settlement outside the reserve, **SAN ANTONIO** on the eastern side of the Macal River, is a good place to learn about traditional Maya practices. It was home to Maya healer Don Elijio Panti, who died in 1996, and his niece María García runs the tiny Tanah Mayan Art Museum (daily 8am–6pm; Bz$8; ☎669 4823), where displays explain local history and culture, and sells slate carvings and other artworks. She also co-owns the *Chichan Ka Guest House* (see below), and can arrange guided tours of the small but breathtaking Elijio Panti National Park (@epnp.org), immediately south of the village.

The reserve

Not far beyond San Antonio, the two approach roads meet and climb steadily to the **reserve**. All visitors have to sign in at the **Mai Gate**, a checkpoint with toilets, drinking water and information, but there are no admission fees or opening hours.

Once in the reserve, pine trees replace the dense, leafy forest. After 3km a road heads off to the left, running for 16km to a point overlooking the **Thousand-Foot Falls** (Bz$2), which despite their name drop around 1600ft (488m). From the overlook, however, roughly 1km distant at the edge of a sheer slope, you can only see perhaps the top third. The spectacular setting makes it worth the trip; across the gorge, the long, slender plume of water disappears into the thickly forested valley below. Don't try to clamber any closer; it's an extremely dangerous climb.

Around 11km beyond the junction to the falls, the **Río On Pools** make a gorgeous spot for a swim. Another 8km on, you reach the reserve headquarters at **Augustine/Douglas Silva**, where you can **camp** and the village store stocks a few basic supplies. The huge **Río Frio Cave** is a twenty-minute walk from Augustine/Douglas Silva, following the signposted track from the parking area through the forest. Sandy beaches and rocky cliffs line the Río Frio on both sides as it flows through the cave.

ARRIVAL AND TOURS

Arrival Two roads lead into the Mountain Pine Ridge Reserve, one from the village of Georgeville, on the George Price (Western) Highway, and the other from Santa Elena, along the Cristo Rey road and through San Antonio. It's possible to rent a mountain bike in San Ignacio and bring it on the bus to San Antonio (Mon–Sat 2 daily).

Tours Tours can be arranged from San Ignacio and with local hotels.

ACCOMMODATION AND EATING

Chichan Ka Guest House Cristo Rey Rd, San Antonio ☎669 4023, @awrem.com/tanah/experience.html. Inexpensive guesthouse, run by the García sisters, who also serve traditional meals using organic produce from the garden, offer courses in the gathering and use of medicinal plants, and are renowned for their slate carvings – their gift shop is a favourite tour-group stop. Buses from San Ignacio stop outside. <u>US$15</u>

Reserve HQ camping You can camp at the reserve headquarters at Augustine/Douglas Silva; ask a ranger at the station for permission to pitch your tent. Camping/ tent <u>US$20</u>

1

CARACOL

Beyond Augustine/Douglas Silva, the Maya Mountains rise to the south, while to the west lies the wild Vaca plateau. Here the ruins of **CARACOL** (daily 8am–4pm; Bz$30), the most magnificent Maya site in Belize, and one of the largest in the Maya world, were lost for over a thousand years until their rediscovery in 1936. Two years later they were explored by A.H. Anderson, who named the site Caracol – Spanish for "snail" – because of its abundant snail shells. Research and restoration has been ongoing since 1985.

Almost all visitors come on guided tours (for San Ignacio options, see p.81); there's no public transport to, or even near, the site. After armed robbers attacked tourists on the road in 2005 and 2006, it was decided that a group convoy would set off with a military escort from the base a few miles south of Augustine/Douglas Silva, at around 9am each day, but there have been no attacks for several years now, and you'll probably just be required to sign in en route.

If you manage to get here on your own, you'll be guided around by one of the guards. The **visitors' centre** is an essential first stop. Of the site itself, only the core of the city, comprising thirty-two large structures and twelve smaller ones grouped round five main plazas, is open to visitors – though even this is far more than you can effectively see in a day.

The most massive structure, **Caana** ("Sky Place"), is 42m high and still one of the tallest buildings in Belize. Each of its three separate tiers is so broad that you can't see the next level from the one below. At the very top a plaza holds three further sizeable pyramids. Hieroglyphic inscriptions have enabled epigraphers to piece together a record of Caracol's rulers from 599 AD. One altar records a victory over Tikal in 562 AD – a triumph that sealed the city's rise to power. At its peak, around 700 AD, Caracol held over thirty thousand structures, covered 144 square kilometres, and had a population of around 150,000.

ALONG THE MOPAN RIVER

Rushing down from the Guatemalan border, the **Mopan River** offers some attractive and gentle **whitewater rapids**. Accommodation here is cheaper than the more upscale Macal River lodges, and all of the places reviewed below can arrange river trips, as well as tours throughout Cayo.

ACCOMMODATION

Clarissa Falls Mile 70, George Price Hwy ☎ 833 3116, ⓦ clarissafallsresort.aguallos.com. Part of a working cattle ranch, 2.5km north of the highway, 7km west of San Ignacio, this restful place is located beside rapids on the Mopan. Simple thatched cottages, all with private bath, plus space for camping. Owner Chena serves great home-cooking, and a quiet bar overlooks the falls. Camping/person US$9, cottages/person US$37.50

Parrot Nest Lodge Bullet Tree Falls ☎ 669 6068, ⓦ parrot-nest.com. Six simple, clean riverside cabins, three of which have private bathrooms, plus two treehouses perched in the branches. Set in beautiful gardens, all have verandas. Great home-cooked meals are served by owner Theo Stevens at a friendly communal table, and there's free tubing and a free daily shuttle to San Ignacio. US$50

XUNANTUNICH

The quiet village of **San José Succotz**, 12km west of San Ignacio, stands across the river from the ruins of **XUNANTUNICH** (pronounced Shun-an-tun-ich), "the Stone Maiden" (daily 8am–4pm; Bz$10). This impressive Maya site is also one of the most accessible in Belize; any bus heading west from San Ignacio can drop you at the cable-winched river ferry (daily 8am–5pm; free). From the far side, a steep road climbs 2km up to the site. Note that the river occasionally floods in the rainy season, so check that the site is open before making a trip.

Your first stop should be the **visitors' centre**, with a scale model of the ruins. The site itself, on an artificially flattened hilltop, includes five plazas, although the surviving structures are grouped around just three. Recent investigations have found evidence of Xunantunich's role in the power politics of the Classic period, during which it probably joined

Caracol and Calakmul in an alliance against Tikal. By the Terminal Classic period, Xunantunich was already in decline, though still inhabited until around 1000 AD.

The track from the entrance brings you out into Plaza A-2, with large structures on three sides. Plaza A-1, to the left, is dominated by **El Castillo**, at 40m the city's tallest structure. The climb can be daunting, but the views from the top are superb, with the forest stretching out all around and the rest of the ancient city beneath you.

ACCOMMODATION AND EATING

★**Nabitunich** San José Succotz, Mile 70, George Price Hwy ☎661 1536, ⓦhannastables.com. Enjoying unbeatable views of the Xunantunich ruins, 10km southwest of San Ignacio, the peaceful San Lorenzo farm makes a wonderful budget base for horseback trips and bird viewing. Accommodation in simple private cottages includes three family-style meals a day in the central lodge, which holds a library and games room. The property also encompasses a long stretch of the Mopan River, which can be explored by kayak, tube, horse or foot. Dorms US$13, cottages/person including meals US$38

★**Trek Stop** San José Succotz, Mile 70, George Price Hwy ☎823 2265, ⓦthetrekstop.com. A wonderful budget option, set in a quiet forest clearing near the highway; shared-bath cabins of varying sizes, with comfortable beds, nets and porches, plus a campsite, with rental tents available for US$10. The restaurant serves large portions and has good vegetarian choices, and there's a shared kitchen, plus rental bikes, kayaks and tubes. Camping/person US$6, cabins US$26

The south

South of Belmopan lies Belize's most rugged terrain. Population density in this part of Belize is low, with most towns and villages located on the water. **Dangriga**, the largest settlement, is home to the **Garífuna** people and is the regional transport hub. Further south, the **Placencia peninsula** is the focus for coastal tourism, boasting some great beaches, and is also the departure point for the south's idyllic cayes. The Southern Highway comes to an end in **Punta Gorda**, from where you can head to Guatemala or visit **ancient Maya sites** and present-day **Maya villages**.

Inland, the **Maya Mountains** form a solid barrier to land travel except on foot or horseback. The Belizean government, showing supreme foresight, has placed practically the whole massif under some form of protection. The most accessible area of rainforest is the **Cockscomb Basin Wildlife Sanctuary**, a reserve protecting the area's sizeable jaguar population.

THE HUMMINGBIRD HIGHWAY

As it heads southeast from Belmopan towards Dangriga, the **HUMMINGBIRD HIGHWAY** passes through magnificent scenery. On the right the eastern slopes of the **Maya Mountains** become visible, part of a ridge of limestone mountains riddled

---

INTO GUATEMALA: BENQUE VIEJO DEL CARMEN

The quiet town of **Benque Viejo del Carmen**, 2km before the Guatemalan border and the westernmost town in Belize, is served by frequent **buses** (which terminate here); to reach the border itself, take a **shared taxi** (Bz$10).

Leaving Belize you pay an exit tax of Bz$37.50/US$18.75. There's no charge to enter Guatemala for North Americans or citizens of the EU, Australia and New Zealand; if you do require a visa (up to US$10), they can sometimes be issued here, but check whether you need one in advance. The Guatemalan border town of **Melchor de Mencos** has little to recommend it, so it is best to continue as soon as you're ready. **Moneychangers** wait either side of the border; you might want to bargain with them to get the best rate.

Minibuses (US$10–15) to **Flores** or **Tikal** usually wait just over the border, while *colectivo* minibuses to Flores wait just over the bridge at the border; regular second-class buses pass the junction just beyond the bridge.

In addition, Mayan Heart World offer a daily shuttle bus between San Ignacio and Tikal (departs San Ignacio 7.30am, Tikal 2pm; US$40 one way; Belize ☎501 824 3328, Guatemala ☎502 2375 7072; ⓦmayanheartworld.net), and can also arrange transfers to and from Flores and El Remate.

1

with underground rivers and **caves**, several of which contain Maya artefacts such as burials, ceramics and carvings.

St Herman's Cave

Shortly after the Hummingbird Highway crosses the Caves Branch River, 19km south of Belmopan, St Herman's Cave is a rarity for Belize: a cave it's possible to visit on your own (daily 8am–4.30pm; Bz$8, includes entrance to the Blue Hole National Park; ☎223 5004, ⓦbelizeaudubon.org). On an unaccompanied visit, however, you'll only get a small glimpse of what caving hereabouts has to offer. It's well worth hiring a guide, which is best arranged in advance through your hotel.

The cave itself is a ten-minute walk from the visitors' centre, beneath a dripping rock face; you'll need a flashlight to enter, heading down steps originally cut by the Maya. Inside, you can clamber over the rocks and splash through the river for about 300m, admiring the vast underground spaces; only with a licensed guide can you continue any deeper, to reach even more stunning formations and ancient sites.

Blue Hole National Park

Two kilometres beyond St Herman's Cave, accessible from the highway or via a trail from its own visitors' centre, **Blue Hole National Park** centres on a beautiful pool whose cool turquoise waters are perfect for a refreshing dip. The "Hole" is actually a short stretch of underground river, whose course is revealed by a collapsed cavern. Be warned, though, that rainy season run-off can turn things a muddy grey.

ARRIVAL AND TOURS

By bus Buses between Belmopan and Dangriga can drop you at St Herman's Cave or the Blue Hole.
Guides The best independent guide to the Hummingbird Highway is Marcos Cucul, based in Belmopan (☎600 3116, ⓦmayaguide.bz).
Cave and rappelling trips The luxurious *Caves Branch Jungle Lodge* (☎822 2800, ⓦcavesbranch.com), 20km south of Belmopan, runs excellent trips – they're not cheap (from US$85/person), but well worth it for the experienced and knowledgeable staff.

ACCOMMODATION

Camping ⓦ belizeaudubon.org. Behind the visitors' centre at St Herman's Cave, trails lead through the surrounding forest and, after 4km, to a campsite. Per person US$10

DANGRIGA

DANGRIGA, the district capital and the largest town in southern Belize, stands on the coast 10km east of the junction of the Hummingbird and Southern highways. Formerly known as Stann Creek, Dangriga is the cultural centre of the **Garífuna**, a people of mixed indigenous Caribbean and African descent, who make up about eleven percent of the country's population. It's also home to many artists, including painters and drum-makers, and you may catch an exhibition or performance. For most travellers, though, Dangriga's prime interest is as a base for visiting **Tobacco Caye** offshore, the **Mayflower Bocawina National Park** (see p.91), and the **Jaguar Reserve** near Hopkins (see p.93).

Gulusi Garífuna Museum

Almost the first building you see as you approach Dangriga, 2km short of the sea, the Gulusi Garífuna Museum is filled with fascinating exhibits on Garífuna history and culture (Mon–Fri 10am–5pm, Sat 8am–noon; Bz$10; ☎669 0639, ⓦngcbelize.org). Displays trace the migration of the Garífuna from St Vincent to Roatán and on to Belize, while artwork, clothing, food and music illustrate their ongoing traditions.

Pen Cayetano's studio gallery

Part art gallery, part performance space, the Pen Cayetano Studio Gallery at 3 Aranda Crescent (Tues–Sat 9am–noon & 2–5pm, Sun 9am–noon; Bz$5; ☎628 6807, ⓦcayetano.de) celebrates the work of Garífuna artist/musician Pen Cayetano, who was awarded an MBE by the British government in 2012. His striking, deep-coloured oil paintings explore themes from Garífuna culture and Belize in general, and he's also renowned as the originator of the calypso-tinged musical genre punta rock. School groups flock through the compound for drumming lessons and demonstrations.

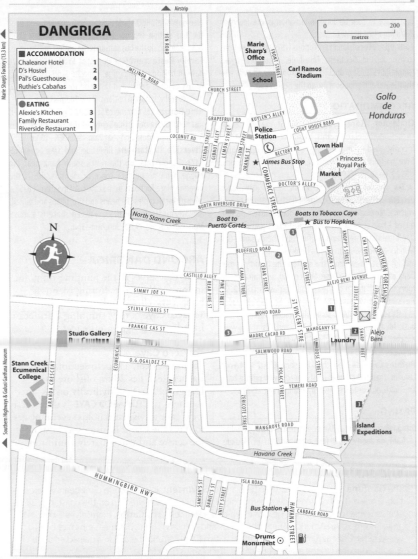

DANGRIGA

Airstrip

ACCOMMODATION

Chaleanor Hotel	1
D's Hostel	2
Pal's Guesthouse	4
Ruthie's Cabañas	3

EATING

Alexie's Kitchen	3
Family Restaurant	2
Riverside Restaurant	1

Marie Sharp's Factory (13.3 km)

Marie Sharp's Office

Carl Ramos Stadium

School

Golfo de Honduras

FEN ROAD

MELINDA ROAD

CHURCH STREET

GRAPEFRUIT RD

KUYLEN'S ALLEY

COCONUT RD

CITRON STREET

GUAVA ALLEY

LEMON STREE

PLUM STREET

ORANGE ST

FRONT STREET

Police Station

COURT HOUSE ROAD

RECTORY RD

Town Hall

Princess Royal Park

RAMOS ROAD

James Bus Stop

Market

DOCTOR'S ALLEY

COMMERCE STREET

NORTH RIVERSIDE DRIVE

North Stann Creek

Boat to Puerto Cortés

Boats to Tobacco Caye
Bus to Hopkins

N

BLUEFIELD ROAD

KNOPP'S STREET

MAGOON ST

CHATUYE ST

CASTILLO ALLEY

CEDAR STREET

CANAL STREET

PINE STREET

REAR PINE ST

OAK STREET

ALEJO BENI AVENUE

SOUTHERN FORESHORE

SIMMY JOE St

SYLVIA FLORES ST

FRANKIE CAS ST

MOHO ROAD

ST VINCENT STRE

GAYETTE STREET

EDWARD STREET

Studio Gallery

MADRE CACAO RD

MAHOGANY ST

Alejo Beni

Stann Creek Ecumenical College

ECUMENICAL

O.G.OGALDEZ ST

SALMWOOD ROAD

MONGOOSE STREET

Laundry

SHARP STREET

ARANDA CRESCENT

ALLAN ST

POLACK STREET

YEMERI ROAD

ZERICOTE STREET

Island Expeditions

Southern Highways & Gulasi Garifuna Museum

MANGROVE ROAD

Havana Creek

HUMMINGBIRD HWY

SAMSON'S ST

DANIEL'S ST

UNITY STREET

ISLA ROAD

Bus Station

CABBAGE ROAD

HAVANA STREET

Drums Monument

0   200
metres

ARRIVAL AND DEPARTURE

By plane Dangriga's airstrip, close to the shore just north of the *Pelican Beach Resort*, is served by at least eight daily flights in each direction on the Belize City–Punta Gorda run. A taxi into town will cost at least Bz$10.

By bus Dangriga's bus terminal, at the south end of town a 10min walk from the centre, is used by all local bus companies. Taxis are usually available for around Bz$5–7. Destinations Belize City, mostly via Belmopan (at least every 2hr, last bus 7.30pm; 1hr 30min–3hr); Hopkins

(Mon–Sat 10.30am & 5.15pm; 30min); Placencia (3–4 daily, last bus 6pm; 1hr 45min); Punta Gorda (8–10 daily, last bus 6.15pm; 2hr 30min).

By boat Boats to Tobacco Caye (40min; from Bz$35) leave from the bridge near the *Riverside Restaurant*; there are no scheduled departures, but if you ask in the restaurant someone should know if one's due to leave.

INFORMATION AND TOURS

Tourist information Dangriga has no tourist office; the

1

best place to pick up local information is the *Riverside Restaurant* (see below).

Tour operators Island Expeditions (⊚ islandexpeditions .com), on the Southern Foreshore, rents sea-kayaks (singles Bz$70/day, doubles Bz$110/day), and will also shuttle you and your boat out to the nearby cayes.

ACCOMMODATION

Chaleanor Hotel 35 Magoon St ☎ 522 2587, ⊚ chaleanorhotel.com. This colonial house holds a friendly, good-value hotel with accommodation ranging from no-frills budget rooms to larger en-suite options. US$23, en suites US$68

★ **D's Hostel** 1 Sharp St ☎ 502 3324, ⊚ valsback packerhostel.com. Simple concrete hostel near the beach, where three plain clean dorms – one male, one female, one mixed – hold eight bunks and private lockers. Rates include free breakfast of fruit and waffles, and there's same-day laundry service, in-room wi-fi, a book exchange, bike rental and lovely sea views from the rooftop. The friendly owner Dana offers lunch and dinner on demand, and can arrange tours and Garífuna language and culture classes. US$12.50

Pal's Guest House 86 Magoon St ☎ 522 2365, ⊚ palsbelize.net. Quiet, somewhat faded hotel. All the basic tiled rooms have private baths and TVs; those with a/c cost more, although only two are in the nicer building on the beach. US$40

Ruthie's Cabañas 31 Southern Foreshore ☎ 502 3184. Four bargain, thatched cabañas on the beach with private bath and porch, plus delicious meals by arrangement. US$28

EATING

Disappointingly few of Dangriga's restaurants specialize in Garífuna food; you'll find more options in Hopkins (see opposite). BBQ stands in the park, market, and near the bus station sell good chicken plates for less than Bz$10; *Elena's* by the bus station is the busiest grill in town.

Family Restaurant 9 St Vincent St ☎ 522 3433. An a/c oasis in baking-hot Dangriga, opposite Scotia Bank, with greasy Chinese dishes and fast food for less than Bz$15, and several vegetarian options. Daily 10am–11pm.

King Burger 135 Commerce St ☎ 522 2476. Simple diner, just north of the creek, that's a round-the-clock rendezvous for locals of all ages. Mon–Sat 7am–3pm & 6–10pm.

Riverside Restaurant Riverside and Oak St ☎ 669 1473. Simple café, on the river's south bank near the bridge, with no outdoor space or views, which is the meeting place for boats to the cayes. All meals cost Bz$8– 10, with local staples like beans and rice, beans and pigtail, and steamed fish. The Bz$3 seaweed shake is a must. Mon–Sat 6.30am–9pm, Sun 7am–3pm.

AROUND DANGRIGA

Dangriga serves as the jumping-off point for one of the most alluring islands a budget traveller could ever afford: **Tobacco Caye**, a tiny, stunning Caribbean island located right on the reef.

Tobacco Caye

Columbus Reef, a superb section of the Barrier Reef, lies 20km offshore from Dangriga. Perched idyllically on its southern tip, **TOBACCO CAYE** is the easiest local caye to visit and holds several places to stay. The island is just a speck: stand in the centre and you're barely a minute's

---

THE GARÍFUNA

The **Garífuna** trace their history to the island of **St Vincent**, in the eastern Caribbean, where two Spanish ships carrying slaves from Nigeria to America were wrecked off the coast in 1635. The survivors took refuge on the island, which was inhabited by **Caribs**, themselves recent arrivals from South America. At first the Caribs and Africans fought, but the Caribs had been weakened by disease and wars against the native Kalipuna, and the Africans gained enough of a foothold to lead to the emergence of the Black Caribs or Garífuna.

While for most of the seventeenth and eighteenth centuries St Vincent fell nominally under British control, in practice it belonged to the Garífuna, who fended off British attempts to assert their authority until 1796. The British colonial authorities, however, would not allow a free black society, so the Carib population was hunted down and transported to **Roatán**, off the coast of Honduras (see p.440). The Spanish Commandante of Trujillo, on the Honduran mainland, took the surviving Black Caribs to Trujillo, where they became in demand as free labourers, fishermen and soldiers.

In the early **nineteenth century** small numbers of Garífuna moved up the coast to Belize. The largest single migration took place in 1832, when thousands fled from Honduras after they supported the wrong side in a failed revolution to overthrow the government. Their arrival is now celebrated as **Garífuna Settlement Day** on November 19 each year.

walk from the shore in any direction, with the unbroken reef stretching north. The reef is so close that you don't need a boat to go **snorkelling** or **diving**.

ARRIVAL AND INFORMATION

By boat Boats to Tobacco Caye (30min; Bz$40) leave daily from near the bridge in Dangriga, though there are no scheduled departures (see p.89).

Diving and snorkelling gear Several of the resorts, including *Reef's End Lodge*, have dive shops that rent gear even to those who are not guests; snorkelling gear costs US$7.50 and diving gear US$25, while a two-tank dive just offshore costs US$100.

ACCOMMODATION AND EATING

Accommodation on the remote caye is increasingly expensive and there are no independent restaurants, but most packages include three meals.

Reef's End Lodge ☎ 670 3919, ⓦ reefsendlodge.com. Dive and adventure resort beside the island's jetty. Stay right on the shore, in simple en-suite rooms that share a balcony, or in separate cabañas. The restaurant/bar, perched over the sea, serves delicious food. Rates include all meals; multi-day dive packages available. Rooms ▓▓▓▓▓ ▓▓▓▓▓▓ **US$115**

Tobacco Caye Paradise ☎ 532 2101, ⓦ tobaco cayeparadisecabin.com. Well-cared-for-family-owned property holding six basic but attractive thatched cabañas with private bath and verandas with hammocks over the sea, plus its own dining room, where lunch and breakfast cost Bz$15 each, dinner Bz$20. **US$54.50**

Mayflower Bocawina National Park

MAYFLOWER BOCAWINA NATIONAL PARK, 16km southwest of Dangriga, off the main road south, is a 7000-acre reserve of broadleaf forest at the base of the Maya Mountains (8am–4pm; Bz$10; ⓦ mayflowerbocawina.tk). The park **visitors' centre**, which stands across from the most accessible of the park's three main Maya sites – a small open plaza surrounded by stone mounds, largely covered by trees – hands out trail maps to two impressive waterfalls, one a simple 5km round trip and the other a more demanding 7km hike. A separate office, 500m in from the entrance station, organizes ziplining and abseiling.

ACTIVITIES

Ziplining Bocawina Adventures and Eco-tours (daily 7am–7pm; ☎ 670 8019, ⓦ bocawina.com) operate what's said to be the longest zipline in central America, with twelve separate platforms and one section that stretches almost half a mile through the jungle, as well as waterfall abseiling. They also offer accommodation in the park's delightful but pricey *Bocawina Rainforest Resort* (US$99).

HOPKINS

Stretching for 3km along a shallow, gently curving bay, 6km east of the Southern Highway, the Garífuna village of **HOPKINS** has, thanks to its sumptuous beach, turned almost entirely to tourism. Its single unnamed main street, a hundred metres inland from the sea, is lined with little guesthouses and cafés, largely catering to independent travellers. These form a continuous strip all the way south to what used to be a separate community known as Sittee Point, but is now effectively a very upscale annexe of Hopkins.

The Garífuna here, most of whom now live in concrete structures, not traditional wood-and-thatch houses, remain proud of their culture – most speak Garífuna as a first language – and Garífuna Settlement Day on November 19 is celebrated enthusiastically with singing, dancing and the beating of drums.

Great beaches plus delicious food and accommodation in all price ranges makes Hopkins a pleasant place to spend a few days relaxing, but it's also well equipped for outdoor activities, from diving and snorkelling to kayaking and windsurfing.

ARRIVAL AND INFORMATION

By bus The 10.30am & 5.15pm buses from Dangriga (Mon–Sat; departing to Dangriga at 7am & 2pm) loop around Hopkins before heading south to the Sittee. Any bus on the Southern Hwy can drop you at the turn-off 4 miles west, from where it's easy and common to hitch a ride into Hopkins, while taxis wait to run tourists into town for Bz$10.

TOURS AND ACTIVITIES

Bike/motorbike rental Several hotels supply free bikes for guests, while Fred's Bikes or Tina's Bicycles, both at the south end of the village, rent for around Bz$20/day. Motorbike Rentals (☎ 665 6292, ⓦ alternateadventures.com), opposite *Thongs Cafe*, rents motorbikes from US$60/day.

Kayaking and windsurfing At the south end of the village, you can rent kayaks for Bz$15/hr at *Tipple Tree Beya* (☎ 533 7006, ⓦ tippletree.com), and windsurfers for Bz$60/day at *Windschief* (☎ 523 7249,

1

ⓦwindschief.com), which also offers windsurfing lessons for Bz$60/hr.

Snorkelling, diving and boat tours Most hotels can arrange snorkelling trips to the reef, while Hopkins Underwater Adventures (ⓣ633 3401, ⓦhopkinsunderwater adventures.com), based at *Parrot Cove Lodge*, runs diving trips to South Water and other cayes (from US$150 for 2 dives, including equipment rental). Motorbike Rentals (see p.91) supplies snorkel gear (US$7/day).

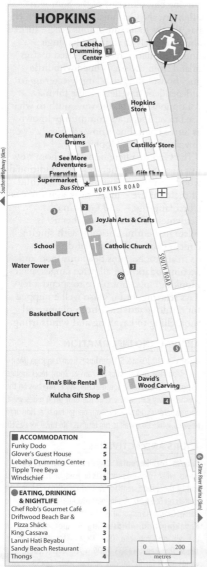

HOPKINS

N

Lebeha Drumming Center **1**

Hopkins Store

Mr Coleman's Drums

Castillós' Store

See More Adventures

Everyday Supermarket

Gift Shop

Bus Stop ★ HOPKINS ROAD

2

JoyJah Arts & Crafts

4

School

Catholic Church

SOUTH ROAD

Water Tower

@ **3**

Basketball Court

5

Tina's Bike Rental

David's Wood Carving

Kulcha Gift Shop

4

Southern Highway (6km)

Sittee River Marina (3km)

■ ACCOMMODATION
Funky Dodo	2
Glover's Guest House	5
Lebeha Drumming Center	1
Tipple Tree Beya	4
Windschief	3

● EATING, DRINKING & NIGHTLIFE
Chef Rob's Gourmet Café	6
Driftwood Beach Bar & Pizza Shack	2
King Cassava	3
Laruni Hati Beyabu	1
Sandy Beach Restaurant	5
Thongs	4

0   200
metres

5 & Sittee River (3km) ▼

ACCOMMODATION

Hopkins holds plenty of accommodation options, with hotels, cabañas and resorts lining the beach.

Funky Dodo Just south of central intersection ⓣ667 0558, ⓦthefunkydodo.com. Friendly Brit-owned "party hostel", very close to the beach and main bus stop, with very basic shared-bath dorms and private rooms. Amenities include a bar, communal kitchen, laundry services, free wi-fi and cosy chill-out spots, and they also run inexpensive tours. Dorms US$10.50, rooms US$26

Glover's Guest House Sittee River ⓣ520 5016, ⓦglovers .com.bz. This very basic budget option, 8km southwest of central Hopkins, serves as the base for travellers taking the Sunday boat out to its sister property, *Glover's Atoll Resort* on Glover's Reef (see opposite). Walk-ins are welcome, with a choice between camping, a bunk bed in the dorm, a shared-bath double room or an en-suite private cabin (which sleeps two). Staying two nights earns you a third free, and there's a riverbank restaurant. Camping/person US$4.50, dorm US$10, doubles US$27, cabins US$43

Lebeha Drumming Center North end of the village ⓣ665 9305, ⓦlebeha.com. Set up to help preserve Garífuna drumming traditions – lessons on request – this offers simple private doubles by the road and some lovely wooden beach cabins with private bath. Doubles Bz$35, cabins US$60

Tipple Tree Beya On the beach, south end of the village ⓣ533 7006, ⓦtippletree.com. Comfortable rooms in a wooden building with private bath, hammocks, fridge and coffeemaker; one private cabin has a kitchen. The beautiful beachside location makes it well worth the price. Doubles US$44, cabin US$60

★ Windschief On the beach, south of the centre ⓣ523 7249, ⓦwindschief.com. Two cabins, one with one double bed and the other with two, both offering private bath, fridge, coffeemaker, and access to the well-stocked beach bar. Windsurfing available (see p.91). Smaller cabin US$33, larger cabin US$49

EATING, DRINKING AND NIGHTLIFE

Hopkins' assorted restaurants serve everything from simple Creole plates to traditional Garífuna meals as well as international cuisine.

★ Driftwood Beach Bar & Pizza Shack At the northern end of the village on the beach ⓣ667 4872. Set on a gorgeous strip of sand, this laidback beach bar serves delicious pizzas (Bz$26–49) and daily dinner specials, and also hosts regular barbecues, full moon parties, drumming nights, volleyball games and jam sessions. Mon, Tues & Thurs–Sun 11am–10pm.

King Cassava At the central junction ⓣ503 7305. Lively largely open-air bar/restaurant that's the social hub of the village. The kitchen serves Mexican food (Bz$10–16) and fry jacks for breakfast, while the bar usually stays open

★**TREAT YOURSELF**

★**TREAT YOURSELF**

Chef Rob's Gourmet Café *Parrot Cove Lodge,* facing the beach in Sittee Point 3km south of central Hopkins ☎ 523 7225, ⓦ chefrobbelize.com. Rob's four-course extravaganza (Bz$59 or Bz$79) is based upon a creative, daily-changing menu with a strong Caribbean influence and fresh local produce. Tues–Sun lunch & dinner.

ⓦ glovers.com.bz. Indulge your Robinson Crusoe fantasy right here, by staying in a simple stilted wood-and-thatch cabin, over the water or on the beach, overlooking the reef. Other options include dorm beds in the main wooden house, or simply camping out. Nightly rates are available, but unless you come for a full week on the resort's catamaran, which leaves the Sittee River on Sun at 9am and returns the next Sat, the boat trip here can be prohibitively expensive. Meals are not included, so you can either bring your own food or eat at the restaurant. The staff pretty much leave you to your own devices – you can choose to enjoy the simple desert-island experience or take part in activities, which are charged separately. Per person per week: camping US$111, dorms US$168, cabins US$280

until midnight, and often puts on live music or drumming at weekends. Mon & Wed–Sun 9am–9pm.

★**Laruni Hati Beyabu** On the beach, north of the centre ☎ 663 0720. Belizean-owned bar/restaurant with a beachfront view, serving delicious local foods from stew chicken or beans and rice to whole grilled fish; most dishes cost around Bz$10. A favourite among locals. Daily 10am–9pm.

Sandy Beach Restaurant On the beach, south end of the village ☎ 650 9183. Run by the Sandy Beach Women's Cooperative, this low-slung green hut serves all kinds of Garífuna specialities, best enjoyed on the beach veranda. Mon–Sat 11am–9pm, Sun 10am–3pm.

Thongo Gafe Two blocks south of central junction ☎ 662 0110. International breakfasts, baked goodies and salads and sandwiches for less than Bz$15, in a cosy coffee-shop setting, with a small gift shop and free wi-fi. Wed, Thurs & Sun 8am–2pm, Fri & Sat 8am–2pm & 6–9pm.

GLOVER'S REEF

GLOVER'S REEF, the southernmost of Belize's three coral atolls, lies 40km offshore from Hopkins. Roughly oval, it stretches 35km north to south, with a number of cayes in its southeastern section. Famous for its wall diving which, thanks to a huge underwater cliff, is among the best in the world, the atoll also hosts a stunning lagoon that offers spectacular snorkelling and diving, as well as a staggering diversity of wildlife, while sailing, sea-kayaking and fishing are also popular. The entire atoll is a **marine reserve** (US$15 entry fee, usually payable to your accommodation or tour guide), with a research station on Middle Caye.

ACCOMMODATION AND EATING

In offering budget accommodation, Glover's is something of an anomaly among the remote atolls.

Glover's Atoll Resort Northeast Caye ☎ 532 2916,

COCKSCOMB BASIN WILDLIFE SANCTUARY

On the mainland, the jagged peaks of the **Maya Mountains** rise west of the Southern Highway. The tallest summits belong to the Cockscomb range, which includes **Victoria Peak** (1120m), the second-highest mountain in Belize. Beneath the ridges is a vast bowl of stunning rainforest, more than four hundred square kilometres of which is protected by the **COCKSCOMB BASIN WILDLIFE SANCTUARY** – better known as the **Jaguar Reserve** (daily 8am–4.30pm; Bz$10; ☎ 666 3495, ⓦ belizeaudubon.org). The basin could be home to as many as eighty of Belize's 800-strong **jaguar population**, but although you may come across their tracks, your chances of actually seeing one are very slim, as they are mainly active at night and avoid humans. More than 290 species of **bird** have also been recorded, including the endangered scarlet macaw, the great curassow and the king vulture.

The sanctuary is at the end of a rough 10km road that branches off the main highway at the village of **Maya Centre**, runs through towering forest and fords a couple of streams before crossing the Cabbage Hall Gap and entering the Cockscomb Basin. Here, you'll find the **reserve headquarters**, where you can pick up maps (they also offer accommodation). Beyond the headquarters, well-maintained trails of varying lengths wind through tropical

1

moist forest, crossing streams and leading to a number of picturesque waterfalls and ridges. For those who have the time – and have made the necessary preparations – it's also possible to take a four- or five-day hike and climb to the summit of Victoria Peak. If you're looking for a more relaxing experience, however, you can float down South Stann Creek in an inner tube, available for rent (Bz$10) at the headquarters.

ARRIVAL AND DEPARTURE

By bus All buses between Dangriga and Placencia or Punta Gorda pass through Maya Centre. To visit the reserve, sign in and pay the entrance fee at the craft centre at the junction of the road leading up to the Cockscomb. From there, you can catch a ride with a taxi or truck the 10km to the reserve headquarters; this usually costs about Bz$30–40 each way for up to five people.

INFORMATION AND TOURS

Information Julio's Store, just beyond the Maya souvenir shop at the highway intersection, sells basic supplies and cold drinks (there's no shop in the reserve). It's also a bar with internet access.

Tours Both Cockscomb Maya Tours, based at the Maya Museum in Maya Centre (☎660 3903, ⓦcockscomb mayatours.com), and *Nu'uk Che'il Cottages*, just up the access road (☎533 7043, ⓦnuukcheilcottages.com), offer guided tours or a simple taxi service into the reserve.

ACCOMMODATION AND EATING

There's camping at the reserve headquarters, and, for the same price, at two other designated sites along the trails – for which you'll need to get a permit at the reserve headquarters. Maya Centre has several inexpensive places to stay, all of which can arrange meals, tours, guides and transport.

Nu'uk Che'il Cottages Maya Centre ☎533 7043 or ☎665 1313, ⓦnuukcheilcottages.com. Maya family compound, 500m up the track to the reserve, where visitors can camp in the garden or sleep either in spartan rooms with private bath, or a large wooden cabin with shared showers and dorm beds. The restaurant serves Maya cuisine (Bz$5–15), and there is a medicinal plant trail out back. Camping/person U̲S̲$̲7̲.̲5̲0̲, dorms U̲S̲$̲1̲1̲, double or triple rooms U̲S̲$̲3̲3̲

Reserve headquarters Cockscomb Basin ⊜base @btl.net, ⓦbelizeaudubon.org. A wide range of accommodation in the park itself, including private furnished cabins for four or six people, wooden dorms and camping space near the visitors' centre; private and shared-bath rooms in a house that also holds a shared kitchen, at

the park entrance 8km off the highway; and additional camping at two designated sites along the trails. There's no restaurant, so bring supplies. Camping/person U̲S̲$̲1̲0̲, dorms U̲S̲$̲2̲0̲, rooms U̲S̲$̲8̲2̲, cabins U̲S̲$̲5̲5̲

★**Tutzil Nah Cottages** Maya Centre ☎533 7045, ⓦmayacenter.com. Two clean, flower-framed cabins, one wood and one concrete, housing four rooms with choice of shared or private bath. Run by the Chun brothers, who also own a small grocery store at the front and offer excellent guided tours of the reserve. Shared-bath rooms U̲S̲$̲2̲0̲, private-bath rooms U̲S̲$̲2̲4̲

PLACENCIA

A slender finger of land, hanging down from the mainland and reached via a road that cuts east from the Southern Highway 16km south of Maya Centre, the Placencia peninsula is the main centre for tourism in southern Belize. Its former fishing villages have merged to form an all-but-unbroken fourteen-mile strip of hotels and resorts, but there's still a lot to like about the area, most of all its beaches – the entire eastern seaboard is lined with a continuous strand of deep, even, white sand.

Friendly, laidback **PLACENCIA** village, at the southern tip of the peninsula, 39km off the highway, holds abundant lodging and dining for budget travellers. There's no real centre; the main road meanders through, passing shops, restaurants and little hotels, before ending at a smart new pier. A short way east, a pedestrian-only wooden boardwalk, known as the Sidewalk, runs parallel to the beach.

More affluent visitors tend to stay in the cluster of charming boutique hotels along the beautiful stretch known as Maya Beach, nine miles north of Placencia.

WHAT TO SEE AND DO

Apart from simply hanging out on the beach, Placencia is a good, if expensive, base for **snorkelling** and **diving** trips to the southern cayes and reef or a day-trip to the **Monkey River**.

Other trips from Placencia can include anything from an afternoon on the water to a week of camping, fishing and sailing. Placencia's lagoon is also ideal for exploring in a **canoe** or **kayak**; you may spot manatees.

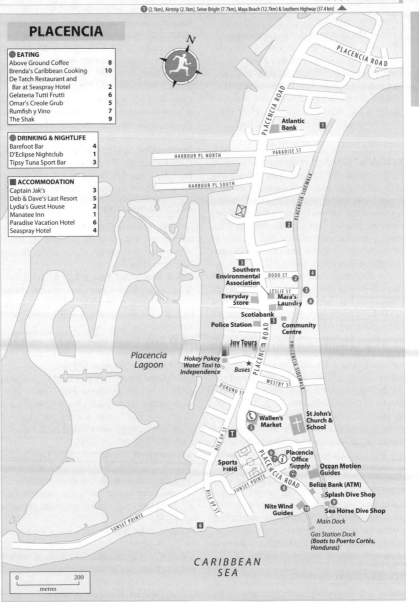

PLACENCIA

① (2.1km), Airstrip (2.1km), Seine Bright (7.7km), Maya Beach (12.7km) & Southern Highway (37.4km) ▲

● EATING	
Above Ground Coffee	8
Brenda's Caribbean Cooking	10
De Tatch Restaurant and	
Bar at Seaspray Hotel	2
Gelateria Tutti Frutti	6
Omar's Creole Grub	5
Rumfish y Vino	7
The Shak	9

● DRINKING & NIGHTLIFE	
Barefoot Bar	4
D'Eclipse Nightclub	1
Tipsy Tuna Sport Bar	3

■ ACCOMMODATION	
Captain Jak's	3
Deb & Dave's Last Resort	5
Lydia's Guest House	2
Manatee Inn	1
Paradise Vacation Hotel	6
Seaspray Hotel	4

N

PLACENCIA ROAD

PLACENCIA ROAD

Atlantic Bank

PARADISE ST

HARBOUR PL NORTH

PLACENCIA SIDEWALK

HARBOUR PL SOUTH

Southern Environmental Association

DODO ST

Everyday Store

LESLIE ST

Mara's Laundry

Scotiabank

Police Station

Community Centre

Joy Tours

Placencia Lagoon

Hokey Pokey Water Taxi to Independence

Buses

PLACENCIA SIDEWALK

WESTBY ST

DUKUNU ST

Wallen's Market

St John's Church & School

BILE UP ST

Sports Field

PLACENCIA ROAD

Placencia Office Supply

Ocean Motion Guides

Belize Bank (ATM)

Splash Dive Shop

Nite Wind Guides

Sea Horse Dive Shop

SUNSET POINTE

BILE UP ST

Main Dock

Gas Station Dock (Boats to Puerto Cortés, Honduras)

SUNSET POINTE

CARIBBEAN SEA

0	200
metres	

Diving and snorkelling

Diving options from Placencia are excellent, but the distance to most dive sites (at least 30km) makes trips here generally more expensive than elsewhere (see p.96). You could visit uninhabited **Laughing Bird Caye National Park**, beyond which lie the exquisite **Silk Cayes**, where the Barrier Reef begins to break into several smaller reefs and cayes, or nearby **Gladden Spit**, a marine reserve that protects the enormous **whale shark**. You can also **snorkel** near Placencia Island, just off the tip of the peninsula.

1

Monkey River

One of the best inland day-trips from Placencia (see p.94) takes you by boat to the virtually pristine **Monkey River**, which teems with fish, birdlife, iguanas and, as the name suggests, howler monkeys. The 20km, thirty-minute dash through the waves is followed by a leisurely glide up the river and a walk along forest trails.

ARRIVAL AND INFORMATION

By boat The *Hokey Pokey* ferry departs for Independence/ Mango Creek from the MnM Dock on the northwest edge of the village, where buses on the Dangriga–Punta Gorda line are usually timed to meet the ferry. *D Express* provides a weekly shuttle between Placencia and Puerto Cortés, Honduras, departing from the Main Dock on Friday morning at 9.30am, and returning from Honduras on Monday; you can buy tickets in advance from the Placencia Tourism Centre (see below).

Destinations Independence (6–7 daily; last boat from Placencia Mon–Sat 6pm, Sun 5pm; last return boat from Independence Mon–Sat 5.30pm, Sun 4pm; 20min; Bz$10; 601 0271); Puerto Cortés, Honduras (Fri 9.30am; 4hr 30min; US$65; ☎ 624 6509, ⓦ belizeferry.com).

By bus Buses from Dangriga (3–4 daily, last bus 2.30pm; 1hr 45min) pull in at the petrol station near the beach at the southern end of the village. In addition, all buses between Dangriga and Punta Gorda stop at Independence/ Mango Creek, from where you can take the *Hokey Pokey* ferry for the short ride to Placencia.

By plane Placencia's airport, 2 miles north of Placencia village, is served by at least a dozen daily flights in each direction on the Belize City–Punta Gorda run (typical one-way fares US$100 to Belize City, US$60 to Punta Gorda; ⓦ tropicair.com and ⓦ mayaislandair.com). Taxis are usually waiting to take passengers into Placencia village (Bz$10).

Tourist information The Placencia Tourism Centre, near the northern end of the main road in Placencia village (Mon–Fri 9–5pm; ☎ 523 4045, ⓦ placencia.com), produces the excellent free *Placencia Breeze* newspaper, with full local listings, transport schedules and a good map, and stocks brochures for accommodation and tour operators.

TOURS AND ACTIVITIES

Diving and snorkelling Splash Dive Center, in the marina north of the village, and with a central office across from Scotia Bank (☎ 523 3058, ⓦ splashbelize.com), is the best-equipped local dive operator. Sea Horse Dive Shop, in town near the petrol station (☎ 523 3166, ⓦ belizes cuba.com), also offers instructions and excursions at competitive rates. Diving trips start around US$125 for a two-tank dive, and US$450 for open-water certification; snorkelling trips start at about US$80/person including

equipment, transport and a snack. Both Pirate's Point Tours (☎ 632 8399, ⓔ shaneyoungbz@yahoo.com) and Ocean Motion Guides (☎ 523 3363, ⓦ oceanmotionplacencia .com) offer snorkelling and manatee-watching trips.

Nature tours Trip'n'Travel, based at Placencia Office Supply at the southern end of the village (☎ 523 3205, ⓦ tripntravel.bz), and Barebones Tours (☎ 677 9303, ⓦ barebonestours.com), who have a base in Monkey River, organize nature tours, overnight jungle adventures, and trips down the Monkey River (around US$65).

Sea-kayaking Saddle Caye South (☎ 523 3207, ⓦ kayakbelize.com) offer excellent kayak rental (single Bz$70/day, double Bz$120/day), as well as guided and self-guided four- to six-day river- and sea-kayaking trips.

ACCOMMODATION

Most budget options in Placencia are clustered around the northern end of the Sidewalk. You could also stay in Monkey River Town, though it's not a good base for Placencia or its beaches.

Deb & Dave's Last Resort Main Rd ☎ 523 3207, ⓔ debanddave@btl.net. Four clean, wooden budget rooms in the heart of the village, with shared hot-water bath, in a secluded annexe to the family home, all set within beautiful gardens. Kayaks for rent. US$27.50

Enna's Guest House Monkey River Town ☎ 720 2033. Basic rooms with shared bath, and a panoramic river view. Enna's brothers are tour guides. US$25

Lydia's Guest House Near the north end of the Sidewalk ☎ 523 3117, ⓦ lydiasguesthouse.com. Twelve clean, secure budget rooms, sharing five bathrooms and a kitchen, in a quiet location near the beach, plus four private beach cottages, each with kitchenette and porch. Rooms US$27.50, cottages US$40

★ **Manatee Inn** At the north end of the Sidewalk ☎ 523 4083, ⓦ manateeinn.com. Timber-frame budget inn, facing the beach, where the two storeys hold six simple but comfortable en-suite rooms, with hardwood floors and ceiling fans. Local tours available, inland and out to sea. US$44

Seaspray Hotel Near the north end of the Sidewalk ☎ 523 3148, ⓦ seasprayhotel.com. Placencia's first hotel, opened in 1964 by the family that still runs it. Excellent accommodation ranging from economy rooms set well back from the beach to a seafront cabaña with veranda and swinging hammock. All have private bath and fridge, some also TV, kitchenette and balcony. Don't miss *De Tatch* restaurant on the beach (see opposite). Economy rooms US$27, standard rooms US$55, cabaña US$71

Sunset Inn Monkey River Town ☎ 720 2028, ⓦ monkeyriverbelize.com. Two-storey wooden building, on a tiny bay at the back of the village. Eight simple rooms, five of them a/c, with comfortable beds, running water and private hot showers, plus tasty Creole food (full board

US$15/person). Owner Clive Garbutt is an excellent guide, and has canoes for rent. No credit cards. **US$30**

EATING

Placencia holds plenty of good restaurants, but things change fast, so ask locally for the latest recommendations. Most places close early; aim to be at the table by 8pm.

Above Grounds Coffee Main Rd ☎634 3212, ⓦabovegroundscoffee.com. Cosy treehouse café, near the south end of the village, with freshly baked cakes and cookies, wi-fi, book exchange and, above all, great Guatemalan coffee (Bz$3–9). Mon–Sat 7am–4pm, Sun 8am–noon.

Brenda's Caribbean Cooking Beside the pier. Simple barbecue shack right by the sea, with shaded open-air seating alongside the grill, where Brenda herself prepares full meals of jerk chicken or seafood gumbo for Bz$15–18, and offers irresistible coconut cookies. Daily 7am–6pm.

★**De Tatch** Sidewalk ☎503 3385. The best Belizean-owned restaurant in town, right on the beach, with a lovely, thatched open-air dining room. Caribbean cuisine at very affordable rates – the Bz$12 lunch specials, such as fish balls with rice and beans, are a real bargain – and delicious seafood mains (Bz$25–30) at all hours. Daily 7am–10pm.

★**Gelateria Tutti Frutti** Main Rd ☎523 4055. Without doubt the best ice cream in Belize, available in dozens of flavours and starting at Bz$4. 9am–9pm; closed Wed.

Omar's Creole Grub Main Rd. Long-standing local favourite. Omar being a fisherman, the speciality is ultra-fresh seafood, grilled or served with Caribbean or coconut curry; shrimp dishes cost Bz$22, whole lobsters are Bz$40. Lunchtime burritos and burgers cost Bz$8–12. 8am–9pm; closed Sat.

The Shak Sidewalk ☎622 1686, ⓦshakbeachcafe.com. Small beachfront restaurant serving smoothies, salads, sandwiches and good all-day breakfasts for Bz$12–25. Mon & Wed–Sun 7am–6pm.

DRINKING AND NIGHTLIFE

Most of Placencia's restaurants serve drinks, but there are also a few places that offer live music and more of a bar atmosphere.

★**TREAT YOURSELF**

Rumfish y Vino Opposite the sports field ☎523 3293, ⓦrumfishyvino.com. Friendly staff, an inventive tapas menu (Bz$12–30) and an extensive drinks list make this self-professed "gastro-bar" the crown jewel in Placencia's dining scene. The candlelit surroundings and atmospheric veranda are as enjoyable as the food. Daily 2–10pm.

Barefoot Bar Sidewalk, Placencia Village ☎523 3515. Very popular, brightly decorated bar, right on the beach, with live music five nights a week, plus great cocktails (happy hour daily 5–6pm), fire dancers and good bar food. Daily 11am–midnight.

D'Eclipse Nightclub Near the airstrip, 2 miles north of Placencia Village ☎523 3288. With its predominantly Caribbean sounds, the peninsula's only true clubbing experience attracts a good mix of locals and visitors. Busy at weekends from midnight. Thurs–Sun 9pm–2am.

Jaguar Lanes & Jungle Bar Maya Beach ☎664 2583. This four-lane bowling alley, 9 miles north of Placencia, makes a fun early-evening rendezvous, serving hot dogs and pizzas in the adjoining open-air bar. Mon, Thurs & Fri 4–8pm, Wed, Sat & Sun 2–8pm.

Tipsy Tuna Sports Bar Sidewalk, Placencia Village ☎523 3089. Lively beachfront bar and restaurant hosting live reggae, soca and punta music. Happy hour (daily 5–7pm) includes free banana chips. Mon 4pm–midnight, Tues, Wed & Sun 11.30am–midnight, Thurs–Sat 11.30am–2am.

DIRECTORY

Banks The main road in Placencia Village holds three banks with currency exchange and 24hr ATMs.

Internet Placencia Office Supply, just south of the village centre, has several computers (Mon–Fri 8am–7pm, Sat 8am–5pm; ☎523 3205); there's also access at *De Tatch Café* and *Tipsy Tuna*.

Laundry Mara's Laundry behind Scotia Bank offers full laundry services for Bz$15/load.

Post office On the road, at the northern end of the village.

TOLEDO

South of the Placencia and Independence junctions, the Southern Highway twists through pine forests and neat ranks of citrus trees and crosses numerous creeks to reach the sparsely populated Toledo District. The highway ends at likeable little Punta Gorda, the southernmost town in Belize, which serves as the base for rewarding visits to inland Maya villages and offers daily skiffs to Puerto Barrios in Guatemala and Lívingston in Honduras.

PUNTA GORDA

Toledo's chief and only town, **PUNTA GORDA**, or "PG", is an appealing blend of village, provincial capital and international ferry port. Set where the

1

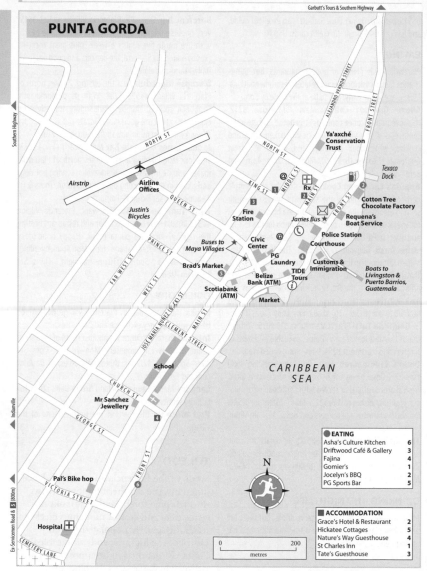

PUNTA GORDA

Garbutt's Tours & Southern Highway

Southern Highway

Indianville

Ex-Servicemen Road & S (800m)

Ya'axché Conservation Trust

Texaco Dock

Airstrip

Airline Offices

Justin's Bicycles

Fire Station

Cotton Tree Chocolate Factory

James Bus

Requena's Boat Service

Police Station

Courthouse

Buses to Maya Villages

Civic Center

PG Laundry

Customs & Immigration

Brad's Market

TIDE Tours

Boats to Livingston & Puerto Barrios, Guatemala

Scotiabank (ATM)

Belize Bank (ATM)

Market

School

CARIBBEAN SEA

Mr Sanchez Jewellery

Pal's Bike hop

Hospital

N

EATING

Asha's Culture Kitchen	6
Driftwood Café & Gallery	3
Fajina	4
Gomier's	1
Jocelyn's BBQ	2
PG Sports Bar	5

ACCOMMODATION

Grace's Hotel & Restaurant	2
Hickatee Cottages	5
Nature's Way Guesthouse	4
St Charles Inn	1
Tate's Guesthouse	3

0   200
metres

Southern Highway ends at the sea, it's a small, unhurried and hassle-free place. On first impression, it's not obvious what there is to do all day, and there's no real beach to speak of, but with a fine crop of hotels and restaurants, and plentiful tours and activities in the vicinity, PG makes a perfect base for a stay in the Toledo District. Home to around eight thousand people, including Garífuna, Maya, East Indians, and Creoles, it's also the business centre for nearby villages and farming settlements, with Saturday its busiest market day.

ARRIVAL AND DEPARTURE

By plane Maya Island Air and Tropic Air operate several daily flights from Belize City (via Dangriga and Placencia),

CACAO AND THE MAYA

The ancient Maya were the first to process cacao into **chocolate**, and these days commercial production and ecotourism are thriving. The environment of Toledo provides ideal growing conditions, and you're likely to see cacao beans drying on concrete pads in the local villages. Almost all the crop is organically produced and used to make the delicious **Maya Gold** chocolate sold abroad by chocolate company Green and Black's.

New, local entrepreneurs have started up, too, including **Cotton Tree Chocolate** at 2 Front St in Punta Gorda (Mon–Fri 8.30am–noon & 1.30–5pm, Sat 8.30am–noon; ☎621 8776, ⓦcottontreechocolate.com), which offers free tastings and tours. **Ixcacao**, a short distance north in the village of San Felipe (☎742 4050, ⓦixcacaomayabelizeanchocolate.com), is a working chocolate farm where you can see the beans growing, watch them being turned into chocolate (US$7.50 for two people), and stay the night in a sixteen-bunk dormitory with electricity and a shared shower room, plus breakfast and dinner for US$25.

The **Chocolate Festival of Belize**, held at the end of May each year, features a Saturday programme of street events and concerts in Punta Gorda, followed by Maya dance and cultural activities at Lubaantun on Sunday.

landing at the rudimentary airstrip five blocks inland, a 5–10min walk from most of the town's hotels.

By bus Buses to and from Belize City stop outside the James Buses office just off Front St, though the express bus departs at 6am from the petrol station northeast of the centre. Buses to the Maya villages leave from the market area.

Destinations Belize City via Belmopan and Dangriga (10 daily, express service at 6am; 4hr 45min–6hr 30min); Jalacte via San Antonio, Río Blanco and Pueblo Viejo (Mon–Sat 3–4 daily, Sun 6am only; 3hr); San Benito Poite, via Blue Creek (4 weekly; 2hr 30min); Silver Creek via San Pedro Columbia for Lubaantun, and San Miguel (Mon–Sat 4–5 daily; 2hr).

By boat Four boats sail each day from the main dock near the centre of the seafront to Puerto Barrios in Guatemala. Requena's Charter Service leaves at 9.30am (☎722 2070, ⓔwater.taxi@btl.net); Memo's at 1pm; Pichilingo at 2pm (☎502 7948 5525); and Marisol at 4pm (☎722 2870). A ferry to Lívingston also departs Tues and Fri at 10am. There's no need to buy your ticket in advance; just turn up at the dock half an hour before departure.

Destinations Puerto Barrios, Guatemala (4 daily; 1hr; Bz$50); Lívingston, Guatemala (2 weekly; 10am Tues & Fri; 1hr; Bz$60).

INFORMATION AND ACTIVITIES

Tourist information The Belize Tourism Industry Association has a large office in a pretty colonial building, just south of the dock on Front St (Mon–Fri 8am–noon & 1–5pm; ☎722 2531); staff can help with transport schedules and set up tours of outlying cayes and sites. Be sure to pick up a copy of the free local newspaper, the *Toledo Howler*.

Garbutt brothers Based at the small marina at the entrance to town, the Garbutt brothers run scuba, snorkel and marine tours, as well as affordable trips to the pristine

Lime Caye. They also rent kayaks and seaside cabins (☎604 3548, ⓦgarbuttsfishinglodge.com).

Maroon Creole Drum School Emmeth Young, co-owner of the *Driftwood Café* (see p.100), offers classes and workshops in making as well as playing drums in a creekside camp a mile out of town (☎668 7733, ⓦmarooncreoledrumschool.com).

ReefCI This research organization, which offers divers the chance to participate in scientific programmes on four-day diving trips to Sapodilla Caye, has an office on Front St, opposite the tourist office (☎629 4266, ⓦreefci.com).

TIDE The Toledo Institute for Development and the Environment, based on the main road a mile out of town, close to *Waluco's* (☎722 2129, ⓦtidetours.org), is involved with many conservation projects. It also offers trips to the cayes and marine reserves; cacao, mountain-bike and kayak tours; and camping trips to Payne's Creek National Park.

ACCOMMODATION

Accommodation in Punta Gorda is generally inexpensive, while it's also possible to arrange guesthouse and homestay accommodation in surrounding villages (see box, p.101).

Grace's Hotel & Restaurant 19 Main St ☎702 2414, ⓔgracemcp@hotmail.com. Functional, clean rooms with private bath in the centre of town; those with a/c cost twice as much. The restaurant, open daily, serves a large menu including hearty Belizean dishes for less than Bz$15. US$27

★**Nature's Way Guest House** 65 Front St ☎702 2119, ⓔnatureswayguesthouse@hotmail.com. The best place in PG to meet other travellers and get information, where eight clean rooms overlooking the sea have shared baths and cold showers. Breakfast (US$6), wi-fi and a book exchange also available. US$25

St Charles Inn 23 King St ☎722 2149, ⓔstcharlespg @btl.net. One of the smarter and larger options in central

1

PG, with friendly staff. All rooms have private bath, and most have TV and a/c. **US$54.50**

Tate's Guesthouse 34 José María Nuñez St, two blocks west of the town centre ☎ 722 0147, ✉ tatesguesthouse @yahoo.com. Quiet, friendly, family-run hotel. Spotless rooms have private bath, TV and wi-fi access; some with a/c. **US$25**

EATING AND DRINKING

Punta Gorda has several excellent places to eat with very reasonable prices.

Asha's Culture Kitchen 80 Front St ☎ 632 8025. Welcoming restaurant in a sleepy seafront spot, serving fresh seafood and BBQ – lobster Bz$30, chicken Bz$10 – on the large deck over the water, and hosting live music and/or drumming most nights. Mon & Wed–Sat 4pm–midnight, Sun 2pm–midnight.

★ Driftwood Café & Gallery 9 Front St ☎ 632 7841. Roomy, friendly café, with free wi-fi, a small art gallery, and a spacious veranda, that serves the best coffee in town, plus great food. Daily specials like fish quesadillas, callaloo omelettes or vegan chocolate chilli cost around Bz$12. Ask here about drum lessons. Daily 7am–4pm.

★ Gomier's Alejandro Vernon St ☎ 722 2929, ⓦ facebook .com/Gomiers. Simple thatched *palapa*, across from the sea at the north end of town, where chef/owner Gomier cooks up wonderful vegetarian dishes and seafood to a gentle reggae soundtrack, and can also teach you how to make your own tofu (Bz$75pp). Fish or tofu burgers Bz$8, garlic shrimp or whole fish Bz$16–18. Mon–Sat 8am–9pm.

Jocelyn's BBQ Front St ☎ 661 9267. This small green shack, with a few plastic tables and chairs scattered at the sea's edge across from the petrol station, serves great jerk chicken and fried fish (with coco-rice and beans) for less than Bz$10. Daily 6am–9pm.

PG Sports Bar Main St ☎ 722 2329. Punta Gorda's liveliest nightspot, opposite the clock tower, with a huge indoor bar; every weekend, locals flock to the dark, sweaty dancefloor to get down to punta, soca, reggaetón and rap. Mon–Thurs 7.30pm–midnight, Fri & Sat 7.30pm–4am.

DIRECTORY

Bank and exchange Belize Bank (with ATM) is on the main square across from the Civic Center. A moneychanger sets up outside the immigration office when international boats are docking.

Internet V-Comp (Mon–Sat 8am–8pm) and KC Photo Shop (Mon–Sat 7.30am–9pm, Sun 4–9pm), both on Main St, charge Bz$6/hr.

Laundry PG Laundry, on Main St beside the Civic Center (Mon–Sat 8am–5pm; ☎ 722 2273).

Post office In the government buildings a block back from the ferry dock.

THE CAYES OFF TOLEDO

Marking the southern tip of Belize's Barrier Reef, the cayes and reefs off Punta Gorda get relatively little attention from visitors. Roughly 130 low-lying mangrove cayes clustered in the mouth of a large bay north of PG are protected in the 600-square-kilometre Port Honduras Marine Reserve, which was established in part to safeguard manatees living in the shallow water. Further out to sea, the Sapodilla Cayes Marine Reserve incorporates another group of irresistible islands.

Snake and Sapodilla cayes

North of Punta Gorda in the **Port Honduras Marine Reserve**, the **Snake Cayes** are idyllic and uninhabited Caribbean islands that draw a small number of visitors for their stunning beaches.

Further out in the Gulf of Honduras, the **Sapodilla Cayes** form a separate **marine reserve** (Bz$20 entrance fee). Guatemalan as well as Belizean day-trippers frequent the largest, **Hunting Caye**; most simply choose to relax on the beach, but the reef, just a few hundred metres offshore, provides excellent opportunities for snorkellers.

Some of these islands already have accommodation, and more resorts are planned, though at present the cayes and reserve receive few foreign visitors and are fascinating to explore on a day-trip from Punta Gorda; contact TIDE (see p.99) for more information.

INLAND TOLEDO

Exploring the Maya heartland of inland Toledo can be a true highlight of a trip to Belize. Roughly half the inhabitants here are descended from the Maya refugees who have fled Guatemala since the late nineteenth century. For the most part, the Mopan Maya from Petén and the Kekchí speakers from the Verapaz highlands keep to their own distinct villages, which look much like their counterparts in Guatemala. Very few speak Spanish, maintaining instead their indigenous languages and Belizean Kriol, and tourism is distinctly low-impact.

Ancient Maya ruins are scattered throughout. The best-known sites are Lubaantun, the supposed home of the famous Crystal Skull, and Nim Li Punit, with its impressive steles. The largest villages are San Antonio and San Pedro Columbia. Simple guesthouses and Maya homestays are available in the rural areas, though a few more luxurious lodges have opened their doors in recent years.

San Antonio

Perched on a small hilltop 32km northwest of PG, the Mopan Maya village of **San Antonio** is the largest Maya settlement in Belize. Its founders came from the village of San Luis, just across the border in Guatemala, and the beautiful church of their patron saint, San Luis Rey, stands in the centre of the village. Most visitors come to relax and learn about Maya village life, but the surrounding area

is rich in wildlife, dominated by jungle-clad hills and swift-flowing rivers, and offers excellent **hiking**.

ACCOMMODATION

Bol's Hilltop Hotel San Antonio ☎702 2144. Basic rooms with shared bath and superb views; also a good place to get information on local natural history and archeology. **US$10**

Blue Creek

The main attraction of the Maya village of **BLUE CREEK**, 40km northwest of PG, is a beautiful stretch of water running through magnificent rainforest. To get to the best swimming spot, a lovely turquoise pool, walk for ten minutes upriver along the right-hand bank. The creek's source, **Hokeb Ha** cave, is another fifteen minutes' walk upriver through the privately owned **Blue Creek Rainforest Reserve**. A guide can take you to Maya altars deep in the cave.

Uxbenka

The ruins of **UXBENKA**, a small Maya site, are superbly positioned on an exposed hilltop 7km west of San Antonio, enjoying great views towards the coast. As you climb the hill, just before the village of **Santa Cruz**, you'll be able to make out the shape of two tree-covered mounds and a plaza, and there are several steles protected by thatched shelters.

Wonderful **waterfalls** lie within easy reach of the road nearby. Between Santa Cruz and Santa Elena, the **Río Blanco Falls** tumble over a rocky ledge into a deep

---

MAYA VILLAGE GUESTHOUSES AND HOMESTAYS

In five Mopan or Kekchí Maya villages in Toledo – Laguna, San Antonio, Santa Elena, San José and San Miguel – basic but clean eight-bed **guesthouses** accommodate overnight guests for Bz$25 per person. Visitors can eat with local families for Bz$7–8 per meal. Each location has its own attraction, be it a cave, waterfall, river or ruin, and offers activities such as guided walks or rental kayaks for around Bz$10–15 per hour. In a further five villages – Barranco, Blue Creek, Medina Bank, Pueblo Viejo and San Pedro Columbia – similar activities are available, but there's no accommodation. The programme is organized by the **Toledo Ecotourism Association** (TEA; ☎722 2531, ⓦteabelize.org). Look out for its logo as you travel around; it's extremely unusual for the guesthouses to be booked out, so in most cases you can just show up in the village and stay. TEA also arranges packages, including accommodation plus all meals and activities, for Bz$85 per person per day, while its website details **bus timetables** for the villages.

In addition, the **Maya Village Homestay Network**, run by Yvonne and Alfredo Villoria (Dem Dats Doin'; ☎722 2470, ⓔdemdatsdoin@btl.net), enables visitors to stay with a Mopan or Kekchí Maya family in one of three villages – Aquacate, San José and Na Luum Ca.

1

pool, while at **Pueblo Viejo**, 7km further on, an impressive series of cascades provides a spectacular sight. Trucks and buses continue 13km further west to **Jalacte**, at the Guatemalan border, used regularly as a crossing point by nationals of both countries, though it's not currently a legal entry or exit point for tourists.

Lubaantun

The Maya site of **LUBAANTUN** (daily 8am–5pm; Bz$10) is an easy visit from Punta Gorda via the bus to **San Pedro Columbia**. To get to the ruins, head through the village and cross the Columbia River; just beyond you'll see the track to the ruins, a few hundred metres away on the left. Some of the finds made at the site are displayed in glass cases at the **visitors' centre**, including astonishing, eccentric flints and ceramics.

Lubaantun ("Place of the Fallen Stones") was a major Late Classic Maya centre, though it was occupied only briefly, from around 750 to 890 AD. The ruins stand on a series of ridges shaped and filled by Maya architects, with retaining walls up to 10m high. The whole site is essentially a single acropolis, with five main plazas, eleven major structures, three ball courts and some impressive pyramids surrounded by forest.

Lubaantun's most enigmatic discovery came in 1926, when the famous **Crystal Skull** was "found" beneath an altar by Anna Mitchell-Hedges, the daughter of the British Museum expedition's leader. Carved from pure rock crystal, the skull's origin and age remain unclear, though much contested.

ACCOMMODATION

Back-a-Bush San Miguel ☎ 631 1731, ⓦ back-a-bush .com. Very simple rooms in a garden compound just off the road to Lubaantun, run by friendly Dutch owner Elsbeth. As well as a dorm holding six bunks, there's also one private room with its own shower, a more comfortable

cabin, and space for camping. Camping/person US$5, dorm US$12.50, room US$30, cabin US$50

Maya Mountain Research Farm 3km upriver from San Pedro Columbia ☎ 630 4386, ⓦ mmrfbz.org. Concealed within the folds of the namesake mountains, this unique set-up offers permaculture students, volunteers and eco-warriors a rare opportunity to fall off the grid. Getting here is an adventure in itself – with a guide from San Pedro Columbia, you either hike or paddle in on a canoe. The rustic wooden cabins barely interfere with the engulfing jungle cacao farm, which borders a pristine stretch of the Río Grande, and meals are cooked on a wood-fired stove and shared in a large *palapa*; wi-fi is available, and other activities include hiking – Lubaantun is less than 3km away – tubing, and exploring unexcavated ruins. They prefer visitors to stay for at least a week. Per person per day, three meals included US$50

Sun Creek Lodge Mile 12 Southern Hwy, Sun Creek ☎ 604 2124, ⓦ suncreeklodge.com. A naturalist's paradise, 3km south of the Dump junction, providing modern conveniences with a rustic feel. Four beautiful thatched cabañas, all with electricity and two with double beds and private bathrooms, and a grander villa with separate living room. The jungle bucket showers make you feel as though you're standing under a waterfall. Local tours and jeep rental (from US$60/day). Rates include breakfast. US$65

Nim Li Punit

Just 1km off the Southern Highway, 73km south of the Placencia junction and an easy day-trip from Punta Gorda, **Nim Li Punit** (daily 9am–5pm; Bz$10) is a Late Classic Maya site that may have been allied to nearby Lubaantun and to Quiriguá in Guatemala (see p.338). The ruins stand atop a ridge, surrounded by the fields of the Maya village of **Indian Creek**.

The **visitors' centre** explains the site, while the adjoining Steles House holds 25 steles found here, eight of them carved. The tallest, among the tallest anywhere in the Maya world, is Stele 14, at more than 9m high. Few of the structures in the site itself have been excavated to any great extent, but the cleared open areas between them are maintained as lush lawns, so it's a lovely place to stroll around.

RANGER FOR A DAY

The **Ya'axche Conservation Trust** (☎ 722 0108, ⓦ yaaxche.org) runs an interesting "ranger for a day" programme from their Toledo HQ. Guests spend the day patrolling the Golden Stream Corridor Preserve, learning about medicinal plants, checking for signs of illegal activity and monitoring biodiversity. The US$45 fee pays the salaries of local park rangers.

TERRAPINS AT TORTUGUERO

Costa Rica

HIGHLIGHTS

❶ Tortuguero Glimpse turtles galore at this isolated village and wildlife-rich surrounding national park. **See p.133**

❷ Puerto Viejo de Talamanca Great surfing and Creole cuisine on the lively Caribbean coast. **See p.139**

❸ Monteverde Hike or zipline in ancient, brooding cloudforest. **See p.143**

❹ Nicoya Peninsula Surf Costa Rica's best waves and find your perfect beach. **See p.157**

❺ Parque Nacional Chirripó Spectacular hiking on the country's highest mountain. **See p.180**

❻ Parque Nacional Corcovado Rainforest treks, amazing wildlife and remote beaches. **See p.188**

HIGHLIGHTS ARE MARKED ON THE MAP ON PP.106–107

ROUGH COSTS

Daily budget Basic US$40/occasional treat US$90

Drink Beer US$2.50, coffee US$1

Food *Casado* US$7

Hostel/budget hotel US$11/US$20

Travel San José–Puerto Viejo de Talamanca (210km) by bus: 4hr 30min, US$10

FACT FILE

Population 4.7 million

Languages Spanish, Creole, Bribrí

Currency Costa Rica colón (CRC; c)

Capital San José (population: 288,000)

International phone code ☎ 506

Time zone GMT -6hr

Introduction

Costa Rica can appear almost unfairly blessed with natural attractions. Within its boundaries lie lush rain- and cloudforests, smouldering volcanoes, mangrove swamps and long sandy beaches, as well as tranquil colonial towns and chilled-out coastal resorts. In sharp contrast to the turbulence experienced by many of its neighbours, the country has become synonymous with stability and prosperity – Costa Ricans, or Ticos, enjoy the best healthcare and education and the highest rate of literacy and (along with Panama) life expectancy in the isthmus. The country has a long democratic tradition of free and open elections, no standing army (it was abolished in 1948) and even a Nobel Peace Prize to its name, won by former president Oscar Arias Sánchez.

Indeed, Costa Rica's past and present are so quiet, comparatively, that the nation is often said to lack a history or identity. This is far from the truth: Costa Rica's character is rooted in its distinct **local cultures**, from the Afro-Caribbean province of Limón, with its Creole cuisine and pidgin English, to the traditional values embodied by the *sabaneros* (cowboys) of Guanacaste.

For travellers, though, Costa Rica is the prime **ecotourism** destination in Central America. Over a quarter of the country is protected, and every year thousands of visitors come to experience the stunning biodiversity offered by its parks and reserves, from **Monteverde** and **Corcovado** to **Chirripó** and **Tortuguero**; hiking, rafting and canopy tours are the most popular activities for exploring the enormous array of exotic flora and fauna. The landscape is incredibly varied: majestic volcanoes, such as Arenal, Irazú, **Poás** and **Rincón de la Vieja**, punctuate the country's mountainous spine, while the beaches on both coasts – **Tamarindo, Santa Teresa, Jacó** and **Puerto Viejo de Talamanca**, among others – provide excellent surfing. And finally, there's cultural diversity; this one small country incorporates the cowboys of **Liberia** and the northwest, the Afro-Caribbean rhythms of **Cahuita** and **Limón** and the indigenous reserves of the Bribrí, Cabécar and Maleku. While the potent combination of sights and activities, accessibility and safety means Costa Rica can sometimes be expensive and crowded, no trip to Central America would be complete without stopping here.

WHEN TO VISIT

The main rainy season runs from May to mid-November, peaking in September and October (on the Caribbean coast, rain falls April to August and November to December). These months are less crowded and generally cheaper, as hotels, tours and activities lower their prices to attract the smaller numbers of tourists. **Peak season** (December, January and Easter) is by and large the driest and the most expensive time to visit – accommodation and transport require advanced bookings during these times.

CHRONOLOGY

10,000 BC First human settlement in Costa Rica.

1000 BC Several autonomous tribes inhabit Costa Rica, the Chorotegas being the most numerous. Foundations are laid at Guayabo, which is mysteriously abandoned around 1400 AD.

100 BC Costa Rica becomes part of the trade network that stretches from Mexico to the Andes.

1502 AD Christopher Columbus lands on the Caribbean coast and allegedly dubs the land "Costa Rica" ("Rich Coast").

1506 Columbus's rival, Diego de Nicuesa, is dispatched by Spain's King Ferdinand to govern the region; expedition fails.

1522 A third Spanish expedition attempts to settle the region. The indigenous people begin a campaign of resistance.

1540 The Spanish establish the Kingdom of Guatemala, which includes most of Central America as well as the Mexican state of Chiapas. After it's discovered that there is no gold in the region, Spain largely ignores Costa Rica for the next several hundred years.

1563 Juan Vásquez de Coronado founds Cartago, the country's first capital.

1723 Volcán Irazú erupts, virtually destroying Cartago in the process.

1737 San José founded.

1779 Coffee is introduced to Costa Rica.

1821 Costa Rica wins independence from Spain.

1823 San José named as capital after a civil war between Josefinos (citizens of San José) and the citizens of Cartago. Costa Rica becomes a state in the Federal Republic of Central America.

1824 Juan Mora Fernández becomes the nation's first elected head of state. He encourages coffee cultivation with land grants, thereby creating an elite class of coffee barons. Guanacaste becomes part of Costa Rica.

1838 Costa Rica withdraws from the Federal Republic, and declares sovereignty.

1843 Coffee becomes the nation's major export crop after British merchant William Le Lacheur establishes a direct trade route between Costa Rica and England.

1856 American adventurer William Walker invades Costa Rica with dreams of annexing Central America to the US, but is defeated in the Battle of Santa Rosa by national hero Juan Santamaría.

1870 General Tomás Guardia Gutiérrez seizes power, ruling as dictator for 12 years. In contrast to his ascent, his policies include curbing military power and free (and compulsory) education for all.

1889 First democratic elections held, though neither women nor blacks are allowed to vote.

1914 The opening of the Panama Canal boosts Costa Rica's economy, now dominated by the banana trade.

1919 Dictator Federico Tinoco Granados violently deposed.

1940 President Rafael Calderón Guardia enacts minimum-wage laws and restricts the working day to eight hours.

1948 Teodoro Picado declares himself president after an annulled election, prompting a six-week civil war and the rise to power of José "Don Pepe" Figueres Ferrer. Figueres famously abolishes the armed forces, establishes citizenship rights for Afro-Caribbeans and institutes the female vote.

1963 Reserva Natural Absoluta Cabo Blanco becomes Costa Rica's first officially protected area.

1981 Economic crisis – Costa Rica defaults on loan interest payments, accruing one of world's highest per capita debts – and instability, caused by civil war in Nicaragua.

1987 Costa Rican President Oscar Arias Sánchez is awarded the Nobel Peace Prize for his efforts in ending the Nicaraguan civil war.

2007 Costa Rica signs controversial CAFTA (a free-trade agreement with the US and Central American neighbours) after several years of fiery debate.

2010 Laura Chinchilla succeeds her political mentor Oscar Arias Sánchez to become the country's first female president.

2012 Major earthquake occurs in Guanacaste, measuring 7.6 on the Richter scale.

2014 The Chinchilla administration receives the lowest approval rating in two decades; Luis Guillermo Solís becomes president.

ARRIVAL AND DEPARTURE

Visitors flying to Costa Rica usually arrive at **Juan Santamaría International Airport** (SJO) near Alajuela (17km northwest of San José). Iberia (Ⓦiberia.com) is the only airline offering direct flights from Europe (Madrid), though these are normally much more expensive than flying via the US; American Airlines (Ⓦaa.com), Delta (Ⓦdelta.com), United (Ⓦunited.com) and US Airways (Ⓦusairways.com) connect Costa Rica to numerous North American cities, including Houston, Miami, New York and Toronto, as well as various Central American destinations. Flights from North America and Nicaragua also arrive at **Daniel Oduber International Airport**, 12km west of Liberia – a convenient jumping-off point for the Nicoya Peninsula. Everyone entering the country technically requires a return ticket, but that's rarely checked at the airport; if entering by land, you are more likely to be asked to produce an onward ticket.

Most travellers entering by **land** arrive with Tica Bus (Ⓦticabus.com) and TransNica (Ⓦtransnica.com), which provide services from Guatemala City,

LAND ROUTES TO COSTA RICA

Costa Rica has several **land borders** with Nicaragua and Panama. The main border crossing with **Nicaragua** is at Peñas Blancas (see box, p.171) via Liberia. Further east, there is another crossing at Los Chiles (see box, p.177), though this also involves a boat trip (and usually an overnight stop).

The main crossing for **Panama** is at Paso Canoas (see box, p.190). Sixaola (see box, p.143), on the Caribbean coast, is a smaller crossing, as is Río Sereno in the southern highlands.

2

2

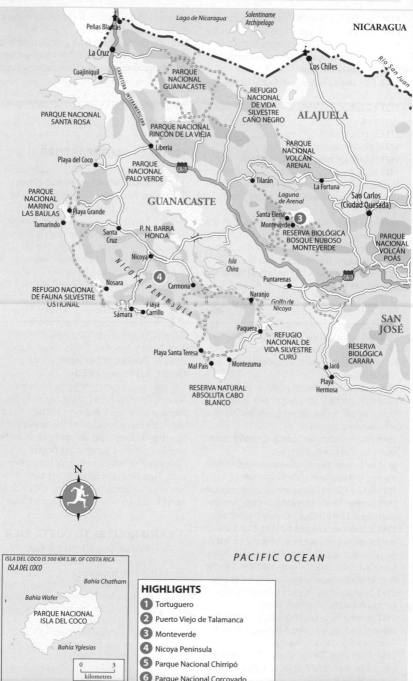

NICARAGUA

Peñas Blancas
La Cruz
Cuajiniquil
Lago de Nicaragua
Solentiname Archipelago
Los Chiles
Río San Juan

PARQUE NACIONAL GUANACASTE

REFUGIO NACIONAL DE VIDA SILVESTRE CAÑO NEGRO

ALAJUELA

PARQUE NACIONAL SANTA ROSA

PARQUE NACIONAL RINCÓN DE LA VIEJA

Liberia

PARQUE NACIONAL VOLCÁN ARENAL

Playa del Coco

PARQUE NACIONAL PALO VERDE

Tilarán

La Fortuna

San Carlos (Ciudad Quesada)

GUANACASTE

Laguna de Arenal

PARQUE NACIONAL MARINO LAS BAULAS

Playa Grande

Tamarindo

P. N. BARRA HONDA

Santa Cruz

Santa Elena
Monteverde

RESERVA BIOLÓGICA BOSQUE NUBOSO MONTEVERDE

PARQUE NACIONAL VOLCÁN POÁS

Nicoya

Isla Chira

Nosara

Carmona

Puntarenas

REFUGIO NACIONAL DE FAUNA SILVESTRE OSTIONAL

Sámara

Playa Carrillo

Naranjo

Golfo de Nicoya

SAN JOSÉ

Paquera

REFUGIO NACIONAL DE VIDA SILVESTRE CURÚ

RESERVA BIOLÓGICA CARARA

Playa Santa Teresa

Mal País

Montezuma

Jacó

Playa Hermosa

RESERVA NATURAL ABSOLUTA CABO BLANCO

N

PACIFIC OCEAN

ISLA DEL COCO IS 500 KM S.W. OF COSTA RICA

ISLA DEL COCO

Bahía Chatham

Bahía Wafer

PARQUE NACIONAL ISLA DEL COCO

Bahía Yglesias

0   3
kilometres

HIGHLIGHTS

1 Tortuguero

2 Puerto Viejo de Talamanca

3 Monteverde

4 Nicoya Peninsula

5 Parque Nacional Chirripó

6 Parque Nacional Corcovado

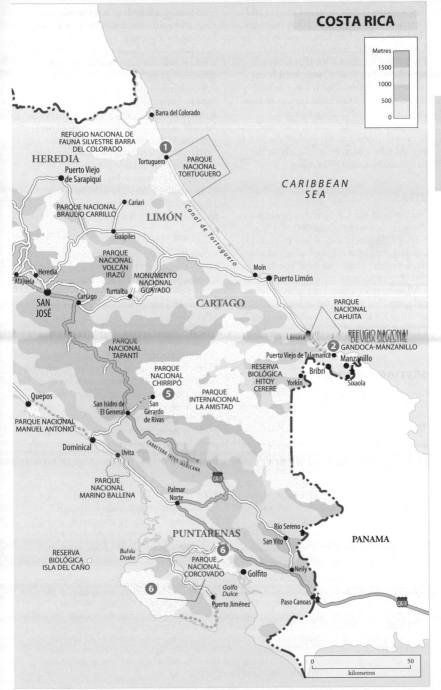

2

Tegucigalpa (Honduras), Managua and Granada (Nicaragua), and San Salvador (El Salvador) to San José, sometimes via Liberia. Services from Changuinola, David and Panama City (Panama) go straight to San José. Cheap local buses run to the borders, but it's worth paying more for an international bus, as it saves you the hassle of finding onward transport across the border; they also tend to cross borders quickly and efficiently. If you do take a local bus, go early in the day to allow time for queuing.

VISAS

Nationals of the UK, Ireland (and most Western European countries), the US, Canada, Australia and New Zealand do not require a **visa** for stays of up to ninety days. For the latest visa info, check out ⓦvisitcostarica.com.

All visitors to Costa Rica must have a **passport** that is valid for at least six months. By law, you should carry your passport on you at all times, though a photocopy suffices.

GETTING AROUND

Costa Rica's inexpensive, comprehensive public **bus** system covers even remote areas.

BY BUS

San José is the hub for virtually all **bus** services in the country; it's often impossible to travel from one place to another without backtracking through the capital. No buses run the three days before Easter Sunday. **Timetables** can be found on ⓦvisitcostarica .com. **Tickets** are cheap – the most expensive journey in the country (San José to Paso Canoas) costs less than US$15

– and are issued with a seat number and a date; make sure the date is correct. If you're heading for a popular destination with few bus connections, book in advance and buy a return ticket as soon as you arrive to guarantee a seat.

A network of more expensive **shuttle buses** – Interbus (ⓣ4100 0888, ⓦinterbusonline.com) and Gray Line (ⓣ2220 2126, ⓦgraylinecostarica.com) – connects San José with Costa Rica's main tourist destinations. These are faster and more comfortable than public buses, and operate door to door. Fares range from around US$40 to US$90; Gray Line also offer various passes, starting from US$198 for a week.

BY PLANE

Costa Rica's two domestic **airlines**, Sansa (ⓦflysansa.com; from Juan Santamaría International Airport) and NatureAir (ⓦnatureair.com; from Tobías Bolaños Airport in Pavas, 7km west of San José), offer scheduled services between San José and destinations such as Tortuguero, Bahía Drake, Golfito, Liberia, Playa Nosara, Tamarindo, La Fortuna Puerto Jiménez and Quepos. Planes are small and highly weather-dependent, so schedules are vulnerable to change. Tickets must be reserved at least two weeks in advance in high season. Rates start from around US$61, though NatureAir offers "*locos*" prices (from US$43) for flights that aren't fully booked.

BY TAXI

Taxis are plentiful in urban areas – look for red vehicles with yellow triangles containing the licence number marked on the front passenger door, and a taxi sign on the roof. In San José, taxis are

---

ADDRESSES IN COSTA RICA

As in most Central American countries, Costa Rica's major cities are laid out in a **grid**, with the main plaza in the middle. Calles run north–south, avenidas east–west. Generally, the calles **east** of the plaza are odd-numbered and those to the **west** even-numbered; the **Calle Central** (sometimes called C 0) is often immediately east of the Parque Central. Avenidas are usually even-numbered **south** of the park, and odd-numbered to the **north**. Exact **street numbers** tend not to exist; a city address written in the Guide as "C 16, Av 1/3", for example, means the place you're looking for is on Calle 16, between avenidas 1 and 3. In smaller towns, addresses tend to be given in terms of landmarks.

metered, while elsewhere, fares are agreed on in advance. In rural areas, 4WDs are often used as taxis, and in some towns you'll also find *colectivos* (shared taxis).

BY CAR

Car rental and petrol in Costa Rica can be expensive, but having your own transport is useful for visiting some of the country's more exciting sights, such as the Valle Central's volcanoes, the Nicoya Peninsula and the Osa Peninsula. Few buses serve these routes, and the timetables of those that do often leave you with little time for exploration.

Road **conditions** are often poor, especially in more remote areas. In dry season, most roads are passable in regular vehicles (though 4WDs are recommended); in the rainy season, most rental companies will insist that you rent a 4WD. Off the Interamericana and other major paved roads, be prepared for potholes, unsurfaced roads, narrow single-lane carriageways lacking hard shoulders, streams to be crossed and obstructions such as cattle.

In peak season, **rental costs** vary from around US$395 per week for a regular vehicle up to US$575 for a 4WD (both including full insurance), and you can expect to pay roughly US$80 a tank on a mid-sized vehicle. Reserving and paying for the car rental online makes for substantial savings. Major international rental companies – Avis, Hertz, Budget, Europcar – are based at and near the international airports; some have other branches in Tamarindo, Jacó and other popular destinations. **Local rental companies** such as Adobe (☎2542 4848, ⓦadobecar.com) and Vamos Rent A Car (☎2432 5258, ⓦvamos4x4.com) offer much better deals.

Buying basic insurance is mandatory, even if you have your own; note that basic insurance in Costa Rica tends only to cover damage by you to other people's vehicles, not to your own car. Full insurance starts at around US$27 per day. **Theft** from vehicles is common, so never leave any valuables in your rental car.

BY BICYCLE

Costa Rica is the easiest of all Central American countries to explore by bike,

and **cycling** is an inexpensive and popular way to get around. Most beach towns have at least one bicycle rental outlet, with prices from around US$10 a day. The quality of the bikes varies greatly, so check the equipment before you pay.

ACCOMMODATION

Although Costa Rica is one of the most expensive countries in Central America, it holds plenty of **budget** B&Bs, hostels and campsites. Most towns have a range of places to stay, and even the smallest settlements have a basic *pensión* or *hospedaje*. In hostels, a dorm bed can cost as little as US$5 a night, and a basic room from around US$20, while from around US$35 a night you'll get a more comfortable en-suite room, with a fan and possibly even a TV and phone, in a B&B environment. Most of the youth hostels that abound all over Costa Rica offer the various amenities backpackers have come to expect – wi-fi, laundry service, book exchange, TV lounge, fans or a/c, tour-booking services and even swimming pools.

When looking at prices, ask if the national **hotel tax** (13 percent) has been added to the published price. Most hostels and hotels price their rooms in US dollars, though you can pay in dollars or colones. Reservations are necessary in high season (Dec–April).

Camping is fairly widespread. In the beach towns, especially, you'll usually find at least one well-equipped private campsite, and many budget hotels let you pitch your tent in the grounds. Although not all national parks have campsites, those that do are generally of high quality, with at least some basic facilities, and cost around US$5 per person per day; all supplies must be carried in, and all rubbish carried out. Never leave valuables in your tent. Camping rough is illegal.

FOOD AND DRINK

The cheapest places to eat are **sodas** – local diner/greasy spoons – which serve three meals a day, with *platos del día* (daily specials) costing around

2

US$5. There's a wide range of **restaurants**, particularly in tourist hotspots; expect to pay from US$10 for a main course in the capital, double that in some coastal towns. A town's central **market** is a good place to stock up on fresh produce, with stalls offering quick and cheap meals. Larger cities boast a full array of American fast-food chains, as well as inexpensive Chinese joints. Generally, restaurants **open** early, around 7am, and most are empty or closed by 10pm. When ordering, check whether or not tax (13 percent) is included in the price.

Costa Rican cuisine (*comida típica*) is economical and filling, with staples such as **gallo pinto** ("painted rooster"), a breakfast dish of rice and beans, and **casados** ("married"), combinations of rice, beans, coleslaw, plantain and meat or fish that are frequently large enough for two to share. Fried/roast chicken is another national favourite. You will also find excellent fresh **fish**, including *pargo* (red snapper), *atún* (tuna) and *corvina* (sea bass), with Tican-style *ceviche* a speciality. Fresh **fruit** is cheap and plentiful – try *mamones chinos* (a kind of lychee), *maracuya* (passion fruit) and *marañón*, whose seed is the cashew nut.

Most menus will have a **vegetarian** option, particularly in international restaurants where the menus are geared towards foreign customers.

DRINK

Costa Rica is famous for its **coffee**, which is a good souvenir to take home – and it's not hard to locate a decent *café negro*. Also good are the **juices** or *refrescos*, combining fresh fruit, ice and either milk (*leche*) or water (*agua*); *batidos* (smoothies) are a thicker, tastier variation, and in Guanacaste you can also get the distinctive corn-based **horchata**. **Tap water** is safe to drink in most places.

Costa Rica has several local brands of lager **beer**. Most popular, and cheapest, is Imperial, but Bavaria Gold is the best of the bunch. Pilsen and Rock Ice (lemon flavoured) are also worth a try; pricier imported beers are available in bars, restaurants and hotels.

SHOP TILL YOU DROP

Costa Rica's indigenous tribes excel when it comes to **crafts**. Look out for colourful Boruca masks – either devil masks or those with jungle motifs – Chorotega pottery, Huetar baskets, coconut-shell carvings by the Bribrí, and cocoa products.

For an after-dinner drink, try creamy, Baileys-style coffee **liqueurs** such as Café Rica. Those with a stronger stomach can try the indigenous sugarcane-based spirit, **guaro**, of which Cacique is the most popular brand.

CULTURE AND ETIQUETTE

Costa Rica is a friendly country, and many Ticos speak at least some English. Though it's officially a **Catholic** nation, the degrees of orthodoxy are hugely varied and many denominations of Christianity are present. Attitudes are still fairly conservative, so do not be tempted to sunbathe topless or nude.

Macho attitudes still exist. **Gay and lesbian** travellers should be discreet, but the increasing number of gay-friendly hotels and nightclubs, particularly in San José and Manuel Antonio, tells of a gradual shift in mentality; ⓦcostaricagaymap.com is a useful website. Solo **women** can travel alone with relative confidence. While gringa-enticement is a rather competitive and popular way to pass the time, it is usually harmless and best ignored.

Prostitution is legal in Costa Rica; underage prostitution is not. Larger beach towns such as Jacó have a reputation as magnets for older foreign men drawn by local underage girls. Do not partake in this socially destructive trade.

TICO PHRASES

¿Cómo amanecío? How did you sleep? – literally "how did you wake up?".
¡Pura vida! Literally "pure life" – a general greeting used to mean "cool", "all right", "all good" and so on.
¡Upe! "Equivalent of "Is there anyone home?" – used when arriving at someone's house, normally in rural areas.

Friendly **bargaining** is worth a try at craft markets but is not the done thing elsewhere. As for **tipping**, most restaurants include a ten-percent service charge in the bill; after a guided tour, a small tip to the guide is the norm.

SPORTS AND OUTDOOR ACTIVITIES

With a national team that has qualified for several World Cups, **fútbol** (or soccer) is Costa Rica's most popular spectator sport. The nation's **surf** – some of the best in Central America – is one of its biggest draws. More than fifty well-known breaks dot the Pacific and Caribbean coasts, and all beach communities offer assorted surf schools and board-companies; Tamarindo, Santa Teresa/Mal País and Puerto Viejo de Talamanca are the most popular beach locations. **Scuba diving** is less of a big deal in Costa Rica than Belize or Honduras, though there is decent **snorkelling** off both coasts; the best areas for exploring brilliant corals are Bahía Ballena and Manzanilla. **Kayaking** makes a good way to explore the country's many lagoons, rivers and mangroves; paddling around Golfo Dulce from Puerto Jiménez, you may even see whales, while Bahía Drake's mangroves are also rich with animal life. Costa Rica also boasts world-class **whitewater rafting** (Class I–V), particularly along the *ríos* Reventazón and Pacuare in the Valle Central, with gentler options near Puerto Viejo de Sarapiquí.

On land, there are some superb **hiking** trails, from short jaunts in the smaller national parks to multiday jungle treks in Parque Nacional Corcovado, while Volcán Chirripó remains the country's most challenging ascent. Costa Rica is also one of the best places in the world for **canopy tours** (the craze started here); the best places to find ziplines, hanging bridges and aerial trams are Monteverde and around Volcán Arenal. **Horseriding** is also frequently offered for volcano tours and elsewhere, but check the condition of the horses before you pay.

COMMUNICATIONS

The Costa Rica postal system is reasonably efficient and reliable. Letters and postcards take around a week to reach the US, and around ten days to reach Europe.

Public **phones** require phonecards (*tarjetas telefónica*), which come in various denominations and are available from most grocery stores, street kiosks and pharmacies; to call abroad, you'll need card number 199. There are no area codes and all phone numbers have eight digits. ☎2 precedes all landline numbers, while mobile phone numbers are prefixed with ☎8.

Top-up **SIM cards** for unlocked mobile phones are readily available from around 2000c and enable you to make inexpensive local calls. A basic mobile phone in Costa Rica can cost less than 10,000c. To buy either a SIM card or a mobile phone, bring your passport.

With the proliferation of **free wi-fi** – most hostels and hotels provide free internet and/or wi-fi – free internet phone calls via Skype are by far the best way to go. The inexpensive **internet cafés**

NATURAL HAZARDS

The downside to the fantastic watersports on offer in Costa Rica is the threat of the sea: powerful **riptides** combined with a lack of lifeguards on many beaches result in around 250 incidents of **drowning** per year. Popular beaches will have signs or flags warning of danger zones, and you should always ask about swimming conditions before jumping in. If you are caught in a riptide, don't struggle against the current – that's how the majority of drownings occur. Instead, let it carry you out beyond the breakers where the riptide ends, then swim towards the shore at a 45-degree angle – not straight in – until the waves can carry you back to the beach.

Costa Rica has a number of active **volcanoes**, and is prone to earthquakes. The last major earthquake occurred in Guanacaste in 2012 (see p.105).

Wildlife in Costa Rica's national parks – venomous snakes, big cats and others – can pose a threat, which is why trekking solo in Parque Nacional Corcovado is not recommended.

2

once commonly found in towns (from around US$1/hr) are becoming rarer.

CRIME AND SAFETY

Costa Rica is a relatively safe country, and crime tends to be **opportunistic** rather than violent. Pickpocketing and luggage theft are the greatest threats, particularly in San José and other large cities (be extra vigilant in bus terminals and markets). If you do have anything stolen, report the theft immediately at the nearest police station (*estación de policía*, or *guardia rural* in rural areas). Tourist-related crime, such as overcharging, can be addressed to the ICT in San José (see p.118).

Car-related crime, particularly involving rental vehicles, is on the rise, so park vehicles securely, especially at night. A common scam is for people to pre-puncture rental-car tyres, follow the car and then pull over to "offer assistance"; beware of seemingly good Samaritans on the roadside.

Drug-trafficking is a growing problem in Costa Rica, and dealers in tourist hangouts such as Jacó and Tamarindo occasionally approach travellers. Drug possession carries stiff penalties.

HEALTH

The quality of **medical care** in Costa Rica is generally very good, with facilities in San José the best in the country, but rather limited in remote corners. Well-stocked **pharmacies** (*farmacias* or *boticas*) are found in most towns; they generally open from 8am to 4.30pm. There are also 24hr pharmacies in private hospitals in San José and several other big towns. Strong insect repellent (50 percent DEET) is a must, since mosquitoes carry dengue fever; there is also a small risk of malaria on the southern Caribbean coast. Vaccinations against typhoid, diphtheria and hepatitis A are recommended.

EMERGENCY NUMBERS

All emergencies ☎911
Cruz Roja (ambulance) ☎128
Fire ☎118
Police ☎117

INFORMATION AND MAPS

One of the best sources of **information** about Costa Rica is the Instituto Costarricense de Turismo, or ICT (Ⓦvisitcostarica.com), whose main office is on the Plaza de la Cultura in San José (see p.118). The handful of smaller regional ICT offices dotted around the country are of limited use; you'll have to rely on local guesthouses and tourist agencies for information.

The best road **map** is the annually updated *Costa Rica Waterproof Travel Map* (Ⓦmapcr.com), available from good bookshops, such as San José's 7th Secret Books (see p.121). The Fundación Neotrópica (Ⓦneotropica.org) 1:500,000 map, available from San José bookshops, shows national parks and protected areas.

MONEY AND BANKS

The official currency of Costa Rica is the **colón** ("c"; plural colones), often colloquially referred to as "pesos". But given the ubiquity of US dollars (US$) – hotels, shops, most restaurants, and tourist sights across the country accept dollars, and many services are priced in dollars – colones are generally only necessary for local transport and food in cheap restaurants. **Coins** come in denominations of 5, 10, 25, 50, 100 and 500, and **banknotes** in denominations of 1000, 2000, 5000, 10,000, 20,000 and 50,000 colones. Many establishments will not accept torn notes, but they can be exchanged at banks.

COSTA RICA ONLINE

Ⓦ**anywherecostarica.com** Useful online resource, with practical advice, destination guides, thematic maps and transport information.

Ⓦ**costarica-nationalparks.com** Detailed guide to the country's parks and wildlife reserves.

Ⓦ**ticotimes.net** Central America's leading English-language newspaper.

Ⓦ**visitcostarica.com** Comprehensive website of the tourist board, including a very handy countrywide bus schedule.

2

STUDENT AND YOUTH DISCOUNTS

Students with ISIC (@isic.org) cards may be entitled to small museum and tour discounts. International Student Exchange (@isecard.com) cards also entitle students to certain discounts.

ATMs (*cajeros automático*) are found in larger towns; some dispense US dollars as well as colones. International Visa and MasterCard debit cards are accepted at any ATM. **Credit cards** are necessary to rent a car, accepted by many hotels, restaurants and businesses, and can be used for obtaining cash advances, though you'll pay a high transaction fee; Visa is more widely accepted than MasterCard. Bring plenty of cash when visiting smaller towns, as banking facilities can be scarce.

OPENING HOURS AND PUBLIC HOLIDAYS

Shops and businesses are open Monday to Saturday from 9am to 6 or 7pm (**malls** usually open daily between 10am and 9pm); in rural areas, they generally close for lunch. **Pharmacies** are open from 8am to 4.30pm. **Banking hours** are Monday to Friday 8.30 or 9am to 3 or 4pm, while **post offices** are open Monday to Friday 8am to 4.30 or 5.30pm, with limited Saturday hours (8am–noon). Many **museums** shut on Mondays, and all banks, post offices, museums and government offices close on the main **public holidays**.

FESTIVALS

Costa Rica celebrates many **festivals**, or *feriados*, throughout the calendar year. Below are some of the highlights:

PUBLIC HOLIDAYS

Jan 1 New Year's Day
March/April Maundy Thursday, Good Friday, Holy Saturday, Easter Monday
April 11 El Día de Juan Santamaría
May 1 Labour Day
July 25 El Día de Guanacaste (Guanacaste Province only)
Aug 15 Mother's Day/Assumption Day
Sept 15 Independence Day
Dec 25 Christmas Day

January Las Fiestas de Palmares is celebrated over two weeks with dancing, music and horse parades.
March Festival Imperial in Alajuela hosts the biggest rock festival in the country, attracting over thirty thousand revellers.
April El Día de Juan Santamaría honours Costa Rica's national hero with week-long festivities including parades and concerts.
August 2 El Día de La Negrita (Virgin of Los Angeles Day) honours the nation's patron saint (La Negrita) with a religious procession from San José to the basilica in Cartago.
September 15 Big parties and events all over the country to celebrate Costa Rican Independence Day.
October 12 El Día de la Raza (Limón Province only) marks Christopher Columbus' landing on Isla Uvita and follows on from the Limón Carnival.
December Las Fiestas de Zapote – the last week of the month is a nonstop street party in San José's southeastern suburb, with music, rodeos, rides and games.

San José

Sitting in the middle of the fertile Valle Central, sprawling **SAN JOSÉ** has a spectacular setting, ringed by soaring mountains and volcanoes on all sides. While not a destination in its own right, San José is, once you get past the chain stores and bumper-to-bumper traffic, a pleasant enough city in which to spend a couple of days. You may well have to, given that it's Costa Rica's major transport hub and the easiest place to organize tours to other parts of the country, as well as day-trips throughout the Valle Central and further afield. A historical centre with attractive colonial buildings, several excellent museums and a lively dining and nightlife scene gives you plenty to occupy your time here, and the temperature – a constant 24ºC or so year-round – is hard to beat.

WHAT TO SEE AND DO

The majority of San José's attractions are within walking distance of each other,

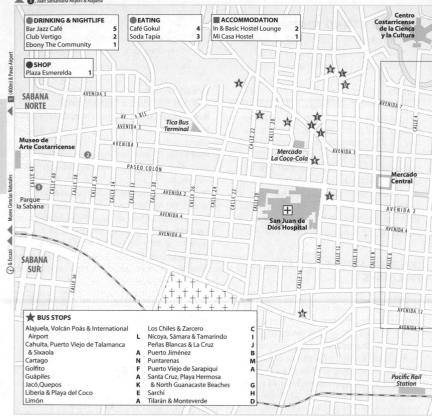

DRINKING & NIGHTLIFE
Bar Jazz Café	5
Club Vertigo	2
Ebony The Community	1

EATING
Café Gokul	4
Soda Tapia	3

ACCOMMODATION
In & Basic Hostel Lounge	2
Mi Casa Hostel	1

SHOP
Plaza Esmerelda	1

Centro Costarricense de la Ciencia y la Cultura

SABANA NORTE

AVENIDA 5

AV 3 BIS

AVENIDA 3

Tica Bus Terminal

Museo de Arte Costarricense

AVENIDA 1

PASEO COLÓN

AVENIDA 7

Mercado La Coca-Cola

AVENIDA 3

Mercado Central

Parque la Sabana

AVENIDA 26

AVENIDA 4

AVENIDA 2

San Juan de Dios Hospital

AVENIDA 6

AVENIDA 4

SABANA SUR

AVENIDA 12

AVENIDA 14

Pacific Rail Station

★ BUS STOPS

Alajuela, Volcán Poás & International Airport	L	Los Chiles & Zarcero	C
Cahuita, Puerto Viejo de Talamanca & Sixaola	A	Nicoya, Sámara & Tamarindo	I
		Peñas Blancas & La Cruz	J
Cartago	N	Puerto Jiménez	B
Golfito	F	Puntarenas	M
Guápiles	A	Puerto Viejo de Sarapiquí	A
Jacó,Quepos	K	Santa Cruz, Playa Hermosa & North Guanacaste Beaches	G
Liberia & Playa del Coco	E	Sarchí	H
Limón	A	Tilarán & Monteverde	D

scattered across the city centre. The **Parque Central** marks the city's epicentre, but the **Plaza de la Cultura** is its social core. Encircling the centre are **barrios**, little neighbourhoods each with their own feel and some great restaurants. A short bus ride from San José, the hillside suburb of **Escazú** is home to expats and wealthy Ticos, and holds picturesque narrow streets with some excellent shops.

Museo de Oro Precolombino

The Plaza de la Cultura conceals one of San José's treasures, a bunker-like underground museum complex containing the **Museo de Oro Precolombino**, or Pre-Columbian Gold Museum (daily 9.15am–5pm; US$11; ⓦmuseosdelbancocentral.org). Featuring priceless gold creations, the vast display includes the largest array of animal-shaped gold ornaments and figurines in Central America – funerary offerings, ceremonial decorations and much more. Displays on regional metallurgy techniques explain which indigenous groups were responsible for which stylistic designs.

Teatro Nacional

San José's heavily columned, Neoclassical **Teatro Nacional** (Tues–Sun 9am–4pm, free guided tours run hourly; US$7; ⓦteatronacional.go.cr), built in 1897, sits on the corner of C 5 and Av 2, behind the Plaza de la Cultura. The theatre's marbled stairways, gilt cherubs and red-velvet carpets would look more at home in Old Europe than in Central America, and remain in remarkably good condition, despite the humidity and a

succession of earthquakes. A vast painting above the staircase, which was reproduced on the 5 colón note in the 1950s, depicts coffee and banana harvests; you can tell that the artist had never actually seen a banana harvest by the awkward way his subjects hold them. During the day you can wander around the post-Baroque splendour, possibly catch a rehearsal or treat yourself to excellent coffee and cakes at the elegant **café**.

Museo del Jade

Three blocks northeast of the Plaza de la Cultura, at Av 7, C 9/11, on the north side of Parque España, is one of the city's finest museums, the **Museo del Jade** (Mon–Fri 8.30am–3.30pm, Sat 10am–2pm; US$8). Jade is the star here, and the displays are subtly backlit to show off the multicoloured and multitextured pieces to full effect. You'll see some **axe-gods** – anthropomorphic bird/human forms shaped like an axe and worn as a pendant – elaborate necklaces, bird and animal representations, and fertility symbols. Besides jade, extensive displays feature fine pre-Columbian gold work, elaborately carved stone *metates* (grinding tables) and stone seats with animal motifs, pottery with jaguar and graphic fertility symbols, shamanic paraphernalia (including a two-pronged clay tube used to inhale hallucinogens), and skulls with unusually serrated teeth.

Museo de Arte y Diseño Contemporáneo

Sprawling across the entire eastern border of the Parque España, the former

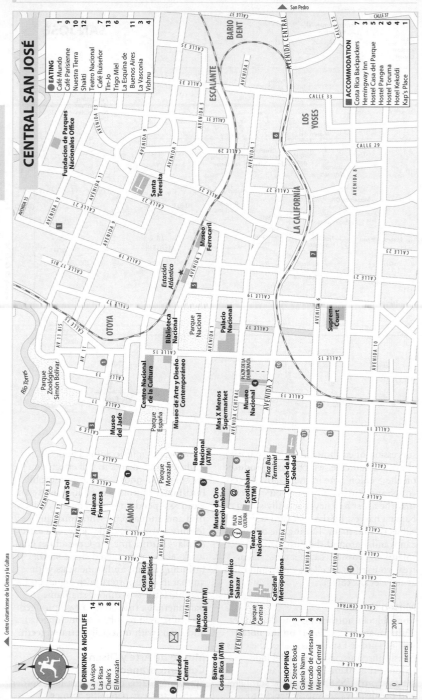

CENTRAL SAN JOSÉ

San Pedro

● EATING

Café Mundo	1
Café Parisienne	9
Nuestra Tierra	10
Shakti	12
Teatro Nacional	7
Café Ruiseñor	13
Tin-Jo	6
Trigo Miel	8
La Esquina de Buenos Aires	11
La Vasconia	3
Vishnu	4

■ ACCOMMODATION

Costa Rica Backpackers	7
Hemingway Inn	3
Hostel Casa del Parque	5
Hostel Pangea	2
Hostel Toruma	6
Hotel Kekoldi	4
Kap's Place	1

● DRINKING & NIGHTLIFE

La Avispa	14
Las Risas	5
Chelle's	8
El Morazán	2

● SHOPPING

7th Street Books	3
Galería Namu	1
Mercado de Artesanía	4
Mercado Central	2

BARIO DENT

ESCALANTE

LOS YOSES

LA CALIFORNIA

Supreme Court

OTOYA

AMÓN

Fundación de Parques Nacionales Office

Santa Teresita

Museo Ferrocaril

Estación Atlántico

Biblioteca Nacional

Parque Nacional

Palacio Nacional

Parque Zoológico Simón Bolívar

Museo del Jade

Centro Nacional de la Cultura

Museo de Arte y Diseño Contemporáneo

Parque España

Parque Morazán

Mas X Menos Supermarket

Museo Nacional

PLAZA DE LA DEMOCRACIA

Banco Nacional (ATM)

Lava Sol

Alianza Francesa

Costa Rica Expeditions

Museo de Oro Precolumbino

Scotiabank (ATM)

PLAZA DE LA CULTURA

Teatro Nacional

Tica Bus Terminal

Church de la Soledad

Teatro Mélico Salazar

Catedral Metropolitana

Parque Central

Mercado Central

Banco Nacional (ATM)

Banco de Costa Rica (ATM)

Río Torres

Centro Costarricense de la Ciencia y la Cultura

N

0   200
     metres

CALLE 37
CALLE 35
CALLE 33
CALLE 29
CALLE 27
CALLE 25
CALLE 23
CALLE 21
CALLE 19
CALLE 17
CALLE 15
CALLE 13
CALLE 11
CALLE 9
CALLE 7
CALLE 5
CALLE 3
CALLE CENTRAL
CALLE 17 BIS

AVENIDA CENTRAL
AVENIDA 1
AVENIDA 2
AVENIDA 3
AVENIDA 4
AVENIDA 5
AVENIDA 6
AVENIDA 7
AVENIDA 8
AVENIDA 9
AVENIDA 10
AVENIDA 11
AVENIDA 12
AVENIDA 13
AVENIDA 15
AV 11 BIS
AV 11

National Liquor Factory, dating from 1887, houses the Centro Nacional de la Cultura (CENAC), home to the cutting-edge **Museo de Arte y Diseño Contemporáneo** (Mon–Sat 9.30am–5pm; US$3; ⓦmadc.ac.cr). Constantly changing exhibits include photography, paintings, abstract sculpture and installations by domestic artists as well as works from across Latin America.

Museo Nacional

Just off the Plaza de la Democracia, the **Museo Nacional** (Tues–Sat 8.30am–4.30pm, Sun 9am–4.30pm; US$8; ⓦmuseocostarica.go.cr) is housed in the old Bellavista Fortress where, after the 1948 civil war, President José Figueres Ferrer proclaimed the abolition of the Costa Rican army. The rooms, arranged in circuitous fashion around a beautiful flowering courtyard, showcase exhibits ranging from the country's most important archeological pieces – ornate mortuary slabs, *metates* covered in elaborate designs and fertility-themed pre-Columbian pottery – to wonderfully intricate anthropomorphic gold figures and the pen with which President Figueres signed the 1949 constitution.

Mercado Central

The majority of Josefinos do their shopping in the **Mercado Central** (Mon–Sat 6am–6pm), which covers the two blocks between Av Central/3 and C 6/8. Upon entering its labyrinthine interior you're confronted by all manner of household goods, bags of coffee, T-shirts and much, much more. In the annexe, colourful arrangements of fruits and vegetables sit alongside dangling sides of beef and silvery ranks of fish. The glut of *sodas* are a good spot to get a cheap bite and watch the world go by. Keep your valuables secure.

Parque la Sabana

At the western end of Paseo Colón – a wide boulevard of shops, restaurants and car dealerships – the vast expanse of green known as **Parque la Sabana** was the site of San José's airport until the 1950s, and is now home to the country's key art museum. Housed in a converted air terminal, the attractive **Museo de Arte Costarricense**, Av 0, C 42 (Tues–Sun 10am–4pm; free; ⓦmusarco.go.cr), has a good collection of contemporary Costa Rican art, as well as the Jardín de Esculturas (Sculpture Garden) and Salón Dorado (Golden Room), which contains a huge mural painted by French artist Louis Ferón in 1940.

ARRIVAL AND DEPARTURE

BY PLANE

Together, Juan Santamaría and Tobías Bolaños airports have comprehensive links to all parts of the country; domestic destinations include Liberia, Tortuguero, Jacó, Puerto Jiménez, Golfito, Tamarindo, Quepos, Puerto Limón, Montezuma and Sámara. The international airport also receives flights mainly from North America (see p.105).

Juan Santamaría International Airport Costa Rica's main airport (☎ 2437 2400, ⓦ aeris.cr) is 17km northwest of San José. Interbus (ⓦ interbusonline.com) runs door-to-door shuttles for US$15; reserve in advance. Red Taxi Aeropuerto (☎ 2221 6865, ⓦ taxiaeropuerto.com) taxis can also be reserved in advance; expect to pay US$35–45 to reach the city centre. Buses to downtown San José depart from the airport bus stop just outside the terminal. Many hostels and guesthouses offer pick-up services (around US$30).

Tobías Bolaños Airport Nature Air uses Tobías Bolaños (☎ 2232 2820), around 7km northwest of the city centre. Buses run to San José every 30min. A taxi into the centre costs around US$20, or else you can get a ride with Interbus (see above) for US$15.

BY BUS

Terminals There is no central bus terminal. The four main bus terminals you're likely to use are La Coca-Cola (Av 1, C 16/18; destinations all over Costa Rica); Gran Terminal del Caribe (C Central north of Av 13; destinations along the Caribbean coast); Terminal Musoc (Av 22, C Central/1; buses to San Isidro and northern destinations); Terminal San Carlos (Av 9, at C 12; destinations in the north and northwest, such as Monteverde and La Fortuna).

Domestic destinations Alajuela (Station Wagon or Tuasa: every 10min, 4.30am–10.45pm; 40min); Cahuita (Mepe: 4 daily, 6am, 10am, noon, 2pm & 4pm; 4hr); Cariari (Gran Terminal del Caribe, for Tortuguero: 8 daily, 6.10am–7pm; 2hr 15min); Cartago (Lumaca: hourly 5.15am–10pm; 45min); Dominical and Uvita (Transportes Morales: 2 daily, 6am & 3pm; 7hr); Golfito (TRACOPA: 2 daily, 7am & 3pm; 8hr); Heredia (MRA: every 10min 5am–11pm; 20min); Jacó (Transportes Jacó: 5 daily, 7.30am, 10.30am, 1pm, 3.30pm & 6.30pm; 3hr); La Fortuna/Arenal (Terminal San Carlos: 3 daily, 6.15am, 8.30am & 11.30am; 4hr); Liberia

2

BUS COMPANIES

Autotransportes San José-San Carlos C 12, Av 7/9 (☎ 2255 4318).

Empresa Alfaro Av 5, C 14/16 (☎ 2222 2666).

Empresarios Unidos C 16, Av 12 (☎ 2222 0064).

Hermanos Rodríguez Terminal Coca-Cola (☎ 2642 0219).

King Quality C 12, Av 3/5 (☎ 2258 8834, ⓦking -qualityca.com).

Lumaca C 13, Av 6/8 (☎ 2537 2320).

Mepe Gran Terminal del Caribe (☎ 2257 8129).

Metropoli Av 2, C 1/3 (☎ 2536 6052).

Microbuses Rapiditos Heredianos (MRA) C 1, Av 7/9 (☎ 2233 8392).

Panaline C 16, Av 3/5 (☎ 2256 8721).

Pulmitán C 24, Av 5/7 (☎ 2222 1650).

Station Wagon Av 2, north of Iglesia de la Merced (☎ 2441 1181).

Tica Bus C 9, Av 4 (☎ 2221 0006, ⓦ ticabus.com).

Tilarán C 12, Av 7/9 (☎ 2222 3854).

TRACOPA Av 5, C 18/20 (☎ 2771 4214).

TransNica C 22, Av 3/5 (☎ 2223 4242, ⓦtransnica.com).

Transportes Blanco C 14, Av 9/11 (☎ 2257 4121).

Transportes Caribeños Gran Terminal del Caribe (☎ 2221 2596).

Transportes Deldú Av 9, C 10/12 (☎ 2256 9072).

Transportes Jacó Terminal La Coca-Cola (☎ 2223 1109).

Transportes Morales Terminal La Coca-Cola (☎ 2223 5567).

Tuasa Av 2, C 12/14 (☎ 2222 5325).

(Pulmitan: hourly 5am–8pm; 4hr 30min); Los Chiles (Terminal San Carlos: 2 daily, 5.30am & 3.30pm; 5hr); Mal País (Hermanos Rodríguez: 2 daily, 7am & 3.30pm; 5hr 15min); Manzanillo (Mepe: 1 daily, noon; 4hr 45min); Monteverde/Santa Elena (Tilarán: 2 daily, 6.30am & 2.30pm; 4hr 30min); Montezuma (Terminal Coca-Cola: 7 daily, 6am–6pm; 6hr); Nicoya (Empresas Alfaro: 5 daily, 6.30am–5pm; 5hr); Nosara (Empresas Alfaro: 1 daily, 6am; 6hr); Palmar Norte for connections to Sierpe and Bahía Drake (TRACOPA: 7 daily, 5am–6.30pm; 5hr); Paso Canoas (TRACOPA: 4 daily, 5am, 1pm, 4.30pm & 6.30pm, Sun also 10pm; 6hr); Peñas Blancas (Transportes Deldú: 7 daily, 4am–4pm; 6hr); Playa del Coco (Pulmitán: 3 daily, 8am, 10am & 4pm; 5hr); Playa Sámara (Empresas Alfaro: daily 12.30pm; 5hr); Puerto Jiménez (Blanco Lobo: 2 daily, 6am & noon; 8hr; book in advance during high season); Puerto Limón (Autotransportes Caribeños: every 30min, 5am–7pm; 3hr); Puerto Viejo de Sarapiquí (Mepe: 9 daily, 6.30am–6pm; 2hr); Puerto Viejo de Talamanca (Mepe: 5 daily, 6am, 10am, noon, 2pm & 4pm; 4hr 30min); Puntarenas (Empresarios Unidos: hourly 6am–7pm; 2hr 30min); Quepos/Manuel Antonio (Transportes Morales: 4 daily, 6am, noon, 6pm & 7.30pm; 3hr 30min–4hr 30min); San Isidro de General (TRACOPA: hourly 5am–6pm; 3hr); Sarchí (from C 18, Av 5/7: 3 daily, Mon–Fri 12.15pm, 5.30pm & 5.55pm, Sat noon; 1hr 30min); Sixaola (Mepe: 4 daily, 6am, 10am, 2pm & 4pm; 6hr); Tamarindo (Empresas Alfaro: 2 daily, 11.30am & 3.30pm; 5hr); Turrialba (hourly 5am–10pm; 2hr); Volcán Irazú (Metropoli: 1 daily, 8am, returning 12.30pm; 2hr); Volcán Poás (Tuasa: 1 daily, 8.30am, returning 2pm; 2hr).

International destinations Changuinola, Panama (daily; 9hr); Guatemala City (Tica Bus: 3 daily, 6am, 7am & 12.30pm; 60hr); Managua, via Antigua, Nicaragua (King Quality: 1 daily, 3am; 8hr; Tica Bus: 3 daily, 6am, 7.30am & 12.30pm; 9hr; TransNica: 4 daily, 4am, 5am, 9am & noon; 9hr); Panama City (Panaline: 1 daily, 1pm; 15hr; Tica Bus: 2 daily, noon & 11pm; 15hr); San Salvador (King Quality: 1 daily, 3am; 54hr; Tica Bus: 3 daily, 6am, 7.30am & 12.30pm; 54hr); Tegucigalpa, Honduras (Tica Bus: 3 daily, 6am, 7.30am & 12.30pm; 48hr; King Quality: daily, 3am; 48hr).

GETTING AROUND

By bus Local buses connect central San José with virtually all of the city's suburbs. Most buses to San Pedro (labelled "Mall San Pedro") leave from Av Central, C 9/15, and those for Paseo Colón and Parque la Sabana (labelled "Sabana-Cementerio") from the bus shelters on Av 2, C 5/7. All buses have their routes clearly marked on their windshields, and usually the fare, too. Buses generally run daily 5am–10pm, with some lines running until 11pm.

By taxi Licensed vehicles are red with a yellow triangle on the side, and have "SJP" licence plates. San José taxis are metered (ask the driver to *toca la maría, por favor*); it's illegal not to use a meter, though some drivers will claim that theirs is broken in an attempt to extract more money, in which case you negotiate the fare upfront. Short rides cost 1500–2500c, and about double that out to the suburbs.

INFORMATION

Tourist information There's a small tourist information stand by the luggage claims in the international airport. San José's tourist office in the Plaza de la Cultura (Mon–Fri 9am–5pm; ☎ 2299 5800, ⓦ visitcostarica.com), C 5, Av Central/2, has free maps and booklets detailing the (ever-changing) national bus schedule. They also hand out a free monthly culture guide, *San José Volando* (ⓦ sanjosevolando.com).

TOUR OPERATORS IN SAN JOSÉ

San José is home to scores of **tour and activity operators**. All those listed here are experienced and reliable, and licensed (and regulated) by the ICT. Be wary of the many fly-by-night operations.

Costa Rica Expeditions C 0, Av 3 ☎ 2257 0766, ⓦ costaricaexpeditions.com. This US-based firm is the most established and experienced of the major tour operators, with an extensive range of tours and multiday packages catering to most budgets.

Costa Rican Trails ☎ 2280 6705, ⓦ costaricantrails .com. Long-running outfitter offering a wide range of sustainable tours, ranging from day-trips throughout the Valle Central to birdwatching and motorcycling tours lasting several days.

Ecole Travel C 7, Av 0/1 ☎ 2234 1669, ⓦ ecoletravel .com. Small agency, popular with budget travellers, offering two-day tours to Tortuguero, a full-day rafting on Río Pacuaré and three-day Corcovado tours, as well as day-trips for US$70–90.

Expediciones Tropicales ☎ 2257 4171, ⓦ costaricainfo.com. Budget traveller favourite with knowledgeable guides, running the popular "combo" full-day tour of Volcán Poás, as well as day-tours to Volcán Irazú, the Valle de Orosí and Lankaster Gardens, Grecia and Sarchí and more.

ACCOMMODATION

Reserve in advance in high season (Dec–May) and on holidays. Most hostels and guesthouses offer free wi-fi and laundry services.

HOSTELS

Costa Rica Backpackers Av 6, C 21/23 ☎ 2221 6191, ⓦ costaricabackpackers.com; map p.116. Lively hostel with simple dorms and facilities including a restaurant and bar (happy hour 5–7pm), and rooms clustered around a garden with outdoor kitchen, hammocks and a pool. Pick-up from bus stations available. Dorms US$12, doubles US$36

Hostel Casa del Parque C 19, Av 1/3 ☎ 2233 3437, ⓦ hostelcasadelparque.com; map p.116. Centrally located, next to the Parque Nacional, this Art Deco house has six spartan rooms and a dorm, an attractive courtyard for socializing, and staff who treat you like old friends, plus a great café serving organic food. Dorm US$13, doubles US$35

Hostel Pangea Av 7, C 3/3b ☎ 2221 1992, ⓦ hostel pangea.com; map p.116. San José's party hostel boasts a pool, rooftop restaurant, bar and dancefloor. As well as simple dorms, there are rooms with private or shared facilities and five posh "suites" with plasma-screen TVs and king-sized beds. Walls are thin, though. Dorms US$14, doubles US$45, suites US$55

Hostel Toruma Av Central, C 29/31 ☎ 2234 8186, ⓦ hostel toruma.com; map p.116. In a colonial building once home to a former Costa Rican president, this San Pedro hostel is smarter than most, with high ceilings, tiled floors and a pool. The dorms are clean and the doubles have safes. No kitchen, but there's a small restaurant on site and the staff are very accommodating. Dorms US$14, doubles US$55

In & Basic Hostel Lounge Los Yoses; take a taxi and ask for 200m Sur y 75m Oeste del Spoon ☎ 2234 2998, ⓦ inandbasic .com; map p.114. Secure and friendly hostel in the suburb of Los Yoses. Owners give plenty of travel advice, rates include all-you-can-eat pancake breakfast and common areas encourage socializing. Dorms US$14, doubles US$36

Mi Casa Hostel Sabana Norte, 150m north of ICE Building ☎ 2231 4700, ⓦ micasahostel.com; map p.114. Close to Parque La Sabana, this chilled-out hostel with a homely vibe lives up to its name. The staff are wonderfully helpful, the vintage furnishings are a nice touch, and you can linger in the garden with a cold beer from the on-site bar. Dorms US$15, doubles US$35

HOTELS AND B&BS

Hemingway Inn C 19, Av 9 ☎ 2221 1804, ⓦ hemingway inn.com; map p.116. Just north of the centre in the quiet Barrio Amón, this rambling 1920s guesthouse features seventeen individually decorated singles and doubles (with safes), each named after a famous American author. Nice garden, too. Singles US$35, doubles US$50

Hotel Kekoldi Av 9, C 5/7 ☎ 2248 0804, ⓦ kekoldi.com; map p.116. Along the city's abandoned railroad tracks, this small, quiet lodge has simple rooms with shared or private baths, plus a kitchen, library, help with tours and car rental, and a lush patio garden. Continental breakfast included. It can be hard to find: tell your taxi driver it's a *calle sin salida* (dead-end road). US$65

★ **Kap's Place** C 19, Av 11/13 ☎ 2221 1169, ⓦ kapsplace .com; map p.116. Run by Karla Arias (an indefatigable source of information), this welcoming hotel has colourful rooms of varying size and price, plus a kitchen, terrace and living room to relax in. Tours, table football, yoga and dance classes are available. Quiet time is 8pm–8am. US$50

EATING

San José has a fairly cosmopolitan eating scene, running the gamut from swanky international restaurants to cheap Tico *sodas* and snack bars, with plenty of American fast-food

2

branches as well. Be aware that in restaurants, the 23 percent tax tends to be added on top of the menu prices. At the Mercado Central you'll find no shortage of small *sodas* serving cheap and filling *tamales*, *casados* and more. There are many American fast-food joints along Paseo Colón and at the food court at the San Pedro mall. Good supermarkets include Más X Menos (Av 0, C 9/11; daily 8am–9pm; another branch in San Pedro on Av 0, 300m north of the church) and Pali (Paseo Colón, C 24/26; Mon–Thurs 8.30am–7pm, Fri & Sat 8.30am–8pm, Sun 8.30am–6pm).

Café Gokul C de la Amargura, Av 3 ☎ 8380 2042; map pp.114–115. This San Pedro restaurant offers the best vegetarian Indian cuisine in the city, including tasty samosas, spicy paneer curries and creamy lassis. Mains around 3500c. Daily 9am–8pm.

★ **Café Mundo** Av 9, C 15; map p.116. Italian-themed restaurant popular with expats, as much for the great location as their extensive wine list and decent pizza and pasta. The half-size portions of pasta (from 3000c) are a bargain, as is the daily lunch special (3700c). There's also a busy bar (attracting a largely gay clientele). Most mains 4000–11,000c. Mon–Thurs 11am–10.30pm, Fri 11am–midnight, Sat 5pm–midnight.

Café Parisienne *Gran Hotel Costa Rica*, Av 2, C 3/5; map p.116. The closest thing in San José to a European street café, with great coffee (from 1000c). While the food isn't cheap (upwards of 4000c), this is a good place to sit and watch the buskers and street performers in the Plaza de la Cultura. Daily 24hr.

Nuestra Tierra Av 2, C 15; map p.116. Close to the National Museum, this well-loved Tico restaurant specializes in two things: a faux-rustic atmosphere and waiters straining under huge platters of *casados* and grilled meats. Mains 5000–11,000c. Daily 24hr.

Shakti Av 8, C 13; map p.116. Peaceful diner with a health-conscious slant: granola for breakfast, veg and fruit juices, herbal teas and numerous veggie options (and fish dishes), as well as a good-value lunch menu (3800–4700c), featuring a soup, salad, vegetarian *casado* and drink. Mon–Fri 7am–7pm, Sat 8am–6pm.

Soda Tapia C 24, Av 2; map pp.114–115. A bright retro-style diner with a huge menu featuring everything from burgers and grilled sandwiches (from 2700c) to large helpings of *casados* and old-style ice-cream sundaes. Mon–Thurs 6am–2am, Fri & Sat 24hr, Sun 6am–midnight.

★ **Teatro Nacional Café Ruiseñor** Av 2, C 3/5 ☎ 2221 3262; map p.116. Coffee (1000c), fruit drinks, sandwiches (2700c) and fantastic cakes (1800c) served amid a Neoclassical decor of marble, crystal and dark wood. Settle in at a window table and check out the goings-on in Plaza de la Cultura. Mon–Fri 9am–5pm, Sat 9am–4pm.

Tin-Jo C 11, Av 6/8; map p.116. Popular Chinese restaurant with an ambitious menu that includes Japanese, Vietnamese, Indian and Thai dishes as well as those from the

mother country. Unsurprisingly, the Chinese favourites stand out: the hot and sour soup and the sizzling platters are great, and portions are very generous. Mains 6000–10,000c. Mon–Thurs 11.30am–2.30pm & 6–10pm, Fri 11.30am–2.30pm & 6–11pm, Sat noon–3.30pm & 6–11pm, Sun noon–9pm.

Trigo Miel C 3, Av 0/1; map p.116. The best-stocked branch of the national bakery chain, with a front window filled with cream cakes. Slices of these, plus sandwiches, pastries and savoury snacks (400–1000c), can be eaten in or taken away. Daily 7am–6pm.

La Vasconia Av 1, C 3/5; map p.116. Get off the tourist trail and dig into cheap breakfasts, *ceviche* and *empanadas* (1700c) alongside Costa Rican workers at this casual *soda*. Adorning the walls are thousands of photos of the national football team (dating as far back as 1905) and there's karaoke nightly, for better or worse. Mon–Fri 9am–1.30am, Sat 11am–2am.

Vishnu Av 1, C 1/3; map p.116. There are no Indian dishes in sight, but this cheery vegetarian *soda* does serve healthy *platos del día*, soy burgers, salads, sandwiches and breakfast options. You can eat well for 2000–3500c. Mon–Fri 8am–7pm, Sat & Sun 9am–6pm.

DRINKING AND NIGHTLIFE

San José's nightlife is varied, with scores of bars. Some of the best are to be found in the *barrios* of Las Yoses and San Pedro – the latter geared towards the university population. Cover charges in clubs average around 3500c and often include a free drink; the action doesn't really kick off until after midnight. Incidentally, in San José, the term "nightclub" generally implies some form of erotic entertainment (prostitution being legal in Costa Rica), while a *discoteca* will be somewhere to dance (with your clothes on). Just so you know.

La Avispa C 1, Av 8/10 ☎ 2223 5343; map p.116. Friendly, landmark gay and lesbian disco-bar, "The Wasp" has three dancefloors and several pool tables housed in a distinct black and yellow building. The big nights are Sunday and

Tuesday, while Thursday is karaoke. There's a varying cover charge at weekends, usually 3500c or less. Thurs–Sat 8pm–6am, Sun 5pm–6am.

Bar Jazz Café Av Central, near the Banco Popular in San Pedro ⓦjazzcafecostarica.com; map pp.114–115. The best place in San José to hear live jazz, blues and Latin, with an intimate atmosphere and consistently good acts. Cover charge 2500–5500c. Doors generally open at 8pm; closed Sun.

Chelle's Corner Av Central, C 9; map p.116. Dating back more than 100 years, *Chelle's* features wood-panelled walls, red leather seats and plenty of local colour. Beers from 1100c, filling *bocas* (appetizers) to absorb the alcohol from 3000c. Daily 24hr.

Club Vertigo Paseo Colón, Av 38/40 ⓦvertigocr.com; map pp.114–115. Swanky European-style club with house, trance and techno keeping the vast dancefloor – both local and international DJs – moving. Upstairs you can sink into a red sofa in the chill-out lounge. Daily 10pm–6am.

Ebony The Community Centro Comercial El Pueblo; map pp.114–115. A young crowd fills *Ebony* to bump'n'grind to salsa, dancehall, hip-hop and reggaetón; Ladies' Night on Thurs is buzzing. Wed 8pm–3am, Thurs–Sun 8pm–6am.

El Morazán C 9, Av 3; map p.116. Classy bar next to Parque Morazán, attracting a trendy, arty clientele with its extensive cocktail list (most mixed drinks around 3000c) and occasional live music on weekends. Daily 5pm–3am.

★ **Las Risas** C 1, Av 0/1 ☎2223 2803; map p.116. One of the best downtown bars, on three floors in a building that once served as the National Library. A young crowd packs the small dancefloor at the popular top-floor disco; the ground-level bar is much more laidback. Bring ID – a copy of your passport will suffice – or the bouncers won't let you in. The cover charge of 1500c usually includes a beer or a shot. Saturday is ladies' night. Mon– Sat 4pm–5am.

Salsa 54 C 3, Av 1/3; map p.116. Great *salsateca* playing a mix of salsa, merengue, cumbia and more. The dancers are seriously good, so if you've got two left feet, you'd better watch from the sidelines. Thurs–Sat 8pm–4am.

ENTERTAINMENT

Josefinos love the theatre, and you often need a strong grasp of Spanish to follow the rapid, colloquial dialogue (though you can find some performances in English). Check the *Tico Times* for listings. Going to the cinema in San José is a bargain, with tickets costing around 2000–3200c. Cinemas generally show subtitled versions of the latest American movies; the few that are dubbed will have the phrase "*hablado en Español*" in the newspaper listings or on the posters.

Cinema CCM (ⓦccmcinemas.com) in Mall San Pedro (Av 0, C 47) is a huge complex screening international films. Sala Garbo (Av 2, C 28; ☎2223 1960, ⓦsalagarbocr.com) is a small venue with two screens showing foreign-language art-house movies.

Theatre Teatro Mélico Salazar, Av 2, C Central/2 (☎2295 6032, ⓦteatromelic.gov.cr), draws great musical talents from Costa Rica and further abroad, along with ballet, theatre and dance performances. Teatro Nacional, Av 2, C 3/5 (☎2010 1111, ⓦteatronacional.go.cr), is the most important theatre in the country, with productions ranging from Shakespeare, symphony orchestra and ballet to Chinese acrobatics and Latin American music.

SHOPPING

7th Street Books C 7, Av 0/1. New and used books, with English literature and a wide range of books on Costa Rica, as well as the best maps of the country. There's an excellent juice and smoothie café attached. Mon–Sat 9am–6pm, Sun 10am–5pm.

Galería Namu Av 7, C 5/7 ⓦgalerianamu.com. Fair-trade gallery stocking quality indigenous crafts and art from all over Costa Rica; come here for Corotega ceramics, Boruca devil masks, Huetar woodcarvings, woven Wounaan goods and more.

Mercado de Artesanía C 22, Av 2 bis in the Plaza de la Democracia. Touristy street market featuring hats, T-shirts, Sarchí ox-carts, jewellery, woodwork, hammocks and fabrics. Daily 10am–5pm.

Mercado Central Av 0/1, C 6/8; map p.116. *The* place to buy coffee beans, but make sure they're export quality – ask for Grano d'oro ("Golden bean"). It's a veritable warren (see p.117), holding a lot of tacky tourist offerings, but there are some decent handmade items; it's just a real hunt to find them. Mon–Sat 8am–5pm.

Plaza Esmerelda Pavas, about 5km northwest of the city centre. Huge crafts co-operative where you can watch cigars being rolled, necklaces set and Sarchí ox-carts painted. Mon–Sat 10am–6pm.

DIRECTORY

Banks All currency exchange in San José is done at banks, of which there are several in the centre. Try Banco de Costa Rica, Av 2, C 4/6; Banco Nacional, Av Central, C 2/4; or ScotiaBank, C 5, Av 0/2 (Mon–Fri 8.30am–6.30pm, Sat 9am–1pm).

Embassies and consulates Canada, Oficentro Ejecutivo La Sabana, 3rd floor, Edificio 3, Sabana Sur (☎2242 4400); UK, 11th floor, Edificio Centro Colón, Paseo Colón, C 38/40 (☎2258 2025); US, opposite the Centro Comercial in Pavas, or Av 0, C 120 (☎2519 2000).

Health The main free public hospital is San Juan de Dios, Paseo Colón, C 14–16 (☎2257 6282). The private hospital, Clínica Biblica, Av 14/16, C 0/1 (☎2522 1000, emergencies ☎2522 1030), is open 24hr, with a pharmacy and English-speaking doctors. Farmacia Fischel has branches at Av 3, C 2 (Mon–Sat 7am–7pm, Sun 9am–5pm), and Av 2, C 5/7 (Mon–Fri 7am–8pm, Sat 8am–7pm, Sun 8am–6pm).

2

Internet If your accommodation doesn't offer free wi-fi or internet, try Café Digital, on the south side of Av Central (Av 0), halfway between C 5 and C 7.

Laundry Offered by most lodgings. Otherwise, try Burbujas, 50m west and 25m south of the Mas por Menos supermarket in San Pedro.

Post office The Correo Central is at C 2, Av 1/3 (Mon–Fri 7am–5pm, Sat 7am–noon).

The Valle Central and the Highlands

Despite its name – literally "Central Valley" – Costa Rica's **Valle Central** is actually an intermontane plateau at an elevation of between 3000 and 4000m. The area supports roughly two thirds of Costa Rica's population, as well as four of its most important cities – San José and the provincial capitals of **Alajuela**, **Heredia** and

Cartago, though none warrants more than a brief visit. Beyond the cities, the region is largely agricultural, with green coffee terraces shadowed by the surrounding mountains and volcanoes. These volcanoes, especially **Irazú** and **Poás** and the national parks around them, are the chief attractions, but there's also excellent **whitewater rafting** (for the time being at least) near **Turrialba**, and the **Monumento Nacional Guayabo**, the country's most important archeological site.

Most people use San José as a base for forays into the Valle Central, but there are plenty of places to stay in the region itself.

ALAJUELA

Costa Rica's second largest city, **ALAJUELA** is close to the airport and just thirty minutes from downtown San José. For the most part, it's a hot urban sprawl, but it's a handy overnight stop if you're flying in late or out early, and also serves as a base for visiting nearby sights.

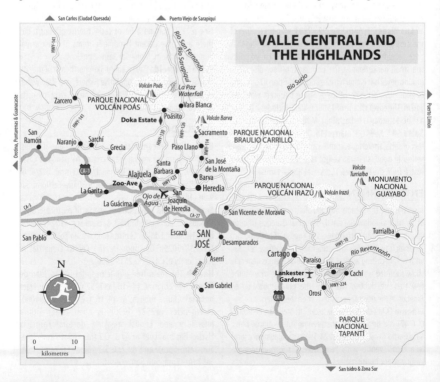

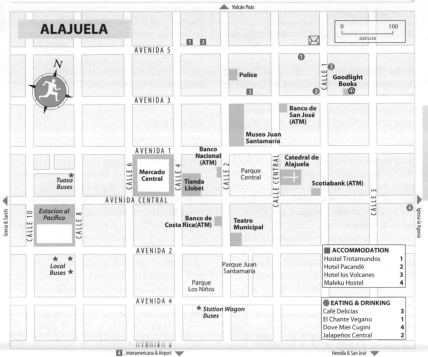

ALAJUELA

Volcán Poás

ACCOMMODATION
Hostel Trotamundos — 1
Hotel Pacandé — 2
Hotel los Volcanes — 3
Maleku Hostel — 4

EATING & DRINKING
Café Delicias — 3
El Chante Vegano — 1
Dove Miei Cugini — 4
Jalapeños Central — 2

2

WHAT TO SEE AND DO

The city's few attractions are close to the **Parque Central**. The most impressive sight is the sturdy former jail, Av 3, C 0/2, which houses the **Museo Juan Santamaría** (Tues–Sat 10am–6pm; free; ⓦmuseojuansantamaria.go.cr). Dedicated to Alajuela's most cherished historical figure – drummer-boy-cum-martyr Juan Santamaría, who sacrificed his life to save the country from American adventurer William Walker in 1856 – the museum's curiously monastic atmosphere is as interesting as its small collection, which runs the gamut from mid-nineteenth-century maps to crumbly portraits of figures involved in the battle of 1856.

Three blocks south of the museum, a small **plaza** that's also named after Santamaría is decked out with murals. On the east side of the Parque Central is the **cathedral**, the final resting place of two of Costa Rica's presidents, which was badly damaged in the 1991 earthquake.

ARRIVAL AND DEPARTURE

By plane Juan Santamaría International Airport is less than 3km south of the city. Many hotels and hostels will arrange a free pick-up/drop-off with notice; otherwise take a bus from outside the airport or a taxi (US$6–9).

By bus Most small terminals are in the streets southwest of the Mercado Central and there are two Tuasa bus terminals across the street from each other.

Destinations Heredia (C 8, Av Central/1: every 10–15min; 45min); Sabanilla, for Doka Coffee Farm (C 10, Av 2/Central: Mon–Fri every 30min; 20min); San José (Tuasa West: C 8, Av Central/1; every 10min 5am–11pm; 45min, via the airport; Station Wagon: Av 4, C 2/4; every 10min 4am–midnight; 45min); Sarchí (C 8, Av Central/1. every 30min, 1hr); Volcán Poás (Tuasa West: C 8, Av Central/1; 9.15am; 1hr 15min); Zoo-Ave (every 30min–1hr; 15min).

INFORMATION

Banks Banco Nacional, C 2, Av 0/1; Scotiabank, C 1, Av Central.

★**Goodlight Books** Av 3, C 1/3 ⓦgoodlight.costari.ca. One of the country's best collections of English-language fiction and nonfiction, including maps, phrase books and travel guides, plus internet access, coffee and cakes. Daily 9am–6pm.

2

ACCOMMODATION

There are several budget digs of comparable quality along Av 3, C Central/2. All the options below provide free airport drop-offs.

Hostel Trotamundos Av 5, C 2/4 ☎2430 5832, ⓦhosteltrotamundos.com. Inexpensive and cheerful, this busy hostel is no palace, but with a communal kitchen and warm and welcoming staff, you won't be complaining. The rooms have shared bathrooms and there are also dorms. Pack your earplugs though – it can get very noisy. Dorms US$13, doubles US$35

Hotel Pacandé Av 5, C 2/4 ☎2443 8481, ⓦhotelpacande .com. This welcoming Tico-run budget hotel offers compact rooms (the cheapest with shared bathrooms), as well as more stylish ones with private facilities, TVs and dark wood furnishings (though most lack natural light). US$35

Hotel los Volcanes Av 3, C Central/2 ☎2441 0525, ⓦhotellosvolcanes.com. Refurbished, rambling 1920s house with spacious, wood-panelled, somewhat musty rooms and an attractive garden and open-air kitchen out back. US$46

Maleku Hostel 50m west of the main entrance of the hospital ☎2430 4304, ⓦmalekuhostel.com. This small and cheerful family-run hostel is one of the town's best budget options: compact dorms and private rooms (with shared bathrooms) are immaculate, and you can get lots of useful travel advice. Dorms US$15, doubles US$38

EATING AND DRINKING

Café Delicias Av 3 at C 1 ☎2440 3681, ⓦcafedelicias .com. A sweet little café, with Café Britt coffee (from 1200c), tempting cheesecakes and pineapple pastries, sandwiches and light meals. There's another branch on the corner of C 9 and Av 6. Mon–Sat 8am–8pm.

El Chante Vegano Av 5, C 3/5 ☎8911 4787, ⓦelchantevegano.com. If you've overindulged, this organic, vegan restaurant is the place to come (mains 3400–5000c). The menu features wholesome soups, salads, sandwiches, burgers and juices. Tues–Sat 11am–8pm, Sun 11am–4pm.

Dove Miei Cugini Av 0, C 5 ☎2240 6893. Family-run restaurant that serves up tasty American-Italian staples (3700–8000c), including minestrone soup, pastas and, of course, pizza (takeaway available). Wash it down with a beer or cocktail at the downstairs bar. Daily 5–10pm.

★**Jalapeños Central** Av 5, C 2. This friendly place, run by a Colombian from New York, gets packed out with expats and locals who come for the excellent Tex-Mex food – enchiladas, burritos and guacamole. Don't miss the *sopa azteca* or the pecan pie. Lunch and dinner specials 3700–5200c. Mon–Sat 11.30am–9pm.

AROUND ALAJUELA

Heading **north** from Alajuela, the road begins to climb, the terrain becomes greener and the air considerably cooler. Along this ascent you'll find great vistas, the **Doka Estate** and access to the nearby Volcán Poás. Travelling **south**, you come across wildlife attractions such as **Zoo-Ave**, while westwards lies Sarchí, famous for its ox-cart.

Doka Estate

Set amid rolling coffee fields 10km north of Alajuela, off the road to Volcán Poás, the **Doka Estate** (tours daily 9am, 10am, 11am, 1.30pm & 2.30pm, Mon–Fri also 3.30pm; 1hr; US$20; ☎2449 5152, ⓦdokaestate.com) is one of the country's most historic coffee farms. The Vargas family have been growing beans here for over seventy years and today produce roasts for Café Tres Generaciones. Guides cover the entire coffee-making process, and finish with a free tasting.

Buses run from Alajuela to the nearby town of Sabanilla, from where a taxi to the estate costs around $5 (a taxi direct from Alajuela will set you back about $25); the estate can also provide transportation (call for details).

Zoo-Ave

The well-run animal park, **Zoo-Ave** (daily 8.30am–5pm; US$20; ⓦzooavecostarica .org), 10km west of Alajuela in La Garita, is an excellent introduction to more than a hundred species of Costa Rican birds, including macaws. Besides the aviary, there's a zoo featuring mostly rescued animals, including monkeys, reptiles and cats, and an animal-breeding centre that aims to reintroduce rehabilitated animals into the wild.

Buses run to Zoo-Ave from Alajuela; to get back, flag down an Alajuela bus on the main road where you arrived.

Sarchí

Touted as the centre of Costa Rican arts and crafts, the commercialized village of **SARCHÍ**, 30km northwest of Alajuela, has a pretty setting. The most famous item produced here is the **Sarchí ox-cart**, a kaleidoscopically painted square cart of Moorish origin; you can check out what is allegedly the world's largest ox-cart in Sarchí Norte, the heart of this spread-out village, and buy small models of it. Large *fábricas* (workshops) line the main road from **Sarchí Sur**, separated from **Sarchí Norte** by the river.

Buses run to Sarchí from Alajuela, with buses back (via Grecia) leaving from Sarchí Norte. (Buses to San José run every 30min 5am–10pm; 1hr 30min).

PARQUE NACIONAL VOLCÁN POÁS

PARQUE NACIONAL VOLCÁN POÁS (daily 8am–3.30pm; US$10), 55km from San José and 37km north of Alajuela, is one of the most easily accessible active volcanoes in the world. Its history of eruptions dates back eleven million years – the last gigantic blowout was on January 25, 1910, when it dumped 640,000 tonnes of ash on the surrounding area – and the last bit of minor activity in 1995 resulted in brief closure of the park. The best time to visit is early in the morning, before the mists sweep in and obscure the view (from as early as 10am). Since tour buses don't arrive until after 10am, it's worth renting a car to get out here. Due to the altitude, it tends to be cold and rain is not uncommon, so dress appropriately.

WHAT TO SEE AND DO

Poás (2704m) has blasted out three craters in its lifetime. Due to more or less constant activity, the appearance of the **main crater** is subject to change – it's 1300m wide and filled with milky turquoise water from which sulphurous gases waft.

Park trails

The park has several well-maintained, short and unchallenging **trails**, which take you through an otherworldly landscape, dotted with smoking fumaroles and tough ferns and trees trying valiantly to hold up against regular sulphurous scaldings.

The paved **Crater Overlook** trail (750m; 15min) winds its way from the visitors' centre to the main crater, along a paved road. Side-trail **Sendero Botos** (1.4km; 30min) heads up through the forest to the pretty, emerald Botos Lake, which fills an extinct crater and makes a good spot for a picnic. Named for the

pagoda-like tree commonly seen along its way, the **Escalonia** trail (about 1km; 30min) starts at the picnic area (follow the signs), then takes you through the forest, where the ground cover is less stunted compared to that at the crater, back to the visitor car park.

Wildlife-watching

A wide variety of **birds** plies this temperate forest, among them the ostentatiously colourful quetzal, robins and several species of hummingbird. Although a number of large mammals live in the park, including coyotes and wildcats, you'll be very lucky to spot them. The small, green-yellow **Poás squirrel**, endemic to the area, is far more common.

Poás is also home to a rare version of cloudforest known as dwarf or **stunted cloudforest**, a combination of pine-needle-like ferns, miniature bonsai-type trees and bromeliad-encrusted cover, all of which have been stunted by an onslaught of cold, continual cloud cover and acid rain from the mouth of the volcano.

ARRIVAL AND DEPARTURE

By bus A daily Tuasa bus leaves San José at 8.30am from Av 2, C 12/14, calling at Alajuela at 9.15am (1hr 30min–2hr). It returns at 2.30pm.

By taxi To reach Poás before both buses and clouds, drive or take a taxi from Alajuela (roughly US$40–50) or San José (around US$65).

INFORMATION AND TOURS

Tourist information The visitors' centre (daily 8.30am–3.15pm), next to the car park at the entrance, has a thorough display on the park's fauna and flora, a trail map, bathrooms and a café.

Tours Many visitors come on tours from San José (approximately US$55/person for a 4–5hr trip).

HEREDIA

Just 11km northeast of San José is lively **HEREDIA**, boosted by the student population of the Universidad Nacional (UNA) at the eastern end of town. The centre has a few historical buildings worth visiting, and can also be used as a base for trips to Volcán Barva and Braulio Carrillo National Park, though the latter can just as easily be visited from San José.

2

WHAT TO SEE AND DO

The quiet **Parque Central**, draped with huge mango trees, is overlooked by the plain **Basílica de la Inmaculada Concepción**, whose unexcitingly squat design – "seismic Baroque" – has kept it standing since 1797, despite several earthquakes. North of the plaza, the old Spanish tower of **El Fortín**, "the Fortress", features odd gun slats that fan out and widen from the inside to the exterior, giving it a medieval appearance; you cannot enter or climb it.

East of the tower on Avenida Central, the **Casa de la Cultura** is a well-maintained colonial house featuring permanent historical displays as well as local paintings and sculpture (opening hours vary).

ARRIVAL AND DEPARTURE

By bus Buses arrive and depart from stops in the southern part of town, mostly near the Mercado Central.
Destinations Alajuela (Av 8, 3 blocks east of the market; every 10–15min; 45min); Paso Llano for Volcán Barva and

PN Braulio Carrillo (southern side of the Mercado Central: Mon–Fri 4.50am, 6.15am, 7.40am, 1pm & 5pm; 1hr 15min); San José (Av 8, a block east of the market: every 30min; 30–45min).

By train The commuter train, the Tren Urbano (ⓦtrenurbano.co.cr), runs between Heredia's railway station on Av 10, C 0, and San José (Mon–Fri every 30min 5.30–8am & 3.30–7pm, returning every 30min 6–8.30am & 4–8pm; 20min).

ACCOMMODATION AND EATING

Given the proximity of San José, there's little point in staying in Heredia, though it does hold some good, central accommodation and dining options.

Café Espigas C 2, Av 2, southwest corner of the Parque Central ⓣ 2237 3275. Serving meal combos that include breakfasts (3500c-plus), *pintos*, *casados*, sandwiches and burgers, as well as Britt Finca coffee. Daily 7am–9pm.

Hotel Las Flores Av 12, C 12/14 ⓣ 2261 8147, ⓦhotel-lasflores.com. Heredia's best budget accommodation option, a 10min walk southwest of the centre, and offering green-hued doubles with private bathrooms, TV and small balconies. Staff are cheerful and there's a small *soda* downstairs. **US$32**

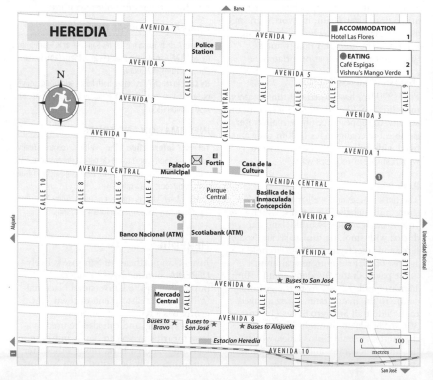

Vishnu's Mango Verde C 7, Av Central/1 ☎ 2237 2526. Bright and bustling vegetarian *soda* with inexpensive salads, sandwiches and pastas, as well as juices and smoothies (dishes 2600–3500c). Mon–Sat 8am–7pm.

PARQUE NACIONAL BRAULIO CARRILLO AND VOLCÁN BARVA

The little-visited **PARQUE NACIONAL BRAULIO CARRILLO** (daily 8am–3.30pm; US$8), 35km northeast of San José, covers 325 square kilometres of virgin rain- and cloudforest. The growth here gives you a good idea of what much of Costa Rica used to look like fifty years ago, when approximately three-quarters of the country was virgin rainforest.

This part of the country receives a lot of **rainfall**, so come prepared for precipitation and some serious mud even during the "dry" season (Jan–April).

The trails

A rather challenging trail ascends the dormant **Volcán Barva** from the Barva ranger station, passing through dense deciduous cover before reaching the cloudforest at the top. It takes around three hours to reach the summit, but you're rewarded by great views and two attractive lagoons. The straightforward **Sendero La Botella** (2.8km) rambles past several small waterfalls from Quebrada González ranger station, while from Zurquí you can either enjoy a gentle hike along the **Sendero Histórico**, which follows Río Hondura to its meeting point with Río Sucio, or else do a short, steep 1km hike to a *mirador*.

ARRIVAL AND DEPARTURE

The Barva ranger station can be accessed from Heredia via Paso Llano; the village of Sacramento, 4km southwest of the entrance, is accessible by bus from Heredia, but there's no public transport beyond here. A 4WD is necessary to drive the rest of the way, or else you have to walk in. Any bus passing between San José and Guápiles will drop you off at either the Zurquí or the Quebrada Gonzáles ranger stations along Hwy 32; it might be difficult to catch a ride back.

INFORMATION

Ranger stations The three most important of the park's five staffed ranger stations – Barva (southwestern entrance), Zurquí (southern entrance) and Quebrada

González (northeast entrance) – have parking (don't leave valuables in the car), picnic areas and well-marked nearby trails. The Volcán Barva climb is accessed via the Barva ranger station (☎ 2266 1883; US$10; 7am–4pm).

Hikes Register at the ranger stations before setting off, and try to arrange a guide for longer hikes, as there have been robberies.

Accommodation and eating Basic huts and camping facilities (US$3) are available, but you need to bring your own drinking water.

CARTAGO

CARTAGO, meaning "Carthage", was Costa Rica's capital for almost three centuries, until the centre of power moved to San José in 1823. Founded in 1563 by Juan Vázquez de Coronado, the city, like its ancient namesake, has been razed a number of times, although in this case by **earthquakes** rather than Romans – two, in 1823 and 1910, practically demolished the place.

WHAT TO SEE AND DO

For the most part, the city is an unattractive, congested concrete sprawl, rebuilt after the last major earthquake with little concern for aesthetics, but is worth a quick stop to visit the **Basílica de Nuestra Señora de Los Ángeles**, particularly in August for the famous La Negrita pilgrimage.

Basílica de Nuestra Señora de Los Ángeles

Cartago's highlight is the **Basílica de Nuestra Señora de Los Ángeles**, C 16 and Av 2, dating back to 1635 and rebuilt in a decorative Byzantine style after the original was destroyed in an earthquake in 1926. Millions of Costa Ricans make an annual pilgrimage here on August 2 to honour the statue of **La Negrita** (or the Black Virgin), the nation's patron saint since 1824. La Negrita is a representation of the Virgin Mary, allegedly found on this spot by a native woman in 1635; legend has it that when the woman tried to take the statuette with her, it reappeared in the spot where it was found. A shrine was built on the spot, where she now resides on a gilded perch at the main altar.

2

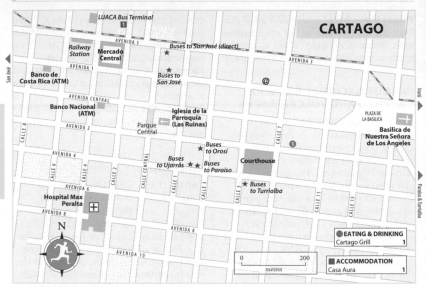

Iglesia de la Parroquia

From the basilica it's a five-minute walk west to Cartago's other attraction – the **Iglesia de la Parroquia** (known as "Las Ruinas"), which sits on the eastern end of the concrete Parque Central. Built in 1575, the church was repeatedly destroyed by earthquakes, but stubbornly rebuilt each time, until the giant quake of 1910 finally vanquished it. Only its elegantly tumbling walls remain, enclosing pretty subtropical gardens. The ruins are not open to the public, but can be viewed from the Parque Central.

ARRIVAL AND DEPARTURE

By bus Buses arrive and depart from various stops around town.

Destinations San José (every 10min; 45min), from the bus station just north of the central market and from Av 4/6, C 2/4; Turrialba (hourly Mon–Fri 6am–10pm; 5 daily Sat & Sun; 1hr 30min), from the corner of C 8 and Av 3; Volcán Irazú (daily 8.30–8.45am, returning 12.30pm; 1hr).

By train The commuter train, the Tren Urbano (trenurbano.co.cr), runs between Cartago's railway station on Av 6, C3, and San José (Mon–Fri 12/day; 45min).

ACCOMMODATION AND EATING

Lodgings in Cartago are limited, so unless you wish to be here for the annual pilgrimage, it's best to visit the city as a day-trip from San José.

Cartago Grill In front of the courthouse, Av 1, C 8/10 ☎ 2591 5342. This popular restaurant with cheerful blue and yellow decor has a crowd-pleasing menu and pile-on-the-pounds portions. Choose between chicken, hamburgers or kebabs, or settle for what they do best – juicy steaks grilled to perfection. Mains 3000–8500c. Daily 11am–9pm, Sat till 10pm.

Casa Aura C 1, Av 6/8 ☎ 2591 8161, casaaura.com. Modest guesthouse, a short walk from the town centre, with four reasonable though spartan rooms (with TVs and private bathrooms), as well as a garden and a small book swap. U̲S̲$̲6̲0̲

PARQUE NACIONAL VOLCÁN IRAZÚ

Around 19km northeast of Cartago, **PARQUE NACIONAL VOLCÁN IRAZÚ** (daily 8am–3.30pm; US$10) makes for a long but scenic trip from the city. The park's blasted-out lunar landscape is dramatic, and Volcán Irazú, its centrepoint, is the tallest (3432m) and largest active volcano in the country. The main crater, 1050m in diameter and 300m deep, is flanked by two smaller craters: the inactive Diego de la Haya is creepily impressive, its deep depression filled with a strange green lake, while the smallest crater, Playa Hermosa, is slowly being taken over by vegetation. On clear days, the viewpoint offers fantastic views to the Caribbean. Two marked **trails** lead to the crater from the entrance, where you'll find the ranger's booth.

ARRIVAL AND INFORMATION

By bus A daily bus runs to the park from the *Gran Hotel Costa Rica* in San José (daily at 8am) – be there early in high season to get a seat – picking up passengers at Las Ruinas in Cartago around 8.30am; it arrives at Irazú at around 10am and returns to San José at 12.30pm.

Tours Tours to the volcano (around US$50–60) can be arranged by a number of San José operators (see box, p.119).

Visitors' centre The park has a visitors' centre with information, toilets and a snack bar.

EATING

La Casona del Cafetal 2km north of the Cachí dam, ☎ 2577 1414, ⓦ lacasonadelcafetal.com This restaurant on a coffee plantation is a worthy lunch stop, with a lavish Sunday buffet and a delicious coffee flan for dessert. Daily 11am–6pm.

TURRIALBA

The pleasant agricultural town of TURRIALBA, 45km east of Cartago on the eastern slopes of the Cordillera Central, has sweeping views over the rugged eastern Talamancas and is Costa Rica's **whitewater rafting** central, with world-class rapids on

the nearby Río Reventazón and Río Pacuaré (see box, p.130). Enjoy the Valle Central rivers while you can, as both are under threat from dams.

ARRIVAL AND DEPARTURE

By bus The bus terminal is at the western entrance of town, off Hwy-10.

Destinations Cartago (9–10 daily; 1hr 20min); San José via Cartago (every 45min 5am–6.30pm; 2hr); Siquirres, for transfers to Puerto Limón (9 daily 6am–6pm; 1hr 45min).

ACCOMMODATION

Casa de Lis Hostel Av Central near C 2 ☎ 2556 4933, ⓦ hostelcasadelis.com. Small, super-central hostel with volcano views from the roof terrace; bright, spotless rooms; and a tranquil vibe. Book ahead, as it fills up quickly. Dorms US$12, doubles US$30

Hotel Interamericano Av 1 near C 1 ☎ 2556 0142, ⓦ hotelinteramericano.com. Experienced and novice rafters alike gravitate towards this basic hotel south of the

---

A TOUR OF THE VALLE DE OROSÍ

If anything is worth renting a car for hereabouts, it has to be the day-trip around the lovely river valley of **Orosí**, a 60km scenic loop complete with coffee plantations, fabulous mountain vistas, a remote national park, Costa Rica's largest dam and artificial lake, and verdant botanical gardens. The road begins in the village of **Paraíso**, 8km south of Cartago. On the way, 3km before you reach Paraíso, it's well worth stopping off at the **Lankester Gardens** (daily 8.30am–5.30pm, last entry 4.30pm; US$7.50; ☎ 2511 7939, ⓦ jbl.ucr.ac.cr) – home to more than 1100 species of orchid, best seen during the dry months of March and April. There are plenty of other tropical species too, and a sculpted Japanese garden.

Heading south from Paraíso, you pass through **Orosí**, where a particularly photogenic 1743 church has survived Costa Rica's umpteen earthquakes. Five kilometres before Orosí, stop at the **Mirador Orosí** (daily 8am–5pm) for the splendid views.

From Orosí, the road runs south for another 10km or so, arriving at **Parque Nacional Tapantí** (daily 8am–4pm; US$10), Costa Rica's wettest national park, with the Cerro de la Muerte (Mountain of Death) looming above it. The park is home to more than 300 bird species; you'll see some if you hike its three trails, the longest of which is a rugged 2km.

Doubling back to Orosí, take the road that runs parallel to the Río Orosí and curves around the **Lago de Cachí**, the lake created by the massive Cachí dam.

Once you pass through the village of Ujarrás, you can double back to Paraíso. Though not technically part of the Orosí loop, it is well worth taking the road towards Turrialba for 2km until you reach **Finca Cristina** (☎ 2574 6426, ⓦ cafecristina.com), an organic coffee farm where you can pick up freshly roasted beans.

2

WHITEWATER RAFTING IN THE VALLE CENTRAL

The two main rivers for whitewater rafting in the Turrialba area are Río Reventazón and Río Pacuaré. While both Costa Rica Expeditions and Expediciones Tropicales (see box, p.119) offer rafting day-trips from San José, they spend a lot of time in transit, and it's cheaper to arrange rafting excursions in Turrialba itself.

Río Reventazón The main river for rafting, with water levels pretty much constant year-round due to water releases from the dam (barring Sundays) and the biggest rafting challenges in Costa Rica. It has four principal rafting sections: El Carmen (Class II float for complete novices), Florida (Class III, scenic float with some whitewater action), Pascua (Class IV, with 15 thrilling rapids that can be tackled by both novices and professionals) and Peralta (Class V, challenging and for pros only; not always available due to safety issues).

Río Pacuaré The Lower Pacuare (Class II–IV) offers a particularly scenic stretch with a good mix of easy floats and challenging rapids. The scenery along the Upper Pacuare is just as gorgeous, though with its Class III–IV runs, you'll be keeping most of your attention on the water. The Pacuare is best rafted between June and October; between October and December, when the water is highest, some Class IV runs become Class V runs, suitable for advanced rafters only.

old train tracks, with inexpensive basic singles (from US$12), doubles, triples and quads on offer. Bilingual Luis can help you organize rafting and other excursions. **US$22**

EATING AND DRINKING

La Feria Av 4, just up from *Hotel Wagelia* ☎ 2556 5550. Decent regional cuisine, including assorted Caribbean dishes – adventurous diners might give the tongue a try (mains around 2600–4500c). Wed–Mon 11am–10pm, Tues 11am–2pm.

La Gaza C 0, Av 6/8 ☎ 2556 1073. Long-standing bar-restaurant serving inexpensive sandwiches and hamburgers (around 2000–3500c), plus the usual range of chicken, meat and seafood dishes. Daily 10.30am–11pm.

Wok'n'Roll C 1, opposite *Turrialba B&B*. Bright, Chinese-run diner serving palatable sushi, though what they do best are the Chinese noodle and rice dishes (around 3500c). You can't go wrong with the Singapore-style fried noodles. Daily noon–10pm.

MONUMENTO NACIONAL GUAYABO

Costa Rica's most important archeological site, the **MONUMENTO NACIONAL GUAYABO** (daily 8am–3.30pm; US$6) lies 19km northeast of Turrialba. Guayabo belongs to the archeological-cultural area known as **Intermedio**, which begins roughly in the province of Alajuela and extends to Venezuela, Colombia and parts of Ecuador. Archeologists believe that Guayabo was inhabited from about 1000 BC to 1400 AD by around twenty thousand people. Then mysteriously abandoned, the city was never found by the conquering Spanish; its remains were only discovered in 1968. Visually, the site is not terribly impressive; what you see are stone residential mounds, some petroglyphs, an aqueduct and cisterns that technically still function after centuries of disuse. At the **visitors' centre** you can see a model of what the city may once have looked like.

ARRIVAL AND DEPARTURE

By bus Buses run to Guayabo from Turrialba from 100m south of the main bus terminal (Mon–Sat 3 daily, 11.15am, 3.10pm & 5.20pm, returning at 5.15am, 7am, 12.30pm & 4pm; Sun 3 daily, 9am, 3pm & 6.30pm, returning 7am, 12.30pm & 4pm; 1hr), though the inconvenient timetable gives you either too much or too little time at the site.

By car Driving from Turrialba takes about 30min. The last 3km is on a bad gravel road – 4WD recommended. Taxis from Turrialba charge around US$20.

Limón Province and the Caribbean coast

Sparsely populated **Limón Province** sweeps south in an arc from Nicaragua down to Panama. Hemmed in to the north by dense jungles and swampy waterways, to the west by the mighty Cordillera Central, and to the south by the even wider girth of the Cordillera Talamanca, the region has a strong Caribbean feel. This is largely due to the presence of the descendants of former

Jamaican slaves and Panamanian and Colombian turtle hunters, and their unique creole – **Mekatelyu** – is still spoken today.

Limón is a haven for ecotourists, having the highest proportion of protected land in the country. At **Parque Nacional Tortuguero** you can watch giant sea turtles lay their eggs, while at **Cahuita** and **Manzanillo** you can snorkel coral reefs and surf at **Puerto Viejo**. In addition, more than anywhere else in Costa Rica, the Caribbean coast exudes a sense of **cultural diversity**: besides the Afro-Caribbean population, the coast is home to several indigenous peoples from the **Bribrí**, **Kéköldi** and **Cabécar** groups. Visits to their communities are some of the most rewarding experiences you may have in Costa Rica.

Limón Province sees a lot of **rain** throughout the year – less so in February/ March and September/ October, but be prepared nonetheless.

GETTING AROUND

Getting around northern Limón Province requires patience. While regular buses follow the one main road from Puerto Limón to the Panama border at Sixaola – Hwy-36 – north of Puerto Limón there is no public land transport at all: instead, private *lanchas* ply the coastal canals connecting Moín, 8km north of Puerto Limón, to Tortuguero and Río Colorado near the Nicaraguan border. Regular boat transfers also run to Tortuguero village from Cariari, a banana town reachable from Guápiles, en route to Puerto Limón. There are also daily flights in tiny planes from San José to Tortuguero.

PUERTO LIMÓN

PUERTO LIMÓN, 165km east of San José, is Costa Rica's main port, with brightly painted houses, a somewhat neglected air

and a reputation as one of Central America's prime drug-trafficking gateways. The police presence is stronger here than in most other parts of the country, but you should still watch your back – mugging and pickpocketing are not uncommon, though most crime does not affect visitors. It's possible to bypass Limón altogether – there are direct buses from San José to Cahuita and Puerto Viejo, with **boats** to Tortuguero from Moín easily organized from Cahuita – but if you're travelling to Tortuguero independently, you may wish to stay in Limón overnight, especially if you coincide with **El Día de la Raza** (see box below).

WHAT TO SEE AND DO

Limón's palm-shaded **Parque Vargas**, by the *malecón* (sea wall), has a certain appeal. The partly pedestrianized **Avenida 2**, known locally as the "market street", is the main drag, touching the north edge of Parque Vargas, at the easternmost end of C 1 and Av 1/2, and the south side of the **Mercado Central**; you can pick up CDs of local reggaetón bands from vendors along the street. The aptly named **Playa Bonita**, 4km northwest of town, is an attractive stretch of sand.

ARRIVAL AND DEPARTURE

By boat Regular (dry season) boats run between Tortuguero and the dock at Moín, 7km northwest of town. Moín is served by buses (US$1) that depart from Terminal Caribeños; taxis cost around US$5.

By bus Grupos Caribeños (⊕2222 0610) services from San José, Siquirres and Guápiles arrive at the Terminal Caribeños at Av 1, C 7/8. Arrivals from the south – Cahuita, Puerto Viejo and Panama (via Sixaola) – terminate at the Transportes MEPE Terminal at C 6, between avs 1 & 2, on the east side of the stadium.

CARNAVAL IN LIMÓN

Though in the rest of the Americas **Carnaval** is usually associated with the days before Lent, Limón takes Columbus's arrival in the New World – October 12 – as its point of celebration. **El Día de la Raza** (Columbus Day), celebrating Columbus's landing on Isla Uvita, is basically an excuse to party.

The carnival features a variety of events, from Afro-Caribbean dance to calypso music, bull-running, children's theatre, colourful *desfiles* (parades) and firework displays. Most spectacular is the **Gran Desfile**, usually held on the Saturday before October 12, when revellers in Afro-Caribbean costumes parade through the streets. This is the most popular time of year to visit Limón, so book rooms well in advance.

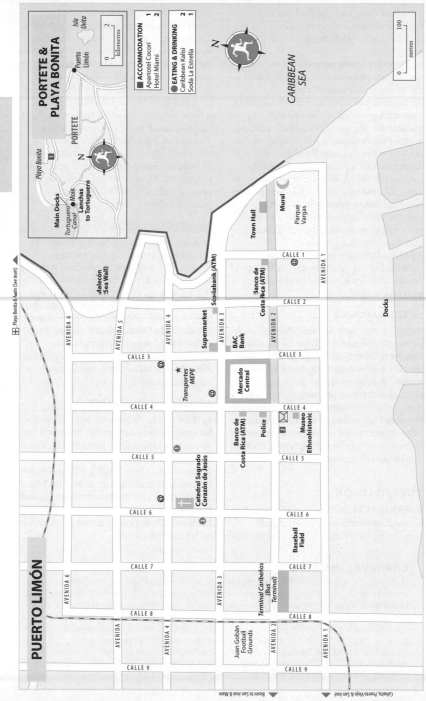

PORTETE & PLAYA BONITA

Isla Uvita

Puerto Limón

Playa Bonita

PORTETE

Main Docks

Tortuguero Canal • Moín

Lanchas to Tortuguero

0 — 2 kilometres

ACCOMMODATION	
Apartotel Cocorí	1
Hotel Miami	2

EATING & DRINKING	
Caribbean Kalisi	2
Soda La Estrella	1

N

CARIBBEAN SEA

0 — 100 metres

PUERTO LIMÓN

Malecón (Sea Wall)

Scotiabank (ATM)

Banco de Costa Rica (ATM)

Town Hall

Mural

Parque Vargas

CALLE 1

AVENIDA 1

Docks

CALLE 2

AVENIDA 2

AVENIDA 6

AVENIDA 5

AVENIDA 4

AVENIDA 3

Supermarket

BAC Bank

CALLE 3

CALLE 3

CALLE 4

Transportes MEPE

Mercado Central

CALLE 4

Banco de Costa Rica (ATM)

Police

Museo Ethnohistoric

CALLE 5

Catedral Sagrado Corazón de Jesús

CALLE 5

CALLE 6

CALLE 6

Baseball Field

CALLE 7

Terminal Caribeños (Bus Terminal)

CALLE 7

AVENIDA 6

AVENIDA 4

AVENIDA 3

AVENIDA 2

Juan Gobán Football Grounds

CALLE 8

CALLE 8

AVENIDA 1

CALLE 9

CALLE 9

Playa Bonita & Moín (See inset)

Buses to San José & Moín

Cahuita, Puerto Viejo & San José

Buses to San José

Destinations from Terminal Caribeños Guápiles (almost hourly 5am–6pm; 2hr); Moín (Mon–Sat hourly 5.30am–6.30pm, Sun every 2hr 5.30am–6.30pm; 30min); San José (hourly 5am–7pm; 3hr).

Destinations from Transportes MEPE Terminal Bribrí & Sixaola (hourly 5am–7pm; 3hr); Cahuita (almost hourly 5am–7pm; 1hr); Manzanillo (5 daily Mon–Fri; 2hr); Puerto Viejo (almost hourly 5am–7pm; 1hr 30min).

By shuttle Interbus (⟨w⟩interbusonline.com) shuttles travelling from San José to Cahuita and Puerto Viejo can drop you off in Limón en route.

ACCOMMODATION AND EATING

Limón is not really a place to go bargain hunting for a night's stay; the more attractive (and safer) options are found along the road between Limón and Moín. A taxi here costs about 1500c, and the bus to and from Moín also runs along the road. Hotel prices rise by as much as fifty percent for Carnaval week. The cheapest places to eat are the *sodas* inside the Mercado Central (Mon–Sat only).

Apartotel Cocorí Playa Bonita ☎ 2798 1670. Don't expect any frills from these barebones self-catering apartments, though they are comfortable and have fan or a/c and have a beautiful leafy setting overlooking the ocean. Pluses include friendly staff and a swimming pool. The lively outdoor bar-restaurant, right by the sea, has lovely views US$51

Caribbean Kalisi C 6, Av 3/4. Family-run cafeteria serving up daily specials of either spicy jerk chicken or beef with generous sides of rice and beans (3000c), as well as the ubiquitous *gallo pinto* breakfasts. Mon–Fri 7.30am–7.30pm, Sat 8am–7.30pm, Sun 8am–5pm.

Hotel Miami Av 2, C 4/5 ☎ 2758 0490, ✉ hmiamilimon @yahoo.com. This friendly, stylish spot near the Mercado Central offers large, clean rooms with cable TV, wi fi and private bathrooms. Most rooms have ceiling fans, though there are a few with a/c (US$10 surcharge) and hot water. US$55

Soda La Estrella C 5, Av 3/4 ☎ 2798 4658. The best lunch in town features excellent *soda* staples, delicious *refrescos*, coffee and snacks like *arreglados* (filled puff pastries; US$3), all accompanied by cordial service. Daily 10am–10pm.

VERAGUA RAINFOREST

Limón is the nearest departure point for **Veragua Rainforest** (Tues–Sun 8am–3pm; full tour US$66, exhibits only US$35; ☎ 4000 0949, ⟨w⟩veraguarainforest.com), a fascinating "research and adventure park" that provides a quick and sleek introduction to the region's rich biodiversity. Owned and operated entirely by Costa Ricans, Veragua holds several smartly designed animal exhibits – including one that mimics a nocturnal habitat for frogs – as well as an aerial tram, a zipline and an elevated trail through the rainforest that leads to a waterfall.

The highlight, though, is the research facility, where you can talk with the resident biologists and learn more about the ongoing study of the park's stunning collection of butterflies.

ARRIVAL AND DEPARTURE

By bus Empresa buses for Siquirres leave Limón's Terminal Caribeños hourly; get off at the Liverpool town stop, about 12km from Limón – let the bus driver know you're going to Veragua. The road leading to Veragua is signposted about 50m from the bus stop. Call in advance to arrange pick-up from here, which is possible most days.

By car If you're driving, a 4WD is necessary to negotiate the bone-rattling gravel road that covers the final 3km to the rainforest.

TORTUGUERO

The peaceful village of **TORTUGUERO** lies on a thin spit of land between the sea and the Canales de Tortuguero, at the corner of one of Costa Rica's great natural attractions – **Parque Nacional Tortuguero**. Despite its isolation – 254km from San José and 83km northwest of Limón – the

---

TURTLE TIME

Every year Tortuguero is overrun with visitors who come for one reason – to see marine turtles lay their eggs (an event called the **desove**). Although Tortuguero is by no means the only place in Costa Rica to see marine turtles nesting, four of the largest kinds of endangered sea turtle regularly nest here in large numbers. Along with the **green** (verde) turtle you might see the **hawksbill** (carey), with its distinctive hooked beak, and the ridged **leatherback** (baula), the largest turtle in the world, which can easily weigh 300kg – some are as heavy as 400kg and reach 3m in length. The rarest of them all is the **loggerhead** (boba); there are only one or two sightings per season. The green turtles and hawksbills nest in the greatest numbers from July to mid-September (August is the peak month); the leatherbacks come ashore (in far smaller numbers) from March to May.

2

national park is extremely popular, mainly because of its spectacular biodiversity. An abundance of species is found here, including fifty kinds of **fish**, more than one hundred **reptiles**, more than three hundred species of **bird** and 160 species of **mammal**, several of which, including the manatee, are under threat of extinction. Most notably, the beach here is one of the world's main nesting sites for **green sea turtles**, as well as the rarer **hawksbill**, **leatherback** and **loggerhead turtles**.

WHAT TO SEE AND DO

While turtle season is the most popular time to visit Tortuguero, the village receives visitors most of the year, since getting here via the **Canales de Tortuguero** – a waterway created by connecting existing rivers and lagoons, allowing sheltered passage to Tortuguero via coastal villages – is an adventure in itself. During the journey you get to see a lot of wildlife, though not as much as you see during guided boat trips at dawn from Tortuguero village itself. Animal- and birdwatching aside, the park also offers hiking and nature walks.

Tortuguero village

Covered in wisteria, oleander and bougainvillea, **Tortuguero village** has the air of a dilapidated tropical garden, with houses protruding from the greenery along the dirt footpaths, and the beach on its eastern side buffeted by rough Atlantic surf. It centres on the main **dock**, or *muelle*, where all the boats arrive. Two dirt paths run north–south through the village – the "main street" and "Avenida 2", or secondary street – from which narrow paths go off to the sea on the eastern side and the canal on the western. The beach is not suitable for swimming due to riptides. At the north end of the village, past the tiny waterfront park with giant bird sculptures, beyond *Miss Junie's* hotel, the **Natural History Museum** (daily 10am–5pm; 1100c; Ⓦconserveturtles .org), run by the Caribbean Conservation Corporation, has a small, informative exhibition on the life cycle of sea turtles and a video explaining the history of turtle conservation in the area.

Parque Nacional Tortuguero

Entrance to **Parque Nacional Tortuguero** (daily 6am–6pm; US$10; ☎2710 2929) is just south of the village and reached by the main path (right from the main dock). You have to pay the entry fee whether you wish to hike in the park or join a guided boat trip. The well-maintained **El Gavilan trail** (2 miles round-trip) starts at the ranger station at the park entrance and heads toward the coast where it turns south, parallelling the beach which remains close at hand for the length of the path. A mostly shaded walk, it gives you a good chance of glimpsing lizards and monkeys. Walking the trail can be a muddy experience and rubber boots are mandatory; numerous places near the park entrance rent or lend them out (US$2/day).

Turtle tours

During turtle season, you can watch the turtles lay their eggs by taking part in a rigorously controlled and extremely well-organized guided **turtle tour** (US$20 for two hours), which leave nightly at 8pm and 10pm from the village. Visitor permits are allocated to guides via a daily lottery at 4.45pm; to guarantee yourself a place, make sure you reserve before 4.30pm on the day in question. The turtle viewing area is divided into five sectors; the two sectors furthest from the village are part of the national park, so you have to pay the US$10 park entry fee on top of the turtle tour fee (unless you already have one from earlier in the day). Since the furthest sectors are the quietest, there's a greater likelihood of seeing turtles there. Visitors must wear dark clothing, refrain from smoking and are not allowed to bring cameras or torches. Tours are conducted in silence, with visitors waiting in special shelter sites close to the beach. When a turtle is spotted by scouts, they radio the guides, who then bring you round the back of the turtle, one by one, to witness the turtle laying its eggs in the nest it has dug. Tours after midnight are illegal.

Boat trips

Worth the trip to Tortuguero in their own right are the **boat trips** (US$20, plus park entry fee) through the area's canals and *caños*, or lagoons, to spot animals including spider, howler and white-faced capucin monkeys, caimans, iguanas and Jesus Christ lizards, and birds including herons, cranes and kingfishers. You're likely to be offered a boat trip as soon as you set foot in Tortuguero. These fall into two categories: canoe trips, where you have to do some of the paddling, and electric boat trips. Canoe guides may tell you that motor boats are not allowed in the narrow Caño Chiquero and Caño Moro – the best for wildlife-watching – which is true of regular boats, but does not apply to the silent electric boats. Bring a poncho for the sudden downpours.

ARRIVAL AND DEPARTURE

Getting to Tortuguero independently requires a bit of forward planning. You can either do a combination bus/boat route, or you can fly (though that means you miss out on half the adventure). If you don't want the hassle of getting there independently, go with one of the numerous companies that offer transfers (around US$60) from San José and La Fortuna (via Cariari) and from Cahuita and Puerto Viejo de Talamanca (via Moín).

From San José to Cariari by bus Take a bus from the Gran Terminal del Caribe at 6.30am, 9am, 10.30am or 1pm to Cariari's *estación nueva*, then walk five blocks north to the Terminal Caribeño (also known as *estación vieja*). On the return journey, buses depart Cariari at 7.30am, 8.30am, 11.30am, 1pm, 3pm and 5.30pm). In peak season, buy bus tickets a day or two in advance.

From Cariari by bus and boat In Cariari you have two options: both Coopetraca (☎ 2767 7590 or ☎ 2767 7137)

and Clic Clic (☎ 2709 8155 or ☎ 8844 0463) charge 3000c for the bus–boat combo. The only difference is that with Clic Clic you pay for the bus to La Pavona in Cariari, and then pay for the boat separately once you get to the dock, with myriad boat companies soliciting your custom, while with Coopetraca, you pay the whole amount up front. Buses (1hr–1hr 30min; 1000c) depart at 6am, 9am, 11.30am and 3pm, returning when the boats from Tortuguero arrive in La Pavona. Boats leave from the La Pavona dock at 7am, 12.30pm and 4pm, returning at 6am, 11.30am and 3pm. A one-way ticket costs 2000c.

From Moín by boat Unlike from La Pavona, boat services from Moín serve tourists rather than locals and, as such, there are no scheduled departures, though during peak season, a number of boats depart daily to and from Tortuguero at around 10am. A return boat ticket costs US$60–70 (4hr). Operators include Tropical Wind (☎ 2798 6059), but there's no real advantage to one operator over another. Even in peak season, it's better to call and ask about departures in advance, though it's possible just to turn up and get a seat on a boat. In low season, it's easier to go via Cariari.

By plane Sansa (☎ 2229 4100, ⌨ flysansa.com) and NatureAir (☎ 2299 6000, ⌨ natureair.com) have daily flights from San José to Tortuguero (departing 6–7am; 30min); fares are in the region of US$125–150. The tiny planes are particularly weather-susceptible, so bad weather can delay or ground the flights. Flights land at the airstrip 4km north of Tortuguero village; water taxis cost US$5/person.

INFORMATION

Tourist information A small, somewhat faded display on the turtles' habits, habitat and history surrounds the information kiosk (daily 9am–6pm) in the village centre. This is the official place to buy tickets for turtle tours; park rangers sell the tickets at the kiosk from 5pm to 6pm. Here you can also get contact info for local guides.

TOUR OPERATORS IN TORTUGUERO

Several **tour operators** in Tortuguero offer competitively priced boat trips. Avoid the beach boys who accost you at the dock or around town.

Casa Marbella See p.136. Excellent trips in an electric boat with knowledgeable Canadian naturalist Daryl Loth and nice extra touches, such as ponchos, provided.

Castor Hunter Thomas ☎ 8870 8630, enquire at *Soda Dona María*. Well-respected guide with more than two decades of experience in leading canoe, turtle and hiking tours.

Iguana Verde Tours Operates out of *Miss Junie's Lodge* ☎ 2231 6803, ⌨ iguanaverdetours.com. Offers a number of tours, including popular canal and national park excursions (from US$20), as well as a village tour

(US$35) that provides an excellent introduction into local and Caribbean culture.

Ross Ballard ☎ 2709 8193 or ☎ 8320 5232, ✉ ballardross1@gmail.com. What you learn from Canadian botanist Ross Ballard during wonderfully informative nature walks around Cerro Tortuguero (US$20) will stay with you forever. Also night tours and overnight stays in the nearby biological station.

Tinamon Tours ☎ 8842 6561, ⌨ tinamontours.com. Biologist Barbara Hartung provides quality canoe, hiking, cultural and several other tours in English, German, French or Spanish.

2

ACCOMMODATION

All accommodation options reviewed here offer free wi-fi. Camping in the wild is not allowed in the village or national park.

Cabinas Balcon del Mar On the beachfront, just south of *Cabinas Icaco* ☎ 2709 8124. Some of the rooms are tiny, dark and inadequately ventilated, while others have private bath and even balconies to catch the sea breeze. The larger apartments come with kitchenettes. Doubles US$8, apartments US$12

Cabinas Tortuguero 200m south of the football pitch ☎ 2709 8114, @ cabinas_tortuguero@yahoo.com. Eleven brightly painted bungalows, some with shared, some with private baths, plus fans and hammocks on the veranda, set in a lovely garden. Shared bath US$25, private bath US$34

★**Casa Marbella** 100m north of the dock ☎ 2709 8011, @ casamarbella.tripod.com. This waterfront B&B, professionally run by Canadian biologist Daryl Loth who is a treasure-trove of local knowledge, boasts airy, spacious rooms with private baths and fans; the corner room upstairs has the best river views. Rates include breakfast. One of the best places for tours (see box, p.135). US$45

El Icaco On the beachfront, east of the village centre ☎ 2709 8044, @ hotelelicaco.com. This popular beachfront place has lime-green rooms, all en-suite with hot water and fan, a communal kitchen, TV lounge and wonderfully relaxing hammock area. Rates include breakfast. Doubles US$30, apartments US$45

Miss Junie's Lodge At the northern end of the village, just before you reach the Natural History Museum ☎ 2231 6803, @ iguanaverdetours.com. Offering a touch more comfort than other options in the village, this attractive lodge, set in lush grounds, has airy wood-panelled rooms with private bathroom, security boxes and fans; those on the first floor at the front are the best of the bunch. Rates include breakfast; the on-site restaurant is a local institution. US$50

Miss Miriam's On the north side of the village football pitch ☎ 2709 8002. Spick-and-span rooms with tiled floors, attractive courtyard with hammocks, a quiet location near the sea and adjacent to the restaurant of the same name. US$17

Princesa Resort Just east of the El Gavilán store ☎ 2709 8131. The most attractive of the three *Princesa* locations in town, with spartan wood-and-concrete rooms on the oceanfront, a garden, two pools and a Tico restaurant. US$30

EATING AND DRINKING

★**Buddha Café** Near the dock. Wonderfully tranquil riverfront setting and an imaginative international menu. Choose from daily specials, such as *ceviche*, pizza, crêpes and more. The home-made brownie with ice cream is to die for. Mains around 3500c. Daily noon–9pm.

Centro Social La Culebra Next to the main dock. This innocuous-looking purple riverfront building becomes the town's most popular watering hole by night: expect a boisterous local crowd and deafening tunes. Beer 1200c. Daily 8pm–late.

Dorling's Bakery Attached to *Cabinas Marbella*. Grab a seat out back in the riverside garden and tuck into a slice of home-made cake – chocolate, carrot, banana and lemon – or a meat-filled pastry or sandwich (2250c). The only spot open before the morning boat tours set off. Daily 5am–7pm.

Miss Junie's *Miss Junie's Lodge*, at the northern end of the village ☎ 2709 8102, @ iguanaverdetours.com. Run by the village matriarch, this local institution is the place to treat yourself to delights such as Caribbean lobster with coconut rice, grilled chicken and fresh whole fish. Mains from 4500c. Daily noon–9pm.

Miss Miriam's On the north side of the football pitch. Run by the daughter of Miss Miriam, this place serves up heaped portions of Caribbean food (mains from 3500c), such as giant river shrimp, fried fish and spicy chicken. Daily 7.30am–9pm.

Soda La Fe Near the entrance to the park. Ideal for pre- or post-park refreshments, this tiny *soda* has filling *pintos* (from 1500c) and *casados* (from 2800c), as well as *empanadas* (750c). Daily noon–9pm.

Wild Ginger Walk towards the beach from the canalfront plaza with the giant birds, then take a left just before you reach it and carry on for 50m. Wonderfully friendly Tico-Californian outpost, with imaginative fusion dishes making the most of local ingredients and great desserts. Mains 5000c. Restaurant daily 6–9pm; bar 6pm–midnight.

DIRECTORY

Banks and exchange There is no bank, and few businesses accept credit cards, so bring plenty of cash.

Health Ebais, across from the dock, serves as a basic clinic, but the doctor only visits once a week.

Internet Most accommodation offers wi-fi and there are a couple of spots with computers around the village. Internet connections can be affected by heavy rains.

CAHUITA

The tiny coastal village of **CAHUITA**, 43km southeast of Limón, comprises just two puddle-dotted, gravel-and-sand roads running parallel to the sea, intersected by a few cross-streets. With its resident Rastas and laidback vibe, it feels more like a Caribbean outpost than part of Central America. Though the principal attraction here is the proximity to **Parque Nacional Cahuita** (see p.139), the fairly empty stretches of sand along the water make the local beaches perfect for relaxing and sunbathing as well.

CAHUITA

■ ACCOMMODATION	
Cabinas Iguana	1
Cabinas Jenny	3
Cabinas Nirvana	2
Secret Garden	4

● EATING & DRINKING	
Café Chocolatte	5
Coco's	4
Miss Edith's	2
Reggae Bar	1
Restaurant La Fé	3

C A R I B B E A N   S E A

N

2

Tree of Life (1.7hr)

Playa Negra

Sloth Sanctuary (100m) & Puerto Limón (44km)

Brigette Tours/
Cabinas Brigitte

Football
Pitch

36

Police

School

Cahuita Tours
& Rentals

Willie's
@ Tours

Supermarket

@

Turística Cahuita

Mr Big J's

CAHUITA MAIN

CALLE PRINCIPAL

Banco de
Costa Rica (ATM)

Kelly Creek
National Park
Entrance

Bus Station

Playa Vargas

0   100
metres

▼ Puerto Viejo de Talamanca (17km) & Bribrí (19km)

WHAT TO SEE AND DO

Cahuita's main street runs from the entrance to **Parque Nacional Cahuita** at **Kelly Creek** to the northern end of the village, marked roughly by the football pitch. Beyond here it continues 2 or 3km north along **Playa Negra** (Black Sand Beach) and beyond to the wonderful **Tree of Life** rescue centre.

Tree of Life

The excellent combined wildlife rescue centre and botanical garden **Tree of Life** (Tues–Sun: Jan to mid-April, Nov & Dec 9am–3pm; July & Aug 11am guided tour only; US$12; ⊛ treeoflifecostarica.com), 2km north of town on the Playa Negra road, takes in wild animals that have been victims of loss of habitat, hunting and the pet trade. Animals that can be are rehabilitated, before being released into the wild, while those that cannot are

given a home here. Resident creatures include coati, capuchin monkeys, an orphaned jaguarundi, howler monkeys, peccaries and more. Todd and Patricia also run breeding programmes for turtles and iguanas, and their twelve acres of botanical gardens include labelled edible plants, such as cinnamon, as well as hundreds of tropical species.

Playa Negra

The blue-flag, black-sand **Playa Negra**, northwest of town, is suitable for swimming and good for anyone learning to surf; boards are available to rent (US$5/hr) from *Cabinas Brigitte*, as well as a couple of other spots.

ARRIVAL AND INFORMATION

By bus Buses pull in at the station next to the Banco de Costa Rica on the main road.

Destinations Bribrí (18 daily; 30–50min); Limón (22 daily;

2

VISIT THE SLOTHS

What creature wears a beatific smile, can turn its head 270 degrees, and moves at a speed of 2m per minute? The sloth, of course. If you've ever seen a sloth cross the road, you'll understand the need for the expertly run **Sloth Sanctuary** (open year-round, the first tour departs at 7am, the last one departs at 2.30pm; ☎ 2750 0775, ⓦ slothsanctuary.com), 11km north of Cahuita, which takes in injured and orphaned sloths, rehabilitates them and reintroduces them into the wild (if possible).

Diurnal, vegetarian three-toed sloths and their omnivorous nocturnal cousins, the two-toed sloths, reside here under the watchful eye of founder Judy, her daughter and grandson, all of whom are actively involved in their care. There are two types of tours to choose from. The **Buttercup Tour** (US$25; 2hr; starts every hour on the hour) consists of an hour-long wildlife-spotting outing in a canoe on the river, followed by an entertaining and educational video about sloths and a tour of the sanctuary. The **Insider's Tour** (US$150 for four people; 7am & 11am; reservations required) adds to that a visit to the sloth hospital and private nursery, where you get to meet the tiniest babies. A fantastic experience. You can get here from Cahuita by taking any of the Limón-bound buses or a taxi.

1hr); Puerto Viejo (22 daily; 30min); San José (5 daily 7am–4.30pm; 4hr); Sixaola (9 daily; 1hr 30min).

By shuttle Interbus shuttles from Puerto Viejo de Talamanca to other popular destinations (see p.239) can pick you up in Cahuita; book in advance.

Tourist information The most useful website is ⓦ cahuita.cr. The tour companies provide the only visitor information in the village itself.

Tours Mr Big J's (☎ 2755 0328), a road back from the main street, offers a range of regional tours, including local jungle hikes; Brigitte Tours at *Cabinas Brigitte* beside Playa Negra (☎ 2755 0053, ⓦ brigittecahuita.com) specializes in horseriding trips; Cahuita Tours (☎ 2755 0000, ⓦ cahuitatours.com), 50m south of the police station, offers national park, kayaking and snorkelling tours as well as tours to indigenous villages.

ACCOMMODATION

There's accommodation along Playa Negra as well as in the village, though that road is poorly lit at night.

IN THE VILLAGE

Cabinas Jenny At the beach end of the side street leading past the tiny plaza ☎ 2755 0256, ⓦ cabinasjenny .com. The beautiful top-floor rooms have high wooden ceilings, mosquito nets, fans and kitchenettes, plus thoughtful touches such as filtered drinking water. Each comes with a private balcony overlooking the sea. The ground-floor rooms are simpler and cheaper, with fans and hammocks on porches. <u>US$27</u>

Secret Garden Down the side street just before Kelly Creek ☎ 2755 0581, ✉ koosiecosta@live.nl. Behind the lush, jungle-style garden, strewn with kitsch statuettes, lie a handful of simple rooms with private bathroom, plus a dorm. The Dutch-run hostel also has a communal kitchen, laundry service and plenty of books to flick through. Dorm <u>US$12</u>, doubles <u>US$33</u>

PLAYA NEGRA

★**Cabinas Iguana** Beyond *Cabinas Brigitte* ☎ 2755 0005, ⓦ cabinas-iguana.com. The lovely wood-panelled *cabinas* on stilts, set back from the beach and surrounding a small, curvaceous pool, have private bathrooms, while rooms in the main lodge, with a screened veranda, share facilities. Extras include laundry, book exchange and bike rental. Doubles <u>US$25</u>, *cabinas* <u>US$45</u>

★**Cabinas Nirvana** About 100m back along the road adjacent to *Reggae Bar* ☎ 2755 0110, ⓦ cabinasnirvana . com. There are four attractive *cabinas*, one airy bungalow and one basic room to choose from at this pretty and inviting property; all have mosquito nets and free wi-fi, while the bungalow also has a/c. There's also a pool and on-site parking. The affable owners are exceedingly helpful and can arrange snorkelling tours to the national park with one of the best local guides. Double <u>US$30</u>, *cabinas* <u>US$45</u>, bungalow <u>US$75</u>

EATING AND DRINKING

Café Chocolatte Main street. Your first stop for great coffee, fresh juices, and mega sandwiches with a variety of fillings (including veggie options) to wrap up for your hike in the park. Sandwiches from 1875c. Mon–Fri 6.30am–2pm.

Coco's At the main junction in the town centre. You'll hear this eye-catching bar, decked out in a Rasta colour scheme, before you see it; a popular spot for a cold beer (1200c) or a potent rum punch (3000c), it attracts a lively clientele after dark. There's also occasional live music, and wonderfully fresh food, from *ceviche* to the squid with *tostones* (mashed, fried plantain). Daily noon–late.

Miss Edith's A block away from the main street, beyond the post office. This simple restaurant is the domain of one of the village's matriarchs, who works her magic daily. Expect mouth-searing jerk chicken, stewed fish (5300c) and other Caribbean delights. Daily 7am–9pm.

Reggae Bar Playa Negra. The location, just opposite the beach, makes this a great place to grab a cold beer (1200c) or enjoy home-cooked food – from the signature prawns in coconut milk to *casados*. Mains from 2500c. Daily noon–midnight.

Restaurant La Fé On the main street, near the main intersection. Popular Tico-run restaurant famous for its spicy coconut sauce (perfect with seafood), offering Tico standards and generous breakfasts. Mains from 3500c. Daily 7am–11pm.

DIRECTORY

Bank Banco de Costa Rica, next to the bus station, a couple of blocks from the main street, has an ATM.
Bicycle rental Bicycles can be rented from *Cabinas Brigitte* or Mr Big J's (5000c/day).
Laundry Mr Big J's, a block from the main street (3500c/bag).

PARQUE NACIONAL CAHUITA

PARQUE NACIONAL CAHUITA (Mon–Fri 8am–4pm, Sat & Sun 7am–5pm; US$10) is one of the country's smallest protected areas, covering the wedge-shaped piece of land from Punta Cahuita back to the main highway and, crucially, the **coral reef** about 500m offshore. Given that this is one of the last living reefs in Costa Rica, snorkelling is only allowed with a guide; local tour operators offer **snorkelling trips** (around US$30). On land, Cahuita shelters the litoral, or coastal, rainforest, a lowland habitat of semi-mangroves and tall canopy cover that backs the white-sand beaches of Playa Blanca and Playa Vargas. **Birds**, including ibis and kingfishers, are in residence, along with white-faced capucin and howler monkeys, coati, raccoons, sloths and snakes.

The park's one **trail** (7km), skirting the beach, is an easy, flat walk, alternating between sandy path and raised boardwalk, with a 1.5km gravel road leading from the Puerto Vargas ranger station to the main road. The Río Perezoso, about 2km from the Kelly Creek entrance, or 5km from the Puerto Vargas trailhead, is not always fordable in the rainy season. Be aware of rip currents at both beaches, and look for green flags indicating safe swimming spots; if starting from Kelly Creek, the first 500m or so of Playa Blanca are not safe.

ARRIVAL AND DEPARTURE

Entrances The park has two entrances: Kelly Creek (south end of Cahuita), and Puerto Vargas (5km south of Cahuita).

EATING

Boca Chica If you do the hike in the morning from Kelly Creek, you will reach this peaceful French-run restaurant at the end of your walk, near the main highway. They offer three set Tico dishes daily (5000c). Daily 9am–6pm.

PUERTO VIEJO DE TALAMANCA

It's **surfing** that really pulls the crowds to the languorous hamlet of **PUERTO VIEJO DE TALAMANCA**, which offers some of the most challenging waves in the country, including the famous "**Salsa Brava**". The **village** itself lies between the thickly forested hills of the Talamanca mountains and the sea, where locals bathe and kids frolic with surfboards. The main drag is crisscrossed by a few dirt streets and an offshoot road that follows the shore. As in Cahuita, many expats have been drawn to Puerto Viejo and have set up their own businesses; and, like Cahuita, most locals are of Afro-Caribbean descent. The village's backpacker and surf-party culture ensures a lively, youthful nightlife, but there is also a **drugs scene**, and **crime**, particularly theft, can be a problem: never take valuables to the beach (and stay off it at night), make sure your accommodation is secure, and take care after dark.

WHAT TO SEE AND DO

It is hard to spend time here without hitting the waves; the best **surf** is from December to March and July to August. There are plenty of places to **rent boards** and book lessons (see p.140) and the surf ranges from beginner waves on Playa Negra to the advanced, reef-side break of Salsa Brava, offering both lefts and rights. For surf **lessons**, Swells Surf Shop has a well-earned reputation.

ARRIVAL AND DEPARTURE

By bus Buses arrive and depart from the stop on the beach road at Puerto Viejo's second cross-street.
Destinations Bribrí (18 daily; 20min); Cahuita (22 daily; 30min); Manzanillo (6 daily; 30min); Puerto Limón (10 daily; 1hr 30min); San José (5 daily; 4hr 30min); Sixaola (9 daily; 1hr).

2

INFORMATION AND TOURS

★**ATEC** On the main road ☎ 2750 0398, ⓦ ateccr.org. An excellent local organization (see box, p.142) offering fascinating trips to nearby indigenous settlements (US$25), as well as private surf lessons (US$60/2hr) and dolphin-watching (US$55).

Exploradores Outdoors In the mini-mall on the main road on the east edge of the village ☎ 2750 2020, ⓦ exploradores outdoors.com. The excellent Exploradores Outdoors runs several tours of the local area, including a kayaking and hiking trip to Punta Uva (US$49). They also lead one of the best day-trips in the country, whitewater rafting on the Río Pacuaré, which includes four hours of rafting on Class III and IV sections of the river – a total of 38 rapids – and lunch (US$99). Tours depart from their rafting centre in Siquirres, with pick-ups from Puerto Viejo, Cahuita or San José: they can drop you off at a different location than pick-up, which is handy if you're moving on to San José or Cahuita.

Terraventuras Main street, 100m south of the bus stop ☎ 2750 0750, ⓦ terraventuras.com. Countrywide adventure tours, plus their own canopy tour (US$55) and overnight trips to Tortuguero.

Tourist information The most useful websites are ⓦ puertoviejosatellite.com and ⓦ greencoast.com, with info on accommodation, activities and eating out. The tour operators listed here can also be helpful.

ACCOMMODATION

If you're staying at or close to *Kaya's Place* and *Rocking J's*, walk with other people or consider taking a taxi back from town after dark, as muggings occasionally occur.

Cabinas Grant On the main road, one block east from the Banco de Costa Rica ☎ 2750 0292. Spotless, locally run hotel with basic but serviceable rooms and dorm beds.

Private rooms on the second floor have balconies and cost slightly more. Dorms US$11, doubles US$35

Cabinas Jacaranda 25m north of the football pitch ☎ 2750 0069, ⓦ cabinasjacaranda.net. Follow the mosaic-tiled floor from the front gate and you discover a mini Eden: simple rooms for between one and four people feature colourful murals, wooden furniture, fans and safes, and most have private baths. There are also verdant gardens, where you can have a massage or take a yoga class, plus a kitchen and free internet. US$35

★**Hotel Pura Vida** Across the street from the football field ☎ 2750 0002, ⓦ hotel-puravida.com. On a quiet street, this fantastic Chilean-German guesthouse oozes tranquillity – from its appealing patio overflowing with greenery, with hammocks, easy chairs and pets sprawled on the tiled floors, to the large, airy, fan-cooled rooms, some with own bathrooms. Hearty breakfast US$7. US$32

Kaya's Place Playa Negra, west of town ☎ 2750 0690, ⓦ kayasplace.com. Arty murals, thatched roofs and carved driftwood give *Kaya's Place* a distinct rustic-chic character; each room is unique, but the ocean-view rooms on the first floor are worth splurging on as the cheapest ones don't get much natural light. Shared bath US$27, private bath US$33

Rocking J's On the main road, 100m beyond Tuanis Bikes ☎ 2750 0657, ⓦ rockingjs.com. The epicentre of backpacker life in Puerto Viejo, *Rocking J's* has a bewildering array of options for shoestringers – including barebones *cabinas* for two and a shoebox-sized treehouse – as well as more upmarket options – the suites and the Stables. The beachside compound also has a big garden, chill-out areas, a restaurant and bar with live music every Friday and frequent parties. You won't get much sleep, but then, that's not the point. Hammocks US$7, camping US$16, dorm US$11, *cabinas* US$26, treehouse US$26

PUERTO VIEJO DE TALAMANCA

■ **ACCOMMODATION**

Cabinas Grant	3
Cabinas Jacaranda	4
Hotel Pura Vida	5
Kaya's Place	6
Rocking J's	1
La Ruka Hostel	2

CARIBBEAN SEA

Buses to Cahuita,
Limón, Sixaola,
Manzanillo &
San José

HWY-36

Cahuita & Bribrí

Playa Negra

HWY-36

La Ruka Hostel 600m along road to Playa Cockles ☎2750 0617, ⓦlarukahostel.com. Staying at *La Ruka* (named after the resident three-legged dog) is like staying at a friend's house; many guests end up lingering longer than they thought. There's a great common area, hung with hammocks, and friendly owners Dani and Dave hold occasional parties. All rooms share facilities. Dorms <u>US$10</u>, doubles <u>US$30</u>

EATING

Bread & Chocolate Half a block off the main street, next to *Cabinas Larry*. Delectable home-made cakes, home-made peanut butter sandwiches — in fact, most things, soups and mains included, are prepared completely from scratch at this lovely café. Don't miss out on the do-it-yourself coffees either. Sandwiches 3000c. Tues–Sat 6.30am–6.30pm, Sun 6.30am–2.30pm.

Chile Rojo First floor of the shopping arcade opposite ATEC. The best way to approach this otherwise budget-busting pan-Asian restaurant/bar is to come with an empty stomach on Monday for the all-you-can-eat sushi and (mostly) Chinese buffet (6750c). The rest of the week, Thai curries and other delights grace the à la carte menu. Thurs–Tues noon–11pm.

Mare Nostrum Main road, not far from *Chile Rojo*. The best budget seafood in town, with an overwhelmingly large menu: the fresh fish (5000–6500c), paella (3700–4800c) and sangria are all specialities. Daily noon–10pm.

Pan Pay On the seafront across from the police station. A popular breakfast spot offering the best croissants in town, plus delicious Spanish omelettes (1500c for a hefty slice with bread), good, low-cost coffee and takeaway sandwiches (1800–2700c). Daily 7am–5pm.

Peace and Love On the seafront near the police station ☎2750 0758. An attractive hippy café specializing in

★**TREAT YOURSELF**

Stashu's Con-Fusion 250m along road to Playa Cockles ☎2750 0530. Chef Stashu is some sort of genius, blending Mexican, Caribbean, Thai and other styles to great effect. Try Thai-style red curry mussels followed by macadamia-encrusted mahi-mahi, and round it off with one of the unbelievably good desserts – chocolate orange brownie with ice cream, perhaps. Mains from 6400c. Mon, Tues & Thurs–Sun 5–10pm.

Italian breads, with a nice mix of fresh seafood and salads (from US$5), too. Daily 8am–8pm.

★**Puerto Pirata Deli** in the centre, across from the beach ☎2750 0459. Cosy local hangout serving Fair Trade coffee, chocolate, pastries (1000c) and vegan-friendly sandwiches (3000c). There's wi-fi too, and an enviable setting across from the beach. Cash only. Daily 9am–6pm.

Soda Mirna Next to ATEC on main road. As well as a token *casado* or two, this great little spot serves up such Caribbean delights as spicy chicken with rice and beans, pork ribs and seafood dishes made fiery by the home-made hot sauce. Mains from 3000c. Daily noon–10pm.

Veronica's Place 100m south of Supermercado El Diamante in the village centre ☎2750 0132. One of the best spots for hearty and reasonably priced Caribbean breakfasts (3000c), using plenty of fresh produce from Veronica's own organic farm. They also serve dinner buffets (4000–5500c). Reservations required, one day in advance. Breakfast served at 8.30am, dinner served from 7pm.

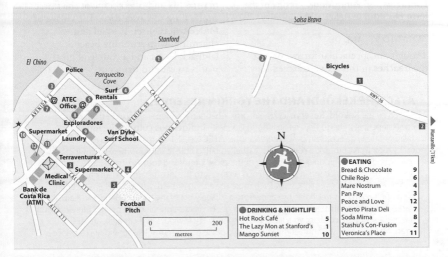

DRINKING AND NIGHTLIFE

Hot Rock Café At the junction of the main street and the road leading to the police station ☎ 2750 0525. One of the town's more openly touristy places, this lively café-bar shows a movie (7pm nightly), usually followed by live Latin or reggae music. Daily 11am–2am.

The Lazy Mon at Stanford's Just east of the main street ☎ 2750 2116. Very popular at weekends, this sports bar serves a small range of snacks and has a large outdoor disco where you can dance to the sounds of reggae and waves crashing on the shore. Daily 10am–10pm.

Mango Sunset 20m from the bus stop. Welcoming bar, with great live rock, reggae and Latin music (notably on Wed) and lots of drinks promotions to get you in the mood (think US$1.50 tequila shots). There are also dartboards and Sky TV for sports events. Mon & Tues 7pm–2.30am, Thurs–Sun 7pm–4am.

DIRECTORY

Bank Banco de Costa Rica, diagonally across from the Super Puerto Viejo supermarket, has an ATM.

Bicycle rental Surf Rentals (☎ 2750 1909), on the main road at the eastern edge of the village, hire out bikes for 7500c a day.

Health The medical clinic, Sunimedica (☎ 2750 0079) is on the main road past the first cross-street as you enter town. Farmacia Amiga, in the small commercial centre next to the post office, is the town pharmacy.

SOUTH TO MANZANILLO

The 12km of coast between Puerto Viejo and **MANZANILLO** village – dotted by the tiny hamlets of **Playa Cocles**, **Playa Chiquita**, **Punta Uva** and **Punta Mona** – is one of the most beautiful stretches in the country.

WHAT TO SEE AND DO

Though not spectacular for swimming, the **beaches** in this area are exceedingly picturesque; a cycle tour from Puerto Viejo along this stretch makes for a fantastic day-trip.

Refugio Nacional de Vida Silvestre Gandoca-Manzanillo

The little-visited but fascinating **Refugio Nacional de Vida Silvestre Gandoca-Manzanillo** (daily 7am–5pm; free), bordering the Río Sixaola and the Panamanian border, incorporates the small hamlets of Gandoca and Manzanillo and covers fifty square kilometres of land and a similar area of sea. It was established to protect some of Costa Rica's last few **coral reefs**, of which **Punta Uva** is the most accessible. You can **snorkel** here, or **dive**, and there are also a couple of good hiking trails. A coastal walk leads east from Manzanillo to **Punta Mona** (5.5km each way), an excellent snorkelling spot; it's straightforward enough, though rain can make sections difficult to navigate. You'll need a guide for the more challenging 9km hike to the village of Gandoca, west of Manzanillo.

The park office (in the green wooden house at the entry to Manzanillo; 8am–noon & 1–4pm; ☎ 2759 9100) can provide trail maps.

Manzanillo

Playa Manzanillo has a large shelf of coral reef just offshore, which teems with marine life and offers some of the finest snorkelling in Costa Rica. The village of **MANZANILLO** itself is small and charming, with stunning beaches, laidback locals and a couple of great places to eat and hang out.

ATEC, THE KÉKÖLDI AND THE YORKÍN RESERVES

Skirted by the **Kéköldi Reserve** (ⓦ kekoldi.org), inhabited by about two hundred Bribrí and Cabécar peoples, Puerto Viejo retains strong links with **indigenous culture**. The Asociación Talamanqueña de Ecoturismo y Conservación, or **ATEC** (see p.140), is a grassroots organization set up by members of the local community. As well as being able to tell you where to buy locally made products, the group arranges some of the most interesting **tours** in Costa Rica. Day-trips to the reserve cost US$35, and include a guided hike, visit to the iguana farm and lunch; these can also be extended for overnight stays. Even more rewarding is the day-trip to the remote Bribrí community of Yorkín, reachable by canoe from a village west of the town of Bribrí. You learn about traditional pursuits, such as cocoa growing, and get to practise grinding the beans before drinking the freshest hot chocolate of your life. If you're spending a few days in the region, an ATEC-arranged trip is a must – contact the Puerto Viejo office (see p.140) at least one day in advance.

INTO PANAMA: SIXAOLA

The **Sixaola–Guabito border** is open daily from 8am to 5pm Panama time or 7am–4pm Costa Rican time (Panama is 1hr ahead); border posts close for lunch for an hour around 1pm, so you'll be hanging around at that time. Get to the border as early as possible, especially since there's nowhere decent to stay in Guabito. Citizens of some nationalities may require a **tourist card** (US$5; valid for thirty days) to enter Panama (see p.518).

In **Panama**, if you're arriving from Bocas del Toro, your best bet is to take the water taxi to Almirante, and then grab a bus to Changuinola (every 30min) and finally a bus to Guabito (every 30min; 30min).

ARRIVAL AND DEPARTURE

By bus Buses depart from along Manzanillo's main street.
Destination Puerto Viejo (6 daily; 30min).
By bike Bicycling to Manzanillo (see opposite for rentals) is a good option; it takes about 90min to cycle from Puerto Viejo.

ACCOMMODATION AND EATING

Cabinas Bucus Behind *Cabinas Manzanillo* ☎ 2759 9143, ⓦ costa-rica-manzanillo.com. Four pristine doubles with wooden shutters, balconies and private stone bathrooms, in a lovely spot backing onto jungle, run by local guide Omar and his German wife Melte, who lead informative tours. US$40
Cabinas Manzanillo On the northern edge of Manzanillo ☎ 2759 9033. Reliable, low-key hotel run by incredibly helpful owners with eight spotless, bright rooms, all with powerful fans, private bath and TV; those upstairs have better jungle views. US$40
★Maxi's Near the beach in central Manzanillo. Manzanillo's – generally thumping – heartbeat, locally renowned *Maxi's* has an upstairs restaurant that attracts visitors from far and wide with its superlative seafood – huge portions of grilled fish, lobster and other delights fresh from the sea. Mains 3000–12,500c. Daily 11.30am–10pm.
Soda Mimi 25m behind Maxi's, set about 100m back from the beach. Simple *soda* with veranda seating serving heaps of Caribbean specialties, like shrimp with rice and Tico staples such as steak with rice and beans (3500c). Daily 11am–8pm.

The Central Pacific

From cool, undulating forests to rolling waves and scorching sands, the physical attributes of the **Central Pacific** region are among the most varied and impressive in the country. Every year thousands of travellers make the rugged 170km journey northwest from San José to the **Monteverde** and **Santa Elena** reserves, to meander on foot through some of the Americas' last remaining pristine cloudforest or take part in one of the famed high-adrenaline canopy tours. Meanwhile, only a hundred or so kilometres away, facing out onto the Pacific, **Jacó** is an unfeasibly popular party town and **surfing destination**. Further south along the coast, tiny **Parque Nacional Manuel Antonio** draws visitors eager to walk its trails in search of monkeys and rare birds, and discover its secluded beaches.

SANTA ELENA AND MONTEVERDE

The hub of the mountainous Monteverde region, and one of Costa Rica's most appealing (and most visited) destinations, is the small Tico village of **SANTA ELENA** and the tiny settlement of **MONTEVERDE**, settled in the 1950s by Quakers who left Alabama to avoid military service. The two nestle in beautiful landscape near three small nature reserves, connected by a narrow, winding, dusty, yet wonderfully picturesque 5km stretch of road that's lined with lodgings, restaurants and craft shops. When walking along it, be very careful of the traffic.

Reserva Santa Elena is easily reachable from its namesake village. In addition to hiking, visitors can join guided animal-spotting night walks, or stop by the snake, frog and butterfly sanctuaries. The forests here are criss-crossed with canopy wires, with enough action-packed activities to satisfy the most jaded of adrenaline junkies. You could also visit **Monteverde cheese factory**, responsible for Costa Rica's tastiest cheese, or a nearby **finca** (coffee farm) to learn about coffee and cocoa production.

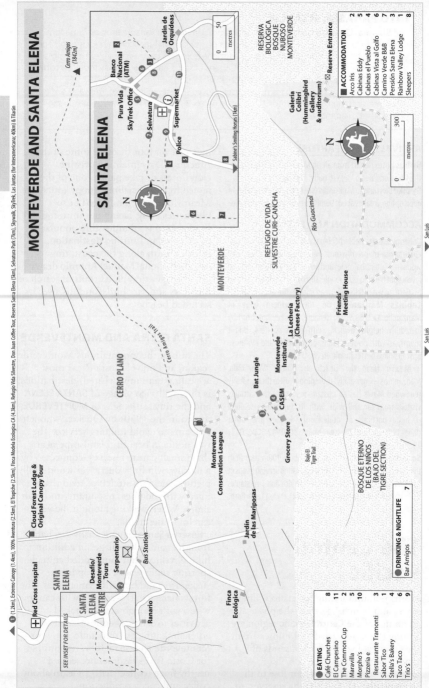

MONTEVERDE AND SANTA ELENA

SANTA ELENA

Cerro Amigos (1842m)

Cerro Amigos (1842m)

Banco Nacional (ATM)
Pura Vida
SkyTrek Office
Selvatura
Supermarket
Police
Jardín de Orquídeas

Sabine's Smiling Horses (1km)

RESERVA BIOLÓGICA BOSQUE NUBOSO MONTEVERDE

Galería Colibrí (Hummingbird Gallery & auditorium)

⊠ Reserve Entrance

■ ACCOMMODATION

Arco Iris	2
Cabinas Eddy	5
Cabinas el Pueblo	4
Cabinas Vista al Golfo	6
Camino Verde B&B	3
Pensión Santa Elena	7
Rainbow Valley Lodge	1
Sleepers	8

Río Guacimal

MONTEVERDE

REFUGIO DE VIDA SILVESTRE CURI-CANCHA

San Luis

San Luis

Friends' Meeting House

La Lechería (Cheese Factory)

Monteverde Institute

Bat Jungle

CASEM

CERRO PLANO

Grocery Store

Bajo El Tigre Trail

BOSQUE ETERNO DE LOS NIÑOS (BAJO DEL TIGRE SECTION)

Cerro Plano Trail

Monteverde Conservation League

Jardín de las Mariposas

Serpentario

Bus Station

Desafío/ Monteverde Tours

Finca Ecológica

Ranario

SANTA ELENA

SANTA ELENA CENTRE

SEE INSET FOR DETAILS

⊞ Red Cross Hospital

Cloud Forest Lodge & Original Canopy Tour

(1.2km) Extremo Canopy (1.4m); 100% Aventura (2.5km); El Trapiche (2.5km); Finca Modela Ecológica C4 (4.3km); Refugio Vida Silvestre, Don Juan Coffee Tour, Reserva Santa Elena (5km); Selvatura Park (7km), Skywalk, SkyTrek, Las Juntas (for Interamericana, 40km) & Tilarán

San José & Hwy 1

● EATING

Café Churches	8
El Campesino	11
The Common Cup	2
Maravilla	5
Morpho's	10
Pizzería e	
Restaurante Tramonti	3
Sabor Tico	1
Stella's Bakery	4
Taco Taco	6
Trio's	9

● DRINKING & NIGHTLIFE

| Bar Amigos | 7 |

0 — 50 metres

0 — 300 metres

CHOOSE YOUR ZIPLINE

Many people visit the Monteverde region purely to experience a high-adrenaline **canopy tour**. Several agencies can take you into the parks to whizz along ziplines far above the ground, or leap into the abyss using an enormous Tarzan swing.

100% Aventura 3km north of Santa Elena towards the reserve ☎ 2645 6388, ⓦ monteverdeadventure .com. For serious zipliners, Aventura (7am–4pm; US$45) offers an excellent array of ziplines (19 platforms in total), a Superman zipline (you're suspended from your back, so you "fly"), included in the entry price, a Tarzan swing that's a little smaller than Extremo Canopy's and a 15m rappel. ATV and horseriding trips are available too.

Extremo Canopy ☎ 2645 6058, ⓦ monteverde extremo.com. True to its name, this extreme ziplining adventure (8am–4pm; US$40) is all about the adrenaline. Highlights include a Superman canopy ride (US$5) and a 45m Tarzan swing – you're practically bungee-jumping before the cable stops your freefall.

Original Canopy Tour In the grounds of *Cloud Forest Lodge* ☎ 2645 5243, ⓦ canopytour.com. The company that started it all (7.30am–4pm; adults US$45), offering thirteen ziplines and a rappel, as well as 5km of hiking trails.

Selvatura Opposite the bus stop ☎ 2645 5929, ⓦ selvatura.com. Besides a host of non-zipline attractions (see below), Selvatura (daily 7am–4pm; US$45) offers 3km of cables, seventeen ziplines and a more modest Tarzan swing than the competition.

SkyTrek Next to the bus stop ☎ 2645 5238, ⓦ skyadventures.travel. One of the most popular canopy tours (7.30am–5.30pm; US$71), with eleven cables, including one that's an incredible 770m long with speeds reaching 64km/h. SkyTram cable car included in the price; more expensive packages include SkyWalk (aerial walkways).

WHAT TO SEE AND DO

The heart of Santa Elena consists of three streets in a triangle, among which sits a plethora of hostels, cafes and tour agencies; east of here, Monteverde spreads along the mountain road. Attractions are found on the outskirts of Santa Elena, along the mountain road and in the forests surrounding the two settlements.

Reserva Santa Elena

Less visited than the Monteverde reserve, **Reserva Santa Elena** (daily 7am–4pm; US$14; ☎ 2645 5390, ⓦ reservasantaelena .org), 6km northeast of Santa Elena village, is an area of exceptional natural beauty, and offers a glimpse of the rich biodiversity of the cloudforest. Established in 1992, the park strives to be self-funding, assisted by donations and revenue from entrance fees, and gives a percentage of its profits to local schools. Much of the maintenance and many of the building projects depend on volunteers, usually foreign students. The trails are well signposted and maintained, but are often muddy, as they're deliberately unpaved and the area is very moist. There's a greater chance of spotting birds and animals early in the mornings; guided tours (daily at 7.30am, 9am & 11.30am; US$15) are available.

Of the five **trails**, the highlights are the 3.4km Sendero Encantado, along which quetzals are frequently spotted, and the longest trail – the Sendero Caño Negro (4.8km; 3hr) loop – a reasonably demanding walk with steep ups and downs, and more chances to spot wildlife. There are boots and rain gear for rent, information about the trails and a small café and gift shop at the **visitors' centre** at the park entrance.

Selvatura Park

A couple of hundred metres down the road towards Santa Elena from Reserva Santa Elena, the **Selvatura Park** (daily 7am–4pm; ☎ 2645 5929, ⓦ selvatura .com) is a catch-all attraction featuring a canopy tour (see box above), treetop walkways (US$30), butterfly garden (US$15), hummingbird garden (US$5) and reptile and amphibian exhibition (US$15). You can choose exactly which activities you want, and while the Serpentario (see p.146), Ranario (see p.146) and the Jardín de las Mariposas (see p.146) are better places to see reptiles, amphibians and butterflies, the hummingbird garden is particularly worth it, with more than a dozen multicoloured species hovering over the

2

sugar water feeders. Several shuttles daily run to and from Santa Elena.

Jardín de Orquídeas
The **Jardín de Orquídeas** (Monteverde Orchid Garden; daily 8am–5pm; US$10; ⓦmonteverdeorchidgarden.com), in the centre of Santa Elena, boasts more than 450 different species of orchid; February is the best month to visit to see them all in bloom. You're given a magnifying glass to appreciate the world's smallest orchid.

Serpentario
On the outskirts of Santa Elena, on the road towards Monteverde, the **Serpentario** (daily 9am–8pm; US$9, US$11 with a guide) showcases a number of scaled, slithering delights, some of which, including the pit viper, are found wild in the area. Highlights include the deadly fer-de-lance, a tangle of boa constrictors and the beautiful eyelash pit viper, with a protrusion above the eyes of which any supermodel would be proud.

Ranario
On the outskirts of Santa Elena, the **Ranario** (Frog Pond) showcases a fascinating array of frogs and toads, including the incredible transparent frog (9am–8.30pm; US$12 including guided tour). Most species are more active in the evenings.

Jardín de las Mariposas
The **Jardín de las Mariposas**, the Butterfly Garden (daily 8.30am–4pm; US$15 includes 1hr guided tour; ⓦmonteverde butterflygarden.com), lets you walk among the butterfly species from Costa Rica's varying climatic regions, including the brilliant turquoise morpho and other eye-catching species. Try to arrive between 10am and 2pm, when the butterflies are most active. It's a ten-minute taxi ride from the main road.

Bosque Eterno de Los Niños
A huge, 220-square-kilometre private reserve, the **Bosque Eterno de Los Niños**, or Children's Eternal Rainforest (☏2645 5003, ⓦacmcr.org), close to the Monteverde settlement, exists thanks to the

Children's Rainforest Movement fundraising initiative that started in 1987, and is a spectacular example of children's pocket money put to good use. Most of the land, covered in primary and secondary rainforest, is set aside for conservation and research, but visitors are allowed to hike along one beautiful trail. Physically separated from the rest of the reserve, the **Bajo El Tigre trail** (daily 8am–4pm; US$12; guided daytime tours 5.30am, 8am & 2pm; 2hr; US$31 including transfers) is a short, easy trek at lower elevations than in the cloudforest reserves, with premontane forest (rare in Costa Rica) and great views out to the Golfo de Nicoya. Sunsets can be spectacular.

For a different experience, join one of the reserve's informative **night walks** (daily 5.30pm; 2hr; US$23 including transfers). These give you a good chance of seeing nocturnal animals, including porcupines, tarantulas, armadillos, agoutis, sloths and a marvellous variety of insects and roosting birds. The trail begins just before the cheese factory (see below).

The Bat Jungle
The **Bat Jungle** (daily 9am–7.30pm; US$11; ☏2645 6566), next to *Stella's Bakery*, fifteen minutes from Santa Elena along the road to Monteverde, is an exceptionally well-run enterprise by biologist Richard Laval. His daily guided tours dispel myths and dole out fascinating facts; for example, the only way to get bitten by a vampire bat is if you sleep naked next to livestock (their preferred meal), and mascara is made from bat poop. You get to see several species of local bats behind glass in a darkened enclosure and hear their excited noises during feeding time (9am, noon & 3pm). Don't miss the excellent *Café Caburé* upstairs, either.

La Lechería
At **La Lechería**, or Monteverde Cheese Factory (1hr 15min tours Mon–Sat 9am & 2pm; US$12; reservations required; ☏2645 5522), informative tours teach you about the Quaker origins of the factory and the traditional processes by which they make their own cheeses

– including their own versions of Edam, Gouda, Cheddar and provolone, among others. It all ends up with a cheese-tasting, and there's a shop and café on the premises.

Refugio de Vida Silvestre Curi-Cancha

The privately owned **Refugio de Vida Silvestre Curi-Cancha** (daily 7am–3pm & 6–8pm; US$10; ☎2645 6915, ⓦreservacuricancha.com), a reserve accessed via a trail behind La Lechería, is the area's newest, with some trails still in construction. A compact area, with narrow forest trails nowhere near as busy as those in the Monteverde and Santa Elena reserves, it offers a better chance of viewing wildlife, with quetzals, coyotes and coatis in residence. You can either sign up for a guided tour (US$17), or ramble along the mostly flat, well-signposted trails – seven of them, ranging from 600m to 2.2km in length – on your own. To get here, take one of the shuttles to Monteverde (see p.148).

Reserva Biológica Bosque Nuboso Monteverde

The world-renowned Monteverde Cloudforest Reserve, or **Reserve Biológica Bosque Nuboso Monteverde** (daily 7am–4pm; US$18; ☎2645 5122, ⓦreservamonteverde.com), a joint conservation effort of the Quakers, the International Children's Rainforest project and others, protects the last sizeable pocket of primary cloudforest in Central America. Stretching over 105 square kilometres, it supports six different **ecocommunities**, hosting an estimated 2500 plant species, more than 100 species of mammal some 490 butterfly species and more than 400 species of bird among them the resplendent **quetzal**. Though the cloudforest cover – dense, low-lit, heavy and damp – can make it difficult to see the animals, the park is nonetheless the most popular of the area's three nature reserves and an essential stop during any Costa Rica trip.

Use the free **map** you're given on arrival to navigate the 13km of well-signposted trails (nine in total). Some are paved, while the more remote trails are unpaved and muddy year-round. **Temperatures** are cool (15° or 16°C). Be sure to carry rain gear, binoculars and insect repellent. It's just about possible to get away without **rubber boots** in the dry season, but you will definitely need them in the wet. The reserve office rents both boots and binoculars (US$2).

Of the **trails**, the most popular option for day-hikes is **El Triángulo**, east of the entrance – this consists of Sendero Pantanoso (1.6km), passing through pine forest and bog and straddling the continental divide; the interpretive Sendero Bosque Nuboso (1.9km), which starts at the ranger station and passes through cloudforest; and Sendero Río (2km), which meanders past several small waterfalls. Keen birdwatchers shouldn't miss **El Camino** (2km), which runs parallel to the Sendero Bosque Nuboso; if you're after a good view, take either **Sendero Mirador La Ventana** to a mesmerizing viewpoint (1550m) overlooking the continental divide, or Sendero Chomogo (1.8km), which crosses El Triángulo to a height of 1680m. If you're fit and serious about wildlife spotting, you may consider the longer, rugged, less developed trails beyond El Triángulo, for some of which you'll need a guide.

The reserve runs highly recommended **guided walks** (7.30am, 11.30am & 1.30pm; US$36; evening walks 5.45pm; 2hr; US$22 including transport; reservations ☎2645 5112), as well as five-hour birdwatching tours (6am, leaving from *Stella's Bakery* in Monteverde; US$64). Additional walks are sometimes put on in high season, but it's worth booking a day in advance, as groups are limited to ten people.

In an attempt to limit human impact and conga-line hiking, a number of **rules** govern entrance to Monteverde, including a quota of 160 visitors at any one time. In high season, consider booking tickets a day in advance (bookings aren't available more than 24 hours in advance). Things get noisy and crowded between 8 and 11am, when the tour groups arrive.

2

ARRIVAL AND DEPARTURE

By bus Buses arrive and depart from the Centro Commercial Monteverde complex, near the MegaSuper supermarket, just east of Santa Elena. It's worth buying tickets for the more popular routes (like San José) in advance. Be aware the timetables are prone to change. Watch your luggage on buses; thefts are common.

Destinations Puntarenas (3 daily, 4.20am, 6am & 3pm; 3hr); San Jose (2 daily, 6.30am & 2.30pm; 4hr 30min–5hr); Tilarán (2 daily; 2hr 30min). From Tilarán there are buses to La Fortuna and Arenal (7hr) – though it's much quicker and better to take the boat-jeep-boat transfer (see box, p.175). For all other destinations, catch any bus to the Interamericana and flag down the bus you want.

By shuttle Two local shuttles can pick you up from your lodgings: one to Santa Elena reserve and another to the Monteverde reserve. Interbus shuttles (ⓦ interbusonline .com) do countrywide transfers (mostly morning departures) to San José, Jacó, La Fortuna, Manuel Antonio, Montezuma, Santa Teresa and Mal País and Tamarindo.

Destinations Monteverde reserve (departing from outside the Chamber of Tourism in central Santa Elena at 6.15am, 7.30am, 1.20pm & 3pm, returning 6.45am, 11.30am, 2pm & 4pm; 30min; US$1 each way). Santa Elena reserve (6.30am, 8.30am, 10.30am & 12.30pm, returning 9am, 11am, 1pm, 3pm & 4pm; 30min; US$2 each way; shuttles will pick you up at your accommodation – book in advance ☎ 2645 6332). Confirm latest schedules at your lodgings.

By taxi 4WD taxis congregate next to the Chamber of Tourism in Santa Elena. Trips from Santa Elena to Monteverde cost around 5000c, to Reserva Santa Elena around 6500c.

By car The roads around Monteverde and Santa Elena are accessed via the Rancho Grande turn-off (18km north of Puntarenas), at the Río Lagarto turn-off around 15km northwest of Rancho Grande in the direction of Liberia, via Las Juntas (another 10km or so towards Liberia), or via Tilarán if coming from the north.

INFORMATION

Tourist information There is a Chamber of Tourism in Santa Elena, but a better bet is *Pensión Santa Elena*, next to Banco Nacional, which offers excellent impartial advice to everyone, not just guests, and may be able to help you save a few dollars by booking things for you.

ACCOMMODATION

The region's budget accommodation is concentrated in and around Santa Elena. Most lodgings offer tourist information and can book tours. In the drier months, advance reservations are essential.

Arco Iris Up a side street just east of the town centre ☎ 2645 5067, ⓦ arcoirislodge.com. Relax in spacious,

well-appointed cabins amid quiet landscaped gardens near the centre. You can also stay in cheaper rooms with double or bunk beds. The delicious breakfast ($7.50) of hearty German bread, granola, fresh fruit, eggs and toast is also available to non-guests (daily 7–9am). Double s US$42, cabins US$88

Cabinas Eddy 100m southwest of the supermarket ☎ 2645 6618, ⓦ cabinas-eddy.com. The well-scrubbed rooms here (some with private bathrooms) can accommodate up to seven and are a cut above most of the region's other budget options. Combine this with friendly owners, free tea and coffee, and mountain views from the wraparound balcony, and you're onto a winner. Breakfast costs extra. US$35

Cabinas el Pueblo Down a dirt track beyond the Super Compro supermarket ☎ 2645 5273 or ☎ 2645 6192, ⓦ cabinaselpueblo.com. Attractive little family-run establishment just far enough away from the centre to miss the traffic noise. The cabins with shared bathrooms are small and pared down; those with private bathrooms have more charm, as well as TVs and fridges. US$24

Cabinas Vista al Golfo A 15min walk up the hill behind the Super Compro supermarket ☎ 2645 6321, ⓦ cabinasvistaalgolfo.com. One of the best-value hotels, offering spick-and-span rooms with shared or private bathrooms; pay extra to get a TV, fridge and balcony. As well as a kitchen and hammocks, there's an upstairs terrace with stunning views of the Gulf of Nicoya. Dorms US$10, doubles US$25

Camino Verde B&B Along the dirt road behind the Super Compro supermarket ☎ 2645 5641, ⓦ hotelcamino verde.com. These simple, bright rooms, surrounding a shared kitchen and with views of the Gulf of Nicoya, make fine use of attractive natural woods, and some have private bathrooms. The rooms nearest the office are the best. US$38

★ **Pensión Santa Elena** Next to Banco Nacional ☎ 2645 5051, ⓦ pensionsantaelena.com. The best and most popular cheapie in town: the staff are extremely knowledgeable, and accommodation runs the gamut from camping to cabins via stylish private rooms (try to get one of the nifty split-level ones), with access to a communal kitchen. Camping US$7, dorms US$12, doubles US$24, cabins US$47

★ **Rainbow Valley Lodge** 15min walk west of Santa Elena ☎ 2645 7015, ⓦ rainbowvalleylodge.cr.com. Run by ultra-helpful Minnesota native Rolf, this wonderfully tranquil retreat consists of two self-contained doubles with coffee makers and fridges, plus killer views down the mountainside. There's also a fully equipped cabin and a visiting coati. Rolf has maps and discount coupons for practically everything. Doubles US$35, cabin US$60

Sleepers 200m southwest of Santa Elena ☎ 2645 7133, ⓦ sleeperssleepcheaperhostels.com. Simple

TOURS IN SANTA ELENA

Operators in town offer various excursions. Note that most hotels and lodges can get you slightly cheaper rates than those listed below.

COFFEE TOURS

Don Juan Coffee Tour On the road out to Tilarán ☎ 2645 7100, ⓦ donjuancoffeetour.com. Monteverde is one of Costa Rica's most important coffee-producing regions; learn all about the process on this well-managed organic farm (2hr; US$30 including transfers). Chocolate- and sugar-themed tours are also available.

★El Trapiche North of Santa Elena ☎ 2645 7780, ⓦ eltrapichetour.com. Tours of this friendly, family-run coffee farm (2hr; US$32) are highly recommended. You'll learn all about the coffee and cocoa processing, ride a traditional ox-cart and watch the oxen work the sugarcane press. You'll also get a cup of some of the best coffee ever, as well as fresh cocoa, sugarcane juice and sugarcane spirit.

HORSERIDING

Desafío/Monteverde Tours Opposite the Super Compro supermarket, Santa Elena ☎ 2645 5874, ⓦ monteverdetours.com. Specializes in horseback tours, including a 2hr 30min ride through forest and farmland, a day-trip to the San Luís waterfalls and an all-day "cowboy" ride (US$85).

★Sabine's Smiling Horses 1km south of Santa Elena cemetery ☎ 2645 6894, ⓦ horseback-ridingtour.com. The multilingual Sabine (English, French, German), whose horses are in excellent condition, arranges horse treks including a popular 3hr waterfall tour (US$60), monthly full-moon tours, and multi-activity combos.

CANYONING

Finca Modela Ecológica North of Santa Elena, en route to La Cruz ☎ 2645 5581, ⓦ familiabrenestours.com. A 2hr tour (8am, 11am & 2pm; US$70) including swimming, bouldering, hiking, ziplining and a rappel down the largest of the six waterfalls on the property.

NIGHT TOURS

★Refugio Vida Silvestre En route to Tilarán ☎ 2645 6996. Given that 70 percent of the local wildlife is nocturnal, wildlife spotting after dark is particularly rewarding. While both the Monteverde reserve (see p.147) and the Children's Eternal Forest (see p.146) offer night walks, Refugio Vida Silvestre (6–9am, 5.30–7.30pm & 7.30–9.30pm; US$27 including transport) specializes in them. During the 2–3hr guided tour, you can expect to see two-toed sloths, kinkajou, tarantulas, pit vipers, frogs and more.

---

accommodation in clean (mixed) dorms and rooms (sleeping up to four) that tick all the boxes for backpackers: low-cost lodgings, communal atmosphere and shared kitchen. Dorms U̲S̲$̲9̲, doubles U̲S̲$̲2̲5̲

EATING

If you're self-catering, stock up at the big Super Compro supermarket in Santa Elena.

Café Chunches Opposite *Pensión Santa Elena*. The short menu at this mellow café, popular with expats, features sandwiches and salads (1500–3000c), excellent breakfasts, daily specials, and sumptuous banana bread and chocolate brownies. The teas and coffees are also top-notch. Local artwork covers the walls and there's plenty of reading material available. Mon–Fri 8am–7pm, Sat 8am–6pm.

El Campesino On the southern side of the Santa Elena triangle ☎ 8704 1867. The menu at this unassuming *soda* may hold few surprises (*casados*, *arroz cons*, etc), but everything is well prepared, portions are large and the service is friendly. Mains 3200–6500c. Daily 6am–8pm.

The Common Cup 50m north of the Serpentario. Ignore the disingenuous name: the coffee (1000–2000c) at this cabin-like café and roastery is anything but average. There's also a good range of breakfasts and cakes. Daily 7am–6pm.

Maravilla Opposite the bus stop ☎ 2645 6623. This bustling, no-frills *soda* is typically packed and for good reason: the food is tasty and the portions generous. For lunch or dinner, you can't go wrong with one of the *arroz cons* (3200–4500c). Daily 7am–9pm.

Morpho's Near *Pensión Santa Elena* ☎ 2645 5607. This stylish split-level restaurant decorated with unusual hanging butterflies and an extravagant wraparound mural serves inventive (and sometimes too inventive) mains (4700–11,000c), as well as less expensive soups and subs. Daily 11.30am–9.30pm.

★Sabor Tico 10min walk along the road to the Santa Elena reserve ☎ 2645 5827, ⓦ restaurantesabortico.com. The best Tico food in town is served at this family-run restaurant; hungry diners pile in for the massive *casados* (around 3000c) and giant fruit juices. However, note that when the place is packed, service is slow. Daily noon–9pm.

Stella's Bakery 500m in the direction of Monteverde from the Bat Jungle ☎ 2645 5560, ⓦ stellasbakery.webs.com. *Stella's* offers freshly baked pastries, pies, brownies,

2

★**TREAT YOURSELF**

Pizzeria e Restaurante Tramonti

Opposite the Paseo de Stella complex on the road to the Monteverde reserve ☎ 2645 6120. Don't leave Monteverde without dining at this divine Italian restaurant. Many of the ingredients are sourced from Italy and you can taste the Mediterranean in everything from the caprese salad to the wood-fired pizzas (5500–10,000c). Daily 11.30am–9.45pm.

muffins and more. Lunch will set you back 1500–3000c. Daily 6am–10pm.

Taco Taco Next to *Pensión Santa Elena*. Great little hole-in-the-wall featuring tacos, quesadillas and burritos, filled with roasted vegetables, chicken or spiced pork (*al pastor*). Mains around 3000c. Daily noon–8pm.

Trio's Near the Super Compro supermarket. Minimalist decor with subdued lighting, black leather seats, huge windows and an inventive menu. Expect unusual soups (such as carrot, sweet potato, coconut and tamarind) gourmet sandwiches and wraps, and standout mains like ribs with guava glaze (mains 5800–9500c). Daily 6–9pm.

DRINKING AND NIGHTLIFE

Bar Amigos Down a side street opposite the church ☎ 2645 5071, ⓦ baramigos.com. Most of Santa Elena's nightlife centres on *Bar Amigos*, which has live bands (every Friday night), DJs, big-screen sports events and locals and visitors slinging back beers. Daily noon–2/3am.

DIRECTORY

Banks Banco Nacional, at the northern apex of the triangle, has an ATM, as do Banco de Costa Rica and Banco Popular.

Health Red Cross (☎ 2645 6128; 24hr); hospital just north of town. Vitosi pharmacy (Mon–Sat 8am–8pm, Sun 9am–8pm) is across the street from the Chamber of Tourism.

Post office Opposite the shopping mall.

PUNTARENAS

Built on a sand spit that's just a few blocks wide, heat-stunned **PUNTARENAS**, 110km west of San José, has the look of raffish abandonment that haunts so many tropical port cities. Most visitors pass through without stopping, as the town is of most use for its transport connections between the southern Nicoya Peninsula and the mainland. While Montezuma-bound travellers can bypass Puntarenas altogether by taking a speedboat from Jacó (see opposite), the city does have a certain decaying charm, and you can spend a couple of relaxing hours here, waiting for your boat or bus, soaking up the sun and local atmosphere, admiring the quaint little **church** (Av Central, C 5/7) and checking out the vibrant **food market** (*mercado*; in the northeast corner of town, off Av 3).

ARRIVAL AND DEPARTURE

By boat The dock for the car and passenger ferries from Paquera and Playa Naranjo, on the Nicoya Peninsula, is on the northwestern point of town (Av 3, C 31/33). Schedules are

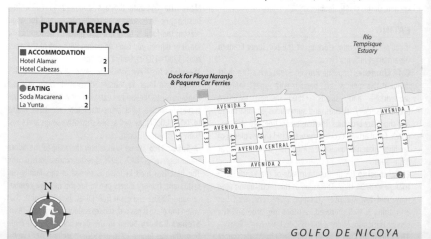

PUNTARENAS

■ ACCOMMODATION	
Hotel Alamar	2
Hotel Cabezas	1

● EATING	
Soda Macarena	1
La Yunta	2

Dock for Playa Naranjo & Paquera Car Ferries

Río Tempisque Estuary

AVENIDA 3

AVENIDA 1

AVENIDA CENTRAL

AVENIDA 2

CALLE 35 · CALLE 33 · CALLE 31 · CALLE 29 · CALLE 27 · CALLE 25 · CALLE 23 · CALLE 21 · CALLE 19

AVENIDA 1

N

GOLFO DE NICOYA

THE CENTRAL PACIFIC **COSTA RICA** 151

subject to change; check times at the ferry office by the dock.
Paquera Naviera Tambor (☎ 2661 2084, ⓦ navieratambor
.com) travels to Paquera (6 daily; $1.50; 1hr 15min), from
where buses run on to Monteverde (2hr), via Tambor (50min)
and Cobano (1hr 30min); the 5pm ferry is the last one that
connects with this service. You'll need to change in Cobano for
Mal País/Santa Teresa (daily 10.30am & 2.30pm; 30min).
Playa Naranjo COONATRAMAR (☎ 2661 1069,
ⓦ coonatramar.com) travels to Playa Naranjo (6.30am,
10am, 2.20pm & 7.30pm, returning 8am, 12.30pm, 5.30pm
& 9pm; 1hr), from where buses head to Nicoya (4 daily; 2hr).
By bus Buses from San José arrive at the bus station on the
corner of C 2 and Paseo de los Turistas. Services to other
destinations depart from across the street. Buses from
Santa Elena/Monteverde (3 daily from Puntarenas: 7.50am,
1.50pm & 2.15pm) pull in at the bus stop on the opposite
side of the *paseo*. If you're heading south along the coast to
Manuel Antonio, you'll need to take the Quepos service
from the bus station; the bus runs via Jacó (1hr 30min).
Destinations San José (hourly; 1hr 30min–2hr); Liberia (9
daily; 3hr); Puntarenas (4.20am, 6am & 3pm; 3hr 30min);
Quepos (8 daily; 3hr).

ACCOMMODATION AND EATING

There's little reason to linger in Puntarenas overnight, but
there are a couple of options. If you do decide to stay. The
cheapest eats are found at the food stands at the Mercado
Central.
Hotel Alamar Paseo de los Turistas, C 31/33 ☎ 2661
4343, ⓦ alamarcr.com. Family-friendly hotel that's one of
the better options on the seafront strip. Its spacious rooms
have a/c, TVs and private bathrooms, and it also has two
pools, a hot tub, and a restaurant. ~~US$72~~
Hotel Cabezas Av 1, C 2/4 ☎ 2661 1045. The town's best

budget option, this bright and sunny hotel offers clean and
compact rooms (private or shared bathrooms and TVs) and
excellent security. The *dueña* is quite the matriarch, but it
adds to the familial ambience. ~~US$25~~
Soda Macarena Opposite the bus station. This small *soda*
with ocean views serves up cheap, delicious fare (from
2500c); try their "Churchills", similar to a crushed-ice
granizado but made with ice cream. Daily 10am–midnight.
La Yunta Paseo de los Turistas, C 19/21 ☎ 2661 3216. As
the mounted bull heads and cattle prints on the walls
suggest, steaks (from 4500c) are the focus here – and are
expertly seared. The seafood is equally appealing, but more
expensive. Mains from 8000c. Daily noon–midnight.

JACÓ

The overdeveloped resort of **JACÓ** can make
no claim to either class or exclusivity:
stretching some 3km along a main road
parallel to the **beach**, it's little more than a
brash strip of souvenir shops, bars,
restaurants and hotels. As the closest beach
to the capital, it's long been a very popular
summer weekend destination for Josefinos,
and now foreign investment is allowing for
almost unrestrained (and generally
unattractive) development. That said, the
long sandy beach is reasonably clean, and
the **surf** is good year-round – the town is
built around the industry. Dozens of places
rent **boards** and give lessons (see p.152).
Alternatively, there's also some nice
snorkelling around **Isla Tortuga**, off the
coast of the Nicoya Peninsula.

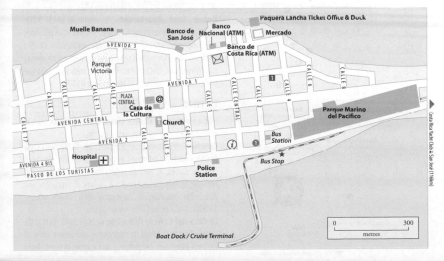

2

ARRIVAL AND DEPARTURE

By boat A taxi-boat from Montezuma runs to Playa Herradura, 7km north of Jacó at 9.30am each day (1hr; $42, including transfer to or from town), returning at 10.45am.

By bus Buses to and from San José, Puntarenas and Quepos stop at Plaza Jacó at the north end of Av Pastor Díaz, the 3km road that constitutes the town's main drag. If you're travelling at a weekend in high season, buy your ticket at least 3 days in advance.

Destinations Puntarenas (8 daily; 1hr 30min); Quepos (8 daily; 1hr 30min); San José (7 daily; 2hr 30min).

By shuttle Interbus (w interbusonline.com) offers daily shuttles to San José, Manuel Antonio, Monteverde, Montezuma, and Santa Teresa and Mal País.

INFORMATION AND TOURS

Tourist information Look for the colourful *Jacó's Map*, printed monthly and complete with tide charts – invaluable for surfers.

Tour operators Drop into Chuck's W.O.W Surf (☎ 2643 3844, w wowsurf.net), on Plaza Palma, at the northern end of town, for tide tables and an excellent free "surf treasure map": board hire is $15–40 a day, and a three-hour lesson will set you back $65.

ACCOMMODATION

Book in advance during the high season (Dec–April), especially at weekends.

Beds on Bohío C Bohío, behind *Papas + Burgers* ☎ 2643 5251, w bedsonbohio.com. Run by young, energetic owners, this is a friendly surfer hangout with lovely staff, a guest kitchen and good amenities. Unfortunately the place could be cleaner and better mattresses wouldn't go amiss. Dorms US$11, doubles US$40

Las Camas Jacó Sol, next to *Sol Dorado* ☎ 8533 7619, w lascamashostel.com. Hungarian-run cheapie that feels more like a friend's house than a hostel. It's not exactly sparkling clean, and the *camas* (beds) themselves could be more comfortable, but it's a good place to socialize. Surfboard rental and lessons available. Dorms US$11, doubles US$30

Hotel de Haan C Bohío ☎ 2643 1795, w hoteldehaan .com. Just off the main strip, *Hotel de Haan* has a great pool area and is particularly popular with a surfing crowd. Rooms are cavernous and pretty rustic; there's a kitchen, free internet and laundry service, and surf lessons are available. Dorms US$10, doubles US$42

Rutan Surf Apartments C Anita ☎ 2643 3328, w rutansurfcabinas.com. A relaxed surfing vibe pervades this unpretentious little spot (also known as *Chuck's Cabinas*) with dorms and simple rooms with battle-weary mattresses and bathrooms. The BBQ area increases the social element. Dorms US$10, doubles US$20

EATING

Más x Menos supermarket, on the main Av Pastor Díaz, is well stocked, and sells imported goods.

Caliche's Wishbone Av Pastor Díaz. Californian-style Tex-Mex with no additives or preservatives but plenty of creative dishes, as well as vegetarian options: tofu salad, monster baked potatoes with a variety of toppings, and pizza. The guacamole's awesome, too. Mains 6000–15,000c. Daily except Wed noon–10pm.

La Casa del Café Av Pastor Díaz ☎ 2643 5915. Cute little coffee shop that roasts its own beans and serves some of the best espressos, cappuccinos and frappes in town (from

Jet boats to Montezuma (2km) ▲   San José ▲

JACÓ

0   100
metres

Playa Herradura (7km) ▶

BOULEVARD

BOULEVARD

Bus Station

CALLE ANCHA

Chuck's WOW Surf

CALLE ANITA

■ **ACCOMMODATION**
Beds on Bohío	4
Las Camas	1
Hotel de Haan	3
Rutan Surf Apartments	2

CALLE BRI BRI

● **EATING**
Caliche's Wishbone	5
La Casa del Café	4
Soda Jacó Rustico	8
Taco Bar	7
Tsunami Sushi	6
The Wok	3

CALLE LAS PALMARAS

● **DRINKING & NIGHTLIFE**
Monkey Bar	2
Wahoos	1

CALLE LAS OLAS

Laundry

AXR

CALLE BOHÍO

PACIFIC OCEAN

CALLE COCAL

Banco Nacional (ATM)

Más x Menos Supermarket

Buses to Quepos ★

★ Buses to Puntarenas

CALLE LA CENTRAL

AV PASTOR DÍAZ

N

CALLE EL HICACO

Aquamatic Coin Laundry

✚ **Cruz Roja (Red Cross)**

CALLE LAS BRISAS

▼ Manuel Antonio, Condor Biker & Quepos

2

SAFETY IN JACÓ

Though in recent years the local council has done much to clean Jacó up, there is still a thriving prostitution and drug scene. While prostitution (for over-18s) is legal in Costa Rica, child prostitution certainly is not, and Jacó has a reputation for attracting middle-aged cruisers who come in search of underage girls. That aside, it's not an unsafe place, and generally the worst that most travellers will encounter is petty thievery, pickpocketing and having items stolen from locked cars. Avoid the **beach** at night, though.

1000¢), as well as tempting cakes and filled panini. Daily 8am–6pm.

Soda Jacó Rústico C Hicaco. The pick of Jacó's *sodas*, packed daily with locals and visitors. An enormous *casado* and a fruit juice or soft drink will leave you with change from 3000¢. Mon–Wed, Fri & Sat 7am–7pm, Thurs 7am–5pm.

★**Taco Bar** Off Av Pastor Díaz, at the start of the road out towards the Costanera Sur ☎ 2643 0222. There are few dishes in the world more perfect than an expertly prepared fish taco (around 4000¢), and that's exactly what you get at this breezy open-air restaurant. Place your order for the type of fish and the number of tacos you want and then help yourself to the salad bar and a variety of sauces. Daily 8am–6pm.

Tsunami Sushi Av Pastor Díaz, near the Banco de Costa Rica. Excellent super-fresh sushi (8000–11,000¢), as well as *gyoza*, spring rolls, noodles and teriyaki, served to a pounding beat; for a quieter meal, opt for seats outside. Nightly specials with many sushi sets going for half-price. Daily 11am–10pm.

The Wok Av Pastor Díaz ☎ 2654 6168. Popular pit stop for a quick Chinese-, Thai- or Indian-inspired stir-fry featuring roasted pork, chicken and tofu with rice or noodles (around 5500¢); the *pad thai* is particularly good. Mon–Sat 11.30am–10pm.

DRINKING AND NIGHTLIFE

Monkey Bar Av Pastor Díaz ☎ 2643 2357. Big bar that draws a boisterous young crowd with pop and dance tracks. There are plenty of promotions and theme nights, including two-for-one drinks on Sunday nights. Daily 9pm–late.

Wahoos Av Pastor Díaz ☎ 2643 1876. This restaurant-bar draws in tourists and expats with its long cocktail list, karaoke nights (in English and Spanish), live music, and big-screen sports. Daily noon–10/11pm.

DIRECTORY

Banks Several banks line the main strip, including Banco Nacional.

Bike/scooter rental There are several bike, scooter and ATV rental outlets; try Jaguar Riders on Av Pastor Díaz (☎ 2643 0180, ⓦ jaguariders.com) for scooters (around $40–50/day).

Health Clinica Jacó, opposite the post office (☎ 2643 1767).

PLAYA HERMOSA

A quieter alternative to Jacó, peaceful **PLAYA HERMOSA** is just 7km south. Offering a long stretch of darkish sand that has a challenging, often fierce, break, the village is pricier than Jacó, however, and geared towards serious surfers.

ARRIVAL AND DEPARTURE

By bus The bus from Jacó to Quepos runs through Playa Hermosa – ask the driver for the right stop – or you can take a taxi (around 4500–5000¢).

ACCOMMODATION

Cabinas Las Arenas ☎ 2643 7013, ⓦ cabinaslasarenas .com. Rustic wooden cabins with private bathrooms, fridges, TVs and fans; an ideal place to meet other surfers, with a family atmosphere. **US$49**

Cabinas Rancho Grande Just south of the football field ☎ 2643 7023, ⓦ cabinasranchogrande.com. The cheapest option on the strip, this sprucely renovated hostel buzzes with friendly surfers who congregate in the outdoor communal kitchen to cook after a hard day battling Hermosa's tubes. Dorms **US$15**, doubles **US$40**

QUEPOS

Backed against a hill and fronted by a muddy beach, compact **QUEPOS** can look pretty ramshackle, but it has a friendly vibe, and its concentration of good inexpensive accommodation, bars and restaurants make it an excellent base for visiting the region's celebrated national park.

THINGS TO SEE AND DO

You can go whitewater rafting, sea-kayaking, horseriding and dolphin watching, but for most visitors, the town's biggest draw is its proximity to Parque Nacional Manuel Antonio and its beaches, 7km south.

Rainmaker Conservation Project

The **Rainmaker Conservation Project** (US$15, US$35 with guide; ☎ 2777 3565,

2

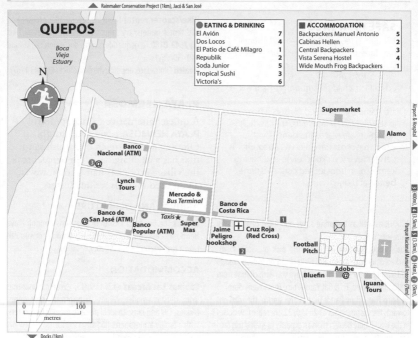

▲ Rainmaker Conservation Project (1km), Jacó & San José

QUEPOS

● EATING & DRINKING	
El Avión	7
Dos Locos	4
El Patio de Café Milagro	1
Republik	2
Soda Junior	5
Tropical Sushi	3
Victoria's	6

■ ACCOMMODATION	
Backpackers Manuel Antonio	5
Cabinas Hellen	2
Central Backpackers	3
Vista Serena Hostel	4
Wide Mouth Frog Backpackers	1

Boca Vieja Estuary

Supermarket

Alamo

Banco Nacional (ATM)

Lynch Tours

Mercado & Bus Terminal

Banco de Costa Rica

Banco de San José (ATM)

Taxis

Super Mas

Banco Popular (ATM)

Jaime Peligro bookshop

Cruz Roja (Red Cross)

Football Pitch

Bluefin

Adobe

Iguana Tours

0   100
metres

▼ Docks (1km)

ⓦ rainmakercostarica.org), 1km northwest of Quepos, is an excellent canopy walk that passes through a privately owned chunk of rainforest. From the platforms high up in the treetops you get great views of the surrounding primary and secondary rainforest, and there's excellent bird-spotting to be had. The canopy walk aside, the reserve also holds several excellent hiking trails.

ARRIVAL AND DEPARTURE

By plane Sansa and NatureAir connect Quepos to San José and Liberia. The airport is 5km east of town; a taxi costs around US$10.

Destinations La Fortuna (2 daily; 40min); San José (7 daily; 25min).

By bus All buses arrive at and depart from the bus terminal in the town centre, next to the Banco de Costa Rica. In high season, buy your tickets to San José in advance.

Destinations Dominical (6 daily; 1hr 30min); Manuel Antonio (every 30min from 7am to 7pm; 20min); Puntarenas (8 daily; 3hr) via Jacó (1hr 30min), San José (9–11 daily; 3hr 30min–4hr 30min); Uvita (3 daily; 1hr 30min).

By shuttle Interbus (ⓦ interbusonline.com) runs shuttles to Jacó, La Fortuna, Monteverde, Montezuma, San José, and Santa Teresa and Mal País.

INFORMATION AND TOURS

Tourist information Jaime Peligro, a block west and then a block south of the bus station, sells new and secondhand books, and is a good source of information (Mon–Fri 9.30am–6pm, Sat 11am–5pm; ☏ 2777 7106, ⓦ queposbooks.com).

Tours There are a couple of good Class III and IV whitewater runs in the area; Iguana Tours (just south of the church; ☏ 2777 2052, ⓦ iguanatours.com) offers horseriding and rafting, plus hiking in Parque Nacional Manuel Antonio and boat and kayak trips around Isla Damas, a wildlife-rich mangrove estuary just north of Quepos.

ACCOMMODATION

Good budget lodgings can be found both in Quepos proper and en route to Manuel Antonio.

Backpackers Manuel Antonio On the main road, halfway between Quepos and Manuel Antonio ☏ 2777 2507, ⓦ backpackersmanuelantonio.com. This sociable hostel boasts spotless dorms, private rooms (with shared bathrooms), a splash pool, communal kitchen, and a good location (handy for the bus, *Angel* restaurant, the supermarket and a laundry). To get here, take a Manuel Antonio bus from Quepos. Dorms US$12, doubles US$35

Cabinas Hellen A block south and east of the bus station ☏ 2777 0504. These secure *cabinas* at the back of a family home are equipped with private bathroom, fridge and fans. They offer decent single rates (US$20), and there's also a small patio and parking. **US$30**

Central Backpackers 500m along the road to Manuel Antonio ☎ 2777 2321, ⓦ centralbackpackers.hostel.com. Small, secure hostel, roughly 15min on foot from Quepos, with a super-helpful and knowledgeable manager who happens to be a good cook to boot. The rooms are spotless and family-style dinners encourage bonding between guests. Dorms **US$12**, doubles **US$38**

★**Vista Serena Hostel** Halfway along the road to Manuel Antonio ☎ 2777 5162, ⓦ vistaserena.com. Run by a helpful, bilingual mother and son, this hillside haven of calm, best reached by bus from Quepos, is a wonderful place to relax and watch the sunset from the hammocks on the terrace. Shoestringers can choose from economy fourteen-bed dorms and premium four-bed ones (all with attached bathroom); if you want more privacy, opt for a fully equipped bungalow. Dorms **US$10**, bungalows **US$45**

Wide Mouth Frog Backpackers Two blocks west of the bus station ☎ 2777 2798, ⓦ widemouthfrog.org. Behind the high security gate is a veritable oasis. Basic, clean rooms form a quad around the pool. Staff are informative, and there's a big kitchen, internet room, TV lounge, book exchange, and friendly dogs underfoot. Some rooms are stuffy, however, as only part of the window will open. Dorms **US$12**, doubles **US$35**

EATING AND DRINKING

Super Mas (opposite the bus terminal) is a well-stocked supermarket with some imported ingredients. The best dining options are along the road to Manuel Antonio.

El Avión 2km from Manuel Antonio village ☎ 2777 0584. If you're wondering how this 1954 Fairchild C-123 plane got here, the story goes that it was due to be passed on to the Nicaraguan Contras in the 1980s, but never made it due to the Oliver North scandal. The Contras' loss is your gain; this airplane-cum-bar, served by Quepos–Manuel Antonio buses, is a great spot for a sunset beer. Daily noon–11pm (low season 1–10pm).

Dos Locos Just southwest of the bus station ☎ 2777 1526. Enjoy the usual range of fajitas, burritos and tacos (4000–9000c), while taking in street views from the open-air dining area. Wash it all down with a margarita or two. Mon–Sat 7am–11pm, Sun 7am–4pm.

★**El Patio de Café Milagro** Facing the sea wall ☎ 2777 0794, ⓦ cafemilagro.com. The coffee (1000–2000c) here is among the best in the country; try the delicious Queppuccino. They also serve *refrescos* and cakes, as well as selling English-language newspapers and magazines. The breakfasts are creative and hearty, and by night it turns into a quality restaurant. There's also a branch on the road to Manuel Antonio. Mon–Sat 7am–5pm.

2

★**TREAT YOURSELF**

Victoria's Quepos–Manuel Antonio road, near the football pitch ☎ 2777 5143, ⓦ victoriasgourmet.com. Upscale Italian restaurant on the Quepos–Manuel Antonio bus route, with delicious, though pricey, pizzas (7000–12,500c) with ingredients including home-made pesto and house mozzarella, as well as similarly priced American-Italian-style pasta dishes such as spaghetti and meatballs. Daily 4–11pm.

Republik On the road parallel to the sea. Swish bar/club with a long list of potent cocktails (the mojitos are particularly good), a chic retro decor and ladies' night on Thurs. Tues–Sat 7pm–4.30am.

Soda Junior Just north of the bus station. This tiny, Tico-run *soda* is the best place in town for inexpensive fried chicken and lip-smacking *casados*. Breakfast from 2000c, mains from 3000c. Daily 8am–9pm.

Tropical Sushi Half a block from the beach, near the fire station ☎ 2777 1710. The Japanese chef at this authentic sushi joint crafts some excellent rolls (3200–4500c; try the dragon roll) and the sashimi is super-fresh. If you favour quantity over quality, go for the all-you-can-eat option. Daily 4–11pm.

MANUEL ANTONIO

The little community of **MANUEL ANTONIO**, 7km southeast of Quepos and the gateway to the ultra-popular **Parque Nacional Manuel Antonio**, enjoys a stunning setting, its spectacular white-grey sand beaches fringed by thickly forested green hills. As you watch the sun set over the Pacific from high up here, you can't help feeling this is one of the most charming places on earth. However, the winding, narrow 7km bottleneck of a road between Quepos and the village suffers from overdevelopment – it's lined with pricey hotels (with a few exceptions), restaurants and tour company offices, which, together with the influx of cars and tour buses, has tainted some of the area's pristine magic. Still, though crowded most of the time, the park remains one of Costa Rica's loveliest destinations, with wildlife-spotting aplenty.

2

WHAT TO SEE AND DO

Tiny Manuel Antonio village is booming, with an ever-increasing stream of visitors heading to the park (see below). Other **activities** include body-boarding and sea-kayaking, with equipment rental along the main sandy swathe of Playa Espadilla; be aware of rip currents. Beginner **surfers** can also take to the waves here, with plenty of surfing instruction (of varying quality) and board rental available. Cross the rocky headland at the western end of Playa Espadilla and you'll find yourself on **La Playita** – Costa Rica's prime gay beach (inaccessible during high tide). Access to the beaches is free, so beware of scammers trying to tell you otherwise, and be particularly cautious with your belongings, as **theft** along the beaches is depressingly common.

ARRIVAL AND DEPARTURE

By bus Buses between Quepos and Manuel Antonio (every 30min 7am–7pm; also 5.45am, 6.45am & 10pm, Sat & Sun also 9.30am; 20min) drop passengers off 200m before the park entrance at the mini-roundabout. There are stops in both directions all along the 7km route.
By shuttle Interbus offers direct shuttle service between Manuel Antonio (via Quepos) and several popular Costa Rican destinations (see p.108).

ACCOMMODATION AND EATING

Backpackers Paradise Near the beach ☎ 2777 0304. Far from a paradise, but okay for the price, given the location. The cell-like rooms are very basic and some are not for the claustrophobic. The sociable bar/restaurant serves great breakfasts. U$\overline{S\$12}$
★**Vela Bar** Near the park entrance ☎ 2777 0413, ⓦ velabar.com. The pick of the village's restaurants, with expertly prepared *mariscos*, including *ceviche* and creole shrimp (from around 8000c), as well as less expensive *casados* and a fine banana split. The service, meanwhile, is as polished as the dark-wood tables, which are set in a peaceful garden terrace. Daily 7am–9.30pm.

PARQUE NACIONAL MANUEL ANTONIO

Despite being Costa Rica's smallest national park, at just 16km square, **PARQUE NACIONAL MANUEL ANTONIO** (Tues–Sun 7am–4pm; US$10; ☎ 2777 5185) is also the most popular. It preserves lovely **beaches**, **mangroves** and humid tropical **forest**. You can also see the *tómbolo* of **Punta Catedral**: a rare geophysical formation, a *tómbolo* is created when an island becomes slowly joined to the mainland through accumulated sand deposits. **Wildlife** – including sloths, snakes, green kingfishers, laughing falcons, iguanas, capuchin, howler and spider monkeys – is in abundance, though you'll be hard pressed to spot the park's shyest primate, the squirrel monkey.

Within the park you'll come across many signs imploring you not to feed the monkeys (or any other wildlife). Take that warning very seriously, as feeding wild creatures leads to their dependence on handouts, sickness and even death.

WHAT TO SEE AND DO

A network of several well-marked trails allows you to explore deep into the park; you can walk the whole lot within half a day. From the entrance, the wide **Sendero Perezoso** (1.8km) leads to the rocky headland of the **Punta Catedral**, preceded by the wide, beautiful crescent of **Playa Manuel Antonio**, popular with swimmers and capuchin monkeys. At the western end of the beach is a semicircle of rocks, visible at low tide and believed to be a **turtle trap** of pre-Columbian origins; at low tide, turtles would be unable to swim out. The **Sendero La Trampa** starts here, linking with the 1.4km loop of **Sendero Punta Catedral** that winds its way around the headland, with several viewpoints overlooking the beaches and rocky islets beyond. The trail exits at **Playa Espadilla Sur**, a long beach with usually very calm waters, just a minute's walk from Playa Manuel Antonio. From the main Sendero Perezoso, instead of heading down to the beaches, you can take the other trail that splits in two: the upper branch heads up to **El Mirador** (1.3km) – a bluff that overlooks Puerto Escondido and a mirage-like beach beyond – while the other fork leads down to the small **Playa Gemellas**, good for sunbathing and swimming. **Playa Puerto Escondido** is only accessible from Playa Gemellas at low tide; sometimes the trail is closed altogether.

Quepos

PARQUE NACIONAL MANUEL ANTONIO

PARQUE NACIONAL MANUEL ANTONIO

Q.Camaronera

Quebrada Azul

Q.Negra

N

Playa Espadilla

Village **Entrance**

Exit ☒

Q.La Catarata

Laguna Negra

Río Naranjo

Sendero Perezoso

Playa Espadilla Sur

Sendero La Trampa

Sendero El Mirador

Playa Puerto Escondido

Punta Catedral

Playa Manuel Antonio

Sendero Playas Gemelas y Puerto Escondido

Isla Olocuita

Sendero Punta Catedral

PACIFIC OCEAN

Playa Playita

Punta Serrucho

Isla

0   500   ------ Main trail

2

ARRIVAL AND INFORMATION

By bus Frequent buses run from Quepos to Manuel Antonio village (see opposite), within walking distance of the park entrance.

By car If you're thinking of driving to the park from Quepos, don't. Parking costs are exorbitant and there have been reports of break-ins and thefts. Take one of the frequent buses instead.

Park information To beat the inevitable crowds, get to the park for opening time. Pay your entrance fee at the Coopalianza office, 75m short of the entrance as you approach from Manuel Antonio village. Guides (US$25 for 2hr), available at the entrance, can be very helpful when it comes to spotting wildlife in the dense foliage; only certified guides are allowed inside the park.

The Nicoya Peninsula

With its wonderful beaches, the Nicoya Peninsula has understandably long ranked among Costa Rica's more popular destinations. The perennial surfing hotspots of **Tamarindo**, **Santa Teresa** and **Playa del Coco** offer some of the country's finest wave action, while quieter stretches like **playas Nosara and Sámara** offer more space for contemplation of the beautiful coastline. Some of the beaches in Guanacaste Province, in the northern section of the peninsula, can be difficult to reach on public transport, but the rewards are great for those with 4WDs who brave the challenge. Similarly, unless you have your own vehicle, pretty much the only way to reach **Montezuma** or Santa Teresa, two lively beach hangouts in the isolated southern part of the peninsula, is by boat from Jacó or Punta Arenas, followed by a bone-shaking ride along rough and rugged dirt roads.

GETTING AROUND

Getting from south to north Nicoya can be tricky. When it comes to public transport, Montezuma, Playa Santa Teresa and Mal País are rather cut off from the rest of the

2

peninsula. Minor beachside roads leading northwest to Sámara are only passable in a 4WD, with rivers to be crossed at low tide only. North of Montezuma, the paved road ends at Paquera; the unpaved road that connects Paquera and Playa Naranjo is dirt-and-gravel, steep and winding in places and potholed. In dry season, a regular vehicle can make it, but in the rainy season, only a 4WD will do. If you're using public transport, you have no choice but to take a ferry from Paquera to Puntarenas (see p.150), and then another to Playa Naranjo.

MONTEZUMA

The colourful beach town of **MONTEZUMA** lies near the southwestern tip of the Nicoya Peninsula, about 40km south of Paquera. Sandwiched between hills covered in lush vegetation and white-sand coves framed by aquamarine sea, the once remote fishing village is still relatively cut off from the rest of the country by bad roads, and attracts a laidback crowd who come here for sun, sea, yoga classes and a more tolerant outlook than in other parts of the country.

WHAT TO SEE AND DO

Lovely **beaches** stretch out in either direction: white sands, dotted with jutting rocks and leaning palms and backed by lush greenery, including rare Pacific lowland tropical forest. Montezuma makes a good base for a day-excursion to the **Cabo Blanco** reserve (see p.160), while for a shorter walk, the environs are laced with **waterfalls**.

Beaches

The beach in front of the football field is excellent for sunbathing, but if you're looking to snorkel, your best bet is **Playa Las Manchas**, 1km southwest of the village (low tide only). Despite the inviting coastline, **swimming** isn't very good on the beaches immediately north of Montezuma – the waves are rough and the currents strong. It's better to continue north towards Playa Grande along an attractive, winding **nature trail** (1.5km; 30min), which dips in and out of several coves. There's reasonable swimming here, and decent surfing, as well as a small waterfall at its eastern edge.

Waterfalls

The trail to a trio of **waterfalls** starts just southwest of the village, towards Cabo Blanco, from a car park opposite the *Hotel Amor del Mar*. The first waterfall is a five-minute walk along a dirt path; in dry season you might only see a few trickles of water here. To reach the second, main, waterfall, follow the footpath along the river, which involves some scrambling up and down boulders (10min). The deep pool that surrounds the second waterfall is perfect for swimming and diving, and, as at the third waterfall, there's a fun rope swing above it. A precarious, narrow footpath also climbs to a smaller waterfall on top of the second one, but, given the sheer drop, it requires the agility and balance of a monkey. Always take care with waterfalls, especially in the wet season, on account of **flash floods**, and under no circumstances try to climb them; several people have died that way in the past.

ARRIVAL AND INFORMATION

By boat The taxi-boat from Playa Herradura, 7km north of Jacó (10.45am; $42; 1hr), is by far the quickest way to get here from the Central Pacific. The return journey (9.30am) is useful for connections south to Manuel Antonio.

By bus Services arrive and depart from across the football field.

Destinations Paquera (for the ferry; 6 daily; 2hr); San José (2 daily; 5hr). For Mal País and Santa Teresa take the 10am or 2pm Paquera bus and change in Cobano (30min) to connect with onward services there (daily 10.30am & 2.30pm).

By car In the rainy season, the steep, unpaved road between Cobano and Montezuma requires a 4WD.

Tour operators Zuma Tours (in the centre, near *El Sano Banano Hotel*; 2642 0024, zumatours.net) offers information and the largest range of tours in town, such as day-trips to Isla Tortuga, horseriding to the Florida Waterfall and trips to Refugio de Vida Silvestre Curú.

ACCOMMODATION

Montezuma is a popular destination, so book in advance. Unfortunately, none of the lodging options is particularly good value. Camping on the beach is illegal.

Hotel Lucy 500m south of the centre 2642 0273. A Montezuma stalwart and one of the village's better cheapies: it has a nice veranda draped with hammocks upstairs, and clean and simple rooms, some with private cold-water bathrooms (those upstairs have sea views);

MONTEZUMA

PACIFIC OCEAN

N

| 0   100 |
| metres |

● EATING & DRINKING		■ ACCOMMODATION	
Cocolores	4	Hotel Lucy	3
Orgánico	2	Luna Llena	2
Puggo's	5	Hotel Los Mangos	4
Soda Naranjo	3	Hotel El Tajalin	1

▼ 5 (200m), Waterfalls (600m), Playa Las Manchas, Cabo Blanco, Cabuya & Mal País

make sure your door locks properly, though. Dorms US$15, doubles US$30

Hotel Los Mangos 500m south of the village ☎ 2642 0384, ⓦ hotellosmangos.com. Split-level hotel set amid mango trees, with brightly decorated rooms, plus expensive-looking but slightly dark bungalows; some

have their own verandas and rocking chairs. There's also a pool and hot tub, and regular yoga classes are held in an airy wooden pavilion. US$40

Hotel El Tajalin Near the church ☎ 2642 0061, ⓦ tajalin .com. In a quiet location just northwest of the centre, this hotel has attractively simple wood-floored rooms with a/c; the airier ones on the top floor have sea views. They also have a communal lounge with television, books and coffee. US$50

Luna Llena On the hilltop above the village ☎ 2642 0390, ⓦ lunallenahotel.com. This friendly German-American-run hostel consists of a mix of rooms (some rather small), most with shared facilities, and a single dorm with mattresses that could do with replacing. It doesn't have a/c, but there are two guest kitchens and a communal space to relax in. Spanish lessons are available. Dorm US$15, doubles US$38

EATING AND DRINKING

Bakery Café Opposite Librería Topsy ☎ 2642 0458. Pretty murals lend a relaxed vibe to this open-walled café, which is particularly good for breakfast: great eggs, French toast,

2

yoghurt and granola, and pancakes (all around 3000c) are on offer. Mon–Sat 6am–10pm.

Cocolores In a garden by the beach. A justifiably popular restaurant offering a varied international menu with European, Middle Eastern and Latino dishes including a great coconut fish curry. Good value considering the excellent quality (mains from around 5000c), though service is not a strong point. There's a happy hour (5–6pm), but you'll have to arrive early to secure one of the prime beachfront tables. Tues–Sun noon–10pm.

Orgánico Next to *Soda Naranjo*, before the *Bakery Café*. This health-conscious café entices you in with its excellent range of healthy (and extremely tasty) falafels, salads, sandwiches and other dishes (try the Thai-spiced burger). The smoothies and milkshakes are not to be missed either. There's live music most nights. Mains 6500–9000c. Mon–Sat 11am–9pm.

Puggo's North of the football field ✆ 2642 0325. Colourful restaurant specializing in Middle Eastern cuisine, so get your fill of falafel, grilled meat kebabs, and *baba ghanoush* here, as well as a few token gringo-pleasers. Service is very slow. Mains from 4500c. Daily except Tues 8am–9.30pm.

Soda Naranjo Opposite *Cocolores*. Hidden behind a wall of leafy foliage, this low-key *soda* serves delicious *casados* and fresh fish dishes at some of the best prices in town (mains around 3500c). The range of fruit juices is excellent, too. Mon–Sat 7am–9.30pm.

RESERVA NATURAL ABSOLUTA CABO BLANCO

Some 7km southwest of Montezuma, the **RESERVA NATURAL ABSOLUTA CABO BLANCO** (Wed–Sun 8am–4pm; US$10; ✆ 2642 0093) is Costa Rica's oldest protected piece of land. Covering the entire southwestern tip of the peninsula, it was established in 1963 thanks to the environmental campaigns of a Danish-Swedish couple. Its natural beauty is complemented by an array of wildlife including howler monkeys, agouti, sloths, peccaries and snakes, while as the islands off the coast provide ideal nesting grounds, sea birds include brown boobies, frigates and brown pelicans.

Hiking, swimming and wildlife-watching are the main activities. There are only two trails. The highlight of the 4.5km **Sendero Sueco**, a demanding and muddy hike that takes around two hours each way, is the **Playa Cabo Blanco**

– a pristine sand-and-pebble beach at the far end, against a backdrop of jungle, jutting headlands and teal waters. The shorter and gentler **Sendero Danes**, a 2km loop, starts and ends on the Sendero Sueco. Be sure to leave around 2pm to make it back to the ranger station for closing time.

ARRIVAL AND INFORMATION

By bus A bus rattles between Montezuma and Cabo Blanco twice daily (8am, 10am, 2pm, 4pm & 6pm from Montezuma, heading back at 1pm, 3pm & 5.30pm; double-check the schedule); fewer departures during rainy season.

By taxi A taxi from Montezuma costs around US$20.

By bike You can cycle down to Cabo Blanco on a mountain bike; there are rental operators in Montezuma (see p.158).

By 4WD or quad bike From Mal País, the park is reached via a beautiful, narrow and steep unpaved road running through the jungle; 4WDs or quad bikes only.

Facilities You can't stay in the park, so have return transport planned, and take plenty of sunblock and water.

MAL PAÍS AND PLAYA SANTA TERESA

The long beach of **PLAYA SANTA TERESA** and neighbouring **MAL PAÍS**, at the tip of the peninsula on the Pacific side, lure ever increasing numbers of travellers with their picturesque setting and some of the best surfing in Costa Rica. Though there's been a fair amount of development in the area as a whole, the atmosphere is still chilled and friendly, with a barefoot surfers' vibe. Despite the villagey feel, the area is pretty cosmopolitan, and you'll find lots of good places to **eat**, even on a budget.

ARRIVAL AND INFORMATION

By bus Buses arrive at and depart from Playa Carmen (the intersection where the right fork takes you to Santa Teresa, and the left to Mal País); services sometimes continue into Mal País and/or Santa Teresa themselves.

Destinations Cobano (for connections to Paquera/ Montezuma; 2 daily; 30–45min); San José (2 daily; 5–6hr).

By car The road between Cobano and Santa Teresa/Mal País is unpaved, and rutted and steep in places, so a 4WD is recommended year-round.

By shuttle Interbus (✆ interbusonline.com) runs shuttles to San José.

By taxi Taxis to Cobano cost around US$35.

Banks Playa Carmen (at the intersection of the roads from Cobano, Mal País and Santa Teresa) is home to a Banco Nacional and a Banco de Costa Rica.

ACCOMMODATION

★**Casa Zen** Around 1.1km north of the intersection ☎ 2640 8523, ⓦ zencostarica.com. The pick of the area's hostels, just 50m from the beach, *Casa Zen* is a stylish wooden house featuring Asian-inspired trimmings and plenty of space. Accommodation options include well-maintained dorms, private rooms and apartments. There are morning yoga classes, movie nights and a restaurant serving mouthwatering Thai cuisine. Dorms US$18, doubles US$40, apartments US$65

Cuesta Arriba 300m north of the football pitch, Santa Teresa ☎ 2640 0607, ⓦ cuestaarribahoste.com. In a peaceful spot, this seems like more of a luxury villa than a hostel, with whitewashed walls, a pool, spacious communal areas festooned with hammocks and large, bright dorms with sturdy bunks and good mattresses. A basic breakfast is thrown in – the only quibble is that the a/c private rooms (separate from the main building) are rather compact. Dorms US$16, doubles US$50

Funky Monkey Around 1.9km north of the intersection ☎ 2640 0272, ⓦ funky-monkey-lodge.com. This hillside lodge with a swish pool and sushi restaurant is part boutique hotel, part swish backpacker hangout. Whether staying in a bungalow (sleeping up to eight), apartment (sleeping up to seven) with ocean views or dorm, you can enjoy the lodge's excellent facilities, which include a yoga/dance studio. Dorms US$17, doubles US$68, bungalows US$90, apartments US$136

★**Hotel Meli Melo** Around 2km along Santa Teresa's main road from the intersection ☎ 2640 0575, ⓦ hotelmelimelo.com. Delightful guesthouse, run by a friendly and attentive French couple. The spacious rooms, surrounded by lush vegetation, good amenities, as well as quirky bathrooms and access to an outdoor kitchen. Bikes, fishing equipment and surfing gear available to rent. US$60

Wave Trotter Surf Hostel Up the hill behind *El Pulpo* in Santa Teresa ☎ 2640 0805, ⓦ wavetrotterhostel.com. Run by two Italian guys (and Coco the dog), this is a surfer's paradise, complete with boards lining the walls and chilled beats echoing through the communal area. The only thing that tops the clean, comfortable (if spartan) dorms and private rooms is the welcoming family atmosphere. Dorms US$16, double s US$38

EATING AND DRINKING

The Bakery 150m north of the intersection ☎ 2640 0560. An appealing stop-off at any time of the day, with delicious pastries for breakfast, light meals like soups, pasta, quiches and salads for lunch, and top pizza for dinner (from 6pm). Picnic baskets and a delivery service are also available, and on Mon evenings there's an all-you-can-eat pizza session (6–8pm; 5500c). Daily 7am–10pm.

Burger Rancho Santa Teresa. The burgers here (from 2500–3000c) are the real deal – unlike in so many places in Costa Rica – and can be washed down with delicious milkshakes or smoothies. Daily 5–10pm.

Caracoles Mal País. The best *soda* in the area, with tables set in the large grounds by a beach overrun with hermit crabs. Choose from classic *casados* or more inventive mains – Caribbean-style prawns, perhaps, or soya-glazed tuna steak. Mains from 3500c. Daily noon–9pm.

★**Chop It** Playa Carmen Mall, near the intersection. Come to this tiny spot for lunch or brunch (3500c plus); choose from over a dozen ingredients to create a mega salad or grilled taco with filling, or opt for a gourmet burger (including the veggie portobello mushroom burger with goat's cheese and red onion jam). Then head next door for some authentic *gelato*. Tues–Sun 11am–4pm.

★**Koji's** Playa Hermosa, 50m south of the Hermosa Valley School ☎ 2640 0815. Who'd have thought that this remote location would play host to some of the best sushi in the country? Chef Koji, a master of his craft, delivers wonderful signature rolls, super-fresh sashimi

---

SURFING IN SANTA TERESA

Santa Teresa and its surrounds have some of the best surfing on the peninsula. **Playa Hermosa** (not to be confused with Playa Hermosa near Playa del Cocos), north of Santa Teresa, is an excellent beach for beginners with consistent right and left breaks. **Playa El Carmen**, straight down from the main intersection, is suitable for beginners also, while **Playa Santa Teresa** boasts a fast break that's the preserve of advanced surfers.

Given the abundance of surf shops and surf schools, **prices** are competitive, and you can expect to pay around US$50 for a 2hr surfing lesson and around US$15/20 for half-/full-day board rental.

Kina Surf Shop 2.2km north of the intersection ☎ 2640 0627, ⓦ kinasurfcostarica.com.

Nalu Surf Shop 1km north of the intersection ☎ 2640 0391 or ☎ 8358 4436, ⓦ nalusurfschool.com.

2

and beautifully grilled and mouthwateringly tender octopus. Wash it all down with a local microbrew. Reserve ahead or else pitch up at the bar. Dishes from 3500c. Wed–Sun 5.30–9.30pm.

PLAYA SÁMARA

PLAYA SÁMARA, one of the more peaceful, though increasingly upmarket, beach resorts on the Nicoya Peninsula, lies 30km southwest of Nicoya. It's more remote than most other Pacific beach towns, which gives the village a pleasantly relaxing atmosphere. The long, dark-sand beach here is one of the country's calmest for swimming – there's a reef about 1km out that takes the brunt of the Pacific's power. The moderate waves also make Sámara a great place to learn to **surf** or paddleboard, and to snorkel to see nearby dolphins.

ARRIVAL AND DEPARTURE

By bus Buses depart from the village's main intersection. Destinations Nicoya (8–12 daily; 1hr); Nosara (3 daily; 40min); San José (1 daily; 4hr 45min).

By shuttle Interbus (@interbusonline.com) runs shuttles to San José via Montezuma (US$50); book ahead.

ACTIVITIES

Surfing Matteo Caretti at the Marea Surf Shop Café, C Principal (☎2656 1181), is a kind, reassuring and professional instructor (private class US$35/hr). Renting boards or taking lessons from C&C Surf School (☎2656 0628) ensures that 10 percent of the proceeds go to a local turtle conservation project. If you don't want to embarrass yourself in front of other novices, opt for private lessons (US$40/1hr lesson).

Paddleboarding and snorkelling The Sámara Adventure Company, in the middle of the beach (☎2656 0920, @samara-tours.com), offers a host of tours, including stand-up paddleboarding (3hr; US$65) and snorkelling (3hr; US$60).

ACCOMMODATION

Cabinas El Ancla On the beachfront road 200m south of the centre ☎2656 0254. Simply furnished rooms, with cold-water bathroom and fan, right on the beach. The upstairs rooms are a bit hotter but still better than the dark and oppressive downstairs rooms. There's a friendly *dueña* and a good, beachfront seafood restaurant. US$40

Camping Los Cocos Beyond *El Ancla* hotel ☎2656 0496. In a fabulous palm-dotted beach location, this

ultra-popular campsite has basic *servicios* and provides electricity until 10pm. Keep an eye on your stuff, as the beach is notorious for thieves at night. US$7

Hostel Matilori First left along the beach road, then first right ☎2656 0291, @isamara.com/matilor.htm. Brightly painted guesthouse with spotless (small) rooms with orthopaedic mattress, TV, safe, fan or a/c and shared bath. There's a well-equipped kitchen and free boogie boards; the friendly multilingual owner is extremely helpful. Dorms US$17, doubles US$42

Tico Adventure Lodge ☎2656 0628, @ticoadventure lodge.com. Stunning American-run lodge built around the trees on the property. There's plenty of greenery, and while the a/c rooms don't benefit from much natural light, they are spotless and comfortable, there's free coffee all day long, and the owner is a great source of local info. US$57

EATING AND DRINKING

El Dorado 150m beyond the Banco Nacional in the *El Dorado Hostel*. Outstanding Italian food (3500–9000c), wine and hospitality. In true Mediterranean style, the Italian owners run things exactly as they would back home, and the dishes are executed with precision and flair. Hours can vary, though generally noon–10.30pm.

Lo Que Hay Just off the beach ☎2656 0811. At this mellow spot, you can watch the game on the big screen while munching your way through awesome tacos (try the delicious fish variety) as well as fajitas and other backpacker-friendly food. Mains from 3000c. Daily 7am–late.

Sámara Organics On the main road in the centre of the village ☎2656 3056. Run by a Californian couple, this cheerful café attached to a health food market offers guilt-free breakfasts and lunches, like potatoes, eggs and toast (2700c) and home-made veggie burgers (3500c). Mon–Sat 7.30am–4.30pm.

★Shake Joe's On the beach ☎2656 0252. Low-key restaurant that attracts students from the language school up the beach. A good spot for a burger (from 3300c) and a shake, and they also do a couple of refreshing salads. Tues–Sun 11am–10pm.

La Vela Latina South of the centre on the beach. Sit in rocking chairs as the friendly staff mix you one of their cracking daiquiris (2500c) or another expertly blended cocktail. Daily 11am–midnight.

PLAYA NOSARA

The stimulating 25km drive from Playa Sámara north to the **PLAYA NOSARA** runs along shady, secluded dirt-and-gravel roads punctuated by a few creeks

– a 4WD is essential year round. Generally referred to collectively, there are three beautiful, rugged beaches hereabouts – Nosara, Guiones and Pelada – of which **Playa Guiones** is the most impressive, and most popular with surfers. The beach settlement itself is spread over a large area; the main **village** of Nosara is 3km inland, home to a small airstrip. Some attempts have been made to limit development – a good deal of the land around the Río Nosara has been designated a wildlife refuge – and the vast majority of people who come to Nosara are North Americans and Europeans in search of quiet and natural surroundings.

ARRIVAL AND INFORMATION

By plane Sansa and NatureAir fly daily to Nosara from San José.

By bus Buses depart from the corner shop by the football field.

Destinations Nicoya (5 daily; 1hr 30min); Playa Sámara (3 daily; 40min); San José (1 daily; 5hr 30min).

By car A dusty, bumpy, potholed dirt road branches off towards Nosara from the paved Nicoya–Sámara road 3km before Sámara; in dry season, a regular car will get you as far as Playa Nosara, but 4WD is required to reach the beaches further along.

Tourist information Useful websites include ⓦnosara .com and ⓦsurfingnosara.com.

ACCOMMODATION

Casa Tucan On the beach road in Playa Guiones, 100m from Banco de Costa Rica ☎2682 0113. This friendly Tico-run place has everything: spacious rooms, relaxing pool area and in-house bar and restaurant, all in a lush garden a stone's throw from the beach. Good for groups. US$70

Gilded Iguana Behind Playa Guiones ☎2682 0450, ⓦthegildediguana.com. There's a lot to like here: large rooms with polished floors and high ceilings, private baths, fridges and colourful paintings, as well as a curvy pool, hammocks and an excellent bar/restaurant. Family rooms are particularly good value for groups. US$60

★Kaya Sol About 100m back from Playa Guiones ☎2682 1459, ⓦkayasolsurfhotel.com. With a mix of clean and airy dorms, spacious, tastefully decorated private rooms in bungalows with their own baths, and longer-stay accommodation with kitchens, *Kaya Sol* is justifiably popular. A lovely pool with mini-waterfall, hummingbirds in the garden and an excellent restaurant complete the package. Dorms US$16, doubles US$58

Nosara Suites At the entrance to Playa Guiones ☎2682 1036, ⓦnosarasuites .com. Five immaculate and positively enormous themed suites with a/c, wi-fi, cable TV and fridge. There's also a fine restaurant and bakery attached, *Café de Paris*, which serves decadent croissants and desserts. US$109

EATING AND DRINKING

If self-catering, try the natural food market Orgánico, at the entrance to Playa Guiones.

Beach Dog Cafe By the beach. Crowd-pleasers at this chilled-out surfers' café include awesome smoothies, killer fish tacos and ample breakfasts – from eggs to French toast. Mains from 3300c. Breakfast and lunch only. Daily 7am–3pm.

Gilded Iguana *Gilded Iguana* hotel. Upmarket gringo bar with Mexican food and well-priced lunch specials, including fish tacos, fajitas and fish and chips. Mains from 3500c. Daily 7.30am–10.30pm.

Robin's Café 50m beyond Banco de Costa Rica. Enjoy delicious organic sandwiches and wraps (2500–3500c), crêpes (from 1500c), pastries, and home-made ice cream in the little garden in front of this café. Raw food fans will appreciate the non-cooked specials. Free wi-fi. Mon–Fri 7.30am–7pm, Sat & Sun 7.30am–5pm.

★Rosi's Soda Tica On a small hill above the road leading into Playa Guiones ☎2682 0728. Small, friendly, family-run restaurant (one of the few in the area that's run by locals) serving excellent *comida típica*, including *casados* (2000–3000c) for lunch and *gallo pinto* (1750–2500c) for breakfast. Mon–Sat 8am–3pm.

REFUGIO NACIONAL DE FAUNA SILVESTRE OSTIONAL

Some 8km northwest of Nosara, Ostional and its chocolate-sand beach make up the **REFUGIO NACIONAL DE FAUNA SILVESTRE OSTIONAL** (☎2682 0400; US$10), one of the most important nesting grounds in the country for **Olive Ridley turtles**, which come ashore here to lay their eggs between May and November. If you're in town during the first few days of the *arribadas* – the mass arrival of turtles to lay eggs – you'll see local villagers carefully stuffing bags full of eggs and slinging them over their shoulders. This is quite legal: villagers of Ostional and Nosara are allowed to harvest eggs, for

2

sale or consumption, during the first three days of the season only. You can't swim here – the water's too rough and there are sharks.

It takes about fifteen minutes to drive the gravel-and-stone road from Nosara to the refuge; alternatively, you can bike it or take a taxi (around 3000c).

NICOYA

Busy **NICOYA** is one of the largest settlements on the peninsula. Located inland, it has little to offer travellers besides being a handy place to change buses. You won't need to spend the night, as onward bus connections are frequent.

ARRIVAL AND DEPARTURE

By bus The bus station is at Nicoya's southernmost point, just before the road bridge leading out of town. Services from Liberia pull into a stand 300m north of the main bus station.

Destinations Liberia (every 30min 6.30am–10pm; 1hr 40min); Playa Naranjo (for connecting ferry to Puntarenas; 4 daily; 2hr 15min); Playa Nosara (6 daily; 1hr 30min); Playa Sámara (8–12 daily; 1hr); San José (8 daily; 4hr).

EATING

Café Daniela C 3 at Av 2. If you're stuck in town for a couple of hours, sate your hunger pangs here with great fajitas (3500c), *casados* (from 2500c) and *pintos* (from 1800c). Mon–Sat 7–9pm.

PLAYA TAMARINDO

Stretching for a couple of kilometres over a series of rocky headlands, **PLAYA TAMARINDO** ("Tamagringo") is one of the most popular Pacific coast beaches, though it couldn't be any less Costa Rican

in character – its dominant features are rampant development and swarms of tourists looking for a good time. There's a decent selection of restaurants, a lively surfing scene and, in high season, a strong party vibe.

WHAT TO SEE AND DO

Tamarindo is the perfect beach for beginner **surfers**: gentle waves push against the grey-white sands on a daily basis, all year round. Intermediates can tackle the wave that breaks in front of the centre of the village, while serious surfers will want to head a few kilometres south to Playa Langosta or north to Playa Grande (see p.166). Numerous places **rent surfboards** – typically US$15–20 per day for a longboard. You can also take river estuary **tours** through the mangroves of nearby Parque Nacional Marino Las Baulas (see p.167) and moonlight turtle tours to the same park (Nov to mid-Feb), as well as windsurfing and snorkelling elsewhere.

ARRIVAL AND INFORMATION

By plane Up to five flights daily from San José and Liberia, with Sansa and NatureAir, arrive at the small airport 4km north of the village.

By boat An estuary separates Tamarindo from Playa Grande; the distance is easily swimmable and the water quite shallow, but it's also home to crocodiles. Take one of the many loitering boats across (US$1).

By bus Buses arrive by the village loop.

Destinations Liberia (9 daily; 2hr); San José (4 daily; 6hr); Santa Cruz, for points south (9 daily; 1hr).

Tours Costa Rica Paradise, Centro Comercial Plaza Conchal (☎ 2653 2251, ⓦ crparadise.com), is one of the most professional and helpful options in the village, offering all the usual tours as well as day-trips to Palo Verde (US$90), horseriding into dry tropical forest (2hr; US$35) and short but exhilarating gyrocopter flights (US$120).

LEARNING TO SURF IN PLAYA TAMARINDO

Several good operators in town offer **surfing lessons** on the beach and in Playa Grande, which should cost US$40–50. Check the student-to-instructor ratio when booking surfing lessons; 2:1 is best.

Mato's Surf Shop In the Sunrise Mall ☎ 2653 0921, ⓦ matossurfshop.com. Going strong since 2001, with bargain 2hr lessons for US$35. Daily 8am–7pm.

Witch's Rock Surf Camp Towards the northern end of the beach ☎ 2653 1262, ⓦ witchrocksurfcamp.com. Regular trips to Ollie's Point and Witch's Rock, and surfing lessons for all abilities (US$45/2hr).

ACCOMMODATION

Wherever you stay, reserve well in advance for high season.

Cabinas Marielos On the main road ☎ 2653 0141, ⓦ cabinasmarieloscr.com. Set back from the main road, among tropical gardens, these charming cabins have floral curtains, security boxes, a/c and bathrooms accessed via saloon-style doors (the bathroom walls don't reach to the ceiling, so they're not the most private). There are also some cheaper rooms with fan. The well-informed owner runs turtle tours. US$45

★**Hostel La Botella de Leche** Across from Plaza Tamarindo ☎ 2653 0189, ⓦ labotelladeleche.com. Excellent backpacker hostel with comfortable bunk-bed accommodation in dorms. It has a/c, wi-fi, a small pool and a well-equipped communal kitchen as well as spick-and-span shared cold-water bathrooms. It's designed with surfers in mind – you can rent and repair boards here, as well as arrange classes. It's very popular, and although the super-friendly owner will do her utmost to squeeze you in, you'd be wise to reserve ahead. Dorms US$20, doubles US$46

La Oveja Negra Next to Tamarindo Adventures ☎ 2653 0005, ⓦ laovejanegrahostel.com. Chilled-out place with a

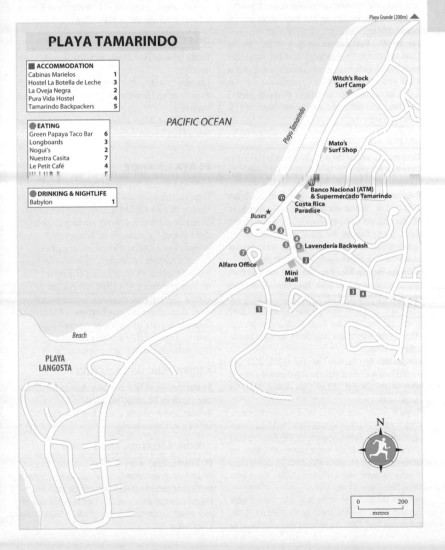

PLAYA TAMARINDO

Playa Grande (200m)

PACIFIC OCEAN

Playa Tamarindo

■ ACCOMMODATION

Cabinas Marielos	1
Hostel La Botella de Leche	3
La Oveja Negra	2
Pura Vida Hostel	4
Tamarindo Backpackers	5

● EATING

Green Papaya Taco Bar	6
Longboards	3
Nogui's	2
Nuestra Casita	7
Le Petit Café	4

● DRINKING & NIGHTLIFE

Babylon	1

Witch's Rock Surf Camp

Mato's Surf Shop

Banco Nacional (ATM) & Supermercado Tamarindo

Costa Rica Paradise

Buses

Lavandería Backwash

Alfaro Office

Mini Mall

Beach

PLAYA LANGOSTA

N

0   200
metres

huge common area decorated with a surfboard collage and sporting a massive TV. Run by a friendly surfer dude, it's not the place to catch up on your snoozing, but if you're looking to surf and party, you're in the right place. Dorms US$14, doubles US$35

★**Pura Vida Hostel** 500m up main road leading up from beach road ☎8368 3508, ⓦpuravidahostel .com. A stand-out hostel – and not just because of the huge thatched *palapa* that shades the communal lounge area. Sociable without being a party hostel, *Pura Vida* is presided over by a knowledgeable hostess; the dorms and doubles are immaculate, there are hammocks and rocking chairs to relax in, and they offer plenty of extras to liven up your stay. Dorms US$15, doubles US$60

Tamarindo Backpackers ☎2653 1720, ⓦtama 6backpackers.com. On a secluded dead-end street, this wonderfully friendly hostel boasts a kidney-shaped pool in a lush garden filled with creeping plants, a/c in dorms as well as rooms, hammocks perpetually filled with relaxing travellers, and a chilled-out atmosphere. Dorms US$15, doubles US$45

EATING AND DRINKING

Tamarindo has one of the most diverse eating scenes in Costa Rica, but prices can be high. There are surprisingly few worthwhile nightspots to choose from, however.

Babylon In the centre about 100m from the beach ☎8939 3588. Spacious reggae bar that is the place to be on Thursday and Friday evenings (2000c including first drink). There's frequent live music, particularly on the weekends and though it's often packed, ocean breezes ensure that it never feels sweltering. Daily 11am–3am.

★**Green Papaya Taco Bar** 50m down the road from *Pasatiempo Hotel* ☎2653 0863. Attractive café and taco bar with reclaimed wood furnishings, terrace seating and plenty of natural light. There's a nice selection of coffee drinks and teas, and the tacos (3500c) and burritos (4000c), made from organic ingredients, are full of flavour. Daily 7am–9pm.

Longboards Near the main T-junction ☎2653 0027. This popular joint is all about BBQ ribs, superb pulled pork and other meaty delights. Mains from 2500c. Mon–Sat 11am–11pm.

Nogui's On the loop ☎2653 0059. Casual restaurant, virtually on the beach, serving excellent breakfasts, decent sandwiches and snacks, though it's the fine fish and seafood that bring in the repeat customers – from the wonderful fish tacos to whole grilled fish. It's a great place to enjoy the sunset with a cold beer (1400c). Mains from 4500c. Daily 11am–11pm.

Nuestra Casita Tucked off the main road. This adorable Tico spot dishes up a brilliant *típico* breakfast for 1500c, and *casados* from 2000c in a secluded area away from the

mad buzz of town. Well worth the time it takes to find it. Daily 8am–9pm.

Le Petit Cafe Plaza Tamarindo ☎2653 4285. A great little spot for breakfast or lunch, this café, on a square, serves an excellent pastrami Reuben (3350c), as well as tasty smoothies and spiced pumpkin lattes. The service can be grumpy, though. Mon–Sat 8am–5pm.

★**Wok N Roll** Opposite Plaza Tamarindo ☎2653 0156. Amazingly, you can find authentic Korean food in Costa Rica – order the house special of sticky ribs with rice and *kimchi* (7000c), or, if chilli-tinged pickled cabbage is not your thing, try the *bulgogi* (5000c), *tom yum goong* (4500c), noodle dishes and – a concession to Western palates – pecan pie. Daily 7.30am–10pm.

DIRECTORY

Banks There are several banks with ATMs, notably on the main road.

Laundry Lavandería Backwash (2000c/kg) is on the left as you turn up towards Playa Langosta from the main beach road.

Supermarket There's a Super Compro on a side street next to Plaza Conchal.

PLAYA GRANDE

Part of Parque Nacional Marino Las Baulas, the long wide crescent of sand that is **PLAYA GRANDE** stretches for nearly 5km. Besides the superb **surfing** beach, the village – a straggle of houses, guesthouses and restaurants spread out along a couple of roads – is a wonderfully low-key place to stay, being the antithesis of Tamarindo's unbridled hedonism across the narrow channel to the south. And then there are the **turtles** – Playa Grande is part of a nature reserve that protects the highly endangered leatherback turtles (see opposite).

ARRIVAL AND INFORMATION

By bus There are no buses from Playa Grande, but you can take a bus from Tamarindo (see p.164).

By boat You can cross the estuary from Tamarindo (US$1) and then walk up the beach.

ACCOMMODATION AND EATING

El Huerto Next door to *Indra Inn*. This excellent Mediterranean restaurant hits the spot with its Spanish tortillas and perfectly *al dente* home-made pasta, but the biggest accolades are reserved for their beautiful melt-in-your-mouth wood-fired pizzas (from 5000c). Daily 11am–10pm.

★**Indra Inn** On main road at the entrance to Playa Grande ⓣ 2653 4834, ⓦ indrainn.com. Run by the friendly team of Matt, Natalya and Marshmallow the dog, this brightly painted guesthouse has spacious a/c rooms and a sociable bar area where guests and staff congregate in the evenings. Rates include an ample breakfast, and the hosts are a great source of local info. **US$60**

★**Mamasa** On main road 200m before *Indra Inn*. Perch on a carved wooden seat under the thatched *palapa* and order a BLT with Cajun mahi-mahi, home-made bagels with cream cheese or granola with yoghurt and lemongrass honey. There's no better place for lunch/brunch/Saturday-night specials, and service is super-friendly. Sandwiches 4000c. Tues–Fri & Sun 10am–2pm, Sat 10am–2pm & 5.30–9pm.

El Manglar & Mi Casa Hostel Near the southern end of the beach ⓣ 2653 0952, ⓦ micasahostel.com. This sociable surfer magnet is two places in one: a hostel with a clean but basic dorm, and a hotel with a/c en-suites and pricier villas, all surrounding a pool in the middle of a lush garden. Dorm **US$20**, doubles **US$55**

Playa Grande Surf Camp South end of the beach ⓣ 2653 1074, ⓦ playagrandesurfcamp.com. Very near the beach, this surfers' haven has cosy A-frame cabañas with a/c sitting by the pool, and fan-cooled cabins with hammocks on the patio. You can grill your own dinner on the barbecue or use the guest kitchen. Dorms **US$15**, cabins **US$45**

★**Rip Jack Inn** ⓣ 2653 0480, ⓦ ripjackinn.com. Homely, relaxed upstairs restaurant, with cats on the bar and imaginative dishes chalked up on the board. For lunch (mains around 4500c), there are sandwiches, fish tacos and big juicy burgers; evening dishes (mains from 7000c) include the likes of clam and mussel linguini and papaya ginger shrimp with softshell crab. Mon–Sat 8am–9pm, Sun 8am–2pm.

PARQUE NACIONAL MARINO LAS BAULAS

On the Río Matapalo estuary between Conchal and Tamarindo, **PARQUE NACIONAL MARINO LAS BAULAS** (daily 9am–4pm; open for guided night tours in season; US$10 out of season, US$25 in season including tour; ⓣ 2653 0470) is less a national park than a reserve, created to protect the nesting grounds of endangered **leatherback turtles**. These wondrous giants, which come ashore to nest from October to mid-February, have laid their eggs at **Playa Grande** for possibly millions of years, and it's one of the few remaining such nesting sites in the world. Turtle sightings are likely on one of the **guided tours**, but not guaranteed on a nightly basis; you wait at the visitor centre, and if a turtle is spotted by a scout, the information is relayed by radio to your guide who will then escort you to the area. Tours are conducted in silence; cameras and smoking are not allowed on the beach.

Around 200m from the park entrance, the **El Mundo de la Tortuga** exhibition (daily 2–6pm, later when turtles are nesting; US$5) includes an audio-tour in English and some stunning turtle photographs. You'll learn about the leatherbacks' habitats and reproductive cycles, along with the threats they face and current conservation efforts. If you come on one of the turtle-watching tours, the exhibition is included in the tour price.

ARRIVAL AND INFORMATION

On foot/by boat There is no public transport to the park, so you can either walk from your lodgings in Playa Grande or visit by boat from Tamarindo, a service that usually comes as part of tour packages, or can be booked when you call to reserve your entrance ticket.

Turtle tours Tours, which run between October and mid-February, typically take place from 9pm until 2am at the latest. Tickets can be bought at the southern entrance, where the road enters the park near the *Villa Baulas*. Booking in advance is highly recommended, as numbers are strictly limited.

PLAYAS DEL COCO

Some 35km west of Liberia, **PLAYAS DEL COCO** was the first Pacific beach to hit the big time with weekending Costa Ricans from the Valle Central. It's turned out to be something of a nightmare: a cross between an upmarket resort filled with brash hotels, casinos and restaurants, and a hotspot for budget travellers in search of Jägermeister and a dancefloor. However, **surfers** use the place as a jumping-off point for nearby Witch's Rock and playas Hermosa and Panamá, the **nightlife** is lively, and there are some good **diving** operators, so it could be worth spending a day or two here.

2

WHAT TO SEE AND DO

The main road down to the beach is a noisy melange of roaring 4WDs and souvenir markets, while the area nearer the beach is a little quieter, with the football pitch and some funky bars that are packed out most nights. The dark-sand beach is not the cleanest, so it's best to take the bus or taxi to the lovely neighbouring **Playa Hermosa**, with its clear blue waters and volcanic sand. Diving is popular; dive centres take you to the islands off the coast, such as **Isla Santa Catalina**, 20km offshore.

ARRIVAL AND INFORMATION

By bus Buses stop at the terminal opposite Deep Blue Diving on the main street.

Destinations Liberia (hourly from 6am–7pm; 1hr); San José (3 daily, 4am, 8am & 2pm; 5hr 30min).

Tour operators Dutch-owned Rich Coast Diving, on the main road about 300m from the beach (☎ 2670 0176, ⓦ richcoastdiving.com), organizes snorkelling (US$50) and scuba trips to Bat Islands, and offers the chance to dive with bull sharks (from US$80) and to frolic with manta rays at Las Catalinas. Summer Salt Dive Centre, next to *Jardín Tropical* (☎ 2670 0308, ⓦ summer-salt.com), is a reputable Swiss-run outfit that also offers dolphin- and whale-watching excursions.

ACCOMMODATION

Cabinas Coco Azul Behind the church ☎ 2670 0431. Friendly cheapie, offering clean rooms with hot-water private bathrooms and fans or a/c set around a garden with mango trees. The rooms on the ground floor get little natural light. US$35

Hotel Coco Palms On the beach, next to the football pitch ☎ 2670 0367, ⓦ hotelcocopalms.com. Like a motel in style, with nice clean rooms with a/c and wi-fi. There's a pool as well as Coco's only sushi spot and the *Lazy Frog* sports bar. Rooms away from the pool are usually quieter. US$28

Hotel Mar & Mar On the waterfront ☎ 2670 1212. Just a few metres from the beach, this breezy motel-style option comes with large, bright, fan-cooled rooms, and hammocks swaying in the breeze on the upstairs terrace. Breakfast is 2500c. US$25

Pure Vibes 200m north of *Lizard Lounge*, 5min from main street. Though the dorms are basic and rather cramped, this large hostel is well geared towards sociable travellers: there's a large L-shaped pool with swim-up bar, the bar staff treat you like friends and the manager holds his famous Jamaican BBQs at the on-site Jamaican-themed restaurant. Other thoughtful touches include bikes for rent. Dorms US$15, doubles US$50

EATING AND DRINKING

Lizard Lounge On the main road, 100m before the beach, on the right ☎ 2670 0181. Relaxing bar and restaurant serving Tico fare and Western burgers (3500c) and steaks (7000c) – all at reasonable prices. It's a pleasant spot to grab a snack, chill out listening to music or catch the latest sporting events and news on the big screen. Daily 4pm–2am.

La Dolce Vita Pueblito Sur shopping centre ☎ 2670 1384. As close as you get to authentic Italian in this town, serving crisp wood-fired pizzas, home-made pasta and fresh fish dishes. Mains from 4500c. Daily 8am–10pm.

Jardín Tropical Overlooking the park at the far end of town. The best breakfast in town – a hearty *gallo pinto* will set you back 2500–3000c – and generous lunchtime *casados*. Daily 8am–4pm.

La Vida Loca At the south end of the beach. Supersized nacho platters, huge burgers, chilli dogs and pizza at this lively gringo heaven. The bar is really hopping in the evenings. Mains from 3000c. Daily 11am–1am.

Guanacaste

Guanacaste Province, bordered to the north by Nicaragua, and by the Pacific Ocean to the west, is distinctly different from the rest of Costa Rica – indeed, if not for a very close vote in 1824, Guanacaste would likely have remained part of Nicaragua. While the traditional **sabanero** (cowboy) culture, music and folklore for which the region is famous have been overtaken by tourism, there is still undeniably something special about the place. The **landscape** has an arid beauty, despite much of it having been essentially shaped by the slaughter of tropical dry forest: the wide, rolling plains and the brooding humps of volcanoes are washed in muted earthy tones. While the province's beaches (roughly two-thirds of the Nicoya Peninsula is in Guanacaste) attract the most visitors, the mud pots and stewing sulphur waters of **Parque Nacional Rincón de la Vieja** and the tropical dry forest cover of **Parque Nacional Santa Rosa** draw scores of nature aficionados to the interior every year, while the town of **Liberia** is seeing more international traffic these days thanks to its expanded international airport and proximity to some hugely popular beaches.

LIBERIA

Most travellers use **LIBERIA** as a jumping-off point for the national parks of **Rincón de la Vieja**, **Santa Rosa** and **Palo Verde**, an overnight stop to or from the **beaches** of the Nicoya Peninsula or a convenient stopover on the way to Nicaragua.

Liberia also boasts several lively **festivals**. In early March **Fiestas Cívicas Liberia** sees ten days of parades, bands, fireworks and bull-running. On July 25, **El Día de la Independencia** celebrates Guanacaste's independence from Nicaragua with parades, rodeos, fiestas and roving marimba bands.

WHAT TO SEE AND DO

The town is arranged around its large **Parque Central**, properly called Parque Mario Cañas Ruiz. One of the loveliest central plazas in the country, it's ringed by benches and tall palms that shade gossiping locals; the startlingly modern **church** seems somewhat out of place.

About 600m away at the eastern end of town, the colonial **Iglesia de la Agonía** is more arresting, with a mottled yellow facade. Once on the verge of collapse, a renovation has given it new life; it's still almost never open, however. The town's most interesting street is **Calle Real** (also

known as Calle Central or Calle 0). In the nineteenth century this was the entrance to Liberia, and practically the entire thoroughfare has been restored to its original – and strikingly beautiful – colonial simplicity.

ARRIVAL AND INFORMATION

By plane Liberia's international airport is 12km west of town. Flights arrive largely from North America. A taxi into Liberia costs around US$10; there are no buses. Destinations include Miami, New York, Atlanta, Denver, Toronto and Brussels, with domestic flights (Sansa and Nature Air) to San José, La Fortuna, Tamarindo and Nosara.

By bus All buses (except those from and to San José and Playa del Coco) arrive at the Terminal Liberia (Av 7, C 12/14) at the northwestern edge of town. The Pulmitan Terminal (Av 5, C 10/12) is one block southeast of Terminal Liberia. International Tica Bus (⊚ ticabus.com) services for Managua via Antigua, Nicaragua, arrive and depart from in front of *Hotel Bromadero* (next to the *McDonald's* by the main crossroads); tickets must be booked in advance through *Hotel Liberia*.

Destinations La Cruz/Peñas Blancas (Nicaraguan border; 6 daily; 2hr); Managua via Antigua, Nicargua (4 daily; 5hr); Nicoya (Mon–Sat every 30min 3.30am–9pm, Sun hourly 8am–6pm; 2hr); Playa del Coco (hourly 5am–11am, then 12.30pm, 2.30pm & 6.30pm; 1hr); Playa Panamá via Playa Hermosa (8 daily 4.30am–5.30pm; 1hr 20min); Playa Tamarindo (6 daily; 1hr 30min–2hr); Puntarenas (5 daily; 3hr); San José (11 daily; 4hr 30min); Santa Rosa (take the

LIBERIA

Mercado Central
Terminal Liberia
Pulmitan Terminal
Police
Parque Central
Banco de Costa Rica (ATM)
Gobernación
Banco Nacional (ATM)
Iglesia de la Agonía
Río Liberia
Tica Bus stop
Bancredito
Banco Popular (ATM) & Banco de San José (ATM)
Toyota Rent a Car
Supermarket
Centro Commercial Santa Rosa

● EATING & DRINKING	
Café Liberia	2
Copa de Oro	3
Jauja	5
Liberia Supremacy	1
Pizza Pronto	4

■ ACCOMMODATION	
Hostal Ciudad Blanca	4
Hotel Liberia	2
Hotel Los Angeles	1
Hotel Posada del Tope	3
Hotel La Siesta	5

0 — 200 metres

N

San José

Nicaraguan Border, Santa Rosa ◀ ▲ Rincón de la Vieja (6km)

◀ Airport, Nicoya & Beaches

▼ San José

2

bus for the Nicaraguan border and ask to be dropped at the park; 40min).

Tourist information Staff at *Hotel Liberia* and *Hotel Posada del Tope* can answer questions on the local area and provide information on a shuttle service to Rincón de la Vieja (US$25 for four people).

ACCOMMODATION

All the accommodation options reviewed below offer free wi-fi.

Hostal Ciudad Blanca Av 4, C 1/3 ☎ 2666 3962. The facade of this restored colonial mansion is grander than its a/c rooms, which are comfortable enough but not all adequately ventilated. US$60

Hotel Liberia C 0, 75m south of the Parque Central ☎ 2666 0161. Well-established, friendly youth-hostel-type hotel with a jolly papaya-orange exterior. The bare and basic rooms with shared cold-water bathroom are set around a sunny courtyard. The newer rooms in an annexe to the rear are better and have their own bath, though they cost an extra US$5. The hotel staff can organize transport to Rincón de la Vieja. The hotel is popular, so a reservation and deposit are required in the high season. US$15

Hotel Los Angeles Av 7, C 2/4 ☎ 2665 5900. Friendly, central motel with secure parking and anonymous, spotless rooms with a/c and TV. Substantial discounts for solo travellers. US$42

Hotel Posada del Tope C 0, 150m south of the municipal government building ☎ 2666 3876. Popular place in a beautiful old house. The bare-bones rooms in the main building are stuffy and could be cleaner; opt for the brighter and only slightly more expensive ones in the annexe across the street, which are set around a charming courtyard. All have fans and share bathrooms. Per person from US$15

★**Hotel La Siesta** C 6, Av 4/6 ☎ 2666 0606, ⓦ hotellasiestacr.com. Attractive hotel with comfortable a/c doubles with private bathrooms and cable TV, set around a courtyard with a fountain and small pool. There are also simpler fan rooms, with TV and private showers and toilets (though, bizarrely, no sinks), in a nearby annexe. Plus laundry, free internet and one of the best restaurants in town. US$60

EATING AND DRINKING

Local treats include *natilla* (sour cream) eaten with eggs or *gallo pinto* and tortillas. For a real feast, try the various *desayunos guanacastecos* (Guanacastecan breakfasts). For rock-bottom-cheap lunches, head for the stalls at the market by the Liberia bus terminal. There's a large supermarket on C 0, Av 3/5.

★**Café Liberia** C 0, Av 2/4 ☎ 2665 1660. In a stunning nineteenth-century property, with grand wooden doors and a frescoed ceiling, *Café Liberia* has perfectly brewed cappuccinos and lattes, plus crêpes, bagels, salads and

sandwiches (including a few vegetarian options). Mains from 1500c. Mon–Sat 10am–6pm.

Copa de Oro C 0, Av 2. Unassuming joint with sport on the TV, quick service and an intriguing mural on the far wall. The menu features hearty *casados* (3500c), *ceviche*, and the house special – *arroz copa de oro* (seafood rice). Mon & Wed–Sun 11am–10pm.

Jauja Av Central, C 8/10 ☎ 2665 2061. One of the better restaurants in town, though very touristy. Large and tasty pasta dishes and pizzas cost around 4500c, and there are also typical steaks and fish dishes. It's all served in a pleasant, outdoor garden setting, although the big-screen TV can be off-putting. Daily 11am–11pm.

Liberia Supremacy Av 1, C 5/7. Reggae on the stereo, cheap beer on tap, a young crowd, and posters of the usual suspects: Che, Marley et al. Tues–Sun 5pm–midnight.

★**Pizza Pronto** C 1, Av 4 ☎ 2666 2098. Rustic-chic locals' favourite where dark-wood tables are covered with Guanacaste topographical maps. Select from over twenty kinds of pizza (from 4500c), all baked in an adobe clay oven. Daily 11am–11pm.

DIRECTORY

Banks Av Central is lined with several banks, including Banco Nacional and Banco de Costa Rica, both across from the Parque Central.

Health Hospital Dr Enrique Baltodano Briceño (☎ 2666 0011, emergencies ☎ 2666 0318) is in the northeastern part of town off C 13, behind the stadium.

Post office Av 3 at C 8, in the white house across from the empty square field bordered by mango trees.

PARQUE NACIONAL RINCÓN DE LA VIEJA

The earth around **PARQUE NACIONAL RINCÓN DE LA VIEJA** (US$10; ☎ 2661 8139), northeast of Liberia, is actually alive and breathing: **Volcán Rincón de la Vieja**, the park's namesake, is very much active. Though it last erupted in 1991, rivers of lava continue to boil beneath the thin epidermis of ground, while **mud pots** (*pilas de barro*) bubble, and puffs of steam rise out of lush foliage, signalling sulphurous subterranean springs. The dramatically dry surrounding landscape, meanwhile, varies from rock-strewn savanna to patches of tropical dry forest and deciduous trees, culminating in the blasted-out vistas of the volcano crater itself. This is great terrain for **camping**, **riding**, **hiking** and **wallowing in mud**, with a comfortable, fairly dry heat

– although it can get damp and cloudy at the higher elevations around the crater. **Birders**, too, will enjoy Rincón de la Vieja, as more than two hundred species are in residence.

WHAT TO SEE AND DO

The park has **hiking trails** for all levels, which begin from one of the two *puestos* (ranger stations) – **Santa María** to the east, and **Las Pailas** to the west. Puesto Santa María is an old colonial house, rumoured to once have been the country retreat of US President Lyndon Johnson, and has some rustic sleeping arrangements (see below).

The hiking trails

Most treks start from Las Pailas, although the main one – the demanding uphill track to the volcano's **crater**, which can be tackled on foot, horseback or a combination of the two – can be embarked on from both. This is one of the best hikes, if not *the* best hike, in the country. A variety of elevations and habitats reveals hot springs, sulphur pools, bubbling mud pots and fields of purple orchids, plus of course the great smoking volcano at the top. It is possible to hike without a **guide**, but should you wish to organize a guided trek ask at Las Pailas (☎2661 8139). Alternatively, several hotels in Liberia offer treks. Ring ahead before you start out, as the trail is often closed due to low visibility or high winds.

From the Las Pailas entrance, the very satisfying 6km circular **Sendero Las Pailas** takes you around some unusual natural features, with bubbling mud pots and a mini-volcano as well as steaming sulphurous vents that make for a highly atmospheric experience. There are more **gentle walks** in the Las Pailas sector, and one in the Santa María sector, that take you to fumaroles and mud pots, and you can also hike to two waterfalls, the *cataratas escondidas*.

ARRIVAL AND INFORMATION

There is no public transport to the park's two entrances. If you drive, a 4WD is recommended year-round, and compulsory in the wet season.

Las Pailas ranger station Las Pailas (daily 8am–4pm) – the western entrance – is the most common gateway. Transfers from *Hotel Posada del Tope* and *Hotel Liberia* (see p.170) cost US$25; a 4WD taxi from Liberia will be around US$40. If you drive yourself, travel through the hamlet of Curubandé, 5km north of Liberia off the Interamericana. The 20km road (1500c/person to pass through a private section) is a decent gravel road, passable by regular car in dry season.

Santa María ranger station Santa María (daily 8am–4pm) is in the east. Transfers are available from Liberia hotels (see opposite); a 4WD taxi from Liberia will cost US$60 or so. Driving, go through Liberia's Barrio La Victoria in the northeast of town (ask for the *estadio* – the football stadium), from where it's a signed, bumpy, 24km drive along a rugged dirt-and-gravel road to the park.

ACCOMMODATION

Most budget travellers stay in Liberia: reasonably priced accommodation around the park is scarce, and there are no restaurants.

Camping There are campsites at both ranger stations Santa María is better equipped, with pit toilets, showers and grills, but you must bring your own food and drinking water. Be prepared for cold nights, strong winds and fog. US$3

INTO NICARAGUA: PEÑAS BLANCAS

Peñas Blancas (daily 7am–8pm) is the main crossing point into Nicaragua and the only one you can cross by land. This is a border post rather than a town, so there's nowhere to stay. Arrive as early as possible and expect to spend at least an hour to get through the procedures. Travellers must fill in exit and entry forms. Some nationalities require Nicaraguan visas; check visa requirements (see p.450) beforehand. Exit stamps are given on the Costa Rican side.

For travellers entering Nicaragua from Costa Rica, there is a fee of US$13; if you're leaving Nicaragua, you pay US$3. Moneychangers are always on hand and have colones, córdobas and dollars; make sure you know roughly what the exchange rate should be in advance. It's 1km between the Costa Rican and Nicaraguan immigration offices; if you've only caught the bus as far as the border, you can either walk across or get a lift in one of the golf carts (tip required). If you're coming from Nicaragua, the last San José bus (5hr 30min) leaves at 5.30pm and the last Liberia bus at 6.30pm (2hr).

2

Rinconcito Lodge In San Jorge, on the road to Santa María ☎ 2666 2764, ⓦ rinconcitolodge.com. The cheapest option close to the park, this eco-farm has simple, good-value *cabinas* with hot-water private baths. Horseriding and trekking tours are also on offer (US$40–55), and the owners are friendly and helpful. Meals and packed lunches are available. US$39

PARQUE NACIONAL SANTA ROSA

PARQUE NACIONAL SANTA ROSA (daily 8am–4pm; US$10; ☎ 2666 5051), 35km north of Liberia, is popular thanks to its good trails, great surfing (though poor swimming) and turtle-spotting opportunities.

Santa Rosa has an amazingly diverse **topography** for its size, ranging from mangrove swamp to rare tropical dry forest and savanna, and a staggering array of mammals, birds, amphibians and reptiles. Jaguars and pumas prowl the park, though you're unlikely to see them; coati, coyotes and peccaries, on the other hand, are often found snuffling around watering holes. Between July and November (peaking in September and October), the spectacle of hundreds of **olive ridley turtles** (*lloras*) nesting on Playa Nancite puts all other animal sightings into the shade; a maximum of twenty visitors is allowed access to the nesting area each day (call ahead to reserve).

Though too rough for swimming, the picturesque **beaches** of Naranjo and Nancite, about 12km down a bad road from the administration centre, are popular with serious **surfers**.

ARRIVAL AND INFORMATION

Park entrance The park's entrance hut is signed from the Interamericana; it's a 7km walk from here to the campsite and administration centre, so it's much more convenient to enter the park if you have your own vehicle.
By bus Buses from Liberia (use the Peñas Blancas/La Cruz service) run past the entrance. Tell the driver well in advance that you want to stop at the park.
Tourist information The visitors' centre at the entrance is effectively the main reception (☎ 2666 5051).

ACCOMMODATION AND EATING

The camping facilities (pay at the administration centre) are among the best in the country. Watch your fires (the area is a tinderbox in the dry season), take plastic bags for your food, don't leave anything edible in your tent (or it will be stolen by scavenging coati) and carry plenty of water. Make sure to stock up on food before entering the park. You can buy drinks at the administration centre, but little else.
La Casona campground About 400m from administration centre. This campsite has bathrooms and grill pits. US$2
Comedor Adjacent to the administration centre. Make reservations at the administration centre (at least 3hr in advance) for a simple lunch in the basic *comedor*. The food – *casados* with fish, chicken or meat and salad (3350c) – is good, and this is a great place to get talking to rangers and other tourists. Daily 11am–4pm.
Playa Naranjo campground On the beach. Camping with picnic tables and grill pits, a ranger's hut with outhouses and showers – and, from time to time, a boa constrictor in the roof. Only open outside the turtle-nesting season. US$2

The Zona Norte

The **Zona Norte** (Northern Zone) spans the hundred-odd kilometres from the base of the Cordillera Central to just short of the mauve-blue mountains of southern Nicaragua. Formerly cut off from the rest of the country by a lack of good roads, the Zona Norte has developed a unique character, with independent-minded farmers and Nicaraguan refugees making up large segments of the population. Many people from the north hold a special allegiance to, and pride in, their area. While less obviously picturesque than many parts of the country, the entire region has a distinctive appeal, with lazy rivers snaking across steaming plains and flop-eared cattle languishing beneath the trees.

Most travellers only venture here to see **Volcán Arenal**. Further north, the remote flatlands are home to the increasingly accessible **Refugio Nacional de Vida Silvestre Caño Negro**, which harbours an extraordinary amount of birdlife. There's a serviceable **bus** network, though if you're travelling outside the La Fortuna or Sarapiquí areas, consider renting a car. The area around Arenal is best equipped for visitors; between Boca de Arenal and Los Chiles in the far north, there is a real shortage of **accommodation**.

LA FORTUNA AND AROUND

That the north attracts the numbers of visitors it does is mainly due to majestic **Volcán Arenal**. However, although the volcano is still considered to be active, it has been slumbering since 2010. On a clear day it remains a majestic sight, but when it's rainy and foggy – which is more often than not – it is almost totally obscured, the summit hidden behind a sombrero of cloud. Just 6km away, **LA FORTUNA** is a compact, simple agricultural town that's become a major tourist hub due to its perfect location as a jumping-off point for a wide range of activities.

WHAT TO SEE AND DO

Besides the **volcano** looming beyond the town, the area around La Fortuna offers ample **outdoor activities** – from rugged cycling tours and canopy tours to nature walks, hot spring spas and paddleboarding on Lake Arenal. Thanks to the proliferation of **tour companies**, it pays to shop around to get a good price; make sure you know exactly what's included in any tour you consider.

Hot springs

Several lodges along the road from La Fortuna to Arenal offer visitors the opportunity to soak in the volcano-tinged sulphurous **hot springs**. **El Tabacón** (daily 10am–10pm; day-pass with lunch or dinner US$85; night-pass with buffet dinner US$70; ⓦtabacon .com) is the most expensive, complete with lush tropical setting, waterfalls gushing down fake cliffs, and a series of beautiful natural pools – both hot and cold – to relax in and numerous spa treatments available. **Baldi Hot Springs** is cheaper (daily 10am–10pm; US$34, with dinner buffet US$56; ⓦbaldihotsprings.cr), and features several hot and warm pools to meander between, as well as two exhilarating water slides. Agencies in town (see box, p.174) can often get you a cheaper price in conjunction with other excursions. **Termales Los Laureles**, 5.5km west of La Fortuna (daily 9am–9pm; US$12; ⓦtermalesloslaureles.com), is cheaper still, and popular with Ticos.

Puentes Colgantes de Arenal

Puentes Colgantes de Arenal (daily 7.30am–4.30pm; ⓦhangingbridges .com; US$24), a popular set of bridges – six suspended and ten regular – is spread along a 3km rainforest trail near the Laguna de Arenal. Even with tour

LA FORTUNA

◼ ACCOMMODATION	
Arenal Backpackers Resort	3
Cabinas La Catarata	6
Gringo Pete's	2
Monte Real	5
Rancho Margot	4
Sleeping Indian Hostel	1

AVENIDA VOLCÁN

AVENIDA FORTUNA

Banco Nacional (ATM)

Fortuna Mountain Bike

School

Eagle Tours

Mercado Artesanía

Parque Central

Taxi Rank

Police

Laundry

Desafío Tours

Banco Popular (ATM)

Aventuras Arenal

AVENIDA CENTRAL

Supermarket

Jacamar

Pura Vida Tours

AVENIDA ARENAL

Bus Terminal

N

● EATING & DRINKING	
Don Rufino	2
Gecko Gourmet	1
Lava Lounge	5
Lava Rocks	6
My Coffee	3
Soda La Parada	4

0   150
metres

Baldi (4km), Termales Los Laureles (5.5km), Puretrek (7km), Tabacón (11km), Volcán Arenal (17km)
Puentes Colgantes de Arenal (20km), Rancho Margot (28km), Tilarán (74km)

San Carlos, San José, Caño Negro & Puerto Viejo

▼ 6 (1.5km), Catarata La Fortuna (4km) & Cerro Chato (9km)

2

TOURS AND ACTIVITIES IN LA FORTUNA

Competition between **tour agencies** in La Fortuna is fierce: for the best experience, make sure you go with an established tour operator, rather than the freelance "guides" who may approach you, some of whom have been involved in serious incidents over the years. The vast majority of operators offer the same standard trips on top of their specialities: guided hikes in Parque Nacional Arenal combined with hot springs visits, canopy tours, rafting, day-trips to Caño Negro, and transfers to Monteverde. The following outfits are particularly recommended.

Aventuras Arenal Av Central ☎ 2479 9133, ⓦ aventurasarenal.com. Long-standing operator offering professionally run biking, horseback and watersports excursions, plus transport to just about anywhere in the country.
★**Desafío Tours** C 2 ☎ 2479 9464, ⓦ desafío costarica.com. Friendly, efficient and community-aware rafting specialists who run trips on the Río Toro and the Río Sarapiquí and guided hikes up Cerro Chato (US$85), among other excursions. Their Monteverde transfer can include a horseriding or mountain-biking

excursion along the way (US$85).
Ecoglide ☎ 2479 7120, ⓦ arenalecoglide.com. The most extensive of the local canopy tours, offering twelve ziplines and a Tarzan swing (US$55).
Jacamar Av Central, next to *Lava Rocks* ☎ 2479 9767, ⓦ arenaltours.com. Volcano tours, trips to Caño Negro (US$96) and a number of nature hikes.
PureTrek Canyoning West of town, en route to *Arenal Nayara Hotel & Gardens* ☎ 2479 1315, ⓦ puretrek.com. Rappelling specialist, offering guided rappels down your choice of four waterfalls.

groups clogging up the trail (odds are you'll be on a tour too), this is a rewarding outing, since your guide will point out wildlife ranging from insects and monkeys to snakes and birds. The trail is pretty gentle, though there's a steep-ish uphill leading to the highest bridge, 25m off the ground, and if you don't have a head for heights you may not like the longest of the suspended bridges.

Catarata La Fortuna and Cerro Chato

You can make an excursion to La Fortuna's stunning waterfall, **Catarata La Fortuna** (daily 8am–5pm; US$10), which sits amid beautiful jungle terrain just 6km south of the church. A taxi (3500–4500c) can take you to the entrance, or it's a good uphill walk on foot (1hr from La Fortuna). Once there, you're in for a steep climb down a winding path and staircase and a gruelling return journey, but the waterfall is spectacular and makes for a wonderfully refreshing swim.

At the entrance to the *cataratas* you'll also find the start of a hardcore 5km, five- to six-hour hike up **Cerro Chato**, a smaller volcanic peak that clings to Arenal's skirts, and offers views of its big brother. You'll be crossing private land and will have to pay US$10.

ARRIVAL AND DEPARTURE

By plane La Fortuna airport is 7km east of town (around $15 by taxi); there are direct daily flights to/from San José (1 daily; 25min) and Quepos (2 daily; 40min).
By bus The bus terminal is at the Centro Comercial, one block south of Av Central.
Destinations Monteverde (take the 8am bus to Tilarán, changing there for the 12.30pm bus to Monteverde; 6–8hr); San Carlos (for frequent San José connections; hourly; 2hr–2hr 30min); San José (2 daily, 12.45pm & 2.45pm; 4hr–4hr 30min); Tilarán (2–3 daily; 3hr 30min).

ACCOMMODATION

Budget accommodation is concentrated in town, with a few possibilities on the road leading to the waterfall and also en route to Arenal.
Arenal Backpackers Resort Av Central ☎ 2479 7000, ⓦ arenalbackpackersresort.com. With its neatly tended lawns, pool lined with palm trees, and wet bar, *Arenal Backpackers* certainly has plenty of amenities. The thin walls, coupled with a lively atmosphere, ensure that you won't be getting much sleep, however. Rooms (with private bathrooms, a/c and TVs) and dorms are spacious, clean and bright, while the deluxe tents (sleeping one to four) come with mattresses and bedding (and that old tent smell). Security is excellent, but staff could be more helpful. Camping US$35, dorms US$15, doubles US$45
Cabinas La Catarata 700m up the road towards the waterfall, a 15min walk from La Fortuna ☎ 2479 7790. This friendly property has four fully equipped cabins (sleeping 3–6), each with a terrace and hammocks overlooking a lush piece of land with a river running

LA FORTUNA TO MONTEVERDE: JEEP–BOAT–JEEP TRANSFERS

The most interesting way to travel between La Fortuna and **Monteverde** (see p.143) is by a **"jeep–boat–jeep" transfer**. This time-saving and spectacularly pretty connection takes 2–3hr, and involves taking a minivan (*not* jeep!) to the Laguna del Arenal, crossing it by boat, and then boarding another minivan for the rest of the journey to Santa Elena/Monteverde. The trip offers both the breathtaking views of the mountain pastures of Monteverde, and your first (or last, depending on the direction) glimpse of majestic Volcán Arenal. The transfer (around US$35) is easily arranged through lodgings and tour agencies –it's best to shop around.

2

through it – ideal for birdwatching. The considerate hosts are super-friendly; breakfast, though, costs extra. US$60
Gringo Pete's C 7, just north of Av Arenal ☎ 2479 8521, ⓦ gringopeteshostel.com. Long-running hostel catering to shoestring travellers. The boxy private rooms have little natural light but the dorm is large and the prices are fantastically low. There are sociable communal areas, kitchen and free coffee, and the staff throw an occasional BBQ. *Gringo Pete's Too*, 225m west of the bus station, has a similar set-up. Dorm US$5, doubles US$12
Monte Real 100m south and 300m east of the Parque Central ☎ 2479 9357, ⓦ monterealhotel.com. This friendly central hotel is set in tranquil garden surrounds alongside a gurgling river. Stylish rooms – some with dead-on volcano views – are well equipped with a/c, fridge and private bath with hot water. There's a small pool. US$62
★**Sleeping Indian Hostel** Av Fort ☎ 2479 8431. Housed above a great little café, this quiet hostel consists of several airy private rooms around a large and appealing common area, complete with hammocks and a guest kitchen. Staff are very friendly and helpful. US$45

★**TREAT YOURSELF**

Rancho Margot Around 28km southwest of La Fortuna, near El Castillo ☎ 2479 7259 or ☎ 8302 7318, ⓦ ranchomargot.org. This terrific self-sufficient eco-retreat encourages a hands-on stay: you can milk the cows; make cheese, wine or marmalade; or help to till the organic gardens. There's a riverside yoga and meditation studio, or you might opt for canyoning, kayaking, horse-riding or one of the other activities on offer; adventurous types can even hike to Reserva Santa Elena, 8km away. Accommodation ranges from basic dormitory-style rooms in the bunkhouse to honeymoon-worthy hilltop bungalows. Rates include full-board, daily yoga classes and a guided tour. A free shuttle bus runs to/from La Fortuna. Dorms US$75, bungalows US$165

EATING AND DRINKING

Gecko Gourmet Just west of the church ⓦ geckogourmet .com. Catering to homesick gringos, this café has breakfast burritos, smoked salmon and cream cheese bagels, meatloaf, BBQ pulled pork and BLTs (around 3500–5000c), as well as fine coffee and smoothies (try the mocha with peanut butter). Daily 7am–3.30pm.
Lava Lounge Av Central, C 2/4. By day this breezy Tiki bar-style restaurant with a *palapa* roof serves excellent fajitas, salads, chunky sandwiches and veggie wraps (3500–6000c), and at night it turns into a relaxed bar with a soundtrack of reggae and chilled beats. Daily 11am–11.30pm.
Lava Rocks Opposite the church. Not to be confused with *Lava Bar and Grill*, this place has wonderfully nice staff and well-executed *comida típica* (*casados* and rice dishes from 4000c). Daily 8am–10.30pm; the bar closes later.
My Coffee Av Central, C 1/2. Besides the ubiquitous *gallo pinto*, breakfast offerings (around 3000c) include French toast, pancakes, eggs done the way you like them and hefty omelettes. Great coffee, too. Daily 8am–8pm.
Soda La Parada Av Central, opposite Parque Central ☎ 2479 9098, ⓦ restaurantlaparada.com. One of the best *sodas* in town, always crowded. It's perfect for an early breakfast of *gallo pinto* or a range of heaped *casados* (around 3500c), which is what they do best; they also offer so-so burgers and pizza. Officially, but not invariably, daily 24hr.

DIRECTORY

Bicycle rental Bike Arenal (☎ 2479 9454, ⓦ bikearenal .com), on Av Central, rents mountain bikes for US$20 a day; one-day tours from US$96.
Health Centro Médico Arenal Vital, C 1, in the *Hotel Las Colinas* (☎ 2479 7027), is a private clinic with English-speaking staff, open around the clock.
Laundry There's a laundry service a block before *La Choza Inn*.
Taxis There's a rank on the east side of the Parque Central. Agree on a price before getting in.

PARQUE NACIONAL VOLCÁN ARENAL

Volcán Arenal is spectacular, whether admired from La Fortuna, where its

2

slopes are still a lush green, or from the barren and desolate western face, where the foliage has been gradually scorched by the ash and lava that once tumbled down the side every day. This volcano was presumed dormant, as it sat there, minding its own business, until 1968, when it spectacularly blew its top, its lava flows wrecking three villages and killing thousands of livestock, as well as eighty people. For many years it spewed molten rock on pretty much a daily basis, before falling quiet in 2010. Even without the lava spills, it remains a spectacular sight, however, and **PARQUE NACIONAL VOLCÁN ARENAL** (daily 8am–4pm; US$10) has several good walking **trails**.

The trails

Easy walks in the park include the **Sendero Los Heliconias** (1km), which starts from the ranger station and leads past the 1968 old lava flow, with the option of a 1.5km trail branch leading to a viewpoint, and **Sendero Las Cascadas** (1km; US$4), in the grounds of the Arenal Observatory Lodge, which leads down to a roaring waterfall. **Sendero Los Coladas** splits off from the Sendero Las Heliconias and skirts the bottom of the volcano for 2km, taking you past the more recent (1993) lava flow and joining the **Sendero Los Tucanes**, an easy 3km through lush rainforest. A little tougher, the misleadingly named **Old Lava Flow Trail** (2km) starts at the park headquarters and rambles up and down along the huge

1993 lava flow. That hike is easily combined with the **Sendero El Ceibo** (1.8km), a jolly ramble through secondary forest. The park's toughest hike is the 4km **Sendero Cerro Chato** (US$4), which runs from the Arenal Observatory Lodge and climbs steeply to the top of dormant Cerro Chato, where you're rewarded with great views of neighbouring Arenal and a stunning 1100m-high volcanic lake. Finally, there's **Arenal 1968** (daily 8am–8pm; US$10), a private network of short trails centred around the 1968 lava flow, located 1.2km before the ranger station.

ARRIVAL AND INFORMATION

Tours Many visitors come to the park on a tour; note that, unlike the full-day tours, half-day tours involve very little hiking.

By bus No buses head into the park, but you can catch the 8am bus from La Fortuna to Tilarán, get dropped off at the park entrance (where you'll find the ranger station/ information centre; several trails start from here) and then catch the return bus at around 2pm.

By car Head west from La Fortuna for 15km, then, at a fork in the road, take a signposted left turn and follow the dirt-and-gravel road for 2km to the entrance. The *Arenal Observatory Lodge* hotel, where several trails set off, is another 3km along that road.

By taxi The 17km taxi ride from La Fortuna to the park entrance costs around US$15–20.

LOS CHILES

LOS CHILES, a humid border settlement 3km from Nicaragua, is becoming more popular with travellers, thanks to its proximity to **Caño Negro**, 25km downstream on the Río Frío (see opposite), and also to the Nicaraguan border, which can only be crossed by boat.

ARRIVAL AND INFORMATION

By boat The boat docks are 1km west of the bus station. Turn left at Cruz Roja on the main street, then head right downhill along Av 0 to the waterfront.

By bus The bus terminal is behind *Soda Pamela* on Av 1, near the intersection with Hwy-35. Bus timetables change frequently, so confirm before setting off.

Destinations San Carlos (Ciudad Quesada; hourly; 2hr–2hr 30min); San José (2 daily, 5.15am & 3pm; 5–6hr); Upala via Caño Negro (3 daily, 5am, 2pm & 4.30pm; 1hr 30min–2hr 30min).

Bank Banco Nacional (with an ATM) is on the north side of the soccer pitch, Av 1, C 0/1.

ACCOMMODATION AND EATING

Cabinas Jabiru One block west and north of the bus station ☎2471 1211 or ☎2471 1496, ✉jcarlos0829 @hotmail.com. The economical rooms here, each with private bathroom, TV, fridge and a/c, may not be the most memorable you'll ever stay in, but they're fine for a day or two. US$30

Rancho Tulipan 100m from the dock ☎2471 1414, ✉sergioca7@hotmail.com. The smartest lodgings in town (which isn't saying much), with comfortable singles, doubles, triples and quads with private bathrooms, TVs and a/c, set amid a garden filled with medicinal plants. There's also a decent restaurant. US$50

REFUGIO NACIONAL DE VIDA SILVESTRE CAÑO NEGRO

The largely pristine 102-square-kilometre **REFUGIO NACIONAL DE VIDA SILVESTRE CAÑO NEGRO** (daily 8am–4pm; US$10; ☎2471 1309), 25km west of Los Chiles, is one of the best places in the Americas to view huge concentrations of both migratory and indigenous birds – over 365 species – along with mammalian and reptilian river wildlife. The protected area consists of wetlands, fed by Río Frío; the river swells up to form a lake during the wet season. Until recently, the park's isolation, 192km from San José, kept it far off the beaten track, but nowadays more visitors are arriving. You can visit on a long day-excursion from La Fortuna (see box, p.174) or from Los Chiles (see opposite), and it

has become much easier to reach the park on your own. Staying overnight gives you an advantage over the day-trippers, as early morning is the best time to see wildlife (get going around 6am).

ARRIVAL AND DEPARTURE

By boat During rainy season (and some of the dry season) it's possible to catch a boat for travel down the Río Frío from Los Chiles (around US$25/person).

By bus Buses arrive and leave from the office of the local guide co-operative Real Tour, in the centre of Caño Negro. There are three buses a day to Los Chiles (at 6am, 3pm & 5.30pm); confirm timetables before setting off.

By car Caño Negro is reachable by rough dirt-and-gravel road between Los Chiles and Upala. It's accessible by regular vehicle during dry season, but a 4WD is mandatory in the rainy season. Coming from Los Chiles, turn before the phone signal tower.

INFORMATION AND TOURS

Tourist Information The entrance fee (US$10) is payable at the Real Tour office (daily 8am–4pm). The ranger station is at Estación Biológica Caño Negro, 6km north of the church.

Tour operators Several agencies in La Fortuna (see box, p.174) offer day-trips here, though these miss out on the best time of day for wildlife-viewing. If you get here under your own steam, hiring an experienced local guide (from US$20) is well worth the money; the local guide co-operative, Real Tour, in the centre of town (☎2471 1621; daily 8am–4pm), can put you in touch with a guide, and you'll find guides waiting around the dock area. Tours cost around US$70–80 for a two-hour excursion along the Río Frío of up to three people, though you can take longer boat tours as well, with guides pointing out birds, caimans, monkeys, iguanas, sloths and other wildlife.

INTO NICARAGUA: LOS CHILES

Currently, the only way to reach Nicaragua from the **Los Chiles** crossing is by **boat** (1hr) on the Río Frío. At least two boats daily (12.30pm & 3.30pm; 1hr 30min) leave the docks in Los Chiles for San Carlos de Nicaragua (see p.500), depending on demand and tides, with return boats at around 10.30am and 4pm. Boats connect with buses for the 14km ride to San Carlos. You need to get an exit stamp from the Costa Rican immigration office, opposite Rancho Tulipan, first. Most nationalities don't need visas for Nicaragua, but check first (see p.450). Make sure the **Nicaraguan border patrol**, 3km upriver from Los Chiles, stamps your passport, as you will need proof of entry when leaving Nicaragua. You'll also need some cash upon arrival in San Carlos; change a few colones for córdobas at the Los Chiles bank. From San Carlos it's also possible to cross the lake to **Granada** and on to **Managua**. There is a US$10 charge to enter Nicaragua. The border crossing is open 8am–5pm.

2

PUERTO VIEJO DE SARAPIQUÍ

Steamy, tropical and carpeted with fruit plantations, the eastern Zona Norte bears more resemblance to the hot and dense Caribbean lowlands than the plains of the north and, despite the toll of deforestation, still shelters some of the country's best-preserved premontane rainforest. The largest settlement, **PUERTO VIEJO DE SARAPIQUÍ**, is principally a river transport hub and a place for the region's banana, coconut and pineapple plantation workers to stock up on supplies. If you're driving from the Valle Central to the Caribbean coast, Puerto Viejo makes a convenient (if not terribly exciting) stopover.

There are two options when it comes to getting here from the Valle Central. The western route, taking just over three hours, goes via Varablanca and the La Paz waterfall, passing the hump of Volcán Barva. This route offers great views of velvety green hills clad with coffee plantations, which turn, eventually, into rainforest. It's faster (1hr–1hr 30min), but marginally less scenic, to travel via the **Guápiles Highway**. The region receives a lot of **rain** – as much as 4500mm annually – so wet-weather gear is essential.

ARRIVAL AND DEPARTURE

By bus The bus station is in the centre of town, on the main road by the football pitch.

Destinations Guápiles (for connections to Puerto Limón; 10 daily, 5.30am–7pm; 1hr); San José (11 daily, 5am–5.30pm; 2hr).

ACCOMMODATION AND EATING

Mi Lindo Sarapiquí On the corner of the football pitch ☎ 2766 6281. A good budget option, with clean, spacious rooms, private hot showers and a friendly atmosphere. The restaurant is very popular too, particularly for its seafood. US$40

★ **Posada Andrea Cristina** 1km west of town on the road to Chilamate ☎ 2766 6265, ⓦ andreacristina.com. A tropical haven, with lovely, quirky cabins, bungalows and a wonderful room in a treehouse set among jungle plants. The hospitable owner has a wealth of information on conservation projects, runs river and trekking tours, offers Spanish classes and serves excellent (mainly vegetarian) food. Double US$55

The Zona Sur

Costa Rica's **Zona Sur** ("southern zone") is the country's least-known and most challenging region. Geographically, it's a diverse area, ranging from the agricultural heartland of the Valle de El General to the high peaks of the Cordillera de Talamanca. South of Cerro Chirripó, one of the tallest peaks in Central America, the cordillera falls away into the lowlands of the Valle de Diquís and the coffee-growing Valle de Coto Brus, near the Panama border.

The region's chief draw is the **Parque Nacional Chirripó**, where the demanding high-altitude trek to **Cerro Chirripó** attracts thousands of hikers. The National Park is accessed through the little mountain town of San Gerardo de Rivas, and getting there is half the adventure. More accessible, the **Playa Dominical** area of the Pacific coast is a surfing destination of tremendous tropical beauty, while tiny **Uvita**, nearby, is the gateway to the whale-watching destination of **Parque Nacional Marino Ballena**.

SAN ISIDRO DE EL GENERAL

An important crossroads for anyone passing through on their way to the Osa Peninsula, Panama or the west coast, **SAN ISIDRO DE EL GENERAL** is a large, hot urban sprawl, reached via a particularly winding and scenic mountain road from Cartago. Odds are you'll only stop here long enough to change buses.

ARRIVAL AND DEPARTURE

By bus From the TRACOPA terminal (☎ 2721 0468), two blocks east of Parque Central on the Interamericana, buses run to San José, Palmar Norte and Paso Canoas (for Panama). From Terminal Quepos (☎ 2771 2550), on the street south of the TRACOPA terminal, buses depart for Quepos, Dominical, Uvita, and Puerto Jiménez via Palmar Norte. To get to San Gerardo de Rivas, go to the local bus terminal on Av 6. Book tickets in advance for popular long-distance buses.

Destinations Dominical (4 daily; 40min–1hr); Palmar Norte (2 daily; 4hr); Paso Canoas (2 daily; 6hr); Puerto Jiménez (3 daily; 5hr); Quepos (4 daily; 3hr 30min); San Gerardo de Rivas (2 daily; 1hr 40min); San José (every 30min; 3hr); Uvita (2 daily; 1hr 30min).

ACCOMMODATION AND EATING

There are a few basic Tico restaurants scattered along C Central.

Hotel Chirripó On the south side of Parque Central ☎ 2771 0529. Your best bet should you need to stay, with the cheapest rooms sharing a bathroom, and the swishest en suites coming with a/c (singles from US$16). **US$57**

SAN GERARDO DE RIVAS

The mountain village of **SAN GERARDO DE RIVAS**, 22km east of San Isidro, is the gateway to the popular **Parque Nacional Chirripó**, home of Costa Rica's

tallest mountain and most demanding climb.

WHAT TO SEE AND DO

While most visitors tend to come for the challenge of tackling Cerro Chirripó, there is much more to the area around San Gerardo de Rivas than just the one mountain. **Cloudbridge Reserve** (daily 8am–5pm; donation suggested), a private swathe of forest accessible by the road that runs past the Cerro Chirripó trailhead, has several attractive, undemanding trails, one of them leading

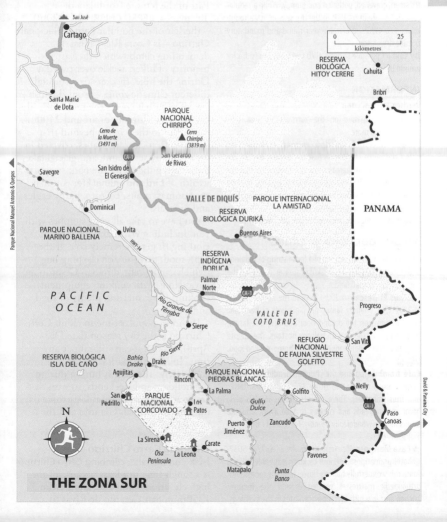

THE ZONA SUR

to a spectacular waterfall (30min). There's also a dramatic **day-hike**, taking in a local art gallery and a trout farm where you can grab some lunch; walk up the Cerro Chirripó trail and take the right fork at the T-junction. *Casa Mariposa* (see below) has the hike details.

ARRIVAL AND DEPARTURE

By bus Buses for San Isidro depart from the football field, around 1.2km short of the Chirripó trailhead (3 daily, 5.15am, 11.30am & 4pm; 1hr 40min).

By car The road from San Isidro to San Gerardo de Rivas is paved for the first 10km up to the town of Rivas. Beyond, it's steep, gravelled, potholed and bumpy. While a regular car can just about make it in the dry season, it's a tough drive, so a 4WD is preferable year-round and mandatory outside dry season.

By taxi It's possible to get a 4WD taxi from San Isidro for around US$40.

INFORMATION

Tourist information *Casa Mariposa* (see below) has extensive information on the surrounding area, bus timetables and more.

Parque Nacional Chirripó ranger station 1km before the football field (daily 6.30am–noon & 1–4.30pm; ☎ 2200 5348). Come here to check in for your hike, find out about current trail conditions and book porters; it is no longer possible to secure park permits or accommodation (see p.181) at the ranger station, however.

Internet All lodgings reviewed below offer free wi-fi.

ACCOMMODATION AND EATING

San Gerardo de Rivas consists of a loose string of lodgings and restaurants, spread over 2km or so. The "centre" of the village is the football field.

Cabinas El Descanso 200m beyond the ranger station ☎ 2742 5061. Friendly, family-run place with rather basic, spartan rooms on the ground floor and brighter, larger, more expensive rooms with balcony upstairs. The on-site restaurant serves generous portions of home-cooked food. U̲S̲$̲2̲2̲

Café Bambú Opposite the church. Friendly café luring hungry hikers with pizzas (from 1750c), pastries, lattes and fruit smoothies. There are also cakes (500c), pies, home-made breads and cookies to take away, and the atmosphere is wonderfully friendly. Fri & Sat 11am–7pm, Sun 9am–6pm.

★ Casa Mariposa 40m from the trailhead ☎ 2742 5037, ⊕ hotelcasamariposa.net. Run by knowledgeable Jill and John, this wonderfully homely hostel has cosy rooms with orthopaedic mattresses centred around the lounge/ kitchen area to which everyone gravitates in the evenings,

a dorm built into the rock face up the garden path, and a large stone bath for that post-hike soak. Your hosts are by far the best source of info on the area, and hikers shouldn't miss out on Jill's famous energy balls. Dorm U̲S̲$̲1̲4̲, doubles U̲S̲$̲3̲5̲

Hotel y Restaurante El Urán Next door to *Casa Mariposa* ☎ 2742 5003, ⊕ hoteluran.com. Conveniently located for hiking in the park, this hostel offers a mix of simple rooms, some with shared facilities, and a popular restaurant serving heaped portions of *casados* and other simple dishes. Shared bathroom U̲S̲$̲1̲8̲

PARQUE NACIONAL CHIRRIPÓ

Part of the remote Cordillera de Talamanca, **CERRO CHIRRIPÓ** (3820m) – the star of the popular **Parque Nacional Chirripó** – is Costa Rica's most demanding **climb**, which the vast majority of hikers tackle over two days. During the hike, trekkers pass through different climatic zones – from the lush cloudforest that covers the mountainsides between the altitudes of around 2400m to 3400m to the *páramo* beyond that point, with rocky landscapes, covered in sparse, hardy scrubland, and glacial lakes dominating the view. The park supports a wealth of **bird and animal life**; you may spot pumas, tapirs, coyotes, harpy eagles and quetzals.

You have to take all your supplies with you, including warm and waterproof clothing (it gets extremely cold at the top), food, three-season sleeping bag (which can be rented in San Gerardo de Rivas along with cooking equipment), cooking stove, fuel and plenty of food and water.

The most popular time to climb Cerro Chirripó is the **dry season** (late Dec– April), though it can still rain at any time. In May the park is closed completely. The park is busiest during the holidays and weekends, so weekdays are your best bet; allow at least three days for your stay in San Gerardo and the two-day hike.

Climbing Cerro Chirripó

Make no mistake: **climbing Cerro Chirripó** is a tough trek, not least because of the high elevation – you'll be going from 1350m in San Gerardo de Rivas to a height of 3820m. The 16km hike to the summit is also mostly steep, with relentless uphills most of the way. However, the trail is beautiful, with sweeping views of the valley below peeking through the trees, and, at the top, a stupendous view of the Caribbean on one side and the Pacific on the other. The hike is usually done over the course of two days; on **day 1** you hike to the *Los Crestones Lodge*, 10km up the mountain, which can take from five to fourteen hours, depending on your general fitness, while on **day 2**, hikers make a push for the summit in the wee hours of the morning in order to watch the sunrise from the top and then make their way down to San Gerardo – the descent often takes as long as the ascent. Super-fit hikers have been known to do the hike in one day, descending to San Gerardo late at night, but it's not recommended, as exhaustion combined with trail hazards can easily lead to injury.

The **trailhead** is around 40m beyond *Casa Mariposa* (see opposite) on your right; the trail entrance is quite narrow, and there are several trails around the lodge, so make sure you don't miss it in the dark (most people begin the hike around 5am).

While the hike to the summit is a wonderful challenge, it's particularly rewarding to linger at the top for an extra day and hike some of the other trails, such as the ones to **Cerro Ventisqueros** (3812m) and **Cerro Terbi** (3760m); enquire about trail conditions at the ranger station.

ARRIVAL AND DEPARTURE

The park entrance is at the trailhead for the hike up Cerro Chirripó. Although it's only a short walk along the dirt road that leads east from the village centre and over the river, it's also possible to follow the same route by car. As for parking, your best bet is *Hotel y Restaurante Urán* (see opposite) or in front of a local's house for a varying fee.

INFORMATION

Permits Reservations for climbing Chirripó for up to three nights are now made by phone only (☎ 2742 5083; Mon–Fri 8am–4pm); no walk-in reservations are available.
Entry fees US$18/day for up to three nights. If you want to hire porters to take your luggage up the mountain, you

need to bring it to the rangers' office before closing time the day before you intend to hike.

ACCOMMODATION AND EATING

Los Crestones Lodge Accommodation resevations must be made in advance via phone after securing your park entrance (☎ 2742 5097 (Mon–Fri 8am–noon & 1–4pm). This basic lodge with solar-powered electricity offers enough simple bunks to sleep sixty people. Buffet meals are provided (from 5000c), and must also be booked in advance at the number above. US$33

DOMINICAL

In spite of large-scale development in the surrounding area, **DOMINICAL**, 44km south of Quepos (see p.153), remains a one-horse town or, rather, a one-street surfing village, where every other person you meet along the main road – a bumpy dirt track running to the beach – seems to be barefoot and carrying a surfboard.

Thousands of (mainly American) **surfers** flock in every year to ride the beach and point breaks and to hit the many beachfront bars. Novice surfers can take lessons from any of several surf shops; Costa Rica Surf Camp (☎2787 0393, ⓦcrsurfschool.com) comes highly recommended for the quality of its instructors and the 2:1 student-teacher ratio, while Green Iguana Surf Camp (ⓦgreeniguanasurfcamp.com) offers lessons and rentals as well. **Swimming** is not a good idea, due to strong riptides; watch for the red flags marking the area, and only swim where lifeguards are present.

ARRIVAL AND INFORMATION

By bus Buses collect passengers along the main strip.
Destinations Palmar, where you can make connections to the Osa Peninsula (2 daily; 2hr); Quepos (5 daily; 2hr–2hr 40min); San Isidro de El General (2 daily, 6.15am & 2pm; 1hr 30min); Uvita (6–8 daily; 20min).
Bank A Banco de Costa Rica stands in the small plaza on Hwy-34, west of the turn-off into the village.
Tourist information There's a small information centre in the central plaza on your right-hand side as you enter the village.

ACCOMMODATION

Cabinas San Clemente On the main road just before the right turn down to the beach ☎ 2787 0158. Simple, clean

2

and secure wooden cabins, ranging from very basic to more spruced up. You pay more for private bathrooms, hot water, a/c and sea views. Dorms US$12, doubles US$68

Posada del Sol Halfway along the main strip ☎ 2787 0082. Adorable, secure guesthouse with just five rooms (including a microscopic single), and surfer-friendly touches, such as sinks for washing wetsuits and clothes lines to dry them. A laidback retreat rather than a party spot. US$32

Tortilla Flats On the beach ☎ 2787 0033. Popular surfers' hotel spread over several buildings. Brightly decorated rooms come with attached baths, and there's a hammock-festooned terrace upstairs. Crowds gather every evening at the beachfront restaurant/bar to party as sun goes down. US$37

EATING AND DRINKING

Chapy's Healthy Subs & Wraps Halfway along the main strip. The most gratifying lunch spot in the village, *Chapy's* does enormous focaccia sandwiches and wraps (from 3000c) with fillings ranging from smoked salmon and cream cheese to spicy hummus and grilled vegetables. Mon–Sat 9am–3pm.

Maracutú Middle of the main strip. Funky Italian restaurant offering mouthwatering vegan, vegetarian and fish dishes (3400–6000c), and surf videos on loop. Wed is reggae night, and on Tues there's an open jam session. Daily noon–11pm.

Soda Nanyoa Tucked away behind the town's fruit stand. You may have to queue for a table at this breezy, open-walled bar/restaurant, but it's probably the freshest orange juice you'll ever taste, and the best *pinto* breakfast (1500c) in town at blissfully low prices. BYOB at night. Daily 8am–9pm.

Tortilla Flats *Tortilla Flats* hotel, on the beach. The prime spot in town to watch the sun set while nursing a cool beer (happy hour 4–6pm), complemented by tacos and foot-long subs (from 2500c). Daily 8am–midnight.

UVITA

Tiny **UVITA**, 17km south of Dominical, and the gateway to **Parque Nacional Marino Ballena**, consists of a few houses, lodgings, shops and restaurants, scattered along a couple of roads. The area just off the Interamericana is referred to as "Uvita", while the street nearest to the beach is "Playa Uvita". You can reach the park by sticking to the main paved road that runs from the Interamericana right up to the entrance, or else by taking the dirt-and-gravel road that heads south (with *Flutterby House* signposted off it)

from that main paved road. The national park aside, the waves here attract novice **surfers**, and the vast deserted beaches make a change from those up north, where you find yourself fighting your fellow sunbathers for a small patch of sand.

ARRIVAL AND DEPARTURE

By bus Buses arrive and depart from the corner where the main road through Uvita meets the dirt road towards *Flutterby House*.

Destinations Dominical (6 daily; 20min); Palmar, where you can connect to Sierpe and Bahía Drake (3 daily; 1hr 15min); Quepos (2 daily; 3hr); San Isidro (2 daily; 1hr 30min).

ACCOMMODATION AND EATING

A couple of small grocery shops, a short walk apart, stock basic foodstuffs.

★ **Flutterby House** Follow the signposts from the main road through Uvita ☎ 2743 8221, ⓦ flutterbyhouse.com. Behind the gates is a ramshackle paradise of treehouses and basic cabins with mozzie nets, the lush grounds alive with surfers, slack rope walkers and dogs. Run by two Californian sisters, this place is as sustainable as it gets, with the innovative toilets due to be used to power the methane stoves in the large guest kitchen. There are surfboards for rent, a lively bar and a wonderfully laidback vibe. Cabins US$40

★ **Sabor Español** Just off the road to the beach, behind *Flutterby House* ☎ 8768 9160. Super-friendly Spanish-run restaurant serving flavourful standards such as gazpacho, *tortilla de patatas*, paella (two-person minimum), and outstanding dishes like whisky-flambéed shrimp. For dessert, there's the non-Spanish but very welcome crêpes with Nutella and ice cream. Mains from 4500c. Daily noon–4pm & 6.30–9.30pm.

Tucan Hotel On the main road just before the right turn down to the beach ☎ 2743 8140, ⓦ tucanhotel.com. A wonderful catch-all, where shoestringers can bed down in a tent, hammock, dorm or private rooms with a/c. The on-site café caters to vegetarians and vegans, and there's free coffee and a beach shuttle thrown in. Camping US$6, hammocks US$6, dorms US$13, doubles US$33

PARQUE NACIONAL MARINO BALLENA

The beautiful **Parque Nacional Marino Ballena** (April–Nov Tues–Sun 8am–4pm; Dec–March Tues–Sun 6am–6pm; US$10), covering the vast beaches that end in Punta Uvita – appropriately enough, given the name of the park, shaped like the tail of a whale – and the waters surrounding Isla Ballena, protects a variety of marine fauna, including bottlenose dolphins, turtles and **migrating humpback whales**. The vast main beach is a spectacular vantage point from which to watch the sunset, and there's good snorkelling to be had off Punta Uvita (best at low tide). During the humpback whale season (Aug–Oct & Dec–April), you may well see pods of the giants breaching off the coast, while turtle season (May–Oct) attracts hawksbill and olive ridley turtles that come to lay eggs on the beach.

ARRIVAL AND INFORMATION

Park entrances The main beach is accessible either from the official entrance next to the ranger stations at the end of the paved road through Uvita (parking US$2), or at the unofficial entrance at the end of the dirt road behind *Hutterby House* (see opposite).

Camping You can bed down at the basic free campsite (cold showers and toilets), 300m from the official park entrance, but you have to bring all supplies with you. US$3

Península de Osa and Golfo Dulce

Costa Rica's **Península de Osa** is the country's remotest and wildest region, and one of the most biologically diverse on earth, making it a hugely exciting destination for birdwatchers and animal lovers alike. While the peninsula's two main settlements – Puerto Jiménez and Agujitas– are linked to the rest of the country by ever-improving roads, they retain an off-the-grid feel, and getting around much of the peninsula is still an adventure. The region experiences **rain** even during the dry season, while during the wettest part of the year (Oct–Dec), when spectacular thunderstorms canter in from the Pacific, travel by road becomes tricky.

Curled around the western shores of the **Golfo Dulce** – a prime spot for spotting whales, whale sharks and other marine fauna – the Osa Peninsula is

covered in dense, pristine rainforest that is part of the **Parque Nacional Corcovado**, the country's top wildlife-spotting and hiking destination. On its western side is the remote and picturesque **Bahía Drake**, home to the village of **Agujitas** and only accessible by boat and rough road. More accessible, **Puerto Jiménez** is the peninsula's main town, sitting directly across the Golfo Dulce from **Golfito**.

GOLFITO

A former banana port, just 33km north of the Panamanian border, gently decaying **GOLFITO** stretches along the water at the cusp of the glorious Golfo Dulce. Golfito's history is intertwined with the **United Fruit Company**, which first set up here in 1938. When it pulled out in 1985 the town became one of the most unsavoury places in Costa Rica. These days, Golfito is a tax-free zone for imports from Panama, with a purpose-built **Zona Americana** – effectively a huge shopping centre – where Ticos come for 24-hour shopping sprees. The tax-free benefit does not extend to foreigners, who typically only come to Golfito if they are into sportfishing or heading straight to Panama from the Osa Peninsula (or vice versa). South of the relatively affluent Zona Americana, the **Pueblo Civil** offers a couple of places to stay if you must, a smattering of restaurants, and the *lancha* across the Golfo Dulce to Puerto Jiménez and the Osa Peninsula.

ARRIVAL AND DEPARTURE

By boat Boats link Puerto Jiménez and Golfito's tiny *muellecito* (little dock) behind *Hotel Golfito*. From Golfito there are five fast boats daily (7.30am, 10am, 1pm, 2.30pm & 3.15pm; 35min; 3000c) and one slow boat at 11.30am (2hr). Boats leave early if full, so get to the dock 20min before departure time (which you should confirm beforehand).

By bus Most services stop at the depot opposite the little park in the northern part of Golfito. Buy your onward ticket in advance, particularly for San José.

Destinations Neilly (hourly 6am–7pm; 1hr 30min); San José (2 daily, 5am & 1.30pm; 7hr; leaves from terminal near Muelle Bananero).

2

2

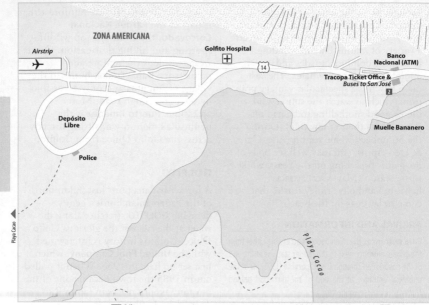

ACCOMMODATION AND EATING

Buenos Días Across the road from the *muellecito*. Cheerful American-diner-style café serving *gallo pinto*, hash browns and more for breakfast (from 2000c), and *casados* and burgers (from 3000c) the rest of the day. Daily 6am–10pm.

Cabinas Princesa del Golfito Opposite the Banco Nacional ☎ 2775 0442. Small and friendly with pleasantly decorated, good-value rooms that have a/c and wi-fi. <u>US$35</u>

Mar Y Luna 500m before the *pueblo civil* on the main road ☎ 2775 0901. Bright, very comfortable doubles with private bath, a/c, TV and sea views, and larger rooms with kitchenettes. It also boasts a renowned seafood restaurant with deck seats virtually on the sea. <u>US$45</u>

Restaurante Hong Kong In the Pueblo Civil ☎ 2775 2383. Renowned for its excellent (and cheap) chow mein dishes (3000c) and a magnet for expat yachters: despite the completely forgettable interior, it serves up some of the best Chinese food to be found in the south. Daily 11am–10pm.

Samoa del Sur Attached to the hotel *Samoa del Sur*, on the main road between the Zona Americana and Pueblo Civil. The beachside bar and restaurant at the *Samoa del Sur* hotel is a pleasant spot for an evening beer or meal, with a menu featuring seafood, such as *ceviche* (7000c) and pizza (from 3500c). Bear in mind that it can get rowdy later in the evening (it's the bar of choice for US marines on shore leave). Daily 11am–midnight.

PUERTO JIMÉNEZ

Most visitors to Parque Nacional Corcovado set off from the tiny town of **PUERTO JIMÉNEZ**, the main gateway for hiking in the park. You're likely to see wildlife in the town itself – from nesting macaws and visiting monkeys to crocodiles in the mangroves. Jiménez has plenty of **activities** of its own to keep you busy for a few days, among them kayaking on the Golfo Dulce, boat trips with dolphin- and whale-spotting possibilities, and day-excursions to various community projects (see opposite).

From Jiménez, *colectivos* (trucks) run to Carate, 43km southwest, from where it's possible to hike straight into Corcovado (see p.188).

ARRIVAL AND DEPARTURE

By bus The bus station is at the western side of the village, a block from the football field.

Destinations San Isidro (2 daily; 5hr); San José (1–2 daily; 8hr).

By car Note that Puerto Jiménez has the only petrol station on the entire Península de Osa, so be sure to fill up before you leave.

By colectivo *Colectivos* depart one block south of the bus

REFUGIO NACIONAL DE VIDA SILVESTRE GOLFITO

PUEBLO CIVIL

Supermarket

Land-Sea
Tours

Muellecito
(Boats to Playa Cacao
& Puerto Jiménez)

Parquecito

Golfo
Dulce

EATING
Buenos Días	2
Restaurante	
Hong Kong	1
Samoa del Sur	3

ACCOMMODATION
Cabinas Princesa	
del Golfito	2
Mar Y Luna	1

GOLFITO

station to Carate (US$9; about 2hr) twice daily (except Sundays in dry season) at 6am and 1.30pm.
By taxi Local 4WD taxis can drive up to four people to Carate for US$80.

INFORMATION AND TOURS

Osa Corcovado On Hwy-245, one block south of the football field ☎ 8632 8150, ⓦ soldeosa.com. One of the newer outfitters in town, Osa Corcovado run a bewildering range of tours; chances are if there's a remote corner of Osa you want to see, they can take you there. Options include birdwatching (4hr; US$40), surfing lessons at Cabe Matapalo (2–3hr; US$40) and sunset kayak tours to see dolphins (3hr; US$40).
Osa Wild Run by experienced tropical biologist Ifi, Osa Wild (☎ 2735 5848, ⓦ osawildtravel.com) is the best source of information on Parque Nacional Corcovado. Guided hikes in the park are arranged (from U$55/person/ day), as are day-trips to community-oriented initiatives around Osa, such as a local coffee farm.
Tourist information The rangers at the Oficina de Área de Conservación Osa, opposite the airstrip (☎ 2735 5036, Mon–Fri 8am–noon & 1–4pm), can answer questions about the national park, recommend local guides, and arrange accommodation and meals at Sirena (see p.190).

ACCOMMODATION

Wherever you want to stay, make sure to book in advance in the dry season.

★ **Bello Horizonte Jungle Hostel** 3km southwest of Puerto Jiménez ☎ 8834 4963. In a lush jungle setting, this superb hostel boasts not only its own organic farm, but also all sorts of sustainable practices, a great common area and bar and walking trails nearby. The owners run a twice-daily shuttle to Jiménez. Camping US$12, dorms US$15, doubles US$35
Cabinas Back Packers Half a block west of main supermarket ☎ 2735 5181. Run by a friendly Colombian, this sparkling-clean budget spot features tiled doubles (some with I Vs) with shared facilities, plus a large kitchen for guest use and free wi-fi. US$20
★ **Cabinas Marcelina** On the main street, near the Catholic church ☎ 2735 5007. This comfortable pink guesthouse is an idyllic hideaway from the dusty streets: all rooms are en suite, and most look onto the sweet breakfast garden filled with tropical flowers. US$45
Cabinas The Corner A block west of the main street and a block south of the bus station ☎ 2735 5328, ⓦ jimenezhotels .com/cabinasthecorner. In addition to the plain fan-cooled four- and five-bed dorms are a couple of rudimentary doubles with private baths – all with free wi-fi. It's a good place to meet other travellers, and the *dueña* is a keen – and vocal – conservationist. Dorms US$6, doubles US$12
Hotel Oro Verde Just off the main road ☎ 2735 5241. Rooms are somewhat musty, with optional hot water and a/c. Bring earplugs, as it can be noisy. Try to nab one of the best rooms with terrace access. In-house tour guide Josh is bubbling with enthusiasm for the national park. US$25

2

San José & Colectivo stop

PUERTO JIMÉNEZ
Golfo Dulce

Jetty for boats to Golfito

EATING & DRINKING
Cafetería Monka	2
Jade Luna	5
Pizzamail.it	1
Restaurante Carolina	3
Soda Veleria	4

Football Field

Bus Terminal
Police
Colectivos
Supermarket
Osa Corcovado
Main Supermarket

N

Osa Wild

Sansa Office
Iglesia Católica de Puerto Jiménez

Banco Nacional (ATM)

Puerto Jiménez Airport

Oficina de Área de Conservación Osa

0   200
metres

ACCOMMODATION
Bello Horizonte Jungle Hostel	5
Cabinas Back Packers	1
Cabinas The Corner	2
Cabinas Marcelina	4
Hotel Oro Verde	3

5 (3km), Carate & Parque Nacional Corcovado

EATING

Cafetería Monka On the main street. The best place for breakfast in town, serving excellent coffee and granola with yoghurt and *huevos rancheros* (Mexican-style eggs with salsa) alongside traditional *gallo pinto*, and sandwiches for lunch. Mains 2700c. Daily 7am–noon.

★**Jade Luna** On the main street. Legendary local ice cream; flavours range from mint Oreo to *dulce de leche* with macadamia (2000c/pot). Daily 10am–5pm.

★**Pizzamail.it** By the football field. Superb, authentic Italian thin-crust pizzas and calzones, with imported ingredients that you may have been hankering for, such as olives and capers. Even the smallest pizza is plenty for one person. Mains from 4000c. Daily 4–10.30pm.

Restaurante Carolina Main street, a block and a half south of the football field. A catch-all restaurant popular with visitors, guides and locals, offering grilled meats, soups and *casados*. Mains from 2800c. Daily 7am–10pm.

Soda Veleria On the main street. Friendly inexpensive *soda*, popular with locals, serving large portions of home-cooked *casados* and fresh juices. Mains from 2000c. Daily noon–9pm.

DIRECTORY

Bank Banco Nacional is on the main road in town.
Health centres The Red Cross (☎ 2735 5109) and medical clinic (☎ 2735 5203) are opposite each other on the side road that leads to the bus station.
Petrol The peninsula's lone petrol station, Bomba Osa, is at the bend of the main road on the south side of the centre.

BAHÍA DRAKE

BAHÍA DRAKE (named after Sir Francis Drake who passed this way in 1579) is one of the most stunning – and remote – areas in Costa Rica, with fiery-orange Pacific sunsets and the blue wedge of **Isla del Caño** floating just off the coast. **Agujitas**, the village, consists of just two streets – the main one running uphill, and the other roughly parallel to the beach. It's a wonderful base for the majority of travellers who come to the area to explore **Parque Nacional Corcovado**.

WHAT TO SEE AND DO

Corcovado's **San Pedrillo** entrance is within hiking distance from Agujitas – 10km (4–5hr each way) along the coastal trail. Upon your return, you can relax in some excellent budget digs (or stay in one of the local upscale ecolodges) and sample surprisingly varied cuisine.

Isla del Caño, 20km west of Agujitas, is one of Costa Rica's top snorkelling and diving destinations, and diving/snorkelling trips are easily arranged through your lodgings. You can also take to the water of **Río Agujitas**, easily reachable from the village; kayaking is a good way to spot the abundant birdlife, as well as caimans. Finally, Bahía Drake is the launchpad for ultra-popular boat trips to **La Sirena**, at the heart of Parque Nacional Corcovado, from where you can go on guided wildlife-spotting rambles in the park without the need for any strenuous hiking (see p.189).

ARRIVAL AND DEPARTURE

By plane The Drake airstrip, 2km north of Agujitas, is served by daily flights from San José with NatureAir and Sansa.

By car and bus There are few bus connections to Agujitas. Your best bet would be to connect with the 11am or 5pm bus that departs from the hamlet of La Palma de Osa on the Golfo Dulce and passes through Rincón de Osa; the bus stops at the end of the road in Agujitas by the beach.

By boat Speedboats ply their way through mangrove channels and along the ocean between Agujitas and Sierpe, a village reachable by minor road off the Interamericana. Once in Sierpe, make your way to the waterfront *Restaurante Las Vegas* (☎ 2788 1082), from where a boatman can take you the 30km downriver on a *lancha* to Bahía Drake (1hr 30min). The going rate for a one-way trip to Drake is about US$15–25/person or around US$60–85/boatload (maximum usually eight). Some hotel *lanchas* will take independent travellers if there's room, but be sure to arrive early; the first regularly scheduled *lancha* departs at 11am. Note that owing to fierce afternoon tides, the second and last scheduled *lancha* leaves around 3pm. If you're driving to Sierpe, it's possible to park your car at *Las Vegas* during your stay at Bahía Drake.

By car Rainfall can make the road into Agujitas impassable at just about any time of year; if you plan on driving to the village, call your lodging first to find out the latest conditions.

INFORMATION AND TOURS

Tourist information ⍟ gringocurtandticoesteban.com.

Fundación Corcovado ☎ 2297 3013, ⍟ corcovadofoundation.org. A volunteer organization set up to maintain the park, improve local amenities and rally against encroaching developers. The beachfront office doubles as an unofficial tourist information office.

Tours Most lodgings offer tours, from snorkelling to horseriding, for US$75–100. Corcovado Expeditions, set back from the beach just next to the Fundación Corcovado (☎ 2775 0916, ⍟ corcovadoexpeditions.net), has trips to Isla del Caño and Corcovado (both US$75), and mangrove and canopy tours. Tracie the "Bug Lady" runs popular nocturnal insect tours (⍟ thenighttour.com; US$35); advance reservations highly recommended.

Banks There are no banks or ATMs in Drake. Some lodgings accept credit cards.

ACCOMMODATION

There are many upscale ecolodges in the Bahía Drake area, with budget accommodation concentrated in Agujitas village. Most places offer wi-fi.

Cabinas Jade Mar In the village ☎ 8384 6681, ⍟ jademarcr.com. A good place to stay if you want to get a taste of local life on a budget, with pleasant, if basic, *cabinas*, kept very clean by the informative Doña Martha. All cabins have private bathrooms (cold water only), and the meals are hearty. Inexpensive tours to Corcovado and Isla del Caño are also available. US$23

Cabinas Murillo On the road running parallel to the beach ☎ 8892 7702, ⍟ drakecorcovadocabins.com. Centrally located, this quiet, Tico-run place offers one of the best bargains in the village. It's worth paying a little extra for the rooms higher up the hillside offering great views of the bay. Guest kitchen and free wi-fi available. Doubles US$30, cabins US$40

Casita Corcovado Up from the road running parallel to the beach ☎ 2775 0627 or ☎ 8996 9987, ⍟ casitacorcovado.com. Up on a bluff, this attractive, ecologically sound three-bedroom cottage offers splendid bay views and hammocks swaying in the sea breeze. Rooms can be rented individually, or the cottage as a whole, and Jamie and Craig make you feel very welcome. Substantial discounts for solo travellers. Doubles US$70, cottage US$175

★**Hotel Finca Maresia** 2km outside Agujitas ☎ 2775 0279, ⍟ fincamaresia.com. On undulating land surrounded by tropical forest, this is a delightful collection of bungalows with orthopaedic mattresses, private baths and balconies, plus simpler rooms with shared baths.

2

There's a wonderfully serene vibe and staff can arrange pick-ups and excellent tours. Rates include breakfast. Doubles US$40, bungalows US$90

Pura Vida Bahía Drake In the centre of the village ☎ 8720 0801, ⓦ puravidadrakebay.com. Locally known as "Martina's Place", this cheerful yellow house offers dorm beds, a fan-cooled double and an apartment for up to four people, as well as a glamping option – double beds set up in large tents outside. German and English spoken. Camping US$22, dorms US$10, double US$30, apartment US$60

EATING

Empanadas Argentinas Main street. True to its name, this friendly place serves up Argentine-style *empanadas* (2000c), as well as more substantial mains. This is also as close as Drake gets to having a nightlife, with the Argentine musician owners occasionally taking to the tiny stage. Daily 4–10pm.

★**Gringo Curt's Seafood and Visitor Center** Main street. This friendly spot does only a handful of dishes, but what a handful! Expect gargantuan portions of fish tacos, an obligatory pasta dish for vegetarians, and the tour de force – a slab of beautifully seasoned fish, baked in a banana leaf and complete with sautéed veggies – a rarity in Costa Rica. A main is enough for two people. Mains 4500–7000c. Daily 11am–9pm.

Restaurante Jade Mar Main street. This open-sided strip-lit place is always busy with locals and visitors. Its catch-all menu features steaks, fresh seafood (including lobster), pizza and pasta. Mains from 4500c.

Soda Mar y Bosque Main street. This lovely, open-air *soda*, run by the descendants of the original Bahía Drake settlers, overlooks a butterfly-filled garden. It's great all day: for breakfast go for a delicious juice or smoothie to wash down your pancakes or *pinto* (2000c); the more substantial *casados* (2500c plus) are equally good. Esteban, the son of the owner, offers informative trips into Corcovado. Mon–Sat 7am–9pm.

PARQUE NACIONAL CORCOVADO

Created in 1975, **PARQUE NACIONAL CORCOVADO** (daily 8am–4pm; US$10; ☎ 2735 5036) protects a fascinating and complex area of land, which houses 2.5 percent of the world's total biodiversity. It's a beautiful park, with deserted beaches, waterfalls, high canopy trees and the best **wildlife-spotting** opportunities in the country. Exploring Corcovado, however, is not for the faint-hearted, due to the heat, distances involved and natural hazards. The **terrain** includes exposed beaches, rivers to be forded, mangroves, *holillo* (palm) swamps and dense forest, although most of it is at lowland elevations. **Trails** are relatively easy to follow, particularly in the dry season, though some hikers have been known to get lost. The coastal areas of the park receive around 3800mm of **rain** a year, with precipitation rising to about 5000mm in the higher elevations of the interior. There is a dry season (Dec–March), but the inland lowland areas, especially those around the lagoon, can be amazingly **hot** during this period.

TREKKING IN CORCOVADO

Don't underestimate the difficulty of hiking in 100 percent humidity and temperatures of at least 26°C (without the benefit of the sea breeze on the Los Patos trail). Plan to hike early – though not before dawn, due to snakes – and shelter during the hottest part of the day. Rangers at each *puesto* always know how many people are on a given trail, and how long those hikers are expected to be. If you are late getting back, they'll go looking for you. Few rangers speak English, so if hiking independently, some knowledge of **Spanish** is essential.

Essentials include sunscreen, insect repellent, a hat and a waterproof bag for your clothes, as you'll have to cross several rivers. Take plenty of **water** – and we mean plenty; several hikers have died in the park due to dehydration – and food; stock up either in Jiménez or Drake. Don't leave any trash in the park or at the ranger stations, as waste is a problem.

Within the park, all ranger stations have camping areas, drinking water, information, toilets and telephone or radio; La Sirena even has (slow) wi-fi. Wherever you enter, jot down the details of the **marea** (tide tables), which are posted at ranger stations. You'll need to cross most of the rivers at low tide; to do otherwise is dangerous. Rangers can advise on conditions.

Finally, although unlikely, there is some chance of getting attacked by wild **animals**. If peccaries display threatening behaviour, climb a tree; if a puma attacks, make yourself as big as possible, shout and fight.

WHAT TO SEE AND DO

The park has three main trails: the most popular starts in the village of **Carate**, 43km southwest of Jiménez, and runs to the **La Sirena** ranger station at the heart of Corcovado via the **La Leona** ranger station, 2.5km from Carate and one of three official entrances to the park. From Bahía Drake, it's a 10km hike to the **San Pedrillo** ranger station – the park's western entrance. From here there's a popular 25km trail to La Sirena, which at the time of writing was closed indefinitely. Finally, there's an 18km trail from the **Los Patos** ranger station to La Sirena.

La Leona to La Sirena

Although the predominantly flat 16km trail from **La Leona ranger station to Sirena** runs mostly inland from the beach, you have to walk on several exposed stretches of beach, including the 2.5km walk from Carate to La Leona, so get an early start. The hike takes 7–8 hours and you are likely to spot such wildlife as scarlet macaws that roost in the coastal trees, monkeys – particularly white-faced capuchins and spider monkeys – and even tapirs and peccaries. There have also been several recent spottings of pumas near La Sirena.

La Sirena to San Pedrillo

The trail from **La Sirena to San Pedrillo** is the toughest of them all. The trail was closed indefinitely at the time of writing, following the deaths of several hikers, but if it reopens, get the latest information from the La Sirena rangers before you set out.

A large part of the 25km stretch runs along the exposed beach, and the two-day hike is exhausting. You have to take more than enough water to last you, as well as a tent, sleeping bag and mosquito net. It is recommended to walk much of the beach trail at night, as the heat during the day must not be underestimated. There are three rivers to ford, the most dangerous just 1km beyond La Sirena. **Río Sirena** is the deepest of all the rivers on the peninsula and can only be crossed with caution at low tide; the brackish water at the mouth of the estuary is home to bull sharks – an aggressive species that occasionally attack humans – and crocodiles. Beyond the third river – La Llorona – the trail splits in two; most hikers follow the shorter beachside trail to San Pedrillo, while the other route runs inland and adds 2km to your hike.

La Palma to Los Patos

The small hamlet of **La Palma**, 24km north of Puerto Jiménez and linked to it by bus, is the starting point for the walk to the **Los Patos** *puesto*. It's a 14km hike, much of it through hot lowland terrain (though it might be possible to arrange a 4WD taxi to take you some of the way).

There are numerous river crossings along the trail, and you need to be careful not to miss the correct turn to the *puesto*. To get to Los Patos from Jiménez, drive 10km north and take the second left, a dirt track, signed to El Tigre and Dos Brazos. Taxis cost around US$20.

Los Patos to La Sirena

The trail across the peninsula from **Los**

WHO'S WHO OF CORCOVADO'S WILDLIFE

Felines All of Costa Rica's cats are represented in Corcovado: the big ones – jaguar, puma, ocelot – and the little ones: jaguarundi, margay and oncilla.

Monkeys You are more likely to spot the white-faced capuchins and spider monkeys, but howlers and squirrel monkeys also reside here.

Other mammals Baird's tapir is the most impressive of the herbivores, but you may also see peccaries, deer, sloths, and several species of anteater, including the ultra-rare and elusive silky (or pygmy) anteater.

Creepy crawlies Insects to beware of are the bullet ant, army ant, tarantula hawk (a wasp with an extremely painful sting) and ticks (though they don't carry Lyme disease here).

Reptiles Besides crocodiles and spectacled caiman that dwell in some of the rivers, you may come across the extremely venomous fer-de-lance snake.

2

INTO PANAMA: PASO CANOAS

The only reason to come to **PASO CANOAS** is to cross the border (usually open 6am–10pm) into Panama. If you're driving, you may find yourself waiting in queues. If taking the international TRACOPA or Tica Bus service, your processing will be quick. For travel into Panama, pick up a **tourist card** (US$5) – check also visa requirements (see p.519). You may be required to show proof of onward travel from Panama.

There are direct Tica Bus services from San José to Panama City (15hr) and daily TRACOPA services between San José and **David**, the first city of any size in Panama, about 90min beyond the border. Buses run from the Panamanian border bus terminal hourly until 5pm. From David it's easy to pick up local services to Panama City.

Patos to La Sirena is 18km long. It is recommended that you hike from Los Patos to La Sirena to get the toughest part out of the way first. It's a demanding walk, with two river tributaries to ford and steep uphills and downhills for the first 6km, taking you into high, wet and dense secondary forest. The remaining 12km or so is flat and easy to follow, and since you're passing through the heart of Corcovado, there's a good chance of seeing some of the park's elusive mammals (or at least their tracks).

ARRIVAL AND DEPARTURE

By air Alfa Romeo Aero Taxi (☎2735 5353, ⓦalfa romeoair.com) is a charter service connecting Puerto Jiménez, Bahía Drake, Golfito, Carate and La Sirena; flights cost around US$100.

★TREAT YOURSELF

Danta Lodge 8km from Los Patos ☎2735 1111, ⓦdantalodge.com. If you want to stay near Los Patos and start the hike to La Sirena early, *Danta Lodge* is an outstanding choice. A friendly, family-run lodge outside La Palma, *Danta* was built entirely from sustainable materials and features intricate woodwork and handmade furniture throughout. Accommodation is in attractive rooms or bungalows, the latter 200m from the main lodge. Rates include breakfast; hearty lunches (6500c) and dinners (8000c) are served in the communal open-air dining area, where there is wi-fi. They rent out horses for the 2hr trip to Los Patos, and lead several well-run tours, including kayaking in Golfo Dulce and night walks on their 70 hectares. Doubles US$122, bungalows US$152

By boat There are regular boat day-trips from Bahía Drake to La Sirena; you can take the boat one-way and then hike from La Sirena to La Palma or Carate, though you will need to get a permit from the park office in Puerto Jiménez.

By colectivo and 4WD taxi Daily *colectivos* run from Puerto Jiménez to Carate (see p.184) along a bumpy, rutted road. If you want to get to Carate earlier in the morning, share a 4WD taxi from Jiménez with other hikers (see p.185).

INFORMATION

Entry and reservations Unless you're coming as part of a tour package, in the dry months, at least, you should reserve at least several days in advance – and ideally longer – with SINAC (☎2735 5036, ⓔpncorcovado @gmail.com). You'll have to specify your group size and dates in advance, plus any meals you require at Sirena (see below); you can do all this at the Oficina de Área de Conservación Osa office in Jiménez (see p.186). You'll be asking the rangers for a lot of crucial information and few, if any, speak English. Bring a phrase book if you're not fluent.

Health Night walks in the jungle are forbidden – there is no way to get you out of the park after dark, and were you to be bitten by a venomous snake, you would die.

Tour operators To increase your chances of seeing wildlife, it's well worth investing in the services of a guide: rates are around US$55/person/day. Osa Wild are particularly good (see p.185).

ACCOMMODATION AND EATING

Book meals in advance at the La Sirena canteen, or bring your own utensils, portable stove and fuel.

Camping You can camp at all the ranger stations. Bring tent, mosquito net, sleeping bag, food and water. US$4

La Sirena accommodation block La Sirena ranger station. Musty dorms and old foam mattresses are provided, but no bedding. US$15

La Sirena canteen La Sirena ranger station. You can eat expensive but good meals here (lunch US$20, dinner US$25); book in advance at the Jiménez office.

PACIFIC SURFING

El Salvador

HIGHLIGHTS

❶ **Pacific beaches** Sample the surf or lounge on the sands. **See p.217**

❷ **Alegría** A scenic mountaintop town with a volcanic lake and stunning views. **See p.231**

❸ **Suchitoto** Stunning lake views in the country's finest colonial town. **See p.240**

❹ **Parque Nacional El Imposible** Pristine mountain forest; a haven for wildlife. **See p.249**

❺ **Ruta de las Flores** Winding mountain road and artistic towns. **See p.250**

❻ **Lago de Coatepeque** Awe-inspiring crater lake hemmed in by volcanoes. **See p.261**

HIGHLIGHTS ARE MARKED ON THE MAP ON P.193

ROUGH COSTS

Daily budget Basic US$26/occasional treat US$40

Drink Coffee US$0.75, Pilsner beer US$1.50

Food *Pupusa* US$0.50

Hostel/budget hotel US$12/US$20

Travel San Salvador–San Miguel (138km) by bus: 2hr 30min, US$2.50

FACT FILE

Population 6.3 million

Language Spanish

Currency US dollar (US$)

Capital San Salvador (population: 2.4 million)

International phone code ☏ 503

Time zone GMT -6hr

Introduction

The smallest and most densely populated country in Central America, El Salvador is also the region's least visited nation. Known less for its world-class surf, volcanoes and stunning forest reserves than the vicious civil war it suffered in the 1980s and gang violence since the 1990s, the country has long struggled to gain tourists' trust. Those who do make it here, though, are well rewarded by the hospitality and honesty of its proud inhabitants and its sheer physical beauty. Almost every journey in El Salvador yields photogenic vistas: towering volcanoes, gorgeous colonial towns, rolling coffee plantations and rugged mountain chains.

Booming **San Salvador** is one of Central America's most developed cities, boasting an enticing spread of galleries, museums, restaurants and sophisticated nightlife. Within easy reach are the fascinating ruins at **Joya de Cerén** and a glorious sweep of the **Pacific coast**, including surfers' favourite **Costa del Bálsamo**. Some beaches offer true seclusion, while others receive the best waves in all of Central America.

Further east is the turtle-rich haven of **El Cuco** and the idyllic islands of the **Golfo de Fonseca**, while inland the small but affable city of **San Vicente** gives access to delightful artistic villages like floral **Alegría**, high above the central plains. Larger **San Miguel** hosts one of the biggest carnivals in Central America,

while the **Ruta de Paz** leads north to the towns of **Perquín** and **El Mozote**, sites of the hardest conflicts of the civil war and some of the only places in the country to make any memorial to it.

In the west, the laidback grandeur of **Santa Ana** lies between the exquisite **cloudforests** of Montecristo and El Imposible. For climbers, the nearby **volcanic peaks** of Izalco and Cerro Verde provide good hiking, while at their base is the mesmerizing deep-blue crater lake of **Coatepeque**; for gastronomes, the **Ruta de las Flores** features **Juayúa**'s famous food festival, as well as other blossom-smothered mountain towns.

The north, though rough and wild, hosts the still unspoiled colonial gem of **Suchitoto**, above the glorious crater lake of Suchitlán. Spotlessly clean and beautifully restored **Metapán** offers visitors a glimpse of rural life at its finest while **La Palma**, near the Honduran border, is famous for its naïf crafts, producing wooden handicrafts, pottery and hammocks.

WHEN TO VISIT

The **dry season** (Nov–March) is the best time to visit El Salvador: northeasterly winds make for less humid air, more accessible dirt roads, sandier beaches and less daunting waves. Humidity builds throughout late March and April into the **wet season** (May–Oct), which is fed by Pacific low-pressure systems and sees clear mornings cloud over to late afternoon and overnight downpours. This is the season for big waves, flowering orchids and spectacular lightning storms, but travel can be difficult and flooding and hurricanes are not unknown. **Temperatures** are always regulated by altitude.

CHRONOLOGY

Pre-8000 BC Paleo-Indian cave dwellers around Corinto are the first known inhabitants.

Pre-1200 BC Maya arrive from Guatemala.

900 AD Maya culture mysteriously collapses.

900–1400 AD Waves of Nahuat-speaking settlers, later dubbed "Pipils", migrate from Mexico, establishing seats of power at Cihuatán, Tehuacán and Cuscatlán.

1524 Pedro de Alvarado crosses the Río Paz to conquer the area for Spain; he names the region "El Salvador" (literally "The Saviour"), in honour of Jesus.

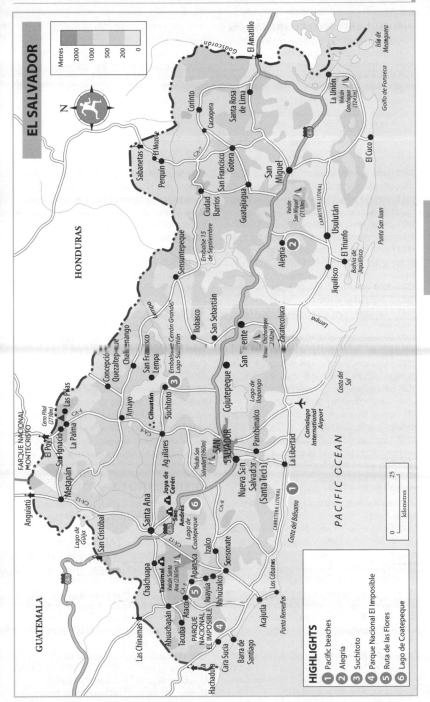

EL SALVADOR

Metres
2000
1000
500
200
0

N

HONDURAS

GUATEMALA

PARQUE NACIONAL MONTECRISTO
Cerro Pital (2730m)

Anguiatú
Metapán
Lago de Güija
San Cristóbal
Chalchuapa
Las Chinamas
Ahuachapán
Tacuba
Ataco
Juayúa
PARQUE NACIONAL EL IMPOSIBLE
Cara Sucia
Barra de Santiago
Punta Remedios
Acajutla
Nahuizalco
Sonsonate
Izalco
Apaneca
Tazumal
Volcán Santa Ana (2365m)
Santa Ana
Lago de Coatepeque
San Andrés
Joya de Cerén
Volcán San Salvador (1960m)
Nueva San Salvador (Santa Tecla)
SAN SALVADOR
La Libertad
Costa del Bálsamo
CARRETERA LITORAL

El Poy
San Ignacio
La Palma
Las Pilas
CA-4
Concepción Quezaltepeque
Chalatenango
Lempa
San Francisco Lempa
Amayo
Cituatán
Suchitoto
Embalse Cerrón Grande
Lago Suchitlán
Ilobasco
San Sebastián
Cojutepeque
Lago de Ilopango
San Vicente
Volcán Chichontepec (2182m)
Zacatecoluca
Panchimalco
Comalapa International Airport
Costa del Sol

Sabanetas
El Mozote
Perquín
Ciudad Barrios
Sensuntepeque
Embalse 15 de Septiembre
San Francisco Gotera
Guatajiagua
Alegría
Volcán San Miguel (2130m)
San Miguel
Usulután
El Triunfo
Jiquilisco
Bahía de Jiquilisco
Punta San Juan
CARRETERA LITORAL
Lempa

Goascorán
El Amatillo
Corinto
Cacaopera
Santa Rosa de Lima
La Unión
Volcán Conchagua (1243m)
Golfo de Fonseca
Isla de Meanguera
El Cuco

CA-7
CA-4
CA-12
CA-8

PACIFIC OCEAN

0   25
kilometres

3

HIGHLIGHTS
1 Pacific beaches
2 Alegría
3 Suchitoto
4 Parque Nacional El Imposible
5 Ruta de las Flores
6 Lago de Coatepeque

3

OVERLAND INTO EL SALVADOR

The main border crossings with **Honduras** are in the east at El Amatillo (see box, p.396), convenient for connections to Tegucigalpa, and at El Poy (see box, p.406) in the northwest.

The main border with **Guatemala** is at La Hachadura (see box, p.249) in the southwest, best for the Pacific beaches and used by international buses from Mexico. Another Guatemala crossing is at Las Chinamas (see box, p.256), near Ahuachapán, used by international buses from Guatemala City. The crossing at Anguiatú (see box, p.338), in the north near Metapán, is used by buses from Esquipulas. A smaller crossing at San Cristóbal (see box, p.338) is close to the city of Santa Ana. Note that you should not be charged a border entry fee, since your Honduran or Guatemalan tourist card is valid in El Salvador (this also applies for leaving El Salvador).

1600–1800 Hacienda feudalism creates a rich Spanish ruling elite and indentured indigenous labour force.

1811 Father José Delgado leads an unsuccessful revolution against the Spanish.

1821 Central American provinces, including El Salvador, declare independence from Spain, but are annexed by Mexico.

1823 Central American countries win independence from Mexico under Salvadoreño Manuel José Arce; Federal Republic of Central America is created.

1840–1931 Coffee becomes main export crop; private interests dominate government.

1841 El Salvador declares independence; Federal Republic is dissolved.

1873 Massive earthquake on March 19 destroys the last vestiges of colonial San Salvador; it gets hit again in 1917.

1927 Liberal candidate Pío Romero Bosque is elected president, takes steps to dismantle oligarchies.

1929 Economy collapses in response to Wall Street crash; Liberal plans for democracy derailed.

1931 General Maximiliano Martínez seizes power in coup, starting fifty years of military rule.

1932 Communist-led rebellion sees thousands killed. Government response is a week-long massacre, "La Matanza".

1961 Right-wing National Conciliation Party (PCN) comes to power after a military coup.

1969 El Salvador attacks Honduras in the six-day "Soccer War" (over immigration and land reform, but sparked by a football match).

1972 Reformist José Napoleón Duarte wins presidential elections; but he is immediately deposed and exiled by the military.

1977 As many as three hundred unarmed civilians shot in front of world media while protesting in San Salvador.

1980 Leftist opposition parties and guerrilla groups form the FMLN-FDR, while right-wing death squads wage terror campaigns. Archbishop Óscar Romero is assassinated; full-scale civil war breaks out.

1981 US pumps aid to military to stem "spread of Communism", despite its links to death squads. El Mozote massacre (see box, p.238). Death squad leader and all-round pathological killer Roberto D'Aubuisson founds ARENA (National Republican Alliance).

1984 Duarte defeats D'Aubuisson to become first civilian president since 1932 (his campaign is financed by the CIA), but he fails to stop human rights abuses by the army.

1986 Another massive quake devastates the nation; between 1000 and 1500 people are killed.

1989 Fighting intensifies; San Salvador is occupied, and six Jesuit priests are assassinated. ARENA candidate Alfredo Cristiani elected president.

1992 Peace accords finally signed, presided over by the UN and the Catholic Church.

2001 US dollar replaces the colón. Two earthquakes kill more than 1000 people and destroy infrastructure.

2005 CA-4 free-trade agreement signed between El Salvador, Honduras, Guatemala and Nicaragua.

2009 Mauricio Funes, ex-journalist and leader of FMLN party, wins presidential elections, ending twenty years of ARENA rule.

2012 Truce between rival criminal gangs (*maras*), the Mara Salvatrucha and Calle 18, results in a 40 percent reduction in crime and a dramatic drop in murder rates.

2014 The country courts international controversy over its strict abortion laws, following the incarceration of a woman who lost her child to a miscarriage.

ARRIVAL AND DEPARTURE

Visitors **flying** to El Salvador will arrive at **Comalapa International Airport (SAL)**, about 50km southeast of San Salvador. The main hub for TACA Airlines (⊕taca .com), it's one of the busiest in Central America, with daily flights from numerous North American cities (principally Dallas, Houston, LA, Miami, New York and Mexico City) as well as the rest of Central America, South America and the Caribbean. The only direct service from Europe is the Iberia (⊕iberia.com) flight from Madrid.

You can enter El Salvador by land from Guatemala and Honduras (see box above). Almost all **international buses** arrive in San Salvador (see p.210), and chicken buses run from border crossings to nearby towns in the daylight hours.

The only international **boats** run from Nicaragua across the Golfo de Fonseca to La Unión (see box, p.228).

VISAS

Visas for El Salvador are not currently required for citizens of the UK, US, Canada, Australia, Ireland, Israel, New Zealand, South Africa and most other European countries. Nationals of Australia, Canada and the US will have to pay a US$10 **entry fee** at the airport. Under the **CA-4 agreement**, there is one tourist card for El Salvador, Guatemala, Honduras and Nicaragua (see box, p.30) – make sure you get a ninety-day allowance rather than a thirty-day one. If you are applying for a formal extension, visit the Dirección General de Migración y Extranjería (Sección de Visas y Prórrogas), 9A Calle Poniente, at 15 Avenida Norte, in the Centro de Gobierno, San Salvador (Mon–Fri 8am–4pm). See @migracion .gob.sv for details.

GETTING AROUND

El Salvador's only form of public transport is the **bus**, which is without doubt the cheapest way to travel. The size of the country, and the efficient road layout around the Carretera Panamericana, mean that you can get from one point to another within the country in less than a day. Most long-distance journeys route through San Salvador, often requiring at least one change of bus if travelling to smaller towns.

BY BUS

Buses are subsidized and extremely cheap: an *especial* bus from San Salvador to Sonsonate (1hr 30min) costs just US$1.30. Centrally placed San Salvador, with its three busy bus terminals (see p.210), is the hub of all bus travel in the country. All other towns of any significant size have at least one bus terminal. Services run in daylight hours, with rare exceptions going just after dusk, so plan your overnight stops carefully.

All routes are covered by the same "**chicken buses**" you'll see in other Central American countries (see box, p.32). More comfortable, **modern buses** are gradually being introduced to major routes, dubbed *especial* and often air-conditioned, though these are less frequent. Best of all are the **coach-style** *super especial* buses that run between San Salvador and San Miguel, which are air-conditioned and rarely stop en route (though quality often varies in both *especial* and *super especial* classes). No buses have toilets on board (that work, at least). In more rural areas, particularly roads where the large buses cannot pass, **pick-up trucks** with cages on the back are the most common form of travel. These are hailed from the roadside and you pay the driver when you dismount (never more than US$0.50).

By shuttle bus and international bus

Special **shuttle bus** services (typically minibuses) for travellers are nowhere near as common in El Salvador as, say, Guatemala, but you'll find several companies running between El Tunco and nearby beaches to San Salvador, the airport and direct to Antigua in Guatemala. If you're looking for a more luxurious ride between San Salvador and Santa Ana, contact Tica Bus or King Quality (see box, p.210), which usually make a stop in Santa Ana on their way to and from Guatemala City – this will cost around US$35, though.

BY TAXI

Licensed **taxis** in El Salvador are yellow and black. They can be hailed or found in large towns and cities around the main plazas, shopping centres or bus stations. There are no meters, so **fares** should be agreed before you set off. Expect to pay US$5–6 for most trips within San Salvador and US$3–5 in other cities, but you can bargain a bit if you are polite. Licensed taxis will also drive **long distance**: ultra convenient, fast, but not cheap unless you have a group. A good trick is to ask a driver how much he charges by the hour (not more than US$10) and then tell them where you're going once you've agreed a rate.

In smaller towns the **tuk-tuk** or **motorcyle rickshaw** abounds; they are generally found at points where buses drop their passengers off. Expect to pay around US$0.50 around town, or a couple of dollars for tourist destinations in the area.

BY CAR

It can be helpful to **rent a car** if you want to explore some of the country's more remote areas, especially stretches of the Pacific coast. Western companies such as Hertz (☎2339 8004) and Avis (☎2339 9268) **rent** at Western prices (from US$45/day with insurance); local garages often charge half those rates (rarely more than US$20/day). Recommended local rental companies include Sandoval (☎2225 0392, ⊛rentacarsandoval.com) and Quick Rent A Car (☎2229 0020, ⊛quickrentacar.com.sv). Note that even if you opt to pay for **insurance** when you rent a car (US$12–15 extra/day), the deductible will still be hefty (typically US$1000) no matter who you rent with, meaning that you'll end up paying for a damaged bumper or a flat tyre.

When driving, look out for abrupt coned-off lanes on the motorway – these are **police stops**, where you may be asked to present your passport, driving licence and car documents. If you need assistance, stop at one of the petrol stations or mechanics that are widespread along the road. Avoid driving at night; **cows** often wander onto main roads, including the Panamericana, and it's hard to see **potholes**. Also, dirt roads can become impassable during the rainy season, even with a 4WD; ask locally about conditions before you set off. Armed **hold-ups** of private cars are extremely rare nowadays (though you shouldn't drive at night on lonely stretches of road, such as the Carretera del Litoral between El Zonte and Sonsonate), but keep US$20 or so aside just in case, and offer no resistance. It's good to rent an old-looking car, so as not to draw attention to yourself – driving solo will also make you a more tempting target. In cities, thefts of cars, or items left in them, do occur, so it's wise to leave your car in a guarded or locked car park overnight.

Hitching is common and you probably won't have to wait more than five minutes for a ride. That said, it carries obvious risks, and we don't recommend it. It helps to speak Spanish, if only to make conversation with the driver.

BY BIKE

Bikes offer great freedom in rural areas, and you can take them on buses as long as they're not too full. There are no formal rental places, but it is possible to do deals with locals, tour operators and at hotels; rates are around US$5 per hour or US$15 per day. Otherwise, a cheap mountain bike shouldn't cost more than US$50 to buy from a general store in any of the bigger towns.

BY BOAT

You can only visit the islands of the Golfo de Fonseca and the Bahía de Jiquilisco by **boat**, and the same obviously applies to

---

ADDRESSES IN EL SALVADOR

Navigating Salvadorian cities is initially confusing but ultimately logical. As elsewhere in Central America, most cities are organized on the **grid** plan: streets running north–south are **avenidas**, those running east–west are **calles**. The main avenida and calle will have individual names (along with a few of the others) and the heart of any city is at their intersection – usually, though not always, at the Parque Central, the main square. North or south of this intersection avenidas are Norte (Nte) or Sur, while east or west calles are Oriente (Ote) or Poniente (Pte). Avenidas lying to the east of the main avenida are numbered evenly, increasing the further you go out; west of the avenida the numbers are odd. Similarly, calles have even numbers south of the main calle and odd numbers north. **Addresses** can be given either as the street name/number, followed by the building number, or as the intersection of two streets. So: "12A C Pte 2330, Col Flor Blanca" is no. 2330, Calle 12 Poniente in the district (*colonia*) of Flor Blanca, while "10A Av Sur y 3 C Pte" is the intersection of 10A Avenida Sur and Calle 3 Poniente.

crossing Lago de Suchitlán. Scheduled services are always much cheaper (US$1–5), but *lanchas* operated by fishermen depart immediately once they've been hired, and need little persuasion to provide private lifts and tours of the country's lakes and mangrove swamps. This is usually done as a set fee for the boat (usually about US$35–45, depending on duration), so getting into a sizeable group reduces the cost.

ACCOMMODATION

El Salvador's **accommodation** industry is slowly waking up to the traveller market: new places are appearing all the time, and very few destinations have nowhere at all to stay. However, the number of **hostels** with dorm rooms is still relatively small, so it's best to budget for cheap **hotels**. Prices are relatively high compared to the rest of Central America: in San Salvador a clean, secure, double room comes to at least US$30, often more, while outside the capital you can expect to pay at least US$13–20, or US$25–30 for air conditioning. Lots of hotels rent multi-bed rooms (intended for Salvadorian families), where you can pack in like sardines – these can be a good way to cut costs if you're with a group. Discounts on longer stays are also often available. Rooms vary within an establishment, so look around. Hotel staff will often try to put you in a room which is outside the wi-fi's range, so be aware if you'll need the internet. Hot water is rare in the cheaper places.

Campsites are available at most lakes, national parks and several towns and beaches. Salvadoreños with spare land may be willing to let you pitch a tent – offer around US$5. Hammock-slinging is possible on some beaches (though steer clear of the sketchier beaches around La Libertad) and at some beach hotels (also for about US$5). The hotels will usually put your bag somewhere safe, if you ask.

Accommodation fills up around Santa Semana (the week before Easter), Christmas, the Fiestas Agostinas (the last week of July and first week of August) and at the time of local festivals; **reserve** in advance around these dates.

FOOD AND DRINK

Eating well in El Salvador is far more about fresh ingredients than refined cooking. The main meal of the day is **lunch** (*almuerzo*), which most locals eat in a *comedor*, where *típicos* (local dishes of meat or fish, rice, vegetable or salad) and coffee go for around US$3–4, or a *pupusería*, where you can get **pupusas** – tortillas served piping hot and filled with cheese (*queso*), beans (*frijoles*), pork crackling (*chicharrón*) or all three – for around US$0.50 (US$0.75–1 in San Salvador). *Pupusas* are normally made fresh from cornmeal, eaten with your hands, and are served with hot sauce, tomato juice and/or *curtido*, a serving of pickled cabbage, beetroot and carrots. The cleanliness and quality of establishments vary, but they're usually OK, though with no frills; if doubtful, choose one that's busy and cooks unfrozen meat.

A standard breakfast (*desayuno*) – it's rare to be offered anything else – is composed of *frijoles* (refried black beans), *queso* (white cheese) and *huevos* (eggs, either fried or scrambled), along with coffee. Although San Salvador's western suburbs are the only place to find the full gamut of international cuisine, most towns have a handful of restaurants. Chinese, Italian, Mexican, and Argentine meat-grilling restaurants are the most widespread, though their authenticity varies. Vegetarians will find dedicated restaurants only in the biggest cities, and should be prepared to eat a lot of beans and cheese. There are also US fast-food chains – set meals for about US$5 – throughout the country, usually clustered along the Panamerican Highway or in the increasingly ubiquitous malls. Fried chicken is the *plat du jour*; the Guatemalan (but US-based) *Pollo Campero* chain is the best of the Central American franchises (ⓦcampero.com).

In addition to *pupusas*, other Salvadoreño **specialities** include *mariscada* (huge bowls of seafood chowder filled with fish and crustaceans), *tamales* (meat or chicken wrapped in maize dough and boiled in a corn leaf), *ceviche* (raw fish and seafood marinated in lime juice) and

3

sopa de frijoles (black or red bean soup). On the coast, *conchas* (cockles or any other shellfish) are served raw with lemon juice, tomato, coriander and Worcestershire sauce (*salsa inglesa*). Try the *ostras* (oysters), especially in popular places to eat by the sea; they are fresher here than in most Western restaurants.

DRINK

Local **coffee** is very good, usually taken black, sweet and strong at breakfast and mid-afternoon with *tamales*. In small villages it will be boiled up with sugar cane and called *lista*. El Salvador's tropical fruits make delicious **juices**. *Jugos* are pure juices – most commonly orange, papaya, pineapple and melon – mixed with ice. *Licuados* (sometimes called *batidos*) blend juice with sugar, ice and sometimes milk, while *frescos* are fruit-based sweet drinks made up in bulk and served with lunch or dinner. Unless you ask otherwise, sugar will be added to *jugos* and *licuados*. *Horchata* is a dense milk drink with a base of rice, sweetened with sugar and cinnamon.

The usual brands of **soft drinks** are available. **Water** from taps isn't safe to drink anywhere in the country, although most accommodation and restaurants provide the filtered stuff. Bottled mineral water and small bags of pure spring water are available almost everywhere. El Salvador produces five good **beers** – the most important decision you will have to make is between Pilsner and Golden Light. True lager followers will go for the excellent and textured former. Most bars offer *baldes* (ice-filled buckets of six cold ones), and these are a cheaper option – usually around US$6 – if you're going to drink more than a couple. **Aguardiente** is a sugar cane-based liquor, fiery but quite smooth, produced under government control and sold through outlets called *expendios*; Tic-Tac is a favourite label.

CULTURE AND ETIQUETTE

Salvadoreños are generally confident, very honest, principled, hardworking and keen to laugh; they will often vie to help travellers. This said, not many tourists pass through the country, especially in rural areas, so you may be regarded as something of a novelty and children especially may stare and touch your hair. While the majority of the population is **Catholic**, Evangelical Protestantism is on the rise.

You should be confident and **polite**: say "Buenos dias" (morning) or "Buenas tardes" (afternoon) when you catch someone's eye or enter a room, shake hands when meeting and do not offend by being paranoid about your safety or belongings. In more informal situations

---

SALVADORIAN SLANG

The Salvadorian slang, called Caliche, is formed from Nahuat and English roots. You'll probably hear it spoken on your travels, particularly by kids and *campesinos*, and you'll always raise a smile if you try a few words yourself.

Ahuevo/caval You got it!
Va! Yes/sure/fine!
Bayunco A joker, immature, crazy
Birria Beer
Brosa/conocido/chero/chera Friend/ friend (m)/friend (f)
Un chingo de… There's a lot of…
Chavo/chava Boy/girl (informal)
Chele/guero A white person/westerner
Chivo/chivisimo Cool/very cool
Chucho/chucha Male dog/female dog
Chuco/chuca Dirty
Cora A quarter of a dollar
La Goma A hangover

Guanaco A native of El Salvador
Huevón/huevonazo/huevonada Lazy/a beggar
Mara Gang or group of friends
Marero Gang member
Paloma Penis, or something cool
Púchica/no chinges! Don't mess around!
Salud/adios Goodbye
Talega Drunk
Vacilar Chill out/have fun/quickie (sexual)
Vergón Cool or amazing (from "verga", penis)
Volo Drunk
Yucca! Calm down!

the greeting is a high-five followed by a fist bump. Women should try not to react to macho male posturing, as this is seen as flirtatious. Remember to remove hats when entering a church. Always ask permission before taking **photos** of people in indigenous areas, though you will generally find lots of eager posers.

Tipping at restaurants is not expected at the cheaper places. More Western-style restaurants (especially in San Salvador) may add around a ten percent service charge, and you can increase this should you want to (or ignore it if the service was poor). Free guides should also be tipped. There is no need to tip anyone else.

Haggling is acceptable and is often a good idea if your Spanish is up to it, especially over hotel prices. Aim generally for two-thirds of the stated price. "Y con mi descuento?" ("And with my discount?") is an effective line if delivered properly.

SPORTS AND OUTDOOR ACTIVITIES

Fútbol (soccer) is by far the biggest spectator sport in El Salvador. There are two domestic seasons every year: the first (the *clausura*) runs every weekend from February to mid-May, the second (called *apertura*) goes from September to mid-December; both are followed by play-offs and finals. The big **teams** of the last few years are Águila from San Miguel, FAS from Santa Ana, Firpo from Usulután and Isidro Metapán. The quality of football is poor, but the crowds are fun and lively; don't bring anything valuable, and always sit with and cheer for the home side. See ⓦfesfut.org.sv for fixtures and information. Great attention is paid to the international scene, too: the whole country has arranged itself behind two Spanish clubs, Barcelona and Real Madrid, though Barcelona is slightly more popular and regarded as the "people's" (ie poor man's) team. **Baseball** is popular as well; San Salvador has a stadium, opposite the Artesan Market on Alameda M.E. Araujo, with games on Sundays. Football, baseball and basketball games take place on wide-spread municipal facilities, in parks and on beaches across the country.

If it is not a training session you will be more than welcome to join in.

El Salvador's 320km of coastline is widely accepted to have the best **surfing** in Central America and is known for several world-famous breaks. The best areas are on the Costa del Bálsamo (see p.220) and the eastern beaches around El Cuco (see p.226). See ⓦsurfingelsalvador .com for surf reports, beach reviews and general information. The best **hiking** is in the national parks. For good challenges try the Parque Nacional Montecristo cloudforest (see p.264), up the volcanoes of the Cerro Verde (see p.262) and through the dramatic, dry rainforest of the Parque Nacional El Imposible (see p.249). **Diving** here is not as good as in the Bay Islands or Belize, and the only Pacific coral diving in Central America is off Los Cóbanos (see p.248), along with a couple of good wreck dives. See ⓦelsalvadordivers.com for more information.

COMMUNICATIONS

Mail (letters), handled by Correos El Salvador, generally takes about one week to the US and nine or so days to Europe; there are parcel services available, but you should use a courier service if sending anything of value. A postcard costs US$0.21 to North America, US$0.61 to Europe and US$0.85 to the rest of the world; leave enough space on your postcards for multiple local stamps as they won't always be stocked with international ones. The use of **mobile phones** is huge in El Salvador (although nano SIM cards for iPhone 5 and upwards are difficult to come by), and unless you have one, you are unlikely to be able to make phone calls other than via expensive hotel phones. By far the cheapest option, though, is web-based calls; almost all internet places are now equipped with headsets.

If you don't want to pay for roaming on your own phone (or don't have one), the cheapest local pay-as-you-go **mobile phone** costs around US$15 and can make and receive international calls. If you have an **unlocked** GSM phone you can just

3

buy a local **SIM card** for US$5 (CDMA phones cannot use SIMs). There are several GSM networks; Movistar (Ⓦmovistar.com.sv), Tigo (Ⓦtigo.com.sv) and Claro (Ⓦclaro.com.sv) are the **primary operators** – Claro also covers the rest of Central America (with the exception of Belize). **Claro** (formerly "Telecom") also has offices in every town, where you can get set up – bring your passport. Forget **public phones**; even if you find one they almost never work. The **telephone code** for the whole of El Salvador is ☎503.

Internet of varying speeds is now available everywhere. Rates range from US$0.50 to US$1 for fifteen to thirty minutes (the range varies wildly, and is often higher in hotels).

CRIME AND SAFETY

Generally, you should be fine if you stay confident and stay in groups in busy areas. This applies in particular to **women travellers**, who should try to ignore the usual catcalls and loud blown kisses, as attempts to scold will be seen as flirtatious; the less attention you pay, the less attention you will receive. Male or female, if you are being pestered, don't show animosity, and head for a busy café or restaurant. Do not respond with insults or aggression to Salvadorians, no matter how unreasonable they are being, as you will cause great offence; the best response to any irritation is to ignore it. In dealing with people who try to sell or beg in the street, the response is "gracias", followed by your attention being turned away.

The **National Civilian Police** (PCN) is one of the best forces in Central America, with little corruption and a good presence in cities, at least until nightfall. Their police stations have 24-hour service and are centrally located in all towns. Crimes should be reported in these offices as quickly as possible. Additionally, an often English-speaking **tourist police** operates nationwide to guide treks, assist and advise (☎2245 5448).

STREET CRIME

El Salvador has a reputation for guns, gangs and danger, which, while not

> ### RIPTIDES
>
> Statistically, the biggest threats to tourists in El Salvador are the **riptides** on its beaches. It is best not to go out too far on your own, and ask locally about the conditions. If you are unable to swim back, try not to panic, swim parallel to the shoreline and wait for the rip to die down. There is no coastguard, so call the police in an emergency or, better still, find the nearest surfer.

unfounded, is no longer a problem in areas frequented by most tourists. The two primary *maras* (**gangs**) are the Mara Salvatrucha 13 and the Calle 18, known informally as "Los Trece" and "Los Dieciocho" respectively, and engage in territory disputes across the country. Gangsters are easily identifiable by their side-shaven haircuts and body art (if a local has tattoos, he's almost guaranteed to be a gangster). The gangs however will generally leave tourists alone, concerning themselves with the more profitable fields of drugs, extortion and human trafficking. You'll frequently be asked for money by beggars, who tend to target the tourists; a firm "no" is usually enough to send them away.

Although muggings are extremely rare, you should avoid wearing expensive clothing and flashing valuables. Don't put up a fight if you are mugged. It's worth keeping US$10–20 in a pocket while travelling, as this will be enough for most *banditos* – highway robbery is rare but does happen on isolated roads. Be especially careful after nightfall in Sonsonate and San Salvador's *centro*; La Unión and San Miguel can also be dodgy.

The area to the east of San Salvador and the slums around Lago de Ilopango should be avoided, as crime and gang-related violence is particularly prevalent in this part of the country.

> ### EMERGENCY NUMBERS
>
> **Cruz Roja** (ambulance) ☎2222 5155
> **Fire** ☎2271 2227 or ☎2271 1244
> **Police** ☎911

HEALTH

Pharmacies are widespread, especially in San Salvador, and most of them will have a wide range of antibiotics for stomach troubles. Two private **hospitals** in San Salvador provide the best medical services in the country (see p.214); in the east, San Miguel's Hospital Clínica San Francisco (see p.236) is another good private hospital. All three have 24hr emergency rooms. Make sure you have comprehensive medical cover in your **insurance policy**; any kind of medical treatment is likely to be expensive, and you will probably be asked to pay up front whether or not you are insured. Have insurance documents or cash at the ready if you need treatment.

INFORMATION AND MAPS

The national tourist board, **Corsatur** (welsalvador.travel), has its main office in San Salvador at Alameda Manuel Araujo, Pasaje y Edificio Carbonel 2, Colonia Roma (Mon–Fri 8.30am–12.30pm & 1.10–4.30pm; ☎2243 7835). The staff (who only speak basic English) will help with enquiries if you persist. Other outposts ("Centro de Amigos del Turista" or CAT) exist in La Palma, Suchitoto, La Unión and Puerto La Libertad, and there's a seldom-manned desk at the airport. Small towns like Apaneca and Perquín have their own kiosks that issue little more than pamphlets in Spanish, but often the best tips come directly from hostel and hotel owners.

Maps of El Salvador are rare and generally terrible, except for those in this guide, and those produced on the second floor of the Centro Nacional de Registros, 1A Calle Poniente and 43 Avenida Norte 2310, San Salvador (Mon–Fri 8am–noon & 1–4pm; ☎2261 8400, ⓦcnr.gob.sv). ITMB's 1: 250,000 *El Salvador* map is also a useful resource, but still carries some inaccuracies.

MONEY AND BANKS

El Salvador has officially used the **US dollar** (US$) since 2001. All US dollar notes and coins are currently in free circulation, but try to stockpile US$1 coins (the bills are rarely seen) and US$5 bills, as anything over US$10 is likely to send the shopkeeper running down the street in search of change. The word "cora" is very important – a bastardization of the "quarter" 25¢ US coin.

ATMs (*cajeros*) are becoming increasingly widespread, particularly in tourist destinations. The Scotiabank machines are the most reliable. However, it's wise to keep a stash of cash for Perquín, Tacuba and the eastern craft towns.

Elsewhere, the main **banks** – Banco Agrícola, Banco Hipotecario, Scotiabank and Citibank – have ATMs, which charge a handling fee of around US$2–3. Payment by **credit card** is unheard of at the budget level, but if you do encounter an establishment that

3

NATIONAL PARK INFORMATION

Officially, there is a permission-granting ritual that must be performed before you enter any of El Salvador's national parks, though if you go with a guide on an organized visit, wardens will usually waive this. Confusingly, parks are administered by three different agencies. All three also allow entry to, and have information about, other preserved areas as well.

Instituto Salvadoreño de Turismo (ISTU) 41 Av Nte & Alameda Roosevelt 115, San Salvador ☎2222 8000, ⓦistu.gob.sv. Manages Parque Nacional Walter T. Deininger, and has information about all the country's national parks. Mon–Fri 8am–4pm, Sat 8am–noon.

Ministerio de Medio Ambiente y Recursos Naturales Edificio MARN (Instalaciones ISTA), 2 C & Colonia Las Mercedes, San Salvador ☎2267 6276,

☎2267 6259, ⓦmarn.gob.sv. Issues permits to the Parque Nacional Montecristo in person or by fax. Mon–Fri 7.30am–12.30pm & 1.30–3.30pm.

SalvaNatura 33 Av Sur 640, Colonia Flor Blanca, San Salvador ☎2279 1515, ⓦsalvanatura.org. Manages the Parque Nacional El Imposible and Parque Nacional Los Volcanes, with books and useful maps for sale, and some free leaflets. Mon–Fri 8am–12.30pm & 2–5.30pm.

3

EL SALVADOR ONLINE

ⓦ**buscaniguas.com.sv** Long-standing portal – in Spanish only – with useful listings, including hotels, restaurants and entertainment, plus interesting blog pages.
ⓦ**elsalvador.travel** The official tourist site, with good information and a directory of businesses, hotels and restaurants , plus a calendar of events in English.
ⓦ**fotosdeelsalvador.com** An appetite-whetting archive holding thousands of photos from across the country (info in Spanish only).
ⓦ**laprensagrafica.com** and ⓦ**elsalvador.com** The websites for the two big conservative daily papers (Spanish only).
ⓦ**luterano.blogspot.com** An excellent English-language blog, updated almost daily, summarizing current affairs and adding well-informed commentary.

will take your card there will be a charge of five percent (more expensive places will not levy this charge). **Travellers' cheques** are less widely recognized, and at present can only be changed in banks. There are **casas de cambio** (generally daily 9am–5pm) along Alameda Juan Pablo II in San Salvador, in Santa Ana and San Miguel and at the borders. There are Western Union and Moneygram outlets in almost every mid-size town.

OPENING HOURS AND PUBLIC HOLIDAYS

Opening hours throughout the country vary. The big cities and major towns generally get going quite early in the morning, with government offices working from 8am to 4pm and most businesses from 8.30 or 9am to 5 or 5.30pm, with some closing for an hour at lunch.

Post offices across the country are generally open Monday to Friday 8am to 5pm and Saturday 8am to noon. **Banks** are open Monday to Friday, from 8.30 or 9am until 4 or 5pm (some of them close from 1 to 2pm). Some banks in the larger cities also open between 8am and noon on Saturday. Hotels in smaller places lock up for the night at around 9 or 10pm, and you may be banging on the door for a while and paying extra if you don't warn them of your late arrival. On **public holidays** everything shuts down, with some businesses also closing on the day of local fiestas. Museums and archeological sites all close on Mondays.

FESTIVALS

Ferías (festivals) in El Salvador, as in the rest of the continent, are very important. Almost every town will have its own annual celebration, honouring the saint most connected to the place in question. The following calendar lists a few highlights.

January 8–15 Cristo Negro and Feria Gastronómica Internacional in Juayúa. Street fiesta with the best range and quality of food.
February Festival Internacional de Arte y Cultura in Suchitoto. A month-long celebration of classical music, opera, art and theatre.
March/April Santa Semana in Izalco. Popularly known as the best place for the Easter processions and street paintings.
May Las Flores y Las Palmas in Panchimalco (second Sun). Celebrates flower and palm-tree cultivation with music, dancing and fireworks.
August 1–5 Fiestas Patronales de San Salvador. Street parties and parades shut down the capital on Aug 1, 3 and 5.
August 1–6 Festival del Invierno in Perquín. Exciting, young and bohemian music and arts festival in this mountain town.
November 14–30 Carnaval celebrated in San Miguel. One of the biggest fiestas in Central America, with processions and music floats, dancing and drinking.

PUBLIC HOLIDAYS

Jan 1 New Year's Day
March/April Easter (Thurs–Easter Sun)
May 1 Labour Day
Aug 1–6 El Salvador del Mundo
Sept 15 Independence Day
Oct 12 Columbus Day
Nov 1 Day of the Dead
Nov 2 All Saints' Day
Dec 24 & 25 Christmas
Dec 31 New Year's Eve

San Salvador

Sprawling across the Valle de las Hamacas at the foot of the mighty Volcán San Salvador is the urban melee of **SAN SALVADOR**, El Salvador's mercurial capital. Established here by the Spanish in 1545, it remained a relatively minor place until 1785, when it was named the first *intendencia* (semi-autonomous governing unit) within the Captaincy General of Guatemala (which nominally controlled all of Central America). Father José Delgado first made the call for independence here in 1811. Not much remains of this illustrious history: a series of earthquakes throughout the nineteenth and twentieth centuries levelled most of the centre. Little you can see predates the nineteenth century.

Today, San Salvador is forward-looking and vibrant; after two progressive mayorships and a more proactive chief of police, the city is going through something of a renaissance. Pleasant suburbs, peaceful little parks, illuminating museums and a thriving historic centre make for an exhilarating place to explore, while a bohemian arts scene, plenty of bars and lively clubs provide fun night-time distractions.

WHAT TO SEE AND DO

San Salvador's social and geographical landscape is conveniently linear. The eastern part of the city – industrial, poor and dangerous – morphs into the crowded **Centro Histórico**, or **El Centro**. The centre's churches and theatre are some of the country's best, though the streets around the main square are completely swamped by markets and *comedores*. The heavy police presence makes this area much safer than it might feel, at least during the day. West of here the roads creep uphill to the more relaxed shops and services around the green acres of **Parque Cuscatlán**, and the heady commercialism of the **Metrocentro**. Heading further west, the climb continues to the trimmed hedges, fancy bars and cultural monoliths of the **Zona Rosa**, before finishing at the fine restaurants, exclusive nightclubs and guarded castles of **Colonia Escalón** – the upscale strip malls and condos now continue all the way into **Santa Tecla**. To the north of this east-to-west progression are the arty, studenty, traveller-friendly cafés, hostels and late-night bars of **Colonia Centroamérica**.

Plaza Barrios

Though at the heart of the raging Centro Histórico, the rejuvenated **Plaza Barrios** remains relatively tranquil. A plaque on a white base on the north side commemorates the six Jesuit priests murdered at La UCA in 1989 (see p.208), while an imperious equestrian statue of **Gerardo Barrios** (president 1859–63) commands the centre. The bronze image was one of several commissions here for Swiss-born sculptor Francisco Durini, better known for his beautification of Quito, Ecuador, in the early 1900s.

Palacio Nacional

On the western edge of the Plaza Barrios stands the **Palacio Nacional** (Mon–Fri 8am–4pm; US$3), built between 1905 and 1911, having replaced an earlier edifice that was destroyed by fire. Briefly home to the president's office and Supreme Court, El Salvador's Legislative Assembly was based here until 1974, and all other government offices – save the National Archives – moved out after the quake of 1986. Since then, restoration of the Neoclassical palace has been ongoing, with the wonderfully ornate upper galleries serving as a **museum** for the building and the history of San Salvador (the ground level remains the National Archives offices). Everything is labelled in Spanish and English.

Catedral Metropolitana

The most imposing structure on Plaza Barrios is the **Catedral Metropolitana** (Mon–Fri & Sun 6am–6pm, Sat 6am–1pm & 4–6pm; donations optional). The cathedral dates back to 1888, but has been severely damaged on a number of occasions, most notably by fire in 1951. Repairs were suspended in 1977 by **Archbishop Óscar Romero**, who

3

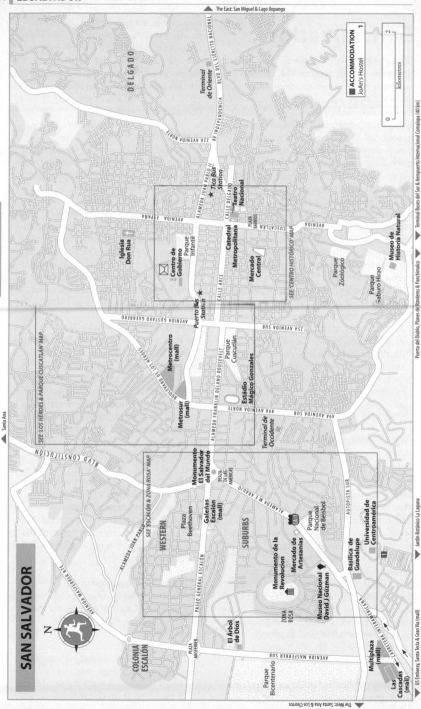

SAN SALVADOR

N

The East: San Miguel & Lago Ilopango

ACCOMMODATION
JoAn's Hostel   1

0   1   2
kilometres

Santa Ana

Terminal de Oriente

BLVD DEL EJERCITO NACIONAL

2A AVENIDA NORTE

AV INDEPENDENCIA

Tica Bus Station

Teatro Nacional

Iglesia Don Rua

Centro de Gobierno

Parque Infantil

ALAMEDA JUAN PABLO II

CALLE DELGADO

AVENIDA ESPAÑA

PLAZA BARRIOS

Catedral Metropolitana

Mercado Central

SEE 'CENTRO HISTÓRICO' MAP

CALLE ARCE

AVENIDA CUSCATLÁN

2A AVENIDA SUR

AVENIDA

Museo de Historia Natural

Parque Zoológico

Parque Saburo Hirao

Terminal Buses del Sur & Aeropuerto Internacional Comalapa (40 km)

SEE 'LOS HEROES & PARQUE CUSCATLAN' MAP

AVENIDA GUSTAVO GUERRERO

Puerto Bus Station

Metrocentro (mall)

BOULEVARD DE LOS HEROES

Parque Cuscatlán

Metrosur (mall)

ALAMEDA FRANKLIN DELANO ROOSEVELT

Estadio Mágico Gonzales

49A AVENIDA NORTE

49A AVENIDA SUR

2A AVENIDA NORTE

Terminal de Occidente

Puerta del Diablo, Planes de Renderos & Panchimalco

BLVD CONSTITUCIÓN

SEE 'ESCALON & ZONA ROSA' MAP

ALAMEDA JUAN PABLO II

Monumento El Salvador del Mundo

PLAZA DE LAS AMÉRICAS

Galerías Escalón (mall)

Plaza Beethoven

WESTERN

SUBURBS

ALAMEDA M E ARAUJO

AUTOPISTA SUR

Parque Nacional de Béisbol

Universidad de Centroamérica

Basílica de Guadalupe

Jardín Botánico La Laguna

PASEO GENERAL ESCALÓN

Monumento de la Revolución

Mercado de Artesanías

Museo Nacional David J. Güzman

ZONA ROSA

El Árbol de Dios

PLAZA MASFERRER

COLONIA ESCALÓN

AVENIDA MASFERRER NTE

Parque Bicentenario

AVENIDA MASFERRER SUR

Multiplaza (mall)

Las Cascadas (mall)

CARRETERA INTERAMERICANA

US Embassy, Santa Tecla & Gran Vía (mall)

The West: Santa Ana & Los Chorros

DELGADO

3

argued that funds allocated for the work should be diverted to feeding the country's poor. Romero's murder in March 1980 (which took place at La Hospital Divina Providencia, in the western suburbs) is widely perceived as the event that sent the country spiralling into civil war: mourners carrying his body to the cathedral were fired upon by government troops stationed on top of the surrounding buildings, and many were slaughtered. Work on the building resumed after the civil war, and was finally completed in 1999. You can visit Romero's resting place in the cavernous *cripta* (Mon–Sat 8–11.45am & 2–4.45pm, Sun 8am–4.45pm; free) below the cathedral, via a separate entrance on the east side of the building. Located behind a small shrine and framed by portraits of the archbishop, the

Modernist bronze **tomb** was designed by Italian artist Paolo Borghi.

Teatro Nacional

Across from the cathedral is the elegant French Renaissance-style **Teatro Nacional**, though the entrance faces the compact **Plaza Morazán**, one block north. Built between 1911 and 1917 and reflecting the global vogue for French culture in the early twentieth century, the restored interior – all red plush, marble and decorative plasterwork – harks back to grander times. The magnificent modern ceiling frieze by Salvadorian artist Carlos Cañas depicts Rubenesque maidens cavorting in the clouds. Regular musical and theatrical events are held here, including performances by the national orchestra most fortnights; tickets are heavily subsidized and sometimes free

3

CENTRO HISTÓRICO

▲ Iglesia Don Rua (2 blocks)

0 — 300 metres

National Stadium

Centro de Gobierno

Parque Infantil

Buses to Lago Ilopango ★

Puertobus Terminal ★

Alealdía

Parque Centenario

ALAMEDA JUAN PABLO II

★ Tica Bus Terminal

Museo Universitario de Antropología (MUA)

Iglesia Sagrado Corazón

Catedral Metropolitana

Market Stalls

Parque San José

Mercado Ex Cuartel

Buses to ★ Los Chorros

Parque Bolívar

Food Stalls

Palacio Nacional

Teatro Nacional

Plaza Centro

Biblioteca Nacional

Iglesia el Rosario

Market

Mercado Sargado Corazón

Banco Hipotecario (ATM)

Centro Commercial Libertad (mall)

Iglesia Calvario

Centro Commercial Union (mall)

Buses to Santa Tecla

Iglesia La Merced

Mercado Central

Police Station

Parque Cuscatlán

N

● **EATING & DRINKING**
Pupsería Doña Isable	2
Pollo Bonanza	3
Del y Arce	1
Panadería Latino	4

▼ Parque Zoológico Nacional & Museo de Historia Natural

(seeing a performance is the only way to get inside). Upcoming events can be found in the Friday edition or website of the national newspaper *Diario del Hoy* (ⓦelsalvador.com).

Iglesia el Rosario

Two blocks east of Plaza Barrios is spacious **Plaza Libertad**, where the central statue of feather-winged *Liberty* (1911), by Francisco Durini, stands watch over the scrappy markets that surround the square. Dominating the east side, the smog-stained, ugly concrete facade of the **Iglesia el Rosario** (Mon–Sat 6.30am–noon & 2–6.30pm, Sun 8.30am–noon & 2–6.30pm) looks like an industrial turbine. Do not let this put you off, as the interior is the most spectacular and original in the country, created in 1971 by artist and architect Rubén Martínez. Sunlight passing through banks of modern stained glass set in the arc of the roof casts acid-bright colour dispersions across the brick walls, contorted metal sculptures, doll-like shrines and the chequered floor.

Iglesia Calvario

One block south and two blocks west of Plaza Barrios, in the jaws of the chaotic street market, is the dark, neo-Gothic **Iglesia Calvario** (daily 7am–5pm), constructed between 1911 and 1950 but managing to look far older. It's a handsome building, with a smattering of blue-and-yellow stained glass from Italy inside, but not much else to see.

Museo Universitario de Antropología (MUA)

West of Plaza Barrios along Calle Arce (at 17 Av Nte), in the campus of Universidad Tecnológica de El Salvador (UTEC), is the enlightening **Museo Universitario de Antropología** (Mon–Fri 9am–1pm & 3–5pm, Sat 9am–noon; free; bus #42). Though smaller than the Museo Nacional, it contains a more focused collection – it also houses some of the most beautifully decorated **Mesoamerican ceramics** in the region. Most of these date from the Classic period (600–900 AD) and are displayed in the ground-floor galleries along with traditional dresses. Upstairs the Sala de Migración contrasts the prehistoric migration of pre-Columbian Americans north to south with the modern, perilous overland migration made by thousands of El Salvadorian workers to the US each year. There's also a fascinating diagram showing what the Spanish regime meant by "mestizo" and "mulatto", and a rare collection of the defunct colón banknotes and coins. Also upstairs, a gallery houses a display of personal effects and music dedicated to the composer **Francisco "Pancho" Lara Hernández** (1900–89), best known for the folk song *El Carbonero*, often regarded as the nation's second national anthem. Labelling is comprehensive throughout the museum, but in Spanish only.

Parque Cuscatlán

Parque Cuscatlán, a short walk west of the Museo Universitario de Antropología, is a large expanse of shady walkways and grass lawns that not only offers respite from the heat and noise, but is also home to several intriguing sights. Engraved into the park's northern embankment, the **Monumento a la Memoria y la Verdad** (Tues–Sun 6am–6pm; free) lists the names of the thousands who died or "disappeared" leading up to and during the civil war of 1980–92. Nearby, the **Sala Nacional de Exposiciones** (daily 9am–noon & 2–5pm; free) hosts high-quality rotating art exhibitions, while at the western end of the park the **Tin Marín Museo de los Niños** (Tues–Sun 9am–5pm; US$2.50; ⓦtinmarin.org) may well be the best kids' museum ever, with fun activities including painting a VW Beetle, sitting in a cockpit of a Boeing 727, or visiting a planetarium (an extra US$1).

Museo de la Palabra y la Imagen

Several blocks north of Parque Cuscatlán via 45 Avenida Norte, the curious **Museo de la Palabra y la Imagen** (Mon–Fri 8am–noon & 2–5pm, Sat 8am–noon; US$2; ⓦmuseo.com.sv) is tucked away on

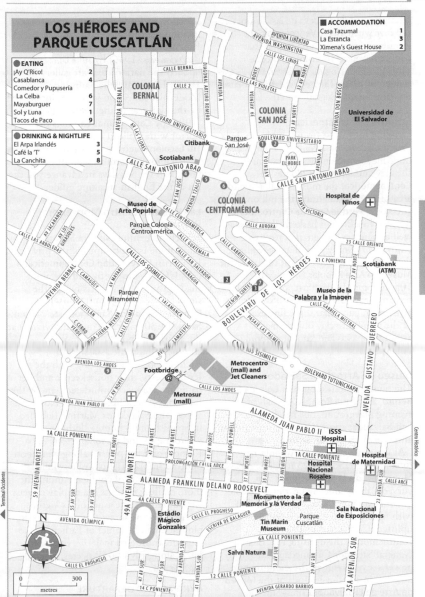

LOS HÉROES AND PARQUE CUSCATLÁN

ACCOMMODATION
Casa Tazumal	1
La Estancia	3
Ximena's Guest House	2

EATING
¡Ay Q'Rico!	2
Casablanca	4
Comedor y Pupusería La Ceiba	6
Mayaburguer	7
Sol y Luna	1
Tacos de Paco	9

DRINKING & NIGHTLIFE
El Arpa Irlandés	3
Café la 'T'	5
La Canchita	8

a side road (at 27 Av Nte 1140). It's nominally a museum of literature dedicated to Salvador Efraín Salazar Arrué (1899–1975), aka **Salarrué**, the seminal Salvadorian writer, poet and painter – displays contain his personal effects and examples of his drawings and writings,

including the much loved *Cuentos de Cipotes* ("Children's Stories") and *Cuentos de Barro* ("Tales of Clay"). Of more interest to foreign visitors are the small galleries at the back containing graphic displays on the civil war. The war photography is moving, shocking and high quality. There's also a re-creation of the "Cueva de las Pasiones", the cave where **Radio Venceremos**, the clandestine guerrilla radio station that counterbalanced government media propaganda during the civil war, was hidden in 1982. The newest exhibit focuses on Salvadorian emigration to the US.

Colonia Centroamérica

Heading northwest from the Museo de la Palabra, across Boulevard los Héroes and up Calle Centroamérica, takes you into the arty and laidback **Colonia Centroamérica**, the most traveller-friendly area of town. Straight up the hill on the street, the **Parque Colonia Centroamérica** has two free floodlit basketball courts, as well as benches and gnarled trees to enjoy; it's the only park that's safe after dark. At the northern end of the park, the **Museo de Arte Popular** (Tues–Sat 10am–5pm; US$1; ⓦartepopular.org) has an engaging collection of Salvadorian folk art, in particular some fine examples of the miniature clay objects made around Ilobasco and known as *sorpresas*, or surprises.

Museo de Arte de El Salvador

The plush western suburb of **Colonia San Benito**, aka **Zona Rosa**, is San Salvador's evening playground, but it's also home to San Salvador's most expressive monument and one of its best museums.

At the northern end of Avenida La Revolución stands the 25m-tall **Monumento a la Revolución**, a vast, curved slab of concrete bearing a mosaic of a naked man (known as "El Chulón") with head thrown back and arms uplifted. Completed in 1954 to commemorate the uprising that ousted General Salvador Castaneda Castro from power six years earlier, the monument now lies inside the grounds of the **Museo de Arte de El Salvador** (Tues–Sun 10am–6pm; US$1.50, free Sun; ⓦmarte .org.sv; bus #34), a superb digest of Salvadorian art from 1870 to the current day. The primary exhibit is "Al Compás del Tiempo", due to run unchanged until mid-2016; highlights include one of **Fernando Llort**'s folksy naïf works, *Domingo en la Plaza* (1979), a good

selection of **José Mejía Vides'** paintings, including a romantic view of Panchimalco, and the vivid realism of *Trabajadores* (1946) by **Julia Díaz** (who opened the nation's first art gallery in 1958). Don't miss the haunting Modernist collection in Sala 3, influenced by the civil war in the 1980s – *El Sumpul* (1984) by **Carlos Cañas** captures the horror with a pile of dead bodies, while **Titi Escalante** reimagines Matisse's dancers with a ghoulish bronze sculpture. If you book two to four days in advance you can get a free English-speaking guide.

La UCA and Centro Monseñor Romero

Stretching behind Nuestra Señora de Guadalupe is the campus of the private, Jesuit-run **Universidad Centroamericana** ("La UCA"), pleasantly laid out amid shady grounds and sports fields. The small but moving **Centro Monseñor Romero** (Mon–Fri 8am–noon & 2–6pm, Sat 8–11.30am; free; ⓦuca.edu.sv/cmr) at the southern end of the campus, commemorates the assassinated Archbishop Romero, along with the six Jesuit priests, their housekeeper and her daughter who were murdered here by the infamous Atlacatl Battalion in November 1989. The Sala de los Mártires (labelled in Spanish only) houses clothing, photographs and personal effects of Romero and the priests, along with those of other human-rights workers killed during the years of conflict. Among the more chilling exhibits is a display of glass jars containing the ashes of six victims, arranged in the shape of a cross, and the bloodied handkerchief of Father Rutilio Grande, murdered in 1977. Enter La UCA along Blvd Los Próceres, or Blvd La Sultana.

ARRIVAL AND DEPARTURE

BY PLANE
Comalapa International Airport The airport (☎2366 9455, ⓦaeropuertoelsalvador.gob.sv) is a 45min drive southeast of San Salvador city centre (note that if you are heading to El Tunco, it's much faster to arrange a pick-up direct from the airport).

By bus Buses displaying their destinations on the windscreens pick up passengers on the other side of the parking lot from the airport terminal (#29 takes you to the Terminal del Oriente in the centre of San Salvador). These buses only cost US$0.60, but can take 1hr to get into the city and are very crowded. After 7pm, taxis are the only way to get to San Salvador.

By taxi Acacya (☎2271 4937 or ☎2222 1202) have a booth at the airport and charge US$30 day or night to the capital, regardless of numbers. They also run a *colectivo*

service (8am, 9am, noon, 1pm, 5pm & 6pm from the airport; 6am, 7am, 10am & 2pm to the airport; 1hr; US$5) leaving and arriving at their offices at 19A Av Nte & 3A C Pte 1107.

BY BUS

San Salvador has three chaotic domestic terminals. International buses depart from individual offices, mostly in the western half of the city (see box, p.210).

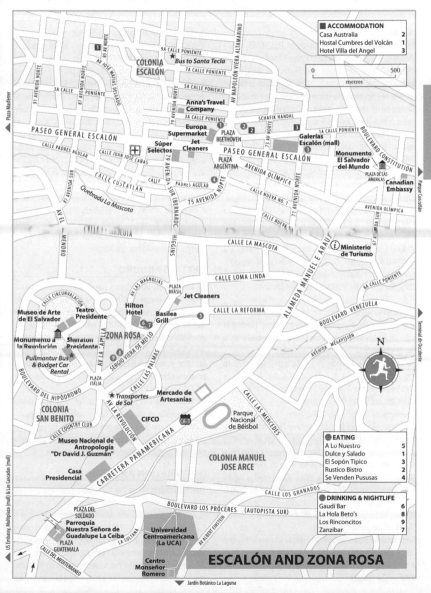

ESCALÓN AND ZONA ROSA

ACCOMMODATION
Casa Australia	2
Hostal Cumbres del Volcán	1
Hotel Villa del Angel	3

EATING
A Lo Nuestro	5
Dulce y Salado	1
El Sopón Tipico	3
Rustico Bistro	2
Se Venden Pususas	4

DRINKING & NIGHTLIFE
Gaudí Bar	6
La Hola Beto's	8
Los Rinconcitos	9
Zanzibar	7

INTERNATIONAL BUS COMPANIES AND STOPS

King Quality Alameda Juan Pablo II & 19 Av Nte; linked to the city centre by bus #52 (☎2271 1361).

Puerto Bus Alameda Juan Pablo II, by the Centro de Gobierno; linked to the city centre by bus #52 (☎2271 1361).

Pullmantur *Hotel Sheraton Presidente*, Av La

Revolución, Colonia San Benito (☎2243 1300, ⓦpullmantur.com).

Tica Bus By the *Hotel San Carlos* at Concepción 121 in the Centro Histórico; linked to the city centre by bus #29 and #34 (☎2222 0848).

Transporte de Sol Av La Revolución (☎2243 1345).

INTERNATIONAL BUSES

Tickets to Guatemala City range from US$30–55, while Managua (Nicaragua) and Tegucigalpa (Honduras) will be US$50–60. Pullmantur runs double-deckers, and, along with King Quality, generally offers the most luxurious service. Buy tickets at the relevant offices (see box above). Shuttle buses also run to Antigua, Guatemala, though it's easier to pick these up in El Tunco (see p.220).

Destinations Guatemala City (King Quality: daily; 5hr; Puerto Bus: 18 daily Mon–Sat, 4 daily Sun; 5hr; Pullmantur: 4 daily; 4hr 30min; Transporte de Sol: daily 7am & 4pm; 4hr 30min); Managua, Nicaragua (Puerto Bus: daily; 11hr; Transporte de Sol: daily 6.15am; 12hr); Panama City via San José, Costa Rica, and Managua, Nicaragua (Tica Bus: daily; 36hr; San José 18hr; Managua 11hr); San José, Costa Rica (Puerto Bus: daily; 18hr); San Pedro Sula, Honduras (Puerto Bus: 2 daily; 6hr); Tapachula, Mexico (Puerto Bus: daily; 10hr; Tica Bus: daily, via Guatemala City; 10hr; Guatemala City 5hr); Tegucigalpa, Honduras (King Quality: 2 daily; 6hr 30min; Puerto Bus: 3 daily; 6hr 30min; Pullmantur: daily; 6hr 30min).

DOMESTIC BUSES

Note that you can also pick up buses to La Libertad and El Tunco at Parque Bolívar, which is much more convenient than the centre than the Terminal de Occidente.

Terminal de Occidente Blvd Venezuela (connected to the centre by buses #4, #27, #34 and #7C; bus #44 goes to Blvd los Héroes and #34 to the Terminal de Oriente). Serves the south and west of the country.

Destinations Ahuachapán (#202; every 30min until 6pm; 3hr 30min); San Juan Opico, for Joya de Cerén (#108; every 20min until 5.30pm; 1hr); La Libertad (#102; 4.30am–8pm; every 10min; 1hr; the *especial* #102A goes all the way to Sunzal via El Tunco 6am–8.15pm; every 30min; 1hr); Metapán (#201A; every 30min until 4.30pm; 3hr 30min); Santa Ana, via San Andrés ruins (#201; 4am–8.10pm; every 10min; 1hr 15min–2hr; *especial* 1hr 15min); Sonsonate (#205; 4.30am–4.15pm; every 15min; 1hr 45 min; *especial* 1hr 15min).

Terminal de Oriente Blvd del Ejército (connected to the centre by buses #3, #5, #7, #8, #9, #28, #29, #34 and #42; and #29 and #54 to Blvd los Héroes). Serves the east and north of the country.

Destinations Chalatenango (#125; 4am–6.30pm; every 10min; 2hr); La Palma/El Poy (#119; every 30min until 4pm; 4hr 30min); La Unión (#304; every 30min until 4pm; 3–4hr; *especial* 1pm; 3hr); San Miguel (#301; hourly 3–11am, less frequent 11am–5.10pm; 3–4hr; *especial* & *super especial* services 3.30am–5pm; every 15min; 2hr 40min); San Vicente (#116; every 30min until 5.30pm; 1hr 30min; *especial* 8 daily; 1hr); Suchitoto (#129; 4.30am–8.15pm; every 20min; 1hr 30min); Usulután (#302; 4 daily; 2hr 30min).

Terminal del Sur On the highway to Comalapa (connected to the centre by buses #11B, #21 and #26). The stop for buses along the eastern Carretera del Litoral to Zacatecoluca and Usulután.

Destinations Costa del Sol (#495; every 30min until 4.30pm; 2hr 30min); Puerto El Triunfo (#185; 6 daily; 2hr); Usulután, for Puerto El Triunfo (#302; every 40min until 4pm; 2hr 30min); Zacatecoluca, for Costa del Sol (#133; every 30min until 5pm; 1hr 30min).

GETTING AROUND

By bus The city bus network runs from 6am until around 8pm and is comprehensive, frequent and cheap – it's US$0.25 to anywhere in the city. Buses are hailed from the side of the road with a flailing arm or whistle. Pay the driver if there is a gate, or the roaming, whistling, shouting driver's assistant if not. Most stops are not marked, so look for large public buildings, shopping centres or groups of people waiting by the road; usually you can also hop on or off if they stop in traffic.

By taxi Yellow city taxis ply the streets and wait around bus terminals, markets and major hotels and shopping areas. They cost US$5–10 depending on how far you go (in the centre trips will be US$5–6), which you should agree on before getting in. Always take taxis after dark.

INFORMATION AND TOURS

Tourist information The Ministero de Turismo (MITUR) and Corsatur offices are at Edificio Carbonell #1, Alameda M.E. Araujo, Colonia Roma (Mon–Fri 8.30am–12.30pm & 1.10–4.30pm; ☎2243 7835, ⓦelsalvador.travel); they give out basic maps and advertisement-laden "guides".

Tour operators Akwaterra (☎7888 8642, ⓦakwaterra .com) speak English and run active ecotours on land and sea – everything from kayaking and surfing to horseriding,

3

USEFUL BUS ROUTES IN SAN SALVADOR

#29 From Terminal de Oriente to Metrocentro via Centro Histórico.

#30B Along Blvd de los Héroes, up Alameda Roosevelt and part of Paseo Escalón, then turning west to run past the Zona Rosa.

#34 From Terminal de Oriente through Centro Histórico to Terminal de Occidente and out along the Carretera Panamericana, past the Mercado de Artesanías.

#42 The length of C 1A from the Centro Histórico to the *Monumento El Salvador del Mundo*, where it turns south towards the University.

#44 Along Blvd de los Héroes, onto 49A Av Sur close to the Terminal de Occidente, past the Universidad de Centroamérica and out past the US Embassy to Santa Elena.

#52 Along Alameda Juan Pablo I, past Metrosur and on to El Salvador del Mundo (opposite the Telecom office), up Paseo Escalón, past the Galerías shopping mall. Note that this route passes the corner of *Hostal Cumbres del Volcán* (see below).

#101A/B/C/D From Centro Histórico up Alameda Roosevelt to Plaza de las Américas, then on to Santa Tecla.

paragliding and mountain biking. El Salvador Divers, 3A C Pte 5020-A, at 99A Av Nte (☎ 2264 0961, ⊛ elsalvador divers.com), offers diving trips along the Los Cóbanos/Los Remedios stretch of the Pacific coast and crater diving at Lake Coatepeque, plus PADI courses and equipment rental.

ACCOMMODATION

The Centro Histórico is not a safe or pleasant place to stay; there is very little to do there at night but wait for a morning bus. The western suburbs are safe, with plenty to see and do, but there are few genuinely budget options apart from in the southern sections. North of Blvd de los Héroes is the middle ground, and much better for travellers: it's safe and with a good amount of nightlife and eating options.

BLVD DE LOS HÉROES AND PARQUE CUSCATLÁN

Casa Tazumal 35A Av Nte 3 ☎ 2235 0156, ⊛ hotel tazumalhouse.com; map p.207. Pricier but homely option with plenty of perks – free wi-fi, airport or bus terminal pick-up, good food and laundry service (US$5) – in addition to clean rooms with cable TV and firm beds. US$43

La Estancia Av Cortés 216 ☎ 2275 3381; map p.207. Relaxed hostel on a quiet residential street just off Blvd de los Héroes, with a large cable-TV area (you'll pay extra for

---

★ TREAT YOURSELF

Hotel Villa del Angel 71 Av Nte 219, Colonia Escalón ☎ 2223 7171, ⊛ villadelangelhotel.com; map p.209. One of the most popular hotels in the city for good reason; the location is excellent (next to Galerías Escalón mall), the owners super-friendly and the rooms superb value, with stylish contemporary design, flat-screen TVs and free wi-fi. US$64

---

basic breakfast, use of the kitchen, water and coffee machine). The dorm bunks spill out into the corridor and the clean en-suite rooms are small and in need of renovation, but great value, especially the room with a private terrace. Dorms US$12, doubles US$30

Ximena's Guest House C San Salvador 202, Colonia Centroamérica ☎ 2260 2481, ⊛ ximenasguesthouse.com; map p.207. The original San Salvador hostel is not necessarily still the best. Beds are lumpy or saggy and the electric hot water (which you pay extra for) is shockingly inconsistent. It remains a travellers' favourite though, not least for the wide range of breakfasts, helpful English-speaking owner and sociable evening atmosphere. Dorms US$7, doubles US$35

COLONIA ESCALÓN AND THE ZONA ROSA

Casa Australia 1A C Pte 3852 ☎ 2224 3931; map p.209. Lacks the atmosphere of the Blvd de los Héroes hostels, but is certainly cleaner and more comfortable; offers free breakfast, the use of computers and wi-fi, and the showers are big and hot. It's incredible value for Escalón, but choose the cheapest rooms, as there is no massive difference in the more expensive ones. US$20

★ Hostal Cumbres del Volcán 85A Av Nte 637 ☎ 2207 3705, ⊛ cumbresdelvolcan.com; map p.209. The backpacker choice in San Salvador, this hostel is surrounded by embassies (read: very safe) and while it's a trek from the main road, bus #52 drops you right on the corner. Comfy dorm bunks or singles (US$15), and private triples/doubles with bathroom and a/c. Free wi-fi (and computers), kitchen and help with transport and tours offered. Dorms US$10, doubles US$30

JoAn's Hostel C del Mediterraneo 12, Colonia Jardines de Guadalupe ☎ 2207 4292, ⊛ joanshostel.hostel.com; map p.204. This newish hostel (just south of La UCA) offers simple modern rooms and dorms, free wi-fi, communal kitchen, lounge with cable TV and a terrace with barbecue. Dorms US$10, doubles US$30

EATING

Cheap eats abound in the Centro Histórico; south of Plaza 17 de Julio (aka Plaza Hula-Hula) is a collection of popular outdoor food stalls (with tables). Prices and quality increase in the western suburbs. The Blvd de los Héroes itself is dominated by fast-food chains (you are never far from a *Wendy's* or a pizza chain in San Salvador), but there are good options off the main drag. Other budget options include the *Eat and Run* chain at petrol stations and the food courts in the malls (see opposite).

CENTRO HISTÓRICO

★ **Del y Arce** C Arce, at 13 Av Sur; map p.205. A classic of the Centro Histórico, this lively cantina does Mexican-style sandwiches (US$2) jam-packed with Salvadorian fillings. Just try to walk past the open-front grill beside the entrance without looking twice. A buzzing atmosphere, and home-made options on the tables like pickled cabbage and hot sauce. Many of the staff are English speaking. Mon–Sat 7am–7pm.

Panadería Latino C Delgado, at Av Providencia Ayala; map p.205. Almost blocked in by market stalls, this local institution is justly popular for its vast ranges of dishes – tacos, chicken, eggs, etc – for under US$1. Daily 6am–8pm.

Pollo Bonanza C Arce, between 7A & 9A Av Sur ☎ 2221 0744; map p.205. A very popular roast chicken joint, and for good reason. The smell of the wood-fire oven at the back wafts through and onto the street outside. Order a whole (US$11), half (US$5) or quarter (US$3) chicken (discounts for takeaway), stack your tray with tortillas and begin to understand why the locals say it's the best chicken in town. Mon–Sat 9.30am–5pm, Sun 9.30am–3.30pm.

BLVD DE LOS HÉROES AND PARQUE CUSCATLÁN

Casablanca C San Antonio Abad, at Av San José ☎ 2235 1489 (no sign); map p.207. A well-staffed lunch joint with large soup portions and freshly fried fish (meals US$1.50 with drink), served by clucking matriarchs in an atmospheric canteen shielded from the traffic by climbing plants. Mon–Sat 7am–2pm.

Comedor y Pupusería La Celba C San Antonio Abad 721 ☎ 2124 2124; map p.207. Best place for a plate of filling *pupusas* in the area, along with tasty but standard *comedor* food, from fried chicken to *tamales* and *tortas* (US$3/head). Mon–Fri 7am–8pm, Sat 7am–1.30pm.

Maya Burguer C G. Cortés, at C Gabriela Mistral; map p.207. This trustworthy hole-in-the-wall burger joint outstrips the big franchises both on price (a two-patty burger, onions and salad are US$4; regular burgers US$1.75) and taste – plus, it's open 24/7. Daily 24hr.

Sol y Luna Blvd Universitario, at Av C ☎ 2521 5927 6637; map p.207. Lovely Ana prepares inventive and tasty vegan food in her quiet restaurant. The buffet (US$6.50/head) includes all the fresh juice you can quaff, and alters daily. Call her up with a day's notice and she'll cook up something special. Mon–Sat noon–5.30pm.

Tacos de Paco C Andes 2931 ☎ 2260 1347; map p.207. Tasty Mexican tacos (US$4–5) served in a room that has original art on the walls and hosts poetry readings on Wed evenings at 6pm. Daily noon–3pm & 5–10pm.

COLONIA ESCALÓN AND THE ZONA ROSA

Dulce y Salado 3A C Pte 3951, at Av Napoleón Viera Altamarino ☎ 2263 2212; map p.209. Decorated like a little girl's bedroom, this small restaurant has good pancake, juice and coffee breakfasts (US$5) and great quiche (US$6.50). Mon–Sat 8am–8pm.

Se Venden Pupusas 75 Av Nte (on the other side of the gate beside the car mechanic); map p.209. This *pupusa* stand on the edge of a mini slum is the real deal. Stuffed with the standard delights of beans, cheese and pulled pork, alongside entire fried plantains and pickled cabbage, Anarudh serves clients who claim it's the best *pupusa* for miles around. You'll eat like a king for two bucks. Mon–Sat 6am–noon.

El Sopón Típico 3A Paseo General Escalón, at 71 Av Nte ☎ 2245 7672; map p.209. A colourful cantina serving up Salvadorian classics and specializing (as the name might suggest) in filling and hearty soups. It also does a passable seafood platter, which at US$12 is big enough for two. A big draw is the US$1.50 lunch menu served at the tables outside the entrance on weekdays. Mon–Sat 11am–8pm, Sun 11am–7pm.

★ **Rústico Bistro** 3A C Pte (aka Shafick Handal), at Av Napoleón Viera Altamarino; map p.209. Local expats judge this the best burger joint in El Salvador (if not Central America), for good reason; the main event is a half-pound, juicy patty of beef seasoned with spices and chipotle sauce and topped with bacon and cheese under a sourdough bun (served with fries). At US$9 it's not cheap, but you'll be glad you coughed up the cash (it's big enough for two to share). Daily noon–4.30pm.

★ **TREAT YOURSELF**

A lo Nuestro C La Reforma 225A ☎ 2223 5116; map p.209. If you want to taste the true potential of what many view as El Salvador's "simple" cuisine, head to this gourmet restaurant. The refined Salvadorian menu is a delight, and the ambience romantic, with table linen and low lighting. Mains US$12–25. Mon–Thurs noon–2.30pm & 7–10.30pm, Fri noon–2.30pm & 7–11pm, Sat 7–11pm.

DRINKING AND NIGHTLIFE

San Salvador's clubs and bars are found mainly in the western suburbs, but there are also small pockets of expat and tourist nightlife, particularly around *La Estancia* in Colonia Centroamérica, behind Blvd de los Héroes. If you fancy mingling with the city's upwardly mobile, head for the cluster of swanky clubs and bars in the shadow of the towering *Hilton Hotel* off Blvd del Hipódromo in Colonia San Benito. Santa Tecla half an hour away also boasts a lively weekend scene along Paseo del Carmen; get a taxi (30min; US$10) to and fro.

BLVD DE LOS HÉROES AND PARQUE CUSCATLÁN

El Arpa Irlandés Av A Col San José 137, on the west side of Parque San José ☎ 2225 0429; map p.207. This laidback bar is the place to come for an ice-cold Guinness (US$4) or a US$6 bucket of Pilsner. There's a pool table, and it livens up on Sat nights with rock bands, which draw a young crowd. No sign – look for the green paint and leprechaun mural. Mon–Thurs 4pm–1am, Fri 3pm–2am, Sat noon–2am.

¡Ay Q'Rico! Blvd Universitario 217, at Av C ☎ 2225 6905; map p.207. Popular among the local students for its cheap daily menus (US$2–3), served with cheaper beers. Also a wide selection of seafood and poultry dishes with a touch of Mexican flavour. Cash only. Mon–Sat 11.30am–3pm & 5pm–2am.

★Café la 'T' C San Antonio Abad 2233, at Av Tzalco ☎ 2225 2090; map p.207. Don't be deterred by the fortress-like security; owner Anna has turned this into an enticing little arty café and bar offering monthly live music and art exhibitions. The *tiramisù* (US$3) is the best in the country and the lemon, honey and vodka-filled "Café Ivanovic" cocktail (US$2.50) is a treat. Tues–Sat 4pm–2am.

La Canchita Pasto 11, al Aconcagua (off C Lamatepec) ☎ 2261 0317; map p.207. This fun and feisty sports bar, one of various drinking dens on the same block (all offering the bucket of six beers for US$6) has the best full-sized pool tables in town (US$1/30min). Part of a mini Zona Rosa which has emerged in recent years, it gets very lively from Thurs onwards. Mon–Sat 10am–1am.

COLONIA ESCALÓN AND THE ZONA ROSA

La Hola Beto's Av Las Magnolias 230, at Blvd del Hipódromo ☎ 2223 6865, ⓦ laholabetos.com; map p.209. Lively restaurant and bar, popular for its tiki-style patio and terrace on the second floor. The mini-chain is known locally for its seafood (mains US$8–15), but this branch is the best for drinks, especially the Salvadorian Cadejo microbrew it has on tap. There's also one close-by *La Canchita* (see above). Daily 8am–midnight.

Los Rinconcitos Blvd del Hipódromo 310 ☎ 2298 9661; map p.209. This no-frills disco and bar makes a good place to start (or end) your evening. Expect live rock music at the weekend, and blaring karaoke most other nights – thankfully, it does promotions on drinks most evenings, too. Daily 5pm–2am.

Zanzibar Blvd del Hipódromo ☎ 2279 0833, ⓦ zanzibar .com.sv; map p.209. Inside the Centro Comercial Basilea complex of shops and restaurants, this stylish open-air bar and restaurant features live music and second-storey views across the boulevard; martinis, margaritas and mojitos from US$4.50. *Gaudí Bar*, a smart wine bar, is also part of the complex. Tues–Fri 5pm–1.30am, Sat 4pm–1.30am.

ENTERTAINMENT

Cinema There are several multi-screen complexes – try Cinemark at the Metrocentro and Gran Vía (☎ 2261 2001, ⓦ cinemarkca.com), or the eleven-screen Cinépolis (ⓦ cinepolis.com.sv) at Galerías Escalón.

Theatre The Teatro Presidente (next to the Museo de Arte) and the magnificently restored Teatro Nacional (see p.205) host everything from ballet to musicals to opera, at anything from free to US$30, while the Teatro Luis Poma, just inside the main arched entrance to the Metrocentro, shows locally produced plays (from US$5). Information can be found in the Friday edition and on the website of *El Diario de Hoy* (ⓦ elsalvador.com). Buy tickets online at ⓦ todoticketsy.com

SHOPPING

Art El Árbol de Dios art gallery, at Av Masferrer Nte 575 & C la Mascota (Mon–Fri 8am–7pm, Sat 9am–6pm; free; ⓦ arboldedios.com), is the shop of El Salvador's emblematic painter Fernando Llort. Everything from prints to cooking aprons in his naïf style can be bought; most items are produced in the workshop in the back. Originals go for about half a million dollars.

Books and newspapers Librería Latinoamérica (Mon–Sat 9am–7pm, Sun 10am–6pm), on the 3rd and 7th levels of the Metrocentro, has English-language titles and US magazines. Librería La Ceiba (Mon–Sat 10am–7pm, Sun 10am–5pm; ⓦ libroslaceiba.com) is the biggest chain of bookstores, branches of which you'll find in Metrocentro, Galerías Escalón and other malls, with a reasonable range, including some books in English (average US$14 for a paperback).

Craft markets There are two good markets for artisan handicrafts: the central Mercado Ex Cuartel (Mon–Sat 7.30am–6pm, Sun 7.30am–2pm), three blocks east of the Teatro Nacional, and the higher-quality Mercado de Artesanías (daily 9am–6pm), opposite the baseball stadium on Alameda M.E. Araujo.

Malls Reputedly the largest mall in Central America, Metrocentro (ⓦ metrocentro.com) at the southern end of Blvd de los Héroes holds three storeys of boutiques, sporting-goods outlets, pricey souvenir shops, a supermarket and a food court. Galerías Escalón (ⓦ galerias.com.sv), at Paseo

3

Gen Escalón 3700, is the same but classier. Multiplaza (ⓦ multiplaza.com) and Las Cascadas (home to Walmart; ⓦ lascascadas.com.sv) on the Carretera Panamericana just outside Santa Tecla have been overshadowed by the pristine Gran Vía mall development (ⓦ lagranvia.com.sv), a few minutes further down the highway – if you want to escape Central America completely for a few hours, this genteel slice of Western consumerism is the place.

Markets Southwest of Plaza Barrios are the ever-expanding street stalls of the Mercado Central (daily 7.30am–6pm), where anything and everything can be bought for about a dollar, even on Sundays.

DIRECTORY

Banks and exchange Most banks ask for the original receipt when cashing travellers' cheques and give over-the-counter cash advances on Visa and MasterCard. Banco Hipotecario, at Av Cuscatlán between 4A & 6A C Ote, and other branches around the city, do not require the receipt. The American Express office is at Anna's Travel Company, 3A C Pte 3737, Colonia Escalón (☎ 2209 8888). Banks and ATMs are ubiquitous around the western suburbs and Blvd de los Héroes.

Embassies Most embassies are located in or around the Paseo Escalón and Zona Rosa districts. The heavily fortified US embassy is on Blvd Santa Elena, Antiguo Cuscatlán (bus #44; ☎ 2501 2999, ⓦ sansalvador.usembassy.gov). Canada is at Centro Financiero Gigante, Alameda Roosevelt y 63A Av Sur (☎ 2279 4655). British citizens should call the embassy at the Torre Futura, Colonia Escalón, on ☎ 2511 5757 (ⓦ ukinelsalvador.fco.gov.uk). Australians should contact the Canadian embassy.

Health The city has two good hospitals: Hospital de Diagnóstico, 21A C Pte at 2A Diagonal (☎ 2226 8878, ⓦ hospitaldiagnostico.com), and its branch, Hospital de Diagnóstico, Escalón, 3A C Pte at 99A Av Nte (☎ 2264 4422). There's also a 24hr pharmacy at Farmacia Internacional, Edificio Kent, Local 6, Alameda Juan Pablo II at Blvd de los Héroes, and a 24hr Farmacia Económica on Hipódromo and Revolución. The Medicentro at 27A Av Nte & 21A C Pte has a number of doctors specializing in different fields (☎ 2225 1312). A consultation will cost around US$40.

Immigration Dirección General de Migración y Extranjería (Sección de Visas y Prórrogas), Centro de Gobierno, off Alameda Juan Pablo II, in the Centro de Gobierno (Mon–Fri 8am–4pm; ☎ 2221 2111), is the place to get stamps, tourist cards and visas extended.

Internet Ciber Morazán, in the Centro Histórico, on Plaza Morazán near the Teatro Nacional (daily 9am–6pm). Webcity Cyber Café, perched on the outer edge of Metrosur (C Los Andes), is also open daily. You'll find a cluster of places around the UTEC campus along C Arce (try La Universitaria Librería y Ciber Café or CompuStar), though these are open Mon–Sat only (usually 9am–7pm). Expect to pay US$0.50–1/hr (the UTEC cafés are the cheapest).

Laundry Jet Cleaners operates several handy branches in the city; Paseo General Escalón; Blvd del Hipódromo 105; and inside the Metrocentro (typically Mon–Sat 7am–7pm; average load US$3).

Police The main station is in the Scottish-castle-like building that occupies an entire block on 10A Av Sur, at 6A C Ote (☎ 2271 4422).

Post office Behind the Centro de Gobierno at 15A C Pte and Diagonal Universitaria Nte; look for the large building with "UPAE" on the side (Mon–Fri 8am–5pm, Sat 8am–noon). There is a smaller office in the lower level of the Metrocentro mall.

Around San Salvador

Northwest of the city, **Volcán San Salvador** looms over the valley, while to the south the **Puerta del Diablo** offers vistas the length of the coast. Tucked beneath the rocks, the village of **Panchimalco**'s splendid colonial church belies its predominantly indigenous populace. To the west are the natural gorge and pools of **Los Chorros**, the exceptionally rare ruins of **Joya de Cerén** and the partially reconstructed pyramids and temples at **San Andrés**.

VOLCÁN SAN SALVADOR

The massive crater which occupies the western side of the **VOLCÁN SAN SALVADOR** (1960m) is well worth the half-day trip from the capital. The **El Boquerón** crater (literally "the Big Mouth") is 558m deep, 1.5km in diameter and was formed around 1000 years ago. Its last eruption was in 1917. Tourists visit the sight through **Parque El Boquerón** (daily 8am–5pm; US$2), a well-maintained park that attempts to give visitors an idea of how the crater came to be through educational videos, although if you want a more colourful history, the locals who hang around the park entrance selling berries will offer their own entertaining spiel for half a buck.

AROUND SAN SALVADOR

3

It's possible to walk down to the **Boqueroncito**, the plug formation in the very centre, although tourists do so at their own risk since the trail is outside the bounds of the park. The descent takes around 45 minutes; the return can take double the time due to the crater's sheer sides. If you plan to descend go early, as it's not a good idea to get caught there in the dark.

The park is at the top of the mountain and access is via **Santa Tecla**, a dilapidated town which was briefly the capital in 1854. The town's central plaza always has market sellers flogging all sorts of bizarre wares, a pleasant diversion for those wanting to break the bus journeys in half.

ARRIVAL AND DEPARTURE

By bus Catch bus #101 (hourly until 6pm; 30min) to Santa Tecla from either the Terminal Occidente or on its route along 79 Av Nte in San Salvador. From there bus #103 (hourly until 5pm) runs up to the top of the volcano. Get off where the bus turns around to descend and walk the final kilometre up the road to the park entrance. The last return journey is around 5pm.
By taxi At least US$25 from San Salvador.

PARQUE ACUÁTICO LOS CHORROS

Six kilometres west of Santa Tecla, just off the Carretera Panamericana (CA-1), El Salvador's most popular *parque recreativo*

familiar, **PARQUE ACUÁTICO LOS CHORROS** (daily 8am–4pm; US$1), is an inviting spot for a swim. Small waterfalls cascade through mossy jungle slopes into four landscaped pools; there are public changing rooms and showers – don't bring valuables – and a couple of *comedores* provide meals.

ARRIVAL AND DEPARTURE

By bus From San Salvador take bus #79 (heading to Lourdes) from 15A Av Sur & C Rubén Darío at Parque Bolívar (every 15min; 30min), or any Santa Ana bus from the Terminal de Occidente, and ask to be dropped at the gate.

JOYA DE CERÉN

Some 14km northwest of Los Chorros (on the road to San Juan Opico, which branches north off the Carretera Panamericana), the Maya site of **JOYA DE CERÉN** (Tues–Sun 9am–4pm; US$3, parking US$1) isn't quite the "Pompeii" it's hyped up to be, but it does offer a totally different perspective to all the other great Mesoamerican ruins. What remains of sites like Copán and Tikal is grand but ceremonial – there is very little evidence of the houses where people actually lived in these cities. Joya de Cerén, on the other hand, is the remains of a humble Maya village buried under

3

more than 6m of volcanic ash around 640–650 AD, left untouched until its accidental discovery in 1976. The site itself is small, with each structure (ten have been excavated) protected in corrugated iron sheds – don't expect giant pyramids. Nowhere else, however, can you see the actual homes of Maya farmers, as well as a sweat bath (*temazal*), *in situ*. The small **Museo Sitio Arqueológico** (general information in English; artefacts labelled in Spanish only) details the development of Maya culture in the region from 900 BC and the excavation project itself; objects found here, including petrified beans, maize, utensils and ceramics, as well as the discovery of gardens for growing a wide range of plants, have helped confirm a picture of a well-organized and stable pre-colonial society, with trade links throughout Central America. As yet, no human remains have been uncovered, which concurs with the hasty departure suggested by the number of artefacts left behind. The guided tours are highly recommended (free; some guides speak English).

ARRIVAL AND DEPARTURE

By bus Bus #108 (every 30min until 5pm) from San Salvador's Terminal de Occidente runs right by the site – get off just after crossing the Río Sucio. If you want to go to San Andrés (see below) in the same trip, start here and take #108 back towards San Salvador as far as the Carretera Panamericana, where you can intercept a #201 (4am–8.10pm; every 10min; towards Santa Ana from the Terminal de Occidente) to San Andrés.

SAN ANDRÉS

A few kilometres southwest of Joya de Céren (32km from San Salvador, on the Carretera Panamericana) lies the elevated Maya ceremonial centre of **SAN ANDRÉS** (Tues–Sun 9am–4pm; US$3, parking US$1). One of the largest pre-Columbian sites in El Salvador, originally supporting a population of about twelve thousand, the site reached its peak as the regional capital around 650–900 AD (it was later used by the Pipils). Only sections of the ceremonial centre have been excavated – seven major structures including the Acropolis and a seventeenth-century

Spanish indigo works – and sadly, they've been preserved using rather too liberal amounts of concrete. You can climb freely around most of the site, though the tallest pyramid ("La Campana") can only be viewed from a distance. The small **Museo Sitio Arqueol** (US$3, some English labelling) includes a good model of what the site would have looked like in the late first millennium.

ARRIVAL AND DEPARTURE

By bus From San Salvador the #201 (every 40min until 5pm) bus between Terminal de Occidente and Santa Ana will drop you by a black ruin on the Panamericana a couple of hundred metres from the site – you will need to tell the driver to stop.

LOS PLANES DE RENDEROS

Overlooking the Valle de Hamacas from the brim of the valley's southern watershed, **LOS PLANES DE RENDEROS** offer fresh air, good food and fine views. The best panoramas of San Salvador are from the *Casa de Piedra* (see below); cheaper, though, is the *mirador* lookout point off the road just before the restaurant as you come up the hill. Jaw-dropping views of the coast are the attraction at the **Puerta del Diablo**, a split rock formation (the three peaks are known as El Chulo, El Chulito and El Chulón), a forty-minute walk from the road through the somewhat grubby **Parque Natural Balboa** (Carretera Los Planes Km 12; daily 8am–6pm; US$0.50, parking $1). The rock's legendary origins – split by a bolt of lightning more than three hundred years ago – have been eclipsed by its very real role in the civil war as a place of death-squad interrogations, executions and body-dumping.

ARRIVAL AND DEPARTURE

By bus Bus #12 (hourly until 6pm) and #17 (every 20min until 5pm) run up the Carretera Los Planes from Av 29 de Agosto (and the Mercado Central) in San Salvador. If you don't fancy walking to the Puerta del Diablo, you can take the bus to the last stop, at Km 14.

EATING AND DRINKING

Casa de Piedra Carretera Los Planes, Km 8.5 ☎ 2280 8822. An open-fronted bar/restaurant serving seafood (mains US$12) and *típicos* with weekend music or karaoke. Daily 11am–2am.

Pupusería Paty Carretera Los Planes, Km 10 ☎2280 8856. Another tempting restaurant, this barn-like place serves some of the best and biggest *pupusas* in the country. Daily 8am–7pm.

PANCHIMALCO

Some 15km south of San Salvador, the largely indigenous town of PANCHIMALCO lies sleepily beneath the Puerta del Diablo. Locals are known as "*panchas*", many of them descendants of the Pipils, though traditional dress is rarely seen nowadays. The baroque **Iglesia Santa Cruz de Roma**, built in 1725, is one of the oldest surviving churches in the country and is also remarkable for its statue of a dark-skinned, indigenous Jesus. There are indigenous **crafts** for sale too, including pre-Hispanic musical instruments, at the **Casa de la Cultura** (Mon–Fri 10am–noon & 2–4pm; ☎2280 8767). Usually a quiet place, things become livelier during the town's annual **festivals** (see p.202). **Bus** #17 runs regularly to the town from outside the Mercado Central in San Salvador (every 20min until 5pm; 30min).

The Pacific coast

El Salvador's **Pacific coast** is a 300km strip of palm-backed beaches, jungle-smothered cliffs, mangrove swamps and exceptional surf breaks. While the tourist potential of many of the beaches is now being developed, most stretches of coastline are still blissfully wild and unspoiled. Indeed, the allure of this part of the country lies in lounging on clean, wide swathes of volcanic sand, catching world-class waves or spending time in relatively untouched fishing villages.

Coming from San Salvador, the most accessible stretch of coast is the **Costa del Bálsamo**, extending around the small fishing town of **La Libertad**. This section boasts some of Central America's most mouthwatering surf breaks, and El Salvador's biggest gringo community. In the extreme east of the region you can watch turtles hatch at **El Cuco**, or catch early-morning *lanchas* to the tranquil islands of the **Golfo de Fonseca**.

The beaches near Acajutla (Los Cóbanos and Los Remedios) and to the west are best accessed via Sonsonate rather than along the coastal road; we've covered them elsewhere (see p.248).

PUERTO LA LIBERTAD

Just 34km south of San Salvador, **PUERTO LA LIBERTAD** (or just "El Puerto"), once a major port and still an important, if shabby, fishing town, has recently grown from surfing haven to tourist junction thanks to its position at the eastern limit of the Costa del Bálsamo. It's a popular place, particularly at weekends, when capital day-trippers join the local and gringo surfers to enjoy the food and sea breezes. The town has a gang presence, although they are strict in leaving tourists alone, and since the construction of a new *malecón* esplanade, it's a lot more welcoming than many of the country's residents make out.

WHAT TO SEE AND DO

The main action in La Libertad occurs along the seafront, not the Parque Central further inland. The focus is the **Muelle** (pier) jutting out into the ocean, which hosts a lively daily fish market, and the *malecón* that stretches from the pier along the town beach, **Playa La Paz**. Playa La Paz itself is quite dirty, and becomes rocky and prone to riptides in the rainy season. For sunbathers, the small and busy **Playa Las Flores** is 1.5km east, reachable by bus #80 (every 20min) or #187 (hourly until 6pm).

Punta Roca

La Libertad's pride and joy is the world-famous **Punta Roca** surf break, which barrels reliably in the early morning and mid-afternoon, a couple of hundred metres to the west of the pier. This is not a beginner's wave, and localism does exist – confrontations are best avoided by hiring a local guide (ask at your hotel or at the tourist office). Even if you don't surf, it's fun just to go and watch experts take on the wave in the morning and evening, or at any of the regular surf events held here.

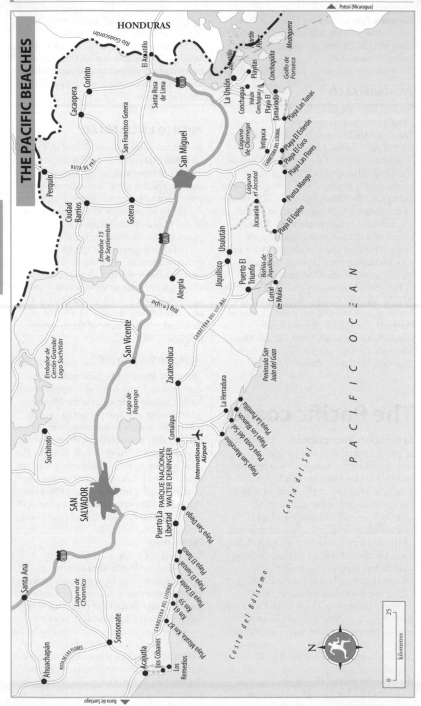

THE PACIFIC BEACHES

HONDURAS

Potosí (Nicaragua)

Rio Goascorán

El Amatillo

Santa Rosa de Lima

Corinto

Cacaopera

San Francisco Gotera

La Unión
Conchagua
Volkán Conchagua
Playtas
Playita
Zacatillo
Martín
Meanguera

Golfo de Fonseca

Playa El Tamarindo

Playa Las Tunas

Playa El Esterón

RUTA DE PAZ

Perquín

San Miguel

Laguna de Olomega

Intipuca

CARRETERA DEL LITORAL

Playa El Cuco
Playa Las Flores

Ciudad Barrios

Gotera

Usulután

Laguna el Jocotal

Jucuarán

Punta Mango

Playa El Espino

Embalse 15 de Septiembre

Jiquilisco

Puerto El Triunfo

Bahía de Jiquilisco

Corral de Mulas

Alegría

Rio (Lempa)

CARRETERA DEL LITORAL

San Vicente

Embalse de Cerrón Grande/ Lago Suchitlán

Zacatecoluca

Península San Juan del Gozo

P A C I F I C   O C E A N

Suchitoto

Lago de Ilopango

La Herradura

Playa La Puntilla
Playa Los Blancos
Playa Costa del Sol

Comalapa

International Airport

PARQUE NACIONAL WALTER DENINGER

SAN SALVADOR

Playa San Marcelino

Costa del Sol

Santa Ana

Puerto La Libertad

Playa San Diego

Playa El Tunco
Playa El Sunzal
Playa El Zonte
Km 59
Playa Mizata, km 87

CARRETERA DEL LITORAL

Costa del Bálsamo

Laguna de Chanmico

Ahuachapán

RUTA DE LAS FLORES

Sonsonate

Acajutla

Los Cóbanos

Los Remedios

N

0   25
kilometres

Barra de Santiago

3

If you need to work on your surf skills before hopping on a board, try some of the better beaches along the coast to the west (see p.220).

ARRIVAL AND DEPARTURE

By bus Services from San Salvador arrive at C Barrios & 4A Av Nte, two blocks inland from the pier. Buses to and from the eastern beaches go from the other side of 4A Av Nte, on Barrios. Further up that road on the corner with 1A C Pte is the stop for Sonsonate and the western beaches.

Destinations Playa San Diego, via Playa Las Flores and Parque Walter Deininger (#187; #80 direct; every 15min; 15–30min); Playa El Sunzal, via El Tunco (#80-A/B, #192, #102-A, #187-A; 4.30am–6pm; every 15min; 35–40min); Playa El Zonte (#192-B to Teotepeque/#192 to La Perla; 7am–7.30pm; hourly; 50min); San Miguel (#324; frequent); San Salvador, Terminal de Occidente (#102: 4.30am–8pm; every 10–15min; 1hr; microbus #102-A: 5am–6.30pm; every 30min; 45min); Sonsonate, via all beaches to the west (#287; daily 6am & 1.55pm; 3hr); Zacatecoluca (#540; 7 daily; 1hr 20min) – change at Comalapa for the airport.

INFORMATION AND ACTIVITIES

Tourist information The extra-helpful Centro de Amigos del Turista (English spoken) is inside the white seafront centre opposite the pier (daily 9am–5pm; ☎ 2346 1634), with clean public toilets opposite the entrance.

Internet You'll find several cybercafés opposite the church on the Parque Central, two blocks inland from the pier.

Surfboards Boards can be bought, sold, rented and repaired at the Hospital de Tablas, on 3 Av Sur, between 2A C Pte and the *malecón* (7am–4pm; rental per board US$12/day).

ACCOMMODATION

Hotel touts abound around the seafront. Aggressive and disrespectful as they may be, it's better to ignore them.

AST Surf Hotel Malecón Turístico, Edificio AST #2-7, Playa La Paz, between 1A Av Sur & 3A Av Sur ☎ 2312 5143,

⊛ astadventures.com. Adventure Sports Travel runs this plush option right on the seafront, with a range of surf packages, airport transfers and three meals daily. *La Terraza*, the open-air rooftop restaurant and bar, is the best place to take in views of the bay. U̲S̲$̲5̲5̲

Hotel Rick 5A Av Sur 30 ☎ 2335 3033, ✉ eldelfin.reyes @gmail.com. This traditional surfers' favourite, managed by the same guys as *El Delfín* (see p.220) is ideally located behind Punta Roca. Rooms are all en suite, with cable TV and space for surfboards. There's a/c in some, but a slightly musty smell in others. U̲S̲$̲2̲8̲

La Posada Familiar 3A Av Sur, at 4A C Pte ☎ 2335 3252. Extremely basic and correspondingly cheap, this family-run set of rooms at the bottom of their overgrown garden come with a choice of a/c or fan and shared or private bathroom, and range accordingly in price. A small *comedor* serves meals and you can see the sea from the roof veranda. U̲S̲$̲1̲2̲

EATING AND DRINKING

The dining scene in La Libertad is relatively pricey but varied, with an inevitable emphasis on seafood. The daily market on the pier sells a good selection from the morning catch, while the cheap seafood restaurants to the east of the pier serve both raw and cooked fish (US$3–5). To the west of the pier along the *malecón* is a collection of much cleaner (and pricier) restaurants, with live music at weekends.

El Delfín 3A Av Sur, Playa La Paz (opposite *Hotel Rick*). A solid seafood joint overlooking the western end of the beach, serving heaps of paella (US$9) for dinner and shrimp omelettes (US$4) for breakfast in pleasant surroundings. Boasts the dubious benefit of Sky TV via satellite. Daily 7am–10pm.

Neto's Beer Malecón, Playa La Paz (just east of the pier). First (and best) of the cheaper places east of the pier – it's clean, and serves fresh seafood and ice-cold beers. Daily 11am–11pm.

Punta Roca 5A Av Sur, Playa La Paz ☎ 2335 4342, ⊛ puntaroca.com.sv. A local institution, after which the break itself is named. There is hearty food with a Western nod ("gringo fry"; US$8), and it is consistently the best place in town for a cold Pilsner (US$1.50). Daily 7am–1am.

DIRECTORY

Banks Banco Agrícola's main branch is on C Barrios, between 4 & 6 Av Nte; it also operates a 24hr ATM opposite the tourist office.

Pharmacy Centro Médico Moises, C Barrios 11-7 (Mon–Fri 7am–6pm, Sat 7am–noon; ☎ 2335 3531).

Post office 2A C Ote, between 2 & 4 Av Nte (Mon–Fri 8am–noon & 12.45–4pm, Sat 9am–noon).

Supermarkets Super Selectos is in the Centro Comercial el Faro, on the Carretera del Litoral east of the centre; Despensa Familiar is at C Calvario and 1A Av Nte (daily 7.30am–7pm).

★ TREAT YOURSELF

Danilo Malecón, Playa La Paz (just west of the pier). If you are going to splurge on quality seafood in Libertad, seek out chef Danilo Ortega's humble-looking place, tucked in among the modern restaurants along the *malecón*. Start with a potent but refreshing *muñeco sour* (US$3), made with local liquor, before tucking into the *ceviche* (US$4.75), fillets of fish (from US$8) or seafood rice (US$6–7). Other mains US$13–15. Daily noon–10pm.

3

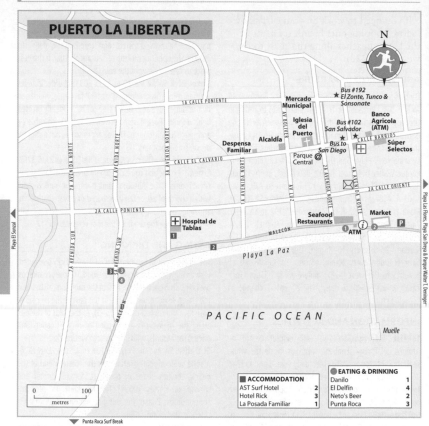

PUERTO LA LIBERTAD

N

Bus #192
El Zonte, Tunco &
Sonsonate

Mercado
Municipal

1A CALLE PONIENTE

AV BOLIVER

Iglesia
del
Puerto

Bus #102
San Salvador

Banco
Agricola
(ATM)

Despensa
Familiar

Alcaldía

Bus to
San Diego

CALLE BARRIOS

Súper
Selectos

CALLE EL CALVARIO

Parque
Central

3A AVENIDA NORTE

5A AVENIDA NORTE

3A AVENIDA NORTE

1A AVENIDA NORTE

2A AVENIDA NORTE

AV LUZ

1A AVENIDA NORTE

4A AVENIDA NORTE

2A CALLE ORIENTE

2A CALLE PONIENTE

Hospital de
Tablas

1

Seafood
Restaurants

Market

ATM

P

2A AVENIDA SUR

2A AVENIDA SUR

MALECÓN

ATM

2

Playa El Sunzal

2

Playa La Paz

Playa Las Flores, Playa San Deiya & Parque Walter T. Deninger

3

4

MALECÓN

PACIFIC OCEAN

Muelle

0   100
metres

Punta Roca Surf Break

ACCOMMODATION	
AST Surf Hotel	2
Hotel Rick	3
La Posada Familiar	1

EATING & DRINKING	
Danilo	1
El Delfin	4
Neto's Beer	2
Punta Roca	3

COSTA DEL BÁLSAMO

Westwards from Puerto La Libertad is the **COSTA DEL BÁLSAMO**, a favourite destination for surfers and day-trippers from the capital. The coast takes its name from the now-defunct trade in medicinal balsam that was once centred here, before tourism took over as the main source of income. More and more expensive beach clubs are now popping up, as international tourists gain confidence in El Salvador, but reasonable accommodation and surfing communities still dominate.

WHAT TO SEE AND DO

West of La Libertad, the Carretera del Litoral runs through thickly wooded hills and tunnels to palm-fringed black beaches. **Playa El Tunco** is by far the most popular beach town in the country, and is

the only stop for many visitors to El Salvador. Further west sit the more tranquil and resort-geared **Playa El Sunzal** and **Playa El Zonte.** To the **east** of La Libertad the only noteworthy stretch of sand is surfer-free **Playa San Diego**, a pleasant beach-stroll surrounded by jungled cliffs. All kilometre distances given are for the Carretera del Litoral, along which there are markers to help you get orientated. La Libertad is the transport hub for the area (see p.217).

Playa El Tunco

Many tourists see nothing more of El Salvador than the colourful sunsets, 200-metre surf breaks and lively party scene at **PLAYA EL TUNCO** (named for a rock offshore which apparently resembles a pig, or *tunco* in the local dialect). The seafront community is geared entirely towards tourism, serving primarily weekend visitors from the capital, surfers and backpackers. Tunco's cappuccino culture paints a sharp contrast to the rest of the country, and will come as a shock for those who have travelled elsewhere in El Salvador. The town is a major stopping point on Central America's beaten track, and for those who don't have the time or desire to explore further inland, it's easily accessible from elsewhere in the region thanks to international shuttle buses direct to and from Antigua, San Salvador and Copán.

The variety of the food on offer plus the amount of English spoken make it a less-demanding destination and Tunco remains relatively tranquil, at least on weekdays. The long stretch of black-sand **beach** is populated by bars and restaurants, from which you can watch the surfers tackle the roaring breaks. The waves here are aggressive, and while lessons are available, beginners are better off getting their bearings at easier spots such as El Cuco (see p.226).

A single one way road (Calle Principal) leads down from the Carretera making a loop through the village; there is parking where it hits the river (US$2/day), and a paved pedestrian-only road down to the beach (aka Calle La Bocana), where most of the action takes place. **Surf shops** will charge around US$10 for a day's board rental (half-days also possible) and US$15 for an hour's lesson; bodyboards are also available for US$10 per day.

ARRIVAL AND DEPARTURE

By plane Most hotels offer pick-ups from the airport for US$30, or US$35 at night (there are no direct public buses; you must take a shuttle to Comalapa, then take bus #187 (hourly until 6pm) to La Libertad).

By bus The easiest option from San Salvador to Playa El Tunco is to catch direct buses #102, #107 or #177 (daily 6am–7pm; every 20min; 1hr) from Parque Bolívar. You can also catch plenty of buses from La Libertad (see p.217). If coming from the west along the Carretera Litoral, buses generally stop at La Perla, where you can change for La Libertad.

ACCOMMODATION

D'rocas C Principal ☎ 2389 6313. The town's best beach resort, which turns into the beachfront's best party on weekends. This mini-resort has clean rooms, all with a/c and private bathroom, plus there's a pool and a decent restaurant. A good option for those looking for the resort experience within the town. **US$20**

La Guitarra C Principal ☎ 2389 6398. Individual cabins with private bathrooms (US$10 extra for a/c) set between the reception and a chilled-out beachfront bar are popular with surfers who come for the discounts on extended stays (generally 3–4 months at a time). Stylish decor, pool, great location and easy beach access make it an excellent option for those looking to avoid the more intense hostel vibe. Also has two complete suites for those who really value their comfort. **US$20**

Hostal Makoi Off C Principal (look for the 'Tortuga Surf Lodge' sign) ☎ 7870 4797. One of three good hostels on this side-street (which the locals have named Calle Jim Morrison) leading down to the beach, a night's stay in this chilled-out spot popular with surfers includes breakfast. The management also give surf lessons, and guests receive reduced rates. **US$10**

Papaya Lodge C Principal ☎ 2389 6027, ⓦ papayalodge .com. The town's most popular hostel, the *Papaya Lodge* has a great location and good communal space, including a treehouse-like roof terrace, a kitchen, a little pool and sitting areas with hammocks, DVDs and books. The large, spotless rooms have a/c or fans with private baths, and the dorms all have roof fans, less a/c, parking, great staff and a shared kitchen and you can't beat it. Dorms **US$10**, doubles **US$25**

Tunco Lodge C Principal ☎ 2389 6318, ⓦ tuncolodge .com. Probably the town's most party-geared hostel, this multilevel place has two six-bed dorms and decent private rooms (the a/c system isn't great, so opt for the fan to save some money), plus a pool, wi-fi and a thatched hangout spot – all in a central location. Airport or San Salvador pick-ups for US$30. Dorms **US$8**, doubles **US$25**

Zuzu's Hangout Guest House Carretera del Litoral Km 42 ☎ 2389 6239, ⓦ zuzusplayaeltunco.com. Bare-bones hostel a long walk from the action, but made more attractive by its discounts during the week. One small dorm and a mix of doubles, free wi-fi and kitchen – not bad if you intend to surf all day, but this is probably a last resort. Rents boards for US$5/hr or US$10/day, with lessons US$8/hr. Dorm **US$10**, doubles with shared bath **US$20**, doubles with private bath **US$40**

EATING AND DRINKING

Comedor Theo C Principal. Proper Salvadorian food at proper Salvadorian prices. This tin-roofed shop offers tables and hammocks inside where you can fill up on local favourites, offering lunch menus, delicious juices and an array of delights displayed behind the counter. Daily 6.30am until the last patron leaves.

Coyote Cojo C La Bocana ☎ 2389 6037. Solid open-fronted restaurant good for people-watching on the road down to the beach. Does good sandwiches (around US$5) and the drinks are cheap. Mon–Thurs & Sun 9am–9pm, Fri 9am–11pm, Sat 9am–2am.

Dale! Dale! Café C La Bocana. The best coffee in town (US$1–2), and the widest choice, with healthy snacks and breakfast options (granola, fresh fruits) from US$3.45. Free wi-fi. Daily 6am–5pm.

D'rocas Beach Bar & Restaurant Off C Principal ☎ 2389 6313. Party central, right on the beach, with cabañas for rent (from US$20) and a large pool (day-use US$3); Thurs is ladies' night, Fri and Sat see live music – you'll pay US$3 cover on Sat. Restaurant daily 8am–6pm; bar Thurs–Sat 5pm–2am.

★**Hotel Mopelia** C Principal ⊛ hotelmopelia-salvador .com. The oldest bar in Tunco which attracts a good crowd, the Belgian owner does justice to his country's brew tradition with a fridge full of imported beer (around US$4 each) and three Cadejo microbrews on draught. His Salvadorian wife runs the extensive kitchen and the couple are rightly proud of their Belgian waffles. The best place in town to spend an evening talking travel with the other patrons. Daily 6pm–midnight.

Restaurante La Bocana C La Bocana ☎ 2389 6238, ⊛ baryrestaurantelabocana.com. Right where the town meets the beach, this two-storey place does a good *mariscada* and ice-cold beers (US$7.50/*balde*). It's a good place from which to watch the surfers beside the rocky outcrop as well as the colourful sunsets over the stretch of black sand. Daily 8am–10pm.

Soya Nutribar C Principal ☎ 7887 1596. Healthy, nutritious meals and drinks, plus their signature "Power-balls" (stodgy protein- and sugar-filled balls of dense cake) to top up your surf mojo; natural *licuados* and smoothies from US$2–2.50, using fresh yoghurt and soy milk, as well as more substantial fish salads (US$5). Daily 8am–5pm.

Sweet Garden C Principal ☎ 2389 6136. This treehouse restaurant overlooking the centre of the Calle Principal specializes in crêpes (from US$3.50) which come savoury or sweet, as well as locally sourced coffee. It's popular in the evening too, especially when they get the candles going. Nice spot for couples. Daily 8.30am–3.30pm & 7–11pm.

Taco Guanaco C La Bocana ☎ 7730 5933. This two-storey *palapa* knocks out delicious and filling Mexican tacos for US$2 and burgers for US$1.50. You'll smell the mouthwatering aromas from the kitchen before you see it. It's usually the last place to close at weekends. Daily 7am–10pm (to sunrise Fri & Sat).

Take a Wok C Principal (at *Hotel Mopelia*). Choose your base (noodles or rice), protein (pork, chicken, tofu etc), extras and one of seven delicious sauces and watch the extremely intense wok-master blend them all together before eating at the bar. Wash it all down with a few Tsing Tao beers (US$2). Good, quick and tasty food which attracts locals and tourists alike. Daily 10am–3pm & 6–10.30pm.

★**Tunco Veloz** C Principal (opposite *Tekuani Ka Hotel*) ☎ 2319 8611. Amazing home-made pizza served in a chilled-out setting – proper thin crusts and local ingredients. The monthly specials are a bizarre and unique treat, featuring toppings like caramelized green apple (surprisingly good). Medium pizzas go for US$8 (enough for one), and large for US$13. Tues–Sun 5–10pm.

DIRECTORY

Banks Banco Hipotecario has an ATM (daily 8am–9pm) inside the *Roca Sunzal Resort*; there's also a Banco Agrícola ATM inside Surfo's & Tiki Travel in the centre of the village.

Internet Most places offer wi-fi. Your best chance of using a computer to get online is at the Mangle store or Sunzal Surf Shop in the centre.

Police Tourist Police, C Principal (☎ 2389 6102).

Playa El Sunzal

Wading across an ankle-deep estuary from El Tunco takes you to the long and wide black sands of **PLAYA EL SUNZAL** (road access at Km 44.5, either side of the Sunzal River). This first section of Sunzal is close to the highway and a few high-priced hotels on the cliffs – there's a cheaper collection of *palapas* further around the headland. For **surfing**, this is the best learners' beach in the country, with long, uncrowded breaks. It's also good for sunbathing, swimming and just lounging on the sand. While this is all easily accessible from Tunco (and Tunco's surf shops are accessible from here), staying here offers the benefit of a distinctly more laidback atmosphere.

EL SALVADOR'S BEST HIDDEN BREAKS

Heading west of El Zonte along the Carretera del Litoral will bring you to three more great and often empty **surfing spots**. **Km 59**, a right-hand beach and point break, tubing when big (though poor at low tide), is often likened to Punta Roca, without the crowds. Around the corner, **Km 61** has equally empty long breaks for longboarders. Further along, **Playa Mizata** at Km 87 is a wave machine, with point and beach breaks going right and left. All three can be reached on the #197 or #287 buses from La Libertad.

INFORMATION

Internet Across the road from *Surfer's Inn* (right on the highway), Ciber Fox (daily 8am–8pm; US$1/hr) has the fastest internet around.

ACCOMMODATION AND EATING

There's a string of *comedores* by the highway near the river, and the basic *Rancho Carolina* and *Rancho Gladys* along the *palapa* strip on the far side of the headland.

San Patricio Carretera del Litoral Km 44.5 (on the highway, 250m from the beach) ☎ 2389 6107, ⓦ ranchosanpatricio .es.tl. More comfortable en-suite rooms than *Surfer's Inn*, with a splash pool and free internet. **US$15**

Sunzal Point Surf Lodge Carretera del Litoral Km 44 (take the road to the beach before the river) ☎ 7842 8886, ⓦ surfsunzal.com. The closest hostel to the waves, right on the jungly point in the middle of Sunzal (it pioneered surfing in the area, opening in 1961). Great-value dorms, plus basic, cheap doubles, fans, hammocks and communal kitchen. Dorms **US$7**, doubles **US$18**

Surfer's Inn Carretera del Litoral Km 44.5 (on the beach) ☎ 2389 6266. Well-shaded camping and basic, concrete en-suite rooms with access to a kitchen and fridge. Camping/tent **US$6**, doubles **US$10**

Playa El Zonte

Down a track just beyond the bridge at Km 53, the small, surfer-dominated **PLAYA EL ZONTE** is a real gem, set apart by its stunning location between two high headlands and its friendly community vibe. Sparkling, grey volcanic sands cover the beach in the dry season (divided by the river), but recede as the waves grow from March to October. The surf here is harder going for beginners than Sunzal and Tunco, better suiting those who are intermediate and above. However, this is no reason for non-surfers to avoid it, as anyone can enjoy the surroundings, swim and join evening games of football.

ACCOMMODATION AND EATING

Costa Brava Carretera del Litoral Km 53.5 (high on the cliffs at the western end of the beach, just off the highway) ☎ 2302 6068 or ☎ 7025 9934. Great food and drinks from Manuel, a Spanish cable-TV chef and local celebrity. His big breakfasts (US$3.25) and excellent seafood dishes (US$6.75–12.50) are great value, though he is only usually there at weekends. Mon–Fri 8am–8pm, Sat 8am–11pm, Sun 7am–7pm.

Esencia Nativa Carretera del Litoral Km 53 (turn off the highway before the bridge) ☎ 7337 8879, ⓦ esencianativa .com. Pleasant rooms around a yard containing a pool, bar

and pizza restaurant, as well as hammocks, airy upstairs terrace, plenty of reading material and table football. The owner, Alex Novoa, really knows his surfing and will organize rental (US$10/day) and surf lessons (US$10/hr). Doubles with fan **US$25**, doubles with a/c **US$35**

Playa San Diego

Some 5km east from La Libertad along the Carretera del Litoral, languid **PLAYA SAN DIEGO**, with its light grey, seemingly endless, scrubby but generally clean stretch of sand, is deserted during the week except for a few fishermen. Views to the sea from the 7km dirt road behind the beach are blocked by ranks of private homes behind locked gates, but get off the bus outside the *Hotel Villa del Pacífico* and you can follow a path just to the left that leads down to the sand.

ACCOMMODATION AND EATING

Cheap accommodation options at San Diego are pretty poor, but there are some good budget places to eat.

Hostal Tortuga Feliz C Principal, Pasaje Ote 15 no. 158 ☎ 2542 2252. Halfway along the seafront similar prices and food to *La Finkita*, with two swimming pools and a chance to see nesting turtles crawling up the beach (tours US$6). Set breakfasts from US$3, lunch and dinner US$6. Daily 8am–10pm.

Hotel Villa del Pacífico C Principal, Pasaje 1 (right by the western end of the beach, nearest the highway) ☎ 2345 5681. The best place to stay: a/c rooms with bath, plus a restaurant and a pool set in manicured gardens. **US$50**

Rancho La Finkita C Principal, Pasaje 16 (halfway along the seafront ☎ 2373 8730. Good-value chicken and steaks (US$3–5) as well as the obligatory fish dishes. Daily noon–10pm.

★ TREAT YOURSELF

El Dorado Surf Resort Playa El Zonte ☎ 7226 6166, ⓦ surfeldorado.com. Welcoming Québécois owners and a great atmosphere make this a top-notch surfer haven, with clean, comfortable rooms and dorms. Surfers (and non-surfers) will find everything they need – board rental, lessons, longboard skateboards, even a training pool – and staff will even help guests plan their travels. One of the country's best treats. Dorms **US$22**, doubles **US$72**

3

COSTA DEL SOL

While it's nowhere near as developed as the Costa del Bálsamo further west, the white-sand 15km peninsula of the **COSTA DEL SOL** is nevertheless still popular with those Salvadorians who are less inclined to spend their holidays alongside raucous gringos. Very close to the airport, the area nevertheless has some decent budget options and some of the best seafood in the country, not to mention a gorgeous beach.

Playa San Marcelino to Playa Los Blancos

Behind **Playa San Marcelino**, the first beach along the main highway, lies a collection of enticing seafood restaurants. More exclusive beach-time is on offer some 3km east at **Playa Costa del Sol**, where a *parque recreativo* (daily 7am–6pm; US$1) rents cabañas for the day. A few kilometres further on, at Km 66, is **Playa Los Blancos**, where there are a couple of cheapish hotels.

ARRIVAL AND DEPARTURE

By bus Bus access to the Costa del Sol usually means a change in the humdrum town of Zacatecoluca, or just Zacate, 45km southeast of San Salvador on the Carretera del Litoral. Bus services finish just before sunset. From here, bus #193 (every 30min; 1hr 30min) serves La Puntilla via all beaches. You can reach Zacatecoluca from La Libertad (#540; 7 daily; 2hr), San Salvador, Terminal del Sur (#133; every 15min; 1hr) and San Vicente (#177; every 15min; 1hr).

ACCOMMODATION AND EATING

At the time of writing Playa Los Blancos and Playa San Marcelino were subject to gang territory disputes. While this should not cause concern for tourists, it makes movement between the towns along the coastal highway after dark extremely difficult.

Kenny Mar Playa San Marcelino ☎ 2332 9041, ⓦ restaurantekennymar.net. Award-winning restaurant serving fresh seafood and sandwiches (US$3–13) and

cheaper breakfasts from US$2.50. Known for its (deceptively) potent frozen strawberry daiquiris. Has awesome views of the sunset. Daily 7am–8pm.

Mini Hotel y Restaurante Mila Playa Los Blancos ☎ 2355 7400. The town's best deal and a safe option, although it's not much to write home about. Nine small but comfortable rooms with fans (four more with a/c inside the main building), a swimming pool and beach access. Sells decent sandwiches for US$2. Doubles without bath $\underline{US\$19}$, doubles with bath $\underline{US\$23}$

Rivera Beach Mar Playa Los Blancos (about 200m west of the *Mila*) ☎ 7282 0067. A basic hotel with a couple of pools, the beach access is good and there is decent food on offer from the basic kitchen at the entrance. $\underline{US\$20}$

★**Sol y Mar** C La Bocana, Playa San Marcelino (no sign, but look for the sun painted on the gate) ☎ 7317 4996. This family-run ranch is the best option in the area, with a large whitewashed building for guests, all rooms with a/c, a palm-fringed pool and direct access to the beach. The restaurant is staffed daily during the high season. $\underline{US\$20}$

Playa La Puntilla

At the far eastern tip of the Costa del Sol (Km 78), **Playa La Puntilla** is a sleepy array of thatch-and-bamboo beach shacks with a dazzling view across the mouth of the **Estero de Jaltepeque** and the Río Lempa – most people come here for the boat trips (see box below). There is inexpensive lodging here, but it is shockingly bad; your best bet is to bring a hammock, as this is a safe place to sling it and sleep. There are plenty of cheap *comedores* along the beach serving fresh seafood, though most only open at weekends.

THE EASTERN BEACHES

Wider and wilder than their western counterparts, the **eastern beaches** tend to be over-visited by Salvadoreños at the weekend but under-visited during the week – the whole stretch offers you the chance to stay in rustic surroundings

---

BOAT TRIPS AROUND THE ESTERO

A **boat trip** around the Estero is really the highlight of this section of coast. *Lancha* owners run trips from La Puntilla across to the **Isla de Tasajera**, around the mangrove swamps of the Estero and up the Río Lempa. You'll be approached by touts as soon as you step off the bus, but don't let yourself be led to a boat or you'll pay the "agent's" commission. It's better to go hunt a boat down yourself; it should cost no more than US$45 per boat for 2–3 hours, so try to get a group together to reduce costs.

where you are unlikely to see another traveller for days on end. The exception is **El Cuco**, where the active beachside community is supplemented by large annual doses of surfers during the wet season.

Puerto El Triunfo

Around 7km south of the Carretera del Litoral (and some 20km southwest of the unexceptional town of **Usulután**), **PUERTO EL TRIUNFO** is a shabby port set on the north shore of the **Bahía de Jiquilisco**, separated from the ocean by the San Juan del Gozo peninsula. Formed by coastal mangrove swamps, the pristine bay features 12km of waterways and a number of jungly islands. A long, fine, sandy beach forms the ocean side of the peninsula, while floating platforms can be swum to from the bay-side beach. There's no accommodation in Triunfo itself – you have to get a speedboat from the town's jetty (US$30 return per boat) out to one of the various hotels on the peninsula. *Restaurante Estefanie* (☎7766 5949, US$50) is a good option and well-known to the boatmen.

Corral de Mulas

From Puerto El Triunfo passenger boats (US$2) cross to El Icaco on **CORRAL DE MULAS**, on the peninsula. Boats leave when full, which happens much more regularly in the early morning (last boat back around 4pm); if you miss these, renting a boat can be costly – expect to pay up to US$45. Corral de Mulas offers the opportunity to engage in old-fashioned, rural Salvadorian life – it's a great place to walk and chat to locals, and as well as camping you can ask to stay with a family when here.

ARRIVAL AND DEPARTURE

By bus Puerto El Triunfo is connected to San Miguel (#377; every 40min; 3hr), San Salvador (#185; 6 daily; 2hr) and Usulutan (#363; every 30min; 30min) – for Playa El Espino, change in Usulután (#363; every 10min; 1hr).

ACCOMMODATION

If you want to stay on Corral de Mulas, either with a local family or camping, ask at Puerto El Triunfo's *alcaldía* (town hall) and they will help you out.
El Jardín 1 Av Nte 4, Puerto El Triunfo ☎ 2663 6089. Between the pier and the bus station, this small, grubby place is the only formal place to stay. <u>US$14</u>

Playa El Espino

Once one of El Salvador's finest swathes of sand, **PLAYA EL ESPINO** is no longer a remote, undeveloped beach, with a 26km paved road from the Carretera del Litoral opening it up to visitors. Sadly, some of this redevelopment is distinctly garish, and even the beach itself has receded in recent years, the water lapping the waterside *palapas* at high tide. Weekends see crowds of day-trippers from Usulután, while during the week many businesses simply close down. What remains of the palm-fringed beach can be magical, and if you are travelling by car Espino is worth a look, but getting here by bus is not worth the hassle – make for El Cuco (see p.226) instead.

ARRIVAL AND DEPARTURE

By bus Access to Playa El Espino is via Usulután on the Carretera del Litoral (from Usulután take #351 or #358B, changing at Jucurán to #358; 7 daily, last one back at 4pm; 1hr 45min). Usulután is connected to Puerto El Triunfo (#363; frequent; 1hr), San Miguel (#373; frequent; 1hr 40min), San Salvador (#302; frequent; 2hr 30min), San Vicente (#417; 6 daily; 2hr) and Santiago de María, for transfers to Alegría (#392C, #35, #348 or #349; every 10min; 45min).

ACCOMMODATION AND EATING

It is best to be in a group of four or five to stay cheaply on Espino, though all accommodation is bare-bones. Book the hotels ahead at weekends. A host of *comedores* and basic restaurants on the beach sell similar dishes, though prices for seafood are high and the quality varies.

TURTLES AND PELICANS AT TORTUGA VERDE

Curious about turtles and pelicans? *La Tortuga Verde* hostel (see p.226) in El Esterón doubles as a **turtle sanctuary and pelican retreat**; pelicans roam the property freely (the owner helps rehabilitate injured birds), and turtles are born on the beach here year-round. Guests get to help release the hatchlings into the sea – a magical experience.

3

BOATS TO NICARAGUA

La Tortuga Verde (see below) arranges taxi/ferry transport across to **Nicaragua** (Potosí) – this is a more reliable alternative to the Cruce de Golfo service (see box, p.228). The fare includes the taxi ride to La Unión, which takes 45min. Boats typically leave between 10am and 11am (Mon–Fri only), and take around 2hr 30min. Although *Tortuga* will not guarantee passage, if you pay for at least one night at the hotel, your room is free for every day you are delayed thereafter (apart from Sat & Sun, when no boats run). For 1–2 people the charge is US$75 per person; it's just US$70 per person for 3–4 people and US$65 for 5–6 people. *Tortuga* can also arrange for a private car to take you all the way to León for an additional US$125.

Taking just the boat back from Potosí to La Unión is much cheaper (see box, p.228). Private boats are also available daily, for US$375 (maximum of eight people).

Arcos del Espino C Principal (at the entrance to the area next to the beach) ☎ 2608 0686. Basic, spotless en-suite rooms (for four people) with a/c, set around a crystal-clear pool. US$38

Natali 300m on right as you reach the beach ☎ 7254 9215. The a/c and en-suite rooms here – with use of a kitchen – sleep five people, including one in an indoor hammock. US$45

Playa El Cuco

Some 30km east of Usulután, the Carretera del Litoral turns south, descending towards the east's most famous beach community, **PLAYA EL CUCO**. The village itself is rather manic, with a beachfront crowded by tourism opportunists. The beaches to either side, however, are ravishing: **El Esterón** to the east is something of a backpacker hub, while the 300m breaks at **Las Flores** to the west are popular with surfers.

Playa Las Flores

A 3km stroll along the beach to the west of town will bring you to **PLAYA LAS FLORES**, home to a 300m surf break which has made the beach popular with tourists. Given its high visibility, lack of rocks and relatively gentle swell it's a very good break for beginners to learn on, and classes (US$20/hour) are offered by the locals who inhabit the grassy area behind the sandbar. The surf is at its best between 6 and 7am or around 3.30 to 5pm.

ARRIVAL AND INFORMATION

By bus The ride from San Miguel to Playa El Cuco is one of the finest bus journeys in the country, with sensational views of the valleys and Volcán San Miguel; sit on the right side of the bus on the way to El Cuco for the best view.
Destinations San Miguel (#320; every 30min; for La Unión

transfer at El Delirio; 1hr 30min); Usulután (#373; every 30min).

Internet There are no internet cafés in El Esterón, but non-guests can use the computer or wi-fi at *La Tortuga Verde* for US$1/hr. There is a small, two-computer internet place in El Cuco next to the police station, and *Leones Marinos* has free wi-fi in its restaurant.

ACCOMMODATION

Most accommodation in El Cuco itself is poor, and the majority of backpackers head east to El Esterón, where a US-expat enclave has developed.

La Bocanna (aka *Munda's Place*), next to *Cruz's Place*, El Esterón ☎ 7338 9646, ⓦ latortugaverderest@yahoo.com. Excellent restaurant (see oopposite) with basic singles and doubles, one of which has a/c (US$25), all with fabulous river views. US$15

Cucolindo Near town along the road, El Esterón ☎ 2619 9012. This beach-fronted place is a decent budget option, with clean rooms. US$30

Estrella del Mar El Cuco (no sign) ☎ 7287 9429. Not so much a hotel as a house with two large and well-kept rooms in the centre of town; look for the "Se Alquilan Cuartos" sign at the southeast corner of the plaza. You'll have the place to yourself, to swing in hammocks, cook your own food and stroll the half-block to the beach. Prices are very negotiable, and you should aim for US$10

Leones Marinos El Cuco ☎ 2619 9015. A large complex with swimming pool, restaurant, more hammocks than you can swing a hammock at and clean rooms (with or without a/c); a good option for those staying in town. There's also a shop by the reception selling everything you could possibly need for a day at the beach. Prices are always negotiable. US$30

Río Mar A house before the end of the beach road, El Esterón ☎ 7338 9646, ⓦ latortugaverderest@yahoo.com. For the best sea views and a pool by the ocean, snag a double room at this great restaurant (see opposite). Some singles available. US$20

★**La Tortuga Verde** C Pacífica, El Esterón ☎ 7774 4855, ⓦ latortugaverde.com, ⓔ latortugaverderest@yahoo.com.

Make sure you book ahead for this excellent American-run hotel, so chilled you might never leave. Featuring arty hidden lighting (so as not to disturb turtles hatching nearby) and a restaurant overlooking the beach serving fresh fish and fruit. They have doubles, some with a/c (for $10 more), a dorm and a good-value "room & board backpacker special": a double bed in the dorm plus breakfast and lunch for US$17. They also have a turtle and pelican sanctuary (see box, p.225), a tiki bar and *lanchas* that will take you to Isla Meanguera, the famous surf break of Punta Mango and Las Flores (which can also be reached by car). They also coordinate with boats to Potosí in Nicaragua (see box opposite). Dorm US$10, doubles US$25

EATING

★ **La Bocanna** (aka *Munda's Place*), next to *Cruz's Place*, El Esterón ☎7338 9646, ⓦlatortugaverderest@yahoo.com. New spot with jaw-dropping views of the ocean and the volcano across in Nicaragua; sit on the shaded patio and enjoy the fresh fish and *conchas* (local black river clams) as the sun sets (mains from US$5). Manager Munda sources her fish daily from local fishermen, and has a secret supply of green coconuts from trees imported from Thailand (much sweeter than the Central American kind). Watch the local kids play football on the beach opposite. Daily 7am–7pm.

Cruz's Place At the end of the beach road and down the right-hand cul-de-sac, El Esterón. This *comedor* has long had a reputation for quality seafood; it's unofficially named after the owner, Cruz, who goes fishing every day, and serves the catch to a faithful bunch of regulars. Enjoy superb views of the ocean while you eat (mains US$4–9). Daily 7am–7pm.

Río Mar A house before the end of the beach road, El Esterón ☎7338 9646, ⓦlatortugaverderest@yahoo.com. Another relatively new place with eye-popping views, right by the ocean. Specializes in seafood and *conchas*, but also serves excellent fried chicken and hamburgers. Day-visitors can use the lovely pool here for US$2. Daily 7am–7pm.

Rocamar On the beach, El Cuco. The most easterly of the various kitchens occupying the three concrete huts with thatched roofs. They all serve prawn cocktails, cold beers and enormous shrimp for low prices. A good lunch option. Daily 9am–10pm.

Siete Mares On the plaza, El Cuco ☎7257 6678. One of the only restaurant owners on the plaza who opted not to name the place after herself, Teresa serves up good *ceviche* with the *urile* clams you'll see displayed in front of many similar restaurants around town, and indeed along the coast. It's also something of a social hub on the weekends. Daily 7am–9pm.

Playa Las Tunas and Playa El Tamarindo

Some 22km east of the El Cuco turn-off along the Carretera del Litoral, another side-road heads along the tooth-like **Península Punta Amapala**, pointing into the mouth of the Golfo de Fonseca. **PLAYA LAS TUNAS**, on the south side, is the first beach you encounter, with a fine dark-sand beach and tides that wash right up into the beachside *ramadas*. It has a friendly atmosphere to it, and, budget-wise, it is your best option for accommodation on a beach between Cuco and La Unión. There's a small village here with several restaurants open for lunch only, right on the beach, selling fresh fish and oysters, and offering plenty of hammocks for a post-prandial lounge.

The final beach at the northern tip of the peninsula, **PLAYA EL TAMARINDO** is a panorama-lover's dream. The huge golden arc of sand, backed by uninterrupted palm trees, curves around the mountainous bay; sitting beneath the Volcán de Conchagua, the islands of the Golfo de Fonseca loom large, and in the distance the mountainsides of Honduras and Nicaragua are clearly visible. The beach faces a protected cove with very little wave action, making it ideal for swimming. On the downside, gangs have been taking over this area in recent years and many locals have moved away – there's not much in the way of places to stay or eat, either, so it's best as a day-trip. Check in La Unión or at *La Tortuga Verde* in El Cuco (see opposite) for the latest situation.

ARRIVAL AND DEPARTURE

By bus Buses to La Unión run along the peninsula, passing through Las Tunas (#383; every 20min); the last one back leaves at 5pm.

ACCOMMODATION AND EATING

Rancho Las Tunas Playa La Tunas ☎2526 5542. The highlight of the restaurants and places to stay at Tunas, perched on a rock that's surrounded by rushing water at high tide, and serving the best oysters (US$7) in the area. They also have two rather pricey rooms on the beach side, with a small pool and stupendous views. US$45

Tropi Tamarindo Playa El Tamarindo ☎2649 5082. The only accommodation on the beach is too pricey for what are little more than standard mid-range rooms, but they will let you use the pool and loungers if you spend US$10, so it's a good spot for beers and food. US$55

3

3

LA UNIÓN

The grimy port town of **LA UNIÓN** sits in a stunning location on a bay at the edge of the Golfo de Fonseca. There are no particular attractions here, but the town is a useful jumping-off point for trips to the beautiful islands of the **Golfo de Fonseca** (see opposite). Shops are scarce on the islands, and prices high, so it's worth stocking up before you go. Budget accommodation is limited, sketchy and not recommended in La Unión; skip the town and stay on the islands or in El Cuco instead, where you can arrange onward travel to Nicaragua (see p.226).

ARRIVAL AND INFORMATION

By bus The main bus terminal is on 3A C Pte, between 4A and 6A Av Nte, two blocks west and one north of the Parque Central. If you're travelling along the coastal highway, you will need the Terminal Los Cantones, two blocks south and one block west of the main terminal, on C San Carlos.
Departures from the main terminal San Miguel (#324; very frequent; 1hr); San Salvador (#304; every 30min until 4.30pm; 2hr 30min); Santa Rosa de Lima (#342; every 15min; 1hr 30min) – change here for the Honduran border at El Amatillo. There are also *especial* buses to San Miguel (#304 and others, frequent departures all day; 40min); and San Salvador (#304; 4am, 6am & 12.30pm; 2hr).
Departures from Terminal los Cantones Conchagua (#382; 4 daily; 30min); El Tamarindo, via Las Tunas (#383; every 20min; 1hr 30min).
Ferries to the Golfo de Fonseca See opposite.
Banks Banco Agrícola, 1A C Pte & Av General Cabañas, or Scotiabank, 3A C Ote & 1A Av Nte, one block downhill from the Parque (both Mon–Fri 8am–4pm, Sat 8am–noon), change money and have 24hr ATMs.

EATING

Cappuccino's 1A C Ote & 3A Av Nte, two blocks down from the Parque ☎ 2605 3091. Freshly brewed coffee and espresso, as well as tasty sandwiches and breakfasts

(from US$2) – the perfect place to chill out while you wait for the boat across to Nicaragua. Mon–Sat 8am–8pm, Sun 9am–5pm.
De Todo supermarket 1A Av Sur between 2A & 4A C Ote. Handily located, just a block south of the Parque. Daily 7am–6pm.

CONCHAGUA

Looming to the south of La Unión is **Volcán de Conchagua** (1225m), with scintillating views across the gulf to Nicaragua and Honduras. The friendly village of **CONCHAGUA**, sitting on its northern slopes, was founded in 1543. The climate is fresher here, a pleasant relief from the heat of La Unión, and the village contains one of the oldest churches in the country, dating back to 1693 and dedicated to Santiago Apóstol.

From Conchagua pick-ups will take you to the lookout point up the volcano (cars pay US$5 to park; locals also charge US$2/car or US$1/person to pass through the gate on the road to the *mirador*), where there are short and long walking routes. If driving, you'll need a 4WD.

ARRIVAL AND DEPARTURE

By bus Bus #382 arrives in Conchagua from the Terminal los Cantones in La Unión (5 daily; 15min).

ACCOMMODATION AND EATING

Note that there are no stores or restaurants on the volcano, so you will need to bring your own supplies.
Pupusódromo Parque Central, Conchagua village. In the evenings you can grab a delicious *pupusa* from the collection of ten *pupusería* along the side of the Parque. Stalls daily 9am–10pm (*pupusas* served from 6pm).
Volcán de Conchagua (CODECA) ☎ 2604 5320, ✉ ongcodeca@yahoo.com. Camping and simple

---

TO NICARAGUA BY BUS AND BOAT

Cruce del Golfo (🌐 crucedelgolfo.com) boats link La Unión with **León** (US$99) and **Potosí** (US$65) in **Nicaragua** every Tuesday and Friday, but only if they have a group of ten to twelve people. You need to arrive at the harbour by 8.30am to complete immigration formalities before the boat departs; after a short break at Isla Meanguera the boat (a covered speedboat) arrives at Potosí around 11.30am. After clearing immigration (1hr), a 4WD car takes you to León in around 3hr (arriving 3.30pm), and will drop off at your hotel. *La Tortuga Verde* in El Cuco can also organize this trip (see p.226), and offers cheaper rates from Potosí back to La Unión: US$45 per person for 1–2 people, US$40 per person for 3–4 people, and US$35 per person for 5–6 people. You'll have to take a taxi (45min; US$35) or bus (see above) to El Cuco from La Unión.

accommodation with shared bathrooms at a stomach-tingling spot near the summit of the volcano. Camping/tent US$5, doubles US$20

ISLAS DEL GOLFO DE FONSECA

Four delightfully secluded **islands** – Conchagüita, Martín Pérez, Meanguera and Zacatillo – sit out in the **GOLFO DE FONSECA** under the stewardship of El Salvador, all a short boat ride from La Unión. **Isla Zacatillo**, the nearest island to La Unión (9km) and once a prison, is just four square kilometres with a small fishing settlement and a few unremarkable beaches; tiny **Isla Martín Pérez** (just half a square kilometre), 1km beyond, has some sandy coves, but no facilities for visitors. Further south, visitor-friendly **Isla Conchagüita** (a circular 8.45 square kilometres) was sacked by English pirates in 1782 and remained deserted until the 1920s, when settlers finally began moving back. In its centre, on the Cerro del Pueblo Viejo, are the remains of a tiny pre-Columbian (Lenca) settlement; a path to the north of the ruins leads up to a large rock bearing engravings that some believe are a map of the gulf. Even now in the two small settlements of Conchagüita and El Líbano you can see fairer, blue-eyed, pirate descendants among the islands' inhabitants.

Legend has it that Sir Francis Drake buried a stash of Spanish silver while at anchor on Isla Meanguera del Golfo, the largest island (23.6 square kilometres) and the furthest away from La Unión (30km). There are still plenty of secluded coves to explore, as well as good swimming and boundless scope for hiking. For fantastic views of the surroundings, climb Cerro de Evaristo, the highest peak on Meanguera. The best beach on the islands, Playa El Majahual, is also on Meanguera (south side). Wide, tranquil and with black sand, it can be reached on foot in 45 minutes by the road south of town and the track it turns into, or by boat in ten minutes if you can persuade a *lancha* owner. For bird lovers, tiny Isla Meanguerita off the southeast coast of Meanguera can only be reached by *lancha*.

ARRIVAL AND DEPARTURE

By ferry Lanchas for the islands of the Golfo de Fonseca arrive and depart in La Unión (see opposite) on the pier jutting out from the northern end of 3A Av Nte. Public lanchas (US$3; 90min) depart La Unión for Meanguera around 10.30am and leave the island for La Unión around 5.30am. There is only one trip per day, so unless you plan to charter a private boat you will have to stay overnight. Lanchas from La Unión to Zacatillo (US$3; 20min) depart when full from the seafront between 9 and 10am, and return in the afternoon any time from 3 to 6pm (agree time with your boatman who will make the return trip to collect you) – it's the only island you can visit as a day-trip. The only way to visit Martín Pérez is by private boat – note also that there are no public lanchas between the islands, so to island-hop you must return to La Unión or hire a private lancha. Schedules are fairly informal; if there are enough people to fill a boat to a specific island, a lancha will be allocated to go direct, but if not, the Meanguera lancha will usually make stops along the way (at Conchagüita, for example). The fare to any of the islands is usually US$3 one way.

By private lancha Local boatmen in La Unión will rent out a lancha for around US$90 100 per boatload to go as far as Meanguera and back, though you can commandeer one on the islands for a little less.

ACCOMMODATION AND EATING

The smaller islands – Conchagüita, Zacatillo and Martín Pérez – have no accommodation, but Meanguera is a terrific getaway spot. The two good backpacker hostels here both have great seafood restaurants with shellfish for less than US$4; they're close enough together to compare. Otherwise, comedores in the villages serve fresh seafood, delivered daily by a fishing fleet that floats in the bay.

El Mirador Isla Meanguera ☎ 2648 0072. This pretty hostel has spotless rooms with hard mattresses, en-suite baths, cable TV and perhaps a fractionally better view than El Paraíso. **US$21**

El Paraíso Isla Meanguera ☎ 2648 0145. Older rooms, cable TV and en-suite baths with the elusive hot-water shower. **US$20**

The east

The rough and wild terrain of **eastern El Salvador** remained relatively unexplored territory for the pre-Columbian Pipils, who did not venture far beyond the natural frontier of the Río Lempa into this land of lofty volcanoes, hot plains and mountain ranges. As a result, its Lenca inhabitants developed their society in isolation from the west, and it was only with some difficulty that the Spanish conquered this frontier in 1537.

Today, coffee production around the flower-filled mountain village of **Alegría** and the region's major cities, languid **San Vicente** and bustling **San Miguel**, create a wealth that contrasts cruelly with the rural poverty found further north. Along the **Ruta de Paz**, refugees from communities devastated by the civil war – this region saw the worst of the fighting – have in the last two decades returned to try and pick up the pieces in this wild and beautiful area. Some have turned to "war tourism" as a viable new occupation, but their ongoing struggle with poverty is often still painfully apparent. The former guerrilla stronghold of **Perquín** contains a moving war museum, while the haunting and unmissably sad village of **El Mozote** was the scene of the conflict's most horrific massacre.

SAN VICENTE

The first major town east along the Panamericana, 60km east of San Salvador, **SAN VICENTE** is a calm, low-slung city with a rich agricultural area producing sugar cane, cotton and coffee. It's a more appealing destination than San Miguel, further along the highway – the one downside is the lack of accommodation. Vicente was sacked during the Insurrection of the Nonualcos in 1833, a doomed indigenous uprising led by Anastasio Aquino (who was later executed here), and the city still has a conspicuous military presence. The barracks are at the southwestern corner of the central Parque Cañas – rivalled only by the number of American Peace Corps trainees, who come here to prepare for forthcoming missions in El Salvador.

WHAT TO SEE AND DO

The centre is compact and laidback with a couple of intriguing sights.

Parque Cañas

The centrepiece of the central **Parque Cañas** is the eye-catching **Torre de San Vicente** (daily 8am–6pm; US$1). Inspired by – and closely resembling – the Eiffel Tower, the 40m clock tower was completed in 1930 and badly damaged by the 2001 earthquake, which killed hundreds here and flattened the entire city centre. It was reopened in 2009 – climb the spiral staircase for the best views of the city.

The **Cathedral** on the Parque was destroyed by the quake, and though it has been rebuilt in the style of the nineteenth-century original, the interior is modern and plain.

Iglesia de Nuestra Señora del Pilar

Two blocks south of the Parque, at Av Crescencio Miranda 2, the **Iglesia de Nuestra Señora del Pilar** (daily 7am–6pm) has far more character than the cathedral. The church was completed in 1769 on the site where a miraculous moving statue of the Virgin Mary persuaded one Manuela de Arce not to stab her husband, or so it's told. Salvadorian independence hero José Simeón Cañas (known as "the liberator of the slaves") was buried here in 1838. The original was restored after earthquake damage, but the modern extension next door remains the primary place of worship (you can enter the older section from a side door).

Dulcería Villalta

Make time for San Vicente's sweetest sight, the **Dulcería Villalta** (Mon–Sat 7.30am–5pm, Sun 7.30am–3pm) north of the Parque at 7A Calle Poniente 4, just off José María Cornejo. Established in 1860, this small shop sells local handmade sweets of all shapes and colours, containing local fruits, milk and molasses, and tasting a bit like fudge. Buy an assorted bag (US$2) to take away or munch in the shady garden at the back.

ARRIVAL AND DEPARTURE

By bus The bus station is on 8A C Pte & 15A Av Sur, a long walk southwest of the centre, but all local buses pass the Parque Cañas going in or out (get out when you see the tower). You can also get a pick-up or local bus (#157; frequent; 10min) 3km up to the Carretera Panamericana to catch the more frequent #301 between San Salvador and San Miguel.

Destinations Costa del Sol (#193E; 4 daily; 2hr 30min); San Salvador, Terminal de Oriente (#116; frequent; 1hr 30min); Usulután (#417; 6 daily; 2hr); Zacatecoluca (#177; every 15min; 50min).

By taxi Local taxis in the Parque Cañas will take you to San Salvador for US$40 or San Miguel US$50.

ACCOMMODATION

Posada Belén 12A C Pte 25, Barrio San Juan de Dios ☎ 2393 6326, ✉ belenmarisol@live.com. The only decent lodgings in town, popular with North American aid workers and presided over by the friendly Ulises and Marisol. Some English spoken. Large, clean rooms with a/c and bathroom, a communal TV lounge, free wi-fi, laundry and a grill in the courtyard. **US$27.50**

EATING AND DRINKING

There are a number of bars around Parque Cañas, while the *comedores* that line the western edge are decent options for a cheap buffet lunch (*Acapulco* is the best), and *Guacamambos* is a much-loved hot-dog stand next to *Rivoly* (dogs US$1; burgers US$1.10). If you have to change buses at the Panamericana turn-off to San Vicente, try one of the *tortillas con carne* sold at the stalls here – a local favourite.

Casa Blanca 2A C Ote, just east of 2A Av Sur ☎ 7883 7086. Meat and fish dishes including cow heart, their speciality – served in a lovely shaded garden that doubles as a good place for an evening drink, though the artsy surroundings are better than the fairly average food. Daily 11am–8pm.

Comedor Rivoly 1A Av Sur, between 2A C Pte & 4A C Pte. A real treat, with big, fresh and tasty meat meals such as *pollo con arroz* (chicken with rice; US$3.50) on spick-and-span tables. Good breakfasts, too. Daily 7am–8.30pm.

La Nevería Parque Cañas. Welcoming ice-cream shop on the main plaza, knocking out all the usual flavours for just US$0.75 per giant scoop. Daily 11am–9pm.

Pupusería Teresita 4A C Pte, just west of 2A Av Sur. Standard but popular *pupusa* canteen serving tasty filled *pupusas* of cheese and *chicharrón* for US$0.50. Daily 6am–9pm.

Taquería Mexicana 4A C Pte, between Av Miranda & 2A Av Sur. This small, clean taco shop serves filling tacos (three per order) – tortillas, refried beans, cheese, pork and chicken – from US$2, with decent salsas on the side. Daily 11am–9pm.

DIRECTORY

Banks Banco Agrícola and Banco Hipotecario on Parque Cañas, both with ATMs and exchange facilities.

Internet Try Cyber Inser or Ciber Life, both on 4A C Pte either side of 1A Av Sur (daily 10am–7pm; US$0.75/hr).

Pharmacy Farmacia Guadalupe II has branches on 4A C Pte, off 1A Av Sur, and also on 2A Av Sur, just north of 2A C (daily 8am–7pm).

Phones Claro (Mon–Fri 8am–5pm, Sat 8am–noon) is at 2A Av Nte 3, just off the southeast corner of the Parque, opposite the Super Selectos supermarket.

Post office C 1 de Julio, one block south of the Parque (Mon–Fri 8am–5pm, Sat 8am–noon).

VOLCÁN CHICHONTEPEC

Looming over San Vicente is one of the most awe-inspiring volcanoes in the country, **VOLCÁN CHICHONTEPEC** (meaning "Hill of Two Breasts" in Nahuatl, and also known as Volcán San Vicente). The second-highest volcano in the country, its twin peaks rising to 2182m, it's considered dormant, with cultivated lower slopes and the steep summit left to scrub and soil. A number of paths lead up the slopes from the village of **San Antonio** on the east side and from **Guadalupe** on the northwest flank. It's a stiff, fairly dull walk of around three to four hours to the top (where there's an old army base) from any of the trails, and good walking shoes, sun protection and lots of water are essential. From the summit, however, there are mind-bending panoramic views north across the Jiboa valley, with San Vicente nestled at the bottom, and west across to Lago de Ilopango. It's possible to do the climb solo, but the paths are unmarked and confusing, so you'd be advised to hire a local guide in either village (ask at the local *alcaldía*; guides are usually free but not always available). Skip the hike altogether in the rainy season (June–Oct). **Buses** to San Antonio and Guadalupe leave daily every hour or so until mid-afternoon from San Vicente's market.

ALEGRÍA

The whole of northern El Salvador seems to unfold below the lofty, floral haven of **ALEGRÍA**, 140km east of San Salvador

3

and the highest town in the country (at around 1240m). It's also home to an extraordinary number of flower nurseries – Alegría simply erupts with blossoms during orchid season.

Laguna de Alegría

The crater of the **Volcán Tecapa** on which the town sits is filled by a lake, the **Laguna de Alegría** (daily 8am–6pm; US$0.25), a body of water fed both by the rain which falls into the enormous crater and the sulphurous eruptions which occur within the depths of the mountain. As a result of the lake's geographical properties, it is filled with volcanic clay – the same stuff you'd be served with back home as facial mud-packs. The awe-inspiring immensity of the crater as you swim through the green water is one of the finest attractions in the entire country.

The lagoon is reached via 3km of cobbled stone road about 40 minutes' walk – the start of which is three hundred metres outside the town entrance. Simply say "La Laguna" to the locals, and they'll point you in the right direction. There's a small shack by the lagoon's entrance that sells cold beers and snacks.

ARRIVAL AND DEPARTURE

Alegría is accessible from the Carretera Panamericana at El Triunfo, 36km east of the San Vicente turning, where a road leads south to Usulután, passing through the pleasant town of Santiago de María; from here a steep but paved road leads 5km up the slopes of Volcán Tecapa into Alegría.

By taxi Taxis charge around US$20 from El Triunfo, and US$15 from Usulután.

By bus Buses drop off and pick up passengers on the northwest corner of the plaza on their routes between Santiago de María and Usulután.

Destinations Santiago de María and Usulután (#348; every 40min until 5pm; 40min); change at Santiago de María for the Carretera Panamericana at El Triunfo (#362; frequent minibuses; 30min).

INFORMATION

Internet There's an internet café just off the Parque (opposite the church), on 1A C Pte, at 2A Av Sur (Mon–Sat 9am–7pm; US$0.80/hr).

Tourist information Alegría has a real, live tourist office (daily 7am–4pm although not reliably; ☎ 2614 7171) at the northwestern corner of the Parque Central, offering all the usual information, but rarely English-speakers or maps.

ACCOMMODATION

Cabañas La Estancia de Daniel C M Araujo, 2A Av Sur (just off the Parque) ☎ 2628 1030, ✉ fredypostecapa @yahoo.com. Inviting home surrounded by trees and flowers, with five cabañas with cable TV and free wi-fi – the amenities are almost as good as at *Entre Piedras* (see below), and prices are lower. Breakfast US$2.50. ̲U̲S̲$̲1̲0̲

Casa Alegre Av C Campos ☎ 7201 8641, ⓦ lacasaalegre .org. The coolest place to stay, with firm beds in clean rooms and a shared bathroom, below the studio of the artists who own it. ̲U̲S̲$̲1̲4̲

Casa del Huéspedes La Palma 1A Ave Nte (on the west side of the Parque Central) ☎ 2628 1012. The friendly old owners here have lovingly maintained the original old-fashioned decor. Bed sizes and firmness vary, but there are hot showers and free wi-fi. Rates are per person (US$10, even if you're in a double room) so it's a better deal for solo travellers. ̲U̲S̲$̲2̲0̲

★**Hostal Entre Piedras** Parque Central ☎ 2605 5886 ✉ entrepiedras.alegria@hotmail.com, ⓦ hostalentre piedras.com. Right on the plaza and offering per-person rates for solo travellers (US$10), this is the best place to stay in town, with wood-panelled rooms with hot water, high-pressure showers, cable TV and free wi-fi. The restaurant is great, too (see below). ̲U̲S̲$̲3̲2̲

EATING AND DRINKING

Café Entre Piedras Parque Central ☎ 2605 5886, ⓦ hostalentrepiedras.com. The best restaurant in town, linked to the guesthouse, serving a vast range of dishes from baguettes and *churrasco* steaks (from US$7), to local "Alegría Bourbon" coffee and delicious pastries (US$1.50) to enjoy on the relaxing terrace. Daily 7.30am–10pm.

★**Cartagena** Two blocks down the hill (north) from the plaza and one block east ☎ 2628 1131. You'll be so blown away by the views from this pleasant open-air restaurant overlooking the expanse of lakes, hills and endless sky, that you won't mind paying a bit over the odds for a stacked plate of deliciously-grilled local meat (US$12) or a few cold ones (US$1.50). Also a hotel, but pricier and less accessible than the other options around town. Daily 8am–7pm.

Casita de mi Abuelo C M. Araujo, just beyond 4A Av Nte. Streetside *comedor* and *tienda* serving sandwiches (US$1.25), ice cream, milkshakes and beers (US$1). Cool off or chill out in the shade. Daily noon–9pm.

Merendero Mi Pueblito C A. Masferrer (just east of the Parque, opposite the *alcaldía* ☎ 2628 1038. The town's most in-vogue restaurant, with jaw-dropping views all the way to the northern border from its own *mirador*, and dishing up big portions (*pollo dorado*; US$4.50) and good vegetarian options. Daily 8am–7pm.

El Portal Parque Central. Decent *carne asada*, *pupusas*, rabbit, deer and *pelibüey* (a local breed of sheep) from US$4.50–7. It's a favourite place for locals to sip beers and enjoy the action on the Parque. Daily 8am–7pm.

SAN MIGUEL

Some 135km east of San Salvador, the chaotic and blisteringly hot **SAN MIGUEL** is the country's third-largest city, though despite being the birthplace of several national heroes and home to some great places **to eat**, it is surprisingly short on sights and attractions. The most exciting time to visit is during the November **Carnaval**, a huge and free event, supposedly the biggest in Central America. San Miguel is a major transportation hub you can't avoid if travelling by bus, but unless you arrive late, frequent connections mean you can pass straight through – you won't miss much.

Initially the least important of the Spanish cities, San Miguel grew wealthy firstly through the profits of gold, and then on the coffee, cotton and *henequén* grown on the surrounding fertile land leading to the nickname "The Pearl of the East". More recently it was a centre of arms trading during the civil war, though today the city's grimy streets hum and rattle with more mundane forms of commerce – downtown resembles the market-smothered Centro Histórico in the capital, albeit on a smaller scale.

WHAT TO SEE AND DO

The city is laid out in the usual quasi-grid system, with the main avenida (Av Gerardo Barrios/Av José Simeón Cañas) and the main calle (C Chaparrastique/C Sirama) intersecting at **Parque Gerardo Barrios**, surrounded by market stalls. However, most of the action – shops, bars, motels and businesses – lies on the seemingly endless strip mall of the Panamericana as it bypasses the centre, best accessed by car.

Parque David J. Guzmán

Although Parque Barrios is technically the central plaza, the heart of San Miguel – and a much better place to sit – is the shady **Parque David J. Guzmán**, a block away to the northeast. It was named after the eminent nineteenth-century Migueleño biologist and member of the French Academy of Science. On the east side sits the **Catedral Nuestra Señora de la Paz** (daily 7am–7pm), started in 1862 and officially completed one hundred years later. Despite its modern elements, it is still an impressive building, with a cast-iron statue of Christ bearing his crown of thorns standing between two red-roofed bell towers. The rather bare interior offers a blissfully cool refuge from the grimy heat outside, with the famed statue of **Nuestra Señora de la Paz** (see box below) above the Italian marble altar.

NUESTRA SEÑORA DE LA PAZ

San Miguel's stately cathedral, with its grand altarpiece and beautiful stained-glass windows, holds a revered wooden statue of **Nuestra Señora de la Paz**, the city's patron (and since 1953, patron of El Salvador). The veneration of the Virgin Mary as "Our Lady of Peace" originated in the Spanish city of Toledo in the seventh century, though accounts differ as to how and when this particular statue arrived in San Miguel (the legend goes it washed up on a beach in 1682). It is generally held that her true moment of glory came during the eruption of Volcán Chaparrastique on September 21, 1787. On seeing a glowing river of lava advancing on San Miguel, the terrified citizens, praying to the Virgin to save them, took the statue to the door of the cathedral and presented her to the volcano. The lava changed course and the city was saved. In honour of these events, San Miguel holds two months of **fiesta**, beginning with the Virgin "descending" the volcano on September 21 and culminating in a procession through the streets, attended by thousands, on November 21. A more recent coda to the fiesta is the annual **Carnaval** held on the last Saturday in November, when free live music, fireworks and street dancing dominate the whole town. Instituted in 1958, it has quickly grown to be the largest carnival in Central America (or so locals like to claim). If you're around during the festival look out for people wandering around holding large plastic iguanas aloft – the locals are nicknamed *garroberos* (iguana eaters) due to their penchant for the lizard's meat.

SAN MIGUEL

ACCOMMODATION
Caleta	4
Hotel del Centro	1
Hotel El Guanaco	3
King Palace	2

● EATING
Bati Jugos Carlitos	3
Comedor y Pupusería Chilita	1
Comedor Vicky	6
Conchadromo Esmerelda	2
Mama Gallina's	8
El Paraiso	4
Pastelería Francesa	5
La Pema	11
Trípicos Grill's	9

● DRINKING & NIGHTLIFE
Maya	7
El Paísa	10

Antiguo Teatro Nacional

Just south of the cathedral is the **Antiguo Teatro Nacional**, a honey-coloured Renaissance-style building completed in 1909. It's closed during the day (the ticket office is usually open just inside the lobby) but evening performances occasionally take place here, particularly during fiesta time; check the *Prensa Gráfica* at weekends.

Capilla de la Medalla Milagrosa

Of the few minor sights within San Miguel, the most appealing is the Gothic **Capilla de la Medalla Milagrosa**, at the western end of Calle 4 Pte where it joins 7A Avenida Sur. The brilliant white chapel was built in 1904 by French nuns working in the hospital that once stood next door, and is known for its pretty blue ceiling and beautiful French stained-glass windows, best seen on a clear evening. Its leafy gardens make an enticing entrance, with the walkway to the main door festooned with bright pink bougainvillea. The chapel is usually open only for services (Sun 5.30am, 8.30am & 5.30pm; usually Mon–Sat 9.30am, check on ☎ 2661 1831).

ARRIVAL AND INFORMATION

By bus Buses arrive at the well-ordered Terminal de San Miguel on 6A C Ote between 8A & 10A Av Nte, four blocks (or a 10min walk) east of the centre.

Destinations Corinto (#327; every 30min; 2hr); El Amatillo, via Santa Rosa de Lima (#330; frequent; 1hr 30min); El Tamarindo, via Las Tunas (#385; hourly; 1hr 30min); La Unión (#324; frequent; 1hr); Perquín (#332 & #426; 9.30am–3.20pm; hourly; 3hr); Playa El Cuco (#320; 3.10am–4pm; every 30min; 1hr 30min); Puerto El Triunfo (#377; every 40min; 1hr); San Salvador (#301; every 15min; 3hr); Usulután (#373; frequent; 1hr 15min). *Especial* and *super especial* services also serve San Salvador (10 daily; 2hr). For San Vicente take one of these latter buses and get off at the Vicente turning on the Panamericana (just over 1hr) – you can get a taxi or local bus into the city from here.

Tourist information There is no official tourist office, but staff at the *alcaldía* (town hall; daily 9am–5pm) on the south side of Parque David J. Guzmán will help you with quick questions (ⓦ alcaldiasanmiguel .gob.sv). During Carnaval, contact the Comite de Festejos de San Miguel for programme details (ⓦ sanmiguelencarnaval.com.sv).

ACCOMMODATION

The majority of accommodation clusters around the bus terminal, inevitably a rather sleazy area. There are posher hotels away from the city centre, mostly along Av Roosevelt Sur, but you'll have to pay a lot more (*Villas San Miguel* and *Comfort Inn* are the most popular).

Caleta 3A Av Sur 601 between 9A & 11A C Pte (get a taxi from the terminal) ☎ 2661 3233, ⓔ hotelcaleta@gmail .com. Clean and quiet hotel, popular with local business travellers during the week. There's a small courtyard with hammocks, and some rooms have private bath. Staff can also help arrange surf trips to secluded beaches. **US$15**

Hotel del Centro 8A C Ote 505, at 8A Av Nte ☎ 2661 5473. This very friendly and helpful hotel is the best of the cheaper options around the bus terminal. The rooms are smallish but well arranged, with cushions on beds and bedside lights; all rooms have bath and TV. There's free wi-fi for guests, although make sure they give you a room within range; US$0.50 laundry washes and US$8 extra for a/c. **US$12**

Hotel El Guanaco 8A Av Nte Pasaje Madrid ☎ 2661 8026. A giant hotel with gaudy green paintwork and kitsch cowboy decor. Its big, airy and clean en-suite rooms all have a/c and cable TV – the oversized three double-bed rooms for US$40 are a great deal for groups. **US$20**

King Palace 6A C Ote ☎ 2661 1086. Good-value and professional hotel opposite the bus terminal, with a glitzy mirrored-window facade. The clean rooms are en suite, some with balcony, cable TV, a/c and telephone. Secure parking, restaurant, fast internet (computers and wi-fi), laundry, swimming pool and rooftop gym and pool also available. **US$25**

EATING

Bati Jugos Carlitos 1A Av Nte, at 4A C Pte ☎ 2661 0606. Carlos serves excellent snacks (US$2.50) and lunches (US$4–7) in an intimate, colourful downstairs and roomier first floor. His speciality is a wide selection of big, fresh fruit *licuados* (US$2), from melon and pineapple to tamarind and papaya. Mon–Sat 8am–5pm.

Comedor y Pupusería Chilita 8A C Ote, just east of 6A Av Nte. A barn of a neighbourhood *pupusería*, particularly popular on Fri & Sat. The *pupusas* are good (4–10pm; US$0.50), but there's also a decent selection of *comidas a la vista* (7am–3pm). Sit inside or on the breezy terrace at the back. Mon–Sat 7am–10pm.

Comedor Vicky 7A Av Nte, at C Chaparrastique. Small, friendly, bare-bones *comedor* that does an ice-cold, freshly squeezed orange juice (US$1.50) and cooked breakfast. The *sopa de gallina india* (US$2.50) is fine for lunch too. Daily 7am–9pm.

Conchadromo Mary 6A Av Nte Bis between 4A & 6A C Ote. The friendlier and cleaner of the two kitchens serving up basic breakfasts and *comidas a la vista* in this parking lot. Serves

3

3

★TREAT YOURSELF

La Pema 5km from town on the road to El Cuco ☎ 2667 6055, ⓦ lapema.com. El Salvador's most renowned restaurant (named after founder "Doña Pema") will set you back around US$20 per head (without alcohol), but the huge servings of *mariscada* (US$12–15), a creamy soup of every conceivable type of seafood, and the bowls of fruit salad served as an accompaniment mean you won't feel like eating again for a while. Credit cards accepted. Daily 10am–5pm.

cheap, cold beers and delicious coconut water (check out the garage full of husks further back). Mon–Sat 7am–10pm.

Mama Gallina's Av Roosevelt Nte 303, at C Chaparrastique ☎ 2661 2123. A popular and well-known restaurant at the crossroads of two of the town's most popular social streets, this pleasant restaurant, decked out with a chicken theme, serves up good seafood and roast chicken. Daily 9am–9pm.

El Paraíso Parque David J. Guzmán. Well-prepared *pupusas* (US$0.50) and *comidas a la vista* (US$3) dished out in an attractive colonial building in a conveniently central location. Prices are low and quality is good. Steer clear of the juices though; they are surprisingly bad. Daily 7am–9pm.

Pastelería Francesa Parque David J. Guzmán ☎ 2661 8054, ⓦ pasteleriafrancesa.com.sv. The best place for a pastry, free wi-fi and decent coffee on the Parque – there is another handy branch of this local chain (they all have blissfully powerful a/c) at 1A Av Nte 302. Both Mon–Sat 7am–6pm, Sun 7am–noon.

★Típicos Grill's Av Roosevelt Sur, at C Chaparrastique ☎ 7910 3918. Don't be scared away by the poor grammar or the probable entire goat roasting out front; this barbecue joint is the real deal. Big racks of ribs, well-marinated chicken, or more exclusive options for exotic meat lovers. Try the venison, rabbit or the *pièce de résistance*: lowland paca (*tepezcuintle*; US$15) – a large rodent, often compared to a beaver, which lives in the mountains around the town. Probably the only place in the country you'll find such food on offer. Daily 9.30am–11pm.

DRINKING AND NIGHTLIFE

By night the focus shifts to the *comedores* and fast-food chains along Av Roosevelt. Think about ordering taxis, not least because the action is quite far out of town. Return journeys can be arranged with the barmen. No journey should be over US$3.

Maya C Chaparrastique 602 ☎ 2635 9347. One of several popular joints along this section of Chaparrastique, a laidback bar and café awash with the sounds of *trova*, salsa and Latin rock. Free wi-fi. Cash only. Mon–Sat 2pm–2am.

El Paisa Av Roosevelt Sur 105 ☎ 2661 0352. Popular Mexican food spot that also does steaks for US$8, though the large tacos are cheaper at US$4. It's used more as an outdoors booze hall with a big screen and a stage for live musicians at weekends. Upmarket *Terraza* and club *New Small Bar* in the same courtyard are also popular and make for a complete night out. Daily 10am–2am.

SHOPPING

Centro Comercial de Artesanías Av Roosevelt between 4A & 6A C Pte. Less artisan than souvenir, but there are some pockets of genuine local crafts. Mon–Sat 8am–5pm.

Mercado Central Parque Barrios. A sprawling affair lined with narrow warrens filled with stalls selling food, clothes and other goods. Daily 6am–6pm.

Metrocentro Av Roosevelt Sur ⓦ metrocentro.com /inicio-SM. At the southern edge of town, this consumer vortex includes stores, banks, bookshop, supermarket, fast-food restaurants and a cinema (Cinemark); any bus heading south down Av Roosevelt will drop you outside. Shops daily 8am–7pm; Cinemark daily 5pm–2am.

DIRECTORY

Banks Banks cluster around the west side of the Parque and along 4A C: Scotiabank is at 2A Av Nte & 4A C Ote 210 (both Mon–Fri 8am–4.30pm, Sat 8am–noon).

Health Farmacia El Progresso, 4A C Ote, at 6A Av Nte (Mon–Fri 8am–6pm, Sat 8am–noon; ☎ 2661 1098); Farmacia Brasil has several branches in the centre, including one on 2A C Ote just off the Parque (Mon–Fri 7am–10pm). Hospital Clínica San Francisco (Av Roosevelt Nte 408; ☎ 2661 1991) is an excellent private hospital with 24hr emergency care.

Internet Cyber Café, 11A Av Nte, between 2A C Ote & 4A C Ote (Mon–Sat 11am–7pm; US$0.80/hr).

Phones Claro, 2A C Ote, at 4A Av Nte (Mon–Fri 8am–6pm, Sat 8am–4pm), at the corner of Parque Guzmán next to the *alcaldía*.

Post office Av José Simeón Cañas Sur & 5A C Ote (Mon–Fri 8am–5pm, Sat 8am–noon).

Supermarket Super Selectos, Galería Jardín, Av Roosevelt at C Almendros (aka 11A C Pte); Despensa Familiar in the centre on Av José Simeón Cañas just north of C Sirama Ote.

GUATAJIAGUA

Lying in the basin of an open valley, peaceful **GUATAJIAGUA** is a wonderfully artistic Salvadorian small town. Like many other craft-based settlements, it has a unified creative output – black clay pottery and sculpture – but the products are of far higher quality than the usual souvenirs. Moreover, the town is very accessible, and as yet untainted by tourism.

Calle Principal, running west of the Parque, is the town's unofficial centre – the many workshops around here include that of Sarbelio Vásquez García, whose sculptures of a kneeling man you'll see imitated throughout town (ask for directions).

ARRIVAL AND DEPARTURE

By bus Buses from San Miguel (#326; hourly; 1hr 20min) can pick up at Chapeltique on the highway if you're coming from the west.

PERQUÍN

Close to the Honduras border, at the start of the Ruta de Paz (CA-7), **PERQUÍN** is a small and, given its history, surprisingly friendly mountain town set in the middle of glorious walking country. During the war the town was the FMLN headquarters, and in later years Radio Venceremos was broadcast to the nation from here. Attempts by the army to dislodge the guerrillas mostly failed, leaving the town badly damaged and deserted. Today, the "town that refused to die" has repaired most of its buildings, although the scars of war are still evident and nearly everyone has a horrendous tale to tell. Recently community action has been moving away from the retrospective outlook that war tourism has created, and instituted new schools, coffee production and a young and hip annual festival, the **Festival del Invierno**, which hosts live music and events in August (since this is the rainy season, it is called the "winter festival").

WHAT TO SEE AND DO

The town itself is clumped around its pentagonal **Parque Central**, where there is a municipal basketball court. One block uphill is Calle de los Héroes, containing most of the town's attractions.

Museo de la Revolución Salvadoreña

Perquín's main draw is the poignant **Museo de la Revolución Salvadoreña** (Tues–Sun 8am–4.30pm; US$1.25), set up by former guerrillas in the wake of the 1992 Peace Accords. The curators travelled throughout the country collecting photographs and personal effects of "disappeared" guerrillas, a collection that is still growing and displayed in the first room. There is a succinct summary (in Spanish) of the escalation to the armed struggle, weaponry and examples of international propaganda aimed at bringing the events in El Salvador to the world's attention, but the most moving exhibits are the anonymous transcripts of witnesses of the El Mozote massacre (see p.239), and drawings by refugee schoolchildren, depicting the war's events as they saw them. A separate room contains the transmitting equipment and studio used by Radio Venceremos, whose clandestine broadcasts every afternoon throughout the war transmitted the guerrillas' view of events, as well as interviews and music. (After the peace accords, the station received an FM licence, and is now a commercial music station based in San Salvador, a status viewed by some as a bit of a sell-out.)

Outside the museum is the crater left by a bomb dropped on the village – standing next to it is a disarmed bomb with "Made in the USA" stencilled on the side. Behind the museum lie the remains of the helicopter that was carrying Domingo Monterrosa, architect of the El Mozote massacre, after it was blown up by the FMLN in 1984. A partial reconstruction of a guerrilla camp lies just down the road from the museum, with more bombs and bullets on display – locals charge US$1 or so to walk through some of the guerrilla tunnels uncovered here.

Cerro de Perquín

Opposite the museum, a track leads up from a parking lot to the panoramic views from the peak of the **Cerro de Perquín**. It's an easy 1km stroll to the top, where climbers can picnic and have their picture taken next to a sign marking the summit.

3

ARRIVAL AND INFORMATION

By bus Buses arrive on the south and west sides of the Parque Central, though it's easier to jump off before town for many of the accommodation options.

Destinations El Mozote (#426; 2 daily; 20min); San Miguel (#332; 4 daily; 2hr).

Tourist information There's a small but enthusiastic tourist office (Mon–Sat 8am–4pm; ☎ 2680 4086) on the outskirts of town, beyond *Posada Don Manuel*. The tourist police (see below) will drive you here if you ask nicely.

ACCOMMODATION

★**Hotel Perkin Lenca** 1.5km south of town on CA-7, Km 205.5 ☎ 2680 4046, ⓦ perkinlenca.com. The owner here, former aid worker Ron Brenneman, built the entire site himself, including the huge barn where excellent meals are served – *La Cocina de Ma' Anita* (US$5–10) – which is worth a visit even if you don't stay. Spotless, spacious rooms in log cabins (all double) or a newer motel-like section, hot-water en suites, firm beds, hammocks and chairs on the porches, great views, table tennis, free internet and a laundry service make this worth every cent. Breakfast is included, and advance booking is recommended; Ron offers a 20 percent discount during the week if enough rooms are available. He also sets up tours to El Mozote with ex-guerrilla guides, and runs a local educational charity. Doubles US$40, cabins US$64

Hotel y Restaurante La Posada Signed at Km 206 on CA-7, 500m south of town ☎ 2680 4037, ⓔ laposada perquin@hotmail.com. This hotel used to be a sawmill, evidenced by the lofty reception area, where simple *típicos* are served. Though the ten rooms are quite dark the beds are firm and good, there's free wi-fi and the shared bathrooms have toilet paper and seats. It stands out for its pool table, in great condition, and gym facilities. Rates include breakfast. US$20

El Ocotal Km 201 on CA-7 ☎ 2634 4083, ⓦ hotelelocotal .com. The cabins with private bath (hot showers), set in a tranquil pine forest several kilometres south of town, are a paler version of those at *Perkin Lenca*, but the restaurant is worth a trip (US$0.25 by Toyota pick-up). Sunday brunch is fun but packed out by locals (see below). US$35

Perquín Real At the southern end of town on CA-7 ☎ 2680 4158, ⓔ xiomvarela@yahoo.com. The best budget option in town has a row of spacious rooms with at least two double beds in each. Shiny new individual shower stalls are a plus, though there is no hot water. Two large (but very friendly) dogs live on site. Per person US$8

EATING

Antojitos Marisol Av los Próceres. Though it looks something like a field hospital, this is the place if you fancy a drink or two, local soups (US$2) and good burgers and fries (US$3). Daily 8am–10pm.

Blanquita Av los Próceres ☎ 2680 4223. The best *comedor* in town, with a small selection but popular *a la vista* and cakes. Breakfast from US$2. Daily 7am–7pm.

La Muralla C de los Héroes, at the foot of the climb to the museum. The evening *pupusa* spot, frying on demand out front while the townsfolk watch dubbed US soaps on the cable TV inside. Around US$2.50 for five *pupusas*. Daily 6–9pm.

El Ocotal CA-7 Km 201. Good *sopas* (US$3) and a mean fried *yuca* on weekends, when it's very popular with locals. It's set in a pine forest, which somehow suits the Eighties power ballads they favour on the stereo. Bring your swimsuit – you can use the pool once you've paid for something. Daily 11am–7pm.

DIRECTORY

Pharmacy Next to the post office on the west side of the Parque.

Police Politur (tourist police) Opposite the church just off the Parque (☎ 2680 4040) are very helpful and friendly.

Post office On the west side of the Parque (Mon, Tues, Thurs & Fri 8am–5pm).

LOS INOCENTES

In December 1981, the elite, US-trained Atlacatl army battalion entered the village of **El Mozote** and rounded up its inhabitants on the suspicion that they had been harbouring FMLN guerrillas. Earlier, the villagers had been warned by guerrillas of the army's intent, but the mayor had been assured by the government that they would be safe staying put. This was not to be: under orders to set an example and obtain information, for three days the soldiers tortured and raped the inhabitants, before **executing** them all, including the children, who were shot in front of their parents. In all, some thousand people were killed, and their bodies subsequently burned or buried in mass graves. Eyewitness testimonies – from soldiers, the (only) survivor, guerrillas who arrived on the scene after the event – were ignored for years, and the bodies of the victims did not begin to be exhumed until 1992. Foreign groups are still working to uncover these mass-burial sites today; in some graves upwards of 85 percent of the bodies belong to children. On the right side of Mozote church, a small garden for "the innocent ones" commemorates the tragedy of their lost lives.

INTO HONDURAS: EL AMATILLO

Beyond Santa Rosa, the road connects with the Carretera Panamericana to run to the border over the Río Goascora at **El Amatillo**. The border crossing is easy and free but busy, and teeming with moneychangers – who give better rates than the banks – and beggars. On the Honduran side, buses leave regularly until late afternoon for Tegucigalpa and Jícaro Galán, and there are also direct buses to Choluteca, for onward connection to the Nicaraguan border along the Carretera Panamericana.

AROUND PERQUÍN

The area around Perquín offers very enjoyable **hiking**, the highlights of which are the route over **Cerro el Pericón** to El Mozote, taking around three hours with a stop to swim in the middle, and a two-hour loop around **Cerro Gigante**. Perquín's tourist office (see opposite) can organize guides a day in advance, some of whom have reasonable English. Paying for a guide (around US$20/group) is tremendously worthwhile, as they are mostly ex-guerrillas who will bring the history of the landscape to life.

El Mozote

A few kilometres south of Perquín (off the CA-7, via Arambala) sits **EL MOZOTE**, the scene of the country's most horrifying wartime massacre (see box opposite). Families are slowly moving back, however, and a **mural** by Argentine artist Claudia Bernard on the left-hand side of the church describes the village's old agricultural life and hopes for the future. On the other side, colourful mosaics of children playing form the backdrop to a heart-rending memorial garden to the young lives lost.

Although the massacre's one survivor, Rufina Amaya, passed away in 2007, newer inhabitants are continuing the guide work she did (no charge, but tipping is expected); these tours are vital to understanding the scars left from the war. You can see a bomb crater, the massacre's mass graves and the hole that Amaya hid in for five days. A moving **monument** to the victims features an iron sculpture of the silhouette of a family and a wall bearing the names of those killed. For a small fee (around US$4), local children will take you to the caves where the guerrillas were hiding out, a pleasant walk of 4–5km through forest and brush,

where wildlife abounds. The caves themselves are not overly spectacular, but it was from here that **Radio Venceremos** ("We Will Overcome") was first broadcast, and as you look out over the densely forested countryside it is easy to see why the army never discovered the guerrillas' hiding place.

ARRIVAL AND DEPARTURE

By bus From Perquín you can take a pick-up to Arambala, 3km down the CA-7, where you change to a Joateca bus that leaves at 8am every morning (the return bus leaves El Mozote at 12.45pm).

On foot El Mozote can be reached on foot from Perquín, via the Cerro el Pericón.

SANTA ROSA DE LIMA

Travelling 50km northeast of San Miguel through hot, low hills, you come to **SANTA ROSA DE LIMA**, a messy but thriving place with a large weekly market, a cheese industry and a well-maintained church. Besides the Wednesday **market** there's not much to do here, but it's a convenient stopover if you're crossing late from Honduras.

ARRIVAL AND INFORMATION

Buses Buses stop at the western end of 6A C Pte.

Destinations El Amatillo (#346; every 20min; 1hr 30min); La Unión (#304 or #342; frequent; 1hr 30min); San Miguel (#330; frequent; 1hr); San Salvador (#306; every 30min; 4hr).

Bank Citibank, Av General Larios 14 (Mon–Fri 8am–6pm, Sat 8am–noon).

ACCOMMODATION AND EATING

Comedor Chayito 6A C Pte & 1A Av Sur. A very clean place which does a good, cheap *comida a la vista* (from US$2). Mon–Sat 7am–4pm.

Taquería El Tabasqueño Carretera Ruta Militar (CA-18), next to the Puente Las Cadenas. Popular taco joint on the main highway, doubling as a car wash. Munch on tacos, *carne asada* and pork ribs (*costilla de cerdo*) from US$2. Daily 7am–10pm.

El Tejano Amigo Colonia Altos de Santa Rosa, 100m north of the Estadio Municipal (just off CA-18) ☎ 2641 4242, ✉ hoteltejanoamigo@hotmail.com. Your best bet for a comfy night's sleep, with a/c, bath and cable TV. US$25

The north

North of San Salvador, hilly pastures and agricultural land give way to the remote, rugged and sparsely populated Chalatenango and Cuscatlán provinces, a region of poverty and pride that was until recently all but closed to outsiders. The Spanish found few natural riches to attract them this far north, and successive generations of *campesinos* have vainly struggled to make a living. This harsh terrain created fertile ground for dissent and support for the FMLN, who controlled large parts of the department of Chalatenango for significant periods during the 1980s. Both army and guerrillas struggled to take control, leaving devastated communities in their wake and refugees fleeing across the border to Honduras. The legacy of the region's wartime status was not exclusively detrimental, however, and the effect of the subsequent repopulation has been the reinvention and modernization of its big towns. Each now has a very singular character: colonial **Suchitoto** is the darling of culture and tourism; **La Palma** is a mountainous escape with a legion of artisans; and bustling **Chalatenango** is a centre of rural commerce.

SUCHITOTO

Cobbled and colonial **SUCHITOTO** perches like a crown on the ridge above the southern edge of Lago de Suchitlán, 47km north of San Salvador. The left-leaning but increasingly gentrified town was made a site of National Cultural Heritage in 1997, and today you will find arts and cultural venues dotted around all Suchitoto's streets. There are food and arts **festivals** every weekend, and the month-long festival of culture in February

draws the country's best painters, orchestras, performers and poets.

During the 1980s, the area was the scene of bitter fighting as the army struggled to dislodge FMLN guerrillas from their nearby mountain strongholds. Upwards of ninety percent of the inhabitants left the town, which was largely resettled by ex-guerrillas after the war. Today life here is generally quiet, with its quality restaurants, bars and luxury hotels offering a welcome respite from rough travelling.

WHAT TO SEE AND DO

Suchitoto has some of the finest examples of colonial architecture in the country, so before getting stuck into the cafés and shops it's worth taking a stroll to admire the low red-tiled adobe houses lining the town's streets and around its tranquil plazas.

Around the Parque Central

Overlooking the Parque Central and inaugurated in 1857, the **Iglesia Santa Lucía** has an impressive Neoclassical facade, a particularly fine wooden altar and strange, hollow wooden columns inside. The quirky **Museo de los 1000 Platos y Más**, 3A Avenida Norte 1, behind the church (Tues–Sat 8am–5.30pm; US$2) contains a gaudy collection of plates, decorated with everything from florid Victorian designs to images of President Lincoln. The **Casa de Cultura** (Mon–Fri 9am–5pm; free), a block north of the church (Pasaje Sta. Lucía 9), has displays on local history and information on local walks.

Museo de la Moneda

The shaded **Parque San Martín**, a couple of blocks northwest of the church, commands stunning views across the blue waters of the lake. Nearby, the **Museo de la Moneda** (Tues–Sun 8am–5pm; US$2; ☎ 2335 1094), 4A Calle Poniente 9, contains examples of **UDIS** ("Unidad de Intercambio Solidario Suchitotense"), the "official" currency of Suchitoto established in 2007 as a sort of voucher system to boost the local economy. It's legal tender (at par with the US$),

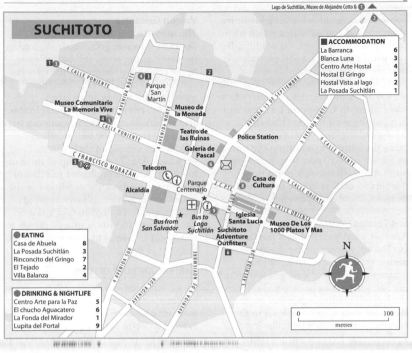

SUCHITOTO

ACCOMMODATION

La Barranca	6
Blanca Luna	3
Centro Arte Hostal	4
Hostal El Gringo	5
Hostal Vista al lago	2
La Posada Suchitlán	1

EATING

Casa de Abuela	8
La Posada Suchitlán	3
Rinconcito del Gringo	7
El Tejado	2
Villa Balanza	4

DRINKING & NIGHTLIFE

Centro Arte para la Paz	5
El chucho Aguacatero	6
La Fonda del Mirador	1
Lupita del Portal	9

though it has never really caught on. The museum also displays coins and notes from all over the world, as well as a comprehensive history of Salvadorian tender. There is also talk of its opening a hostel in 2016.

Museo de Alejandro Cotto

Northeast of town, Avenida 15 de Septiembre leads down to the lakeshore, passing the **Museo de Alejandro Cotto** (Sat & Sun 2–6pm, although hours are unpredictable due to the artist's infirmity; US$4), a beautifully restored colonial house with a fine collection of local paintings, sculpture, indigenous artefacts and musical instruments. The owner, Cotto himself, is a famous Salvadorian writer and film-maker, and is often in residence. The entrance price, while relatively steep for El Salvador, goes towards funding the February arts and culture festival.

Museo Comunitario La Memoria Vive

The small **Museo Comunitario La Memoria Vive** (Tues–Sun 8am–3pm; US$2;

☎2335 1080), 2A Calle Poniente 5, was opened in 2010, dedicated to the history, culture and art of Suchitoto. Small exhibitions highlight the effect of the civil war, Pipil civilization, the creation of Lago de Suchitlán in 1976 (it's actually a reservoir), the local Festival del Maíz and fiesta of the Virgen de Santa Lucía.

Lago de Suchitlán

Like many lakes in El Salvador (and arguably on a global scale) the **Lago de Suchitlán** is better and more expansively viewed from afar, best done from the north side of town. However, recent local investment has gone into the **Puerto de San Juan**, where eight lakeside restaurants offer tasty staples and ice-cold Pilsners around a pretty courtyard. A clean and cooling swimming pool is on offer – a nice place to escape the intense midday heat. Boat tours also leave from the dock (7am–4pm; 1hr; US$30) and take in various spots around the lake, the best of which is the bird-lovers' haven of **Isla de los Pájaros** in the middle of the lake, the

3

home of a range of fish-eating birds; it's always best if you go with a guide who can explain more about the wildlife. If you get the *lancha* (US$5/boat) across the lake to the northern side at San Francisco Lempa, *Tao Tao* restaurant (see p.245) offers more extensive tours of the lake (taking in Copapeyo, La Presa and San Juan as well) for less (US$10).

To get to the lake, buses (US$0.35) make the journey to and from the market in Suchitoto every twenty minutes until 4pm. Alternatively, walk north on Avenida 15 de Septiembre from the Parque Central and keep going.

Los Tercios

Another worthy excursion is the **Cascada Los Tercios**, a waterfall that flows over unusual hexagonal basaltic columns – note that the water level gets low in the dry season. You can be dropped off by the Lago de Suchitlán minibus on the lakeshore, near a trail that leads to the waterfall, or walk to it by following the signposts south out of town (30min). Another option is to join the police escort which leaves from the main plaza every day at 3pm, although it's a good idea to inform them at the Amigos de Turista office in the main square earlier in the day, so they know they'll have someone to take.

Salto El Cubo

Salto El Cubo, with its chilly twin pools, is a better waterfall for swimming than Los Tercios. It's a pleasant twenty-minute walk west of town – go to the western end of Calle Morazán, then follow the signs down the track.

Volcán Guazapa

The roads up and around **Volcán Guazapa**, a former guerrilla stronghold to the south of the town, still bear witness to the crumbling remains of the trenches and dugouts used by both sides, now quietly submerged beneath green vegetation. **Horseriding** is popular in this area and hacks across the volcano can be organized through the tourist office (US$17 for a group of three on horseback, US$15 for a group of three on foot; 6hr; requires minimum number of participants). Check the condition of the horses before you go, as some aren't in great shape. You'll need to take a taxi or bus #107 or #163 (to Aguilares; get off at La Clínica La Mora) to the starting point, 8km out of town.

ARRIVAL AND DEPARTURE

Hostal El Gringo (see opposite) runs collection services from Comalpa airport (US$65), San Salvador (US$35) and other places in the country.

By boat From San Francisco Lempa on the northern shore, twelve-man speedboats (US$5/boat; 10min) and a four-car ferry (US$25/boats; 40min) make the crossing to the Puerto de San Juan, ten minutes north of Suchitoto. From there minibuses (US$0.35; every 20min) take passengers to and from the town hall in the centre. From San Francisco Lempa buses travel on to Chalatenango at around 6am, 7.25am, noon & 2.45pm (40min).

By bus Buses stop at 1A C Pte, beside the municipal market.

Destinations Aguilares (#163; every 40min; 1hr) for transfer to Chalatenango (#125) & La Palma (#119); San Martín (#129; 10 daily; 1hr) for San Miguel (#301); San Salvador, Terminal de Oriente (#129; every 15min; 1hr 30min).

By tuk-tuk Tuk-tuks ply the Suchitoto streets, and will not only take passengers anywhere in town (around US$0.50) but also down to the ferry (around US$3).

INDIGO

A blue dye used primarily today in the manufacture of jeans, Suchitoto is one of the few places in the world that still produces real natural indigo (most used in the textile industry today is synthetic). Classes are available in the town, at which you can learn about the ancient art of dyeing and even make your own hand-dyed garments, including hand-spun shawls, handkerchiefs or any of your own clothes you care to bring along for a colour change. The **Taller de Indio de la Mujer** beside the theatre offers a two-hour class for US$17, while Irma Guadrón of **Arte en Añil** on 2A Av Sur, went as far afield as Japan to perfect her art, and produces amazing work, some of which you can commission specially from her if you've got a few days to spend in town. She charges slightly more (around US$25) for a class, but you leave with better stuff. Classes are in Spanish.

INFORMATION

Tourist information Centro de Amigos del Turista Suchitoto, southwest corner of main plaza (daily 9am–5pm; ☎2335 1782, ⓦ suchitoto.travel).

TOUR OPERATORS

El Gringo Roberto Broz Moran at *Hostal El Gringo* (☎7860 9435, ⓦelgringosuchitoto.com; see below) organizes tours covering everything from how to make *pupusas* (US$12; 45min) to city walking tours (US$25/person, or US$50/group of three) and boat tours of the lake (US$35/person; minimum three people; 2hr 30min). He also runs a pick-up service to the airport (see below).

Suchitoto Adventure Outfitters Based in the *Lupita del Portal* café on the main square, Suchitoto Adventure Outfitters (☎23351429, ⓦsuchitotoadventureoutfitters .com) organize waterfall jumping during the rainy season (US$80/group of 1–4; 3hr 30min), as well as tours of the town (US$100/group of 1–4; 3hr), kayaking, horseriding and excellent tours of guerrilla battlefields. Owner René Borbón speaks good English and is a mine of information.

ACCOMMODATION

La Barranca Opposite Parque San Martín ☎2335 1408. Very clean, wood finished rooms down the hill behind a restaurant (run by the same people) beside the park. The en-suite rooms have a splendid view of the lake, there's a shared kitchen for guests and good free wi-fi. **US$25**

Blanca Luna One block south of Parque Centenario ☎2313 9685, ⓔblancaluna21@hotmail.es. The most central of the cheap hotels has two or three double beds in the basic rooms, as well as fan, cable TV and en suites. None too clean but not bad value, and an airy roof terrace makes up for the scruffy rooms, with hammocks and climbing bougainvillea. The artist manager's paintings decorate the walls. **US$16**

Centro Arte Hostal 2A C Pte 5 ☎2335 1080, ⓦcapsuchitoto.org. In their quest to expand, renovate and restore this beautiful old chapel, the current owners (who include an American missionary who came to help during the civil war and then stayed) have built a modern and inviting dormitory, as well as two fully equipped apartments with queen-sized beds. The chapel itself is being converted into a performing arts centre, due to open in 2016. Dorms **US$12** doubles **US$20**

Hostal El Gringo C Francisco Morazán 27 ☎2335 1371, ⓦelgringosuchitoto.com. Cosy and secure hostel with two private rooms and one dorm (five single beds), free wi-fi (and two computers), cable TV in the lounge, kitchen, laundry (US$5/load) and a restaurant (see opposite). El Gringo himself is one of the country's best tour guides and

can offer advice on your travels if you're lucky enough to catch him at home. Discounts for longer stays. Dorm **US$7**, doubles **US$18**

Hostal Vista al Lago 2A Av Nte 18 ☎2335 1357. A homestay hotel that does exactly what it says on the tin, with stunning views northwards over the lake below. The rooms here are small and pretty cosy (no a/c and shared bathrooms) but the family that runs it is relaxed, the courtyard has a bar and serves food, and the bench overlooking the lake is possibly the best spot in town for an evening drink. **US$30**

EATING

Casa de Abuela Northeast side of main square beside cathedral. What started out as an artisanal gift shop with good (and cheap) merchandise from all over the country now offers great coffee and comfort food – you can't beat the bagel and cream cheese – with seating both inside and out. Daily 9am–6pm.

★**Rinconcito del Gringo** C Francisco Morazán 27 ☎2327 2351. From the same gringo, Roberto Broz Moran, who runs the *Hostal El Gringo*, this largely Tex-Mex restaurant offers fresh juice smoothies (US$2.50), massive *pupusas* (US$0.75) with the option of rice or corn dough, and big, spicy portions (meals US$2.50–7). Admire the expressive paintings by artist Trudy Myrrh in the on-site gallery. Free wi-fi. Daily 7am–8pm.

El Tejado 3A Av Nte 58 ☎2335 1769. Big meat and chicken dishes (US$6) are served in a pleasant garden with an unrivalled lake view. The best thing is the giant and clean swimming pool where you can cool off on hot days; you may be asked for a US$3 supplement for this. Mon–Fri 10am–5pm, Sat 9am–9pm, Sun 9am–5pm.

Villa Balanza At *La Barranca* hotel, Parque San Martín ☎2335 1408, ⓦvillabalanzarestaurante.com. This open-sided barn restaurant has rustic antique-ranch decor, with romantic tables in a corner alcove overlooking the lake. The food is good, with breakfasts and lunches (chicken *suprema* US$7) served by waitresses in "traditional" milkmaid outfits. Hosts dance nights which attract the locals every other Saturday. Daily 10am–9pm.

3

DRINKING AND ENTERTAINMENT

Suchitoto is a great place to go out – largely safe and with lots of choice. There are also plenty of excellent cultural events on throughout the year.

Centro Arte para la Paz 2A C Pte 5 ☏ 2335 1965, ⓦ capsuchitoto.org. This pleasant bar in a secluded spot is the venue for the Museo Comunitario La Memoria Vive (see p.241), and also hosts a range of arts events, including film, theatre and concerts. Mon–Fri 7.30am–4.30pm, Sat 7.30am–2pm.

El Chucho Aguacatero One block north of the plaza on the western side ☏ 2335 1008. The coolest bar in town, with a laidback bohemian theme and centred around a courtyard shared with the Galería de Pascal art gallery (see below), this bar is a staple hangout spot for locals and tourists alike. The name is the Salvadorian expression for a street dog. Does food until 8pm. Daily 5pm until late.

La Fonda del Mirador Av 15 de Septiembre 85 ☏ 2335 1126. The largely expensive menu has some cheap and filling treats (seafood salad; US$4), but it really comes into its own as a spot for early evening drinks with stunning sunset views of the lake. Daily 11am–7pm.

Lupita del Portal Parque Central ☏ 2335 1429. Laidback café and bar with outdoor tables, specializing in gourmet pupusas (roasted garlic and basil or cheese and spinach; US$1.50), tasty sweet pasties and a potent chaparro (aguardiente, or cane liquor). Owner René Barbón runs Suchitoto Adventure Outfitters (see p.243) from here, one of the best tour operators in the country. Daily 7am–9pm.

SHOPPING

Galería de Pascal 4A C Pte 2B (same building as El Chucho Aguacatero, see above) A large exhibition space that sells original paintings, which are naturally very expensive, as well as local artisanal work. Mon–Fri 10am–6pm, Sat 10am–7pm, Sun 9am–6pm.

DIRECTORY

Banks There are two standalone ATMs on the southern side of the plaza (of which the Scotiabank unit is the more reliable).

Internet Hostal El Gringo (see p.243) offers free wi-fi and two internet computers for restaurant and hostal clients.

Pharmacy Farmacia Santa Lucía (daily 8am–noon & 2–6pm), on the corner of C Francisco Morazán and Av 5 de Noviembre, is well stocked.

Police The tourist police have a good presence in town; the office on the corner of Av 15 de Septiembre and 4A C Pte (☏ 2335 1141) is open 24hr.

AGUILARES AND CIHUATÁN

Some 35km north of the capital, on the border-bound Troncal del Norte (CA-4), the pleasant workaday town of **AGUILARES** has nothing more to offer than a relaxing snack in the garden at *Río Bravo* on the Parque. Archeology buffs might want to pass through, however, as 4km to the north sit the ruins of **CIHUATÁN** (Tues–Sun 9am–4pm; US$3; ⓦ cihuatan.org), the most important Postclassic site in the country. Originally covering an area of around four square kilometres, Cihuatán (meaning "Place of Women" in Nahaut) was founded sometime after the first waves of Pipils (or Toltecs) began arriving in El Salvador in the tenth century and destroyed for reasons unknown around 1200 AD. The excavations, which include stepped pyramids and a pelota court bearing a clear Mexican influence, were officially opened in 2007, along with a very informative bilingual museum. To really get into it, it's worth reading the information on the website before going.

ARRIVAL AND DEPARTURE

Take any **bus** from Aguilares (20min) or the capital (around 1hr) to Chalatenango or La Palma and ask to be dropped at the gates – they're right on the highway.

CHALATENANGO

Around 18km north of Aguilares, on the Troncal del Norte, is a major crossroads at the scrubby junction of **Amayo**.

The road east from here (CA-3) leads through agricultural and pasture lands along the northern fringes of Lago de Suchitlán to **CHALATENANGO** (known to the locals as Chalate), an important centre of rural trade. The town has the rough-and-ready feel of a frontier settlement, an atmosphere enhanced by the fortress-like army barracks on the main square. During the early 1980s it was under FMLN control, and though much of the town's physical damage has been repaired, the barracks still has bullet holes in its walls. Nowadays, though, Chalatenango is a bustling and very friendly place.

WHAT TO SEE AND DO

While not a particularly beautiful town, Chalatenango lies in a very attractive setting – southeast of the La Peña mountains, overlooking the distant Cerro Grande to the west and Lago de Suchitlán to the south – and much of its attraction lies in day-trips to the surrounding area (see below). However, the daily **market** that seals off Calle San Martín every morning from 5am to 1pm is full of fresh, locally grown produce and cowboy attire, which you'll see even more of when the Friday horse fairs come to town. Twenty minutes to the east of the centre is the **Parque Recreativo Agua Fría** (daily 8am–5pm; US$1), with artificial pools, a water slide and a café in a pleasant park.

ARRIVAL AND DEPARTURE

By boat If you're crossing the lake from Suchitoto to the south, ferries arrive at the San Fernando de Lempa jetty, from where buses (US$0.80) make the round trip to Chalate every 2–3 hours. Taxis will make the trip into town for US$15. Ask the staff in *Tao Tao* restaurant on the jetty when the next bus is, or to call you a cab.

By bus All buses arrive and depart from along 3A Av Sur, a couple of blocks south of the Parque Central.

Destinations Concepción Quetzaltepeque (#300B; every 30min; 20min); La Palma – take the San Salvador bus and change at Amayo (#119; every 30min; 3hr); San Francisco Lempa (#542; 5 daily; 45min); San Salvador, Terminal de Oriente (#125; frequent; 2hr).

ACCOMMODATION

Hotel La Ceiba Behind the garrison building and down the hill on 1A C Pte ☎ 2301 1080. Standard features for the price (cable, en suite, a/c), though the six rooms are a bit run-down. US$12

La Posada del Jefe (El Instituto ☎ 7335 7450. The furthest option from the centre is just about adequately clean, though rooms are dark and poky, and – despite its enviable hilltop location – there are no views over the town. At the price and at ten blocks' slog uphill beyond the church to the east of the centre, it's a bit steep. US$20

EATING AND DRINKING

For an evening drink, the stall on the south side of the church on C San Martín does cheap beer as well as burgers, and stays open until 11pm. There are plenty of open-air pizzerias among the craft stalls on the square, with eat-in tables or takeaway (US$4–5).

Comedor Blanquita C Morazán & Av Libertad. A good *comedor* serving the usual *comida típica*, though a visit to the toilet might put you off your food. Daily 7am–7pm.

Comedor Carmary 3A Av Sur. This *comedor* is popular at lunchtime, serving the locally favoured *a la vista* (US$3–4), with vegetarian options too. Daily 7–10am, 11.30am–5pm.

Sarita 1A Av Sur. The countrywide ice-cream chain offers plenty of different flavours – or try a Giga, their cheaper but just as tasty version of a Magnum (US$1.25). Daily 11am–7pm.

AROUND CHALATENANGO

The villages **north of Chalatenango** are spread across forested mountains and rarely visited. More adventurous travellers may want to explore beyond the artisan town of **Concepción Quetzaltepeque**; find out more beforehand by asking the tourist office or local experts in Suchitoto (see p.243). By the Lago de Suchitlán, **San Francisco Lempa** is a great little stop before crossing the lake to Suchitoto.

Concepción Quetzaltepeque

Some 12km northwest of Chalatenango, the village of **CONCEPCIÓN QUETZALTEPEQUE** is notable for its **hammock** industry. Workshops lining the village's main street and homes around the village turn out colourful items in nylon and, less commonly, cotton and *mezcal* fibres for prices at about half those in San Salvador. Most producers sell in the market at Chalatenango at roughly the same bargain rate as in the workshops here. The annual hammock festival takes place November 10–12.

San Francisco Lempa

The little lakeside town of **SAN FRANCISCO LEMPA** is home to the pier for ferries to and from Suchitoto (see p.240). The town itself is very pleasant for a dock community, but holds no real interest. In the vicinity, however, are an excellent restaurant and a great camping spot.

ACCOMMODATION AND EATING

Hacienda Grande 3km west of San Francisco Lempa along the shore ☎ 2375 1447, ⊕ haciendagrande.webs .com. Probably the nicest camping in the country (they have tents to lend out), next to a swimming pool and restaurant. They also have horses you can take out on your own (US$4/hr). Camping/person US$5

Tao Tao At San Francisco Lempa's jetty ☎ 2399 3118. This restaurant, worth a visit even if you're not getting a ferry, serves tasty, big, predominantly seafood dishes such as the enormous *camarones* (US$7), grilled with or without garlic butter, on its lakeside veranda. The boatmen operating the crossings can be found lounging in hammocks underneath the building. They also give advice on how to walk, or get a boat, to *Hacienda Grande* (see p.245). Daily 8am–8pm.

LA PALMA

Beyond Amayo, the Troncal del Norte (C-4) winds up the Cordillera Metapán Alotepeque to the Honduran border through an abundance of vertiginous, pine-clad mountain vistas (for the best views sit on the left-hand side of the bus on the way up). Some 8km short of the border lies the serene village of **LA PALMA**, supposedly named after the indigenous custom of building houses out of palms. The climate is cooler here and the peace is only broken during the annual fiesta of **Dulce Nombre de María**, in the third week of February. But under the surface the village's plentiful *artesanías* are hives of industry, reproducing the brightly painted, naïf-style representations of people, villages and farming life and religion made famous by Salvadoreño artist **Fernando Llort** (Llort lived here 1971–80), on wooden and ceramic handicrafts and toys, which are now sold all over the world.

WHAT TO SEE AND DO

The **crafts industry** is the economic mainstay of the village, with **workshops** lining the main road. Most sell their goods on the spot and are pretty relaxed about visitors turning up to watch; prices are cheaper than in San Salvador and the items make great gifts. The **Museo Fernando Llort**, at the western end of town, displays a selection of Llort's colourful paintings (Mon–Fri 8am–4pm, Sat 8am–noon; free; ☎2335 9076).

Hiking trails

North of La Palma are several fine **hiking trails**, including El Salvador's highest mountain, **Cerro Pital** (2730m), 10km away on the Honduran border. A rough

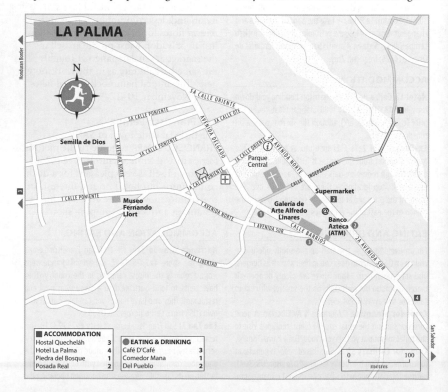

LA PALMA

N

5A CALLE ORIENTE

5A CALLE PONIENTE

5A AVENIDA NORTE

5A CALLE ORIENTE

5A CALLE OTE

AVENIDA DELGADO

Semilla de Dios

3A CALLE PONIENTE

1A CALLE ORIENTE

Parque Central

1A AVENIDA NORTE

INDEPENDENCIA

CALLE

1A CALLE PONIENTE

1A CALLE PONIENTE

Museo Fernando Llort

1A AVENIDA NORTE

1A AVENIDA NORTE

Galería de Arte Alfredo Linares

Supermarket

@

Banco Azteca (ATM)

1A AVENIDA SUR

CALLE BARRIOS

2A AVENIDA SUR

CALLE LIBERTAD

Honduran Border

San Salvador

0   100
metres

■ **ACCOMMODATION**
Hostal Quecheláh	3
Hotel La Palma	4
Piedra del Bosque	1
Posada Real	2

● **EATING & DRINKING**
Café D'Café	3
Comedor Mana	1
Del Pueblo	2

road branches east just before La Palma to run to Las Pilas on the lower slopes of the mountain; a dirt road also leads up from the village of **San Ignacio**. Hiking to the summit is an adventure of two or three days, for which you will need to be fully equipped – the owners of the *Hotel La Palma* (see p.247) are a good source of information on shorter walks and guides, and run their own excursions around the hillsides.

ARRIVAL AND INFORMATION

By bus There is no bus station as such. You can ask to get off at either end of town or in the centre; the bus goes along 2A Av Nte on the way up to the border, and calles Delgado and Barrios on the way back down. To get to Chalatenango change at Amayo and walk over to the bus stop where the #125 to Chalatenango passes every 20min. Destinations Amayo (#119; every 30min; 1hr); El Poy, Honduras border (#119; every 30min; 30min); San Ignacio (#119; every 30min; 15min); San Salvador, Terminal de Oriente (#119; every 30min; 3hr 30min).

Tourist information The Centros de Amigos del Turista (daily 9am–5pm; ☎ 2335 9076) is on the north side of the Parque Central.

ACCOMMODATION

★ **Hotel La Palma** Barrio el Tránsito, Troncal del Nte Km 84 ☎ 2335 9012. Supposedly the oldest functioning hotel in El Salvador (since 1944), this friendly and good-value place at the entrance to town has clean and bright rooms, with hot-water en suites, nicely decorated with huge Llortist murals. Singles cost US$18. There's a reasonably priced restaurant (specializing in *gallina india*, a local chicken dish), free wi-fi and a pool and hammock area. __US$35__

Piedra del Bosque C a La Loma Larga (across the river from C Independencia) ☎ 2335 9067 or ☎ 7722 2465. Charming owner Óscar built this entire eco-complex, with extremely basic hillside cabins (with double rooms), a river-fed swimming pool, restaurant, hammocks, camping space, collection of archeological finds, craft shop, and bonfires in the evening. Óscar will talk you through everything stone by stone. It's a bit out of the way, what with your having to cross the funky suspension bridge, but a cool place nonetheless. Camping/tent __US$10__, doubles __US$25__

Posada Real 2A Av Nte ☎ 2335 9009, ☺ posadarealla palma@hotmail.com. This well-run hotel and restaurant (daily 7.30am–7pm) just up from the Parque is slap-bang in the centre of town and a good option if you're on a tight budget. Bustling matriarch Berthalidia offers en-suite rooms set around a charming flowered courtyard. __US$10__

EATING

Café D'Café C Gerado Barrios. A good little coffee-shop serving up locally sourced produce, as well as chai and frozen concoctions. Does good food (mains US$5–8) and is a nice place to stop for a rest in the middle of all the souvenir shops that surround it. Daily 8am–7pm.

Comedor Mana C Barrios (no sign) ☎ 7918 8009. A proper Salvadorian diner in a green-painted house (within and without) with murals on the walls. Serves up classic dishes (around US$4 for a full meal), all made fresh to order with local ingredients. Daily 7am–8pm.

Del Pueblo 2A Av Sur. A family-run establishment with bags of character, carved wooden chairs and handmade candles, *Del Pueblo* serves a good-value menu featuring mostly meats and one of the best *típico* breakfasts around (US$4–5). Daily 8am–9pm.

SHOPPING

Artesanía shops abound in La Palma, mainly concentrated around the Parque; bargaining is acceptable.

Semilla de Dios 3A C Pte at 5A Av Nte ☎ 2335 9098. A little out of the way and not very well signposted but well worth the expedition (all the locals will point you in the right direction), this artistic production line built around Llort's iconic, colourful naïf style is probably the best *artesanía in town*. Most of what they make here is exported, but much of the best stuff they keep behind on display in the shop. Wander into the back and the artists will happily show how it's all made. Mon–Sat 7am–5pm, Sun 9am–4pm.

DIRECTORY

Bank Banco Azteca, C Barrios 34 (Mon–Fri 8am–4pm, Sat 8am–noon).

Internet Palma City Online, next to the supermarket on 2A Av Sur, has a fast connection (daily 11am–7pm; US$0.50/hr).

Pharmacy Farmacia San Rafael, C Barrios, at 1A C Pte (Mon–Fri 8am–12.30pm & 1.30–6pm).

Post office On 1A C Pte (Mon–Fri 8am–5pm, Sat 8am–noon).

★ **TREAT YOURSELF**

Hostal Quecheláh 500m west of town in Colonia Monte María, C La Tejera ☎ 2305 9328. This arty B&B is a 15min walk uphill from town, but the tasteful bedrooms with amazing beds, hot-water bathroom (shared) and free wi-fi, not to mention the bar, lovely artwork, mountain views and friendly owners, make it a real treat. Only three rooms, so advance booking advisable. __US$45__

The west

The rich landscape of **western El Salvador** is in many ways the most enticing part of the country, with rolling mountain chains and valleys dominated by vibrant green expanses of coffee plantations. Spared from the most violent hardships of the conflict of the 1980s, the friendly towns and cities of the west have a relatively well-developed tourist infrastructure that makes travelling here easier than in other regions.

The Carretera Panamericana runs between San Salvador and the main city of the west, **Santa Ana**, but the primary access route to the southern part of the region leads through the sweaty town of **Sonsonate**, 65km west of the capital. From here, buses head off in several directions: down to the coast for the untouched beaches of **Los Cóbanos**, **Los Remedios** and **Barra de Santiago**; to the tranquil forest reserve at **Parque Nacional El Imposible**; and northwest into the mountains. High above the plains, **Apaneca**, **Ataco** and **Juayúa** are picture-perfect Salvadorian towns, harbouring talented communities of local and foreign artists. Closer to Santa Ana lie the peaks of **Cerro Verde**, **Volcán Santa Ana** and **Volcán Izalco**, the sublime crater lake of **Lago de Coatepeque**, and the pre-Columbian site of **Tazumal**. In the north of the region, near the Guatemalan border, the accommodating little town of **Metapán** gives access to the **Bosque Montecristo**, where hiking trails weave through unspoilt cloudforest amid some of the most remote and perfectly preserved mountain scenery in the region.

> ## INTO HONDURAS: EL POY
>
> Crossing the border to **Honduras** at **El Poy** (daily 6am–6pm), 11km from La Palma, is straightforward and quick: the #119 bus from La Palma and San Salvador drops you within sight of the gate. Many trucks use this route, but private traffic is light; crossing early in the day is advisable. The last bus #119 from the border for La Palma and San Salvador leaves at 4.15pm. On the Honduran side, buses run the 10km to Nueva Ocotepeque (see box, p.406) every 40min or so from 7am until 5pm, departing from just the other side of the gate that marks the beginning of Honduras.

LOS CÓBANOS AND LOS REMEDIOS

With idyllic white sands, warm water and gentle waves, **LOS CÓBANOS** is the ideal place for just lounging on the beach, though it's also the only **reef-diving** spot in the country. Just 25km south of Sonsonate, via a fast highway, it is a favourite weekend destination for Salvadoreños, when it is better to round the headland at the west end of the small bay to the quieter beach of **LOS REMEDIOS**. Although rather rocky, the pretty, gently curved beaches here make a nice contrast to the dark, palm-fringed expanses further down the coast.

> ## THE WEST BY BUS: SONSONATE CONNECTIONS
>
> **SONSONATE**, set in tobacco and cattle-ranching country, prickles with heat in the day and menace at night. It has a history of gang problems, and since there is nothing here to see, its main feature is the **bus terminal**.
>
> Destinations Ahuachapán, via all towns on the Ruta de las Flores (#249; 6.15am–5pm; every 15min; 2hr); Barra de Santiago (#285 direct: 2 daily; 1hr 20min; #259 getting off at the turning off the Carretera del Litoral: frequent; 1hr); Parque Nacional El Imposible main entrance (#259; frequent; 1hr 20min); La Perla (#261; 4.30am–4.30pm; hourly; 2hr); Los Cóbanos (#257; 5.30am–6pm; every 30min; 40min); La Libertad, via the Costa del Bálsamo (#287; daily 5.55am & 3.30pm; 3hr; US$1.50); La Hachadura, Guatemala border (#259; 4.30am–7.30pm; every 10min; 1hr 45min); San Salvador (#205; 4.30am–5pm; every 15–20min; 1hr 30min); Santa Ana (#216 via Los Naranjos: every 20min; 1hr 15min; #209B via El Congo; hourly; 1hr 45min).

ARRIVAL AND DEPARTURE

By bus #257 leaves Sonsonate every thirty minutes for Los Cóbanos until around an hour before sunset, and there are also occasional direct buses from San Salvador (#207); the last bus leaves the beach at 5pm.

TOURS

Los Cóbanos Tours (☎ 2417 6825) runs boat trips which leave when there's a large enough group – usually enough to charge US$20 – (8am–3pm; 3hr; US$37) off the coast into the Área Natural Protegida Complejo Los Cóbanos in search of dolphins, sea turtles and humpback whales (best Nov–Jan).

El Salvador Divers (ⓦ elsalvadordivers.com) runs dive trips out to the reef – arrange these in advance or in San Salvador.

Grupo Calle Real (☎ 2260 4314, ⓦ senderoselsalvador .com) arranges cheap packages for groups of eight or more and a variety of tours for just two people or more (snorkelling US$12; boat tours US$37).

ACCOMMODATION AND EATING

Budget accommodation is limited along the beaches. The best places to eat are the fishermen's restaurants that line the shore. The delicious fish is caught in the morning and cooked at lunch.

Los Cóbanos Village Lodge Los Remedios ☎ 2420 5248, ⓦ loscobanosvillagelodge.com. Clean *palapas* with balconies onto the beach and a dorm with seven beds. They also provide breakfast, offer use of the pool, and rent out snorkel gear and kayaks. Dorm US$12, doubles US$59

BARRA DE SANTIAGO

West of the colourful port town of Acajutla, the Carretera del Litoral runs on to the Guatemalan border at La Hachadura (see box below), with the slopes of the Cordillera Apaneca rising to the north and rolling pasturelands to the south. After 35km an unmarked track leads south to **PLAYA BARRA DE SANTIAGO**, a gorgeous, sandy strip of land separating the ocean from a protected estuary and mangrove reserve inland. The peninsula is occupied by a scruffy fishing village, but the expanse of beach is delightfully empty and the locals still seem a little surprised to see visitors. Barra de Santiago is also a major **turtle-nesting** area – visit between August and November and you can see giant sea turtles laying eggs along the beach.

ARRIVAL AND DEPARTURE

By bus Bus #259 from Sonsonate passes the turning from the Carretera, where pick-ups go to the village; or Lena of *Capricho Beach House* can organize a lift. You can also wait for direct buses (#285) that go twice a day from Sonsonate.

TOURS

Julio César Local expert Julio (☎ 7783 4765) runs illuminating birdwatching boat trips (US$45) around the mangroves and to a small archeological site, Isla El Cajete, where obsidian arrowheads, ceramics and other remains have been found dating from the Postclassic period (700–1524); he is also very knowledgeable on local flora and fauna.

Canoe trips *Capricho Beach House* can organize canoe trips into the nature reserve.

ACCOMMODATION AND EATING

As with Los Remedios, the best places to eat are local fishermen's shacks that line the shore.

Capricho Beach House Final C Principal, at 39 Av Sur, 3km from Barra de Santiago village ☎ 7860 8632, ⓦ ximenasguesthouse.com/en-capricho.html. The place to stay, related to *Ximena's* in San Salvador (see p.211). Choose between firm metal beds in the dorms, and en-suite doubles with fan or a/c. There's an outdoor kitchen for guests and a restaurant (6am–9pm). Free wi-fi. Dorms US$12, doubles US$47.20

PARQUE NACIONAL EL IMPOSIBLE

One of El Salvador's greatest hidden glories, the forest reserve of **PARQUE NACIONAL EL IMPOSIBLE** takes its name from a perilous gorge within the park which made the transportation of coffee harvests out of the coastal mountain range almost impossible. Covering more

---

INTO GUATEMALA: LA HACHADURA

From the Barra de Santiago turning the Carretera del Litoral continues the last few kilometres to **La Hachadura**, a 24hr border crossing used by international buses heading for Mexico and reached via bus #259 from Sonsonate (1hr 45min). There's a small *hospedaje* on the Guatemalan side, and buses to Guatemala City (4hr; 6am–3pm), stopping at Esquintla along the way, leave from a point 1km down the road.

3

than 31 square kilometres and rising through three climatic zones across the Cordillera de Apaneca, the reserve contains more than four hundred species of tree and 1600 species of plant, some unique to the area. You may glimpse some of the more than three hundred bird species here, including the emerald toucanet, trogons, hummingbirds and eagles, while the park provides a secure habitat for a diverse range of animals, including anteaters, *tepezcuintle*, white-tailed deer and ocelot, plus more than five hundred different species of butterfly, including the dazzling blue morpho.

The gorge itself was bridged properly over fifty years ago, but a weathered plaque commemorates those beasts of burden who never made it across the rope bridge which once hung there.

There are two main guided tours, both easily organized either by the loitering guides at the park entrance or by the owners of *Hostal Mama y Papa* (see p.257) in Tacuba. The first is a walking tour (around US$25) of around six hours, culminating in the highest point in the park, from where panoramic views of the Pacific Ocean to the south, Guatemala to the west and lush coffee, rice and fruit plantations to the north are visible. The second tour (around US$40) takes in a series of hidden waterfalls at the eastern end of the park, which tourists can abseil down before leaping into deep pools below.

Clearly marked **trails**, offering a variety of walks lasting from two hours to a full day, set off from the park's visitors' centre (see below). It's not advisable, however, to try to explore deeper within the densely forested park without a **guide** (see below).

ARRIVAL AND DEPARTURE

The park has two main access points. The main entrance is at the southern limit of the park, at the end of a bone-shaking road which splits northwards from the Carretera Litoral east of Cara Sucia. The other way to enter is from Tacuba on the northern side of the park (accessed via Ahuachapán), a far better option for backpackers since the pretty village has better accommodation, and hotels will arrange tours for their guests into the park.

By bus The main park entrance is accessed from the Desvío Ahuachapío turn-off on the Carretera del Litoral, halfway between the Sonsonate–Acajutla road and Cara Sucia, and about 13.5km from the park itself on a gravel road. Bus #259 from Sonsonate stops at the turn-off to the park (5km before Cara Sucia) on its way to the Guatemalan border (at La Hachadura) – get off here and catch the 11am or 2pm pick-up, or 3.30pm bus (#811) to San Miguelito (daily), a short walk from the park gate. Pick-ups make the return journey at 5.30am and 6.30am; the bus departs at 7.30am.

By tuk-tuk Motorcycle rickshaw drivers in Cara Sucia will take passengers up to the park entrance for around US$20/ ride: expensive but avoids a lot of hassle.

INFORMATION

Entry fee and guides There's a US$6 entry fee (parking is an additional US$1/day) to enter the reserve from the south, which is managed by SalvaNatura (33 Av Sur 640, Col Flor Blanca, San Salvador; ☎ 2279 1515, ⊛ salvanatura .org). If coming from Tacuba there's no fee, although you'll be with a guide most likely organized by your hotel. Guides at the south entrance are free, but will ask for a tip – US$5 is a reasonable fee for two hours.

Visitors' centre In the old Hacienda San Benito, 100m inside the main entrance, is the solar-powered Centro de Visitantes Mixtepe (daily 7am–5pm; free) with information boards about the park's wildlife, tour guides on hand and a small souvenir store.

RUTA DE LAS FLORES

Beginning at the northern edge of the Parque Nacional El Imposible and stretching east for more than 70km from the Guatemalan border, the glorious mountains of the Cordillera Apaneca are covered in a hedge-patchwork of coffee plantations and lush pine forest. The so-called "**Ruta de las Flores**", covering the area between Concepción de Ataco and Nahuizalco, is named after the abundant white coffee flowers visible during May and the wild flowers that colour the hills and valleys from October to February. This stretch is one of the country's biggest attractions, due mainly to the beautiful and friendly towns with good accommodation, *artesanía*, restaurants and sights, the highlights of which are **Juayúa**'s now-famous *ferias gastronómicas*, the high Laguna Verde and the strongly artistic community of **Ataco**.

ACCOMMODATION AND EATING

There are *comedores* inside the park, and a restaurant in the *hostal*. *Hostal Mamá y Papá y Manolo* is the best option in Tacuba (see p.257).

Camping SalvaNatura allows camping on three sites, with small campfires and rinsing (but not washing) possible in the river. The campsite near the visitors' centre offers grills, picnic tables and toilets. Camping/person <u>US$5</u>

Hostal El Imposible Inside the park, 800m from the main entrance ☎ 2279 1515. A comfy, eco-neutral (solar-powered) hostel, with five comfortable cabañas, a springwater pool and a very good restaurant, *Restaurante El Ixcanal*. <u>US$30</u>

NAHUIZALCO

The population of the village of **NAHUIZALCO**, 10km north of Sonsonate on the Ruta de las Flores (see box opposite), is mostly descended from the region's indigenous peoples, although few wear traditional dress any longer. The town thrives on the manufacture of **wicker** and **tule** (a type of plant) handicrafts, with workshops lining the main street. Some of the pieces are small enough to take home, and gentle bargaining is acceptable. The government arts organization **CEDART**, 3A C Pte 3 (in front of the Parque), is a helpful place to start and has a shop (Mon–Fri 7.30am–4.30pm; ☎ 2453 0618). There's also a candlelit **night market**, with food and craft stalls open until around 10pm.

ARRIVAL AND INFORMATION

By bus Bus #249, which runs the length of the Ruta de las Flores from Sonsonate to Ahuachapán (every 15min), stops at the highway turn-off, which is a 500m walk downhill to the centre; bus #53D goes direct to the village from Sonsonate.

Services Travellers are better lodged in nearby Juayúa, where the accommodation is cheaper and the town livelier. The cheap food stalls in the market around the Parque are usually open during the day.

JUAYÚA

Beyond Nahuizalco, the air freshens as the road winds its way up to the enchanting colonial town of **JUAYÚA** (pronounced "why-YOU-ah"), once in the heart of a major coffee-producing area. When coffee prices slumped in the early 1990s, Juayúans started the **food festivals** (*ferias gastronómicas*) that now dominate the centre every weekend. The town itself is safe at night, clean and crammed with traditional adobe houses adorned with florid street murals by local painters, while the coffee-growing countryside offers plenty of activities to work off the weekend's indulgences.

WHAT TO SEE AND DO

On Saturdays and Sundays the main plaza and roads leading onto it are lined with the **feria gastronómica**'s food stalls; look out for iguana, paella, snake, Chinese and Mexican dishes, frogs, excellent seafood and chocolate-covered frozen fruit on sticks (US$1). The festival has been so successful with day-trippers that half of Juayúa seems to own a stall or food cart – if you can't visit on a weekend you'll still find a few plying their wares during the week.

Templo del Señor de Juayúa

On the west side of the main plaza (Parque Unión) stands the magnificent **Templo del Señor de Juayúa** (daily 6am–noon & 2–6pm; free). It was rebuilt in colonial style in 1956, and houses the Black Christ of Juayúa, thought to have been carved around 1580 by Quiro Cataño, sculptor of the Black Christ of Esquipulas in Guatemala (see box, p.337). Consequently, the town is something of a pilgrimage site, particularly during the January 8–15 festival.

Reptilandia

Reptilandia (daily 9am–6pm, usually closed noon–1pm; US$0.50, parking US$1), one block south of the church on 6A C Pte, is an enthusiastic if slightly amateurish mini-zoo containing reptiles and insects from El Salvador and elsewhere in the tropics. More than twenty snakes, bearded dragons and Australian lizards slither around glass cases, while scary-looking tarantulas and scorpions pose for photographs.

Los Chorros de la Calera

Just 2km out of town (take the street to the left of the mermaid statue), **Los**

3

3

Chorros de la Calera (free) is the town's local swimming spot, featuring three waterfalls with two artificial pools, the top one deep enough to jump in, and connected by a couple of water-filled tunnels. You can walk there (a steep twenty-minute hike down a rocky jungle hillside), or take a tuk-tuk (motorcycle taxi; US$1). On weekdays locals recommend you organize a free tourist police escort (see below).

ARRIVAL AND DEPARTURE

By bus Buses drop off and pick up passengers beside the Scotiabank at the entrance to the town, two blocks west of the main square. Red motorcycle rickshaws (US$0.50) will take you direct to your hotel, although none of the accommodation options listed are more than a few blocks away.

Destinations Ahuachapán, stopping at Apaneca and Ataco (#249; every 30min; 1hr 15min); San Salvador, Terminal de Occidente (#205, normal 1hr 45min; *especial* 1hr 15min); Santa Ana (#209 via Cerro Verde, frequent, 1hr); Sonsonate (via Nahuizalco #249; every 30min; 45min; direct #53; every 30min; 15min).

INFORMATION AND TOURS

Tourist office The well-stocked and enthusiastic tourist office, on the eastern side of the Parque (daily 8am–5pm), offers excellent maps, but has limited English.

Police The tourist police office (Politur) is at 1 Av Nte, just north of C Merceditas (☎ 2469 2510).

Tours There are trekking, horseriding, geysers and coffee tours to be enjoyed locally – organize trips with your accommodation.

ACCOMMODATION

The town is largely quiet during the week, but at weekends you should book ahead.

Casa de Huespedes "Doña Mercedes" 2A Av Sur, at 6A C Ote 3–6 ☎ 2452 2287. A quiet hotel presided over by the clucking Doña Mercedes, this cheerful place has comfortable beds, hot water and cable TV. The shared bathrooms are very clean, and en suites cost just US$5 more. US$20

Hostal Casa Mazeta 2A Av Nte, at C 1 Ote ☎ 2406 3403, ⓦ casamazetajuayua.blogspot.com, ⓔ casamazeta @hotmail.com. British owner Darren Clarke has run this lively and party-friendly hostel since 2008, and is an expert on getting the most out of the region. Two blocks from the Parque, it offers clean rooms (shared or private bath), dorms and cheap hammock space (US$4) under cover – although hammocks should be avoided in the rainy season due to ravenous mosquitoes. Accommodation is arranged around

a leafy little garden. There's a lounge area, DVDs, free wi-fi, laundry and kitchen. Dorm US$9, doubles US$20

Hotel Anáhuac 1A C Pte, at 5A Av Nte ☎ 2469 2401, ⓦ hotelanahuac.com. The other popular hostel in town, *Anáhuac* is the option for the more peace-and-quiet-minded backpacker, and boasts what are probably the best showers in the country. Immaculately clean rooms, wall art which turns crumbling plaster into a display, comfortable beds, a lovely courtyard with hammocks, free wi-fi, a good DVD collection, book exchange and tours organized. Dorm US$9, double US$20

EATING AND DRINKING

El Cadejo Café 4A C Pte, between 2 Avs Sur & Daniel Cordón Sur. The coolest bar in town, named after the Salvadorian legend of a nocturnal dog which will appear in the paths of lost travellers. This bohemian spot serves up locally grown coffee (US$2), microbrewed beers (US$3.50) and specially-shaken *mojitos*, and it has live music on Saturdays. Also serves food, although it's not much to write home about. Thurs–Sun 11am until late.

El Mirador 4A C Pte (at the western end of town) ☎ 2452 2432. Come here for breakfast on the third floor. They have pancakes (US$1.50) and fruit salads as well as the *típicos* (try the *frijoles borrachos*, "drunken beans") and the panoramic views – only slightly marred by the glass – are a good morning eye-opener. Mon–Fri 7am–10pm, Sat & Sun 7am–2.30pm.

Panadería Festival 4A C Ote (south side of the Parque). This basic canteen serves good local coffee, traditional Spanish cakes (US$1.50 with a coffee) and fine breakfasts (from US$2.50). Daily 8am–7pm.

Pupusería Doña Cony 2 Av Sur, at 6A C Ote ☎ 2452 2256. A popular evening spot with the locals, Doña Cony makes fresh *pupusas* to order (US$0.60 each), and stuffs them full of delicious things like *ayote* (calabasa squash). Also makes other regional dishes. Daily 5pm–9pm.

★ TREAT YOURSELF

Restaurante R & R C Mercedes 1–2, at 1 Av Nte (a block north of the Parque) ☎ 2452 2083. Don't miss this fantastic restaurant, surely one of the country's finest, on your visit. Burly chef Carlos Cáceres, who trained in Canada, cooks up a storm in his well-ordered kitchen, and will probably be out to check everything was fine. It's amazingly cheap (think US$15/ head) for the fantastic food he serves up. Top-cuts of beef, wonderful "Granny's Recipe Ribs" and delicious seafood, all prepared with local organic produce. Mon–Fri 11am–9pm, Sat & Sun 8am–9pm.

Taquería Guadalupana C Merceditas Cáceres, at Av Daniel Cordón ✆ 2452 2195, ⓦ taqueriaguadalupana .com. Big portions of top-notch Mexican food – daily deals for US$2.99. *Tacos al pastor* (three for US$2.75) are a favourite. Tues–Sun 9.30am–10pm.

DIRECTORY

Bank Scotiabank (Mon–Fri 8am–4pm, Sat 8am–noon), by the weekend bus stop at the western end of 4A C Pte, has an ATM.

Supermarkets Selectos supermarket, C Merceditas, at Daniel Cordón; Despensa Familiar, 2A C Ote, at Daniel Cordón (both daily 8am–7pm).

Post office Two blocks south of the supermarket on Av Daniel Cordón, at C Óscar Romero (Mon–Sat 9am–4pm).

APANECA

A short ride further along CA-8 from Juayúa lies **APANECA**, another captivating mountain town, founded by Pedro de Alvarado in the mid-sixteenth century. Despite being popular with weekend visitors, tourism is far less developed here than in Juayúa or Ataco – there are fewer cafés and hotels, and the town is a little shabby around the edges.

WHAT TO SEE AND DO

There's little to do in Apaneca itself, and during the week you're likely to have the place – and the wonderful surrounding mountain scenery – all to yourself.

Laguna Verde

It's an enjoyable and not too strenuous walk through woods and fincas to the **Laguna Verde**, a small crater lake 4km northeast of town. Fringed by reeds and surrounded by mist-clad pine slopes, the lake is a popular destination, and at weekends you're likely to share the path with numerous families and groups of walkers. From the highway on the southern edge of town, follow the well-signed dirt road, and keep going straight up. The hamlet just above the lake, reached after about ninety minutes, has gasp-inducing views from Ahuachapán to Cerro Artillería on the Guatemalan border.

Adventure sports

Apaneca has become the unlikely base for a couple of adventure sports outfits in recent years. **Apaneca Aventura Buggy Tours** (✆ 2614 7034) operates off-road buggy rides (*cuadrimoto*; 2–5hr; from US$50/person) from its office at 4A Avenida Norte and Calle Los Platanares (Tues–Sun 8.30am–5pm). **Apaneca Canopy Tours**, Avenida 15 de Abril at Calle Central, offers zipline tours (Tues–Sun: June–Oct 9.30am, 11.30am, 3pm & 7pm; Nov–May 9.30am & 11.30am; US$35/person; ✆ 2433 0554) over lush forests and coffee plantations (with a plantation tour included) – its longest cable runs for 280m and the highest is 125m off the ground. Make reservations in advance for buggy and canopy tours.

ARRIVAL AND INFORMATION

By bus Services to and from Ahuachapán, via Ataco (#249; every 30min; 1hr); San Salvador, Terminal de Occidente via Sonsonate (#205; 1hr 45min); Nahuizalco, terminating in Sonsonate (#53D; every 30min; 30min).

Internet Cibernautica, on the far side of the Parque (daily 8am–6.30pm; US$0.50/hr).

Tourist office 3A Av Norte (daily 9am–5pm). Constantly manned by very helpful staff offering ideas on how to get the best out of the whole of the Ruta de las Flores.

ACCOMMODATION

Hotel Colonia 1A Av Sur by 6A C Pte ✆ 2433 0662. This pretty hotel at the north end of town does indeed have a colonial-looking courtyard. The hotel is furnished with sofas and hammocks, and the good en-suite rooms have sturdy mattresses. __US$20__

Laguna Verde Guest House 3.5km from town, in the hamlet by Laguna Verde, left of the school ✆ 7859 2865. In a magnificent position on the edge of the El Cuajusto crater and a short walk from Laguna Verde, the "guest house" is in fact two delightfully remote structures: the white igloo with four bunks and a kitchenette is a good, if slightly damp-smelling, novelty, but the cabin (sleeps two) is a better pick, with views down to Ahuachapán that are beautiful at night. No one lives on site, so calling ahead is essential. Dorm __US$14__, cabin __US$35__

EATING

Cheap eats are on offer at the Mercado Municipal on 1A Av Sur, opposite the small *parque*; other than *Comedor y Pupusería Edith* (see below), however, most of the food stalls tend to open at lunch or weekends only. There's also an excellent *pupusería* on the corner where the buses collect and drop passengers.

Comedor y Pupusería Edith Mercado Municipal, 1A Av

3

Sur. The market food stall with the longest hours, serving *pupusas*, snacks and locally made meringues. Daily 9am–7pm.

El Jardín de Celeste Km 94 CA-8 (the road to Ataco) ☏ 2433 0281, ⓦ eljardindeceleste.com. Don't believe the hype: Ataco's renowned *La Cocina de mi Abuela* on 1A Av Nte is not what it once was and most people now rate this hotel's restaurant to be the best around. It's not as expensive, serving very well-prepared *típicos* like *pollo con arosa* as well as international dishes for under US$10, and with its own plant nursery on site, the surroundings are pretty good too. Daily 7am–6.30pm.

ATACO

Unlike its quiet neighbour Apaneca (twenty minutes away), **ATACO** (full name Concepción de Ataco) is vibrant and lively, with an artistic community unlike anywhere else in the country. Some good, cheap accommodation and restaurants have emerged over recent years, giving it the feel of an up-and-coming destination. The sunset chorus of the birds nesting in the trees of the main square is wonderful.

WHAT TO SEE AND DO

You'll see artisans at work throughout the town, and vast, exuberant murals daubed on adobe walls and homes.

Diconte & Axul

The lauded **Diconte & Axul** handicraft store, on the corner of 2A Avenida Sur and Calle Central Ote 8 (Mon–Fri 8am–6pm, Sat & Sun 8am–8pm; ☏ 2450 5030), is owned by Álvaro Orellana and Cristina Pineda, whose boldly coloured, manga-influenced **paintings** of cats, moons and fish cover several buildings both here and in San Salvador (under the name "Axul"). The shop, in a house built in 1910, sells stylish canvases, masks, wooden figures and boxes for surprisingly little – it's best known for fabrics produced using traditional treadle looms (you can see the looms at the back). It also has a good café (see below).

On the opposite street corner is **Artesanías Madre Tierra** (Mon–Sat 9am–6pm), its exterior walls painted in similar day-glo designs and selling a

similar mix of local and Guatemalan handicrafts, souvenirs and weavings.

Swimming spots

Hotels can arrange guides to take you to the enticing swimming spots of the 50m **Salto de la Chacala** (on the Río Matala between Ataco and Apaneca), as well as the **Balnerario Atzumpa** (daily 7am–4pm; US$0.25), 2km from town on the road to Ahuachapán, for around US$10 per person.

ARRIVAL AND DEPARTURE

By bus Buses come and go from the town entrance on the main road at the southeast end of the town. Tuk-tuk drivers charge passengers US$0.50 to go anywhere in town from here. Bus #249 takes in the town on its route from Ahuachapán to Sonsonate (and vice versa). The #205 (1hr 45min; *especial* 1hr 45min) makes the journey from San Salvador.

ACCOMMODATION

Posada de Don Oli 1A Av Sur ☏ 2450 5155. This family-run hotel has swings in its pretty courtyard, hot water, and breakfast included. It's a great deal for groups – two of the eight rooms sleep four. <u>US$35</u>

Segen Hostel 3A C Pte 1 (a block north of the main plaza) ☏ 2450 5832, ⓔ segenhostel@hotmail.com. Rooms here are small but neat and tidy. There's one room with five beds, but the management rents it to groups rather than as a dormitory. Prices are always negotiable, but more so during the week. <u>US$15</u>

EATING AND DRINKING

The weekend capital trade means food and drinks here can be relatively pricey. The *portales* on the north side of the Parque are lined with bars and restaurants, while there's a tiny market selling fresh fruit and veg on 2A Av Sur, one block down from the Diconte & Axul store.

Café del Sitio At the back of the Diconte & Axul store, 2A Av Sur, at C Central Ote 8. Drinks and snacks (the spaghetti is a speciality; US$2–7) served in a lovely little garden. Daily 8am–6pm.

Cevichería Albamar C Central, at 1A Av Sur (opposite Portland). A proper local bar in an ivy-walled garden, boasting an arcade game shack, decent food (US$3 for a burger and fries) and ice-cold beers (US$1). Officially daily 10am–10pm, although it stays open later at weekends.

Doña Mercedes Av Central Sur (opposite the market). A large canteen with smart wooden tables that does an excellent range of *pupusas* (US$0.50 each), as well as good *tortas* and imported beers. Daily 7am–3pm.

★ **House of Coffee** Av Central Sur 13 ☏ 2450 5353. By

far the best place for an espresso or cappuccino, with coffee sourced directly from the Escalón family's local plantation – order a fluffy crêpe with your drink (from US$2). Tues–Sun noon–6pm.

Portland Grill Bar C Central Pte, 1A Av Sur 1 **☎**2450 5823. The coolest place to drink in town, with a vast menu of beers, cocktails and wines (US$1.50 specials), a pool table and an extensive menu of international dishes from US$4.75. Mon–Thurs & Sun 11.30am–10pm, Fri & Sat 11.30am–11pm.

Sibaritas C Emilia Aguilera, Av Central Sur **☎**2450 5756. Gorgeous restaurant in an old house, but not as expensive as you might think: US$2.50 drink specials and breakfasts from US$5. Shame it's only open at the weekend. The theme is Latino-Caribbean fusion, combined with Mediterranean flavours and dishes (pastas, marinated fish and pork). Fri noon–8pm, Sat 8am–10pm, Sun 8am–8pm.

Xochikalko Northeast corner of the plaza **☎**2541 6593. Top-notch Salvadorian restaurant serving traditional dishes such as *gallo en chichi* and *sopa de gallina india* as well as pizzas, burgers and soups (mains US$8–15). Mon–Fri 11am–7.30pm, Sat & Sun 9am–10pm.

AHUACHAPÁN

From Apaneca the CA-8 tumbles down 15km or so to the city of **AHUACHAPÁN**, the western terminus of the Ruta de las Flores. It's one of the oldest Spanish settlements in the country, and, like most towns in the area, its wealth grew from the coffee trade. Lauded Salvadorian poet **Alfredo Espino** was born here in 1900, during the coffee boom – his only book, *Jícaras Tristes*, is one of the most published collections of poetry in the country.

Today the main industry is geothermal electricity generation, at one time supplying seventy percent of the country's power, while the city centre retains an air of peaceful charm, with tight streets and elegant *parques*. Nonetheless, Ahuachapán is principally a springboard for surrounding attractions.

WHAT TO SEE AND DO

Confusingly, the **Parque Central** is not at the exact centre, but along the main road into town (6A C Pte) and Avenida Francisco Menéndez (three blocks north of the intersection of the two main streets, calles Gerardo Barrios and Menéndez). A bronze statue of Menéndez (the ex-President was born here in 1830)

graces the southern side of the plaza under the palm trees, while across the street an arcade of cobblers ply their trade. On the east side is the indoor Mercado Municipal.

Iglesia Parroquia de Nuestra Señora de la Asunción

The imposing white edifice of the **Iglesia Parroquia de Nuestra Señora de la Asunción** on the Plaza Concordia (five blocks south of Parque Central on Av Menéndez), with intricate stained glass and a wooden ceiling, dominates the centre of the city and acts as the focus for the annual fiesta in the first week of February. By the side of the church you can view the famously whimsical **murals** of local artists Fabio and Bruno Jiménez, along the **Pasaje La Concordia**.

The ausoles

Some 5km east of town, near the hamlet of El Barro, are the **ausoles** (geysers) that form the basis of the local geothermal industry. The plumes of steam hang impressively over the lush green vegetation and red soil – particularly photogenic in the early morning light. Access to the area is via the turn-off signed "Los Ausoles" on the road to Apaneca – get a pick-up or take the bus that leaves twice daily from the market. The power plant itself is off-limits, but locals will allow you access to their land for a small fee, from where you can get a better view. **Eco Mayan Tours** (Paseo General Escalón 3658, Colonia Escalón, San Salvador; **☎**2298 2844, **⊛**ecomayan tours.com) provides tours to the *ausoles*, including a chance to roast corn over them, and a tour of the plant (US$30 from Ahuachapán or U$75 to and from San Salvador).

Termales Santa Teresa

At the **Termales Santa Teresa** (daily 8am–6pm; **☎**2413 2173, **⊛**termalesde santateresa.com), hot springs just 2km outside Ahuachapán (off the road to Ataco) have been fed into three gorgeous tiled pools. It costs US$10 to soak all day long, and most weekdays you'll have the place to yourself.

3

3

ARRIVAL AND DEPARTURE

By bus The terminal, a chaotic affair, is on Av Comercial, between 10A and 12A C Pte, eight blocks from the Plaza Concordia. Little moto-taxis (tuk-tuks) are a cheap way to get around town (pay no more than US$1).

Destinations Chalchuapa, for Tazumal (#210; frequent; 30min); Las Chinamas–Guatemala border (#263; 6am–5pm; every 15min; 30min); Santa Ana (#202/#210; frequent; 1hr); San Salvador (#202; frequent; 3hr 30min); Sonsonate (#249; every 15min; 2hr 30min); Tacuba (#264/#15; every 30min; 45min).

ACCOMMODATION

La Casa Grande 4A Av Nte, at 4A C Ote ☎7185 7171. Not for light sleepers on the weekends, but this friendly restaurant rents out its six clean rooms for some of the cheapest rates in town. Just a few paces from the bar, it's nevertheless a safe option given the zealous entry security. US$12

Casa de Mamapán 2A Av Sur, at Pasaje La Concordia (in front of Parque Concordia) ☎2413 2507, ⓦ lacasademamapan.com. Housed in a beautiful and immense colonial mansion built in 1823, this cosy hotel has a prime location on Plaza Concordia, with seven homely en-suite rooms all with a/c, cable TV and free wi-fi. The small café opens onto the mural-smothered Pasaje La Concordia (the hotel is similarly adorned). US$53

EATING AND DRINKING

Café El Imposible Pasaje La Concordia. This no-frills local café (don't let your tuk-tuk driver confuse it with the brothel of the same name) is a cool place to hang out amid the wild murals on this stretch of the *pasaje* – grab a coffee, pastry or cold beer. Daily 7am–10pm.

La Casa Grande 4A Av Nte 2, at 4A C Ote ☎7185 7171. There's plenty of character in this restaurant, with loud music blaring and a standard menu featuring some game specialities including venison (*venado*) and rabbit (*conejo*) for under US$6. Daily 10am–2am.

La Estancia 1A Av Sur 1–3, at C Barrios ☎2443 1559. Housed in an elegantly decaying former coffee mansion built in 1910, this bizarrely decorated *comedor*, with

stuffed exotic animals and colonial-era machinery as adornment, serves up tasty Salvadorian staples in a time warp back to the colonial era. Daily 7am–6pm.

Mixtas 2A Av Sur, just north of the Parque Concordia. Serving "*mixtas*" – flatbreads stuffed with meat, cheese or vegetables (US$2.20) – this clean canteen with plastic tables also offers *pupusas* (US$0.65), *churrasco* (steak) plates (US$4.75) and a big selection of fruit juices. Daily 9am–11pm.

Pastelería Roxana 2A Av Sur 1–2 ☎2413 3410, ⓦ pasteleriaroxana.com.sv. One of two branches in the town, this is a great place for cakes and coffee – local specialities include *semitas* (bran or pineapple cakes) and *salpores de almidón* (small biscuits). The local chain was founded in 1969, down the road in Chalchuapa. Daily 8am–6pm.

DIRECTORY

Banks Scotiabank and Citibank face each other on the corner of C Gerardo Barrios & Av Francisco Menéndez, with money exchange, travellers' cheque-cashing and ATMs (both Mon–Fri 8am–4pm, Sat 8am–noon).

Internet Ciber Sharks, 2A Av Sur, just north of Parque Concordia (daily 10pm–6pm; US$0.75/hr).

Pharmacy Farmacia Central, 2A Av Sur & C Barrios (daily 8am–noon & 2–6pm; ☎2443 0158).

Post office 1A C Ote & 1A Av Sur (Mon–Fri 8am–5pm, Sat 8am–noon).

Supermarket Despensa Familiar, Av Central Sur Lote 1 (daily 7am–7pm), is by the bus terminal.

TACUBA

Some 15km west of Ahuachapán lies the tranquil mountain village of **TACUBA**, reached via a winding and scenic road with tantalizing views of coffee plantations and the Parque Nacional El Imposible (see p.249). An important settlement existed here long before the Spaniards arrived, and the village retains strong folkloric traditions, although you'll only really notice these at fiesta time.

INTO GUATEMALA: LAS CHINAMAS

From Ahuachapán, a reasonably good and very scenic road (CA-8) runs the 20km or so to the **Guatemalan border** on the Río Paz, just past **Las Chinamas** (local bus #11AH from Ahuachapán; every 15min; 1hr). You'll have to walk across the bridge and up the hill to reach the buses that run to Guatemala City from Valle Nuevo (see box, p.338) on the Guatemalan side (500m), though moto-taxis will whisk you there for a small fee. International buses between Santa Ana, San Salvador and Guatemala City also pass through this border crossing; passports are normally checked on the bus, but there will be a short wait on both sides of the border. The mobs of moneychangers on the Guatemalan side will take hefty commissions if they can, so make sure you know the current exchange rate before agreeing on an amount.

IMPOSIBLE TOURS

Based in Tacuba, **Imposible Tours** (☎ 2417 4268, ⊛ imposibletours.com) is one of the best tour operators in the country, due in most part to good-humoured and charismatic leader Manolo González, whose ceaseless enthusiasm comes from a genuine desire to get to know everyone he guides. The company's hallmark tour takes you along the back route through **Parque Nacional El Imposible** along a series of occasionally staggering waterfalls and sheer-walled canyons, though the set-up is flexible. Other options include **mountain biking** along ridges to the coast, several day-treks and wallowing in hot **volcanic springs** with a beer or two. Tours start from US$25–30 per person.

WHAT TO SEE AND DO

The village is small and welcoming, but the only thing to see is the ruined colonial **church**, the **Iglesia Santa María Magdalena de Tacuba**, which was much less ruined before the 2001 earthquake. Built between 1605 and 1612 in an elegant Baroque style, it was flattened for the first time by an earthquake in 1773. Either the guard or Manolo of Imposible Tours (see box above) will let you in to walk through and climb up the remaining structure. The real draw of Tacuba is, however, its back route into the dramatic **Parque Nacional El Imposible** (see p 249).

ARRIVAL AND DEPARTURE

By bus Tacuba can be reached by bus #264 or minibus #15 (every 30min; 45min) from Ahuachapán.

ACCOMMODATION AND EATING

Hostal Mamá y Papá y Manolo 10A C Pte, at 1A Av Sur 1, Tacuba ☎ 2417 4268. Well known in town, the family owners of this excellent guesthouse will go out of their way to ensure you leave town with a good impression. Breakfasts are hearty, especially when accompanied by the El Imposible-grown coffee which will knock your socks off. Hammocks throughout, a cosy dorm and shared bathroom sit next to spacious and homely doubles. Watch out for the cute (and territorial) resident ducks. Dorm US$0, doubles US$20

Miraflores 2A Av Nte, at 7A C Ote ☎ 2417 4746, ✉ miraflores@hotmail.com. A good option if *Mamá y Papá* is full, this bright and breezy place has a flower-filled courtyard ringing with birdsong. Try to get an en-suite room (cold water only) – they're brighter (with two windows). Rates include two meals. US$20

Pupusería Milna 8A C Pte, at 1A Av Sur. Top-notch *pupusas* (three for US$1) with a wide range of fillings, all made fresh to order at the street-front kitchen. Make sure you let them cool down after they come piping hot off the griddle. Can't go wrong. Daily 6am–8pm.

TAZUMAL AND CHALCHUAPA

Northeast from Ahuachapán, the road drops down onto a broad and scenic plain to the town of **CHALCHUAPA** and the towering archeological site of **Tazumal** (Tues–Sun 9am–4pm; US$3; ☎ 2444 0010), the most impressive Mesoamerican ruin in the country, which lies on the southern edge of Chalchuapa – the highway passes on the north side, so if driving you must pass through the town to get to the ruins. The main showstopper is a vast fourteen-stepped ceremonial pyramid, influenced by the style of Teotihuacán in Mexico. Though the site certainly possesses its own enigmatic beauty and is easily the most impressive ancient ruin in El Salvador, as a whole it is – by comparison with sites in Honduras and Guatemala – fairly small, and parts have been rather sloppily restored. The site was occupied for more than 750 years, mostly in the Late Classic period (600–900 AD). Earlier remains, dating back to 100–200 AD, have been found beneath the pyramid. The Maya abandoned the city around the end of the ninth century, during the collapse of the Classic Maya culture, and, unusually, Pipils moved in and occupied the site, building a pyramid dating back to the Early Postclassic (900–1200 AD) and another pelota court, in the northwest corner of the site. Tazumal was finally abandoned around 1200 AD. The **Museo Sitio Arqueológico** (same hours; Spanish only) displays artefacts discovered during excavations, including some stunning ceramics.

Casa Blanca

Aficionados should check out the smaller, grassy ruins of **Casa Blanca** (Tues–Sun

9am–4pm; US$3; US$1 parking; ☎2408 4641), an important Maya centre between 200 BC and 250 AD, just a five-minute taxi ride from Tazumal (it's right on the main highway on the north side of Chalchuapa). Visit in mid-winter and the site is smothered in pink *madrecacao* blooms. There's also a small exhibit here on traditional indigo production and tie-dye cloth making – enthusiastic women provide demonstrations (Spanish only).

ARRIVAL AND DEPARTURE

By bus #218 from Ahuachapán drops passengers off at a small plaza a few blocks from the centre of Chalchuapa; from here, walk uphill for about four blocks and follow the sign for Tazumal (you'll see the souvenir shops before the ruins). If driving, just park on the street outside (ask anyone for directions if you miss the signs).

SANTA ANA

El Salvador's second city, sweltering **SANTA ANA** lies in a superb location in the Cihautehuacán valley. Surrounded by jungle-smothered peaks, with the slope of Volcán Santa Ana rising to the southwest, the gently decaying colonial streets exude a restrained, provincial calm that is generally only ruptured during the July fiesta, when a host of events bring the streets to life. It's the most relaxed of El Salvador's cities, with the most elegant and lively Parque Central in the country and a decent nightlife, though the natural attractions of **Lago de Coatepeque**, the forest reserve of **Cerro Verde**, and the **Santa Ana and Izalco volcanoes** all beckon.

WHAT TO SEE AND DO

Santa Ana's **historic centre** possesses arguably the finest main plaza in the country: the **Parque Libertad** is neatly laid out with a small bandstand, where people gather to sit and chat in the early evening.

Catedral de Santa Ana

On the eastern edge of Parque Libertad is the magnificent **Catedral de Santa Ana** (Mon–Sat 6.30am–noon & 2–6.30pm, Sunday Mass 6.30am, 7.30am, 8.30am, 10am & 11am; free), an imposing neo-Gothic edifice completed in the early twentieth century. It's the second cathedral to occupy this site: a Spanish settlement was initially founded here in July 1569, when Bishop Bernardino de Villapando arrived en route from Guatemala. Completed seven years later, this church occupied the site of the present cathedral until it was destroyed in the early twentieth century to make way for the new building.

Inside the cathedral, the high naves, rather unsympathetically painted in pink and grey, soar upwards, and images – some dating back four hundred years – line the walls to the altar. Check out the snazzy rosaries sold just inside the entrance by the cathedral's rector. Inset into the walls are plaques from local worshippers giving thanks to various saints for miracles performed.

Teatro Nacional

On the northern edge of the Parque, the **Teatro Nacional**, completed in Renaissance style in 1910, was funded by taxes on local dignitaries. Once the proud home of the country's leading theatre companies, the building became a cinema in the 1930s before falling into disuse. Now restored to something resembling its former glories, it once again hosts recitals and concerts, as well as exhibitions and plays (see p.260). Guided tours (US$1.50) are in Spanish; you can usually wander around unaccompanied (Mon–Sat 8am–noon & 2–6pm).

Museo Regional del Occidente

On the second block down Avenida Independencia from the Parque, the **Museo Regional del Occidente** (Tues–Sun 9am–noon & 1–5pm; US$1) provides a comprehensive introduction to the region's history and archeological sites, though the best bit is the room dedicated to the various evolving forms of legal tender in the country, from 1828 right up to the dollar – fitting, considering this was once the local office of the Banco de Central de Reserva.

ACCOMMODATION
Casa Frolaz	3
Casa Verde	2
Hotel Libertad	1

EATING
Ban Ban	2
Expresión Cultural	4
Lovers' Steak House	5
Quattro Estaciones	7
Simmer Down	1
El Sin Rival	3

DRINKING & NIGHTLIFE
Chevy's	6
Drive Inn El Molino	8

SANTA ANA

ARRIVAL AND DEPARTURE

By bus The main Terminal Mercado Colón is on 10A Av Sur between 13A & 15A C Pte. Buses for Metapán (#325) arrive and depart two blocks west of the main terminal, in front of the Despensa Familiar supermarket, and international Puerto Buses to and from Guatemala arrive and depart from 25A C Pte between 6A & 8A Av Sur, just north of *Casa Frolaz*. King Quality and Ticabus (to and from Guatemala) usually stop at the Shell petrol station on the outskirts of the city (confirm before you leave; taxis will take you to the petrol station for US$4–5).

Destinations Ahuachapán (#210; frequent; 1hr 30min); Chalchuapa (#218; frequent; 30min); Guatemala City, Guatemala (standard: hourly; 4hr; first class: 2 daily; 3hr 30min); Juayúa (#238; daily 6.45am, 9.50am, 12.30pm, 2.30pm, 4pm, 5.35pm; 2hr); Lago de Coatepeque (#220; every 30min; 1hr 30min); Metapán (#235; every 40min; 1hr 15min); Parque Nacional Los Volcanes (#248; 6 daily; 1hr); San Cristóbal (#248; every 20min; 1hr); San Salvador (#201; 4am–8.10pm; every 10min; 2hr); Santa Elena, Belize, via Flores, Guatemala (daily; 9hr); Sonsonate (#216: frequent; 1hr 15min; #209: frequent; 1hr 45min).

GETTING AROUND

By bus Bus #51 runs between the centre and the bus terminal, and you can take any bus going up and down Av Independencia to get between the centre and the Metrocentro (US$0.25).

By taxi There are stands on the Parque, outside the Metrocentro and on 10A Av Sur, by the market, or you can hail one on the street. They should cost US$4–5, which you should politely agree beforehand.

ACCOMMODATION

The area around 8A and 10A Av Sur has the highest concentration of cheap and basic places to stay, co-dependent on the vice industry operating on the streets at night. Book ahead for *Casa Frolaz* or *Casa Verde*.

Casa Frolaz 29A C Pte 42B, between 8A & 10A Av Sur ☎ 2440 5302, ✉ casafrolaz@yahoo.com. One of the country's finest accommodation options is in the house of Javier Díaz, who is a descendant of one of the city's oldest families, a painter of international repute and a perfect host. With a private kitchen, laundry, hot water and a fruit-filled garden, a stay here could be three times the price. Free wi-fi but no computers. Shuttle buses to Copán (US$30). Camping/tent US$5, dorms US$8, double US$20

★**Casa Verde** 7A C Pte, between 8A & 10A Av Sur ☎ 7856 4924, ⓦ hostalverde.wordpress.com, ✉ casaverde _santaana@hotmail.com. Certainly the best hostel in the country, the *Casa Verde* has thought of everything. USB-charger ports inside your personal locker, bedside fans and lights, rucksack racks, spotlessly clean rooms and beers on the honour system. There's a cinema room, pool with volleyball, laundry service, wi-fi throughout, free water and coffee, board games and a rooftop terrace. Book ahead. Dorms US$10, doubles US$25

Hotel Libertad Libertad 4A C Ote 2, at 1A Av Nte ☎ 2441 2455, ✉ javal@navegante.com.sv. Airy and cool, this colonial monolith right by the cathedral has gigantic, clean and basic rooms with TV, some with bathroom. Free wi-fi. Bring your own padlock for the doors. Dorms US$10, doubles US$15

EATING

Ban Ban Av Independencia Sur 52 ☎ 2447 1865. The best bakery in town (opened in the 1970s) with a blissfully potent a/c. Serves sandwiches for lunch, and cakes, pastries and coffee all day. Indoor and outdoor seating. Free wi-fi. Daily 8am–7pm.

Expresión Cultural 11A C Pte, between 6A & 8A Av Sur ☎ 2440 1410. An arts and cultural centre, bookshop and internet café in a bohemian, leafy courtyard. They do especially good sandwiches (including a veggie option), as well as full meals (US$7–8) and desserts (US$3–4). Mon–Sat 7am–9pm, Sun 8am–6pm.

Lovers' Steak House 4A Av Sur, at 17A C Pte ☎ 2440 5717. A meat grill and Santa Ana institution that serves huge portions of steak and seafood, accompanied by a *bocadillo* (appetizer), as well as wine or beer. Mains cost around US$12, but you will definitely be full when you leave. Daily noon–10pm.

★**Simmer Down** Next to the cathedral on Parque Libertad ☎ 2455 4899. Amazing two-storey pizza joint with treehouse-like views over the main plaza. The pizza (personal size US$3, large US$10–13) is made from scratch in a wood-fired oven, as are all the condiments they use in their original and delicious toppings. A beautiful spot to

hang out and study the beautiful facade on the cathedral next door. Expect to pay about US$6/head. Tues–Sun 11am–10pm.

El Sin Rival C Libertad Ote ☎ 2441 0042, ⓦ elsinrival .com.sv. A cool place to chill out in the centre, this *sorbetería* serves original flavours of sorbet (two scoops US$1.25). The mini-chain started out as a *sorbetes* cart opened in 1951 by Emiliano Rivera Landaverde, soon dubbed "without rival". Also has a full restaurant one block to the east. Daily 10am–8pm.

DRINKING AND NIGHTLIFE

The only area with any nightlife in the centre is around Parque Libertad, the rest of the bars are located to the south of the city, and it's wise to take a taxi (US$5) to and from each location. Heading out of town, taxis are easily found on Av Independencia; on the way back, get the barman to arrange one.

Chevy's Av Moraga Sur, 1km south of town. A fun open-air bar with karaoke (even if the host reserves all the English songs for himself), cold beers and a snack menu that includes rabbit, chicken wings and fries. A fun place to spend an evening. Mon–Thurs noon–10pm, Fri & Sat noon–3am, Sun noon–9pm.

Drive Inn El Molino 25A Av Sur, at Carretera Antigua ☎ 2447 9035, ⓦ driveinnelmolino.com. A little out of town and best reached by taxi, this big and well-known bar has pool tables, live music, food and dancing. The party starts to kick off around midnight and there's a US$5 cover charge. The best night is Thurs, but it's lively all weekend. Wed–Sat 11am until the early morning.

ENTERTAINMENT

Cinema Cinemark, in the Metrocentro, shows dubbed or subtitled Hollywood blockbusters.

Theatre The beautifully restored Teatro Nacional (see p.258) has a calendar of classical music, theatre and performance arts (☎ 2447 6268). Check listings in the Friday *Prensa Gráfica* or stop by to find out times. Tickets should be under US$4 a show.

★TREAT YOURSELF

Quattro Estaciones 29A C Pte & 10 Av Sur 42B ☎ 2440 1564. This smart local favourite distinguishes itself from the pricier options nearby by its fine cooking rather than the size of its portions. It has an Italian influence, with good bruschette and spaghetti dishes, as well as a fine wine menu and coffee selection. US$18–20 per head. Mon–Thurs noon–9pm, Fri & Sat noon–10.30pm.

DIRECTORY

Banks There is a clump of banks around 2A Av Nte behind the *alcaldía*.

Internet Time Out (10am–7 or 9pm; US$1/1hr) is on 10A Av Sur & 29A C Pte.

Market The Mercado Central (daily 7am–5pm) is on 8A Av Sur between 1A & 3A C Pte, and the Mercado de Artesanías (Mon–Sat 8.30am–6pm), with a range of national crafts, is on 1A Av Sur.

Phones Claro, C Libertad Ote, at 5A Av Sur (Mon–Fri 8am–6pm, Sat 8am–4pm).

Post office Av Independencia at 7A C Pte (Mon–Fri 7.30am–5pm).

Supermarkets La Despensa de Don Juan (8am–8pm), on the southeast corner of the Parque (1A Av Nte, at C Libertad Ote), has a good selection; there is also a Despensa Familiar at 8A C Ote 1–3 (daily 7am–7pm).

LAGO DE COATEPEQUE

From El Congo junction, 14km southeast of Santa Ana, a winding branch road descends to the truly stunning crater lake of **LAGO DE COATEPEQUE**. The views are so mesmerizing that it's worth getting off the bus at the *mirador*, 4km from the water's edge, to take your time soaking them in, and then walking down the rest of the way. As much of the shore is bounded by private houses, access to the water itself is difficult. **Boat rides** are available at *Rancho Alegre* (see below), costing from US$20 per person for a thirty-minute trip around the lake, while jet skis are US$25 per 30min.

ARRIVAL AND DEPARTURE

By bus Bus #220 leaves the Santa Ana terminal for the lake (every 30min until 7pm; 1hr). If you're heading back to San Salvador, take the Santa Ana bus as far as El Congo then walk down the slip road to the main highway and catch any bus running from Santa Ana to the capital.

ACCOMMODATION AND EATING

Accommodation on the lake is limited and poor – you are better off visiting as a day-trip.

Mirador La Pedrera 2km out of El Congo on road down to the lakeside. The last of a series of bars looking out over the lake on the road down to the waterside, this green-painted shack is a peaceful retreat from the rowdier and more expensive bars on the waterside. Commanding stunning views over the lake, it's the perfect place to spend a lazy afternoon. Also does delicious food with local ingredients – try the crab bisque, made with crustaceans fished five hundred metres away. Daily 9am–10pm.

Rancho Alegre Cantón La Laguna, Caserío La Bendición (along the lake) ☎ 2441 6071, ⓦ restauranterancho alegresv.com. This waterside restaurant and hotel rents simple rooms for four or six people, all with a/c and hot water bathrooms. The restaurant (daily 9am–8pm) serves the usual mix of local and international dishes (breakfasts from US$4.50; mains US$7.50), with lively bands playing at the weekend (margaritas US$4.25). <u>US$40</u>

PARQUE NACIONAL LOS VOLCANES

Around 14km southeast of Santa Ana on the Panamericana, a narrow road rises up from the El Congo junction through coffee plantations, maize fields and pine woods to the **PARQUE NACIONAL LOS VOLCANES** (daily 8am–5pm; US$1; wsalvanatura.org). Here you can conquer the three dizzying volcanic peaks of Cerro Verde, Santa Ana and Izalco, or just enjoy the flora and fauna on a more relaxing hike through pristine mountain forests.

WHAT TO SEE AND DO

The oldest volcano in the park, **Cerro Verde**, is now a softened, densely vegetated mountain harbouring a wealth of wildlife – park activities centre around the car park near the top. **Santa Ana**, the highest volcano in the country at 2365m, has erupted out of its dormant state, while **Izalco**, one of the youngest volcanoes in the world, is an almost perfect, bare lava cone of unsurpassed natural beauty, and a very

---

INTO GUATEMALA: SAN CRISTÓBAL

Crossing to **Guatemala** at **San Cristóbal** is quick and easy: it's open 24hr, and there are frequent buses from Santa Ana (#36; 1hr) to the crossing. There are no official exchange facilities, but the touting moneychangers can offer reasonable rates. On the Guatemalan side, buses run to Asunción Mita, with connections to Guatemala City.

novel climb (the best views of it are from Santa Ana). The climb up Santa Ana is much easier than Izalco, and has more shade.

Volcán Cerro Verde

Dense forest fills the crater of the long-extinct **Volcán Cerro Verde**, inside of which a now-rare mix of Salvadorian flora and fauna combine, like a big bowl of nature soup. The numerous species of **plants**, including pinabetes and more than fifty species of orchid, are best viewed in season (for most species, between November and March), while armadillos and white-tailed deer are shy and hard to see year-round. Agoutis, which look like long-legged guinea pigs, can be found rummaging in the forest floor, but it's the **birds** that are most regularly spotted. Hummingbirds and toucans are commonly seen, as is the turquoise-browed motmot (torogoz – El Salvador's national bird), identifiable by its pendulous, racketed tail.

From the main car park, go clockwise along the main trail, the *sendero natural*, for an enjoyable walk of around 45 minutes through the green calm of the forest. *Miradores* along the way overlook Volcán Santa Ana and, far below, Lago de Coatepeque. Smaller trails branch off through the trees if you want to explore. The trails are clear and very well managed, but can get busy at weekends.

Volcán Santa Ana

A path branches left from a signed turn ten minutes into the *sendero natural* from the car park, and leads eventually to the summit of **Volcán Santa Ana**, known also as "Ilamatepec" (Nahuat for "old lady mountain"), with a sulphurous crater lake at the summit. In October 2005 the old lady turned out to be a bit more vigorous than her name suggests, erupting violently, killing two people in a boiling mudslide that broke off down its side and spitting rocks, some the size of cars, in a 2km radius. A second eruption was predicted, though has never materialized, and evacuated communities have long since moved back. The trail to the summit was closed for several years, but is

now open; guided climbs follow the same format as Volcán Izalco (see below), but check with Corsatur (☎2243 7835) for an update in case of further eruptions. Tours depart at 11am sharp from the Caseta de Guías in the car park, with a mandatory guide and a couple of uniformed policemen, costing around US$5.

Volcán Izalco

Sitting in contrast to the green slopes around it, the bleak, black volcanic pile of majestic **Volcán Izalco** began as a small hole in the ground in 1770. The volcano formed rapidly over the next two centuries, during which time its lava plume, known as the "lighthouse of the Pacific", was used by sailors to navigate. Then in 1966, just as a new hotel was built at its base, the plume dried up. Now guided tours leave daily at 11am from the car park for the steep climb to the top (3–4hr; tip US$5–8); be there at 10.30am for the tour briefing. The guides are compulsory, for your safety, set up in response to muggings. A marked trail leads from the lookout down for about thirty minutes to a saddle between Volcán Santa Ana and Volcán Izalco. From here it takes at least an hour to climb the barren moonscape of volcanic scree to the summit. Bring water and good shoes.

ARRIVAL AND DEPARTURE

By bus Sonsonate-bound bus #248 runs to the car park (daily 7.30am; returning daily 3pm) from Santa Ana's Vencedora terminal. The last bus from the car park leaves at 5pm but runs to El Congo only, from where you can pick up services to Santa Ana or San Salvador.

ACCOMMODATION

Camping If you have your own tent, you can camp for free around the visitors' centre in the car park, though there are no dedicated facilities, so bring food and water; ask a warden to tell you where to set up.

METAPÁN

Some 40km north of Santa Ana, the beautifully restored town of **METAPÁN** is scenically situated on the edge of the mountains of the Cordillera Metapán–Alotepeque, and is probably the cleanest town in the entire country. Metapán was one of only four communities that supported Delgado's first call for independence in 1811; the town is the birthplace of **Isidro Menéndez** (1795–1858), a key figure in El Salvador's independence movement and often credited with drafting the country's first constitution. With low-set, gently whitewashed buildings, it is one of the more pleasant of Salvadorian provincial towns, the market less unsightly than most and confined to the outskirts well away from the centre. The main reason for staying in Metapán, however, is as a base for the international reserve of **Parque Nacional Montecristo**, jointly administered by the governments of El Salvador, Honduras and Guatemala.

WHAT TO SEE AND DO

At the Parque Central, the **Iglesia de la Parroquia San Pedro Apóstol**, completed in 1743, is one of El Salvador's finest colonial churches, with a beautifully preserved facade. Inside, the main altar is flanked by small pieces worked in silver from a local mine, while the ornately decorated cupola features paintings of San Gregorio, San Augustín, San Ambrosio and San Gerónimo. On the south side of the plaza, the colonnaded **alcaldía** is an attractive building in its own right, watched over by two statues of teeth baring jaguars symbolizing the strength and suffering of the indigenous people of the department. The west side, rather bizarrely, forms one of the stands of the town's football stadium, though it's cunningly disguised with a neo-colonial colonnaded facade and balcony restaurant, which also offers a good people-watching perch over the square.

Parque Acuático Apuzunga
Just outside Metapán on the nearby Guajoyo River (on the road to Santa Ana), the **Parque Acuático Apuzunga** (Sat & Sun 7am–5pm; ☎2483 8952, ⓦapuzunga.com) offers five naturally fed swimming pools (US$3), ziplining (US$10), camping (US$48/tent) and rafting with professional river guides (US$50/person).

ARRIVAL AND DEPARTURE

By bus Buses arrive at the main terminal on the Carretera Internacional, five or six blocks from the centre down C 15 de Septiembre, which heads past the market and most of the hotels towards the centre.

Destinations Anguiatú and the Guatemalan border (#211A/#235; every 30min; 30min); El Poy/Citalá (#463; Mon–Sat 5.20am & noon; 3hr); San Salvador (#201A; 6 daily; 2hr); Santa Ana (#235; every 20min; 1hr 30min).

ACCOMMODATION

Hostal de Metapán One block down the hill from the bus terminal ☎2402 2382, ⓔhostaldemetapan @hotmail.com. Rafael and Estrella have created a spotless, central guesthouse with eight rooms including en-suite doubles with a/c, free wi-fi, parking, free coffee and breakfast. US$18

Hostal Villa Limón Carretera Internacional (near the border, get bus #21) ☎2442 0149, ⓔhostalvillalimon @hotmail.com. Three rustic but pleasant log cabins (for up to 6 people) equipped with kitchens and grill (wood fire), fridge and microwave. There's also a camping area with grills and toilets. The owners operate a zipline through the jungle (US$15), and offer meals (US$4–7). Camping/ person US$5, cabins US$55

EATING

Antojitos La Nueva Esperanza Off the Parque on Av Benjamin Valiente. Excellent, lofty food hall in a colonial building, with seven dishes of *comida a la vista* a day (US$2–3) and offering *El Sin Rival* ice cream. Tues–Sun 11.30am–10pm.

Balompié Café 3A Av Nte ☎2416 4140, ⓦbalompiecafe .com. Soccer-themed restaurant (*balompié* means soccer) overlooking the main plaza to one side and the town football pitch to the other. The balcony kitchen specializes in meat (mains US$8) – pork comes from pigs they farm

3

INTO GUATEMALA: ANGUIATÚ

Some 13km north of Metapán, **Anguiatú** is a generally smooth border-crossing to **Guatemala**. Open from 5am–10pm, it's the most convenient crossing if you're heading for Esquipulas in Guatemala or the Copán ruins in Honduras. Regular buses run from the Guatemalan side to Chiquimula until 5.30pm. If you're coming in the other direction note that the last bus to Metapán leaves at 6.30pm.

themselves – and offers a bucket of beer for US$6.50. Mon & Wed–Sun 10.30am–10pm.

Taquería Guadalajara Carretera Internacional (one block west of the terminal) ☎ 2402 4399. Quality Mexican food – beef tacos, *al pastor*, quesadillas and burritos, as well as giant *tortas* (grilled baguettes), from US$2.50. Daily 4.30pm–midnight.

DIRECTORY

Banks Scotiabank, with ATM, at Av Ignacio Goméz & C 15 de Septiembre (Mon–Fri 8am–4.30pm, Sat 8am–noon); Citibank, Av Isidro Menéndez & 3A C Pte (Mon–Fri 8.30am–6.30pm, Sat 8.30am–noon).

Supermarket Super Selectos (7am–7pm) is near the bus terminal on Carretera Internacional.

Tourist information On the southeast corner of the Parque Central. The helpful staff (often managed by American Peace Corps volunteers) can offer good insight into more than just Parque Montecristo, such as the lakes and hiking trails to the southwest.

PARQUE NACIONAL MONTECRISTO

The enchanting **PARQUE NACIONAL MONTECRISTO** reserve (daily 7am–3pm) rises through two climatic zones to the **Punto Trifinio**, the summit of Cerro Montecristo (2418m), where the borders of Honduras, Guatemala and El Salvador converge. The higher reaches of Montecristo, beginning at around 2100m, are home to an expanse of virgin **cloudforest**, with an annual rainfall of 2m and one hundred percent humidity. Orchids and pinabetes thrive in these climatic conditions, while huge oaks, pines and cypresses, some towering to higher than 20m, swathed in creepers, lichens and mosses, form a dense canopy preventing sunlight from reaching the forest floor. **Wildlife** abounds, with howler and spider monkeys the most visible (and audible) mammals, and jaguars and other large mammals hiding out. **Birds**, including hummingbirds, quetzals, toucans and the regional endemic bushy-crested jay, are more easily seen. Walking straight to the summit is a truly rewarding climb of around four hours; the path from Los Planes leads through the cloudforest, however, and you can branch off in any direction – bring warm clothing and good footwear. Note that the upper reaches of cloudforest are closed to visitors from May to October. Trails also lead from just below **Los Planes** (1890m) to the peaks of Cerro El Brujo and Cerro Miramundo.

ARRIVAL AND INFORMATION

By tour Various operators in San Salvador (see p.211) run tours (US$30–50/person) to the park.

By taxi or pick-up Occasional pick-ups make the 5km journey up from Metapán for a negotiable fee; the best place to catch them is at the turning to the Parque Central, by *Hotel San José* on the Carretera Internacional. You could also try to get into a group of four and organize a taxi from around Metapán's Parque (US$45 return).

On foot You're not allowed to enter Parque Nacional Montecristo on foot.

Entrance fee and registration The park entrance is 5km from Metapán. Pay the entrance fee (US$6, plus US$1.50 for a vehicle) here. After another 2km you come to the Casco Colonial, formerly Hacienda San José, where the wardens are based and where you have to register; it has an interesting collection of natural history and archeological exhibits, as well as a small orchid garden. In theory, you need permission to enter the park from the Ministerio de Medio Ambiente in San Salvador (☎ 2223 0444), but if you're on an organized tour your guide will take care of this; otherwise you can call the Ministerio or just turn up and plead ignorance.

ACCOMMODATION AND EATING

Camping There are free camping areas at Los Planes, 14km from the Casco Colonial (with toilets and picnic tables, but no equipment, so bring food and water), and two simple cabins sleeping up to eight each. Camping free, cabins US$35

Restaurant Also at Los Planes is a small restaurant serving *típicos* (US$3).

CHICHICASTENANGO MARKET

Guatemala

HIGHLIGHTS

❶ Antigua The former capital, boasting colonial buildings and ruined churches. **See p.288**

❷ Lago de Atitlán Breathtaking, steep-sided crater lake. **See p.299**

❸ Highland villages Traditional highland villages offering insight into Maya life. **See p.309**

❹ Río Dulce gorge Stunning jungle-clad river system with numerous tributaries. **See p.342**

❺ Semuc Champey Idyllic turquoise waters and caves to explore. **See p.352 & p.353**

❻ Tikal Once a great Maya metropolis, now an incomparable site. **See p.364**

HIGHLIGHTS ARE MARKED ON THE MAP ON PP.268–269

ROUGH COSTS

Daily budget Basic US$25/occasional treat US$40

Drink Beer (330ml) US$2, coffee US$1

Food Tostada US$0.50

Hostel/budget hotel US$8/US$16

Travel Quetzaltenango–Guatemala City (194km) by public bus: 4hr, US$8

FACT FILE

Population 15.4 million

Languages Spanish, 23 indigenous languages

Capital Guatemala City (population: over 3 million)

Currency Quetzal (Q)

International phone code ☎502

Time zone GMT -6hr

Introduction

Guatemala is simply loaded with natural, historical and cultural interest. In established destinations – Antigua, Lago de Atitlán, Flores – you'll have your choice of Western comforts and convenient transport options. Get off the beaten track and opportunities for activities like jungle trekking, exploring ancient Maya ruins and cooling off in crystalline pools and waterfalls abound. Whatever preconceived notions you have, throw them away – you'll be surprised by the variety of beguiling experiences the country has to offer.

Guatemala's landscape, defined by extremes, is dramatic and wildly beautiful. Rising steeply from the Pacific coast, and contributing to the country's status as the most mountainous Central American nation, is a chain of volcanoes (some still smoking). In many **highland villages** these behemoths are just a fact of life. Then there are the **lowlands** – on the flat, steamy Pacific side you'll find black-sand beaches, turtles and mangroves, while the tropical Caribbean coast is fringed with coconut palms. **Petén**, the country's least populous yet largest department, fosters everything from savanna to rainforest, and is extraordinarily rich in both **Maya ruins** and wildlife. Guatemala also has some superb cities: **Antigua** is home to irresistible colonial architecture and a plethora of restaurants, cafés and Spanish schools, while **Quetzaltenango** is the de facto capital of the highlands and another important study centre. Even **Guatemala City**, avoided by many, possesses its own gritty charm

The country's landscape has had an undeniable effect on the history and lifestyle of its people. **Indigenous groups** (mostly Maya) are in the majority here, especially in the highlands; villages such as Todos Santos Cuchumatán, Chichicastenango and Nebaj are renowned for riotously coloured textiles and some of the most sense-assaulting **markets** in the world. Throughout the country you'll find that Guatemalans (or Chapines, as they call themselves), while perhaps more reserved than some of their neighbours, are polite, helpful and welcoming at every turn.

WHEN TO VISIT

As with all mountainous countries, Guatemala's **climate** is largely governed by **altitude**. Many places of interest (including Antigua, Lago de Atitlán, Cobán and the capital) are between 1300 and 1600m, where the climate is temperate: expect warm days and mild evenings. Low-lying Petén is a different world, with steamy conditions year-round, and the Pacific and Caribbean coasts are equally hot and humid.

The rainy season is roughly between May and October. Precipitation is often confined to the late afternoon, and the rest of the day is frequently warm and pleasant. As a rule, it's only in remote areas that rain can affect travel plans. The **busiest times** for tourism are during July and August, between Christmas and mid-January, and around Easter, when Holy Week (Semana Santa) celebrations are quite a spectacle to behold.

CHRONOLOGY

c. 2500 BC Proto-Maya period. Agricultural communities are formed and an early Maya language spoken.

1800 BC Preclassic Maya culture emerges in the forests of Petén.

1000 BC Early settlement at sites including Nakbé and El Mirador.

300–150 BC Colossal temple construction at El Mirador, which enters its greatest era as 70m-high temples are built.

150 AD Preclassic cities in the Mirador Basin are abandoned.

300–900 AD Classic Period of Maya culture sees astounding advances in architecture, astronomy and art, and development of political alliances.

378 AD Tikal defeats Uaxactún; Teotihuacán influence permeates the Petén.

682 AD Hasaw Chan K'awil begins 52-year reign at Tikal, which becomes a "superpower" of Maya world. Vast temple construction programmes commence.

750 AD Population peaks at around 10 million in Maya region.

780 AD Warring increases and Maya cities gradually decline.

1200s Toltecs invading from Mexico institute a militaristic society that fosters highland tribal rivalries.

1523 Conquistador Pedro de Alvarado arrives, and takes advantage of tribal rivalries to bring the Maya under Spanish control.

1540 The last of the highland tribes are subdued.

1541 Guatemala's capital (today's Antigua) presides over the provinces of modern-day Costa Rica, Nicaragua, El Salvador, Honduras and Chiapas.

1773 Antigua is destroyed by an earthquake; the capital is relocated to its present-day site.

1821 The Captain-General of Central America signs the Act of Independence and Guatemala briefly becomes a member of the Central American Federation.

1847 Guatemala declares itself an independent republic.

1871 Rufino Barrios starts a liberal revolution, which heralds sweeping social change but crushes dissent and marginalizes the rural poor.

1901 The United Fruit Company begins to grow bananas in Guatemala. It monopolizes railway and port facilities, and establishes a pervasive political presence.

1944 Guatemala embarks on a 10-year experiment with "spiritual socialism".

1952 Law redistributing United Fruit Company land is passed, to the benefit of 100,000 peasant families.

1954 The CIA sets up an invasion of Guatemala to overthrow its "communist-leaning" government.

1955–85 Military governments send the country into a spiral of violence, economic decline and corruption.

1976 Huge earthquake leaves 23,000 dead, 77,000 injured and a million homeless. Presence of guerrilla groups increases in the wake of the destruction.

1978 Lucas García takes over, escalating the civil war and massacring some 25,000 peasants, intellectuals, politicians, priests and protesters.

1982 Efraín Ríos Montt stages a successful coup. His Civil Defence Patrols polarize the country, trapping peasants between armed forces and guerrilla groups.

1985 The first legitimate elections in thirty years are won by Vinicio Cerezo, but the army is still clearly in control.

1992 Civil war rumbles on. Rigoberta Menchú is awarded the Nobel Peace Prize for campaigning on behalf of Guatemala's indigenous population.

1996 Peace accords are signed on December 29.

1998 Bishop Juan Gerardi is assassinated two days after publishing an investigation of wartime atrocities.

1999 Alfonso Portillo takes office. His reign is plagued by corruption, and the country is left virtually bankrupt.

2004 Newcomer Oscar Berger is inaugurated president; the economy makes some teetering progress.

2007–11 Guatemala's first left-leaning president in fifty years, Alvaro Colom, is elected. Drug traffickers and street gangs challenge the rule of law.

2012 Ex-general Otto Pérez begins presidency with iron-fist mandate to tackle crime. Huge celebrations mark the start of new cycle in the Maya Long Count calendar on 21st December.

2013 Ex-military ruler Efraín Ríos Montt is found guilty of genocide during Guatemala's civil war; the conviction is later overturned.

2015 Remittances from Guatemalans living abroad rise to form more than ten percent of the nation's GDP

4

LAND AND SEA ROUTES TO GUATEMALA

Mexico borders Guatemala at Ciudad Hidalgo–Tecún Umán and El Carmen–Talismán (see box, p.331), both close to the Mexican city of Tapachula. Ciudad Cuauhtémoc–La Mesilla (see box, p.329) is convenient when travelling from San Cristóbal de Las Casas. There are also two routes connecting Palenque and Flores: Frontera Corozal–La Técnica/Bethel via the Río Usumacinta and El Ceibo–El Naranjo (see p.373).

Entering Guatemala from **Belize**, there's either the land crossing in Petén at Benque Viejo del Carmen–Melchor de Menchos (see box, p.87) or two boat routes: Punta Gorda to Puerto Barrios and Punta Gorda–Lívingston (see p.99).

Coming from **El Salvador**, most Guatemala City-bound traffic uses the Las Chinamas–Valle Nuevo border (see box, p.256), while the La Hachadura–Ciudad Pedro de Alvarado (see box, p.249) route is convenient for Guatemala's Pacific coast. There are also two border crossings at Anguiatú (see box, p.263) and at San Cristóbal Frontera (see box, p.261); both access the eastern highlands.

415Copán with Chiquimula, and Corinto–Entre Ríos (see box, p.120), which links Puerto Cortés with Puerto Barrios.

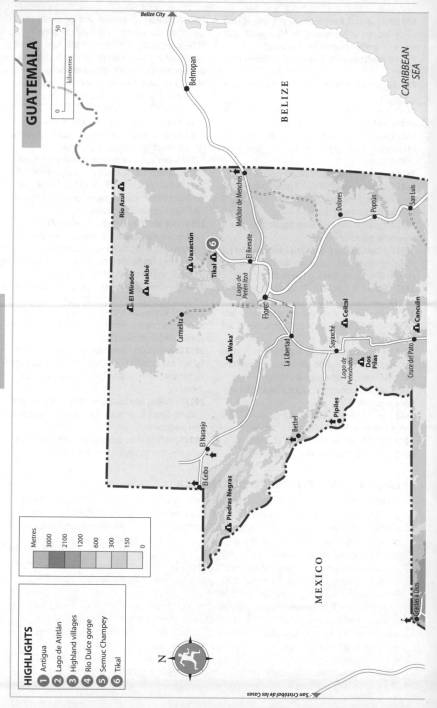

GUATEMALA

HIGHLIGHTS

1. Antigua
2. Lago de Atitlán
3. Highland villages
4. Rio Dulce gorge
5. Semuc Champey
6. Tikal

Metres
3000
2100
1200
600
300
150
0

kilometres
0   50

CARIBBEAN SEA

BELIZE

Belize City

Belmopan

Río Azul

Uaxactún

Nakbé

El Mirador

Tikal — 6

El Remate

Melchor de Mencos

Dolores

Poptún

San Luis

Lago de Petén Itzá

Flores

Carmelita

Waka'

La Libertad

Sayaxché

Ceibal

Cancuén

Cruce del Pato

Lago de Petexbatún

Dos Pilas

El Naranjo

Bethel

Pipiles

El Ceibo

Piedras Negras

MEXICO

Gracias a Dios

San Cristóbal de las Casas

N

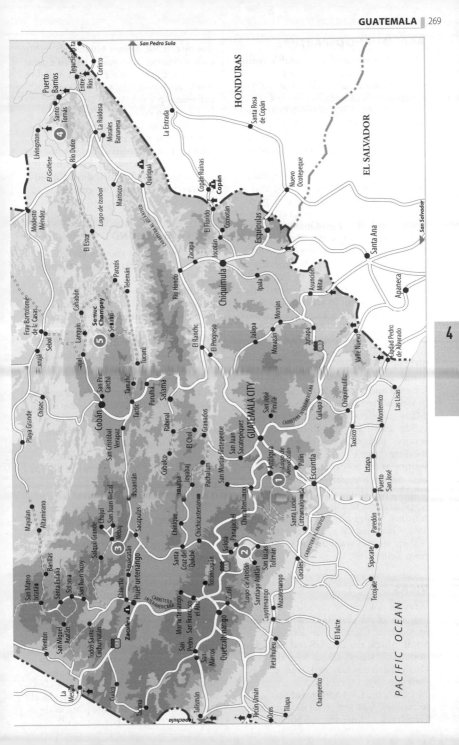

4

ARRIVAL AND DEPARTURE

The vast majority of Guatemala's visitors arrive at the modern **La Aurora International Airport** (GUA) in the southern suburbs of Guatemala City. Most long-haul flights arrive from the US: Delta (⊕delta.com) flying from Atlanta/Los Angeles/New York; United (⊕united.com) from Houston/Newark/Washington; and American Airlines (⊕aa.com) from Dallas–Fort Worth/Miami. Avianca (⊕avianca.com) also connects Los Angeles, Miami, Bogotá and all the Central American capitals (Belize excepted) with Guatemala City, while Spirit Airlines (⊕spirit.com) fly from Fort Lauderdale. Interjet (⊕interjet.com.mx) and Aeroméxico (⊕aeromexico.com) both fly from Mexico City. Iberia (⊕iberia.com) offers direct flights from Madrid and San Salvador and there are also connections to Roatán and with TAG airlines (⊕tag.com.gt). **Flores airport** in Petén is served by Tropic Air (⊕tropicair.com) and TAG airlines from Belize City.

You can enter Guatemala by **land** from Chiapas and Tabasco in Mexico, as well as Belize, Honduras and El Salvador. Many travellers choose to take cross-border shuttles or long-distance **bus** services, though it's also possible to use local transport – you'll always find buses waiting at the border to take you to the next town (cross early in the day to ensure more choice of departures). Unofficial fees of a dollar or two are routinely charged by border officials to enter Guatemala at all land borders.

There are two **sea routes** to Guatemala from Belize.

VISAS

Visas are not currently required by the majority of travellers (including citizens of Australia, Canada, New Zealand, South Africa, the UK, US and most, but not all, EU states). Check with the closest Guatemalan embassy well in advance of your trip.

In 2006 the **CA-4 agreement** was set up to facilitate visa-free travel in Guatemala, Honduras, El Salvador and Nicaragua (see box, p.30). If your Guatemala tourist card is coming to an end, you can extend it by travelling to either Mexico or Belize, which are outside the CA-4, or get an extension in Guatemala City at the immigration office (see p.288).

The Guatemala and Honduras governments have announced a commitment to abolish border checkpoints and customs posts from 1 December 2015, which should speed up travel between the two countries considerably.

GETTING AROUND

Expect to get what you pay for when it comes to Guatemalan **transport**: options available range from the country's "chicken buses" (see box, p.321) to privately operated shuttles. If you're in a hurry, you can also expect to be frustrated – despite frequent services and an improved road network, delays are still common. An epidemic of speedbump-building (even on major highways like the CA-13 between Río Dulce Town and Flores) means that journey times can be painfully slow. Be aware, too, that safety remains a major issue when travelling in Guatemala; premium services are not necessarily more secure. Highway robberies have decreased markedly in recent years due to an increase in highway patrols, but tourist vehicles remain occasional targets.

Traffic accidents are also common. If you're feeling uncomfortable with your driver, consider asking him to slow down (if a private shuttle), or if on public transport, get off and wait for the next bus.

BY BUS

Buses in Guatemala are incredibly crowded, but they're also cheap and the easiest way to get around. In urban and rural areas alike, **second-class buses** – known as *camionetas* to Guatemalans and "chicken buses" to foreigners (see box, p.32) – are numerous. Second-class buses generally start and stop at the local terminal (often in the same place as the local market) and will drop you off wherever you like en route. They don't generally have schedules (except on more remote routes), instead leaving every thirty minutes or when full. Pay your **fare** (expect it to be about Q8/hr) to the *ayudante* (conductor) on the bus. It pays to be open to help from locals when trying to negotiate your passage – the *ayudantes* are invariably friendly, knowledgeable and for the most part honest.

In many areas **microbuses**, or *micros*, supplement (or have replaced) chicken buses. They cost roughly the same. These minibuses can depart from a central bus station, private terminal or just a bus stop.

First-class, or **Pullman**, buses are more comfortable and make fewer stops. Each passenger has a seat, and tickets can be bought in advance. Some Pullman companies stop en route to pick up passengers if they have space, but most only pause very infrequently at designated bus terminals. Pullmans usually leave from the bus company's office rather than a town's main bus terminal. Expect to pay about Q12–16 per hour of travel.

All the main tourist routes are also served by convenient **shuttle buses** that will whisk you around for a price (Antigua–Panajachel, for example, costs Q80–100). Tickets are booked (best the day before) through a travel agent or your hotel. You'll be picked up from your accommodation and dropped off where you choose.

Shuttles are best used for relatively short journeys – for longer trips Pullmans are far more comfortable. Some shuttle bus operators (the Lanquín–Flores route is notorious) pack passengers in the aisles between seats on little stools – not much fun when the journey time is more than eight hours and there are twenty people aboard a non-air-conditioned minibus.

BY CAR

Driving in Guatemala is not for the faint-hearted, though if you prepare yourself for some alarming local practices it can be a highly enjoyable way to get around. The main routes are paved, but minor roads are often extremely rough and landslides are common in the rainy season. **Parking** and **security** are the main problems; in the larger towns you should always use a guarded car park. **Petrol** costs around Q23 a gallon, **diesel** a little less. **Renting a car** costs from Q260 a day for a small vehicle, but watch out for extra charges (excesses on any damage caused can be huge). All major rental firms have an office at the airport in Guatemala City (see p.284).

If you plan to visit the more remote parts of the country, then you might **hitch a ride** with a pick-up or truck from time to time. You'll usually have to pay for your lift – around the same as the bus fare. This said, hitching is never entirely safe, and carries obvious risks.

Motorcycle taxis, or tuk-tuks, are common in most towns and villages, but not in big cities (including the capital and Quetzaltenango). A short ride usually costs Q5, a longer trip Q10 or so. Clarify that the price is for the journey, not per person. **Taxis** are also readily available,

---

ADDRESSES IN GUATEMALA

Like the majority of towns and cities in Central America, Guatemala's streets generally follow a **grid system**, with the occasional diagonal thrown in for variety. In most towns, **avenidas** run north–south and are numbered from 1 Avenida (on either the west or east side of town), while **calles** run east–west (and will start at 1 Calle in the north). Even small towns will centre on a plaza (with the exception of waterside settlements such as Panajachel and Lívingston). In larger towns the ever-expanding street network is divided into **zonas**, each of which may have its own separate set of numbered calles and avenidas (ie, 1 Calle may exist in more than one *zona*). **Addresses** in Guatemala are given listing first the calle or avenida that the property is on, followed by a number signifying the calle/avenida that intersects to the north/west. The final number given is the property number. For example "6 Av 9–14, Zona 1" is in Zona 1, on 6 Avenida south of 9 Calle, house number 14.

but cost more (around Q40 for a 3km trip). Except in Guatemala City, meters are nonexistent so it's essential to **fix a price** before you set off.

BY BIKE

Cycling is the most exhilarating way to see Guatemala, but the country's mountainous terrain makes it very challenging. If you set out and it all gets too much, you can change to a bus – most buses will carry bikes on the roof. You can rent mountain bikes in Antigua, Panajachel and Quetzaltenango, as well as several other cities. Repair shops are fairly widespread.

Several tour agencies, including in Antigua, Santa Cruz La Laguna and Quetzaltenango, offer escorted mountain bike tours, which are an excellent way to see the countryside.

BY BOAT

Small, speedy, motorized boats called **lanchas** are the main form of water transport. The two definitive boat trips in Guatemala are through the Río Dulce gorge system, starting in either Livingston or Río Dulce Town, and across Lago de Atitlán. The Monterrico, Lago de Petexbatún and Lago de Petén Itzá regions also offer the possibility of excellent boat excursions.

BY PLANE

The only internal **flight** most tourists are likely to take is from Guatemala City to Flores (from Q1700 return), with two airlines, TACA (⊛taca.alternativeairlines .com) and TAG (⊛tag.com.gt), offering daily services. Virtually any travel agent in the country can sell you a ticket, or you can book via the airlines' websites.

ACCOMMODATION

Accommodation in Guatemala comes in different guises: *pensiones*, *posadas*, *hospedajes* and hotels. The names don't actually mean much, however, as they're approximately the same thing, although in general hotels are towards the top end of the price scale and most *hospedajes* and *pensiones* towards the bottom. Budget

options are plentiful and even in tourist centres you can sleep for as little as Q30 in a dorm. **Hostels and lodges** tailored to backpackers are springing up across the country; most have dorms and camping facilities as well as private rooms. Wherever you stay, **room prices** are fixed by Inguat, the tourist board (see p.276), and there should be a tariff posted by the door of your room. You should never pay more than the posted rate.

Rates rarely include breakfast; however, many moderately priced rooms (Q130– 250) come with cable TV and hot-water showers (though actually only emit a trickle of lukewarm water). Only on the coasts and in Petén will you need a **fan** or **air conditioning**, while you'll need heavy-duty blankets in the highlands. A **mosquito net** is sometimes provided in lowland areas, but if you plan to spend time in Petén or on either coast it's probably worth investing in one.

Camping facilities are rare and it's not worth bringing a tent unless you're a complete canvas addict. Lanquín, Laguna Lachúa, Poptún, El Remate and Tikal have campsites.

FOOD AND DRINK

You can be well fed in Guatemala for just a few dollars a day. Cheap eats are abundant, from fresh produce at markets to street stalls selling tasty snacks. **Lunch** is the main meal for locals; you'll get a two-course lunch, with a drink, for Q20–30 in *comedores* throughout the country. These *menú del día* or *almuerzo* set menus are usually served from noon to 3pm. **Breakfast** is also good value, if fattening, with traditional *desayunos* including a combination of eggs, beans, tortillas, cheese, fried plantains and cream. Most places in tourist centres also offer continental options for slightly more money. Alternatively, fresh fruit can be bought from street vendors, and muffins and breads from bakeries, cutting your breakfast bill considerably. **Evening meals** in restaurants are generally more expensive (from Q40).

Maya cuisine is at the heart of Guatemalan cooking. Maize is an essential ingredient, appearing most commonly as a **tortilla**, which is like a small, thick corn wrap. **Beans** (*frijoles*) are served either refried (*volteados*) or whole (*parados*). Chillis, usually in the form of a spicy sauce (*salsa picante*), are the final ingredient. When Guatemalans talk about "*comida típica*" you can be sure that these three ingredients will feature on the plate.

Popular **market snacks** include *pupusas* (thick stuffed tortillas topped with crunchy, grated salad vegetables) and tostadas (corn crisps smeared with avocado, cheese and other toppings). On the Caribbean coast there is a distinct **Creole cuisine**, heavily based on fish, seafood, coconuts, plantains and banana. *Tapado* (a coconut-based fish or shellfish soup) is the signature dish in these parts. In small towns and rural areas across the country, you can expect your choice to be confined to rice, tortillas and beans, and fried chicken or grilled beef. Vegetarians receive a mixed bag; Guatemala City offers some gems (even for vegans) and tourist hubs such as Flores, Antigua and Lago de Atitlán present interesting veggie menus too. Elsewhere, options can be quite limited.

DRINK

Bottled water (*agua pura*) is available almost everywhere and cheapest if bought in 500ml plastic bags (*bolsitas*), which cost Q1 each in shops.

Guatemalan **coffee** is great – unfortunately, most of it is exported. In tourist centres espresso machines are becoming very common – expect to pay Q12–18 for a cappuccino – but off the gringo trail very weak or instant coffee is the norm. During the day locals drink water or **refrescos**, water-based drinks with some fruit flavour. **Fizzy drinks** like Coca-Cola or Fanta (all called *aguas* or *gaseosas*) are also popular. For a healthy treat, order a **licuado**: a thick, fruit-based smoothie made with either water or milk (milk is safer).

The national **beer** (*cerveza*) is Gallo, a medium-strength, bland lager that comes in 330ml or litre bottles (around Q15 and Q30 respectively in a bar; much less

in a supermarket). Brahma, another lager, is also widely available, while Moza, a dark brew with a slight caramel flavour, is worth trying, too. Better still, and served in traditional bars, is a *mixta* – a mix of draught clear (*clara*) and dark (*obscura*) beers. **Rum** (*ron*) and **aguardiente**, a clear and lethal sugar-cane spirit, are also popular and cheap. Ron Botran Añejo is an acceptable brand (around Q55 a bottle), or for a real treat order a glass of the fabulously smooth Zacapa rum. Hard drinkers will soon get to know Quetzalteca, a local *aguardiente*. Chilean and Argentine **wines** are popular in tourist centres: a glass costs from Q25 in a bar; bottles start at about Q75.

CULTURE AND ETIQUETTE

Perhaps more than in other Central American countries, **religious doctrine** – Catholic, Evangelical Protestant, indigenous spiritual beliefs – continues to influence cultural behaviour in Guatemala. Consequently, Guatemalans are fairly modest, reserved folk. This is particularly true of the Maya, who can be suspicious of outsiders; tradition rules in indigenous communities. The dominant Ladino (Latin American) culture is generally less rigid, thanks to the more immediate effects of globalization. Women show more skin, and the Latin American **machismo** is more obvious. Even this, though, is pretty inoffensive – the odd comment or whistle from men trying to impress their friends – and can be ignored by female travellers.

Homosexuality is not illegal, though it is frowned upon by many. There are small gay communities in Guatemala City, Antigua and Quetzaltenango, but few public meeting places.

It would be a mistake to take Guatemalan reserve for unfriendliness, and you're likely to receive gracious hospitality from all levels of society. **Politeness** is valued highly by Ladino and Maya society alike, and there is a pleasantry for nearly every occasion – you will endear yourself to locals by returning these. "*Buen provecho*", for example, is usually exchanged among strangers

4

4

GUATEMALAN WORDS AND PHRASES

Baa Right! (often used at the start of sentences, or on its own as an affirmative)
Buena onda Cool
Fijase It's like this… (often used to preface why something hasn't gone according to plan)
Chapín/Guatemalteco/Guatemayan Guatemalan/Ladino/Maya

… AND GESTURES

Rubbing one's elbow signifies that somebody is cheap.
Pulling one's collar signifies that someone has clout/power.

---

in restaurants; it literally translates to "I hope your meal is of good benefit to you!" Be prepared, though, for the fact that **noise pollution** and **personal space** are almost foreign concepts: it is quite usual to be woken by firecrackers at 5am, evangelical PA systems blare for hours, and you can expect a good deal of pushing and shoving on buses and around markets.

Tipping in restaurants and *comedores* is not expected, but is certainly appreciated.

SPORTS AND OUTDOOR ACTIVITIES

Football (soccer) is the country's top spectator sport, by far. The two big local teams, both from Guatemala City, are Municipal and Communications. Admission to games is inexpensive (starting at Q25 or so). Football also provides for easy cross-cultural conversation, as most Guatemalan men are well versed on the topic and have a favourite team in the Spanish Primera Liga. The website ⓦguatefutbol.com (Spanish only) details fixtures and results.

Guatemala is a paradise for outdoor activities. With a sturdy pair of shoes, you can **hike** volcanoes, jungles and national parks, and sections of Lago de Atitlán. **Caving** is also popular, especially in the area north of Cobán where there are great caverns and underground rivers to explore: Lanquín (see p.352), Kan'ba

(see box, p.353) and Finca Ixobel (see p.357) are the places to head for. Finca Ixobel, Antigua and San Pedro La Laguna also make good bases for exploring the countryside on horseback. Wildlife- and **birdwatching** can be very rewarding in Guatemala, as the nation is home to ten percent of the world's registered species and encompasses twenty ecosystems and some three hundred microclimates. National parks and reserves good for wildlife include Tikal (see p.364), Monterrico (see p.334), Cerro Cahuí (see p.363), the Biotopo del Quetzal (see p.347), Waka' (see box, p.370) and the vast Reserva de la Biosfera Maya around El Mirador (see p.371). Other activities include **cycling** in the highlands, **altitude diving** in Lago de Atitlán's volcanic lake (see p.307) and **surfing** on the Pacific coast (see p.330). You can also **sail** from Río Dulce – one popular route takes you to Belize's more remote cays.

COMMUNICATIONS

Guatemalan **postal services** are fairly efficient by Latin American standards, and even the smallest of towns has a *correo* (post office); hours are generally Monday to Friday 8am to 5pm. Airmail letters generally take around a week to the US, and a couple of weeks or so to Europe. Post coming into Guatemala is fairly reliable too, though note that there is no longer any **poste restante** service.

There are no **area codes** in Guatemala. To call a number from abroad simply dial the international access code, followed by the country code (ⓣ502) and the number (all of which are eight-digit). The cheapest way to make an **international phone call** from Guatemala is usually from an internet café set up with Skype or web-phone facilities. Some places include Skype calls in the cost of renting a terminal, but most charge a little extra. Local calls are cheap, and can be made from either a communications office or a phone booth (buy a phonecard).

Many North American and European **mobile phones**, if unlocked, will work in Guatemala; all you'll need is a local SIM

EMERGENCY NUMBERS

PROATUR (tourist assistance) ☎ 1500
Fire ☎ 122 or ☎ 123
Police ☎ 110 or ☎ 120
Red Cross Ambulance ☎ 125

ATM SCAMS

A number of travellers have reported **ATM scams** in Guatemala, particularly in Antigua. Card holders are finding their bank accounts drained of cash, days or even months after they've used a cash machine. It's probable that scammers are "skimming" or using cloned cards. Check your balance regularly and consider changing your PIN when you return to your home country.

card (Tigo and Claro are the most popular networks and have excellent coverage). Note that all SIMs have to be officially registered (for security purposes), and you'll have to show your passport to get one. Cheap phones can also be bought locally from as little as Q150 (including around Q75 of calling credit). Keep an eye out for "*doble*", "*triple*" and even "*cuádruple*" offer days, when you get several times the top-up credit you pay for.

The country is very well connected to the **internet**, though don't expect lightning connection speeds. Wi-fi is very common in all the main tourist centres, where most hotels, hostels and cafés provide complimentary access. You'll find virtually every small town in the country has an internet café or two; rates are usually Q3–10 per hour.

CRIME AND SAFETY

Personal safety is a valid concern for visitors to Guatemala. The vast majority of the nearly two million tourists who come every year experience no problems at all, but general crime levels are high, and it's not unknown for criminals to target visitors.

Ask before taking **photographs** in indigenous areas, and be particularly careful not to take pictures of children without permission from their parents. (In remote regions wild rumours circulate that tourists steal children, or their organs.) **Muggings** and acts of **violent crime** are common in Guatemala City; there's not too much danger in daylight, but use taxis at night. There have also been a few cases of armed robbery in Antigua and around Lago de Atitlán.

All this said, relatively few tourists actually have any trouble. However, it's essential that you minimize your chances of becoming a victim. **Petty theft** and **pickpocketing** are likely to be your biggest problems – as anywhere, theft is most common in bus stations and crowded markets. As a rule, ask for local advice on safety issues. If you do plan to be in a risky spot, don't take more than you can afford to lose – many travellers carry "decoy" wallets with just a small amount of cash to satisfy muggers. You could also consider buying pepper spray, which is available locally in camping stores and Los Próceres mall in Guatemala City (see p.288).

If you become a victim of crime you should first contact **PROATUR** (see box below) who will assign a representative to help you out. You'll also have to file a

PROATUR

PROATUR (☎ 1500, ⊛ proatur.visitguatemala.com) is a nationwide network of English-speaking staff (see website for contact information, including mobile phone numbers) employed to help tourists. **PROATUR** employees are extremely helpful and will liaise with local police. Some can also organize a police escort to accompany travellers along highways known for banditry. In addition, there's a 24-hour call centre, staffed by English speakers who can assist with anything from updates on road conditions and bus timetables to security issues, and their Facebook and Twitter feeds give live updates about travel, traffic and security in Guatemala.

report with the police, though be aware that the force has a poor reputation for efficiency and crime solving. In Antigua there's a well-established **tourist police** force.

Drugs (particularly marijuana and cocaine) are quite widely available. Don't partake: **drug offences** are dealt with severely – even the possession of marijuana could land you in jail.

HEALTH

Guatemala's **pharmacies** can provide many over-the-counter medications, and some pharmacists can diagnose ailments and prescribe the appropriate pills. However, pharmacists are not qualified medics – so make sure your Spanish is correct.

Even in remote communities there are basic **health centres**, although you may find only a nurse or health worker available. In case of serious illness, head for a city and a private **hospital**. Guatemala's doctors often speak English, and many were trained in the US. You must travel with medical insurance (see p.42), as without it you'll need to pay for any hospital treatment up front.

INFORMATION AND MAPS

The national **tourist board**, Inguat (ⓦvisitguatemala.com), with offices in Guatemala City, Panajachel, Antigua, Flores and Quetzaltenango, gives out glossy brochures and will try to help you with your trip, but don't expect too much independent travel advice. The main office in Guatemala City (see p.285) has a library of information about tourism and can also provide you with a good country map.

Specialist travel agents and hostels are often excellent sources of information.

MONEY AND BANKS

The Guatemalan currency, the **quetzal** (Q), has been very stable against the dollar for the last decade. The **exchange rate** at the time of writing was Q7.5 to US$1. **US dollars** are also accepted in many of the main tourist centres; prices for hotels and tours are often quoted in dollars. That said, you certainly can't get by with a fistful of greenbacks and no quetzals. Euros and other foreign currencies are tricky to cash; try foreign-owned hotels or stores.

Debit and credit cards are very useful for withdrawing currency from bank ATMs but are not that widely accepted elsewhere, so don't count on paying with them except in upmarket hotels and restaurants. Beware expensive surcharges (5 to 10 percent is sometimes added) if you do want to pay by a card in many places.

ATMs are very widespread, even in small towns – though note that in Antigua, especially, there have been reports of ATM scams (see box, p.275). Charges of Q15–20 per withdrawal are common, but those using the 5B network, including Banrural, did not charge at the time of research. **Travellers' cheques** are almost impossible to cash these days. Note that currency exchange counters at Guatemala City airport offer appalling rates (see p.284). At the main land-border crossings there are usually banks and a swarm of moneychangers who generally give fair rates for cash.

Bank hours are extremely convenient, with many opening until 7pm (and some as late as 8pm) from Monday to Friday and until 12.30 or 1pm on Saturdays.

GUATEMALA ONLINE

ⓦ**fhrg.org** Website of the Foundation for Human Rights in Guatemala, offering comprehensive coverage of the current human rights situation, plus news reports.

ⓦ**lanic.utexas.edu/la/ca/guatemala** The University of Texas provides a comprehensive Guatemala portal offering access to news sources and academic resources.

ⓦ**revuemag.com** The *Revue*'s website has fully downloadable files of the monthly magazine, including back copies.

ⓦ**visitguatemala.com** Official Inguat site.

Student discounts are rare in Guatemala but some museums do offer reduced entry rates. You'll need an International Student Identity Card (ISIC).

OPENING HOURS AND HOLIDAYS

Most offices and shops are **open** between 8am and 5pm, though some take a break for lunch. **Archeological sites** are open every day, usually from 8am to 5pm (Tikal maintains longer hours), while most museums open Tuesday to Sunday from 9am to 4pm. **Sundays** remain distinguishable – many businesses close and transport is less frequent, though tourist centres such as Antigua keep buzzing. On **public holidays** (see box below) virtually the entire country shuts down, and though some buses do run it's not the best time to be travelling.

FESTIVALS

Traditional **fiestas** are one of the great excitements of a trip to Guatemala, and every town and village, however small, devotes at least one day a year to celebration. Many of the best include some specifically local element, such as the giant kites at **Santiago Sacatepéquez** (see p.298), the religious processions in Antigua and the wild horse race in **Todos Santos Cuchumatán** (see p.328). At times virtually the whole country erupts simultaneously. The following is a selection of some of the most interesting regional and national festivals.

PUBLIC HOLIDAYS

Jan 1 New Year's Day
March/April Semana Santa – Easter Week
May 1 Labour Day
June 30 Army Day, anniversary of 1871 revolution
Aug 15 Guatemala City fiesta (capital only)
Sept 15 Independence Day
Oct 12 Discovery of America (only banks are closed)
Oct 20 Revolution Day
Nov 1 All Saints' Day
Dec 25 Christmas

January 23–24 The town fiesta in Rabinal, in Baja Verapaz, renowned for pre-colonial dances.

March/April Semana Santa (Easter week) is celebrated nationwide. Particularly impressive processions take place in Antigua, Guatemala City, Santiago Atitlán and San Cristóbal Verapaz. Every Sunday of Lent sees massive street processions in Antigua, which culminate with the main event on Easter Sunday.

July 25 Cubulco, Baja Verapaz, hosts the Palo Volador, a bungee-jump-style ritual.

July 31–Aug 6 Cobán celebrates the national folklore festival.

August 15 Guatemala City fiesta.

November 1 All Saints' Day, with celebrations all over, but most dramatic in Todos Santos Cuchumatán and Santiago Sacatepéquez, where massive kites are flown.

December 7 Bonfires (the Burning of the Devil) take place throughout the country.

December 21 Huge traditional fiesta in Chichicastenango.

Guatemala City

Spilling across a highland basin, surrounded on three sides by jagged hills and volcanic cones, **GUATEMALA CITY** is the largest city in Central America, home to more than three million people. Characterized by an intensity and a vibrancy that simultaneously fascinate and alarm, Guatemala's capital is a shapeless and swelling metropolitan mass, and the undisputed centre of the country's politics, power and wealth. Not even a wild imagination will be able to make it out as a pleasant environment – indeed, for many travellers time spent in the capital is an exercise in damage limitation, struggling through bus fumes and crowds. However, once you get used to the pace, Guatemala City can offer some surprises, including a satisfying variety of restaurants, authentic bars and a sprinkling of interesting sights, as well as multiplex cinemas and shopping plazas. It is important to note, though, that the city's **crime rate** is one of the highest in Central America. While daytime is relatively safe, conditions deteriorate after dark, when you should be vigilant and take taxis to get around.

4

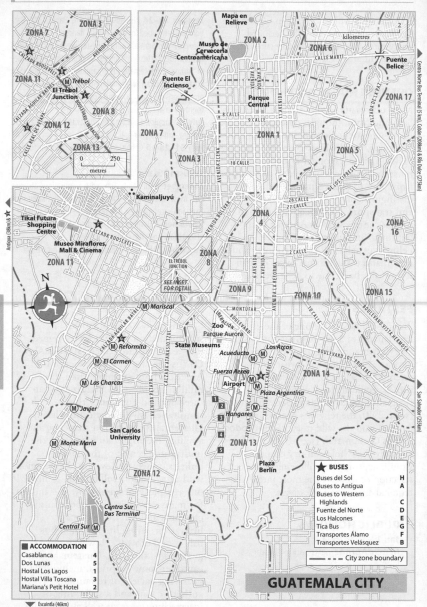

Mapa en Relieve

Museo de Cervecería Centroamericana

Puente El Incienso

Parque Central

Puente Belice

ZONA 2

ZONA 3

ZONA 7

ZONA 11

Ⓜ Trébol
El Trébol Junction

ZONA 8

ZONA 12

ZONA 13

ZONA 6

CALLE MARTÍ

ZONA 17

ZONA 1

8 CALLE

9 CALLE

ZONA 7

ZONA 3

18 CALLE

ZONA 5

C. DE LOS CIPRESES

26 CALLE

27 CALLE

ZONA 4

ZONA 16

ZONA 8

EL TRÉBOL JUNCTION

SEE INSET FOR DETAIL

• Kaminaljuyú

Tikal Futura Shopping Centre

Museo Miraflores, Mall & Cinema

CALZADA ROOSEVELT

ZONA 11

ZONA 9

ZONA 10

ZONA 15

Ⓜ **Mariscal**

C. MONTÚFAR

BOULEVARD VISTA HERMOSA

Ⓜ **Reformita**

Zoo
Parque Aurora

State Museums

Acueducto

Los Arcos

BOULEVARD LOS PRÓCERES

Ⓜ **El Carmen**

Fuerza Aérea

Airport

ZONA 14

Ⓜ **Las Charcas**

Plaza Argentina

Ⓜ **Javier**

1 2

3 **Hangares**

San Carlos University

Ⓜ **Monte María**

4 5

ZONA 13

ZONA 12

Plaza Berlín

Centra Sur Bus Terminal

Central Sur Ⓜ

★ **BUSES**

Buses del Sol	H
Buses to Antigua	A
Buses to Western Highlands	C
Fuente del Norte	D
Los Halcones	E
Tica Bus	G
Transportes Álamo	F
Transportes Velásquez	B

– – – City zone boundary

GUATEMALA CITY

■ **ACCOMMODATION**

Casablanca	4
Dos Lunas	5
Hostal Los Lagos	1
Hostal Villa Toscana	3
Mariana's Petit Hotel	2

▼ Escuintla (46km)

Antigua (38km) & ★

Centra Norte Bus Terminal (5 km), Cobán (208km) & Río Dulce (275km)

San Salvador (255km)

0 — kilometres — 2

0 — metres — 250

N

WHAT TO SEE AND DO

Despite the daunting scale of Guatemala City – it consists of 25 sprawling zones – the key areas of interest are quite manageable. Broadly speaking, the city divides into two distinct halves. The northern section, centred on **Zona 1**, is the old part of town, and undeniably the most exciting part of the capital. It's characterized by crumbling nineteenth-century townhouses, faceless concrete blocks,

ADDRESSES IN GUATEMALA CITY

The system of street numbering in the capital can be confusing – and is often complicated by the fact that the same calles and avenidas can exist in several different zones. Always check the zone first and then the street. For example, "7 Av 9–14, Zona 10" is in Zona 10, on 7 Avenida between 9 and 10 calles, house number 14.

broken pavements and parking lots, but there are also some architectural gems. Signs of regeneration are evident here and there as cafés and bars popular with students open and streets are pedestrianized. South of 18 Calle, Zona 1 merges into **Zona 4**, home to the Municipalidad, tourist and immigration offices and the Teatro Nacional.

The southern half of the city, beyond the Torre del Reformador, begins with **zonas 9 and 10** and is the modern, wealthy part of town, split in two by **Avenida La Reforma**. Here you'll find exclusive offices, international hotels, private museums and, in the **Zona Viva**, Guatemala's most expensive clubs, boutiques, restaurants and cafés. Continuing south, **zonas 13 and 14** are rich leafy suburbs and home to the airport, zoo and the state museums.

Parque Central

The windswept expanse of the vast **Parque Central**, at the northern end of Zona 1, is full of life, especially on Sundays and public holidays as people and pigeons, shoe-shiners and raving Evangelicals jostle for space.

On the west side of the square is a concrete bandstand, the Concha Acústica, where you can enjoy a variety of marimba and classical music performances (Wed 4–6pm & Sat 3.30–5pm; free). Most of the city's major sights – including the cathedral, Palacio Nacional and two semi-restored colonial arcades, the Pasaje Aycinena and Pasaje Rubio (leading off the park's south side) – lie nearby.

Palacio Nacional

Just north of the Parque Central is the striking **Palacio Nacional** (entrance by guided tour only, conducted in Spanish or English; daily 9.30am–4pm; hourly; 30min; Q40), a lavish, pale-green palace built in the 1940s by president Jorge Ubico and nicknamed "El Guacamole" by locals. It housed the government's executive branch for about fifty years but today hosts cultural exhibitions.

The tour gives you a brief look at the interior, with its two Moorish-style interior courtyards (one containing an eternal flame dedicated to the heroes of Peace Accords). You'll also see striking murals depicting warring Spaniards and Maya and the principal state reception room, complete with a suitably grandiose chandelier embellished with four cut-glass quetzals.

Cathedral

On the east side of the Parque Central sits the blue-domed **cathedral** (daily 7am–noon & 2–7pm), completed in 1868. Its solid, squat design was intended to resist the force of earthquakes and has, for the most part, succeeded. Inside there are three main aisles, austere colonial paintings and intricate altars housing an array of saints. The cathedral's most poignant aspect is outside, however: etched into the twelve pillars that support the entrance railings are the names of thousands of the dead and "disappeared" victims of the country's civil war.

Mercado Central

Guatemala City's best market, the **Mercado Central** (Mon–Sat 6am–6pm, Sun 9am–1pm), spreads out underground beneath a car park east of the cathedral between 8 and 9 avenidas and 6 and 8 calles. The place is a riot of colour, with the obligatory handicrafts, souvenirs, fruit and vegetable displays and some impressive fresh-flower arrangements. On the lowest level there's a fine selection of cheap and authentic food stalls, snack stands and juice bars.

■ ACCOMMODATION
La Coperacha	1
Hotel Ajau	5
Hotel Colonial	3
Hotel Spring	2
Theatre	
International Hostel	4

★ BUS STOPS
ADN Mayan World	D
Fuente del Norte	E
Línea Dorada	C
Litegua	B
Rutas Orientales	G
Transportes Galgos	F
Transurbano buses	A
to Centra Norte	

● EATING
Café de Imeri	1
Café León	12
Café Saúl	11
Long Wah	2
La Luna	4
Rey Sol	9
Rocque Rosito	6

● DRINKING & NIGHTLIFE
Black and White	10
Las Cien Puertas	5
Genetic Majestic Club	13
El Gran Hotel	7
El Portal	3
Soma	8

GUATEMALA CITY:
ZONAS 1 AND 4

1 (700m)

Parque Minerva & Mapa en Relieve (1.75km)

Parque del Centenario
Palacio Nacional
Mercado Central
Biblioteca Nacional
Parque Central
Parque Centenario
ATM
Mercado Central
Cathedral
@Cyber
Teatro Lux
San Agustín
San Miguel de Capuchinas
Palacio de Correos
Iglesia de San Francisco
Police Headquarters
Casa Mima
Gómez Carrillo
Parque Concordia
Belén
ZONA 1
Tipografía
Plaza Barrios
El Amate Plaza
El Calvario
Mercado Sur
CENTRO CÍVICO
Museo del Ferrocarril
Teatro Nacional
Municipalidad
Banco de Guatemala
Banco de Guatemala
Centro Comercial
Estadio Nacional Mario Flores
Bolívar
4 Grados Sur
4 Grados Norte
Migración
CUATRO GRADOS NORTE
Centro Cultural de España
Santa Cecilia
Trovajazz
Exposición
Plaza de la República
ZONA 4
Iglesia Yurrita
Jardín Botánico
Torre del Reformador
Torre del Reformador
Terminal

Trébol Junction (1.25km) & Kaminaljuyu (3km)

N

0   250
metres

Sexta Avenida

Sexta Avenida (6 Av) was the city's main commercial artery for decades, lined with glamorous department stores, cinemas and cafés. People from all over the city would promenade the Sexta to see and be seen. But the character of the street took a downturn in the 1980s, as stalls choked the pavements and many businesses closed.

In 2009, the city authorities implemented a regeneration programme, clearing the street traders, planting trees and pedestrianizing the avenida (except for cycles) between the Parque Central and 18 Calle, making Sexta a delight to stroll once again. Be sure to stop by the well-kept **Parque Concordia**, the fabulously elaborate facade of the **Iglesia de San Francisco** and renovated Art Deco splendour of the **Teatro Lux** as you explore the heart of Zona 1.

Palacio de Correos

The Baroque **Palacio de Correos**, south of the Parque Central on 7 Avenida between 11 and 12 calles, is one of the city's most arresting buildings, with an elaborately restored terracotta-and-cream facade. Don't miss the adjoining decorative bridge, built in the same Baroque style, which spans 12 Calle.

Casa Mima

South of the post office, at the corner of 8 Avenida and 14 Calle, **Casa Mima** (Mon–Sat 10am–5pm; Q20; ⊛casamima .org) is an immaculately restored, late nineteenth-century Guatemalan townhouse with original furnishings from various design movements. The decor offers a fascinating glimpse into a wealthy household, with lavish rooms kitted out with gilded mirrors, chandeliers, oriental rugs, hand-painted wallpaper and curios including a gloriously detailed dolls' house and a ninety-year-old "talking machine" (a gramophone). The house even has a private chapel complete with a fabulous wooden altar.

Museo del Ferrocarril

An excellent museum dedicated to the history of Guatemalan railways, the splendidly renovated **Museo del Ferrocarril** at 9 Avenida and 18 Calle (Tues–Fri 9am–4pm, Sat & Sun 10am–4pm; Q2; ⊛museofegua.com) is located in Guatemala City's former train station. You'll find several old steam engines and carriages to clamber over and examine, plus rooms stuffed with railway curiosities, including staff uniforms and tickets.

Mapa en Relieve

North of the Parque Central, in Zona 2's Parque Minerva, the **Mapa en Relieve** (daily 8am–6pm; Q25; ⊛mapaenrelieve.org) is a huge, open-air relief model of Guatemala. The map's vertical scale has been somewhat exaggerated, but still highlights the dramatic landscape of the highlands, shedding new light on those perilous mountain bus journeys.

Museo de Cervecería Centroamericana

Just to the south of the Mapa on 3 Avenida Norte Final, **Cervecería Centroamericana** (Mon–Thurs 8.30am–5pm; free tours 9am, 11am & 2.30pm; book on ☎2289 1555; ⊛museocerveceria.com) is Guatemala's largest brewery. Beer has been produced here for 125 years; today, around a dozen varieties are brewed, including Dorada, Victoria and Gallo (Guatemala's most popular). The museum, containing some interesting antique curios and photographs related to the history of beer-making in Guatemala, is interesting enough, but the highly informative tour allows you access to the plant, gazing into the vast stainless-steel vats and viewing the bottling process. The tour finishes, appropriately, with a complimentary glass or two of Gallo.

Centro Cívico

At the southern end of the old city, beyond sleazy 18 Calle and around 6 and 7 avenidas, the distinctively 1960s architecture of the **Centro Cívico** area marks the boundary between zonas 1 and 4. Looming over

4

**GUATEMALA CITY:
ZONAS 9 AND 10**

● EATING	
Kacao	5
Paco's Café	1
Pitaya	4
Resko	7
Sopho's	3
Tacontento	6

■ ACCOMMODATION		● DRINKING & NIGHTLIFE	
Quetzalroo	1	The Box Lounge	8
		Kahlua	9
		One Club	2
		Rattle & Hum	10

7 Avenida is the **Banco de Guatemala** building, bedecked with bold modern murals and stylized glyphs recounting the history of the nation and the conflict between Spanish and Maya. Just south of here is the main Inguat office (see p.285). On a small rise to the west of 6 Avenida is the futuristic **Teatro Nacional**, designed to resemble a ship (see p.287).

Jardín Botánico

The city's **Jardín Botánico** (Mon–Fri 8am–3pm, Sat 9am–noon; Q10), at the northern end of Avenida La Reforma, is a beautiful evergreen space with quite a selection of species, all neatly labelled in Spanish or Latin. An anachronistic natural history museum, the **Museo de Historia Natural** (same hours), also sits within the grounds; the collection, mainly mangy stuffed animals, is pretty dull.

Torre del Reformador

South of the Centro Cívico, at the junction of 7 Avenida and 2 Calle, in Zona 9, is the landmark **Torre del Reformador**, Guatemala's stunted version of the Eiffel Tower. The steel structure was built in honour of President Barrios, whose liberal reforms transformed the country between 1871 and 1885. Just to the north, at the junction with Ruta 6, is the **Iglesia Yurrita** (Tues–Sun 8am–noon & 3–6pm), built in a weird neo-Gothic style reminiscent of a horror-movie set.

Museo Ixchel and Museo Popol Vuh

The campus of the University Francisco Marroquín, reached by following 6 Calle Final off Avenida La Reforma, is home to two excellent private **museums** (both Mon–Fri 9am–5pm, Sat 9am–1pm; combined ticket Q50). The **Museo Ixchel** (Ⓦmuseoixchel.org) shouldn't be missed if you're a fan of textiles, or just can't get enough of Guatemalan traditional dress: its collection is dedicated to Maya culture, with emphasis on traditional weaving. Stunning hand-woven fabrics include some impressive examples of ceremonial costumes, with explanations in English, plus information about techniques, dyes, fibres and weaving tools.

The excellent **Museo Popol Vuh** (Ⓦpopolvuh.ufm.edu.gt) next door is home to an outstanding collection of archeological artefacts collected from sites all over the country. The small museum is divided into Preclassic, Classic, Postclassic and colonial rooms, and all the exhibits are top quality. Particularly interesting is a copy of the Dresden Codex, one of very few surviving written and illustrated records of Maya history.

Parque Aurora

In Zona 13, **Parque Aurora** houses the city's **zoo** (Tues–Sun 9am–5pm; Q30; Ⓦaurorazoo.org.gt). Here you can see African lions, Bengal tigers, hippos, giraffes, elephants, monkeys and all the Central and South American big cats, including some well-fed jaguars. As zoos go, it's not bad and the grounds are a delight. It's also open on full-moon nights, the ideal time to see nocturnal animals.

Museo Nacional de Arqueología y Etnología

Opposite the Parque Aurora is a complex of three state-run museums, of which the **Museo Nacional de Arqueología y Etnología** (Tues–Fri 9am–4pm, Sat & Sun 9am–noon & 1.30–4pm; Q60; ⓦmunae.gob.gt) is the best. The collection includes a world-class selection of Maya treasures, though the layout and displays are very much in need of an update. Noteworthy pieces include spectacular jade masks from Takalik Abaj, a stunning wooden temple-top lintel from Tikal and priceless artefacts from Piedras Negras, one of the remotest sites in Petén. Stele 12, dating from 672 AD, depicts a cowering captive king begging for mercy, and there's an enormous carved stone throne from the same site, richly engraved with glyphs and decorated with a two-faced head.

Museo Nacional de Arte Moderno

Opposite the archeological museum, the **Museo Nacional de Arte Moderno** (Tues–Fri 9am–4pm, Sat & Sun 9am–noon & 1.30–4pm; Q50) also suffers from poor presentation, but does boast some imaginative geometric paintings by Dagoberto Vásquez, and a collection of startling exhibits by Efraín Recinos, including a colossal marimba-cum-tank sculpture. There's also a permanent collection of Cubist art and massive murals by Carlos Mérida, Guatemala's most celebrated artist.

Kaminaljuyú

Way out on the western edge of the city lies Zona 7, which wraps around the ruins of pre-colonial **Kaminaljuyú** (daily 9am–4pm; Q50). Archeological digs have uncovered more than three hundred mounds and thirteen ball courts here, though unlike the massive temples of the lowlands, these structures were built of adobe, and most of them have been lost to erosion and urban sprawl. Today the site is little more than a series of earth-covered mounds; to learn more about the city, visit the Museo Miraflores (see below).

Museo Miraflores

The modern **Museo Miraflores** (Tues–Sun 9am–7pm; Q40; ⓦmuseomiraflores.org), a ten-minute walk south of the Kaminaljuyú ruins on Calzada Roosevelt, is dedicated to the ancient city and its importance as a trading centre. Exhibits include striking stone sculptures and stele

---

FIRST-CLASS BUS COMPANIES IN GUATEMALA CITY

ADN Mayan World (ADN) 8 Av 16–41 Zona 1 (☏2251 0610, ⓦadnautobusesdelnorte.com).

Buses del Sol (BS) *Hotel Crowne Plaza*, Av Las Américas 9–08, Zona 13 (☏2422 5000 ⓦbuses delsol.com).

Fuente del Norte (FN) has two terminals: 17 C 8–46, Zona 1, for Petén and Honduras, and Calzada Aguilar Batres 7–55, Zona 12, for Tecún Umán border (☏7447 7070, ⓦgrupofuentedelnorte.com).

Hedman Alas (HA) 2 Av 8 73, Zona 10 (☏2362 5072, ⓦhedmanalas.com).

Linea Dorada (LD) 16 C 10–03, Zona 1 (☏2415 8900, ⓦlineadorada.com.gt).

Litegua (L) 15 C 10–40, Zona 1 & Centra Norte (☏2326 9400, ⓦlitegua.com).

Los Halcones (LH) Calzada Roosevelt 37–47, Zona 11 (☏7963 3000).

Monja Blanca (MB) Centra Norte (☏2238 1409, ⓦmonjablanca.com).

Platinum/King Quality (KQ) Based at *Biltmore Hotel*, 15 C 0–31, Zona 10 (☏2369 7070, ⓦplatinum centroamerica.com).

Pullmantur (P) Based at *Holiday Inn*, 1 Av 13–22, Zona 10 (☏2363 6240, ⓦpullmantur.com).

Rutas Orientales (RO) 21 C 11–60, Zona 1 & Centra Norte (☏2503 3100, ⓦrutasorientales.com.gt).

Tica Bus (TB) Calzada Aguilar Batres 22–55, Zona 12 (☏2473 3737, ⓦticabus.com).

Transportes Álamo (TA) 12 Av A 0–65, Zona 7 (☏2471 8626).

Transportes Galgos (TG) 7 Av 19–44, Zona 1 (☏2232 3661, ⓦtransgalgosinter.com.gt).

Transportes Velásquez (TV) 0 C 31–70, Zona 7 (☏2439 5553).

4

pieces, ceramics, impressive jade jewellery, obsidian flints and a scale model of Kaminaljuyú. The grounds encompass several temple mounds, one of which has been penetrated by a tunnel that leads to a chamber boasting a noble's tomb and some spectacular artefacts. To get there from the city centre, take any bus headed to "Tikal Futura" or Antigua.

ARRIVAL AND DEPARTURE

Arriving in Guatemala City is always a bit disconcerting. Wherever you arrive, you should *always* take a taxi to your destination in the city (unless it's a block or two away), or use the Transmetro (see below).

BY PLANE

Aurora airport The modern and efficiently run airport (☎ 2334 7680) is in Zona 13 some way south of the centre, but close to Zona 10.

Transport into the city The easiest way to get from and to the airport is by taxi. You can pre-pay your fare from a taxi desk; Zona 10 costs about Q75, Zona 1 around Q90. Note, however, that most guesthouses in Zona 13 offer free pick-ups. Don't risk taking the city buses that leave from outside the airport because of security concerns.

Getting to Antigua Regular shuttle buses run to Antigua (Q80/person, three minimum) until about 10pm. A taxi to Antigua is about Q275.

Currency exchange All the official-looking Global Exchange currency exchange booths offer derisory rates (25 percent lower than the banks') and represent a total scam. Seek out a Banrural bank (daily 8am–9pm) instead – there are branches in the Arrivals and Departures areas – where you can change US dollars and euros at fair rates. There are no ATMs in Arrivals, but two in the Departures hall.

BY BUS

First-class buses Travelling by first-class (Pullman) bus, you'll arrive at the private depot of the company you're using (most are in Zona 1 or 10; a few use the huge Centra Norte terminal, 8.5km northeast of Zona 1). Centra Norte is secure and well organized, with buses leaving from designated bays below an upmarket shopping mall. However, it's a long, long way from the centre of town (Q120 in a taxi, or Q2 in a Transurbano bus #311 to the Parque Colón or 18 C in Zona 1) along heavily congested roads – allow 1hr for the journey. Note that many Zona 1 bus depots are located in an unsavoury part of the city; be on your guard for petty thieves. There's no regular first-class bus service to Antigua – most travellers use shuttle buses (Q70–90) – but it is possible to connect with second-class services at Trébol Transmetro stop.

Second-class buses "Chicken buses" use two main transport hubs. Buses for the western highlands use bus stops (there's no terminal) at 41 C between 7 Av and 11 Av, Zona 8, which is very close to Trébol Transmetro stop. All buses for southern Guatemala (including the border with El Salvador, Monterrico, Retalhuleu and the Mexican border) plus Santiago Atitlán use a large terminal called Centra Sur (also known as Centro de Mayorio) in Zona 12, 14km south of the Parque Central. This has a Transmetro stop directly above it and security guards.

Domestic destinations Antigua (second-class from 21 C & 2 Av, Zona 3, via Trébol junction, every 10min until 6.30pm; 1hr–1hr 30min); Chichicastenango (second-class from 41 C Zona 8, every 30min; 3hr); Chiquimula (RO every 30min; L 2 daily; 3hr 30min); Cobán (MB hourly; 5hr); El Florido border (L 1 daily at 2.45pm; 4hr 45min); Esquipulas (RO every 30min); Flores (FN 16 daily, LD 4 daily, ADN 2 daily; 8–9hr); Huehuetenango (LD 2 daily, LH 6 daily, TV 5 daily; 5hr 30min); La Mesilla (LD 2 daily, LH 2 daily; 7hr 30min); Monterrico (second-class from Centra Sur, 2 daily; 3hr 30min; or travel via Iztapa which has hourly onward connections); Nebaj (second-class from 41 C, Zona 8, 5 daily; 5hr 15min); Panajachel (second-class from 41 C, Zona 8, hourly until 4pm; 3hr); Puerto Barrios (L 21 daily, 5hr 30min–6hr 30min); Poptún (take a Flores bus; 7hr); Quetzaltenango (ADN 2 daily, TA 6 daily, LD 2 daily, TG 2 daily; 4hr); Río Dulce Town (L 5 daily; 5hr – or catch a Flores bus); San Pedro La Laguna (second-class from 41 C, Zona 8, 8 daily; 3hr 45min); Santiago Atitlán (second-class from Centra Sur, 9 daily; 3hr); Tecún Umán (FN 6 daily; 6hr).

International destinations Copán, Honduras (HA 2 daily, 5am & 8am; 5hr); La Ceiba, Honduras (HA 2 daily 5am & 8am; 12hr); Managua, Nicaragua (BS 1 daily at 3am, TB 2 daily; 18–28hr); San Pedro Sula, Honduras (FD 1 daily, HA 2 daily, RO 2 daily; 8–9hr); San Salvador, El Salvador (BS 2 daily, TB 2 daily, P 3–4 daily, KQ 2 daily, TG 1 daily; 5hr), Tapachula, Mexico (KQ 1 daily, LD 1 daily, TB 1 daily, TG 2 daily; 6hr); Tegucigalpa, Honduras (HA 2 daily 5am & 8am; 12–13hr; or the following all involve a stopover in San Salvador, around 36hr in total: KQ 2 daily, P 1 daily, TB 1 daily).

BY CAR

Car rental Two good local companies are Tabarini, 2 C A 7–30, Zona 10 (☎ 2444 4200, ⓦ tabarini.com), and Adaesa, 4 C A 16–57, Zona 1 (☎ 2220 2180, ⓦ adaesa .com). Rates start at about Q300/day.

GETTING AROUND

Avoid all city buses other than the **Transmetro** and Transurbano due to security concerns, and always take **taxis** after dark rather than walk.

BY BUS

Guatemala City has an excellent rapid transit bus network, the Transmetro, which operates on dedicated bus lanes that are closed to all other traffic, making it by far the fastest way around the city. The bad news is that there are currently only four routes (and the fourth, connecting Plaza Barrios in Zona 1 with Zone 6 to the northeast, is not particularly useful for travellers); more routes are planned, so that by 2020 the capital will have a comprehensive and efficient bus network. Transmetro articulated buses are modern, air-conditioned, wheelchair-friendly and only stop every kilometre or so. Transport police provide security. No food or drinks are permitted on board.

Orange line (Line A) Connects Plaza Barrios and the Centro Cívico with points to the southwest, along Av Bolívar via the Trébol junction and down to the Centra Sur bus terminal. It's useful for passengers on second-class buses to and from the highlands who want to connect with Zona 1 (Mon–Fri 4.30am– 10pm, Sat & Sun 4.30am–9pm).

Green line (Line B) Runs north–south from Plaza Barrios, 18 C in Zona 1, along 6 Av through zonas 4 and 9 to Zona 13, returning along 7 Av. It connects with the purple line at Tipografía station (Mon–Fri 5am–9pm, Sat & Sun 5am–8pm).

Purple line (Line C) This does a loop through Zona 1 north of the Tipografía station, heading up 5 Av on the west side of the Parque Central and returning along 7 Av.

Transurbano buses do not run on designated lanes, are slower and not as modern, but are considered safe by citizens. To use them you have to obtain a SIGA travel card (free; available at stations including Plaza Barrios and Centra Norte), for which you'll have to present your passport. You can check routes at ⓦ transurbano.com.gt; one of the most useful is Ruta 311V which connects the Centra Norte bus terminal with Parque Colón, Zona 1 (five blocks east of the Parque Central).

BY TAXI

There are both metered and non-metered taxis. Metered taxis are comfortable and fairly cheap; Amarillo (☎ 2470 1515) is highly recommended and will pick you up from anywhere in the city. The fare from Zona 1 to Zona 10 is about Q45. Always take taxis after dark.

INFORMATION AND TOURS

Tourist information The main Inguat tourist office (Mon–Fri 8am–4pm; ☎ 2331 1333, ⓦ visitguatemala .com) is at 7 Av 1–17, Zona 4, and has English-speaking staff and plenty of brochures.

Tours *Quetzalroo* (see below) offer an excellent bike tour of the city for US$7.50/person. Non-guests are welcome to join; book ahead.

ACCOMMODATION

The capital is much more expensive than the rest of Guatemala. Firstly choose the zone where you want to base yourself. Zona 1 is not a great area to be hunting for a room late at night, but it's safe enough in the day and early evening. Zona 13, very near the airport, has some good options (and most places offer free airport pick-ups and drop-offs) but it's a quiet, suburban location with no restaurants close by. Zona 10 is a relatively safe upmarket part of town with a glut of restaurants and bars. All the places listed have free wi-fi.

ZONA 1 AND 2

La Coperacha 4 Av 2–03 ☎ 2232 1414; map p.280. A fifteen-minute walk north of the Parque Central, this sociable hostel is run by welcoming Guatemalans. It has an arty feel, bikes for rent, a guests' kitchen, good travel information and a filling complimentary breakfast. Dorms Q75, doubles Q175

Hotel Ajau 8 Av 15–62 ☎ 2232 0488, ⓔ hotelajau @hotmail.com; map p.280. This Art Nouveau-era hotel has an impressive lobby, old-school ambience and very helpful staff. The 45 rooms, all with TVs, are well scrubbed, if a little bare; many are en suite. There's a *comedor* for breakfast and evening meals. Q140

Hotel Colonial 7 Av 14–19 ☎ 2232 6722, ⓦ hotelcolonial.net; map p.280. Offering good value, this Spanish-style hotel has some classy tiling and wrought ironwork. The three classes of rooms (some without private bathroom) have solid dark-wood furniture. Q160

Hotel Spring 8 Av 12–65 ☎ 2230 2858, ⓦ hotelspring .com; map p.280. A reliable choice, this large, rambling, secure place has been hosting travellers and Peace Corps workers for decades. Most of the 43 rooms are spacious but would benefit from a little more love and attention; many have private bathroom and cable TV. The pretty central courtyard is a nice focal point for meeting other guests. Breakfast is available, plus laundry and free drinking water. Q170

Theatre International Hostel 8 Av 14–17 ☎ 4202 5112, ⓦ theatreihostel.com; map p.280. New place that styles itself as a "party hostel"; it has some good things going for it, including a hot tub, ample lounging areas, a kitchen and a courtyard. However, old-timers should note its ageist rules – over-45s are barred! Dorms Q60, doubles Q160

ZONA 10

Quetzalroo 6 Av 7–84, Zona 10 ☎ 5746 0830, ⓦ quetzalroo.com; map p.282. This hostel (in an apartment block) has quality accommodation, three shower rooms, a guests' kitchen, TV lounge, laundry room and a fun, communal vibe. The location is good and airport

4

(or bus terminal) transportation and fast wi-fi are gratis. Excellent bike tours (see p.285) of the city are offered. Dorms **Q120**, doubles **Q265**

ZONA 13

Casablanca 15 C C 7–35 ☎ 2261 3129, ⓦ hotelcasablancainn.com; map p.278. Tasteful, stylish guesthouse with light, airy and spacious rooms, most en suite. There's a well-stocked bar and an attractive sitting room. Breakfast, airport transfers and wi-fi are included. **Q360**

★ **Dos Lunas** 21 C 10–92 ☎ 2261 4248, ⓦ hoteldoslunas.com; map p.278. A very welcoming and efficient guesthouse in a leafy gated community managed by Guatemalteca Lorena Artola and her Dutch husband Hank, who take great care of guests. The attractive rooms are spotless, and rates include airport transfers and breakfast. Tourist advice is second to none; book well ahead. Dorms **Q112**, doubles **Q250**

Hostal Los Lagos 8 Av 15–85 ☎ 2261 2809, ⓦ loslagoshostal.com; map p.278. A good B&B just 400m from the airport with inviting rooms and dorms. Staff are friendly and informative; free airport transfers and drinking water are offered. Dorms **Q120**, doubles **Q320**

Hostal Villa Toscana 16 C 8–20 ☎ 2261 2854, ⓦ hostalvillatoscana.com; map p.278. For a splurge, this upmarket B&B is ideal. Offers stylish, very well presented rooms, with neutral colour schemes contrasting with vibrant Maya textiles; all have cable TV, no.9 has a balcony, and the suite has a private terrace. **Q480**

Mariana's Petit Hotel 20 C 10–17 ☎ 2261 4105, ⓦ marianaspetithotel.com; map p.278. Welcoming guesthouse very close to the airport with inexpensive rates, a quiet location and free airport transfers. **Q320**

EATING

You'll find affordable places to eat scattered around Zona 1, while in Zona 10 the emphasis is more on refined dining. Wherever you are, street vendors and fast-food chains are never far away. For really cheap eats head to the stalls inside the Mercado Central (see p.279).

ZONA 1

Café de Imeri 6 C 3–34 ☎ 2232 3722; map p.280. Popular European-style café with alpine decor and filling breakfasts, pasta, sandwiches, baguettes and an excellent *menú del día* (Q38). The adjacent store sells baguettes, cakes and *pan integral*. Mon–Sat 8am–6pm.

★ **Café León** 8 Av 9–15 ☎ 2251 0068, ⓦ cafeleon.net; map p.280. Atmospheric old-school café with gleaming espresso machines and vintage photographs that's a downtown hotspot for Guatemala's chattering classes. Linger over a treacle-thick espresso, milky *café con leche* or one of the regional coffees (from across Guatemala),

though there are also good breakfasts, cakes (*cubiletes*, *empanadas*), sandwiches and refreshing *raspado* (iced lime juice). There's a second Zona 1 branch at 12 C 6–23. Mon–Fri 8am–6pm, Sat 9am–1pm.

Café Saúl Teatro Lux, 6 Av & 11 C ☎ 2379 8718; map p.280. Hip café in an old cinema foyer complete with movie theatre-style seats, classic film posters and vintage projection equipment. The menu is a bit pricey but includes nutritious juices, good crêpes (around Q50), salads and a tasty antipasti selection (Q64) that's enough for two. Daily 8am–8pm.

Long Wah 6 C 3–75 ☎ 2232 6611; map p.280. One of the better budget Chinese restaurants in this neighbourhood, consistently recommended by locals, with a menu that includes won tons and chow mein. They also offer food to go. Daily 11.30am–3pm & 6–9.30pm.

Rey Sol 11 C 5–51 ☎ 2232 3516; map p.280. Vegetarian café-restaurant serving a good choice of lunch dishes that might include lasagne (Q24), a stir-fry or Mexican-style options. Doubles as a health-food store, selling good bread, *empanadas*, granola, soya milk, herbal teas and veggie snacks. Mon–Sat 7.30am–7pm, Sun noon–4pm.

Rocque Rosito 8 Av & 9 C ☎ 2232 7343; map p.280. A spacious café with banquette seating and stylish sofas that's ideal for a coffee or juice and a quick bite – try a crêpe or a sandwich. Mon–Sat 7.30am–6pm.

ZONA 10

Kacao 1 Av 13–51 ☎ 2337 4188, ⓦ kacao.com.gt; map p.282. Set under a giant *palapa* (thatched) roof, this restaurant is a great setting in the evening – you enter through a bamboo forest, to find the dining room illuminated by hundreds of candles. The menu is refined *comida guatemalteca*, with excellent *suban-ik* (spicy curry-style Maya dish with peppers and chicken, beef and smoked pork). Portions are generous; expect to pay upwards of Q100 a head. Daily noon–3pm & 6–11pm.

Paco's Café 1 Av 10–43; map p.282. Tiny, very welcoming *comedor* that's a winner for a traditional breakfast, snack (tacos are just Q7) or a filling set lunch: Q20 buys you a bowl of soup, grilled meat with rice, vegetables and tortillas, a drink and a dessert. Mon–Fri 7am–3pm.

Pitaya 13 C Av 2–75 ☎ 2334 3884; map p.282. Hip juice bar, with amazing selection of healthy blends (including wheatgrass shots, lots of smoothies and supplements including Omega 3 and ginseng) as well as salads, wraps and breakfasts. Mon–Fri 7.30am–6.30pm, Sat 9am–5pm.

Resko 14 C 4–12 ☎ 2363 4150; map p.282. Inexpensive, welcoming *comedor*, popular with office staff, which offers fine-value meals for the location and a menu that changes daily. Breakfasts are just Q15 and the Q25 lunch deal includes soup, tortillas and a drink. Daily 7am–3pm.

Sopho's Fontabella Plaza, 12 C & 4 Av ☎ 2419 7070; map p.282. This bookstore café is a delightfully civilized (if pricey) place to browse a book or magazine, sip a *café con leche* and snack on a sandwich or cake. The set lunch changes daily, and there's a little outdoor terrace. Daily 8am–7pm.

Tacontento 2 Av & 14 C ☎ 2360 2815, ⓦ tacontento .com; map p.282. Offers decent tacos and Mexican classics: eat in the lively dining room or on the streetside terrace. The lunch special (Q30) includes soup, three tacos and a drink. Mon–Wed & Sun noon–midnight, Thurs–Sat noon–1am.

DRINKING AND NIGHTLIFE

Nightlife in the capital essentially comes down to two choices: gritty Zona 1, which has some highly atmospheric old bars and raucous student places, and Zona 10's Zona Viva, largely the domain of wealthy Guatemaltecos, and bursting with upmarket bars and clubs. It's best not to stroll around Zona 1 late at night, but Zona 10 is considered safe enough. For information on Guatemala's small but growing club and DJ scene consult ⓦ electronik.net.

ZONAS 1 AND 2

Black and White 11 C 2–54, Zona 1 ⓦ blackandwhitebar .com; map p.280. In the heart of the city, this well-established bar-club is an intimate space and attracts a lively gay crowd with themed nights, go-go dancers and events. Wed–Sat 7pm–1am.

Las Cien Puertes Pasaje Aycinena, 9 C 6–47; map p.280. Guatemala City's definitive bohemian bar is in a beautiful run-down arcade – it's popular with artists, students and political activists. Expect graffiti-splattered walls, good sounds and moderate prices. Mon–Sat 5pm–1am.

El Gran Hotel 9 C 7–64 ☎ 2232 9478; map p.280. A key destination in Zona 1, this bar/cultural centre draws a young crowd with indie, alt rock and electronica acts, film and poetry evenings and stand-up comedy. On weekend nights, or when a popular band is playing, the atmosphere is raucous. Cover charge is US$2.50–6, with two or three live bands per week. Tues–Sat 5pm–midnight.

★ El Portal Pasaje Rubio, 9 C between 6 & 7 avs; map p.280. One of Che Guevara's old drinking haunts, and the decor (and clientele) is little changed since the revolutionary era. Order a *chibola* of *cerveza mixta*, munch on a few (complimentary) *boquitas* and soak up the scene: hard drinkers glued to bar stools and wandering *tríos* of musicians prowling the tables, mariachi style. Mon–Sat 11am–10pm.

Soma 11 C 4–27 ☎ 2253 0406; map p.280 Gregarious bar that's a magnet for the city's young artistic crew. Regularly features live acts (mainly indie and alternative, with bands influenced by the likes of Bowie, Talking Heads and REM). Also operates as a cultural centre and café. Tues–Sat 6pm–1am.

ZONA 4

Genetic Majestic Club Vía 3 & Ruta 3; map p.280. The capital's premier (mainly) gay club has three floors and a VIP section, and plays pumping house music. There are themed nights and go-go dancers. Thurs–Sat 8pm–1am.

ZONA 10

The Box Lounge 15 C 2–23; map p.282. One of the capital's electronic hubs, with an underground vibe and sociable atmosphere. Features live house, electro, funk and techno DJs every night; check their Facebook page for events. Tues–Sat 8am–1am.

Kahlua 1 Av 15–07 ☎ 4736 2278; map p.282. Well-established, four-storey club that draws a young, party-minded crowd. Musically, things are pretty mainstream, including the latest Latin dance hits. Thurs–Sat 7pm–1am.

One Club 1 Av 11–37 ⓦ onegt.club; map p.282. Leading club that features credible tech-house and progressive and electro DJs from Central America and Europe. It draws a cool crowd – dress up. Thurs–Sat 8pm–1am.

Rattle & Hum 4 Av 16–11 ☎ 2366 6524; map p.282. Upmarket Australian-owned bar, popular with both expats and locals, with a sociable atmosphere and live music and bar grub. There's a huge selection of shots and cocktails. Mon 5–10pm, Tues–Sun 5pm–1am.

ENTERTAINMENT

For full listings of cultural events in the city, see ⓦ cultura .muniguate.com or consult supplements in the national press (best are *Prensa Libre* and *El Periódico*).

Centro Cultural de España 6 Av 11–02, Zona 1 ⓦ cceguatemala.org. In a spectacular location inside an old Art Deco cinema, showcasing an innovative selection of arthouse, European and independent Latin American movies, plus occasional classics. Also hosts plays and concerts.

Cinépolis Oakland Mall, Diagonal 6 13–01, Zona 10 ⓦ cinepolis.com.gt. This multiplex has the best-quality audiovisuals in the city, and even offers "butler service" tickets, which get you a leather seat and drinks brought over to you.

Teatro Nacional Off 6 Av, Zona 1 ⓦ mcd.gob.gt; map p.280. The national complex has several theatres, including an amphitheatre, and stages some diverse and prestigious events. You can find out what's on via the website.

Trovajazz Vía 6 3–55, Zona 4 ⓦ trovajazz.com. Intimate venue with a good reputation that showcases quality jazz, blues, acoustic and *trova* (Latin American folk). Entrance is around US$5 for most acts.

SHOPPING

For souvenirs, foodstuffs and everyday items check out Zona 1's Mercado Central (see p.279).

Fontabella Plaza 12 C 12–59, Zona 10 ⓦ plazafontabella.com; map p.282. A classy shopping

4

centre, with boutiques and restaurants scattered around little courtyards. Check out Sopho's bookstore for English titles, the iStore for Apple goodies or Vinoteca for a glass of wine. Daily 8am–10pm.

Los Próceres 16 C 2–00, Zona 10 ⓦ proceres.com; map p.282. Conveniently located mid-range mall, with four floors and more than two hundred stores, including many budget clothes, electrical and phone shops, some food stalls, a spa and a multi-screen cinema. Daily 8am–10pm.

Oakland Mall Diagonal 6 13–01, Zona 10 ⓦ oaklandmall .com.gt; map p.282. Upmarket mall with stores including Diesel and Zara, a good food court and free wi-fi. Daily 8am–10pm.

DIRECTORY

Banks ATMs and banks are very widespread, and there are several inside Los Próceres mall. You can exchange euros at Banco Internacional, avs Las Américas 12–54, Zona 13, and Banrural, at the airport.

Embassies Most embassies are in the southeastern quarter of the city, along Avs La Reforma and Las Américas: Australia, contact the Canadian embassy; Belize, 5 Av 5–55, Zona 14 (ⓣ 2367 3883, ⓦ embajadadebelize .org); Canada, 13 C 8–44, Edificio Edyma Plaza, Zona 10 (ⓣ 2363 4348, ⓦ canadainternational.gc.ca); Germany, Edificio Reforma 10, Av La Reforma 9–55, Zona 10 (ⓣ 2364 6700, ⓦ guatemala.diplo.de); Honduras, 19 Av A 20–19, Zona 10 (ⓣ 2366 5640); Mexico, 2 Av 7–57, Zona 10 (ⓣ 2420 3400, ⓦ embamex.sre.gob. mx/Guatemala); New Zealand (honorary), 13 C 7–85, Zona 10 (ⓣ 2431 1705); South Africa (honorary), 11 Av 30–24, Zona 5 (ⓣ 2332 6953); Sweden, Edificio Reforma 10, Av La Reforma 9–55, Zona 10 (ⓣ 2384 7300, ⓦ swedenabroad.com); UK, Torre Internacional, 16 C 0–55, Zona 10 (ⓣ 2380 7300, ⓦ ukinguatemala.fco.gov .uk); USA, Av La Reforma 7–01, Zona 10 (ⓣ 2326 4000, ⓦ guatemala.usembassy.gov).

Health The Centro Médico, 6 Av 3–47, Zona 10 (ⓣ 2332 3555), is a private hospital with 24hr cover and English-speaking staff.

Immigration The main immigration office (*migración*) is 6 Av & Ruta 3, Zona 4 (Mon–Fri 8.30am–2.45pm; ⓣ 2411 2411). Visas can be extended here; you'll need copies of your passport, proof of funds (such as a credit card) and a passport-style colour photograph.

Internet Wi-fi is widespread. Cyber (7 Av & 9 C, Zona 1) has quick connections. You'll find two internet cafés inside Géminis Diez mall (12 C & 2 Av, Zona 10). Expect to pay around Q5/hr.

Laundry Lavandería el Siglo, 2 C 3–42, Zona 1 (Q40 for wash and dry; Mon–Sat 8am–6pm).

Police The police headquarters are in the fortress building on 6 Av, Zona 1. In an emergency, dial ⓣ 120.

Post office The main post office is at 7 Av and 12 C, Zona 1 (Mon–Fri 8.30am–5.30pm, Sat 8.30am–1pm).

Antigua

A visit to the colonial city of **ANTIGUA** is a must for any traveller in Guatemala. Nestled in a valley between the Agua, Acatenango and Fuego volcanoes, the city was founded in 1541 and built on a grand grid pattern as befitting a capital. Antigua grew in importance over the next two hundred years, peaking in the mid-eighteenth century, before being largely destroyed by an earthquake in 1773. Since then, it's become something of an open-air architectural museum, with many of its major remaining structures and monuments preserved as ruins – the impressive churches and magnificent buildings on view today date back to the Spanish empire. Local conservation laws are strict, ensuring that the city will remain in its current

---

SEMANA SANTA IN ANTIGUA

Antigua's **Semana Santa (Holy Week)** celebrations are some of the most impressive and remarkable in all Latin America. The celebrations start on Palm Sunday with a procession representing Christ's entry into Jerusalem, and continue through to Good Friday, when processions re-enact the progress of Christ to the Cross. Setting out at about 8am from La Merced, Escuela de Cristo and the village of San Felipe, and accompanied by solemn dirges and clouds of incense, penitents carry images of Christ and the Cross on massive platforms. Initially garbed in either purple or white, after 3pm, the hour of the Crucifixion, the penitents change into black. Some of the images they carry date from the seventeenth century, and the procession itself is thought to have been introduced in the early years of the Conquest. Check the exact details of events with the tourist office (see p.293), and reserve a hotel well in advance if you want to stay in the city.

ANTIGUA

EATING
Angie Angie	3
Toko Baru	5
Y tu Piña Tambien	2

DRINKING & NIGHTLIFE
Café No Sé	1
Café Sky	4

■ ACCOMMODATION
La Casa de Gloria	4
Earth Lodge	1
Hobbitenango	2
El Hostal	3

San Juan del Obispo & Santa María de Jesús

atmospheric state, and continue to draw in thousands of visitors every year. Long favoured by travellers as an antidote to hectic, nearby Guatemala City, in recent years Antigua has seen its population joined by both large numbers of Guatemaltecos from "la capital" and many expats attracted by the city's sophisticated and relaxed ambience. Tourists of every nationality fill the town, along with numerous foreign students attending the city's language schools. With smart restaurants and wine bars catering to this international, cosmopolitan crowd, Antigua's civilized world can at first seem quite bourgeois, but like most travellers, you will probably end up staying a lot longer than planned.

WHAT TO SEE AND DO

Antigua is laid out as a grid, with avenidas running north–south, and calles east–west. Each street is numbered and has two halves, either a north (*norte/nte*) and south (*sur*) or an east (*oriente/ote*) and west (*poniente/pte*) with the city's main plaza, the **Parque Central**, at their centre. Despite this apparent simplicity, most people get lost here at some stage. If you're confused, remember that Volcán Agua, the one closest to town, is almost directly south.

Parque Central

Antigua's focal point is its main plaza, the **Parque Central**. It's a popular hangout, with both visitors and locals congregating, chatting and relaxing on its many benches around the central **Fuente de Las Sirenas** fountain, built in 1739.

Catedral de San José

Of the structures surrounding the plaza, the **Catedral de San José**, on the east side, is the most arresting. Built in 1670, the cathedral was quite elaborate for its time and location – it boasted an immense dome, five aisles, eighteen chapels and an altar inlaid with mother-of-pearl, ivory and silver – but the 1773 earthquake almost destroyed the building. Today only two of the original interior chapels remain; take a peek inside and you will find a gold cloister and several colonial images. To get some idea of the vast scale of the original building, check out the ruins to the rear (enter from 5 C Ote; daily 9am–5pm; Q5) where you'll find a mass of fallen masonry and rotting

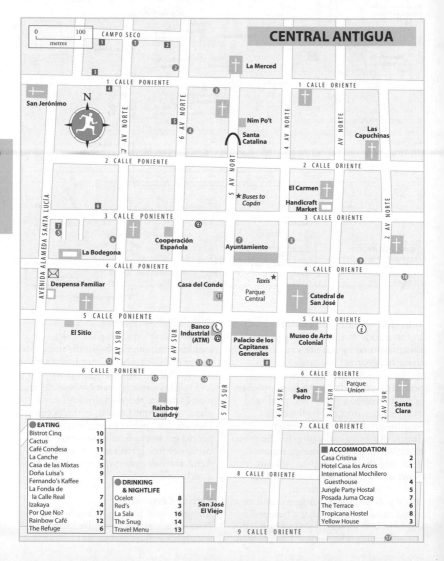

CENTRAL ANTIGUA

La Merced

San Jerónimo

Nim Po't

Santa Catalina

Las Capuchinas

El Carmen
Handicraft Market

★ Buses to Copán

Cooperación Española

Ayuntamiento

La Bodegona

Despensa Familiar

Casa del Conde

Taxis ★
Parque Central

Catedral de San José

El Sitio

Banco Industrial (ATM) @

Palacio de los Capitanes Generales

Museo de Arte Colonial

Rainbow Laundry

San Pedro

Parque Union

Santa Clara

San José El Viejo

● **EATING**
Bistrot Cinq	10
Cactus	15
Café Condesa	11
La Canche	2
Casa de las Mixtas	5
Doña Luisa's	9
Fernando's Kaffee	1
La Fonda de la Calle Real	7
Izakaya	4
Por Que No?	17
Rainbow Café	12
The Refuge	6

● **DRINKING & NIGHTLIFE**
Ocelot	8
Red's	3
La Sala	16
The Snug	14
Travel Menu	13

■ **ACCOMMODATION**
Casa Cristina	2
Hotel Casa los Arcos	1
International Mochilero Guesthouse	4
Jungle Party Hostal	5
Posada Juma Ocag	7
The Terrace	6
Tropicana Hostel	8
Yellow House	3

beams, broken arches and hefty pillars. Buried beneath the floor are some of the great names of the Conquest, including Bishop Marroquín, Pedro de Alvarado and his wife. At the very rear of what was once the nave, steps lead down to a burial vault that's regularly used for Maya religious ceremonies – an example of the coexistence of pagan and Catholic beliefs that's so characteristic of Guatemala.

Palacio de los Capitanes Generales

One of the oldest buildings in Antigua, the **Palacio de los Capitanes Generales** takes up the entire south side of the Parque Central. Dating to 1558, it's been rebuilt more than once, and been through several incarnations, serving as the Mint for all of Latin America, the home of the colonial rulers, dragoon barracks, stables, law courts, ballrooms and more. It's currently undergoing a lengthy renovation project.

Ayuntamiento

On the north side of the plaza is the **Ayuntamiento**, the city hall. Dating from 1740, its metre-thick walls balance the solid style of the Palacio de los Capitanes Generales opposite. Unlike most others, this building survived earlier rumblings and wasn't damaged until the 1976 earthquake, although it has since been repaired. The city hall was abandoned in 1779 when the capital moved to Guatemala City, but it was later reclaimed for use by the city's administration. The Ayuntamiento also holds a couple of minor museums, the Museo del Libro Antiguo (daily 9am–4pm, Q30) and the **Museo de Santiago** (closed for renovation at time of writing).

Iglesia de San Francisco

Southeast of the Parque Central on 1 Avenida Sur is the colossal **Iglesia de San Francisco** (daily 6am–6pm). One of the oldest churches in Antigua, dating from 1579, during the colonial period it served as a vast religious and cultural centre that included a school, a hospital, music rooms, a printing press and a monastery. All of this was lost, though, in the 1773

earthquake. Restoration of the chapel started in 1960, and today very little remains of what was once the original monument.

Inside the church is the tomb of **Hermano Pedro de Betancourt**, a Franciscan from the Canary Islands who founded the Hospital of Belén in Antigua, and is credited with powers of miraculous intervention. Pope John Paul II made him Central America's first saint in 2002.

The **ruins** (daily 9am–4.30pm; Q5) of the monastery to the rear are among the most impressive in Antigua, with colossal fallen arches and pillars strewn over extensive gardens and grassy verges. Don't miss the curious museum here and its "hall of miracles" which contains dozens of crutches and walking sticks left behind by grateful pilgrims, who credit Hermano Pedro with divine healing.

Casa Popenoe

The grand colonial mansion **Casa Popenoe** (Mon–Fri 8am–4pm, Sat 8am–11am; entrance by guided tour only, book in advance at ☎2413 3258, ⓦ casapopenoe.ufm.edu; US$10) on 1 Av Sur dates from 1634. The structure was in ruins when, in 1932, Dr Wilson Popenoe, a United Fruit-company scientist, began its comprehensive restoration, which took decades. Inside there's an incredible collection of furniture and art, including portraits of Bishop Marroquín and a menacing-looking Alvarado himself. The kitchen and servants' quarters have also been carefully renovated, and you can see the bread ovens and pigeon loft (which would have provided the original occupants with their mail service).

Parque Unión

One block west and one block north of San Francisco is **Parque Unión**, flanked on each end by a church (both daily 8am–4.30pm). The one on the western side is **San Pedro**, dating from 1680, and the one to the east is **Santa Clara**, a former convent with a fine ornate facade. In colonial times the latter was a popular place for aristocratic ladies to take the veil

4

– the hardships were not too extreme, and the nuns gained a reputation for their fine cooking. In front of Santa Clara is a large open-air *pila* (washhouse).

Las Capuchinas

At the junction of 2 Calle Oriente and 2 Avenida Norte are the remains of **Las Capuchinas** (daily 9am–5pm; Q40), dating from 1726, once the largest and most beautiful of the city's convents. These ruins are among Antigua's best preserved, and yet least documented: the Capuchin nuns who lived here were not allowed any contact with the outside world. Food was passed to them by means of a turntable, and they could only speak to visitors through a grille. You should wander through the ruins – they are beautiful, with fountains, courtyards, massive pillars and a unique tower, or "retreat", which has eighteen tiny cells set into the walls on the top floor and a cellar that probably functioned as a meat storage room. The convent was damaged following the 1751 earthquake, and in 1773 the sisters left the premises.

The impressive new **museum** here beautifully showcases some terrific religious art and ecclesiastical artefacts including colonial-era sculptures and portraits.

Santa Catalina and La Merced

A couple of blocks west of Las Capuchinas, spanning 5 Avenida Norte, the **arch of Santa Catalina** is all that remains of yet another convent, this one founded in 1609. The arch was built so that the nuns could walk between the two halves of the establishment without being exposed to the outside world. At the end of the street, just to the north, the church of **La Merced** boasts one of the most intricate facades in the entire city. The church is still in use, and the cloisters and gardens, including a monumental fountain, are open to the public (daily 8am–5pm; Q5).

Cerro de la Cruz

Northeast of Antigua, the **Cerro de la Cruz**, a hilltop with a giant cross, has commanding views of the city and Volcán Agua. It was something of a mugging hotspot for years, but an increased police presence has meant it's now considered perfectly safe. A tuk-tuk here costs Q20.

Santo Domingo

Once forming the largest monastery in Antigua, the immense complex of **Santo Domingo** is today largely occupied by a luxury hotel. Substantial parts of the gorgeous grounds have been sensitively converted into a **cultural zone** (Mon–Sat 9am–6pm, Sun 11.45am–6pm; Q50), which includes several small museums, the monastery ruins, various subterranean crypts, artisans' workshops, exhibitions of local textiles and crafts, a re-creation of an early pharmacy and an art exhibition space.

LANGUAGE SCHOOLS IN ANTIGUA

Antigua is an extremely popular place to attend **language school**. Listed here are only a few of the many schools offering Spanish courses.

Antigüena Spanish Academy1 C Pte 10 (☎7832 7241, ⊛spanishacademyantiguena.com).

Centro Lingüístico Maya 5 C Pte 20 (☎7832 0656, ⊛clmaya.com).

Christian Spanish Academy 6 Av Nte 15 (☎7832 3922, ⊛learncsa.com).

Guate Linda Language Center 7 Av Nte 76 (☎4360 5238, ⊛guatelindacenter.com).

Ixchel Spanish School 4 Av Nte 32 (☎7832 3440, ⊛ixchelschool.com).

Ixquic 7 Av Nte 74 (☎7832 2402, ⊛ixquic.edu.gt).

Probigua 6 Av Nte 41B (☎7832 2998, ⊛probigua.org).

San José El Viejo 5 Av Sur 34 (☎7832 3028, ⊛sanjoseelviejo.com).

Spanish Academy Sevilla 1 Av Sur 17 C (☎7832 5101, ⊛sevillantigua.com).

Tecún Umán Spanish School 6 C Pte 34A (☎7832 2792, ⊛tecunuman.centramerica.com).

The **Museo Colonial** harbours an exquisite array of religious artefacts and treasures from the Spanish era including a breathtaking collection of golden crowns, silver lecterns and chalices. You can then tour the monastery's four **crypts**, including the Calvary crypt which has an impressive mural of Christ and the crucifixion. The crypts are dotted around the ruined remains of Santo Domingo's 68m-long **church**. Inside the complex's **Archeological Museum** are some impressive Maya ceramics, including intricately painted drinking vessels, funerary urns and incense burners in an exhibition room that has walls painted with scenes from the famous murals of Bonampak. The neighbouring **Museum of Maya Art and Modern Glass** has exhibitions of Maya artefacts and ceramics together with contemporary glassworks that are supposed to have been influenced by them – a slightly bizarre concept.

ARRIVAL AND DEPARTURE

By bus Antigua's second-class bus terminal is beside the market. Very few travellers now take local buses to Guatemala City, partly due to security concerns and partly because they use an inconvenient terminal in the capital in Zona 3, 1.5km west of the centre. If you're heading to the western highlands catch the first bus to Chimaltenango and transfer there. The following buses all leave from the main terminal, except the Panajachel bus (which leaves from 4 C Pte 34) and Hedman Alas (ⓦ hedmanalas.com) buses to Copán, Honduras, which leave from *Hotel de Don Rodrigo*, 5 Av Nte 17.

Destinations Chimaltenango (every 15min; 40min); Ciudad Vieja (every 20min; 15min); Escuintla (every 45min; 1hr 15min); Guatemala City (every 15min; 1hr–1hr 30min); Panajachel (7am daily; 2hr 30min); San Antonio Aguas Calientes (every 30min; 20min); San Juan Del Obispo (hourly; 15min); Santa María de Jesús (every 30min; 30min).

By shuttle bus Minibuses can be booked through most travel agents, including Atitrans and Adrenalina Tours (see below). Shuttles typically cost triple the price of public buses, but they are much more comfortable and a bit quicker.

Destinations Chichicastenango (2 daily, more on market days; 2hr 30min); Cobán (daily; 6hr); Copán, Honduras (daily; 6hr); El Tunco, El Salvador (3–4 weekly; 5hr); Guatemala City (7 daily; 1hr–1hr 30min); Lanquín (daily; 8hr 30min); León, Nicaragua (3–4 weekly; 15hr);

Monterrico (8am daily; 2hr 30min); Panajachel (2–3 daily; 2hr 30min); Quetzaltenango (daily; 3hr 30min); San Cristóbal de las Casas, Mexico (daily; 12hr); San Marcos la Laguna (3 daily; 3hr 15min); San Pedro La Laguna (3 daily; 3hr).

TRAVEL AGENTS

Adrenalina Tours 3 C Pte 2D ⓣ 7832 1108, ⓦ adrenalina tours.com. Good for shuttle buses and bespoke tours across the country.

Atitrans 6 Av Sur 8 ⓣ 7832 3371, ⓦ atitrans.net. Runs shuttle bus connections all over Guatemala and has a good reputation for reliability.

Viajes Tivoli 4 C Ote 10 ⓣ 7832 4274, ⓦ viajestivoli.com. A recommended all-rounder for flights and tours.

GETTING AROUND

By taxi On the east side of the Parque Central, or call ⓣ 7832 0479. A short trip is about US$5. For a female cab driver, call Chiqui on ⓣ 5715 5720.

By tuk-tuk Rides cost Q10.

Bike rental Guatemala Ventures and Old Town Outfitters (see below) rent quality mountain bikes for Q150/day.

Car and motorbike rental Tabarini, 6 Av Sur 22 (ⓣ 7832 8107, ⓦ tabarini.com), has cars from Q295/day. CA Tours, 6 C Oriente 14 (ⓣ 7832 9638, ⓦ catours .co.uk), rents scooters for Q300/day.

INFORMATION

Tourist information Inguat, 5 C Ote 11 (Mon–Fri 8am–4pm, Sat & Sun 9am–4pm; ⓣ 2421 2800 ext. 610, ⓔ info-antigua@inguat.gob.gt). Staff are pretty clued up and English is spoken.

Tourist assistance PROATUR (ⓣ 5978 9835, ⓦ proatur .visitguatemala.com) helps victims of crime and will also escort tourists around Antigua, including up to Cerro de la Cruz.

ACTIVITIES AND TOURS

Guatemala Ventures 1 Av Sur 15 ⓣ 7832 3383, ⓦ guatemalaventures.com. An excellent range of biking trips (from Q250 for a few hours exploring Antigua's villages) plus bike rental. Horseriding, caving, birdwatching and volcano climbs are also offered.

Niños de Guatemala Casa Convento Concepción, 4 C Ote 41 ⓣ 7832 8033, ⓦ ninosdeguatemala.org. Superb tours of non-touristy villages in the Antigua area, taking in niche industries like a chicken bus workshop as well as the NGO's own school.

Old Town Outfitters 5 Av Sur 12 ⓣ 7832 4171, ⓦ adventureguatemala.com. Runs volcano hikes including Acatenango (from Q560), mountain-bike excursions, rock-climbing trips for all levels (from Q600) and sea-kayaking, and rents tents, sleeping bags, packs and bikes.

4

ACCOMMODATION

Antigua has lots of excellent budget accommodation, including many good hostels. You'll also see rooms and apartments advertised on café noticeboards. During Semana Santa the whole town is fully booked, but even if you haven't reserved you can usually find a room in a family home. All the following places have free wi-fi.

HOSTELS

★**Earth Lodge** ☎5664 0713, ⓦearthlodgeguatemala .com; map p.289. A highland rural retreat (and avocado farm), owned by a Canadian-American family, which enjoys sweeping views of the Panchoy valley and its volcanoes. Accommodation options include A-frame cabañas, a wood-cabin dorm and treehouses. Wholesome meals are served, and there's a Maya-style sauna and good walking trails. Consult their website for transport information (you can arrange a pick-up from Antigua). Dorms Q56, cabañas Q195

Hobbitenango 9km northeast of Antigua ☎5909 9106, ⓔhobbitenango@gmail.com; map p.289. High, high up in the hills above Antigua, this is a quirky, artistically designed place with amazing volcano views (five can be seen on clear days from a lookout nearby), good grub and stellar cocktails. They also host an annual music festival here. Shuttles (US$2) connect the lodge with Antigua four times a day. Dorms Q56, cabins Q412

El Hostal 1 Av Sur 8 ☎7832 0442, ⓦelhostal.hostel.com; map p.289. Spacious rooms and dorms that offer comfort and style in an elegant converted colonial house. The communal bathrooms (with superb hot-water showers) are spotless, and there's a great central courtyard for chilling. Rates include an excellent breakfast. Dorms Q75, doubles Q240

International Mochilero Guesthouse 1 C Pte 33 ☎7832 0520, ⓦinternacionalmochilero.com; map p.290. This long-running place has cheap rates, especially for private rooms (very basic but doable for a night or two), as well as a large garden. Dorms Q50, doubles Q125

Jungle Party Hostal 6 Av Nte 20 ☎7832 0463, ⓦjunglepartyhostal.com; map p.290. A huge hostel that attracts a young backpacking crowd. Dorm accommodation varies (the cheapest is a no-frills crash pad). The bar/café and roof terrace are good for socializing; breakfast is included. Q62

The Terrace 3 C Pte 24B ☎7832 3463, ⓦterracehostel .com; map p.290. Very popular with young travellers, this well-run party hostel has an amazing roof terrace, which is the perfect spot to take advantage of the all-day happy hour and barbecues (Wed & Sun). If you want to meet people and have fun, look no further. Dorms Q68, doubles Q195

★**Tropicana Hostel** 6 C Pte 2 ☎7832 0462, ⓦtropicanahostel.com; map p.290. Raising the bar very high, this luxe hostel has it all: a pool, hot tub, ping-pong table, garden, terrace, bar, full menu and welcoming vibe. The cheaper dorms (with triple-deck bunks) have fifteen beds, but the high ceilings and fine-quality mattresses help compensate. Dorms Q75, doubles Q195

Yellow House 1 C Pte 24 ☎7832 6646, ⓔyellow houseantigua@hotmail.com; map p.290. This welcoming solar-powered hostel is a good choice, boasting a lovely rustic-style roof terrace with hammocks, greenery and views. The four bathrooms mean that you shouldn't have to wait long for a *ducha*. Accommodation varies: the three-bed dorms are the best value, while the cabin-like upstairs rooms are lovely. Rates include use of kitchen and a good buffet breakfast. Dorms Q75, doubles Q190

HOTELS AND GUESTHOUSES

Casa Cristina Callejón Camposeco 3A ☎7832 0623, ⓦcasa-cristina.com; map p.290. This little hotel offers fine value, with fourteen very clean and attractive rooms, all with private hot-water bathrooms; those on the upper floors enjoy more natural light and privacy. There's a rooftop sun terrace, free coffee, drinking water and wi-fi. Q210

La Casa de Gloria C San Luquitas 3B ☎4374 1391, ⓔlacasadegloria@yahoo.com; map p.289. Sociable guesthouse about a 10min walk southwest of the Parque Central, with five private rooms (singles are just Q70), a kitchen and free drinking water. Run by a welcoming Guatemalteca (a salsa and Spanish teacher), it's a great option if you're after a local experience. Q105

Hotel Casa los Arcos Callejón Camposeco (off 7 Av Nte) ☎7832 7813, ⓔcasa_losarcos@hotmail.com; map p.290. A family-owned guesthouse with a good choice of modern, spotless rooms (nine en suite), all with hand-woven bedspreads and cable TV. It's a great deal for singles (rooms are Q125/person), and there's a guests' kitchen. Q250

★**Posada Juma Ocag** Alameda Santa Lucía Nte 13 ☎7832 3109, ⓦposadajumaocag.com; map p.290. A very hospitable and efficiently managed place with eight immaculately presented, if smallish, rooms decorated with local fabrics; all have good beds, a wardrobe or clothes rack, private bathroom and reading lights. There's a small patio ideal for relaxing, and free drinking water. Q190

EATING

CAFÉS

Café Condesa West side of the Parque Central ☎7832 0038; map p.290. This classy café has a gorgeous cobbled patio, smart dining rooms and gurgling fountains. Great for breakfasts (from Q30) and superb salads – order the green leaves with toasted macadamia nuts and outstanding home-made corn bread. Mon–Thurs & Sun 7.30am–8pm, Fri & Sat 7.30am–9pm.

Doña Luisa's 4 C Ote 12 ☎ 7832 2578; map p.290. One of Antigua's most renowned café-restaurants, set in a historic colonial mansion. Offers a straightforward menu of sandwiches, burgers and salads, but the in-house bakery (there's a shop next door) really is the best in town. Daily 7.30am–9.30pm.

Fernando's Kaffee 7 Av Nte 43D ☎ 7832 6953, ⓦ fernandos-kaffee.com; map p.290. Courtyard café owned by a java freak who selects and roasts (on the premises) his own arabica coffee from small estates and also makes gourmet chocolate. Breakfasts (from Q20), sandwiches (Q22), light lunches and wonderful juices, smoothies and cakes are also available. Mon–Sat 7am–7pm, Sun 7am–1pm.

Rainbow Café 7 Av Sur 8 ☎ 7832 1919, ⓦ rainbow cafeantigua.com; map p.290. Long-running travellers' hangout with a wide choice of imaginative salads, Mexican and vegetarian dishes and filling breakfasts, with a daily set lunch for Q35. There's live music every night, regular political and social lectures and it's also home to a good secondhand bookshop. Daily 7am–11pm.

The Refuge 7 Av Nte 18A ☎ 4118 4904, ⓦ refuge coffeeroasters.com, map p.290. Stylish little café which proudly states that "coffee is our main focus" though you can also grab a cup of *mate* (Argentinian tea) or a cupcake should the urge arise. Free wi-fi. Mon–Fri 7.30am–7pm, Sat 8am–6.30pm.

Y Tu Piña También 1 Av Sur 10B ⓦ ytupinatambien .com; map p.289. This arty hangout has appealing blended fruit juices and excellent breakfast options (from Q24). Also scores for salads and sandwiches, which are all served with sweet potato fries. Free wi-fi. Mon–Fri 7am–8pm, Sat & Sun 8am–8pm.

RESTAURANTS

Angie Angie 1 Av Sur 11A ☎ 7832 3352; map p.289. On the east side of town, this garden restaurant is superb for grilled meats, imaginative salads, fresh pasta (try the ravioli with gorgonzola) and tasty tapas-style options (Q30–40). Tables are set around a log fire at night and there's live music (blues, jazz, latin) on weekends too. Daily 8am–10pm.

Cactus 6 C Pte 21 ☎ 7832 2163; map p.290. Mexican-owned, this great new place specializes in tacos (try the shrimp and bacon) which are prepared to perfection, as well as filling burritos (the fish is excellent) and the like. There's a full bar and live music some nights. Daily 11am–10pm.

La Canche 6 Av Nte 42; map p.290. For a very local experience, chow down at one of the lino-topped tables inside this humble store-cum-*comedor*. Filling Guatemalan *comida típica* (Q12–20 a meal). Tables are shared. Mon–Sat 11am–8.30pm.

Casa de las Mixtas 1 Callejón, off 3 C Pte; map p.290. Authentic, filling Guatemalan *comedor* grub: extensive breakfast options and hearty portions of grilled meats and *caldos* (soups) at reasonable prices. Daily 8am–4pm.

La Fonda de la Calle Real 3 C Pte 7 ☎ 7832 0507, ⓦ lafondadelacallereal; map p.290. Flavoursome, authentic Guatemalan food with specialities including *caldo real* (chicken soup with rice, spices and lemon). There are two additional branches at 5 Av Nte 5 and 5 Av Nte 12. Daily noon–10pm.

Izakaya 6 Av Nte 19A ☎ 7832 1984; map p.290. For a gourmet experience, head to this exceptional restaurant (owned by a *Nobu*-trained chef and her partner) that has an understated feel: the menu (Japanese fusion) is short and premises are quite simply furnished. There's an open kitchen, so you can watch the tempura (Q35), *ceviche* (Q45) and delectable fillets of mahi-mahi and meats being expertly prepared. Not cheap (around Q200 a head) but worth it. Daily noon–10.30pm, closed Mon lunch.

Por Que No? 2 Av Sur & 9 C Ote ☎ 4324 5407; map p.290. Quirky hole-in-the-wall complete with wacky decor and graffiti-enriched walls run by a friendly, very welcoming couple. There's a short menu (try the burritos or peppercorn steak); it's also good for a casual beer. Mon–Sat 6–10pm.

Toko Baru 1 Av 17A ☎ 4079 2092; map p.289. A popular, inexpensive place that serves pretty authentic Middle Eastern favourites (particularly falafel) plus Asian dishes including curries, satay and spring rolls. The daily special is just US$4.50. Tues–Sat noon–9pm, Sun 1–8pm.

DRINKING AND NIGHTLIFE

Bars are spread throughout Antigua. Two of the main areas are around the arch on 7 Av Nte and over on 1 Av Sur. There's not really a nightclub scene, but if you want some dancefloor action *La Sala* is your best bet.

BARS

★**Café No Sé** 1 Av Sur 11C ☎5501 2680, ⓦcafenose
.com; map p.289. The most satisfying bar in town is a
crepuscular affair, barely illuminated by candlelight. Draws
a good mix of characters – local artists and creative types,
wasters and wannabes, travellers and hard-drinking
expats spinning tall tales – plus the odd stray dog. There's
good acoustic music virtually nightly, comfort food and a
(semi-) secret *mescal* bar serving the house brand: Ilegal.
Can get very smoky. Daily 1pm–1am.

Café Sky 1 Av Sur ☎7832 7300; map p.289. On the top
deck of a sky-blue structure on the east side of town, this
bar is the best bet for sunset, with volcano views *par
excellence*. Daily 8am–11pm.

Ocelot 4 Av Nte 3 ☎5658 9028; map p.290. Probably
Antigua's classiest bar, *Ocelot* is a great place for a relaxed
drink, with elegant furnishings, gingham floor tiles,
seductive cocktails (around Q30) and live music most
nights. There's an excellent quiz (trivia) on Sunday
evenings. Daily 12.15pm–1am.

Red's 1 C Pte 3; map p.290. Large British-owned sports
bar with pool tables and a dart board, good beer selection
and a pub grub menu that takes in local, Mexican, Indian
curries and English comfort food like shepherd's pie. Daily
10am–midnight.

La Sala 6 C Pte 9 ☎7832 9524; map p.290. Lively dance
bar where DJs spin electronica and house music, mixed
party anthems on Saturday nights and salsa on Sundays.
At the weekend it can be a riot, with table-top dancing and
lots of shot-downing. Daily noon–1am.

The Snug 6 C Pte 14 ☎4215 9601; map p.290. As the
name suggests, this Irish bar is small but perfectly formed,
an intimate spot to sip a beer or two. There's live music on
weekend nights. Daily noon–11pm.

Travel Menu 6 C Pte 14 ☎7832 2937; map p.290. Newly
renovated, this sociable bar-grill now has live music every
night. The bar is well stocked and the menu features
comfort grub like burgers and fish 'n' chips. Daily 4–11pm.

ENTERTAINMENT

Cinemas Cooperación Española, 6 Av Nte (☎7832 1276,
ⓦaecid-cf.org.gt), and El Sitio (see below) show Western
and Latin American films daily. Listings are posted on
noticeboards all over town.

Cultural institutes Cooperación Española (see above)
promotes all manner of cultural events: films, exhibitions,
lectures and workshops, and its library is a terrific resource.
El Sitio, 5 C Pte 15 (☎7832 3037, ⓦelsitiocultural.org),
has an active theatre, art gallery and café and regularly
hosts exhibitions and concerts.

SHOPPING

Good supermarkets include La Bodegona, 4 C Pte &
Calzada Santa Lucía, and Despensa Familiar, Calzada Santa
Lucía between 4 and 5 C.

Casa del Conde West side of Parque Central ☎7832
3322, map p.290. Bookstore with a good selection of
new English-language books about Guatemala as well
as travel guides, novels and photography titles. Daily
8am–7.30pm.

Dyslexia Books 1 Av Sur 11; map p.289. The best
secondhand bookstore in town, with informed staff and
lots of interesting fiction and non-fiction in English,
Spanish and other European languages. Daily 1–6pm.

Nim Po't 5 Av Nte 29 ⓦnimpotexport.com; map p.290.
Selling fine textiles at fair prices, this warehouse-like store
is something of a museum of contemporary Maya
weaving, with a stunning array of complete costumes, plus

VOLCÁN PACAYA

Volcán Pacaya, one of Guatemala's many cones, is a spectacular Strombolian volcano
(characterized by low-level, intermittent explosions). Though technically closer to Guatemala
City than to Antigua, it's nonetheless more commonly reached from the latter – indeed, it is
the trip to make in the area. Depending on Pacaya's activity level, you may be able to scale its
slopes.

You can only visit the volcano on a **guided tour** (prices start at Q75 for budget tours), which
are offered daily (leaving at 6am and 2pm) by virtually all travel agents and tour operators in
town. Tours entail an hour's climb up the volcano where you can, quite literally, poke at the
lava flows with a stick (make sure you wear good shoes, as thin soles can melt). Bring
marshmallows for toasting. The views at sunset are breathtaking – remember to bring a torch,
as it will be nearly dark when you walk down. The volcano sits inside Pacaya National Park, for
which entry is an additional Q50. Note that sulphurous fumes and high winds can occasionally
make the ascent impossible.

The budget tours described here can feel impersonal and rushed, as you're herded in a large
group from a packed minibus up the crater and back again. If you want to experience the
volcano differently, contact the recommended tour operators (see p.293), who can organize
bespoke trips.

other *artesanías* including wooden masks, basketry and useful stuff like handmade iPad cases. Daily 8am–6pm.

Markets The main *mercado* (daily 7am–5.30pm) by the bus terminal is fascinating. Browse the Latino CDs and Hollywood DVDs and shop for unusual tropical fruit or fake footie gear. Just south of here, the Mercado de Artesanías is a tad touristy, so bargain hard. There's another handicraft market next to the El Carmen church on 3 Av Nte.

DIRECTORY

Banks There are many ATMs in town, including at Banco Industrial, 5 Av Sur 4, just south of the plaza.

Crime If you're a victim of a crime in Antigua, contact English-speaking PROATUR rep Abraham Martínez (☎ 5578 9835), who will help you deal with the police and file a report. The police headquarters are outside town.

Internet and phones Free wi-fi is very common in Antigua's cafés and hotels. Internet cafés charge around US$0.75/hr. *Funky Monkey*, 5 Av Sur 6, is a good place for fast surfing speeds, Skype and cheap international calls. Daily 8am–10pm.

Laundry Rainbow Laundry, 6 Av Sur 15 (daily 7.30am–8pm).

Medical care Hospital Privado Hermano Pedro, Av Recolección (☎ 7832 1190), offers 24-hour emergency service.

Post office Av Alameda Santa Lucía (Mon–Fri 8am–5.30pm).

AROUND ANTIGUA

The countryside **around Antigua** is extremely beautiful. The valley is dotted with small villages, ranging from the *ladino* coffee centre of Jocotenango to the *indígena* village of Santa María de Jesús. For the more adventurous, Agua and Acatenango volcanoes offer strenuous but

CRIME AROUND ANTIGUA

Visitors to the areas around Antigua should be aware that **crime against tourists** – including violent robbery and rape – is not common but does occur. Keep informed by taking local advice, and try to avoid walking alone at night, or to isolated spots during the day. PROATUR (see box, p.275) will often accompany you, or even give you a ride to many sites.

superb hiking, best done with a specialist agency (see p.293). Northwest of Antigua is **Santiago Sacatepéquez**, renowned for its annual Festival of the Day of the Dead, when beautiful, intricately decorated kites – some with a diameter of up to 7m – soar through the skies. Further west are the ruins of **Iximché**, the "Place of the Maize Tree", where you can visit what remains of a pre-Columbian archeological site. All of these sites (except the last) are less than an hour from Antigua.

Santa María de Jesús and Volcán Agua

Heading south from Antigua, a good paved road snakes through the coffee bushes and past the village of San Juan del Obispo before arriving in **SANTA MARÍA DE JESÚS**. Perched on the shoulder of **Volcán Agua**, the village is some 500m above the city, with brilliant views over the Panchoy valley and east towards smoking Volcán Pacaya. Though the women wear beautiful purple

THE CULT OF MAXIMÓN

Despite being just 18km from Antigua, few tourists visit the shrine of the "evil saint" **San Simón** (or Maximón), in San Andrés Itzapa, and you may feel more welcome here than at his other places of abode, which include Zunil (see p.324) and Santiago Atitlán (see p.303). To reach the saint's "house" ("Casa de San Simón") – which is only open from sunrise to sunset – head for San Andrés' central plaza, turn right when you reach the church, walk two blocks, then up a little hill, where you should spot street vendors selling charms, incense and candles.

Once you've tracked down the shrine, you'll find that Maximón lives in a peculiar world, his image surrounded by drunken men, cigar-smoking women and hundreds of burning candles, each symbolizing a request. You may be offered a *limpia*, or soul cleansing, which, for a small fee, involves being beaten by one of the resident women with a bushel of herbs. A bottle of *aguardiente* is also demolished: some is offered to San Simón, some of it you drink yourself and the rest is consumed by the attendant, who may spray you with alcohol (from her mouth) for your sins.

4

huipiles, the village itself is of minimal interest – most people come through here on their way up Agua, the easiest and most popular of Guatemala's major cones to climb. It's an exciting ascent with a fantastic view to reward you at the top. The trail starts in Santa María de Jesús: it's a fairly simple climb on a clear (often rubbish-strewn) path, taking five to six hours, and the peak, at 3766m, is always cold at night. There is shelter (though not always room) in a small chapel at the summit, and the views certainly make it worth the struggle.

As there have been (occasional) robberies reported on the outskirts of Santa María, it's best to team up with an Antigua adventure sports outfit (see p.293) and not attempt the hike on your own.

Buses run from Antigua to Santa María (every 30min or so 6am–6pm).

Jocotenango

Despite being rather unattractive, the suburb of **JOCOTENANGO**, just 3km north of Antigua, does boast a couple of interesting sights, both of which are grouped in the **Centro La Azotea** cultural centre (Mon–Fri 8.30am–4pm, Sat 8.30am–2pm; Q50, including tour in English; Ⓦcentroazotea.org). **Casa K'ojom**, which forms one half of the centre, is a purpose-built museum dedicated to Maya culture, especially music. Displays clearly present the history of indigenous musical traditions, beginning with its pre-Columbian origins and moving through sixteenth-century Spanish and African influences – which brought the marimba, bugles and drums – to today. Other rooms are dedicated to the village weavings of the Sacatepéquez department and the cult of Maximón (see box, p.297). Next door, the 84-acre **Museo de Café** plantation dates from 1883, and offers the chance to look around a working organic coffee farm. All the technicalities of husking, sieving and roasting are explained, and you can sample a cup of the home-grown brew after the tour. A free hourly **shuttle bus** runs between the cathedral in Antigua and the Azotea.

San Andrés Itzapa

Beyond Jocotenango, the Antigua–Chimaltenango road ascends the Panchoy valley, past small farming villages, before a side road branches off to **SAN ANDRÉS ITZAPA**. San Andrés is known as the home of the cult of **San Simón** (or Maximón), the "evil saint" – a kind of combination of Judas Iscariot and Pedro de Alvarado – who is housed in his own pagan chapel (see box, p.297).

There are direct **buses** from the Antigua terminal to San Andrés (hourly). Alternatively, catch a bus to Chimaltenango (every 20min) and ask to be dropped off at the entrance to the town.

Santiago Sacatepéquez

SANTIAGO SACATEPÉQUEZ, 20km northeast of Antigua on the Carretera Interamericana, is renowned for its fiesta honouring the **Day of the Dead** (Nov 1). On this day, colourful, massive kites with bamboo frames – some take months to create – are flown in the town's cemetery, symbolizing the release of the souls of the dead from agony. Teams of young men struggle to get the kites aloft while the crowd looks on with bated breath, rushing for cover if a kite comes crashing to the ground. At other times of the year, there's little to see or do here – if you find yourself passing through on a Tuesday or a Sunday you might visit the town market, but that's about it.

To reach Santiago Sacatepéquez, catch a **bus** to San Lucas Sacatepéquez (buses running between Antigua and Guatemala City pass through), and then change there – many buses shuttle back and forth between the two.

Chimaltenango

The grim, traffic-plagued town of Chimaltenango is an ugly transport hub on the Interamericana. Frequent **buses** arrive from both Guatemala City and Antigua; you can change here for buses to destinations in the highlands. Services to Antigua leave every twenty minutes between 6am and 7pm from the turn-off on the highway.

Iximché

The Maya site of **Iximché** (daily 8am–5pm; Q50) sits on a beautiful exposed hillside about 5km south of the small town of **TECPÁN**, northwest of Antigua. These are the ruins of the pre-Conquest capital of the Kaqchikel Maya, who allied themselves with the conquistadors in the early days of the Conquest. Time and weather have taken their toll, though, and the majority of the buildings – which once housed more than ten thousand people – have disappeared, and just a few low pyramids, plazas and ball courts are left. Nevertheless, the site – protected on three sides by steep slopes and surrounded by pine forests – is quite peaceful; the grassy plazas make excellent picnic spots and you may have the place to yourself during the week. George W. Bush stopped here in 2007 on a visit to Guatemala to take in a Maya ceremony, though not all the locals were impressed; after he'd left, Maya shamans performed a cleansing ritual to rid the site of what they called "bad energy". The ruins are still used for Maya worship: ceremonies, sacrifices and offerings take place down a small trail behind the final plaza.

Take any **bus** travelling along the Carretera Interamericana between Chimaltenango and Los Encuentros and ask to be dropped at Tecpán, which is just off the highway. Regular buses shuttle back and forth from Tecpán's plaza to the ruins.

Lago de Atitlán

Lago de Atitlán, one of the most visited destinations in Guatemala's western highlands, was described by Aldous Huxley in 1934 as one of the most beautiful lakes in the world – and it really is exceptionally scenic. Atitlán is of interest both for its majestic setting (it's hemmed in by three volcanoes and steep

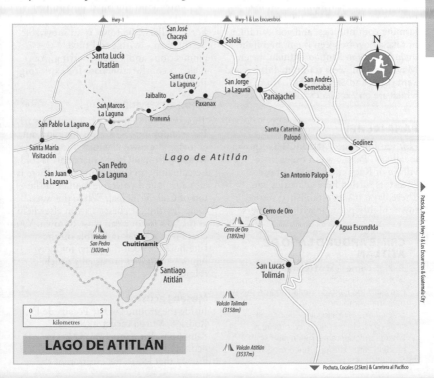

LAGO DE ATITLÁN

PARADISE IN PERIL

Atitlán's beauty remains overwhelming, although recent pressures are decidedly threatening. Sediment analysis has shown that the lakewater has risen and fallen in cycles for thousands of years, but after the tropical storm Stan in 2010 Atitlán rose 5m in eighteen months, an unprecedented event that caused businesses to flood and beaches to disappear, and threatened livelihoods. The once-idyllic lakeside pathway in Santa Cruz (a village particularly badly affected) is no more, and docks in San Pedro and San Juan had to be rebuilt. Theories rage as to why the lake is rising so quickly but for the Maya, with centuries of local knowledge, it was less of a surprise: their villages sit high above the shore, and many sold lakefront land to foreigners. By 2015, with the lake continuing to rise, more businesses were being affected and owners were planning to rebuild at higher levels.

Cyanobacteria is another huge issue. This blue-green algae occurs in lakes worldwide, feeding on pollution from agricultural run-off and human waste, and its toxins can pose a danger to the health of humans and animals.

In 2009, following a period of warm, settled, sunny weather, a smelly, gooey green mass of algae began to carpet the surface of Atitlán, at times affecting around thirty percent of the lake, and only fading as the temperature cooled and high winds broke it up. Smaller patches have returned in subsequent years, and the threat lingers for years as phosphorus- and nitrogen-rich nutrients remain in the lake.

---

hills) and for its cultural appeal – the lake's shores are dotted with thirteen diverse yet traditional Maya villages. With the exception of cosmopolitan **Panajachel** and **San Pedro La Laguna**, most of the pueblos are subsistence farming communities, and you can hike or take a boat between them; highlights include visits to **Santiago Atitlán**, where Maya men still wear traditional dress, and **Santa Cruz** and **San Marcos**, both of which are on excellent walking trails.

PANAJACHEL

Not too long ago **PANAJACHEL**, known locally as "Pana", was a quiet little village of Kaqchikel Maya, whose ancestors settled here centuries ago. These days, it's an established resort town, highly popular with foreigners

---

CRIME AROUND LAGO DE ATITLÁN

Though **crime** against tourists is rare, hikers have been sporadically robbed on paths around Lago de Atitlán and on the trails that climb the volcanoes. Take precautions: hire a local guide or walk in a large group. In the more remote areas, where foreigners are a much rarer sight, incidents are extremely uncommon.

---

and holidaying Guatemalans. Yet somehow it has retained a traditional feel in spite of its worldly nature: the river delta behind the town continues to be farmed, and the bustling Sunday market is a decidedly non-touristy affair. For travellers, the town is an inevitable destination – with good travel connections and a lovely setting, it makes a comfortable base for exploring the lake.

WHAT TO SEE AND DO

There are two main daytime activities in Pana: **shopping** and simply **hanging out**, enjoying the town's lakeside location. **Weaving** from all over Guatemala is sold here, mainly on Calle Santander. There is also a fruit and vegetable **market** at the top of Calle Principal. While the water looks inviting, it's best to swim elsewhere, as the lake is not clean close to town. You could rent a **kayak** (available on the lakeshore between the piers) for a few hours – mornings are usually much calmer.

Museo Lacustre

Inside the grounds of the Posada de Don Rodrigo, **Museo Lacustre** (Sun–Fri 8am–6pm, Sat 8am–7pm; Q35) is dedicated to the turbulent geological history that led to the creation of the

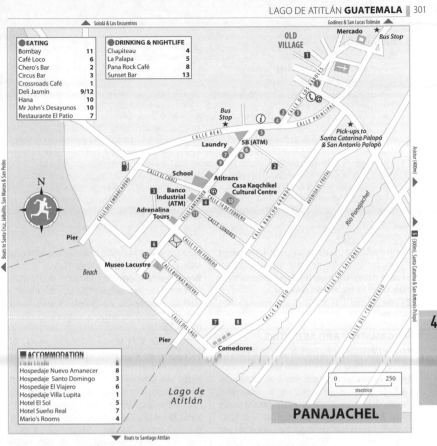

PANAJACHEL

lake. There's also a fascinating room dedicated to the underwater Maya site of Samabaj (see box, p.302) that re-creates what it's like to dive the site with the aid of high-tech gadgetry.

Casa Kaqchikel Cultural Centre

The handsome **Casa Kaqchikel Cultural Centre** (daily 8am–9pm; ⓦcasacakchiquel.com; free) on C 14 d e Febrero was originally built as a luxury hotel by a Swiss countess (guests included Che Guevara, Ingrid Bergman and Klaus Kinski). Today there's a fascinating collection of old photographs, postcards and documents relating to the lake displayed here. It's also home to two good restaurants (see p.303), and occasionally hosts musical events, readings and art exhibitions.

ARRIVAL AND DEPARTURE

By bus Buses to/from Sololá stop on C Principal and continue to the marketplace. The bus to/from Antigua departs from a separate stop on C Principal.
Destinations Antigua (Mon–Sat 10.45am; 2hr 30min); Chichicastenango (4–6 daily; 1hr 30min); Cocales (6 daily; 2hr); Guatemala City (8 daily; 3hr); Quetzaltenango (7 daily; 2hr 30min).

GETTING AROUND

By tuk-tuk Tuk-tuks (Q5/person) are everywhere in Pana.
By boat Most lakeside villages are served by *lanchas* – small, fast boats, which depart about every 30min. Panajachel has two piers. The main pier, at the end of C del Embarcadero, serves the villages on the northern side of the lake: Santa Cruz (about 15min), Jaibalito (20min), Tzununá (30min) and San Marcos (40min). This pier is also home to direct (15min) and non-direct (50min) boats to San Pedro, from where you can easily get to San Juan. The second pier, at the end of C Rancho Grande, is for Santiago Atitlán (25min by *lancha*) and

SAMABAJ

In December 2011 news emerged that the remains of an important ceremonial Maya settlement, dubbed **Samabaj**, had been discovered opposite the tiny village of Cerro de Oro on the south side of Lake Atitlán.

Samabaj is highly unusual on many fronts. Most of the Maya remains found in the Atitlán region date back 500 years or so, but Samabaj was a Preclassic Maya site that thrived more than 2000 years ago and was a place of pilgrimage, located on an offshore island. Around 250 AD, an abrupt rise in Atitlán's lakewater flooded Samabaj, preserving the monuments (including several steles and altars) around 18–30m below the surface. Links have been established with the Preclassic Maya superpower of El Mirador, way to the north in Petén.

Officially it's forbidden to dive the site, but Guatemala City-based scuba schools regularly ignore regulations and dive Samabaj most weekends, threatening its archeological integrity as divers pick over the ruins. ATI Divers based in Santa Cruz (see p.309) will know the latest situation, and whether diving at the site has been officially authorized. You can view many of the discoveries for yourself in Panajachel's Museo Lacustre (see p.309).

lake tours. The last boats on all routes leave around 7.30pm. Tourists pay Q10 for a short trip, or Q15–20 for a longer journey. Locals pay less. Some *lancheros* try to charge more for the last boat of the day.

By bike Emanuel, C 14 de Febrero, rents mountain bikes (Q75/day).

INFORMATION AND ACTIVITIES

Tourist information You can find some good historical and cultural information about Atitlán on ⓦatitlan.com.

Travel agents Atitrans, *Anexo Hotel Regis*, C Santander (☎7762 0146, ⓦatitrans.net), is a professional nationwide agency offering tours of the region and shuttle buses; Adrenalina Tours, C Santander (☎7762 6236, ⓦadrenalinatours.com) has shuttle bus connections and highland tours.

Yoga and fitness Panajachel Center, C Principal (☎7762 2936, ⓦthepanajachelcenter.com). Experienced hatha and vinyasa instructors, plus dance classes and fitness sessions. Also home to a café with a healthy menu.

ACCOMMODATION

There's no shortage of cheap accommodation in Pana, although most places are *hospedajes* as opposed to hostels with dorms.

Casa Linda Down an alley off the top of C Santander ☎7762 0386. A traditional, family-managed place in a quiet location with a gorgeous, fecund central garden to enjoy. There are 21 neat, simple, well-priced rooms, with balcony or veranda – they're priced per person, so solo travellers get a great deal. Q120

Hospedaje Nuevo Amanecer C Ramos, opposite the Santiago dock ☎7762 0636. This *hospedaje* has pleasant rooms and sparkling bathrooms with hot water and cable TV. Q200

Hospedaje Santo Domingo Off C Monterrey ☎7762 0236. A travellers' stronghold with a very tranquil setting

and a garden ideal for chilling. Rooms are simple but good value, some with en-suite bathrooms. Q120

Hospedaje El Viajero Off C Santander ☎7762 0128. Close to the lakeshore and set off the road, this attractive place has en-suite rooms with cable TV and a guests' kitchen. It's priced per person so singles are a steal at Q85. Q170

★**Hospedaje Villa Lupita** Callejón El Tino ☎7762 1201. Superb *hospedaje*, run by a welcoming family, in an old town location. Everything is beautifully set up: the pretty, very clean and good-value rooms (many with private bathroom) boast highland rugs and blankets and come with reading lights and good mattresses. Q110

Hotel El Sol Ctra Santa Catarina Palopó ☎7762 6090, ⓦhotelelsolpanajachel.com. Japanese-owned hotel with super-clean accommodation: an eight-person dorm with lockers plus four immaculate rooms. The bathrooms have reliable hot showers. The only slight drawback is the location, 1km east of the centre. Dorm Q65, doubles Q195

Hotel Sueño Real C Ramos, opposite the Santiago dock ☎7762 0608, ✉hotelsuenoreal@hotmail.com. Excellent little family-run guesthouse with immaculate rooms, each with *ikat* curtains and highland blankets. It's located very close to the lakeshore and breakfast is included. Q200

Mario's Rooms C Santander ☎7762 1313. This welcoming place maintains high standards and the accommodation has character, with attractive if smallish rooms (some with private bathroom) overlooking a slim, sunny garden courtyard bursting with pot plants. Free breakfast and drinking water. Q130

EATING

Panajachel has an abundance of restaurants. For really cheap, authentic Guatemalan food, head to the *comedores* close to the market.

Bombay Halfway along C Santander ☎7762 0611. An

★**TREAT YOURSELF**

Mr John's Desayunos Casa Kaqchikel Cultural Centre, C 14 de Febrero ☏4298 1415, ⓦmister-jon.com. Taking the morning shift inside Casa Kaqchikel, this is the place for an American-style breakfast in Pana, with excellent pancakes, omelettes, granola and all the hearty sides you could desire. Tues–Sun 8am–noon.

inviting vegetarian place where the menu features a hit-list of global classics: falafel, Indonesian *gado-gado*, pasta and Mexican dishes, most priced at around Q50. Mon & Wed–Sun 11am–9pm.

Café Loco C Santander ☏5029 2195, ⓦbrownholic.com. Hip Korean-owned café, where every imaginable coffee combo is available from an assortment of high-tech coffee machinery, prepared by a couple of complete java-istas. Incongruously enough, their other branch is in Gangnam. Asian and local meals are also offered. Daily 9am–8pm.

Chero's Bar C de los Árboles ☏7762 0254. Simple *pupusería* where the Salvador-style healthy snacks are made right in front of you. A good feed is around Q25. Always lively as it doubles as a sociable bar with lots of drink specials. Daily 11am–10pm.

Circus Bar C de los Árboles ☏7762 2056, ⓦcircusbar .com.gt. Serving the best pizza in Pana (from Q50), this atmospheric restaurant offers good salads, bruschettas, pasta and grilled meats. There's a full bar including cocktails (and mocktails) and live music (jazz, salsa, flamenco, bolero, *trova*) every night at 7.30pm. Daily noon–midnight.

★**Crossroads Café** C del Campanario 0–27 ☏5292 8439, ⓦcrossroadscafepana.com. A real find, this simple yet very welcoming little place is run by an American perfectionist who selects, blends and roasts his own beans from the Guatemalan highlands and far beyond. Also offers herbal teas, rich hot chocolate and delicious fresh pastries and cakes. Tues–Sat 9am–1pm & 2.30–6pm.

★**Deli Jasmín** Bottom of C Santander ☏7762 2585. The most delightful garden setting for a bite to eat in Pana, and also serves some of the best food. Healthy breakfasts, sandwiches, salads, Mexican dishes and *tempeh* (an Indonesian soybean product, somewhat similar to tofu); most dishes are Q30–45. There's a second branch halfway up C Santander with the same menu. Mon & Wed–Sun 7am–6pm.

Hana Casa Kaqchikel Cultural Centre, C 14 de Febrero ☏4298 1415, ⓦrestaurantehana.com. Terrific new Japanese-owned restaurant in a historic courtyard setting, ideal for sushi (around Q60 for a big plate), udon dishes, donburi and tempura. There's a good beer selection, and

sake and green tea is available. Also offers takeaway with free delivery. Tues–Sun noon–9pm.

Restaurante El Patio Towards the top of C Santander ☏7762 2041. The menu here offers pretty standard Guatemalan grub, but it's famous for its Monday *caldo*. Portions are massive and the *licuados* (shakes) are cheap (Q10). Daily 8am–9pm.

DRINKING AND NIGHTLIFE

Pana's mini Zona Viva (around the southern end of C de los Árboles) buzzes on weekend nights. The *Circus Bar* (see above) has live music nightly.

Chapiteau Southern end of C de los Árboles ☏7762 2056, ⓦpanajachel.com/chapiteau. Disco with a lively dancefloor on weekend nights. Salsa instructors are often at hand early in the evening to sort out your steps. Cover around Q25. Wed–Sat 7pm–1am.

La Palapa C Santander ☏4568 8033, ⓦlapalapa.com.gt. Large, open-sided bar-restaurant with live music (blues, rock, *trova* and acoustic) several times a week. Food (everything from breakfasts to a great Saturday barbecue) is also served and trivia (quiz) nights are popular. Daily 7am–1am.

Pana Rock Café Towards the top of C Santander ☏7762 2144, ⓦpanarockcafe.com. A kind of *Hard Rock Café* tribute bar with an old American school bus converted into sitting areas. Popular for sports games, and there's live rock music on weekend nights. Daily 8am–1am.

Sunset Bar By the lake ☏7762 0003. For a sundowner this bar can't be beat, with fine volcano and lake views; overpriced food is also served. Daily 11am–midnight.

DIRECTORY

Banks Banco Industrial, C Santander, has an ATM, and there's a 5B ATM at the northern end of the road too.

Emergencies Contact the local English-speaking PROATUR rep (☏5874 9450) if you need assistance.

Internet ICC, C Santander (daily 8am–10pm).

Laundry Lavandería Santander, C Santander (Mon–Sat 7am–8pm), charges Q5 for a pound of washing, drying and folding.

Medical care Dr Edgar Barreno speaks good English; his office is down the first street that branches to the right off C de los Árboles (☏7762 1008).

Pharmacy Farmacia La Unión, C Santander.

Post office C Santander and C 15 de Febrero.

Telephone Get Guated Out, C de los Árboles, has very inexpensive rates to landlines and mobiles worldwide (and has internet access).

AROUND PANAJACHEL

It's well worth taking the time to explore the area **around Pana**, the best connected

4

of all the lake towns. The landscape surrounding the different villages is so diverse that it's easy to forget they all look over the same lake.

Sololá

Perched on a natural balcony overlooking Lago de Atitlán, **SOLOLÁ** is a fascinating settlement, largely overlooked by the majority of travellers. It is probably the largest Maya town in the country, with a majority of residents still wearing traditional costume – the women covered in striped red cloth and the men in their outlandish "space cowboy" shirts, woollen kilt-like aprons and wildly embroidered trousers. Although the town itself is nothing much to look at, its Friday **market** is one of Central America's finest, drawing traders from all over the highlands, as well as thousands of local Maya. There's also another, smaller, market on Tuesdays.

To **get to** Sololá, take a bus from Panajachel (every 30min 5am–7pm).

SANTIAGO ATITLÁN

SANTIAGO ATITLÁN, a microcosm of Guatemala's past, sits sheltered on the side of an inlet on the opposite side of the lake from Panajachel. The largest of the lakeside villages, it's one of the last bastions of traditional life, serving as the main centre for the Tz'utujil-speaking Maya. During the day it's a fairly commercial place and you should expect some sales pressure from vendors, but by mid-afternoon, when the boats have left, things become much quieter.

It's worth taking a few hours to wander around – and if you want to get away from the foreign crowds that pervade other parts of the lake, consider staying for a night or two.

WHAT TO SEE AND DO

There's not much to do in Santiago other than stroll around and soak up the atmosphere. During the day the town's main street, which runs from the dock to the plaza, is lined with weaving shops and souvenir stands.

Market day is Friday, with a smaller event on Sunday.

Museo Cojolya

The one museum in town, the **Museo Cojolya** (Mon–Fri 9am–5pm; free; ⓦcojolya.org), about 300m up the main drag from the dock on the right, takes textiles as its subject. Inside you'll find excellent displays about the tradition of backstrap weaving in Santiago. You can see local women in action here, weaving classes can be arranged (contact them two days in advance) and a range of very good quality shirts, bags and souvenirs are sold. Guided tours of weavers' homes and workshops can also be arranged (Q75/person).

Santiago church

Santiago's whitewashed Baroque Catholic **church**, which dates from 1571, is an essential visit. The huge central altarpiece culminates in the shape of a mountain peak and a cross, which symbolizes the Maya world tree. On the right as you enter, there's a stone memorial commemorating **Father Stanley Rother**, who died here in 1981, defending his parishioners against the military and death squads.

Casa de Maximón

Folk Catholicism plays an important role in the life of Santiago – one of the few places where Maya still pay homage to **Maximón**, the "evil" saint (see box, p.297), known locally as Rilej Mam. Every May he changes residence – any child will take you to see him: just ask for the "Casa de Maximón". It costs a few quetzales to enter his current home and take his picture.

ARRIVAL AND INFORMATION

By boat *Lanchas* link Santiago with both San Pedro (15min) and Panajachel (20min); they leave when full.

By bus The town is well connected by bus to Cocales and Guatemala City's Centra Sur terminal (8 daily, 3am–4pm; 3hr). Microbuses also leave very regularly for San Lucas Tolimán.

Tourist information Consult the excellent website ⓦsantiagoatitlan.com for history and information in English.

ACCOMMODATION

Hospedaje Colonial Rosita Just south of the church ☎ 5397 7187. An old-fashioned *hospedaje* with basic rooms, a vigilant owner and communal bathrooms. **Q110**

Hotel Chi-Nim Ya On the left uphill from the dock ☎ 7721 7131. Long-running place with simple rooms (some with private bath) set around a courtyard. **Q120**

EATING

Café Rafa 400m up from the dock ☎ 7721 7896. A casual café with street tables ideal for people-watching, fast wi-fi and a fine line-up of coffee creations (beans are sourced from the owner's farm), smoothies and snacks. Mon–Sat 9am–9pm.

Comedor Brendy By the main square. *Comedor* specializing in filling set lunches (from Q20), including rich *caldos*. Daily 7am–7pm.

CHUITINAMIT

Opposite Santiago Atitlán, on the lower flanks of the San Pedro volcano, the Postclassic Maya ruins of **Chuitinamit** are worth a quick visit. This modest site, originally called Chiya, was the fortified capital of the Tz'utujil before the conquistador Alvarado and his Kaqchikel allies laid waste to the place in 1524 – arriving in a flotilla of three hundred canoes. Sadly, the site is in pretty poor shape today as locals have re-carved the stone monuments, creating cartoon-like figures, and have even added a Virgin Mary! That said, Chuitinamit is still actively used by shamans for ceremonies, and its position high above the lake affords panoramic views. The paths around the site are littered with Maya ceramic fragments and obsidian arrowheads and blades.

ARRIVAL AND DEPARTURE

By boat To get to Chuitinamit you'll need to hire a boat (around Q100 for a return trip of 1hr) from the dock in Santiago; it's a steep 10min hike up to the ruins.

SAN PEDRO LA LAGUNA

Around to the west of Volcán San Pedro lies the village of **SAN PEDRO LA LAGUNA**, considered by many travellers as the place to be. It's *the* party destination on the lake, with bars pumping out reggae and trance, which upsets some locals (most of whom

are evangelical Christians). Periodically, crackdowns curtail the party action.

If you've no interest in the high life, you'll still find plenty to do in San Pedro, with yoga classes, some good language schools and plenty of hiking trails. It's the kind of place people love or hate – come and make your own mind up.

WHAT TO SEE AND DO

As the lake water is quite polluted around San Pedro, the town's two **swimming pools**, both close to the Santiago dock, are popular places to cool off. You'll also find **thermal pools** between the two boat docks for relaxing. **Volcán San Pedro**, which towers above the village at some 3020m, can be climbed in around four hours. Drop by the visitors centre on the lower slopes of the peak, and hire a **guide** (Q100), which is essential as the foliage is dense and the route very difficult to find. There's another great hike to **Indian Nose**, with arguably an even better perspective of Atitlán – contact the Excursion Big Foot and Casa Verde tour operators (see below) for a guide. For something less strenuous, consider taking out a **kayak**.

ARRIVAL AND DEPARTURE

By boat There are two docks in San Pedro. All boats from Panajachel and villages on the north side of the lake, including Santa Cruz and San Marcos, arrive and depart from the Panajachel dock on the north side of town. Boats from Santiago Atitlán use a separate dock to the southeast, a 10min walk away.

By bus The public bus stop is in front of the church. Buses connect San Pedro with Quetzaltenango (7 daily; 2hr 15min) and Guatemala City (9 daily; 3hr 30min). Minibuses (about every 20min) link the town with San Juan, San Pablo and San Marcos, or you can hire a tuk-tuk. Casa Verde Tours (see below) run shuttles to Antigua (2hr 45min), Chichicastenango (1hr 30min), Cobán (9hr), Guatemala City (3hr 45min), Huehuetenango (4hr), Lanquín (11hr), Quetzaltenango (2hr 15min) and San Cristóbal de las Casas in Mexico (11hr).

INFORMATION AND TOURS

Tourist information There's no tourist office. The website ⊛ tzununya.com offers plenty of online guidance.

Casa Verde Tours Up from the Panajachel dock ☎ 5837 9092. Offers horseriding, hikes to Indian Nose and community walks; precise prices depend on numbers but rates are reasonable.

4

Excursion Big Foot Left of the Panajachel dock ☎7721 8203. Organizes treks up San Pedro volcano and to Indian Nose, horseriding and bicycle rental at Q60/day.

ACCOMMODATION

San Pedro has some of the cheapest accommodation in Latin America, with lots of choice.

Casa Elena Left from the Panajachel dock ☎5310 9243. No frills, just spartan, cheap rooms; you pay more for a private bath. There's a dock at the rear for swimming and a guests' kitchen. Q70

Hostal Fé Right from the Panajachel dock ☎5273 6688, ⓦhostelfe.com. This party hostel occupies one of the ugliest buildings in town, a Soviet-style concrete monster, and the formula is pretty simple: basic digs and a bar-resto by the lake with lots of drinking games and organized entertainment to rev up the young punters. Rates include breakfast. Dorms Q60, doubles Q225

Hotel Gran Sueño Left from the Panajachel dock ☎7721 8110. Run by a welcoming family, this likeable place has clean, smallish rooms all with private bathrooms and TV. Some have nice touches like wall maps, and those on the upper level have lake views. Q135

Hotel María Elena Left from Panajachel dock ☎5098 1256. Two-storey block with spacious rooms, all with private bathrooms. The communal balconies have hammocks at the front for quality swinging time. Q100

Hotel Pinocchio Between the docks ☎5845 7018. Yes, it's a large concrete block, but the rooms are kept tidy, the huge garden is lovely, staff are welcoming and there's a guests' kitchen. Prices are flexible according to demand, so you should be able to bargain at quiet times. Q100

Mr Mullet's Left of Panajachel dock ☎4419 0566. A popular party hostel with simple, clean rooms with good mattresses and four-bed dorms with huge lockers; bathrooms (with hot water) are shared. There's a garden at the rear for chilling, and a bar area. Dorms Q35, doubles Q100

Zoola Between the docks ☎5547 4857. Love-it-or-hate-it Israeli-owned lakeside hostel popular with young travellers. There's a great chill-out space shaded by canvas and a (tiny) lakeside pool, dorms are pleasant enough and there's tasty Middle Eastern food. However, the stoner vibe won't appeal to all. Minimum two-night stay; no advance reservations. Dorms Q35, doubles Q100

EATING

Vegetarians are well catered for in San Pedro, and there are also a few typical Guatemalan *comedores* in the centre of the village.

★**Café La Puerta** Between the docks ☎5098 1272. A lovely garden setting and the best food in San Pedro: an inventive menu of freshly prepared, healthy food including home-made pasta, delicious sandwiches, salads, guacamole and lots of great breakfast choices (Q20–35), smoothies and juices. Daily 7.30am–9pm.

D'Noz Panajachel dock ☎5578 0201, ⓦdnozsanpedro .com. This bar/restaurant offers a global menu – Mexican, Indian and Chinese – friendly service, free films (8.30pm every night) and a long happy hour (5–8pm). Daily 8am–1am.

Home Between the docks ☎4255 2314. Vegetarian restaurant that enjoys a leafy garden setting with tables under trees and a wide choice of curries, burritos, tofu stir-frys, wraps, lentil dishes and great set lunches (Q30). Wed–Sun 9.30am–4.30pm.

Idea Connection Between the docks ☎7721 8356. Superb, very welcoming Italian-owned garden café with delicious breakfasts (from Q25), pasta and pizza. It also operates as a bakery; check out their delicious bread and croissants. Fast wi-fi, and live music some evenings. Mon–Wed & Fri–Sun 7am–5pm & 6–9.30pm.

Nick's Place By the Panajachel dock ☎7721 8065. Popular, locally owned restaurant with a superb-value menu of international and Guatemalan food (many meals are below Q30) and a fine lakefront location. Daily 7am–11pm.

Zoola Between the docks ☎5547 4857. This hotel/restaurant has low tables set under a tent and serves commendable Middle Eastern food. Service is very slooooow, so take a good book or play backgammon while you wait. Daily 8am–10pm.

DRINKING AND NIGHTLIFE

San Pedro's vibrant bars are concentrated on the trail between the docks, and around the Pana dock. Most places have happy hours. After the 1am curfew "after parties" start up in private homes.

Alegre Pub Above Panajachel dock ☎7721 8100. Pub showing European football, NFL and NBA games, and serving comfort grub such as Sunday roasts and shepherd's pie. Also hosts darts and pool tournaments. Daily 9am–1am.

El Barrio Between the docks ☎4424 6941. An intimate little bar with a garden that has something on most nights of the week: Tuesdays are LGBT-friendly, and there's a quiz (trivia) on Wednesdays. Also serves reasonable grub. Mon–Fri 5pm–1am, Sat & Sun 10am–1am.

Buddha Bar Between the docks ☎4178 7979, ⓦthebuddhaguatemala.com. This scruffy multistorey American-owned bar is popular for live music (everything from country to reggae; open-mike night is Monday), DJ and comedy events, pool tables, dart board, films and general craic. Daily noon–1am.

DIRECTORY

Banks Banrural (Mon–Fri 8am–5pm, Sat 9am–12.30pm) has an ATM, and there's a second ATM by the Panajachel dock.

Internet Wi-fi is very widespread in San Pedro. Head to *Idea Connection* café (see opposite) for fast connections and Skype calls.

Language schools Casa Rosario, south of Santiago Atitlán dock (☎5613 6401, ⍟casarosario.com); Cooperativa Spanish School, 400m south of Panajachel dock (☎7721 8214, ⍟cooperativeschoolsanpedro .edu.gt); Corazón Maya, south of Santiago Atitlán dock (☎7721 8160, ⍟corazonmaya.com); San Pedro Spanish School, between the piers (☎5715 4604, ⍟sanpedro spanishschool.com).

SAN JUAN LA LAGUNA

Just 2km west of San Pedro, the tranquil village of **SAN JUAN LA LAGUNA** specializes in the weaving of *petates*, lake-reed mats and textiles: two large co-ops, Las Artesanías de San Juan, signposted on the left from the dock, and the Asociación de Mujeres de Color, on the right, have weaving for sale. There's also a shrine to **Maximón** (see box, p.297) dressed in local garb in the village centre, next door to *Restaurant Chi'nimaya*.

Contact the community guide association, Rupalaj K'istalin (☎4772 2527, ✉rupalajkistalin@gmail.com; tours US$15–18/person) to visit natural dye-weaving co-ops, local forests for

---

★ TREAT YOURSELF

Café El Artesano ☎4555 4773. This delightful garden café-restaurant in the village centre is owned by Ditres, a chef from the capital who tired of city life. His platters of cheese and cured meats (around Q150 for two people) are simply sublime, featuring a dozen or more artisan products that he's sourced from across Guatemala, which he serves with olives, nuts, home-made bread and a pickle or two. Uncork a bottle of wine and you're set. The rest of the menu takes in smoked fish, delicious salads (from Q25) and grilled meats. Nov–April Mon–Wed 10am–7pm, Thurs 10am–10pm, Fri 10am–4.30pm; shorter hours in rainy season.

---

birdwatching, coffee plantations, archeological remains, local craftsmen and Maya ceremonies.

ARRIVAL AND INFORMATION

Regular pick-ups and minibuses run between San Pedro and San Juan, tuk-tuks are around Q15, or you can walk. Consult the excellent community website ⍟sanjuanlalaguna.org for all things San Juan.

ACCOMMODATION AND EATING

Hospedaje Estrella del Lago Next to Asociación de Mujeres de Color. A well-run place with attractive, simple rooms and a guests' kitchen. Rates are charged per person. **Q150**

SAN MARCOS LA LAGUNA

SAN MARCOS LA LAGUNA, on the northwest shore of the lake, is the most bohemian place around Atitlán, home to legions of foreigners of an artistic and spiritually minded persuasion. If you're enticed by holistic centres, rebirthing classes and all things esoteric, this is the place for you. The village has a decidedly relaxed feel – there's no real bar scene – so it's a perfect place to read a book in your hammock and enjoy the natural beauty of the lake. The bulk of hotels and restaurants are close to the water, while the Maya village sits on higher ground further away from the shore.

WHAT TO SEE AND DO

Apart from a huge stone **church**, built to replace the colonial original destroyed in the 1976 earthquake, there are no sights as such (though the sartorial tastes of some of the gringo residents are amusing). The **San Marcos Holistic Centre** (⍟sanmholisticcentre.com) offers massage, reflexology, kinesiology and natural remedies. Activities include meditation at the long-established *Las Pirámides* (⍟laspiramidesdelka.com) and hatha yoga (drop-in classes US$5) at the impressive new Kaivalya (⍟yoga retreatguatemala.com). Yoga Forest (⍟theyogaforest.org), twenty minutes' walk above the village, has a stunning location for its classes (daily rate US$40) and courses.

There are wooden jetties by the shore for swimming. On a clear day, views of the lake's three **volcanoes** (including double-coned Tolimán) are sublime, while in the distance you can glimpse the grey peak of Acatenango near Antigua.

ARRIVAL AND DEPARTURE

By boat *Lanchas* from other lakeside villages, including San Pedro (10min), Santa Cruz and Pana (40min), pull up at the dock, which is about a 5min walk from the centre of town. The last boats leave at 5pm.

By bus and shuttle bus If you're travelling by public bus to Quetzaltenango travel via San Pedro; to Guatemala City and Antigua it's quickest via Panajachel. Casa Verde (☎5837 9092), inland from the dock, organizes shuttle bus connections to destinations across Guatemala (all via San Pedro).

ACCOMMODATION

San Marcos has some good accommodation, though few places with rock-bottom rates. All the following are signposted from the dock.

Aaculaax 300m west of the dock ☎5803 7243, ⓦaaculaax.com. This fantasy eco-hotel is built from thousands of recycled bottles and wood, incorporating lots of stained glass and artistic touches. It's quite upmarket, but the budget choices here are very attractive. Breakfast is included. $\overline{Q120}$

Circles Uphill from dock ☎3327 8961, ⓦcircles-cafe .com. Above a pretty café, the accommodation here is clean and well-presented, and there's a little terrace and garden for relaxing. Dorms $\overline{Q75}$, rooms $\overline{Q150}$

Eco-Hotel La Paz Uphill from dock ☎5061 5316, ⓦlakeatitlanlapaz.com. Very spacious, rustic cottages, a superior six-bed, two-storey dorm, good home-cooking and yoga classes. Guests get the run of a lovely leafy garden with hammocks. Dorms $\overline{Q70}$, doubles $\overline{Q160}$

Hospedaje Panabaj In the village ☎5678 0181. Two-storey block in a quiet location, with basic rooms that face a garden. The shared bathrooms are kept tidy. $\overline{Q80}$

Hostal del Lago 150m east of dock ☎5898 9872. Social, boho hostel with simple, basic dorms and reasonable rooms. There's lots going on: yoga sessions by the lake, a popular bar, live music and film and theatre nights; a good breakfast is included. Dorms $\overline{Q60}$, doubles $\overline{Q160}$

Hostel San Marcos West of dock ☎3009 5537, ⓦhostelsanmarcos.com. Just steps from the shore, this backpackers' stronghold has decent dorms and rooms and an in-house café-restaurant (with a wood-fired pizza oven). Rates include breakfast. Dorms $\overline{Q70}$, doubles $\overline{Q170}$

El Paco Real Uphill from the dock ☎5723 5426. Very well-built thatched bungalows, some sleeping up to four

and many with private bathrooms, dotted around a shady garden. There's a good bar/restaurant too. $\overline{Q150}$

El Tul y Sol Short walk west of the dock ☎5293 7997, ⓦeltulysolatitlan.jimdo.com. Very spacious, superb-value rooms at the rear of a lakeside. You get a huge bed, nice wooden furniture, private bathrooms, lake views from a shared balcony and even a free breakfast for very little here. It's a total bargain for single travellers. $\overline{Q120}$

EATING AND DRINKING

Allala By the football field. Authentic Japanese-owned garden restaurant ideal for delicious noodle dishes, veggie tempura, sushi, *onigiri*, miso soup and sake. Daily 6–10pm.

Comedor Mi Marquensita Susi In the village. Simple local place, just off the Parque Central, ideal for eating your fill of *comida típica* at very reasonable prices. Daily 7am–7pm.

La Fé Inland from the dock ☎5994 4320. Well-regarded restaurant with an eclectic menu of home-made soups, burritos, burgers and kebabs. It's renowned for its authentic Indian curries, and the *nan* breads are stupendously good. The English owner plans to open a tapas place across the lane. Daily 7.30am–10.30pm.

Hostal del Lago 150m east of the dock ☎5898 9872. This hostel's bar is the busiest spot in town, with different drink specials every night, and live music. Daily noon–10pm.

Il Giardino Inland from the dock ☎4902 5915. This (vegetarian) garden restaurant serves fresh pasta, great crêpes and breakfasts, and bakes its bread in house. They play classical music until noon here, offer fine juices and also have a full bar. Daily 8am–9pm.

JAIBALITO

JAIBALITO, an isolated lakeside settlement nestling between soaring slopes clad with *milpa* (corn), remains resolutely Kaqchikel – very little Spanish is spoken, and few of the local women have ever journeyed much beyond Lago de Atitlán – though the opening of a few hotels means that outside influence is growing.

From Jaibalito it's a thirty-minute walk to Santa Cruz along a glorious, easy-to-follow path that parallels the steep hillside.

ACCOMMODATION AND EATING

La Casa del Mundo ☎5218 5332, ⓦlacasadelmundo .com. Excellent lodge that sits pretty on a little peninsula with panoramic lake views from its cute cottages, and great food. $\overline{Q300}$

★**Posada Jaibalito** ☎5598 1957, ⓦposadajaibalito .com. A superb guesthouse owned by an ethically minded

German. It has a fine six-bed dorm (with lockers and en-suite bathroom), great private rooms, tasty and inexpensive Guatemalan and European food (Q15–27) and very cheap drinks. Dorm <u>Q38</u>, doubles <u>Q75</u>

SANTA CRUZ LA LAGUNA

Set well back from the lake on a shelf 100m or so above the water, **SANTA CRUZ LA LAGUNA** is the largest of the lake's northwest villages, with a population of around four thousand. There isn't much to see in the village itself, apart from a fine sixteenth-century church, and most people spend their time by the bucolic lakeshore, which is fringed by mature trees, dotted with holiday homes and a handful of lovely hotels.

It's a good base for swimming, chilling out with a book, or exploring the tough but spectacular inland **hiking** trails. Tours Atitlán (☏ 5355 8849, ⓦ tours-atitlan .com), owned by Maya guide Pedro Juan Solis, offers lots of tours including excellent mountain-bike trips (around Q375), birdwatching walks and treks. You can rent **kayaks** for Q15 per hour from Los Elementos (west of the dock; ☏ 5359 8328, ⓦ kayakguatemala.com), and dive the lake with ATI Divers (based at the *Iguana Perdida*; ☏ 5706 4117, ⓦ atidivers.com).

ARRIVAL AND DEPARTURE

By boat *Lanchas* connect Santa Cruz with Panajachel (6am–7pm; about every 30min).

ACCOMMODATION AND EATING

★**Café Sabor Cruceño** Maya village ☏ 5287 1391. Offers truly spectacular views and memorable food, featuring local specialities like *jocón* (meat cooked with sesame and pumpkin seeds, peppers and *tomatillos*). The café benefits the community, providing training for the Maya residents of Santa Cruz. Mon–Fri 11am–3pm.

★**Iguana Perdida** On the shore ☏ 5706 4117, ⓦ laiguanaperdida.com. The hub of the community, the *Iguana* has a really convivial atmosphere. There are basic dorms and budget rooms, but it's the lakefront location and social vibe that really make this place. Dinner is a three-course communal affair. The hotel also offers yoga classes, an open-mike night (Thurs), TV lounge, book exchange, kayak rental, scuba diving and great travel advice. Dorms <u>Q35</u>, doubles <u>Q100</u>

The western highlands

Guatemala's **western highlands** are home to some of the most dramatic and breathtaking scenery in the country. The area also has the highest concentration of one of the Americas' largest indigenous groups, the **Maya**. Languages and traditional costume still remain largely intact – probably the most striking dress of all is that worn in **Todos Santos Cuchumatán**. From the wild mountains surrounding **Nebaj** to the bustling colourful market of **Chichicastenango**, you are bound to be captivated by the region's sublime scenery, culture and colour. The western highlands are also home to the country's second most populous city, **Quetzaltenango**, which draws numerous language students and voluntary workers. Travelling in remote parts of the highlands can be arduous, but the main highways are all paved.

4

CHICHICASTENANGO

CHICHICASTENANGO, Guatemala's "*mecca del turismo*", is known best for its twice-weekly **markets**, which are some of the most colourful in the country. It also offers an insight into indigenous Maya society in the highlands. Over the years, Maya culture and folk Catholicism have merged here, with indigenous rituals continuing often under the wings of the Church. You'll also see traditional weaving, mostly by the women, who wear beautiful, heavily embroidered *huipiles*. For the town's **fiesta** (Dec 14–21), and on Sundays, a handful of *cofrades* (elders of the religious hierarchy) still wear traditional clothing and carry spectacular silver processional crosses and incense burners.

WHAT TO SEE AND DO

Although Chichi's main attraction is undoubtedly its vibrant markets, the town also offers other sights of cultural interest.

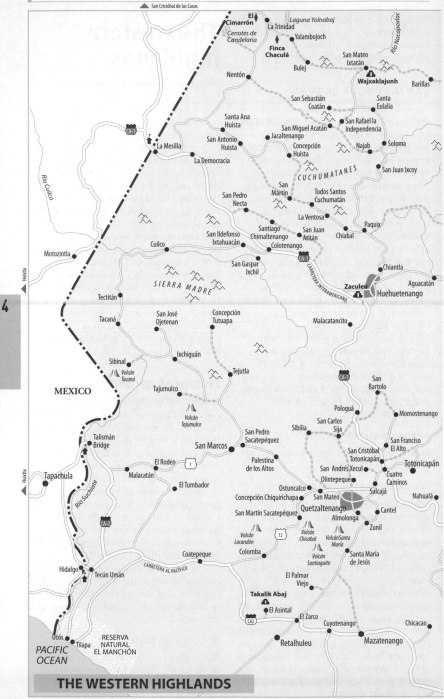

THE WESTERN HIGHLANDS

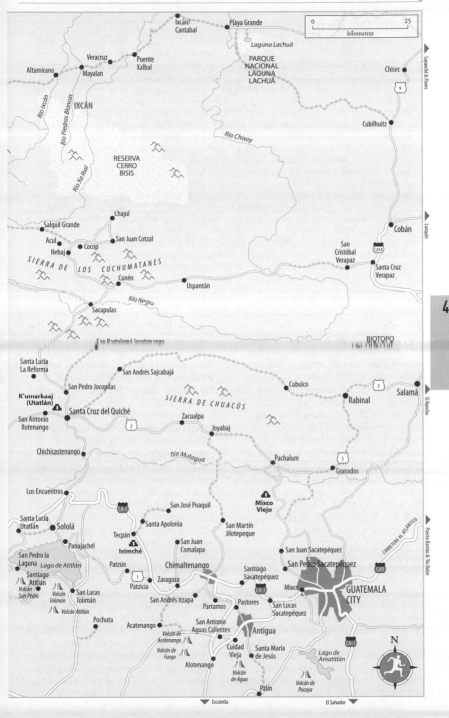

4

HIGHLAND HISTORY

The **Maya** have lived in the Guatemalan highlands for some two thousand years. The Spanish arrived in the area in 1523, making their first permanent settlement at **Iximché** (see p.299), the capital of their Kaqchikel Maya allies. Not long after, conquistador **Pedro de Alvarado** moved his base to a site near modern-day Antigua, and gradually brought the highlands under a degree of Spanish control. Eventually, **Antigua** also served as the administrative centre for the whole of Central America and Chiapas (now in Mexico). In 1773, however, the city was destroyed by a massive earthquake and the capital was moved to its present site.

The arrival of the Spanish caused great hardship for the native Maya. Not only were their numbers decimated by Spanish weaponry, but waves of infectious diseases also swept through the population. Over time, indigenous labour became the backbone of the Spanish Empire, with its **indigo** and **cacao** plantations. The departure of the Spanish in 1821 and subsequent **independence** brought little change at village level. Ladino authority replaced that of the Spanish, but Maya were still required to work the coastal plantations and at times were press-ganged to work, often in horrific conditions.

In the mid-1960s, **guerrilla movements** began to develop in opposition to Guatemala's military rule, seeking support from the highland population and establishing themselves in the area. The Maya became the victims in this process, caught between the guerrillas and the army. Some 440 villages were destroyed; around 200,000 people died and thousands more fled, seeking refuge in Mexico. Despite the harsh conditions and terrific adversity, the Maya survived: traditional costume is still worn in many areas (particularly by women), a plethora of indigenous languages is still spoken and some remote areas even still observe the 260-day Tzolkin calendar.

Markets

Most visitors come to Chichicastenango for its **markets**, which fill the town's central plaza and all surrounding streets on Sundays and Thursdays. Fruit and vegetable vendors congregate inside the covered Centro Comercial (which adjoins the plaza); most of the other stalls sell textiles and souvenirs. The crowds are eclectic – you'll be surrounded by myriad foreigners and commercial traders, as well as Maya weavers from throughout the highlands – but many of the goods are geared to the tourist trade, so initial prices are high and haggling is essential. The trading starts early in the morning, and goes on until mid-afternoon.

Iglesia de Santo Tomás

The **Iglesia de Santo Tomás**, on the southeast corner of the plaza, was built in 1540 and is now a local religious centre, home to a faith that blends pre-Columbian and Catholic rituals. For the faithful, the entire building is alive with the souls of the dead, each located in a specific part of the church. Before entering, it's customary to make offerings in a fire at the base of the steps or to burn incense. Don't enter the building by the front door, which is reserved for *cofrades* and senior church officials; use the side door instead and be warned that **taking photographs** inside the building is considered deeply offensive – don't even contemplate it.

Beside the church is a former **monastery**, now used by the parish administration. It was here that a Spanish priest, Francisco Ximénez, became the first outsider to be shown the Popol Vuh, the Maya holy book; it is said that the Maya became interested in Christian worship here in the early eighteenth century, after Ximénez showed respect for their own religion by reading the book.

Museo Rossbach

On the south side of the plaza, often hidden by stalls on market day, the **Museo Rossbach** (Tues, Wed, Fri & Sat 8am–12.30pm & 2–4pm, Thurs 8am–4pm, Sun 8am–2pm; Q5) houses a broad collection of pre-Columbian artefacts, mostly small pieces of ceramics (including some demonic-looking incense burners), jade necklaces and earrings, and stone carvings (some of which are two

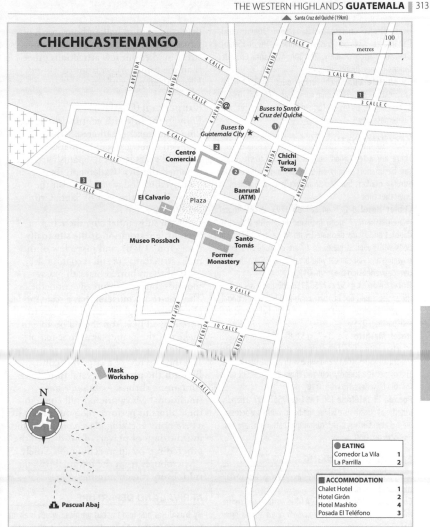

Santa Cruz del Quiché (19km)

CHICHICASTENANGO

Buses to Santa
Cruz del Quiché

Buses to
Guatemala City

Centro
Comercial

Chichi
Turkaj
Tours

Banrural
(ATM)

El Calvario   Plaza

Museo Rossbach   Santo
Tomás

Former
Monastery

9 CALLE

Mask
Workshop

N

EATING
Comedor La Vila   1
La Parrilla   2

ACCOMMODATION
Chalet Hotel   1
Hotel Girón   2
Hotel Mashito   4
Posada El Teléfono   3

Pascual Abaj

Los Encuentros & Hwy-1 (18km)

4

thousand years old). Also on show are some interesting old photographs of Chichi and local weavings, masks and carvings.

Pascual Abaj

Many of the hills that surround Chichicastenango are topped with shrines. The closest of these, **Pascual Abaj**, is less than 1km south of the plaza and regularly visited by outsiders. The shrine comprises small altars facing a stern pre-Columbian sculpture. Offerings are usually overseen by a shaman, and range from flowers to sacrificed chickens, always incorporating plenty of incense, alcohol and incantations. Be sensitive about taking photographs. To get to Pascual Abaj, walk down the hill beside Santo Tomás, take the first right, 9 Calle, and follow this as it winds its way out of town then uphill through a pine forest.

ARRIVAL AND INFORMATION

By bus Chichi doesn't have a bus terminal, but all buses stop by the corner of 5 C and 5 Av north of the centre.

Destinations Guatemala City (every 20min; 3hr); Panajachel (4–6 buses daily; 1hr 15min); Quetzaltenango (7 daily; 2hr 30min); Santa Cruz del Quiché (every 20min; 30min).

By shuttle bus Chichi Turkaj Tours (☎ 5070 6580, ✉ chichiturkajtours@yahoo.com) at 7 Av 05–31 offers shuttle buses to Lago de Atitlán, Antigua and Guatemala City.

ACCOMMODATION

There are a few good budget hotels in town. These can be in short supply on Saturday nights before the Sunday market, but you shouldn't have a problem at any other time.

Chalet Hotel 3 C 7–44 ☎ 7756 1793, 🖥 chalethotel guatemala.com. A good highland inn, with attractive doubles and twins decorated with Maya *artesanías* and beds with woollen blankets; all are en suite. It's solar-powered and you can eat your breakfast (Q25) on the roof terrace overlooking the town. Q195

Hotel Girón 6 C 4–52 ☎ 7756 1156. This hotel, set just off the street, could not be more central. It offers functional, spacious, pine-trimmed rooms with clean bathrooms and safe parking. Q150

Hotel Mashito 8 C 1–7 ☎ 5168 7178. Lime green structure with a selection of simple, clean, well-presented rooms, all with cable TV and some with private bathrooms. The owner is a friendly soul and there are excellent rates for solo travellers. No wi-fi. Q80

Posada El Teléfono 8 C 1–64 ☎ 7756 1197. Friendly, functional guesthouse where the basic rooms are accessed via rickety stairways. The communal bathrooms are kept pretty clean. Q60

EATING AND DRINKING

Many restaurants are quite pricey as they're geared to day-tripping Westerners.

Comedor La Vila 6 Av & 5 C. A little north of the centre, this clean *comedor* scores for *comida típica* at low rates. Daily 7.30am–6pm.

La Parrilla 6 C & 5 Av ☎ 7756 1321. Set in a small courtyard, this is a good place to get away from the market crowds. It offers great breakfasts (from Q20); all mains come with vegetables, rice and a soup starter. Daily 7am–9pm.

DIRECTORY

Banks Banrural, 6 C (Tues–Sun 9am–5pm), has an ATM.
Internet Comser Cyber, 5 C & 4 Av (daily 8am–8pm; Q5/hr).

SANTA CRUZ DEL QUICHÉ

SANTA CRUZ DEL QUICHÉ, known locally as "Quiché", is capital of its eponymous

department, and half an hour north of Chichicastenango. The town has a busy street market but few attractions other than the minor Maya ruins of K'umarkaaj nearby.

K'umarkaaj (Utatlán)

Early in the fifteenth century, the K'iche' king Gucumatz (Feathered Serpent) founded a new capital, **K'umarkaaj**. A hundred years later, the Spanish arrived, renamed the city **Utatlán** and then destroyed it. Today you can visit the ruins, 3km to the west of Santa Cruz del Quiché.

Once a substantial city, there has been little restoration at **the site** (daily 8am–5pm; Q40), and just a few of the main structures are still recognizable, most of them buried beneath grassy mounds, but it is impressive nonetheless. The one-room **museum** has a scale model of what the original city is thought to have looked like. You should be able to make out the main plaza, three temple buildings, foundations of a circular tower and the remains of a large ball court. Beneath the plaza are several tunnels containing shrines – *costumbristas* (traditional Maya priests) still come to these altars to perform **religious rituals**. If a ceremony is taking place you'll hear the murmurings of prayers; don't disturb the proceedings by approaching too closely.

Microbuses from the terminal pass the ruins every fifteen minutes.

ARRIVAL AND DEPARTURE

By bus Buses pull into the bus terminal, which is about four blocks south and a couple east of the central plaza. The street directly north of the terminal is 1 Av, which takes you into the heart of the town.

Destinations Guatemala City (every 20min; 3hr 30min) via Chichicastenango (30min); Nebaj (6 daily; 2hr 30min); Quetzaltenango (9 daily; 3hr); Totonicapán (6 daily; 1hr 30min); Uspantán (7 daily; 2hr 30min).

By microbus Microbuses supplement the chicken bus services to Sacapulas (every 45min; 1hr 15min), Totonicapán (hourly; 1hr 15min) and Uspantán (hourly; 1hr 15min).

ACCOMMODATION AND EATING

Café San Miguel Opposite the church ☎ 7755 1488. Long-running café-restaurant with filling local food, including *empanadas*, sandwiches (from Q12) and snacks. Daily 7am–9pm.

Hotel San Andrés 0 Av 9–04 ☏ 7755 3057, ✉ hotelsan _andres@hotmail.com. Three-storey hotel on a quiet street with spacious, clean rooms, all with private bathroom. **Q150**

SACAPULAS

Just over an hour from Quiché, spectacularly situated on the Río Negro and beneath the foothills of the Cuchumatanes, lies the little town of **SACAPULAS**, with a small colonial church and a good market every Thursday and Sunday. A two-minute walk outside of town, upriver, takes you to some small **salt flats**; several roadside stallholders will sell you bags of black salt (Q2), which is said to have medicinal properties.

ARRIVAL AND DEPARTURE

By bus and microbus These run to Quiché (every 30min; 1hr) until around 5.30pm. There are also services to Nebaj (6 daily; 1hr 15min), Uspantán (7 daily; 2hr) and Aguacatán (7 daily; 1hr 30min), from where there are excellent connections to Huehuetenango.

ACCOMMODATION AND EATING

Comedor y Hospedaje Tujaal ☏ 4383 7657. This friendly riverside place has eleven basic rooms with private bathrooms and TV. The food here includes the local *mojarra* river fish and dishes like *pollo dorado* (fried chicken) or *bistek* (steak), both around Q25. Food daily 7am–8.30pm. **Q100**

NEBAJ

NEBAJ, a bustling market town with a dwindling number of attractive old adobe houses and plenty of new concrete structures, is the centre of Ixil country (see box below). Though the pretty central plaza is well kept, the surrounding streets are riddled with potholes and none too clean. Nebaj is remote, but it's well worth a visit for the glimpse it affords of the traditional **Ixil** way of life. The weaving, especially, is spectacular, with the women's *huipiles* an artistic tangle of complex geometric designs in superb greens, yellows, reds and oranges. There are some wonderful **hikes** in the surrounding region, too.

WHAT TO SEE AND DO

The **plaza** is the community's focal point, lined by its major shops and municipal buildings. The **market area**, which sprawls southeast of the plaza, is worth investigating. On Thursdays and Sundays the town explodes, as out-of-town traders visit with secondhand clothing from the US, stereos from Taiwan and Korea, and chickens, eggs and produce from across the highlands. The town **church** on the plaza is also worth a look – inside its door on the left are dozens of crosses, forming a memorial to those killed in the civil war. Three blocks north of the plaza, the town's small **museum** (5 Av & 2 C; Mon–Fri 9am–noon & 1–6pm, Sat 8am–1pm; Q20) has modern displays

4

THE IXIL REGION

The three small towns of **Nebaj**, **Chajul** and **Cotzal**, high in the Cuchumatanes, form the hub of the **Ixil-speaking region**, a massive area of over 140,000 inhabitants whose language is not spoken anywhere else. For all its charm and relaxed atmosphere today, the region's history is a bitter one. After many setbacks, the Spanish finally managed to take Nebaj in 1530, but by then they were so enraged that not only did they burn the town to the ground, but they condemned the survivors to slavery. Independence didn't improve conditions – the Ixil people continued to be regarded as a source of cheap labour, and were forced to work on the coastal plantations. In the late 1970s and early 1980s, the area was hit by horrific violence when it became the main theatre of operation for the **EGP** (the Guerrilla Army of the Poor). Caught up in the conflict between the guerrillas and the military, the civilians suffered terribly.

After the 1996 peace accords a degree of normality steadily returned, but the region remains desperately poor. Opportunities are so limited that in some villages the majority of men leave to live and work in "el Norte", their remittances forming a vital part of the local economy. Despite its troubled legacy, the region's fresh green hills are some of the most beautiful in the country and the three towns are friendly and accommodating.

that chart the region's history and culture; exhibits include Postclassic Maya ceramics.

There are several beautiful **hikes** in the hills around Nebaj, for which guides can be arranged at *El Descanso* (see below).

ARRIVAL AND INFORMATION

By bus The main terminal is two blocks southeast of the plaza.

Destinations Acul (roughly hourly 5.30am–5pm; 30min); Chajul (regularly 5.30am–6pm; 45min); Cobán (daily microbuses 5am and 1pm from 4 Av & 2 C; 6hr – or take any bus to the Cunén junction and catch an onward connection there); Cotzal (regularly 5.30am–6pm; 40min); Guatemala City (5 daily; 6hr); Huehuetenango (take a Quiché-bound bus and change in Sacapulas); Santa Cruz del Quiché (7 daily; 2hr 30min).

Tourist information *El Descanso* restaurant (☎4516 2059, ⓦnebaj.com), an excellent community tourism initiative, can arrange numerous treks (from Q150/day) as well as cooking classes, Spanish lessons and weaving instruction.

ACCOMMODATION

Gran Hotel Ixil 2 Av 9–15, Zona 5 ☎7756 0036. It's not actually very grand, but the owners, the Briz family, are hospitable and helpful and it's a comfortable, relaxed place to stay. All the rooms are spacious and well kept, with private bathroom and TV, and overlook a central garden. No wi-fi. **Q122**

Hospedaje Ilebal Tenam Calzada 15 de Septiembre ☎7755 8039. An efficiently run *hospedaje* with dozens of rooms, ranging from the small and functional to the attractive and comfortable – those in the rear block have TVs and private bathrooms. The hot water is reliable. No wi-fi. **Q70**

Hotel Villa Nebaj Calzada 15 de Septiembre 2–37 ☎7755 8115, ⓦhotelvillanebaj.com. This garish hotel has extremely comfortable rooms – all have quality beds, bedside lights and cable TV, and the Ixil fabrics add a splash of colour. Those without private bathroom are a real bargain. **Q100**

Media Luna Media Sol 3 C 6–15 ☎5311 9100. The entrance is run down (and there's rarely anyone around apart from a cleaner) so don't expect a hostel vibe, but the rooms are reasonable enough and shared bathrooms adequately clean. There are basic cooking facilities. No wi-fi. Dorms **Q35**, doubles **Q90**

Popi's 5 Av 3–35 ☎7756 0092. Founder Popi has moved on, but this guesthouse remains a good place to meet other travellers, and has pretty fast wi-fi (a rarity in these parts). However, the rooms are very basic, set around a yard. Dorms **Q35**, doubles **Q110**

EATING

Local specialities include *boxboles* (maize dough steamed in *güisquil* – squash – leaves with herbs) and *pollo pulique* (chicken cooked with *tomatillos* and spices).

Comedor Elsin East side of the Parque. Classic *comedor*, humble and filled with cooking smoke, offering hearty food at low prices. Daily 7.30am–9pm.

★ **El Descanso** Two blocks northwest of the plaza on 3 C ☎5847 4747. Huge café-restaurant-hub that's a popular hangout for backpackers and development workers, with sofas, free wi-fi, and a long menu, including good breakfasts (from Q22) and mains including pasta, Mexican dishes, sandwiches and grilled meats. There's also beer and wine by the glass. Daily 8am–10pm.

El Rinconcito del Acul Calzada 15 de Septiembre ☎4006 9678. Something really different, this excellent little place only offers one thing – thick tortillas (Q30) stuffed with Chancol cheese (made in nearby Acul) or smoked chorizo. They'll also serve you a good coffee or glass of wine, or you can buy a whole cheese from the store next door. Daily 7.30am–7.30pm.

DIRECTORY

Bank Banco Industrial, 3 Av, has an ATM.

Internet Surf (slowly) at *El Descanso*, 3 C, for US$0.75/hr (daily 8am–10pm).

Language school Nebaj Language School, based at *El Descanso* (☎7756 0207, ⓦnebaj.com). A week of one-on-one tuition and a family homestay with meals is US$150.

ACUL

One of the most interesting hikes from Nebaj takes you to the village of **ACUL**, about a ninety-minute walk away. Starting from the church in Nebaj, cross the plaza and head along 5 Calle past *Hotel Turansa*. At the bottom of the dip, beyond *Tienda y Comedor El Oasis*, the road divides: take the right-hand fork and head out of town along a dirt track. This switchbacks up a very steep hillside, and heads over a narrow pass into the next valley, where it drops down into Acul. The village was one of the country's original so-called "model villages" into which people were herded after their homes had been destroyed by the army during the civil war.

ACCOMMODATION AND EATING

Hacienda San Antonio On the outskirts of the village ☎5305 6240, ⓦquesochancol.com. One of the best rural lodges in the country, run by an Italian–Guatemalan family who make some of the country's best cheese, Chancol, which they sell at pretty reasonable prices. They also rent out delightful rustic rooms. **Q310**

Posada Doña Magdelena ☏ 5782 0891. Charming little place with simple rooms (one has a private bathroom) and a pretty garden; the owner also serves tasty, inexpensive meals. **Q100**

SAN JUAN COTZAL

SAN JUAN COTZAL, the second of the three Ixil towns, is about forty minutes from Nebaj. The town sits in a gentle dip in the valley, which is sheltered somewhat beneath the Cuchumatanes and often wrapped in a damp blanket of mist. Intricate turquoise *huipiles* are worn by the Maya women here, who also weave bags and rope from the fibres of the maguey plant.

The **community tourism** project Tejidos Cotzal (☏ 5428 8218 or ☏ 4621 9725, ⊕ tejidoscotzal.org), just behind the marketplace, can hook you up with a guide (Q200/head, minimum two people) to show you around this lovely region, the waterfalls, hilltop Maya shrines and cottage industries (including candle making), and introduce you to local weavers. **Market days** (Wed & Sat) are a particularly good time to visit, when there's more transport and life in the town.

ARRIVAL AND DEPARTURE

By bus Regular buses connect Cotzal for Nebaj until 5.30pm. It's possible to also visit Chajul the same day if you get an early start from Nebaj.

ACCOMMODATION AND EATING

El Maguey ☏ 7765 6199. A basic place where the rooms have TVs; bathrooms are shared. They also serve good meals. **Q100**

CHAJUL

CHAJUL, made up mainly of old adobe houses, with wooden beams and red-tiled roofs blackened by the smoke of cooking fires, is the most determinedly traditional and least bilingual of the Ixil towns. The women wear earrings made of old coins strung up on lengths of wool, and dress in bright reds and blues, while some boys still use blowpipes to hunt small birds, a skill that dates from the earliest of times. The colonial church is home to the **Christ of Golgotha** and the focus of a large pilgrimage on the second Friday of Lent, a particularly good time to be here. Staff at the office of charity Limitless Horizons (☏ 5332 6264, ⊕ limitlesshorizonsixil .org), next to the Salon Municipal, can direct you to local guides for **hiking**.

ARRIVAL AND DEPARTURE

There are regular bus, microbus and pick-up connections between Nebaj and Chajul until around 6pm (40min). There are fewer transport options from Cotzal, but you shouldn't have to wait too long for a ride.

ACCOMMODATION AND EATING

You can stay with a local family – many rent out beds – or at the *posada*.

Posada Vetz K'aol 500m southwest of the plaza ☏ 7765 6114. A friendly inn that has bunk beds in large dorms and tasty, cheap grub. Espresso coffee is usually available too. **Q60**

QUETZALTENANGO

QUETZALTENANGO, Guatemala's second city, sits in a beautiful mountain valley ringed by volcanoes. In pre-Columbian times the town belonged to the Mam Maya people, who named the town Xelajú, meaning "under the rule of the ten mountains" – hence the name, **Xela** (pronounced "Shay-La"), by which the city still goes. It was the Spaniards who dubbed the city Quetzaltenango, roughly translated as "the land of the quetzal". Xela went on to flourish during colonial times, thanks in large part to the area's abundant coffee crops, but a massive earthquake in 1902 destroyed nearly the entire city. Subsequently almost completely rebuilt (all the Neoclassical buildings you can see today date to this time), Xela is once again one of the country's major centres. Nonetheless, it manages to preserve an air of subdued, dignified calm, and remains popular among travellers, especially language students looking for more of an authentic Guatemalan experience than their counterparts in Antigua.

4

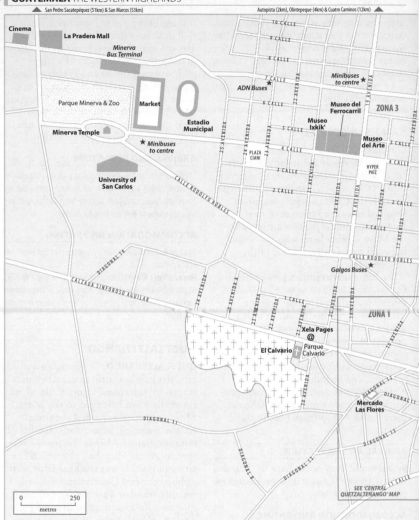

Cinema

La Pradera Mall

Minerva
Bus Terminal

Parque Minerva & Zoo

Market

Minibuses
to centre

Museo del
Ferrocarril

ZONA 3

ADN Buses

Museo
Ixkik'

Estadio
Municipal

Minerva Temple

Museo
del Arte

★ Minibuses
to centre

PLAZA
CIANI

HYPER
PAÍZ

University of
San Carlos

CALLE RODOLFO ROBLES

CALLE RODOLFO ROBLES

DIAGONAL 14

CALZADA SINFOROSO AGUILAR

Galgos Buses

ZONA 1

Xela Pages
@

El Calvario

Parque
Calvario

DIAGONAL 11

DIAGONAL 11

Mercado
Las Flores

DIAGONAL 11

DIAGONAL 13

DIAGONAL 8

DIAGONAL 12

SEE 'CENTRAL
QUETZALTENANGO' MAP

0   250
metres

WHAT TO SEE AND DO

There aren't many sights in the city itself, but if you have an hour or two to spare then it's worth wandering through the streets, soaking up the atmosphere and taking in a museum or a market. The city is divided into zones; you'll primarily be interested in zonas 1 and 3, home to the central plaza and the (second-class) bus terminal, respectively. Most places are within walking distance, except the bus terminal and railway terminal museums.

Parque Centro América

The **Parque Centro América**, with a mass of mock-Greek columns and imposing bank facades, is at the centre of Xela. There's none of the buzz of business that you'd expect, though, except on the first Sunday of the month when the plaza hosts a good artisan market with blankets, baskets and piles of weavings for sale. On the west side of the plaza is the impressive **Pasaje Enríquez**, planned as a sparkling arcade of upmarket shops

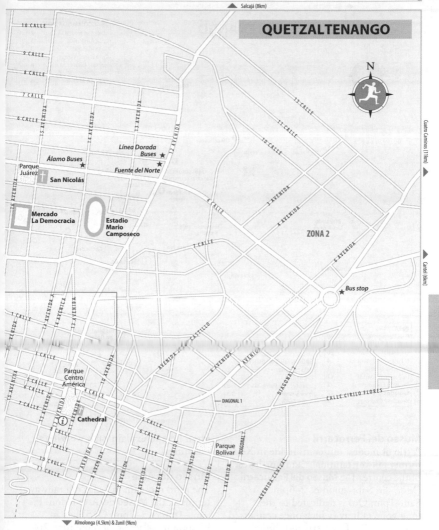

QUETZALTENANGO

but now home to a number of good bars and restaurants.

Casa de la Cultura

At the southern end of the plaza is the **Casa de la Cultura** (Mon–Fri 8am–noon & 2–6pm, Sat & Sun 9am–5pm; Q7), the city's blatant architectural homage to ancient Greece. On the ground floor you'll find a room dedicated to the marimba, along with assorted documents, photographs and pistols from the liberal revolution and the state of Los Altos. Upstairs are modest Maya artefacts, historic photographs and a bizarre natural-history room that has curious displays of stuffed bats, pickled snakes and assorted freaks of nature including a four-horned goat.

Mercado La Democracia

Around 750m northwest of the plaza, the **Mercado La Democracia** is a vast covered complex with stalls daily selling local produce and lots of inexpensive clothing.

Museo del Ferrocarril

A trio of modest museums reside in Xela's former railway terminal, 2km northwest of the centre. The **Museo del Ferrocarril** (Mon–Fri 8am–noon & 2–6pm, Sat 8am–1pm; Q6) is dedicated to the long-gone railway (which once connected Xela to the Pacific coast), and though exhibits are not particularly well presented you will find curiosities, including some original train seats and tickets.

Museo Ixkik'

Next door to the Museo del Ferrocarril the more impressive **Museo Ixkik'** (daily 9am–1pm & 3–6pm; Q25; ⓦmuseoixkik.org) concentrates on Maya costume, with examples of fine *traje* from across the highlands and one room devoted to Xela itself. Guides are often here to explain each weaving's meaning.

Museo del Arte

The third museum in Xela's old railway terminal, the **Museo del Arte** (Mon–Fri 9am–1pm & 3–7pm; Q15) has an important collection of more than 200 paintings from artists including Efraín Recinos.

The Minerva Temple and around

Out on the northwestern edge of town, the **Minerva Temple** is a Greek-influenced structure built to honour President Barrios's enthusiasm for education. Below the temple are the sprawling daily produce **market** and the **Minerva Bus Terminal**. It's here that you can really sense the city's role as the centre of the western highlands, with

TOURS FROM QUETZALTENANGO

Xela has several excellent tour operators offering some fascinating trips around the region. Exact prices depend on numbers taking tours.

Adrenalina Tours Inside Pasaje Enríquez, Parque Centro América ☎7761 4509, ⊚adrenalinatours.com. Long-established, professionally run company with some excellent tours around Xela. Also runs shuttle buses and offers volcano climbs (Chicabal and Volcán Santa María).

Altiplano's 6 C & 7 Av ☎4748 6952, ☎5247 2073, ⊚altiplanos.com.gt. Reliable, locally owned operator with trekking and tour programmes to villages around Xela and beyond. They also buy and rent camping gear.

Diversity Tours 15 Av 3–86 ☎7761 2545. Contact them for shuttle buses, and tours of sights including the Santiaguito viewpoint and Tajumulco (Q525).

Quetzaltrekkers *Casa Argentina*, 12 Diagonal 8–37 ☎7765 5895, ⊚quetzaltrekkers.com. Offers several outstanding hikes, including a three-day trek from Xela to Atitlán (minimum donation Q750) and a day-hike to Fuentes Georginas (Q340), plus rock climbing. All profits go to a charity for street children.

---

indígena traders from all over the area doing business.

ARRIVAL AND INFORMATION

By bus Unfortunately, most buses arrive and depart from nowhere near the centre of town. Second-class buses pull into the chaotic Minerva Bus Terminal on the city's northwestern edge; to get to the main plaza, walk 300m through the market stalls to 4 C and catch a microbus marked "Parque". There are five companies operating first-class buses to and from the capital (4hr), each with their own private terminal: Álamo, 14 Av 5–15, Zona 3 (☎7767 4582); ADN, 23 Av 5–06, 3 (☎6649 2089); Galgos, C Rodolfo Robles 17–43, Zona 1 (☎7761 2248) and Línea Dorada, 12 Av 5–13, Zona 3 (☎7767 5198, ⊚lineadorada.info). For the latest schedules check out ⊚xelawho.com. For Antigua, take any Guatemala City-bound bus and change in Chimaltenango.

Destinations Chicken buses leave for Chichicastenango (7 daily; 2hr 30min); Guatemala City (every 20min; 4hr); Huehuetenango (every 30min; 2hr); La Mesilla (6 daily; 3hr 45min); Momostenango (every 30min; 1hr 15min); Panajachel (6 daily; 2hr 30min); Retalhuleu (every 30min; 1hr 15min); San Francisco El Alto (every 30min; 45min); San Pedro La Laguna (7 daily; 2hr 15min); Santa Cruz del Quiché (7 daily; 3hr); Tecún Umán (hourly; 3hr); Totonicapán (every 20min; 1hr), Zunil (from Minerva via 10 C and 9 Av, Zona 1, every 30min; 30min).

By shuttle bus Shuttle buses are offered by travel agents (see box above); destinations include Chichicastenango (market days only; Q180), Panajachel (Q150), Antigua (Q225), Cobán (Q360), Guatemala City (Q260), San Pedro La Laguna (Q120) and San Cristóbal de las Casas in Mexico (Q260).

Tourist information The Inguat tourist office, Parque Centro América (Mon–Fri 9am–5pm, Sat 9am–1pm; ☎7761 4931, ⊚info-xela@inguat.gob.gt), is not particularly helpful; tour operators (see box above) are

better informed. To find what's on, pick up a copy of *Xela Who* (⊚xelawho.com), available in many of the popular bars and cafés.

ACCOMMODATION

All these places are in Zona 1, located within a ten-minute walk of the Parque Centro América.

Black Cat Hostel 13 Av 3–33 ☎7761 2091. This is a deservedly popular hostel, with a sociable vibe and a hip bar area with retro sofas. The dorms are fine, shared bathrooms are clean, but the private rooms are overpriced. Rates include a massive breakfast. Dorms Q50, doubles Q170

Casa Argentina 12 Diagonal 8–37 ☎7761 2470, ⊕casargentina.xela@gmail.com. Long-standing backpackers' hangout that has seen better days. Dozens of small rooms (most with TVs and a few with en-suite bathrooms), a "dorm city" (with more than twenty beds!) and guests' kitchen. Also home to Quetzaltrekkers (see box above). Dorms Q30, doubles Q50

★Casa Renaissance 9 C 11–26 ☎3121 6315, ⊚casarenaissance.com. Welcoming Dutch-owned place in a fine old townhouse with five huge rooms, gorgeous original floor tiles, free tea, coffee and water, sunny patios, a guests' kitchen, fast wi-fi, good bathrooms and a TV lounge stocked with DVDs. Q130

Hostal Miguel 12 Av 8–31 ☎7765 5554, ⊚learn2speak spanish.com. Nine very simple rooms in a slightly ramshackle old house that are basic but inexpensive. There's a living room (with TV) and cooking facilities, and it's also home to a language school. Q80

Hostal Siete Orejas 2 C 16–92 ☎7768 3218, ⊚7orejas .com. Flashpacker place with very high-quality, spacious rooms, each with hand-carved beds, good mattresses and a wooden chest of drawers. Dorms Q80, doubles Q315

Pensión Andina 8 Av 6–07 ☎7761 4012. Offers good value, with plain, smallish, well-scrubbed rooms, all with private bathrooms and reliable hot water, set around a covered courtyard. Q110

4

★ **TREAT YOURSELF**

Casa Mañen 9 Av 4–11 ☎7765 0786, ⓦcomeseeit.com. Attractive B&B with a good selection of spacious rooms, which have plenty of local charm thanks to the use of highland textiles and tasteful furnishings. Rooms 8 and 9 have fireplaces. There's also a rooftop terrace and the breakfast (included) is a veritable banquet. <u>Q465</u>

EATING

CAFÉS

Café Lounge 13 Av 6–16 ☎7765 8418. This smart little café scores for espresso and meals and snacks including paninis, crêpes, cakes and sandwiches. The set lunch is Q25 and wi-fi is reliable. Mon–Sat 7am–9.30pm, Sun 3–7pm.

Café La Luna 8 Av 4–11 ☎5174 6769. Crammed with curios including a collection of 1930s radios and antiques, *La Luna* has seven different varieties of drinking chocolate (Q6) – though note that they're (outrageously) pre-sweetened to local tastes. Snacks are also served (Q25–30). Mon–Fri 10am–9pm, Sat 4–9pm.

El Cuartito 13 Av 7–09 ⓦelcuartitocafe.com. Xela's hippest little café/bar has a Mediterranean-influenced menu with options for breakfast including Spanish toast with tomato, garlic and olive oil. Good smoothies and cocktails, too. The decor is quirky and the clientele bohemian. Daily 8am–11pm.

Xela Café Gourmet 6 C Av 9–26. This smart café has a broad choice of espresso-based coffees and a menu that takes in panini and burgers. Daily 8am–8pm.

RESTAURANTS

La Esquina Asiatica 9 Av 6–79 ☎5214 7829. Offers authentic East Asian classics like *pad thai*, *satay*, Vietnamese spring rolls and noodle dishes. Prices are very reasonable (mains Q25–35) and the surroundings are attractive. Mon & Wed–Sat 12.15–9pm, Sun 12.15–3.15pm.

El Pasaje Mediterraneo Pasaje Enríquez ☎3001 3441. A classy tapas restaurant with two attractive dining rooms and an appealing menu of dishes from Spain, Greece, Turkey and Italy; there's a decent wine list, too. Reckon on three or four tapas (most are Q30–40) for two people. Mon–Sat noon–10pm.

Sabor de la India 15 Av 3–64 ☎7765 0101. This Indian-owned place serves up filling and pretty authentic dishes and lots of vegetarian options including a good *thali* (Q60). The premises lack atmosphere, though. Tues–Sat noon–10pm, Sun 5–9pm.

Sagrado Corazón 1 14 Av 3–08. Small, informal place that's a great spot to try Guatemalan specialities like *pepián* or *jocón* (meat cooked with peppers and *tomatillos*). Daily 8am–7.30pm.

Sagrado Corazón 2 9 C & 11–16. Head here for honest Guatemalan grub, particularly dirt-cheap breakfasts. The set lunch (around Q20) is a winner too, and there's always a veggie version available. Daily 8am–8pm.

DRINKING AND NIGHTLIFE

The main areas for nightlife and dancing in central Xela are 14 Av A (which is lined with bars) and Pasaje Enríquez.

Bajo La Luna 8 Av 3–72 ☎7761 0125. In an atmospheric cellar, this wine bar is perfect for a relaxed drink (though they do have occasional parties). You can nibble on snacks while you sip. Tues–Sat 7–11pm.

El Cuartito 13 Av 7–09 ⓦelcuartitocafe.com. Popular with Xela's artistic community, this small, happening bar with shabby-chic decor (including lighting made from old beer bottles) has live music and DJs some nights. Doubles as a café in the day. Daily 8am–11pm.

Discoteca La Parranda 14 Av 4–47. Strut your stuff (and perfect those salsa steps) on Wed (when there are free classes) at this bar/club. From Thurs to Sat it's a mix of reggaetón, Latin, electronica and r'n'b. Wed–Sat 6pm–1am.

Pool & Beer 12 Av 10–21 ☎5025 1329. Pool tables and table football are available in this spacious bar with friendly staff. On Saturdays there's a DJ and dancing, and the place gets rammed with young Quetzaltecos. Tues–Sun 6pm–midnight.

★ **Salón Tecún** Pasaje Enríquez. Xela's most dependable and popular bar, this atmospheric pub-like drinking institution is a favourite with both locals and travellers. There's a sociable interior and bench seating outside in the arcade. Daily 8am–1am.

ENTERTAINMENT

Casa N'oj Parque Centro América ☎7768 3139. Art exhibitions, films and lectures in a wonderful restored building.

Cinemas Blue Angel, 7 C 15–79, Zona 1, has a daily video programme (Q10) at 8pm with a large selection of movies (mainly Hollywood blockbusters and cult films). There's a multiscreen cinema by La Pradera mall, near the Minerva terminal.

Teatro Municipal 14 Av A & 1 C ☎7761 2218. Dance and theatre performances, concerts and exhibitions.

North & South 12 Av 3–43 ☎7761 7900. This bookshop stocks cultural and political books and guidebooks, and has a café (for espresso coffee and a bagel). Daily 8am–8pm.

La Pradera Just behind the Minerva market, Zona 3, ☎7767 7884, ⓦcentroscomercialespradera.com. Shopping mall with more than a hundred stores. Daily 9am–9pm.

LANGUAGE SCHOOLS IN QUETZALTENANGO

Quetzaltenango has many excellent **language schools**, and if you're looking for a full-immersion experience it's ideal, as few people speak English in town. Good schools include the following:

Casa de Español Xelajú Callejón 15, Diagonal 13–02, Zona 1 ☎ 7761 5954, ⓦ casaxelaju.com.

Celas Maya 6 C 14–55, Zona 1 ☎ 7765 8204, ⓦ celasmaya.com.

Centro Bilingüe Amerindia (CBA) 8 C 6–28, Zona 1 ☎ 7765 2521, ⓦ cbaspanishschool.com.

La Democracia 9 C 15–05, Zona 3 ☎ 7767 0013, ⓦ lademocracia.net.

Inepas 15 Av 4–59, Zona 1 ☎ 7765 1308, ⓦ inepas .org.

Juan Sisay 15 Av 8–38, Zona 1 ☎ 7765 1318, ⓦ juansisay.com.

Kie Balam Diagonal 12 4–46, Zona 1 ☎ 7761 1636,

ⓦ kiebalam.com.

Madre Tierra 13 Av 8–34, Zona 1 ☎ 7761 6105, ⓦ madre-tierra.org.

Miguel de Cervantes 12 Av 8–31, Zona 1 ☎ 7765 5554, ⓦ learn2speakspanish.com.

La Paz 2 C Callejón 16 2–47, Zona 1 ☎ 4018 2180, ⓦ xelapages.com/lapaz.

Pop Wuj 1 C 17–72, Zona 1 ☎ 7761 8286, ⓦ pop-wuj .org.

Proyecto Lingüístico Quetzalteco de Español 5 C 2–40, Zona 1 ☎ 7765 2140, ⓦ plqe.org.

Sakribal 6 C 7–42, Zona 1 ☎ 7763 0717, ⓦ sakribal .com.

Uwachulew 14 Av A 3–33 ☎ 5594 1890. Eco-store run by a hip crew that stocks lots of organic and fairtrade products, from jams and chocolate to wine. Doubles as a café and wine bar, with occasional events featuring soul, funk and latin DJs. Mon–Sat 8am–11pm.

Vrina 15 Av 3 64 ☎ 7177 0320. Excellent bookshop with thousands of used titles; it buys and trades as well, and offers bike rental. Mon–Sat 9am–6pm.

DIRECTORY

Bank Banrural (Mon–Fri 9am–6pm, Sat 9am–1pm) on the Parque Centro América has an ATM.

Bike rental The Bike House, 15 Av 5–22, Zona 1, has mountain bikes (Q45/24hr or Q100/week).

Health Hospital San Rafael, 9 C 10–41, Zona 1 (☎ 7761 4414 or ☎ 7761 2956).

Internet Xela Pages, 4 C 19–48, Zona 1 (Mon–Fri 8am–8pm, Sat 10am–6pm; Q3–6/hr). Also offers cheap calls.

Laundry Lavandería Tikal, Diagonal 13 8–07 (Mon–Sat 8am–5pm; Q25 for a typical load, washed and dried in 2hr).

Police If you're in trouble or have been the victim of crime, first contact the PROATUR rep (☎ 4149 1104) for the Xela area.

Post office 15 Av & 4 C (Mon–Fri 8.30am–5.30pm, Sat 9am–1pm).

Supermarket Despensa Familiar, 3 Av & 7 C, in the centre of town (daily 7.30am–8pm).

AROUND QUETZALTENANGO

Based in Quetzaltenango, you could easily spend a week or two exploring the highlands, perhaps on a guided tour (see box, p.321). There are numerous smaller towns and villages nearby, mostly indigenous agricultural communities and weaving centres with colourful weekly markets, as well as some lovely hot springs. The area also offers excellent **hiking**. The most obvious climbs are **Volcán Santa María**, towering above Quetzaltenango itself, and up **Volcán Chicabal** to its sublime crater lake. Straddling the coast road to the south is **Zunil** and the hot springs of **Fuentes Georginas**, overshadowed by more breathtaking volcanic peaks; while to the north are **Totonicapán**, capital of the department of the same name, and **San Francisco El Alto**, a small town perched on an outcrop overlooking the valley. Beyond that lies **Momostenango**, the country's principal wool-producing centre and a centre of Maya culture.

Volcán Santa María

Due south of Quetzaltenango the perfect cone of **Volcán Santa María** (3772m) looms over most of the Xela valley. The view from the top is, as you might expect, truly spectacular, with nine other volcanoes visible on clear days, including the smoking summit of Santiaguito directly below. You can climb the volcano as a day-trip, but for the best views you need to be on top at dawn, either sleeping on the freezing peak, or camping at the site below and climbing the final section in the dark by torchlight. Either way, you need to make sure you're acclimatized to the altitude for a few days before attempting the climb. It is highly recommended you go with a guide; they can be organized at most of the tour operators in Quetzaltenango (see box, p.321).

Laguna Chicabal

One spectacular excursion (and less strenuous than the trip to Volcán Santa María) is to **Laguna Chicabal**, a crater lake set in the cone of the Chicabal volcano, about 25km southeast of Xela.

The hike, a two-hour trek from San Martín Sacatepéquez, starts just before the village; get your bus driver to drop you off at the right spot on the highway, where you'll see a sign to the lake. On the way you'll pass the entrance to the reserve (Q25). Once you enter the reserve, a signposted route to the left leads to a *mirador* (from where there are stunning views of the emerald lake and the volcanoes of Santa María and Santiaguito, Tajumulco and Tacaná), or, alternatively, you could take the precipitous path straight down to the shore. Small sandy bays bear charred crosses and bunches of fresh-cut flowers, marking sites of ritual sacrifice. Every May 3 *costumbristas* gather here for ceremonies to mark the fiesta of the Holy Cross; never disturb any rituals that are taking place. Swimming is not permitted.

ARRIVAL AND DEPARTURE

By bus Get a Coatepeque-bound bus (every 30min; 40min) from Quetzaltenango's Minerva terminal to the town of San Martín Sacatepéquez.

ACCOMMODATION

Cabins There are rustic cabins at the entrance to the reserve. Per person Q40–75
Camping You can camp for free on the Laguna Chicabal shore, though you'll have to bring your own supplies.

Zunil

Some 10km south of Quetzaltenango is the village of **ZUNIL**, a vegetable-growing market town hemmed in by steep hills and a sleeping volcano. The main plaza is dominated by a beautiful white colonial church with a richly decorated facade; inside, an intricate silver altar is protected behind bars. The women of Zunil wear vivid purple *huipiles* and carry bright shawls – the plaza is awash with colour during the Monday market. Just below the plaza is a **textile co-operative**, where hundreds of women market these weavings. **Maximón**, the "evil saint" (see box, p.297), has a strong following locally; his mannequin is usually paraded through the streets during Holy Week, dressed in Western clothes and smoking a cigar. Virtually any child in town will take you to his current abode for a quetzal.

ARRIVAL AND DEPARTURE

By bus Buses to Zunil run from Quetzaltenango's Minerva bus terminal (every 30min or so), though some also leave from closer to the centre of town, stopping beside the Shell petrol station at 10 C & 9 Av in Zona 1.
Tours Tour operators in Xela (see box, p.321) run trips to Zunil.

Fuentes Georginas

High in the hills, 8km from Zunil, are the **Fuentes Georginas** (Mon–Fri 8am–6pm, Sat & Sun 7am–6pm; Q40), a set of luxuriant hot springs. Surrounded by fresh green ferns, thick moss and lush forest, the baths are sublime, and to top it all there's a restaurant and bar. It's a blissful place to spend a few hours soaking away the chicken-bus blues or recovering from a volcano climb in the heavenly steaming pools.

ARRIVAL AND DEPARTURE

By bus There's a dedicated shuttle bus service from Xela: buses (Q140 return; daily 9am & 2pm; 30min) leave from the Fuentes office, 14 Av & 5 C, Zona 1. Otherwise, minibuses (Q80 one way) head up from Zunil on demand.

ACCOMMODATION AND EATING

Bungalows ☎ 5704 2959. Stone bungalows are available for the night, complete with bathtub, two double beds, fireplace and barbecue. Q320
Restaurant The springs have their own restaurant – meals around Q60, snacks Q30 – and a well-stocked bar.

Totonicapán

A one-hour bus journey from Xela, **TOTONICAPÁN** is capital of one of the smaller departments, a pleasant if unremarkable provincial town. As you enter Toto you pass one of the country's finest *pilas* (communal washing places), ringed with Gothic columns. Surrounded by rolling hills and pine forests, the town stands at the heart of a heavily populated and intensely farmed region. Toto's Tuesday and Saturday morning **markets** fill its two plazas to bursting. The town is an important centre of commercial weaving, producing much of the cloth worn as skirts by indigenous women throughout the country. Totonicapán is best done as a day-trip from Xela; **buses** shuttle from the Minerva terminal and back every fifteen minutes or so, via the Cuatro Caminos junction.

San Francisco El Alto

The small town of **SAN FRANCISCO EL ALTO** overlooks the Quetzaltenango valley from a lovely hillside setting just north of Totonicapán. The view alone is worth a visit, with the great plateau stretching out below and Volcán Santa María on the horizon, but the main reason for a trip here is the **Friday market**, possibly the biggest in Central America and attended by traders from every corner of Guatemala – many arrive the night before, and some start selling by candlelight from as early as 4am. By noon the market is at its height, buzzing with activity; things start to thin out in the early afternoon.

The market is separated into a few distinct areas. At the very top of the hill is an open field used as an **animal market**, full of everything from pigs to parrots. Buyers inspect the animals' teeth and tongues, and at times the scene degenerates into a chaotic wrestling match, with livestock and men rolling in the dirt. Below, around the town's plaza, the stalls are dominated by textiles and clothing, mainly *ropa americana* (secondhand clothes), as well as vegetables, fruit and pottery. For really good views of the market and the surrounding countryside, pay the church caretaker a quetzal and climb up to the church roof.

Buses connect Quetzaltenango and San Francisco every twenty minutes from the Minerva terminal; the first is at 6am, and the last bus back leaves at about 5pm (45min).

Momostenango

Some 22km from San Francisco is **MOMOSTENANGO**, a small, isolated town and the centre of wool production in the highlands. The main reason for visiting is to take in the town's **Sunday market**, which fills the town's two plazas. Momostecos travel throughout the country peddling their blankets, scarves and rugs – years of experience have made them experts in the hard sell and given them a sharp eye for tourists. The town is also famous for its unconventional folk-Catholicism, and there are many Maya **shamans** working here. While you're here you could also walk to the *riscos*, a set of bizarre pumice pillars, or beyond to the **hot springs** of Pala Chiquito, about 3km away to the north.

Visits are best done as day-trips from Quetzaltenango, or you could head on to Huehuetenango. **Buses** run from the Minerva terminal in Quetzaltenango, passing through Cuatro Caminos (every 30min, 6am–5pm; 1hr 45min). There are additional services on Sundays, for the market.

HUEHUETENANGO

Bustling **HUEHUETENANGO**, capital of the department of the same name, lies at the foot of the Cuchumatanes mountain range. A small city, it's pretty relaxed, but heavy traffic, much of which thunders through the town centre, reduces this appeal somewhat. There are no real sights, but the area around the central square is attractive, surrounded by shaded walkways and administrative offices. A few blocks east, around 1 Avenida, the **market area** is always alive with activity, its streets packed with Maya from remote corners of the highlands. Few travellers

4

HUEHUETENANGO

■ ACCOMMODATION	
Hotel Gobernador	1
Hotel Mary	3
Hotel Zacaleu	2
Todos Santos Inn	4

● EATING	
Café Bougambilias	1
Cafe La Tinaja	4
Cafetería Las Palmeras	2
Museo del Café	3

Bus Terminal (2km) & Carretera Interamericana (4km)

stay long in Huehue, but if you're heading to or from Mexico or Todos Santos Cuchumatán you'll probably find yourself here to change buses. While you're in town, it's easy to take in the minor ruins of **Zaculeu** close by (see opposite).

ARRIVAL AND INFORMATION

By bus The bus terminal is halfway between the Carretera Interamericana and the centre. Minibuses make constant trips between the town centre and the bus terminal until about 8pm. Buses to Zaculeu leave from the corner of 2 C and 7 Av. There's also a bus stop at the El Calvario church, 1 Av and 1 C, for services to Todos Santos Cuchumatán (hourly; 2hr 15min) and Cobán (daily 1.30pm; 5hr 30min). Some first-class buses use their own private terminals.

Destinations from main terminal Aguacatán (every 30min; 40min); Barillas (9 daily; 6hr 30min); Gracias a Dios border (3 daily; 4hr 30min); Guatemala City (every 30min; 5hr 30min); La Mesilla, Mexican border (second-class, every 30min; 2hr); Quetzaltenango (every 30min; 2hr); Sacapulas (daily 11.30am & 12.30pm; 2hr).

Destinations private buses Linea Dorada, Calzada Kaibil Balam 8–70 (1 daily pullman to Guatemala City, 1 daily to La Mesilla; ☎7768 1566, ⓦlineadorada.info); Los Halcones, 10 Av 9–12 (5 daily to Guatemala City, 2 daily to La Mesilla; ☎7765 7986, ⓦtransportesloshalcones.com); Transportes Velásquez, main terminal (5 daily to Guatemala City; ☎7764 7594).

Information and tours There is no tourist office in Huehue. Adrenalina Tours is based in Quetzaltenango (see box, p.321) but offers the best tours of the Huehue region, including a two-day trip to remote sites near the Mexican border (Q1100/head).

ACCOMMODATION

Hotel Gobernador 4 Av 1–45 ☎7764 1197. A warren of basic, bare rooms (some en suite), none of them fancy, but all of them cheap. The shared bathrooms are clean enough. **Q80**

Hotel Mary 2 C 3–52 ☎7764 1618. It would benefit from a little TLC, but this basic, secure place has adequate budget rooms that will suffice for a night. There's a *comedor* too. **Q140**

Hotel Zacaleu 5 Av 1–14 ☎7764 1086, ⓦhotelzaculeu .com. A classy colonial-style hotel with spacious if old-fashioned rooms set around a lovely leafy courtyard (and a less appealing newer section). Don't miss the fantastic old bar. Good rates for solo travellers (from Q125). **Q250**

Todos Santos Inn 2 C 6–74 ☎5432 3421. This budget place has clean, well-scrubbed rooms and bathrooms. Those upstairs are fairly bright and cheery, those downstairs a bit gloomy. Singles cost just Q60; no wi-fi. **Q120**

ZACULEU'S HISTORY

The site of **Zaculeu**, first occupied in the fifth century, is thought to have been a religious and administrative centre for the Mam, and the home of the elite; the bulk of the population most likely lived in small surrounding settlements or else scattered in the hills.

In 1525 conquistador Pedro de Alvarado dispatched an army to conquer the area; the approaching Spanish were met by about five thousand Mam warriors, but the Mam leader, **Kaibal Balam**, quickly saw that his troops were no match for the Spanish and withdrew them to the safety of Zaculeu, where they were protected on three sides by deep ravines and on the other by a series of walls and ditches. The Spanish army settled outside the city and besieged the citadel for six weeks until starvation forced a surrender.

EATING

Café Bougambilias Opposite the church ☎ 7764 0105. This large *comedor* is a good place for breakfast – try the highland-style *mosh*: porridge with cinnamon, wheat and sugar. Daily 7am–9.30pm.

Café La Tinaja 4 C 6–51 ☎ 7764 1513. A hip little café/restaurant/store with quirky decor and an arty vibe. Check out the board for the specials of the day, which might include Mexican quesadillas and baguettes. They serve fine Huehue coffee and it's also good for a beer in the evenings. Daily noon–11pm.

Cafetería Las Palmeras Opposite the church ☎ 5783 2967. Very popular, clean and efficiently run restaurant that offers fine-value lunch deals (from Q25), which all include soup and a *refresco*. Daily 7am–9.30pm.

Museo del Café 4 C 7–40 ☎ 7764 1125. A veritable temple to the arabica and robusta beans, this garden café has its own roastery, coffee sacks on the walls, photographs of coffee fincas and lots of café curios. Great cappuccino, espresso and filter coffee is served, and it's also a good choice for breakfast (from Q25), lunch or dinner – the *menú del día* (Q25) is satisfyingly filling. Mon–Sat 7am–9.30pm.

DIRECTORY

Bank G&T Continental on the main square (Mon–Fri 8am–7pm, Sat 8am–1pm) has an ATM.

Internet Ciber Sky, 3 C & 7 Av charges Q5 per hour.

Language school Xinabajul, 4 Av 14–14, Zona 5 (☎ 7764 6631, ⊛ spanishschoolinguatemala.com).

ZACULEU

A few kilometres west of Huehuetenango are the ruins of **Zaculeu** (daily 8am–5pm; Q50), once the capital of the **Mam**, who were one of the principal pre-Conquest highland Maya tribes. Zaculeu includes several large temples, plazas and a ball court, all restored pretty unfaithfully by the United Fruit Company in 1946–47. Nonetheless, Zaculeu has a unique atmosphere – surrounded by pines, and with fantastic views of the mountains, its grassy plazas make excellent picnic spots. To get to Zaculeu from Huehuetenango, take one of the **buses** that leave every thirty minutes from close to the school, at 7 Avenida between 2 and 3 calles – make sure it's heading for "Las Ruinas".

AGUACATÁN

4

It's 22km east from Huehue to **AGUACATÁN**, a small agricultural town strung out along a very long main street, and the only place in the country where the Akateko and Chalchitek languages are spoken. It is best done as a day-trip, preferably in time to see Aguacatán's huge Sunday **market**, which actually gets under way on Saturday afternoon, when traders arrive early to claim the best sites.

WHAT TO SEE AND DO

On Sunday mornings, a steady stream of people pours into town, cramming into the **market** and plaza, and soon spilling out into the surrounding area. Around noon the tide turns as the crowds start to drift back to their villages, with donkeys leading their drunken drivers home.

Aguacatán's other attraction is the source of the **Río San Juan**, 1km east of the centre, which emerges fresh and cool from beneath a nearby hill, making a good place for a chilly dip.

ARRIVAL AND DEPARTURE

By bus Buses and microbuses connect Huehuetenango to Aguacatán (6am–6pm, roughly every 30min; 40min).

THE CUCHUMATANES

The largest non-volcanic peaks in Central America, the **Sierra de los Cuchumatanes** rise from a limestone plateau close to the Mexican border, reaching their full height of more than 3800m above Huehuetenango. This is magnificent mountain scenery, ranging from wild, exposed craggy outcrops to lush, tranquil river valleys. While the upper slopes are almost barren, scattered with boulders and shrivelled cypress trees, the lower levels are fertile, planted with corn, coffee and sugar. In the valleys are hundreds of tiny villages, simply isolated by the landscape. These communities are still some of the most traditional in Guatemala, and a visit, either for a market or fiesta, offers one of the best opportunities to see Maya life.

The most accessible of the villages in the vicinity, and the only one which receives a steady trickle of tourists, is **Todos Santos Cuchumatán**. Mountain trails from Todos Santos lead to other villages, including the equally traditional pueblo of **San Juan Atitán**.

Be wary of taking pictures of people in this region, particularly children. Rumours persist locally that some foreigners steal babies, and a tragic misunderstanding led to the death of a Japanese tourist here in 2000.

Beyond Aguacatán the road runs out along a ridge, with fantastic views stretching out below, eventually dropping down to the riverside town of Sacapulas, 90min away (see p.315); very regular microbuses ply this route until 5pm.

4 TODOS SANTOS CUCHUMATÁN

The village of **TODOS SANTOS CUCHUMATÁN** is many travellers' favourite place in Guatemala. The beauty of the alpine surroundings is a key attraction: the entire region is crisscrossed with excellent trails, offering fantastic **hiking**. Highland Maya culture is all-pervading here: the vast majority of Todosanteros are indigenous and speak Mam as their first language, and the ancient 260-day Tzolkin calendar is still observed. Most houses have a low mud-brick structure outside, called a *chuj*, which is similar to a sauna, with a wood fire lit under the rocks; family members use the steam generated to cleanse themselves. The local costume is incredible: the men wear straw hats, red-and-white-striped trousers and pinstripe shirts decorated with pink and blue collars, while the women wear dark blue *cortes* and intricately woven purple *huipiles*.

WHAT TO SEE AND DO

The village itself is pretty – a modest main street with a few shops, a plaza and a church – but is totally overshadowed by the looming presence of the Cuchumatanes mountains. Todos Santos sits at an altitude of 2460m, and it can be very chilly up here when the mists set in. Most of the fun of this place is in simply hanging out, but if you want to take a shirt, pair of trousers or *huipil* home, be sure to visit the excellent co-op selling quality **weavings** next to the *Casa Familiar*.

Museo Balam

The **Museo Balam** (Mon–Sat 8am–5pm; Q5), 300m east of the plaza, is definitely worth a visit, with lots of fine old photographs to admire and such eclectic local objects as a wet weather "raincoat" made from leaves and a hundred-year-old marimba.

ALL SAINTS' DAY IN TODOS SANTOS

The **All Saints' Day** fiesta (Nov 1) in Todos Santos Cuchumatán is one of the most famous in the country. The all-day horse race on All Saints' Day attracts large crowds, and is characterized by a massive stampede as the inebriated riders tear up the course, some still slugging on liquor bottles. On the "**Day of the Dead**" (Nov 2), the action moves to the cemetery, with marimba bands and drink stalls set up among the graves – a day of intense ritual that combines grief and celebration. By the end of the fiesta, the streets are littered with drunken revellers and the jail packed with brawlers.

Tucumanchum

Above the village – follow the track that goes up behind the *Comedor Katy* – is the small Maya site of Tucumanchum where you'll find a couple of mounds sprouting pine trees. The site is used by *costumbristas* for the ritual sacrifice of animals.

ARRIVAL AND INFORMATION

By bus Buses and microbuses from Huehuetenango (hourly; 2hr 15min) pass right through the centre of town.
Information The community website ⊛todossantos cuchumatanes.weebly.com is dedicated to the Todos Santos region.

ACCOMMODATION AND EATING

Plenty of families rent out rooms very cheaply, and *comedores* are scattered around the market.
Casa Familiar 100m uphill from the plaza ☎7783 0656 or ☎5737 0112, ✉wovent@gmail.com. A hospitable highland hotel with renovated rooms that have TVs, woven bedspreads and private hot-water bathrooms. They'll prepare a *chuj* sauna for you here, and offer excellent cooking in the restaurant (meals are great, though a little pricier than other places in town at around Q75). There's an on-site store selling local weavings, too. **Q200**
Comedor Evelin 150m east of the plaza, then just up a steep lane ☎5721 2121. Run by an industrious Ladina, this place offers inexpensive grub (meals Q20–25) including filling breakfasts. Daily 6am–8pm.
Hotelito Todos Santos Up a lane on the left before you reach *Casa Familiar* ☎5327 9313 or ☎7783 0603. A good cheap choice with basic but bargain-priced singles (Q50) and clean doubles with private bathrooms and TV. **Q150**

DIRECTORY

Bank The Banrural bank on the plaza has an ATM.
Internet Access is available from a couple of places on the main drag.
Tours Rigoberto Pablo Cruz (☎5206 0916, ✉rigoguiade turismo@yahoo.com) is a good local tour guide who

HIGHLAND MARKET DAYS

Make an effort to catch as many highland market days as possible – they're second only to local fiestas in offering a glimpse of the traditional Guatemalan way of life.
Mon Chimaltenango; Zunil.
Tues Chajul; Nebaj; Totonicapán.
Wed Chimaltenango; Santiago Sacatepéquez; Todos Santos Cuchumatán.
Thurs Chichicastenango; Nebaj; Sacapulas; San Juan Atitán; San Lucas Tolimán.
Fri Chajul; Chimaltenango; Nebaj; San Francisco El Alto; Santa María de Jesús.
Sat Todos Santos Cuchumatán; Totonicapán.
Sun Chichicastenango; Momostenango; Nebaj; San Juan Atitán; San Lucas Tolimán; San Martín Sacatepéquez; Santa María de Jesús.

offers trips and leads hikes around Todos Santos; he speaks Mam, Spanish and English. The guide Roberto Bautista (☎4384 4379, ✉roberbautista@yahoo.es) is also recommended.

AROUND TODOS SANTOS

It would be a real shame to miss out on one of the many **hikes** that can be done around Todos Santos – make sure you spend some time exploring the surrounding areas, home to some of the country's most breathtaking and dramatic scenery.

San Juan Atitán

The village of **SAN JUAN ATITÁN** is five to six hours on foot from Todos Santos via a wildly beautiful, isolated highland trail. It's an easy route to follow: take the track past the ruins and high above the village

INTO MEXICO: LA MESILLA

From Huehuetenango the Carretera Interamericana runs for 79km to the **Mexican border** at **La Mesilla**. There are buses (every 30min, 5am–8pm; 2hr). The two sets of customs and *migración* are 3km apart, connected by shared (*colectivo*) taxis. At **Ciudad Cuauhtémoc** on the Mexican side you can pick up buses to Comitán (1hr 15min) and even direct to San Cristóbal de las Casas (2hr 30min). Linea Dorada runs a first-class service to Guatemala City at 8pm. Most travellers use shuttle bus connections between San Cristóbal de las Casas and towns in Guatemala including Quetzaltenango, Panajachel and Antigua; consult Adrenalina Tours (⊛adrenalinatours.com) for the latest schedule.

through endless muddy switchbacks until you get to the ridge overlooking the valley. If the skies are clear, you'll be rewarded by an awesome view of the Tajumulco and Tacaná volcanoes. Take the easy-to-follow central track downhill from here past some ancient cloudforest to San Juan Atitán. Market days are Mondays and Thursdays. There is irregular **transport** back from San Juan Atitán to Huehue (around 6 daily pick-ups; 1hr).

You can **stay** in San Juan Atitán, in a couple of cheap *hospedajes*, or continue west along the valley from Todos Santos to **San Martín** and on to **Jacaltenango**, a route which also offers superb views. There's basic accommodation in Jacaltenango, so you could stay the night and then catch a bus back to Huehuetenango in the morning. Some buses from Huehue also continue down this route.

The Pacific coast

The **Pacific coast**, a strip of 250km of black volcanic beaches, is known in Guatemala as La Costa Sur. Once as rich in wildlife as the jungles of Petén, it's now the country's most intensely farmed region, with coffee grown on the volcanic slopes and entire villages effectively owned by vast cotton, sugar cane, and African palm plantations. A few protected areas try to preserve some of the area's natural heritage; the **Monterrico Reserve** is one of the most accessible of these, a swampy refuge for sea turtles, iguanas, crocodiles and an abundance of birdlife. It also encompasses a beachside village with a near-endless stretch of clean, dark sand. Close to the Mexican border, the empty sands at the tiny beach resort of **Tilapita** are another good alternative for some hammock time, and perhaps the odd boat excursion through the coastal mangrove forest.

Due to the powerful undertow surfing is pretty limited, but tiny **Paredón** has the most reliable waves as well as a fine oceanic beach and a travellers' vibe. Away from the coast, you can glimpse the impressive art of the Pipil around the town of **Santa Lucía Cotzumalguapa**, and the Maya site of **Takalik Abaj** is worth a detour on your way to or from Mexico, or as a day-trip from Quetzaltenango.

The main route along the coast is the **Carretera al Pacífico**, which runs from the Mexican border at Tecún Umán into El Salvador at Ciudad Pedro de Alvarado. It's the country's swiftest highway and you'll never have to wait long for a bus. Off this road, however, things slow down considerably.

TILAPA AND TILAPITA

Most travellers arriving in Guatemala's extreme west forgo the beaches in these parts and head straight from the border to Quetzaltenango or Guatemala City. But for total relaxation, a day or two in tranquil **Tilapita** will be time well spent.

Tilapa

South of Tecún Umán (see box opposite), a paved road paralleling the border passes endless palm-oil and banana plantations to the humble little village of **TILAPA**. The dark-sand beach here has a relatively gently shelving profile; lifeguards are only posted on weekends, though.

The coastline forms part of the **Reserva Natural El Manchón**, which covers some 30km of prime turtle-nesting beach and extends around 10km inland to embrace a belt of swamp and mangrove, which is home to crocodiles, iguanas, kingfishers, storks, white herons, egrets and an abundance of fish. Speak to one of the local boatmen in Tilapa or Tilapita about taking a tour (around Q120/hr) of the canals and lagoons.

Tilapita

On the other side of an estuary from Tilapa is the even tinier, and more agreeable, beach settlement of **TILAPITA**. Here there's a real opportunity to get away from it all and enjoy a superb stretch of clean, dark sand and the ocean (with not too much undertow). Just next to the *El Pacífico* hotel is a small **turtle hatchery**, with protected

INTO MEXICO: EL CARMEN AND TECÚN UMÁN

There are two border crossings with **Mexico** in the coastal region, both open 24hr. The northernmost is the **Talismán Bridge**, also referred to as **El Carmen**. On the Mexican side, a constant stream of minibuses and buses leaves for Tapachula (30min). Coming from Mexico, there are regular buses to Guatemala City until about 7pm; if heading towards Quetzaltenango or the western highlands, take the first minibus to Malacatán or Coatepeque and change there.

Further south and leading directly onto the Carretera al Pacífico, the **Tecún Umán–Ciudad Hidalgo** crossing is favoured by most Guatemalan, and virtually all commercial, traffic. If you're Mexico-bound, there are very frequent bus services to Tapachula (40min) over the border. There's a steady flow of buses to Guatemala City along the Carretera al Pacífico via Retalhuleu, and also regular direct buses to Quetzaltenango until 3pm (3hr 30min).

Four companies – Galgos, Platinum King Quality, Tica Bus and Linea Dorada – run direct buses (5 in total; 6hr) between Tapachula in Mexico and Guatemala City (see p.283).

enclosures where eggs are buried until they hatch, and some information boards (the Olive Ridley turtle is the main visitor here, between June and October).

ARRIVAL AND INFORMATION

By bus Regular buses connect Coatepeque on the Carretera al Pacífico and Tilapa (every 30min, last bus returns at 6pm; 2hr). If you're travelling along the Pacific highway, just wait at the Tilapa junction on the highway for a connection.

By boat Boatmen buzz you up the canal that connects Tilapa and Tilapita (10min; Q10); it's possible to wade over at low tide.

Information ⓦ playatilapa.com.

ACCOMMODATION AND EATING

There's a row of beach *comedores* dispensing surf-fresh prawns and deep-fried fish (around Q50 a meal), plus Gallo beer in Tilapa.

El Pacífico Just off Tilapita beach ☎ 5940 1524. This small hotel, popular with travellers, has large, bare rooms with decent mattresses, fans and showers – though you might want to bring your own mosquito net. The pool is filled most weekends. Good food, including fresh fish, is served (a huge meal is about Q50) and the beers are ice cold. It's run by a welcoming local couple; no advance reservations. **Q100**

RETALHULEU

RETALHULEU, usually referred to as **Reu** (pronounced "Ray-oo"), may be one of the largest towns in the area, but that doesn't mean it's exciting. However, it is something of a transport hub, with many **buses** running along the coastal highway

stopping at the Retalhuleu terminal, a ten-minute walk from the plaza. If you find yourself with time on your hands, take a look at the **Museo de Arqueología y Etnología**, on the plaza (Tues–Sat 8am–5.30pm; Q15), home to an amazing collection of anthropomorphic figurines, mostly heads, and some photographs of the town dating back to the 1880s.

ARRIVAL AND DEPARTURE

By bus From Reu there are buses to Guatemala City (every 30min; 3hr), the Mexican border (every 30min; 1hr 30min) and Quetzaltenango (every 30min; 1hr 15min), plus regular buses to Champerico (1hr) and the beach at El Tulate (1hr 45min) until about 6.30pm.

ACCOMMODATION AND EATING

Cafetería La Luna 5 C & 8 Av. Two blocks south of the plaza, this dependable place has satisfying *comida típica*, including tasty breakfasts. Daily 7.30am–10pm.
Hotel América 8 Av 9–32 ☎ 7771 1154. An inexpensive place to stay with well-kept rooms with fan and private bathrooms. **Q135**

TAKALIK ABAJ

TAKALIK ABAJ (daily 7am–5pm; Q50) is among the most important Mesoamerican sites in the country and one of the few that has both Olmec and Maya features. Though the remains of two large **temple platforms** have been cleared, it's the sculptures and steles found carved around their base, including rare and unusual representations of frogs and toads (monument 68) and an alligator (monument 66), that make a trip here worthwhile. Among the finest carvings is stele 5, which features two standing figures separated by a hieroglyphic panel that has been dated to 126 AD. Look out for giant Olmec-style heads too, including one with great chipmunk cheeks. Royal tombs unearthed in 2002 and 2012 confirmed that following the Olmec, the site was later occupied by the Maya.

To get to Takalik Abaj, take a local **bus** from Reu 15km west to the village of El Asintal, from where you can take a pick-up (Q5) to the site, 4km away.

CHAMPERICO

A fast highway runs the 40km or so south from Reu to the beach at **CHAMPERICO**, which is best visited as a day-trip. The town enjoyed a brief period of prosperity many decades ago when it was connected to Quetzaltenango by rail, though there's little sign of this now apart from a rusting pier. The dark-sand **beach** is impressive for its scale (though watch out for the dangerous undertow), but perhaps the best reason for visiting is **seafood**; there are rows of beachside *comedores*, all offering deep-fried prawns and fresh fish for around Q60 a head. Don't wander too far from the busiest part of the beach – muggings have occurred in isolated spots here. **Buses** run between Champerico and Quetzaltenango every hour or so until 6pm (2hr 15min), and there are also very regular connections to Retalhuleu.

SANTA LUCÍA COTZUMALGUAPA AND AROUND

The nondescript coastal town of **SANTA LUCÍA COTZUMALGUAPA** functions as a good base to explore three mysterious Pipil **archeological sites** that are scattered around the surrounding cane fields. Bear in mind, though, that getting to them all isn't easy unless you have your own transport or hire a taxi.

WHAT TO SEE AND DO

Four **archeological sites** around Santa Lucía are all that remains of the Pipil civilization, an indigenous non-Maya culture with links to Mexico known for their intricate stone carvings. Don't attempt to visit the sites on foot, as muggers hide in the cane fields. Hire a **taxi** in the plaza in Santa Lucía – to visit all four sites in an hour or so reckon on at least Q100.

Bilbao

Unearthed in 1860, the site of **Bilbao** (on the northern edge of town) has four sets of stones visible *in situ*, two of which perfectly illustrate the magnificent precision of the Pipil carving techniques, beautifully preserved in slabs of black volcanic rock. The carved bird-like patterns, with strange circular glyphs, are arranged in groups of three.

El Baúl

This hilltop site, about 3km beyond Bilbao, has two stone monuments. One is a standing figure wearing a skirt and a spectacular headdress, the other a massive half-buried stone head (known as Dios Mundo) with a wrinkled brow – this is possibly Huhuetéotl, the fire god of the Mexicans. Local people make animal sacrifices, burn incense and leave offerings of flowers here.

Finca El Baúl

Finca El Baúl lies about 3km beyond the hilltop site. Its modest **museum** (admission free) has carvings including some superb heads, stone skulls, a massive jaguar and an extremely well-preserved stele of two boxers (monument 27) dating from the Late Classic period. Alongside all this antiquity is the finca's old steam engine, a miniature machine that used to haul the cane along a system of private tracks.

Finca Las Ilusiones

Around 1.5km east of town, **Finca Las Ilusiones** has a collection of artefacts and some stone carvings in its **Museo Cultura Cotzumalguapa** (Mon–Fri 8am–4pm, Sat 8am–1pm; Q25). Two of the more striking figures are the pot-bellied statue (monument 58), probably from the middle Preclassic era, and a copy of monument 21, which bears three figures, the central one depicting a ball player. To **get here**, head east out of town along the highway and follow the signs on the left.

ARRIVAL AND INFORMATION

By bus Pullmans now use a new bypass that avoids the centre of town. Most second-class buses running along the highway will drop you at the entrance road to Santa Lucía. From Centra Sur terminal in Guatemala City, second-class buses (every 30min; 1hr 45min) run to Santa Lucía's terminal, which is a few blocks from the plaza.

ACCOMMODATION AND EATING

There are plenty of places to eat near the main plaza.
Hotel Internacional Just south of the main highway ☏ 7882 5504. There are no decent budget options in the centre, but this hotel has spacious rooms with either fan or a/c. Q160

SIPACATE AND PAREDÓN

The low-key village of **SIPACATE** is located inside the **Parque Natural Sipacate-Naranjo**, a mangrove coastal reserve. Some of the best **surf** in the country here is about 5km to the east on the empty sands of neighbouring **Paredón** beach, where there's a growing surf scene. Waves average 2m and are most consistent between December and April, though conditions are usually tough for beginners.

Many travellers linger longer in Paredón than they'd anticipated, investing in quality hammock time during the day and combing the beach at night for nesting turtles. Do be very careful swimming in the always-powerful ocean: riptides are common and there are no lifeguards. There are no banks or ATMs nearby, so stock up beforehand, and bring suncream and insect repellent as the Paredón mosquitoes are notoriously hungry.

ARRIVAL AND DEPARTURE

By bus Regular buses to Sipacate (8 daily; 2hr) leave Siquinalá, just west of Santa María Cotzumalguapa, on the Carretera al Pacífico. There are also two daily buses from the Centra Sur terminal in Guatemala City to Sipacate

(4hr). Once you're in Sipacate village you need to catch a public boat to reach the beach. (It's a little complicated to reach Paredón from Sipacate, but the *Paredón Surf House* website has clear instructions.)
By shuttle bus From Antigua direct shuttles are operated by both *Paredón Surf House* and *Driftwood Surfer* (2hr).
By car If you've got your own wheels, you can reach Paredón via Puerto San José. Take the coast road past Juan Gaviota and El Carrizal; the last section is a dirt/sandy track.

ACCOMMODATION AND EATING

Driftwood Surfer Beachside in Paredón ☏ 5783 5946, ✉ thedriftwoodsurfer@gmail.com. This exciting new English-American-owned travellers' favourite has dorms and rooms (all accommodation has a/c and en-suite bathroom), a pool and a great elevated bar that catches the sea breeze. There's a social vibe, roast dinners on Sundays and surfboards for rent. Dorms Q80, doubles Q270
El Paredón Surf Camp Beachside in Paredón ☏ 4593 2490, ⊛ surf-guatemala.com. This simple set-up has dorms (with mosquito nets and lockers) and basic accommodation. Food is prepared by a local family and Rafa, the welcoming manager, is on hand for surf lessons (Q110/hr); boards and kayaks can be rented. Dorms Q75, doubles Q165
Paredón Surf House Beachside in Paredón ☏ 5691 3096, ⊛ paredonsurf.com. This beautifully constructed place has lovely thatched bungalows with Bali-style outdoor bathrooms, a loft dorm with quality mattresses and some very pretty new seafront *casitas*. There's a small oceanside pool, tasty grub (lunch from Q35, dinner Q75), a full bar, surf lessons and boards for rent. Cash only. Dorms Q80, suites Q560

ESCUINTLA

Sitting at the junction of the two main coastal roads from the capital, **ESCUINTLA** is the largest of the Pacific towns, typified by relentless heat and traffic. Unfortunately, it's also dangerous, and the only reason you should find yourself in town is to change buses.

ARRIVAL AND DEPARTURE

By bus Buses to Guatemala City leave from 8 C & 2 Av. For other destinations, there are two terminals: for places en route to the Mexican border, buses run through the north of town and stop by the large Esso station (take a local bus up 3 Av); buses for the coast road are best caught at the main terminal on the south side of town, at the bottom of 4 Av. Buses leave every 30min for the eastern border and hourly for Antigua.

4

ACCOMMODATION

Hotel Costa Sur 12 C 4–13 ☏ 5295 9528. If for some reason you're stuck here, check into this good-value, clean and orderly place. **Q145**

MONTERRICO

The tiny beachside settlement of **MONTERRICO** enjoys one of the finest settings on the Pacific coast. Scenically, things are reduced to a strip of dead-straight sand, a line of powerful surf and an enormous curving horizon. The village is scruffy but friendly and relaxed, separated from the mainland by the waters of the Chiquimulilla canal, which weaves through a fantastic network of **mangrove swamps**. Be sure to take care in the waves as there's a vicious **undertow**.

If you're looking for a really tranquil experience, try to avoid visiting on a weekend when Monterrico is much busier with visitors from Guatemala City.

WHAT TO SEE AND DO

Monterrico's long stretch of **beach** is perfect for kicking back with a book and watching one of the many beautiful sunsets that tinge the sky pink. Squadrons of pelicans – flying in formation and nicknamed the "Monterrico air force" by locals – skim over the ocean, angling their wings to clip the crest of the wave as they glide along the coastline.

Biotopo Monterrico-Hawaii nature reserve

Natural beauty aside, Monterrico's other attraction is the **Biotopo Monterrico-Hawaii nature reserve**, which embraces the village, the beach – an important

4

MONTERRICO

● EATING

Hotel Playa Saltamonte	3
Johnny's Place	2
Pez de Oro	4
Taberna El Pelícano	1

■ ACCOMMODATION

Brisas del Mar	1
Café del Sol	2/6
Hotel El Delfin	3
Hotel Playa Saltamonte	5
Johnny's Place	4

La Avellana

Bus Depot

★ Minibuses/buses to Iztapa & Guatemala City

Itzapa (25km)

Airstrip ✈

Farmacia

High School

★ Pick-ups & Buses to Hawaii

Banrural (ATM)

CALLE PRINCIPAL

Proyecto Lingüístico Monterrico

Super Monterrico

CECON Turtle Hatchery

Parque

Hawaii (8km)

N

0   500
metres

PACIFIC OCEAN

turtle nesting ground – and a large slice of the mangrove swamps behind. The reserve is actually home to four distinct types of mangrove, which act as a kind of marine nursery, offering small fish protection from their natural predators, while above the surface live hundreds of species of bird and a handful of mammals, including raccoons and armadillos, plus iguanas, caimans and alligators. The best way to explore the reserve is in a small *cayuco* (kayak); these are best organized via your guesthouse or down at the dock itself. The reserve's **visitors centre** (daily 8am–noon & 2–5pm; Q40), just off the beach between *Hotel El Mangle* and the *Pez de Oro* hotel, has plenty of information about the environment (Spanish only), and sections where endemic species including sea turtles, caimans, iguanas and other lizards are bred for release into the wild. There's a short interpretive **trail** through the grounds of the centre to explore too.

ARRIVAL AND INFORMATION

By bus The bus stop is just south of the dock, a 5min walk from the beach. From Guatemala City's Centra Sur terminal buses leave for Monterrico (2 daily; 3hr 30min), Iztapa (6 daily) and Puerto San José (every 20min). There are very regular bus links between Puerto San José and Iztapa (every 30min; 30min) and Iztapa and Monterrico (every 30min; 1hr) until 6pm.

By shuttle bus Most visitors arrive on the daily shuttle buses that link Antigua with Monterrico (2hr 15min; Q80).

By boat Boats leave for La Avellana (8 daily; 40min; passengers Q7, cars Q100), from where there are connections to Taxisco (see box, p.336) on the coastal highway.

Tourist information There is no tourist office. Consult ⓦ monterrico-guatemala.com.

ACCOMMODATION

At weekends it's best to book ahead (and price rises of 20 percent are common). All places listed below are right on or just off the beach.

Brisas del Mar Turn left just before the beach; it's on the left ☏ 5500 0811. This motel-like place has forty keenly priced bungalows (with fan or a/c) that are in decent shape, with private bathrooms, mosquito nets and good beds. All face a garden and pool, and there's a restaurant. Fan **Q120**, a/c **Q195**

Café del Sol Turn right at the beach, 250m to the west ☏ 5050 9173, ⓦ cafe-del-sol.com. Boasts a lovely beach-facing frontage, with sunloungers facing the ocean. It's a well-run hotel with a wide choice of accommodation divided between inland and beachside blocks and you'll find a restaurant, hot tub and three pools. **Q300**

Hotel El Delfín On the right at the beachfront ☏ 5702 6701, ⓦ hotel-el-delfin.com. This rambling place is owned by an enthusiastic, welcoming British-Guatemalan couple. Some rooms are awaiting renovation, but all have fans and mosquito nets, and a couple have a/c (Q225). There's an international vibe, pool, bar, cheap food, semi reliable wi-fi, and complimentary coffee and iced water. Your fourth night is free. Dorms **Q35**, doubles **Q100**

Hotel Playa Saltamonte Just off the beach ☏ 5456 9854, ⓔ hotel.playa.saltamonte@gmail.com. The Swiss-German owners of this new addition offer four clean, stylish rooms (Q375 with a/c); rates include breakfast. There are two (small) pools and a restaurant; *Bar Bambas* is on the upper level. **Q300**

Johnny's Place Turn left at the beach and walk for 150m ☏ 5812 0409, ⓦ johnnysplacehotel.com. A backpacking favourite, with an enticing beachside location and nice chill-out zone (a *palapa* with hammocks). It offers a well-designed new beachside block, bungalows (some ancient, some recently renovated), plus a/c rooms and a family-sized apartment. There's a main pool, and several bungalows have tiny private pools too. The party vibe has been turned down a notch recently but the bar here still rocks on weekends. Dorms **Q40**, doubles **Q210**

EATING AND DRINKING

You'll find a row of traditional Guatemalan places on C Principal just before you hit the beach, all offering huge portions of fried prawns and fresh fish for about Q50–60 a plate.

Hotel Playa Saltamonte Turn left at the beach and walk for 150m ☏ 5456 9854. This hotel's bar-restaurant serves good breakfasts, fresh fish, shrimp and pasta dishes. On the upper level *Bar Bambas* (Thurs–Sat

4

INTO EL SALVADOR: CIUDAD PEDRO DE ALVARADO

Very regular buses run along the coastal highway to the border with **El Salvador** at **Ciudad Pedro de Alvarado**. From Taxisco the border is just over an hour away. The crossing is fairly quiet but there are onward buses (every 30min) and a few basic *hospedajes* on both sides of the frontier.

5–11pm, Sun 9am–9pm) has great ocean views and a good vibe. Daily 7am–10pm.

Johnny's Place Turn left at the beach and walk for 150m. Waveside café that's renowned for its *ceviche*, which is available in four different styles, and also offers an extensive menu. It doubles as a bar and there's some DJ and dance action most Saturdays. Daily 7am–10pm.

Pez de Oro Turn left at the beach and walk for 350m ☎7920 9785. This restaurant has a pretty beachfront dining area with checked tablecloths and Italian food including fresh fish, salads, pasta and sandwiches (Q35). Daily 7am–9.30pm.

DIRECTORY

Banks There are two banks; Banrural has an ATM.
Language school Proyecto Lingüístico Monterrico (☎5475 1265, ⓦmonterrico-guatemala.com/spanish-school), on the main drag, offers inexpensive one-on-one Spanish instruction (20hr for Q750).
Police Contact PROATUR first on ☎5460 7045 or ☎1500.

The eastern highlands

The **eastern highlands**, southeast of the capital, are probably the least-visited part of Guatemala. The landscape lacks the appeal of its western counterpart – the peaks are lower and the towns, whose residents are almost entirely Latinized, are nearly universally featureless. You're unlikely to want to hang around for long. **Esquipulas** is worth a visit, though, for its colossal church, home to the Cristo Negro Milagroso (Miraculous Black Christ), and the most important pilgrimage site in Central America. It's conveniently positioned very close to the border with Honduras and El Salvador. There's also the attractive crater lake on top of the **Volcán de Ipala**, whose isolation adds to its appeal.

CHIQUIMULA

Perennially hot and dry, the town of **CHIQUIMULA** is an unattractive, bustling *ladino* stronghold. Few travellers spend the night – if you've just arrived in Guatemala, things only get better from here. Although the centre itself is nothing to boast about, the little **Parque Calvario** square, a couple of blocks south of the main plaza, is a pleasant enough spot with a few cafés and restaurants.

ARRIVAL AND INFORMATION

By bus The sprawling bus terminal is a 10min walk northeast of the central plaza, near 1 C and 11 Av, Zona 1. Destinations Anguiatú (every 30min; 1hr); Esquipulas (every 20min; 1hr); El Florido border (every 30min; 1hr 30min); Guatemala City (hourly; 3hr 30min); Ipala (every 45min; 1hr); Puerto Barrios (hourly; 4hr 30min); Santa Elena, for Flores (5 daily; 7hr 30min).
Facilities Banks and internet cafés are dotted around the main plaza.

ACCOMMODATION AND EATING

Inexpensive *comedores* are around the central market, just east of the plaza.
Hostal María Teresa 5 C 6–21 ☎7942 0177. Located a block south of the Parque Ismael Cerna, this hotel has a lovely garden courtyard and well-presented rooms with a/c and TV. Q180
Parrillada de Calero 7 Av 4–83 ☎7942 5639. For sizzling *churrascos*, this lively place excels at barbecued *lomito*, *pollo* and *carne de res* (beef); meals start at around Q40. Also a good bet for breakfast. There's live music here on Sundays. Daily 7am–10pm.
Pensión Hernández 3 C 7–41 ☎7942 0708, ⓔchapin54@yahoo.com. A warren of a place run by a friendly family, with dozens of basic rooms in several different price categories – you pay a lot more for a/c and TV. There's safe parking and a small concrete pool for cooling off. Q120

VOLCÁN DE IPALA

Reached down a side road off the main highway between Chiquimula and Esquipulas, the **VOLCÁN DE IPALA**

THE BLACK CHRIST OF ESQUIPULAS

In 1595, following the indigenous population's conversion to Christianity, the town of Esquipulas commissioned famed colonial sculptor Quirio Cataño to carve an image of Christ. Sculpted in a dark wood, the image acquired the name **Cristo Negro** (Black Christ). Rumours of its miraculous capacities soon spread – according to the religious authorities, the first miracle took place in 1603, but it wasn't until 1737, when the archbishop Pardo de Figueroa was cured of an illness, that its healing properties were recognized. It has ever since been the object of the most important religious pilgrimage in Central America.

(1650m) may at first seem a little disappointing – it looks more like a hill than a grand volcano. However, the cone is filled by a beautiful little **crater lake** ringed by dense tropical forest – you can walk round the entire lake in a couple of hours. It's well worth heading here if you're looking for some peace; if you visit on a weekday it should be pretty quiet.

ARRIVAL AND INFORMATION

By bus Buses between Chiquimula and Agua Blanca pass the trailhead at El Sauce (Km 26.5), from where it's a 90min hike to the summit.

By car If you've got a (high clearance) vehicle you can access the lake via a steep, rough track from Agua Blanca.

Entrance fee Staff at the visitors centre on the volcano's slope collect a Q15 entrance fee.

ESQUIPULAS

ESQUIPULAS is home to the most important Catholic shrine in Central America. For the past four hundred years pilgrims from all over the region have flocked here to pay their respects to the **Cristo Negro Milagroso** (Miraculous Black Christ), whose image is found in the town's magnificent basilica. The principal day of **pilgrimage** is January 15; if you're in town at this time make sure you book accommodation in advance (or commute from Chiquimula). The rest of the town is a messy sprawl of cheap hotels, souvenir stalls and restaurants that have sprung up to serve the pilgrims.

WHAT TO SEE AND DO

The **Black Christ** is the focus of the town, and is approached through the church's side entrance, beyond a little area full of candles that are lit upon exiting the building. Pilgrims stand reverently in line, slowly making their way towards the image. The walls are plastered with anything and everything – golden plaques with engraved messages to Christ, passport-sized photos that the pious slip into large picture frames, interwoven gold and silver necklaces that, viewed from a distance, form the image of Jesus. Pilgrims mutter prayers as they approach the image: some kneel, while others briefly pause in front of it, before getting moved on by the crowds behind. They leave walking backwards so as to show their respects to Christ by not turning their back on him.

ARRIVAL AND DEPARTURE

By bus All buses leave from 11 C, the main drag. Rutas Orientales runs a reliable bus service between Guatemala City and Esquipulas; Transportes María Elena has buses to Santa Elena (near Flores, Petén) via Río Dulce Town and Poptún. Microbuses head to the borders with El Salvador and Honduras at Agua Caliente until 6pm. For Copán, catch a microbus towards Chiquimula and change buses at the junction on the highway that leads to El Florido (see opposite).

Destinations Agua Caliente (every 30min; 30min); Anguiatú (every 30min; 1hr); Chiquimula (every 20min; 1hr); Guatemala City (every 30min; 4hr 15min); Santa Elena (3 daily; 8hr 15min).

ACCOMMODATION

Hotels in Esquipulas fill up quickly on weekends, when prices (which are always negotiable) increase. Cheap places are clustered just north of the main road, 11 C.

La Favorita 2 Av 10–15 ☎ 7943 1175. Basic, cell-like and very inexpensive rooms; pay a little more for a private bathroom. It's a 2min walk from the church. **Q90**

Hotel Posada Santiago 2 Av 11–58 ☎ 7943 2023. This

4

INTO EL SALVADOR: ANGUIATÚ, SAN CRISTÓBAL FRONTERA AND VALLE NUEVO

There are three border crossings with El Salvador in the region of Esquipulas.

ANGUIATÚ

Buses run to the **Anguiatú** crossing from Chiquimula (every 30min, 6am–6pm; 2hr) and Esquipulas (from 6 Av & 11 C, Zona 1; every 30min, 6am–6pm; 1hr). From the Anguiatú border, buses go to **Metapán** (every 30min, 6am–6pm; 20min), where you can get a connection to San Salvador and Santa Ana.

SAN CRISTÓBAL FRONTERA

Buses connect El Progreso and Jutiapa with the San Cristóbal border crossing (2hr), from where you can get a bus to Santa Ana (1hr). Regular buses travel between Guatemala City and El Progreso.

VALLE NUEVO

Several companies operate very regular bus connections from Guatemala City (see p.284), travelling via **Valle Nuevo** for El Salvador.

---

hotel offers decent value; rooms come with private bathrooms and there's a restaurant too. **Q160**
Hotel Villa Edelmira 3 Av 8–58 ☎ 7943 1431. A reliable family-run hotel with excellent rates for singles. **Q120**

EATING AND DRINKING

Many of the cheaper restaurants and *comedores* are on 11 C and the surrounding streets.
Cafetería La Rotonda 1 Av 10–30 ☎ 7943 2361, ⓦ cafeterialarotonda.com. Popular for Western and Mexican grub (tacos, burritos, burgers) and coffee (including cappuccinos), and they sell beers and spirits too. Daily 7.30am–10pm.
Restaurante Calle Real 3 Av & 10 C ☎ 7943 2405. A large *comedor* serving up generous portions of grilled meats, soups and filling breakfasts. Daily 7am–9pm.

Izabal

The eastern section of Guatemala, the department of **Izabal**, has a decidedly sultry, tropical feel, with rainforest reserves, a Caribbean coastline, a vast lake and a dramatic gorge system to explore. As you approach the coast, skirting the Maya ruins of **Quiriguá**, the landscape dramatically changes from dry, infertile terrain to lush, green vegetation. Although **Puerto Barrios** is nothing more than a port town, the relaxed settlement of **Lívingston**, home to the black Garífuna people, has a unique blend of black Caribbean and Guatemalan cultures.

QUIRIGUÁ

Sitting in an isolated pocket of rainforest, surrounded by a forest of banana trees, the small Maya site of **QUIRIGUÁ** is home to some of the finest Maya carvings anywhere. Only Copán, across the border in Honduras (see p.412), offers any competition to the site's magnificent steles, altars and so-called "zoomorphs", covered in well-preserved and superbly intricate glyphs and portraits.

WHAT TO SEE AND DO

Entering the site (daily 8am–4.30pm; Q80), you emerge at the northern end of the **Great Plaza**. By the ticket office is a small **museum** (daily 8am–4.30pm; free), which explains the site's history (see box, opposite) and discovery. Quiriguá is famous for the **steles** scattered across its

★ TREAT YOURSELF

Posada de Quiriguá Hillside above Quiriguá village ☎ 5349 5817, ⓦ geocities .jp/masaki_quirigua. Japanese-owned guesthouse with immaculately clean rooms in a fertile garden setting. The doubles are very spacious. You'll find the food a real highlight, with fine Guatemalan and Japanese meals (dinner is US$10), good vegetarian choices and wonderful home-made drinking chocolate. It's not signposted, but tuk-tuk drivers know the place. **Q160**

THE HISTORY OF QUIRIGUÁ

Quiriguá's **early history** is still relatively unknown, but during the Late Preclassic period (250 BC–300 AD) migrants from the north established themselves as rulers here. In the Early Classic period (250–600 AD), the area was dominated by Copán, just 50km away, and doubtless valued for its position on the banks of the Río Motagua, an important trade route, and as a source of jade. It was during the rule of the great leader **Cauac Sky** that Quiriguá challenged Copán, capturing its leader 18 Rabbit in 738 AD and beheading him, probably with the backing of the "superpower" city of Calakmul. Quiriguá was then able to assert its independence and embark on a building boom: most of the great steles date from this period. For a century Quiriguá dominated the lower Motagua valley. Under **Jade Sky**, who took the throne in 790, Quiriguá reached its peak, with fifty years of extensive building work, including a radical reconstruction of the acropolis. Towards the end of Jade Sky's rule, in the middle of the ninth century, the historical record fades out, as does the period of prosperity and power.

Central Plaza, seven of which (A, C, D, E, F, H and J) were built during the reign of Cauac Sky and depict his image. The nine steles are the tallest in the Maya world – the largest of all is Stele E, elevated 8m above ground and weighing 65 tonnes. Note the vast headdresses, which dwarf the faces, as well as the beards, an uncommon feature in Maya life. As you make your way towards the acropolis, you will be able to make out the remains of a **ball court** on your right, before reaching six blocks of stone carved with images representing animal and human figures: the **zoomorphs**. Have a look at the turtle, frog and jaguar.

1880s, the port fell into the hands of the United Fruit Company and was used to ship UFC bananas to the US. Puerto Barrios fell into a long decline in the late twentieth century, but a new container facility has revived its fortunes to a degree. However, the town retains a seedy feel, with potholed streets, a clutch of strip bars and iffy characters. The one sight worth a peek is the remarkable **Hotel del Norte** (see p.340), Barrios' last surviving Caribbean architectural landmark, with timber corridors warped by a century of storms and salty air – be sure to take a look at the colonial-style bar and dining room.

ARRIVAL AND DEPARTURE

By bus The ruins are some 70km beyond the junction at Río Hondo, and 4km down a turn off from the main road. All buses travelling between Guatemala City and Flores or Puerto Barrios pass by. From the turn-off tuk-tuks and motorbikes (both Q10) shuttle passengers back and forth to the archeological site.

ACCOMMODATION AND EATING

The village of Quiriguá, just south of the turn-off, has a few places to stay.

Hotel y Restaurant Royal ☎ 7947 3639. Basic place with simple, spacious rooms (some with private bathroom) and a good *comedor* (meals Q25–30). **Q80**

PUERTO BARRIOS

PUERTO BARRIOS is not somewhere you'll want to hang around for too long – probably just long enough to hop on a boat to your next destination. Named after President Rufino Barrios in the

ARRIVAL AND INFORMATION

By boat All boats use the dock at the end of 12 C. If you're heading to Belize, remember to clear *migración* (7am–7pm) first and pay your Q80 exit tax; the office is on 12 C, a block inland from the dock.

Destinations Lívingston (5 scheduled daily, additional services leave when full; 30min; US$5); Punta Gorda, Belize (daily 10am, 1pm & 2pm; 1hr 15min).

By bus There's no purpose-built bus station in Puerto Barrios but all buses leave from near the central market. Litegua buses (☎ 2326 9595, ⌨ litegua.com), some of the best in Guatemala, serve all destinations along the Carretera al Atlántico from a terminal at 6 Av, between 9 and 10 calles. Note that *directos* (some double-deckers) don't leave the highway, but non-direct buses travel via Morales, which adds at least 30min to the journey. Second-class buses to Chiquimula and microbuses to Río Dulce arrive and depart from a stop opposite Litegua's depot.

Destinations Chiquimula (hourly; 4hr 30min); Guatemala City (21 daily; 5hr 30min–6hr 30min); Río Dulce Town (every 40min; 2hr). Microbuses for the Entre Ríos

4

INTO HONDURAS: ENTRE RÍOS

Microbuses (every 30min, 6.30am–4.30pm; 1hr) for the border crossing to Honduras at **Entre Ríos** depart from the Puerto Barrios marketplace. Once there, you may be asked for an unofficial "exit tax" (Q20 or so). Buses leave the border post of **Corinto** for Puerto Cortés (hourly; 2hr) via Omoa. The border crossing is open 24hr. Note border formalities may change if Honduras and Guatemala proceed with a customs union, planned (at the time of writing) for December 2015.

Honduran border (every 30min; 1hr) leave from the market area.

Tourist information There's no tourist office.

ACCOMMODATION

Barrios is not very backpacker-friendly: there are few good cheap places.

Hotel Europa 2 3 Av & 12 C ☎7948 1292. Very close to the dock, this motel-style place has decent (if ageing) clean rooms with two beds and TV with either fan or a/c. It's priced per person, so single travellers get a fair deal and the owners are very helpful. Q160

★ **Hotel del Norte** 7 C & 1 Av ☎7948 0087. A landmark, highly atmospheric Caribbean hotel, built entirely from wood. Unfortunately the facilities are pretty historic too, and many of the rooms lack bathrooms, but with this much faded style and heritage on offer the comfort levels are adequate enough. There's a swimming pool, and the sea-facing location is magnificent. Meals, served in a mahogany-panelled restaurant, are disappointing though. There's also a modern block with bland a/c rooms. Q165

Hotel Xelajú 8 Av between 8 & 9 C ☎7948 1117. Yes, it looks like a prison, but the manager is friendly, rooms (some with bathroom) are clean and it's very secure and cheap. Q80

EATING

For *comedores* and juice stands head to the market where you'll find *pan de coco* (coconut bread) and *tortillas de harina* (wheat tortillas stuffed with meat and beans).

La Habana Vieja 13 C between 6 & 7 avenidas ☎5617 8193. Run by Cubans, and offering excellent meat dishes (from around Q55), a set lunch for Q28, good mojitos and coffee. There's an a/c interior and small street terrace. Mon–Sat 7am–11pm.

Rincón Uruguayo 7 Av & 16 C ☎7948 6803. Head here for *parrilladas* (South American-style barbecues); about Q80 or so for a serious gut-busting feast. Mon–Sat 10am–10pm.

DIRECTORY

Banks Banco Industrial, 7 Av & 7 C, and Banco G&T Continental, 7 C between 6 & 7 avs, both have ATMs.

Internet Red Virtual, 17 C & 9 Av, offers access for Q5/hr (daily 8am–9.30pm).

LÍVINGSTON

Lying at the mouth of the Río Dulce and only accessible by boat, **LÍVINGSTON** is unlike anywhere else in Guatemala – it's largely inhabited by the **Garífuna** (see box, p.90), or black Carib people, whose communities are strung out along the Caribbean coast between southern Belize and northern Nicaragua. The town is a little scruffy, and has a slightly edgy vibe at times, with a few resident hustlers eager to scrounge a beer or sell you ganja. But the vast majority of the population is relaxed and welcoming, and the local culture is certainly fascinating: a unique fusion of Guatemalan and Caribbean life, with a lowland Maya influence for good measure. Be sure to try the delicious *tapado* (seafood soup) and other local treats while you're in town.

WHAT TO SEE AND DO

Lívingston is a small place with not much to do other than kick back and relax. The local **beaches**, though safe for swimming, are not the stuff of Caribbean dreams, with dark sand and greyish water. The sole exception is wonderful, white-sand **Playa Blanca**, though this is privately owned and can only be visited on a tour (see opposite).

The most popular trip around town is to **Las Siete Altares**, a group of waterfalls about 5km to the northwest, a good spot to take a dip and have a picnic. Robberies have occurred here occasionally, however, and though no incidents have been reported for some time, it's best to hire a local guide or visit as part of a tour.

ARRIVAL AND DEPARTURE

The only way to get to Lívingston is by boat from Puerto Barrios, the Río Dulce or Belize; they arrive at the main dock on the south side of town.

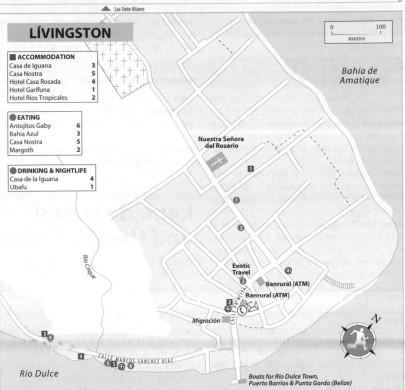

LÍVINGSTON

Las Siete Altares

Bahía de Amatique

ACCOMMODATION
Casa de Iguana	3
Casa Nostra	5
Hotel Casa Rosada	4
Hotel Garífuna	1
Hotel Ríos Tropicales	2

EATING
Antojitos Gaby	6
Bahía Azul	3
Casa Nostra	5
Margoth	2

DRINKING & NIGHTLIFE
| Casa de la Iguana | 4 |
| Ubafu | 1 |

Nuestra Señora del Rosario

Río Chɔque

Exotic Travel

Banrural (ATM)

Banrural (ATM)

Migración

CALLE PRINCIPAL

Río Dulce

CALLE MARCOS SÁNCHEZ DÍAZ

Boats for Río Dulce Town,
Puerto Barrios & Punta Gorda (Belize)

4

For the Río Dulce Boats for Río Dulce Town leave daily at 9am and 2pm. Tickets (Q135/person) for the river trip up the *río* can be booked by any travel agent or hotel in Lívingston. The journey takes around 2hr 30min – all boats stop at some hot springs, Isla de los Pájaros (a bird sanctuary) and cruise past the Castillo de San Felipe – but are otherwise eager to get to Río Dulce Town quickly. To really get the most out of the stunning gorge scenery you need to do a more leisurely cruise.

For Puerto Barrios *Lanchas* leave for Puerto Barrios (5 daily; additional services leave when full; 30min; Q35).

For Belize Boats run to Punta Gorda in Belize (Tues & Fri 7am; 1hr; Q200). Get your exit stamp at the *migración* (see p.342) the day before you leave; there's a fee of Q80.

For Honduras Combined boat/shuttle bus tickets are sold by Exotic Travel (see below) and other agencies to Copán (Q350), San Pedro Sula (Q375) and La Ceiba (Q500).

INFORMATION AND TOURS

Tours If you want an educative, highly informed walking tour of the Garífuna *barrio*, contact Philip Flores (also known as Polo) on ☎ 4806 0643.

Travel agents Exotic Travel (☎ 7947 0049, ⓦ bluecaribbeanbay.com), in the same building as the *Bahía Azul* restaurant (see p.342), is the best travel agent in town. They can arrange trips (minimum six people) around the area, including Playa Blanca (Q140) and the Sapodilla Cayes off Belize for snorkelling (Q450 plus exit fees).

ACCOMMODATION

Make sure you book ahead during holidays; at other times you should easily be able to find a bed.

Casa de la Iguana C Marcos Sánchez Díaz ☎ 7947 0064, ⓦ casadelaiguana.com. It's now under new management but this hostel remains a party hotspot with drinking games, hedonism and all-round merriment. All accommodation – dorms and cabañas with shared (or private) bathrooms – is set around a large grassy plot. There's local and Western grub. Dorms Q35, cabañas Q140

Casa Nostra C Marcos Sánchez Díaz ☎ 7947 0842, ⓦ casanostralivingston.com. A small welcoming guesthouse ably run by gringo Stuart. His rooms are simple and clean, and rates include free drinking water and coffee. Bigger premises are under construction next door with a fine river frontage. The food is excellent, too (see below). **Q130**

★**Hotel Casa Rosada** C Marcos Sánchez Díaz ☎7947 0303, ⓦhotelcasarosada.com. A lovely waterfront hotel run by a very hospitable couple from Guatemala and Belgium. The small, cheery wooden cabins are kept immaculately clean and have twin beds, nets and nice hand-painted detailing. Bathrooms are all shared but kept very clean. There's a huge, lush garden to enjoy and a private dock for sunbathing. Excellent, wholesome meals are served too. **Q160**

Hotel Garífuna Off C de la Iglesia ☎7948 1091. Secure Garífuna-owned guesthouse with neat, clean and good-value rooms, all with fans and private showers. **Q100**

Hotel Ríos Tropicales C Principal ☎7947 0158 or ☎5755 7571, ⓦmctropic.webs.com. Prices have risen here, but these well-presented rooms – some very spacious and with tasteful furniture and art, others much simpler – are still a good deal. There's a sunny patio at the rear with sofas and a little espresso bar at the front. **Q130**

EATING

Prices tend to be higher than in most parts of Guatemala. Make sure you try *tapado* (seafood soup with coconut, the local speciality) – reckon on about Q70–80 for a huge bowl.

Antojitos Gaby C Marcos Sánchez Díaz. Busy, cheap little *comedor* with streetside tables serving local grub and good seafood (including *sopa caracol* and *tapado*). Daily 7am–9.30pm.

Bahía Azul C Principal ☎7947 0151. Popular café-restaurant in a fine old Caribbean building, with an inexpensive menu (try the *coco burguesa* – burger in *pan de coco*) and an excellent terrace for watching the world go by. Daily 6.30am–11pm.

★**Casa Nostra** C Marcos Sánchez Díaz ☎7947 0842, ⓦcasanostralivingston.com. For food with a home-cooked flavour, look no further than this guesthouse restaurant. Breakfast options include granola, hot cakes and vegan pancakes; there's lots of seafood (try the garlic shrimp) and fish, and the pizzas are definitely the best in town. Daily 7am–10pm.

Margoth C de la Iglesia ☎7947 0019. Try *tapado* and a wide array of Garífuna dishes in this large Garífuna-owned restaurant. Daily 7am–10pm.

DRINKING AND NIGHTLIFE

Casa de la Iguana C Marcos Sánchez Díaz. The bar scene here (happy hour 6–8pm) is nearly always lively, and it's really popular with young travellers. Daily until 1am.

Ubafu C de la Iglesia. This intimate bar is a key place for live music, especially Garífuna punta. Bands play at weekends and the odd weekday too. Daily 6pm–1am.

DIRECTORY

Bank Banrural on C Principal has an ATM.
Immigration About 200m up the main drag (daily 6am–6pm). Get your exit and entry stamps and pay your departure tax (Q80) here.
Internet Most places have wi-fi. Rapid Internet is 400m north of the dock (daily 8am–9pm).

Lago de Izabal and the Río Dulce

Fringed by lush forests, wetlands and some outstanding natural attractions, **Lago de Izabal** is a beautiful tropical area with plenty to keep you occupied for a few days. The lake empties into the spectacular **Río Dulce** gorge system, which you can explore by boat from a jungle guesthouse. **El Estor** serves as a good base to access the beautiful nature reserve to the west of the lake, which is home to numerous species of wildlife and secluded spots. The area also encompasses one of the country's most curious natural phenomena, the Finca El Paraíso **hot-spring waterfall**.

THE RÍO DULCE GORGE

From Lívingston, the river leads into an astonishingly beautiful system of **gorges**. Tropical vegetation and vines cling to the walls, and the birdlife is outstanding, with white herons, sea eagles, pelicans and parrots darting over the water.

WHAT TO SEE AND DO

To really get the most out of the stunning region around these gorges you need to **stay locally**, and explore the myriad tributaries slowly – not glimpse it from the speeding *lanchas* that zip between Lívingston and Río Dulce Town. Fortunately there are a couple of excellent ecolodges (both with kayaks for rent), which allow you to do just that.

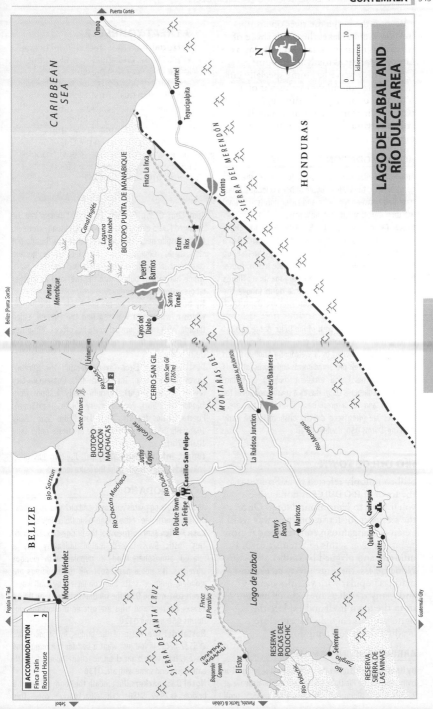

LAGO DE IZABAL AND
RÍO DULCE AREA

N

0   10
kilometres

CARIBBEAN SEA

HONDURAS

BELIZE

Puerto Cortés

Omoá

Cuyamel

Tegucigalpita

Corinto

Entre Ríos

Finca La Inca

BIOTOPO PUNTA DE MANABIQUE

Canal Inglés

Laguna Santa Isabel

Punta Manabique

Puerto Barrios

Santo Tomás

Cayos del Diablo

Livingston

Siete Altares

Río Dulce

BIOTOPO CHOCÓN MACHACAS

El Golfete

Lagito Cayos

Río Chocón Machaca

Río Dulce

Río Dulce Town

San Felipe

Castillo San Felipe

CERRO SAN GIL

Cerro San Gil (1267m)

MONTAÑAS DEL MICO

CARRETERA AL ATLÁNTICO

Morales/Bananera

La Ruidosa Junction

Río Motagua

Mariscos

Denny's Beach

Lago de Izabal

Quiriguá

Los Amates

RESERVA BOCAS DEL POLOCHIC

Selempim

Río Zarquito

Río Polochic

El Estor

Boquerón Canyon

Finca El Paraíso

SIERRA DE SANTA CRUZ

RESERVA SIERRA DE LAS MINAS

SIERRA DEL MERENDÓN

Río Sarstún

Modesto Méndez

Belize (Punta Gorda)

Poptún & Tikal

Sebol

Panzós, Tactic & Cobán

Guatemala City

ACCOMMODATION
Finca Tatin   1
Round House   2

4

Beyond the gorge the river opens up into the **Golfete** lake, the north shore of which has been designated the **Biotopo de Chocón Machacas** (daily 8am–5pm; Q50). This reserve has some specially cut trails where you might catch sight of a bird or two, or, if you've time and patience to spare, a tapir or jaguar. If you're very lucky you may even see a **manatee** here; dawn is the best time.

ACCOMMODATION

Around 7km inland from Lívingston, just west of the main gorge section, there are a couple of fine ecolodges. Boats travelling between Río Dulce and Lívingston (see below) will drop you off at either of these places.

Finca Tatín 400m up the Río Tatín from Río Dulce ☎ 4148 3332, ⊛ fincatatin.centroamerica.com. On a tributary of the Río Dulce, this jungle lodge is well set up for travellers, offering healthy food, table tennis, tubes, hammocks, walking trails, a gym and yoga space. There's a wide choice of accommodation: a dorm (above the bar), private rooms and two-storey cabins. Dorm Q50, doubles Q150, cabins Q225

★ **Round House** 1km west of Río Dulce gorge ☎ 4294 9730, ⊛ roundhouseguatemala.com. Right on the *río*, this sociable place is owned by a welcoming English-Dutch couple and has well-presented dorms and rooms (all beds have mossie nets) and excellent cooking (a filling, flavoursome dinner is Q55). There's a small pool (ideal for volleyball) and it's a great base to explore the area. Manatees are often seen directly offshore in the early morning. Dorms Q50, doubles Q120

RÍO DULCE TOWN

Still commonly referred to as Fronteras, the town of **RÍO DULCE** is not a place you'll want to hang around long. Once the stopover for ferries on their way to El Petén – a gargantuan concrete bridge now spans the river – this tiny transit town is unlovely and plagued by traffic. Nonetheless, there are pretty creeks and marinas popular with yachties nearby, and many travellers find a hotel away from the town itself and explore the sights around Lago de Izabal before heading down to Lívingston.

ARRIVAL AND INFORMATION

By boat The dock is under the north side of the bridge. For Lívingston via the Río Dulce gorge, *colectivo* boats leave at 9.30am and 1.30pm; there are additional services until

4pm (2hr; Q135). Pick-ups from local hotels can be arranged for no extra cost. The boatmen usually cruise up to the Castillo de San Felipe for photographs (but do not stop there), slow down at an islet to see nesting cormorants and pelicans; then stop for 15min at a place where hot springs bubble into the river and at another where water lilies are profuse.

By bus All buses stop on the north side of the bridge, which is where you will also find the Litegua, Linea Dorada, ADN and Fuente del Norte bus offices. Minibuses to El Estor leave from a side road just north of the Río Dulce bridge.

Destinations El Estor (every 45min; 1hr 30min); Flores (every 30min; 3hr 30min–4hr); Guatemala City (every 30min; 5–6hr); Lanquín (daily 1.30pm from *Sundog Café*; 5hr); Poptún (every 30min; 1hr 45min); Puerto Barrios (hourly; 2hr); San Pedro Sula (daily 10am; 8hr); San Salvador (Fuente del Norte only, daily 10am; 7hr).

Tourist information ⊛ mayaparadise.com has good links and listings covering the Río Dulce region.

ACCOMMODATION

All the following places will come and pick you up by boat from the north side of the bridge in Río Dulce Town.

Casa Perico 3km northeast of the bridge ☎ 5930 5666. This rustic Swiss-owned jungle hideaway has a relaxed atmosphere and is popular with budget travellers. It's not a party spot. All the buildings are wooden, built on stilts and connected by walkways. Meals cost around Q30, the set dinner is Q55. You'll find kayaks for rent and trips are offered around the *río*. Dorms Q50, rooms Q120

Hostal del Río North of the bridge, by *Sundog Café* ☎ 5527 0767. If you just want a bed for the night, this place is fine, with eight clean, functional rooms all with bathrooms and some with a/c. Q130

Hotel Backpackers Underneath the south side of the bridge ☎ 7930 5480, ⊛ hotelbackpackers.com. This huge, rickety wooden structure has large dorms and some mediocre doubles. Unfortunately it's looking pretty shabby these days (which is a shame as it's owned by the nearby Casa Guatemala children's home, and many of the young staff are former residents). Dorms Q40, doubles Q150

Hotel Kangaroo On a creek opposite the Castillo ☎ 5363 6716, ⓦ hotelkangaroo.com. Owned by an Australian-Mexican couple, this timber-and-thatch lodge has a six-person dorm and attractive rooms, some with private bathrooms. There's a jacuzzi, a fully stocked bar and filling tucker (though meals are pricey for backpackers). Dorm Q50, doubles Q160

EATING AND DRINKING

There's a strip of undistinguished *comedores* on the main road close to the bus stop.

Benedición a Dios Down a little side road off the main drag ☎ 5797 1120. Famous for its huge wheat tortillas, a local speciality topped with cabbage and marinated beef (there are veggie options, too). Daily 7am–9pm.

Bruno's Under the north side of the bridge ☎ 7930 5721. Yachtie hangout, with a wide menu of local and international grub. The happy hour (4–7pm) features beer for a buck. Free wi-fi and a pool. Daily 8am–11pm.

★ Sundog Café Down a lane on the north side of the bridge ☎ 4865 0035. A social hub for travellers, this Swiss-run place offers great thin-crust pizza (from a wood-fired brick oven, starting at Q55), baguettes and sandwiches (on delicious home-made bread) and espresso coffee. Also offers wine, and all spirits are double shots. Mon & Wed–Sun noon–10pm.

DIRECTORY

Banks Banrural and Banco Industrial have ATMs.
Internet Access the internet at the *Río Bravo* restaurant north of the bridge.

CASTILLO DE SAN FELIPE

Looking like a miniature medieval castle, the **CASTILLO DE SAN FELIPE** (daily 8am–5pm; Q25), 1km upstream from the Río Dulce bridge, marks the entrance to Lago de Izabal, and is a tribute to the audacity of British pirates, who used to sail up the Río Dulce to raid supplies and harass mule trains. The Spanish were so infuriated by this that they built the fortress to seal off the entrance to the lake, and a chain was strung across the river. Inside there's a maze of tiny rooms and staircases, plenty of cannons and panoramic views of the lake.

LAGO DE IZABAL

Guatemala's largest lake, the **LAGO DE IZABAL**, is most definitely worth a visit – not only does it boast great views of the highlands beyond its shores, but the west of the lake on the Bocas del Polochic is also home to untouched forests and bountiful wildlife. Most hotels in Río Dulce Town (see opposite) will organize a lake cruise taking in the main sights, or you can explore the north shore by bus along the road to El Estor.

The **hot-spring waterfall** (daily 8am–5pm; Q12) near the *Finca El Paraíso*, 25km from Río Dulce and 300m north of the road, is a truly remarkable phenomenon, with near-boiling water cascading into cooled pools, creating a steam-room environment in the midst of the jungle. There is also a series of caves above the waterfall, their interior of different shapes and colours (remember to bring a torch). Buses and pick-ups travel in both directions until about 6pm.

Some 7km further west is the hidden **Boquerón canyon**, with near-vertical cliffs rising more than 250m; villagers (including Hugo, a *campesino*-cum-boatman) will paddle you upstream in a canoe for a small fee. Hiking trips into the canyon can be organized too; speak to *Casa Perico* or *Sundog Café* in Río Dulce Town (see p.344) or tour operators in El Estor (see p.346).

EL ESTOR

Supposedly given its name because of the English pirates who came up the Río Dulce to buy supplies at "the store", the tranquil lakeside town of **EL ESTOR** lies 6km west of El Boquerón. Few tourists make it to this corner of the lake, so it's a great place to escape the gringo trail. The town is ideally positioned to capitalize on the vast **ecotourism** possibilities of the lake and its surrounding areas.

ARRIVAL AND INFORMATION

By bus Buses arrive and depart from 3 C west of the Parque Central. Microbuses (every 45min; 1hr 30min) connect El Estor with Río Dulce Town until 6pm. There are 6 daily buses to Cobán (7hr) via Tactic. Some public transport

(1–2 daily) struggles up towards Lanquín via Cahabón, though this route is very mountainous and can be near-impossible to drive during heavy rains. The one guaranteed departure for Lanquín is a private 4WD truck (Q150; 4hr), which passes through town around 2.30pm. You can check all schedules at *Café El Portal* on the main square.

Tour operators Hugo at *Hotel Ecológico* and Óscar Paz at *Hotel Vista del Lago* can organize tours, boats and guides.

ACCOMMODATION AND EATING

Chaabil 3 C, lakeshore ☎ 7949 7272. The cabaña-style rooms here have fans, chunky wooden beds and private bathrooms, and some have beautiful lake views. Their restaurant (daily 7.30am–9.30pm) offers a fine setting for meals (Q35–70) of grilled meats and lots of seafood. **Q160**

Hotel Ecológico Cabañas del Lago 1.5km east of the centre ☎ 7949 7245 or ☎ 4037 6235. Set in a tranquil shady lakeside plot, these wooden bungalows could be better presented and maintained. However, the location and excellent food (huge meals of fresh fish, shrimp or local grub are Q45–80) help compensate. **Q200**

Hotel Vista del Lago Lakeside ☎ 7949 7205. This beautiful old wooden building by the lakeshore is claimed to be the original "store" that gave the town its name. Small, clean rooms with private bathrooms; those on the second floor boast superb views of the lake. **Q160**

DIRECTORY

Bike rental You can rent bikes at 6 Av 4–26 (Q80/day).
Bank Banrural on C Principal has an ATM.

RESERVA BOCAS DEL POLOCHIC

The **RESERVA BOCAS DEL POLOCHIC** is one of the richest wetland habitats in Guatemala, and shelters around 300 species of bird and a large number of mammals, reptiles, amphibians and fish. The ecosystem is one of the few places in the country where you can find manatees and tapirs, and you're bound to spot (or certainly hear) howler monkeys.

ARRIVAL AND INFORMATION

By boat To get to Selempím catch a public *lancha* from El Estor (Mon, Wed & Sat noon; Q40 one way; 1hr 15min) or rent a private *lancha* (around Q700). *Lanchas* should return to El Estor at 7am the same days, but check schedules at Defensores' office (see below). Day-trips to Bocas cost around Q550; ask Hugo or Óscar in El Estor (see above) to recommend a local boatman.

Information Defensores de la Naturaleza, 5 Av & 2 C in El Estor (☎ 7949 7130, ⓦ defensores.org.gt), manages the reserve and can help with information.

ACCOMMODATION

Selempím Lodge Bookings via Defensores (see above). This large mosquito-screened wooden house has bunk beds with mosquito nets. Guides are available to lead you on walks up into the foothills of the Sierra de las Minas and conduct kayak tours of the river delta. Rates include three substantial meals. **Q150**

The Verapaces

The twin departments of the **Verapaces** harbour some of the most spectacular mountain scenery in the country, yet attract only a trickle of tourists. **Alta Verapaz**, in particular, is astonishingly beautiful, with fertile limestone landscapes and mist-soaked hills. The mountains here are the wettest and greenest in Guatemala – ideal for the production of the cash crops of coffee, cardamom, flowers and ferns. To the south, **Baja Verapaz** could hardly be more different: a low-lying, sparsely populated area that gets very little rainfall.

Many travellers completely bypass Baja Verapaz, whizzing through on Carretera 14 from Guatemala City to Cobán and

---

VERAPACES HISTORY

The history of the Verapaces is quite distinct from the rest of Guatemala. The Maya here resisted the Spanish so fiercely that eventually the conquistadors gave up, and the Church, under the leadership of **Fray Bartolomé de las Casas**, was given the role of winning the people's hearts and minds. By 1542 the invincible **Achí** Maya had been transformed into Spanish subjects, and the King of Spain renamed the province Verapaz (True Peace). Nonetheless, the Verapaces remain very much *indígena* country: Baja Verapaz has a small Achí outpost around the town of Rabinal, and in Alta Verapaz the Maya population is largely **Poqomchi'** and **Q'eqchi'**.

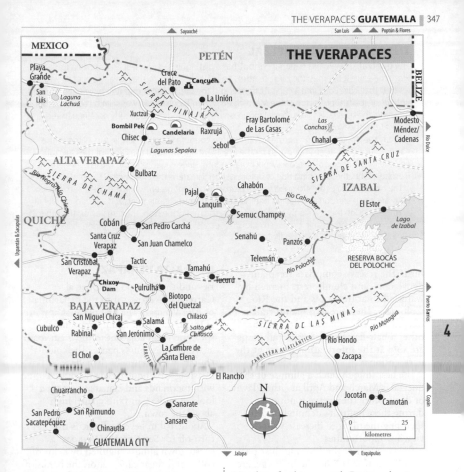

THE VERAPACES

MEXICO
PETÉN
BELIZE

Sayaxché · San Luis · Poptún & Flores

Playa Grande · San Luis · Laguna Lachuá · Cruce del Pato · Cancuén · La Unión

Xuctzul · Bombil Pek · Chisec · Candelaria · Raxrujá · Lagunas Sepalau · Sebol

Fray Bartolomé de Las Casas · Las Conchas · Chahal · Modesto Méndez/Cadenas · Río Dulce

SIERRA CHINAJÁ

ALTA VERAPAZ
Río Negro/Río Chixoy · SIERRA DE CHAMÁ · Bulbatz · Pajal · Lanquin · Cahabón · Semuc Champey · Río Cahabón · El Estor · SIERRA DE SANTA CRUZ · IZABAL · Lago de Izabal

QUICHE · Uspantán & Sacapulas
Cobán · San Pedro Carchá · Santa Cruz Verapaz · San Juan Chamelco · San Cristóbal Verapaz · Tactic · Tamahú · Senahú · Panzós · Telemán · Río Polochic · RESERVA BOCAS DEL POLOCHIC

Chixoy Dam · Purulhá · Tucurú · Biotopo del Quetzal

BAJA VERAPAZ
San Miguel Chicaj · Salamá · Chilascó · Saltó de Chilascó · SIERRA DE LAS MINAS · Río Motagua · Puerto Barrios
Cubulco · Rabinal · San Jerónimo · La Cumbre de Santa Elena · Río Hondo · Zacapa
El Chol · CARRETERA AL ATLÁNTICO · El Rancho · Copán

Chuarráncho · Sanarate · Jocotán · Camotán
San Pedro Sacatepéquez · San Raimundo · Sansare · Chiquimula
Chinautla · GUATEMALA CITY

N
0 — 25 kilometres

Jalapa · Esquipulas

4

the rest of Alta Verapaz. However you should certainly consider stopping off at the **Biotopo del Quetzal**, a forest reserve that's home to large numbers of Guatemala's national bird.

North of here the large town of **Cobán** has some intriguing attractions, some great cafés and restaurants and a good range of budget accommodation.

MARKET DAYS IN THE VERAPACES

Mon Salamá, Senahú, Tucurú
Tues Chisec, Cubulco, Lanquín, Purulhá, Rabinal, San Cristóbal Verapaz
Fri Salamá
Sun Chisec, Cubulco, Lanquín, Purulhá, Rabinal, San Jerónimo, Santa Cruz, Tactic

Heading further towards Petén, take time to check out some of the interesting community tourism projects that showcase Alta Verapaz's limestone landscape, as well as its living Maya heritage. The star attraction in the area, however, has to be the natural wonder of **Semuc Champey**, just outside the village of **Lanquín**.

BIOTOPO DEL QUETZAL

The CA-14 highway towards Cobán sweeps around endless tight curves below forested hillsides. Just before the village of **Purulhá** (km 161) is the **BIOTOPO DEL QUETZAL** (daily 7am–4pm; Q30), an 11.5-square-kilometre nature reserve designed to protect the habitat of the endangered

THE RESPLENDENT QUETZAL

The **quetzal**, Guatemala's national symbol, has a distinguished past but an uncertain future. From the earliest of times, the bird's feathers have been sacred: to the Maya the quetzal was so revered that killing one was a capital offence, and the bird is also thought to have been the *nahual*, or spiritual protector, of the Maya chiefs. When Tecún Umán was slain by conquistador Alvarado, the quetzal is said to have landed on his chest, and consequently obtained its red breast from the Maya's blood.

Today the quetzal's image permeates the entire country: as well as lending its name to the nation's currency, citizens honoured by the president are awarded the Order of the Quetzal, and the bird is also considered a symbol of freedom, since caged quetzals die in confinement. Despite all this, the sweeping tide of deforestation threatens the existence of the bird.

The heads of males are crowned with a plume of brilliant green, while the chest and lower belly are a rich crimson and trailing behind are the unmistakeable oversized, golden-green tail feathers, though these are only really evident in the mating season. The females, on the other hand, are an unremarkable brownish colour. Quetzals can also be quite easily identified by their strangely jerky, undulating flight.

bird. The reserve comprises steep and dense rain- and cloudforest, pierced by waterfalls, natural pools and the Río Colorado. There are two **hiking** trails, one an easy one-hour circuit, and the other a half-day Stairmaster. Trail maps are sold at the information centre at the park entrance.

The best time to catch a glimpse of the quetzal is March and April at either dawn or dusk. Since the reserve is not open during these hours it's definitely worth spending the night to increase your viewing opportunities.

To the north of the Biotopo, just past Purulhá at Km 167 on the highway, are the sacred **Chicoy Caves** (daily 9am–5pm; Q25), where there are towering stalagmites of up to 20m. Maya religious rituals are still regularly performed here.

ARRIVAL AND DEPARTURE

By bus Buses to and from Cobán pass the reserve entrance every 30min.

ACCOMMODATION AND EATING

Ranchitos del Quetzal Km 160.5 ☎ 4130 9456, ⓦ ranchitosdelquetzal.com. Very close to the *biotopo* entrance, this rural lodge has well-furnished accommodation (singles Q175) that fringes cloudforest and a good café-restaurant (you have to pay a Q40 entrance fee to eat here unless you're a guest, as it's deemed inside the hotel's private reserve). The owners are a delight, and will help you spot quetzals in the trees around the hotel. **Q250**

INTO ALTA VERAPAZ

Beyond the Biotopo del Quetzal, Carretera 14 crosses into the department of Alta Verapaz. The first place of any size is **Tactic** – a small, mainly Poqomchi'-speaking town adjacent to the main road, at which most buses pause. The colonial **church** in the centre of the village, boasting a Baroque facade decorated with mermaids and jaguars, is worth a look, as is the Chi-Ixim chapel high above the town.

About 10km beyond Tactic is the turn-off for **San Cristóbal Verapaz**, a pretty town almost engulfed by fields of coffee and sugar cane, set on the banks of the Lago de Cristóbal. From here a (mostly) paved road continues to **Uspantán** in the western highlands.

COBÁN

Though not as visually impressive as other Guatemalan colonial cities, the welcoming mountain town of **COBÁN** is the perfect base for some fantastic day-trips to surrounding forests, rivers, caves and natural swimming pools. The town's microclimate is such that locals say that it rains for thirteen months a year here – heavy downpours are actually quite rare, but Cobán is famous for its drizzle (known as *chipi chipi*). Cobán is also an important coffee-growing centre; you can tour fincas that provide beans for the town's cafés.

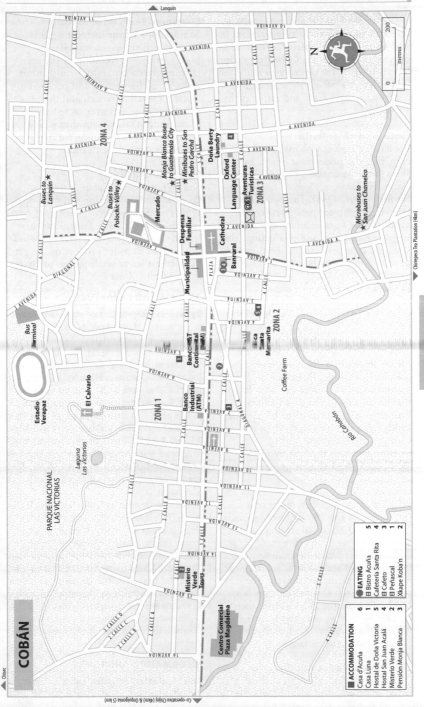

COBÁN

Lanquin

ZONA 4

ZONA 3

ZONA 2

ZONA 1

Buses to Lanquin ★
Buses to Polochic Valley ★
Monja Blanca buses to Guatemala City ★
Minibuses to San Pedro Carchá ★
Doña Berry Laundry
Oxford Language Center
Aventuras Turísticas
Microbuses to San Juan Chamelco ★

Mercado
Despensa Familiar
Municipalidad
Cathedral
Banrural
PLAZA

Bus Terminal
Estadio Verapaz
El Calvario
Banco Continental
Banco Industrial (ATM)

Coffee Farm

Río Cahabón

Laguna Las Victorias
PARQUE NACIONAL LAS VICTORIAS

Misterio Verde Tours

Centro Comercial Plaza Magdalena

Chirrepeco Tea Plantation (4km)
Co-operativa Chijol (4km) & Okjuigonía (5 km)
Chisec
Lanquin

ACCOMMODATION
Casa d'Acuña	6
Casa Luna	1
Hostal de Doña Victoria	5
Hostal San Juan Acalá	4
Misterio Verde	2
Pensión Monja Blanca	3

● EATING
Bistro Acuña	5
Cafetería Santa Rita	4
Cafeto	3
Peñascal	1
Xkape Koba'n	2

4

WHAT TO SEE AND DO

There are several interesting attractions in and around town. Cobán is centred on an elevated **plaza**, with the **Cathedral** gracing its eastern side. The central area is divided into four zones, which are separated north–south by 1 Calle and east–west by 1 Avenida.

Finca Santa Margarita

For a closer look at Cobán's principal crop, take the guided tour offered by the **Finca Santa Margarita**, 3 C 4–12, Zona 2 (Mon–Fri 8am–12.30pm & 1.30–5pm, Sat 8am–noon; Q35). The interesting tour (in English or Spanish) covers the history of the finca, examining all the stages of cultivation and production. You also get a chance to sample the crop and, of course, buy some beans.

El Calvario

A short stroll northwest from the town centre on 3 Calle is the church of **El Calvario**, one of Cobán's most intriguing sights. Steep steps lead up via the Stations of the Cross – blackened by candle smoke and decorated with scattered offerings. There's a commanding view over the town from the whitewashed church, which has a distinctly pagan aura, often filled with candles, incense and corn cobs. The Calvario attracts many Maya worshippers, and the Sunday services are in the Q'eqchi language.

Orquigonia

Six kilometres southwest of the centre, **Orquigonia** at Km 206 on Hwy 14 (daily 7am–6pm; Q30) is well set up for visitors, with an interpretive trail, excellent complimentary guided tour (Spanish only) and a terrific collection of rare orchids, plants and flowers. The wooded grounds also attract many birds and butterflies. The orchids are at their best between November and February. All transport heading south along the highway passes the entrance.

Chirrepeco Tea Plantation

Coffee is not the only crop in these parts, and 6km southeast of town the

Chirrepeco Tea Plantation (daily 8am–4.30pm; tour including guide Q30; ⓦtechirrepeco.com) offers a highly enjoyable roundup of the tea farming process: planting, cultivation techniques, harvesting and packaging. There's a small museum, and the tour also takes in some caves sacred to the Maya and, of course, finishes with a brew. Microbuses heading for San Juan Chamelco pass the entrance.

Co-operativa Chijoj

Some 7km west of Cobán is the **Co-operativa Chijoj** (Mon–Fri 8am–4pm; Q50; ⓦcoffeetourchicoj.com), a community-run coffee farm. Tours here include ziplining across a river and a full explanation of coffee production. To get here, take a *micro* heading west to **Chijoj** from 3 Calle, Zona 2 (Q2).

ARRIVAL AND DEPARTURE

By bus Most public transport arriving in Cobán drops you on the outskirts of town (with the exception of Monja Blanca buses from Guatemala City). The muddy main bus terminal in the north of the city, also known as Campo Dos terminal, has services to Chisec, Sayaxché, Flores, Uspantán, Nebaj, Salamá and Playa Grande. From Campo Dos it's a 20min walk or US$3 taxi ride to the Parque Central. Buses for Lanquín use a bus stop at the junction of 3 Av and 6 C on the northeast side of town. Buses down the Polochic valley to El Estor leave from 3 Av and 3 C, Zona 4. For San Juan Chalmeco *micros* leave from 1 Av A, Zona 3. Monja Blanca pullman buses for Guatemala City use a terminal at 2 C 3–77, Zona 4 (☎7951 1793, ⓦmonjablanca.com). For the Biotopo del Quetzal catch a Salamá bus.

Destinations Chisec (every 30min; 1hr 30min); El Estor (hourly; 7hr); Flores (daily 1pm, or change in Sayaxché; 6hr); Guatemala City (every 30min 2am–6pm; 4hr 30min); Lanquín (hourly 6am–6pm; 2hr 15min); Nebaj (2 daily, or travel via Uspantán; 6hr); Playa Grande (every 30min; 4hr); Raxrujá (every 30min; 2hr); Salamá (every 45min; 1hr 30min); San Juan Chalmeco (every 10min; 15min); Sayaxché (hourly; 4hr); Uspantán (hourly; 3hr).
By shuttle bus Contact Aventuras Turísticas (see below). Destinations Antigua (3 daily; 6hr); Flores (2 daily; 6hr); Guatemala City (3 daily; 4hr 30min); Lanquín (3 daily; 2hr 15min).

INFORMATION AND TOURS

Tour operators Aventuras Turísticas, *Hostal de Doña Victoria*, 3 C 2–38, Zona 3 ☎7951 2008,

ⓦaventurasturisticas.com. Trips include Semuc Champey and Laguna Lachúa. Misterio Verde 2 C 14–36, Zona 1 ☎7952 1047, ⓦecohostalmisterioverde .jimdo.com. Cultural tourism specialist offering ecotourism trips, including visits to the Sierra Caquipec cloudforest (Q1125 for two days) that benefit poor communities.

Tourist information There is no tourist office in town; the tour operators listed above are the best sources of information.

ACCOMMODATION

Casa d'Acuña 4 C 3–11, Zona 2 ☎7951 0449, ⓦcasadeacuna.com. A splendid place to stay, with excellent four-bed dorms and a couple of (small) doubles, all with shared bathrooms, set to one side of a simply gorgeous colonial-style courtyard restaurant (see box below). Make sure you indulge in a meal while you're here. Dorms Q60, doubles Q120

Casa Luna 5 Av 2–28, Zona 1 ☎7951 3528, ⓦcobantravels.com. This backpacker haunt is well run by Lionel, a fluent English-speaker, and his family. Spacious rooms and a dorm (none with private bathrooms) are set around a pleasant courtyard garden with hammocks. There's a TV lounge, tours are offered and rates include breakfast. Dorm Q60, doubles Q150

Hostal de Doña Victoria 3 C 2–30, Zona 3 ☎7951 4213, ⓦhotelescoban.com. This place, decorated with antiques and artefacts, oozes character. The bedrooms all have private bathrooms (though avoid the noise-prone streetside rooms), and there's an internet café and a tour agency on site. Q200

Hostal San Juan Acalá 6 Av 2–50, Zona 3 ☎7952 1528. Dependable little hotel where cleanliness is taken very seriously. All the eleven rooms have good beds, highland blankets and wooden furniture, private bathroom and TV. Q175

★ TREAT YOURSELF

El Bistro Acuña Casa d'Acuña, 3 C 3–17, Zona 2 ☎7951 0449, ⓦcasadeacuna.com. A very classy restaurant in colonial premises with tables dotted around a lovely garden courtyard and several atmospheric dining rooms. It's fantastic for breakfast (from Q30), lunch or dinner, with mains costing Q50 for pasta up to around Q120 for exquisite fish and meat dishes. Waiters in starched white uniforms and classical music add to the refined atmosphere and the wine list includes many tempting half-bottles. Daily 8am–10pm.

Misterio Verde 2 C 14–36, Zona 1 ☎7952 1047, ⓦecohostalmisterioverde.jimdo.com. Fine new hostel with inexpensive rates, attractive accommodation, a great café for socializing and a garden. It's also the base of Misterio Verde tours (see above). Rates include a good breakfast. Dorms Q90, doubles Q180

Pensión Monja Blanca 2 C 6–30, Zona 2 ☎7951 1900 or ☎7952 0531. Agreeably old-fashioned place with plenty of rooms, many with private bathrooms; the hot water is reliable. The courtyard gardens are lovingly tended, and don't miss the Victorian-style tearoom for breakfast. Q160

EATING

Cobán has European-style restaurants and cafés and basic *comedores*. You'll find the cheapest food around the market, but as it's closed by dusk, in the evening you should head to the street stalls set up around the plaza.

Cafetería Santa Rita 2 C 1–36, Zona 2 ☎7952 1842. An archetypal *comedor*, ideal for cheap, filling *comida típica*, including huge breakfasts, with friendly service. Daily 8am–8pm.

El Cafeto 2 C 1–36, Zona 2 ☎7951 2850. This cosy little place serves coffee (from the local Chijoj finca, see opposite), including cappuccinos. It's a good bet for breakfast: a full-on Guatemalan fry-up is around Q24. Sandwiches, burgers, hot dogs and pastas are also served. Daily 7.30am–8pm.

El Peñascal 5 Av 6–21, Zona 1 ☎7951 2102. A new restaurant whose authentic local dishes – *jocon*, steak in cardamom sauce – are widely acclaimed and nicely presented, many of them served in ceramic bowls. Also good for breakfast or a *menú del día* (Q30). Daily 8am–10pm.

Xkape Koba'n Diagonal 4 5–13, Zona 2 ☎7951 4152. Stylish café/restaurant in a gorgeous old house where the walls are decorated with *huipiles* and local art. There's a very inventive menu with snacks and many local recipes including the famous local *kak-ik* turkey soup (Q55), and *kakaw-ik* (a chocolate milk drink flavoured with vanilla, chilli and honey). Mon–Sat 10am–7pm.

DIRECTORY

Banks G&T Continental and Banco Industrial are both on 1 C, west of the Parque Central; both have ATMs.

Internet Inside *Hostal Doña Victoria*, 3 C 2–38, Zona 3.

Laundry Doña Berty, 2 C 6–10, Zona 3. Wash and dry service for US$3.50.

Language schools Oxford Language Center, 4 Av 2–16, Zona 3 (ⓦolcenglish.com), is well regarded.

Shopping The lively daily market is centred on the junction of 3 C & 1 Av at the meeting of zonas 1 & 4, and

4

extends uphill to the streets behind the cathedral, where you can find cheap street food. For supermarket shopping head to Despensa Familiar just north of the cathedral, or Plaza Magdalena on the town's western outskirts.

AROUND COBÁN

The area surrounding Cobán is both craggy and lush, with limestone bedrock and a surface of patchwork fields. There are still some areas of forest, mainly to the southeast, but the Maya population of Alta Verapaz has turned most of the land over to the production of maize, coffee, cardamom and ferns. It's worth venturing into this rural heartland of Guatemala to explore traditional market towns and their surrounding villages, as well as freshwater swimming pools and stalactite caves.

San Juan Chamelco

A few kilometres southeast of Cobán, easily reached by regular *micros*, **SAN JUAN CHAMELCO** is the most important Q'eqchi' settlement in the area. However, Chamelco's focal point is its hilltop **church**, a huge, open-plan space with timber-frame roof and several Jesus effigies with bloody stigmata. The best time to visit the village is the week preceding its annual **fiesta** (June 23), when celebrations include folk dancing in traditional dress and the arrival of numerous saints from neighbouring San Pedro Carchá, brought to greet the holy effigies from Chamelco's own church.

Just outside Chamelco are the **Grutas del Rey Marcos**, an extensive cave network (daily 7am–5pm; Q40, including the services of a guide, hard hat and boot rental). You can take a tour that explores up to 100m into the caverns, which are full of stalagmites that uncannily resemble various familiar objects. To reach the caves, catch a *micro* from the church in Chamelco headed for Santa Cecilia.

Microbuses congregate behind the church on the hilltop and head to Cobán and the surrounding Maya villages.

Balneario las Islas

At the town of San Pedro Carchá, 5km east of Cobán, is the **Balneario las Islas**, a natural pool with a river tumbling into it. To get to Carchá there are regular departures from the car park opposite the Monja Blanca terminal in Cobán. The Balneario is about fifteen minutes east of town – locals should be able to direct you.

LANQUÍN

From Cobán a paved road heads east, almost as far as the Q'eqchi' village of **LANQUÍN** (the last 11km are along a painfully slow and bumpy dirt track). The journey is stunningly beautiful, in spite of the evident deforestation – sit on the right side of the bus for the best views. The nearby natural wonder of **Semuc Champey** is a prime stop on the backpacker trail, and consequently has some excellent accommodation. Most visitors stay at least two nights (either in Lanquín or around Semuc), with weekends and holidays being especially busy.

WHAT TO SEE AND DO

Lanquín itself is a sleepy place, superbly sheltered beneath towering green hills.

Grutas de Lanquín

As you enter Lanquín from Cobán you pass the impressive cave system, the **Grutas de Lanquín** (daily 8am–6pm; Q30), from where the Río Lanquín emerges. You should refrain from using flash photography inside (or outside) the cave as it unsettles the bats that live here. At dusk every day thousands fly out of the cave to feed – you can watch them for free from the entrance car park or anywhere along the riverbank. Tubing down the river from the cave is very popular and a blissful way to experience a tropical river; all the hostels organize tours – after heavy rains the river can be fairly feisty.

ARRIVAL AND DEPARTURE

By bus Public microbuses connect Cobán with Lanquín (hourly 6am–6pm; 2hr 15min). A few buses also struggle north between the Pajal junction and Fray Bartolomé de las Casas (every 90min; 2hr) via a rough road, though ongoing road improvements should speed things up. Heading east, there are buses to Cahabón (roughly hourly; 1hr 15min), from where one daily bus (4am; 4hr) and irregular pick-ups head down to El Estor.

By shuttle bus There are connections from Antigua (2 daily, 8am & 2pm; 8hr) and Cobán (3 daily; 2hr). Note that service standards on these routes are poor, and minibuses are run-down and uncomfortable. The Antigua buses are particularly bad; the 2pm departure involves travelling at night (which is not recommended). On arriving in Lanquín don't listen to what local hustlers tell you about hotels being full; some of these guys board shuttle buses. There's also one daily 4WD shuttle pick-up truck (Q160) at 7.30am to Río Dulce Town.

Destinations Antigua (3 daily; 8hr 30min); Cobán (3–4 daily; 2hr); Flores (2 daily; 9hr).

INFORMATION AND TOURS

Bank and exchange Banrural, just south of the Parque, changes dollars but has no ATM. Many lodges will give you a cash advance (for a hefty commission of around 7 percent).

Tour operators Most of the lodges offer tours, including tubing down the Río Lanquín (Q50) and Semuc (Q170 including entrance).

Tourist information El Retiro and Zephyr Lodge offer good practical information.

ACCOMMODATION AND EATING

Comedor Shalom In the village. Excellent comedor with three or four daily-changing set-meal deals (Q20–30), friendly local staff and clean surrounds. Daily 7am–8pm.

Posada Ilobal Beyond the market in the village centre ☎ 7983 0014. The best of the village cheapies, with a nice garden and five plain, clean rooms in an old wooden house, some with valley views. A good option if you'd rather not be surrounded by gangs of gap-year students. **Q100**

La Poza Riverside Guesthouse A 15min walk east of Lanquín ☎ 4685 5766, ✉ lapoza@rocketmail.com. Beautiful four-bedroom riverside house that's a great deal for groups, with a deck overlooking the Río Lanquín, tubes, table tennis, a sauna and extensive grounds. There are discounts for longer stays. House **Q725**

El Muro In the village ☎ 5413 6442, ⊚ elmurolanquin .com. A sociable new hostel with dorms, doubles and hammock space (Q30), good tours and lots of bar business. Dorms **Q45**, doubles **Q150**

El Retiro On the banks of the Río Lanquín ☎ 4513 6396, ⊚ elretirolanquin.com. This long-running riverside lodge has a lovely setting, and accommodation is well designed,

consisting of four-bed dorms, cabins, suites and rooms, some with private bathrooms. Still draws backpackers, though the vibe is quite not what it was. Dorms **Q50**, doubles **Q100**

★ **Zephyr Lodge** Just north of Lanquín centre ☎ 5168 2441, ⊚ zephyrlodgelanquin.com. This expertly designed hostel-lodge offers stunning views over the Lanquín river valley and evergreen Verapaz hills and has a great pool. The fine accommodation – "luxe" dorms are Q100 – is well-designed and comfortable, and staff are switched on to travellers' needs. The food is great, with plenty of veggie choices, and it's a sociable place with a lively bar scene. Reserve ahead. Dorms **Q70**, doubles **Q300**

PARQUE NACIONAL SEMUC CHAMPEY

One of the most beautiful natural destinations in Guatemala, **SEMUC CHAMPEY** (daily 8am–6pm; Q50), 12km southeast of Lanquín, is a shallow staircase of sublime turquoise pools suspended on a natural limestone bridge. This idyllic spot sits at the base of a towering jungle-clad valley and makes a wonderful destination for a blissful day's wallowing and swimming. Just a few years ago very few visitors made it to this remote part of Guatemala, but the secret is now definitely out, and the pools are very much a key stop on the backpacking trail between Tikal and the western highlands. That said, you can usually find a peaceful corner without too much difficulty.

THE KAN'BA CAVES

It's well worth a visit to the privately owned **KAN'BA CAVES** (guided tour only, 8am, 10am, 1pm & 3pm; Q60), on the riverbank close to the entrance to the Semuc Champey National Park. Best for adrenaline junkies, tours here are run without hard hats and torches – you swim one-handed while holding stubby candles aloft. Sharp rocks and slippery surfaces add to this treacherous assault course, which will leave you shivering and happy to emerge into the daylight. Some tubing is usually included at the end of the tour.

Most travellers choose to visit Semuc as part of a **tour**, which avoids having to wait for infrequent public transport.

There are security guards at the site, but it's best not to leave your belongings unattended. You'll find a small café (reasonable meals are around Q40) and there are vendors selling drinks and snacks at the entrance.

ARRIVAL AND DEPARTURE

By pick-up To get to Semuc Champey without a tour you'll need to catch a pick-up or truck from Lanquín (roughly hourly until 4pm; 45min).

ACCOMMODATION

El Portal 100m before Semuc ☎4091 7878, ⓦ elportaldechampey.com. Community-owned lodge, just a short walk from Semuc, which enjoys river views. The accommodation is inviting, with well-built screened wood cabañas with hammocks and balcony, cosy private rooms and a dorm. There's great birding and a restaurant, but electricity only between 6 and 10pm. Dorms **Q50**, doubles **Q130**

Utopia Eco Hotel 3km before Semuc ☎3135 8329, ⓦ utopiaecohotel.com. Terrific ecolodge in a remote, beautiful location that enjoys a lovely riverside plot on the banks of the Cahabón. There's rustic accommodation and camping, inexpensive (vegetarian) food, a communal vibe and lots to do including hikes, tubing and Spanish lessons. Dorms **Q50**, cabañas **Q150**, cabins **Q375**

CHISEC

CHISEC is a small town, bisected from north to south by CA-14. There's not much here – in fact, the huge plaza seems to account for half the town. However, it makes a convenient base for visiting nearby attractions and has several hotels.

WHAT TO SEE AND DO

Just outside Chisec are a couple of wonderful natural attractions.

B'omb'il Pek

Some 2km north of town, with an office on the highway, is the entrance to the **B'omb'il Pek** caves, accessible on community-run tours (daily 8am–3.30pm; 2hr; Q80). The first "cave" is actually a sinkhole, with vertical sides clad in jungle. Maya ceremonies are performed here. The second cave is only accessed via a tiny entrance, which you'll have to squeeze through horizontally; those with a larger physique will not be able to make it. Inside there's an ancient painting of two monkeys, thought to represent the hero twins of the Popol (see p.312). A pleasant addition to the tour involves inner tubing for thirty minutes (Q30) on the nearby **Río San Simón**, which cuts a tiny gorge through the rock. Very regular *micros* pass the tour office on the highway, shuttling between Chisec and Raxrujá.

Lagunas Sepalau

Some 10km east of Chisec are the beautiful **Lagunas Sepalau** (daily 7am–5pm; Q60 including guide). Set among a protected forest reserve, these three lovely lagoons are ringed by towering rainforest. Guides escort you along a trail, pointing out wildlife (iguanas and monkeys are sometimes seen) and medicinal plants, and can provide you with canoes for paddling across the lakes. The pristine lake waters are perfect for swimming. To get here from Chisec either catch the 10am microbus or hitch a ride with a pick-up (Q5). There's more traffic returning in the afternoon, when you shouldn't have to wait too long for a ride.

ARRIVAL AND DEPARTURE

By micro From Cobán, *micros* run right past the plaza, then continue north past *La Estancia*.

Destinations Cobán (every 30min; 1hr 30min); Playa Grande (hourly; 1hr 30min); Raxrujá (every 30min; 30min). Some northbound *micros* also continue on to Sayaxché.

ACCOMMODATION AND EATING

Café La Huella On the main road, just off the north side of the plaza. For filling, tasty meals. Reckon on Q25 for lunch or dinner; breakfast is less. Daily 7am–8pm.

Hotel La Estancia 800m north of the centre ☎5514 7444, ⓦ hotelestanciadelavirgen.com. Huge concrete hotel with four floors of plain, functional, fairly clean rooms with cable TV and either a/c or fan. There's a good restaurant and small swimming pool. **Q155**

RAXRUJÁ

The small town of **RAXRUJÁ** provides a handy base for visiting the nearby **Candelaria cave network** and the Maya ruins of **Cancuén**. The town itself, however, is no beauty: little more than a sprawl of buildings along the roadside, centred at the junction where the paved road ends and rough tracks lead to La Unión and **Fray Bartolomé de las Casas**.

ARRIVAL AND DEPARTURE

The direct road south to the Pajal junction (for Lanquín) is being upgraded. When finished, it'll be a shortcut to Semuc Champey.

By micro Micros to and from Cobán (every 30min; 2hr) via Chisec (30min); Playa Grande (hourly; 2hr); and Sayaxché (every 30min; 2hr 30min).

ACCOMMODATION AND EATING

Doña Reyna Just north of the main junction in the centre. A simple but satisfying comedor where meals (from Q20) are freshly prepared and portions are generous. Daily 6.30am–9pm.

★ **Hotel Cancuén** Towards the western end of town ☎ 5764 0478, ⓦ cuevaslosnacimientos.com. Excellent place with broad selection of fine value, clean, neat rooms; bathrooms have cold water in the cheaper options, but as this is a tropical-hot town, that won't matter. Dr César, the friendly owner, also offers great tours to the Cuevas de los Nacimientos (see below) and to Cancuén ruins. There's a small comedor on site, plus internet access (Q10/hr). **Q80**

AROUND RAXRUJÁ

The limestone hills around Raxrujá are riddled with **cave** networks and subterranean rivers. Also nearby is the rarely visited Maya ruin of **Cancuén**.

The Candelaria caves

Forming a core section of 22km, the spectacular **Candelaria cave system** is the longest underground complex in Latin America. (If subsidiary streams, galleries and systems are included then it measures more than 80km.) It's quite straightforward to visit part of this cave network, but rather confusingly, there are four possible entrances. Two are community run (**Candelaria Camposanto** and **Mucbilha'**) and two – the most impressive sections – are privately owned (**Cuevas de Candelaria** and **Cuevas de los Nacimientos**).

The Cuevas de Candelaria contain some truly monumental caverns, including the 200m-long Tzul Tacca cave. To reach this cave complex, hop on a *micro* heading west from Raxrujá. At the large "Cuevas de Candelaria" sign, about 5km from town, a path leads south towards a resort complex containing some overpriced rustic bungalows. You don't have to be a guest to visit the caves. A one-hour group tour on foot is Q35 per person, or by inner tube Q100. Usually you can tag onto a group if they have one visiting and simply pay per head. Otherwise, you need a minimum of three to obtain the above rates.

Hotel Cancuén in Raxrujá (see above) offers a full-day tour (Q160; minimum four people) to Los Nacimientos (ⓦ cuevaslosnacimientos.com), where you can visit the crystalline Cueva Blanca, as well as float for several hours through creepy bat-filled caverns on a tube.

Cancuén

North of Raxrujá is the large Maya site of **CANCUÉN** (daily 8am–4pm; Q80), where a huge Classic-era palace, which had 170 rooms, has been unearthed. You can also see the remains of an impressive bathing pool (which was used for ritual purification). Uniquely, Cancuén seems to have lacked the usual religious and defensive structures characteristic of Maya cities, instead existing as an essentially secular trading city. The vast amounts of jade, pyrite, obsidian and fine ceramics found recently indicate that this was actually one of the greatest trading centres of the Maya world, with a paved plaza (which may have been a marketplace) covering two square kilometres. Cancuén is thought to have flourished because of its strategic position between the great cities of the lowlands, like Tikal and Calakmul, and the mineral-rich highlands of southern Guatemala. There's a trail with good information panels (in English), and a visitors centre.

4

ARRIVAL AND DEPARTURE

By pick-up and lancha To get to Cancuén, pick-ups (approximately hourly) leave Raxrujá for the *aldea* of La Unión, 12km to the north, where boatmen will take you by *lancha* for the 30min ride along the Río Pasión to the site. Unfortunately it's an expensive trip – around Q350 for the whole boat – but it can accommodate up to sixteen people. It's also possible to travel via the village of La Isla, but connections here are not as good.

PARQUE NACIONAL LAGUNA LACHUÁ

In the far northwest corner of Alta Verapaz is the frontier town of Playa Grande and the nearby natural attraction of **PARQUE NACIONAL LAGUNA LACHUÁ** (daily 7am–4pm; Q40; ☎5861 0088 or ☎7861 0086), a sublime spot to get off the beaten track for a day or two of tranquillity and swimming in pristine water. The lake is a near-perfect circle of crystal water, ringed by a tropical forest reserve that's home to a host of wildlife, including jaguars, ocelots, otters and tapirs.

ARRIVAL AND INFORMATION

By bus From Cobán *micros* bound for Playa Grande pass the entrance (every 30min; 2hr 45min), and there are good links from both Chisec and Raxrujá.

Visitors centre You pay your entrance fee and accommodation costs at the visitors centre on the road. It is also possible to leave your backpack here and take just a smaller bag on the sweaty 4km walk through the jungle to the lakeside lodge. There's absolutely no access into the reserve by vehicle.

ACCOMMODATION

Park accommodation The well-maintained national park provides camping facilities and a lodge with mosquito-netted bunks. There are good cooking facilities and drinking water, but you need to bring your own food. Camping/person Q30, lodge Q60

Petén

The low-lying northern department of **Petén**, once the Maya heartland, occupies about a third of Guatemala's territory but is home to just three percent of its population. In the last thirty years there has been a wave of immigration to the area, initially encouraged by the government in an attempt to cultivate this wild land. Vast swathes of rainforest have been cleared for ranching and commercial logging, despite the fact that forty percent of the department is officially protected by the **Maya Biosphere Reserve**. However, most sights of note, at least, are still shrouded in jungle, and you will doubtless witness some of Petén's remarkable wildlife.

Petén also boasts an incredible number of **Maya sites** – several hundred ruined cities have been mapped in the region, though most are still buried beneath the forest. The superstar attraction is **Tikal**, but other, less-visited highlights include atmospheric **Yaxhá** and the immense **El Mirador**.

The lakeside towns of **Flores** and **Santa Elena** form the hub of the department, while to the east is the peaceful alternative base of **El Remate**. The caves and scenery around **Poptún**, on the main highway south, also justify exploration, while down the other road south, **Sayaxché** is surrounded by yet more Maya sites.

FLORES' COYOTES

Many travellers experience the hard sell on arrival in Flores from local **ticket touts**, known as **coyotes**. These guys (many speak good English) try to get you to book hotel rooms, tours and transport with them, so they can earn a commission. Some lie about hotels being full (even faking phone calls to popular hotels) and sell bogus tickets. Several travellers every week purchase expensive shuttle/bus tickets to distant destinations (such as Río Dulce or Copán) only to find their tickets are not valid. Be especially wary when arriving on tourist shuttles from Belize and Mexico, when you are likely to be travel-weary and new to the country. Only book direct through reputable agencies and hotels, and if you do get fleeced, report any trouble to PROATUR (see p.275).

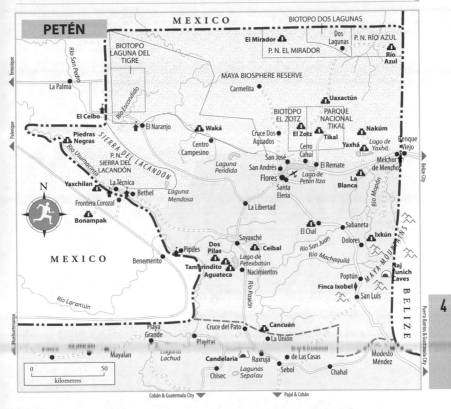

POPTÚN AND AROUND

Heading north from the Río Dulce the paved highway to Flores cuts through a degraded landscape of small *milpa* farms and cattle ranches. Many travellers choose to stop along the way at the sublime *Finca Ixobel* (see below) outside the small town of **POPTÚN**. There's no reason to stay in the town itself, but you may well pause to top up the finances (there are several banks with ATMs). The area **around Poptún** also offers excellent opportunities to visit little-known attractions, including the Naj Tunich caves, Las Cataratas waterfalls near the village of Mopán, and the minor archeological sites of El Chal, Ixcún and Ixtontón.

ARRIVAL AND DEPARTURE

By bus and minibus Minibuses shuttle between Poptún and Santa Elena (for Flores) until 6.30pm, while a constant stream of buses and minibuses heads south to Río Dulce and on to Guatemala City all day and night.

Destinations Guatemala City (every 30min; 7hr) via Río Dulce Town; Santa Elena (every 30min; 1hr 45min).

ACCOMMODATION

★**Finca Ixobel** 5km south of Poptún ☎5410 4307, ⓦfincaixobel.com. This farm and ecolodge is a legendary travellers' meeting point. It's a supremely beautiful and relaxing place where you can swim in the pond, walk in pine forests and enjoy delicious (mostly organic and home-grown) food. The finca uses solar power and natural composting. You run a tab (dinner costs Q30–70), paying when you leave – which can be a rude awakening. Volunteer workers are usually needed. Activities include horseriding (Q100) and a famous river cave trip (Q80). Microbuses and chicken buses will drop you off at the entrance gate, from where it's a 15min walk; after dark, take a tuk-tuk from Poptún (Q15). Camping/person Q35, dorms Q40, doubles Q145, tree houses Q145

FLORES

Lago de Petén Itzá

Lanchas/water-taxis

Museo Santa
Barbara
Isla
Santa
Barbara

CALLE FRATERNIDED

Boats to
San Miguel & Tayasal

Handicrafts
Market
Theatre
Banrural
PARQUE
AVENIDA FLORES
Catholic Church
Gobernación
Departmental
CENTRAL
CALLE
EL ROSARIO

Martsam Travel
Supermarket
& ATM
Beto's
INGUAT
CALLE CENTRAL
Mayan
Adventure

CALLE CENTRO AMERICA

San Juan
Travel
CALLE SUR
Bus
Stop

Causeway to Santa Elena (750m)

● EATING

Café Arqueológico Yaxhá	4
Cool Beans	2
Mijaro	5
Terrazzo	1
La Villa del Chef	3

N

■ ACCOMMODATION

Los Amigos	5
Chaltunha Hostal	1
Doña Goya's	2
Hospedaje Yaxhá	6
Hotel Casa Amelia	4
Hotel Mirador del Lago	3
Hotel Petenchel	7

0		200
	metres	

SANTA ELENA

1 CALLE
Maya
Mall

CALLE PRINCIPAL

SAN
BENITO

SANTA
ELENA

1 CALLE A
San Juan
Travel
2 CALLE
3 CALLE
3 CALLE

Turismo
Aventura
Banco
Agromercantil (ATM)
4 CALLE (CALLE PRINCIPAL)

N

Banco
Industrial
(ATM)
Market
Terminal
Viejo
4 CALLE A

5 CALLE

Terminal Nuevo (500m)

Airport, Tikal & Belize

0		200
	metres	

FLORES AND SANTA ELENA

Despite the legions of tourists that pass through, the charming town of **FLORES** – gateway to the Mundo Maya and the capital of Petén – has retained an easy pace and a sedate, old-world atmosphere. This tiny island (joined by a 500m causeway to the shore) on Lago de Petén Itzá has historically been a natural point of settlement. It remained the capital of the Itzá Maya until 1697, when the Spanish finally forced the town (then known as Tayasal) under their control. Across the causeway, **SANTA ELENA** and adjoining San Benito are home to the gritty business of

Guatemalan life, with sprawling markets and multiple hardware stores.

Flores boasts the lion's share of quality restaurants and decent budget accommodation, while Santa Elena is the region's transport hub and home to several banks and characterless expensive hotels. You will inevitably pass through Santa Elena on your way in and out of Flores, but there is no particular reason to visit here other than to check out the market, which chaotically surrounds the old (still partly used) bus terminal, Terminal Viejo.

ARRIVAL AND DEPARTURE

By plane The airport is 3km east of the causeway. Tuk-tuks/taxis charge Q15–20 for a ride between the airport and town. Note that demand for flights to Guatemala City is heavy in peak periods, and over-booking is common. Reserve well in advance and arrive promptly for check-in.

Destinations Guatemala City (3 daily; 2 with Avianca ⓦ avianca.com and 1 with TAG ⓦ tag.com.gt; 50min). Belize City (2 daily with Tropic Air ⓦ tropicair.com; 45min)

By bus Most buses use Santa Elena's large, modern Terminal Nuevo on 6 Av about 2km south of the causeway (Linea Dorada buses continue on to Flores). There are also some services around Lago de Petén Itzá, to San Andrés and San José from here. For Copán in Honduras, catch a bus heading for San Pedro Sula. Some local buses also use bus stops at the market in Santa Elena – there are buses from here to destinations across Petén, including Poptún and Sayaxché. Tuk tuks from Santa Elena to Flores cost Q5.

Destinations from Terminal Nuevo Belize City (daily 7am, with Linea Dorada; 5hr); Chiquimula (5 daily; 7hr 30min); El Ceibo border (6 daily; 4hr); El Naranjo (every 30min; 4hr); El Remate (every 30min; 45min); Guatemala City (3 daily with ADN; 4 daily with Linea Dorada; 15 daily with Fuente del Norte; 2 daily with Rápidos del Sur; most services stop in both Poptún and Río Dulce en route; 8–9hr); La Técnica via Bethel (5 daily; 4hr 30min); Melchor de Menchos (*micros* every 30min; 2hr 15min); Poptún (hourly; 2hr); San Pedro Sula, Honduras (daily 5.45am, with Fuente del Norte; daily 6am & 10am, with María Elena; 12–14hr); San Salvador (daily 5.45am, with Fuente del Norte; 12hr); Sayaxché (every 30min; 2hr); Tikal (6 daily; 1hr 30min); Uaxactún (1 daily; 2hr 30min).

Destinations from Terminal Viejo Carmelita (daily 1pm; 3–4hr); San Andrés (every 45min; 30min); San José (every 45min; 35min).

By shuttle bus You should only book shuttle buses and tours through recommended travel agents or hotels. Don't buy tickets from freelance guides, as scams are common. Note that San Juan Travel uses its own private terminal on 6 Av in Santa Elena, but will collect you from your accommodation.

Destinations Belize City (daily 5am, with San Juan Travel; 5hr); Chetumal (daily 5am, with San Juan Travel; 8hr); Cobán (3 daily, in the morning; 5hr 30min); Lanquín (3 daily, in the morning; 8hr); Palenque (daily 5am; 8hr); Tikal (several daily; 1hr).

GETTING AROUND

Canoes La Villa del Chef (see p.361) rents canoes for Q20/hr.

Lanchas You can hop across to the Tayasal Peninsula by *lancha* for a quetzal or two; they run on a regular basis until 11pm from the dock on Flores's northeast shore. Boatmen also offer day and half-day trips to explore the lake by *lancha*. They tend to hang out around the southwest corner of the island, close to *Hotel Petenchel* and near the dock for San Miguel.

TOUR OPERATORS IN FLORES

Flores has dozens of tour operators, many of them pretty average. For **Tikal**, it's easiest to book your bus via your hotel, as no matter who you book with you're likely to end up on a shuttle operated by San Juan Travel, 6 Av, Santa Elena (ⓣ 5847 4729). This agency does not have the best reputation, but has recently improved a little; however, it's best to use them for shuttle buses only. Three of the best agencies are:

Martsam Travel C 30 de Junio, Flores ⓣ 7867 5093, ⓦ martsam.com. A professional outfit offering well-organized trips to sites including Tikal, Yaxhá and Aguateca.

Mayan Adventure Inside *Café Arqueológico Yaxhá*, C 15 de Septiembre, Flores ⓣ 5830 2060, ⓦ the-mayan-adventure.com. Archeologist owner Dieter offers great trips to Yaxhá and La Blanca (Q400/head for four people) and the ruins of El Zotz, Nakúm and Nixtun Ch'ich'.

Turismo Aventura 6 Av & 4 C, Santa Elena ⓣ 7926 0398, ⓦ toursguatemala.com. A good all-rounder with visits to Maya ruins, tailor-made trips and airline tickets.

Taxis and tuk-tuks For short hops, tuk-tuk drivers charge Q5–10 for anywhere in the Flores/Santa Elena/San Benito area.

INFORMATION AND TOURS

Tourist information *Los Amigos* hostel is probably the best source of advice for budget travellers. Otherwise Inguat has an office on C Centro América in Flores (Mon–Fri 8am–4pm; ☎7867 5365, ✉peten@inguat.gob.gt), and two booths: one on Calle Sur in Flores, the other at the airport.

ACCOMMODATION

There are several good budget places in Flores itself, making it unnecessary to stay in noisier and dirtier Santa Elena. For even more tranquillity, try sleepy San Miguel just across the lake.

★ **Los Amigos** C Central ☎7867 5075 or ☎4495 2399, ⓦamigoshostel.com. Flores's main backpacker base has been upgraded recently but retains its sociable vibe. There's a pretty courtyard garden, an eclectic veggie menu, DVD collection, secure charge points for mobile phones and a reliable travel agency with excellent transport info. Accommodation options have expanded across the road and there are now posher dorms (with a/c available and also a late-night (sound-proofed) lounge bar and movie room. Dorms <u>Q55</u>, doubles <u>Q160</u>

Chaltunha Hostel Across the lake in San Miguel village ☎4219 0851, ⓦchaltunhahostel.com. The welcoming vibe and stunning lake views are the plus points at this hotel, located in tranquil San Miguel. It offers comfortable-enough screened rooms, basic dorms and excellent travel advice and there's a small pool. Rates include breakfast; boat transfers are US$0.75. There's a second, less attractive branch in Flores. Dorms <u>Q50</u>, doubles <u>Q160</u>

Doña Goya's C La Unión ☎7867 5513, ✉hospedajedonagoya@yahoo.com. Budget hotel offering no-frills but spacious dorms (which lack lockers) and reasonably large doubles (you pay more for a view). The rooftop terrace, with hammocks, is a bonus. Dorms <u>Q35</u>, doubles <u>Q95</u>

Hospedaje Yaxhá C 15 Septiembre ☎5830 2060, ⓦcafeyaxha.com. Simple, clean rooms above the recommended *Café Arqueológico Yaxhá* (see below), all with private bathroom and powerful fans. <u>Q160</u>

Hotel Casa Amelia C La Unión ☎7867 5430, ⓦhotelcasamelia.com. A four-storey green-and-white hotel with twelve good-value, very spacious rooms with cable TV, six of which have great views of the lake. Single rooms are well priced. <u>Q320</u>

Hotel Mirador del Lago C 15 Septiembre ☎7867 5409. The basic rooms at this friendly place have fan, screened windows and bathroom but no views, while those facing the lake also have cable TV. They also offer inexpensive water refills, a laundry service and a small restaurant. <u>Q80</u>

Hotel Petenchel C Sur ☎7867 5450. This place has a row of good, clean, double rooms with hot-water bathroom, fan and TV. There's a little café here, too. Expect some street noise from tuk-tuks and traffic, particularly on weekends. <u>Q150</u>

EATING AND DRINKING

You'll find a good selection of restaurants in Flores, though prices are high compared to the rest of Guatemala. Be aware that some local restaurants still serve wild game (such as *venado*, *pavo silvestre*, *coche de monte* or *tepesquintle*) – this is best avoided, as it is most likely to be poached from reserves. For economical eats, head for the stalls on the plaza (7am–10pm).

Café Arqueológico Yaxhá C 15 Septiembre ☎5830 2060, ⓦcafeyaxha.com. This intimate place has an unusual menu that features many pre-Hispanic dishes of Maya origin, using ingredients like yucca and squash. Main dishes are in the Q40–60 range. The walls of the café are covered with posters and photos relating to local Maya sites, to which Dieter, the German owner, runs excellent tours. Evening slide shows about the Maya are well worth attending, too. Daily 7am–9pm.

Cool Beans C 15 Septiembre ☎5571 9240. A fine café-restaurant with tables that spill down to the lakeside garden. They're trying a lot harder than most here: the breakfasts are excellent (featuring home-made bread, home-made jam and real butter), sandwiches are huge (try the shredded carrot, bacon and guacamole) and mains are delicious (most Q35–50). Draught beer, espresso coffee and cocktails are available. Mon–Sat 7am–10pm.

★**TREAT YOURSELF**

Terrazzo C La Unión ☎7867 5479. Flores's best restaurant boasts an unrivalled upper-level covered deck that catches the breeze, and the cooking is top drawer: chef Juan Pablo has many years of experience in different corners of the globe and he cooks here from an open kitchen. Savour his *saltimbocca* or fettuccini prepared with grated courgette and shrimps (Q70). The decor is quirky too, with retro sofas and artwork. Get here early for a sundowner; the superb cocktails are a bargain during happy hour (5–7pm). Mon–Sat 11am–10pm.

INTO BELIZE: MELCHOR DE MENCOS

There is regular transport from Santa Elena to the **Belize** border at **Melchor de Mencos** (every 30min; 2hr 15min) from the Terminal Nuevo; most buses make a stop in the market area on their way west. It is also possible to take direct services to Belize City and beyond (see p.359). The border is fairly straightforward, although you'll probably be charged a Q20 unofficial exit tax. Moneychangers should give you a fair rate. Once in Belize you'll need to take a taxi (US$3) for the short journey to Benque Viejo del Carmen, from where it's a thirty-minute bus journey to the pleasant town of San Ignacio, or three hours to Belize City (last bus leaves at 6pm).

Mijaro South of the causeway, Santa Elena ☎ 7926 1615. Offers good *comida típica* and plenty of meat dishes at local prices. The daily special is Q24. Daily 7am–10pm.

La Villa del Chef C La Unión ☎ 7926 0296. Elegant place with a lovely vista over the lake from its huge windows and terrace seating. Food presentation, portions and quality are all very good: both the beef and veggie burgers are wonderfully flavoursome, or try the lake fish. There are extra charges for bread and water, but they do at least benefit development projects in Petén. Popular for happy hour drinks (Q10). Daily 8am–10pm.

DIRECTORY

Banks and exchange In Flores, there's an ATM inside the supermarket on C 20 de Junio. You'll find many more banks in Santa Elena, including Banco Agromercantil at the main junction on 6 Av and 4 C. There's also an ATM inside the Terminal Nuevo bus station. Petén Net (see below) will cash euros, Belizean dollars and Mexican pesos.

Doctor Centro Médico Maya, 4 Av near 3 C, in Santa Elena (☎ 7926 0180) is a professional place; some staff speak a little English.

Internet and telephone Tikal Net and Petén Net, both on C Centro América in Flores, offer fairly quick connections, Skype and discounted international calls.

Laundry The cheapest is Beto's on Av Barrios, Flores (wash and dry Q25). It's open daily but often closed until noon.

Shopping As well as the plethora of tourist shops, there is a handicrafts market on the Parque Central (9am–9pm).

LAGO DE PETÉN ITZÁ

While the majority of visitors to Flores rightly prioritize a visit to Tikal, there are other worthwhile day-trip excursions in the region surrounding **LAGO DE PETÉN ITZÁ**.

From Flores it's possible to visit a number of nearby attractions by *lancha*. The tiny **museum** (daily 9am–5pm; Q10), on an island just off Flores's western shores, houses a collection of Maya pottery, while at **ARCAS**, an animal rescue NGO 5km east of San Miguel village (daily 8am–3pm; Q15; ⏿arcasguatemala .com), you can volunteer and learn about wildlife protection in Petén, walk an interpretive trail and view animals that cannot be released into the wild. For the best *lancha* prices you'll need to get a group together and haggle fairly fiercely. Estimate about Q100 per hour.

Península Tayasal

Incredibly, this attractive peninsula, just a five-minute *lancha* ride across the lake from Flores, is largely overlooked by the tourist dollars flooding into that town. The village of **San Miguel** and nearby **El Mirador** and **Playita El Chechenal** make for an easy excursion. Regular *lanchas* leave from the northeast shores of Flores

LANGUAGE SCHOOLS IN SAN ANDRÉS AND SAN JOSÉ

Most visitors come to San Andrés and San José to study or volunteer at one of the local **language schools**. You'll pay Q1500–1700 per week for twenty hours of one-to-one lessons, food and lodging and a homestay with a local family. Very few locals here speak English so you can progress quite quickly. Good schools include:

Eco Escuela de Español ☎ 5940 1235 or ☎ 3099 4846. A community-run, well-established school in San Andrés.

Escuela Bio Itzá ☎ 7928 8056, ✉ bioitza@yahoo

.com. Based in San José, part of a project for the conservation of the Itzá biosphere and culture. Activities include volunteer work in the botanical garden.

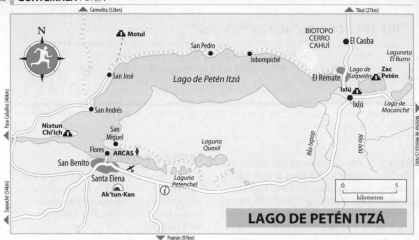

LAGO DE PETÉN ITZÁ

to San Miguel. To reach the *mirador* it's a twenty-minute, fairly isolated walk. Follow the lakeshore west past the village, turn uphill after the last buildings, then follow the track up until it evens out to a shaded trail and take the left branch (keeping the lake to your left). Eventually you'll reach a clearing and lookout tower, from where there are fantastic views of the lake. Back down at the clearing you can follow another trail for ten minutes around the northern side of the peninsula (keeping the lake to your left), until you reach a signposted left turn for La Playita. You can see the turquoise water beckoning you and there is a quiet beach area with picnic benches and toilets. To return to San Miguel village, simply turn left at the end of the beach road and follow the track for fifteen minutes to complete your circuit.

Nixtun Ch'ich'

Spread over a peninsula about 4km west of Flores, the extensive Maya ruins of **Nixtun Ch'ich'** have barely been touched by archeologists. It's an enormous site, with dozens of small temple mounds and a triadic temple complex (ZZ1) more than 30m in height that was a magnificent ceremonial centre. The 60m-long **ball court** ranks as one of the largest ever found in the entire Maya world. A 2007 dig revealed millennia of occupation, beginning before 1000 BC and extending into the early eighteenth century. Nixtun Ch'ich' is situated on private land used for cattle ranching. Virtually all the mounds you see were once temples, but there's been no excavation or restoration, so the site looks like a series of grassy hillocks. Wear good boots and expect to encounter cow dung and plenty of mud after heavy rains. The only access to this intriguing site is via one of the late-afternoon boat tours (Q150/person) offered by Mayan Adventure (see box, p.359) in Flores.

San Andrés and San José

Across the lake from Santa Elena and Flores are the quiet villages of **SAN ANDRÉS** and **SAN JOSÉ**, both of which have good language schools. The villages' roads slope steeply up from the shore, lined with colourful buildings. San José, in particular, has an impressive array of facilities (including a water park), and a lovely public beach. The village is also undergoing a cultural revival: Itzá, the pre-Conquest Maya tongue, is being taught in the large school.

ARRIVAL AND INFORMATION

By microbus Regular microbuses connect Santa Elena with both villages (every 30min to both; 30min to San Andrés, 40min to San José).

Facilities San José has a bank with ATM and several *comedores* serving *comida rápida*.

EL REMATE

The tranquil village of **EL REMATE** lies midway between Flores and Tikal on the northeastern corner of Lago de Petén Itzá. The lake is a beautiful turquoise blue here and many of the budget hotels offer swimming access – extremely welcome after a sweaty morning climbing Tikal's jungle temples. The village itself is a lovely place to take a break from the rigours of the road, with little traffic and a lot of nature to enjoy.

WHAT TO SEE AND DO

On the north shore of the lake, fifteen minutes' walk from the centre of El Remate, the **Biotopo Cerro Cahuí** (daily 7am–4pm; Q35) is a 6.5-square-kilometre wildlife conservation area comprising lakeshore, ponds and some of the best examples of undisturbed tropical forest in Petén. There are hiking trails (4km and 6km), a couple of small ruins and two thatched *miradores* on the hill above the lake; pick up maps and information at the gate where you sign in. It's best to visit the park in the early morning, when it's cooler and wildlife is most active.

ARRIVAL AND DEPARTURE

By bus Getting to El Remate is easy: every minibus to Tikal heads through the village, while minibuses from Santa Elena pass through about every 30min or so. Coming from the Belize border, get off at the Ixlú junction – from here you can walk (it's 2km away) or wait for a ride to El Remate.

Destinations Flores (around 15 daily; 45 min); Tikal (around 10 daily; 40min). San Juan Travel (see box, p.359) operates two daily shuttles buses for Belize City (Q160) and onward connections to Chetumal, Mexico.

INFORMATION AND TOURS

Exchange There are no banks. You can change dollars (US and Belize) at *La Casa de Don David* in the village centre.

Internet There's a little internet place right by the junction in the heart of the village.

Tourist information Several hotels, including *La Casa de Don David* and *Mon Ami*, provide good information.

Tours Santiago Billy, owner of *Mon Ami* (see below), offers

good tours in his 4WD to Maya sites including Yaxhá and Aguateca as well as horseriding. Prices depend on numbers, but if you can get a group together rates per person drop considerably.

ACCOMMODATION

El Remate has plenty of budget places and a few mid-range options, too. You'll pay slightly more for lake views or access, but the setting is so idyllic it's probably worth it.

La Casa de Don David Centre of El Remate ☏ 7928 8460, ⌨ lacasadedondavid.com. A large, efficiently run guesthouse offering spotless rooms (most with a/c) facing a huge garden that extends down towards the lakeshore. Meals are served on an elevated deck that makes the most of the views, and the birdlife is outstanding. There's excellent independent travel advice. Rates include a meal. __Q350__

Casa de Doña Tonita 800m down the road to Cerro Cahuí ☏ 5701 7114. One of the cheapest deals in town, this no-fuss place has four basic clapboard rooms, built above the lake, with great views, and a reasonable six-bed dorm. There's tasty budget-friendly food in the *comedor*. The lakeside location is superb. Dorm __Q30__, doubles __Q80__

Hostal Hermano Pedro Up a lane opposite the football pitch ☏ 2261 4181, ⌨ hhpedro.com. This large wooden house feels like a youth hostel, and has a profusion of rooms (most with private bath) that open onto a communal decked balcony. Rates include breakfast. __Q100__

Hotel Sun Breeze Lakeside, in the centre of El Remate ☏ 7928 8044, ✉ sunbreezehotel@gmail.com. The *Sun Breeze* no longer has lake views, but it remains an excellent budget choice with very well presented, screened rooms. The owners are friendly and offer tours, transport and a laundry service. Doubles __Q80__, doubles with private bath __Q120__

★ Mon Ami 300m beyond Doña Tonita's guesthouse, down the road to Cerro Cahuí ☏ 3010 0284. Superb French-owned guesthouse with rustic well-constructed rooms and bungalows scattered around a tranquil, forested plot of land. All the accommodation has style and character, enhanced by the use of local textiles and artistic flourishes; even the dorm is very spacious and comfortable. There's excellent swimming from the dock, and the restaurant offers some of the best food in Petén. Dorm Q55, doubles Q210

Posada del Cerro 300m beyond *Mon Ami* guesthouse ☎5376 8722, ⊚posadadelcerro.com. Above the lakeshore, this stylish German-owned guesthouse has rooms and apartments (some lack en-suite bathrooms) that blend modern fittings with natural materials in a jungle setting. Fine meals are offered (Q30–110); breakfast is not included. There are bikes for rent too. Dorm Q100, doubles Q350

EATING

You'll find a good selection of simple *comedores* in the village centre, and most hotels have restaurants.

Mon Ami 300m beyond *Dona Tonita's* ☎7928 8413, ⊚hotelmonami.com. This lovely hotel restaurant is not cheap, but the quality is outstanding and if you choose carefully (pasta is Q30–40 and the lunch special is Q55) you won't break the bank. Wine is available by the glass. Free wi-fi. Daily 7am–9pm.

Restaurant Cahuí Near the football pitch. Offers breakfasts (from Q20), *comida típica*, burgers and pasta (meals from Q30). The fine lake-facing terrace makes a great place for a sundowner too. Daily 8am–9pm.

Restaurant El Muelle South of *Restaurant Cahuí*

☎5514 9785. This smart restaurant's menu is not cheap, though there are snacks (sandwiches, burgers and nachos) for less than Q30, and you get free use of the fantastic lakeside swimming pool if you eat here. Daily 7.30am–9.30pm.

TIKAL

Towering above the rainforest, **TIKAL** is possibly the most spectacular and visually impressive of all Maya ruins. The site is dominated by six giant temples, steep-sided pyramids that rise up to 64m from the forest floor. In addition, literally thousands of other structures, many half-strangled by giant roots and still hidden beneath mounds of earth, demand exploration. The site itself is deep in the jungle of the **Parque Nacional Tikal**, and the forest is home to all sorts of wildlife, including howler and spider monkeys, toucans and parakeets, coatis and big cats. Perhaps early explorer Sylvanus Morley coined the most fitting description of Tikal: "Place Where the Gods Speak". The sheer scale of the place is astounding and its jungle location spellbinding. Whether you can spare as little as an hour or as long as a week, it's always worth the trip.

THE RISE AND FALL OF TIKAL

900 BC First known settlement at Tikal.

500 BC Evidence of early stone buildings at the site.

250 BC Early pyramid built in the Mundo Perdido.

c.10 AD Great Plaza begins to take shape and Tikal is an established major site with a large permanent population.

c.250 AD Continuous eruption of the Ilopango volcano causes devastation and disrupts trade routes.

292 AD First recorded date on steles at Tikal.

378 AD Tikal, aligned with Teotihuacán, defeats rival Uaxactún.

550 AD Tikal conquers neighbouring city-states and establishes an influence reaching as far as Copán in Honduras.

562 AD Caracol defeats Tikal in a "star war", probably in alliance with the city of Calakmul, a formidable new power to the north.

682–810 AD Tikal's legendary leader Hasaw Chan K'awil revives the city with a series of incredible victories deposing sequential kings of Calakmul. The Great Plaza is remodelled and five great temples built.

869 AD Ceremonial construction ceases at Tikal; the population dwindles.

1000 AD Tikal abandoned.

1848 Ruins of Tikal officially rediscovered by a government expedition.

1956 Project to excavate and restore the buildings started.

1984 Most major restoration work completed.

Tikal is vast. The **central area**, with its five main temples, forms by far the most impressive section; if you start to explore beyond this you can wander seemingly endlessly in the maze of smaller, unrestored structures and complexes. Whatever you do, Tikal is certain to exhaust you before you exhaust it. Rather too many visitors congregate to witness the sunrise from Temple IV when the forest canopy bursts into a frenzy of sound and activity, but as a vantage point it can't be beaten. There are two official park **museums**, the Museo Lítico (daily Mon–Fri 9am–5pm, Sat & Sun 9am–4pm; Q10) and the Museo Tikal (Mon–Fri 9am–5pm, Sat & Sun 9am–4pm; Q10), which house some of the artefacts found in the ruins, including jade jewellery, ceramics and obsidian flints, as well as numerous steles.

From the entrance to the Great Plaza

From the site map at the entrance, a path branches right to **complexes Q and R**. The first pyramid, with a line of eight steles in front of it, is also known as the Temple of Nine Mayan Gods. Bearing left after Complex R, you approach the **East Plaza**; in its southeast corner stands an imposing temple, beneath which were found the remains of several severed heads, the victims of human sacrifice. From here a few short steps bring you to the **Great Plaza**, the heart of the ancient city. Surrounded by four massive structures, this was the focus of ceremonial and religious activity at Tikal for around a thousand years. Beneath the grass lie four layers of paving, the oldest of which dates from about 150 BC. **Temple I** (or Jaguar Temple), towering 44m above the plaza, is the hallmark of Tikal. The skeleton of ruler Hasaw Chan K'awil (682–721 AD) was found in the tomb at the temple's core, surrounded by an assortment of jade, pearls, seashells and stingray spines. There's a reconstruction of the tomb (*tumba* 116) in the Museo Tikal. Standing opposite, like a squat version of Temple I, is **Temple II**, known as the Temple of the Masks for the two grotesque masks, now heavily eroded, which flank the central stairway. The **North Acropolis**, which fills the whole north side of the Great Plaza, is one of the most complex structures in the entire Maya world. In true Maya style it was built and rebuilt on top of itself, and beneath the twelve temples that can be seen today are the remains of about a hundred other structures.

Central Acropolis

On the southeastern side of the Great Plaza is the **Central Acropolis**, a maze of tiny interconnecting rooms and stairways. The buildings here are usually referred to as palaces rather than temples, although their precise use remains a mystery. Behind the acropolis is the palace reservoir, which was fed with rainwater by a series of channels from all over the city.

From the West Plaza to Temple IV

Behind Temple II is the **West Plaza**, dominated by a large Late Classic temple on the north side, and scattered with various altars and steles. From here the Tozzer Causeway leads west to **Temple III** (60m), still covered in jungle vegetation. Around the back of the temple is a huge palace complex, of which only the **Bat Palace** has been restored.

At the end of the Tozzer Causeway is **Temple IV**, at 64m the tallest of all the Tikal structures, built in 741 AD. Twin ladders, one for the ascent, the other for the descent, are attached to the sides of the temple. Its summit, with stupendous views over an ocean of rainforest, is unmatched, with the roof combs of the great temples piercing the canopy and intermittent roars of howler monkeys resonating across the jungle.

Mundo Perdido and Plaza of the Seven Temples

Southeast of Temple IV, a trail passes some Maya kilns before winding round down to the **Mundo Perdido**, or Lost World. This magical and very distinct section of the site has its own atmosphere and architecture, its buildings designed as an astronomical observatory. The main feature is the **Great Pyramid**, a 32m-high

4

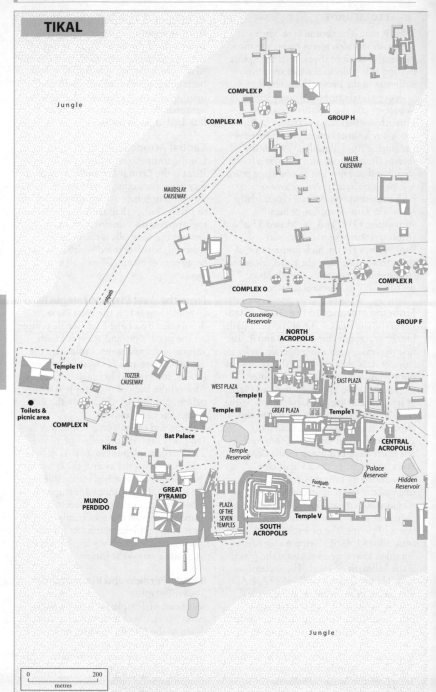

TIKAL

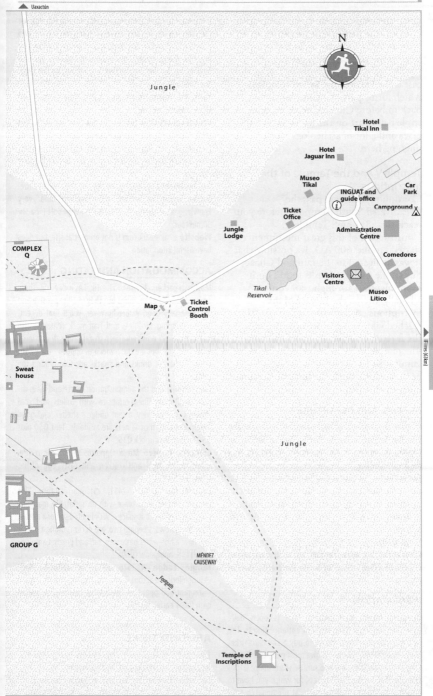

Uaxactún

Jungle

N

Hotel
Tikal Inn

Hotel
Jaguar Inn

Museo
Tikal

INGUAT and
guide office

Car
Park

Campground

Ticket
Office

Administration
Centre

Jungle
Lodge

Comedores

COMPLEX
Q

Visitors
Centre

Museo
Litico

Tikal
Reservoir

Map

Ticket
Control
Booth

Flores (63km)

Sweat
house

Jungle

GROUP G

MÉNDEZ
CAUSEWAY

Footpath

Temple of
Inscriptions

4

structure whose surface hides four earlier versions, the first dating from perhaps as early as 500 BC. After accidents on the steep stone staircase, it is usually not possible to climb this temple. Just to the east is the **Plaza of the Seven Temples**, which forms part of a complex dating back to before Christ. There's an unusual triple ball court on the north side of the plaza and a lot of archeology work ongoing here.

Temple V and the Temple of the Inscriptions

Continuing east, you pass the unexcavated South Acropolis before you reach the 58m-high Temple V. Construction of this great monument started around 600 AD. It's possible that it was dedicated to the rain god Chaac, due to the six large masks found on its monumental 13m-high roof comb. Finally, there's the **Temple of the Inscriptions**, also known as Temple VI, reached via a ten-minute hike through the forest along the Méndez Causeway. The temple (only discovered in 1951) is famous for its 12m roof comb, at the back of which is a huge but rather faint hieroglyphic text.

ARRIVAL AND DEPARTURE

It's wise to arrive early at Tikal when the air is fresh and heat less intense, but note that it's rare to witness an impressive sunrise over the ruins due to mist rising from the humid forest.

From Flores The easiest way to reach the ruins is via one of the tourist minibuses (Q70 return) that pick up passengers from every hotel in Flores, Santa Elena and El Remate, as well as Flores airport, starting from 3.30am.

From Belize If you're travelling from Belize, change buses at Ixlú, the three-way junction at the eastern end of Lago de Petén Itzá, from where there are plenty of passing minibuses (Q35 one way) all day long.

INFORMATION

Opening hours and tickets Tikal is open daily 4am–8pm, and has three kinds of entrance tickets. The vast majority of visitors choose to buy a standard ticket (6am–6pm; Q160) which will give most people sufficient time at the site. There are also sunrise (4am–8am; Q100) and sunset (6–8pm; Q100) tickets, for which you have to be accompanied by an official guide, at additional cost. So

if you want to arrive at dawn, catch the sunrise (though see the warning above) and leave at 4pm, you'll need two tickets (Q100 and Q160). Note that if you're staying at a hotel (or the campsite) inside the national park you still have to pay for entrance tickets (even if you do not enter the ruins area).

Tourist information Inguat has a desk (6am–4pm) close to the ticket office.

Visitor centre Close to the entrance there are shops and stalls (which sell souvenirs, hats, sun cream, memory cards for cameras, film, batteries and water) and a visitor centre, where you'll find a café-restaurant, toilets and luggage storage.

Guides There's a licensed guide office in the visitor centre. Guides, most of whom are excellent and very knowledgeable, charge Q350 for up to five people for a 3hr 30min tour.

Website ⓦ tikalpark.com is not an official site, but does have useful information.

ACCOMMODATION AND EATING

Most backpackers choose to visit Tikal as a day-trip. There are three hotels at the ruins but they're all expensive and not especially good value; however, you'll find decent, secure camping facilities, and hammock rental is also possible. There's nowhere cheap to eat inside the national park. Your best bet are the *comedores* opposite the visitor centre. Cold soft drinks and snacks are sold around the ruins.

Camping Behind the administration centre and main car park. Well-maintained campsite with toilets and cold showers. You can rent a tent under a shelter, and good hammocks with mossie nets are available. Tent Q50 plus Q50/person, hammock Q35

Comedor Impero Maya Opposite the visitor centre. Offers grilled beef and chicken and tasty egg dishes (from Q35).

Jaguar Inn ⓣ 7926 2411, ⓦ jaguartikal.com. This upmarket hotel rents tents with an inflatable mattress, sheets and pillow, but space is very limited so book ahead. Their bungalows, sleeping two, are decent, though pricey, and have a hot-water bathroom, fan and porch. Camping/tent Q135, bungalow Q670

Jungle Lodge ⓣ 2476 8775 or ⓣ 7861 0447, ⓦ junglelodgetikal.com. This attractive lodge with a good restaurant and pool has a few basic rooms with shared bath (book early). Q360

AROUND TIKAL

Dotted throughout the Petén jungle are literally hundreds of **Maya ruins**. With tourism booming in the region many of these are becoming more accessible via a selection of trips offered by Flores- and El Remate-based operators. To see these more remote sites independently you will need plenty of time to account for sporadic transport schedules. In addition, some larger, still unexcavated sites require a local guide simply to navigate the ruins themselves.

Uaxactún

Some 23km north of Tikal, strung out by the side of a disused airstrip, are the village and ruins of Uaxactún (pronounced "Wash-ak-toon"). The overall impact of the place may be a little disappointing after the grandeur of Tikal, but you'll probably have the site to yourself. The most interesting buildings are in **Group E**, east of the airstrip, where three low, reconstructed temples, built side by side, are arranged to function as an observatory. Viewed from the top of a fourth temple, the sun rises behind the north temple on the longest day of the year and behind the southern one on the shortest day. On the other side of the airstrip is **Group A**, a series of larger temples and residential compounds, some of them reconstructed, a ball court and some impressive steles.

ARRIVAL AND DEPARTURE

By bus One daily bus (2pm; 2hr 30min) from Santa Elena passes through Tikal (around 3.30pm) en route for Uaxactún. It returns at 5am.

ACCOMMODATION AND EATING

The village is *very* isolated, and as there's no mobile phone coverage everyone uses a community phone (☎7783 3931). Internet access is by satellite only.

Aldana's Friendly, family-run place with bare-bones wooden rooms and camping. Tours of the region and meals (Q30–40) offered. Camping/person Q20, doubles Q50

Campamento Ecológico El Chiclero ☻campamento elchiclero@gmail.com. A good base for travellers, this welcoming place offers simple rooms with mossie nets, camping and hammock space; bathrooms are shared but clean. Owner Antonio Baldizón organizes 4WD trips (in the dry season Feb–June) to ruins of Río Azul, Naachtun and El Mirador. His wife Neria prepares excellent food – huge meals cost Q50. Hammock Q30, camping/person Q30, doubles Q140

Yaxhá

Midway between El Remate and Melchor de Menchos, some 12km off the highway, is the partly restored site of Yaxhá (daily 6am–5.30pm; Q80). The site is rarely visited, but is very well managed with an impressive collection of reconstructed temples and palaces, and numerous steles. Yaxhá's greatest attraction is its stunning location on the northern shores of the tranquil **Yaxhá lagoon** (no doubt the site was originally chosen with this in mind). Many of the remains are from the Preclassic period, and there's a terrific example of triadic temple arrangement at the North Acropolis where you'll probably have a 2000-year-old ceremonial centre to yourself. Views over the lake from the top of **Temple 216**, the site's largest structure, are unforgettable, with 360-degree vistas over an intact rainforest. You ought to be lucky enough to see (and hear) plenty of monkeys too.

ARRIVAL AND DEPARTURE

By road The main Flores–Belize road passes 12km south of the clearly signposted turn-off for Yaxhá. If you're not on a tour, then it's possible to get a ride in a pick-up or *colectivo* (around Q5) from the main road as there's regular traffic to La Máquina village, 2km before the lakes.

On a tour Many Flores-based tour operators offer trips to the Yaxhá area; highly recommended tours run by Mayan Adventure (see box, p.359) include La Blanca and cost Q1500 (based on four people).

ACCOMMODATION

Camping The campsite by the lakeshore has a (cold) shower block.

Nakúm

The substantial ruins of **Nakúm**, which have been the subject of extensive investigation in the last few years, are 18km north of Lago de Yaxhá. This site now has the second largest number of restored buildings in Guatemala after Tikal.

It's thought that Nakúm was a trading post in the Tikal empire. Settlers first arrived in the Middle Preclassic, but it rose to prominence in the **Late Classic** and was only abandoned around 950 AD.

4

Nakúm's ceremonial centre is split between northern and southern sections, connected by a causeway. The **northern sector** is largely unrestored but contains a plaza surrounded by low platforms, Structure X (a towering pyramid-temple topped with a building arranged in a triadic pattern) and Structure W (a fourteen-roomed palace).

The **southern section** is highly impressive; it's here you'll find Nakúm's iconic roof combs – large, elaborate and defining the site's architectural style. The section contains three large plazas surrounded by temples: thirteen steles and ten altars dot the Central Plaza. Its grand **acropolis** contains a **palace** (Structure D) of 44 rooms and myriad interior patios. Clear evidence of Teotihuacán influence has been found around Patio 1, where Central Mexican green obsidian and *Talud-Tablero* – or "slope-and-panel" style – platforms have been unearthed.

ARRIVAL AND DEPARTURE

By road Access from Yaxhá is along a rough track that is usually impassable between July and January (unless the road is improved). The rest of the year you'll need a 4WD, though it could still take 1hr 30min to drive.

Tours Flores tour operators, including Mayan Adventure (see p.360), run trips here.

La Blanca

La Blanca is a small, unusual site close to the Belize border, primarily of interest because it was occupied much later than most Maya settlements, at least until 1050 AD. Most of the buildings date from the Late Classic period; archeological work is ongoing.

The entire site is dominated by a huge, ostentatious **palace** built round a square patio. Intriguing features include a 6m-high arch, fine murals and ancient graffiti.

There's a small **information centre** here with informative panels in English about the site and its history.

ARRIVAL AND DEPARTURE

Tours La Blanca is 12km south of the Flores–Belize highway, the turn-off is 11km before Melchor de Mencos; the dirt access road is in good condition. There's very little

transport from the highway, so a tour makes sense. Combined trips to La Blanca and Yaxhá are offered by Mayan Adventure (see box, p.359) in Flores, costing Q400 (minimum four people).

El Zotz

Some 25km southwest of Uaxactún, along a rough track passable by 4WD, is **El Zotz**, a mid-sized Maya site set in its own nature reserve. A royal tomb, dating from around 400 AD, was discovered here in 2010 beneath the El Diablo pyramid, containing the king buried with the tiny corpses of six infants (possibly sacrificial victims). In addition, many impressive stucco **masks** have been uncovered around the site in recent years by ongoing archeological investigations.

Smothered by vegetation, El Zotz had been systematically looted, although there are guards on duty today. Zotz means "bat" in Maya and each evening at dusk you'll see tens, perhaps hundreds, of thousands of **bats** of several species emerge from a cave near the campsite – one of the most remarkable natural sights in Petén. From the tops of El Zotz's jungle-shrouded temples it's also possible to see the roof combs of Tikal.

To **get here** you take a tour (around Q2000/head) from Flores – ask at *Los Amigos* (see box, p.359) to form a group. This usually involves approximately six hours of walking per day and two nights' camping in the jungle, and finishes at the ruins of Tikal.

Waka' (El Perú)

It's possible to reach the Maya ruins of **Waka'** (previously known as El Perú) independently but you'll need a tent, a good grasp of Spanish and plenty of initiative. The ruins are largely unreconstructed but mainly date from the Classic period when the city was allied to Calakmul. A royal tomb unearthed here in 2004 contained the remains of a queen, who was buried along with stingray spines (used for ritual bloodletting). A second tomb (accompanied by jade jewellery and figurines) was found in

WAKA' WILDLIFE

Close to the Waka' site, at the confluence of the San Pedro and Sacluc, there's a **biological research station** (with good accommodation) at which rangers monitor forests that contain the largest concentrations of **scarlet macaws** in northern Central America. You've also an excellent chance of observing spider and howler monkeys, crocodiles, river turtles and the Petén turkey, and may even see a tapir on the banks of the Sacluc River. The best time to see scarlet macaws is between February and June when they nest in hollows of larger trees, but there are exotic birds in the Waka' region at all times of year.

2012 and is thought to belong to Lady K'abel, a princess originally from Calakmul.

A chicken bus leaves Santa Elena's market terminal at 10am for **Paso Caballos** (4hr), from where you can hike or take a boat to the site, and where local guides may also be hired. It's easier to take a **tour**; companies based in Flores (see box, p.359) offer tours of Waka', often dubbed the "Scarlet Macaw Trail" (see box above). These exciting two- or three-night trips are by 4WD, pick-up and boat along rivers and through primary forest, staying at the research station or camping at the ruins. You can also book tours directly (☏ 5699 3669 or ☏ 4890 9797, ⓦ lasguacamayas.org) with the station.

El Mirador

Only accessible by foot, mule or helicopter, the colossal Preclassic site of **El Mirador** is perhaps the most exotic and mysterious of all Petén's Maya sites. Still buried in the forest, way north of the remote village of Carmelita, this massive city matches Tikal's scale, and may even surpass it. By 1000 BC a settlement was thriving here, and by 450 BC impressive temple construction had begun, the city peaking in influence between 350 BC and 100 AD when it was unquestionably the superpower of Mesoamerica, eclipsing the Olmecs in Mexico and lording it over the entire Maya region. Fittingly, Mirador's name in Preclassic Maya times is thought to have been Te Tun ("The Birthplace of the Gods").

The core of the site covers some sixteen square kilometres, stretching between two massive pyramids that face each other across the forest. One of these, **La Danta**, sits on a vast stone base platform measuring 600m by 300m, the pyramid itself reaching 79m above the forest floor – the tallest pre-Columbian structure in the Americas.

The area around El Mirador is riddled with smaller Maya sites, and as you look out across the forest from the top of either of the main temples you can see others rising above the canopy on all sides – including giant Calakmul in Mexico. Although much of the site is still buried, archeologists are currently

4

TOURS TO EL MIRADOR

For the time being, **getting to El Mirador** is a substantial undertaking, with most backpackers opting to take a five- or six-day **tour** from Flores (although during the rainy season this may not be possible). Tours involve up to eight hours of arduous jungle-trekking per day; you'll need plenty of repellent to kill off the mosquitoes, ticks and other nasties. Tours usually include horses or mules to carry your food and equipment.

Some travellers have successfully organized their own expeditions using freelance guides in the village of Carmelita (which is connected by a daily 1pm bus from Santa Elena; 3–4hr). Doing it this way can work out as cheap as US$220–250 per head (depending on numbers) but most independent trekkers (and tour agencies) use the guide association **Cooperativa Carmelita** (☏ 7861 2641) which has steep rates (upwards of US$350/head).

Contact *Los Amigos* in Flores (see p.360) first before you start planning an expedition. Owner Matthias has been to El Mirador several times, will know the latest situation and organizes budget-conscious trips.

excavating and have already uncovered fantastic Maya artwork inside some temples.

Engulfed by some of the densest tropical forests in the Americas, you're sure to encounter some spectacular **wildlife** around El Mirador, including the resident troops of howler and spider monkeys, bats (including vampires), toucans, plenty of bugs, spiders, scorpions and quite possibly snakes too. Wildcat numbers are healthy, with an estimated four hundred jaguars, as well as ocelots, *jaguarundi* and pumas. You're quite likely to see jaguar pug marks, though the big cats themselves are very elusive.

SAYAXCHÉ

The small town of **SAYAXCHÉ**, on the banks of the Río de la Pasión, is a handy base for visiting the nearby archeological sites of Ceibal, Aguateca and Dos Pilas. The complex network of rivers and swamps that cuts through the surrounding area has been an important trade route since Maya times and there are several ruins in the area. There's no bridge, so all road transport has to use a ferry to shuttle across the river.

WHAT TO SEE AND DO

The Maya sites of **Ceibal**, **Aguateca** and **Dos Pilas** are in an isolated pocket of the country and are seldom visited. If you only have the time (or finances) for one ruin, Aguateca is the most impressive. Whether you choose to arrive by boat or by trekking, the journey through the jungle gives all these ruins a special *Heart of Darkness* aura. Trips can be organized via Flores tour operators (see box, p.359).

Ceibal

Surrounded by forest and shaded by huge ceiba trees, the ruins of **Ceibal** (daily 7.30am–5pm; Q50) are a mixture of cleared open plazas and untamed jungle. Though many of the largest temples lie buried under mounds, Ceibal does have some outstanding and well-preserved carving: the two

main plazas are dotted with lovely **steles**, centred around two low platforms. During the Classic period Ceibal was unimportant, but it grew rapidly between 830 and 930 AD, apparently after falling under the control of colonists from what is now Mexico. This is evident in the intriguing Mexican-influenced carving displayed here.

Lago de Petexbatún: Aguateca and Dos Pilas

To the south of Sayaxché is **Lago de Petexbatún**, a spectacular expanse of water ringed by dense forest and containing plentiful supplies of snook, bass, alligator and freshwater turtle. The shores of the lake abound with birdlife and animals (including howler monkeys) and there are a number of Maya ruins.

Aguateca (daily 8am–4.30pm; Q50), perched on a high outcrop at the southern tip of the lake, is the furthest away from Sayaxché but the most accessible. Extensive restoration work is still ongoing at this intriguing site, which is split in two by a natural chasm. The atmosphere is magical, surrounded by dense tropical forest and with superb views of the lake from two *miradores*. Throughout the Late Classic period, Aguateca was closely aligned with (or controlled by) nearby Dos Pilas, and military victories were celebrated at both sites with remarkably similar steles – look out for Stele 3 here, which shows Dos Pilas ruler Master Sun Jaguar in full battle regalia. In the late eighth century, these Petexbatún cities began to lose regional control, and despite the construction of 5km of walls around the citadel (the remains are still visible today), Aguateca was overrun in 790 AD.

The resident guards will provide you with stout walking sticks – essential as the slippery paths here can be treacherous – before escorting you around the steep trails, past palisade defences, steles, temples and palaces (including the residence of Aguateca's last ruler, Tante K'inich) and a barracks.

Dos Pilas is buried in jungle west of the Lago de Petexbatún. Once the centre of a formidable empire in the early part of the eighth century, with a population of around ten thousand, it has some tremendous steles, altars and four short **hieroglyphic stairways** decorated with glyphs and figures around its central plaza.

ARRIVAL AND DEPARTURE

By bus and minibus Getting to Sayaxché from Flores or Raxrujá is very straightforward, with regular minibuses and buses plying the smooth highway. A ferry (US$0.40/head) takes you over the Río de la Pasión.

Destinations Cobán (2 daily; 6hr); Flores (every 30min; 2hr); Raxrujá (every 30min; 2hr 30min).

Boats and tours There are plenty of boatmen offering trips to the ruins – but you'll have to be patient and bargain hard to get a good deal. Try Viajes Don Pedro (☎7928 6109), its office is on the riverfront; or the owners of *Restaurant Yaxkín* (see p.347) and *Yaxkín Chel Paraíso*.

Getting to Ceibal Ceibal is reachable by land or river. It's easy enough to make it here and back to Sayaxché in an afternoon by boat; haggle with the boatmen at the waterfront and you can expect to pay around Q450 (for up to five people). The boat trip is followed by a short walk

through towering rainforest. By road, Ceibal is just 17km from Sayaxché. Any transport heading south out of town passes the turn-off, from where an 8km track leads to the site through the jungle. Alternatively, hire a pick-up for the full journey for around Q300 return – ask at *Restaurant Yaxkín* (see p.374).

Getting to Aguateca A beautiful 2–3hr boat ride (Q500, up to six people) can get you to within a 20min walk of the ruins. Alternatively, it's usually possible to access the site via the village of Nacimientos (no facilities other than *tiendas*), from where it's an hour or so's walk; the trail may not be passable in the rainy season, however. A *micro* leaves Sayaxché at 2pm directly to Nacimientos, and from the highway junction of Las Pozas, south of Sayaxché, there's more transport.

Getting to Dos Pilas To get to Dos Pilas from the lakeshore you have to trek 12km on foot (or on horseback).

INFORMATION

Banks There are several ATMs in town.

Internet Head to the internet café on Sayaxché's plaza.

Tourist information *Restaurant Yaxkín* (see p.374) offers free travel advice and has a big map of the area painted on the wall. If you're staying for a few days, head to the hotel *Yaxkín Chel Paraíso*, where Don Rosendo Girón is an authority on the region.

CROSSING THE MEXICAN BORDER: BETHEL/LA TÉCNICA/EL NARANJO

It's a straightforward trip to Mexico via **Bethel**, on the Río Usumacinta; travelling via **La Técnica** will cost less. There's also now a paved road right to the Mexican border at **El Ceibo,** close to the frontier town of **El Naranjo**; this route is popular with travellers.

BETHEL

Buses (roughly hourly, 5am–3pm; 4hr) leave Santa Elena's Terminal Nuevo for **Bethel**, where there's a Guatemalan *migración* post, and a good cheap *posada*. At Bethel it's relatively easy to find a shared *lancha* heading downstream (around Q60/person; 30min) to Frontera Corozal (see p.359).

LA TÉCNICA

A cheaper option is to get off the bus in Bethel, obtain your exit stamp there, and then continue on the same bus for 12km to the tiny settlement of **La Técnica**, where you can cross the Usumacinta (boats leave when full; 5min; Q10) to Corozal on the opposite bank. La Técnica lacks accommodation or other facilities. Agencies in Flores (see box, p.359) offer cross-border tickets direct to Palenque using the La Técnica route (about Q225/person).

EL CEIBO

Very regular buses connect Santa Elena with **El Naranjo** (every 30min; 4hr), from where microbuses run to the border post at **El Ceibo** (every 30min; 15min). Note the border is only open from 9am to 5pm. Get an early start and avoid getting stuck for the night in El Naranjo, which is a rough place with little to recommend it. On the Mexican side, buses leave for Tenosique in Tabasco (every 40min; 1hr 15min).

ACCOMMODATION AND EATING

Hotel La Pasión 50m up from the dock, Sayaxché ☎ 4056 5044. Spacious, well-presented rooms with cable TV, bathroom and fan. **Q110**

Restaurant Yaxkín One block up from the dock, on the left, Sayaxché. A family-run restaurant that serves up *comida típica* and good burgers (Q25) and sandwiches. Offers impartial tourist information too. Daily 7am–8pm.

Yaxkín Chel Paraíso Barrio Esperanza, six blocks up and five across (southeast) from Sayaxché dock ☎ 4053 3484. Rustic place with bungalows and a restaurant (serving good Mexican food and fish); the garden is also a delight, bursting with tropical flowers. Owner Chendo is a local fixer who can arrange tours and transport. **Q100**

4

MAYA RUINS, COPÁN

Honduras

HIGHLIGHTS

❶ Parque Nacional La Tigra Trails through pristine cloudforest, close to the capital. **See p.393**

❷ Lago de Yojoa Caves, cloudforest hikes and the stunning Pulhapanzak falls. **See p.400**

❸ Gracias Among Honduras's oldest towns, and gateway to Parque Nacional Celaque. **See p.402**

❹ Copán Step back in time at these spectacular Maya ruins. **See p.412**

❺ La Mosquitia Isolated and unspoiled reserves of wetlands and rainforest, accessible by boat. **See p.432**

❻ Bay Islands A unique culture, beaches and world-famous diving. **See p.435**

HIGHLIGHTS ARE MARKED ON THE MAP ON P.377

ROUGH COSTS

Daily budget Basic US$35/occasional treat US$55

Drink Nacional beer US$1.50–2.50, coffee US$1–2

Food *Almuerzo típico* US$5

Hostel/budget hotel US$12/US$20

Travel Copán–San Pedro Sula (140km) by bus: 3hr, US$8 (local), US$20 (*ejecutivo*)

FACT FILE

Population 8.25 million

Languages Spanish, English in the Bay Islands

Currency Honduras lempira (L)

Capital Tegucigalpa (population: 1.3 million)

International phone code ☎ 504

Time zone GMT -6hr

5

Introduction

One of Central America's most beguiling (and best-value) destinations, Honduras has been plagued by soaring crime rates in recent years: most visitors either race to see the mind-bending Maya ruins at Copán or the palm-fringed beaches of the Bay Islands, and skip the rest of the country. While the statistics are scary, much of Honduras remains safe, friendly and sprinkled with exceptional sights – from the wetlands of La Mosquitia to the subtropical shore of the Golfo de Fonseca, this is a land of inspiring, often untouched natural beauty.

The capital, **Tegucigalpa**, is somewhat underwhelming, but home to some decent museums, Spanish colonial remnants, restaurants and services, while 100km south lies the volcanic **Isla El Tigre**, a little-visited but worthwhile getaway. An essential detour on the way north is the **Lago de Yojoa** region, which offers birdwatching, caves and a gorgeous waterfall. To the west, colonial towns like **Santa Rosa de Copán** and **Gracias** offer a surprising variety of restaurants, hot springs and access to indigenous villages, while the sparsely populated region of **Olancho** – Honduras's "Wild East" – contains the **Sierra de Agalta** national park, which has the most extensive stretch of virgin cloudforest in Central America. On the Caribbean coast, **Tela** and **Trujillo** are lively towns with attractive beaches, while **La Ceiba**, larger and with thriving nightlife, is the departure point for the **Bay Islands**, a Caribbean outpost that seems like another country – with world-class diving, sandy coves, a rich cultural mix and international tourism to match.

Gradually, Honduras is waking up to its potential as an **ecotourism** destination – its network of national parks and preserves is extensive – as well as the likely benefits of an increased tourist infrastructure for the country's struggling economy (it's the second-poorest country in Central America after Nicaragua, with more than half the population living below the poverty line). The pick of Honduras's natural attractions is the biosphere reserve of the **Río Plátano** in **La Mosquitia**. Encompassing one of the finest remaining stretches of unspoiled tropical rainforest in Central America, the region is largely uninhabited and a trip here really does get you off the beaten track.

Nevertheless, the country's development has been stymied by political instability and the headline-grabbing violence of its **drug gangs**, which use the country as a staging post. Security in parts of Honduras, notably **San Pedro Sula**, remains a serious issue (see p.383).

WHEN TO VISIT

The **climate** in Honduras is generally dictated by **altitude**. In the central highlands, the weather is pleasantly warm in the daytime and cool at night. The hot Pacific and Caribbean coasts offer the relief of breezes and cooling rain showers, while San Pedro Sula and other lowland towns can be positively scorching in summer.

Honduras's **rainy season**, "winter" (*invierno*), runs from May to November (most markedly June and July). In much of the country it rains for only a few hours in the afternoon, though along the northern coast and in Mosquitia rain is possible year-round. October and November are the only months you might want to avoid in these parts – they fall in the middle of the **hurricane season** (generally said to begin in August), and are when you're most likely to be affected by storms.

CHRONOLOGY

1000 BC Maya settlers move into the Río Copán valley.
100 AD Construction of the city of Copán begins.
426 AD Maya royal dynasty is founded. Copán, the civilization's centre for artistic and scientific development,

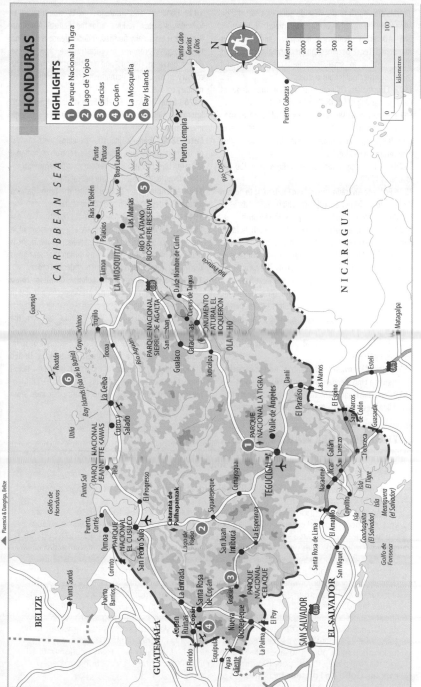

HONDURAS

HIGHLIGHTS

1. Parque Nacional la Tigra
2. Lago de Yojoa
3. Gracias
4. Copán
5. La Mosquitia
6. Bay Islands

Metres
2000
1000
500
200
0

N

0   100
kilometres

▲ Placencia & Dangriga, Belize

BELIZE

GUATEMALA

EL SALVADOR

NICARAGUA

CARIBBEAN SEA

Golfo de
Honduras

Golfo de
Fonseca

Punta Gorda
Puerto Barrios
Corinto
Omoa
Puerto Cortés
San Pedro Sula
PARQUE
NACIONAL
EL CUSUCO
Punta Sal
Tela
PARQUE NACIONAL
JEANNETTE KAWAS
El Progresso
Cuero y
Salado
La Ceiba
Utila
Bay Islands (Isla de la Bahía)
Roatán
Guanaja
Cayos Cochinos
Trujillo
Jocoa
Río Aguán
Limón
Punta
Patuca
Guamaja
Puerto Lempira
Bus Laguna
Rais Ta Belén
Palacios
Las Marías
RÍO PLÁTANO
BIOSPHERE RESERVE
LA MOSQUITIA
PARQUE
NACIONAL
SIERRA DE AGALTA
Gualaco
San Esteban
Catacamas
Cuevas de Talgua
Dulce Nombre de Culmi
Juticalpa
MONUMENTO
NATURAL EL
BOQUERÓN
OLANCHO
Río Patuca
Punta Cabo
Gracias á Dios
Río Coco
Puerto Cabezas
El Florido
Copán
Ruinas
Esquipulas
Agua
Caliente
La Entrada
Santa Rosa
de Copán
Gracias
PARQUE
NACIONAL
CELAQUE
Nueva
Ocotepeque
La Palma
El Poy
Cataratra de
Pulhapanzak
Lago de
Yojoa
PARQUE
NACIONAL EL CUSUCO
Siguatepeque
Comayagua
San Juan
Intibucá
La Esperanza
TEGUCIGALPA
PARQUE
NACIONAL LA TIGRA
Valle de Angeles
El Paraíso
Danlí
Las Manos
El Espino
San Marcos
de Colón
Guasaule
Nacaome
Alcar Galán
San Lorenzo
Choluteca
Coyolito
El Amatillo
Santa Rosa de Lima
San Miguel
Isla
Meanguera
(El Salvador)
Isla
Conchaguita
(El Salvador)
Isla
El Tigre
SAN SALVADOR
Estelí
Matagalpa

5

controls area north to the Valle de Sula, east to Lago de Yojoa and west into present-day Guatemala.

900 AD Maya civilization collapses, and Copán is abandoned. Lenca becomes the predominant indigenous group, settling in small, scattered communities and absorbing other indigenous cultures.

1502 Christopher Columbus arrives on the island of Guanaja, naming it "Isla de Pinos" (Island of Pines).

1524 Hernán Cortés sends Cristóbal de Olid from Mexico to claim the isthmus in Cortés's name; the man arrives himself one year later, founds Puerto Cortés and Trujillo, then returns to Mexico.

1524–71 Indigenous population declines from 400,000 to around 15,000.

1536 Pedro de Alvarado arrives from Guatemala to govern the territory. Lempira, a Lenca chieftain, amasses a 30,000-man force, which rebels against the Spanish.

1537 Lempira is assassinated and the Spanish hold on Honduras is assured with the founding of Comayagua (capital of Honduras Province). Gold and silver are discovered in the country's interior and mining begins. The *encomienda* labour system is put in place, assuring social stratification.

1800 With mines failing and droughts destroying agricultural harvests, the economy enters a crisis period. Society is deeply divided, and the country still has no national printing press, newspapers or university.

1821 Honduras gains independence from Spain, but is annexed by Mexico.

1823 United Provinces of Central America declare themselves an independent republic. Civil war begins.

1830 Honduran Francisco Morazán elected president of the Republic after defeating Conservative forces in Guatemala.

1839 Honduras and Nicaragua go to war against El Salvador. Morazán resigns, and the Central American Republic is essentially finished. Independence is not kind to Honduras's economy or infrastructure, and intense rivalry between Liberals and Conservatives keeps the country in an almost permanent state of political and military conflict.

1876 Liberal Dr Marco Aurelio Soto is elected president. Improves infrastructure and encourages foreign investment.

Late 1800s Banana industry develops with arrival of US fruit companies, which gain control of national infrastructure; private interests dominate government.

1880 Tegucigalpa becomes national capital.

1904 American writer O. Henry coins the term "Banana republic" to describe his parody of Honduras.

1941 Honduras joins the Allies in World War II.

1956 A coup introduces the military as a new element in the country's hierarchy of power. Civilian government is reinstated in 1957, but a new constitution that year gives the military the right to disregard presidential orders.

1963 Another coup brings Colonel Oswaldo López Arellano to power as provisional president; he remains in power for twelve years.

1969 So-called "Football War" breaks out on the Honduras–El Salvador border (see box below).

1975 The "Bananagate" scandal (the payment of more than US$1 million to government officials by United Brands Company in return for reductions on export taxes) forces López to resign. Under his successors – all high-ranking military officials – the country becomes even more stratified.

THE FOOTBALL WAR

In one of the more bizarre conflicts in modern Latin American history, the "Football War" broke out between Honduras and El Salvador on **July 14, 1969**. Ostensibly caused by a disputed result in a **football match** between the two countries, the conflict also stemmed from tensions generated by a steady rise in **illegal migration** of *campesinos* from El Salvador into Honduras in search of land.

In April 1969 the Honduran government had given settlers 30 days to return to El Salvador, and then began forced expulsions – the result was the breakout of sporadic violence. In June, the two countries began a series of qualifying matches for the 1970 World Cup. The first game, held in Tegucigalpa, was won by Honduras, with a score of 1–0. At the second game (won 3–0 by El Salvador), held in San Salvador, spectators booed the Honduran national anthem and attacked visiting Honduran fans. El Salvador won the decisive third game 3–2 in Mexico City, then promptly cut diplomatic ties with Honduras. On July 14, El Salvador bombed targets in Honduras without warning, and advanced up to 40km into Honduran territory.

After four days, around 2000 deaths and a complete breakdown of diplomatic relations, the Organization of American States (OAS) negotiated a ceasefire, establishing a 3km-wide demilitarized zone along the border. Tensions and minor skirmishes continued, however, until 1980, when a US-brokered peace treaty was signed. Only in **1992** did both sides finally accept an International Court of Justice ruling demarcating the border in its current location (ratified in 1998). Incredibly, the dispute has rumbled on regardless, with military action threatened over the **Golfo de Fonseca** by both sides as recently as 2013.

5

LAND AND SEA ROUTES TO HONDURAS

Honduras has land borders with Guatemala, El Salvador and Nicaragua, and sea crossings with Belize. There is a US$3 exit tax at each one.

From **Guatemala**, there are three crossings. The most frequently used is at El Florido for Copán (see box, p.415); there is also a crossing at Agua Caliente (see box, p.406), used by buses from Esquipulas, and one at Corinto–Entre Ríos (see box, p.340), which connects Puerto Barrios and Puerto Cortés.

El Salvador has two crossings: El Amatillo (see box, p.239) in eastern El Salvador, and El Poy in western El Salvador (see box, p.248).

There are three crossings from **Nicaragua**. The easiest is Las Manos (see box, p.476), for Tegucigalpa; the others are at El Espino and Guasaule (see box, p.473).

From **Belize**, there are weekly boats from both Placencia and Dangriga to Puerto Cortés (see p.96).

1981 Honduras becomes focus for US-backed Contra war in Nicaragua; relationship between military and government grows closer; human rights violations rise.
1989–98 Following US withdrawal, the economy collapses completely, but power is slowly wrested back from the military.
1998 Hurricane Mitch hits Honduras, killing more than 7000.
2005 Manuel Zelaya of the Liberal Party is elected president.
2006 Honduras signs the Central America Border Control Agreement (see box, p.30).
2009 Manuel Zelaya is ousted from government in a move seen by many as a coup and by others as a legitimate action. Porfirio Lobo Sosa of the conservative National Party is elected president in November. Honduras is suspended from the Organization of American States (OAS).
2011 Zelaya and Lobo sign an agreement that allows the former to come out of exile and return to the country. The move leads to Honduras's re-entry into the OAS.
2013 National Party candidate Juan Orlando Hernández wins the presidential election, defeating Xiomara Castro, wife of deposed president Zelaya.
2015 San Pedro Sula declared most violent city in the world for third year running.

ARRIVAL AND DEPARTURE

Visitors **flying** to Honduras have a choice of airports. The three most commonly used are: **Toncontín International (TGU)**, outside Tegucigalpa; **Ramón Villeda Morales International (SAP)**, southeast of San Pedro Sula; and **Juan Manuel Gálvez International (RTB)**, on Roatán. All three are served by direct flights from other Central American capitals, as well as North American (namely Miami, Houston and Atlanta) and South American destinations. Airlines such as United (⊕united.com) and Avianca (⊕avianca.com) ply these routes. In addition, Air Transat (⊕transat.com) operates flights between Toronto and Montréal to Roatán, and SOSA (⊕aerolineassosahn.com) operates flights between La Ceiba and Grand Cayman, from where you can connect to the UK and elsewhere in Europe. From 2015 the departure tax should be incorporated into your air ticket price.

You can enter Honduras by **land** from Guatemala, El Salvador and Nicaragua. International services such as Tica Bus (⊕ticabus.com) offer long-haul trips from other Central American cities, but you can also travel via slower, cheaper local transport. If you do come by local bus, you'll have to disembark, cross the border on foot and change buses on the other side. The only **sea routes** to Honduras are from Belize.

VISAS

Citizens of Australia, Canada, New Zealand, the UK, the US and most European countries do not need visas for stays in Honduras of up to ninety days. **Tourist cards**, given on entry, are good for stays of between thirty and ninety days (you'll usually get thirty days). The card is a yellow slip of paper that needs to be returned when you leave. Extensions (L500) on a month-by-month basis can be obtained from local *migración* offices. After four months you must leave the country for a minimum three days before returning and starting the process again.

5

Honduras is part of the **CA-4 border control agreement**, which means you can move freely within Honduras, Guatemala, El Salvador and Nicaragua for up to ninety days (see box, p.30).

GETTING AROUND

Most budget travellers in Honduras depend on the bus, though there are security issues to be aware of (see box below). To reach the Bay Islands you will need to fly or take a boat.

BY BUS

Bus services in Honduras are fairly well organized, with frequent departures from the main transport hubs of Tegucigalpa, San Pedro Sula and La Ceiba, as well as a network of local services. These local, or **"chicken" buses** (see box, p.32) are the cheapest, but also get packed and stop frequently, so can be quite slow. **Rapiditos** also serve local routes. Usually minibuses, they are much quicker but a little more expensive than chicken buses. On the longer intercity routes there's usually a choice of services, with an increasing number of luxurious air-conditioned **express buses** (*ejecutivos* or *lujos*), plus comfortable services with a few scheduled stops (*directos*). **Fares** are extremely low on most routes, at around US$2–3 an hour or less, though they can triple on some of the really smart services – travelling between Tegucigalpa and La Ceiba can cost as much as US$40. For the express buses (notably Hedman Alas, the smartest operator: ⓦhedmanalas.com), you should buy tickets in advance when possible; if you are getting on at smaller destinations the conductor will come through and collect the fare.

BUS SAFETY

It is important to be aware of the **security** situation when travelling by bus in Honduras. In some of the bigger cities, notably San Pedro Sula and to a slightly lesser extent Tegucigalpa, local buses are not safe to use. Intercity buses have been subject to armed robberies to such an extent that many services have a soldier on board. Always take a taxi to/from bus terminals, and don't travel on any buses after dark.

The frequency of buses slows down considerably after lunch, so you should try to be at your final destination by 4pm to avoid getting stranded.

BY TAXI

Taxis are generally the safest way to travel around the bigger towns and cities, and should always be used after dark; they can also be hired for longer journeys – negotiate a price up-front. They operate in all the main towns, tooting when they are available. Meters are nonexistent, so always agree on a price before getting in.

Three-wheeled moto-taxis (similar to tuk-tuks or auto-rickshaws) are available in some parts of the country.

BY CAR

If your budget will stretch to it, **renting a car** can open up the country's more isolated areas. Including insurance and emergency assistance, **rates** start at around US$55 a day for a small car, and US$90 for larger models and 4WDs. The highways connecting the main cities are well looked after, but the numerous dirt roads in the highlands can be impassable

ADDRESSES IN HONDURAS

Honduras's major cities are mainly laid out in a **grid**, with a park or plaza at the centre. Here calles run east–west, and avenidas north–south. In some towns, such as Santa Rosa de Copán Ruinas, street names are followed by the designation "**NO**", "**NE**", "**SO**" or "**SE**" (northwest, northeast, southwest and southeast respectively), depending on their location around the central park. Note that smaller towns (including Copán) don't have **street names**, so addresses tend to be given in terms of landmarks. Exact **street numbers** tend not to exist anywhere; a city address written in the Guide as "C 16, Av 1–3", for example, means the place you're looking for is on Calle 16, between avenidas 1 and 3, while "Av 1, C 11–13" means it's on Avenida 1, between calles 11 and 13.

at certain times of the year, so always seek local advice on conditions before starting out. Rental agencies can be found at the airports in San Pedro Sula, Tegucigalpa and Roatán as well as in San Pedro Sula and Tegucigalpa towns. As with bus travel, however, it's important to be aware of the safety issues: car-jackings and armed robberies are not uncommon; intercity routes are not safe after dark, and it's important to seek local advice before setting off.

Hitching is very common in rural areas, but – as everywhere else in the world – carries inherent risks and is not advisable.

BY PLANE

Internal flights in Honduras are fairly affordable. A small number of domestic airlines offer competitive fares, with frequent departures between Tegucigalpa and San Pedro Sula, La Ceiba and the Bay Islands; the most established airlines are SOSA (waerolineassosahn.com) and CM Airlines (wcmairlines.com), while Avianca (wavianca.com) also operates domestic flights. A one-way ticket between Tegucigalpa and San Pedro costs around US$110, while La Ceiba to Utila or Roatán is US$75.

BY BOAT

Boats are the most budget-friendly option when it comes to reaching the Bay Islands: La Ceiba is linked to Roatán and Utila by daily ferries; Trujillo has less regular services to/from Guanaja.

ACCOMMODATION

That Honduras is slowly waking up to tourism is reflected in the country's **accommodation** options. The larger cities – Tegucigalpa, San Pedro Sula – offer the widest range of places to stay, with something to suit all budgets. **Hostels** are beginning to spring up across the country, generally representing excellent value for money; Copán has some of the best budget hostels on the mainland. Of the Bay Islands, Utila is the cheapest and Roatán has a few places catering to backpackers, while Guanaja is aimed more at luxury tourists. On the mainland,

US$10–20 gets you a basic room; more than US$20 will secure a well-furnished room, with extras such as TV, a/c and hot water. A 16 percent tax is occasionally added to the bill. Usually the only time you need to **reserve** in advance is at Semana Santa or during a big local festival, such as the May Carnaval in La Ceiba.

The only formal provisions for **camping** are at Omoa, Copán Ruinas and in some of the national parks. Elsewhere, pitching a tent is very much an ad hoc affair. If you intend to camp, make sure you ask permission from the landowner. Tempting though they may seem, the north-coast beaches are not safe after dark and camping here is highly inadvisable.

FOOD AND DRINK

Budget travellers can eat very well in Honduras. The best way to start the day is with a **licuado**, a sort of fruit smoothie. Many places mix them with bananas and cornflakes, so they're very filling. Most towns have **markets** where you can pick up a huge amount of fresh produce. With an eye on your budget, you'll find that eating a big **lunch** is a better option than waiting for dinner. Market areas tend to be where you will find the cheapest *comedores*, where typical *almuerzos* of rice, beans, tortillas and meat can be had for around US$3–4.50. The larger cities have a decent range of **restaurants**, including an increasing number of fast-food chains. On the whole, you'll pay US$5–6 for a good-sized lunch at a restaurant. The ever-popular Chinese restaurants routinely have portions big enough for two, making them a reliable budget option. Note that most shops and facilities close from noon to 2pm so that families can eat lunch together.

Some of the highlights of *comida típica* (local cuisine) in Honduras include **anafre**, a fondue-like dish of cheese, beans or meat, or a mixture of all three, sometimes served as a bar snack, and **tapado**, a rich vegetable stew, often with meat or fish added. The north coast has a strong Caribbean influence, with lots of seafood. **Guisado** (spicy chicken stew) and **sopa de caracol** (conch stew with

5

coconut milk, spices, potatoes and vegetables) should both be tried at least once. Probably the most common street snack, sold all over the country, is the **baleada**, a white-flour tortilla filled with beans, cheese and cream; two or three of these constitute a reasonable meal.

DRINK

Licuados or **batidos** are a mix of fruit juice and milk. **Tap water** is unsafe to drink; bottled, purified water is sold everywhere and many hotels have water machines. The usual brands of **fizzy drink** are ubiquitous.

Honduras produces five brands of **beer**: Salvavida and Imperial are heavier lagers, Port Royal slightly lighter and Nacional and Polar very light and quite tasteless. **Rum** (*ron*) is also distilled in the country, as is the Latin American rotgut, **aguardiente**. Adventurous connoisseurs of alcohol might wish to try **guifiti**, an elixir of various plants soaked in rum, found in the Garífuna villages of the north coast.

CULTURE AND ETIQUETTE

Catholicism is the main **religion** in Honduras – though American Evangelical missionary groups are having an impact – and with it come traditional values and roles. Family is very important, and children tend to grow up and settle close to their parents, though increasingly Honduran youngsters are going to the US in order to send back some money. Anti-gay attitudes are prevalent, and while not illegal, public displays of affection between **same-sex couples** are frowned upon.

Women can travel alone with relative confidence in Honduras. While *gringa*-enticement is a rather competitive and popular way to pass the time, it is usually harmless and best ignored. Common-sense precautions apply; take taxis at night, leave expensive jewellery and electronic equipment at home and never flash money/cameras/phones around (see opposite).

Hondurans are very friendly, and, on the whole, glad to have visitors in their country and keen to tell you about where they

---

HONDURAN SLANG

Ando hule I'm broke
Bola A dollar
Jalón A pick-up
Birria A beer
Macizo Cool
La riata Something/someone useless

---

come from. Greeting shop assistants is polite, and in smaller towns a simple "buenos días" can win you new friends in no time. Of Honduras's population, 85–90 percent are ladino (a mix of Spanish and indigenous people). The rest of the country is made up of a mixture of **ethnic minorities**. Prominent groups include the Maya Chorti in the department of Copán; the Lenca, with their traditional clothing, found along the Ruta Lenca in the area around Santa Rosa de Copán; and the Miskitos in La Mosquitia.

A ten percent **tip** is the norm for waiters and tour guides, but is not expected in taxis. **Haggling** is not widespread, but a bit of gentle negotiation can earn you a discount at a hotel or a lower price with a taxi driver.

SPORTS AND OUTDOOR ACTIVITIES

The largest spectator sport in Honduras is **football** (soccer), and the Honduran national league and the major European leagues are all keenly followed. Olimpia and Motagua from Tegucigalpa, Marathón and Real España from San Pedro Sula, and Victoria from La Ceiba are the biggest teams and usually pull in a fairly decent crowd. **Tickets** don't need to be bought in advance, as most games don't sell out.

With a number of **national parks** – most of which have accommodation and/or camping and well-marked trails – Honduras is a fantastic place to **hike**. Parque Nacional Celaque, with the highest peak in the country, is a great place to start. Meanwhile, the Bay Islands offer some of the cheapest places in the world to take PADI **diving** certification courses – both the diving and the **snorkelling** are excellent – while Lago de Yojoa has **fishing** and **birdwatching** trips.

COMMUNICATIONS

There are **post offices** in every town; letters generally take a week to the US and up to two weeks to Europe. Opening hours are usually Monday to Friday 8am to noon and 2 to 5pm, Saturday 8am to 1pm.

International **phone** calls can be made from Hondutel offices (there's a branch in every town), but are very expensive to Europe (around L60/min) – you are much better off visiting an internet café with web-phone capabilities. Many public telephones are out of use or damaged, so for local calls (eight-digit numbers) it's better to buy a cheap **mobile phone** (US$25–30) and periodically top up the credit (*recarga*), which can be done in most small shops. Alternatively, you could visit an office of mobile-phone provider Claro (the largest provider in Latin America – ⓦ claro.com /hn) or rival Tigo to see if your GSM phone will accept a foreign SIM card, though the process for registering these has become complicated in recent years (most need a Honduran identity card).

All landline numbers start with a 2, while mobile numbers start with different digits (3, 8 or 9) according to the provider.

Internet cafés can be found in most towns; the average rate is L20–30/hr, or more on the Bay Islands. Many hotels provide internet/wi-fi access for guests, usually for free.

CRIME AND SAFETY

The security situation in Honduras has deteriorated dramatically in recent years, largely thanks to the activities of violent **drug gangs** ("*maras*"). San Pedro Sula has been dubbed the most violent city in the world (2013–15), thanks to a horrifically high murder rate, and Tegucigalpa is not far behind.

The Bay Islands are considered safer than the mainland, and rural areas are generally safer than urban areas, though far from crime-free; taking the usual precautions and seeking advice from locals are vital. Hiking alone or walking on isolated stretches of beach (or indeed any stretch of beach at night) is inadvisable.

> ### EMERGENCY NUMBERS
> **Cruz Roja** (ambulance) ☏ 195
> **Fire** ☏ 198
> **International operator** ☏ 197
> **Police** ☏ 199 (☏ *199 from a mobile)

5

If you are the victim of a crime the **police** are unlikely to be of much help, but any incidents of theft should be reported for insurance purposes (ask for a *denuncia*).

The websites of the British Foreign Office (ⓦ fco.gov.uk) and the US Department of State (ⓦ state.gov) have up-to-date security information and advice on Honduras; check both before travelling.

STREET CRIME

Street crime is a real concern throughout the country; as well as numerous cases of pickpocketing and robberies, some tourists have been killed (sometimes as a result of resisting a mugging). That said, the murder rate finally started to drop in 2014 and 2015 (by 20 percent), and the vast majority of travellers who visit Honduras do so safely.

You can reduce the likelihood of being a victim of crime by using **common sense** and caution. Leave your valuables at home (or in the safe of your hotel). Don't walk around cities or bigger towns unless you're very sure of your surroundings, and take care with **bus travel** (see box, p.380). After dark take a taxi, even for short distances. Steer well clear of rough neighbourhoods (local advice on where not to go is invaluable): for example, the Comayagüela district in Tegucigalpa, particularly around the market, and the streets south of the old railway line in San Pedro Sula are both considered very dangerous. Going around in groups is safer than exploring on your own.

HEALTH

The Honduras Medical Centre, Av Juan Lindo in Tegucigalpa, is considered one of the best **hospitals** in the country; in San Pedro Sula head for the Hospital Centro Médico Betesda at Av 11A NO, C 11A–12A NO. Facilities in rural areas tend to be much more limited, though most

5

towns have at least one **pharmacy** (some of which are open 24hr), and staff, who can issue prescriptions, tend to be very helpful.

In general, it's worth trying to learn a little emergency Spanish, as English is not widely spoken. Basic medical care is relatively inexpensive (certainly when compared with the US); for serious problems or emergencies it's best to head for a **private hospital** (or even, if possible, one in your home country).

Malaria is present in Honduras, predominantly along the coast (including Roatán and the other Bay Islands), as is dengue fever and **chikungunya**. This viral infection is transmitted to humans through the bite of the same mosquitos that carry dengue; once rare in the Americas, a major outbreak hit the region in 2014. Honduras suffered its first death in 2015, with 6700 contracting the disease by the time of research. The disease is present in most cities in the country, and all along the Honduran coast. Like dengue, there is no cure (so bite prevention is the best defence), but though unpleasant, the disease is rarely fatal in healthy adults.

Honduras also has one of the highest rates of **AIDS** in Central America, so it is especially important to take all the usual precautions when it comes to sex. Make sure, too, if you seek medical help that all instruments are sterilized.

INFORMATION AND MAPS

The national tourist office, the **Instituto Hondureño de Turismo** (⊕honduras .travel), is fairly helpful. The main office in Tegucigalpa (see p.380) can provide general **information** about where to go and what to see in the country. Most towns you'll visit will have a municipality-run tourist office. These vary in helpfulness; the better ones sell maps, can arrange homestays and can tell you the cheapest places to stay. **National parks** and reserves are overseen by the government forestry agency, **ICF** (⊕icf.gob.hn). If you intend to spend much time in any of the parks, it's worth visiting one of their offices for detailed information on flora and fauna.

Honduras Tips (⊕hondurastips.hn), a free bilingual magazine found in the

better hotels and tourist offices, has fairly up-to-date information on hotel **listings** and bus routes – it is updated every few months. The magazine also has maps of most towns in the country.

The best **map** of Honduras is published by Reise Know-How (⊕reise-know-how .de), and can be bought in bookshops or online; unfortunately, the chance of finding it in Honduras is unlikely.

MONEY AND BANKS

Honduras's currency is the **lempira** (L), which consists of 100 centavos; at the time of writing, the exchange rate was L21.5 to US$1. Coins come as 1, 2, 5, 10, 20 and 50 centavos and notes as 1, 2, 5, 10, 20, 50, 100 and 500 lempiras. In heavily touristed areas – Copán, the Bay Islands – **US dollars** are widely accepted, but on the whole lempiras are the standard currency.

You will need **cash** for day-to-day expenses, though credit/debit cards are accepted at smarter hotels and restaurants (there is often a hefty charge levied for credit/debit card payments, especially on the Bay Islands). ATMs are widespread, though acceptance of foreign **debit cards** can be hit-and-miss. Make sure before you leave home that your PIN is four digits or fewer; your card will be rejected if it is longer. As a rule Visa is more widely accepted than other cards. Beyond the usual charges for using your card abroad, there are no additional ATM charges. Visa cardholders can also get **cash advances** in several banks, including Banco Atlántida; MasterCard is sometimes accepted but not to be relied upon. Honduras has a number of national **banks**, of which the biggest are Banco Atlántida, Banco de Occidente and BAC/Credomatic.

OPENING HOURS AND PUBLIC HOLIDAYS

Business hours for **shops** are generally Monday to Friday 9am to noon and 2pm to 4.30 or 5pm, and Saturday from 9am to noon. **Banks** in larger towns are generally open from 8.30am to 4.30pm (until noon on Saturdays), while those in smaller towns shut for an hour at lunch; moneychangers generally operate longer hours. **Museums** often stay open at lunch, but close at least one day each week. On **public holidays** (see box below), almost everything closes, and public transport generally operates on a reduced schedule.

FESTIVALS

Honduras's calendar is full of **festivals** featuring everything from small local events to major national parties. The following are just a few highlights.

January 25–February 4 Pilgrims flock to Tegucigalpa to worship and celebrate the Virgen de Suyapa.
March–April Semana Santa (Easter) is a major celebration throughout Honduras, with many of the cities hosting sizeable parades.
April 6–12 Punta Gorda celebrates the arrival of the Garífuna.
May La Feria de San Isidro or Carnaval in La Ceiba, during the week leading up to the third Saturday. Festivities culminate in a street parade through the city centre, followed by live music until the early morning.
June 29 San Pedro Sula holiday.

PUBLIC HOLIDAYS

Jan 1 New Year's Day
Easter week Semana Santa
April 14 Day of the Americas
May 1 Labour Day
Sept 15 Independence Day
Oct 3 Birth of Francisco Morazán
Oct 12 Discovery of America
Oct 21 Armed Forces Day
Dec 25 Christmas

Tegucigalpa and around

Situated 1000m above sea level, deep in a mountain valley, the traffic-choked Honduran capital of **TEGUCIGALPA** (known as "Tegus") isn't totally without charm, its colonial feel, museums, mountain viewpoints and cool climate making it far more pleasant than most Central American capitals. Indeed, surrounded by reminders of its past – crumbling colonial buildings and decaying nineteenth-century mansions – the city today is a vibrant, noisy place. A handful of churches and a decent history museum will easily keep you entertained for a day or two.

Tegucigalpa was founded by the Spanish in 1578, when silver deposits (*tegucigalpa* means "silver mountain" in the Nahuatl language) were found in the hills to the east. With wealth from the silver mines pouring in, the city's location at the centre of key trade routes became highly advantageous, and Tegucigalpa soon rivalled the then capital, Comayagua, sharing government status with its northern rival from 1824. In 1880, President Soto officially shifted power to Tegucigalpa. Since the 1920s, the nation's economic focus has moved northwards to San Pedro Sula, but Tegucigalpa continues to function as the nation's political and governmental centre. Today, **street crime** is a serious problem (see p.383), so take common-sense precautions.

WHAT TO SEE AND DO

The heart of Tegucigalpa's **old city** is the shady Parque Central, known as **Plaza Morazán**; a number of interesting churches and museums, plus many hotels, lie within easy walking distance of the square. East from the centre, two major roads, Avenida Jeréz (which becomes Avenida Juan Gutemberg and then Avenida La Paz) and Avenida Miguel Cervantes (which becomes Avenida República de Chile), skirt the edges of upmarket **Colonia Palmira**.

5

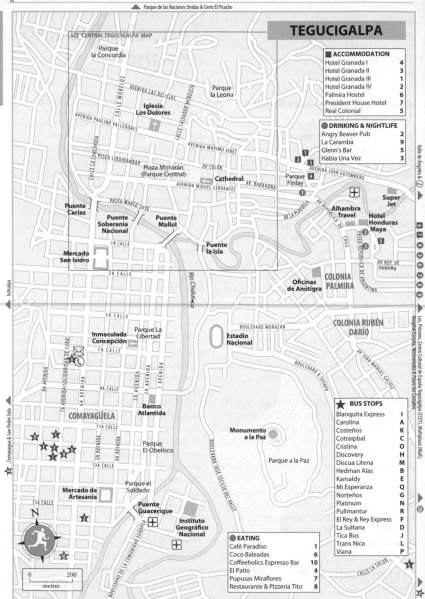

Parque de las Naciones Unidas & Cerro El Picacho

TEGUCIGALPA

SEE 'CENTRAL TEGUCIGALPA' MAP

Parque la Concordia

AVENIDA LAS DELICIAS
CALLE MORELOS
AVENIDA PAULINO VALLEDORES
CALLE LA CONCORDIA
PASEO LIQUIDÁMBAR

Iglesia Los Dolores
CALLE SALVADOR MENDIETA
AVENIDA MAXIMO JEREZ

Parque la Leona

Plaza Morazán (Parque Central)
PASEO MARCO SOTO
AVENIDA MIGUEL CERVANTES
AV COLON
AV. BARAHONA
Cathedral

AVENIDA JUAN GUTEMBERG
Parque Finlay

Super Jet

Puente Carías
Puente Soberania Nacional
Puente Mallol
1A CALLE
Puente la Isla

Alhambra Travel
Hotel Honduras Maya
AV LA PLATUELA
AV REPUBLICA DE
AV REP. DE CHILE
PASEO REPUBLICA DE PANAMÁ

Mercado San Isidro
3A CALLE

Río Choluteca

Oficinas de Amitigra

COLONIA PALMIRA

5A CALLE
Parque La Libertad

BOULEVARD MORAZÁN

COLONIA RUBÉN DARÍO

Inmaculada Concepción
7A CALLE
8A AVENIDA (SOLIDARIDAD DE CUBA)
6A AVENIDA
9A CALLE
3A AVENIDA
2A AVENIDA
1 AVENIDA

Estadio Nacional

AV JUAN MANUEL GÁLVEZ

BOULEVARD A SUYAPA

Banco Atlantida

11A CALLE
5A AVENIDA
4A AVENIDA

Parque El Obelisco
13A CALLE

Monumento a la Paz
Parque a la Paz

BOULEVARD JOSE CECILIO DEL VALLE

COMAYAGÜELA

Mercado de Artesanía
15A CALLE

Parque el Soldado
Puente Guacerique
Instituto Geográfico Nacional

BOULEVARD DE LA COMUNIDAD EUROPEA

N

0   200
metres

Royeri, Viana Clase Oro, King Quality & Toncontín International Airport (7km)

CALLE LA SALUD

ACCOMMODATION
Hotel Granada I	4
Hotel Granada II	3
Hotel Granada III	1
Hotel Granada IV	2
Palmira Hostel	6
President House Hotel	7
Real Colonial	5

DRINKING & NIGHTLIFE
Angry Beaver Pub	2
La Caramba	9
Glenn's Bar	5
Había Una Vez	3

BUS STOPS
Blanquita Express	I
Carolina	A
Costeños	K
Cotraipbal	C
Cristina	O
Discovery	H
Discua Litena	M
Hedman Alas	B
Kamaldy	E
Mi Esperanza	Q
Norteños	G
Platinum	N
Pullmantur	R
El Rey & Rey Express	F
La Sultana	D
Tica Bus	J
Trans Nica	L
Viana	P

EATING
Café Paradiso	1
Coco Baleadas	6
Coffeeholics Espresso Bar	10
El Patio	4
Pupusas Miraflores	7
Restaurante & Pizzeria Tito	8

Parque de las Naciones Unidas & Cerro El Picacho

Valle de Ángeles &

Juticalpa

Comayagua & San Pedro Sula

Los Próceres, Centro Cultural de España Tegucigalpa (CCET), Multiplaza (Mall), Hospital Escuela, Metrocentro & Paseo los Castaños

Running west from Plaza Morazán, the pedestrian-only **Paseo Liquidámbar** is lined with shops, cafés and the Museo para la Identidad Nacional (see opposite). Further west, the character of the city rapidly becomes more menacing as you approach the banks of the Río Choluteca and Tegucigalpa's twin, **Comayagüela**, which sprawls away through down-at-heel business districts into industrial areas and poor *barrios*.

Plaza Morazán

Plaza Morazán is the centre of life for most people who live and work in the capital. Shaded by a canopy of trees and populated with shoe-shiners and other vendors, it's an atmospheric, if not particularly peaceful, place. A **statue** at the centre of the square commemorates national hero Francisco Morazán, a soldier, Liberal and reformer who was elected president of the Central American Republic in 1830. On the eastern edge of the plaza, the beautifully restored peach-coloured facade of the **Catedral de San Miguel** (daily 6am–6pm; free), originally built in 1786, is one of the best preserved colonial buildings in Central America. Inside, look out for the magnificent Baroque-style gilded altar and the baptismal font, carved in 1643 from a single block of stone by indigenous artisans.

Museo para la Identidad Nacional

The permanent exhibition at the illuminating **Museo para la Identidad Nacional** (Paseo Liquidámbar, at Calle El Telégrafo; Mon–Sat 9am–5pm, Sun 11am–5pm; L70; ☎2238 7412, ✆min .hn), inside the former Palacio de los Ministerios, charts the history of Honduras. Starting with the geographical formation of Central America, the displays move chronologically through the Maya civilization and colonial era to the various post-colonial presidents and their influence on the country. The museum's highlight is a 3D audiovisual presentation of Copán ("Copán Virtual"; Tues–Fri 10am, 11.30am, 2pm & 3.30pm, Sat 10am, 11.30am, 1pm, 2pm & 3.30pm, Sun 11.30am, 1pm, 2pm & 3.30pm; L35) that re-creates how the Maya kingdom would have looked at the height of its power.

Museo Histórico Militar de Honduras

Three blocks east of Plaza Morazán at Parque Valle (between Avs Paz Barahona and Cristóbal Colón) is the Cuartel de San Francisco, completed in 1735 on the site of the sixteenth-century colonial convent of San Diego. The adobe-walled barracks now contain the **Museo Histórico**

Militar de Honduras, a mildly interesting museum dedicated to the Honduran armed forces (Mon–Fri 8am–4pm, Sat & Sun 9am–4pm; L10; ☎2237 9729). The signage is all in Spanish.

Next door lies the **Iglesia de San Francisco** (daily 9am–4pm; free), a plain-looking church built at around the same time as the Cuartel complex but containing a much older, beautiful gilded altar smothered in gold leaf.

Iglesia y Convento de Nuestra Señora de la Merced

Just south of the Parque Morazán on smaller Plaza de La Merced, the **Iglesia y Convento de Nuestra Señora de la Merced** (or just "La Merced"; Mon–Fri 9am–4pm; free) is a relatively small colonial church and convent rebuilt and added to many times since the late seventeenth century. Inside the church you'll find a timber coffered ceiling and ornate, Rococo altarpiece dedicated to La Virgen del Rosario. The adjacent convent building was formerly home to the **Galería Nacional de Arte**, controversially relocated to Comayagua in 2014 after funding problems (see p.398). Its Neoclassical facade sits rather uncomfortably alongside the stained concrete bulk of the **Congreso Nacional**, the country's seat of government next door.

Iglesia Los Dolores

A few blocks northwest from the central plaza, the white-domed **Iglesia Los Dolores** (daily 7am–noon & 3–6pm; free), completed in 1732, sits next to the small **Plaza Los Dolores**. Its Baroque facade is decorated with a representation of the Passion of Christ, featuring a crowing cock and the rising sun; inside, the elaborate gold altar dates from 1742. A choir usually sings at 6pm on Saturdays and Sundays.

Colonia Palmira and around

The upscale **Colonia Palmira** neighbourhood is home to most of the capital's foreign embassies, luxury hotels, top restaurants and swanky residences. A particular landmark, the high-rise, Modernist **Hotel Honduras Maya** opened

5

on the Avenida República de Chile in 1970. A kilometre beyond the hotel, an overpass gives access to eastward-bound **Boulevard Morazán**, Tegucigalpa's major commercial and entertainment artery. No city buses run along here, so you'll have to walk or take a taxi. On Calle 1, the **Centro Cultural de España Tegucigalpa (CCET;** Tues–Sun 10am–8pm; ☎ 2238 2013), housed in a stylish modern building, puts on a stimulating programme of music, art exhibitions and talks.

Cerro El Picacho

Some 5km north of Plaza Morazán, older suburbs – previously home to the wealthy middle classes and rich immigrants, now long gone – edge up the pine-studded slopes of **Cerro El Picacho** (1327m), mostly protected within the **Parque Naciones Unidas El Picacho** (Mon–Fri 8am–3pm, Sat & Sun 9am–4.30pm; L30). With its spectacular views over the city, bike rentals (L50/hr) and faux Maya stone steps, the park is a popular place for picnics (and is safe during the day), though the shabby **zoo** (Zoológico Metropolitano Rosy Walther: Mon–Fri 8.30am–3pm, Sat & Sun 8.30am–5pm; L25) is best avoided. At the top of the hill soars the open-armed 32-metre-tall **Cristo del Picacho** (statue of Christ; daily 8am–5pm; L10), illuminated at night in a dazzle of coloured lights. Take a bus from in front of *Hotel Granada 2* or a taxi (around L150–200); it's usually a thirty-minute journey, depending on traffic.

ARRIVAL AND DEPARTURE

By plane Toncontín International Airport, 7km south of the city, handles international (see p.379) and domestic flights. Taxis (around L150–200; US dollars are generally accepted) wait outside the terminal. Bus #24 also passes the airport, running through Comayagüela and Tegucigalpa.

Domestic destinations La Ceiba (Avianca & SOSA, 3 daily; 50min); Roatán (Avianca & CM Airlines, 1–2 daily; 1hr 10min); San Pedro Sula (Avianca/SOSA/CM Airlines, 2 daily; 50min).

By bus There is no main bus station; each international or intercity bus company has its own terminal (see box opposite), most of them scattered around Comayagüela. Whichever station you use, take a taxi to your drop-off point.

Domestic destinations Choluteca (B 3.30am–4pm, hourly; luxury ME 6am, 10am, 2pm & 6pm; normal ME 4am–6pm, hourly; R, S 4am–5.45pm, 1–2 hourly; 2hr 30min–3hr 30min); Comayagua (LS 6am–1.30pm, hourly; 1hr 30min–2hr); Copán Ruinas (HA 5.30am, 5.45am & 10am, via San Pedro Sula; 8hr); Juticalpa (direct D 6.15am–4.15pm, hourly; 2hr; normal D 6.45am–5pm, hourly; 3hr); La Ceiba (CR 6.15am, 7.30am, 9.30am, 12.30pm & 3.30pm; HA 5.30am, 5.45am, 10am & 1.30pm; K 7.15am, noon & 3.15pm; V 6.30am, 9.30am & 1.30pm; 5hr 30min–7hr); La Esperanza (CA 5am–4.50pm, hourly; 4hr); La Guama (for Lago de Yojoa) (N 6am–2.30pm, 1–2 hourly; ER 7.30am, 9.30am, noon & 2pm; 2hr 30min); San Pedro Sula (CN 5am–5.15pm, hourly; CR 7 daily; ER 7.30am, 9.30am, noon & 2pm; HA 5.30am, 5.45am, 10am, 1.30pm & 5pm; N 6am–2.30pm, 1–2 hourly; RE 5.30am–6.30pm, hourly; V Mon–Fri & Sun 6.30am, 9.30am, 1.30pm, 4pm & 6.15pm, Sat 6.30am, 9.30am & 1.30pm; 3hr 45min–4hr 15min); Santa Rosa de Copán (HA 5.30am, 5.45am & 1.30pm; LS 6am, 7.30am, 8.30am & 10am; 7hr); Siguatepeque (N 1–2 6am–2.30pm, hourly; ER 7.30am, 9.30am, noon & 2pm; 2hr); Tela (CR 6.15am, 7.30am, 9.30am, 12.30pm & 3.30pm; HA 5.30am, 5.45am & 10am; 5hr); Trujillo (C daily 6.10am & 8.20am; 5hr 30min).

International destinations Guatemala City (IIA daily 5.30am, 5.45am & 10am; PL daily 5.30am; P daily 6.15am; TB daily 6am, with overnight in El Salvador; 11–12hr); Managua (PL Tues, Wed & Sat 2pm; TB daily 9.30am; TN daily 5am; around 8–10hr); Panama City (TB; daily 9.30am with overnights in Nicaragua and Costa Rica; 2 days); San José (TB daily 9.30am with overnight in Managua; 1 day); San Salvador (PL daily 6am; P daily 6.15am; TB daily 6am; 7hr).

GETTING AROUND

By bus Chicken buses run the urban routes. Route names and numbers are painted on the front, and you pay your fare on the bus (L12–15). No buses pass close to Plaza Morazán or Blvd Morazán. However, buses are not especially safe (see box, p.380), and tourists are often targeted by pickpockets. Don't use the buses after dark; take a taxi instead.

By taxi Taxis are usually white with numbers painted on the side. A short ride within the city costs around L100–150 during the day, a little more at night, though they'll ask you for a lot more. *Colectivo* taxis gather at predetermined stops (*puntos*); the most central one is on C Palace just north of Plaza Morazán. They generally leave when full with passengers going to a similar area of the city. Though you may have to wait a bit, they are cheaper than standard taxis. Always use a taxi to get around after dark.

INFORMATION

Tourist information The Instituto Hondureño de Turismo has an office in Edificio Europa, Av Ramón Ernesto Cruz, Colonia San Carlos (Mon–Fri 8am–5pm; ☎ 2222 2124).

BUS COMPANIES AND STOPS

Tegucigalpa does not have a central bus terminal. Instead, each bus company has its own office and bus stop – most are in Comayagüela (see p.386). Take a taxi when travelling to and from this area. The following are the main operators.

Blanquita Express (B; ☎ 2225 1502) Direct to Choluteca from its stop in Barrio Villa Adela (Av 6, between calles 23 and 24), Comayagüela.

Carolina (CA) To La Esperanza from Av 7 (Solidaridad de Cuba), C 7–8.

Costeños (CN; ☎ 2225 2934) Normal services to San Pedro Sula from Av 6, at C 18 in Barrio Villa Adela, Comayagüela.

Cotraipbal (C; ☎ 2237 1666) Direct to Trujillo from Av 7, C 11–12.

Cristina (CR; ☎ 2225 1446, ⓦ transportescristina .com) Direct to La Ceiba, San Pedro Sula and Tela from Blvd Fuerzas Armadas, at Colonia Tiloarque.

Discovery (D; ☎ 2222 4256) Normal services to Juticalpa from Av 7, C 12–13.

Discua Litena (DL; ☎ 2230 2939) Direct services to El Paraíso (for Nicaragua) from Colonia Kennedy, near Mercado Jacaleapa.

Hedman Alas (HA; ☎ 2231 0378, ⓦ hedmanalas .com) Direct and luxury services to La Ceiba, Copán via San Pedro Sula, Tela and Guatemala City from Centro Comercial Centro América, Blvd Centroamérica (just south of Blvd Suyapa), to the east of central Tegucigalpa.

Kamaldy (K; ☎ 2220 0117) Services to La Ceiba from Av 8, at C 12.

Mi Esperanza (ME; ☎ 2225 1502) Luxury and normal services to Choluteca from Blvd Comunidad Económica Europea (between calles 23 and 24), Barrio Villa Adela, Comayagüela.

Norteños (N; ☎ 2237 0706) Normal services to La Guama and San Pedro Sula from C 12, Av 6–7.

Platinum (PL; ☎ 2225 5415, ⓦ platinumcentroamerica .com) Formerly King Quality, with luxury services to Guatemala City (Guatemala), Managua (Nicaragua) and San Salvador (El Salvador) from Blvd Comunidad Económica Europea, Barrio La Granja, Comayagüela.

Pullmantur (P; ☎ 2232 0216, ⓦ pullmantur.com) Luxury services to San Salvador (El Salvador) and Guatemala City from *Hotel Marriott Tegucigalpa*, Blvd Juan Pablo II.

El Rey (ER; ☎ 2237 1462) Normal services to La Guama and San Pedro Sula from C 12, Av 7–8, Barrio Concepción, Comayagüela.

Rey Express (RE; ☎ 2237 8561) Direct services to San Pedro Sula from the same spot as El Rey.

La Sultana (LS; ☎ 2237 8101) Normal services to Santa Rosa de Copán and Comayagua from Av 8, C 11–12.

Tica Bus (TB; ☎ 2291 0022, ⓦ ticabus.com) Luxury services to Guatemala City (Guatemala), Managua (Nicaragua), Panama City (Panama), San José (Costa Rica) and San Salvador (El Salvador) from Centro Comercial Plaza Toncontín in Lomas de Toncontín (on the Anillo Periferico 2 ring road south of the airport). Taxis will charge at least L150 from the centre.

Trans Nica (TN; ☎ 2239 7933, ⓦ transnica.com) Luxury services to Managua (Nicaragua) from *Hotel Alameda*, Boulevard Suyapa.

Viana (V; ☎ 2225 6583, ⓦ vianatransportes.com) Luxury services to La Ceiba and San Pedro Sula from Gasolinera Esso Presidencial (Esso petrol station), on Blvd Fuerzas Armadas.

Travel agent Alhambra Travel (☎ 2220 1704) on Av República de Chile, in the "*area comercial*" connected to the *Hotel Honduras Maya*, is quick, friendly and efficient (Mon–Fri 9am–5pm, Sat 9am–noon).

ACCOMMODATION

As the capital, Tegucigalpa's accommodation is generally pricier than elsewhere in Honduras. All the options below offer free wi-fi unless otherwise stated. It's worth noting that airbnb (ⓦ airbnb.com) lists at least forty properties in and around the city, starting at US$35 per night, and ⓦ couchsurfing.com also has a presence here.

Aparthotel ROS Av El Dorado 346, Residencial Las Colinas ☎ 2235 4807, ⓦ aparthotelros.hn; map p.390. Excellent-value hotel with modern, comfy rooms, cable TV and free shuttle to the airport or bus terminals. Breakfast (on the roof deck) included. __US$58__

Hotel Granada I Av Juan Gutemberg at Av Cristóbal Colón ☎ 2237 2381, ⓦ hotelgranadahn.com; map p.386. A consistently popular budget option, open since 1971, *Hotel Granada I* has basic but clean rooms, with private bathrooms and cable TV. __L585__

Hotel Granada II & Hotel Granada III Opposite each other on Paseo Casamata Subida Casa Martín, just off Av Juan Gutemberg *Granada 2* ☎ 2238 4438, *Granada 3* ☎ 2237 8066, ⓦ hotelgranadahn.com; map p.386. Just around the corner from the original *Hotel Granada*, and under the same management, these hotels are both solid choices. Free water and coffee. All rooms, which include several triples and quads, are en suite and have fans; add L100 for a/c. __L600__

5

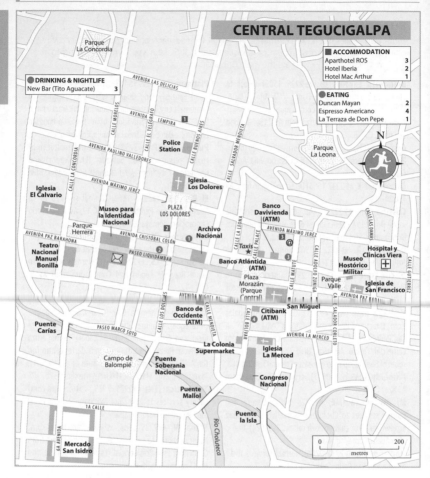

CENTRAL TEGUCIGALPA

■ **ACCOMMODATION**
Aparthotel ROS	3
Hotel Iberia	2
Hotel Mac Arthur	1

● **DRINKING & NIGHTLIFE**
New Bar (Tito Aguacate)	3

● **EATING**
Duncan Mayan	2
Espresso Americano	4
La Terraza de Don Pepe	1

Hotel Granada IV Av Juan Gutemberg at Paseo Casamata (facing *Granada III*) ☎ 2237 4004, ⓦ hotelgranadahn.com; map p.386. The newest and most comfortable of the *Granada* hotels, which opened in 2007. All rooms have cable TV and private bathroom, and computers with free internet are available in the lobby area. <u>L800</u>

Hotel Iberia Plaza Los Dolores ☎ 2237 9267; map p.390. Rooms are basic but very clean. There's little natural light, no a/c, and hot water is only available 6–8am, but sharing a bathroom makes things very cheap. <u>L360</u>

Hotel Mac Arthur Av Lempira 454 ☎ 2237 9839, ⓦ hotelmacarthur.com; map p.390. Neat en-suite rooms with TVs and fans (a/c costs around US$10 extra) at this lower mid-range hotel, which also boasts a nice pool area. Rates include breakfast. <u>US$50</u>

★ **Palmira Hostel** Av Juan Lindo 412, Colonia Palmira ☎ 2236 9143, ⓦ palmirahostel.com; map p.386. The only real hostel in the capital offers plain but clean rooms (with bathroom) and bright six-bed dorms, with common kitchen. Great, safe location opposite the French Embassy, close to supermarket and ATMs. Dorms <u>US$10</u>, doubles <u>US$25</u>

★ **Real Colonial** Calzada San Martín 458, Colonial Palmira ☎ 2220 7497, ⓦ realcolonialhotel.hn; map p.386. It may cost a bit more, but this B&B is a real treat, with plush a/c rooms featuring bold, contemporary artwork and flat-screen TVs with cable. <u>US$60</u>

EATING

The centre has all the usual fast-food chains and cheap and cheerful cafés, as well as a few good-value restaurants with meals for less than L100; smarter restaurants are to be found in Colonia Palmira and along Blvd Morazán.

CAFÉS

★ **Café Paradiso** Av Paz Barahona 1351 ☎ 2237 0337; map p.386. Attractive café-bar, popular with local artists, in a colonial-era building with art on the walls and a relaxed outdoor seating area. The menu runs from Honduran coffee (from Marcala and Santa Bárbara) and croissants to beer and pastas (from around L100–150). It's gay-friendly, and film (Tues & Thurs) and literary events are often staged in the evenings. Try the *carajillo* (coffee with cognac). Mon–Sat 10am–10pm.

Coco Baleadas Centro Corporativo Los Próceres (Blvd Morazán and Av La Paz) ☎ 2222 2626; map p.386. This mini-chain is a Honduran take on the classic sandwich bar, offering coconut *baleadas* (see p.382) with a choice of twenty or so fillings. You can get a *baleada* and a soft drink for under L80. Daily 7am–10pm.

Coffeeholics Espresso Bar Plaza Las Lomas, Lomas del Guijarro ☎ 2263 2047; map p.386. Fashionable café which serves delectable, creamy cakes (with names like "frozen turtle peanut butter pie"), potent coffee, wholesome salads, sandwiches and even pizzas. Spectacular views from the outdoor deck. Mon–Fri 9.30am–10pm, Sat & Sun 9.30am–11pm.

Espresso Americano Edificio Midence Soto, C Bolívar (just off Plaza Morazán); map p.390. Burgeoning local chain specializing in high-quality Honduran coffee, established here in 1994, with the full range of cappuccinos, lattes, espressos and snacks such as ham and cheese brioche (from L80). Daily 7am–8pm.

RESTAURANTS

★ **Duncan Mayan** Av Cristóbal Colón, at C Adolfo Zuniga ☎ 2237 2672; map p.390. Legendary local restaurant, operating since the late nineteenth century, especially good for a leisurely breakfast (from L75). Dinner mains are L100–160 – be warned, horse steak is a popular dish. Mon–Sat 8am–10pm, Sun 8am–9.30pm.

El Patio Far eastern end of Blvd Morazán ☎ 2221 4141; map p.386. Meat may not be Honduras's strong point, but they make a good stab at it in this cavernous banqueting hall, patrolled by waiters in traditional garb since 1977. Try the *pincho olanchano*, a skewer of roast beef, chorizo and pork – the cowboys from Honduras's own Wild East would be proud. Mains L160–320. Daily 9am–2am.

Pupusas Miraflores 2 Blvd Suyapa (east of Blvd Miraflores) ☎ 2239 2985; map p.386. Good, inexpensive restaurant (another mini-chain), crammed with locals, specializing in *pupusas* (from L20), tacos and *flautas* ("flute" tacos). Try the *loroco* flower-filled *pupusa* when it's in season. Take a taxi here – drivers should know it. Daily 11am–10pm.

Restaurante & Pizzeria Tito Blvd Morazán 101 at Av Juan Lindo ☎ 2231 1917; map p.386. No-frills restaurant serving the best slice in the city. Reasonably authentic, with small but good-value crusty pizzas (from L120): try the shrimp or the *capricciosa* (cheese, ham, mushroom, artichoke and tomato). Check out the old bank notes from around the world on the walls (it opened in 1976). Daily 11.30am–10pm.

La Terraza de Don Pepe Av Cristóbal Colón 2062 ☎ 2237 1084; map p.386. On two floors above a fried-chicken chop, this *comida típica* restaurant has plenty of character with once-grand, now faded dining rooms and a slip of a balcony (plus a bizarre shrine to the Virgen de Suyapa). The dishes of the day (around L80–100) are good options. Mon–Sat 8am–10pm.

DRINKING AND NIGHTLIFE

Use taxis when going out at night. Most bars in the centre are fiercely local, so you're best off heading to Colonia Palmira and Blvd Morazán. *Café Paradiso* (see above) is also worth stopping by for an early evening drink

★ **Angry Beaver Pub** Av República de Brasil, Colonia Palmira (opposite *Honduras Maya Hotel*); map p.386. This Canadian–Honduran venture serves a vast range of beer and has a pleasant outdoor area perfect for lounging. Also serves good coffee and sandwiches, and offers free wi-fi. Good place to meet English-speaking locals. Daily 4pm–2am.

La Caramba 2/F, Centro Comercial Lomas del Bulevar, Av Morazán; map p.386. Live music specialists, with "salsa Saturdays", jazz, reggae and rock nights. Drinks from L35. Thurs–Sat 7pm–2am.

Glenn's Bar C 4A, off Av 1A, Colonia Palmira; map p.386. Better than its bland name might suggest, this is a tiny, satisfyingly grungy place. It's not easy to spot – look out for it just beyond the triangular traffic island with trees. Cash only. Mon–Sat 6pm–2am.

Había Una Vez Near *Hotel Honduras Maya*, Paseo República de Argentina (Plaza San Martín); map p.386. An artsy café-bar with original work displayed on the brightly

5

painted walls (and colanders for lampshades). A beer will set you back around L40, and there's some decent food on offer too, including large, fresh salads. Tues–Thurs 6pm–midnight, Fri & Sat 6pm–2am.

★**New Bar (Tito Aguacate)** Av Cristóbal Colón, at C Matute (across from Plaza Morazán); map p.390. A classic Tegucigalpa experience. A local bar in an old adobe building nicknamed after the current owner Don Fernando's father, it's celebrated for its *calambre* (L60). This cocktail of lemon juice, sugar, red wine and gin was invented here by José "Tito" Valentín in the 1960s (the bar was founded in 1945); apparently it's a hangover ("*la goma*") cure, but is drunk at any time. Also sells beers and serves small bar snacks. Mon–Sat 11am–11pm.

SHOPPING

La Colonia Parque La Merced on C Bolívar ⓦ lacolonia.hn. Supermarket selling everything you need to make lunch, as well as toiletries and alcohol. Daily 7am–8pm.

Metromedia Av San Carlos beyond C República de Mexico; smaller branch in Multiplaza ⓦ metromedia.hn. Bookstore with a wide range of fiction, nonfiction and travel titles in Spanish and English, as well as secondhand books and US newspapers and magazines. There's a café on site. Mon–Sat 10am–8pm, Sun noon–6pm.

Multiplaza Av Juan Pablo II, 1.5km southeast of Colonia Rubén Darío ⓦ multiplaza.com. Mall with international shops, a huge food court with the usual fast-food chains and a Cinemark cinema. Tigo and Claro (both Mon–Sat 10am–8pm, Sun 11am–7pm) stores here sell SIM cards and mobile phones. Daily 8am–10pm.

DIRECTORY

Banks Most banks will change dollars and travellers' cheques. Banco Atlántida, on Plaza Morazán (with 24hr ATM) and elsewhere, gives advances on Visa cards. ATMs are commonplace.

Car rental Autos Corporativo (ⓣ 2234 3183, ⓦ hondurasrentacar.com) at the airport and in Colonia Palmira; Xplore Rent a Car (ⓣ 2239 0134, ⓦ xplorerentacar .com), on C Principal in Colonia Tres Caminos.

Embassies Belize, ground floor of *Hotel Honduras Maya*, Área Comercial del Hotel Honduras Maya, Av República de Chile (Mon–Fri 9am–1pm; ⓣ 2238 4616); Canada, Edificio Financiero CITI, Blvd San Juan Bosco, Colonia Payaquí (Mon–Fri 9am–3pm; ⓣ 2232 4551, ⓦ canadainternational.gc.ca); Costa Rica, Residencial El Triángulo, C Principal 3451 (Mon–Fri 8am–3pm; ⓣ 2232 1768); El Salvador, Diagonal Aguan 2952, Colonia Altos de Miramontes (Mon–Fri 8.30am–noon & 1–3pm; ⓣ 2232 4947); Guatemala, C Londres 0440, Colonia Payaquí (Mon–Fri 8.30am–3pm; ⓣ 2231 1543); Mexico, Av Eucalipto, at Av Berlin, Colonia Lomas de Guijarro (Mon–Fri 8–11am; ⓣ 2232 0141); Nicaragua, Bloque M1, off C Real de Minas,

Colonia Tepeyac (Mon–Fri 8.30am–1pm; ⓣ 2232 1966); Panama, Edificio Palmira 200, by the *Hotel Honduras Maya*, Colonia Palmira (Mon–Fri 8am–1pm; ⓣ 2239 5508); US, Av La Paz (Mon–Fri 8am–5pm; ⓣ 2236 9320, ⓦ honduras .usembassy.gov). The nearest UK embassy is in Guatemala City (ⓣ 502 2380 7300). Citizens of Australia, Ireland, New Zealand and South Africa should contact their respective embassies in Mexico City.

Hospitals Hospital y Clínicas Viera (ⓣ 2237 3160, ⓦ hospitalyclinicasviera.hn), Av Colón, by C Las Damas, is a reliable private healthcare provider. There are emergency departments (24hr) at the public Hospital Escuela, Blvd Suyapa (ⓣ 2232 6234), and Hospital General San Felipe, C La Paz by the Bolívar monument, though neither has the best reputation.

Immigration Dirección General de Migracíon, off CA 5 (Blvd Comunidad Económica Europea) near the airport (Mon–Fri 9am–5pm; ⓣ 504 2234 1996), Carretera al Batallón 1404, in Colonia Los Torres is the only place you can extend visas (see ⓦ migracion.gob.hn).

Internet Cybercafé Colonial, C Matute. Prices are around L25 per hour. There's also Multinet Cyber Café in Multiplaza mall (daily 8am–8pm).

Laundry Superc Jet, Av Juan Gutemberg beyond Parque Finlay (Mon–Sat 8am–6.30pm; around L40 /load).

Police Go to the FSP office on C Buenos Aires, behind Los Dolores church, with any problems.

Post office The post office is on Paseo Liquidámbar at C El Telégrafo, three blocks west of Plaza Morazán (Mon–Fri 8am–7pm, Sat 8am–1pm).

AROUND TEGUCIGALPA

There are several places a short bus ride away from Tegucigalpa where you can while away an afternoon, or even a day or two. The venerated **Basílica de Suyapa** takes only twenty minutes to reach, or for a really adventurous couple of days you could take yourself off to **Valle de Ángeles** for a morning before going on to the **Parque Nacional La Tigra** to hike.

Basílica de Suyapa

Some 6km east of Tegucigalpa's centre, the monolithic white bulk of the **Basílica de Suyapa** (daily 9am–5pm; free) rises from the flat plains. Built in the 1950s, it is home to the **Virgen de Suyapa**, patron saint of Honduras. The statue of the Virgin was discovered by two *campesinos* in 1747. The story goes that after bedding down for the night, one of them noticed he was lying on something, but without looking to see what the offending object was, threw it to one side. Within a few minutes, however, the object had returned. The next day, the two carried the little statue down to Suyapa where, placed on a simple table adorned with flowers, the Virgin began to attract worshippers.

Today you can see the tiny statue (just 6cm tall) behind the wooden altar in **La Pequeña Iglesia**, the original eighteenth-century chapel behind the Basílica. According to legend, each time she is placed in the larger Basílica, the Virgin mysteriously returns to the simple chapel, built 1777–80 by one Captain José de Zelaya y Midence in thanks for the recovery of his health.

City **buses** to Suyapa run hourly from the Mercado San Isidro in Comayagüela (20min).

Valle de Ángeles
Continuing east from the Basílica de Suyapa, the road rises gently amid magnificent scenery, winding through forests of slender pine trees. Some 22km from the capital is **VALLE DE ÁNGELES**, a former mining town now reincarnated as a handicraft centre and scenic getaway for *capitalanos*, with red-tiled roofs and narrow cobbled streets. Surrounded by forested mountains, the small town slumbers during the week, then explodes with activity at weekends. The town is chiefly noted for its quality carved wooden goods and delicious *pupusas*, and it's an alluring place to while away a couple of hours.

ARRIVAL AND DEPARTURE
By bus Buses leave Tegucigalpa for Valle de Ángeles from a car park near the San Felipe Hospital at the eastern end of San Felipe (daily, every 45min until 6pm; 45min–1hr) and terminate a couple of blocks from the town's Parque Central. The last return bus leaves around 5.30pm.

EATING
★Café La Estancia C Principal ☎3393 2137. Wonderfully rich coffee served in colonial surroundings, full of antique furniture and the aroma of freshly roasted beans. The house was once owned by Honduran president Marco Aurelio Soto. Mon–Sat 7am–6.30pm.
Café Los Holandesas Barrio Arriba (next to the police

station) ☎2262 6364, ⓦ lasholandesas.com. Opened in 2013, this cosy place specializes in *stroopwafels* (Dutch caramel waffles) and strong Honduran coffee. Wed–Fri 2–6pm, Sat & Sun 10am–8pm.
Virginia's Pupusas Just off the Parque Central. Local ladies make and grill fresh *pupusas* outside this small restaurant, the traditional tortilla typically stuffed with cheese and beans (or pork) from L30. The *tajaditas* (fried plantains with salsa and salad) are also good, especially when washed down with some fresh blackberry juice. Traditional *sopa de mondongo* (tripe soup) served on Sundays. Small seating area inside. Daily 7am–6pm.

Parque Nacional La Tigra
The oldest reserve in Honduras, **Parque Nacional La Tigra** (daily 8am–4pm; US$10) is also one of the best, offering a relatively easy – and safe – taster of untrammelled Central American cloudforest. Just 22km from Tegucigalpa, its accessibility and well-maintained system of trails make it a justly popular destination. Much of the original cloudforest here was destroyed through heavy logging, so what you see today is generally secondary growth; parts of the park still shelter oak trees, bromeliads, ferns, orchids and other typical cloudforest flora, along with a huge amount of tropical birdlife and **wildlife** such as deer, white-faced monkeys and ocelots – though they tend to stick to parts of the park that are out of bounds to visitors. The **trails** provide some relatively straightforward hiking, either on a circular route from the visitors centre or across the park between the two entrances on the 6km Sendero Principal. **Guides** (US$15–20/trail) are also available, though they tend to only speak Spanish. You can visit the park as a day-trip but it's worth staying a couple of nights.

The park has two entrances. The western side is reached via the village of **Jutiapa**, 17km east of Tegucigalpa, with its own accommodation and visitor centre. The eastern entrance at **El Rosario** is accessed via the old mining town of **San Juancito** from where you can walk (45min) or get a pick-up for the 1km to the park's visitor centre. The old hospital in Rosario serves as the main park visitor centre and hostel.

INTO NICARAGUA: LAS MANOS

The **Las Manos** border crossing, some 120km from Tegucigalpa, is the most convenient place to enter **Nicaragua** from the capital. Buses run to the town of El Paraíso (Discua Litena; hourly 6am–6pm; 2hr 15min), 12km from the border, from where minibuses and pick-ups shuttle to the border every thirty minutes or so. With an early enough start, it's possible to reach Managua (see p.457) the same day. Taxi drivers hawking for business may well tell you that no buses run to the border from El Paraíso, but this is not true. However, if you don't want to wait around for one of the buses, you could take a taxi for about US$6.

The border post itself is a collection of huts housing the immigration and customs officials. Both sides are open daily until 5pm and crossing is generally straightforward. There are no banks, but eager moneychangers accept dollars, lempiras and Nicaraguan córdobas. There's a US$3 exit tax to leave Honduras. On the Nicaraguan side, trucks leave every hour for Ocotal, from where you can pick up buses to Estelí and Managua.

Note that the foundation charged with overseeing the park, **Amitigra**, ran into serious financial difficulties at the end of 2014 and at the time of writing the effects of budget cuts were hard to predict – the park is unlikely to close, but ask your accommodation in Tegucigalpa about the latest situation.

ARRIVAL AND INFORMATION

If you plan to take public transport to the park, it's important to confirm the latest bus information and departure times with your hotel first – these often change.
Via Jutiapa Take the El Hatillo bus from C Finlay, at C Cristóbal (daily every 45min; 1hr 30min) in Tegucigalpa, or from Parque Herrera, 500m west of Plaza Morazán (Mon–Fri 7am, 9am, 2pm, 4pm & 5pm, Sat & Sun 8am, 10am, noon, 1pm & 3pm; 1hr 30min–2hr); the bus will drop you at El Chaparro, from where it's a 15–20min walk uphill to the visitor centre. Buses return daily at 5.30am, 5.45am, 6am, 7am, 9am, 11am, noon & 3pm.
Via San Juancito Direct buses to San Juancito originate at the Mercado San Pablo in Barrio El Manchen, Tegucigalpa, but you can also pick them up at the San Felipe petrol station, in front of Hospital San Felipe (at the end of Av La Paz) daily at around 2pm, 3pm and 5pm (*colectivos* run between the Plaza Morazán and San Felipe); you can also pick up these buses in Valle de Ángeles. It's a steep 1km up to the park's visitor centre from the last stop (45min); pick-ups are sometimes available for around L300. Buses depart San Juancito daily at 5.30am, 6.30am and 8am.
Visitor centres Both El Rosario and Jutiapa have visitor centres (both daily 8am–4pm) with small exhibition areas, toilets, basic cafeteria and information (trail maps) provided by guides and rangers.

ACCOMMODATION

Eco-Albergue El Rosario Centro de Visitantes El Rosario ☎ 2238 6269. Simple but clean accommodation for up to

40 people in the form of shared and private rooms, with shared bathrooms and basic cafeteria. Per person <u>US$25</u>
Eco-Albergue Jutiapa Centro de Visitantes Jutiapa ☎ 2265 1891. Six basic but modern private rooms, each with three beds and private bathrooms, with one additional cabin for three people. Camping is also available (bring your own tent). Camping/person <u>US$10</u>, rooms/person <u>US$25</u>

Southern Honduras

Stark, sun-baked coastal plains stretch **south** from Tegucigalpa all the way to the Pacific Ocean. Though a world away from the clean air and gentle climate of the highlands, this region is nonetheless beautiful in its own right, defined by a dazzling light and ferociously high temperatures. Traditionally a poor region, it's also a little-visited one, with the foreigners who do pass through usually in transit to Nicaragua or El Salvador. If you're really looking to get off the gringo trail, this is the place to do it.

The chief attraction in the area – and well worth a visit – is **Isla El Tigre**, a volcanic island set in the calm waters of the **Golfo de Fonseca**, while the colonial city of **Choluteca** offers a change of pace from the frenzy of the capital and makes a convenient stopover en route to Nicaragua.

The main transport junction in this part of the country is the village of **Jícaro Galán**, at the intersection of Highway CA-5 and the Carretera Panamericana, some 70km south of Tegucigalpa. Buses stop here to exchange passengers before continuing west to the border with El Salvador at El Amatillo, 42km away (see box, p.396), or east to Nicaragua.

ISLA EL TIGRE

Volcanic **ISLA EL TIGRE** lies in the heart of the Golfo de Fonseca, its dramatic conical peak rising sharply against the sky and across the sparkling water. With inviting beaches, calm waters and constant sunshine, it's an ideal spot to hide away for a couple of days.

WHAT TO SEE AND DO

The island's only town is **AMAPALA**, once the country's major Pacific port and now a decaying relic of the nineteenth century. Looking up from the dock, you'll see ageing wooden houses clustered along the hillside, while the restored nineteenth-century church in the **Parque Central** shows signs of the island's desire to get on the tourist map – cruise ships now stop here. Nonetheless, during the week there's every chance you'll be the only visitor on the island.

From the southern side of the island there are stunning **views** across the gulf to Volcán Cosiguina in Nicaragua, and in some places to Isla Meanguera and mainland El Salvador. The island's own (extinct) volcanic peak (783m) can be climbed in a steep and very hot two- to three-hour **walk**; ask for directions to the start of the trail, opposite the naval base, about 15 minutes' walk southwest of Amapala.

Beaches

An 18km dirt road circumnavigates the island, giving access to some glorious deserted **beaches**; it takes four or more hours to walk the whole thing, or you can take one of the moto-taxis that hang around the end of the dock in Amapala (around L300 for a trip around the island, or L20 for a short one-way drop-off).

A 45-minute walk or short moto-taxi ride (avoid the overpriced car taxis that may be waiting at the end of the pier)

east from the Parque Central takes you to **Playa El Burro**, where you can while away the afternoon people-watching – children and taxi drivers play football on the beach before cooling off in the sea. The popular black volcanic sands at **Playa Grande**, a short ride west of the plaza, is backed by rows of *comedores* serving freshly barbecued fish at the weekend. A further ten minutes west is **Playa Negra**, another pretty volcanic sand beach with the clearest water.

ARRIVAL AND INFORMATION

By bus and boat Mi Esperanza runs buses from Tegucigalpa to Choluteca (daily 1–2 hourly; 3hr 30min), which can drop you off at Jícaro Galán on the Carretera Interamericana (look out for the Dippsa fuel station). Local buses (daily every 30min 6am–5pm; 1hr; L40) shuttle between here and the fishing village of Coyolito (30km). Transportes Juan Ché runs one direct bus daily from Tegucigalpa to Coyolito at 10am, returning at 2am (L100). From Coyolito, regular taxi boats run 24hr (20min) to and from Amapala's dock for around L30 (reckon on US$10 or L250 for a private boat; rates increase at night). You can also be dropped off at Playa El Burro (10min) for L25/person (or L90 for a small private boat for four people).
Bank The nearest ATM is in San Lorenzo, between Coyolito and Choluteca. Bring plenty of cash (small notes).
Tourist information The tourist office on the pier (Mon–Fri 8am–noon & 2–5pm, Sat 8am–noon; ☏ 9823 8579) has a basic hand-drawn map of the island on the wall that you can copy or photograph.

ACCOMMODATION AND EATING

Budget accommodation standards are fairly low, though a good option is to contact the tourist office to arrange a homestay (from L250/person/night).
Casa de las Gárgolas Barrio Nuevo (Paseo a Playa Grande) ☏ 2795 8529. This large, modern stucco hotel, studded with whimsical gargoyles, is a short ride out of town, with a relaxing pool and spacious a/c rooms (with a choice of one double bed, two double beds or triples with space for six) – definitely worth paying the extra to stay here, if you can. No wi-fi at the time of writing. L833
El Faro Victoria At the end of the Amapala dock ☏ 2795 8543. Atmospheric place with a terrace that sits over the water. There's good food, including fried fish and *curiles* cocktail (local clams marinated in their own blood, lime juice and *chismol*, which is similar to salsa). Most mains L75–200. Mon–Thurs 7–10pm, Fri–Sun noon–3pm & 7–10pm.
Veleros Casa de Huéspedes Playa El Burro ☏ 2795 8040. Friendly guesthouse with three spick-and-span

5

INTO NICARAGUA AND EL SALVADOR: EL ESPINO, GUASAULE AND EL AMATILLO

Choluteca is a transport hub for most of the country's border crossings with Nicaragua and El Salvador. There's a US$3 exit tax at each of the crossings.

INTO NICARAGUA

For **Nicaragua**'s **El Espino** border, Rey Express buses (3 daily; 1hr) run the 110km from Choluteca to San Marcos de Colón. From there frequent *colectivo* taxis (around L25) go to El Espino and the border, 10km away. The border post itself (daily 8am–5pm) is quiet and straightforward, with moneychangers on both sides. On the Nicaraguan side, regular buses run to Somoto, 20km from the border. White *rapiditos* leave Choluteca for **Guasaule** (6am–5pm, every 30min; 40min). There's regular transport from Guasaule on to Chinandega, León and Managua.

INTO EL SALVADOR

For **El Salvador**, local buses run from Choluteca to **El Amatillo** (3.15am–5.45pm, hourly; 2hr 15min). This point of entry (open 6am–10pm) teems with border traffic, moneychangers and opportunistic beggars. Crossing, however, is straightforward. A bank on the El Salvadoran side changes dollars and lempiras, but you'll get slightly better rates from the moneychangers as long as you're careful. If coming **from Tegucigalpa** you don't need to go all the way to Choluteca – just change at Jícaro Galán onto the Choluteca–El Amatillo service. Over the border in El Salvador, buses (daily every 10min from 6am until around 6.30pm) leave for Santa Rosa de Lima – 18km away, and the closest place offering accommodation (see p.239) – and San Miguel, 58km away (see p.361).

---

rooms. The attached *palapa*-roofed beach café (mains around L100–150) is a great place to watch the world go by; try the shrimp *ceviche*. **L520**

CHOLUTECA

Honduras's fourth-largest city, with a population of around 145,000, **CHOLUTECA** boasts a handsome colonial centre – its main draw. Most sights are grouped around the **Parque Central** (or Parque Valle), itself a charming spot to enjoy the evening air. Dominating the square, the imposing seventeenth-century **Catedral de la Inmaculada Concepción** is worth a look for its elaborately constructed wooden ceiling and font, carved in 1640. On the southwest corner of the square is **Casa Valle** (☎2882 2792), the birthplace of **José Cecilio del Valle** (1780–1834), one of the authors of the Central American Act of Independence in 1821. Built around 1777, the colonial house is slowly being restored, serving as a library, tourism office and small museum of Lenca and Chorotega pottery, as well as period antiques from Valle's era. It is Valle's statue that stands in the middle of the square.

This was another site having problems with funding at the time of writing, so check for updates before visiting.

ARRIVAL AND INFORMATION

By bus The main terminal is ten blocks northeast of the Parque Central (a 20min walk or L40 taxi ride). Mi Esperanza also has a stop down the street from the main terminal. Both Mi Esperanza and Blanquita Express run regular buses to/from Tegucigalpa (daily 2–3 hourly; 2hr 30min–3hr 30min). There are also buses to Nicaragua and El Salvador (see box above).

Banks Banco Occidente, one block south of the Parque Central, has a 24hr ATM, as does Banco Atlántida (Av J.C. del Valle, at C F.D. Roosevelt).

Internet Try Global Cyber (Mon–Sat 7.30am–6pm) in Pasaje Sarita, near *Espresso Americano*.

ACCOMMODATION AND EATING

Bonsai Av Valle, half a block south of Parque Central ☎2782 2648, ✉hotelbonsai@ymail.com. The rooms vary quite widely at this low-cost hotel, so make sure you look at a few before checking in; the better ones have private bathrooms and a/c. The grassy courtyard that most rooms open onto saves the place from drabness. **L425**

Café Café Carretera a Frontera El Guasaule, Barrio Los Fuertes (in front of Gasolinera Puma) ☎2782 2515. Gourmet coffee comes to Choluteca, with this modern café offering iced coffees and frappes, as well as pastries and light snacks. Reliable wi-fi and refreshingly cold a/c. Mon–Fri 7.30am–7.30pm, Sat 7.30am–7pm.

The central highlands

In stark contrast to gritty San Pedro Sula to the north and the sprawl of Tegucigalpa to the south, Honduras's central highlands are blessed with a rich array of natural and historic attractions. Take an early-morning birding trip on **Lago de Yojoa**, a twilight stroll around former capital **Comayagua**, or a tour of spectacular **Cataratas de Pulhapanzak**, a dazzling waterfall and one of the region's highlights.

COMAYAGUA

The first capital of Honduras, the enchanting colonial city of **COMAYAGUA** lies just 85km north of Tegucigalpa. Santa María de Comayagua, as it was first known, was founded in 1537 and quickly gained prominence thanks to the discovery of **silver** nearby, becoming the administrative centre for the whole of Honduras. Following independence, however, the city's fortunes began to decline, particularly after Tegucigalpa was designated alternative capital of the new republic in 1824, and especially when President Soto permanently transferred the capital to Tegucigalpa in 1880. Although Comayagua is today a relatively rich and important provincial centre, the main reason to visit is the architectural legacy of the colonial period, in particular the dazzling cathedral overlooking the Parque Central.

WHAT TO SEE AND DO

Most sights of interest are within a few blocks of the large, tree-lined **Parque Central**, which is graced by a fountain and

▲ Bus Terminal

Hotel América Inc	4
Hotel Casa Grande B&B	1
Hotel Norymax Colonial	5
Hotel Morales	2
Hotel Santa Lucia	3

COMAYAGUA

0   100
metres

Museo de Comayagua

Iglesia San Francisco — PLAZA SAN FRANCISCO

Galería Nacional de Art

CALLE 6 NO

BOULEVARD 4 CENTENARIO

CALLE 5 NO

@ •

Iglesia de la Inmaculada Concepción

Centro Medico Comayagua Colonial

Parque Central

Casa de Cultura

CALLE 4 NO

Museo Historico Civico Comayagua Casa Cabañas

Supermarket

CALLE 3 NO

Banco Davivienda (ATM)

CALLE 2 NO

General Market

AVENIDA 1 NO / CALLE DEL CARMEN

CALLE 1 NO

PLAZA LA MERCED

Iglesia de la Merced

N

EATING & DRINKING

Comidas Rápidas Venecia	5
Gota de Limón	1
La Princesita	4
Villa Real	3
Viva Café & Lounge	2

CERO CALLE ESTE

CALLE MANUEL BONILLA

▼ Hospital Regional Santa Theresa

5

a handsome bandstand. It's a great place to watch city life, especially in the evenings, when music booms out of speakers. The centre is relatively compact, with a spate of new projects leading Comayagua to be dubbed the "city of museums"; at the time of writing work was progressing on the latest attraction next to the Alcaldía on the central plaza, the former home of conquistador **Alonso de Cáceres** (who was the founder of the city).

Catedral de Comayagua

On the southeast corner of the Parque Central is the artfully restored **Catedral de Comayagua** (Mon–Sat 9.30am–noon & 2–5pm, Sun 9.30am–5pm; free), whose intricate facade consists of tiers of niches containing statues of the saints. Constructed 1685 to 1715 and more properly known as **Iglesia Catedral de la Inmaculada Concepción**, it was the largest church of its kind in the country during the colonial period, housing sixteen altars, though only four of these survive today. The cathedral's bell tower is considered one of the outstanding examples of colonial Baroque architecture in Central America, and is home to the twelfth-century **Reloj Arabe**, one of the oldest clocks in the world. Originally made for the Muslim emirs of the Alhambra in Granada, Spain, the timepiece was presented to the city in 1582 by King Philip II.

Casa de Cultura

Housed inside the seventeenth-century Portal de los Encuentros on the south side of the Parque Central, the **Casa de Cultura** (Mon–Fri 9am–5pm, Sat & Sun 9am–noon; free; ☎2772 2028, ⟨w⟩municomayagua.com) hosts changing exhibitions, usually related to the city's history. Its location makes it a convenient place to take refuge from the sun for a while.

Museo de Comayagua

One block north of the Parque Central, on Plaza San Francisco, the **Museo de Comayagua** (daily 8am–4pm; US$4; ☎2772 0386) occupies the sixteenth-century colonial home of one Don

Francisco del Barco y Santiponce, confiscated by the state in 1860 to act as the first Casa Presidencial and briefly the Congreso Nacional de Honduras. Today its small but absorbing range of permanent exhibits chronicles local history from the pre-Hispanic period through to the Colonial and Republican eras. Highlights include a pre-Columbian Lenca stele, some terrific jade jewellery and a colourful Semana Santa display.

Museo Histórico y Cívico "Casa Cabañas"

One of the city's newer projects, the **Museo Histórico y Cívico "Casa Cabañas"** (daily 9am–5pm; US$5; ☎2771 8377) charts Honduran history between 1824 and the present day. The first gallery is dedicated to the Federation period and the county's first head of state **Dionisio de Herrera** (1824–27), while the second room explores the life of nineteenth-century military hero and former president **José Trinidad Cabañas**. The final room covers the presidencies of Ricardo Maduro (2002–06) and Porfirio Lobo Sosa (2010–14). The museum occupies the former home of Cabañas, behind the old Casa Episcopal on Calle 3 NO, at Av 1 NE.

Galería Nacional de Arte

In 2014 the **Galería Nacional de Arte** (Mon–Sat 9am–3pm, Sun 9am–2pm; L30; ☎2772 1575, ⟨w⟩galerianacionalde artehonduras.org), with its extensive and illuminating collection of Central American art, was controversially relocated from the capital to Comayagua (C 5 NO, at Av 1 NE, one block east of the main square). Its new home is the restored **Caxa Real** ("Royal Exchange"), built 1739–41 but mostly destroyed by fire in 1840. The building's original purpose was to levy the Quinto Real ("King's fifth"), the 20 percent tax imposed by Spain on the mining of precious metals (principally the tonnes of silver being produced around here at the time).

Displays range from prehistoric petroglyphs and Maya stone carvings to religious art, while special rooms house an ambitious selection of modern and contemporary Honduran art, including some works by Pablo Zelaya Sierra, one of the country's leading twentieth-century artists.

Iglesia de la Merced

Three blocks south of the Parque Central is another colonial church, the **Iglesia de la Merced** (daily 7am–8pm; free). Built between 1550 and 1558 (though its facade dates only to the early eighteenth century), this was the city's original cathedral, holding the Reloj Arabe (see opposite) until 1715, when the new cathedral was consecrated. In front of the church is the delightful **Plaza La Merced**.

ARRIVAL AND INFORMATION

By bus In early 2015 the new bus terminal finally opened, around 900m northwest of Parque Central on C 7 NO and Blvd 4 Centenario – either a L40 taxi ride (L60 at night) or 15min walk. All buses should now be using this terminal, but some may still drop closer to the centre or the highway around the town, so check when you get on. There are daily buses to/from Tegucigalpa (with La Sultana daily; hourly; 1hr 30min–2hr) and San Pedro Sula (with La Sultana & Mirna daily; 1–2 hourly; 2hr 30min–3hr 15min). For Lago de Yojoa, catch any San Pedro Sula-bound bus and ask for La Guama.

Bank Banco Davivienda on C del Comercio (Av 1NO), next to Supermercado Carol, has a reliable ATM (daily 6am–8pm).

Hospitals Hospital Regional Santa Theresa (Av 2 NO at 2A C S) is the only major public hospital in the city with a 24-hour emergency department. Better for foreigners is the private Centro Médico Comayagua Colonial (☎ 2772 1126) (ⓦ centromedicocolonial.com), on C 3 NO (towards Barrio Suyapa).

Internet La Red, on the Parque Central, is a conveniently located cybercafé; its computers have Skype.

Tourist information Tourist information and a map are available at the Casa de Cultura (Mon–Sat 9am–5pm; ☎ 9749 3086).

ACCOMMODATION

Hotel América Inc Av 1 NO, just south of C 1 NO ☎ 2772 0360, ⓦ hotelamericainc.com. A big, faded mid-range hotel with welcoming staff, pool, 24hr hot water and cable TV. Cheaper rates (around L700/US$35) are available if you forego breakfast (usually included) and switch the a/c for a fan. Free wi-fi. **L835**

Hotel Norymax Colonial C Manuel Bonilla, Av 1 NE–2 NE ☎ 2772 1703. One of the better budget hotels in town: rooms vary in quality (some have more natural light, cable TV and better furnishings) so ask to look at a few. Free wi-fi, but usually only in common areas. **L650**

Hotel Morales C Colonia El Inva ☎ 2772 5035. Doubles with a/c (with fan about L100 cheaper) and breakfast hosted by the friendly Wendy Morales and her family. There's also free wi-fi, cable TV, hot water, a lovely pool, restaurant and guaranteed 24hr electricity. **L950 (US$45)**

Hotel Santa Lucía C 2 NO, Barrio Santa Lucía ☎ 2772 9011, ⓦ hotelsantaluciacomayagua.com. This excellent mid-range hotel with clean, modern rooms offers superb value. Rates include wi-fi and breakfast. **L780**

EATING AND DRINKING

An extensive general market three blocks south of the Parque Central sells meat and fish, with stalls around the main building for fresh fruit and vegetables. You can easily pick up an *almuerzo* for around L60 in the surrounding *comedores*.

Comidas Rápidas Venecia Av 1 NO (C del Comercio) at C 3 NO, one block south of the Parque Central ☎ 2772 1734. A simple café, but clean and friendly with low-cost mix-and-match breakfasts, buffets and lunches (mains around L50–70). Mon–Sat 8.30am–8pm.

Gota de Limón C 5 NO, one block east of the Parque Central ☎ 2772 8446. There's a vibrant, clubby feel to this restaurant bar, which serves economical *comida típica* (from L90) and has live DJs (mainly playing reggaetón) at night. Beers around L40. Sun–Wed 10.30am–7pm, Thurs–Sat 10.30am–2pm.

La Princesita Blvd 4 Centenario, C 4 NO–5 NO ☎ 2772 5660. This bakery and cake shop may be decorated with a princess-themed wallpaper border, but their *baleadas* are definitely for grown-ups. Try the "super" with beans, cheese, egg, chorizo, shredded chicken and *encurtido* (pickles). You can have a good meal here for less than L60. Mon–Sat 8am–6.30pm, Sun 8am–2pm.

Villa Real A block southeast of the Parque Central on Av 1 NE ☎ 2772 0101. The restaurant serves a tasty chicken stew, but this bar and *discoteca* is best for a drink (buckets of Miller Lite from around L140) and the club scene at the weekends. It's set in a beautifully restored colonial home with a large garden courtyard; note the shrine to Barcelona FC in a display cabinet. Tues–Thurs 11am–2.30pm & 5–10pm, Fri & Sat 11am–2.30pm & 5pm–2am.

5

Viva Café & Lounge Av 1 NO (at Parque Central) ☎ 2772 0779. Artsy café and live music space, also serving breakfast, coffee and sandwiches. In the evenings DJs spin electro and house in the upstairs room while the ground floor pays host to classic rock and karaoke. Mon–Thurs & Sun 8am–10pm, Fri & Sat 8am–2am.

LAGO DE YOJOA

Beyond Comayagua, the highway descends from the mountains and the air becomes appreciably warmer. Some 67km north of Comayagua sits the dazzling blue **LAGO DE YOJOA**, a lake approximately 17km long and 9km wide. Its reed-fringed waters, sloping away to a gentle patchwork of woods, pastures and coffee plantations, are overlooked by the mountains of **Cerro Azul Meámbar** to the east and **Santa Bárbara** to the north and west. Both of these contain small but pristine stretches of **cloudforest** and are protected as national parks. The bowl of the lake is a microclimate and attracts more than four hundred species of **bird**, one of the highest concentrations in the country.

During the week, the waters – and surrounding hotels – are virtually empty, making this a supremely tranquil place for a couple of days of rowing, birdwatching and general outdoor exploring. However, at weekends the lake is a favourite with middle-class Hondureños, and the peace can be shattered by the crowds and the buzz of jet skis.

WHAT TO SEE AND DO

The area around Lago de Yojoa offers some of the most **adventurous activities** of the region: you can hike through the cloudforests of the national parks, get wet crawling behind a plunging waterfall, explore some dark and mysterious caves

or get up close to the local wildlife (see box below).

Cuevas de Taulabé

The jagged stalactites, fruit bats and bizarre limestone formations (dubbed "Angel Wing", "Buddha" and "Shark", among others) at the **Taulabé caves** (daily 8.30am–4pm; US$4; ☎ 3179 1201), just off the CA-5 at km 140 (12km south of the lake), were only discovered in 1969. More than 12km of tunnels and caverns have so far been explored, but only 300m have paths and (multicoloured) lighting. You can walk through the caves on your own, but local guides also hang around for "extreme" tours on all fours, in some of the side passages (negotiate a "tip" beforehand – generally L150, includes helmets and flashlights; prepare to get muddy). The caves can be slippery, so make sure you wear suitable shoes. All local **buses** running along the CA-5 (between Lago de Yojoa and Siguatepeque) will drop you off here; it's also easy to catch a bus on to La Guama for the lake or back to the junction at Siguatepeque for connections to the west.

Parque Nacional Cerro Azul Meámbar

Continuing north beyond the Taulabé caves and along the east side of the lake to the small town of **La Guama**, a dirt road splits off the main highway to run east for another 7km to the entrance to **Parque Nacional Cerro Azul Meámbar** (daily 7am–5pm; US$7; ☎ 9865 9082 or ☎ 2608 5506, ⓦ paghonduras.org). Named after its highest peak, the blue-hued Cerro Azul Meámbar (2047m), this is one of the smaller and more accessible national parks, with a core of untouched cloudforest. Anyone

---

NATURE TOURS OF LAGO DE YOJOA

If it's nature you're after, contact D&D Adventures (☎ 9994 9719, ⓦ ddadventures.com) from the folks at *D&D Brewery* (see opposite), who run fantastic early-morning **tours** on the lake (6am from *D&D Brewery*; L350). Offering the chance to see several species of bird – including herons, kingfishers and hawks – as well as bats, iguanas and otters, this is a great introduction to the lake. They also run guided day-hikes up the summit of Santa Bárbara mountain (US$25), and the Cloud Forest Loop trail (US$75/person for two), exploring the dense cloudforest at 1400–2000m, with the possibility of spotting quetzals. Half-day kayak rental on the lake is US$11 (US$15 for two people).

planning to hike should be prepared for precipitously steep gradients in the upper reaches of the reserve, with dense vegetation and tumbling waterfalls.

The **visitors centre** at the park's entrance has information on two short walking trails: Los Vencejos (300m) to the Vencejos falls, and El Venado (700m), which passes one of the park's two fourteen-metre **birdwatching tower**'s where you'll spot toucans, hummingbirds, hawks, flycatchers and woodpeckers (Nov–March is best for birdwatching). The 5.1km **El Sinaí Trail** is a lot tougher, rising to 1120m via hanging bridges and taking in stellar views of Yojoa lake far below. You don't really need a guide for any of the trails, which are suitable for day-trips, though it is worth staying overnight so that you can see the forest in the early morning.

Buses that ply the route from La Guama to Santa Elena (a small community halfway along the road to the park) may also take you on to the park entrance for around L200 (acting like taxis). Alternatively, *D&D Brewery* (see below) offers private return transport for US$55 (up to 4 people), including 4 to 5 hours at the park. It is money well spent, given the steep one-hour walk from Santa Elena, and the occasional assaults that have been reported along this route.

Peña Blanca

The village of **PEÑA BLANCA**, north of the lake, is the commercial focus for the area. Approaching from the south on CA-5, ask for the *desvío* (turn-off) to Peña Blanca, just after La Guama; from here you can catch one of the frequent *rapiditos* or local buses to Peña Blanca itself. The El Mochito bus from San Pedro Sula also passes through Peña Blanca.

There are various useful services here: Banco Occidente (on Calle Principal, next to the canal; Mon–Fri 8am–3.30pm, Sat 8am–noon) changes dollars and travellers' cheques, though there is currently no ATM; and *El Dorao* is a coffee shop selling excellent local coffee, espressos and snacks, with free wi-fi (there's also a small internet café across the street).

Cataratas de Pulhapanzak

5

The absolute highlight of this region is the privately owned **Cataratas de Pulhapanzak** (daily 7am–6pm; L60), a mesmerizing, 43m-high cascade of churning white waters on the Río Blanco. The waterfall is at its most dazzling in the early mornings, when rainbows form in the rising sun. It's easy enough to explore on your own, but to really get the most out of your visit take advantage of the fantastic **guided tours** run by the staff (L250/US$12; wear sturdy shoes), which are not for the faint-hearted. They'll take you jumping or diving in and out of pools, ducking behind the falls and climbing through the caves behind the curtain of water. River **tubing** is available as well (L500). The **canopy tour** (L500/US$25) is also recommended: a network of five ziplines works its way down the river until you are flying through rainbows above the waterfall. Do not be tempted to swim in the area of water immediately above the falls, as there have been fatalities.

The falls are an easy, partly uphill, fifteen-minute walk (300m) from the village of **San Buenaventura**, 8km north of Peña Blanca; **buses** between El Mochito and San Pedro Sula run hourly (Mon–Sat; less frequently Sundays), passing through both Peña Blanca and San Buenaventura en route. A football field inside the waterfall site entrance fills with locals at the weekend and a restaurant offers cheap fish or fried chicken.

ACCOMMODATION AND EATING

Cataratas de Pulhapanzak cabins ⊕ 3319 7282, ⊚ pulhahn.com. A collection of (pricey) wood cabins with a/c, cable TV, free wi-fi and hot water, in a great location close to the falls. You can also camp (bring your own gear), and there's a café-restaurant for refreshments (daily 7am–9pm; breakfast included). Camping/person US$10, cabin (for two) US$80

El Cortijo del Lago On the road to Peña Blanca, 2km from La Guama ⊕ 9906 5333, ⊚ airbnb.com. This lodge run by a US-Honduran couple can accommodate up to sixteen people in quiet dorms (with a/c and free wi-fi). A good restaurant serves dishes such as tilapia fillet with *chismol*, rice and vegetables picked fresh from the garden. Dorms US$10

★**D&D Brewery, Lodge & Restaurant** Los Naranjos, just outside Peña Blanca on the road to San Pedro Sula; take

5

the El Mochito bus from San Pedro Sula until you see the *D&D Brewery* sign ☎ 9994 9719, ⓦ ddbrewery.com. This marvellous microbrewery/restaurant/lodge, set in a thickly wooded area near the lake, is a real treat. There's a pool, the tropical garden teems with birds and plants, and the home-brewed beer packs a tangy punch. Accommodation ranges from dorms and basic but well-maintained rooms to atmospheric cabins sleeping up to five; if you have a tent, you can also camp in the grounds. Free wi-fi in common areas. Camping/person US$3.50, dorms US$6.50, doubles US$17.50, cabins (for two) US$35

Panacam Lodge 7km from the highway between San Pedro Sula and Tegucigalpa, La Guama turn-off ☎ 9865 9082, ⓦ panacamlodge.com. The park has some fantastic accommodation, from simple dorms (which require groups of ten to sixteen people) to wooden cabins with hot-water bathrooms, free wi-fi and satellite TV, and is well signposted from La Guama. Bring your own equipment if you want to camp. Rates include breakfast and free entry to park trails. Camping/person US$8, dorms US$13, doubles US$60

The western highlands

The **western highlands** of Honduras present a picturesque landscape of pine forests, sparsely inhabited mountains and remote villages. The departments of **Lempira** and **Intibucá** contain the highest concentration of indigenous peoples in the country, and many of the towns in the region make up the so-called **Ruta Lenca**. Around the village of **La Esperanza** particularly, look out for Lenca women wearing traditional coloured headdresses while working in the fields.

Cobbled, colonial **Gracias** makes a relaxing base for hikes in the protected cloudforest of the **Parque Nacional Celaque**. An easy bus ride away is **Santa Rosa de Copán**, which is also a peaceful place to stay and still unspoilt, despite its growing popularity with tourists and its proximity to the famous **Copán ruins**.

LA ESPERANZA

Just west of the busy commercial centre of Siguatepeque, a good paved road (N-22) winds its way 65km southwest

from CA-5 to the small Lenca city of **LA ESPERANZA**, the centre of commerce for western Honduras and the capital of the department of Intibucá (it essentially merges into its twin city of Intibucá). La Esperanza is the highest city in Honduras (1700m) and is known for its cool climate (average lows are just 11ºC in Dec/Jan), but during the week there's nothing much to see – the town livens up considerably during the colourful **weekend market** (Sat & Sun), when Lenca farmers from surrounding villages pour into town; the daily market (Mon–Fri) is far less busy.

ARRIVAL AND INFORMATION

By bus Buses running between Tegucigalpa and San Pedro Sula can drop you off at the *desvío* (turn-off) to La Esperanza, just west of Siguatepeque. Buses (daily; every 2hr; 2hr) run between the *desvío* and the main bus terminal at the eastern edge of central Esperanza until mid-afternoon. Alternatively Transportes Carolina runs hourly to/from Tegucigalpa and San Pedro Sula, direct (with stops). San Juan Intibucá and Gracias minibuses also arrive and depart at the bus terminal.

Bank Banco de Occidente, in the centre of town (Av El Calvario) has one ATM that only takes Visa cards; Banco Atlántida also has a branch and ATM in the centre on Av Los Próceres.

ACCOMMODATION AND EATING

Casa Vieja Parque López ☎ 2783 1189. Congenial bar and restaurant right on the main square, with wood-beam ceiling (the building dates from the 1880s), bilingual staff, ice cold beer and TVs showing US and European sports. The huge burgers (from L80) are hard to resist. Daily 11am–1am.

El Fogón Two blocks west and one block north of Parque López ☎ 2783 0111. Popular restaurant-bar with a hearty mix of Honduran and international dishes, as well as live music (and sometimes karaoke) in the evenings. Mains from L120. Sun–Thurs 9am–10pm, Fri & Sat 9am–midnight.

Posada Papá Chepe Parque López ☎ 2783 0443. Beautiful colonial hotel with relatively good deals and cosy rooms, though it's more of a mid-range option than a budget place. Free wi-fi and excellent on-site restaurant. US$35

Wawa's Hotel At the entrance to town, on highway from Siguatepeque ☎ 2783 4005. Comfortable, clean rooms with hot water, free wi-fi and cable TV (but not breakfast) on the edge of town. Owner Nimia speaks English. US$20

SAN JUAN INTIBUCÁ

A bumpy 52km northwest of La Esperanza, the village of **SAN JUAN INTIBUCÁ** is trying to develop its tourist potential thanks to a local *cooperativa* promoting the area's deep-rooted **Lenca** traditions. Information about tours and craft demonstrations is available from *Hotel Guancascos* in Gracias (see below). Options include participating in the roasting of coffee beans, hikes to nearby waterfalls and cloudforests, and observing the production of traditional handicrafts. San Juan Intibucá is linked by fairly regular **buses** to both Gracias (daily; every 1–2hr; 45min–1hr) and La Esperanza (daily; hourly; 1hr–1hr 30min).

GRACIAS

Founded in 1536 by Spanish conquistador Juan de Chávez, some 36km northwest of San Juan Intibucá, **GRACIAS** lies in the shadow of the nearby **Parque Nacional Celaque** (see p.404). It's a historic but hot and dusty cobbled town, well located for day-trips to surrounding natural attractions.

WHAT TO SEE AND DO

Shady **Parque Central** lies at the centre of town, with San Marcos church on its southern side. Built in 1840, the old colonial mansion opposite San Sebastián church on Calle Alberto Galeano is **Casa Galeano**. It serves as the local museum (daily 9am–6pm; L30), with exhibits on Lenca culture, though labels are in Spanish only. Rising above the town (three blocks west of the square), the **Fuerte de San Cristóbal** (daily 9am–4pm; L30) is an old fort built in 1865, with a small museum inside, though the views are the main reason for the hike up.

Balneario Aguas Termales Arcilaca

The **Balneario Aguas Termales Arcilaca** (also known as Termales Presidente; daily 8am–midnight; L100; ☎9738 4777) are hot springs about an hour's walk southeast (4km from town, on the road between Gracias and La Esperanza), or around L60–100 each way in a moto-taxi – you can arrange for one to come and

collect you for the return leg. These are small pools purpose-built for bathing in the 33–36° waters; an on-site *comedor* serves basic meals.

La Campa

Around 16km south of Gracias, via a gravel road, the old mining town of **La Campa** is far more atmospheric than its bigger neighbour, though tourist development has also taken off here. It's known for shops selling Lenca-style pottery (there's a small museum that displays the various types) and **Canopy Extremo** (daily 9am–4pm; US$25; ☎9521 4681), a 600m-long zipline that shoots over a precipitous canyon just outside town. One bus departs Gracias for La Campa daily at noon, but it only returns at 7am; taxis and moto-taxis (L400–500) are easy to find.

ARRIVAL AND INFORMATION

By bus The bus terminal is four blocks west of the Parque Central on the main highway (CA-11A). There are buses to/from Santa Rosa de Copán (with various companies daily every 20–30min; 1hr 15min) and San Pedro Sula (with Gracianos, Toritos & Cooperative Transportes Lempira 4 daily; 4–5hr). There are also small local buses to San Juan Intibucá and La Esperanza.

Bank Banco Occidente, one block west of the Parque Central (Mon–Fri 8am–4pm, Sat 8–11.30am), changes dollars and travellers' cheques, and has an ATM.

Shopping Envasados y Dulces Lorendiana (☎2656 1058), two blocks southwest of the Parque Central on Av Principal Dr Juan Lindo, sells beautifully bottled pickles, preserves and other food delicacies.

Tourist information An office in the centre of the Parque Central (daily 8am–noon & 1–4.30pm) sells maps and provides basic information, though staff at *Hotel Guancascos* (see below) are more helpful. ⓦ mancomunidadcolosuca.org is also worth a look.

ACCOMMODATION

Hotel Guancascos Av Eleuterio Galeano Trejo, Barrio San Sebastián (east side of Fuerte San Cristóbal) ☎2656 1219, ⓦ guancascos.com. Dutch-owned ecofriendly hotel in a former coffee farm, with two dorms and fifteen well-kept rooms (all have TVs, fans and private bathrooms with hot water). There's a good restaurant (see p.404; breakfast included with rooms, not with dorms) and guided tours of the national park are offered. Free wi-fi. Dorms __L200__, doubles __L800__

Hotelito Josue Av Principal Dr Juan Lindo ☎2656 0076.

5

No-frills hotel with variety of rooms including singles and doubles with either shared or private bathrooms (cold showers), some with cable TV. The staff are extremely friendly and there's a decent shared kitchen and narrow garden courtyard to lounge in. **L250**

EATING AND DRINKING

El Gran Cogolon Av Juan Lindo at C Jeremia Cisneros ☎ 2656 0080. Fashionable juice and smoothie bar, which also serves good coffee, beers and cocktails on the roof of the *Hotel Real Camino Lena*, with fine views of the city and mountains. Live music Fri & Sat evenings. Daily noon–10pm.

Guancascos *Hotel Guancascos*, Av Eleuterio Galeano Trejo (east side of Fuerte San Cristóbal) ☎ 2656 1219, ⒲ guancascos.com. Diners enjoy a superb view from the terrace, especially if you make it for an early breakfast. Highlights include the home-baked bread and the chocolate brownies. Expect to pay around L75–150 for a meal. Daily 7am–10pm.

Kandil Kafe Pizzería Av José María Medina 34, Barrio La Merced (three blocks north from Parque Central) ☎ 2655 9768. An unexpectedly fashionable café, given the town's sleepy and traditional feel. It's crisply painted, with minimal furnishings, and the pizzas with prosciutto or *loroco* (a local flower that is used as a herb) are particularly recommended. Mains L80–200. Tues–Sun 11.30am–10pm.

El Señor de la Sierra Parque Central (in the bandstand). The name of this café refers to Lempira (the heroic chief of the Lenca in the 1530s), whose image graces their drinks menu. There's free wi-fi, the coffee's good, and there are usually one or two snack options (about L45). Daily 8am–10pm.

PARQUE NACIONAL CELAQUE

PARQUE NACIONAL CELAQUE (daily 8am–4pm; L120) protects one of the largest and most impressive expanses of virgin cloudforest in Honduras. Thousands of years of geographical isolation have resulted in several endemic species of flora. Locals also claim that the park is home to more quetzals than all of Guatemala (never mind Honduras), though you'll still have to keep a sharp eye out to see one. The focus of the park is the nation's highest peak, **Cerro Las Minas** (2870m).

WHAT TO SEE AND DO

Inside the park, there are rambles and hikes of all experience levels to choose from. The most exciting and scenic option is the 6km marked **trail** up to the summit of **Cerro Las Minas** (2870m;

elevation gain around 1450m). In the upper reaches of the park much of the main trail consists of 40-degree slopes, so this is not a hike for the unfit. Experienced hikers go up and down in around seven to eight hours, but most end up **camping** at one of the two designated spots along the way (see below). The cloudforest proper doesn't begin until after *Campamento El Naranjo*, so try to make it this far. **Guides** aren't necessary for the main trail, but you'll need one if planning to undertake the more difficult treks on the southern slopes. An easier hike is the five-mile round-trip (from the park gate) to the **Mirador de la Cascada** (view over the falls), which takes around four to five hours at a moderate pace (there's still a 700m elevation gain).

ARRIVAL AND INFORMATION

The park is best approached from Gracias, the entrance is an 8km walk west from town.

On foot Take the dirt road from Gracias through the village of Mejicapa (around 1.5–2km from Gracias), from where a marked track leads uphill to the entrance.

By pick-up Pick-ups or moto-taxis (L150 one way or L300 return) from Gracias are sometimes available; *Hotel Guancascos* (see p.403) can also arrange transport.

Entrance fee and opening times The park is open daily 8am–4pm. Pay your entrance fee (L120 or US$6) at the visitors centre, which is near the Río Arcagual.

Information and guides *Hotel Guancascos* in Gracias (see p.403) functions as an unofficial information centre for the park. As well as selling maps, they can arrange lifts up to the lodge, gear and guides. A recommended guide is Luis Melgar (☎ 9971 5114 or ☎ 9949 6681), who only speaks Spanish; guides typically charge US$20–50/day depending on the route and group size.

ACCOMMODATION

Camping There are two designated camping spots on the way to the peak, the basic but well-sheltered *Campamento Don Tomás* and *Campamento El Naranjo* (the latter is the best overnight for the Minas climb), with covered fire pits and drinking water. You need to bring everything else with you. There are showers at the visitors centre. Per person **L100**

SANTA ROSA DE COPÁN

It's an easy ninety-minute bus ride 45km northwest from Gracias to **SANTA ROSA DE COPÁN**, a colourful colonial relic built on the proceeds of the tobacco industry. Unusually for a town of this size, the majority of its streets are still cobbled, which gives it a traditional feel. While fresh in the mornings and evenings, the town heats up steadily during the day.

WHAT TO SEE AND DO

In the centre of town is the charming, shady **Parque Contreras**, the Parque Central, with the elegant **Catedral de Santa Rosa** on its eastern side. **Calle Real Centenario**, lined with shops and restaurants, runs along the southern edge of the Parque, past the town's central **market** a couple of blocks east.

Flor de Copán Cigar Company factory

Santa Rosa de Copán was chosen in 1765 as the headquarters of the Royal Tobacco Factory and the "golden weed" continues to play a role in the local economy. The **Flor de Copán Cigar Company** maintains offices in the town centre – in the original Royal Tobacco building on Calle Real Centenario – but their **factory** is 2km northwest of the town centre, about 300m after turning right out of the bus station. Around thirty thousand hand-rolled cigars are produced daily, and **tours** in Spanish and English are available, but you'll need to book with the tourist office (see p.406) a day ahead (Mon–Fri 10am & 2pm; US$3; ☎ 2662 0185).

Beneficio Maya

Some 2km northwest (just six blocks from the bus terminal and close to the cigar factory), a short taxi ride from the Parque Central, is the home of the **Beneficio Maya** coffee company (☎ 2662 1665; ⓦcafecopan .com). A family-run business responsible for producing the Café Copán brand, they offer tours of local coffee farms such as Las Granadinas during the coffee season (Nov–Feb; US$2), which should be booked via the tourist office (see p.406). They welcome visitors year-round for coffee roasting (Mon & Tues 2–5pm; free if you buy a cup of coffee or roasted beans).

EATING & DRINKING
Café La Taza	2
Kaldi's Koffee Shop	3
El Rodeo	5
La Taquiza	4
Ten Napel Café	1

ACCOMMODATION
Alondras Tu Hotel	2
Blanca Nieves	1
Karolina Boutique	3

SANTA ROSA DE COPÁN

5

ARRIVAL AND DEPARTURE

By bus The main bus terminal is just off the highway, 2km northwest of the centre on Blvd Bueso Arias (with Hedman Alas and La Sultana stops nearby). Taxis (around L20–25) and the yellow buses marked *urbanos* (city buses; L7) run daily; every 30min to the Parque Contreras.

Destinations Copán (travel via La Entrada); La Entrada (local services; daily every 30min; 45min); Gracias (various companies daily every 20–30min; 1hr 15min); Nueva Ocotepeque (La Sultana; daily; hourly; 2hr); San Pedro Sula (Hedman Alas, La Sultana, Congolón and local services; daily 2–3 hourly; 3hr 30min); Tegucigalpa (Hedman Alas and La Sultana; 6 daily; 7hr).

INFORMATION

Internet You can get online at the tourist office (see below) and Bonsay Cyber Café on C Real Centenario (Mon–Sat 9am–9pm, Sun 10am–6pm; L6/15min or L23/1hr).

Tourist information The tourist office in the centre of the Parque Contreras (Mon–Sat 7am–noon & 1.30–5.30pm, Sun 10am–5.30pm; ☎ 2662 2234, ⓦ visitesanta rosadecopan.com) has city maps and helpful staff.

Tour operators Max Elvir of Lenca Land Trails (☎ 9997 5340, ⓔ lencatours@gmail.com), a local English-speaking guide, offers a number of excellent tours, including trips to Parque Nacional Celaque, indigenous villages and hot springs, all for around US$50–75.

ACCOMMODATION

A great option in Santa Rosa de Copán is to organize a homestay through the tourist office (around L250–300/night). Airbnb (ⓦ airbnb.com) also lists a handful of basic apartments in Santa Rosa, from around L315/night.

Alondras Tu Hotel Av 2 SO, C 1 –2 SO ☎ 2662 1194, ⓦ alondrastuhotel@gmail.com. The ground-floor rooms are a little dark at this lower-mid-range hotel in the centre, but those upstairs are much brighter (hot water and cable TV included in all rooms). There's a spacious communal area, free wi-fi and coffee, and juice and pastries at breakfast. L550

Blanca Nieves Av 3 NE, at C 2 NE ☎ 2662 1312. A decent budget option – the simple en-suite rooms are larger and better value than those with shared facilities. L400

Karolina Boutique Av 1 SE, at C 2 SE ☎ 2662 2210, ⓔ hotelkarolinaboutique@hotmail.com. This mid-range option is a great deal, with very comfy doubles with private bath, cable TV, free wi-fi and breakfast included. L550

EATING AND DRINKING

Santa Rosa has a glut of eating establishments. Cheap *comedores* line the bus station and upstairs in the Mercado Central, where filling *almuerzos* can be had for around L60. In the evenings street vendors sell *tamales* and tortillas around the market and Parque Contreras. There are several places to sample the excellent local coffee.

Café La Taza C Real Centenario, Av 3–4 NO ☎ 2662 7161. Small, homely café proudly displaying their certification of good coffee practice ("high grown") – most of it is produced and roasted locally by the owners. Free wi-fi. Coffee L30–40. Mon–Sat 8am–7pm.

Kaldi's Koffee Shop Av 1 NE, just south of the cathedral ☎ 2662 6202. The perfect place for a cake and a stimulating coffee (from L25) with varieties from as far away as Ethiopia and Thailand, as well as – of course – Honduras. Free wi-fi. Cash only. Mon–Sat 10.30am–7pm.

El Rodeo Av 1 SE, C 1–2 SE ☎ 2662 0697. Huge steakhouse serving the best barbecued meat in town:

INTO EL SALVADOR AND GUATEMALA: EL POY AND AGUA CALIENTE

Buses to both El Salvador and Guatemala pass through **Nueva Ocotepeque** (daily; hourly from Santa Rosa de Copán; 2hr 30min). It's a dirty, busy town, and most people change buses and move on quickly, but if you get stuck, the *Hotel Turístico*, up from the bus stop (☎ 2653 3639; L500), is a solid choice. The Banco de Occidente, near the bus stop, changes currencies and travellers' cheques, but you'll get better rates for Guatemalan quetzales at the border.

TO EL SALVADOR

For **El Poy** (**El Salvador**), *rapiditos* run the 7km from Nueva Ocotepeque (6am–6pm, every 15min; 10min; L50/person). El Poy itself is drab and dusty, but the crossing is straightforward, as the immigration windows are next to each other in the same building just a short walk from where the bus drops you. Banpaís (Mon–Fri 8am–noon & 1–5pm) will change currencies. There are buses to La Palma, the nearest town over the border, and San Salvador (daily every 30min; 6am to 4.30pm).

TO GUATEMALA

For **Agua Caliente** (**Guatemala**), yellow local buses make the trip from Nueva Ocotepeque (daily from 6am to 6.30pm; every 30min; 30min). There are no banking or accommodation facilities on the Honduran side. Over in Guatemala, minibuses (daily 6am to 6pm; every 20min) leave for Esquipulas (see p.337).

a mixed grill comprising steak (including *puyaso*, or top sirloin), chorizo, pork chop, chicken and sides, plus drinks, feeds four and costs around L500. Mon–Sat 10am–1am.

La Taquiza C 1 SE, at Av 4 SE ☎ 2662 5161. Congenial sports bar with plenty of TV screens for major sports events (football) and a decent menu of Mexican food – the beef tacos are especially good. Lunch specials from L90. Happy hour Tues–Thurs 4–7pm. Tues–Sun 11am–11pm.

Ten Napel Café C 1, Av 2–3 NO ☎ 2662 3238. A lovely café with a fantastic garden, free wi-fi, and bags of coffee, cigars and maps of the town for sale, plus good sandwiches, bagels and cakes. If you fancy a treat, try the tiramisu or the passion fruit cheesecake (around L65). Cash only. Mon–Sat 8am–noon & 2–7pm.

DIRECTORY

Banks Banco Occidente, south of the Parque, has a 24hr Visa/Plus ATM and also changes cash dollars and travellers' cheques. There's a second ATM opposite Manzanitas supermarket.

Post office On the west side of the Parque (Mon–Fri 8am–noon & 2–5pm, Sat 8am–noon).

COPÁN RUINAS TOWN

A charming town of steep cobbled streets and red-tiled roofs set among green hills, **COPÁN RUINAS** has more to offer than just its proximity to the famous archeological site of Copán (see p.412). Despite the weekly influx of visitors, Copán Ruinas has managed to remain largely unspoilt. Many travellers are seduced by the relaxed atmosphere, clean air and rural setting, and end up staying longer than planned, studying Spanish, eating and drinking well or exploring the region's other minor sites, hot springs and beautiful countryside. US dollars are accepted everywhere in town along with lempira, but bring lots of small bills.

(see p.412)

WHAT TO SEE AND DO

The **Parque Central** is lined with banks, municipal structures and the simple, whitewashed Baroque-style church of San José Obrero, while the only major sight in town is the archeological museum.

Museo Regional de Arqueología

On the west side of the plaza is the **Museo Regional de Arqueología** (daily 9am–5pm; US$3), housing some impressive Maya carvings from the Copán region, including glyph-covered altars T and U and **Stele 7**, discovered just 100m from the Parque Central. There are also two remarkable **tombs**, one of which contains the remains of a female shaman, complete with jade jewellery, an entire puma skeleton, the skull of a deer, and two human sacrificial victims.

ARRIVAL AND DEPARTURE

By plane The new domestic airport at Copán Ruinas (in Río Amarillo, about 15km from the centre) was inaugurated in 2015; at the time of writing, CM Airlines looked set to start flights from San Pedro Sula. Taxis will shuttle to and from the centre.

By bus Buses from the east generally terminate by a small football field at the entrance to town; Hedman Alas (☎ 2651 4037) has its own terminal on the main CA-11 highway (Av Copán). Taxis into town from the latter should be just L20/person, though drivers will almost certainly try to overcharge you.

Destinations Agua Caliente (daily; hourly 5am–4pm; last return to Copán at 4pm; 1hr); Antigua, Guatemala (with Hedman Alas, via Guatemala City, 2.20pm; 6hr); La Entrada (local buses daily 6am–5pm, every 45min; 1hr); Guatemala City (Hedman Alas daily 8.00 & 4.30pm; 7hr); San Pedro Sula (Hedman Alas & Casasola, 8 daily; 3hr). For Tegucigalpa, Tela and La Ceiba, you have to travel via San Pedro Sula. For Santa Rosa de Copán and Gracias, you have to go via La Entrada.

By shuttle bus Basecamp (see below) runs daily 6am & noon shuttle buses to Guatemala (Guatemala City & Antigua; US$20); and to El Salvador on Tues, Thurs & Sat at 12.30pm (several destinations including San Salvador, Suchitoto and El Tunco; US$36).

INFORMATION AND TOURS

Internet There are several internet cafés in town, including Maya Connections (just south of the plaza on Av Centroaméricano, at C La Independencia) and *La Casa de Todo* restaurant (L10/30min, L20/1hr), on Av Sesesmiles at Calle 18 Conejo.

Tourist information Copán Connections and Basecamp (see below) are both excellent sources on the local area and the country as a whole.

Tour operators Basecamp (☎ 2651 4695, ⓦ basecamp honduras.com), in the *ViaVia* café (see p.409), offers a range of hikes (US$10–45) lasting up to 8hr, horseriding trips (from US$15), including to *Finca El Cisne* (see box, p.412), canopy tours (US$45), and excursions to Macaw Mountain Bird Park (US$10) and Luna Jaguar hot springs (US$55 for up to eight people). The town tour (US$10) is particularly good: English-speaking owner Gerardo explains what really makes Copán Ruinas tick, politically

(see p.409)

5

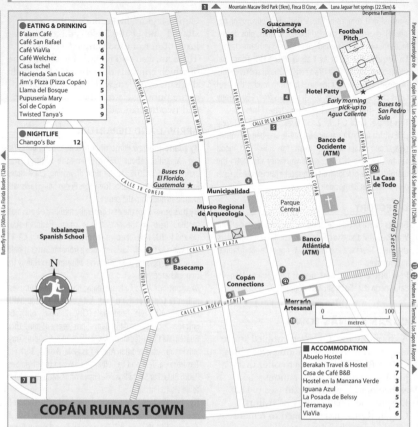

COPÁN RUINAS TOWN

● EATING & DRINKING

B'alam Café	8
Café San Rafael	10
Café ViaVia	6
Café Welchez	4
Casa Ixchel	2
Hacienda San Lucas	11
Jim's Pizza (Pizza Copán)	7
Llama del Bosque	5
Pupusería Mary	1
Sol de Copán	3
Twisted Tanya's	9

● NIGHTLIFE

Chango's Bar	12

■ ACCOMMODATION

Abuelo Hostel	1
Berakah Travel & Hostel	4
Casa de Café B&B	7
Hostel en la Manzana Verde	3
Iguana Azul	8
La Posada de Belssy	5
Terramaya	2
ViaVia	6

and economically. Copán Connections (☎ 2651 4182, ⓦ copanconnections.com) at *Twisted Tanya's* (see opposite) is a one-stop source of information on Copán and popular destinations like Lago de Yojoa and the Bay Islands. They also offer wider tours of Honduras, transfers, house rentals, flight bookings, and numerous tours including one that combines Macaw Mountain with the Miramundo coffee farm (US$70).

ACCOMMODATION

Abuelo Hostel Av Buena Vista (five blocks from Parque Central) ☎ 9772 7884. Private rooms and dorms (with fan) a short walk from Parque Central (via Av Centroamérica) in a quiet neighbourhood. Free shuttle to the ruins and bus station, pleasant terrace, hot water and free wi-fi. Dorms **L120**, doubles **L500**

Berakah Travel & Hostel Av Copán (one block north of Parque Central) ☎ 9951 4288, ⓦ berakahtravel.com. Same folks as *Abuelo* (see above), with this central location offering a mix of comfy private rooms and dorms, an

enticing terrace and basic shared kitchen. Free wi-fi. Dorms **L140**, doubles **L320**

★Casa de Café B&B Five blocks southwest of Parque Central, overlooking the Río Copán valley ☎ 2651 4620, ⓦ casadecafecopan.com. Charming B&B with comfortable and airy rooms, all with nice individual touches, fans, and sparkling private bathrooms. There's a fabulous garden where you can lie in a hammock and enjoy the views, and a spacious communal lounge with a TV, small library and wi-fi access. An excellent breakfast and unlimited coffee and tea are included in the rates. **US$58**

Hostel en la Manzana Verde Av Copán (one and a half blocks north of the Parque Central) ☎ 2651 4652, ⓦ viaviacafe.com. Under the same ownership as *ViaVia* (see p.409), this clean hostel has six-bed dorms, a communal kitchen, free laundry facilities and free wi-fi. **L120**

Iguana Azul C Rosalila (five blocks southwest of Parque Central, overlooking the Río Copán valley, next to the *Casa de Café B&B*) ☎ 2651 4620, ⓦ iguanaazulcopan.com. An excellent, spotless budget choice, with four private rooms and two very pleasant dorms, all with shared bathrooms and ceiling fans. Amenities include a pretty garden, hot showers, free purified water, laundry facilities and free wi-fi. Dorms **L160**, doubles **L320**

La Posada de Belssy C de la Entrada (one block north of the Parque Central) ☎ 2651 4680, ⓦ laposadadebelssy .com. With a small pool and relaxing hangout area at the top of the building, hot-water bathrooms, communal kitchen and free coffee, this is a solid budget choice. Rooms (with fan, or a/c for another L100) are small and old-fashioned, but adequate. Breakfast costs L50. **L400**

ViaVia C de la Plaza (two blocks west of the Parque Central) ☎ 2651 4652, ⓦ viaviacafe.com. This hotel-cum-café-cum-tourist office, part of an international chain and under hospitable Belgian management, has simple but spotless rooms with private bathrooms (hot water) and fans. Bottled water, wi-fi and salsa classes are free, and they offer yoga and movie screenings for a fee. Double **L265**

EATING

There's a food market one block west of the Parque, and Copán's wide range of cafés and restaurants generally maintains high standards. Most places open daily around 7–8am and stop serving at 10pm.

CAFÉS

B'alam Café C La Independencia, one block south of Parque Central ☎ 2651 4338. An intimate café attached to the *Yat B'alam* hotel, with a tiled floor and tiny terrace. It serves coffee and a tasty quesadilla cake, as well as snacks such as bagels with cream cheese and jalapeño jelly and pittas with chicken, cheese, tomatoes and *papalinas* (potato chips), plus a Middle Eastern take on the *baleada*. Snacks from L70. Daily 7am–7pm.

Café San Rafael Av Centroamérica (one and a half blocks south of Parque Central) ☎ 2651 4546, ⓦ cafesanrafael .com. Owner Carlos Guerra, who studied cheese making in

California, produces his own camembert, brie, gouda and mozzarella – to name just a few – which feature in a variety of dishes here (sandwiches L100–160). The coffee, grown, harvested and roasted on Guerra's *finca*, is excellent too (L30–40). Daily 8am–8pm.

Café ViaVia C de la Plaza (one and a half blocks west of Parque Central) ☎ 2651 4652. Attached to the hotel of the same name (see above), this café-bar is the town's social hub, with a streetside terrace, a leafy garden and a menu featuring an array of breakfast dishes, sandwiches and main meals (L110–130), including plenty of vegetarian options. There's a daily happy hour (5–7pm) and a range of evening activities such as film screenings and salsa classes. Daily 7am–midnight.

Café Welchez Parque Central (northwest corner, next to *Hotel Marina Copán*) ☎ 2651 4202, ⓦ cafehonduras.com. Boasts some of the world's smallest balconies, which offer great views of the square. Inside, wood panelling adds a distinguished feel. Local gourmet coffee (L30–40) and desserts (try the German chocolate cake) are the focus. Coffee tours can be arranged (US$40). Daily 6am–10pm.

Casa Ixchel Av Los Sesesmiles (one and a half blocks northeast of Parque Central) ☎ 2651 4515. Just behind the church, this coffee shop is supplied by its own organic coffee farm and offers plenty of vegan options as well as burgers (L160), big American-style cooked breakfasts and free wi-fi. Daily 8am–6.30pm.

RESTAURANTS

Jim's Pizza (Pizza Copán) Av Centroamérica (half a block south of Parque Central) ☎ 2651 4381. Locals and tourists flock to this Texan-run joint to indulge in delicious, generous pizzas and pasta (from L170). Takeaway is available, and live US sport is shown on the big screens. Daily 11am–9pm.

Llama del Bosque Av La Cuesta, at de La Plaza (one and a half blocks west of Parque Central) ☎ 2651 4431. Slightly old fashioned Honduran restaurant (the first to open in Copán, back in 1975) with a reasonably priced menu including local breakfasts, meat and chicken dishes, *baleadas* and snacks (most dishes L80–120). Daily 6.30am–10pm.

Pupusería Mary Av Los Sesesmiles (one and a half blocks north of Parque Central, opposite the football field) ☎ 2651 4673. This great local restaurant specializes in *pupusas* served with pickles made from everything from cauliflower to chilli. A drink and a couple of *pupusas* costs under L60. Daily 7am–10.30pm.

Sol de Copán Av Mirador (one block northwest of Parque Central) ☎ 2651 4758. German microbrewery (seriously) and restaurant helmed by Munich native Tomas, who knocks out authentic home-made Bavarian sausages and brewed-on-site craft beers (on tap). Wed–Sun 1–11pm.

★ Twisted Tanya's C Independencia, at Av Mirador (one block southwest of Parque Central) ☎ 9770 1599, ⓦ twistedtanyas.com. Some of the best food in town, with

5

> **★TREAT YOURSELF**
>
> **Hacienda San Lucas** 1.8 km southeast of Parque Central ☎ 2651 4495, ⓦ haciendasanlucas.com. Wonderful converted farmhouse set in the hills south of town (taxi L50), with sensational views over the valley. In the evening, hundreds of candles are lit all over the grounds and you can watch the night unfold over the ruins. The food, meanwhile, is some of the best you'll find in Honduras: five-course traditional Maya-inspired meals (from US$30) featuring dishes such as *tamales* and *adobo* sauce are on offer, as well as dishes such as a *tamale* plate which includes home-made cheese, *encurtido* (pickles), beans and fresh tortilla. Reservations essential for lunch and dinner. Daily 7am–10pm.

mains such as slow-roasted pork, spicy chicken curry and seafood pasta. Three courses cost L160; individual dishes are L120 upwards. The "backpackers' special" menu (3–6pm; L120–200) has offerings such as home-made beef ravioli, as well as two-for-one cocktails. Mon–Sat 2–10pm.

BARS

In addition to *Chango's* (see below), *Café ViaVia* (see p.409) and *Twisted Tanya's* (see p.409) are also excellent nightspots. All bars have to close before midnight (those on the outskirts can open later at the weekends).

Chango's Bar 10min walk southeast of Parque Central ☎ 2651 4525. Things don't really get going much before 10pm, when they start playing a mix of merengue and other Latin beats. Drinks L30 during happy hour (Fri 7–11pm). Thurs–Sat 6pm–3am.

SHOPPING

La Casa de Todo Av Los Sesesmiles, at C 18 Conejo (one block east of Parque Central). Shop and internet café with a selection of English-language books for sale or exchange, and every souvenir imaginable including jewellery and ceramics. Daily 8am–9pm.

Mercado Artesanal C Independencia, one block south of the Parque. Tourist-friendly market selling T-shirts, handicrafts and the like. Open daily in the afternoon.

Supermarket Despensa Familiar on Av Los Sesesmiles, at C Las Gradas. Daily 8am–9pm.

DIRECTORY

Banks Banco de Occidente (Mon–Fri 8.30am–4.30pm, Sat 8.30–11.30am & 1–4pm) and Banco Atlántida (Mon–Fri 9am–5pm, Sat 9am–noon) both have 24hr ATMs.

Language schools Guacamaya (☎ 2651 4360, ⓦ guacamaya.com), Av Copán, two blocks north of the plaza, offers a week-long course for US$260 which includes 20hr of one-on-one tuition, homestay accommodation, a day-trip and university credits. Without the homestay it's US$160. Ixbalanque (☎ 2651 4432, ⓦ Ixbalanque.com), three blocks west of the Parque, is another option; a week-long course, including a homestay, costs US$300. Both schools can also organize volunteering opportunities.

Laundry La Casa de Todo (see above) has a one-day service.

Post office Behind the Museo Regional de Arqueología (Mon–Fri 8am–4pm, Sat 8am–noon).

AROUND COPÁN RUINAS

While the main draw for travellers to Copán is the nearby ruins, there's a lot more on offer. **Nature parks** give visitors the chance to walk among beautiful butterflies and exotic birds, a local family-run farm can show you how your morning cup of coffee came into existence, and lesser-known archeological sites like **Las Sepulturas** can be gratifyingly devoid of tourists.

Macaw Mountain Bird Park

Around 3km north of Parque Central (around L20–30 each way in a moto-taxi), the **Macaw Mountain Bird Park** (daily 9am–5pm; US$10 or L200; ☎ 2651 4245, ⓦ macawmountain.org) is normally home to over twenty bird species, including types of parrot, scarlet macaws, owls and toucans rescued from captivity. Your ticket gives you a free guided tour (recommended) and entry for three days – with walk-through aviaries, a restaurant, a stunning forest location and a natural pool for swimming, it's worth the entrance fee.

Las Sepulturas

Some 2km east of Copán along the highway (L30 by moto-taxi) and 1.4km from the main ruins lies the smaller archeological site of **Las Sepulturas** (daily 8am–4pm; US$15, includes entrance to Copán), the focus of much interest in recent years because of the information it provides on daily domestic life in Maya times. Eighteen of the forty-odd residential compounds at the site have

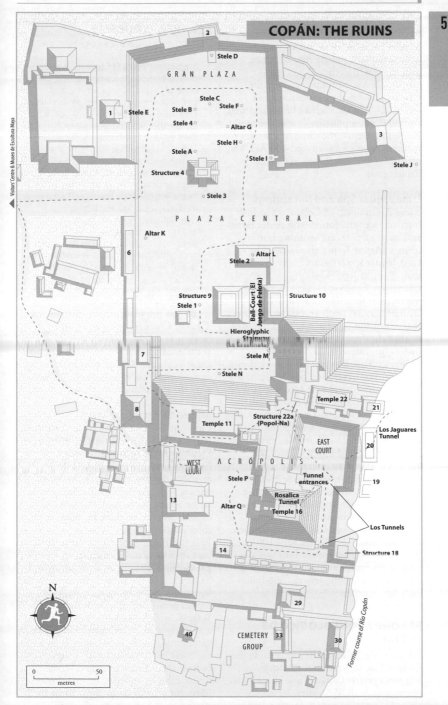

COPÁN: THE RUINS

GRAN PLAZA

○ Stele D

Stele C ○

Stele B ○   ○ Stele F

Stele 4 ○   ○ Altar G

Stele H ○

Stele A ○

Stele I ○

Stele J ○

1

Stele E ○

2

3

Structure 4

○ Stele 3

PLAZA CENTRAL

Altar K ○

6

○ Altar L

Stele 2 ○

Structure 9   Structure 10

Stele 1 ○

Ball-Court 'El Juego de Pelota'

Hieroglyphic Stairway (La Escalinata)

7

Stele M

Stele N ○

Temple 22

21

Structure 22a (Popol-Na)

8

Temple 11

Los Jaguares Tunnel

20

EAST COURT

19

WEST COURT

ACRÓPOLIS

Stele P ○

Tunnel entrances

13

Rosalica Tunnel

Altar Q ○   Temple 16

Los Tunnels

14

Structure 18

29

40   33   30

CEMETERY GROUP

N

0   50
metres

Visitor Centre & Museo de Escultura Maya ◄

Former course of Río Copán

5

been excavated, yielding one hundred buildings that would have been inhabited. Smaller compounds on the edge of the site are thought to have housed young princes, as well as concubines and servants. It was customary to bury the nobility close to their residences, and more than 250 tombs have been excavated around the compounds. One of the most interesting finds – the tomb of a priest or shaman, dating from around 450 AD – is on display in the museum in Copán Ruinas town.

Luna Jaguar Spa and hot springs

Some 22km north of Copán, set in lush highland scenery dotted with coffee farms and tracts of pine, are soothing hot springs (Aguas Termales) managed by **Luna Jaguar Spa & Resort** (daily 9am–9pm; ☎ 2651 4746, ⓦlunajaguarspa.com) – here thermal waters pour into the cold-water river, creating natural pools and showers. Note that admission to what's dubbed the **Area Popol Nah**, the two enticing thermal pool baths (plus cafeteria), is only L60 – there's no need to pay for the spa across the river. For L200 (or US$10), though, you can enter this spa, **El Acrópolis**, the more exclusive area fit for a Maya king, with thirteen treatment stations variously offering foot massages, whirlpools, mud treatments and steam baths (entry rises to L240 1–5pm, and L300 5–9pm). **El Templo** is the massage centre (US$25/30min). Most people visit on tours (*ViaVia* charges US$10), but the spa runs a shuttle from *Hotel Patty* in Copán Ruinas (on Av Los Sesesmiles, next to the football field) at around 1pm, returning around 5.30pm, for L100 one way (confirm in advance). Local moto-taxis charge as much as US$35–45 (return) for the bone-jarring, one-hour-each-way journey.

PARQUE ARQUEOLÓGICO DE COPÁN

Set in serene, rolling hills just outside the town of Copán Ruinas, the **Parque Arqueológico de Copán** is one of the most tantalizing of all Maya sites. Its

> ### ★ TREAT YOURSELF
>
> If you want to get a real insight into the local way of life, take a day-trip or stay overnight at **Finca El Cisne** (☎ 2651 4695 or ☎ 9920 4836, ⓦfincaelcisne.com), 24km north of Copán Ruinas. Owner Carlos Castejón's family has worked the land here since 1885, and they now invite guests to explore their working farm, which is involved in the production of cardamom, coffee and cattle. Day-long tours with English-speaking guides (from US$82 or L1700) include transport to and from the finca, fantastic scenic horseriding, swimming in the Río Blanco and a trip to the Luna Jaguar Spa and hot springs. Overnight tours (from US$95 or L1974) include accommodation, breakfasts and dinners. Visits can be arranged through the finca office (Mon–Sat 8am–noon & 4–8pm; ☎ 2651 4695) in *Café ViaVia* (see p.409).

pre-eminence is not due to size – in scale it's far less impressive than ruins such as Tikal or Chichén Itza – but to the overwhelming legacy of artistic craftsmanship that has survived over so many centuries. Copán now ranks as the second most visited spot in the country after the Bay Islands.

Museo de Escultura Maya

Opposite the visitors centre at the ruins (see p.416) is the illuminating **Museo de Escultura Maya** (Museum of Maya Sculpture; daily 8am–4pm; US$7), arguably the finest in the entire Maya region, with a tremendous collection of steles, altars, panels and well-labelled explanations in English. Entrance is through an impressive doorway made to look like the jaws of a serpent; you then pass through a tunnel signifying the passage into *xibalba*, or the underworld.

Once out of the tunnel you are greeted by a full-scale, flamboyantly painted replica of the magnificent **Rosalila Temple**, built by Moon Jaguar in 571 AD and discovered intact under Temple 16. A vast crimson-and-jade-coloured mask of the Sun God, depicted with wings outstretched, forms the main facade. Other exhibits concentrate on aspects of Maya beliefs and cosmology, while the

COPÁN

Once the most important **city-state** on the southern fringes of the Maya world, Copán was largely cut off from all other Maya cities except **Quiriguá**, 64km to the north in Guatemala (see p.338). Archeologists now believe that settlers began moving into the Río Copán valley from around 1400 BC, taking advantage of the area's rich agricultural potential, although construction of the city is not thought to have begun until around 100 AD. For those interested in finding out more, *Vision del Pasado Maya* by Fash and Fasquelle, available from the museums, is an excellent historical account of the site's history in Spanish.

426 AD Yax K'uk Mo' (Great Sun First Quetzal Macaw), a warrior-shaman, establishes the basic layout of the city. Yax K'uk Mo's son Popol Hol creates a cult of veneration for Yax K'uk Mo' which continues for more than fifteen generations.

553 AD Golden era of Copán begins with the accession of Moon Jaguar, and the construction of his magnificent Rosalila Temple.

578–628 AD Reign of Smoke Serpent.

628–695 AD Reign of Smoke Jaguar.

695–738 AD 18 Rabbit reigns and oversees the construction of the Gran Plaza, the final version of the ball court and Temple 22 in the East Court, creating much of the stonework for which Copán is now famous. Following 18 Rabbit's capture and decapitation by Quiriguá's Cauac Sky, construction at Copán comes to a halt for seventeen years.

749–763 AD Smoke Shell reigns and completes the construction of the Hieroglyphic Stairway.

760 AD Copán's population booms at around 28,000, the highest urban density in the entire Maya region.

763–820 AD Yax Pasaj, Smoke Shell's son, commissions Altar Q, which illustrates the entire dynasty from its beginning.

776 AD Yax Pasaj completes the final version of Temple 16.

822 AD Ukit Tuuk' assumes the throne: the only monument to his reign, Altar L, was never completed. Skeletal remains indicate that the decline of the city, which began around this time, was provoked by inadequate food resources created by population pressures.

1576 Don Diego de Palacios, a Spanish court official, mentions the ruins of a magnificent city "constructed with such skill that it seems that they could never have been made by people as coarse as the inhabitants of this province" in a letter.

1834 Explorer Juan Galindo writes an account of the ruins.

1839 John Stephens, the US ambassador to Honduras, buys the ruins. Accompanied by Frederick Catherwood, a British architect and artist, he clears the site and maps the buildings. *Incidents of Travel in Central America, Chiapas and Yucatán* is published by Stephens and Catherwood, and Copán becomes a magnet for archeologists.

1891 British archeologist Alfred Maudsley begins a full-scale mapping, excavation and reconstruction of the site, sponsored by Harvard University's Peabody Museum.

1935 Washington's Carnegie Institution diverts the Río Copán to prevent it carving into the site.

1959–60 Archeologists Heinrich Berlin and Tatiana Proskouriakoff begin to decipher the site's hieroglyphs, leading to the realization that they record the history of the cities and the dynasties.

1977 Instituto Hondureño de Antropología e Historia starts running a series of projects, including tunnelling, with the help of archeologists from around the world.

1989 Rosalila Temple, buried beneath Temple 16, is discovered.

1993 Papagayo Temple, built by Popol Hol and dedicated to his father Yax K'uk Mo', is discovered.

1998 Yax K'uk Mo's tomb is discovered.

2004 Excavation of Yax K'uk Mo's tomb is completed – bone analysis proves he was from Tikal.

2005 Oropéndola Temple, also buried beneath Temple 16, is discovered; discovery made public when excavation begins in 2007.

2012 The Núñez Chinchilla group is located on the north side of the park (around 145 burials have been discovered).

upper storey houses many of the finest original sculptures from the Copán valley, comprehensively displaying the skill of the Maya craftsmen.

Plaza Central and Gran Plaza

Straight through the avenue of trees from the warden's gate lie the **Plaza Central** and **Gran Plaza**, large, rectangular arenas strewn with the magnificently carved and exceptionally well preserved steles that are Copán's outstanding features. The northern end of the Gran Plaza was once a public place, the stepped sides bordered by a densely populated residential area.

5

Structure 4 in the centre of the two plazas is a modestly sized pyramid-temple.

Dotted all around are Copán's famed **steles** and altars, made from local andesite. Most of the steles represent **18 Rabbit**, Copán's "King of the Arts" (steles A, B, C, D, F, H and 4). **Stele A** (731 AD) has 52 glyphs along its sides including the emblem glyphs of the four great cities of Copán, Palenque, Tikal and Calakmul – a text designed to show that 18 Rabbit saw his city as a pivotal power in the Maya world. The original is now in the museum. **Stele B** (731 AD) depicts 18 Rabbit bearing a turban-like headdress intertwined with twin macaws, while his hands support a bar motif, a symbol designed to show the ruler holding up the sky. **Stele C** (730 AD) is one of the earliest stones to have faces on both sides. Two rulers are represented here: facing the turtle-shaped altar (a symbol of longevity) is 18 Rabbit's father Smoke Jaguar, while on the other side is 18 Rabbit himself. **Stele H** (730 AD), perhaps the most impressively executed of all the sculptures, shows 18 Rabbit wearing the latticed skirt of the Maize God, his wrists weighed down with jewellery, while his face is crowned with a magnificent headdress.

Ball court (El Juego de Pelota)

South of Structure 4, towards the Acrópolis, is the I-shaped **ball court** (738 AD), one of the largest and most elaborate of the Classic period, and one of the few Maya courts still to have a paved floor. Dedicated to the great macaw deity, both sloping sides of the court are lined with three sculptured macaw heads. The rooms overlooking the playing area are thought to be where priests and the elite watched the game.

Hieroglyphic Stairway (La Escalinata Jeroglífica)

Protected by a vast canvas cover just south of the ball court is the famed **Hieroglyphic Stairway**, perhaps Copán's most astonishing monument. The stairway comprises the entire western face of the Temple 26 pyramid, and is made up of some 72 stone steps; every block forms part of the glyphic sequence – around 2200 glyph blocks in all, forming the longest known Maya hieroglyphic text. Since their discovery at the end of the nineteenth century and a well-meaning reconstruction in the 1930s, the blocks have become so jumbled their true meaning is unlikely ever to be revealed. It is known that the stairway was initiated to record the dynastic history of the city; some of the lower steps were placed by 18 Rabbit in 710 AD, while Smoke Shell rearranged and completed most of the sequences in an effort to reassert the city's dignity and strength in 755 AD. At the base of the stairway the badly weathered **Stele M** depicts Smoke Shell and records a solar eclipse in 756 AD.

Temple 11

Adjacent to the Hieroglyphic Stairway, and towering over the extreme southern end of the plaza, are the vertiginous steps of **Temple 11** (Temple of the Inscriptions). At its base, **Stele N** (761 AD) represents Smoke Shell. The depth of the relief has protected the nooks and crannies, and in some of these you can still see flakes of paint – originally the carvings and buildings would have been painted in a whole range of bright colours, but only the red has survived.

Acrópolis

South of the Hieroglyphic Stairway monumental temples rise to form the

---

LOS TUNELES

You can now view the brilliant original facade of the buried Rosalila Temple by entering through a short **tunnel** – an unforgettable, if rather costly (an extra US$15), experience. The admission price also includes access to two further tunnels, which extend below the East Court and past some early cosmological stucco carvings – including a huge macaw mask – along with more buried temple facades and crypts including the Galindo tomb. Only ten people are allowed in at a time, with a guide.

Acrópolis. This lofty inner sanctum was the reserve of royalty, nobles and priests where religious rituals were enacted, sacrifices performed and rulers entombed. For over four hundred years, the temples grew higher and higher as new structures were built over the remains of earlier buildings. A warren of excavated tunnels, some open to the public, bore through the vast bulk of the Acrópolis to the Rosalila Temple and several tombs.

Popol-Na

A few metres east of Temple 11 are the **Popol-Na** (Structure 22A), a governmental building with interlocking weave-like brick patterns, and **Temple 22**, which boasts some superbly intricate stonework around the door frames and was the site of religious blood-letting ceremonies. The decoration here is unique in the southern Maya region, with only the Yucatán sites such as Kabáh and Chicanna having carvings of comparable quality.

East Court

Below Temple 22 are the stepped sides of the **East Court**, a graceful plaza with life-sized jaguar heads – the hollow eyes would have once held jade or polished obsidian. Dominating the Acrópolis, **Temple 16**, built on top of the **Rosalila Temple** (see box opposite) is the tallest structure in Copán, a 30m pyramid completed by the city's sixteenth ruler, Yax Pasaj, in 776 AD. It was Maya custom to ritually deface or destroy obsolete temples and steles. Yax Pasaj's extraordinary care to preserve the Rosalila Temple beneath illustrates the importance of the previous centre of

worship during a period that marked the apogee of the city's political, social and artistic growth. The discovery of the Rosalila Temple (and its twin, the Oropéndola Temple), has been one of the most exciting finds of recent years.

At the southern end of the East Court is **Structure 18**, a small, square building with four carved panels, and the burial place of Yax Pasaj, who died in 821 AD. The diminutive scale of the structure reveals how quickly decline set in. The tomb, empty when excavated by archeologists, is thought to have been looted on a number of occasions. South of Structure 18, the **Cemetery Group** was formerly thought of as a burial site, though it's now known to have been a residential complex for the ruling elite.

West Court

The second plaza of the Acrópolis, the **West Court**, is confined by Temple 16 and the south side of Temple 11. At the base of Temple 16 and carved in 776 AD, **Altar Q** celebrates Yax Pasaj's accession to the throne on July 2, 763 AD. Six hieroglyphic blocks decorate the top of the altar, while the sides are embellished with sixteen cross-legged figures representing previous rulers of Copán. All point towards a portrait of Yax Pasaj, which shows him receiving a ceremonial staff from the city's first ruler, Yax K'uk Mo', thereby endorsing Yax Pasaj's right to rule.

ARRIVAL AND INFORMATION

On foot From Copán Ruinas centre the ruins are an easy 20min walk along a shaded pavement following the highway. Bring lots of water – you won't be able to buy any in the park and after two hours of wandering around the site you'll need to rehydrate.

INTO GUATEMALA: EL FLORIDO

The **Guatemalan border** is just 12km west of Copán, and crossing at the **El Florido** border post – usually busy with travellers coming to and from the Copán ruins – is pretty easy, though it can be slow. Minibuses and pick-ups leave for El Florido (daily; about every 30min from 6am to around 4pm) from just west of the Parque Central in Copán Ruinas (Av Mirador, at C 18 Conejo). Hedman Alas, Copán Connections (see p.408) and Basecamp (see p.407) in Copán Ruinas have direct daily shuttles to Antigua and Guatemala City, with connections to Río Dulce. The ever-present moneychangers at the border handle dollars, lempiras and quetzales at fairly good rates. From the border, buses leave (daily every 30min; from 6am to around 4pm; 1hr 15min) for Chiquimula (see p.336), 57km away down a smooth paved road.

5

By moto-taxi You can grab a moto-taxi from Parque Central to take you to the ruins (5min; L20–30).

Hours and admission The site is open daily 8am–5pm (last entry 4pm). The US$15 admission fee includes entrance to the complex of ruins as well as to the smaller site of Las Sepulturas (see p.410). The ticket is now valid for just one day. It's another US$15 for the tunnels and US$7 for the Museo de Escultura Maya.

Tourist information On entering the site, the visitors centre, where you pay your entrance fee, is to your left. From here it's a 200m walk east to the warden's gate, where your ticket will be checked and you'll be greeted by squabbling macaws.

Tour guides Guides are available and are generally well worth the fee – they do an excellent job of bringing the ruins to life; get together with other visitors to spread the cost (around US$25–40/2hr, depending on group size).

Olancho

Stretching east of Tegucigalpa to the Nicaraguan border and north into the emptiness of La Mosquitia, the sparsely populated uplands of **Olancho** are widely regarded as the "Wild East" of Honduras: an untamed frontier region with a not entirely undeserved reputation for lawlessness and a long-running problem with drug smuggling. Over time, everyone from the first Spanish settlers to the Honduran government has had trouble imposing law and order here, and in many respects today is no different: the region's profitable cattle-ranching industry (which has encroached into national parks and other protected areas) and the logging of its massive forests (much of which is done illegally) have led to the creation of a powerful local oligarchy supported by military and police connivance. Travelling here can be challenging – you should check the current security situation before making plans – but incredibly rewarding.

Despite Olancho's size – it makes up a fifth of Honduras's total territory and is larger than El Salvador – conventional tourist attractions are few, and its high, forested mountain ranges interspersed with broad valleys make getting from place to place difficult and slow. However, these same ranges harbour some of the country's last untouched expanses of tropical forest and cloudforest: the national parks of **El Boquerón** and **Sierra de Agalta** are awe-inspiring. Along the valleys, now given over to pastureland for cattle, are scattered villages and towns. Both **Juticalpa**, the department capital, and **Catacamas**, 43km east at the end of the paved highway, are good bases for exploring the region.

Olancho's **climate** is generally pleasant, with the towns at lower altitudes hot during the day and comfortably cool at night; up in the mountains it can get extremely cold after dark.

ARRIVAL AND DEPARTURE

Once off the main highway, travelling in Olancho becomes arduous, with the dirt roads connecting villages served by infrequent and invariably slow public transport; unless you have a group, driving a rented car is not advisable because of security concerns.

Destinations to/from Catacamas Juticalpa (daily every 30–40min; 40min); Tegucigalpa (daily every 30min; 3–4hr).

Destinations to/from Juticalpa Catacamas (daily every 30–40min; 40min); Gualaco (daily 4am; 1hr 30min); La Ceiba (2 daily; 9hr); San Esteban (daily 4am; 3hr 30min); Tegucigalpa (hourly; 3hr); Trujillo (daily 4am; 8hr).

GETTING AROUND

By bus Monumento Nacional El Boquerón is about halfway between Juticalpa and Catacamas, so any bus going between the two towns can drop you near the start of the main trail, by the Boquerón bridge (moving on, just flag them down on the main highway). For Parque Nacional Sierra de Agalta take the daily bus from Juticalpa to Trujillo (see above) and get off at Gualaco or San Esteban; accessing the park trails from either town requires a significant hike.

By pick-up Pick-ups from the market in Juticalpa also make the trip to the Parque Nacional Sierra de Agalta.

INFORMATION AND TOURS

Tourist information The ICF agency (formerly COHDEFOR) in Juticalpa is set back from the road on Av 7 near C 14 (erratic hours, but in theory Mon–Fri 9am–5pm ☎ 2785 2253).

Tour operators Olancho Tours (☎ 9811 7451, ✉ olancho tours@yahoo.com) offers excursions throughout the region; contact them by phone or email. Beaks and Peaks (based at *Hotel Guancascos*, Av Eleuterio Galeano Trejo in Gracias) also run excellent wildlife tours of the area (☎ 9966 5163, ⊕ beaksandpeaks.com).

5

OLANCHO: THE HIGHLIGHTS

Olancho's attractions may require a fair degree of effort to reach, but they're worth it – you'll often have sights to yourself.

CUEVAS DE TALGUA

Located 8km northeast of Catacamas on the banks of the Río Talgua, the Cuevas de Talgua (daily 9am–5pm; US$6) are notable for the discovery in 1994 of a prehistoric **burial ground** (800–1400 BC), featuring hundreds of skeletons arranged in chambers deep underground. Though the burial ground itself is out of bounds to visitors, the rest of the site has been developed for tourists, with a **museum** telling the tale of the finds and trails leading through the caves. To get here, take the local **bus** from Catacamas to Talgua (daily 7am, 11am & 3pm; 20min). The last return bus leaves Talgua at 4pm. Taxis generally quote around L200–250, but try to pay no more than L150.

MONUMENTO NACIONAL EL BOQUERÓN

Some 20km east of Juticalpa is one of the last remaining tracks of **dry tropical forest** in Honduras, home to a wide variety of wildlife, including more than 250 species of bird. Hike the moderately strenuous main trail through the **reserve**, which runs from where the bus drops you off (near the Puente Boquerón bridge) to a point a few kilometres west of the main entrance; the walk is manageable in one day if you get an early start. The trail can be hard to follow, especially after heavy rainfall, and there are no rangers or information facilities once you reach the park. Bring your own food and water.

PARQUE NACIONAL SIERRA DE AGALTA

The most extensive stretch of virgin **cloudforest** remaining in Central America. Though the area has been designated a protected area since 1987, large stands of pine and oak in the lower parts of the park have nonetheless still been logged, and much of the land cleared for ꞏꞏꞏꞏ ꞏꞏꞏꞏꞏꞏ. The higher reaches of the mountain, however (including Honduras's fourth-highest peak, La Picucha), are so remote that both vegetation and wildlife have remained virtually untouched. Here a typical cloudforest of oaks, liquidambar and cedar, draped in vines and ferns, covers the slopes up to about 2000m, where it gives way to a dwarf forest. Tapirs, jaguars, ocelots, opossums and three types of monkey are among the species of mammal recorded. More evident are the birds, of which more than four hundred species have been sighted. Hiring a **guide** is highly recommended, and pretty much essential for hiking the difficult trails: ask at the IHAH office in Catacamas, Gualaco or San Esteban.

ACCOMMODATION AND EATING

Eating out in Olancho usually means simple Honduran canteens serving basics such as chicken, rice and beans, though tilapia is heavily farmed here and appears frequently on menus. The region is also famed for its spicy sauces: tabasco chilli peppers are grown here (the D'Olancho Añejo brand is marketed globally), but local places often have their own, fiery concoctions. Local coffee, produced in small fincas, is also good. You'll get more choice in Catacamas and Juticalpa, where there are supermarkets and decent cafés, but beyond the towns most travellers eat at their lodgings.

CATACAMAS

Hotel Papabeto C de los Blancos ☎ 2899 5006. Modern hotel with comfy a/c rooms, pool, cable TV and free wi-fi (breakfast included). The on-site restaurant is open daily serving mostly Honduran food. **L945**
Hotel Plaza María Av 3 (C Independencia), C 3–4

☎ 2799 4832, ⓦ www.hotelplazamaria.com. *Plaza María* offers comfortable en-suite rooms with TVs, a pool, a decent restaurant and free wi-fi. The helpful manager speaks English. Breakfast included. **L1100**

JUTICALPA

Hotel El Paso Blvd Los Poetas (in front of the Claro office) ☎ 2785 2311. A decent budget choice with a mix of rooms: all have private bathrooms, but only the more expensive options (L650) have a/c and hot water. Noise can be a problem, so bring earplugs. **L450**

The north coast

Honduras's **north coast** stretches for some 300km along the azure fringes of the Caribbean. A magnet for Hondurans and

5

foreign tourists alike, the region provides sun, sea and entertainment in abundance, especially in the coastal towns of **Tela**, **La Ceiba** and **Trujillo**, with their broad expanses of beach, clean warm waters, plentiful restaurants and buzzing nightlife. Dotted along the north coast between these main towns are a number of laidback **villages** blessed with unspoilt **beaches**. Populated by the **Garífuna** people, descendants of African slaves and indigenous peoples (see box, p.91), these villages are often very much removed from the rest of Honduran culture and society, and can feel like visiting an entirely different country.

When beach life loses its appeal, there are several **natural reserves** to visit in the region. The national parks of **Cusuco**, **Pico Bonito** and **Capiro y Calentura**, whose virgin cloudforest shelters rare wildlife, offer hiking for all levels; the wetland and mangrove swamps at **Punta Sal** and **Cuero y Salado** require less exertion to explore.

The region's **rainy season** generally runs from November to January, while the hurricane season is August to October. Obviously it's best to visit outside of these times, but you won't necessarily be battered incessantly by rain or winds if you do visit during this period. Temperatures rarely drop below 25–28°, but the heat is usually tempered by ocean breezes.

SAN PEDRO SULA

The country's second city and driving economic force, **SAN PEDRO SULA** sprawls across the fertile Valle de Sula ("Valley of the Birds" in Usula dialect) at the foot of the Merendón mountain chain, just an hour from the coast. Flat and uninspiring to look at, and for most of the year uncomfortably hot and humid, it has also been dubbed the most violent city in the world since 2013, primarily due to the murderous activities of Honduran **drug gangs**. There's little point in visiting at present, especially if you're on a budget (though tourists are rarely targeted, the high crime rate can make staying here an edgy experience for newcomers, and there's little to see in any case). Having said that, San Pedro Sula is the **transport** hub for northern and western Honduras, meaning you may have to pass through. Take authorized taxis to get around and avoid walking about after dark.

ARRIVAL AND DEPARTURE

By plane Aeropuerto Internacional Ramón Villeda Morales, the north coast's main point of arrival for both domestic and international flights (see p.379), lies 12km southeast of the city. There is no public transport between the city centre and the airport; taxis cost around L300–400 (US$15–20). Hedman Alas (whedmanalas.com) offers convenient bus pick-ups from the airport en route to La Ceiba, Copán and Guatemala; check the website for times.

Domestic destinations La Ceiba (CM Airlines, EasySky, Lanhsa, SOSA, 2–3 daily; 30min); Roatán (CM Airlines, EasySky, Lanhsa, SOSA & Avianca, 2–3 daily; 2hr 35min); Tegucigalpa (CM Airlines, SOSA & Avianca, 2–3 daily; 50min).

By bus The Terminal Metropolitana de Autobuses is 5km south of the town centre; all services listed below leave from here. The city buses are dangerous and not recommended, so take a taxi from the terminal to the centre; they should cost less than L100–150 (set the price before getting in).

Destinations La Ceiba (daily; hourly; 3hr); Comayagua (daily; 1–2 hourly; 2hr 30min–3hr 15min); Copán Ruinas (8 daily; 3hr); La Entrada (25 daily; 1–2hr); Gracias (4 daily; 4–5hr); Guatemala City & Antigua (5 daily; 7–8hr); Managua (1 daily; 12hr); Ocotopeque (5 daily; 5hr); Puerto Cortés (daily; every 30min; 1hr); Pulhapanzak & Lago de Yojoa (14 daily; 1hr 30min); San Salvador (1 daily; 6hr); Santa Rosa de Copán (daily; 2–3 hourly; 3hr 30min); Siguatepeque (daily; 1–2 hourly; 3hr); Tegucigalpa (daily; every 30min; 3hr 30min–4hr); Tela (daily; 1–2 hourly; 1hr 30min); Trujillo (daily; hourly; 5–6hr).

ACCOMMODATION AND EATING

San Pedro, the second-largest city in Honduras, is one of the fastest-growing in Latin America. Don't be tempted by any of the super-cheap hotels – most aren't secure and can be dangerous.

★**Cafetería Pamplona** South side of Parque Barahona (Parque Central) ☎2550 2639. A San Pedro institution, with wood, brick and tiled decor and a Spanish flavour. Tasty and inexpensive breakfasts, snacks such as *baleadas*, and more substantial meals are available (dishes from L45–120). Mon–Fri 7am–7pm, Sun 8am–2pm.

★**Guaras Hostal** Residencial Andalucía Casa 6, C 13 SO, at Av 13 SO ☎9650 4431, wtheguarashostal.com. Friendly hostel close to the bus terminal (the owners will usually pick up and drop off from the bus station and the airport), with secure and clean dorms and modern a/c rooms with cable TV and hot showers. Free wi-fi. Dorms US$12, doubles US$40

SAN PEDRO SULA

ACCOMMODATION
Guaras Hostal 2
Tamarindo 1

EATING & DRINKING
Caféteria Pamplona 2
Peco's Bill (Chedrani's) 1
Power Chicken 3

Peco's Bill (Chedrani's) Av 15, at C 6 NO ☎ 2557 5744. This rambling, open-sided place feels like an overgrown tree house, and is as popular with drinkers as it is with diners. Grilled meat (from L120), from steaks to pork chops, is the order of the day here; adventurous diners can sample the *mondongo* (tripe) stew. Tues–Sun 11am–11pm.

Power Chicken Near the junction of Avs 15 and Circunvalación ☎ 2553 5353. Residents of the city will not hear a bad word said about this place, and they're right: this is fast food at its finest. Spicy chicken, ribs, steak, fried plantain, *yuca* – it's all here, with mains around L75–120. Mon–Thurs 9am–9.30pm, Fri–Sun 9am–9pm.

Tamarindo C 9A NO 1015, between avs 10 and 11 ☎ 2557 0123, ⓦ tamarindohostel.com. Older hostel, a five-minute drive from the centre, with slightly stuffy dorms, clean bathrooms, a communal kitchen, a barbecue area and a swimming pool. The private rooms are basic but adequate. Dorms US$13, doubles US$30

DIRECTORY

Banks Banco Atlántida has a number of branches downtown, including one on the Parque Central with an ATM; Banco Davivienda (with ATM) is at C 1 and Av 7 NO.

Consulates Belize, Industrias Global, Km 5, on the road to Puerto Cortés (☎ 2551 6247); El Salvador, Edificio Park Plaza (Local 10), Av 11, C 5–6 NO, Barrio Guamilito (☎ 2557 5591); Mexico, Av 18 SO, at C 7 SE (☎ 2552 3672); Nicaragua, Av 23, C 11B–11C, Colonia Trejo (☎ 2550 0813); UK, Honorary Consul only, ⓔ Edgardo.Dumas-HonCon @fconet.fco.gov.uk; US, in the Banco Atlántida building on the northern side of the Parque Central (☎ 2236 9320 or ☎ 2238 5114).

Hospital The Hospital Centro Médico Betesda is at Av 11, C 11–12 NO.

Post office C 9, at Av 3 SO (Mon–Fri 7.30am–5pm, Sat 8am–noon).

5

PUERTO CORTÉS: BELIZE BY BOAT

In theory, several companies run **boats** between **Belize** (see p.96) and Puerto Cortés in Honduras, some 60km north of San Pedro Sula, although in reality the timetables are inconsistent and boats rarely leave on time. One-way tickets cost around US$65.

The Nesymein Neydy service (☎2223 1200, ✉mundomayatravels@yahoo.com) to Dangriga (5hr) is scheduled to leave from Puerto Cortés's Laguna de Pescadería (3km southeast of town under the bridge near the fish market) every Monday at 8.30am and Tuesday at 9am, but you should be at the dock at least two hours before. Return trips depart 9.30am on Thursday and 9am on Saturday. The D-Express (☎2665 0726, ⱳbelizeferry.com) leaves from the same spot every Monday at 11am, for Big Creek (2hr) and Placencia (3hr 30min) – again, it's best to get there in plenty of time. The return journey from Placencia Shell Gas Dock is on Friday at 9.30am.

GETTING TO PUERTO CORTÉS

Several companies run buses between San Pedro Sula and Puerto Cortés (daily; every 30min; 1hr), arriving at terminals one block north of the main plaza on Av 4 , between C 3 and C 4. Take a taxi to the ferry dock, or get the bus driver to drop you off on the way into town. Buses also run between Cortés and Corinto (for Guatemala; daily; every 45min; 4hr), and Omoa (daily; every 30min; 1hr).

OMOA

Spreading inland from a deep bay at the point where the mountains of the Sierra de Omoa meet the Caribbean, **OMOA** was once a strategically important location in the defence of the Spanish colonies against marauding British pirates. Its popularity with travellers has waned in recent years, thanks to a Mexican gas company's decision to construct breakwaters here in 2006 to protect their storage tanks. This has altered the current of Omoa bay, causing the beach to shrink – it is estimated that 60 percent disappeared over the course of four years.

WHAT TO SEE AND DO

Omoa's one outstanding sight, the restored **Fortaleza de San Fernando de Omoa** (Mon–Fri 8am–4pm, Sat & Sun 9am–5pm; US$4), stands amid tropical greenery in mute witness to the village's colourful history. Now isolated 1km from the coast, having been beached as the sea has receded over the centuries, the triangular fort was originally intended to protect the port of Puerto Barrios in Guatemala. Work began in 1756 but was never fully completed due to a combination of inefficiency and a labour shortage. The steadily weakening Spanish authorities then suffered the ignominy of witnessing the fortress being temporarily occupied by British and Miskito military forces in October 1779. A small museum on site tells the story of the fort and

displays a selection of military paraphernalia including cannons and period weaponry.

ARRIVAL AND INFORMATION

By bus Buses between Puerto Cortés and Corinto pass the southern end of the village at a crossroads, though some go all the way to the beach, where you'll find most of the action.
Destinations Corinto (for Guatemala; daily; every 20min 8am–4pm; 1hr); Puerto Cortés (daily; every 30min; 1hr).
By moto-taxi Moto-taxis ply the 2km stretch from the crossroads to the beach.
Bank Banco de Occidente, just off the highway, can advance cash on your cards but doesn't have an ATM.

ACCOMMODATION AND EATING

Roli's Place Along the main road about 200m from the sea ☎2658 9082, ⱳomoa.net. Simple budget place with comfortable rooms as well as camping, though the dorms are usually rented out to students; they also have kayaks,

---

INTO GUATEMALA: CORINTO

Moving on from Omoa to **Guatemala** is an excruciatingly slow journey along the notoriously bumpy road leading southwest to **Corinto**, 2km from the border. Corinto has its own *migración* (daily 8am–5.30pm). Pick-ups shuttle to and from the border, from where you can catch a minibus (daily; every 30min) into Guatemala; there's usually an exit fee of US$3 charged. Minibuses pass through the village of Entre Ríos, for Guatemalan *migración*, to Puerto Barrios, an hour from the Honduran border.

5

free bikes, free wi-fi and laundry facilities. There's a useful map of Omoa on the website. Doubles L300

Sueños de Mar At the western end of the beach road (turn right at the beach) ☎ 3331 4506, ⊛ suenosdemar .com. You'll find hearty, home-cooked food, Canadian style, at this guesthouse-restaurant. Breakfasts (L100–120) include imported Virginia ham, while "smokies" in a bun are well worth a try. Rooms are also worth considering, all with cable TV, a/c and free wi-fi. Breakfast and lunch 8am–5pm, bar open until 8pm. Doubles US$35. Note that the property was up for sale at the time of writing, so check the current status before you arrive.

TELA

Sitting midway around the Bahía de Tela, surrounded by sweeping beaches, **TELA** has a near-perfect setting. In the past, the town has suffered from a reputation for violence, but a force of tourist police has substantially cleaned up its image. Whether you choose to partake in the nightlife or not, the wealth of alluring **natural reserves** – including Punta Sal – within minutes of the town makes Tela well worth a visit. The town is also one of the favourite destinations for Hondurans during **Semana Santa** (Easter Holy Week): it's best to book several weeks or months ahead for that period.

WHAT TO SEE AND DO

Today's Tela is a product of the banana industry. In the late nineteenth century United Fruit built a company town – **Tela Nueva** – here, on the west bank of the Río Tela; the old town became known as **Tela Vieja**. These distinctions still stand. The old town, which lies about 2km north of the highway and two blocks from the beach on the east bank of the river, encompasses the **Parque Central** and main shopping area. Five blocks west from the Parque Central is the Río Tela, beyond which lies Tela Nueva. A fifteen-minute stroll covers practically everything there is to see.

Beaches

It's the **beaches** that most people come for; those in Tela Vieja, though wide, are more crowded than the stretch of pale sand in front of the *Telamar Resort* in Tela Nueva. Even better beaches can be found along the bay outside town – if you walk far enough in either direction you should be able to have one entirely to yourself.

ARRIVAL AND INFORMATION

By bus Most local bus services use the terminal on Av 9, at C 9 NE. Buses to the surrounding villages use the terminal two blocks north on C 11, at Av 8 NE. There are buses to La

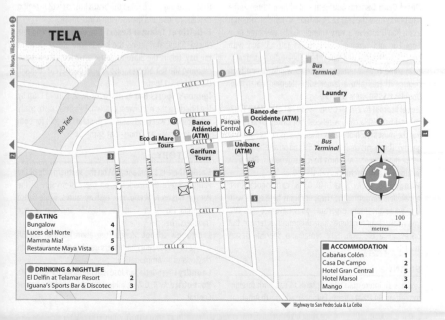

TELA

Bus Terminal

Laundry

Banco de Occidente (ATM)

CALLE 11

CALLE 10

@ Banco Atlántida (ATM)

Parque Central (i)

Eco di Mare Tours

CALLE 9

Garífuna Tours

Unibanc (ATM)

@

Bus Terminal

N

Río Tela

AVENIDA 2 · AVENIDA 3 · AVENIDA 4 · AVENIDA 5 · AVENIDA 6 · AVENIDA 7 · AVENIDA 8 · AVENIDA 9

CALLE 8

CALLE 7

CALLE 6

0   100
metres

● EATING
Bungalow	4
Luces del Norte	1
Mamma Mia!	5
Restaurante Maya Vista	6

● DRINKING & NIGHTLIFE
El Delfín at Telamar Resort	2
Iguana's Sports Bar & Discotec	3

■ ACCOMMODATION
Cabañas Colón	1
Casa De Campo	2
Hotel Gran Central	5
Hotel Marsol	3
Mango	4

Tel. Nueva, Villas Telamar &

Highway to San Pedro Sula & La Ceiba

5

Ceiba (daily; every 30min; 2hr 30min) and San Pedro Sula (8 daily; 2hr). You can also get to San Pedro Sula by taking a taxi out to the highway south of town (L100) and flagging down one of the buses coming from La Ceiba.

Tourist information The tourist office is in the municipal building off the southeast corner of the Parque Central (Mon–Fri 8am–6pm, Sat 8am–noon; ⓦ telahonduras.com).

Tour operators Garífuna Tours, just off the Parque Central (ⓣ 2448 2904, ⓦ garifunatours.com), organize trips to Punta Sal (US$36), Punta Izopo (US$32) and Laguna de los Micos (US$39). They also run an "EcoPass" tour, which includes visits to both Punta Sal and Punta Izopo plus Cayos Cochinos (see p.429), for US$109.

ACCOMMODATION

Many of Tela's older hotels are quite run down. There are, however, a number of newer, better-value places opening up as the town becomes more of a fixture on the backpacker trail. Many of these tend to get busy at weekends, when it pays to book ahead.

Cabañas Colón Triunfo de la Cruz ⓣ 9989 5622. Garífuna-owned, no-frills beach bungalows a short ride from town, right by the water. The functional rooms have private bathrooms (with showers) and there's a restaurant serving local dishes. US$34

Casa De Campo C 25 SE Barrio Venecia ⓣ 3326 3752. Nine a/c self-catering apartments with hardwood floors, garden, free wi-fi and cable TV. Some units feature full kitchens and private bathrooms (cheaper rooms have shared bathrooms and no kitchens). Breakfast US$5 extra. Double US$80

Hotel Gran Central Southern end of Av 6 (three and a half blocks from the sea) ⓣ 2448 1099, ⓦ hotelgrancentral .com. You'll receive a very friendly Gallic welcome here from Luc and Véronique. The rooms (all a/c and with private bathrooms and safes) have been decorated with flair; some have a terrace, shuttered windows and high ceilings. There's also a larger suite sleeping up to five. Doubles US$50, suite US$120

Hotel Marsol Av 2, near C 9 ⓣ 2448 1781 or ⓣ 2448 1782, ⓦ hotelmarsoltela.com. A reliable but pricey choice, and not the most stylish of places (the curtains are particularly gaudy). The rooms come with a/c, TV and private bathrooms – the more expensive rooms have kitchenettes. Breakfast included, but no internet as yet. US$80

Mango C 8, at Av 5 ⓣ 2448 0338, ⓦ mangocafe.net. A travellers' favourite. The cheaper rooms here come with fan, while the more expensive ones have a/c and TVs. Rooms are clean and there's a small communal terrace, but prices are a bit high. Bike rental and Spanish classes available. US$25

EATING

Tela has an interesting mix of places to eat, with foreign-run restaurants that cater to European and North American visitors competing with locally owned seafood places. One staple that shouldn't be missed is the delicious *pan de coco* (coconut bread) sold by Garífuna women and children on the beach and around town.

★**Bungalow** C 9, three and a half blocks east of the Parque Central. An eight-sided wooden affair decorated with American memorabilia, perhaps because owner and chef Norman Taylor grew up in New Orleans. Barbecue ribs, spaghetti with shrimp and pork chops with Cajun rice are among the dishes (from L100) on offer. Mon, Tues & Thurs–Sun 11am–1am.

Luces del Norte C 11, at Av 5. Popular with tourists and locals alike, *Luces del Norte* offers a good range of seafood dishes (L100–250), including an array of conch-based meals. Daily 7am–10pm.

Mamma Mia! Av 4, between C 9–10 ⓣ 2448 2222. Very friendly Italian-owned pizza and pasta spot with some seafood and meat dishes as well as a wide range of breakfast options. Mains from L120. Mon–Sat 8am–9pm, Sun 11am–9pm.

Restaurante Maya Vista C 9, three and a half blocks east of the Parque Central ⓣ 2448 1497. Attached to a hotel on a hillside, so you can enjoy dazzling ocean views as you dine, and the best sunset in town. The menu features a mix of fish, seafood, steaks and pasta (breakfast from L85, dinner mains from L170). Daily 7am–9pm.

DRINKING AND NIGHTLIFE

Tela has a thriving nightlife, at weekends at least, when the bars along C 11 behind the beach host crowds listening to salsa, reggae and mainstream dance music.

El Delfín at Telamar Resort 1km west of town, in Tela Nueva. Situated right on the beach with stellar views of the bay, this is the place to go for a tranquil drink while enjoying the sea breezes. Also knocks out decent seafood. Daily 11am–11pm.

Iguana's Sports Bar & Discotec Av 2, C 10–11, up by the bridge in the northwest of town. This lively disco really gets going at weekends and is a popular hangout for both locals and travellers. Thurs–Sat 8pm–late.

DIRECTORY

Banks There is a Unibanc ATM on the southern side of the Parque. Banco de Occidente, on the eastern side of the Parque, has an ATM and does cash advances, while Banco Atlántida (Av 4, at C 9) has an ATM and can change travellers' cheques.

Language school *Mango* (see above) has a Spanish school (US$139/20hr) and offers good combined deals on classes and accommodation.

Laundry Lavandería San José is at the eastern end of C 10.

Post office Av 4, C 7–8, a block southwest of the Parque Central.

AROUND TELA

Tela is a good base for a number of attractions. These include the **Garífuna villages** along the bay on pristine beaches on either side of town, the **Punta Sal** wildlife reserve, and **Lancetilla**, probably the finest botanical reserve in Latin America, just 5km south of town. To get to any of these places, you can take taxis or rely on local buses, but renting a bike is probably the most enjoyable way to get around; ask at Garífuna Tours (see opposite) for rental information.

Garífuna villages

The **Garífuna communities** of the north coast have an entirely different history and culture from the mestizo people who represent the majority of Hondurans. The villages, located on quiet and expansive stretches of beach, can be a fascinating getaway for a few hours. Weekends are the best time to visit them, when people congregate to perform the traditional, haunting and melodic drum-driven rhythms of Garífuna music.

Heading west from Tela, a dirt road edges the bay between the seafront and the **Laguna de los Micos**, which forms the eastern edge of Punta Sal (see above). Some 7km along this road is the sleepy village of **Tornabé**, and, beyond that, **Miami**, which is set on a gorgeous stretch of beach at the mouth of the lagoon. Though Tornabé has a few brick-built houses, Miami consists of nothing but traditional palm-thatched huts.

ARRIVAL AND DEPARTURE

By bus Buses (daily 6am–5pm; hourly; 30min) run to Tornabé to/from the eastern end of C 10 in Tela. From Tornabé pick-ups (Mon–Sat 6.30am & 12.30pm, returning 8am & 2pm; 30min) run to Miami.

ACCOMMODATION

Rooms Local families in Tornabé and Miami may rent out basic rooms if you ask around, but otherwise accommodation is limited.

Parque Nacional Jeannette Kawas (Punta Sal)

The **Parque Nacional Jeannette Kawas** (daily 6am–4pm; US$5; ⓦprolansate .org), commonly known as **Punta Sal**, is a wonderfully diverse **reserve** encompassing mangrove swamps, coastal lagoons, wetlands, coral reef and tropical forest, which together provide habitats for an extraordinary range of flora and fauna. Jeannette Kawas, for whom the reserve is named, was instrumental in obtaining protected status for the land, in the face of intense local opposition; her murder, in 1995, has never been solved.

Lying to the west of Tela, curving along the bay to the headland of Punta Sal (176m), the reserve covers three lagoons: **Laguna de los Micos**, on the park's eastern side; **Laguna Tisnachí**, in the centre; and the oceanfront **Laguna El Diamante**, on the western side of the headland. More than one hundred species of bird are present, including herons and storks, with seasonal migratory visitors bumping up the numbers; animals found in the reserve include howler and white-faced monkeys, wild pigs, jaguars and, in the marine sections, manatees and marine turtles. Boat trips along the Río Ulúa and the canals running through the reserve offer a superb opportunity to view the wildlife at close quarters. Where the headland curves up to the north, the land rises slightly to Punta Sal; a **trail** over the point leads to small, dazzling **beaches** at either side.

It's possible to visit parts of Punta Sal independently – you can rent a **boat** in Miami (see above) to explore the Laguna de los Micos and surrounding area – though most people opt to join an organized **tour** (see opposite). You could also **hike** the scenic 8km from Miami to the headland along the beach, though you should check the security situation first and certainly not attempt it alone.

Jardín Botánico de Lancetilla

The extensive grounds of the **Jardín Botánico de Lancetilla** (Mon–Fri 7.30am–3pm, Sat & Sun 8am–3pm; US$8), 5km south of Tela, started life in 1925 as a United Fruit species research and testing station, and over time has grown into one of the largest collections of fruit and flowering trees, palms, hardwoods and tropical plants in the world. There are also 365 recorded species of bird. Guided **tours** of the

5

arboretum and birdwatching tours are available, and visitors are also free to wander along the marked **trails**; maps are available at the **visitors centre** at the entrance to the park. A small, refreshing swimming hole in the Lancetilla River is at the end of one of the trails.

ARRIVAL AND INFORMATION

By bus To get to Lancetilla, take a San Pedro Sula-bound bus from Tela for a couple of kilometres to the signposted turn-off; ask the driver to drop you there. From here, the park is a further 3km.

By taxi or bike A taxi from Tela costs around L100 each way. You could also rent a bike from *Mango* (see p.422).

Visitors centre Park entrance (☏ 2448 1740).

LA CEIBA

Some 190km east along the coast from San Pedro Sula, steamy **LA CEIBA**, the lively capital of the department of Atlántida, is the gateway to the Bay Islands. Although the town is completely bereft of architectural interest and its sandy beaches are often strewn with rubbish, it does enjoy a remarkable setting at the steep slopes of the Cordillera Nombre de Dios. La Ceiba is home to a cosmopolitan mix of inhabitants, including a large Garífuna community, and really comes into its own at night, with visitors and locals gathering to take part in the city's vibrant **dance scene**.

Ceiba, as it's generally known, owes its existence to the banana industry: the Sicilian-American Vaccaro Brothers (whose company later became Standard Fruit and now Dole) first laid plantations in the area in 1899 and set up their company headquarters in town in 1905. Although fruit is no longer shipped through La Ceiba, the plantations are still important to the local economy, with crops of pineapple and African palm now as significant as bananas.

WHAT TO SEE AND DO

Most things of interest to visitors lie within a relatively small area of the city, around the lush **Parque Central**, with its busts of Honduran historical heroes. The unremarkable, twin-towered **Catedral San Isidro** sits on the Parque's southeast corner. Running north from the Parque almost to the seafront, Avenida San Isidro, together with Avenida Atlántida and Avenida 14 de Julio, frame the main commercial district, with shops, banks, a couple of supermarkets and the main municipal market. Stroll a block west of the Parque and you'll find the **Oficinas del Ferrocarril Nacional** (the old train station), which is planted with tropical vegetation and dotted with museum-piece train carriages, many dating from the days of the peak of the banana trade.

All the **beaches** within the city limits are too polluted and dirty, even for the most desperate. It's better to head east to the much cleaner beaches a few kilometres out of town (see p.427).

ARRIVAL AND DEPARTURE

By plane Domestic and international (see p.379) flights land at Aeropuerto Internacional Golosón, 9km southwest of the centre, off the main highway to San Pedro Sula. A taxi to/from the centre costs around L200–350 depending on time of day, number of people and luggage – confirm the rate before getting in. Drivers will accept US dollars but will give change in lempira.

Domestic destinations Brus Laguna (AeroCaribe de Honduras 6 weekly; 1hr); Guanaja (SOSA 2 daily Mon–Sat; 30min; Lanhsa 2 daily Mon–Sat; 30min); Puerto Lempira (AeroCaribe de Honduras 1 daily; 1hr 20min, via Ahuas; SOSA 6 weekly; 1hr 10min; Lanhsa 1 daily Mon–Sat; 1hr 10min); Roatán (SOSA 2–3 daily; 15min; Lanhsa 3 daily; 15min); San Pedro Sula (SOSA 1 daily; 30min; Lanhsa 1 daily Mon–Sat; 30min); Tegucigalpa (Avianca 1 daily; 50min; SOSA 2 daily Mon–Sat; 45min; Lanhsa 1 daily Mon–Sat; 45min); Utila (SOSA 3 weekly; 10min).

By boat Ferries to and from Roatán and Utila in the Bay

CARNAVAL IN LA CEIBA

The most exciting time to be in La Ceiba (book well in advance) is during **Carnaval**, a week-long bash held every year leading up to the third Saturday in May to celebrate the city's patron saint, **San Isidro**. Dances and street events in various *barrios* around town culminate in an afternoon parade on the third Saturday. The 200,000 or so partygoers who attend Carnaval every year flock between the street events and the clubs on Calle 1 in the Zona Viva, where the dancing continues until dawn.

LA CEIBA

CARIBBEAN SEA
Old Dock

■ ACCOMMODATION	
Hotel Caribe	2
Hotel Casa de España	1
Hotel Catracho	4
Hotel El Estadio	3
Tornabé Hostel	5

BARRIO INGLÉS

● EATING	
Café Ki' bok	5
Cafetería Cobel	4
Super Baleada	6
Sushi Totemo	9
Xpats Bar & Grill	7

● DRINKING & NIGHTLIFE	
Garage Café	8
El Guapo's Bar & Grill	1
Hibou	3
La Palapa	2

Parque Bonilla

BARRIO EL CENTRO

Banco Credomatic

Banco Atlantida (ATM)

Market

Oficinas de Ferrocarril Nacional

Centro Comercial Panayotti

Bank

Parque Central

Banco de Occidente

Aero Caribe

Cathedral San Isidro

Ceiba Municipal Stadium

Mercado San José Bus Station (1.5km), Viana & Hedman Alas bus terminals

Megaplaza & Plaza Premier (malls)

Airport (9km), San Pedro Sula, Museum of Butterflies and Insects, Uniplaza (mall), La Moskitia & Ecoaventuras

& Dock for Ferries to Bay Islands (5km)

0   200 metres

N

Islands use the Muelle de Cabotaje municipal dock, about 5km east of the city (the terminal has an ATM). A shared taxi to the dock should cost L60/person or L120–200 total.

Destinations Roatán (☎ 2445 1775, ⊚ roatanferry.com; daily 9.30am & 4.30pm to Roatán, 7am & 2pm to La Ceiba; 1hr 10min; tickets from L644 or US$31 one way); Utila (☎ 2425 3390, ⊚ utilaprincess.com; daily 9.30am & 4pm to Utila, 6.20am & 2pm to La Ceiba; around 1hr; tickets from L472 one way).

By bus or taxi Most long-distance and local buses arrive at and depart from the main terminal at Mercado San José, 1.5km west of the centre on Blvd 15 de Septiembre; local buses run into town, while taxis, usually shared, charge around L30–50/person (or L100–200 total). The Viana and Hedman Alas terminals are a bit further along the same road. The Cotuc/Contraibal bus stations (for La Mosquita) are slightly closer to the entrance to town (coming from Tela) across from the "Santa Marta" petrol station.

Destinations Guatemala City (2 daily; 11hr); Olanchito (for Juticalpa; 12 daily; 3hr); San Pedro Sula (20 daily; 3hr); Tegucigalpa (daily; hourly; 5hr 30min–7hr); Tela (daily;

every 30min; 2hr 30min); Tocoa (for La Mosquita; daily every 45min; 2hr); Trujillo (20 daily; 3hr–4hr 30min).

By shuttle There is a nonstop a/c shuttle service between La Ceiba and León, Nicaragua, for US$70 one way. The price includes breakfast and wi-fi (from La Ceiba Mon, Wed & Sat 8am; 14hr; ☎ 8995 9293, ⊚ leonlaceibashuttle.com). Omar at *Tornabé Hostel* (see p.426) offers the same service, plus a direct route to Río Dulce and Puerto Barrios in Guatemala, for US$50.

INFORMATION

Internet La Ceiba is crammed with internet cafés, with rates around L20/hr and most open Mon–Sat 8am–9pm. Try the cafés in the Megaplaza and Centro Comercial Panayotti malls.

Taxis Expect to pay L30–50/person for a taxi ride in La Ceiba during the day, a bit more after 8pm.

Tourist information There's a tourist office on C 8, in the Banco de Occidente building on Parque Central; some staff speak English. ⊚ visitalaceiba.com has information on the city.

5

LA CEIBA TOUR OPERATORS

A couple of well-run companies offer tours to the surrounding area and further afield.

La Moskitia Ecoaventuras ☎ 2441 3279 or ☎ 9929 7532, ⊛ lamoskitia.hn. Jorge Salaverri is an expert on La Mosquitia and the Río Plátano, and his company also offers tours to Pico Bonito (from US$45/two people), Cuero y Salado (from US$73) and Cayos Cochinos (from US$80), plus rafting (from US$45) and sea-kayaking (from US$45). Its office is located in Colonia Toronjal 2 close to Megaplaza mall: turn right at *Pollitos La Cumbre*, continue for two blocks then turn right again.

Omega Tours Río Cangrejal valley, 19km from La Ceiba ☎ 2440 0334 or ☎ 9631 0295, ⊛ omegatours .info. Extensive range of tours including rafting, kayaking, horseriding (from US$76) and trips to Cayos Cochinos and La Mosquitia. All start at their lodge, which borders both Pico Bonito and Nombre de Dios parks, and prices include a night's stay.

ACCOMMODATION

La Ceiba has a range of budget places to stay. The only problem is deciding whether you want to be near the centre or closer to the nightlife along C 1. Prices rise around Carnaval time in May, when reserving ahead is essential.

Hotel Caribe C 5, between Avs San Isidro and Atlántida ☎ 2443 1857. Cheap accommodation two blocks from Parque Central, with simple but adequate doubles, free wi-fi, cable TV and shared bathrooms. Cash only. <u>US$16</u>

★ **Hotel Casa de España** Av 14 de Julio, C 4–5 ☎ 2454 0210, ⊛ hotelcasadeespana.com. Impeccably clean hotel, dotted with plants and other homely elements. The comfortable en-suite rooms, with a/c, can be a bargain if you're able to haggle the price down a bit (singles pay US$40). Opt out of breakfast, though, which adds more than L100 to the cost. Budget rooms are also available (no breakfast, fan only; US$20/ person). Free wi-fi. <u>US$50</u>

Hotel Catracho C 12, at Av Ramón Rosa ☎ 2440 2312 or ☎ 2440 2313, ⊛ hotelcatracho.com. An aging hotel with basic rooms (with fan; a/c L100 extra) at a fair price, this place is saved from blandness by the pool and deck area. Only a minute's walk from *Xpats Bar & Grill* (see below), too. No breakfast, but free wi-fi in the lobby. <u>L350</u>

Hotel El Estadio Av Las Américas (C del Estero), C 6–7 ☎ 6226 3310, ⊛ hotelelestadio.com. Helmed by English-speaking Peter, this bare-bones hostel near the football stadium offers a ten-bed dorm and several private rooms (with a/c, bathroom and satellite TV). Breakfast usually US$5 extra. Free wi-fi. Dorm <u>US$10</u>, doubles <u>US$24</u>

Tornabé Hostel Bloque 4, No. 13, Colonia Monteverde ☎ 9813 8998, ⊛ tornabe.com. Small, cosy dorms with a/c and free wi-fi on the outskirts of town. Doubles as tour agency and runs a León, Nicaragua, shuttle service (US$80). <u>US$12</u>

EATING

★ **Café Ki'bok** Two blocks east of the Parque C 8–9, Barrio El Iman ☎ 2442 2673. A friendly, good-value little café with art on the walls and a homely feel. The menu ranges from burgers to spaghetti with shrimps, with several vegetarian options. Dishes from L120. Mon–Fri 7am–7pm, Sat & Sun 8am–noon.

Cafetería Cobel C 7, at Av Atlántida ☎ 2442 2192. This Ceiba institution features a simple, meat-heavy menu offering the usual steaks and chops plus a range of soups, and a selection of cakes and pastries. Lunch/dinner from L80–100. Mon–Sat 7am–6pm.

Super Baleada Av Colón, at C 12. The cheapest meal you're likely to have in La Ceiba and surely one of the best. *Baleadas* from L12. Daily noon–9pm.

★ **Sushi Totemo** Uniplaza Mall 2/F, C del Hospital D'Antoni ☎ 2443 8100. Superb sushi restaurant, with owner-chef Jaime incorporating ingredients from Manchego to plantain in his Japanese cuisine. Start with edamame or *gyoza*, then try the San Pedro Sula roll with a fried tempura and sesame coating, filled with crispy breaded shrimp and spicy avocado salsa. Dishes from L120. Mon–Sat noon–9pm.

Xpats Bar & Grill End of C 12, near Av 14 de Julio ☎ 9698 1985. A huge, thatched bar-restaurant with food ranging from the healthy organic to the tastily stodgy (such as German sausage plates for L115). Mains from L170–250. Good beers and cocktails too; happy hour is 7–9pm. Mon & Tues 11am–midnight, Wed 11am–1am, Thurs–Sat 11am–2am, Sun 11am–11pm.

DRINKING AND NIGHTLIFE

La Ceiba has long had a reputation as the place to party, though the economic downturn in the city in recent years means it's not as lively as it was and you need to take care at night – get your hotel to call a taxi. Still, there are several good options for a night on the town. The action takes place along C 1, which runs parallel to the seafront. Nicknamed the *Zona Viva* due to its preponderance of bars and clubs, the area hums several nights a week, though weekends are really explosive. Just stroll down the street to see what's going on and where the crowds are. *Xpats Bar & Grill* (see above) is a good place outside the Zona Viva for an evening drink.

Garage Café Av Morazán (between calles 14 and 15) ☎ 2442 0185. American-themed sports bar (with TV screens to show major games), cold beer and friendly service. Has air-conditioned interior and outdoor seating. Beer is only L42 if you're there before 8pm (more afterwards). Tues–Sun 11am–10pm.

El Guapo's Bar & Grill C 1, at Av La Bastilla ☏ 3355 6823. This is right next door to the sprawling *Snake* bar and shares the same *palapa* feel. Hugely popular on Fri and Sat nights, it has a fantastic atmosphere, especially when the karaoke takes over. Daily happy hour 5–7pm; the food's a bit pricey though. Mon 4–11pm, Tues–Sun 11am–1am.

Hibou C 1, Av Dionisio de Herrera–Manuel Bonilla ☏ 9975 4134. This plush dance club has teenagers and twenty-somethings patiently queueing for entry (from L100–200); dancefloor, several bars, and DJs spinning top 40 reggaetón and rock inside, and *palapa* beach bar outside. Wed, Fri & Sat 8pm–5am.

La Palapa C 1, at Av 15 de Septiembre (opposite *Hotel Quinta Real*) ☏ 2440 3525. Very popular bar and restaurant in the Zona Viva, known for its large dancefloor. Sat nights are especially exciting: live bands perform a mix of merengue, reggae and rock. Sun–Wed 11am–11pm, Thurs–Sat 11am–2am.

DIRECTORY

Banks Most of the banks are on C 9 and Av 14 de Julio one block east of the Parque. The Megaplaza mall also has several banks and ATMs.

Health Hospital D'Antoni (☏ 2443 2264) is at the southern end of Av Morazán. Two good pharmacies are Auto Farmacia Zaz (24hr) and Farmacia Mary Ann (daily 8am–11pm), both on C 13, near Av 14 de Julio.

Immigration Immigration is between C 17 & 18 on Av 14 de Julio.

Post office Av Morazán, C 13–14.

Shopping The main general market is on Av Atlántida, C 5–7. The huge Megaplaza mall (daily 10am–8pm) is in the southern outskirts of town at the end of Av Morazán (at C 22).

AROUND LA CEIBA

The broad sandy beaches and clean water at **Playa de Perú** and the village of **Sambo Creek** are easy day-trip destinations east of La Ceiba. A trip to explore the cloudforest within the **Parque Nacional Pico Bonito** requires more planning, although the eastern edge of the reserve, formed by the **Río Cangrejal**, is still easily accessible, and also offers opportunities for swimming and whitewater rafting. Finally, a trip to the serene islands of the **Cayos Cochinos** is highly recommended.

Playa de Perú

Some 10km east of the city, **Playa de Perú** is a wide sweep of clean sand that's popular at weekends. Any local **bus** running east up the coast (towards Trujillo) will drop you at the highway-side turn-off, from where it's a fifteen-minute walk to the beach. About 2km beyond the turning for Playa de Perú, on the Río María, there's a series of **waterfalls** and **natural pools** set in lush, shady forest. A path leads from Río María village on the highway, winding through the hills along the left bank of the river; it takes around thirty minutes to walk to the first cascade and pool, with some muddy sections and a bit of scrambling during the wet season.

Sambo Creek

There are deserted expanses of white sand at the friendly Garífuna village of **Sambo Creek**, 8km beyond the Río María. As well as the beach and a clutch of low-key seafood restaurants, there is **Sambo Creek Canopy Tours and Spa**, 500m beyond the village, which offers ziplining (US$45) and a hot spring spa for US$25 (both daily 8am–4pm; ☏ 3355 5481). Boats to Cayos Cochinos also depart from Sambo Creek.

ARRIVAL AND DEPARTURE

By bus Olanchito or Juticalpa buses from La Ceiba will drop you at the turn-off to Sambo Creek on the highway, a couple of kilometres from the village; slower buses run all the way to the village centre from La Ceiba's terminal (daily; every 30min; 45min).

ACCOMMODATION AND EATING

★**Paradise Found** Playa Helen ☏ 9861 1335, ⓦ paradise foundlaceiba.com. An excellent accommodation option, also with great food – try the ribs smoked with fruitwood – and it becomes a congenial bar popular with locals and visitors in the evenings. Breakfast included. Rooms are US$79 during Easter week. <u>US$59</u>

Parque Nacional Pico Bonito and Río Cangrejal

Directly south of La Ceiba, the Cordillera Nombre de Dios shelters the **Parque Nacional Pico Bonito** (daily 6am–4pm; US$8), a remote expanse of tropical broadleaf forest, cloudforest and – in its southern reaches, above the Río Aguan valley – pine forest. Taking its name from

5

the awe-inspiring bulk of Pico Bonito (2435m), the park is the source of twenty **rivers**, including the Zacate, Bonito and Cangrejal, which cascade majestically down the mountains' steep, thickly tree-smothered slopes. The park also provides sanctuary for an abundance of wildlife, including armadillos, howler and spider monkeys, pumas and ocelots. The lower fringes are the most easily accessible, with a few **trails** laid out through the dense greenery.

Most visitors take tours from La Ceiba or stay at the very expensive *Lodge at Pico Bonito* (ⓦ picobonito.com), but it is possible to go it alone. The entrance at the **Río Cangrejal**, which forms the eastern boundary of the park just south of La Ceiba, features a visitors centre and loop trail (3–4hr) to the El Bejuco waterfall. The river also boasts some of the best rapids in Central America; **whitewater rafting** and **kayaking** trips are organized by tour companies (see box, p.426). There are some magnificent swimming spots, backed by gorgeous mountain scenery, along the river valley.

The second entrance is accessed via the village of El Pino, 18km west of downtown La Ceiba, where another loop trail leads to the less impressive Cascada Zacate.

ARRIVAL AND DEPARTURE

By bus Buses and *rapiditos* (daily; every 30min; 30–45min) run between La Ceiba and the village of El Pino, from where you can hike into the park. The Río Cangrejal entrance, 11km south of downtown La Ceiba via the Yaruka road, is much easier to get to by taxi; buses also run up here from the junction on the Trujillo road (just across the main Cangrejal bridge, known as "La Cuenca" del Río Cangrejal). *Jungle River Lodge* (see below) offers free transport with

any activity. Alternatively, tour companies in La Ceiba (see box, p.426) operate day- and overnight trips.

ACCOMMODATION

Jungle River Lodge Km 8, Río Cangrejal ☎ 2416 5009, ⓦ jungleriverlodge.com. Excellent lodge that has clean dorms and rooms (more expensive with hot showers), a restaurant-bar and a full roster of tours and activities. Dorms US$12, doubles US$30

Refugio de Vida Silvestre Cuero y Salado

Some 30km west from La Ceiba, the **Refugio de Vida Silvestre Cuero y Salado** (daily 8.30am–3.30pm; US$10; ☎ 2440 1990) is one of the last substantial remnants of wetlands and mangrove swamps along the north coast. The reserve is home to a large number of endangered animal and bird species, including manatees, jaguars, howler and white-faced monkeys, sea turtles and hawks, along with seasonal influxes of migratory birds. The refuge now enforces a sixty-person-per-day visitor limit, so it's best to make a reservation in advance with FUCSA (see p.428).

ARRIVAL AND INFORMATION

By bus, moto-taxi and motocarro By far the easiest way to visit the reserve is on an organized tour from La Ceiba. To get here independently, catch a bus (6.20am–3.30pm, hourly; 30min; L20) from La Ceiba's San José bus terminal, to the village of La Unión, 20km or so west. From here take a moto-taxi (10min; around L30) to the El Bambú Estación del Motocarro then take a *motocarro* or *burra de línea* (a very rudimentary train – a little like a tuk-tuk on rails; daily 7am–3.30pm; 45min; US$10/L200 return; ☎ 9904 4610) 9km to the visitors centre (daily 6am–6pm) at Salado Barra. Most visitors hire boats (*lanchas*) or kayaks from here to go further into the park.

Tours It's best to arrange canoe or boat tours through a travel agency or FUCSA (see p.428). Kayaks are L60/hr; guides are an extra L200/hr. Students get a 10 percent discount on entry and boat tours Mon–Wed. Boat tours (2hr) start at L400 for two people, or L160 per person for three or more people. Guides are an additional L150/boat.

Fundación Cuero y Salado FUCSA is a good source of information on the park, and can organize boat trips, guides and accommodation for independent travellers; its La Ceiba office (generally Mon–Fri 9am–5pm) is in Barrio La Merced on C 15, Av Ramón Rosa, Edificio Daytona (☎ 2443 0117 or ☎ 2440 2707, ✉ cuero_salado@yahoo.com).

ACCOMMODATION

Fundación Cuero y Salado It is possible to stay inside the reserve, but you must bring plenty of water, rubbish bags and insect repellent. You can either bring your own tent, rent one through FUCSA (sleeping bags also available, L50) or stay in one of their very basic cabins. If you stay overnight, the *burra* costs L300 return. Camping/person (own tent) L80, camping/tent (rented) L150, cabins/person L150

Cayos Cochinos

Lying 30km offshore, the alluring **Cayos Cochinos** (US$10 if visiting independently, US$5 with a tour group) comprise thirteen privately owned cays, and two thickly wooded islands – **Cochino Grande** (or **Cayo Mayor**) and **Cayo Menor**. Cayo Mayor features hiking trails, a lighthouse and the rare pink boa constrictor, while Cayo Menor is home to a scientific research station (where most tours stop for orientation). The only settlements are two small Garífuna fishing villages established in the 1960s: **Chachauate** on tiny Lower Monitor Caye and **East End** on Cayo Mayor. Fringed by a reef, the whole area was designated a **marine reserve** in 1993, with anchoring on the reef and commercial fishing both strictly prohibited. The small amount of effort it takes to get to the islands is well worth it for a few days' utter tranquillity.

ARRIVAL AND DEPARTURE

By bus and boat You will have to shell out a bit to travel to the islands, especially if you're on your own. The only feasible way to get there is with the fishermen who sail from the Garífuna villages of Sambo Creek (see p.427) or Nueva Armenia (40min; around US$30/person return). Buses from La Ceiba run to Sambo Creek (daily; every 30min; 45min) and Nueva Armenia (6 daily; 2hr).
Tours Several tour companies in La Ceiba offer day-trips and overnight stays, starting from around US$40/person

> ### DIVING IN THE CAYOS COCHINOS
>
> Based in Sambo Creek (see p.427), **Pirate Islands Divers** (☎ 3228 0009 or ☎ 9563 9172, ☻pirateislandsdivers.com) is run by PADI Master Instructor Tony Márquez and offers two-tank diving trips (from US$95/person for two people), open-water courses (from US$336) and snorkelling trips (US$40).

(see box, p.426). If arranging a tour, ask whether the price quoted includes the entrance fee. Lunch is usually extra.

ACCOMMODATION AND EATING

Cabañas Laru Beya East End, Cayo Mayor ☎ 9489 6058, ☻reservaciones@recouth.com. Posh accommodation on the two main islands is limited to the expensive *Turtle Bay Eco Resort* on Cayo Mayor (from U$119), but for a cheaper alternative try these two well-maintained nine-bed dorms, which have electricity. Meals are L100–160. Cash only. L650

Chachauate Villagers in the traditional Garífuna fishing village of Chachauate on Lower Monitor Caye offer budget accommodation, including *Hotel Aba Ouchaja Tiñu* (with two bare-bones rooms and shared showers) and thatched beachfront cabins (shared showers, no electricity). They will also cook meals for you (mains L140–160). Basic groceries are available in the village, but there is no running water and toilets are latrines. Cash only. Per person L160

TRUJILLO

Perched above the sparkling waters of the palm-fringed Bahía de Trujillo, backed by the awe-inspiring Cordillera Nombre de Dios, **TRUJILLO** immediately seduces the small number of tourists who make the 90km trip from La Ceiba. Wonderfully relaxed, the city has a very different feel from its big north-coast neighbours, La Ceiba and Tela, though since 2014 the town has become a regular cruise-ship destination, so things are changing.

The area around present-day Trujillo was populated by a mixture of Pech and Tolupan indigenous peoples when Columbus first disembarked here on August 14, 1502; the city itself was founded by one of Hernán Cortés's lieutenants, Juan de Medina, in 1525, though it was frequently abandoned due to attacks by European pirates. Not until the late eighteenth century did repopulation begin in earnest, aided by the arrival, via Roatán, of several hundred Garífuna. In 1860, US filibuster and adventurer William Walker, who had briefly ruled Nicaragua (see p.449), landed in Trujillo en route to the Bay Islands. Disgruntled British settlers, unhappy at the recent treaty making them Honduran subjects, had invited him, but a British naval commander apprehended Walker and handed him over to the Honduran authorities. He was

5

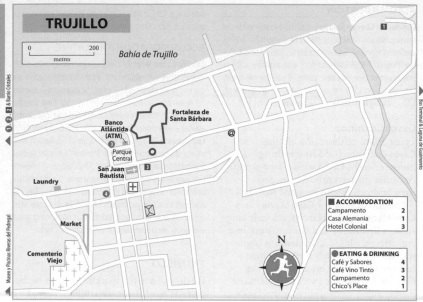

promptly executed by firing squad, and is buried in Trujillo's old cemetery.

WHAT TO SEE AND DO

Apart from its enchanting **beaches**, much of Trujillo's appeal lies in meandering through its languid, crumbling streets, though things can get temporarily animated when cruise ships dock. The town proper stretches back five or so blocks south of the **Parque Central**, which is just 50m from cliffs overlooking the sea. On the north side of the square is a bust of Juan de Medina. Southwest from the centre, a couple of blocks past the market, is the **Cementerio Viejo**, where Walker's grave lies overgrown with weeds – collect the key to the gate from the office in the fort.

Beaches

The town's most outstanding attractions by far are its **beaches**, which have long stretches of glittering sand. The glorious sweep of the **Bahía de Trujillo** is unaffected by excessive tourist development (as yet), and its calm, blue waters are perfect for effortless swimming. The beaches below town, lined with *champas* (thatch-roofed,

open-sided huts), are clean enough, but the stretches to the east, beyond the disused airstrip, are emptier. It's also possible to walk east along the beach to the reserve of **Laguna de Guaimoreto** or west to the Garífuna village of **Santa Fé**.

Fortaleza de Santa Bárbara

In town, near the Parque Central, is the sixteenth-century **Fortaleza de Santa Bárbara** (daily 8am–noon & 1–4pm; US$3), site of William Walker's execution. The low-lying fort hangs gloomily on the edge of the bluffs, overlooking the coastline that it singularly failed to protect against pirates. The museum charts the town's often-colourful history, and has an exhibition room on Garífuna culture (Spanish labels only).

Museo y Piscinas Riveras del Pedregal

Turn right beyond the Cementerio Viejo and a ten-minute stroll brings you to the privately run **Museo y Piscinas Riveras del Pedregal** (daily 7am–5pm; L50), an eccentric collection of rusty junk. Almost all of the original pre-Columbian ceramics once held by the museum have been sold off, though the replacement replicas are pretty convincing. Outside, the wheels of an American jumbo jet that crashed in the area in 1985 can be seen. Behind the building are a couple of small, naturally fed swimming pools.

Parque Nacional Capiro y Calentura

Directly above the town lies the dark-green swathe of the **Parque Nacional Capiro y Calentura** (daily 6am–5pm; US$3.50). The reserve's huge cedars and pines tower amid a thick canopy of ferns, flowering plants and vines. As a result of the devastation wrought by Hurricane Fifi in 1974, much of the cover is secondary growth, but it still provides a secure habitat for howler monkeys, reptiles and colourful birdlife and butterflies. You can walk into the reserve by following the dirt road past the *Villa Brinkley* – it winds, increasingly steeply, up the slope of Cerro Calentura to the radio towers just below its summit; a 10km walk, this is best done in the relative cool of early morning. Alternatively, you could negotiate with a taxi driver to take you to the top and then walk down. Unfortunately there aren't any trail maps, so you'll have to do a bit of exploring.

ARRIVAL AND DEPARTURE

By bus The main bus terminal is to the east of town, at the bottom of the hill leading into the centre. From here infrequent urban buses head up the hill to the Parque Central, or you can take a taxi (around L50).

Destinations La Ceiba (daily; hourly; 3hr–4hr 30min); Puerto Castilla (7 daily, last one 6pm; 45min); San Pedro Sula (daily; hourly; 6–10hr); Tocoa (daily; hourly; 2hr 30min).

ACCOMMODATION

There's not much in the way of budget accommodation in town, but there are a couple of excellent places in glorious settings just outside the centre.

Campamento Campamento 3km west of town, on the road to Santa Fé ☎ 9991 3391, ⓦ campamentoresort.com. Helmed by the congenial Noel, this simple but tranquil spot features comfy a/c rooms and cabins with cable TV and access to a decent pool. Free wi-fi. Doubles L1200, cabins L1600

★**Casa Alemania** 1km east of town ☎ 2434 4466, ⊜ hotelcasaalemaniatrujillo@gmail.com. An extraordinary range of options is on offer here, from tiny backpacker rooms and camping all the way up to a penthouse. There's also a book exchange, housed in an attractive library-like room, excellent meals and free wi-fi. Camping/person L175, doubles L750

Hotel Colonial Just east of the Parque Central ☎ 2131 4011. Best deal in town, with basic but adequate rooms, hot showers, TV, balconies overlooking the square and free wi-fi (which is a bit patchy). L400

LA MOSQUITIA HISTORY AND POLITICS

Dramatized in *The Mosquito Coast* (1981) by Paul Theroux (and the 1986 movie starring Harrison Ford), the relationship between tradition and modernization has always been a troubled one in La Mosquitia, with indigenous tribes, European settlers and missionaries battling each other and the harsh, tropical climate.

Before the Spanish arrived, La Mosquitia belonged to the **Pech** and **Sumu**. Initial contact with Europeans was comparatively benign, as the Spanish preferred to concentrate instead on the mineral-rich lands of the interior. Relations with Europeans intensified when the **British** began seeking a foothold on the mainland in the seventeenth century, establishing settlements on the coast at **Black River** (now Palacios; see p.433) and **Brewer's Lagoon** (Brus Laguna; see p.435), whose inhabitants – the so-called "shoremen" – engaged in logging, trading, smuggling and fighting the Spanish.

Britain's claim to La Mosquitia – made nominally to protect the shoremen, though really intended to ensure a transit route from the Atlantic to the Pacific – supposedly ended in 1786, when all Central American territories except Belize were ceded to the Spanish. In the 1820s, however, taking advantage of post-independence chaos, Britain again encouraged settlement on the Mosquito Coast and by 1844 had all but formally announced a protectorate in the area. Not until 1859 and the British–American Treaty of Comayagua did Britain formally end all claims to the region.

The initial impact of mestizo Honduran culture on La Mosquitia was slight. Since the creation of the administrative department of Gracias a Dios in 1959, however, indigenous cultures have gradually become diluted: Spanish is now the main language, and the government encourages mestizo settlers to migrate here in search of land. Pech, Miskito and Garífuna communities have become more vocal in recent years in demanding respect for their cultural differences and in calling for an expansion of health, education and transport infrastructures.

5

EATING AND DRINKING

Café y Sabores Two blocks south of the Parque ☎ 3235 4620. Doors and windows are propped wide open in this diner-like place, allowing for nice, breezy breakfasts, lunches and (early) dinners (mains from L90, *baleadas* from L16). Good *licuados* too. Mon–Sat 6am–9pm, Sun 6am–1pm.

Café Vino Tinto Just north of the Parque Central. This enticing café has an open-sided seating area overlooking the bay, hung partly with white drapes. Try the delicious *tostones rellenos* – slices of fried plantain with various toppings – or the beef kebabs. Mains from L90. Free wi-fi. Tues–Sun 9am–11pm.

Campamento 3km west of Trujillo on the road to Santa Fé ☎ 9991 3391, ⊛ campamentoresort.com. In a lovely beach location, shaded by palm trees, this restaurant (part of a hotel; see p.431) serves up fresh fish and seafood, as well as a few more unusual dishes such as agouti steaks. Daily 7am–10pm.

Chico's Place Beach Rd, west of town. Super clean, fun beach bar and restaurant, helmed by Kyle and his team, with L45 beers and free wi-fi – it's gaining a following among cruise ship passengers but in the evenings you'll have it to yourself. Daily 11am–11pm.

DIRECTORY

Bank Banco Atlántida, on the Parque Central, gives Visa cash advances and has a 24hr ATM.
Laundry A block northwest of the market.
Pharmacy Two blocks south of the Parque.
Post office Three blocks south of the southeast corner of the Parque.

La Mosquitia

Occupying the northeast corner of Honduras is the remote and undeveloped expanse of **La Mosquitia** (often spelt "Moskitia"). Bounded to the west by the mountain ranges of the Río Plátano and Colón, with the Río Coco forming the border with Nicaragua to the south, this vast region comprises almost a fifth of Honduras's territory. With just two peripheral roads and a tiny population divided among a few far-flung towns and villages, entering La Mosquitia really does mean leaving the beaten track. There are few phones in the region (mobile phone coverage is virtually nonexistent), and all accommodation is extremely basic, often without electricity and with latrine-style toilets. Food is usually limited to rice,

beans and the catch of the day, so if you're making an independent trek, bring enough food with you for your party and guides. Getting around requires a spirit of adventure, but the effort is well rewarded.

To the surprise of many who come here expecting to have to hack their way through jungle, much of La Mosquitia is composed of marshy coastal wetlands and flat savanna. The small communities of **Palacios**, **Batalla** and **Brus Laguna** are access points for the **Río Plátano Biosphere Reserve**, the most famous of five separate reserves in the area, set up to protect one of the finest remaining stretches of virgin tropical rainforest in Central America. **Puerto Lempira**, to the east, is the regional capital.

The largest ethnic group inhabiting La Mosquitia is the **Miskitos**, numbering around 30,000, who spoke a unique form of English until as recently as a few generations ago. There are much smaller communities of **Pech**, who number around 2500, and **Tawahka** (**Sumu**), of whom there are under a thousand, living around the Río Patuca.

ARRIVAL AND DEPARTURE

By plane There are regular flights between La Ceiba and Brus Laguna (AeroCaribe, Mon–Sat 1 daily; 2hr), and between La Ceiba and Puerto Lempira (AeroCaribe, CM Airlines, Lanhsa, SOSA, 2–3 daily; 1hr 5min–1hr 20min). You can also fly between Puerto Lempira and Tegucigalpa (CM Airlines Mon, Wed & Fri, 1 daily; 1hr 30min). Timetables are not strictly observed and routes often change; take local advice as to their reliability at the time of your visit.

By land Getting to the region overland – the cheapest option – is possible, but progress is extremely slow, especially during the rainy season (Oct–Jan). Take the earliest bus from La Ceiba or Trujillo to Tocoa, then a pick-up (*paila*) to Batalla (hourly 7am–noon; 4–5hr; L500), a small village on the coast. Returning, stay overnight in Batalla to catch the early-morning trucks for Tocoa (daily from 6am).

TOURS

A number of companies in La Ceiba, San Pedro and Tegucigalpa offer tours to La Mosquitia.

Tour operators The excellent La Moskitia Ecoaventuras in La Ceiba (see box, p.426) offer tours starting from US$994 (five days; includes air transport to the region). Mesoamérica Travel (⊛ mesoamerica-travel.com), based in San Pedro Sula, offer a relatively "budget" five-day tour (excluding flights) from US$350. Another option is Omega Tours, near

La Ceiba (see box, p.426). La Ruta Moskitia (☎ 2406 6782, ⓦ larutamoskitia.com) offers excellent advice on visiting the region, as well as a range of tours and lodges throughout the region that bring real benefits to the local communities.

GETTING AROUND

Travelling around the region independently rather than as part of a tour is by no means impossible, as long as you're prepared to go with the flow. Transport to and within La Mosquitia is mainly by air or water: Puerto Lempira and Brus Laguna are currently connected to La Ceiba by regular flights (see above), while *lanchas* ply the waterways connecting the scattered villages. Bear in mind that all schedules, especially those of the boats, are subject to change, delay and cancellation; transport on the rivers and channels is determined by how much rain has fallen.

By plane There is a daily flight between Brus Laguna and Puerto Lempira (AeroCaribe; 30min), and La Ceiba and Brus Laguna (AeroCaribe; Mon–Sat 1 daily; 2hr).

By land *Colectivos* run from Río Plátano to Brus Laguna (L250/person; 2hr) and Rais Ta/Belén (L50/person; 45min).

By boat Travelling around the region by boat is pricey, with *expreso* boats much more expensive than multiple-stop *colectivo* boats. From Batalla, *colectivo* boats leave for destinations within La Mosquitia such as Palacios (see below), just across the lagoon, where you can change for communities a bit further along the coast. If heading for Las Marías (see p.434), you will need to spend the night in one of these communities; note also that there are no *colectivo* services to Las Marías. Some Spanish makes negotiating the various connections and inevitable delays much easier. Prices to Las Marías include the charge for the driver spending two nights with you there.

Destinations from Brus Laguna Las Marías (*expreso*: L3500 4000/boat, 4 5 people; 6hr); Rais Ta/Belén (direct: L1500–2000/boat; 4–5 people; 2hr).

Destinations from Palacios Batalla (*colectivo*: daily every 30min; 15min; L250); Rais Ta/Belén (*expreso*: L800–1000/boat, up to ten people; 1hr 30min; *colectivo*: L200/person; 2–3hr).

Destinations from Rais Ta/Belén Las Marías (*expreso*: L4000–5000/boat, 4–5 people; 5hr); Brus Laguna (direct: L1500–2000/boat; 4–5 people; 2hr); Palacios (*expreso*: L800–1000/boat, up to ten people; 1hr 30min; *colectivo*: L200/person; 2–3hr).

BATALLA AND AROUND

Scattered along the Caribbean shoreline, the Garífuna village of **BATALLA** lies at the end of the road, just west of one of the Río Plátano Biosphere Reserve's three coastal lagoons, Laguna Ibans. It's where the pick-ups from Tocoa drop you (see p.432), and, for independent travellers, a logical place from which to begin exploration of the region. Local boatmen will offer tours of Laguna Bacalar from here (where there's usually plenty of wildlife in the mangroves) from L200– 350 per trip, depending on group size.

WHAT TO SEE AND DO

East of Batalla is a cluster of absorbing **Miskito** and **Garífuna villages**, including **Palacios**, just across the Bacalar lagoon (which has a mixed Miskito and mestizo population). Remnants of the British settlement of Black River can still be seen here (rusting cannons, ruins of mills), a colony established in 1732 and abandoned in 1787 (a subsequent Spanish attempt to settle the area was ended by a massacre by the Miskitos in 1800). It's still possible to find the grave of the settlement's founder, William Pitt, in the overgrown cemetery near the village.

About 8km to the east, a **turtle project** has been established at the Garífuna village of **Plaplaya** (boats between Palacios and Rais Ta/Belén will stop here if you ask). Highly endangered giant leatherbacks, the largest species in the world (reaching up to 3m in length and 900kg in weight), nest in the beaches around the village between April and June.

On the other side of Laguna Ibans, **Rais Ta** and **Belén** are tranquil, laidback Miskito villages lined with virtually empty beaches, linked by boat with Palacios (see opposite) or by pick-up truck with Plaplaya. From here it's a two-hour hike (or a pick-up ride) to the village of **Río Plátano**, where *colectivo* boats chug up the lagoon to Brus Laguna (see p.435).

ACCOMMODATION

Palacios has garnered a sketchy reputation in recent years (in part due to drug smuggling) and at the very least local bars with blaring sound systems will keep you awake most nights. As yet there's no alternative in Batalla (other than hammocks on the beach), but if you leave La Ceiba/Trujillo early enough you can get to Rais Ta/Belén in one day, a much more enticing prospect.

Pawanka Beach Cabañas Belén ☎ 433 8220. Near a small lagoon just off the beach, these three basic but cosy cabañas are managed by the friendly Mario Miller, with mosquito nets and on-site restaurant (meals L70–85). Per person **L250**

5

Raista Ecolodge Rais Ta ☏ 433 8216. This beautiful ecolodge is owned by the Bodden family and helmed by Doña Elma, with eight traditional cabins on stilts, with hammocks on their porches, shared cold-water bathrooms and clean toilets. No electricity (candles supplied). Purified water is included, and meals provided for an extra charge (L70–85). Per person **L250**

Río Tinto In the centre of Palacios. You'll find adequate rooms at this ramshackle place run by local Don Felix Marmol. **L200**

RÍO PLÁTANO BIOSPHERE RESERVE

The **RÍO PLÁTANO BIOSPHERE RESERVE** is the most significant nature reserve in Honduras, sheltering an estimated eighty percent of all the country's animal species. Visitors usually come to experience the tropical rainforest, but the reserve's boundaries – which stretch from the Caribbean in the north to the Montañas de Punta Piedra in the west and the Río Patuca in the south – also encompass huge expanses of coastal wetlands and flat savanna grasslands. Sadly, even its World Heritage status hasn't prevented extensive destruction at the hands of settlers: up to 60 percent of forest cover on the outer edges of the reserve has disappeared in the last three decades.

To get the most out of the park you should head for the small Pech and Miskito village of **Las Marías**, where plenty of prospective **guides** are available to help you explore the river and surrounding jungle for L150–250 a day. One rewarding, if rather wet, trip you can make is by *pipante* (pole-propelled canoe), five hours upstream to rock **petroglyphs** at Walpaulban Sirpi, carved by an unknown people – these are more or less at the heart of the reserve. The journey itself is the main attraction, along channels too shallow for motorized boats to pass; in sections you'll be required to leave the boat and make your way through the undergrowth. *Pipantes* require three guides each, but carry only two passengers and cost around US$30 (excluding guides).

ARRIVAL AND INFORMATION

By boat Getting to the heart of the Río Plátano reserve requires travelling 10km up the Río Plátano by boat to the village of Las Marías, from Rais Ta/Belén or Brus Laguna (see opposite).

Tourist information For general information about the reserve, contact the tour operators who work within the region (see box, p.426).

ACCOMMODATION

Hospedaje Doña Justa Las Marías (near the health centre). Simple *palapa*-style guesthouse, with spacious rooms (with mosquito nets) and shared bathroom set around a blossom-filled garden and patio. Meals are served on request (extra L90–150). **L200**

Hospedaje Don Ovidio Las Marías (near the old airstrip). Basic *hospedaje* with slightly rougher rooms than *Doña Justa*, but better shared bathrooms (and cold showers), and cheaper meals served on request (extra L70–100). **L200**

THE LOST CIVILIZATIONS OF LA MOSQUITIA

The legendary "White City" (**La Ciudad Blanca**), also known as the "City of the Monkey God", has been the dream of Western explorers since the days of the Spanish conquistadors in the sixteenth century, but it wasn't until relatively recently that archeologists started to probe deep into the vast wilderness of La Mosquitia. In 2015 *National Geographic* magazine announced that an expedition into the region, guided by former SAS soldiers and accompanied by Honduran troops, had discovered a previously unknown **ruined city**: plazas, earthworks, mounds, an earthen pyramid and a cache of 52 stone sculptures and artefacts from between 1000 and 1400 AD (the site was documented but not excavated, its exact location kept a secret).

The ruins were actually identified in 2012 from the air and, rather than there being only one "White City" for explorers to find, La Mosquitia is now known to be riddled with ancient, **unexcavated sites** ranging from large ceremonial centres to abandoned villages – some scholars criticized *National Geographic* for exaggerating the 2015 expedition at the expense of ongoing research in the region. The term "lost city" is now being discouraged: the ruins were most likely built by ancestors of the **Pech** indigenous people who still live in the area, and have always known about them.

Until the ruins are properly excavated and protected, visitors will not be permitted near these sites – likely to be many years in the future.

5

BRUS LAGUNA

Some 30km east along the coast from Batalla, on the southeastern edge of the Laguna de Brus, is the friendly Miskito frontier settlement of **BRUS LAGUNA**. The town is mostly seen by visitors as they are coming or going – regular **flights** (see p.424) connect the town with Puerto Lempira, and guides and boats can be hired for multiday trips, travelling up the Río Sigre into the southern reaches of the Río Plátano reserve.

ACCOMMODATION

La Estancia Main street, near the water ☎ 2433 8043 or ☎ 2898 7959. Basic but clean rooms all with fans and cable TV, and some with en-suite bathroom and a/c. **L350**

Laguna Paradise Centre of Brus Laguna ☎ 2433 8039 or ☎ 2898 7952. Small guesthouse with simple but adequate rooms, cable TV and private bathrooms. **L300**

PUERTO LEMPIRA

Capital of the department of Gracias a Dios, **PUERTO LEMPIRA** is the largest town in La Mosquitia, with a population of eleven thousand. Set on the southeastern edge of the biggest of the coastal lagoons, Laguna de Caratasca, some 110km east of Brus Laguna, the town survives on government administration and small-scale fishing and shrimping. Like Brus Laguna, Puerto Lempira is mostly used by travellers as a transit hub – flights connect it with the rest of Honduras, and it's close to the border with Nicaragua.

INFORMATION

Bank Banco Atlántida (Mon–Fri 8–11.30am & 1.30–4pm, Sat 8–11.30am), next to *Hotel Flores*, changes travellers' cheques and gives Visa cash advances.

Information Mopawi (☎ 2433 6022, ⊕ mopawi.org), the Mosquitia development organization, has its headquarters in the town, three blocks south of the main dock.

ACCOMMODATION

Gran Hotel Flores In the centre of town ☎ 2433 6421. The best of the accommodation options, with small rooms all with a/c and bathroom. **L400**

The Bay Islands

Strung in a gentle curve 60km off the north coast, the **Islas de la Bahía**, with their clear waters and abundant marine life, are the country's main tourist attraction. Fringed by a coral reef, the islands are the perfect destination for inexpensive, water-based activities – diving, sailing and fishing top the

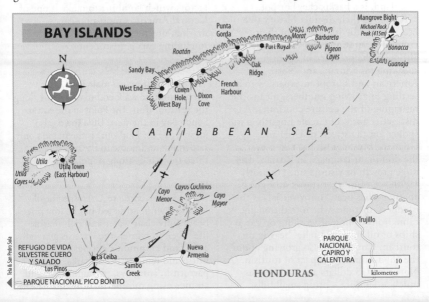

5

BRITS & BUCCANEERS – A HISTORY OF THE BAY ISLANDS

The Bay Islands' history of conquest, pirate raids and constant immigration has resulted in an unusual society. The original inhabitants were recorded by Columbus in 1502, but the indigenous population declined rapidly as a result of enslavement and forced labour. Following a series of English **pirate** attacks launched from here, the Spanish invaded the islands in 1650 and evacuated the whole population, including the remaining indigenous tribes. Port Royal, on the island of Roatán, was occupied by **English settlers** in 1742, but after Spanish attacks this too was abandoned in 1788. Roatán was left deserted again until the arrival of the **Garífuna** in 1797. These 300 descendants of African slaves and indigenous tribes, forcibly expelled from the British-controlled island of St Vincent following a rebellion, were dumped at Punta Gorda on Roatán's north coast. In 1821, the newly-founded Central American Federation claimed the Bay Islands, but made no attempt to settle them.

Further waves of settlers arrived after the British Slavery Abolition Act came into force in 1834 (abolishing slavery throughout most of the British Empire), when white Cayman Islanders and freed slaves arrived first on Utila, later spreading to Roatán and Guanaja. From around 1839 Britain effectively controlled life on the "**Colony of the Bay Islands**", though its political status remained uncertain. After pressure from the US, the islands were finally relinquished to a now independent Honduras in 1859 (in return for a free hand in Belize), and sovereignty established two years later. Descendants of British settlers were generally unhappy with the move, some claiming British citizenship (illegally) right up to the 1950s. Spanish became the official language in 1872, but the islands remained mostly English-speaking until mainland immigration ramped up in the 1990s. The biggest event in recent decades was **Hurricane Mitch**, which ravaged the islands in 1998.

list – or just lounging on the beach. Comprising three main islands and some 65 smaller cays, the chain lies on the **Bonacca Ridge**, an underwater extension of the Sierra de Omoa mountain range. **Roatán** is the largest and most developed of the islands, while **Guanaja**, to the east, is a bit posher. **Utila**, the closest to the mainland, is a backpacker hotspot.

Thanks to their distinct history (see box above), the islands retain their **cultural separation** from the mainland, although the presence of Spanish-speaking Hondurans and North American and European expats, who are settling in growing numbers, means the reshaping of the culture continues. A distinctive form of Creole English is still spoken on the streets of Utila and Guanaja, but Spanish has taken over as the dominant language in Roatán. The huge growth in visitors since the early 1990s – a trend that shows no signs of abating – has been controversial, as the islanders' income, which traditionally came from fishing or working on cargo ships or oil rigs, now relies heavily on tourism. Concern is also growing about the environmental impact of tourism. Note that US dollars are used here as much as lempira – bring small bills.

UTILA

The smallest of the three main Bay Islands (it's only 4km wide), **UTILA** is also the cheapest and one of the best places in the world to learn to dive (and even if you don't want to don tanks, the superb waters around the island offer great swimming and snorkelling possibilities), factors which combine to make it one of Central America's most popular destinations for budget travellers (including gap-year students).

WHAT TO SEE AND DO

The island's principal **main road**, a twenty-minute walk end to end, runs along the seafront from **The Point** in the east to **Sandy Bay** in the west. **Utila Town** (also known as East Harbour) is the island's only settlement and home to the majority of its three-thousand-strong population.

Diving

Most visitors come to Utila specifically for the **diving**, attracted by the low prices, beautifully clear water and rich marine life. Even in winter, the water is generally calm, and common sightings include nurse and hammerhead sharks, turtles, parrotfish, stingrays, porcupine fish and an increasing number of dolphins. **Whale**

sharks also continue to be a major attraction – the island is one of the few places in the world where they frequently pass close to shore.

In contrast to Roatán, the reef here does not come close to the shore and you need to take a boat to dive sites (the whale sharks swim in the deep channel between the islands); most sites here involve wall diving, though there are also several wrecks (including the cargo ship *Halliburton*, sunk on purpose to create an artificial reef in 1998).

On the less-developed north coast of the island, **Blackish Point** and **CJ's Drop Off** are both good sites; on the south coast the best spot is **Airport Caves**. The dive schools (see box, p.439) will be happy to spend time talking to you about the merits of the various sites.

It's worth spending a morning walking around checking out all the schools. You want to feel comfortable with your decision, as diving can be dangerous – it is imperative that you get along with your instructor.

Swimming and snorkelling

Close to the centre on the western side of town, where the road ends beyond *Driftwood Café*, busy **Chepes Beach** offers a narrow strip of sand, shallow water and a bar. The best **swimming** near town is further along the bay at **Blue Bayou Beach**, a twenty-minute walk west of the centre, which also boasts a small sandy beach (the excellent snorkelling here is US$1.50). At the far end of the eastern side of the bay, man-made **Bandu Beach** offers good snorkelling just offshore (admission US$3/L60).

The best beaches on the island – white-sand **Treasure Beach** (southwest), **Pine Point** (west) and **Rock Harbour** (north) – take a little more effort to reach, as they're usually only accessible by water taxi from town.

Iguana Station

The **Iguana Station** (Mon–Fri 9.30am–noon & 1.30–5pm; L60; ☎ 2425 3946, ⓦ utila-iguana.de), signposted from the road five minutes west of the dock, is a

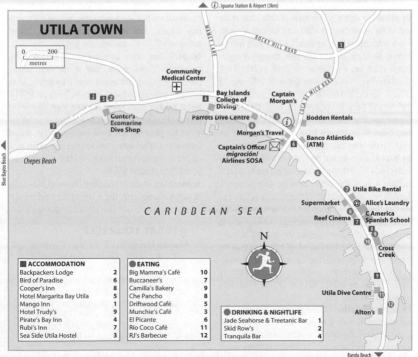

▲ ⓘ, Iguana Station & Airport (3km)

UTILA TOWN

0 — 200 metres

Community Medical Center ✚

MARET LANE

ROCKY HILL ROAD

Bay Islands College of Diving

Captain Morgan's

COLA DE MICO ROAD

Gunter's Ecomarine Dive Shop

Parrots Dive Centre

Morgan's Travel

Bodden Rentals

Banco Atlántida (ATM)

Captain's Office/ migración/ Airlines SOSA

Chepes Beach

Blue Bayou Beach

CARIBBEAN SEA

N

Utila Bike Rental

Supermarket

@ Alice's Laundry

Reef Cinema

C America Spanish School

Cross Creek

Utila Dive Centre

Alton's

■ ACCOMMODATION	
Backpackers Lodge	2
Bird of Paradise	6
Cooper's Inn	6
Hotel Margarita Bay Utila	5
Mango Inn	1
Hotel Trudy's	9
Pirate's Bay Inn	4
Rubi's Inn	7
Sea Side Utila Hostel	3

● EATING	
Big Mamma's Café	10
Buccaneer's	7
Camilla's Bakery	9
Che Pancho	8
Driftwood Café	5
Munchie's Café	3
El Picante	6
Río Coco Café	11
RJ's Barbecue	12

● DRINKING & NIGHTLIFE	
Jade Seahorse & Treetanic Bar	1
Skid Row's	2
Tranquila Bar	4

Bandu Beach ▼

5

breeding centre for the endangered Utila spiny-tailed iguana, found only on the island and facing extinction. Guided tours explain the life cycle of the species. It's worth a visit, especially if you need a break from all the diving.

Utila Cays

The **Utila Cayes** (or Cayolitos) – eleven tiny outcrops strung along the southwestern edge of the main island – were designated a wildlife refuge in 1992. **Jewel Cayes** and **Pigeon Cayes**, connected by a narrow causeway, are both inhabited, and the pace of life is even slower than on Utila. Small *lanchas* regularly shuttle between Pigeon Cayes and Utila (US$10), or can be rented to take you across for a day's snorkelling (US$20). Ask at *Buccaneer's* (see opposite).

Water Cay, a blissful stretch of white sand, coconut palms and a small coral reef, is even more idyllic. Captain Hal charges around US$45 for return trips to Water Cay; ask for him at Parrots Dive Center (see opposite).

ARRIVAL AND INFORMATION

By plane The airstrip is 3km north of Utila Town at the end of the island's second main road, Cola de Mico Rd, which heads inland from the dock. Tuk-tuks (L60) wait for arriving flights. SOSA (you can book through Morgan's Travel, which has an office at the dock; ☎ 2425 3161, ⓦ utilamorganstravel.com) flies between Utila and La Ceiba (3 weekly; 20min); CM Airlines (ⓦ cmairlines.com) flies to and from Tegucigalpa (Sat only; 1hr 25min). Charter operator Island Air (ⓦ islandairhonduras.com) runs between Roatán and Utila on Saturdays only for US$125; other days it's US$500 for up to four people.
By boat All boats dock in the centre of Utila Town. Daily ferries (☎ 2425 3390, ⓦ utilaprincess.com) run to La Ceiba (6.20am & 2pm; 1hr; depart La Ceiba daily 9.30am & 4pm). Tickets (one way L448–472) are usually available on the day. There were no scheduled boat services between Roatán and Utila at the time of writing, but it is possible to catch infrequent charters making the trip: ask at travel agents or head to the East End, where noticeboards at the supermarket might advertise upcoming trips (usually US$50–95/person) to West End, Roatán. You could also try Captain Dillard on ☎ 2425 3241 or ☎ 3216 5366, who sometimes makes the trip.
Tourist information Captain Morgan's dive shop (see box opposite) is often used as an unofficial information point. ⓦ aboututila.com is another useful source of information about the island. The Bay Islands Conservation

Association runs an information office on New Airport Rd, inland from the centre via Cola de Mico Rd (Mon–Fri 9am–noon & 2–5pm; ☎ 2425 3260, ⓦ bicautila.org).

GETTING AROUND

Scooters and quad bikes Scooters cost around US$35–40/day, golf carts and quad bikes go for around US$60/day; try Bodden Rentals (Mon–Sat 8am–noon & 1–4pm; ☎ 2425 3245, ⓔ boddenlance@yahoo.com), near the dock on Cola de Mico Rd.
Bikes Bodden Rentals (Cola de Mico Road), *Rio Coco Café* (see p.440) and Utila Bike Rental (southeast of the dock) rent out bikes (L75–100/day).

ACCOMMODATION

Utila has more than enough affordable accommodation. With the exception of Semana Santa and parts of the high season, there's always somewhere available. Most of the dive schools (see box opposite) have affiliated lodgings, and enrolling in a course invariably gets you a few free or discounted nights. There are no designated places to camp except on the cays. Electricity is expensive on the island so opting out of a/c will make things cheaper

EAST OF THE DOCK

Bird of Paradise Main St, near the dock ☎ 2425 3190. Simple rooms with private or shared bathrooms in a traditional wooden house right in the heart of town, with fans (no a/c), free wi-fi and shared kitchen. Shared bathroom US$18, private bathroom US$23
Cooper's Inn 5min from the dock ☎ 2425 3184, ⓦ tonicooper15@yahoo.com. One of the best budget places on the island, with orderly rooms (all with fans, some with a/c), some with private bathrooms. Free wi-fi. US$18
Hotel Trudy's South end of the main road, west of the dock ☎ 2425 3103, ⓦ underwatervision.net. Right on the water, this place has smart four-bed dorms (fan, shared bathrooms and hot water) and some private rooms with a/c and bathroom. The bar area is one of Utila's social hubs. Dorms US$8, doubles US$40
★ **Rubi's Inn** Next door to the Reef Cinema ☎ 2425 3240, ⓔ rubisinn@yahoo.com. This is one of the most popular

---

★ **TREAT YOURSELF**
Mango Inn 5min inland from the dock on Cola de Mico/Airport Rd ☎ 2425 3335, ⓦ mango-inn.com. A beautiful, well-run place, timber-built and set in shady gardens. They offer thatched, a/c cabins sleeping up to four, plus pleasant dorms (only available to divers from Utila Dive Centre). There's a good pizza restaurant on site. Doubles US$68, cabins US$105

DIVE SCHOOLS IN UTILA

Open-water courses cost around US$295–300; prices are supposed to be fixed but in reality some schools charge more and some less (plus fifteen percent tax). The price normally includes accommodation for at least part of the course, and discounted accommodation afterwards. Fun dives cost around US$35–40. There's a US$3 daily reef-conservation fee to pay too.

Alton's Main St (southeast of the centre) ⓣ 2425 3704, ⓦ diveinutila.com. Accommodation on site (discounted following courses), and use of kitchen. It has a conch nursery and a stringent ecological policy.

Bay Islands College of Diving 5min west of the dock on Main St, next to *Utila Lodge* ⓣ 2425 3291, ⓦ dive-utila.com. Professional school, with an indoor training pool and the island's only hyperbaric chamber on site.

Captain Morgan's On the corner opposite the dock ⓣ 2425 3349, ⓦ divingutila.com. Accommodation provided at *Pirate's Bay Inn* and the *Lonestar Hotel*.

Gunter's Ecomarine Dive Shop 8min west of the dock ⓣ 2425 3350, ⓦ ecomarineutila.com. A small, relaxed operation that offers a "lazy boat" for late risers. Its dock is a favourite haunt of sea horses.

Parrots Dive Center 2min west of the dock ⓣ 2425 3772, ⓦ parrotsdivecenter.com. Professional facilities, friendly staff and a dynamic environment.

Utila Dive Centre Near the end of the road east of the dock, close to the bridge ⓣ 2425 3326, ⓦ utiladivecentre.com. Perhaps the best reputation for quality and safety, and courses are a bit pricier as a result. Accommodation at *Mango Inn*.

mid-range places on the island. There are twelve comfortable rooms with private bathrooms and fans, a communal kitchen, hot water, free wi-fi (with a strong signal), a pleasant beach and lots of trees dotted around the grounds. US$25

WEST OF THE DOCK

Backpackers Lodge Down an alley opposite Gunter's Dive Shop ⓣ 2425 3350. Ten passable rooms (eight private rooms and two dorms) with shared bathrooms. Enquire at Gunter's Ecomarine Dive Shop – divers with Gunter's get a fifty percent discount (over Easter the lodge is reserved for divers only). Dorms US$6, doubles US$10

Hotel Margarita Bay Utila Main St, opposite *Driftwood Café* ⓣ 2425 3366, ⓦ margaritabayutila.com. Very pleasant, big rooms, plus six large waterside cabins with kitchenettes, a wide terrace all around the house and hot water and a/c throughout. Doubles US$35, cabins US$70

Pirate's Bay Inn Main St, 4min from the dock ⓣ 2425 3818, ⓦ piratesbayinn.com. This hostel has clean, sparsely furnished dorms as well as spick-and-span private rooms with fans and hot showers (a/c costs US$10 extra) – the latter are normally reserved for divers on Captain Morgan package deals, but are available to non-divers during quiet periods. Dorms US10, doubles US$39

★ **Sea Side Utila Hostel** Main St, opposite Gunter's Ecomarine Dive Shop, 8min from the dock ⓣ 2425 3150. Just about the best budget accommodation on the island. Three-person dorms come with spotless bathrooms, and there are also a few private rooms (with fans, a/c US$15 extra). There's a communal kitchen and a nice balcony upstairs, where you can take in the Caribbean sunsets. Dorms US$7, doubles US$15

UTILA CAYS

Camping Water Cay. Camping is allowed here – a caretaker turns up every day to collect the fee. You'll need to bring a tent, food, equipment for a fire and water. US$2

EATING

Lobster and fish are excellent on the islands (though it's a good idea to ask about the reef-friendliness and sustainability of what's being served), and then there's the usual rice, beans, chicken, and US and European food. Prices are higher than on the mainland: for low-cost eating, head for the evening stalls on the road by the dock, which do a thriving trade in *baleadas*. Many restaurants stop serving at around 9.30pm.

EAST OF THE DOCK

Big Mamma's Café Main St, 5min from the dock. Clean, inexpensive and popular with the nearby dive shops, with some dishes (such as pizza slices) on display at the counter. *Baleadas* from L20, but often sells out. Thurs–Tues noon–2pm & 6–9.30pm.

Buccaneer's Main St, 3min from the dock ⓣ 2445 5455. Also known as the *Bundu Café*, this barn like place has a good range of breakfast options (specials from L99), plus burgers, sandwiches and nachos, ice-cream sundaes and alcoholic coffees. The sofa by the book exchange is a good place to park yourself on a rainy afternoon. Daily 8am–10pm.

Camilla's Bakery Main St, 5min from the dock. A good spot for a snack or picnic supplies, this bakery has everything from croissants and bagels to banana bread and pecan pie (all around L60–70). It shares the premises with *Pizza Nut* restaurant, which opens in the evening from 5pm. Tues–Sat 8.30am–2pm.

★ **Che Pancho** Main St, 4min from the dock. Underneath

5

Reef Cinema in a shady courtyard, this friendly little café serves huge, top-notch smoothies, hot dogs (try the Argentine *choripan* with *chimichurri* sauce), sandwiches and snacks. There's normally also a home-baked cake or two. Mon–Sat 8.30am–6pm.

El Picante 2min from the dock. One of the smarter restaurants in town, *El Picante* produces tasty Mexican food (L100–200) – from fajitas to enchiladas. Sun–Thurs 11am–10pm, Fri 11am–5pm, Sat 6–10pm.

★ **Río Coco Café** Beside the bridge, 8min from the dock ☎ 9800 3495. The best coffee (L20–40) in Utila is served at this café, alongside delicious home-made chocolate chip cookies, banana bread, smoothies and savoury muffins. Free wi-fi. Mon–Fri 7am–2pm, Sat 8am–noon.

RJ's Barbecue Beside the bridge, 8min from the dock. You can have anything you want – snapper, marlin, wahoo, king fish, steak, burgers – as long as it's barbecued. Get there early as it fills up quickly. Mains around L140–200. Wed, Fri & Sun 5.30–10pm.

WEST OF THE DOCK

Driftwood Café 10min from the dock, right at the end of Main St. The food here is excellent, and they have one of the most peaceful jetties on the island. Menu highlights include pork chops, burgers, baja fish tacos, pulled pork sandwiches, and fish soup (all around L100–200). Try the house drink, the "Monkey Ball" shot (made with Kahlúa). The kitchen is open until 9pm, the bar until 10pm. Tues–Sun 11am–10pm.

Munchie's Café 1min from the dock. A real mix of dishes – from local breakfasts to seafood kebabs – served in an 1864 house with an iguana garden out back and a nice porch. Mains L100–200. Daily 6am–10pm.

DRINKING AND NIGHTLIFE

Despite its tiny population, Utila is a hedonistic party island. A Honduran beer will set you back around L35. Most of the restaurants (including *Driftwood Café*) double as bars, and some of the hotels (notably *Mango Inn*) are also good drinking spots.

★ **Jade Seahorse & Treetanic Bar** A short walk up Cola de Mico Rd ☎ 3291 8694. The most eccentric place on the island. Run by American artist Neil Keller, this hotel/restaurant/bar is a maze of glass, colour and reflective surfaces that really comes alive at night. *Treetanic*, the bar section (Tues–Sat 6pm–1am), is an old boat up in a mango tree. Restaurant Tues–Sat 5–9pm.

Skid Row's Main St, next door but one to *Sea Side Utila Hostel*. Though it feels a little like somewhere they repair boat parts, the "best dive in Utila" is a small, friendly place full of expat seadogs boozing throughout the day. Some of the cheapest beers on the island, plus good food. Daily 10am–midnight.

Tranquila Bar Behind Parrots Dive Center, 2min west of the dock ☎ 9958 3538. Lively, low-lit open-air bar over the water,

packed with locals and backpackers most nights. Tequila is only L10 on "Tequila Tuesdays", and on Thursdays vodka is L25. Mon–Wed & Sun 4pm–1am, Thurs–Sat 4pm–4am.

DIRECTORY

Bank Banco Atlántida (Mon–Fri 8.30am–3.30pm, Sat 8.30–11.30am), opposite the dock, has an ATM but it's not that reliable – try to bring cash. US dollars are used everywhere on the island along with lempira.

Books *Buccaneer's* and *Che Pancho* (see p.439) both have book exchanges, though choices are limited.

Cinema Reef Cinema (☎ 2425 3754), above *Che Pancho*, has one screening daily at 7.30pm (tickets around L50).

Health The Community Medical Center is 2min west of the dock (Mon–Fri 10.30am–3.30pm).

Immigration At the captain's office (Mon–Fri 9am–noon & 2–4.30pm).

Internet Mermaids Internet (Sun–Thurs 8am–10pm, Fri 8am–3pm, Sat 6–10pm), on main street, 5min east of the dock.

Language school Central America Spanish School has an outpost on Utila (☎ 2443 6453, ⓦ ca-spanish.com).

Laundry Alice's Laundry (daily 7am–8pm) is next to Mermaids Internet.

Post office At the main dock.

Meditation If you're after an immersive meditation experience, Float Utila (☎ 2425 3827, ⓦ floatutila.com), 4min west of the dock, offers reportedly the world's largest sensory deprivation floatation tank. A 60min session costs US$50.

ROATÁN

Some 50km from La Ceiba, **ROATÁN** is the largest of the Bay Islands, a curving ridged hump almost 50km long and 5km across at its widest point. A popular stopoff for cruise ships and major destination for holidaying North Americans, Roatán can be a bit of a shock if you've been travelling off the beaten path in Central America. With a large expat population, US dollars the de facto currency and much higher prices than mainland Honduras, it can seem like another country (though not crime free, it's also much safer here).

The island's accommodation mostly comes in the form of all-inclusive luxury resort packages, although there are a few good deals to be found in **West End**. Like Utila, Roatán is a superb **diving** destination, and also offers some great hiking, as well as the chance to do nothing except laze on a beach. **Coxen**

Hole is the island's commercial centre and largest settlement.

Roatán's abundance of great diving and superb beaches often takes away from the charm of the island's smaller towns and **villages**, which are worth exploring to get a sense of what it would have been like before the tourists and cruise ships arrived.

Coxen Hole

COXEN HOLE (also known as Roatán Town) is uninteresting and run down; most visitors come here only to change money or shop. All of the town's practical facilities and most of its shops are on **Main Street**, near where the buses stop.

Sandy Bay

Midway between Coxen Hole and West End, **SANDY BAY** is an unassuming community with a number of attractions. The **Roatán Institute for Marine Sciences** (daily 7am–5pm; US$5; ☎9556 0212, ⊕roatanims.org), based at *Antony's Key Resort*, has exhibitions on the marine life and geology of the islands and a museum with useful information on local history and archeology. There are also **bottlenose dolphin** "encounters" in waist-deep water with 24 captive dolphins (some wild caught and some captive born), housed in two large natural enclosures penned off from the rest of the bay around adjacent Bailey's Key; naturally, the usual ethical considerations about captive dolphins apply (daily 8am, 10am, 1pm & 2.30pm; US$69 for 30min).

Across the road, several short nature trails weave through the jungle at the **Carambola Botanical Gardens** (daily 8am–5pm; US$10; guided tours cost an extra US$5; ☎2445 3117, ⊕carambolagardens.com), a riot of beautiful flowers, lush ferns and tropical trees. A thirty-minute hike to the summit of Carambola Mountain gives a view of the coral in the ocean beyond.

West End

With its calm waters and incredible sandy beaches, **WEST END**, 14km from Coxen Hole, makes the most of its ideal setting at the southwest corner of the island. From

ROATÁN: WEST END

Wordy's Grceries

Roatán Institute
for Deep Sea
Exploration Book Nook

Native Sons
Laundry

Banco
Davivienda
(ATM)

Half Moon Bay

Coconut Tree Divers

Captain Van's
Rentals

Roatán
Divers

Roatán Rentals
Ocean Connections

CARIBBEAN
SEA

Water Taxi to
West Bay

West End
Divers

Barefoot Charlie's

■ ACCOMMODATION	
Buena Onda Hostel	5
Chillies	4
Hidden Garden Cabins	6
Mariposa Lodge	8
Posada Arco Iris	3
Posada Las Orquídeas	1
Sea Breeze Inn	7
Splash Inn Dive Resort	9

0   200
metres

Airport

Coxen Hole & ATM

West Bay

● EATING			
C Level Cafe & Bar	5	Rudy's	12
Café Escondido	6	Tong's Thai	
Cannibal Café	4	Island Cuisine	8
Creole's Rotisserie		● DRINKING & NIGHTLIFE	
Chicken	11	Blue Marlin	7
Deliciosa Creamery	3	Foster's (aka Barking Monkey)	13
Fresh Bakery	2	Nova	9
Por Qué No	10	Sundowners	1
		Tita's Pink Seahorse Bar	14

the beautifully sheltered **Half Moon Bay** at the northern end of town, a sandy track runs 1km or so along the water's edge, past guesthouses, bars and restaurants geared towards independent travellers of all budgets. The year-round community of sun-worshippers and dive shops gives the village a laidback charm during the day and a vibrant, party feel after dark.

West Bay

Around 2km from West End, towards the extreme western tip of Roatán, is the stunning white-sand beach of **West Bay**, fringed by coconut palms and washed by

5

crystal-clear waters. There's decent snorkelling at the southern end of the beach, though the once-pristine reef has suffered in recent years from increasing river run-off and the close attentions of unsupervised day-trippers – if a cruise ship is in town West Bay will be mobbed. Note also that the beach is free; resorts do try to charge fees of US$10–15 to enter their property but whatever the staff may tell you, there is no "private beach".

From West End, it's a pleasant 45-minute stroll along the beach and over a few rock outcrops; alternatively, you can take one of the small *lanchas* that leave regularly from the jetty near West End Divers (L60/person each way, prices go up after 6pm; three-person minimum).

French Harbour

Leaving Coxen Hole, the paved road runs northeast past the small secluded cove of Brick Bay to **FRENCH HARBOUR**, a busy fishing port and the island's second-largest town. Less run down than Coxen Hole, it's a lively and interesting place to spend a few hours.

Oak Ridge

From French Harbour the road cuts inland along a central ridge to give superb views of both the north and south coasts of the island. After about 14km the road reaches **OAK RIDGE**, a fishing port with wooden houses strung along its harbour – it's attractive in a bleak sort of way. There are some nice, unspoiled beaches to the east of town, accessible by *lanchas* from the main dock, and other nearby communities can be reached by boat cruises through the mangroves. Boatmen offer trips to Port Royal, the mangroves and Morat for US$50 per boat or to Pigeon Caye for US$200 per boat (up to ten people).

Punta Gorda

About 5km from Oak Ridge on the northern coast of the island is **PUNTA GORDA**, the oldest Garífuna community in Honduras. The best time to visit is for the anniversary of the founding of the settlement on April 12, when Garífuna from all over the country attend the celebrations. At other times it's a quiet

and slightly dilapidated little port with no buildings of note, though the black, white and yellow of the Garífuna flags brighten things up.

Port Royal

The road ends at **PORT ROYAL**, on the southern edge of the island, where the faint remains of the eighteenth-century **Fort George**, built by the English, can be seen on **Fort Morgan Caye** offshore. The village lies in the **Port Royal Park and Wildlife Reserve**, the largest refuge on the island, set up in 1978 in an attempt to protect endangered species such as the yellow-naped parrot.

The eastern tip of Roatán is made up of mangrove swamps, with a small island, **Morat**, just offshore. Beyond is **Barbareta Caye**, which has retained much of its virgin forest cover.

ARRIVAL AND DEPARTURE

By plane Regular domestic and international flights (see p.379) land at Roatán's international airport, on the road to French Harbour, 3km east of Coxen Hole. There are information and hotel reservation desks, car rental agencies (Avis ☎ 2445 0122) and a bank at the airport. A taxi to/from West End costs US$25 (US$30 to West Bay); evening and night rates are US$5–20 extra.

Domestic destinations La Ceiba (EasySky, Lanhsa, SOSA; 4–5 daily; 30min); San Pedro Sula (EasySky, CM Airlines, SOSA & Avianca; 2–3 daily; 2hr 35min); Tegucigalpa (EasySky, CM Airlines, SOSA & Avianca; 2–3 daily; 1hr 10min). Island Air (☎ 9558 8683, ⊚ islandairhonduras .com; contact for timetables) also operates flights on small planes between Utila, Roatán and Guanaja, as well as San Pedro Sula and La Ceiba.

By boat Roatán's main ferry terminal is now located on the main road in Dixon Cove, about 5 minutes from the Mahogany Bay cruise-ship dock (15min by taxi to the airport). Best Car Rental (☎ 2445 2268, ⊚ roatanbestcarrental.com) has a desk at the terminal. A taxi to/from West End or West Bay (both 45min–1hr) costs US$30, or L90/person if sharing (*colectivo*). Daily ferries run to La Ceiba (7am & 2pm; from La Ceiba daily 9.30am & 4.30pm; 1hr 10min; US$30/L620 one way; ☎ 2445 1775, ⊚ roatanferry.com). You can usually buy tickets on the day, if you turn up about an hour in advance.

GETTING AROUND

By bike, moped, motorbike or car Captain Van's Rentals (☎ 2445 4076, ⊚ captainvans.com), at the southern end of Half Moon Bay, rents scooters (US$39/day), motorbikes (US$55–65/day) and cars (US$55–65/

5

WATERSPORTS AROUND WEST END

The waters around West End offer fantastic watersports – primarily **diving**, and superb **snorkelling** in the reef just offshore, but with plenty of other activities available. **Roatán Marine Park** (ⓦroatanmarinepark.com) is a grassroots nonprofit organization created to protect the island's reef; the group charges divers a pass fee of US$15 for one year, US$10 for one week and US$3 for one day.

DIVING

Diving courses in West End are available for all levels, and prices are officially standardized. The four-day PADI Open Water course costs US$230–350 depending on the school, plus US$170 for the PADI eLearning course, with some schools offering discounted accommodation. Fun dives cost US$35–45 per dive, with ten-dive packages around US$300. Recommended West End-based **schools** include: West End Divers (ⓣ2445 4289, ⓦwestenddivers.info), Ocean Connections (ⓦocean-connections.com), Coconut Tree Divers (ⓣ2445 4081, ⓦcoconuttreedivers.com), Native Sons (ⓣ2445 4003, ⓦnativesonsroatan.com) and Roatán Divers (ⓣ8836 8414, ⓦroatandiver.com).

SNORKELLING

The best **snorkelling** spots around West End are at the mouth of Half Moon Bay and at the Blue Channel (access via the beach, 100m south of *Foster's* bar). You can rent equipment (around US$10/day) from many of the dive schools and some shops along the main road.

KAYAKING

You can rent **sea kayaks** from the *Sea Breeze Inn*, close to the entrance road; expect to pay US$5 per hour for a single kayak (US$14/half-day, US$18/day), and US$7 per hour for a double kayak (US$18/half-day, US$21/day).

day); add nineteen percent tax to these rates. You'll need a credit card (not debit card) for a security deposit, and you'll have to bring your driving licence.

By minibus There are three minibus routes covering all of the island's main settlements; all tend to run from around 6am to 6pm Mon–Sat, with limited service on Sundays. Bus #1 (every 30min; L40) goes from Coxen Hole to French Harbour, stopping in Oak Ridge; the last bus from Oak Ridge leaves between 4.30pm and 6pm. Buses from Oak Ridge go via Punta Gorda. Bus #2 (every 15min; L40) goes from Coxen Hole to Sandy Bay, stopping in West End.

By taxi It's never hard to find taxis and *colectivos* in Roatán, though as with everything else, it is often a lot more expensive than on the mainland.

By water taxi Water taxis run from West End to West Bay, leaving from the jetty near *Splash Inn Dive Resort* (L60 each way).

ACCOMMODATION

In the low season (April–July & Sept to mid-Dec) discounts may be available, particularly for longer stays. Note that taxes and "fees" can add 20–25 percent to the quoted room rate in Roatán. Airbnb (ⓦairbnb.com) lists over one hundred properties on the island, starting at US$15/night.

WEST END

Buena Onda Hostel Next to the petrol station ⓣ9770 0158, ⓔbuenaondaroatan@gmail.com. While the mixed dorms can get a little messy when busy, the vibe is always friendly, owner Sophie Segui is a great host and this is the cheapest bed in the West End area. Shared kitchen, games room, hot showers and free wi-fi. Short walk down to the beach. Laundry US$5. Rates go up to US$17 during peak periods. U̲S̲$̲1̲2̲

Chillies Half Moon Bay ⓣ445 4062, ⓦnativesonsroatan .com/chillies. *Chillies* is a well-set-up budget choice owned by English/Roatanian couple Michele Akel and Alvin Jackson, with a range of accommodation options (all but the most expensive cabins, which sleep up to six, have cold-water bathrooms) and a communal kitchen. Pay with cash and you can avoid the 23 percent surcharge on credit cards. Dorms U̲S̲$̲1̲1̲, doubles U̲S̲$̲2̲4̲, cold-water cabins U̲S̲$̲3̲0̲, hot-water cabins U̲S̲$̲3̲4̲

Hidden Garden Cabins Carretera Principal ⓦhiddengardencabins.com. These studio-size wooden cabins (that sleep two) are superb value, set in lush gardens a short walk from the main drag, with basic kitchens, ceiling fans and private bathrooms. U̲S̲$̲4̲5̲

Mariposa Lodge On a side street halfway down the main beach road ⓣ2445 4460, ⓦmariposa-lodge.com. A quiet and very comfortable mid-range place with a mix of a/c double rooms and fan-only apartments (which sleep up to four). Doubles U̲S̲$̲7̲4̲, apartments U̲S̲$̲6̲9̲

Posada Arco Iris Half Moon Bay ⓣ2445 4264, ⓦroatanposada.com. Set in attractive gardens just off the beach, with excellent, imaginatively furnished and spacious rooms, studios and apartments, all with fridge and hammocks; a/c is US$15 extra per night. There's also

5

an attached Argentine restaurant. Doubles US$48, studios US$54, apartments US$66

Posada Las Orquídeas At the northern end of the main beach road ☎ 2445 4387, ⓦ posadalasorquideas.com. There's a serene feel to this rather smart, secluded hotel. Rooms all have fridges and fans; those with a/c and sea views cost extra, and #14 is the pick of the bunch. US$67

★ **Sea Breeze Inn** Just south of Half Moon Bay, behind the *Cannibal Café* ☎ 2442 4026, ⓦ seabreezeroatan.com. Popular place, offering a mix of (rather cramped) a/c rooms, and better-value studios and apartments with kitchenettes. Avoid the noisy ground-floor rooms. Doubles US$40, studios US$60, apartments US$90

Splash Inn Dive Resort South of Half Moon Bay ☎ 2445 4110, ⓦ roatansplashinn.com. A reliable mid-range hotel providing spotless rooms with TVs and a/c, plus a decent Italian-inspired restaurant and a dive school. Breakfast US$8. US$59

EATING

There's a good range of places to eat in West End, with fish and seafood featuring heavily – take advice from the dive shops as to the most reef-friendly choices – though prices are high compared to the mainland. Prices quoted below are in the currency used by each establishment; you can pay with either US dollars or lempiras at all.

WEST END

C Level Cafe & Bar Next to Reef Gliders Dive Shop ☎ 9839 8267. Best pizzas on the island (wood-oven, thin-crust), lionfish tacos, views right over the water from the upper deck and friendly staff. Large pizzas (not available Sat) from US$10. Also does a decent breakfast and infamous "pour-yourself Bloody Mary" (or the Canadian version known as a "Caesar", with added clam broth) for just US$5. Mon, Tues, Thurs & Fri 4–9pm, Wed noon–9pm, Sat noon–6pm.

Café Escondido Just south of Half Moon Bay, above West End Divers ☎ 9952 0813, ⓦ cafeescondido.com. Breezy

first-floor café with good breakfast (including filled muffins, French toast and massive banana pancakes) and lunch specials from L100 (sandwiches and "rice bowls"), plus good Honduran coffee (you can even get a flat white). Mon & Thurs–Sun 7.45am–2.30pm; bar 3–10pm.

Cannibal Café Just south of Half Moon Bay, in front of the *Sea Breeze Inn* ☎ 2442 4026. This split-level Mexican joint is famous for its filling "Big Kahuna" burritos (L200–300) – if you can eat three in an hour they're on the house. Tacos, quesadillas, fajitas and chimichangas (mains L220) are also available, plus decent margaritas. Mon–Sat 10.30am–10pm.

★ **Creole's Rotisserie Chicken** Towards the southern end of the main beach road ☎ 2445 4275. If you're looking for value for money, this is the place. As the name suggests, lip-smacking roast chicken (L120 for a quarter chicken and two sides) is the focus here, though the huge quesadillas (L150) and rum cake are also good. Get there early or be prepared to wait. Daily 3–10pm.

Deliciosa Creamery Carretera Principal, opposite *Cannibal Café* ☎ 9812 2416. Addictive ice cream has finally arrived in the West End, with this justly popular shop knocking out half a dozen fresh flavours (the salted caramel and coconut are mouthwatering). Daily 11am–9pm.

Fresh Bakery Alba Plaza, a 20–30min walk from West End in Gibson Bight, just before Sandy Bay. Well worth the stroll from West End, this café serves excellent coffee (L35–60), sandwiches and bagels (L100–120), and fresh bread, cakes, pastries and cookies to eat in or take away. Mon–Sat 7am–2pm.

Por Qué No Between Eagle Ray and *Foster's* ☎ 9631 5483. German and Austrian classics such as sauerkraut, *Leberkäse Schnitzel* and fresh potato salad (mains US$4.50–16; breakfast US$3.50–9). German owners Peter and Conny even serve *weizen* (wheat) beer. Hummingbirds collect around their special feeder. Dinners by reservation only (minimum four people). Sun–Fri 8am–3pm.

Rudy's Towards the southern end of the main beach road ☎ 2445 4205. Locally renowned spot for breakfast (US$3–5) – the banana pancakes are particularly good. *Rudy's* also serves shots and smoothies of the local so-called "miracle fruit", *noni*. Sun–Fri 7am–midnight.

DRINKING AND NIGHTLIFE

Drinking in West End can drain your pocket fast, so seek out half-price happy-hour deals, some of which last until 10pm. Expect to pay around L45 for a beer. Note that the 2014 Honduran law prohibiting alcohol sales between Sun 5pm and Mon 7am is enforced in Roatán, meaning bars sometimes shut completely on Sun evenings (there may be an exemption for the Bay Islands in the future).

WEST END

Blue Marlin Just south of Half Moon Bay ⓦ bluemarlinroatan.com. A popular bar-restaurant that

★ **TREAT YOURSELF**

Tong's Thai Island Cuisine Just south of Half Moon Bay. For something a little different, try this Thai restaurant, which knocks up tasty (if sometimes slightly oversweet) red, green and penang curries, pad thai, fried rice, spicy soups and a range of other dishes. The candlelit tables out on the jetty are particularly romantic in the evening. Mains US$12–20. Daily noon–3pm & 5.30–9.30pm.

often serves as the first stop after *Sundowners* (see below) closes and the crowds start heading down the beach. Mon–Thurs noon–midnight, Fri & Sat noon–2am.

Foster's (aka Barking Monkey) At the second of the big piers to the south of town ☎9869 0779. Set on its own pier, *Foster's* is a West End institution. There's a daily happy hour (4–7pm), and Fri nights are particularly rowdy. Also known for its three-tail lobster dinners (L300). Mon–Thurs 10am–midnight, Fri & Sat 10am–2am, Sun 10am–10pm.

Nova A 5min walk south of Half Moon Bay ☎9719 1208. With fluorescent strings dangling from the ceiling and swinging chairs at the bar, this atmospheric place sees DJs play electro, breakbeat and drum'n'bass, but also latin and 80s music. Fri night is especially lively. Mon–Thurs 11am/noon–midnight, Fri & Sat 11am/noon–2am.

★ **Sundowners** Half Moon Bay ☎9907 7700. The happy hour (daily 5–7pm) at this tiny but always buzzing beach bar, popular with both locals and tourists, is a good way to kick off the night. Daily 10am–10pm.

★ **Tita's Pink Seahorse Bar** Sueno Del Mar ☎2445 4343. Beach bar with wooden stools right on the beach next to a volleyball court, helmed by the indomitable Tita herself. Best "Monkey La La" on the strip (the island cocktail made from Kahlúa, Bailey's, vodka, rum and coconut juice). Daily 11.30am–9pm.

DIRECTORY

Banks In Coxen Hole, Banco Atlántida and the Banco Davivienda near the small square have ATMs (24hr). In West End there is a Banco Davivienda ATM (24hr) at the Coconut Tree store, right by the mini roundabout triangle. None are particularly reliable.

Books Book Nook in West End (Half Moon Bay; Thurs–Tues 11am–5pm) has a good selection of novels and travel books (including a few *Rough Guides*) to buy or rent.

Immigration The *migración* is near the small square (Parque Central) on Main Street in Coxen Hole, in a green building (Mon–Fri 9am–noon & 1.30–4pm).

Internet Most hotels, restaurants and bars offer free wi-fi.

Laundry There's a small laundry (Sun–Fri) close to *Linga Longa* restaurant in West End.

Post office In a blue building near the *migración* and the small square on Main Street in Coxen Hole (Mon–Fri 8am–noon & 2–4pm).

Supermarkets Woody's Groceries is a small supermarket in West End (next to *Posada Arco Iris* at the northern end). Venerable HB Warren (now owned by Sun Grocery), near the Parque Central in Coxen Hole, is the best supermarket in town, plus there's a small and not too impressive general market (Mercado Municipal) just behind Main Street. The biggest supermarkets on the island are the Eldon's Sun Grocery stores in French Harbour and Coxen Hole, and the Plaza Mar near the airport.

Hospitals Wood Medical Center in Coxen Hole (☎2445 1080) offers emergency care as well as inpatient and outpatient services.

GUANAJA

GUANAJA, some 25km long and just 4km wide at its largest point, is divided into two unequal parts by a narrow canal and surrounded by pristine coral reef. The only way to get around the island is by water taxi, which adds both to the atmosphere and, unfortunately, to the cost of living. The island is very thinly populated and receives relatively few travellers, though it's only 12km northeast of Roatán; this is one of the more idyllic, hidden treasures of Honduras, but it's not really a budget destination, at least as yet. Note that sandflies and mosquitoes are endemic throughout the island, so arrive prepared to deal with them.

WHAT TO SEE AND DO

Most of Guanaja's 10,000 inhabitants live in **Bonacca** (also known as **Guanaja Town**), a crowded settlement on a small caye a few hundred metres off the east coast. It's here that you'll find the island's shops, as well as the bulk of the less unreasonably priced accommodation. The only other settlements of any substance are **Savannah Bight** (on the northeast coast) and **Mangrove Bight** (on the northwest coast), connected by the only road on the island.

Bonacca

Wandering around the warren of tight streets, walkways and canal bridges in **BONACCA** makes for an interesting half-hour or so – though government plans to eliminate the town's tiny

5

waterways for new roads means it may not be the Honduran Venice for much longer. Virtually all the houses in town are built on stilts – vestiges of early settlement by Cayman Islanders – with the main causeway running for about 500m east–west along the cay.

Hiking

Though Guanaja's Caribbean pine forests were flattened by Hurricane Mitch in 1998, there's still some decent hiking to be found. A wonderful trail leads from Mangrove Bight up to **Michael Rock Peak**, the highest point in the Bay Islands (412m), and down to Sandy Bay on the south coast, affording stunning views of Guanaja, Bonacca and the surrounding reef. Fit walkers can do the trail in a day, or you can camp on the summit, provided you bring your own provisions.

Beaches

Some of the island's finest white-sand beaches lie around the rocky headland of **Michael's Rock**, near *Bo's Island House Resort* on the north coast, with good snorkelling close to the shore.

Diving

Diving is spectacular all around the main island, but particularly off the small cayes to the east, and at **Black Rocks**, off the northern tip of the main island, where there's an underwater coral canyon. The **Mestizo Dive**, off Soldado Beach, south of Michael's Rock, was opened in 2002 to mark the 500th anniversary of Christopher Columbus's visit, with sunken statues of the explorer and national hero Lempira on a reef surrounded by genuine Spanish colonial artefacts, including a cannon.

ARRIVAL AND DEPARTURE

By plane The Guanaja airport is on the larger, northern section of the island, next to the canal. If you have pre-booked a resort on the island you will be met at the airport. Aerocaribe, SOSA and Lanhsa (Mon–Sat 4–6 daily; 30min) have regular flights to/from La Ceiba (usually no flights Sunday); at the time of writing Lanhsa was also operating a once-weekly (Sat) flight from Roatán, but check the website or your hotel for the latest. Island Air (☎9558 8683, ⏾islandairhonduras .com) also operates flights on small planes between Utila, Roatán and Guanaja, as well as San Pedro Sula and La Ceiba.

INFORMATION AND TOURS

Bank You can change dollars and get cash advances at Banco Atlántida, southeast of the dock in Bonacca, though the ATM only dispenses L4000/day/card.

Tour operators To get to some of the underwater sites you'll have to contact one of the island's dive schools: *Bo's Island House Resort* usually has the best rates (single dives US$30–45), but there's also Guanaja Divers (⏾guanaja divers.com), on private Graham's Cay, a short boat ride (2.5km) from the main island (two-tank dives US$80).

ACCOMMODATION AND EATING

Bo's Island House Resort Near Michael's Rock ☎9991 0913, ⏾bosislandhouse.com. *Bo's* has clean, well-ventilated rooms, all with hot-water bathrooms. Rates include full board; good week-long diving packages available too. No TV, internet or phone reception, but free kayak use. Per person **US$90**

Manati Sandy Bay ☎2408 9830. Run by Roland's parents (see below) this German restaurant and bar is the best place to eat on the island, with excellent schnitzel, sausages and sauerkraut. Free wi-fi. Daily 11am–9pm.

Roland's Garden Guesthouse ☎9527 6880, ⏾rolandsgardenguesthouse.com. Popular B&B in a quiet, jungle location on Fruit Harbour Bight, powered by solar energy (including hot water) and run by German-born Roland (who also runs fabulous island tours). Rooms are clean and cosy, with bathrooms, kitchenette and breakfast on the balcony included. **US$80**

Nicaragua

HIGHLIGHTS

❶ León Hot sun, black volcanoes and a revolutionary past. **See p.467**

❷ Granada A tourist-friendly colonial jewel. See p.484

❸ San Juan del Sur Surf by day, party by night. See p.491

❹ Isla de Ometepe Hike mysterious twin volcanoes in Lago de Nicaragua. **See p.495**

❺ Río San Juan Pristine tropical forest and the El Castillo ruins. **See p.502**

❻ Little Corn Perfect, pint-sized Caribbean getaway. **See p.509**

HIGHLIGHTS ARE MARKED ON THE MAP ON P.449

ROUGH COSTS

Daily budget Basic US$20/occasional treat US$50

Drink Beer US$1, coffee US$0.50

Food *Comida corriente* US$3

Hostel/budget hotel US$7/US$16

Travel Managua–Chinandega (130km) by bus: 2hr, US$3

FACT FILE

Population 6 million

Languages Spanish, Creole and indigenous

Currency Nicaraguan córdoba (C$)

Capital Managua (population: 1.8 million)

International phone code ☏ 505

Time zone GMT -6hr

Introduction

Wedge-shaped Nicaragua may be the largest nation in Central America but, despite recent growth, it remains one of the least visited. Still, many travellers who spend any time here find that Nicaragua's extraordinary landscape of volcanoes, lakes, mountains and vast plains of rainforest helps make it their favourite country on the isthmus. Compared to the Maya ruins of Guatemala or the national parks of Costa Rica, Nicaragua offers few traditional tourist attractions – almost no ancient structures remain, and years of revolution, civil war and natural disasters have laid waste to museums, galleries and theatres – and a chronic lack of funding, high inflation and unemployment have impoverished the country's infrastructure. It's these same qualities, though, that make Nicaragua an incorrigibly vibrant and individualistic country, with plenty to offer travellers prepared to brave its grubby highways, cracked pavements and crammed public transport.

Virtually every visitor passes through the capital, **Managua**, if only to catch a bus straight out – while the city has an intriguing atmosphere and a few sights, it's hard work, and many quickly head for **Granada**, with its lakeside setting and wonderful colonial architecture. A smattering of **beaches** along the Pacific coast, notably cheery **San Juan del Sur**, continues to attract the **surfing** and backpacking crowds, while the beautiful **Corn Islands**, just off the coast of **Bluefields**, offer idyllic white-sand beaches framed by windswept palm trees and the azure Caribbean Sea. Culture and the arts are very much alive in Nicaragua, too; visit **Masaya**'s Mercado Nacional de Artesanía to find some fantastic-value high-quality crafts, or stay on the **Solentiname archipelago** and learn about the primitive painting traditions that have flourished there.

Buzzing **León** is often considered the country's cultural capital – look for the famous **murals** depicting Nicaragua's turbulent political history. Ecotourism, volcano-viewing and hiking are the attractions of the **Isla de Ometepe**, with its thrilling twin peaks rising out of the freshwater lake, while further east, up the lush Río San Juan, sits **El Castillo**, a small town with a great fortress. In the central region, where much of the country's export-grade coffee is grown, the climate is refreshingly cool; hiking and birdwatching are the main activities near the mountain town of **Matagalpa**.

Stepping off Nicaragua's beaten track is appealingly easy – the peaceful waters of the **Pearl Lagoon** and lush highlands of **Miraflor** reserve are fine spots for exploration, but really are just the tip of the iceberg. More than anything, the pleasures and rewards of travelling in Nicaragua come from interacting with its inhabitants

> **WHEN TO VISIT**
>
> Nicaragua has two distinct **seasons**: the dry summer (*verano*) and the wet winter (*invierno*). **Summer** (Dec–April) can be extremely hot and often uncomfortably dry. Fewer travellers come in the **rainy season** (May–Nov) – which alone could be a reason for choosing to put up with the daily downpour. On the **Pacific coast**, rain often falls in the afternoons from May to November, although the mornings are generally dry. The **central mountain region** has a cooler climate with sporadic rainfall all year, while the **Atlantic coast** is wet, hot and humid year-round, with September and October the height of the tropical storm season.

– who tend to be engagingly witty and very hospitable. This is a country where a bus journey can turn into a conversational epic and a light meal into a rum-soaked carnival, a stroll round the street can be interrupted by a costumed giant and a marching band, and a short boat ride can seem like a trip into another world.

CHRONOLOGY

1000 AD Aztec migrate south after the fall of Teotihuacán (Mexico), following a prophecy that they would settle where they found a lake with two volcanoes rising from it – Isla de Ometepe.

1522 The Spanish arrive and name the region "Nicaragua", after the indigenous groups living there.

1524 Spanish establish the settlements of Granada and León.

1821 Nicaragua gains independence from Spain as part of the Central American Federation.

1838 Nicaragua becomes an independent nation (save the Atlantic coast, which is claimed as British territory).

1855 American adventurer William Walker takes control of the government.

1857 Walker is overthrown by joint efforts of Nicaragua, Costa Rica, Guatemala and the US. He is later executed in Honduras.

1857–93 "The Thirty Years": a period of relative prosperity. US companies come to dominate the Nicaraguan government.

1893 General José Zelaya seizes control, establishing a dictatorship.

1909 Civil war breaks out. Four hundred US marines land on the Caribbean coast. Zelaya resigns.

1912–25 US military bases are established.

1927 Augusto Sandino leads a guerrilla campaign in protest at the US military presence. US takes over Nicaraguan military and develops Nicaraguan National Guard.

1934 Under orders of National Guard commander General Anastasio Somoza, Sandino is assassinated.

1937 Somoza "elected" president, commencing forty-year dictatorship.

1956 Somoza is assassinated by Rigoberto López Pérez. One of Somoza's sons, Luis, becomes interim president, and another, Anastasio, head of the National Guard.

1961 Frente Sandinista Liberación Nacional (FSLN), or Sandinista National Liberation Front, is founded.

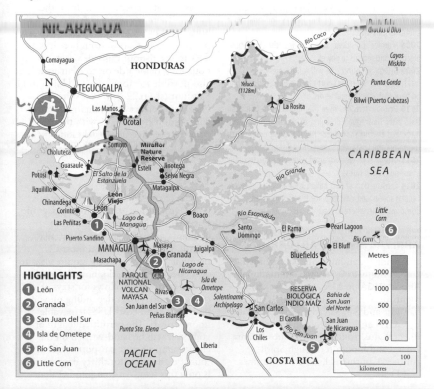

6

1967 Luis Somoza dies; his brother Anastasio becomes president.

1972 Massive earthquake flattens Managua, killing some 10,000.

1978 Opposition leader Pedro Chamorro is assassinated by National Guard; demonstrations and fighting spread across the country.

1979 Sandinistas gain control of the country, and Somoza is forced to flee. Revolution is officially won on July 19. Liberal Sandinistas are in control of government.

1981 Unhappy with Nicaragua's left-wing policies and communist ties, the US funds Contra troops in an anti-Sandinista campaign.

1984 FSLN's Daniel Ortega wins presidential election.

1988 FSLN and Contras sign a ceasefire.

1990 Violeta Chamorro defeats Daniel Ortega to become Latin America's first female president. US cuts off aid to Contras.

1996 Right-wing ex-lawyer Arnoldo Alemán, former mayor of Managua, becomes president.

1998 Hurricane Mitch devastates the region.

2001 Alemán's vice president, Enrique Bolaños, is elected.

2002–03 Alemán is jailed on charges of embezzlement and money laundering.

2004–05 The World Bank and Russia clear much of the country's debts, as part of the Heavily Indebted Poor Countries Initiative.

2006 Former president Ortega wins the November elections and returns to power.

2009 Ortega announces he will run for president in late 2011, after the Supreme Court lifts the constitutional ban on back-to-back electoral terms.

2010 Periodic tensions over the disputed Río San Juan flare after Nicaraguan dredging of the river. Troops are mobilized but no shots fired; the UN ruling orders both Nicaragua and Costa Rica to keep their distance.

2011 Ortega is re-elected, amid widespread accusations of voting irregularities.

2014 Construction of $50 billion Nicaragua Interoceanic Canal is announced, despite protests and many unanswered questions about where the financing is coming from.

ARRIVAL AND DEPARTURE

If arriving on an international flight, you'll land at **Augusto C. Sandino International Airport (MGA)** in Managua. As well as flights from neighbouring capitals such as San José and San Salvador (served mainly by COPA and TACA), Managua receives direct flights from major US hubs Atlanta, Miami and Houston through Spirit Airlines, Continental, American Airlines and Delta.

LAND AND SEA ROUTES TO NICARAGUA

Nicaragua shares borders with Costa Rica and Honduras. The busiest Nicaraguan land entry/exit point is at Peñas Blancas (see box, p.171), on the southern border with **Costa Rica**. Los Chiles in Costa Rica provides a water crossing further east, to San Carlos on the Río San Juan, and at the time this guide went to print, a land crossing at San Carlos was on schedule to be opened in 2015. The two main border crossings with **Honduras** in the north, meanwhile, are at Guasaule and El Espino (see box, p.396) and Las Manos (see box, p.394), with the latter providing the quickest access to Tegucigalpa.

You can enter Nicaragua by land from Honduras and Costa Rica (see box, above). International **buses** pull into Managua, often via Granada and Rivas (if coming from the south); it's also possible to take local services to and from the border. There is a **water crossing** from the border at Los Chiles, Costa Rica (see box, p.177), to San Carlos; from here it is a five- to seven-hour bus ride or an hour-long plane ride on to Managua. It is also possible to cross from La Unión in El Salvador (see p.228) to Potosí in Nicaragua, either by arranging to cross with local fishermen, or with the passenger service Cruce del Golfo (US$65; ⊛rutadelgolfo.com).

VISAS

As part of the **CA-4 agreement** (see box, p.30), visitors are granted ninety days of travel within Nicaragua, Honduras, Guatemala and El Salvador. Australian, British, Canadian, US and most EU nationals do not currently require **visas** to visit Nicaragua. You do, however, need a **tourist card**, which allows for stays of thirty to ninety days depending on your nationality and costs US$10 (payable upon arrival). The permitted length of your visit will be hand-written on the entry stamp in your passport; while all tourist cards allow for thirty days' entry, it is only this hand-written number that counts. If coming on a one-way ticket from the US you may be asked to provide proof of when you will be leaving Nicaragua (eg, a bus ticket to Costa Rica).

GETTING AROUND

Public transport, especially buses, is geared toward the domestic population. It's very cheap but quite uncomfortable.

BY BUS

The standard local **buses** in Nicaragua are the usual old North American school buses, though an increasing number of express minibuses and coaches also serve the more popular routes – only a few córdobas more, they are less crowded, stop less frequently and occasionally even have air conditioning. Most **intercity buses** (regular, non-express services are called *ruteados*) begin running between 4am and 7am, departing about every thirty minutes, or when the bus is full, with last buses leaving by 5 or 6pm. **Bus stops** are usually at the local market – only Estelí and Managua have anything approximating a modern terminal – and fares are very cheap. You'll pay US$1–4 for anything up to three or four hours, with longer journeys to the Atlantic coast costing up to US$20. There is often a list of fares displayed at the front of the bus. You can usually keep your **luggage** with you, although especially on busy services it may end up on the roof or in a pile at the back of the bus. It should be safe, but it's worth keeping valuables on your person. Most buses have a conductor and a helper (*ayudante*) as well as a driver – in most instances, you'll pay the conductor once the bus is moving. If you

SHUTTLES

Nicaragua's buses are cheap and safe, but if you're in a group, in a rush, or want to travel later in the day you may want to consider a **shuttle** – cars or minibuses that head between the tourist hotspots. The trip from Managua airport to San Juan del Sur, for example, will set you back around US$65 between two or US$130 among six – compared to US$2.50 on the slow bus (though you'd also need to make your way across town from the airport to the bus station – around US$5 per person in a taxi, whereas a shuttle will take you straight to/from the airport). Most tour companies can arrange this, or try the shuttle companies direct at ⓦtravel jinotega.com, ⓦadelanteexpress.com or ⓦpaxeos.com.

have a lot of luggage, you may be charged extra, but it should never be more than the price of a single fare to your destination.

Timetables for key routes can be viewed on ⓦthebusschedule.com. Alternatively, your accommodation should be able to fill you in.

BY TAXI

Taxis – many on their last legs – are most often seen in cities, but they also make long-distance journeys; a good deal, especially if in a group. In Managua, most taxi fares are US$2–4 during the day and US$3–7 at night. Outside the capital, in-town fares vary, but are usually around US$0.50–1. Always agree on the fare before getting into the cab, and don't be afraid to haggle if the rate seems high – at Managua's bus terminals, overcharging foreigners is the norm.

ADDRESSES IN NICARAGUA

Nicaraguan towns are usually set up on a vague **grid system**, with a commercial build-up around the *parque central* and main streets, and residential neighbourhoods sprawling outwards from the centre. Only main streets are labelled with signs, and smaller towns do not have any street names at all, depending instead on their direction from the main square: calles go east–west and avenidas north–south, with a central calle and avenida acting as the grid's axis. Calles and avenidas **northeast** of the main park are generally designated *noreste* (NE), those **northwest** are *noroeste* (NO), **southeast** are *sureste* (SE) and southwest *suroeste* (SO). There is also no set numbering system for streets in Nicaraguan towns. Addresses refer to locations' proximity to **local landmarks**, such as churches, roundabouts, shopping centres, banks, restaurants and petrol stations.

6

BY CAR

Renting a car is probably the best way to explore the country's many beaches. Rates average US$40 a day for the cheapest models (including basic, obligatory insurance). Outside Managua and the main west-coast highway, you'll want something robust and preferably 4WD. Rental is most reliable in Managua – Alamo, Avis, Hertz and Thrifty all have offices at the airport. You need a valid licence, passport and a credit card. Make sure you take out full-cover **insurance**. Bear in mind when driving that road signage is quite poor, and you'll need to ask directions frequently. And as with other Central American countries, don't drive at night – it's less a question of crime than the lack of lighting, which disguises potholes, sudden deviations in the road or even the road disappearing altogether, as well as cattle straying onto the highway.

Although it's generally safe to **hitch** a ride with a pick-up truck (but not advisable otherwise), it's only common among locals in the countryside where there is little or no other transport. Most pick-up trucks will happily stop and let you jump in the back – just bang on the roof when you want to get off. If you're driving in the countryside yourself, it's almost rude not to stop and pick up people walking in the same direction.

BY BOAT

Boats provide vital links around Nicaragua's numerous waterways and two large lakes. On the Atlantic coast, they are the main means of transport. For travellers the most useful routes are those between Bluefields and either Pearl Lagoon or El Rama (both of which are served by small boats called *pangas*), and the cargo boat which goes between Granada and San Carlos, stopping at Ometepe. San Carlos can also be accessed by boat from the border crossing at Los Chiles.

BY PLANE

Nicaragua's domestic airline, La Costeña (☎ 2298 5360, ⊚ lacostena.online.com .ni), operates fairly reliable **flights** around the country, with Managua the inevitable hub. Routes run from the capital to locations including San Carlos, Bluefields, the Corn Islands and Puerto Cabezas (the latter two are hard to reach *without* flying), and also run from Bluefields to the Corn Islands and Puerto Cabezas. A return will set you back US$120–180, and can be bought by phone or online, as well as at the airport.

If the flight is full, there's a chance you'll be **bumped** – rare but not inconceivable, especially if you're travelling to or from the Corn Islands around Christmas or Easter. To be safe, call the airport you're departing from (numbers are given throughout the Guide) the day before you fly to confirm your booking. If you are bumped, your reservation will be valid for the next flight. Luggage occasionally gets left behind, especially on the smallest planes, but is almost always on the next scheduled arrival.

ACCOMMODATION

Most budget travellers to Nicaragua at some point find themselves in a Nicaraguan **hospedaje** – a small and usually pretty basic *pensión*-type hotel, most often family-owned and -run. Simple *hospedajes* charge around US$10–15 for a double. For this you get a bed and fan; in many places you'll have to share a bathroom, and breakfast is not normally included. **Hostels** (US$5–10 for a dorm bed) are common in backpacker hotspots like León and Granada but rare elsewhere. **Hotels** (from US$20) tend to be more luxurious, with air conditioning, cable TV and services like tours and car rental; you are less likely to see these in very small towns. **Camping** is pretty rare thanks to the low cost of accommodation. If you're determined to camp, the most promising areas are beach spots around San Juan del Sur, Isla de Ometepe and the Corn Islands.

FOOD AND DRINK

As in the rest of Central America, **lunch** (around 11.30am–1.30pm) is the main meal. Central markets in Nicaraguan towns are guaranteed to have snack spots, with several small **comedores** or **cafetines** offering cheap **comida corriente** (everyday food) – a set lunch of meat, rice and salad, for around US$3. Throughout the country **street-side kiosks** sell hot meals; you'll soon become familiar with their plastic tablecloths, paper plates and huge bowls of cabbage salad. The food is cheap – around US$2 – but generally well prepared. **Restaurants** are more expensive (around US$6), and generally open daily for lunch and dinner from noon to 9pm in smaller towns and until 11pm in cities.

Nicaraguan **cuisine** is based around the ubiquitous **beans**, **rice** and **meat**, and everything is cooked with oil. Lunch usually includes **chicken**, **beef** or **pork**, most deliciously cooked *a la plancha*, on a grill or griddle, and served with beans, rice, plantain and shredded cabbage salad. For breakfast and dinner the rice and beans are generally fried together to make **gallo pinto**, served with an egg for breakfast or **cuajada** (curd cheese) for dinner. Roast chicken, pizza and Chinese food also crop up in the bigger towns.

On the Atlantic coast the cuisine becomes markedly more **Caribbean**. Here rice is often cooked in mild coconut milk, and the staple fresh **coconut bread** is delicious. **Rondon** is a stew of *yuca*, *chayote* and other vegetables cooked in coconut milk, usually with fish added, which is traditionally eaten at weekends. In the rest of the country weekends are the time to eat **nacatamales**, parcels of corn dough filled with vegetables, pork, beef or chicken, which are wrapped in a banana leaf and steamed for several hours, or **baho** – beef, plantain and *yuca* slow-cooked in a huge pot.

Tropical **fruit** is abundant, cheap and delicious, and throughout the country you'll see **ice cream**-sellers pushing their Eskimo carts. The quality isn't great, but you will find an extraordinary range of flavours, including many made with local fruits and nuts.

DRINK

Given Nicaragua's heat, it's just as well that there's a huge range of cold drinks, or **refrescos** (usually shortened to *frescos*),

available. These are made from grains, seeds and fruits, which are liquidized with milk or water. Some unusual ones to look for include *cebada*, a combination of ground barley and barley grains mixed with milk, coloured pink and flavoured with cinnamon and lots of sugar; *pinolillo*, a spiced corn and cacao drink; and *semilla de jícaro* (or "hickory seed"), which looks and tastes a bit like chocolate. Just about every fruit imaginable is made into a *fresco*, including watermelon, passion fruit, papaya, *pitaya* (dragon fruit) and melon.

You might want to ask whether your *fresco* is made with purified water, as **tap water** is generally worth avoiding, especially outside major cities. Alongside a fairly standard mix of soft drinks, **bottled water** is found everywhere; if you buy a drink to take away it will usually come in a plastic bag – bite off the corner, and you're off. Nicaragua has two local brands of **beer**, Victoria and Toña, both light and refreshing lagers. For spirits, it is common in bars to buy local Flor de Caña **rum** by the bottle. It comes in dark and white, gold, old, dry and light, and is an excellent buy at just US$5–10 per bottle. It's usually brought to the table with a large bucket of ice and lemons, but you can mix it with soft drinks for something a little less potent.

CULTURE AND ETIQUETTE

Nicaraguans are generally courteous and appreciate this trait in visitors, and it is considered polite to address strangers with "Usted" rather than "Tú" (or its local form "Vos"). You will often hear the term *Adiós* (literally, "to God") used as a greeting – hardly surprising in a country where ninety percent of the population is Christian. The older generations in particular are often religiously conservative in appearance and manner. *Machista* attitudes are still prevalent, and female travellers, especially those travelling solo, may be harassed by catcalls from local (usually young) men; this is best ignored.

With regard to **tipping**, posher restaurants, especially the tourist dens of

6

NICARAGUAN WORDS AND PHRASES

Adiós Used as a greeting in passing, as well as the standard "goodbye"

Chele/a ("che-le"/"che-la") White or pale-skinned person

Dale pues ("dah-leh pweh") Literally, "give it, then", it's used to say "OK", "go on", "fine", "it's on", etc

Naksa/Aisabi "Hello"/"Goodbye" in the Miskito language

Granada and León, will add a ten- to fifteen-percent service charge to the bill – you don't have to pay it. If someone carries your bag, they'll probably expect C$5–10 for their trouble. Outside of the tourist areas, most Nicaraguans don't tip and taxi drivers don't expect a tip.

Haggling is the norm in markets and with street vendors, but not in shops.

SPORTS AND OUTDOOR ACTIVITIES

Nicaragua's national sport is **baseball**, and every town has a field and numerous, active leagues. Ask your local taxi driver about league games, for which most of the town will turn out in support. **Football** (soccer) is played by children in the street, but lacks the popularity here that it has in other Latin countries.

Visiting **surfers** are drawn to the country's Pacific coast, where there seems to be an endless run of deserted beaches with great breaks; the most popular area (with good tourist amenities) is around **San Juan del Sur**, near the Costa Rican border – you'll find the most surf camps, teachers, and board sales or rentals in this area. Nicaragua also offers excellent **hiking**, with stunning volcanoes, like those on **Isla de Ometepe** and mountains around Estelí and Matagalpa. On the Atlantic coast, **diving** and **snorkelling** are a must, particularly on the **Corn Islands**, where you can reach wrecks and reefs from right off the beach. Nicaragua is also the only country in the world currently offering **volcano-boarding** – using a customized plank to ride the ashes on the Cerro Negro volcano near León.

COMMUNICATIONS

Most towns have **post offices** (generally Mon–Fri 8am–5pm, Sat 8am–noon), although there are few on the Atlantic coast. A postcard to the US is C$15, C$20 to Europe.

There are virtually no coin-operated **phones** in Nicaragua, and you're best off using phones in internet cafés or *pulperías* (small neighbourhood shops), where the shop owner will "hire" use of his phone out to you. Phone numbers within Nicaragua changed from seven to eight digits a few years back, but you'll still see some in the old format – just add a "2" (landline) or "8" (mobile) to the number. Calling Nicaragua from abroad, the **country code** is ☏ 505.

If you decide not to bring your own phone, you could buy a **mobile phone** for as little as US$15; Movistar (Ⓜ movistar .com) and Claro (Ⓦ claro.com.ni) have pay-as-you-go packages. Both have an outlet in the airport.

You'll find **internet cafés** in even the smallest towns. Rates – generally C$10–15 per hour – often rise in smaller or more remote towns, where connections can also be painfully slow. **Wi-fi** is increasingly common, even in cheaper accommodation, and is usually free for customers. If you bring a laptop, you might want to buy a **surge protector**, as power surges can happen. As a precaution, unplug anything electrical if the electricity goes off; most surges happen when it comes back on.

CRIME AND SAFETY

Nicaragua is the second-poorest country in the Americas, and unemployment is rife. You'll almost certainly encounter street kids, but you're far more likely to be greeted with courtesy than aggression, and Nicaragua remains **safer** than many of its neighbours. You should take care in Managua, however (see box, p.457).

The **police** in Nicaragua are generally reliable, but watch out for the traffic police (*policía de tránsito*), who are infamous for targeting foreigners and who will take any chance to threaten you with a fine (*multa*) in the hope that you'll

6

pay them off. Often even ordinary police officers will try stopping you, but if they are not traffic police, they can't fine you, so stand your ground. To **report a crime** you must go to the nearest police station. If you need a police report for an insurance claim, the police will ask you to fill out a *denuncia* – a full report of the incident. If the police station does not have the *denuncia* forms, ask for a *constancia*, a simpler form, signed and stamped by the police. This should be sufficient for an insurance claim.

Visitors to Nicaragua should in theory carry their **passports** on them at all times, though checks are rare and a photocopy is usually acceptable.

STREET CRIME

Petty theft can be a problem – keep an eye on your bags and pockets, especially on buses. **Muggings** have occurred in tourist stretches like the beaches of San Juan del Sur and at day-trip destinations around Granada – your accommodation should be able to advise you, and cabs are plentiful. Larger hotels will have safes where you can leave valuables.

Wherever you are, **women** should be wary of going out alone at night, though the chief threat is being verbally harrassed by groups of drunken men; while unpleasant, if you ignore this the situation is unlikely to escalate.

HEALTH

Serious medical situations should be attended to at a **hospital** – most towns and cities have one. In an emergency, if possible, head to Managua. Failing this, find a Red Cross (Cruz Roja) post, health centre (*centro de salud*) or pharmacy (*farmacia*) for advice. **Pharmacies** are generally open daily between 8am and 5pm, and in each town they take turns to stay open all night; in an emergency out of hours ask which pharmacy *esta de turno* (is on duty).

INFORMATION AND MAPS

The national tourist board, **INTUR** (🌐 intur.gob.ni), has **information** offices throughout the country, with the largest in Managua. Although staff are usually friendly, they generally only speak Spanish and can't offer much besides colourful leaflets. They may stock *Anda Ya!*, a free quarterly booklet that's packed with advertorial, but also has some useful maps and details of bus times. Tourist information centres and most hotels have free **maps** which come with lots of advertisements but are generally accurate.

MONEY AND BANKS

Nicaragua's **currency** is the **córdoba** (C$), which is divided into 100 centavos; at the time of writing, the exchange rate was C$26.5 to US$1, but it devaluates at a set rate each day; check the current rate at 🌐 bcn.gob.ni. Notes come in denominations of 10, 20, 50, 100, 200 and 500 córdobas; coins come in denominations of 1, 5 and 10 córdobas, and 25 and 50 centavos. Get rid of C$500 notes when you can, as they can be difficult to change. Small US dollar bills are accepted for most transactions, as long as they are not marked or torn, and accommodation and tour prices are usually quoted in dollars – although US$100 bills can usually only be changed at a bank.

6

Banks are usually open Monday to Friday from 8am to 4pm; many are also open on Saturday mornings until noon. Most will change US dollars, and some change euros, and colones (from Costa Rica) but no other currency.

Moneychangers (*coyotes*) operate in the street, usually at the town market, and are generally reliable – though it helps to have an idea of what you expect to get back before approaching them.

Travellers' cheques are only changed by the Banco de América Central (**BAC**) – even here you'll struggle with anything but US-dollar cheques – and they're probably not worth bothering with.

Credit cards such as Visa, MasterCard and Amex are generally accepted in more expensive hotels and restaurants and can also be used to pay for car rental, flights and tours. BAC, Bancentro, Banco ProCredit and Banpro's **ATMs** all accept foreign-issue cards, and in most reasonable-sized towns you will find at least one of these, distributing cash in dollars or córdobas. That said, you can't rely on ATMs alone and, especially out of the major centres, you'll have little alternative but to carry a decent amount of cash. There are currently no ATMs on Little Corn Island or Solentiname, or in Pearl Lagoon or San Juan de Nicaragua.

OPENING HOURS AND PUBLIC HOLIDAYS

Many shops and **services** in Nicaragua observe Sunday closing: on weekdays you'll find most places open from 8am to 4pm, and on Saturdays from 8am to noon. **Businesses**, **museums** and **sites**

---

close for lunch, normally between noon and 2pm, before reopening again until 4 or 5pm. Supermarkets, smaller grocery shops and the small neighbourhood shops called *pulperías* or *ventas* generally stay open until 8pm.

Bars and **restaurants** tend to close around 11pm or midnight, except for nightclubs – most of which are in Managua – which stay open until 2am or later. Public holidays (see box above) see almost everything shut down, so don't plan on visiting tourist attractions over those dates.

FESTIVALS

Nicaragua's calendar includes plenty of **festivals**, from local events to national fiestas and raucous *hípicas* (horse parades). In addition, each town in Nicaragua has its own patron saint whose saint's day is observed with processions and celebrations – these may well combine old customs inherited from the Aztecs with mestizo traditions, including the masked *viejitos* ("old ones" – young and old alike wearing masks of old men and women). Nicaraguans also love to dance, and you will probably see folkloric dances in the streets, usually performed by children. The calendar here lists just a few highlights.

March–April At Easter the whole country packs up and goes to the beach: buses are crammed, hotel rooms are at a premium, and flights to the Corn Islands are fully booked. Semana Santa (Holy Week) processions, in which crowds follow *pasos* (depictions of Christ and the Virgin), are the biggest in Granada.

May The Atlantic coastal town of Bluefields celebrates Palo de Mayo, an adapted May Day fiesta flavoured with Caribbean reggae and soca – a fusion of dance and folklore.

July 19 The holiday marking the Revolution is still celebrated ardently by Sandinistas and is usually accompanied by parades and marches. In Managua, the Plaza de la Revolución fills with Sandinista supporters, who gather in memory of the historical events.

December 31 Throughout much of the country, New Year's Eve is mainly celebrated in the home, although San Juan del Sur is known for drawing a crowd of young revellers. Bear in mind you'll find most things closed on January 1.

PUBLIC HOLIDAYS

Jan 1 New Year's Day
Easter week Semana Santa
May 1 Labour Day
May 30 Mother's Day
July 19 Anniversary of the Revolution
Sept 14 Battle of San Jacinto
Sept 15 Independence Day
Nov 2 All Souls' Day (Día de los Muertos)
Dec 7 & 8 Inmaculada Concepción
Dec 25 Christmas

Managua and around

Hotter than sin and crisscrossed by anonymous highways, there can't be a more visitor-unfriendly capital than **MANAGUA**. Less a city in the conventional sense than a conglomeration of neighbourhoods and commercial districts, Managua offers few sights and cultural experiences – in fact, most visitors are so disturbed by the lack of street names and any real centre that they get out as fast as they can.

Not even the city's setting on the southern shore of **Lago de Managua** is particularly pleasant: the area is low lying, swampy and flat, relieved only by a few eroded volcanoes. It also, unfortunately, sits on top of an astounding eleven **seismic faults**, which have shaken the city severely over time. The result has been a cycle of ruin and rebuilding, which has created a bizarre and postmodern mixture of crumbling ruins inhabited by squatters, hastily constructed concrete structures and gleaming new shopping malls and hotels. The old city centre, damaged further in the **Revolution** of 1978–79 and never thoroughly repaired, remains eerily abandoned.

All this said, there *are* things to enjoy here, although being a tourist in Managua does require a good degree of tenacity. As Nicaragua's largest city and home to a quarter of its population, the city occupies a key position in the nation's economy and psyche, and offers more practical services than anywhere else in the country.

WHAT TO SEE AND DO

For the visitor, sprawling Managua can thankfully be divided into a few distinct areas. The **old ruined centre** on the lakeshore is the site of the city's tourist attractions, including the few impressive colonial-style buildings that have survived all the earthquakes. **Lago de Managua**, which forms such a pretty backdrop to this part of the city, is unfortunately severely **polluted** from sewage and regular dumpings of waste.

Just to the south is the city's main landmark, the **Crowne Plaza Hotel**, whose white form, reminiscent of a Maya pyramid, sails above the city. Walking just west of the *Crowne Plaza* and twelve or so blocks south of the old ruined city centre brings you to the backpacker-frequented **Barrio Martha Quezada**, home to tech bottom units and international bus connections. A further 1km south, around **Plaza España**, you'll find many of the city's banks, airline offices and a well-stocked La Colonia supermarket. In the southeast of the city, a new commercial district has grown up along the **Carretera a Masaya**, the main thoroughfare through the southern part of the city. East of here lie the **Metrocentro** shopping centre and upmarket residential suburb of **Altamira**.

6

SAFETY IN MANAGUA

Managua has its problems with poverty, theft and violence. The areas around the **Carretera a Masaya** are relatively clean and safe, while many locals will warn you away from hostel-packed **Barrio Martha Quezada**. Like most of the city, however, that district is safe enough to **walk around** in the daytime, if sketchy in the evening. **Cabs** are a good idea anyway, given Managua's perplexing layout and their low prices, and are worth investing in at night, especially if you're on your own.

That said, cab-based **express muggings** have occurred. If in doubt, don't get into a packed cab or one without a red-and-white number plate, try to sit in the front and, if you don't like the look of something, don't be afraid to find another vehicle – the vast majority of drivers want nothing more than to overcharge you slightly, and seeking one out yourself is a better bet than letting yourself be directed into one. Away from the main terminals you're on safer ground catching a cab, and if they open the door to let another passenger in, don't panic – shared rides are the norm.

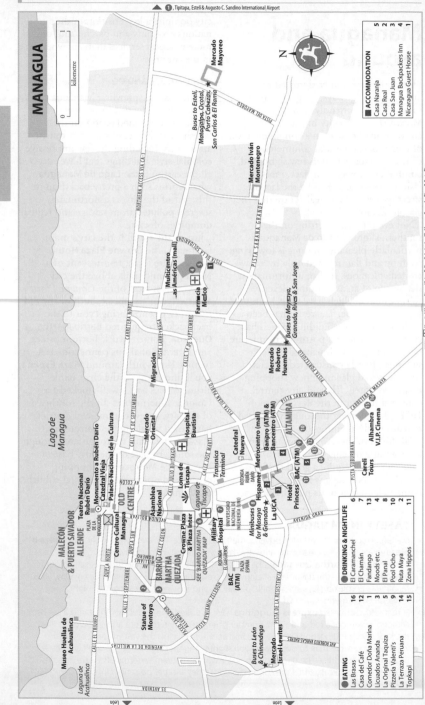

MANAGUA

0 — kilometre — 1

1, Tipitapa, Estelí & Augusto C. Sandino International Airport

Lago de Managua

Laguna de Acahualinca

Museo Huellas de Acahualinca

MALECÓN & PUERTO SAVADOR ALLENDE

Teatro Nacional Rubén Darío

Monumento a Rubén Darío

Catedral Vieja

Palacio Nacional de la Cultura

Centro Cultural Managua

Asamblea Nacional

OLD CENTRE

Statue of Montoya

Mercado Israel Lewites

Buses to León & Chinandega

BARRIO MARTHA QUEZADA

Military Hospital

Crowne Plaza & Plaza Inter

Laguna de Tiscapa

Loma de Tiscapa

Mercado Oriental

Migración

Hospital Bautista

Catedral Nueva

La UCA

Hotel Princess

Transnica Terminal

Minibuses for Masaya & Granada

Hispamer

Banpro (ATM) & Bancentro (ATM)

Metrocentro (mall)

BAC (ATM)

ALTAMIRA

Careli Tours

Alhambra V.I.P. Cinema

Mercado Roberto Huembes

Buses to Moyogalpa, Granada, Rivers & San Jorge

Multicentro as Américas (mall)

Farmacia Medco

Mercado Iván Montenegro

Mercado Mayoreo

Buses to Estelí, Matagalpa, Ocotal, Porto Cabezas, San Carlos & El Rama

Hospital Metropolitano Vivian Pellas, Galerías (mall), Masaya, Granada, Rivers & Costa Rica

● **EATING**

Las Brasas	16
Casa del Café	12
Comedor Doña Marina	1
Licuados Ananda	3
La Original Taquiza	5
Pizzería Valenti's	9
La Terraza Peruana	14
Topkapi	15

● **DRINKING & NIGHTLIFE**

El Caramanchel	6
El Chamán	7
Fandango	13
Moods etc.	4
El Panal	8
Pool Ocho	10
Ruta Maya	2
Zona Hippos	11

■ **ACCOMMODATION**

Casa Naranja	5
Casa Real	2
Casa San Juan	3
Managua Backpackers Inn	4
Nicaragua Guest House	1

6

Plaza de la Revolución

At the heart of the old centre is **Plaza de la Revolución**, a battered, intriguing and often eerily empty square flanked by city landmarks, including the cathedral ruins, the Palacio Nacional and the park containing **Carlos Fonseca's tomb** (marked by an eternal flame). The tomb, which serves as a memorial to the FSLN founder, is fringed by a row of huge black-and-red flags. Each year on July 19 thousands of Sandinista supporters make a pilgrimage to the area, paying homage to the Revolution and the ensuing movement.

Catedral Vieja

On the eastern side of the Plaza de la Revolución stands the wreckage of the ash-grey Catedral Santiago de los Caballeros. Known as the **Catedral Vieja**, the ruins are a compelling and oddly romantic monument to a destroyed city. Birds fly through the interior, where semi-exposed murals and leaning stone angels with cracked wings still line the walls. Plans to restore the cathedral are continually being shelved; for now, the building remains officially closed to visitors.

Palacio Nacional de La Cultura

The lovely blue-marble and cream-stucco exterior of the **Palacio Nacional**, on the south side of the plaza, holds a darker history. During the long years of Somoza rule the columned building was the seat of government power: Colombian writer Gabriel García Márquez called it "*el partenón bananero*" – the banana parthenon. Then, on August 22, 1978, Sandinista commandos disguised as National Guard soldiers ran through its corridors to capture the deputies of the National Assembly, a cinematic coup d'état that effectively brought down the Somoza dictatorship.

Today, the Palacio, still a functioning government building, also houses the national library and archives, while the ground floor intersperses small, relaxing gardens with a **museum and art gallery** (Tues–Fri 8am–5pm, Sat & Sun 9am–4pm; C$80). There's a good display of Nicaraguan handicrafts, colourful murals and large sculptures, plus a few pre-Columbian artefacts. The museum frequently holds dance, poetry and *artesanía* events; ask at reception.

Teatro Nacional Rubén Darío

Perched like a huge white futurist bird north of the Plaza de la Revolución, the **Teatro Nacional Rubén Darío** (show times vary; **⊙** 2222 7426, **⊛** tnrubendario.gob.ni) is Managua's main cultural venue, hosting foreign and Nicaraguan theatre, dance and opera groups. It's worth going inside just to see the massive chandeliers, marble floors and stirring view out to the lake from the enormous windows upstairs. There is a small permanent art exhibition in the foyer (free), and theatre buffs might be interested in a tour (Mon–Fri

---

NAVIGATING MANAGUA

In a city where nobody uses **street names** (if they actually exist) or addresses, it's helpful to have your destination given to you in terms of neighbourhood and distance from a **landmark** – taxi drivers will most easily find places in relation to a well-known city fixture. For destinations around Barrio Martha Quezada, use the *Crowne Plaza*, Tica Bus terminal or Montoya statue as a reference point; the Metrocentro shopping centre and La Unión supermarket are useful landmarks around Zona Hippos and Los Robles.

Distances are measured in metres as much as in blocks – in local parlance, 100m is a city block, or **cuadra**. Sometimes an archaic measure, the **vara**, is also used: one vara (a yard) is interpreted as roughly equivalent to a metre. To confuse the issue still further, many Managuans do not use the cardinal points in their usual form: north becomes *al lago* – towards the lake; *al sur* is south; *arriba* – literally, "up" – is to the east (where the sun rises); and *abajo*, "down", is to the west (where the sun sets). So, *del Inter* (*Hotel InterContinental*, now the *Crowne Plaza*, although many people still use its old name) *una cuadra arriba y dos cuadras al lago*" means one block east and two blocks north of the *Crowne Plaza*.

9am–noon & 1-4pm; call ahead), which takes you around otherwise closed parts of the building. South of the theatre is the **Monumento a Rubén Darío**, a striking sculpted memorial to the famous poet (see box, p.469).

Malecón

North of the theatre, an attempt has been made to spruce up the previously seedy lakeshore boardwalk, or **malecón**, with bars and food kiosks, plus a couple of fairground rides. A statue of Latin American liberator **Simón Bolívar** sits in the middle of the nearby roundabout, guarding the shorefront's entrance. The area gets quite lively at weekends, though it's fairly deserted during the week except for ambling teenage couples. There are pleasant views to the north, where **Volcán Mombotombo** and **Mombotombito** sit side by side against the horizon on the far shore of the lake, 50km away. Just south of the *malecón* is the **Plaza de la Fe San Juan Pablo II**, a large square whose central obelisk commemorates Pope John Paul II's two visits to Nicaragua.

El Puerto Salvador Allende

Carry on along the waterfront and you come to the shiny new area of El Puerto Salvador Allende. There is a C$5 charge and the area is patrolled by security guards for extra safety, which makes this area great for an evening out. There are a number of restaurants serving similar local dishes (chicken or beef C$200; fish C$250; beer C$26). On weekends a ferry service takes passengers on a cruise on the lake (3, 5 & 7pm; 1hr 30min; C$180).

Museo Huellas de Acahualinca

Volcán Mombotombo's capacity for destruction is evoked in the **Museo Huellas de Acahualinca** (daily 8.30am–4pm; US$4, $1 to take photos), 1.5km west of the *malecón* in Barrio Acahualinca (take a taxi or bus #112). A rudimentary affair, it nonetheless offers a fascinating glimpse into the area's history. Alongside fragments of pottery and boards on fauna and geology, a series of great pits reveals animal and human footprints from prehistoric nomads – preserved in volcanic ash, the footprints have been dated to around 6000 years ago.

Loma de Tiscapa

Directly behind the landmark *Crowne Plaza*, you can get some perspective on both Managua's dramatic history and its weird, battered cityscape in the **Loma de Tiscapa**, or Tiscapa Historical National Park (Mon–Sat 7am–5.30pm, Sun 9am–5.30pm; US$1). The fifteen-minute walk up the hill takes you via a series of

BARRIO MARTHA QUEZADA

Old Centre

N

Montoya Statue

CALLE COLON

CALLE 27 DE MAYO

@ Cine Dorado (closed)

CALLE 8A

AVENIDA WILLIAMS ROMERO

AVENIDA 10A

CALLE 9A

AVENIDA 8A

AVENIDA 7A

AVENIDA 5A

CALLE 9A

Tica Bus terminal

CALLE 10A

AVENIDA 4A

AVENIDA 3A

King Quality bus terminal

AVENIDA 2A

AVENIDA BOLIVAR

Crowne Plaza Hotel

ℹ️

Monumento Roosevelt

0   300
metres

Plaza España

Loma de Tiscapa

ACCOMMODATION
Apartamentos Los Cisneros	3
Casa Castillo	1
Casa Gabrinma	7
Casa de Huéspedes Santos	2
Los Felipe	5
Hostal Dulce Sueño	6
Hostal Palmerita	4

● EATING				● DRINKING & NIGHTLIFE			
Café Mirna	8	Jimmy 'Three Fingers'		La Casa de Los		El Viajero	4
Comida a la Vista	3	Alabama Rib Shack	7	Mejía Godoy	5		
El Grillito	6	Típico Doña Pilar	2	Q	1		

posters detailing the rise and fall of Somoza's National Guard, then past the elegant white pillars of the Monumento Roosevelt and a decapitated statue of Justice before winding round and up to a silhouetted statue of **Sandino**. Nearby lie a tank and statue donated to Somoza by Mussolini. Photos detail the disastrous earthquakes of 1931 and 1972, while a display in the tunnels of the former prison goes into gory details of Somoza's infamous *noches de tortura* (torture nights).

The **views** of the city from here are excellent, stretching north to Lago de Nicaragua and the distant volcanoes and south beyond the new cathedral towards Masaya. Adventurous types can enjoy them on a so-called **canopy tour** (Tues–Sun 8.30am–5pm; US$17.25; ☏ 8872 2555) from the top of the hill. Three cables cover more than 1km, allowing you to glide high above the city and the picturesque – but polluted – **Laguna Tiscapa**, which sits below the Loma de Tiscapa's summit.

Carretera a Masaya and the Metrocentro

About 1km south of the laguna lies Managua's biggest concentration of residential and commercial neighbourhoods and most of its westernized nightlife. The main thoroughfare through this part of the city is the **Carretera a Masaya**, hemmed in to the east by the embassy neighbourhood of Altamira and to the west by La UCA, or the Universidad Centroamericana. It's on this road, just south of Pista Juan Pablo II, where you'll find the bland but blissfully cool **Metrocentro** shopping centre, which offers shops, ATMs, a food court, banks, a cinema and the *InterContinental Metrocentro* hotel. Further south along the carretera you'll come to the newer and bigger Galerías Santo Domingo, complete with a cinema with a VIP screen which has reclining seats and waiter service, and a selection of restaurants and bars.

Catedral Nueva

A short walk from the Metrocentro shopping centre, in the middle of a field, is the Catedral Metropolitana de la Purísima Concepción, known simply as the **Catedral Nueva** (usually daily 6.30am–6pm), a striking and brutal piece of architecture whose roof resembles a collection of large concrete hand-grenades. Inside there's a bleeding figure of Christ encased in glass, but the milling worshippers are more compelling than the cavernous interior.

ARRIVAL AND DEPARTURE

As the transport hub of the country, Managua is virtually impossible to avoid. From here you can get almost anywhere by bus, while flights put the otherwise inaccessible parts of the country on the map.

BY PLANE

Airport The Augusto C. Sandino International Airport is 11km east of Managua; on arrival, you'll have to pay US$10 for a tourist card (see p.29). Designated airport taxis wait just outside the terminal doors; reportedly safer than normal taxis, and always a/c, these charge US$15–20 for journeys to most parts of the city. If you cross the street from the airport you can catch a normal taxi, which shouldn't cost more than US$9. There are also a couple of tour operators in the arrivals hall offering expensive but efficient transport to other parts of the country. There are several ATMs, and the BAC bank has a window where you can change dollars, but not travellers' cheques. You'll find car rental agencies in the arrivals hall. The domestic terminal sits at the main terminal's western end.

International flights Copa (☏ copaair.com) and Taca (☏ taca.com) between them have international flights to San José, Panama City, Guatemala, San Salvador and Tegucigalpa. American carriers Spirit, Delta, United and AA fly to Fort Lauderdale, Atlanta, Houston and Miami International respectively. Nature Air runs small, direct flights to Costa Rica.

Domestic flights Domestic airline La Costeña (☏ 2263 2142, ☏ lacostena.com.ni) runs one or more flights a day to San Carlos, Bluefields, Puerto Cabezas and the Corn Islands; advance reservations are recommended, either at the airport office, online or via agencies across the city.

BY BUS

Domestic buses Domestic buses arrive at one of the several crowded, noisy and generally chaotic urban marketplaces that also serve as bus terminals: from Masaya, Granada, Rivas or other southern destinations, chicken buses come into the Mercado Huembes near the Carretera a Masaya on the southeastern edge of the city and express minibuses arrive and depart from La UCA, near Metrocentro; buses from the north and east – including

6

6

TOUR OPERATORS IN MANAGUA

Organized tours are generally best arranged locally – we've listed operators throughout the Guide. If you've only got a short spell in the country and don't fancy the rigours of Nicaragua's clamorous bus terminals and ramshackle taxis, though, various places can arrange trips from Managua. These are usually pricey, but can get you to remote areas fast and will pick you up from your hotel or the airport. **Careli Tours**, opposite Colegio La Salle, Planes de Altamira (☎ 2278 6919, ⊛ carelitours.com), are good for expensive best-of-Nicaragua-type packages (US$200–1200), lasting up to a fortnight, as well as trips combining Nicaragua and Costa Rica. Otherwise, operators in León and Granada can help – try the likes of Green Pathways and Va Pues (see box, p.470) or Tierra Tour and Nicaragua Adventures (see box, p.486).

Estelí, Matagalpa, Ocotal, San Carlos and El Rama – arrive across town at the terminal in the Mercado Mayoreo; chicken buses from the northwest towns of León and Chinandega use the busy Mercado Israel Lewites in the southwest of the capital and express minibuses use La UCA. Taxis crowd the arriving buses; it is more expensive but safer (see box, p.457) to get a taxi from inside the terminal. Leaving Managua, the busiest domestic bus routes run to the provincial cities, particularly León in the northwest and Granada in the south. Other main routes run to Matagalpa, Estelí, Masaya and Rivas, the last for connections to the Costa Rican border and the beach town of San Juan del Sur. Buses to the Atlantic coast can be grievously affected by the weather – in the rainy season in particular, times are elastic and journeys can be decidedly wearing. Below, where we list buses as having regular departures (hourly or more frequent), these run from 5am–6pm unless otherwise stated.

Domestic destinations Bluefields (from Mercado Iván Montenegro; express departure daily 9pm, arriving in Rama around 3am for the early-morning *panga* to Bluefields; 10hr); Chinandega (from Mercado Israel Lewites; standard departures daily 5am–7pm every 30min, 2hr 30min; express departures every 30min, 1hr 40min); El Rama (daily from Mercado Mayoreo; 7 daily 4am–9pm, 7hr); Estelí (daily from Mercado Mayoreo; standard departures daily every 30min 3am–5pm, 3hr; express departures hourly 5am–5pm, 2hr); Granada (daily from Mercado Huembes second-class departures every 15min 5.30am–10pm, 1hr 20min; from Mercado Huembes express departures every 15–20min, 1hr); León (daily second-class departures every 15–30min, 2hr from Mercado Israel Lewites; express departures every 15–20min 6am–9pm, 1hr 30min from La UCA); Masaya (daily from Mercado Huembes second-class departures every 20min, 5.30am–9.30pm 1hr; from La UCA express services every 15–20min, 40min); Matagalpa (daily from Mercado Mayoreo; second-class departures every 30min, 3.30am–6.30pm 3hr; express services hourly, 4am–6pm 2hr); Ocotal (daily from Mercado Mayoreo; second-class departures hourly, 3am–6pm, 3hr 30min); Puerto Cabezas (daily from Mercado Mayoreo; second-class departures

noon & 5pm, 18–25hr); Rivas (daily from Mercado Huembes; second-class departures every 25min, 5am–5pm, 2hr 25min; express services every 30min, 6am–9pm, 2hr); San Carlos (daily from Mercado Mayoreo; 7 daily 5am–6pm, second-class departures, 5–7hr); San Jorge (daily from Mercado Huembes; express departures every 30min, 6am–9pm, 2hr).

International buses Two major companies serve Managua. The Tica Bus station (☎ 2222 6094, ⊛ ticabus .com) sits two blocks east and one block south of the old Cine Dorado in Barrio Martha Quezada. Transnica buses (☎ 2277 2104, ⊛ transnica.com) depart from 300m north and 50m east of the Rotonda Metrocentro, behind the cathedral.

International destinations Panama City (Tica Bus 1 daily, noon, with overnight in San José; 32hr); San José (Tica Bus 3 daily, 6am, 7am & noon, 10hr; Transnica 4 daily, 5am, 7am, 10am & 1pm, 9hr); San Salvador (Tica Bus 1 daily, 4.45am, 11hr; with Transnica 2 daily, 3.30am & 11.30pm, 10hr); Tegucigalpa (Tica Bus 1 daily, 5am, 8hr; Transnica 3 daily, 3.30am, 5am & 11.30am, 8hr).

GETTING AROUND

By bus Buses, generally labelled with a route number, cover the main city routes. The fares are dirt cheap (C$2.5–5) but pickpocketing is common, so be alert. A new pre-paid card has been introduced and some buses will have a sign saying 'solo tarjetas' indicating they only take cards, whereas others saying 'uso mixto' accept cash and cards. Cards cost C$50 to buy and are difficult to get hold of, so unless you're going to be in Managua for a long time it's not worth the hassle. As ever, enterprising Nicaraguans have found a solution – every time a bus which only takes cards pulls up people with pre-paid cards will rush over to swipe theirs for you for a fee. Normal cash or card fares are C$2.5, or it will cost C$5 for someone to swipe you in. If unsure of your destination ask the driver to point out stops, which are unmarked. Services start at 5am and continue until 10pm, becoming less frequent from about 6pm onwards. Useful buses include #109 (running from the *malecón* to Mercado Huembes), #110 (Mercado Israel Lewites, La UCA and Mercado Iván Montenegro), #114 (El

Mayoreo to Metrocentro and La UCA) and #112 (Mercado Israel Lewites to the *malecón*).

By taxi Legitimate taxis have red-and-white striped licence plates and are officially registered. Cheap and plentiful, they will probably be your main mode of transport, with most trips costing around C$30–80 and the journey from Barrio Martha Quezada to the airport around C$150 (agree on a price before setting off and do your best to haggle, especially with taxis waiting at bus terminals). Drivers always like to have more than one passenger at a time, and will stop to pick up and drop off people en route – if travelling alone, it's safest to sit next to the driver. Taxis will honk at you as a matter of course, whether you want one or not.

INFORMATION

Tourist information There is an under-stocked INTUR desk at the airport. The INTUR headquarters (Mon–Fri 8am–1pm & 2–5pm; ☏ 2254 5191, ⓦ intur.gob.ni) are in central Managua, one block west of the *Crowne Plaza*. The staff are well intentioned and some speak English, but don't have much in the way of hand-outs or information on accommodation or tours. You should be able to pick up a free map of the city, if available – for everything else, your hotel will probably be of far more use. You can also try the CIT office opposite, but it's much of the same.

ACCOMMODATION

Barrio Martha Quezada, where most international buses arrive, is the place for backpacker-friendly *hospedaje*-type accommodation; most places are scattered in the quiet streets on either side of the Tica Bus terminal. Elsewhere in the city, you'll find more secure and modern districts than Martha Quezada, notably in the relatively swish area around the Metrocentro.

★ TREAT YOURSELF

Casa Naranja Planes de Altamira ☏ 2277 3403, ⓦ hotelcasanaranja.com; map p.458. Smart, quiet and charming upmarket option, its cool corridors dotted with furniture and musical instruments. Rooms have hot water and TVs, and some come with nice little outdoor areas too. Breakfast included. US$100

Casa Real Two blocks west and two blocks south of the Rotunda Rubén Darío ☏ 2278 3838, ⓦ casareal.com; map p.458. Spotless, family-run hotel with spacious, clean rooms (with TV, a/c and private bath) grouped around a leafy inner lounge with huge hammocks; the upstairs rooms are brighter, with balconies. Breakfast included. US$75

BARRIO MARTHA QUEZADA AND AROUND

Apartamentos Los Cisneros One block north and one and a half blocks west of the Tica Bus terminal ☏ 2222 3535, ⓦ hotelloscisneros.com; map p.460. The sole upmarket option in the heart of Martha Quezada, offering bright standard rooms and chalet-style apartments with hot water, fridge, cooker and optional fan or a/c. It's an extra US$5 to use the kitchen appliances, but the fee is waived for stays of a week or more. Doubles US$30, two-person apartments US$40

Casa Castillo One block west and one and a half blocks north of Tica Bus ☏ 2222 2265; map p.460. Hospitable, family-run *hospedaje* with seven basic, clean rooms with private bath; those right at the back and upstairs are larger and quieter. US$14

Casa Gabrinma One block south and half a block east of Tica Bus ☏ 2222 6650; map p.460. Welcoming guesthouse with a chatty owner whose cute, vaguely monastic rooms – all with ceiling fans – are set around a series of leafy inner courtyards. US$20

Casa de Huéspedes Santos One block north and one and a half blocks west of Tica Bus ☏ 2222 3713, ⓦ casadehuespedessantos.com.ni; map p.460. Big, ramshackle *hospedaje* that feels like a youth club when it's full and a shed when it's empty, with hammocks, easy chairs, funky art on the walls and an indoor patio with cable TV. Some of the 28 scruffy rooms are on the gloomy side – try to get one upstairs, where ventilation is better. All have ceiling fans, and some come with private bath. US$14

★ Los Felipe One and a half blocks west of Tica Bus ☏ 2222 6501, ⓦ hotellosfelipe.com.ni; map p.460. This clean, peaceful hotel has 27 clean and compact rooms nestled amid an urban jungle of foliage. All come with private bath and TV, and there's wi-fi and laundry available alongside optional a/c and a swimming pool (9am–5pm). Dorms US$8, doubles US$20

Hostal Dulce Sueño Half a block east of Tica Bus ☏ 2228 4125, ✉ hospedajedulcesueno@yahoo.es; map p.460. Helpful budget place in a secure courtyard. Try to get one of the two brighter upstairs rooms, which sit alongside a rooftop area with hammocks where you can squint over Martha Quezada's tin roofs and ponder your next excursion. There's a kitchen and fridge too. US$20

Hostal Palmerita One block west and half a block north of Tica Bus ☏ 2222 5956; map p.460. Simple, faded hostel that draws a mostly Nica clientele. Nothing special, but the seven rooms are a reasonable deal. US$20

ELSEWHERE IN THE CITY

Casa San Juan C Esperanza 560, behind La UCA ☏ 2278 3220, ⓦ casasanjuan.net; map p.458. Welcoming mid-range guesthouse in a quiet neighbourhood. The spotless

6

rooms come with a/c, cable TV and well-equipped modern, private bathrooms. Breakfast is included and other meals are available with advance notice. The hotel is popular, so reserve in advance. US$55

Managua Backpackers Inn 100m south of the old *Chamán* nightclub, Los Robles ☎2267 0006, ⓦmanaguahostel.com; map p.458. A well-located, friendly hostel with tidy dorms and private rooms, some with en-suite bathroom. The courtyard garden with a pool, shaded by a mango tree and surrounded by deck chairs and hammocks, is tranquil, although the nearby nightlife can be noisy. There's a large communal kitchen and TV room, free wi-fi and laundry services. Dorms US$10.50, doubles US$29

Nicaragua Guest House Two blocks south and two and a half blocks west of Rotonda La Virgen ☎2249 8963, ⓦ3dp.ch/nicaragua; map p.458. A small guesthouse in a good location for the airport and most buses, with basic rooms, all en suite with TV and a fan or a/c (US$10 extra), and a cool courtyard garden. The upside is that it's a safe three-block walk away from the new Multicentro Las Américas shopping centre, the downside is the 11pm curfew. US$20

EATING

Wherever you walk in Managua – on the street, at the bus stop or even under a shady tree – you will find someone selling a drink or *comida corriente*. Good, cheap food on the hoof is also easy to get in any of the major markets – look out for *pupusas*, a Salvadoran concoction of cheese, tortillas, sauce and meat. Managua also has a surprisingly cosmopolitan selection of restaurants: Chinese, Spanish, Mexican, Japanese, Italian, Peruvian, North American – even vegetarian. Americanized fast food is virtually everywhere, but cafés are thin on the ground and tend to be frequented by expats and wealthier locals. As for picnic food and self-catering, well-stocked supermarket chains La Colonia and La Unión sell a large selection of local and imported food including organic produce. You can also buy a lot of the basics at local *pulperías*, small shops set up in people's houses. Fruit and vegetables are cheapest at the weekend markets, when the growers come into town to sell their produce.

BARRIO MARTHA QUEZADA AND AROUND

Café Mirna One block west and south of the Tica Bus terminal; map p.460. This compact, likeable, family-run place has become something of an institution over its thirty-year history, though the service can be uneven. Come for decent *típica* or gringo breakfasts, or the *comida casera* buffet (C$70) at lunchtime. Mon–Sat 6.30am–2pm, Sun 7am–2pm.

Comida a la Vista Two blocks west of the Tica Bus station; map p.460. Definitive lunch-only buffet joint – the only thing bigger than the huge plates of satisfying *comida típica*

(around C$80 with a drink) is the queue, which can sprawl from the busy counter through the restaurant hall and out into the street. If the buzz of the main room isn't to your taste, try the pleasant area upstairs. Mon–Sat 7am–3pm.

El Grillito Just north of the INTUR office; map p.460. There aren't too many spots in Martha Quezada that might tempt you in for both a meal and a drink: *El Grillito* won't win any prizes, but with bright murals, reasonably priced beers (C$39) and seafood and grilled meat (from C$200) served on its open terrace, it's a reasonable place to while away one of Managua's hot nights. Daily noon until late.

Jimmy 'Three Fingers' Alabama Rib Shack One block east and half a block south of Tica Bus (☎8861 0791). The father ran an Irish bar, the son has decided to make it a rib shack – good ideas clearly run in the family. A great little spot to come for beer (C$27) and a snack (from C$35) or, of course, a delicious plate of ribs (C$265). Daily noon–10pm.

Licuados Ananda Next to the Montoya statue; map p.458. This restaurant and juice bar, set around a covered patio and garden, is a veritable oasis in Managua's concrete chaos. The varied veggie menu includes a good-value *plato del día*, nice bread and superb smoothies (C$55) – try the papaya. A meal plus *fresco* will cost C$70–80. Mon–Sat 7am–3pm.

Típico Doña Pilar One block east of *Casa de Huespedes Santos*; map p.460. Simple plastic chairs and a large grill set up on the sidewalk every evening, offering quesadillas, enchiladas and lip-smacking grilled chicken for a mere C$100 (drink included). Daily from 6pm.

METROCENTRO AND AROUND

Casa del Café One block north of Carretera a Masaya, by the Mexican Embassy ⓦcasadelcafe.com.ni; map p.458. This branch of a local chain serves reasonable coffee (from C$45), breakfasts (C$130) and snacks (cheese croissant C$90); the draw is the foliage-shaded balcony, a rare bit of tranquillity in this achingly modern stretch of town. Mon–Fri 7am–9pm, Sat 8am–9pm, Sun 8am–4pm.

Pizzeria Valenti's One block east of *Domino's Pizza*, house no. 6 ☎2278 7474, ⓦpizzavalenti.com; map p.458. The outside patio is a decent place to enjoy a thin-crust pizza – they're filling and good value considering the area. A lunch combo of a meal and a beer is on offer for C$150.

La Terraza Peruana Planes de Altamira No. 14, 150m south of *Ola Verde* ☎2278 0013, ⓦlaterrazaperuana.com; map p.458. Upmarket Peruvian restaurant with a relaxing shaded terrace. The tasty and substantial dishes include seven varieties of *ceviche* (C$179–339), Chinese chicken (C$149) and rice with seafood (C$309).

ELSEWHERE IN THE CITY

Las Brasas Around the corner from *Topkapi* ☎2277 5568, ⓦrestaurantelasbrasas.com; map p.458. The popular buffet lunch, serving good Nica food, is a bargain at C$140 (drink included). Dinner is more expensive (C$200–300), but it's worth coming for a drink (beer C$35).

Comedor Doña Marina Opposite the airport, one block east of *Las Mercedes Hotel*; map p.458. There's no sign, so look out for the green-and-brown *comedor* full of airport workers filling up on chicken, beef (both C$60) or whole fish (C$70); these include a drink if eating in, and they can pack to go if you're running for your flight. Twice as filling and half the price of a sandwich at the airport. Daily 5am–8pm.

La Original Taquiza Half a block west of La Virgen roundabout; map p.458. You can't miss this place right on the highway. It keeps expanding, but you can still expect to queue on a weekend for their tasty Mexican tacos (around C$125 for a filling portion). Daily 11am–midnight.

Topkapi Opposite the Alhambra cinema; map p.460. Simple fast food at a good price (thin-crust pizza C$90, beer C$30), including national dishes such as *caballo bayo* (C$450 for 4 people; you get a tortilla and a dish and help yourself to food from communal plates). It's been open since 1974, so it must be doing something right.

DRINKING AND NIGHTLIFE

Managua's nightlife is given a shot in the arm with the continuing return of the "Miami Boys" – wealthy families who fled Revolutionary Nicaragua – who have helped drive the demand for upmarket bars and discos. As well as the plusher options, the city offers a reasonable choice of cheaper places to drink and dance – most places only charge a few dollars cover and drinks are either included or cost around C$20–60. You can expect to hear merengue, salsa, reggaetón, pop, house and even Nica rancho music (not unlike American country). Most bars shut between midnight and 2pm, and clubs start filling up from 10pm – Saturday is the busiest evening of the week.

BARS

El Caramanchel Three blocks south and half a block west of Plaza Inter ☏ 8931 4199; map p.458. Frequented by a lively international crowd, this "cultural bar" is decorated with Mexican tapestries, old beer ads and odd artworks. It hosts several live gigs a month as well as occasional poetry readings, theatre and photography exhibitions, but it's worth a visit just for a drink or for the tasty local food (from C$50). Free entry, beer from C$30. Wed–Sun 6pm–3am.

La Casa de Los Mejía Godoy Colonia Los Robles, opposite the *Crowne Plaza* ☏ 2222 6610, ⊛ losmejiagodoy .zonaxp.com; map p.460. The brainchild of Nicaraguan guitarist and song-writing brothers Luis Enrique and Carlos Mejía Godoy, this is a cultural centre and bar rolled into one. There's an art gallery, a CD/bookstore and a café/bar selling *comida típica* (around C$200). Thurs sees young local musicians jam, and if the brothers aren't performing on Fri

& Sat, there's likely to be a quality replacement. Cover from US$10. Mon & Tues 8am–4.30pm, Wed–Sat 8am–1am.

★**Fandango** Half a block north of *La Terraza Peruana*, Planes de Altamira; map p.458. This is where the pros from Managua's dance schools come to let off steam. Grab a beer (C$38) and maybe some tapas (very limited menu; from C$100) and watch in awe. Wed–Sat 3pm–2.30am.

El Panal Opposite the Universidad Nacional de Ingeniería, tucked away behind the copy shops in a disused container; map p.458. There's live music on Sat afternoons and Wed evenings, but it's worth popping in for a beer (C$26) any day to mingle with the young poets and writers of Managua. *Comida corriente* is less than C$100. Take a taxi. Mon–Sat noon–11pm or midnight.

Pool Ocho Los Robles, behind the Casa Pellas building; map p.458. While visiting pool halls is not generally a good idea in Nicaragua, this one is safe and well lit. Bar food costs around C$130, beer C$35 and the pool tables cost C$40/30min – less than US$2, but expensive enough to attract only serious players. Mon–Sat 2pm–2am, Sun 3pm–midnight.

Ruta Maya 150m east of the Montoya statue ☏ 2268 0698, ⊛ rutamaya.com.ni; map p.458. Long-standing cultural centre/bar that hosts a diverse cross section of the city's musical and artistic talent and tends to attract an older, more sophisticated crowd. Seating is outdoors under a big marquee; traditional Nica food is also available (C$100–200). Gig tickets are usually C$130. Open daily; gigs Thurs, Fri & Sat.

El Viajero C 9A, a block west of the Tica Bus terminal; map p.460. Come for an unfussy beer or four (C$44/litre) or cheap seafood *ceviche* (from C$80). Expect cheesy Nica pop and some uproariously drunk locals. Tues–Sat noon–2am.

Zona Hippos Av Gabriel Cardenal, a block west of the *Hilton Princess* hotel; map p.458. Not one bar but a whole street-full. The Americanized joints, including *Woody's* and *Hippos*, are good for the daily 5–7pm happy hour, but walk further down the street for some artier establishments. The new *Embassy Bar* is British owned and does European dishes from US$5.50; *El Garabato*, down the street, offers a lunchtime buffet for less than C$100. Generally daily noon–11pm.

CLUBS

El Chamán 200m south of the *Tiscapa* restaurant, off Av Simón Bolívar ⊛ chamanbar.net; map p.458. One of the biggest clubs in town, and arguably the most iconic: it's built in the shape of a Maya pyramid. Caters to a younger crowd, with Latin, hip-hop and pop playing on the three nicely decorated floors. There's regular live music and the occasional rock-centric talent contests are worth a look. Ladies' night Thurs & Fri (women free, men C$100), Sat C$130 for women and C$200 for men; Thurs–Sat 8pm–4am.

6

6

Multicentro Las Américas 500m south of Rotonda La Virgen; map p.458 A shopping mall by day, with a decent selection of food outlets, this is one of the safest places to experience the mixture of Nicaraguan cultures that co-exist in Managua. Old favourite *Moods* is now here with its slightly upmarket crowd and classic disco music (entry C$100), along with six other clubs – try *Nicarabbean Roots* for a taste of the Atlantic coast then move on to the nearby karaoke or sports bars if the fancy takes you. Mon–Wed noon–midnight, Thurs–Sun noon–2am or later.

Q C 27 de Mayo, two blocks north of the Tica Bus terminal; map p.492. Friendly, relaxed gay club, playing mainstream US and Latin pop, which can be heaving at the weekend. It's one of only three gay clubs in town: nearby *Lollipop* and *Tabú* have a similar vibe. Entry around C$100. Thurs–Sun 9pm until late.

Cinema Alhambra V.I.P. (see box above), Cinemark Metrocentro (☎ 2271 9037, ⓦ cinemarkca.com), Cinemas Inter in Plaza Inter (☎ 2222 5122), Cinemas Galerías in Galerías Santo Domingo (☎ 2276 5065). American blockbusters (usually with subtitles).

Teatro Nacional Rubén Darío ☎ 2222 7426, ⓦ tnrubendario.gob.ni; map p.458. One of the best theatres in Central America (see p.459), with a main auditorium seating 1200 people, exhibition space and occasional experimental theatre in the basement. Events are scheduled most weekends. Bus #109 stops right in front.

SHOPPING

Hispamer One block east, one block south and then one block east again from UCA ☎ 2270 4409, ⓦ hispamer.com .ni. The largest selection of academic, fiction and nonfiction titles (in Spanish) in Nicaragua. There's a decent selection of classic and modern English-language fiction too. Mon–Fri 9am–6pm, Sat 9am–noon.

Mercado Oriental A few blocks southeast of the old centre. A small, lawless city-within-a-city where you can buy just about anything, but need to keep a close eye on your pockets and an even closer eye on your back – Nicaraguans will tell you that this is one of the most dangerous places in the country. If you must go, take someone with you and leave your valuables in your hotel. In the streets around the entrance to the market are many shops selling furniture – including beautiful rocking chairs – and electrical goods.

Mercado Roberto Huembes Near the Carretera a Masaya in the south of the city. Safer than the Mercado Oriental to wander around, with an excellent crafts section. There's a huge range of hammocks – everything from a simple net one (C$140) to a luxury, two-person, woven cotton option (from C$800). Products made of leather and skins are in abundance, but choose carefully as many of the species used are endangered. Paintings in the style of the artists' colony on the Solentiname islands are available here, along with many fine pen-and-ink drawings and abstract works. You can buy Nicaraguan cigars as well as pottery and wicker products (*mimbre*) such as baskets, mats, chairs and wall-hangings.

DIRECTORY

Banks Central banks that exchange foreign currency include Banpro and Bancentro, both on the Carretera a Masaya near the *Hotel Princess*, and BAC (Banco de América Central), Plaza España. ATMs accepting foreign cards (Visa, MasterCard and Cirrus) can be found at these banks and in most malls, as well as in many petrol stations and at the airport.

Embassies and consulates Canada, C El Nogal 25, Bolonia (☎ 2268 0433, ✉ managua@international.gc.ca); UK, one block north of the Military Hospital (☎ 2254 5454); US, Km 5.5, Carretera Sur (☎ 2252 7100, ⓦ nicaragua.usembassy.gov).

Health Hospital Bautista, in Barrio Largaespada (☎ 2264 9020, ⓦ hospitalbautistanicaragua.com), is your main option; Hospital Metropolitano Vivian Pellas, Km 9.75, Carretera a Masaya, 250m west (☎ 2255 6900, ⓦ metropolitano.com.ni), is more sophisticated and more expensive. Both are private, with 24hr emergency departments. Medco is one of the larger pharmacy chains, with branches at Bello Horizonte and Plaza España. Alternatively, try the 24hr pharmacy at the Hospital Bautista.

Immigration The main office is two blocks north of Los Semáforos de la Colonia Tenderí (Mon–Fri 8am–1pm; ☎ 2244 3989), and there's another in the Metrocentro and Multicentro Las Américas (Mon–Fri 10am–4pm, then 4–6pm for picking up passports only; Sat & Sun 10am–1pm; ☎ 2244 3989). All can renew visas (US$10 for thirty days).

Internet There are plenty of internet cafés around town – in Barrio Martha Quezada, try Sistema Internet, Av Williams Romero, one block north of Cine Dorado (C$16/hr).

Post office Palacio de Correos, Plaza de la Revolución (Mon–Fri 8am–5pm, Sat 8am–noon).

The northwest

Nicaragua's Pacific **northwest** is hot and dry, with grassy plains punctuated by dramatic volcanoes. The largest city in the northwest, and once the capital of Nicaragua, is **León**, the birthplace of the Sandinistas and a lively town with a dynamic tourist scene. The northwest's sweeping **coastline** is just as appealing, with surf beaches and breezes that relieve the sometimes vicious heat. **Chinandega** offers no such relief, but is a convenient base near the Honduran border.

LEÓN

The capital of Nicaragua until 1857, **LEÓN**, 90km northwest of Managua, is now a provincial city, albeit an energetic, architecturally arresting one. A significant element in the city's healthy buzz is the presence of the **National University** (the country's premier academic institution) and its large student population, swelled by the ranks of young people studying at León's various other colleges. León's colonial architecture is arguably as impressive as Granada's; there's also a wide range of tours, an entertaining backpacker scene and the best **art gallery** in the country.

Yet for all its buzz, León has a violent history. The original León was founded by Hernández de Córdoba in 1524 at the foot of Volcán Momotombo, where its ruins – now known as **León Viejo** (see p.472) – still lie. The city was moved northwest to its present-day location after

6

LEÓN

EATING
Asados Pelibuey	2
Café la Rosita	1
Casa Abierta	9
Cocinarte	10
Pan y Paz	4
Taquetzal	8

DRINKING & NIGHTLIFE
El Alamo etc	3
La Olla Quemada	6
Oxygen	7

ACCOMMODATION
Bigfoot	5
Hostal Guardabarranco	4
Hostal d'Oviedo	7
Hostal Sonati	1
Hotel Azul	2
Lazy Bones	3
La Tortuga Booluda	6

Bus Terminal

Subtiava & Las Peñitas

Managua & Discoteca Dilectus

6

León Viejo's destruction by an earthquake and volcanic eruption in 1609. In 1956, the first President Somoza was gunned down in León by the martyr-poet Rigoberto López Pérez. During the Revolution in the 1970s, the town's streets were the scene of several decisive battles between the Sandinistas and Somoza's forces, and many key figures in the Revolution either came from León or had their political start here. Although many years have passed since then, and most of the Sandinista graffiti has been painted over, the city continues to wear its FSLN heart on its sleeve: the street signs read "León: ciudad heroica – primera capital de la revolución", and a few fine examples of the city's famous murals remain.

WHAT TO SEE AND DO

León's heart is the **Parque Central**, which is shadowed by the largest cathedral in Central America. **Calle Central Rubén Darío** runs along the Parque's northern edge, cutting the city in two from east to west, while **Avenida Central** runs between the Parque and Cathedral north to south. Splendidly and unusually, León has street signs, though people will usually still give you directions in relation to a landmark.

Parque Central

The **Parque Central** lies at the intersection of Calle Central Rubén Darío and Avenida Central. Centring on a statue of General Máximo Jeréz guarded by four lions, it's visited by a constant stream of locals, street vendors and tourists. If you value your hearing, avoid the square at 7am and noon, when a ludicrously loud siren wails across the city – a throwback to the days when workers flocked in to León's booming cotton factories.

Cathedral

The city's most obvious attraction is its colossal **Cathedral** (open from sunrise to late evening), a gorgeous, battered, cream-coloured structure whose volcano-blackened turrets tower over the heart of León. Now a UNESCO World Heritage Site, the building was begun in 1747 and took more than a century to complete. You can climb up to the roof (Mon–Sat

8.30–11.30am & 2–4pm; US$3; access via a door on the north side) for stunning views across to the surrounding volcanoes. Inside, don't miss the tomb of local hero **Rubén Darío**, Nicaragua's most famous writer and poet, which is guarded by a statue of a mournful lion.

Museo de la Revolución de León

On the western side of the park is one of the city's Sandinista strongholds, the **Museo de la Revolución de León** (daily 7am–5pm; C$50). You'll be shown around the airy, decaying building by an FSLN combat veteran, who'll talk you through the extensive collection of photos, articles and news clippings documenting the Revolution, its historical antecedents and its aftermath. It's an affecting tour, though you'll need some Spanish to make sense of things. You may be allowed onto the roof, which has crackling views of León.

Mausoleo Héroes y Mártires

The northeast corner of the Parque is home to the **Mausoleo Héroes y Mártires**, a star-shaped monument dedicated to those who died fighting for freedom during the civil war, surrounded by a large mural colourfully detailing Nicaragua's history from pre-Columbian times to the ending of the civil war.

La Recolección

Two blocks north and one block east of the Parque is one of Nicaragua's finest colonial churches, **La Recolección**, with a beautiful Mexican Baroque facade dating from 1786, and some fine mahogany woodwork inside.

Parque Rubén Darío

Followers of Nicaragua's second religion, poetry, might want to head for the **Parque Rubén Darío**, a block west of the Parque Central, which is home to a statue of the rather sombre-looking poet dressed in suit and bow tie.

Centro de Arte Fundación Ortiz-Guardián

Sitting on Calle Central Rubén Darío, a little to the west of Parque Rubén Darío,

RUBÉN DARÍO

Born in 1867 in a village outside Matagalpa, the writer **Rubén Darío** is one of Nicaragua's most famous sons. *Azul ...*, published in 1888, became particularly influential and is often cited as a cornerstone for the birth of Spanish-language modernism. A century after his death in 1916, he remains one of the region's most influential poets.

is the **Centro de Arte Fundación Ortiz-Guardián** (Tues–Sat 9am–5pm, Sun 9am–4pm; US$1), an expansive art gallery in two renovated colonial houses. The collection features an engrossing cross section of Latin American art, including pre-Hispanic and modern ceramics and some impressive modern art.

Museo Archivo Rubén Darío

A few blocks west of the Centro de Arte Fundación Ortiz-Guardián is the **Museo Archivo Rubén Darío** (Mon–Sat 8am–noon & 2–5pm, Sun 8am–noon; donations requested), housed in a substantial León residence that was the home of the poet's aunt, Bernarda. Inside, the lovingly kept rooms and courtyard garden are home to wonderfully frank plaques detailing Darío's tempestuous personal life and diplomatic and poetic careers, along with personal possessions and commemorative items, such as Rubén Darío lottery tickets.

Casa Rigoberto López Pérez

A block west and half a block north of La Merced (being refurbished at the time of going to press). A simple yet striking look at the spot where President Somoza was assassinated by the young Rigoberto López Pérez, who was, in turn, promptly gunned down by the National Guard. Photos taken at the scene hang at the entrance to the dancefloor where these events leading up to the Revolution took place.

La Veinte Uno

Three blocks south of the cathedral lie the ruins of **La Veinte Uno**, the National Guard's 21st garrison and scene of heavy fighting in April 1979. The garrison now houses two very different museums, which together go by the long-winded title of **Museo de Leyendas y Tradiciones Coronel Joaquín de Arrechada Antigua Cárcel de La Veinte Uno** (daily 8am–5pm; C$50). One half of the building houses a collection of ghoulish figures from Nicaraguan folklore, including a chariot-riding grim reaper and a giant crab, while the other focuses on the garrison's ugly past, with a small collection of revealing black and white photos taken during and after the Somoza era. Captions in Spanish document the torture that went on inside.

Subtiava

Four kilometres west of the city centre is the *barrio* of **Subtiava**, which long predates León and is still home to much of the city's indigenous population. It is also the site of one of the oldest **churches** in the country. Recently renovated, the small adobe building is not always open, but worth a visit if you're catching a bus to or from the beach at Las Peñitas (see p.472).

ARRIVAL AND INFORMATION

By bus Buses arrive at the anarchic, traffic-clogged terminal, eight blocks northeast of the centre, from where you can hop in a taxi (standard fare anywhere in town is C$20) or walk into town.

Destinations Chinandega (frequent, from 5am; leaves when

THE GIGANTONA Y EL ENANITO OF SUBTIAVA

In November and December, be sure not to miss the posses of young boys hammering away at snare drums while a huge **gigantona** (a papier-mâché figure of an elegant colonial-era woman, directed from underneath by a teenager and accompanied by El Enanito – the big-headed dwarf directed by a smaller child) weaves among them. Traditionally, the boys are given a few córdobas for a recital of poetry, typically that of national bard Rubén Darío. The *gigantonas* are judged during the festivities of La Purísima (a festival celebrating the Virgin Mary's conception) on December 7, with the best winning a prize.

6

TOURS IN LEÓN

As you might expect from a backpacker-friendly city with volcanoes, beaches and mangroves within striking distance, León is packed with tour operators. The headline activity is **volcano-boarding**, in which you'll truck off to the ash-covered slopes of Cerro Negro in the morning, spend a good hour slogging up its alien, gas-belching curves and then skid down on a board that generally moves at a fairly gentle pace despite the fierce gradient, although some boards are faster – and damp days can be especially quick. Almost every operator offers it – Quetzaltrekkers give you two runs (most operators only offer one), Bigfoot has the fastest boards and are experts, since they invented the sport.

Trips from León can also take in the wet ride through the canyon at **Somoto**, near the Honduran border, treks up the **San Cristóbal and El Hoyo volcanoes**, the ruins of **León Viejo** (see p.472) and more; Spanish lessons can also be arranged. Rates for excursions are fairly standard (from US$30/day) and most require a minimum of four people to run, though you may be able to haggle, especially with a larger group. The companies below are all established and reliable.

Bigfoot Tours *Bigfoot* hostel, Av 2 NE ☎ 2315 3863, ⓦ bigfoothostels.com. Fun firm mostly focusing on volcano-boarding and surf trips to Isla Los Brasiles, though other trips can be arranged.
Green Pathways Av 2 NE ☎ 2315 0964, ⓦ greenpathways.com. Country-wide adventures, including turtle-watching and volcano-scaling. One of the more upmarket and reliable options, with good connections around the country. Their night tour of Telica volcano (US$50) is well worth it – you're almost sure to see lava here, and the tour ends with supper with a local family in the village at the foot of the volcano, a great chance to interact with people from outside the city.

Quetzaltrekkers 3A C NO ☎ 2311 7388, ⓦ quetzaltrekkers.com. Friendly, reliable bunch offering volcano treks around the country. All profits go towards supporting street children in León. Food and drink is included in tour prices. Office open daily 10am–6pm.
Sonati 3A C NE ☎ 2311 4251, ⓦ sonati.info. Non-profit-making company, operating from the hostel of the same name, whose volcano trips are supplemented by visits to the swamps of Isla Juan Venado and various birdwatching trips.
Va Pues 2A C SO ☎ 2315 4099, ⓦ vapues.com. This moderately upmarket operator has country-wide tours, trips to local fincas and – of course – volcano-boarding.

full; 50min); Estelí (3 daily, roughly 7am–3pm; leaves when full; 2hr 30min); Guasaule (1 daily, 4am; 3hr 30min); Las Peñitas (14 daily; 50min); Managua (every 15min 6am–9pm; 1hr 15min–2hr); Matagalpa (daily 5.20am, 2.45pm & 3.10pm; 3hr); San Isidro (for more frequent Matagalpa and Estelí connections; 24 daily 5.20am–3.10pm; 2hr).
Tourist information INTUR, AV Central (Mon–Fri 8am–4pm), has a few leaflets and maps and general tour information – the hostels and tour companies are usually more helpful.

ACCOMMODATION

Budget accommodation in León has really taken off in the last few years, and there is now an abundance of good-value hostels.
Bigfoot Av 2 NE ☎ 2315 3863, ⓦ bigfoothostels.com. This sociable place is popular with a younger backpacker crowd. The huge dorms are clean, and there's a large kitchen and a small foot-shaped pool. The *Volcano Café* out front does omelettes (C$90) and bacon sandwiches (C$100) for breakfast and 'build your own' pasta for lunch and dinner (C$125). Dorms US$6, doubles US$13
★**Hostal Guardabarranco** Av 2 NE ☎ 2311 7124, ⓦ hostalguardabarranco.net. Just a few doors up from

Bigfoot, but much quieter, this clean, family-run place offers the best of both worlds – you can party down the street, and still get a good night's sleep. Free wi-fi and use of kitchen. Dorms US$8, doubles US$20
Hostal d'Oviedo Av 1 SO ☎ 2311 3766. Small, quiet hostel downhill from the town centre with friendly Nica owners and a homely front room with easy chairs. There's wi-fi, a kitchen and a fridge too. Dorms US$7, doubles US$18
Hostel Sonati 3A C NE ☎ 2311 4251, ⓦ sonati.info. Non-profit hostel linked to the tour operator of the same name, with animal-themed rooms and dorms, a flower-filled courtyard, a kitchen and a quieter atmosphere than some places in town. Dorms US$7, doubles US$18
Lazybones Av 2 NO ☎ 2311 3472, ⓦ lazybonesleon.com. The clean and comfortable dorms at this large hostel are arranged around an airy courtyard with hammocks and a pool table, while the mellow back-courtyard boasts a swimming pool. The doubles and triples are pretty good too – try to get one of the upstairs rooms with a balcony. There's free organic coffee and tea, plus wi-fi. Dorms US$8, doubles US$20
La Tortuga Booluda 1A C SO ☎ 2311 4653, ⓦ tortugabooluda.com. Great little hostel that's a lovely place to relax during the day as well as lay your head down

at night. Just a few blocks from the centre, it still feels set apart, and the free pancake breakfasts, kitchen facilities, wi-fi and pool table complete the package. Dorms U$$7, doubles U$$18

EATING

León boasts a cosmopolitan and ever-increasing range of places to eat and drink, from pizza joints and seafood restaurants to chic café-bars and bohemian hangouts. Most of the restaurants close around 10pm, while the trendier places stay open until the small hours, especially at weekends. For cheap eats at lunchtime try the stalls behind the market selling traditional *baho* (made with beef, plantain and *yuca*) plus a drink for C$100, or in the evening the stalls behind the cathedral serving barbecued chicken or beef with plantain chips and a drink for C$90.

Asados Pelibuey 2A Av NO. A handful of tables and platefuls of delicious chicken, beef and other *comida corriente* (from C$65) at this excellent little place, run by a women's co-operative. Daily 7am–9pm.

Café La Rosita Av Central. It's worth getting a coffee here just for the views from the roof terrace. Free wi-fi, good breakfast selection, lunch and a *fresco* C$85. Daily 7am–10pm.

Cafetín San Benito 2A Av NE. Tasty juices and a solid buffet will set you back a paltry C$60 in the café out front or courtyard out back. There's Chinese food (from C$40) too. Closed Sun.

Casa Abierta 3A C SE, at the back of Colibri Connexion. An organisation which serves as a meeting point for all NGOs in León, this place focuses on organic food and sells things you won't find anywhere else. Sit by the pool (or have a dip, US$2) and enjoy their healthy shakes (US$2) or a vegetable kebab with yoghurt sauce (US$5). Mon & Wed–Sun 9am–7pm.

Cocinarte 4A C SO. Housed in the oldest building in León, this is the city's original vegetarian restaurant, serving a variety of international food such as curry (C$185), falafel (C$195) and a vegetarian take on the Nicaraguan classic *indio viejo* (C$170). Mon & Wed–Thurs 11am–10pm.

★TREAT YOURSELF

Hotel Azul Av Central ☎ 2315 4519, ⓦ hotelazulleon.com. In the sweltering heat of León you'll be forgiven for craving a night or two with a/c and a swimming pool. This new contemporary hotel is centrally located and has a laidback, European feel about it. Even if you don't stay here, it's worth popping in to treat yourself to a meal in the top-notch restaurant (deliciously rich *boeuf bourguignon* C$250; lunchtime specials available). Breakfast included. U$$60

Pan y Paz 1A C NO ⓦ panypaz.com. The French owner grew up in a bakery, and you won't find better bread in Nicaragua. Prices are reasonable (quiche and salad C$60, sandwiches from C$50, coffee from C$10), and there's free wi-fi and a relaxing courtyard where you can while away the afternoon. Mon–Sat 7am–7pm.

Taquezal 1A C SO. Rustic but stylish café-bar with candlelit tables and a good menu featuring decent vegetarian pasta dishes, Chinese food, wonderful iced tea with lemon and a fine selection of espresso drinks. Mains from C$190. It gets dancier later in the evening. Daily 9am–2am.

DRINKING AND NIGHTLIFE

León is second only to Managua in the party stakes, thanks in large part to its many students, and Fridays and Saturdays are usually fairly happening. Most of the restaurants are good for a beer too.

El Alamo/Don Señor/La Cabaña/El Mirador 1A Av NO. Not one, not two, but (confusingly) four bars in one! Choose a different entrance to the same building and you could find yourself in a sports bar, chill out room, karaoke bar, or disco. The best bet for food is the sports bar, *El Alamo*, where you can get a reasonable steak (C$180) and beer (C$31). Daily 5pm–midnight; happy hour 5–7pm.

★**La Olla Quemada** C Central, Rubén Darío ⓦ laollaquemada.com. You'll find big speakers and a lively, mostly local crowd at this scruffily funky bar, which is busiest on Wed (live music), Thurs (Salsa night) and Sun (films). Open daily, hours vary.

Oxygen (ask for Oxigeno) 1A C SO. Slightly upmarket and usually with a cover charge of around C$50 at weekends, but there are often offers on beers for around C$20. The sign says *Oxygen*, but everyone calls it *Oxigeno*. Open from 8pm Wed–Sun, dancing gets going around 10pm and keeps going until late.

DIRECTORY

Banks There's a cluster of banks on the corner of 1 C NE and 1A Av, all with ATMs.

Internet There are scores of internet cafés: CyberFlash .com, next to *Bigfoot*, has a quick connection (C$10/hr) and can also burn pictures from your camera to disk.

Language schools Most of the hostels and tour companies, including Va Pues (see box opposite), offer lessons and homestays; Nicaragua Spanish Language Schools (NSLS; ⓦ nicaraguaspanishschools.org) are an established institution.

Laundry Most hostels will wash clothes, or try the friendly Laundry Express, Av Central, at 4A C NO (washing C$60/load, drying C$$30/10min). Mon–Fri 7am–9pm, Sat & Sun 8am–4pm.

Post office 3 Av NO, C 3–4. Mon–Fri 8am–5pm, Sat 8am–noon.

6

AROUND LEÓN

Worthwhile day-trip destinations from León include the Pacific beach of **Las Peñitas**, west of the city and easily accessible by bus, and more out-of-the-way UNESCO World Heritage Site of **León Viejo**.

Las Peñitas and Poneloya

Surfers come to **Las Peñitas**, 20km west of León, for reliable Pacific waves, although the village's relaxed vibe is enjoyable whether you're bound for board or hammock. The water here is fairly rough, due to a combination of powerful waves and riptides, but you can swim reasonably safely. **Poneloya**, 2km north, is a different story: ask locals about riptides (*corrientes peligrosos*) before venturing into the water, and never swim alone. Nearby **Isla Juan Venado** is a nature reserve and turtle-nesting site.

ARRIVAL AND DEPARTURE

Most travellers come to Las Peñitas as a day-trip from León. Buses leave León's Subtiava Terminal (see p.469) every hour (6am–6pm; 45min). The last bus back to León leaves at 6.45pm. A taxi will cost around US$12.

ACCOMMODATION AND EATING

Accommodation in town is limited, but there are several simple places right on the black-sand beach. Both *Barco de Oro* and *Bigfoot* offer surfboard rental and can help arrange fishing trips and excursions to Isla Juan Venado. Get Up Stand Up Surf in *Bigfoot* offers surf lessons.

Barco de Oro On the beach ☎ 2317 0275, ⓦ barcadeoro .com. Formerly a nightclub frequented by Somoza, this place is now a tranquil travellers' haven. The basic rooms have rustic wooden beds, en-suite bathrooms and a lovely upstairs balcony for sunset-watching. There's quality seafood on offer in the restaurant (Mains C$150–300; beer C$35). Dorms U̲S̲$̲7̲, doubles U̲S̲$̲2̲4̲

Bigfoot Las Peñitas On the beach ☎ 2310 2658, ⓦ bigfoothostels.com. The new party hostel with swimming pool, restaurant and a great beachfront location. Daily shuttles (book at Get Up Stand Up Surf shop, opposite hostel) leave from outside the *Bigfoot* in León (see p.470) at 3pm. Mon is beach party night and there's a free shuttle to/from the León hostel especially for it. Dorms U̲S̲$̲6̲, doubles U̲S̲$̲1̲8̲

Surfing Turtle Lodge Isla Los Brasiles, just across from Poneloya beach ☎ 23102748, ⓦ surfingturtlelodge.com. The main draw here is the opportunity to see sea turtles lay their eggs, so check if it is the right time of year. It's well

signposted in Poneloya – you need to get the boat (US$1) from next to *Chepe's* bar (clean, reasonably priced and friendly). Camping/person (tent provided) U̲S̲$̲5̲, dorms U̲S̲$̲1̲0̲, doubles U̲S̲$̲3̲5̲, cabins U̲S̲$̲5̲5̲

León Viejo

Founded in 1524, **León Viejo** (Mon–Fri 9am–5pm, Sat & Sun 9am–4pm; C$45), 32km east of the modern city and now designated a UNESCO World Heritage Site, was the original site of León, before it was destroyed by an earthquake and volcanic eruption on December 31, 1609. Among the ruins excavated since the site's discovery in 1967 are a cathedral, monastery and church; the graves of Nicaragua's first three bishops and of the country's founder, **Francisco Fernández de Córdoba**, were also uncovered. It's a modest site, although a wander around the half-restored buildings and accompanying plaques gives you a good idea of just how bloody Nicaragua's colonial history was. The surroundings are almost as fun: for much of the year the woods are rich with birds and butterflies, and the old fort, located just east of the main ruins, offers tremendous views of Lago de Managua and brooding Volcán Momotombo.

ARRIVAL AND DEPARTURE

Unless you visit with a tour, getting to the site is half the fun. You'll first need to head to La Paz Centro, a village about 60km north of Managua – buses leave León every 30min or so 5.30am–7.30pm. Some will drop you off on the motorway just outside town: from there get a motorized rickshaw to La Paz Centro's bus terminal for a few córdobas. Buses run (roughly hourly) from the terminal via various small villages to the site itself, which sits a few hundred metres from the route's terminus, Puerto Momotombo. The total journey from León to León Viejo can take anything from 90min to double that – set off early.

CHINANDEGA

CHINANDEGA, 35km northwest of León, is primarily a working city. Set on a plain behind looming Volcán San Cristóbal, the area's dry, kiln-like climate is ideal for growing cotton, the area's main economic activity, along with Flor de Caña **rum**, Nicaragua's export-grade tipple, produced in a distillery on the outskirts of town. Chinandega is generally visited on the

6

INTO HONDURAS AND EL SALVADOR

Crossing into **Honduras** via **Guasaule** (buses from Chinandega) can be chaotic. Exit tax is US$2 (it's US$10 to enter Nicaragua), and the border post is open 24 hours. It's just under 1km between the Nicaraguan border post and the Honduran side, across an impressive bridge, and it's easily walkable, though you'll be repeatedly offered bicycle taxis (C$20) from Guasaule bus station. From the border there's a direct bus to Tegucigalpa every 2 hours.

There's another crossing at **El Espino**, which is connected to the small town of Somoto by frequent buses. Somoto, home to a smattering of accommodation and a canyon (which you can visit on tours from León and Estelí), is served by regular buses from Estelí and hourly departures from Managua's Mercado Mayoreo. Exit tax is US$2 (it's US$10 to enter Nicaragua), and the crossing relatively quiet.

To skip Honduras altogether, you can cross the Gulf of Fonseca from Potosí in Nicaragua to La Unión, **El Salvador**. There is an official border post at each side – exit tax is US$2, and it's US$10 to enter Nicaragua – but no regular public transport. You can either take your chance on finding a fishing boat heading that way and haggle (not easy, as they have to get permission to take you) or book a shuttle service. Established players Ruta del Golfo (ⓦrutadelgolfo.com) offer a range of packages depending on how far you need to travel, starting at US$65 per person for just the water crossing. To get to Potosí take a bus from Chinandega's main terminal (daily 9.30am and 1pm; 2hr).

way to the Honduran border and, with wildlife-rich volcanoes nearby and a decidedly untouristed vibe, it's not a bad place to stop off. Most action centres on the **Parque Central**, which has an odd miniature fort at its centre and Parroquia Santa Ana, a faded but peaceful church opposite its northern end.

The **coast west** of here is truly beautiful and unspoilt, with great surfing and kayaking. There is some laidback accommodation in the village of **Jiquilillo** – check out ⓦrancho-esperanza.com.

ARRIVAL AND DEPARTURE

By bus Buses arrive at the market southeast of the centre. Destinations Guasaule (regular daily service, leaving when full; 1hr); Jiquilillo (5 daily from the El Mercadito terminal – get a taxi from the main terminal; 1hr 30min); León (daily, every 15min; 50min–1hr 30min); Managua (every 20min; 1hr 40min–2hr 30min).

INFORMATION

Banks There are several ATMs, including a BAC a block east and half a block south of the Parque Central.
Tourist information There's an INTUR office (Mon–Fri 8am–noon & 1–5pm) four blocks south and half a block east of the park, where you can get info on climbing volcanoes and visiting the area's quiet beaches. Don Alvaro at *Hotel Casa Grande* (closed for refurbishment at the time of writing) can organize walking trips to San Cristóbal (US$25/person) and a stay in his family farm on its slopes. Ibis Kayaking (ⓣ 8961 8548, ⓦ ibiskayaking .com) offer trips for a day or more to the spectacular

mangrove estuaries of the Padre Ramos reserve, on the coast to the west of Chinandega.

ACCOMMODATION

Don Mario Two blocks north and one block east of the Parque Central ⓣ P311 1091. This lovely, relaxing little place is the best option in town, with welcoming rooms, neat en suites, wi-fi and a shared kitchen. __US$20__

EATING AND DRINKING

The competing sound systems of a series of bars at the northeast end of the Parque Central play everything from folk laments to Euro pop, and are your best bet for an evening drink.
Comedor La Parrillada One block south of the Parque Central. Classic *comida corriente* café, its deliciously smoky meats cooked on a barbecue on the pavement. Meal and drink C$65 at lunchtime. Daily 9am–9pm.
Kfé los Balcones Two blocks east and half a block south of the park. An air-conditioned haven in sunny Chinandega with free wi-fi, what more could you ask for? Breakfasts C$85, sweet and savoury crêpes C$60–100, smoothies C$60. Mon–Fri 7.30am–9pm, Sat & Sun 9am–9pm.

The central highlands

North of Managua, the **central highlands** sweep up from sea level in a lush procession of mountainous hillsides, bright-green coffee plantations and

6

cattle-flecked alpine pastures, stretching north to the Honduran border and east to the jungles and mines of the interior. The climate here is fairly temperate and the soil productive, with plenty of tobacco plantations and an economy based on coffee, grains, vegetables, fruit and dairy farming. The 150km journey north from Managua to **Estelí**, the northeast's largest city, is one of the most inspiring in the country, as the Carretera Panamericana winds through the grassy Pacific plains, skirting the southern edge of Lago de Managua before climbing slowly into a ribbon of blue mountains. East of here is **Matagalpa**, a town of steep slopes and coffee shops, while around the two sit fincas and reserves that merit deeper exploration.

ESTELÍ

The largest town in the north, at first sight **ESTELÍ** can seem downtrodden. But this low-key city is an engaging place and a hotbed of political activity. Notorious for its staunchly leftist character, Estelí saw heavy fighting and serious bloodshed during the Revolution. Somoza bore a particular grudge against the town's inhabitants, and waged brutal offensives on the city. The scars have not really healed, either on the bombed-out buildings that still dot the streets or in people's minds, and the region remains a centre of Sandinista support.

Estelí's relatively rural setting makes it a good base for trips. **El Salto de la Estanzuela** – a secluded waterfall within walking distance of the centre – makes for a great day out, while the wonderful **Miraflor nature reserve** is just under 30km away.

WHAT TO SEE AND DO

Although Estelí lacks the stunning mountain views of Matagalpa, the centre of town is a nice place to wander, and the climate is refreshingly cool. Much of the pleasure lies in soaking up the atmosphere, particularly along **Avenida Central**, whose southern end sees shops' wares spill out onto the street, including cowboy boots and the local farmers' favourite, Western-style hats.

Parque Central

The town's **Parque Central** isn't as nice as some others in the country, but is nonetheless busy from dawn until dusk. The **cathedral** on the eastern side of the Parque has a rather austere facade but an interesting interior, with bright windows and lots of artwork. The south side of the

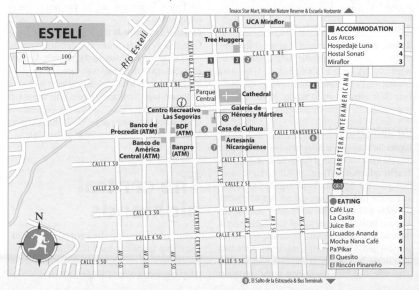

ESTELÍ

0 — 100 metres

Texaco Star Mart, Miraflor Nature Reserve & Escuela Horizonte ▲

UCA Miraflor

Tree Huggers

CALLE 4 NE
CALLE 3 NE
CALLE 2 NE

Parque Central
Centro Recreativo Las Segovias
Banco de Procredit (ATM)
BDF (ATM)
Banco de América Central (ATM)
Banpro (ATM)

Cathedral
Galería de Héroes y Mártires
Casa de Cultura
Artesanía Nicaragüense

CALLE 1 NE
CALLE TRANSVERSAL

Río Estelí

AVENIDA CENTRAL

CARRETERA INTERAMERICANA

CALLE 1 SO
CALLE 2 SO
CALLE 3 SO
CALLE 4 SO
CALLE 5 SO

CALLE 1 SE
CALLE 2 SE
CALLE 3 SE
CALLE 4 SE
CALLE 5 SE

N

■ ACCOMMODATION	
Los Arcos	1
Hospedaje Luna	2
Hostal Sonati	4
Miraflor	3

● EATING	
Café Luz	2
La Casita	8
Juice Bar	3
Licuados Ananda	5
Mocha Nana Café	6
Pa'Pikar	1
El Quesito	4
El Rincón Pinareño	7

8, El Salto de la Estnzuela & Bus Terminals ▼

Parque is dominated by the **Centro Recreativo Las Segovias**, which puts on regular music and sporting events, particularly basketball games.

Galería de Héroes y Mártires

Just south of the Parque Central is the tiny **Galería de Héroes y Mártires** (officially daily 9am–5pm but can be sporadic; C\$20), a simple yet moving museum devoted to the Revolution and to the many residents of Estelí who died fighting in it. The women who work at the Galería are, for the most part, mothers and widows of soldiers who were killed.

Casa de Cultura

The **Casa de Cultura** (☎2713 3021), a cultural venue a block south of Parque Central, hosts local art exhibitions, dancing and music events. Across the street, the **Artesanía Nicaragüense** has a reasonable selection of crafts, pottery and cigars.

ARRIVAL AND DEPARTURE

By bus Estelí has two bus terminals: Cotran Sur, at the southern entrance to town, serves destinations south of Estelí; while Cotran Norte, 100m north, serves destinations north of Estelí, plus most express buses to León and one daily Managua bus. Some buses may also drop you at the Shell Estelí or the Shell Esquipulas (in true Nica style, they are no longer Shell garages, but the name is still used to give directions). You can also catch buses to the Miraflor reserve (see p.476).

Destinations León (daily 5.45am and 3:10pm from Cotran Norte; 6.45am from Cotran Sur; all 2hr 30min; alternatively get on any bus to Matagalpa and get off at San Isidro); Managua (15 daily from Cotran Sur 3.30am–6pm; 2–3hr); Masaya (2 daily from Cotran Norte; 2pm & 3pm; 2hr 30min); Matagalpa (every 30min from Cotran Sur 5.15am–5.45pm; 1hr 45min); Ocotal (12 daily 6.30am–5pm from Cotran Norte; 2hr).

By taxi A taxi into town from any of the main bus stops should cost around C\$10–15/person.

INFORMATION AND TOURS

Tour operators UCA Miraflor, Av 4 NE, at C 4 NE (☎2713 2971, ⓦmiraflor.org), can, in theory, arrange accommodation in the Miraflor reserve (see p.476) and give you information on getting there independently. The friendly TreeHuggers (☎8496 7449), opposite *Hospedaje Luna* (see below), is a better option, with more English spoken. They can arrange homestays with local families in Miraflor, offer general advice, bike rental, information on

Spanish classes and cigar tours and can also help organize trips to other destinations including the canyon at Somoto, near the Honduran border.

Tourist information INTUR, C 1 NE, half a block west of Parque Central (Mon–Fri 8am–5pm; ☎2713 2468, ⓔesteli@intur.gob.ni), has some information on transport links and tours.

Banks There's a bank on every corner of C Transversal and Av 1 SO.

Internet There are plenty of places in town; try Cyber on Av 1 SE (C\$10/hr; Mon–Sat 8am–6pm).

Spanish lessons Estelí is a good spot to immerse yourself in the Spanish language and Nicaraguan culture. Escuela Horizonte has 25 years' experience in providing Spanish for all levels (☎2713 4117, ⓦescuelahorizonte.edu.ni).

ACCOMMODATION

Budget accommodation is mostly on the simple side, with a few decent options around the Parque Central.

★**Hospedaje Luna** Av 2 NE ☎8441 8466, ⓦcafeluzyluna.org. Estelí's main backpacker hostel is a likeable place with a social conscience and what is probably the town's most useful information office ("TreeHuggers") across the road. The dorms and private rooms are clean, if basic, there's a good book exchange and wi-fi and the associated *Café Luz*, opposite, is a decent hangout too. Dorms US\$9, doubles US\$25

Hostal Sonati 3 blocks east of the Cathedral ☎2713 6043, ⓦsonati.org. Nonprofit organization with another hostel in León. New, clean dorms, plus doubles with private bathroom and hot water. Dorms US\$7, doubles US\$25

Miraflor Av Central ☎2713 2003. Small hotel with homely, terracotta-coloured rooms, overhead fan and decent bathroom. There's also a restaurant and bar on site. It's a good deal, especially if you're travelling in a group (a five-bed room costs US\$30). C\$500

EATING

Café Luz Av 2 NE ⓦcafeluzyluna.org. Civilized tourist den, and a good place to socialize. Most produce is organic and grown by local co-operatives, and everything is on offer, from good black coffee (C\$10), yoghurt (US\$1), the

6

popular *gallo pintado* (a spiced-up version of the national favourite *gallo pinto*, US$2.50) and *nacatamales* (US$2) to juices and beer. Daily 7am–10pm.

La Casita 5min walk past the hospital on the right ☎ 2713 4917. Right on the southern edge of town, and a convenient stop if you're visiting El Salto, this charming café has beautifully carved tables, a botanic garden out back and some fairly slow service. Sit by the tinkling stream (surprisingly tranquil despite the nearby motorway), snack on small loaves of bread with honey (C$28) and drink lassis (C$20), pots of chai (C$2520) and the like. Tues–Sun 9am–7pm.

Juice Bar Av Central ☎ 2713 5822. Don't be confused by the huge cakes on display – this locally run establishment was the first juice bar in Nicaragua and still serves delicious juices and smoothies using locally produced fresh fruit and vegetables (C$25–35). Mon–Sat 7.30am–5.30pm.

Licuados Ananda C Transversal. Arranged, rather surreally, around a disused swimming pool, this relaxing outdoor café has mostly veggie mains (dish of the day C$60), a reasonable range of smoothies (C$30) and filling breakfasts. Daily 8am–5pm.

Mocha Nana Café C Transversal ☎ 2713 3164. This laid-back café, with outdoor seating, is one of the few places in the country you can get a decent cup of real English tea (C$30). Frequent live music at the weekend – look out for posters around town (panini C$75, bagel with hummus C$40).

Pa'Pikar Two blocks north of the Cathedral ☎ 2713 2959. Eccentric, colourful place serving sandwiches, gyros, curly fries and all sorts of treats you won't find elsewhere (C$40–100). Mon & Thurs–Sun 6–11pm.

El Quesito One block east of the Cathedral ☎ 2713 0547. Try local dairy-based specialities, such as *quesillo* (string cheese) and *cuajada* (curd cheese), as well as the ubiquitous tacos and *nacatamales*. Breakfasts C$15–50; lunch C$120–130; supper C$45–60. Yoghurt (C$30) and other treats also available to take away.

★**El Rincón Pinareño** Av 1 SE. Popular Cuban restaurant, serving filling sandwiches with chips and well-cooked steaks (C$70–370). Head upstairs for a balcony seat. Daily noon–10.30pm.

AROUND ESTELÍ

Estelí is blessed with beautiful natural surroundings, some – like the appealing waterfall of **El Salto de la Estanzuela** – an easy day-trip. The gorgeous **Miraflor** reserve to the north is worth staying in for a night or more.

El Salto de la Estanzuela

El Salto de la Estanzuela is one of the few waterfalls in Nicaragua easily accessible

INTO HONDURAS: LAS MANOS

The **Las Manos** border crossing for **Honduras** is less busy and less hassle-prone than the trip via Guasaule (see box, p.473). The exit fee is US$2; there is a US$10 fee to enter Nicaragua. The post is open 24hr, but vehicles can only cross between 8am and 5pm. To get here, take one of the regular buses from Managua or Estelí to the small town of Ocotal, and change for the bus to Las Manos (every 45min 5am–4pm; 30min). Continuing on, there are regular buses from Las Manos to the nearest town, El Paraíso (every 30min; 30min), where buses leave to Tegucigalpa (every 15min). There are two direct buses a day from the border to Tegucigalpa (9.20am & 2.20pm).

on foot from a major centre of population. Located in the **Reserva Natural Tisey-Estanzuela**, it's reached on a lovely two-hour walk through green, rolling hills – although it's also possible to drive right to the foot of the falls. The path begins just beyond the hospital at the southern edge of town – it's a fairly dull forty-minute walk to get here, and you may want to get a bus (C$4) from the eastern end of the Parque Central. Turn right at the *Kiosko Europeo* and follow the path around to the left for 4km or so until you see a sign for "Comunidad Estanzuela"; go through the gate on the right-hand side and follow the path for another 1km (you can cut off early if you want to explore the lovely but litter-strewn stretch above). The falls themselves – 35m or so in height – are located at the bottom of a steep flight of steps and cascade spectacularly into a deep pool perfect for swimming in. Don't go directly underneath the falling water as rocks do occasionally fall down, especially after heavy rainfall. Nearby is **El Mirador**, one of the most spectacular viewpoints in all Nicaragua; on a clear day it's possible to see volcanoes as far away as El Salvador.

Miraflor nature reserve

The wonderful **Miraflor nature reserve**, 28km northeast of Estelí, covers 206 square kilometres of forest, part of which is farmed by a group of agricultural co-ops – more than five thousand locals currently produce coffee, potatoes, milk, cheese and exotic flowers in and around the protected area. One of the project's main aims is to find sustainable ways in which farming and environmental protection can coexist; the emphasis is firmly upon community-centred tourism.

The reserve itself comprises several different **ecosystems**, ranging from savanna to tropical dry forest and humid cloudforest. To best appreciate this diversity it's advisable to stay for at least two or three days, either walking or horseriding between the zones and staying with different families each night – a very satisfying back-to-basics experience. Guides can take you to waterfalls, swimming spots, viewpoints, flower gardens and caves once inhabited by the ancient Yeluca and Ceballoi mountain peoples. In terms of flora and fauna, Miraflor is one of the richest reserves in the country, with over three hundred species of bird including quetzal, guardabarranco (the national bird of Nicaragua) and urraca, a local type of magpie, as well as howler monkeys and reclusive mountain lions. There are also over two hundred species of orchid.

ARRIVAL AND INFORMATION

By bus To get to the reserve, take a bus from Estelí. For El Coyolito, La Pita and El Cebollal, all villages within the reserve, head to the Texaco Star Mart (on the Interamericana just north of the centre – any taxi can take you) for 6am or 1pm; for Yalí, La Rampla or Puertas Azules, head to Cotran Norte for 6am, noon or 3pm.

Guides and accommodation UCA Miraflor and *Hospedaje Luna* in Estelí (see p.475) can arrange your trip and advise you on different areas' strengths. Both can book good, Spanish-speaking local guides (US$15/group) and accommodation (US$20 for three starchy but delicious meals a day, plus a bed in a farmhouse). Due to the altitude, it gets chilly of an evening – come prepared.

MATAGALPA

Known as "La Perla del Septentrión" – "Pearl of the North" – **MATAGALPA** is spoken well of by most Nicaraguans,

principally, perhaps, because of its relatively cool climate: at about 21–25°C, it's considered *tierra fría* in this land of 30°C-plus temperatures. Located 130km northeast of the capital, this small, quiet town is a gateway to the blue-green mountains and coffee plantations that surround it, whether you fancy a short hike into the hills or a longer trip to fincas like the famous **Selva Negra** to the north.

WHAT TO SEE AND DO

Matagalpa's services, hotels and restaurants are spread out between the seven blocks that divide the town's two principal squares: **Parque Morazán** to the north and the smaller **Parque Darío** seven blocks to the south. The town's main thoroughfares, **Avenida José Benito Escobar** and **Avenida Central**, link the two.

6

Parque Morazán

At the northern end of town, sunny **Parque Morazán** fronts the **Catedral de San Pedro**, dating from 1874. Unusually, the cathedral was constructed side-on, with its bell towers and entrance facing away from the Parque. A large **Sandinista monument**, consisting of three men firing guns, stands on one corner of the eastern side, with a monument to Matagalpino Tomás Borge, one of the founders of the Sandinista party, on the opposite corner.

Museo del Café

One and a half blocks south of the Parque Morazán, the **Museo del Café** (Mon–Fri 8am–12.30pm & 2–5.30pm; free) houses some old photos of Matagalpa life and explanations of the coffee-growing process. The museum sells quality coffee and is also behind Matagalpa's new **Feria Nacional del Café** (held in November), a festival celebrating the town's coffee expertise with talks and traditional music and dance.

Casa Museo Comandante Carlos Fonseca

The **Casa Museo Comandante Carlos Fonseca** (Mon–Fri 8am–5.30pm; donations welcomed), 100m southeast of the Parque Darío, documents the life of martyred local hero Carlos Fonseca (co-founder of the Sandinista National Liberation Front), who was gunned down by Somoza's National Guard in 1976.

Cerro Apante

Matagalpa is not a city of intoxicating beauty, but several day-hikes take you out into the inspiring scenery that surrounds it. The most accessible explores **Cerro Apante**. From Parque Darío head south up the hill for thirty minutes, following the road into the reserve itself. Turn left at the rangers' cottage, where you'll probably have to pay the C$30 entry fee, and climb the (at times steep) path through pleasant woodland to a *mirador* offering cracking views of the town and the crown of mountains that surrounds it. You can continue along the ridge, but the summit proper is private property – signs warn you off the final climb up

some wooden stairs. The walk should take less than three hours in total. Guides are available for C$250 for the three hours, but need to be arranged in advance (Arcenio Brenes; ☎ 8651 3727).

ARRIVAL AND DEPARTURE

By bus Matagalpa's south bus terminal is southwest of the city centre; it's about a 10min walk to Parque Darío.
Destinations Estelí (daily every 30min 4am–6pm; 1hr 30min); León (daily 6am, 2pm & 3pm; 3hr; for a more frequent service, take any bus towards Estelí and change at San Isidro); Managua (daily every 20min 3.30am–6.45pm; 2–3hr); Masaya (2pm & 3.30pm daily; 3hr).

INFORMATION AND TOURS

Tourist information INTUR (Mon–Fri 8am–noon, 1–5pm; ☎ 2772 7060) on Av Central can offer a few fliers and maps.
Tour operators Helpful Matagalpa Tours, one block southeast of Parque Morazán (☎ 2772 0108, ⊚ matagalpatours.com), offers excursions to the surrounding area, including tours of local coffee and chocolate farms and treks in the hills. Nativos, based in *La Buena Onda* hostel (✉ nativotour@hotmail.com), can organize city tours, walks up Cerro Apante and trips to waterfalls and fincas.

ACCOMMODATION

Alvarado Just north of Parque Darío on Av José Benito Escobar ☎ 2772 2830, ✉ hotelalvarado@gmail.com. This charming, family-run hotel above a pharmacy has en-suite wood-panelled rooms with TV, wi-fi and fan; some are on the small side (and two lack windows). C$450
Apante East side of Parque Darío ☎ 2772 6890. Tasteful rooms with TV, wi-fi, and beds, and colourfully tiled, hot-water bathrooms. Some are a lot larger than others, for the same price, so ask to see a few before choosing. C$450
★ **La Buena Onda** One block north and two blocks east of the Cathedral ☎ 2772 2135, ⊚ hostelmatagalpa.com. Smart, welcoming hostel with solid facilities – wi-fi, book exchange, hot water, free coffee and kitchen for guests' use. Nativos tours are based here too (see above). Dorms US$8, doubles US$30
Hotel Vizcaino Two and a half blocks east and one and a half blocks north of *La Buena Onda* ☎ 8121 8468. Brand new hotel offering wi-fi, private parking, hot water (Matagalpa mornings are cold), and good service. Breakfast included. US$45

EATING

Artesanos Next to Matagalpa Tours. Appealing café-bar with a relaxed daytime vibe (lunch C$75 including drink) and a nice buzz at night, when it's pretty much *the* place to come. Fri is salsa night. Daily 7.30am–2am.

Barista Café Nica Av José Benito Escobar ☎ 2772 6338, ⓦ baristacafenica. Modern coffee shop with free wi-fi and good service. Decent cappuccino C$50, panini C$100–130.

Cafetería Don Chaco One and a half blocks south of Parque Morazán on Av José Benito Escobar ☎ 2772 2982. Intimate little restaurant serving up a range of Nicaraguan dishes. The breakfasts (C$45) will set you up nicely for a day's walking and there are healthy smoothies (C$30–50) and mains (around C$125) too. Mon–Fri 7am–6pm, Sun 7am–3pm.

★ **El Mexicano** One block north and two blocks east of the Cathedral, opposite *La Buena Onda* ☎ 2772 3732. Authentic, reasonably priced (starters C$40, mains C$80–100) Mexican food on regularly changing seasonal menus. The Mexican chef/owner and his Nicaraguan wife are very accommodating – just ask if you fancy something that's not on the menu, or want to eat vegetarian food. Free wi-fi. Mon–Sat 11am–9pm.

★ **La Vita è Bella** Tucked down an alleyway behind *La Buena Onda* ☎ 2772 5476. The chef is from Tuscany, the lasagne (C$140), pasta (C$80-12070–100) and bread are all home-made and the pizza is perhaps the best in the country (C$70–150). There's a relaxing courtyard at the back. Tues–Sun noon–10pm.

DIRECTORY

Banks You'll find a couple of banks with ATMs on Av Central just south of Parque Morazán.

Internet Ciber Center (C$12/hr) on Av José Benito Escobar, has reasonably fast connection (Daily 9am–8pm).

Laundry Cuenta Conmigo, 2.5 blocks north of *La Buena Onda* (C$80 for up to 3kg; Mon–Fri 8am–noon & 2–5pm; ☎ 2772 6713, ⓦ lavanderiacuentaconmigo.info). Charitable organization providing help for people with mental illnesses. Volunteer opportunities also available.

AROUND MATAGALPA

Matagalpa has an exceptional natural setting, and most of the area is only accessible on tours (see opposite). You can get a good feel for it in the grounds of the **Selva Negra**, where footpaths weave through the thick tropical forest.

Selva Negra

North of Matagalpa, the **SELVA NEGRA** (US$2.50, US$5 if staying overnight) is a stretch of dark blue, pine-clad mountains named by the area's German immigrants in the nineteenth century after their homeland's Black Forest, thanks to the physical resemblance and its spring-like climate. An amazing variety of **wildlife** flourishes in these pristine tropical forests, including more than eighty varieties of orchid, many birds, sloths, ocelots, margay, deer, snakes, mountain lions and howler monkeys.

The **trails** range from short strolls around the central lake to the thigh-burning La Mosquitia, which ascends to 1570m. It's perfectly feasible to come up from Matagalpa early in the morning and pack most of them into a day's hiking.

The owners of the *Selva Negra* hotel (see below) have grown **coffee** here since 1891, and the finca still produces some of the best export-grade coffee in the country; the estate employs 250 workers, most of whom live nearby. Various **tours** of the operation run daily, including horseback treks (US$10/hr), and there's a small museum too.

ARRIVAL AND DEPARTURE

By bus To get here from Matagalpa, hop on one of the buses to Jinotega (daily 4am–6pm every 30min) and ask to be let off at Selva Negra (after about 30min). The hotel and office is a 20min walk away – head 100m uphill, turn right at the tank and continue up the track.

ACCOMMODATION AND EATING

Selva Negra 10km north of Matagalpa ☎ 2772 3883, ⓦ selvanegra.com. Many visitors to the area stay in this faded but prestigious hotel, which offers an accessible route to the forest and mountains. Options include good-sized doubles, individually designed cabañas and perfectly adequate dorms. There's a pricey restaurant on site (though your entry fee doubles as a voucher for food and drink), serving good coffee and traditional German food as well as local options – avoid the disappointing Sunday buffet. Dorms U̲S̲$̲1̲5̲, double̲ U̲S̲$̲6̲5̲, cabañas U̲S̲$̲8̲5̲

The southwest

The majority of Nicaragua's population lives in the fertile **southwest** of the country. Bordered by Lago de Nicaragua to the east and the Pacific to the west, and studded with **volcanoes** – Volcán Masaya, Volcán Mombacho and the twin cones of Ometepe's Concepción and Maderas – the southwest is otherwise a flat, low, grassy plain, home to what is

6

6

left of Nicaragua's beef industry, while coffee plantations can be found at higher altitudes.

Masaya, 29km south of Managua, and **Granada**, 26km further south, are the region's key cities; Masaya's excellent crafts market attracts virtually everyone who comes to Nicaragua, while the nearby **Parque Nacional Volcán Masaya** offers the most accessible volcano-viewing in the country. The picturesque "**Pueblos Blancos**", or White Towns, lie on the road connecting Managua, Masaya and Granada; the latter, with its fading classical-colonial architecture and lakeside setting, is Nicaragua's most beautiful and touristy city, and makes a good base for exploring nearby attractions such as the **Isletas de Granada** and **Volcán Mombacho**. Some 75km south of Granada, **Rivas**, the gateway to Costa Rica, is of little interest in itself, though many travellers pass through on their way to Isla de Ometepe (see p.495) and the popular beach town of **San Juan del Sur**.

MASAYA

Set midway between Managua and Granada and shadowed by the hulking form of Volcán Masaya, **MASAYA**'s stirring geography and regular festivals would make it an enjoyable stop even if it weren't also the centre of Nicaragua's **artesanía production**. During the Sandinista years, Masaya developed its crafts tradition into a marketable commodity, and the city is now the best place in the country to buy hammocks, rocking chairs, traditional clothing, shoes and other souvenirs. Most visitors come here on day-trips from Managua or Granada, easily manageable on the bus, but Masaya is a pleasant place to overnight too.

WHAT TO SEE AND DO

Masaya is an attractive place to explore on foot: there's not too much traffic in the streets and all the sights are within walking distance of each other.

Parque Central

What little action there is in downtown Masaya takes place in the local hangout,

the **Parque Central**, where – with the help of Spanish finance – **La Parroquia de La Asunción** church (daily 6am–7pm) has been renovated. Its cool interior boasts a lovely wooden ceiling and images of various Central American saints, swathed in coloured satin and wilting gold lamé.

Iglesia de San Jerónimo

The ramshackle **Iglesia de San Jerónimo**, 600m north of the Parque Central (opening hours vary but there should be someone to let you in), is the best example of colonial architecture in Masaya. The statue of San Jerónimo on the altar depicts an old man wearing a loincloth and a straw hat, with a rock in his hand and blood on his chest, evidence of self-mortification. The tower is officially closed to the public awaiting renovation, but it's worth asking if they'll let you up to see the panoramic views of the city and surrounding area, with volcanoes rearing grandly from the plains.

Mercado Nacional de Artesanía

Two blocks east of the Parque Central sits the **Mercado Viejo** (daily 8am–6.30pm), which has been converted into the grandly named **Centro Cultural (Antiguo Mercado de Masaya) – Mercado Nacional de Artesanía**. Behind the large, fortress-style walls lies a complex network of stalls selling paintings, many in the naïf-art tradition of the Solentiname archipelago, as well as large, excellent-quality hammocks, carved wooden bowls, utensils and animals, simple wood-and-bead jewellery, cotton shirts, straw hats and leather bags and purses. It's a fun place for a potter even if you're not going to buy anything – safe, not too hustly and dotted with drinks stalls and restaurants. The weekly **Jueves de Verbena** party night (see box, p.482) takes place here too. Check out the giant wall map of the country, which shows the places in Nicaragua where crafts are produced. If your Spanish is up to it, ask about visiting artisans at work in their homes and workshops. Many of the crafts on sale come from designs that originated in the indigenous *barrio* of **Monimbó**, fifteen minutes' walk south of the market,

MASAYA

● NIGHTLIFE	
Coco Jambo	4
Ritmo de la Noche	3
El Toro Loco	7

● EATING	
Baho Vilma	5
Cafetín la Criolla	6
La Jarochita	1
La Ronda	8
Tele Pizza	2

■ ACCOMMODATION	
Hostal Santamaría	3
Hotel Regis	2
Madera's Inn	1

6

▼ Iglesia de San Sebastián & Monimbó

where you'll find more produce on sale
▲▲▲▲▲ ▲ ▲ ▲ ▲ ▲ ▲▲ ▲ ▲.

Museo del Folclor

Inside the Mercado Nacional de
Artesanía, the **Museo del Folclor**
(Mon–Sat 9am–5pm, Sun 9am–noon;
US$2) is a modern building displaying a
variety of national costumes and masks
from around the country. Interesting
information (in Spanish only, but there
are plans to offer tours in English)
explains the origin and meaning of many
of the traditional dances and costumes
you'll doubtless come across on your
travels.

Laguna de Masaya

On the western side of town, seven
blocks from the Parque Central, **Laguna
de Masaya** beckons. Despite its crystalline
appearance and appealing, forested
slopes, the lake is heavily polluted with
sewage effluent from the town. It's still
worth the walk, though, as the waterfront
malecón has stunning views of the
smoking cone of Volcán Masaya (see
p.483) and most of the town's late-night
bars and clubs.

(see p.483)

ARRIVAL AND INFORMATION

By bus Chicken buses from Managua (daily 5am–9.30pm
every 20min; 1hr) and Granada (daily 6am–6pm, every
20min; 45min) arrive at the dusty, chaotic terminal next to
Masaya's main market (Mercado Nuevo) to the east of
town; it's a 15min walk to the centre from here, so ask to
be let off earlier, at the Iglesia San Jerónimo. There is one
bus daily from the main terminal to Estelí (6am; 3hr).
Minibuses from Managua (daily 5.30am–6pm, every
15min; 40min) arrive at and depart from the street in front
of the small Parque San Miguel, three blocks east of the
Parque Central.

By taxi It's fairly easy to negotiate a taxi between Masaya
and Granada for around C$200.

Tourist information The INTUR office (Mon–Fri
9am–5pm; ☎2522 7615), half a block south of the
Mercado Nacional, can provide information on local hotels
and volcano tours.

ACCOMMODATION

There are several reasonable budget options, most of
which are clustered a few blocks north of the Mercado
Nacional.

Hostal Santamaría Half a block southeast of the
Mercado Nacional ☎2522 2411. The 22 small, tidy rooms
here, all en suite with cable TV, are quiet and cool and just
a stone's throw from the old market. Popular with Nica
travellers. __US$20__

Hotel Regis Av Sergio Delgadillo ☎2522 2300,

6

@ hotelregismasaya@hotmail.com. A spotless bargain with cell-like, wood-panelled rooms with thin partition walls, and a neat little courtyard. 10pm curfew. C$260
★**Madera's Inn** One block north of *Hotel Regis* ☎ 2522 5825, ⓦ hotelmaderasinn.com. Probably the best of the lot in Masaya, with bright and cosy rooms, including a dorm, spread over a tidy and welcoming family house with interesting nooks and knick-knacks and a nice dining area. Rooms come with shared or private bath and either fan or a/c. Breakfast is included for the private rooms, but so is an 11pm curfew. Dorms US$6, doubles US$20

EATING, DRINKING AND NIGHTLIFE

Masaya's social scene is fairly low-key. If you fancy a boogie later on head to one of the three clubs – *Coco Jambo*, *Ritmo de la Noche* (both clubs play Eighties music and salsa) and *El Toro Loco* (younger reggaetón crowd) – which get going on the *malecón* until around 3am Fri–Sun. You'll pay a cover change of C$60 (ladies free Fri & Sat) at all three; get a taxi there and back at night.
Baho Vilma South side of the Parque Central. As good a place as any to try the delicious national dish *baho* – beef, green plantain and *yuca* cooked in a huge pot (C$80). Daily from noon until they sell out, at around 2pm.
Cafetín La Criolla Southwest corner of the Mercado Nacional. Hearty, popular market cheapie – stuff yourself on chicken, plantain, rice and a drink for C$110 and watch tourists and locals browse and haggle. Daily 9am–6pm.
La Jarochita Av Sergio Delgadillo, north of La Asunción ☎ 2522 0450. A charming Mexican restaurant where you can dine on fajitas, burritos and quesadillas (C$100–150), all washed down with tequila or a cold beer (C$35). Head upstairs to the pleasant balcony. Daily 11am–10pm.
La Ronda Overlooking La Asunción and the Parque Central. An airy bar and restaurant drawing a local crowd with cheap beer (C$24, C$42 for a litre) and televised sport. The food (steak with jalapeños C$215) is pretty decent too.
Tele Pizza Av San Jerónimo. Tasty, decent-sized pizzas for C$120–200, as well as pastas (from C$140) served from a pink front room and restful courtyard.

DIRECTORY

Banks Banks and ATMs are plentiful in Masaya; there's a handy Banpro machine by the Mercado Nacional de Artesanía, and a branch of BAC opposite the police station where you can change dollars and travellers' cheques.
Internet There are various spots around town: try Cyber M&G, on the south side of the Parque Central (C$12/hr).
Post office There's a tiny office one block north of the Mercado Nacional next to the BAC (Mon–Fri 8am–4pm, Sat 8–11am).

AROUND MASAYA

Attractions around Masaya include the town's namesake **volcano** and a crater lake, **Laguna de Apoyo**, which can be explored on foot and with a guide. The nearby **Pueblos Blancos**, meanwhile, are famous for artisanal crafts, including pottery, which is made in small workshops throughout the villages, while the historical site of **Coyotepe** is a must for anyone interested in the nation's political history.

Coyotepe

Three kilometres out of town on the road to Managua is the old fort of **COYOTEPE** (daily 8am–5pm; US$2 plus tip for guide). Built on a hilltop by the Somoza regime to house political prisoners, the abandoned structure commands stunning views of Masaya and the volcanoes of Masaya and Mombacho, and also offers an eerie reminder of the atrocities carried out here by Somoza's National Guard: when Sandinistas stormed the fort during the Revolution, the National Guard responded by slaughtering all those inside. It's now administered by Nicaragua's Boy Scouts, who will illuminate the tunnels on a torchlit tour and tell you grim tales about Nicaragua's recent past.

ARRIVAL AND DEPARTURE

By bus From Masaya, take any Managua-bound bus and ask to be let off at the entrance, from where a winding path leads up to the fort. On your return, simply flag any Masaya-bound bus down from the roadside.

By taxi A cab from Masaya will cost C$50 or so.

Parque Nacional Volcán Masaya

Just outside Masaya, the **PARQUE NACIONAL VOLCÁN MASAYA** (daily 9am–4.45pm; C$100; ☎2528 1444) offers you the chance to peer into the smoking cone of a volcano, as well as some stunning long-distance views. Gazing warily over the smoke-blackened rim into the crater's sulphurous depths, you can well imagine why the Spaniards considered this to be the mouth of hell itself – the large white cross above the crater marks the spot where a Spanish friar placed a cross in the sixteenth century to exorcize the volcano's demonic presence. This is still one of the most active volcanoes in the world; the last eruption of note occurred in 2001, but plumes have been spotted since then, and signs advise drivers to park their cars facing downhill in case a quick getaway is required.

From the entrance (see below), it's a 1.5km walk up the road to the **Centro de Interpretación Ambiental** (daily 9am–4pm), home to an exhibition outlining the area's geology, agriculture and pre-Columbian history, along with an interesting 3D display of the country's chain of volcanoes. From the centre you're best off hitching or getting a spot in one of the regular minibuses going up to the **crater** (C$25 each way – they are less frequent in the afternoon so arrive early if you can), as it's a fairly steep 5km hike up a paved road. Walking down is more pleasant, although in theory (and despite the lack of any kind of danger) you must be accompanied by a guide along this stretch – if you're not, a ranger will probably follow you down, at a discreet distance, on a bike. The rangers at the crater can point out a few short walks around the area that you can take unaccompanied, and also offer guided **tours** of two trails, Sendero Los Coyotes and Sendero de Las Pencas, as well as

highly recommended **night hikes** (5–7/8pm; US$10; book in advance), including a visit to the subterranean **Cueva Tzinancanostoc**, where you'll see bizarre lava formations and a bat colony and, if you're lucky, the lava glowing deep in the main crater. Look out for the stunted bromeliads common to high-altitude volcanic areas, and the famous *chocoyos del cráter*, small green parrots that have thrived in an atmosphere that should be poisonous.

ARRIVAL AND DEPARTURE

By bus The park entrance lies between Km 22 and Km 23 on the Managua–Granada highway, about 4km north of Masaya. You can get off any bus (except the express) between Managua and Masaya or Granada at the entrance – you'll pass Coyotepe (see p.482) on the way.

By taxi Alternatively, you could hire a taxi from Masaya (about C$200 return). Arrive early if you want to catch a minibus to the crater (see above).

Pueblos Blancos

Scattered within 15km of Masaya are the "Pueblos Blancos" or White Towns: **Nindirí**, **Niquinohomo**, **Masatepe**, **Catarina**, **Diriá** and **Diriomo**. The name comes from the traditional whitewash used on the villages' houses – called *carburo*, it is made from water, lime and salt – as well as a past tradition of practising white magic in the area. The white buildings are pretty, but there's not much more to see: although each town has its own specific artisan traditions and fiestas, and local identity is fiercely asserted, they seem remarkably similar, sleepy towns with a few people hanging out around nearly identical central squares. **CATARINA** is the prettiest, the main draw being **El Mirador** (US$1), a lookout at the top of the village that stares right down into the blue waters of the collapsed crater lake of Laguna de Apoyo, with Volcán Masaya looming behind it. Restaurants, cafés and *artesanía* stalls have sprung up around the viewpoint.

ARRIVAL AND DEPARTURE

By bus A regular local bus runs from Masaya's main bus terminal to Catarina (daily 5am–8.30pm, roughly every 30min; around 30min). From Granada (daily 6am–6pm;

6

around 25min), buses to Niquinohomo pass through the town, or alternatively you can take any Masaya or Managua bus and ask to be let off at the Catarina turning, from where you'll need to take another short bus ride to the edge of the village.

Laguna de Apoyo

The volcanic **Laguna de Apoyo** draws tourists with its mineral-rich waters, tropical rainforest and stunning views. Nature-lovers will be entranced by the rare **flora and fauna**, including howler monkeys, armadillos and toucans, and divers can check out the lake's unique fish, but it's a pleasant place just to relax and sip a few beers, too. Its popularity means stretches get a bit party-centric on busy days, and others are under threat from developers despite its natural reserve status, but it remains a stunning place.

ARRIVAL AND DEPARTURE

By bus Masaya has direct buses part way to the lake (daily around 10am & 3pm; 1hr).
From Granada Most tourists visit from Granada, whether on a tour (see box, p.486), or using the *Bearded Monkey* or *Hostel Oasis* shuttles which leave Granada daily around 10am and return around 4pm (C$40–60 return).

ACCOMMODATION

Monkey Hut ☎2520 3030 or ☎8366 9986, ⓦthemonkeyhut.net. Many backpackers head to this place for day-trips, paying US$7 to use the hammocks, kayaks, kitchen and buzzing bar, which means the accommodation can feel like an afterthought. Dorms US$16, doubles US$49

GRANADA

Set on the western shore of Lago de Nicaragua, some 50km southeast of Managua, **GRANADA** was once the jewel of Central America. The oldest Spanish-built city in the isthmus, it was founded in 1524 by Francisco Fernández de Córdoba, who named it after his hometown in Spain. During the colonial period Granada became fabulously rich, its wealth built upon exploitation: sited just 20km from the Pacific, the city was a transit point for shipments of gold and other minerals mined throughout the Spanish Empire. In the mid-nineteenth century Granada fell to American

adventurer William Walker, who briefly gained control of the city – and, by default, the entire country. Granada paid dearly for the eventual overthrow of Walker; as he retreated in the face of international resistance, he burned the city practically to the ground.

Today Granada is central to the Nicaraguan government's tourism ambitions. Its popularity with foreign visitors has led to a large-scale restoration of the stunning old colonial **buildings**, many of them repainted in pastel shades, and a burgeoning network of foreign-owned bars, restaurants and hostels has sprung up. This manageable, gringo-packed city also makes a **good base** from which to explore the lake, volcanoes, Zapatera archipelago and Isla de Ometepe; while more adventurous travellers might head from here to San Carlos, the Solentiname islands (see p.501) and beyond.

WHAT TO SEE AND DO

There are few "must see" attractions in Granada itself, but most of the pleasure is simply in strolling the streets and absorbing the colonial atmosphere – be sure to take a peek through open front doors along Calle La Calzada to see the magnificent interior courtyards that adorn some of the private houses.

Parque Central

At the centre of town sits the attractive, palm-lined **Parque Central**, peopled by an engaging mix of tourists, stalls, itinerants and horses. A few small kiosks sell snacks, and an ice-cream seller wanders around ringing his handbell in search of trade. On the east side of the Parque is the large, graceful **cathedral** (open daily to the public as a house of worship), built in 1712 and damaged in the 1850s during William Walker's violent reign.

As well as the cathedral, many of the city's most captivating historic houses line the square. The palatial red house with white trim on the corner of Calle La Calzada, across from the cathedral, is the **Bishop's Residence**, with a columned upstairs veranda typical of the former homes of wealthy Granadino burghers.

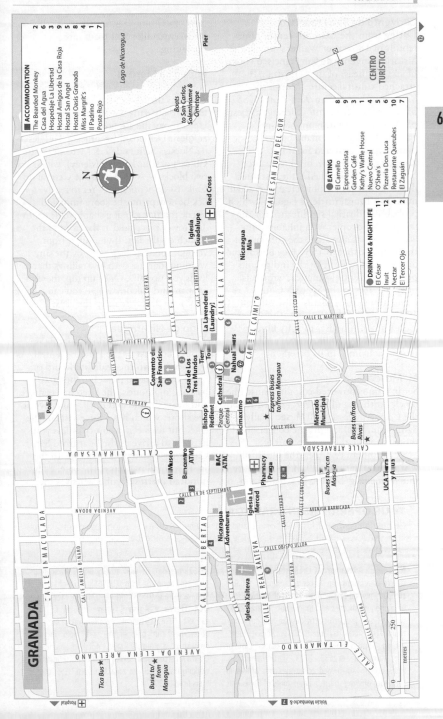

GRANADA

ACCOMMODATION

The Bearded Monkey	2
Casa del Agua	6
Hospedaje La Libertad	3
Hostal Amigos de la Casa Roja	9
Hostal San Angel	5
Hostel Oasis Granada	8
Miss Margrit's	4
Il Padrino	1
Poste Rojo	7

EATING

El Camello	8
Espressionista	9
Garden Café	3
Kathy's Waffle House	1
Nuevo Central	4
O'Shea's	5
Pizzería Don Luca	6
Restaurante Querubes	10
El Zaguán	7

DRINKING & NIGHTLIFE

El César	11
Inuit	12
Nectar	4
El Tercer Ojo	2

Lago de Nicaragua

Boats to San Carlos, Solentiname & Ometepe

Pier

CENTRO TURISTICO

6

6

Convento de San Francisco

Dating from the sixteenth century but rebuilt in 1867 after Walker's attack, the historic **Convento de San Francisco** is two blocks northeast of the cathedral. The attached **cultural centre** (Mon–Fri 8am–5pm, Sat & Sun 9am–4pm; US$2) has been converted into Nicaragua's best pre-Columbian museum, housing various displays and many of the **petroglyphs** recovered from Isla Zapatera. Hewn from black volcanic basalt in about 1000 AD, these statues depict anthropomorphic creatures – half man, half lizard, turtle or jaguar – which probably had ritual significance for the indigenous peoples who inhabited the islands. It was also from the confines of this convent that in 1535 **Frey Bartolomé de Las Casas**, apostle of the indigenous peoples of Central America, wrote his historic letter to the Spanish Court, condemning the Indians' mistreatment at the hands of the Spanish. The Convento also houses the city **library**; many of Walker's filibusterers are buried in the catacombs in its basement.

Mi Museo

Set in a fine converted colonial house one block northwest of the Parque Central on the Calle Atravesada, **Mi Museo** (daily 8am–5pm; free) is a private collection of more than five thousand pieces of pre-Columbian ceramics, the oldest of which dates back to 500 BC. There's not much labelling, but the jars, plates and urns of various sizes, mostly depicting birds, crocodiles and toads, are intriguing.

Iglesia La Merced

For panoramic views of Granada's rooftops, as well as the lake and volcano, climb the **tower** (daily 8am–12.30pm & 2–6pm; US$1 – pay the attendant in the stairwell) at **Iglesia La Merced** (technically La Iglesia de Nuestra Señora de Las Mercedes – the Church of Our Lady of Mercy), which sits two blocks west of the Parque Central on Calle 14 de Septiembre. Yet to receive a lick of new paint, the sooty front and serene interior give it a shabby-chic charm. The tower is accessed at the front of the church on the left. If you suffer from vertigo, you may be put off by the tiny winding staircase with low railings that leads you upstairs. Once up top, there's a wraparound balcony where you can take photos or simply soak up the view.

Lago de Nicaragua

The shoreline of **Lago de Nicaragua** is about 1km east of the Parque Central. As you head down the wide boulevard of Calle La Calzada, past churches and baseball diamonds, the stretch gets more and more dilapidated until you arrive at the shore, which has a huge vista of the lake, but feels eerily empty unless you happen to arrive as the boat from San Carlos or Ometepe is docking. To the south a small park lines the lake, a few hundred metres beyond which is the

---

TOUR OPERATORS IN GRANADA

Guides hang around the larger hostels, and can be a reasonable bet as long as you ensure you know what you're getting for the price. The established operators below offer greater experience and professionalism, though.

Nicaragua Adventures C La Libertad ☎ 2552 8461, ⓦ nica-adventures.com. Long-standing, reliable company owned by European expats that offers trip-planning and shuttles and tours across Nicaragua, as well as Granada-specific activities like half-day kayak tours of Las Isletas, day-trips to Masaya and city tours.
Tierra Tour C La Calzada, two blocks east of the cathedral ☎ 2552 8723, ⓦ tierratour.com. Professional, Nica-owned company (with offices in León too) offering shuttles, kayak tours of the Isletas

(US$25/person), as well as city and volcano tours, diving in Laguna de Apoyo (US$65), and night tours of Masaya volcano (US$35 including entrance fee).
UCA Tierra y Agua C Atravesada, at C Nueva ☎ 2552 0238, ⓔ turismo@ucatierrayagua.org. This government-run co-operative can help organize homestays around Granada, notably around the Charco Muerto region, taking in crafts, horseriding and walking trails (bed and breakfast from US$5, guided tours from US$5).

entrance to the **Centro Turístico** (C$10 entry occasionally imposed), a group of lakeside bars and cheap restaurants that's ironically far more popular with locals than visitors. It's deserted on weekdays but popular at weekends, especially in the evenings, when the nightlife gets going. If heading here after dark, get a taxi back into town.

ARRIVAL AND INFORMATION

By boat The boat from San Carlos (14hr) and Ometepe (4hr) docks at the pier at the bottom of C La Calzada (leaves Granada Mon & Thurs 2pm; leaves San Carlos Tues & Fri 2pm). A/c first-class tickets – the only ones that can officially be sold to foreigners – are C$104 to Ometepe, C$219 to San Carlos. They're available on the day of travel from the dock office at the bottom of C La Calzada – arrive by noon to be safe or call ahead (☎2552 2966). The journey is notoriously cold and uncomfortable – come prepared.

By bus Buses from Managua (daily 5.30am–9pm, every 20min; 40min) come into the terminal west of town, 700m from the Parque, from where you can walk or grab a taxi into the centre (C$10). Services from Rivas (daily 6am–3pm, every 45min; 1hr 30min) and points south pull up at the market, a short walk southwest of the centre. Buses from Masaya (daily 6am–6pm, frequent; 45min) pull up a block west of the market. If you're travelling from Costa Rica, the Tica Bus for Managua will stop and let you off at its Granada office on Av Elena Arellano, 1km northwest of the centre, but you may not be able to board there. Check when you buy your ticket.

Tourist information Granada's better-than-average (in the sense that it might actually prove useful) INTUR office (Mon–Fri 8am–5pm; ☎2552 6858, ✉granada@intur .gob.ni) is on C Corral, and stocks information on climbing local volcanoes and other attractions. There is also a kiosk on C La Calzada.

GETTING AROUND

Several hostels and tour agencies rent out bikes for a standard US$1/hr or US$6/day.

By taxi Taxis line up in the northwest corner of the Parque. Any trip in Granada should cost C$10–20.

ACCOMMODATION

The Bearded Monkey C 14 de Septiembre ☎2552 4028, ✇thebeardedmonkey.com. Granada's best-known backpacker hostel is worth visiting for its cool, verdant courtyard bar even if you don't stay here. The large dorms are perfectly decent, and there are private rooms and hammocks too. It's a big, busy place – expect some noise. Dorms US$6, doubles US$15

★**Casa del Agua** Av Guzmán ✇casadelaguagranada .com. Dinky, smart place with a handful of rooms and a kitchen encircling a cool little pool. It's small enough that you'll end up talking to everyone and offers a surprisingly mellow experience given its just-off-the-square location. US$34

Hospedaje La Libertad C 14 de Septiembre ☎8408 0003, ✇la-libertad.net. A pleasant set of dorms, this one distinguished by some nice old baños and free use of the kitchen, but the big draw is that guests get free use of the nearby gym. It's Nica-owned, with tours including trips to a few remote beaches. Dorms US$5, doubles US$12

Hostal Amigos de la Casa Roja C Estrada ☎2552 2085, ✇nicaraguamiahostal.com. Well-run, central hostel. Guests have use of the communal kitchen and wi-fi, and laundry services are also available (US$4–6). Dorms US$7, doubles from US$15

Hostal San Angel Av Guzmán ☎2552 4591, ✉mariacampos118@hotmail.com. This welcoming, family-run hostel, which stretches either side of Casa del Agua, offers quiet and tidy (if slightly dark) rooms, all en suite with good mattresses and fans. Breakfast included. US$28

Hostel Oasis Granada C Estrada, 100m north of Masaya bus terminal ☎2552 8006, ✇nicaraguahostel.com. A self-proclaimed "backpackers' paradise", this imaginatively conceived hostel offers comfortable dorm beds and private rooms in a restored colonial house. There's also free wi-fi, plus DVDs, tours, a bar and even a tiny swimming pool. Dorms US$9, doubles US$20

Il Padrino 2 blocks north of El Convento de San Francisco ☎8777 4478, ✇lamesadelpadrino.com. Elegant hotel with a laidback arty vibe, spacious doubles and a beautiful garden. Even if you don't stay, it's worth popping by to see if the Italian owner has opened his long-planned restaurant. US$50

Poste Rojo Pozo del Oro ☎8903 4563, ✇posterojo.com. Located 10km out of Granada near Volcán Mombacho, this funky collection of treehouses offers hammocks, dorms and doubles on the edge of the rainforest, with some great

6

★**TREAT YOURSELF**

Miss Margrit's C La Libertad ☎8983 139, ✇missmargrits.com. The owner and his staff go out of their way to make you feel like this place is home. Use the kitchen, just ask if you need to do laundry – nothing is too much trouble. An easy walk into the centre but just far enough away from the noise, and it comes complete with a swimming pool. All rooms have hot water and a/c. Breakfast included. US$75

6

views. They also run yoga classes (Tues) and full-moon parties, and can organize tours to nearby Mombacho and beyond. Take a bus from Granada's market to Rivas, Nandaime or Diriomo, or get the free daily noon shuttle from *The Bearded Monkey*. Hammocks US$7, dorms US$8, doubles US$20

EATING

Granada offers an increasingly cosmopolitan variety of places to eat, with lots of Italian and Spanish food. Most places have wi-fi. Budget travellers can grab a quick but basic bite at the town market, and in the early evening a couple of small food stands open up on the Parque, selling cheap and filling meat and rice dishes. Most of the gringo-orientated places sit at the western end of C La Calzada, where prices are higher, but there's a nice buzz most evenings.

El Camello C El Camito. Food from the Mediterranean and further east. Most ingredients (including the lamb) are grown on the owner's farm. Kafta sandwich (C$110) and Thai green curry (C$190) are not to be missed. Beer C$35. Mon & Wed–Sun noon–10pm.

A Garden Café C La Libertad and C El Cisne. This cool haven from the bustling streets is tucked inside yet another colonial conversion. There's an extensive breakfast menu (*huevos al pesto* C$95) as well as tasty and imaginative smoothies (C$70), salads and sandwiches (around C$125), and free wi-fi, and the leafy courtyard comes complete with tinkling fountain. Daily 7am–9pm.

Kathy's Waffle House Opposite the San Francisco convent on C El Arsenal ⓦ kathyswafflehouse.com. A breakfast institution in Granada offering good coffee and tasty grub; expect to queue for a seat. The waffles (C$120), omelette, bacon and fries (C$130) and filling lunches (BLT C$115) are served on a beautifully shaded terrace looking across to the convent. Daily 7am–2pm.

Nuevo Central C La Calzada. The interior, dominated by a long bar, is nice enough, but like most people on La Calzada you'll probably be on the paved street breathing in the night air and ignoring the hawkers. The food and drink – omelettes (C$90), burgers (C$90) and lovely, juicy burritos (C$110) – is decent and relatively cheap for the location.

O'Shea's C La Calzada ⓦ osheaspubgranada.com. So you didn't come to Nicaragua to eat fish and chips, but when it's on the menu along with shepherd's pie and Irish stew for the same price as your average rice and beans in Granada's Parque Central (all C$160), why not? Wash it down with Guinness (C$145) and/or Jameson (C$100), or start early with a full Irish breakfast (C$150). Daily 8am until late.

Pizzeria Don Luca C La Calzada, opposite *Zoom*. Popular and unpretentious, with pleasingly authentic Italian food. Be warned, though: the *pequeña* size is just that. Pizza from C$80, pastas from C$165. Open Tues–Sun for lunch and dinner.

Restaurant Querubes Half a block north of the market on C Atravesada. A *buffet típica*, where hefty portions of rice, beans, plantain, salad and *churrasco* or grilled chicken come to C$130. The lunch menu has fewer options than the evening one; both offer food comparable in quality to La Calzada's offerings, for half the price. Daily 7am–6pm.

DRINKING AND NIGHTLIFE

Most travellers in search of alcohol and company tend to head either to the buzzing bar at *The Bearded Monkey* or to C La Calzada (for a super-cheap night, buy your drinks from the supermarket on La Calzada – they will open bottles for you, lend you glasses, and even have a couple of tables). There are also some great venues for a night out, with music ranging from acoustic Nicaraguan folk to the ever-present strains of reggaetón. The Centro Turístico (see p.487) is the place to head later on – take a taxi.

El César On the lakefront in the Centro Turístico. Granada's largest club has a party setting under an open-air *rancho*. Latin and disco dominate. Cover charge C$20–30. Daily noon–midnight (Fri–Sun until 3am).

Inuit On the lakefront in the Centro Turístico. When *El César* shuts, around 3am, the party usually heads to this place at the other end of the lakefront. Daily noon–midnight (Sat & Sun 24hr).

Nectar C La Calzada. Small cocktail bar with groovy art and a quiet courtyard which provides some much-needed calm on C La Calzada. Decent juices, sandwiches, soups and salads for under C$150 and cold beer (C$35). Happy hour 4–7pm. Tues–Sun 11am–11.30pm.

El Tercer Ojo C La Calzada. Tapas bar and deli with a funky, cushion-strewn interior set in a lovely colonial building. The global food isn't cheap, and you might prefer to stick to the booze – beer is C$36 but happy hour (6–8pm) offers good deals on rum, sangría and wine. Daily 7am–11pm (later if busy).

DIRECTORY

Banks All banks in town change dollars. The Banco de América Central (BAC), on the corner of C Atravesada and La Libertad, will change travellers' cheques, and also has one of many ATMs in the city.

Health The Praga pharmacy on C Real Xalteva is well stocked (daily 7am–10pm), while the Hospital Privado Cocibolca (☏ 2552 2907) is just outside town on the highway to Managua.

Internet Most hotels and cafés offer free wi-fi, and you can also try Ciber El Chele on C El Camito (daily 9am–10pm; C$14/hr).

Language schools There are plenty of places to learn Spanish in Granada – UCA Tierra y Aqua (see box, p.486) can set you up with a rural homestay for the full cultural experience. Ask at tour offices or your accommodation for options in the city or try the highly recommended Nicaragua Mia, C El Caimito (☏ 2252 0347, ⊚ nicaraguamiaspanish.com), who offer one-on-one and group lessons.

Laundry Try Mapache on the corner of C La Calzada and C El Cisne (☏ 2522 6711), or La Lavandería (☏ 2252 0018) just north on C El Cisne. Both also offer pick-up and delivery.

Post office C El Arsenal (Mon–Fri 8am–5pm, Sat 8am–noon).

AROUND GRANADA

Although Granada is a jumping-off point for trips to Ometepe (see p.495) and Solentiname (see p.501), there are a couple of worthwhile **day-trips** closer to town.

Isla Zapatera and Las Isletas

About 20km south of Granada, scattered about Lago de Nicaragua, are more than three hundred and fifty islands all believed to have been formed from the exploded top of Volcán Mombacho. Many of the pre-Columbian artefacts and treasures you find in museums throughout the country came from this group, which must have been of religious significance for the Chorotega-descended people who flourished here before the Conquest. The smaller islands, **Las Isletas**, make for a varied boat tour. Some are home to monkeys, one has a small fortress built by the Spanish conquistadors; one or two have private mansions, and on others you will see women washing their clothes in the lake in front of their ramshackle houses.

At 52 square kilometres, **Isla Zapatera** is the largest of the islands, skirted by attractive bays and topped by a much-eroded extinct volcano. Guides should be able to show you **El Muerto** (The Dead), a site full of the remains of tombs, several **petroglyphs** and the scant remains – a few grassy mounds and stones – of **Sozafe**, a site sacred to the Chorotegas. These apart, there's really very little to see, bar lovely views of the lake.

ARRIVAL AND DEPARTURE

Tours Every tour operator in Granada (see box, p.486) runs half-day boat tours to Las Isletas from US$25/person – some can also arrange more tranquil kayak trips. The easiest way to visit Zapatera is with a travel agency, such as Tierra Tour in Granada (see box, p.486), who offer informed but costly archeological excursions.

Lanchas Cabaña Amarilla Cheaper than the tour operators is Lanchas Cabaña Amarilla (☏ 8878 0763) at the far southern end of the Centro Turístico, a 20min walk beyond the entrance – unless you're on the waterfront anyway it's easiest to get a taxi down here. From here tours of Las Isletas cost US$20/hr (not/person) for groups of 1–8 people. They even have a bar where you can stock up before heading out.

Volcán Mombacho

The slopes of the rather lovely **RESERVA NACIONAL VOLCÁN MOMBACHO** (daily 8am–5pm; US$20 including transport on the eco truck or US$5 to walk to the summit, plus US$4–6 for entrance to certain trails at the summit which require a guide) are home to one of only two **cloudforests** in Nicaragua's Pacific region (the other is at Volcán Maderas on Isla de Ometepe). The reserve is run by the **Fundación Cocibolca** (⊚ mombacho.org), whose interesting **research station and visitors centre** at the volcano's summit acts as the centre for the study and protection of the reserve's flora and fauna

6

6

– which includes three species of monkey, 22 species of reptile, 87 species of orchid, 175 species of bird and some fifty thousand species of insect. The air is noticeably cooler up here, the views of the lakes and volcanoes around are tremendous, and several **trails** skirt the four craters at the top of the volcano.

ARRIVAL AND TOURS

By bus To get to the volcano take any bus from Granada bound for Rivas or Nandaime and ask to be let off at the turn-off for the park (at Intersection El Guanacaste). From the turn-off it's a 2.5km walk to the entrance, from where it is a further 5.5km to the top. Alternatively, you can take the "eco-truck" to the summit from the reserve entrance (Mon–Wed 8.30am & 10.30am, Thurs–Sun 8.30am, 10am, 1pm & 3pm).

Tours Most visitors choose the easier option of a tour from Granada (see box, p.486), which start from around US$35/person and typically include a visit to a coffee finca. For canopy tours Miravalle, at the volcano entrance (☏ 8872 2555, ✉ canopymiravealle@yahoo.com), is your best bet (US$28/person).

ACCOMMODATION

Fundación Cocibolca Ecoalbergue ☏ 2552 5858, ⓦ mombacho.org/eco.htm. Simple rooms where you can bunk down, and some space for camping (tents not provided). Dinner, breakfast and transport from Granada are included in the room rates. Camping/tent US$17, doubles US$100.

RIVAS

Most travellers, experiencing **RIVAS** as a dusty bus stop on the way to or from Costa Rica, San Juan del Sur or Ometepe, are unaware of the pivotal role it played in Nicaraguan history. Founded in 1736, it became an important stop on the route of Cornelius Vanderbilt's Accessory Transit Company, which ferried goods and passengers between the Caribbean and the Pacific via Lago de Nicaragua – the town's heyday came during the California Gold Rush, when its streets were full of prospectors travelling with the Transit Company on their way to the goldfields of the western US. Modern-day Rivas isn't anything special, and can seem scarily deserted at night, but it's not a bad place to get stuck, especially if you fancy a taste of the real Nicaragua between gringo-tastic Granada and San Juan del Sur.

WHAT TO SEE AND DO

The colonial church near the Parque Central, **La Parroquia San Pedro**, is worth a visit, primarily for a fresco featuring a maritime-themed depiction of Catholicism triumphing over the godless communists. The desperately underfunded **Museo de Antropología e Historia de Rivas** (Mon–Fri 8am–noon & 2–5pm, Sat 8am–noon; US$1) sits four blocks west and two north of the Parque, with fine views of the rest of the town. Inside you'll find artefacts of the local Nahua Nicarao people dating from the fourteenth to sixteenth centuries, prehistoric bones (thought to be from a mammoth), some frightening stuffed animals and a few dusty 78rpm records from the early twentieth century.

ARRIVAL AND DEPARTURE

By bus Chicken buses pull into the ragged station in the market, a few blocks northwest of the town centre. Express buses to/from Managua (daily 5.45am–9pm every 20min; 1hr 45min) stop on the highway, just outside town (get a bike taxi for C$10). Both Transnica and Tica Bus pass through Rivas (by the Texaco station) en route to San José, Managua and beyond.

Destinations Granada (daily 6am–3pm, every 45min; 1hr 30min); Managua (*ruteado* 6am–9pm, every 20min; 3hr); Peñas Blancas (daily 5am–5.30pm, every 40min; 45min); San Juan del Sur (daily 7am–7pm, every 30min; 45min–1hr).

By taxi A taxi anywhere in town will set you back around C$10. A shared taxi from the market to San Jorge (see below) should be about C$15 and to San Juan del Sur C$50 (all/person).

To Isla de Ometepe The quickest route out to Isla de Ometepe (see p.495), in Lago de Nicaragua, is via San Jorge, which is just east of Rivas on the lakeshore. From Rivas, San Jorge is best reached by shared taxi (see above) and is accessible on direct buses (daily 6am–9pm, every 30min) from Managua's Mercado Huembes. There's not much to the town, although it does have a small beach and a reasonable hotel (see below).

ACCOMMODATION

Hospedaje Lidia One block north and two and a half blocks east of Parque Central ☏ 2563 3477. Rooms (some with private bath), sleeping up to five, spin off two pleasant courtyards at this decent family-owned option.

It's convenient for the Tica Bus, if further from the market than most. Traditional breakfast US$3. **US$20**

Hostal El Chinica Half a block south of Parque Central ☎ 2563 1109, ✉ hostalelchinica@gmail.com. A haven in this grubby town: central, clean and well run. All rooms are en suite, with a/c and cable TV. You can also order room service from the family's Chinese restaurant round the corner. **C$600**

Hotel Hamacas San Jorge, east of Rivas on the lakeshore ☎ 2363 0048, ⓦ hotelhamacas.com. A short walk from the ferry terminal, this is a pleasant place to lay your head. Rates include breakfast. **US$32**

EATING AND DRINKING

A quick, cheap meal can be picked up at any of the *comedores* in the market, where you'll find good chicken, pork or beef and rice dishes for around C$55. Daily from around 6am–6pm.

El Mesón Four blocks south of the market, behind Iglesia San Francisco. Classic lunch-only buffet joint, serving good daily specials for around C$50. Daily noon–6pm.

Repostería Don Marcos 100m east of the Parque Central's northern edge. Excellent for breakfast or stocking up for a long bus ride; a coffee and a piping-hot pastry will set you back C$20. Mon–Sat 7am–4pm.

Vila's Rosti-Pizza On the southwest corner of the Parque. Probably your best bet for an evening, with a giant kids' playground inside and great people-watching from the tables outside. Chow down on *pollo a la plancha* (C$175) or beef with jalapeño sauce (C$$180). Daily noon–10pm.

DIRECTORY

Banks There is a handful of banks in town: BAC (Mon–Fri 8.30am–4.30pm, Sat 8.30am–noon), two blocks west of the Parque, will change travellers' cheques and dollars. There are several ATMs around the Parque.

Health Clinica María Inmaculada, on the north side of the Parque, is open daily.

Internet Cafés are all over Rivas; try Cyber Plus (C$10/hr) just off the northwest corner of the Parque.

Tourist information There's an INTUR office one block south and half a block east of the museum. Mon–Fri 8am–5pm, Sat 8am–noon.

SAN JUAN DEL SUR

In the mid-1800s the sleepy fishing village of **SAN JUAN DEL SUR** was a crucial transit point on Cornelius Vanderbilt's trans-isthmian steamboat line, on which people and goods were transported to Gold Rush-era California. The town is enjoying a second wave of prosperity, thanks to its popularity with wave-hunting Westerners, and you'll find few places in Nicaragua more geared up to backpackers.

Located in a lush valley with a river running down to the town's beach, the setting is beautiful; the beach itself is a long, wide stretch of fine dark sand running between two cliffs. With excellent seafood restaurants, gringo-packed bars and an increasing number of good places to stay, San Juan is the kind of place where a two-day stay can turn into a two-week reverie. The locals are mostly happy with the attention, but there are occasional reports of muggings on the quieter beaches – get local advice before heading off on your own.

WHAT TO SEE AND DO

The lack of conventional sights in San Juan del Sur means that most people are engaged either in sunning themselves on the beach or undertaking something more energetic in the surrounding azure seas. While the waters around town aren't the cleanest, the stunning cliffs round the and beaches just along the coast are easily accessible.

Watersports

Surfing is the most popular sport in town, and you can easily rent boards and arrange transport – the town beach is surfable but not spectacular, and the good beaches are too far to walk to. Head for **Remanso** (to the south, and good for beginners), **Maderas** (to the north, popular with experienced surfers) or a number of further-flung options. Almost anywhere in town can arrange this – transport should set you back around US$5 and board hire about US$10. Water taxis to *playas* Maderas and Majagual (12km to the north) leave from the area in front of *Hotel Estrella* at 10 or 11am daily, returning at 4 or 5pm (40min; US$10 return) a taxi will cost about the same.

The beaches, inlets and bays of the coast are ripe for exploration, and **sailing** and **fishing** trips are almost as popular as surfing – *Casa Oro* arrange backpacker-oriented fishing tours, and local tour companies (see box, p.493) all have trips of their own. San Juan isn't quite the

SAN JUAN DEL SUR

0 — 100 metres

N

EATING
"Chicken Lady"	6
El Gato Negro	3
San Juan Steak Grill	7
V.I.P	5

DRINKING & NIGHTLIFE
Arribas	2
Crazy Crab Beach Club	1
Iguana Bar	4

BAC (ATM)

@

Arena Caliente

Neptune Watersports

San Juan del Sur Surf and Sport

Mercado

Tica Bus Ticket

@

Bus stop

Bike Rental

AVENIDA MERCADO

ACCOMMODATION
Casa 28	3
Casa Oro	6
Hostel Esperanza	8
Hotel Estrella	4
The Naked Tiger	1
Pacha Mama	2
Rebecca's Inn	7
Sueños del Mar	5

Banco Pro Credit (ATM)

Farmacia Santa Ana

Bancentro (ATM)

AVENIDA DEL PARQUE

Parque Central

BDF (ATM)

Andrea's Laundry

Bampo (ATM)

INTRADA SAN JUAN

1 & Refugio de Vida Silvestre La Flor

Corn Islands, but there's still plenty of diving here: try Neptune Watersports.

Other activities

Da Flying Frog (⊚daflyingfrog.com, ☎8465 6781) on the road out to Maderas beach has a zipline canopy tour which offers great views of the San Juan bay in the distance (US$30). *Surf Ranch* (⊚surfranchnicaragua.com, ☎8816 8748), a popular surf camp located 5km out of town at Gigante beach (free shuttle from *Barrio Café* in town), offers everything from wall climbing to paintballing and a twenty-foot-high airbag drop to get your adrenaline pumping. **ATV** rental can be arranged through a few hostels, including *Casa 28* (see opposite).

Refugio de Vida Silvestre La Flor

The **Refugio de Vida Silvestre La Flor**, 19km south of San Juan del Sur (C$200 entrance fee; if travelling direct, contact the national environment agency, MARENA ☎2563 4264), is a guarded reserve dedicated to protecting the **sea turtles**, primarily the Olive Ridley species, that nest here in large numbers between July and February. The night-time nestings themselves are an amazing spectacle, and the reserve also has good surf, a beautiful white sandy beach and a stand of shady trees, plus more great empty beaches within walking distance. Most hostels and operators can organize a trip here from San Juan – getting here independently (either via one of the water taxis opposite *Hostel Estrella*, or by bus from the main stop) can be tricky and you're best asking in town about the frequency of buses. Mosquitoes and sandflies are abundant – take repellent. Camping overnight (there are a few tents here to rent) is an expensive C$500 per tent.

ARRIVAL AND INFORMATION

By bus Buses from/to Rivas (daily 7am–7pm, every 30min; 45min–1hr) and Managua (3 express daily 10am–4pm, 3hr; *ruteados* daily every hour 10am–4pm, 4hr) pull up outside the market.

By taxi A shared taxi from/to Rivas should only cost you C$50/person.

TOUR OPERATORS IN SAN JUAN DEL SUR

There's plenty of competition in San Juan del Sur, and most operators offer similar deals at similar prices. It's easy to organize trips via accommodation – if in doubt, try *Casa Oro*, *Hostel PachaMama*, *Casa 28* or *La Casa Feliz* – but several other tour and rental companies are worth considering.

Arena Caliente Next to the market ☎ 8815 3247, ⓦ arenacaliente.com. Friendly place offering surf lessons, rental and transport, plus fishing trips (US$30). Lodging and packages can also be arranged.

Neptune Watersports A block west of the market ☎ 2568 2752, ⓦ neptunenicadiving.com. San Juan's diving specialists can take you below the waves (US$85 for a two-tank dive) and also run fishing trips (US$45/hr for a group of up to eight).

San Juan del Sur Surf and Sport Half a block west of the market ☎ 2568 2022, ⓦ sanjuandelsursurf.com. This long-standing local operator offers fishing trips (a boat of your own from US$275/half-day), tours to Refugio La Flor (US$30), ATV rentals and a nearby canopy tour (US$30) plus – of course – surf rental and lessons.

6

Tourist information The INTUR office (Mon–Fri 9am–1pm) is a block east of the cathedral. Various websites offer news and information – ⓦ sanjuansurf.com is the pick of the bunch.

Bike rental Bikes can be rented at many hotels, including *Hospedaje Elizabeth* (opposite the bus stop) for US$6–8/day.

ACCOMMODATION

Like Granada, San Juan del Sur is witnessing a major expansion of tourist accommodation, with big, sociable places bunched on the waterfront and mellower, smaller establishments tending to sit a few streets back. Bear in mind that many places raise their prices in high season (around Christmas and Easter), when it might be worth reserving in advance.

Casa 28 Half a block south of *El Gato Negro* ☎ 2568 2441, ⓔ marvincalde@hotmail.es. A reasonable, chilled-out budget option offering fifteen basic rooms with a fan, shared bath and optional a/c. U̲S̲$̲2̲0̲

★ **Casa Oro** One block west of the Parque ☎ 2568 2415, ⓦ casaeloro.com. Sprawling backpacker den offering everything the homesick surfer might require, from pizza delivery and DVD nights to wave reports, board rental, a beach shuttle (US$5 return) and a funky rooftop terrace. Dorms are decent, there's a kitchen, and beach, sailing and surf trips can be arranged. Dorms U̲S̲$̲1̲0̲, doubles U̲S̲$̲3̲2̲

Hostel Esperanza Three blocks west and half a block south of the Parque ☎ 8760 4343, ⓦ hostelesperanza .com. Relaxed, somewhat chaotic hostel with unexceptional rooms but a tremendous beachfront location. There's a barbecue, hammocks and wi-fi too. Breakfast included. Dorms U̲S̲$̲1̲0̲, doubles U̲S̲$̲2̲5̲

Hotel Estrella On the beachfront, two blocks west of the market ☎ 2568 2210, ⓔ hotelestrella1929@hotmail.com. With a downstairs area devoted to selling on secondhand ovens and fridges, this hotel may be quirky, but it also has a plum location right on the beachfront and reasonable prices. The rooms at the back are nothing special and bathrooms are shared, but snag yourself a front balcony and you're sorted. Breakfast is included. Numerous tours are run from here too, including fishing trips for US$40/hr. U̲S̲$̲3̲0̲

The Naked Tiger On the hills to your right as you come into town, behind Barrio Auxiliadora ⓦ thenakedtigerhostel .com, ☎ 8621 4738. Relatively new but already a San Juan institution, they don't do reservations – once you arrive you're welcome to stay for as long as you want. If the dorms are full, it's not uncommon for people to be willing to doss on the sofas. Set on the hills behind San Juan, there's a free shuttle from outside *Barrio Café*. Wed is pool party night, complete with resident DJ and only topped by the legendary Sunday Funday. Tickets for this, in the form of T-shirts (US$30; US$15 for guests), go on sale at 9.30am on Sun, at the hostel and also at *Pacha Mama* hostel; get there early to be sure of getting in. The event is a mad "pool crawl" around town with free transport and a free shot at each location. Dorms U̲S̲$̲3̲0̲0̲

Pacha Mama ☎ 2568 2043. Perfectly located just a block from the beach, this is a real surfers hostel. Has a more chilled vibe but works with *The Naked Tiger* in organizing events such as Sunday Funday. Breakfast included for all guests. Dorms U̲S̲$̲1̲0̲, doubles U̲S̲$̲2̲5̲

Rebecca's Inn Just off the northwestern edge of the Parque ☎ 8675 1048. A family-run inn with colourful, clean, wood panelled rooms (fan and shared bath) and friendly service. U̲S̲$̲2̲0̲

Sueños del Mar Just southeast of the market ☎ 2568 2079. Cosy TV room, kitchen and outdoor bamboo shower. The rooms are small but the vibe is friendly. Continental breakfast included. Dorms U̲S̲$̲8̲, doubles U̲S̲$̲1̲6̲

EATING

San Juan del Sur is a great place to eat seafood – a whole baked fish costs about C$270, while fresh lobster starts at around C$350. There are plenty of bars and restaurants along the beachfront, though the same dishes are

6

INTO COSTA RICA: PEÑAS BLANCAS

Crossing the border at **Peñas Blancas**, 35km from San Juan del Sur, can be a time-consuming process when countless migrant workers head back to see their families; don't be surprised if it takes up two hours – you'll be there most of the day if you try to do it around Christmas or Semana Santa.

Local buses from Rivas go all the way to the border; if you're leaving from San Juan del Sur, take the Rivas bus only as far as the highway at La Virgen and then catch a connecting bus – there's no need to go all the way back to Rivas. If you're travelling on to a Central American capital, you can also head back to Rivas and catch a Transnica or Tica Bus as it passes through (see p.490).

The crossing is open daily 6am to 8pm, and packed with touts offering money-changing and to fill out your forms for you. You'll be charged an exit tax of US$2. There is a US$10 fee to enter Nicaragua. It's a fairly easy 1km walk (a moto-taxi will charge around C$20, a taxi a bit more) to the Costa Rican *migración* where you'll have to pay a US$3 municipal tax before hopping on the regular onward transport to San José.

If entering Nicaragua from Costa Rica there is a new US$7 exit tax on the Costa Rican side. In theory you pay at a machine, but at the time of writing it was out of order, in which case you are at the mercy of the touts, who add on a US$1 admin fee to give you a receipt.

---

considerably cheaper and often equally tasty at the *comedores* inside the market (C$70 for chicken or beef, C$150 for fish or lobster).

★**"Chicken Lady"** *Asados Juanita*, at the central market. A word-of-mouth travellers' favourite, this street-side BBQ serves lip-smacking chicken plates to eat in or take away from C$140. Daily, evenings only.

El Gato Negro 50m east of *Iguana Bar*. A colourful, mellow café and bookshop with a reasonable menu (muffins C$40, sandwiches from C$100) and organic coffee (C$40 with refills). Daily 7am–3pm.

San Juan Steak Grill Half a block south of the park, look for the chef tending the BBQ out front. Order a mixed grill and they bring it to your table on its own mini BBQ (C$$350 – great for sharing). For something smaller, try their tasty tacos (2 for C$$80) or a healthier bacon salad (C$$160). Mon–Wed & Fri 5–10pm, Sat & Sun 5pm–midnight.

V.I.P (La Vecchia Signora) Half a block south of *Casa 28*. The best pizza in town (C$140–200), nothing more, nothing less. Beers C$30. Wed–Sun 4–10pm.

DRINKING AND NIGHTLIFE

The seafront bars are perfectly located for soaking up the sunset with a cold beer. As well as *Crazy Crab*, several clubs and bars are open as late as 3 or 4am – all cater to a lively mix of locals, tourists and resident surfers.

Arribas 100m north of *Iguana Bar*. Buzzy beachside place where you can sip your beer (C$35) on the sands. Open daily from 9pm until the early hours.

Crazy Crab Beach Club 500m north of *Iguana Bar*. Salsa classes from 9pm, but it only really gets busy after 1am, when everyone who hasn't gone to bed yet shakes their stuff to a merry mix of salsa and pop. Beer C$25. Entry C$30 on Sat, free otherwise. Thurs–Sun 9pm until sunrise.

Iguana Bar On the beachfront square, a block north of

Hotel Estrella. This place is booming at night, when the huge bamboo balcony overlooking the beach and bay fills with flirting locals and foreign beach bums. There's reasonable food during the day (clams C$150, fish C$230), while a beer is C$40. Ladies' night with cheaper drinks for women after 10pm Mon–Thurs.

DIRECTORY

Banks Banks have popped up all over town, and there are several ATMs. Bancentro, south of the market, and Banco Pro Credit, one block east of *Hotel Estrella* (both Mon–Fri 8am–4.30pm, Sat 8am–noon), will change US dollars and euros.

Health Farmacia Santa Ana, half a block south of the market, is open daily.

Internet Connexion Cyber, opposite *El Mercado* (Mon–Sat 7am–10pm, Sun 7am–9pm), and Cyber Manfred, opposite *El Gato Negro* (daily 8am–9pm), both charge C$20/hr and have phones.

Laundry Several hostels have DIY facilities (washboards, not machines) and there are several independent laundries charging about C$60/load; try Andrea's, just south of *Casa Oro*.

Lago de Nicaragua

Standing on the shore and looking out onto vast **Lago de Nicaragua**, it's not hard to imagine the surprise of the Spanish navigators who, in 1522, nearly certain they were heading towards the Pacific, found the lake's expanse instead. They weren't too far off – merely a few thousand years – as both it and Lago de Managua were probably once part of the Pacific, until seismic activity created the plain that now separates the lake from the ocean. Several millennia later, by the time the Spanish had arrived, the Lago de Nicaragua was the largest **freshwater sea** in the Americas after the Great Lakes: fed by freshwater rivers, the lake water gradually lost its salinity, while the fish trapped in it evolved into some of the most unusual types of fish found anywhere on earth, including freshwater shark and swordfish. Locally, the lake is still known by its indigenous name, Cocibolca ("sweet sea").

It's easy to be captivated by the natural beauty and unique cultures of the **islands** that dot the southwest sector of the lake, including twin-volcanoed **Isla de Ometepe** and the scattering of small islands that make up the **Solentiname archipelago**. On its eastern edge the lake is fed by the 170km **Río San Juan**, which you can boat down to the remote **El Castillo**, an old Spanish fort surrounded on all sides by pristine jungle. The Río San Juan and El Castillo are reached via the largest town on the east side of the lake, **San Carlos**, a

bug-ridden settlement mainly used by travellers as a transit point.

Making your way around the lake can be quite an undertaking: Lago de Nicaragua is affected by what locals call a "short-wave phenomenon" – short, high, choppy waves – caused by the meeting of the Papagayo wind from the west and the Caribbean-generated trade winds from the east. Crossing can be hell for those prone to seasickness. You'll need to be prepared for the conditions and patient with erratic boat schedules.

Now could be the time to visit, as work has officially begun on a canal to rival Panama's. It will run north of the river and right through the lake, though up to now work has been limited to the beginning of an access road.

ISLA DE OMETEPE

Almost everyone who travels through Nicaragua comes to **ISLA DE OMETEPE**, Lago de Nicaragua's largest island, to experience its lush scenery and tranquil atmosphere. Ometepe's name comes from the Nahuatl language of the Chorotegans, the original inhabitants of Nicaragua, who called it Ome Tepetl – "the place of two hills" – for its two volcanoes. The island

6

has probably been inhabited since the first migration of indigenous groups from Mexico arrived in this area, and a few stone sculptures and **petroglyphs** attest to their presence on the island. Even from the mainland, taking in the sight of its two cones, you can tell it's a special place.

The higher and more symmetrical of the two is **Volcán Concepción** (1610m), Nicaragua's second-highest volcano. Much of the island's 40,000-strong population live around the foot of Volcán Concepción, where you'll find the main towns of **Moyogalpa** and **Altagracia**. Smaller, extinct **Volcán Maderas** (1394m) is less perfectly conical in shape, but clothed with precious **cloudforest**, where you're likely to spot such **wildlife** as white-faced (*carablanca*) and howler (*mono congo*) monkeys, green parrots (*loro verde*) and blue-tailed birds called *urracas*. Almost all activities on the island are based in the outdoors: walking, hiking, **volcano-viewing**, **volunteering** and **horseriding** are among the most popular.

WHAT TO SEE AND DO

Most people are here to visit Ometepe's iconic twin volcanoes, but there's plenty to do elsewhere, from chilling at lodges and stretching out on beaches – notably **Playa Santo Domingo** – to exploring waterfalls and pre-Columbian remains.

Moyogalpa

Moyogalpa, the largest town on the island, sits on the northwest side of Volcán Concepción. It's convenient for the ferry and has a few decent bars and restaurants, while its popularity with backpackers means it's not a bad place to arrange a tour or spend a lazy evening. After you've walked up the hill and looked at the dock, there's not much sightseeing to do – the **museum** (☏2569 4225; Mon–Fri 8am–5pm, Sat & Sun 9am–5pm; US$2), on the right just before the church at the top end of town, through the back of a souvenir shop, houses a few artefacts and petroglyphs.

Altagracia

While there's also little to detain travellers in **Altagracia**, a sleepy town set slightly inland on Ometepe's northeastern side, it is quieter and less touristed than Moyogalpa. The **Parque Central** is ringed by several pre-Columbian statues found

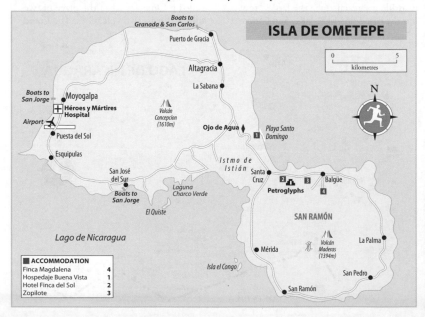

SAN DIEGO DE ALCALÁ

Every year during the third week of November, Altagracia celebrates the week-long **fiesta of San Diego de Alcalá**, in honour of the village's patron saint. If you're passing through on November 17 you may be lucky enough to see one of the highlights of the festival, the **Baile del Zompopo** ("dance of the leaf-cutter ant"). The locals set out from the church in a traditional procession through the streets, parading aloft an image of San Diego. Participants act out the distinctive dance with tree branches held aloft – representing the indigenous leaf-cutter ant – while moving to traditional drum rhythms.

on the island, while the **Museo de Ometepe** (Mon–Fri 8am–noon & 1–4pm, Sat 9am–3pm, Sun 9am–1pm; US$2 plus C$30 photography fee), off the west side of the park, houses a few more local archeological finds.

Volcán Concepción

The main hike (8–10hr return) up Volcán Concepción starts from just outside Altagracia. Much of the climb is extremely steep and it's compulsory to hire a **guide** (see p.498) for the upper sections. Several **trails** wind up, and all are quite an exercise – start early and bring plenty of water – with an exposed and rocky stretch towards the summit that gets very windy. The cloudforests of the lower slopes are gorgeous (keep an ear out for howler monkeys), and the dramatic views from the top, encompassing neighbouring Volcán Maderas and the expanse of surrounding Lake Nicaragua and right over San Juan del Sur and out to the ocean, are genuinely breathtaking.

Playa Santo Domingo

Stretching for more than 1km on the east side of the narrow isthmus separating the two volcanoes is the grey-sand **Playa Santo Domingo**. This is the best place to swim on the island, and many volcano-climbers and hikers spend a day soaking up some sun here. The beach is accessed from the recently resurfaced main road circling Concepción.

Volcán Maderas

The **hike** (7–8hr return) up the verdant slopes of dormant **Volcán Maderas** is less arduous than the steep climb up and down Concepción, though it can nonetheless be a muddy and slippery walk – guides are mandatory (see p.498). The final stretch down into the crater is not for the faint of heart; the rocks are almost sheer and you'll have to use a rope. Birds and monkeys can be heard (if not seen) all the way up, and the summit gives stunning views of Concepción and the lake. The crater itself is eerily silent and still, its lip covered by a mixture of dense, rainforest-like vegetation and a few bromeliad-encrusted conifers. Make sure you take plenty of water, sunscreen and perhaps a swimming costume; the crater lagoon is swimmable, if pretty mucky.

The rest of the island

If you have time, it's worth exploring the quiet villages dotted around the lower slopes of Maderas. **Petroglyphs** are scattered over this part of the island, with one group clustered between the hamlets of Santa Cruz and La Palma – ask at *Finca Magdalena* (see p.499) for a guide (US$6). A two- or three-hour hike from the *Finca Magdalena* will take you to the pleasant, but extremely cold, **San Ramón waterfalls**. The naturally fed pools at **Ojo de Agua** (the waterhole), a twenty-minute hike from Villa Paraíso near Playa Santo Domingo, also merit a visit. If you've just hiked a volcano, there's nothing more refreshing than climbing on the rope swing and diving in to one of the rainforest-shaded pools.

ARRIVAL AND DEPARTURE

BY BOAT
The boat journey between Isla de Ometepe and the mainland can be fairly bumpy. Moyogalpa's dock is at the bottom of the town's steep and narrow main street and Altagracia's is 2km out of town ($10/person in a minivan). The third port, at the village of San José del Sur, is less convenient – you'll probably have to get a taxi.
From San Jorge The majority of travellers arrive by ferry (C$50–75) or less comfortable *lancha* (C$40–60) via San Jorge, northeast of Rivas (see p.491). There are roughly hourly departures every day between San Jorge and Moyogalpa (7am–5.45pm) and three ferries from San

6

Jorge to San José del Sur (9.30am, 2pm & 5pm), though itineraries change regularly – check at the INTUR office in Granada (see p.487) or on ⓦepn.com.ni.

From Granada There are currently two boats a week from Granada to Altagracia (Mon & Thurs 2pm; 4hr; C$220; return Wed & Sat 12.30am). The journey is not great, however – the lake is often very choppy and tourists have to buy a "first class" ticket, sitting in an icily cold a/c section of the boat.

From San Carlos Two boats a week run from San Carlos to Altagracia (Tues & Fri 2pm, arriving midnight; C$230; return Mon & Thurs 7.30pm). The same caveats apply to this trip as to the boats from Granada.

GETTING AROUND

The roads around the island have been resurfaced, so getting around is not the nightmare it once was. There is also an airport with flights (Tues, Thurs & Sun only) to/from Managua, San Carlos and San Juan de Nicaragua.

By bike and motorcycle Ometepe is one of the best places in Nicaragua to cycle. Ask at your accommodation or UGO (see below) for the best place to rent bicycles or motorbikes and check the condition of your bike carefully before you get on it – some operators have been known to claim you've wrecked their machines and refuse to give you back your deposit.

By bus Buses connect Moyogalpa and Altagracia (Mon–Sat roughly hourly 8.30am–5.30pm; 1hr–1hr 30min), taking in Playa Santo Domingo. A handful of services connect the two towns with Mérida and Balgüe (2 daily) and Mérida (3 daily) – check with your accommodation, as schedules fluctuate.

By taxi Minibus taxis are mostly found in Moyogalpa, but charge a whacking C$600 for a trip to Mérida or Balgüe – a good option if travelling in a group. You can also hire these drivers/minibuses for the day; beware, however, of drivers telling you that the last bus has already left in order to get your custom.

INFORMATION

Tour operators There's no INTUR office on the island but you won't be short of advice – all accommodation will be able to point you towards a tour and in some you'll be approached by informal guides. These can be a reasonable bet for a simple trip – but in all cases, check exactly what you're getting. For something more substantial it's worth speaking to UGO (on the left, just as you exit the dock at Moyogalpa; ☎2827 7714), a confederation of guides who can take you all over the island – trips cost US$10–40/person, depending on how large your group is and what you're after.

ACCOMMODATION

In Moyogalpa and Altagracia, most rooms are simple, concrete and dry-wall cubicles, while those at the various fincas and haciendas can be charmingly rustic, with lots of polished wood and hammocked balconies. Many of the latter are splendidly located – but you may have to rely on their catering, as many are pretty isolated.

MOYOGALPA

Hospedaje Central Three blocks east (uphill) and one south of the dock ☎2569 4262, ⓦhostelometepe.com. Likeable, creaky hostel with a lively on-site bar and restaurant, *El Indio Viejo* (see opposite). There are reasonable doubles (a/c and bath US$3 extra), wi-fi throughout, and a relaxing, hammock-bedecked courtyard. Most work is done by volunteers and there are links to ecological and spiritual projects that the grizzled owner will fill you in on if you ask. Dorms US$5.50, doubles US$17

★**The Landing Hotel** 50m east (uphill) from the dock ☎2569 4113, ✉hbsaussy@gmail.com. Smart hotel with a decent downstairs bar and restaurant (pasta C$100, fillet of fish C$120), helpful staff and splendid views from the upstairs terrace. The comfortable rooms – either en suite or with shared bath – are a stone's throw from the dock, and good value too. Dorms US$7, doubles US$20

ALTAGRACIA

Hotel Castillo 100m south and 50m west of the Parque Central ☎2552 8744. Basic but spotless rooms, some with private bath, as well as a good restaurant, large hammocks, an internet café (C$15/hr) and a bar showing sports. The latter gets busy when there's sport on, but the courtyards remain mellow enough with their hammocks and rocking chairs. You pay US$5 extra for private bath, another US$25 for a/c. US$10

Hotel Central Two blocks south of the Parque Central ☎2552 8770. Probably the best choice in town, with excellent-value rooms, some with a balcony and private

---

PUESTA DEL SOL HOMESTAYS

For an authentic Ometepe experience, consider arranging a homestay with a local family. For US$25 per night (including all meals), one of ten families in the **Puesta del Sol** collective will take you in and share their home with you. The group (☎8619 0219, ⓦpuestadelsol.org) has small plots of land growing organic herbs, fruits and other plants from its base 2km from Moyogalpa, and makes wine and tea from hibiscus. Visitors can learn about cultivation, experience life with a typical Nica family and arrange visits to Ometepe's sights – bike and canoe rental can also be arranged. The families don't speak English, so this is a good option if you want to practice your Spanish.

bath and sweet little cabañitas. There's also a restaurant and bicycle rental (US$1/hr, US$6/day). Doubles US$12, cabañas US$24

THE REST OF THE ISLAND

Finca Magdalena Take the bus from Altagracia to Balgüe, from where it's a 30min hike up a signposted path ☎8418 5636, ⓦfincamagdalena.com. This welcoming old hacienda, converted by the Sandinistas into an organic coffee co-operative (and still going strong), has stunning views across the lake. The no-frills accommodation consists of hammocks or camping, large dorm rooms, partitioned private rooms, and a private en-suite hut. A restaurant serves hearty meals and organic coffee, while tours take you round the plantations and to nearby waterfalls and petroglyphs. Dorms US$4, doubles US$12, hut US$23

Hospedaje Buena Vista Playa Domingo ☎2569 4868. Probably the best budget bet on lovely Playa Domingo, with simple rooms, a cheap and cheerful *comedor* next door and a more tranquil vibe than the boozier options elsewhere on the island. Dorms US$7, doubles US$25

El Zopilote On the road between Santa Cruz and Balgüe, about 300 metres from Santa Cruz; look for the old school bus converted into a farm shop on your right ☎8369 0644, ⓦometepezopilote.com. Eco-farm, growing its own organic food and serving it in their great restaurant (Tues, Thurs & Sat is pizza night – worth going for, even if you're staying elsewhere). As well as dorms and cabins, you have the option of a simple hammock under a cabin (locker provided). Dorms US$7, doubles (cabins) US$16, hammocks US$4

EATING AND DRINKING

The best choice of places to eat and drink is in Moyogalpa; Altagracia has a handful of others, with a shack on the north side of its Parque Central offering classic, hearty fodder for

around C$50. Out of town, most of the fincas and haciendas have excellent on-site restaurants. There's not a huge party scene on Ometepe; Moyogalpa is the liveliest after dark.

MOYOGALPA

★**The Cornerhouse** A block uphill from the dock, opposite the petrol station ☎2569 4212, ⓦthecornerhouseometepe.com. A cool vibe, due mainly to the friendly staff. Breakfast menu (C$50–130), delicious sandwiches (around C$140) and smoothies (C$50). There are also four rooms for rent on a first-come-first-served basis. Daily 7am–5pm.

El Indio Viejo Three blocks east (uphill) and one south of the dock ☎2569 4262, ⓦhostelometepe.com. This bar and restaurant is a sociable joint, but a little rough, a definite backpacker hangout, offering breakfast for C$50–100, mains for C$95–175 and beer for C$25.

Esquina Caliente Three blocks east (uphill) from the dock. Cute little café with a cool vibe and the option of sitting at tables inside or bar stools outside. Breakfasts are C$75–100, and lunch of burger, fries and a drink is C$115. Free wi-fi. Mon–Sat 8am–10pm.

Timbo al Tambo 100m uphill (east) from docks. A funky little café-bar with a cool half-raised dancefloor playing latin music to a lively local crowd. Beer C$19, mojito C$30.

ALTAGRACIA

Hotel Kencho Opposite *Hotel Castillo*. Reasonable, airy restaurant below the hotel of the same name, where you can chomp down on chicken (C$115), grilled fish (C$115) or *desayuno típico* (C$80). Open daily 7am–late evening.

ELSEWHERE ON THE ISLAND

★**Café Campestre** On your left as you arrive in Balgüe ☎8725 8447, ⓦcampestreometepe.com The British owner bought a farm here twelve years ago and now serves his organic produce in the restaurant. If you need a curry fix, it's worth making the trip to Balgüe just to eat here (Thai and Indian curries C$125–145), and if you're lucky, there'll even be some home-brewed beer ('hooch' C$30). There are also local tours available. Mon–Sat noon–7pm.

DIRECTORY

MOYOGALPA

Banks Banpro, Bancentro and Banco ProCredit have branches in Moyogalpa; all change US dollars and have an ATM.

Health Emergencies can be attended to at the Héroes y Mártires Hospital, just outside Moyogalpa on the road to Altagracia.

Internet Ciber Café, one block uphill (east) from the dock on the left (C$16/hr), or Garcia Cyber, 1.5 blocks east of *The Cornerhouse* (C$15/hr), which is super clean and has a/c. Most hotels and restaurants have wi-fi.

6

ELSEWHERE ON THE ISLAND

ATM There is an ATM at *Hotel Central* in Altagracia.

Internet Altagracia's only option is Cyber Vajoma, in the *Hotel Castillo* (C$15/hr). Most of the fincas and haciendas also offer (often slow) internet access.

Laundry Services are provided by many hotels.

SAN CARLOS

Sleepy **SAN CARLOS**, at the southern end of Lago de Nicaragua and the head of the Río San Juan, has to be one of the most unprepossessing towns in the whole country. Despite its position as one of the main transit towns for the lake area, and the odd bit of renovation work around the dockfront, an air of apathy pervades its ramshackle buildings and battered streets. That said, the people are friendly and most visitors end up spending at least one night here – generally en route to the **Solentiname archipelago**, to **El Castillo** and points further south along the **Río San Juan** or to Costa Rica via Los Chiles, although San Carlos itself is an access point to the wild and relatively untouched Los Guatuzos reserve.

ARRIVAL AND DEPARTURE

By plane La Costeña (☎2583 0048) flies from Managua to San Carlos (40min), landing at the tiny airstrip just north of town. It's a 20min walk into town; a taxi (5min) should cost about C$20.

By boat Solentiname boats (see p.502) use the main dock in San Carlos, while those for Granada, El Castillo, Sabalos, San Juan del Norte, Ometepe and Los Chiles use the dock on the east side, by the Petronic station – pay your US$2 exit fee at *migración*, just west of the municipal dock. Boats from Granada arrive in San Carlos around 4am at the eastern dock by the Petronic station; from here it's a 10min walk or 2min taxi ride to any of the town's accommodation. You can either strike out to find a hotel, or wait around (for about 1hr) for boats on to El Castillo – they use the same dock. Boats back to Altagracia/Granada currently leave on Tues and Fri at 2pm (10hr/14hr) – arrive early to pick up tickets.

By bus The bus station is by the eastern dock, opposite a cluster of *comedores*.

Destinations Chinandega (Sun & Thurs 3pm 8.5hr); El Rama (1 daily, 8am; 6hr); Granada (leaves San Carlos Tues & Fri 3pm & 4pm; leaves Granada Mon & Thurs 11am & 3pm); Managua (7 daily 5am–6pm; 5–7hr).

INFORMATION

Tourist information There's a small but unusually helpful INTUR office in the main dock building (Mon–Fri 8am–1pm; ☎2853 0301), where you can get up-to-date information on Solentiname and points south on the Río San Juan. They post a boat timetable with current prices outside. The CANTUR office (Mon–Fri 8am–5pm; ☎2583 0266), one block west of *Hotel Carmina*, also provides tourist information, along with a free map of town.

Tour operators *Hotel Cabinas Leyko* can organize wildlife trips and tours, including a combined tour of *Los Guatuzos* and the river crossing to Costa Rica, or try Ryo Big Tours (☎8828 8558, ✉ryobigtours@hotmail.com), in the same office as CANTUR, for excursions to the Los Guatuzos reserve or further up the river.

ACCOMMODATION

San Carlos has a lot of transient traffic, which is reflected in its spartan hotels. There's little to choose between the few vaguely acceptable and not overly bug-ridden, sinister or noisy places in town.

Hotel Cabinas Leyko Two blocks west of the Parque ☎2583 0354, ✉leykou7@yahoo.es. The best budget rooms in town, which isn't saying much. The decent, if slightly damp, wooden rooms come with wall fan or a/c

---

INTO COSTA RICA: LOS CHILES AND SANTA FÉ BRIDGE

Boats (Mon–Sat 10.30am, 1.30pm & 4pm, Sun 11am & 1.30pm; US$10) leave from the east *muelle* (dock) in San Carlos for the scenic hour-plus chug to **Los Chiles** in Costa Rica. It's best to aim for one of the earlier services, as the later ones can be unreliable, and it's easiest to get your exit stamp from the customs office at the dock before departure (US$2). Coming the other way the charge is US$10. The actual border post is just outside Los Chiles; you'll need to walk a few hundred metres down to the immigration office to get an entry stamp to Costa Rica at the Los Chiles *muelle*, then either hop in a taxi or walk a further kilometre to the bus stop. It's a world away from the chaos of Nicaragua's other borders.

Before you reach the town of San Carlos the road forks, heading off to the new bridge over the San Juan River with a highway continuing right into Costa Rica. At the time of going to print transport has not been properly established as only the Nicaraguan border post is open, but the Costa Rica side should open soon and bus services are planned from San Carlos bus station.

(a/c costs extra), screened windows and shared or private bath. There's also a balcony with rocking chairs and lake views. US$13

Hotel Santa Lucía Half a block east and one and a half blocks north of *Hotel Cabinas Leyko* ☏ 2583 0385, ✉ santalucia.hostal@yahoo.es. A relatively new hotel run by a friendly family who keep the place spotlessly clean. Meals can be arranged. C$550

Hotelito Carmina Opposite *Restaurante Kaoma*. Quiet, safe and clean family-run hostel. All rooms are en suite with cable TV and there is wi-fi, though it doesn't reach all the rooms. 10pm curfew. C$500

EATING

Criollo del Lago Right opposite the plaza by the waterfront. A popular spot for simple, well-priced food. Breakfast (C$40–60), lunch (C$70–80) and supper (C$50 for *gallo pinto*, eggs and cheese). They don't sell beer, but nor do they mind if you shout over to the waitress and buy one from the *comedor* next door.

Restaurante Don Leo Next to and part of the same business as *Cabinas Leyko*. Attentive staff for such a simple café, with English spoken. Breakfast C$75, sandwiches C$40–100, mains from C$200. They can also arrange tours.

Restaurante el Granadino One block uphill from the *muelle municipal*. Probably the best restaurant in town, set on a huge wooden balcony overlooking the main square and dock. Steaks, fish and chicken from C$170.

Restaurante Kaoma On the waterfront, a block up from the *muelle municipal*. Good, filling seafood and vegetarian (on request) plates for C$100–250, with a bit of a buzz come the evening. Mon–Fri 10am–midnight, Sat & Sun 10am–1am

DIRECTORY

Banks There's a Bancentro with an ATM a block up from the waterfront and a Banpro ATM in one of the hexagonal huts on the waterfront.

Internet A couple of internet cafés sit near the Parque Central, two blocks up from the waterfront and most accommodation has wi-fi.

SOLENTINAME ARCHIPELAGO

Lying in the southeast corner of Lago de Nicaragua, the **SOLENTINAME ARCHIPELAGO** is made up of 36 islands of varying size. For a long time it was the islands' colony of naïf-art **painters** that brought it fame – priest and poet Ernesto Cardenal lived here for many years before becoming the Sandinistas' Minister of the Interior in the 1980s, and it was his promotion of the archipelago's primitive

ACCOMMODATION
Hotel Cabinas Leyko	2
Hotelito Carmina	3
Santa Lucía	1

EATING & DRINKING
Criollo del Lago	4
Restaurante Don Leo	1
Restaurante el Granadino	2
Restaurante Kaoma	3

SAN CARLOS

art and artisan skills that led to the government declaring Solentiname a national monument in 1990 – but today the islands are better known for their unspoilt natural beauty and remarkable wildlife. The archipelago's **isolation** keeps all but the most determined travellers away, so it's a nice departure from the backpacker trail.

WHAT TO SEE AND DO

The archipelago's largest islands are also the most densely inhabited: **Mancarrón, La Venada, San Fernando** (also referred to as Isla Elvis Chavarría) and **Mancarroncito**. Most people stay on Mancarrón, home to a simple church whose interior holds vibrant paintings of birds, trees and houses, and make trips to San Fernando and other nearby islands. It's worth paying a visit to the small MUSAS **museum** on San Fernando (Mon–Sat 8am–12.30pm & 2.30–5pm; US$2), where you'll find

6

information on the local wildlife, petroglyphs, medicinal plants and, of course, the local artisanal process. Make sure you bring plenty of cash with you – there's no ATM on the islands. Other than that, you're best off interspersing long periods of relaxation with the odd hike along the many trails – where you'll see plenty of birdlife – and a few spots of fishing.

ARRIVAL AND DEPARTURE

By boat A "ferry" goes to Mancarrón (also calling at La Venada and San Fernando) from San Carlos twice a week (Tues & Fri 1pm; 2hr; C$80), although it's best to check departure times at the dock. Returning to San Carlos, boats depart from Mancarrón at 4.30am on Tues and Fri. There is also a daily "tourist" service between San Carlos and Solentiname, but this is subject to change (check ⓦ transol.com.ni or ☎ 8828 3243 before travelling).

ACCOMMODATION AND EATING

Almost all accommodation offers meals; failing that, owners will point you to the nearest hotel that has a dining room – there are no dedicated restaurants on the islands. All accommodation listed is on the circular path that loops round to/from the dock: take the fork to the left to come to Sueño Feliz first, take the path uphill to reach *Hotel Mancarrón* first.

MANCARRÓN

El Buen Amigo ☎ 8869 6619. A clean, basic and friendly *hospedaje* located around the middle of the path round "town". Traditional food from C$80. <u>US$8</u>

Hostal Sueño Feliz ☎ 8876 5573, ⓔ esperanzarosales .29@gmail.com. Family-run *hostal* – all rooms with shared bathroom. Also a great place to buy local arts and crafts, and they offer different activities such as "artist for a day", where you can make your own balsa wood carving (US$10/person). Price includes breakfast. <u>US$20</u>

★ TREAT YOURSELF

Hotel Mancarrón Just before *El Buen Amigo* ☎ 8852 3380, ⓦ hotelmancarron .com. Solentiname's luxury option, with en-suite rooms in beautiful gardens. Even if you don't stay, it's worth treating yourself to a meal here (C$180), as the owner's creative use of local ingredients makes a welcome change from the staple rice and beans you'll get elsewhere. <u>US$70</u>, with all meals <u>US$110</u>

SAN FERNANDO

Hotel Familiar Vanessa Just left of the main dock ☎ 8680 8423, ⓔ jose.sequeirapineda@gmail.com. Simple, friendly, family-run *hostal* with shared bathroom. Meals can be cooked to order. <u>US$15</u>

Mire Estrellas Beside the lake ☎ 8894 7331. Cheap, simple rooms with a hammocked balcony on the lake. You can eat at the restaurant of the pricey *Hotel Cabañas Paraíso*, opposite. <u>US$20</u>

RÍO SAN JUAN

The mighty 170km-long **RÍO SAN JUAN** is one of the most important rivers in Central America. In colonial times it was the route by which the cities of Granada and León were supplied by Spain and emptied of their treasure by pirates. It's the site of regular squabbles between Nicaragua and Costa Rica (see p.450), although you wouldn't know it while drifting down its sinuous and gloriously verdant length: the only settlements nearby are remote and sleepy villages whose inhabitants make their living by fishing and farming. **Ecotourism** offers one of the few sources of income: pack a waterproof, insect repellent and a stout pair of boots, and get ready for grand castles, intriguing tours and giant grilled river shrimp.

WHAT TO SEE AND DO

Most travellers see the Río San Juan from a boat between **San Carlos** (see p.500) on the eastern shore of Lago de Nicaragua and the old Spanish fort and town of **El Castillo**, the only real tourist attraction in the area. **Wildlife** is abundant along the river, and travellers who venture up- or downstream will certainly spot sloths, howler monkeys, parrots and macaws, bats, storks, caimans and perhaps even a tapir.

El Castillo

The full name of the Río San Juan's historic fort is La Fortaleza de la Inmaculada Concepción de María, though everyone refers to it simply as **El Castillo**. Lying on a hillock beside a narrow stretch of the Río San Juan, the fort was built by the Spanish as a defensive measure against the pirates who continually sacked Granada in the seventeenth century. It was more or less effective for a hundred years, until a British force led by a young Horatio Nelson finally took it in 1780, after which it was abandoned for nearly two centuries. The neatly restored structure boasts an interesting small **museum** (daily 8am–5pm; C\$45, plus C\$25 to take photos or C\$50 for video, tickets valid for the length of your stay) with dusty armaments of the period, information on the area's history and a few random artefacts found during the restoration of the castle, and a **library** (closed at weekends) with more than a thousand books on the history of the castle and the Río San Juan area.

Reserva Biológica Indio Maíz

Downstream from El Castillo, heading out towards the Caribbean, the northern bank of the Río San Juan forms part of the 3000-square-kilometre **Reserva Biológica Indio Maíz**, the largest nature reserve in Nicaragua. The climate here is very wet and hot, with the vast expanses of dense rainforest sheltering many species, including the elusive manatee, jaguars, tapirs, scarlet macaws, parrots and toucans. The pristine Indio Maíz vegetation stands in sharp contrast with the Costa Rican side, where agriculture and logging have eroded the forest.

San Juan de Nicaragua

Located at the mouth of the mighty Río San Juan, just as the Río Indio branches off northwards, Greytown was one of the first places European explorers/ pirates (depending on your point of view) arrived. Nearby **San Juan de Nicaragua** (aka San Juan del Norte, aka Greytown), however, is perhaps the youngest town in Central America, established in the early 1990s when a mishmash of families displaced by the war decided to return to Nicaragua. All that is left of old Greytown is an overgrown graveyard and a dredger brought by Cornelius Vanderbilt in the 1800s with hopes of creating an interoceanic canal.

ARRIVAL AND DEPARTURE

BY PLANE

La Costeña (☎ 2263 2142) runs flights from Managua and San Carlos on Thurs & Sun, which arrive at the tiny airport where the old town of Greytown once stood. The only way to/from the airport is by private *panga*. Arrange in advance through your accommodation, or call *Hotelito Evo* (US\$10/ person; ☎ 2583 9019). Planes are small and flights regularly sell out, so if you're planning to travel along the river and then hop on a plane back to Managua, you'd be better off booking the flight before you set off – or be prepared to spend a few more days in San Juan. There is a US\$2 airport tax payable at all national airports.

BY BOAT

El Castillo Boats travel between El Castillo and San Carlos (see p.500) daily (leaving San Carlos Mon, Tues & Fri 8am, noon, 2.30pm & 3pm, Wed & Thurs 8am, noon & 3pm and Sun 8am &1.30pm; leaving El Castillo Mon–Sat 5am, 6am, 7am, & 2pm, Sun 5am & 2pm; 2–3hr; C\$90), stopping off at Sábalos en route. Lodges can also organize transport. During the week there may be more daytime departures, while on Sunday afternoon departures are unreliable – check at the docks.

Reserva Biológica Indio Maíz You can hire a private boat from El Castillo (around US\$25 one way; around 20min) to get to the research station, or board any boat travelling between San Carlos and San Juan de Nicaragua (they have to stop here as there is a checkpoint, but for the return journey you may find that boats are already full by this point). A couple of operators in El Castillo also offer tours (see below).

San Juan de Nicaragua *Pangas* to/from San Carlos arrive/leave from the dock at the north end of town (fast boats Mon & Fri 6am, Thurs & Sun 5am; 7hr; C\$630; slow boats Thurs, Sat & Sun 5am; 10–12hr; C\$330). All boats make the return trip from San Carlos the following day. At the time of writing there is a regular service between San Juan de Nicaragua and Bluefields with Transporte Oporta (☎ 8830 3696) leaving San Juan on Wed at 8am and Bluefields on Fri at 9am (3–5hr; C\$900). It's a rough, wet ride so come prepared and call ahead, as this service is subject to change.

INFORMATION AND TOURS

EL CASTILLO

Tourist information The Asociación Municipal de Ecoturismo El Castillo runs a small tourist office just up from the dock (Mon–Sat 8am–6pm; ☎ 8652 6020). They offer canoe trips (US\$15/person; 3–4hr) and walking tours in the Indio Maíz biological reserve, and atmospheric sunset cayman-spotting trips (US\$45 for four people). Nena Tours (☎ 8821 2135, ⊛ nenalodge.com), operating from the lodge of the same name (see p.504), offers an

English-speaking alternative, with tours of the reserve (from US$75 for four people), trips in a traditional dug-out canoe (US$15/person) and cayman-spotting (US$45 for four).

ACCOMMODATION

6

The trip to and from El Castillo can be completed in a day, but the small and friendly village around the fort offers several accommodation options and is a charming place to rest up, especially if you've been travelling hard and fast via San Carlos. Just over halfway between San Carlos and El Castillo, the small riverside town of Sábalos offers several rather wonderful lodges – the only drawback is that you'll be dependent on their food and tours, which are more expensive than those in El Castillo.

SÁBALOS

Grand River Lodge Along the river, roughly 2km before Sábalos ⓣ8936 3919, ⓦhotelgrandriverlodge.com. Tiny wooden cabins with charming open-roofed shower rooms. There's a real family atmosphere, with the owner happy to show guests around his cocoa plantation, and horseriding and kayaking can be arranged. Rates include breakfast; other meals C$70. Cabins US$20, camping/hammocks/person (with own equipment) US$3

★**Hotel Kateana** One block north of the dock, on the right-hand side. The sweet owner will go out of her way to accommodate you. If you've had your fill of rice and beans, she can tell you where to find cheap vegetables and lend you her kitchen. Laundry service available. Doubles with shared bath C$400, with private bath C$450

Hotel Sábalos ⓣ2271 7424, ⓦhotelsabalos.com.ni. A great hotel just up the river from *Sábalos Lodge*. The en-suite rooms are rather plain, but immaculately tidy, set over the river and accessed from a large, wooden porch. A wide variety of tours can be arranged, too. Price includes breakfast. US$42

EL CASTILLO

Albergue El Castillo On the hill by the entrance to the ruins ⓣ8924 5608. Simple, comfortable rooms with mosquito nets and fans in a huge, wooden cabin-style hotel with balcony and great river views – get a room upstairs. Breakfast is included. US$25

Hospedaje Universal Just left of the dock ⓣ8666 3264. This family-run hostel has small, clean wood-partitioned rooms and shared showers, along with a wooden balcony with hammocks right on the river. US$10

Nena Lodge 5min from the dock, on the left ⓣ2583 3010, ⓦnenalodge.com. Neat, tidy rooms in a friendly, family-run hostel that also offers tours. US$20

RESERVA BIOLÓGICA INDIO MAÍZ

★**Refugio Bartola** ⓣ8376 6979 or ⓣ8873 8586. A scientific research station offering eleven comfortable en-suite wooden rooms. Rates include three good meals a day. US$110

SAN JUAN DE NICARAGUA

Hostal Familiar On the left, 200m along the riverside from the dock ⓣ8446 2096. The friendly and helpful owner is also a good cook – a big bonus in this town, where your options are limited. The waterfront location is great, but there is a bar opposite, so it can be noisy at night (the cabins on the waterfront are quieter than the rooms). Waterfront cabins US$20, standard rooms C$400

Hotelito Evo Fourth street back from the waterfront, three blocks west of the mobile phone tower ⓣ2583 9019, ⓦhostalevo.com. The town's first hostel, with the parents gradually handing the business down to their sons. It's the best place in town for tours – the boys grew up on the river and know all the waterways. Rates include breakfast; other meals are available. US$20

EATING AND DRINKING

Options are limited in Sábalos but El Castillo has a few decent spots. In San Juan de Nicaragua, there are some pleasant places to eat along the waterfront.

EL CASTILLO

Borders Coffee Signposted down a small path near *Hotel Victoria*. Small café making an effort to offer something different. Sip beer (C$25), great milkshakes and proper coffee (C$20), and dine on reasonable food ("American" breakfast C$80, seafood pasta C$150); the chef's special is pasta with various sauces. Open daily 7am–around 8pm, depending on demand.

Restaurante Victoria At the end of the street, left from the dock ⓣ2583 0188, ⓦhotelvictoriaelcastillo.com. The hotel is pricey, but you can be forgiven for deciding to splash out on a clean restaurant with efficient service. Set meals of chicken, fish or pasta are all C$200 and there's a good selection of drinks. Daily 7am–9pm.

Soda La Orquidea 30m on the right from the dock. Has a sweet little upstairs balcony for typical breakfasts (C$50), tasty chicken (C$120) and the chef's speciality river shrimp (C$300).

SAN JUAN DE NICARAGUA

Most places offering accommodation can also make you meals, but these need to be ordered in advance.

Bar El Rama 200m along the riverside from *Hostal Familiar*. Not much on offer in the way of food, but this local bar has a friendly crowd and cheap drinks. Mon–Fri noon–midnight, Sat & Sun 10am–1am.

Tucan 1.5 blocks south (along the river) from the dock and one block west. No set times, but if you ask and are patient they can always rustle something up. All meals C$130 including drink.

The Atlantic coast

Nicaragua's low-lying **Atlantic coast** makes up more than half the country's total landmass. It's mostly composed of impenetrable mangrove swamps and jungle, and as such only a few places in the region attract visitors in any number: **Bluefields**, a raffish port town, the idyllic **Pearl Lagoon** just to the north, and the **Corn Islands**, which boast sandy beaches, swaying palm trees and a distinctly Caribbean atmosphere. Outside these areas, the coast remains an untouristed tangle of waterways and rainforests, and should be approached with caution and negotiated only with the aid of experienced locals and good supplies of food, water and insect repellent. Indeed, there is only one actual town in the northern half of the coast – **Puerto Cabezas**. Few travellers make the trip (flying is the only real transport option), but the impoverished town has a unique feel and is the best access point for the Miskito-speaking wildernesses of the northeast.

The possibilities for ecotourism in this vast, isolated coastal region are obvious, though a scarcity of resources and a lack of cooperation between central and local government have so far stymied all progress; while the long-discussed highway linking Managua and Bluefields has failed to leave the drawing board.

6

EL RAMA AND JUIGALPA

If you are travelling to Bluefields and beyond via land and river there are few options for breaking up the journey, and since you can buy a combined bus and boat ticket right from Managua to Bluefields, many don't bother. If you do decide to have a stopover the obvious choice is El Rama, where the road ends and the river begins and you have to change transport anyway. However, Juigalpa is a bigger, cleaner and more prosperous town where you can find fast food, get a taste of farming life in this cattle farming district and even visit a museum.

HISTORY AND POLITICS ON THE ATLANTIC COAST

The Atlantic coast never appealed to the Spanish conquistadors, and repelled by disease, endless jungle, dangerous snakes and persistent biting insects, they quickly made tracks for the more hospitable Pacific zone. As a result, Spanish influence was never as great along this seaboard as elsewhere. English, French and Dutch buccaneers had been plying the coast since the late 1500s, and it was they who first made contact with the **Miskito**, **Sumu** and **Rama** peoples who populated the area. Today the **ethnicity** of the region is complex, and the east can feel like another country. The indigenous peoples mixed with slaves brought from Africa and Jamaica to work in the region's fruit plantations, and while many inhabitants are Afro-American in appearance, others have Amerindian features, and some combine both with European traits. **Creole English** is still widely spoken.

During the years of the **Revolution** and the Sandinista government, the FSLN met with suspicion on the Atlantic coast, which had never really trusted the government in Managua. The region was hit hard by conflict, and half the Miskito population went into exile in Honduras, while a much smaller number made their way to Costa Rica. In 1985 the Sandinistas tried to repair relations by granting the region political and administrative autonomy, creating the territories **RAAN (Región Autonomista Atlántico Norte)** and **RAAS (Región Autonomista Atlántico Sur)**, though this only served to stir up further discontent, being widely seen as an attempt to split the Atlantic coast as a political force. Improvements to infrastructure (notably the resurfacing of the road to El Rama and the extension of the route right the way to Pearl Lagoon) show that the government has not forgotten the east coast, and tourism offers a route out, of sorts, but its profits remain focused on a handful of accessible destinations. As the jungles of the northeast are sacrificed for farmland and more Spanish-speakers from the west move to the Atlantic, this damp, diverse region is losing some of the qualities that make it so distinctive and appealing – but for now, this great, troubled region remains a land apart.

6

ARRIVAL AND INFORMATION

In El Rama the bus station sits in the town's low-key centre, and *pangas* leave from the small jetty two blocks south and one block west of here. Buses continuing between El Rama and Managua will drop you on the highway at the edge of Juigalpa, from where you can get a taxi to your accommodation (C$10 to the town centre).

By boat High-speed *pangas* (2hr; C$250) run daily between El Rama and Bluefields from 5.30am, with several departures in the early morning and a couple more heading downstream until around 1pm – with sufficient demand another may leave later in the afternoon. There are also boats to Big Corn Island (see p.509).

By bus There are services from Managua to El Rama via Juigalpa (8 daily from 4am–9pm; Juigalpa 3hr, El Rama 5–7hr), Pearl Lagoon to El Rama (daily 4pm; 5hr) and San Carlos to El Rama (daily 4.10pm; 5hr).

Facilities In El Rama continue north from Año Santo church (two blocks east of the bus station) to the crossroads and you'll spot a Bancentro bank to your left and an internet café down the road to your right. In Juigalpa banks can be found on C de los Bomberos one block north of the Parque Central.

ACCOMMODATION AND EATING

In both towns the cheapest food is to be found in the market, serving typical dishes of rice, beans and meat with a drink for around C$60.

Eco-Hotel El Vivero A couple of kilometres outside El Rama on the road from Managua ☎2517 0281, ⓦ ecohotelvivero.com. The best option if you're intending to spend any time in El Rama, with nice a/c rooms in a large wooden building set in the jungle. Ask the bus to drop you off or get a cab (C$20). **US$30**

El Expresso One block west and three blocks north of the bus station in El Rama. A cool and somewhat clinical refuge from grubby El Rama, this big-windowed restaurant offers tender chicken and decent shrimp (both C$180).

Hospedaje El Nuevo Milenio 1.5 blocks north of the Parque Central in Juigalpa ☎2512 0646. Clean rooms with TV and fan. The owners speak English. **US$12**

Pizza Lylleana Two blocks north of the Parque Central, Juigalpa ☎2512 2873. Pretty good pizza baked in a wood-fired oven to eat in or take away. Individual pizzas for under C$100 (depending on toppings). Tues–Sun 11am–10pm.

BLUEFIELDS

There are no fields, blue or otherwise, near steamy **BLUEFIELDS**, the only town of any size on the country's southern Atlantic coast. It acquired its name from a Dutch pirate, Abraham Blauvelt, who holed up here regularly in the seventeenth century, and it still has something of the fugitive charm of a pirate town, perched on the side of a lagoon at the mouth of the Río Escondido, though this is about the only allure it holds. Indeed, listen to some travellers' tales of constant rainfall, murderous mozzies and menacing streets, and you might never come here at all.

But despite being undoubtedly poor, frequently wet and utterly beachless, Bluefields can be an intriguing place to stop over on your travels around the area. Fine river views and a hospitable, partly Creole-speaking population reward those who do visit. Avoid the portside "hotels" and hustlers and get a taxi if you head out of the small central area, and you should be just fine – indeed, Bluefields' karaoke-, country- and reggae-based nightlife can be pretty engaging if you keep half an eye out.

The few streets in Bluefields are named, though locals resort to the usual method of directing from landmarks: the Moravian church, the mercado at the end of Avenida Aberdeen and the Parque to the west of town are the most popular ones.

WHAT TO SEE AND DO

Take a *panga* from behind the market to **El Bluff** (leave and return when full; 30min; C$50). There are few amenities here, but there is a beach on the far side and a *comedor*. **Bluefields Museum** on Calle Central (Mon–Fri 8am–noon & 2–5pm; $2) has an interesting collection around the history of the indigenous communities on the Atlantic coast, as well as a library and bookshop.

ARRIVAL AND INFORMATION

By plane The small airport (☎2572 2500) is about 3km south of town – take a taxi (around C$20). There are daily flights to and from Managua and Big Corn Island and flights (Mon, Wed & Fri) to Puerto Cabezas.

By boat Boats arrive and leave from the dock about 150m north of the town's Moravian church, although you may be dropped at the market too. There's a C$5 port fee on top of ticket prices. *Pangas* head to Rama (daily from 5.30am, with several departures in the early morning and a few more heading upstream until around noon and occasional afternoon departures; 2hr; C$250) and Pearl Lagoon (Mon–Sat 9am, or when full, with sporadic departures until around 4pm, Sun 9am only; 1hr; C$170). Several ferries head to Big Corn – the *Bluefields Express* (Wed 9am; 5–7hr; C$210) is your best bet, as the rest leave from El

Bluff, outside Bluefields, making connections tricky. In theory Captain D does the return journey to/from Bilwi every two weeks but the schedule often changes, so it's best to call in advance. ☎ 8850 2767 (approx 4hr; C$800).

Tourist information The small INTUR office, in a small building next to the airport (Mon–Fri 8am–5pm; ☎ 2572 0221), has a few brochures and is friendly enough but don't expect too much help.

ACCOMMODATION

Lodging in Bluefields is underwhelming, with gloomy, noisy, overpriced rooms the norm. The cheaper, more basic establishments attract a rough local clientele – one reason why some places have a curfew. You can walk to all accommodation in Bluefields' small centre from the docks.

Hotel Aeropuerto By the airport ☎ 2572 2862. Perfectly located if you're flying out the next day. The rooms are large, but some are dark and musty while others have wood panelling and windows leading onto a balcony with great views of the lagoon – ask to see a selection. US$1 extra for a/c. There's a fair range of food on offer at the downstairs restaurant too. US$25

Hotel Caribbean Dream C Central ☎ 2572 0107, ✉ reyzapata1@yahoo.com. The snazziest option in the centre, not that that's saying a huge amount: all rooms are en suite, with TVs and optional a/c. Bag one of the brighter rooms upstairs, which lead onto a pleasant balcony. US$26

EATING

Except for seafood, which is as plentiful and fresh as anywhere along the coast, Bluefields doesn't offer a great deal of choice on the eating front. The cheapest eats are, naturally, found in the market.

Chez Marcel One block south of the Parque. The tablecloths, plastic flowers and a/c indicate that this is one of the fanciest restaurants in town, but the prices aren't too bad – try the chicken in wine (C$190) or fried snook (C$205), or push the boat out towards lobster thermidor (C$380). Open daily for lunch and dinner.

Galería Aberdeen A block west of the market. This sprawling coffee shop trying hard to be modern is a good place to come if you fancy a change. Spinach and feta cheese salad (C$120), steak, salad and hash browns (C$200) and good range of national and international beers and wines available. Daily 7am–9pm.

La Ola A block west of the market. Munch on tasty *ceviche* (C$120), chicken and chips (C$100) and *pescado a la plancha* (C$180) on the breezy balcony or in the functional downstairs space, which comes complete with "*no hay credito*" signs and groggy-looking men sipping beer (C$22). Daily 8.30am–midnight.

★**Pelican Bay** Beyond *Tia Irene's*, overlooking the bay right at the end of the street ☎ 2572 2089. Packed with locals eating whole fish (C$230) or seafood stew (C$391).

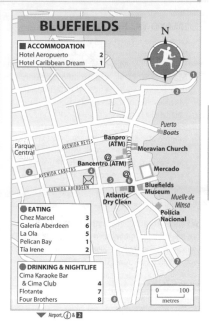

BLUEFIELDS N

■ ACCOMMODATION
Hotel Aeropuerto 2
Hotel Caribbean Dream 1

● EATING
Chez Marcel 3
Galería Aberdeen 6
La Ola 5
Pelican Bay 1
Tia Irene 2

● DRINKING & NIGHTLIFE
Cima Karaoke Bar
 & Cima Club 4
Flotante 7
Four Brothers 8

Puerto Boats
Banpro (ATM)
Parque Central
AVENIDA REYES
Moravian Church
Bancentro (ATM)
Mercado
AVENIDA CABEZAS
AVENIDA ABERDEEN
Atlantic Dry Clean
Bluefields Museum
Muelle de Minsa
Policia Nacional
0 100 metres

▼ Airport. ⓘ & 2

There's no dance floor, but it's a decent place to listen to music and sink a few beers (C$29).

Tia Irene *Bluefields Bay Hotel*, Barrio Pointeen ☎ 2572 2143. This tropical, bamboo-clad *rancho* sits on the water and is packed to the rafters with locals on the weekends, when the small dancefloor comes alive. You can eat anything from whole fish (C$205) to lobster (C$330), and gaze upon the rusty hulks and palm trees that surround Bluefields while sipping a beer (C$25). Closed Mon; karaoke nights Thurs–Sat.

DRINKING AND NIGHTLIFE

Bluefields' nightlife features an interesting mix of promenading couples, likely lads, drunken policemen, pool halls and karaoke. Country and western, soca and reggae dominate the dancefloors. Travel in groups at night.

Cima Karaoke Bar 50m west of Bancentro. You'll probably hear this popular bar, a reggae and soca stronghold with speakers blasting into the street, before you see it. Cover charges (C$30) only apply on weekends. (*Cima Club*, next door, has no cover charge, but a slightly rougher crowd.) Upstairs bar & club daily; downstairs karaoke Thurs–Sun.

Flotante Five blocks south of the Moravian church. This waterfront building on stilts has an indoor dancefloor and cracking views over the (almost) unspoilt bay. With beer from C$23 and piña coladas at C$50, this is a popular spot on the weekends but it's a good idea to take a taxi at night. There's music in the evenings and food from 2pm (plate of mixed snacks for sharing C$380).

6

¡MAYO YA! FESTIVAL

During the month of May, particularly in the last week, the streets of Bluefields are taken over by **¡Mayo Ya!** or **Palo de Mayo**, one of the most exciting fiestas in the country. Derived from the traditional May Day celebrations of northern Europe and celebrating the arrival of spring, ¡Mayo Ya! features a mixture of reggae, folklore and indigenous dance that young Blufileños pair ingeniously with the latest moves from Jamaica. The celebrations wrap up with the election of the Mayaya Goddess, the queen of the festivities.

★ **Four Brothers** On the southern side of town (a short taxi ride). This big, groovy shed is the granddaddy of the Caribbean music scene in Bluefields, and commands a loyal, largely Creole crowd. Thurs–Sun 10pm–early hours.

DIRECTORY

Banks There are several ATMs in town, with a Banpro opposite the Moravian church and a Bancentro just around the corner.

Internet Cyber Central next to Bancentro (Mon–Fri 8am–7.30pm) offers internet access for C$10/hr.

PEARL LAGOON

Mellow, manageable and just a short hop from Bluefields, **PEARL LAGOON** (Laguna de Perlas) is a slowly growing spot on Nicaragua's tourist map. It's connected to El Rama and thence Managua by road, but most visitors arrive on a bouncy boat ride that takes you through tangled mangroves into a vast, shallow lagoon. In its southern corner, the village of Pearl Lagoon has sandy streets, quality seafood and a friendly Creole populace who make their living from fishing and tourism. Once you've seen the **big gun** that looks out over Pearl Lagoon's small wharf, you've seen the sights, but it makes a fine base for fishing trips, longer excursions and sitting happily on your backside, sinking beer and lobster and watching the sun set.

Those who fancy exploring can head out to the remote **Pearl Cayes** where the water really is crystal clear (for all its charms, Pearl Lagoon is a little more silty), or walk/cycle inland to **Awas**, a Miskito village about 3km west with a small beach and a decent restaurant. (It's best to head back before dark.)

ARRIVAL AND DEPARTURE

By boat *Pangas* to/from Bluefields take about 1hr. One leaves the small wharf at 6.30am and there are sporadic departures later in the day, often at 1pm. Arrive early to put your name on the passenger list, or call by the day before.

By bus The bus from El Rama arrives at the basketball court around 9pm daily and leaves at 5.30am (5hr). Try to get there around 5am if you want a seat.

INFORMATION AND TOURS

Tourist information INTUR office in the green building by the wharf (Mon–Fri 8am–5pm, though opening times can be sporadic).

Tours For tours, you are best off dealing direct with operators. Fishermen at the dock offer trips, and most accommodation can point you in the right direction, but there are a couple of established players too. The friendly *Queen Lobster* restaurant (contact Pedro on ☎ 8499 4403) offers fun combined fishing and cooking classes (US$25); trips to the Pearl Cayes (US$200 for 2–4 people) and sports fishing in Top Lock Lagoon with a stay on the family farm. George Fox (☎ 5749 8992; head right from the dock towards *Casa Ulrich* and his house is on the left) has trips to Orinoco and the Wawashang Reserve, and out to the Pearl Cayes – a group of four will pay around US$200 for the day.

Bike rental *Queen Lobster* rents bicycles (C$20/hr).

ACCOMMODATION

Cool Spot Turn left out of the wharf and left again back down to the waterfront to a yellow house with no sign; ask for Doña Cherry ☎ 8662 4270. No-frills accommodation with shared bath. The friendly owner may show you how to bake coconut bread and make *rondon*. **C$200**

Green Lodge 100m south of the wharf ☎ 2572 0507, ✉ williamsdes60@yahoo.com. This popular choice offers creaking rooms in the main house and newer lodgings in a modern annexe in an overgrown garden. All rooms have TV, and there are fine hammocks for chilling. **C$400**

Hospedaje Ingrid One block west and three blocks south of *Green Lodge*, set back from the path ☎ 2572 5007 or ☎ 8725 6606. Several small but pleasant cabins alongside a family home. All have private bathrooms and TV. **C$250**

Queen Lobster 200m north of the wharf ✆ queenlobster .com. This excellent restaurant (see opposite) offers two beautiful cabins over the water with TV and hot water – a good option if you fancy a treat. Free wi-fi for guests. **US$30**

EATING AND DRINKING

Spices and seafood make Pearl Lagoon a fine place to eat. Just south of the dock are two bakeries (open early until they sell out), offering delicious soda cake, coconut and cheese pasties from C$5. Most restaurants are also decent options for a sundowner, and there are a couple of proper bars with the Atlantic coast's traditional soundtrack of country and reggae.

Bar Relax A block west (inland) from *Green Lodge*. This groovy bar is a decent place to see the locals shake their stuff on the dancefloor and guzzle beer (C$20) in the covered outdoor area.

Casa Ulrich 300m north of the dock. The filet mignon (C$300), grilled fish (C$180) and other main meals get plaudits at this hostel/restaurant, and the elevated deck is a good place to sink a few beers (C$25) too. They also have dorms for US$10/person, and free wi-fi for customers.

★**Queen Lobster** 200m north of the wharf ⓦ queenlobster.com. This charming round hut over the water offers excellent Creole cuisine – it's one of the few places you can get *rondon* (C$250) without pre-ordering – plus crab in breadcrumbs (C$160) or a tasty chicken salad (C$160). Tours and cooking classes are on offer, along with accommodation (see opposite). Free wi-fi for customers.

THE CORN ISLANDS

Lying 70km off the country's Atlantic coast, the **CORN ISLANDS** (Las Islas de Maíz) offer white beaches, warm, clear water and a Caribbean vibe – the kind of place you come to intending to stay for a couple of days and end up hanging around for a week or more.

Like many parts of the Caribbean coast, during the nineteenth century both larger **Corn Island** and tiny **Little Corn** were a haven for **buccaneers**, who used them as a base for raiding other ships in the area or attacking the inland towns on Lago de Nicaragua. These days it's **drug-runners** who use the islands, unfortunately, as part of the transportation route for US- and Europe-bound cocaine.

WHAT TO SEE AND DO

Big Corn is home to virtually all the islands' services, has a reasonable selection of hotels and restaurants, and is large enough to ensure that – if you're prepared to head far enough – you can get your own patch of beach. More backpackers head straight to idyllic **Little Corn**, though if you have time you might want to try them both out. Reached by a quick but bouncy *panga* from the bigger island, "La Islita" is extremely quiet, with **rustic** tourist amenities – bring sunscreen, mosquito repellent, a torch and money. Set on just

three largely undeveloped square kilometres, with a population of just over a thousand, the island boasts lush palm trees and beautiful **white-sand beaches**, great snorkelling and diving, good swimming and, above all, plenty of peace and quiet – with no cars on the island, traffic consists of bikes, dogs and wheelbarrows.

Big Corn

It's possible to walk round the entire island of **BIG CORN** in about three hours. **Brig Bay** stretches south from the dock and main town past shacks and perfectly serviceable sands. **Long Bay**, across the airstrip heading east, is quieter and less populated, and there are plenty of places to swim in either direction. North of Long Bay is **South End**, where there's some coral reef good for snorkelling – there's more on the northeast corner near the village of Sally Peachy. The southwest bay, **Picnic Center**, is a fine stretch of sand near a loading dock – there's a huge party here during Semana Santa, when crowds of people come over from Bluefields and the locals set up stalls to sell food and drink.

About 1.5km offshore to the southeast, in about 20m of clear water, is the wreck of a Spanish galleon, while the beach in front of *Paraíso Beach Hotel* boasts three newer wrecks, lacking the historical excitement of the galleon but with excellent marine life within wading distance of the shore.

Little Corn

If you're going to work up the energy to do anything at all on **LITTLE CORN**, it's likely to be **diving** or **snorkelling**; the island has around nine square kilometres of glorious, healthy reef to explore. Little Corn is even easier to navigate than its larger neighbour; all *pangas* arrive at and depart from **Pelican Beach**, while most backpackers stay on **Cocal Beach** on the east side of the island. The north end is even more remote and quieter than the rest of the island, and best suited to couples or families. There's great snorkelling both here and off Iguana Beach, just south of Cocal Beach – ask your accommodation for advice, as some reefs are a fair swim away.

6

6

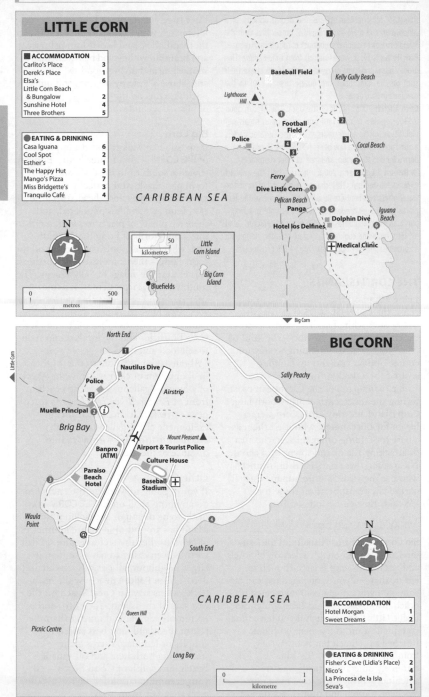

LITTLE CORN

■ ACCOMMODATION

Carlito's Place	3
Derek's Place	1
Elsa's	6
Little Corn Beach & Bungalow	2
Sunshine Hotel	4
Three Brothers	5

● EATING & DRINKING

Casa Iguana	6
Cool Spot	2
Esther's	1
The Happy Hut	5
Mango's Pizza	7
Miss Bridgette's	3
Tranquilo Café	4

Baseball Field

Kelly Gully Beach

Lighthouse Hill

Football Field

Police

Cocal Beach

Ferry

Dive Little Corn

Pelican Beach

Panga

Dolphin Dive

Iguana Beach

Hotel los Delfines

Medical Clinic

CARIBBEAN SEA

N

0 — 500
metres

0 — 50
kilometres

Little Corn Island

Big Corn Island

Bluefields

Big Corn

BIG CORN

North End

Little Corn

Nautilus Dive

Police

Airstrip

Sally Peachy

Muelle Principal

Brig Bay

Mount Pleasant

Banpro (ATM)

Airport & Tourist Police

Culture House

Paraiso Beach Hotel

Baseball Stadium

Waula Point

South End

Picnic Centre

Queen Hill

CARIBBEAN SEA

Long Bay

N

■ ACCOMMODATION

Hotel Morgan	1
Sweet Dreams	2

● EATING & DRINKING

Fisher's Cave (Lidia's Place)	2
Nico's	4
La Princesa de la Isla	3
Seva's	1

0 — 1
kilometre

ARRIVAL AND DEPARTURE

BIG CORN

By plane The easiest and quickest route takes you in an often-tiny plane to/from Managua (1hr) or Bluefields (30min), both offering great views. La Costeña (☎ 2263 2142, ⊛ lacostena.com.ni) operates four flights daily from Managua to Corn Island (daily 6.15am, 11am, 2.30pm & 3.35pm). Depending on the number of passengers, the same flights will stop at Bluefields, or there will be separate departures around the same time. There is a US$2 airport tax payable at all national airports. Taxis await incoming flights and can take you to your hotel or the jetty for Little Corn (10min); a taxi to anywhere on the island costs US$1.

By boat Cargo boats and freight ferries head to the island. The *Bluefields Express* (Wed 9am; 5–7hr; C$210) leaves from docks in Bluefields, while the *Río Escondido* (☎ 8437 7209; 5–7hr; C$210) departs El Bluff on Wed at 9am (returning Thurs at 9am). If you want to miss out Bluefields, try *Captain D* (☎ 8202 0306; 12hr; C$400 with bed), which leaves El Rama at 8pm on Tues and Corn Island at 11pm on Sat, with a brief stop at El Bluff. Boats arrive at the *muelle principal* on the west side of the island. A harbour tax of C$3 must be paid at the harbour entrance on Big Corn.

LITTLE CORN

By boat A regular *panga* leaves the *muelle principal* at the northern end of Brig Bay on Big Corn (10am & 4.30pm daily, returning from Little Corn 6.30am & 1.30pm; 30min; C$140) – flights generally wait for the *panga*, and vice versa, so you're unlikely to miss your connection. The ride is rough and can be very wet – waterproof your bag if you can. The boat drops you off on Little Corn's western side, amid the island's only real cluster of population and facilities.

INFORMATION AND TOURS

BIG CORN

Tourist information There's a small INTUR office opposite the *muelle principal* but opening times are sporadic and you can probably get more information from your hotel.

Tour operators Trips can be arranged through *Paraíso Beach Hotel*, the small resort on the west of the island (☎ 2575 5111, ⊛ paraisoclub.com), who also rent scuba gear and golf carts. Nautilus Dive (☎ 2575 5077, ⊛ nautilus -dive-nicaragua.com) offer dives with boat, guide and complete equipment for US$85/person, as well as fishing trips and snorkel tours for US$25 (min 2 people). Dorsey Campbell (☎ 8909 8050) lives in the relaxed hamlet of Sally Peachy; US$20 will get you equipment for as long as you want, plus Dorsey's formidable expertise.

LITTLE CORN

Tour operators Two friendly, PADI-certified dive outfits offer a similar range of activities and prices – from single-tank dives (US$35) to trips to Blowing Rock (US$95) and five-day packages (US$150). Dolphin Dive (⊛ dolphin divelittlecorn.com) is run from the fancy *Hotel Los Delfines* and also offers kitesurfing (⊛ kitelittlecorn.com), while Dive Little Corn is just south of *Miss Bridgette's* (see p.512). Snorkel and kayak rental costs around US$10/day – you can also rent snorkels at most accommodation on the island.

ACCOMMODATION

6

Things get busy, and prices rise, during the Christmas/New Year period and around Semana Santa. If you're here at quieter times, it may be worth haggling.

BIG CORN

Much of Big Corn's accommodation is rather anonymous, with options spread between built-up Brig Bay and the quieter beaches that sprawl around the island – you'll need taxis to get to these.

Hotel Morgan 20m north of the Nautilus Dive shop ☎ 2575 5052, ⊛ bigcornislandhotelmorgan.com. Located right opposite the beach with a range of accommodation options; you might want to splash out on one of the sweet wooden cabins which boast TV, a/c and hot water. There's also a decent restaurant with free wi-fi for customers. Doubles US$15, cabins US$40

Sweet Dreams Right by the harbour ☎ 2575 5105. The location makes this orange-hued hotel a good bet for those heading off to Little Corn. The first-floor rooms are smallish but tidy, mostly en suite and all with TV, and there's a restaurant attached. Doubles with shared bath US$20, with private bath US$25

LITTLE CORN

Head to the east and north sides of Little Corn if you want tranquillity and great snorkelling on your doorstep. A 20min walk away, in the main village, a couple of relatively inexpensive options vie for your custom, though prices all over the island have risen steeply following the opening of a five-star resort in 2014. Many places only have electricity in the evenings and at night.

Carlito's Place Cocal Beach ☎ 2570 0432, ⊛ carlitosplacelittlecorn.com. A friendly beachfront backpacker hangout with individual en-suite *cabinas*. Meals are served in a cheery pink space from around US$6, and they are home to the Karma Massage Shack – worth a visit, if you can find room for more relaxation. US$30

Elsa's Cocal Beach ☎ 2575 5014. An island institution, with simple, clean double cabañas and smaller rooms in thatched huts on the beach. One of the islands' cheaper options. Rooms from US$15, cabañas US$25

Sunshine Hotel 200m north of the ferry ☎ 8495 6223. Hostel-style accommodation in a rather grand building (in Little Corn terms), offering ten rooms (with two double beds in each), pool and ping-pong tables, wi-fi, a kitchen

6

for guests, a cool shared balcony and among the cheapest snorkel hire on the island (US$3/day). US$20

Three Brothers 150m north of the ferry on the right ☎8658 8736. This simple guesthouse is just a short walk from the beachfront bars and restaurants. Rooms are clean and secure, there's an on-site grocery, and you can use the kitchen. Guests are offered a discount at both dive shops on the island. US$15

EATING AND DRINKING

It's easy to fill up on fish, prawns or lobster for reasonable prices (C$150–250), although service can be slow and opening times erratic. For inexpensive meals, there are several nameless *comedores* in Big Corn by the dock, which serve large plates of *comida típica* for C$150. On Little Corn, *Elsa's* (see below), *Cool Spot* (next to *Elsa's*) and *Carlito's Place* (see p.511), on the east side, all serve up cold beer and dishes for C$150–250.

BIG CORN

Fisher's Cave, aka Lidia's Place Beside the harbour entrance. Seafood specialists in the thick of Big Corn's action. Perch in the courtyard dining area and go for classic Caribbean *rondon* (C$280, order in advance), lobster in tomato sauce (C$280) or a land-lubbing dish of chicken breast (C$200). Open daily.

Nico's On the east side of the island. Popular beachside nightspot, with a small waterfront balcony and heaving dancefloor where you join locals in "sexy dancing" to reggaetón and Caribbean rhythms, or swaying to country music. Beer C$30. Thurs, Sat & Sun, evenings only.

★**Seva's** Sally Peachy. Locally renowned restaurant with a veranda facing the azure sea, serving tasty grilled fish (C$200), and a big and tender plate of fish, chicken and lobster (C$330), as well as standard breakfasts (C$60). Open daily.

LITTLE CORN

Casa Iguana On the lower east side of the island ⓦcasaiguana.net. A busy little bar-restaurant offering US$6 breakfasts, lunch for US$8, snacks and hot food during the day, as well as family-style US$15 three-course dinners (which need to be reserved in advance – they will tell you the time). Most food comes from their farm and garden, which also provides the mint for their mojitos (US$3.50). Free wi-fi for customers. A range of *cabinas* (US$65) is also available. Breakfast served from 7am–9am, small snacks available all day until 9 or 10pm.

Cool Spot Cocal Beach, next to *Elsa's*. On the beach at the heart of the east side's backpacker accommodation, *Cool Spot* serves up chicken with pasta (C$130), chilli prawns (C$280) and more, and has more buzz and more tables than anywhere else on the east side of the island. They also have rooms (US$40).

★**Esther's** The small pink house on the path from the school to the baseball field. *Esther's pan de coco*, or coco bread, is famous on the island, and comes out of the oven here at about 1pm daily.

The Happy Hut In the "village" behind *Tranquilo Café*. The name pretty much nails it – this simple club is the place to dance to reggae at weekends. Evenings only, stays open as long as people keep dancing.

Mango's Pizza Just south of Dolphin Dive. A (possibly welcome) change from rice, beans and all things coconut: the cheesy pizzas (C$150–200) are also available for takeaway.

★**Miss Bridgette's** Opposite the dock. Renowned for good seafood at the best prices on the island, *Miss Bridgette's* is always busy; lobster C$250 and *rondon* C$300 (requires advance notice), while big breakfasts are C$110. Open daily from 6.30am.

Tranquilo Café Just north of Dolphin Dive. This likeable (if not cheap) place is one of the island's main hangouts. There's wi-fi (free for customers), reasonable diner food, tasty organic coffee and a range of beers (US$2) and cocktails. There's a gift shop and book exchange too. Things can get busy in the evenings (especially on bonfire nights – usually Wed and Sat), when the music gets turned up and wide-eyed divers knock back mojitos. Daily 8am–late.

DIRECTORY

Bank On Big Corn, the Banpro, south of the centre on the road from the airport, has an ATM. There's no bank at all on Little Corn but Tranquilo does cash-back on card payments.

★**TREAT YOURSELF**

Derek's Place North Little Corn ⓦdereksplacelittlecorn.com. A handful of rustic-chic, wood-and-bamboo *cabinas* on stilts, complete with solar panels, ingenious fold-out tables and walls built from bright glass bottles, set among palms overlooking the beach. A treat for anyone after relaxed privacy. Hearty communal meals cost US$8.50 for lunch or from US$12 for dinner (must be ordered in advance). Derek also runs snorkelling and diving trips. Double with shared bath US$65

Little Corn Beach & Bungalow Cocal Beach, Little Corn ☎8333 0956, ⓦlittlecornbb.com. This neat place, set at the mellow north end of Cocal Beach, offers neat shipwreck-themed bungalows with nice touches (from the recycled rainwater to the little foot-baths by the door), and a friendly and professional restaurant (breakfast US$3.50, dinner US$9–15) that's a great place to chill, with coffee and free wi-fi for guests. Cabins US$79, bungalows US$209

6

La Princesa de la Isla Just south of *Paraíso Beach Hotel*, Big Corn ☎8854 2403 ⓦlaprincesadelaisla.com. Serving delicious, authentic Italian meals, including superb home-made pastas and desserts like *pannacotta* (four courses from US$18–22), plus tasty breakfasts (US$6), all concocted by an Italian chef. Lunches and dinners are cooked upon request – pop by or call and arrange your menu and time. The *Princesa* also offers nicely rustic rooms (US$55) and *cabinas* (US$70). Daily 8am–10pm.

Health Assistance can be found at the hospital on Big Corn, or the medical clinic just south of Dolphin Dive on Little Corn.
Internet Apart from hotels offering wi-fi, the only access on Big Corn is at the internet café in *El Comisario*; it's a little out of the way so you might want to get a taxi. On Little Corn, higher-end places to stay and many bars, including *Tranquilo Café*, offer free wi-fi for customers.

BILWI (PUERTO CABEZAS)

Small and scruffy **PUERTO CABEZAS**, or **BILWI**, as it's been officially named in defiance of central governmental control (the name means "snake leaf" in the Mayangna-Sumo indigenous tongue), is the most important town north of Bluefields and south of La Ceiba in Honduras. Everyone seems to have come to this town of thirty thousand people in order to do some kind of business, whether it be a Miskito fisherman walking the streets with a day's catch of fish dangling from his hand, a lumber merchant selling planks to foreign mills, or the government surveyors working on the all-season paved road through the jungle that may one day link the town with Managua. The people are mostly welcoming, but this is an impoverished and often lawless corner of the country and travellers are advised to take a taxi if venturing even a few blocks from the town centre.

WHAT TO SEE AND DO

The town's amenities are all scattered within a few blocks of the Parque Central, a few hundred metres west of the seafront. The water at the small local **beach** below the hotels can be clear and blue if the wind is blowing from the northeast, although the townspeople usually head to Bocana beach a few kilometres north of town; taxis can take you here for about C$15. The river water is not safe to bathe in and you need to watch your belongings as there are often a few dodgy characters around.

The southern horizon is broken by the atmospheric outline of the **muelle viejo** (old pier), a twenty-minute walk through the *barrios* (take a taxi), where you'll find fishermen and rusting ships. It was built in 1924 and saw guns delivered for the civil war and trussed-up

THE RAAN: NORTHERN NICARAGUA

The northern reaches of Nicaraguan Mosquitia – the famous **Mosquito Coast** – is one of the most impenetrable and underdeveloped areas of the Americas. No roads connect the area with the rest of the country, and the many snaking, difficult-to-navigate rivers and lagoons, separated by thick slabs of jungle, prevent the casual traveller – or any non-local, for that matter – from visiting the area. Bordered at its northern extent by the **Río Coco**, Nicaragua's frontier with Honduras, La Mosquitia is dotted by small settlements of the indigenous – mainly Miskito – peoples. The area was highly sensitive during the war years of the 1980s, when Contra bases in Honduras sent guerrilla parties over the long river border to attack Sandinista army posts and civilian communities in La Mosquitia and beyond. The Sandinistas forcibly evacuated many Miskitos from their homes, ostensibly to protect them from Contra attacks, but also to prevent them from going over to the other side.

Few travellers come to **Bilwi/ Puerto Cabezas**, the only town of any size and importance in the area. Heading out beyond Cabezas is difficult, but with determination, a big budget, a good guide, a water purification kit and a good mozzie net, you can use it as a springboard to get even further from the tourist routes and into isolated Miskito communities – Waspám, near the Honduran border, is the biggest.

6

turtles pulled in for their meat; now access is limited by a wire fence.

Puerto Cabezas is also the headquarters for **YATAMA** (Yapti Tasba Masraka Nanih Aslatakanka, which translates roughly as "Children of the Mother Earth"), a political party which fights for the rights of the indigenous Atlantic coast peoples, and which is fiercely opposed to central government, whether Conservative, Liberal or Sandinista.

ARRIVAL AND DEPARTURE

By plane Flights from Managua (1hr 30min) and Bluefields (50min) touch down at the airstrip (☎2792 2282) 2km north of the town centre. Taxis will cost no more than C$20/person. Drivers wait at the airport when flights are due to arrive.

By bus The bus terminal is a taxi ride (C$15) west of town. The bus journey to/from Managua (2 daily; 18–30hr depending on how much it's been raining) is notoriously hellish, and impossible after very heavy rain.

By boat In theory *Captain D* does the return journey to/from Bluefields every two weeks but the schedule often changes, so it's best to call in advance on ☎8850 2767 (approx 4hr; C$800) and expect a rough ride.

INFORMATION AND TOURS

Banks The Banpro, a block south of the Parque Central, has an ATM, and there are Bancentros at the airport and just east of the market.

Health Clinica y Farmacia Sukia, 100m south of Banpro (Mon–Fri 8am–6.30pm, Sat 8am–noon).

Internet Access is available at several cafés; try Comunicaciones Saballes, just south of Banpro (C$15/hr).

Tourist information The INTUR office (Mon–Fri 8am–1pm) behind the market can provide information about local hotels and restaurants.

Tour operators AMICA (Mon–Fri 8am–noon & 2–5.30pm; ☎2792 2219, ❿asociacionamica@yahoo.es), four blocks south of the Parque Central, focus their energies on improving the lives of the region's indigenous women. They're your best bet for local trips, heading to the lagoon-side fishing village of Haulover, the long black-sand beach at Wawa Bar and the small community of Karata, most of whose members were displaced in Honduras and Costa Rica during the war but many of whom have now returned.

ACCOMMODATION

Puerto Cabezas is one place where it's worth spending a bit – there's a real jump in quality and it's nice to have comfortable digs in this shabby town.

★**Hotel Casa Museo Judith Kain** 400m north of the INTUR office ☎2792 2225, ❿casamuseojudithkain@ hotmail.com. One of the prettier options in town, offering bright rooms with high ceilings, folksy bedspreads, hot water, wi-fi and a choice of fan or a/c. A free museum (donations welcome) details the history of the Mosquito Kingdom from when the British educated and crowned kings to rule this part of Nicaragua, to its integration into the rest of Nicaragua and subsequent autonomy following the civil war. It also houses examples of the art, clothes and traditional tools and implements used by the various indigenous groups. US$16

Hotel Cortijo 1 100m north of the Parque and **Hotel Cortijo 2** on the street behind ☎2792 2659, ❿cortijoaa @yahoo.com.mx. Both have cool and comfortable wooden rooms (all with fan or a/c and private bath). #1 has wi-fi (which guests at #2 can come and use for free), while #2 has a wooden jetty running down to the sea and balconies in the back rooms (US$2 extra) overlooking the ocean. They also have a laundry service and do decent breakfasts with real coffee. US$25

Hotel Liwa Mair On the small cliffs that overhang the beach ☎2792 2225. Under the same management as *Casa Museo*, with well-equipped and generally spacious rooms. Those upstairs have wonderful private balconies with hammocks. US$15

Hotel Pérez 100m north of *Hotel Cortijo 1* ☎8615 4000. This ageing place boasts carpeted floors, European-style glass windows and a quirky reception. The best rooms, which you'll pay more for, are out back around the old wooden balcony. US$18

Hotel Tangney A block and a half east of the Banpro ☎8943 9891. Ramshackle guesthouse with slightly shabby rooms, a cool balcony and fans but no mozzie nets – if you want cheap prices, it's adequate. US$6

EATING AND DRINKING

Comedor Abril Opposite Banpro. Cheap, home-style restaurant serving a decent, filling lunch for C$70. Open Mon–Sat, breakfast and lunch only.

Comedor Aqui Me Quedo Opposite the Parque Central. Classic beef, chicken and *gallo pinto* done well for C$80 including *fresco*, in this simple pit stop that's well set for gazing over the market.

★**Kabu Payaska** On a bluff 2km north of town ☎2792 1620. This great sweep of a terrace over the beach is a cracking place to feast on delicious lobster *a la plancha*, fresh fish or chicken (C$250), or to just enjoy a beer (C$20) or two. Get a taxi here and back – they will call one for you. Daily noon–midnight.

Restaurante Malecón 300m south of *Hotel Liwa Mair*. Appealing beachfront restaurant and bar specializing in seafood; lobster and shrimp dishes cost around C$300, while the cold beers are C$28. A good place to view the Old Pier. Things get funkier at night, when there are sometimes DJs and karaoke. Daily noon–midnight or later.

VOLCÁN BARÚ, CHIRIQUÍ HIGHLANDS

Panama

HIGHLIGHTS

❶ **Casco Viejo** Panama City's captivating old quarter seeps faded grandeur. **See p.527**

❷ **Panama Canal** Explore this incredible engineering feat by boat or train. **See p.541**

❸ **Guna Yala** Experience the traditional culture of the Guna. **See p.558**

❹ **Azuero Peninsula** Join the revelry at one of the Azuero's riotous festivals. **See box, p.566**

❺ **Chiriquí Highlands** Cool mountain air, fine coffee and untouched cloudforest. **See p.573**

❻ **Bocas del Toro** Dive, surf and snorkel in the warm Caribbean. **See p.583**

HIGHLIGHTS ARE MARKED ON THE MAP ON PP.518–519

ROUGH COSTS

Daily budget Basic US$35/occasional treat US$50

Drink Beer US$1.50, *café con leche* US$2

Food *Arroz con pollo* US$4

Hostel/budget hotel US$13/US$30

Travel Panama City–Bocas del Toro by bus (600km): 10hr, US$29

FACT FILE

Population 3.7 million

Language Spanish

Currency US dollar (US$)

Capital Panama City (population: 1.4 million)

International phone code ☏ 507

Time zone GMT -5hr

Introduction

A narrow, snake-shaped stretch of land that divides oceans and continents, Panama has long been one of the world's greatest crossroads – far before the construction of its famous canal. Though its historical ties to the US have led to an exaggerated perception of the country as a former de facto American colony, Spanish, African, West Indian, Chinese, Indian, European, and several of the least assimilated indigenous communities in the region have all played a role in the creation of the most sophisticated, open-minded and outward-looking society in Central America. The comparatively high level of economic development and use of the US dollar also make it one of the more expensive countries in the region, but the wildlife-viewing and adventure-travel options are excellent.

Cosmopolitan and contradictory, **Panama City** is the most striking capital city in Central America, its multiple personalities reflected in the frenzied energy of its international banking centre, the laidback street-life of its old colonial quarter, its polished nightlife and the antiseptic order of the US-built former Canal Zone. Located in the centre of the country, it is also a natural base from which to explore many of Panama's most popular destinations, including its best-known attraction, the monumental **Panama Canal**. The colonial ruins and Caribbean coastline of **Colón Province** are also within reach of the capital. Southeast of Panama City stretches **Darién**, the infamously wild expanse of rainforest between Central and South America, while to the north, along the Caribbean coastline, **Guna Yala** is the autonomous homeland of the Guna, who live in isolation on the coral atolls of the **Guna Yala Archipelago**. West of Panama City, the Carretera Interamericana runs through the Pacific coastal plain, Panama's agricultural heartland. This region lures travellers intrigued by the folkloric traditions and nature reserves of the **Azuero Peninsula**, also a major surf destination, and the protected cloudforests of the **Chiriquí Highlands** on the Costa Rican border. The mostly uninhabited Caribbean coast west of the canal meets Costa Rica near the remote archipelago of **Bocas del Toro**, a popular holiday destination thanks to its largely unspoiled rainforests, beaches, coral reefs, surfing hotspots and easy-going vibe.

WHEN TO VISIT

Panama is well within the tropics, with temperatures hovering at 25–32°C throughout the year, and varying only with **altitude** (the Chiriquí Highlands are generally 15–26°C). Visiting Panama during the **dry season** (late Dec to April; known as *verano*, or summer) maximizes your chance of finding sunny days. However, seasonal climatic variation is really only evident on the Pacific side of the country's mountainous spine. The average annual rainfall here is about 1500mm; on the Caribbean, about 2500mm falls, spread more evenly throughout the year. From May to December, the storms of the Pacific's winter (*invierno*) **rainy season** are intense but rarely extended.

CHRONOLOGY

1501–02 European explorers Rodrigo de Bastidas and Christopher Columbus visit modern-day Panama.

1510 Conquistador Diego de Nicuesa establishes Nombre de Dios, one of the earliest Spanish settlements in the New World.

1513 Vasco Núñez de Balboa crosses Panama, becoming the first European to see the Pacific Ocean.

1519 Panama City is founded on August 15 by conquistador Pedro Arias de Ávila (known as Pedrarias).

1596–1739 Spanish colonies and ships, loaded with treasure from indigenous Central and South American empires, are attacked several times by British privateers. Henry Morgan sacks Panamá Viejo in 1671.

1746 Spain re-routes treasure fleet around Cape Horn, but trade remains Panama's dominant economic activity.

1821 Panama declares independence from Spain, and joins the confederacy of Gran Colombia (Bolivia, Peru, Ecuador, Venezuela, Colombia and Panama).

1830 Panama becomes a province of Colombia after the dissolution of Gran Colombia.

1851 US company begins building railroad across Panamanian isthmus; project is completed in 1855.

1881 French architect Ferdinand de Lesseps begins excavations for the Panama Canal, which turns out to be an unmitigated disaster. Some 20,000 workers die before the venture is abandoned in 1889.

1903 Backed by the US, Panama declares separation from Colombia. French engineer Philippe Bunau-Varilla signs a treaty with the US, essentially selling rights to the canal, and giving the US control of the Canal Zone "in perpetuity".

1914 The canal is completed. More than 75,000 people have a hand in its construction.

1939 Panama ceases to be a US protectorate, but tensions continue to build between Panama and the US territory of the Canal Zone.

1964 "Martyrs' Day" flag riots, precipitated by a student protest, leave 21 Panamanians dead and over 500 injured in the Canal Zone.

1968 General Omar Torrijos Herrera, Chief of the National Guard, overthrows president Arnulfo Arias and imposes a dictatorship.

1977 Torrijos signs new canal treaty with US President Jimmy Carter, who agrees to transfer the canal to Panamanian control by December 31, 1999.

1983 Colonel Manuel Noriega becomes de facto military ruler. He is initially supported by the US, but also cultivates drug-cartel connections.

1988 US charges Noriega with rigging elections, drug smuggling and murder; Noriega declares state of emergency, dodging a coup and repressing opposition.

1989 Guillermo Endara wins the presidential election, but Noriega seizes presidency. US troops invade Panama and oust Noriega, but also kill and leave homeless thousands of civilians.

1992 US court finds Noriega guilty of drug charges, sentencing him to forty years in prison.

1999 Mireya Moscoso, the widow of former president Arnulfo Arias, is elected as Panama's first female president. US closes military bases and hands full control of the canal to Panama in December.

2003 A country-wide strike over mismanagement of the nation's social-security fund shuts down public services and turns violent.

2004 Martín Torrijos, son of former dictator Omar Torrijos, is elected president. Under Panamanian management, the canal earns record revenues of one billion US dollars.

2006 Referendum on a US$5.2 billion plan to expand the Panama Canal is passed by an overwhelming majority. Panama and the US sign a free-trade agreement.

2008 Noriega is released from prison in the US but following extradition to France is sentenced to seven more years in prison for money laundering.

2009 Right-wing supermarket multimillionaire Ricardo Martinelli is elected president in landslide victory; initially popular for increasing the minimum wage and introducing pensions, his presidency ends mired in corruption scandals

7

LAND AND SEA ROUTES TO PANAMA

Panama has three land routes from **Costa Rica**: the main border crossing along the Interamericana is at Paso Canoas (see box, p.190), while a less-frequented border outpost is at Guabito, on the Caribbean coast (see box, p.143), which allows for access to the Bocas archipelago. There's a rarely used border post in the Chiriquí Highlands at Río Sereno (8am–5pm; reached by bus from Volcán).

Though you can take local transport and switch buses at the Paso Canoas border, the slightly costlier fares on international services from Panama City to San José (Costa Rica) run by Tica Bus (Ⓦ ticabus.com; US$12 one way) give you a better shot at an efficient and hassle-free passage (though border waits can be long). In addition to official documents, travellers at the border crossing will often be asked to show an onward or return ticket. If travelling on a one-way ticket, *migración* is likely to require advance purchase of your bus fare back to San José.

TO AND FROM COLOMBIA

Crossing by land to or from **Colombia** is both forbidden and dangerous. However, there is a new ferry service (see box, p.546) – for cars and foot passengers – between Cartagena, Colombia, and Colón, Panama. It is also possible to book passage on private yachts and passenger boats heading for Colombia, stopping in Guna Yala on the way (see box, p.550), or to fly to Puerto Obaldía, a town at the far eastern end of Guna Yala on the Caribbean coast, and make a short trip by speedboat to Capurganá, just over the border in Colombia (see box, p.562).

7

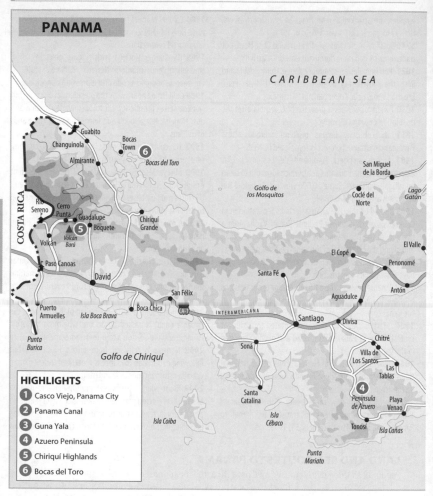

PANAMA

CARIBBEAN SEA

Guabito
Changuinola
Bocas Town ⑥
Almirante
Bocas del Toro
San Miguel de la Borda
Golfo de los Mosquitos
Coclé del Norte
Lago Gatún

COSTA RICA

Río Sereno
Cerro Punta
Guadalupe ⑤
Boquete
Volcán Barú
Volcán
Chiriquí Grande
El Copé
El Valle
Penonomé
Paso Canoas
Santa Fé
Antón
David
San Félix
Aguadulce
CA-1 *INTERAMERICANA*
Santiago
Divisa
Chitré
Puerto Armuelles
Isla Boca Brava
Boca Chica
Soná
Villa de Los Santos
Las Tablas
Punta Burica
Golfo de Chiriquí
Santa Catalina
Isla Coiba
Isla Cébaco
④ *Península de Azuero*
Playa Venao
Tonosí
Isla Cañas
Punta Mariato

HIGHLIGHTS

① Casco Viejo, Panama City
② Panama Canal
③ Guna Yala
④ Azuero Peninsula
⑤ Chiriquí Highlands
⑥ Bocas del Toro

and violent clashes with indigenous populations, as the cost of living soars.

2011 Noriega is extradited back to Panama to serve another twenty years for murder and money laundering.

2014 The canal's centenary celebrations are marred by strikes over the spiralling costs of the canal expansion project. Juan Carlos Varela is voted in as the new president.

ARRIVAL AND DEPARTURE

The vast majority of international **flights** arrive at **Tocumen International Airport (PTY)** in Panama City. Services arrive daily from the US (most are routed through Atlanta, Dallas/Fort Worth,

Houston or Miami) and other Central and South American cities; KLM and Iberia fly from Amsterdam and Madrid, respectively. Flights from San José, in neighbouring Costa Rica, often stop in David before continuing on to Panama City. The recently upgraded airport in David is expected to see direct international flights from and to the US at some point but in the meantime there are two daily direct flights a week by Copa to Tocumen, which connect with their other international flights.

You can cross into Panama by **land** from Costa Rica (see box, p.517), but due to

security concerns it's not possible to do so from Colombia. Instead, backpackers are increasingly booking passages by **boat** (see box, p.550).

VISAS

Travellers from Australia, Canada, Ireland, New Zealand, the UK or the US **do not require a visa** to enter Panama. Passports are generally stamped for three or six months and extensions cannot be granted unless applying for a different kind of visa, such as a residency permit.

GETTING AROUND

Although the canal corridor and the western Pacific region are covered by a comprehensive road network served by regular **public transport**, eastern Panama, Guna Yala and Bocas del Toro are each linked to the rest of the country by just a single road. Access to the islands of Bocas del Toro is by plane or boat, whereas you can reach Guna Yala by shared 4WD transport and boat or by plane. Boats also provide the main means of transport between the islands in both archipelagos, as well as along the rivers of the Darién region. Crossing the isthmus by train is also possible between Panama City and Colón.

BY BUS

Where there are roads, **buses** are the cheapest and most popular way to travel. Panama City is the hub of the network, with regular buses to Colón, Metetí in Darién, Almirante (for Bocas del Toro) and all the western cities and towns. Buses vary in comfort and size, from modern, a/c Pullmans to smaller "coaster" buses and old US school buses – Central America's ubiquitous "chicken buses" (see box, p.32). Smaller towns and villages in rural areas tend to be served by less frequent minibuses, pick-up trucks and flat-bed trucks known as **chivas** or *chivitas*, converted to carry passengers, while Colón and David are also served by express buses, which are more expensive, more comfortable and faster. ⓦthebusschedule.com/pa is a fairly reliable source to check **bus timetables**.

Most buses are owned either by individuals or private firms, and even when services are frequent, **schedules** are variable. Cities and larger towns have bus terminals; otherwise, buses leave from the main street or square. You can usually flag down through-buses from the roadside, though they may not stop if they are full or going a long way. In general, you can just turn up shortly before departure and you should be able to get a seat, though the express buses to and from David, buses from Bocas del Toro, and international buses to Costa Rica, are definitely worth **booking in advance**.

ADDRESSES IN PANAMA

Panama's towns are mainly laid out in a **grid pattern**. Calles run north–south, and avenidas east–west. Both calles and avenidas are generally numbered in order, calles north to south and avenidas west to east. In larger cities – Panama City and David in particular – roads, especially major thoroughfares, usually have two or more names. In smaller towns and villages exact **street numbers** or even names tend not to exist, so addresses are frequently given in terms of landmarks.

Fares, as elsewhere in Central America, are good value: bank on paying around US$2 per hour of travel, more for the more luxurious long-distance buses; the most you'll have to pay is US$27.80 for the overnight, ten-hour ride from Panama City to Almirante.

BY TAXI

In larger cities, like Panama City and David, **taxis** are plentiful and inexpensive. Most intra-city rides will cost US$2 (US$3–5 in the capital). There are many unlicensed cab drivers patrolling the streets who are willing to negotiate on prices, but who may engage in unscrupulous practices. Even licensed cab drivers won't hesitate to exploit an obviously unsavvy, lost or needy tourist. Specifically, be wary of price hikes on the Amador Causeway in Panama City.

BY CAR

Starting at around US$30–35 a day or US$200 a week, including taxes and insurance (almost double for 4WD), **car rental** is reasonably priced but not cheap. However, having your own vehicle is a good way of seeing parts of the country not well served by public transport, especially the canal corridor and the Azuero Peninsula. All of the main rental companies are based at Tocumen International Airport, and also in the city centre; some also have offices at Albrook airport and the airport in David; National Panamá (ⓦnationalpanama.com) is popular with locals as it offers some of the cheapest rentals in the country.

Driving in Panama is pretty straightforward, though even the paved roads in the canal corridor and the west can be badly maintained. The main roads on the Azuero Peninsula are in good condition, however, as is the road across the cordillera to Bocas del Toro, and the secondary roads to Cerro Punta, Santa Fé, Boquete and El Valle. **4WD** is rarely necessary except during the rainy season and in more remote rural areas. Police **checkpoints** appear throughout the country, mainly on provincial borders, and normally you are only required to slow down. If the police ask you to stop, in most cases they will just want to know your destination and see your licence and/or passport.

Hitching is possible, but carries all the obvious risks. Private cars are unlikely to stop for you on main roads, though in more remote areas, hitching is often the only motor transport available, and there is little distinction between private vehicles and public transport – drivers will pick you up, but you should expect to pay the same fares you would for the bus.

BY BOAT

Scheduled **ferries** run from Panama City to Isla Taboga and the Pearl Islands, as well as from Bocas del Toro to Almirante and Colón. Motorized **water-taxis** and **dugout canoes** are important means of transport in Bocas del Toro, Darién and Guna Yala. Where there isn't a scheduled water taxi, you'll either have to wait for somebody going your way, or hire a boat. Hiring a dugout canoe, though it can be expensive, also opens up possibilities for wilderness adventure – up jungle rivers to isolated villages or out to uninhabited islands.

BY PLANE

Cities and larger towns are served by regular **flights** with Air Panama (ⓦairpanama.com), the only domestic carrier, which flies to David, Bocas and parts of Darién, as well as to Guna Yala and to the Pearl Islands. With the exception of the more isolated areas, though, most destinations are so close to Panama City that it's scarcely worth flying, not least because it's very expensive (at the time of writing, high-season return flights between Panama City and Bocas were available from around US$205). Flights can theoretically be bought online but the website is temperamental; it's better, if you can, to try their office on Avenida Balboa.

BY BIKE

Cycling is a popular way to get around in western Panama, where roads are generally paved and traffic scarce (away from the Interamericana and other major routes), and towns usually have a shop offering parts and simple repairs. Other good roads

for cycling include all those on the Azuero Peninsula and the roads to Cerro Punta and El Valle, off the Interamericana.

BY TRAIN

The **Panama Canal Railway** (ⓦpanarail .com), which runs alongside the canal between Panama City and Colón, offers an excellent way of seeing the canal and the surrounding rainforest (see p.543).

ACCOMMODATION

Most areas in Panama offer a wide choice of places to stay. In general, the cheapest **hotel** rooms, normally a simple en-suite double (with one double bed – *cama matrimonial*) with cable TV and a/c costs US$30–40 a night, although **hostels** – most common in well-travelled spots like Bocas Town, Boquete, David and Panama City – will put you up for around US$12–15 per person. In **Panama City**, where many hotels target business travellers, prices tend to be slightly higher, while at the very low end of the market some hotels – euphemistically termed **drive-in motels** and auto-hotels – cater largely to Panamanian couples, with hourly rates. Locally referred to as a "Push", each unit is accessed by a push-button garage door to provide couples with privacy. These are often the least expensive lodgings, but not recommended for a solid night's sleep.

For popular hostels, particularly in the city, you will need to **book in advance**, especially during public holidays, fiestas, Carnaval and even right through the high season (Dec–April). During these times hotel prices can double, and many places are booked out months in advance. The ten percent **tourist tax** charged on hotel accommodation is not always included in the quoted price but has been factored into the prices that we have quoted throughout the chapter.

There are no official **campsites** in Panama, but you will find several hostels that allow you to pitch your tent from around US$6 per person, and you can camp in the national parks, though facilities will be limited. That said, camping is never really necessary – even in

7

the smallest villages there's almost always somewhere you can bed down for the night. If you do camp, either a **mosquito net** or mosquito coil (*mechita*) is essential in the lowlands. Almost all the national parks have ANAM (see box, p.525) **refugios** where you can spend the night for around US$15, though this fee is not always charged. These refuges are usually pretty basic, but they do have bunk beds, cooking facilities and running water.

FOOD AND DRINK

Street vendors are less common in Panama than elsewhere in Central America. The cheapest places to eat are the ubiquitous canteen-like **self-service restaurants** (sometimes called *cafeterías*), which serve a limited but filling range of Panamanian meals for around US$4–5; these usually open for breakfast and stay open late. Larger towns generally have several more upmarket **restaurants** with waiter service, where a main dish may cost upwards of US$7 (from US$10 in Panama City), as well as US-style fast-food places. There is often a seven percent **tax** to pay on meals; some also add on a ten percent service charge. These costs have been factored in when we have quoted prices throughout this chapter. Large **supermarkets** in the major cities offer a good range of cold and hot snacks to eat in or take out.

Known as **comida típica**, traditional Panamanian cooking is similar to what you find elsewhere in Central America. Rice and beans or lentils served with a little chicken, meat or fish form the mainstay, and *yuca* (cassava) and plantains are often served as sides. The national dish is **sancocho**, a chicken soup with *yuca*, plantains and other root vegetables flavoured with cilantro – similar to coriander though more pungent. **Seafood** is plentiful, excellent and generally cheap, particularly *corvina* (sea bass), *pargo rojo* (red snapper), lobster and prawns. Fresh tropical **fruit** is also abundant, but rarely on the menu at restaurants – you're better off buying it in local markets. Popular **snacks** include *carimañolas* or *enyucados* (fried balls of manioc dough filled with meat), *empanadas, tamales, patacones* (fried, mashed and refried plantains) and *hojaldres* (discs of deep-fried leavened bread). Toasted sandwiches called *emparedados* or *derretidos* are also very popular, appearing on most menus, from humble cafeterias to high-end cafés.

The diverse **cultural influences** that have passed through Panama have left their mark on its cuisine, especially in Panama City, where there are scores of international restaurants – Italian, Greek and Chinese being the most numerous. Almost every town has at least one Chinese restaurant, often the best option for **vegetarians**. Perhaps the strongest outside influence on Panamanian food, though, is the distinctive **Caribbean** culture of the West Indian populations of Panama City, Colón Province and Bocas del Toro. Speciality dishes involve seafood and rice cooked with lime juice, coconut milk and spices

DRINK

Coffee is excellent where grown locally (in the Chiriquí Highlands) and generally good throughout Panama, made espresso-style and served black or with milk as *café americano*. Iced water, served free in restaurants, along with tap water in all towns and cities except Bocas del Toro, Guna Yala, Darién and remote areas, is perfectly safe. **Chichas**, delicious blends of ice, water and tropical-fruit juices, are sometimes served in restaurants and by street vendors, and are not to be confused with *chicha fuerte,* a potent, fermented maize brew favoured by *campesinos* and indigenous populations, who prepare it for ceremonial occasions. **Batidos**, delicious when prepared with fresh fruit, are thick milkshakes. Also popular are **pipas**, sweet water from green coconuts served either ice-cold or freshly hacked from the palm tree. Fresh **fruit juices** are highly recommended, but it's best to make sure not too much sugar is added.

Beer is extremely popular in Panama. Locally brewed brands include Panamá, Atlas, Soberana and Balboa; imported beers such as Budweiser, Heineken and Guinness are available in Panama City and other major tourist centres. For a quicker buzz, many Panamanians turn to locally produced **rum** – Carta Vieja and Abuelo are the most common brands – though the national drink is Seco Herrerano (known as *seco*), an even more potent sugar-cane spirit established by the family of the current president. Imported whiskies and other spirits are widely available and you can get **wine** in most major towns.

CULTURE AND ETIQUETTE

Panama, like much of the rest of Latin America, is **socially conservative**, with a vast majority of the population reported to be Roman Catholic. Thanks to the country's history, more religions are present than in other parts of the region, but the combination of a largely Catholic cultural identity, marked economic stratification and other ingrained colonial legacies has produced a country and people who appreciate rules and accept established social castes. This is not to say, however, that Panamanian society is stagnant. The history of a US presence, widespread access to global media and entertainment, and relatively diverse demographics as well as recent economic expansion, have all contributed to making Panama a country familiar with change.

Macho attitudes, however, do prevail. For women travelling in Panama, unsolicited attention in the form of whistles and catcalls is almost inevitable, though easily ignored. Overall, the Caribbean and indigenous areas of Panama hold less macho and more relaxed attitudes, though revealing clothing is not tolerated (except on the beach). Though attitudes toward homosexuality are gradually softening – it was decriminalized in 2008 – by and large same-sex relationships are kept under wraps.

Tipping is only expected in more expensive places, where a tip is sometimes included in the final bill, or where service has been particularly good. It's not usual to **haggle** in shops, but prices are more negotiable in markets, especially if you're buying a lot, and you'll often need to bargain when organizing transport by boat or pick-up truck.

SPORTS AND OUTDOOR ACTIVITIES

European and Latin American **football** (soccer) leagues have a broad fan base and are closely followed in Panama, but **baseball** (*beisbol*) is the country's official national sport. There are twelve teams in the national league, and home teams are sacred to their impassioned fans, making the experience of attending a game lively and culturally rich (see ⓦfedebeis.com.pa). The season runs from January to April. Panama City's stadium, 8km northeast of the city centre – and named after Major League Baseball Hall-of-Fame player and Panamanian native Rod Carew – is never full, other than during the play-offs; tickets cost around US$5.

Hiking, rafting, surfing and diving are probably the most common and easily accessible of the outdoor activities. Boquete, in the Chiriquí Highlands, provides an ideal departure point for **hikes** up Volcán Barú (see p.582), Panama's highest point, as well as for **rafting** trips down ríos Chiriquí and Chiriquí Viejo (see p.579). Isla Coiba is a world-renowned **dive** site for experienced divers (see p.572), while Bocas del Toro also has a good reputation, with trips ranging from all-day snorkel tours to underwater exploration of shipwrecks and spectacular reef walls. Bocas can also have excellent **surf**, though it is seasonal and less consistent than on the Pacific coast, where Santa Catalina has the most popular break, and is considered world class. ⓦwannasurf.com lists the best breaks.

Panama is also one of the world's top destinations for **birdwatching;** areas in the former Canal Zone (see p.541) and the Chiriquí Highlands (see p.573), for example, are home to numerous colourful exotic species. It's well worth engaging the services of an expert on birding trips; local Spanish-speaking guides charge around US$40 per half-day, not including transport. You'll pay up to three times that for a bilingual naturalist guide, though the price will usually include use of a telescope and private transport.

COMMUNICATIONS

Other than in remote areas, Panama's **communications** network is good. **Letters** posted with the Correo Nacional (COTEL) cost US$0.45 (US$0.35 for postcards) to both the US and Europe, and should reach their destination within a couple of weeks. Even though **post offices** can be found in most small towns, it's best to post mail in Panama City.

Panama's privatized telephone company is owned by Cable & Wireless. **Local calls** are cheap, and there's a wide network of payphones that take phonecards sold in shops and street stalls; a *Telechip* card allows you to make both local and international calls. Local numbers should have seven digits; local mobile numbers have eight digits and begin with a "6" or a "5". Many internet cafés also provide international phone calls for around US$0.10 per minute to North America or Europe. You can make **international reverse charge calls** from payphones via the international operator (✆ 106).

Mobile phone coverage is growing, and even covers remote stretches of the Darién and Guna Yala, with the Más Móvil and Digicel networks having the best coverage outside of the capital. It's easy to buy a local SIM card in Panama City (around US$3) and replace the card in your own phone with it, although you may need a "hacker" to unlock your phone for use of the Panamanian networks.

You should be able to find an **internet** café almost anywhere you go; rates are normally US$1 per hour. Wi-fi is commonly available and free in hostels and most hotels, especially in Panama City.

CRIME AND SAFETY

Panama has something of an unjust reputation as a dangerous place to travel. Although **violent crime** does occasionally occur, it is usually in particular city areas, as in most countries, and Panama is far safer than most other countries in Central America. Nonetheless, you should take special care in **Colón** and some districts in **Panama City**, and more generally late at night in cities, or when carrying luggage; take a taxi. Outside these two cities, the

only other area where there is any particular danger is near the **Colombian border** in Darién and Guna Yala. This frontier has long been frequented by guerrillas, bandits and cocaine traffickers, and several travellers attempting to cross overland to Colombia have been kidnapped or killed – or have simply disappeared. It is possible to visit some areas of Darién safely, including parts of the national park, but always seek advice before travel (see p.553). Note, too, that some of the boats that ply the coast may be involved in smuggling.

If you become the victim of a crime, report it immediately to the local **police** station, particularly if you will later be making an insurance claim. In Panama City and Colón the **tourist police** (*policía de turismo*) are better prepared to deal with foreign travellers and more likely to speak some English – in Panama City they wear white armbands.

Although by law you are required to carry your **passport** at all times, you will rarely be asked to present it except when in transit; the tourist police recommend that when walking around the towns and cities it's better to carry a copy of your passport (including the page with the entry stamp).

HEALTH

Medical care in Panama is best sought in the two largest cities: Panama City and David. Panama City has a handful of top-notch **hospitals** with many US- and European-trained doctors and English-speaking staff (see p.539). As most doctors and hospitals expect payment up front, frequently in cash, check your health insurance plan or buy supplementary travel insurance before you leave home.

PANAMA ONLINE

ⓦ almanaqueazul.org A green portal (in Spanish), promoting ecological and sustainable tourism within Panama.

ⓦ anam.gob.pa Official ANAM website page (click on the icon for *Áreas Protegidas*) with links to info in Spanish on all the national parks and many of the other reserves.

ⓦ extremepanama.com A great portal, with links to independent tour operators, organized by region and activity.

ⓦ thevisitorpanama.com Website of *El Visitante/The Visitor*, a dual-language, weekly publication.

ⓦ visitpanama.com Panamanian Tourist Authority (ATP) site, with some information on attractions and links to hotels, airlines and tour agencies.

Pharmacies are numerous and often stay open late; in addition, 24hour supermarkets Rey, Romero and Super 99 usually have 24-hour pharmacies. Hospitals and occasionally health clinics have pharmacies on site, and many types of medicines are available over the counter, without a prescription.

INFORMATION AND MAPS

Good, impartial information about Panama is hard to come by once you're in the country. The biggest network of information is the **Panamanian Tourist Authority** (ⓦvisitpanamav2.com) or the **Autoridad de Turismo Panamá** (ATP; ⓦatp.gob.pa), which has its main office in Panama City and many provincial branches; their ATP offices offer flyers and pamphlets but the quality of information varies enormously and staff rarely speak English. *The Visitor/El Visitante* (ⓦthevisitorpanama.com), a free, weekly **tourist promotion magazine** in English and Spanish, is available online and at ATP offices and tourist venues throughout Panama, and lists attractions and upcoming events. Several **tour operators** based in Panama City (see box, p.535) can give you advice on the rest of the country, in the hope of selling you a tour.

Panama's **national parks** and other protected areas are administered by the National Environment Agency, **ANAM** (ⓦanam.gob.pa). Their regional offices are often very helpful – though again you'll need some Spanish – and are an essential stop before visiting areas where permission is needed, or if you want to spend the night in a *refugio* and/or hire a guide.

The best **maps** of Panama are the *International Travel Map of Panama* and the *National Geographic* one (both available online). The *Rutas de Aventura* series of maps (ⓦrutasdeaventura.com), covering most cities and tourist areas in Panama, are widely available in bookshops and souvenir stores throughout the country for around US$4.

MONEY AND BANKS

Panama adopted US dollars (referred to interchangeably as dólares or balboas) as its currency in 1904, and has not printed any paper currency since. The country does, however, mint its own coinage: 1, 5, 10, 25 and 50 **centavo** pieces plus a US$1 coin, which are used alongside US coins. Both US$100 and US$50 bills are often difficult to spend, so try to carry nothing larger than a US$20 bill. It is difficult to **change foreign currency** in Panama – change any cash into US dollars as soon as you can. Foreign banks will generally change their own currencies.

Travellers' cheques are impossible to change, so you're better off with a credit card, and a debit card for ATM withdrawals, though you are likely to be charged by your bank at home. The three major **banks** are Banco Nacional, Banco General and Banistmo. Almost all branches have **ATMs**, as do many large supermarkets. Major **credit cards** are accepted in most hotels and restaurants in Panama City and the larger provincial towns, though hardly anywhere in Bocas del Toro. Visa is the most widely accepted, followed by MasterCard. Some shops will charge an extra five percent if you pay by credit card.

7

OPENING HOURS AND PUBLIC HOLIDAYS

Opening hours vary, but generally government **offices** are open Monday to Friday from 8.30am to 3.30pm. **Post offices** are open Monday to Friday 8am to 5pm, and Saturday 8am to noon, while the major **banks** are generally open from 8am to 3pm Monday to Friday, and from 9am to noon on Saturday. **Shops** are usually open Monday to Saturday from 9am to 6pm, though large supermarkets are often open 24 hours.

Panama has several national **public holidays** (see box below), when most government offices, businesses and shops close. Panama City and Colón also each have their own public holiday, and there is one public holiday for government employees only. When the public holidays fall near a weekend, many Panamanians take a long weekend (known as a *puente*) and head to the beach or the countryside – it can be difficult to find hotel rooms during these times. Public holidays that fall midweek are sometimes moved to a Monday or Friday to avoid disrupting the working week. Several of these public holidays also coincide with **national fiestas** that continue for several days.

FESTIVALS

The following lists a few highlights on Panama's festivals calendar. There are even more festivals on the Azuero Peninsula (see box, p.566).

January Feria de las Flores y del Café in Boquete (date varies).

February Comarca de Guna Yala (Feb 25) celebrates the Guna Revolution of 1925, their independence day; Carnaval (Feb/March) is celebrated all over the country, but especially in Las Tablas and Panama City, with an aquatic version in Penonomé; Festival de los Diablos y Congos, biennially in Portobelo (2015, 2017; date varies).

March/April Semana Santa. Celebrated everywhere, but most colourfully in La Villa de Los Santos, Pesé and Guararé, on the Azuero Peninsula.

April Feria de las Orquideas in Boquete (date varies); Feria International del Azuero in La Villa de Los Santos (date varies).

June Corpus Christi (date varies) in La Villa de Los Santos.

July Nuestra Señora del Carmen (July 16) on Isla Taboga; Patronales de La Santa Librada and Festival de la Pollera in Las Tablas (July 20–22).

August Festival del Manito Ocueño (date varies) in Ocú.

October Festival of Nogagope (Oct 10–12) on Isla Tigre, Comarca de Guna Yala; Feria Guna (mid-Oct) on Isla Tigre; Festival de la Mejorana (five days mid-Oct) in Guararé; Fiesta de Cristo Negro (Oct 21) in Portobelo.

November 10 The "First Cry of Independence", Independence Day, celebrated as part of "El Mes de la Patria". Cities and towns across the nation put on parades featuring school drumming troupes and majorettes, which the whole population comes out to watch.

PUBLIC HOLIDAYS

Jan 1 New Year's Day
Jan 9 Martyrs' Day
Feb/March (date varies) Carnaval
March/April Good Friday
May 1 Labor Day
Aug 15 Foundation of Panama City (Panama City only)
Nov 2 All Souls' Day
Nov 3 Independence Day
Nov 4 Flag Day (government holiday only)
Nov 5 National Day (Colón only)
Nov 10 First Cry of Independence
Nov 28 Emancipation Day
Dec 8 Mother's Day
Dec 25 Christmas

Panama City

Few cities in Latin America can match the diversity and cosmopolitanism of **PANAMA CITY**: polyglot and postmodern before its time, its atmosphere is, surprisingly, more similar to the mighty trading cities of Asia than to anywhere else in the region. The city has always thrived on commerce; its unique position on the world's trade routes and the economic opportunity this presents has attracted immigrants and businesses from all over the globe. With nearly a third of the country's population living in the urbanized corridor between Panama City and Colón, the capital's metropolitan melting pot is a study in contrasts.

The city's layout, too, encompasses some startling incongruities. On a small peninsula at the southwest end of the Bay of Panama stands the old city centre

---

STREET NAMES IN PANAMA CITY

Getting around Panama City can be disconcerting, so it's often best to take a taxi to your accommodation. Confusingly, many streets have at least two names: Avenida Cuba, for instance, is also Avenida 2 Sur, and the road commonly known as Calle 50 is also Avenida 4 Sur or Avenida Nicanor de Obarrio. We have used the most common names throughout this account.

---

of **Casco Viejo**, a breezy jumble of ruins and restored colonial buildings. Around 4km to the northeast rise the shimmering skyscrapers of **El Cangrejo**, the modern banking and commercial district, which now extend down the coast as far as the eye can see, entrapping the ruins of **Panamá Viejo**, the first European city on the Pacific coast of the Americas, and its surrounding slum areas. West of the old centre, the former US Canal Zone town of **Balboa** retains a distinctly North American character. Isles of tranquillity far from the frenetic squalor of the city include **Isla Taboga**, the "Island of Flowers", some 20km off the coast; the islets of the Amador Causeway alongside the Pacific entrance to the canal; and the **Parque Nacional Metropolitano**, an island of tropical rainforest within the capital. Panama City is also a good base for day-trips to the canal and the Caribbean coast as far as Portobelo, as well as to Isla Contadora in the Pearl Islands (see box, p.541).

WHAT TO SEE AND DO

The old city centre of **Casco Viejo** (also known as Casco Antiguo or San Felipe) is the most picturesque and historically interesting part of Panama City and houses many of its most important buildings and several museums. Declared a UNESCO World Heritage Site in 1997, it is gradually being restored to its former glory after decades of neglect. For views of the modern city and ships waiting to cross the canal, head for the bougainvillea-shaded **Paseo Las Bóvedas**, running some 400m along the top of the old city's defensive wall between the Plaza de Francia and the corner of Calle 1 and Avenida A, although the recent extension of the Cinta Costera has somewhat obstructed the vista.

To the west, the **Amador Causeway** (Calzada de Amador) marks the entrance to the canal and the former Canal Zone, comprised of the causeway and the town of Balboa. Halfway down the causeway is the unmistakeable rainbow-coloured rooftop of the impressive Frank Gehry-designed **biodiversity museum**. East along the bay from the old city centre, the pulsing and chaotic commercial heart of the capital lies in the neighbouring districts of **Bella Vista**, **El Cangrejo** and **Punta Paitilla**, where the majority of hotels, restaurants and tourist shops can be found.

Casco Viejo and El Cangrejo are joined by **Avenida Central**, the city's main thoroughfare. Running north of the old centre, its name changes to **Vía España** as it continues through the downtown districts of Calidonia and La Exposición and the residential neighbourhood of Bella Vista. Several other main avenues run parallel to Avenida Central: Avenida Perú, Avenida Cuba, Avenida Justo Arosemena and, along the seafront, **Avenida Balboa**, which has now been subsumed into the six-lane **Cinta Costera**.

Plaza Catedral

Elderly men chat amiably among the shaded benches and gazebos of cobblestoned **Plaza Catedral**, which sits at the heart of Casco Viejo and the old city. It's also known as Plaza de la Independencia, in honour of the proclamations of independence from both Spain and Colombia that were issued here. The western side of the plaza is dominated by the classical facade of the **cathedral** (closed for restoration). Built between 1688 and 1796, it was constructed using stones and three of the bells from the ruined cathedral of Panamá Viejo (see p.540).

Across the square from the cathedral towers the half-restored facade of the **Hotel Central**, built to replace the Grand Hotel, which was, in its time, the

7

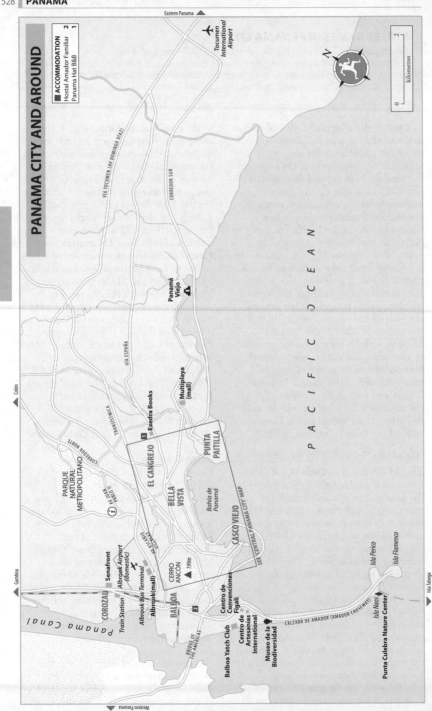

PANAMA CITY AND AROUND

ACCOMMODATION
Hostal Amador Familiar   **2**
Panamá Hat B&B   **1**

Eastern Panama ▲

Tocumen International Airport

VÍA TOCUMEN (AV DOMINGO DÍAZ)

CORREDOR SUR

Panamá Viejo

N

0   kilometres   2

P A C I F I C   O C E A N

VÍA ESPAÑA

Multiplaza (mall)

Colón ▲

TRANSÍSTMICA

Exedra Books

CORREDOR NORTE

EL CANGREJO

1

PUNTA PAITILLA

PARQUE NATURAL METROPOLITANO

AV DE LOS MÁRTIRES

BELLA VISTA

Bahía de Panamá

CASCO VIEJO

SEE 'CENTRAL PANAMA CITY MAP'

CERRO ANCON
▲ 199m

Gamboa ▲

AV DE LOS MÁRTIRES

Senafront
Albrook Airport (domestic)

Albrook Bus Terminal

Albrook (mall)

BALBOA

2

Centro de Convenciones Figali

Centro de Artesanías International

CALZADA DE AMADOR (AMADOR CAUSEWAY)

Balboa Yacht Club

Museo de la Biodiversidad

BRIDGE OF THE AMERICAS

Panama Canal

COROZAL

Train Station

Western Panama ▲

Isla Naos

Isla Perico

Isla Culebra Nature Center

Isla Flamenco

Isla Taboga ▲

plushest hotel in Central America. Southeast of the cathedral is the Neoclassical Palacio Municipal, whose small **Museo de Historia Panameña** (Mon–Fri 9.30am–3.30pm; US$2) offers a cursory introduction to Panamanian history.

Museo del Canal Interoceánico

The excellent **Museo del Canal Interoceánico** (Tues–Sun 9am–5pm; US$2; ☎211 1649, ⓦmuseodelcanal .com), on the south side of the Plaza Catedral, explains in great detail the history of the country's transisthmian waterway. Photographs, video footage and historic exhibits – including the original canal treaties – document everything from the first Spanish attempt to find a passage to Asia to the contemporary management of the canal. All displays are in Spanish, but there are audio guides in English (US$5, including entry), or you can hire an English-speaking guide (US$5/person for 3–10 people); book **tours** in advance.

Palacio Presidencial

On the seafront two blocks north of the Plaza Catedral along Calle 6, the **Palacio Presidencial**, built in 1673, was home to several successive colonial and Colombian governors. In 1922 it was rebuilt in grandiose neo-Moorish style under the orders of President Belisario Porras, who also introduced white Darién herons to the grounds, giving the palace the nickname of "Palacio de las Garzas". The birds and their descendants have lived freely around the patio fountain ever since and have now been joined by a couple of cranes, donated by the South African government. The streets around the palace are closed to traffic and pedestrians, but the presidential guards allow visitors to view the exterior of the palace between 8am and 5pm daily via a checkpoint on Calle 4.

Plaza Bolívar

Two blocks east of the Palacio Presidencial is **Plaza Bolívar**, an elegant square dedicated in 1883 to Simón Bolívar, whose statue, crowned by a condor, stands in its centre.

Bolívar came here in 1826 for the first Panamerican Congress, held in the chapter-room of the old **monastery** on the northeast corner of the square, now the **Salón Bolívar**, a small museum whose centrepiece is a replica of the Liberator's bejewelled ceremonial sword. The whole building has been beautifully restored and currently houses government offices, but you can visit for free (Mon–Fri 9am–4pm); go through the door marked "Ministerio de Relaciones Exteriores", to the right of the building's main courtyard entrance.

Next door stands the church and monastery of **San Francisco de Asís**, with its distinctive bell tower. Built in the seventeenth century, it was extensively modified subsequently and is currently closed for renovation.

Teatro Nacional

Just south of Plaza Bolívar on Avenida B is the **Teatro Nacional** (Mon–Fri 9.30am–5pm; US$1), designed by Genaro Ruggieri, the Italian architect responsible for La Scala in Milan. Extensively restored in the early 1970s, the splendid Neoclassical interior is richly furnished and decorated in red and gold, with French crystal chandeliers, busts of famous dramatists and a vaulted ceiling painted with scenes depicting the birth of the nation by Panamanian artist Roberto Lewis. Official opening hours are rarely adhered to, but if the door is unlocked – it's rarely actually open – you can usually take a look around (US$1); alternatively, try to catch a performance here (see p.539).

Plaza de Francia

The **Plaza de Francia** lies at the southeastern tip of the peninsula. Enclosed on three sides by seaward defensive walls, it's the site of a **monument** dedicated to the thousands of workers who died during the disastrous French attempt to build the canal (see p.541). The Neoclassical **French Embassy** building, fronted by a statue of former president Pablo Arosemena, stands on the north side of the square. During the colonial period the square was a military centre, with the now restored vaults

7

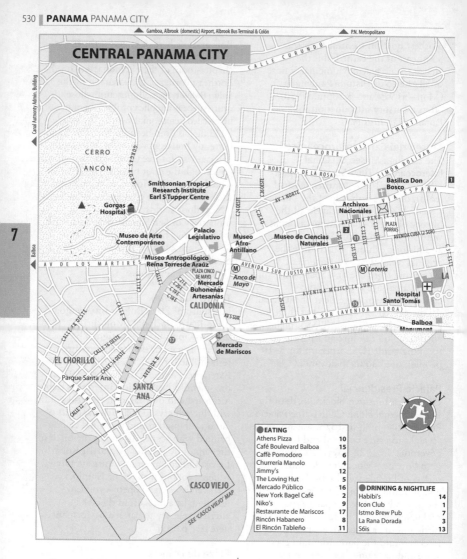

CENTRAL PANAMA CITY

CALLE CURUNDU

Canal Authority Admin. Building

◄ Balboa

CERRO ANCÓN

AV 3 NORTE LUIS F. CLEMENT

AV 2 NORTE (J.F. DE LA ROSA)

Basilica Don Bosco

Smithsonian Tropical Research Institute Earl S Tupper Centre

AV 1 NORTE

VIA SIMÓN BOLIVAR

VIA ESPAÑA

Gorgas Hospital

Archivos Nacionales

PLAZA PORRAS

AVENIDA PERÚ (1 SUR)

Palacio Legislativo

Museo de Arte Contemporáneo

Museo Afro-Antillano

Museo de Ciencias Naturales

AVENIDA CUBA (2 SUR)

Museo Antropológico Reina Torres de Araúz

AVENIDA 3 SUR (JUSTO AROSEMENA)

Lotería

LA

PLAZA CINCO DE MAYO

AV DE LOS MÁRTIRES

Mercado Buhoneras Artesanías

Anco de Mayo

AVENIDA MÉJICO (4 SUR)

Hospital Santo Tomás

CALIDONIA

AV S SUR

AVENIDA 6 SUR (AVENIDA BALBOA)

Balboa Monument

EL CHORILLO

Parque Santa Ana

CALLE 16 OESTE
CALLE 14 OESTE

AVENIDA CENTRAL

AVENIDA B

Mercado de Mariscos

SANTA ANA

CALLE 12

N

CASCO VIEJO

SEE 'CASCO VIEJO' MAP

● EATING	
Athens Pizza	10
Café Boulevard Balboa	15
Caffè Pomodoro	6
Churrería Manolo	4
Jimmy's	12
The Loving Hut	5
Mercado Público	16
New York Bagel Café	2
Niko's	9
Restaurante de Mariscos	17
Rincón Habanero	8
El Rincón Tableño	11

● DRINKING & NIGHTLIFE	
Habibi's	14
Icon Club	1
Istmo Brew Pub	7
La Rana Dorada	3
S6is	13

under the seaward walls – known as **Las Bóvedas** – serving as the city's jail; built below sea level, it is claimed that they would sometimes flood at high tide, drowning the unfortunate prisoners within.

Iglesia y Convento de Santo Domingo
Two blocks west along Avenida A from the corner with Calle 1 stands the ruined **Iglesia y Convento de Santo Domingo** (irregular opening hours), completed in 1678 and famous for the **Arco Chato**

(flat arch). Just 10.6m high but spanning some 15m with no external support, the Arco Chato (open irregular hours) was reputedly cited as evidence of Panama's seismic stability when the US Senate was choosing whether to build an interoceanic canal through Nicaragua or Panama.

Iglesia de San José and Plaza Herrera
On Avenida A at the corner with Calle 8 is the **Iglesia de San José**. Built in 1673 and since remodelled, the church is exceptional only as the home of the

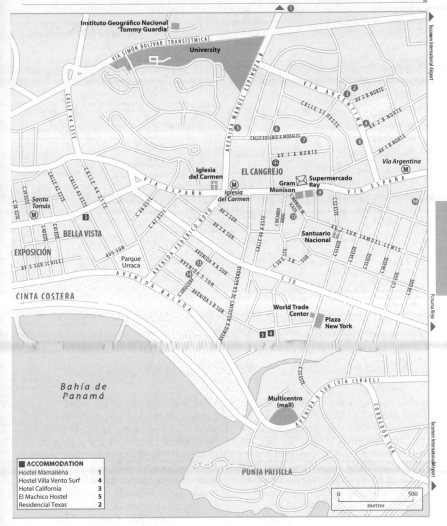

ACCOMMODATION

Hostel Mamallena	1
Hostel Villa Vento Surf	4
Hotel California	3
El Machico Hostel	5
Residencial Texas	2

legendary Baroque Golden Altar, one of the few treasures to survive Henry Morgan's ransacking of Panamá Viejo in 1671 – it was apparently painted or covered in mud to disguise its real value.

One block west of San José, Avenida A emerges onto **Plaza Herrera**, a pleasant square lined with nineteenth-century houses. This was originally the Plaza de Triunfo, where bullfights were held, but was renamed in 1922 in honour of General Tomás Herrera, whose equestrian monument is at its centre. Herrera was the military leader of the short-lived independence attempt in 1840; he went on to be elected president of Colombia, but was assassinated in 1854. Note that beyond the plaza lies the no-go slum area of **El Chorrillo**, which was devastated during the US invasion of Panama, leaving hundreds dead and thousands homeless.

Avenida Central

Avenida Central runs north all the way from the waterfront in the old city centre,

CASCO VIEJO

through the scary, off-limits *barrios* of Santa Ana and El Chorillo – so don't venture down the side streets – towards the more modern portion of the city. The pedestrianized, ten-block stretch between **Parque Santa Ana**, a small park, and Plaza Cinco de Mayo is the liveliest and most popular **shopping** district for the city's less wealthy residents. Blasts of air conditioning and loud music pour from the huge superstores that line the avenue, while hawkers with megaphones attempt to entice shoppers inside with deals on clothing, electronics and household goods. Nowhere is the diversity and vitality of the city more evident.

Plaza Cinco de Mayo

As Avenida Central emerges onto **Plaza Cinco de Mayo**, the pedestrianized section ends and the maelstrom of traffic takes over again. The plaza is actually two squares rolled into one. The first has a small monument to the volunteer firemen killed while fighting an exploded gunpowder magazine in 1914. To the south of the plaza stands a forlorn Neoclassical building that was once the Panama Railroad Pacific terminal, and is about to house (for the second time) the **Museo Antropológico Reina Torres de Araúz**, which will only reopen once funding has been made available. The second square, Plaza Cinco de Mayo proper, borders the legislative palace compound, identifiable by a black, monolithic monument. Heading north from here, under the flyover, Avenida Central splits, with the north fork called Avenida Central and the south called Avenida Justo Arosemena (Av 3 Sur).

Museo Afro-Antillano

At the corner of Avenida Justo Arosemena and Calle 24 is a wooden former church, now the **Museo Afro-Antillano** (Tues–Sun 9am–4pm; US$1; ☎262 5348), dedicated to preserving the history and culture of

Panama's large West Indian population. It's very small, but the exhibits – photographs, tools and furniture – give a good idea of the working and living conditions of black canal-workers.

Mercado de Mariscos

Even if you don't smell the **fish market** from a distance, the vultures circling outside are a sure indication that you've reached the city's seafood hub, on Avenida Balboa close to the entrance to Casco Viejo. Inside you'll find a fantastic selection of Panama's marine life on ice, with lime, and ready to consume. The market is open daily (6am–5pm) but usually closed for fumigation on the first Monday of the month.

Balboa

To the southwest of Calidonia and El Chorillo, Panama City encompasses the former Canal Zone town of **Balboa**, administered by the US as de facto sovereign territory from 1903 to 1979. Balboa retains many of the characteristics of a US provincial town: clean and well ordered, it stands in stark contrast to the chaotic vitality of the rest of the city, though it conceals a troubled past.

Along the border of the former Canal Zone runs **Avenida de Los Mártires**, named in honour of the young Panamanians, mostly students, killed by the US military during the flag riots of 1964. A sculpture by González Palomino, depicting three people climbing a flagpole, was erected here in 2004 as a tribute to the fallen; above it rises **Cerro Ancón**, crowned by a huge Panamanian flag that is visible throughout the city. An early morning or late afternoon walk to the top (30min from the gate; US$6 taxi ride) will reward you with great **views** of both the canal and the city and likely sightings of **toucans** in the treetops.

Museo de Arte Contemporáneo

On the west side of Avenida de Los Mártires, close to the legislative palace, the **Museo de Arte Contemporáneo** (Tues–Sat 10am–5pm, Sun 10am–4pm; US$5; ☏262 2012, ⊛macpanama.org), housed in a former Masonic temple, has a small collection of modern paintings and engravings by Panamanian and Latin American artists, as well as temporary international exhibitions.

Canal Authority Administration Building

On Gorgas Road in Balboa Heights, the **Panama Canal Authority Administration Building** (daily 8am–11pm; free) was built during canal construction and is still home to the principal administration offices. Inside, four dramatic murals by US artist William Van Ingen depict the story of the canal's construction under a domed ceiling supported by marble pillars.

7

THE AFRO-ANTILLANOS

Some five percent of Panama's population are **Afro-Antillanos** – descendants of the black workers from the English- and French-speaking West Indies who began migrating to Panama in the mid-nineteenth century to help build the railroad and canal. Widely considered second-class citizens or undesirable aliens, Afro-Antillanos worked and lived in appalling conditions under French and American control. Most of the twenty thousand workers who died during the French canal attempt were West Indians, and the mortality rate was four times higher among black workers than white during US construction.

Throughout the twentieth and into the twenty-first century, successive Panamanian governments have ignored the needs of Afro-Antillanos, and they remain among the most marginalized segments of the population. In spite of this, they maintain a vibrant and distinct **culture** whose influence is widely felt in contemporary Panamanian society. Many second- and third-generation Afro-Antillanos still speak the melodic patois of the West Indies, and the street Spanish of Panama City and Colón is peppered with Jamaican slang. Unique Protestant beliefs imported from the West Indies continue to thrive, heavily spiced Caribbean dishes permeate Panamanian cuisine, and the music, from jazz in the 1950s to "reggaespañol" in the 1990s, has made an indelible mark on the region.

7

At the rear of the building, where a Panamanian flag now flutters, a broad stairway runs down to the **Goethals monument**, a white megalith with stepped fountains that represent the canal's different locks, erected in honour of George Goethals, chief engineer from 1907 to 1914 and first governor of the Canal Zone. Beside the monument is **Balboa High School**, whose ordinary appearance belies the dramatic events it has witnessed. It was here in 1964 that Zonians attacked students attempting to raise the Panamanian flag, triggering the **flag riots** that left a group of young Panamanians dead. During the 1989 invasion, the school was used as a detention camp for Panamanian prisoners, some of whom were allegedly executed by US soldiers.

Calzada de Amador (Amador Causeway)

West of Balboa, the **Calzada de Amador**, originally designed as the canal's Pacific breakwater, runs 6km out into the bay, linking the mainland with the tiny islands of **Naos**, **Perico** and **Flamenco**. It's a popular weekend escape for the city's wealthier residents, who come here to jog, swim, stroll, rollerblade or cycle – you can rent bikes (see p.536) – and to enjoy the sea air and views of the city and the canal. It is here that the much vaunted **Museo de la Biodiversidad** (Mon & Wed–Fri 10am–4pm, Sat & Sun 10am–5pm; US$22; ☎830 6700, ⓦbiomuseopanama.com), a "biodiversity exhibition centre" designed by architect Frank Gehry, has finally opened after almost twenty years of construction. Visually stunning, with state-of-the-art interactive screens and large-scale audiovisual presentations, the museum also incorporates aspects of the history of Panama. It is by far the city's best museum but has a hefty price tag to match the hype. The northern sector of the causeway is currently an unpleasant construction site, being redeveloped into a complex that will comprise luxury bars, restaurants and hotels, and a marina.

At the southern side of Punta Culebra, a small promontory at the end of Naos,

4km along the Causeway, and next to the unexciting **Punta Culebra Nature Center** (Tues–Thurs & Sun 10am–6pm, Fri & Sat 10am–8pm; US$5; ⓦstri.org), is the departure point for passenger ferries to Isla Taboga (see p.541) and for some of the canal transit tours (see p.543). Beyond, Perico and Flamenco are home to more shops, bars, restaurants and a marina.

Parque Natural Metropolitano

A couple of kilometres north of central Panama City, the 2.65-square-kilometre **Parque Natural Metropolitano** (daily 7am–4pm; ☎232 5552, ⓦparque metropolitano.org; US$4) is an unspoilt tract of tropical rainforest that is home to more than two hundred species of bird and mammal, including Geoffroy's tamarin monkeys, white-tailed deer, sloths and agoutis. It's possible to complete the four main **trails** in just a few hours; the best of these is the combined La Cienaguita and Mono Titi trail (3km), which leads to a *mirador* with views across the forest to the city. As elsewhere, the best time to see wildlife, particularly birds, is early in the morning – there's nothing to stop you from coming in earlier than the official opening time. The **park office** and main entrance are on Avenida Juan Pablo II; no buses pass the entrance, though buses from Albrook bound for Corundú can drop you nearby, and a taxi from El Cangrejo should cost about US$4.

ARRIVAL AND DEPARTURE

BY PLANE

International flights Tomucen International Airport (☎238 4322) lies about 24km northeast of Panama City. Taxis to the city centre cost US$30 for one or two people, or US$15/person with three or more people sharing. When leaving Panama, save the taxi fare to Tomucen by taking the Metrobus labelled "Tomucen vía Corredor Sur" from inside the Albrook bus terminal (5.20am–10pm; every 20min; hourly between 10am and 5.20pm; 30–40min; US$1.25), picking up passengers at a stop just opposite the artisans' market off Plaza Cinco de Mayo, and dropping them off just outside the international airport. Some hostels participate in Hostel Ride (ⓦhostelride.com), a shared hostel shuttle service that runs three times a day (US$9).

Domestic flights Almost all domestic flights (Air Panama; ☎316 9000, ⓦairpanama.com) leave from Albrook airport (☎315 0241), whose official name,

Marcos A. Gelabert Airport, is rarely used. It lies roughly 3km, or a 15min taxi ride, northwest of the centre. Taxis from Albrook to the city should cost around US$6 from just outside the terminal building, but are much cheaper if flagged down on the road across from the terminal.

Destinations Bocas del Toro (3 daily; 1hr); Contadora, Pearl Islands (1 daily; 20min); David (5 daily, and 2 with Copa Airlines from Tocumen; 1hr); Guna Yala (daily flights to Achutupo, Corazón de Jesús, El Porvenir, Mulatupo, Playón Chico; 30min–1hr 15min); Jaqué (Mon & Fri; 1hr 15min); also to Puerto Obaldía (6 days a week; 1hr); Sambú via Garachiné (Wed & Sat; 1hr).

BY BUS

International buses International services from Costa Rica, with Ticabus (☎ 314 6385, ⓦ ticabus.com), arrive at and depart from the Albrook bus terminal (simply referred to as "*el terminal*"), 3km northwest of the city centre and very near the domestic airport. Taxis, which can take you into town from around US$4–5, and local city-bound buses (US$0.30) leave from the ground floor, in front of the terminal. Ticket offices for onward domestic travel (you can buy a ticket, in person, in advance of travel, on long-distance buses) are inside the building, along with toilets, ATMs and a 24hr cafeteria. Buses depart from the back of the terminal; for the turnstiles, you'll need a 3-in-1 card (*tarjeta; see below*).

Destinations Paso Canoas, on the border (Panachif: 10 daily 7.30am–10.30pm; 9hr): San José (Ticabus: 2 daily; 11am [executive class]: 16hr; 11pm [economy class]: 18hr).

Domestic buses The Albrook bus terminal (see above) is also the transport hub for all domestic buses.

Destinations Almirante and Changuinola, for Bocas (2 daily, 8pm & 8.30pm; 10/11hr); Chitré (hourly; 4hr); Colón

(local departures every 20min; 2hr; express departures every 30min; 1hr 30min); David (hourly; 7hr, plus 2 express departures daily; 5hr 30min); El Valle (every 30min; 2hr 30min); Gamboa (8 daily; 45min); Las Tablas (every 2hr; 4hr 30min); Metetí (every 40min until 4.15pm; 5–6hr); Miraflores Locks (take Miraflores, Paraíso or Gamboa bus; 20min); Paraíso (every 30–45min; 20min); Paso Canoas (10 daily; 9hr, plus 2 express departures daily; 7hr); Penonomé (every 15min; 2hr 15min); Santiago (every 30min; 3hr 30min); Soná, for Santa Catalina (8 daily; 5hr); Yaviza (2 direct, otherwise change in Metetí; 6–7hr).

GETTING AROUND

By bus Buses head almost everywhere in the city from Albrook bus terminal, many passing through Plaza Cinco de Mayo, the nearest point to Casco Viejo, before heading towards El Cangrejo and Bella Vista. There are two types of public buses. Best known, but being phased out, are the chicken buses (see p.31) – known in Panama as *diablos rojos*, or red devils, because of the devil-may-care attitude of many of the drivers. These cost just US$0.30/ride, payable on exit, and operate from 6am to midnight. Though they operate fixed routes, there are no fixed timetables; destinations are painted on the windscreen. Newer, a/c metrobuses (ⓦ mibus.com.pa) operate the same hours and also cost US$0.30 – except for the airport bus, which costs US$1.25. You need a pre-paid 3-in-1 card (US$2) for which you buy credit, which can be used to pay for access through the turnstiles to the buses at the terminal, and for rides on the metrobus or the new metro (see p.536). Cards are available at supermarkets (such as El Rey on Vía España and El Machetazo on Av Central) as well as at the Albrook bus terminal and the new metro stations.

TOUR OPERATORS IN PANAMA CITY

Panama City boasts a number of decent tour operators, though many are only really worth considering for excursions in the former Canal Zone, along the central Caribbean Coast and to Darién, and few are budget. For trips west, it's often more convenient, and cheaper, to engage a local operator in the nearest tourist centre – highlighted in the relevant sections of this chapter. Several hostels also organize inexpensive tours.

Ecocircuitos Albrook Plaza, 2nd Floor, No 31, Ancón ☎ 315 1305, ⓦ ecocircuitos.com. Actively promotes sustainable tourism and offers a range of day- and multiday tours with multilingual, naturalist guides, including trekking across the isthmus, kayaking and birdwatching.

Embera Tours ☎ 250 1165 or ☎ 6519 7121, ⓦ embera tourspanama.com. Run by Garceth Cunampio, an English-speaking Embera guide who organizes excursions to villages up the Chagres (from US$110 for a day-excursion, up to 6 people; US$200 for an overnight trip).

Panamá Orgánica ☎ 6079 6825 or ☎ 6725 0799,

ⓔ panamaorganica@gmail.com. Small outfit offering customized budget tours to hard-to-access areas such as Darién and Guna Yala, working with local communities and independent operators. Can also help arrange transport to Colombia and day-trips from Panama City. At least one week's notice needed.

Scuba Panamá Av 6 Norte at C 62A ☎ 261 3841, ⓦ scubapanama.com. The country's oldest dive outfit offers countrywide diving excursions – including the popular and gimmicky two oceans in one day (US$200) – equipment sale and rental, and diving instruction. They also have accommodation in Portobelo (see p.549).

By metro Panama City has one new metro line – the first in Central America – which leaves from Albrook bus terminal (follow the escalator up from the main entrance hall) and heads northeast towards Los Andes. For tourists, the most useful stops are likely to be at Plaza Cinco de Mayo, Iglesia del Carmen (on Vía España at the junction with Federico Boyd) and Vía Argentina, at the junction with Vía España. Journeys are currently US$0.35 (though set to increase soon), payable via the 3-in-1 card (see above).

By taxi Taxis are plentiful and cheap, if prone to hiking prices for tourists and in rush hour. Fares are theoretically based on a zone system, though few taxi drivers adhere to it. Most city rides will cost about US$4–5 for one or two people, maybe closer to US$5–6 to the bus terminal. Taxis from Albrook bus terminal into town tend to be pricier, especially at night. No trip should cost more than US$6, except to the Amador Causeway (often around US$10), where drivers do not expect to get a client for the return journey, and to Tocumen International Airport (US$30).

By bike The safest places to ride a bicycle in Panama City are on the Amador Causeway or along the Cinta Costera. For rentals head to *Las Pencas* restaurant, close to the Museo de la Biodiversidad (see p.534), where *Bicicletas Moses* (daily noon–6pm in high season; otherwise weekends only) will kit you out for US$3–4/hr. Rali-Carretero, Vía España at Av Argentina (☎263 4136) and on Av Balboa (☎263 4136), has spare parts and a maintenance centre.

INFORMATION

Tourist information For simple queries, ask at the international or domestic airport booths. The central tourist office, Av Samuel Lewis & Ortega, Edif. Central, 2nd Floor (☎526 7000, ⓦatp.gob.pa), is not geared up to actually dealing with tourists; you'll get more information from the city's hostels, where you'll also be able to book travel and accommodation for trips including to Guna Yala, the canal and beyond, and boat trips to Colombia.

ACCOMMODATION

A growing number of budget travellers bed down in Casco Viejo. The restoration of many of the area's colonial buildings makes it a pleasant retreat from the congestion and the pollution of the rest of the city – though there's constantly some construction noise to contend with – and the nightlife is pretty good. The Calidonia/La Exposición area offers unexceptional but affordable modern hotels and *residenciales*, while further northeast along Vía España, the districts of Bella Vista, Marbella and El Cangrejo, the other hub of the city's nightlife and commercial activity, have a couple of hostels, some mid-range options and the expensive chain hotels. In high season (Dec–April) it's highly advisable to book in advance no matter where you're staying; hostels, in particular, are almost always booked up. It's also best to exercise caution in all neighbourhoods after dark.

CASCO VIEJO

Hospedaje Casco Viejo C 8A 8–31 by Iglesia San José ☎211 2127, ⓦhospedajecascoviejo.com; map p.532. Currently being renovated, this well-kept and surprisingly spacious *hospedaje* may be lacking in colonial charm and the staff often speak only limited English, but its rates are rock bottom. There's a small, shared kitchen, free basic breakfast (toast and coffee) and wi-fi, though the place suffers from periodic water problems. Dorms <u>US$13</u>, doubles <u>US$30</u>

Luna's Castle C 9A Este between Avs B & Alfaro ☎262 1540, ⓦlunascastlehostel.com; map p.532. Perfect for partying 'packers, but not the best option for a weary traveller in need of sleep, this colonial maze of high-ceilinged rooms has a busy kitchen, loads of chill-out spaces with wi-fi, and a cinema, framed by a kaleidoscope of vibrant artwork. Experienced gringo owners and friendly young staff will arrange your onward travel (including boats to Colombia). The *Relic* bar is downstairs (see p.538). Pancake breakfast included. Dorms <u>US$15</u>, doubles <u>US$32</u>

Magnolia Inn C 8 & Boquete, behind the cathedral ☎202 0872, ⓦmagnoliapanama.com; map p.532. Lovingly restored, two floors of this colonial mansion are part hotel, part luxury hostel. The deluxe four- and six-bed dorms offer excellent value, boasting a/c, fans, excellent mattresses and reading lights, plus a beautifully furnished dining and lounge area to relax in. Dorms <u>US$15</u>, doubles <u>US$80</u>

Panamericana Hostel ☎202 0851, ⓦpanamericana hostel.com. Moving to a new location in Casco Viejo and due to reopen in late 2015, it promises to feature the same artistic flourishes as its previous incarnation.

CALIDONIA AND LA EXPOSICIÓN

Residencial Texas C 31 between avs Perú & Cuba beside the national lottery ☎225 1467, ⓔhoteltexas@mixmail.com; map pp.530–531. Friendly, secure place offering good-value rooms with spotless tiled bathrooms, decent hot showers and good mattresses, though the furniture is tired. <u>US$38</u>

BELLA VISTA, EL CANGREJO & MARBELLA

Hostel Mamallena C Primera, Casa de la Junta Comunal por el Colegio Javier, Perejil ☎6676 6163, ⓦmamallena.com; map pp.530–531. Popular, well-run hostel with clean dorms and small private rooms (all with a/c), as well as a communal kitchen – where you can make your free breakfast pancakes all day! – and a funky courtyard garden with hammocks. Good info and travel assistance. Dorms <u>US$13</u>, doubles <u>US$33</u>

Hostel Villa Vento Surf Av 5 B Sur ☎397 6001, ⓦhostelvillaventosurf.com; map pp.530–531. Modern hostel in the heart of the banking district, but within reach of restaurants and nightlife. There are six basic fan-ventilated en-suite private rooms, and four rather small dorms (with fan; a/c costs an extra US$5) with comfortable bunks. The pool and BBQ patio area are the big draws and the place has a kitchen, lockers and wi-fi. Dorms US$15, doubles US$45

Hotel California Vía España, at C 43 Este ☎ 263 7736, ⓦ hotelcaliforniapanama.net; map pp.530–531. Not the most convenient location but this is a very popular hotel, offering excellent-value rooms (single, double and triple), free wi-fi and a rooftop jacuzzi. US$44

El Machico Hostel C 47 Este, Casa 2 ☎ 203 9430, ⓦ elmachicohostel.com; map pp.530–531. New, vibey hostel in the heart of the banking sector, with plenty of places to lounge around inside, or outside by the pool and terrace area – the star features. Dorms have a/c, and are enlivened by brightly coloured sheets and modern artwork. Dorms US$17

ELSEWHERE IN THE CITY

★**Hostal Amador Familiar** C Akee, off Av Amador, behind *Tamburelli's*, Balboa ☎ 314 1251, ⓦ hostalamadorfamiliar.com; map p.528. Converted three-storey Canal Zone building attracting foreign and Panamanian visitors. Simple, compact dorms (with a/c) and en-suite rooms (with fan or a/c) with hot showers, plus a back patio kitchen area for the DIY breakfast (included in the price). Special airport transfer rates and wi-fi. Dorms US$17, doubles US$33

Panama Hat B&B (formerly Casa del Carmen) C Primera El Carmen 32 ☎ 263 4366, ⓦ lacasadecarmen.net; map p.528. Attracts a wide age range with their restful patio and garden, and free services including breakfast, internet, shared kitchen, laundry, hot water and barbecue area. Strongly recommended, with rooms for one to five people. Dorms US$17, doubles US$55

EATING

Panama City's cosmopolitan nature is reflected in its restaurants: anything from US fast food to Greek, Italian, Chinese, Japanese and French can easily be found, and excellent seafood is widely available. Cheap takeaway meals are also available from the Rey supermarket (open 24hr) on Vía España – get a whole roast chicken for US$7.

CASCO VIEJO AND SANTA ANA

Café Coca-Cola Plaza Santa Ana, C 12 at Av Central; map p.532. The self-proclaimed "oldest restaurant in Panama" and something of an institution among the city's older residents, who gather to drink coffee, read the paper and discuss the news. Filling Panamanian staples (*ceviche*, chicken with rice, soups) from US$4.50, and generous breakfasts. The people-watching is fabulous; the food is variable. Daily 7am–11pm.

★**Caffè Per Due** Av A, at C 3 ☎ 6512 9311; map p.532. Cosy café that keeps its prices affordable: thin, crispy pizzas (from US$8), salads and cakes. Tues–Sat 9am–10pm, Sun from 9.30am.

> ★**TREAT YOURSELF**
>
> **René Café** Plaza Catedral, at C 7 ☎ 262 3487; map p.532. Provided a 4WD isn't parked out front, the outdoor tables provide a splendid vantage point for admiring the cathedral while savouring a good-value set menu lunch (US$11) washed down with a glass of wine. The more substantial dinner menu is pricier (US$27) but still excellent, and better enjoyed in the homely ambience inside. Expect tapas-style appetizers. Mon–Sat 10am–3pm & 6–10pm.

Casa Sucre Av B, at C 8 ⓦ casasucrecoffeehouse.com; map p.532. Laidback arty café decked out with eclectic antiques and a similarly eclectic spread of coffee-table books, from Chinese World Heritage Sites to Maya architecture. Serves gourmet coffees, deli sandwiches, all-day breakfasts and its signature dish, a filling soup served in a bread bowl (US$9). Free wi-fi. Mon–Wed 8am–6pm, Thurs–Sat 8am–8pm, Sun 9am–6pm.

★**Diablo Rosso Café** C 6, at Av A ☎ 262 1957; map p.532. Also home to the Diablo Rosso Art Gallery, this trendy boutique café has a varied Mediterranean-influenced menu of large and delicious panini and quinoa-rich salads (US$7–10). Displaying a collection of quirky furniture, art, designer clothing and accessories – all of which are for sale – the place also hosts Tuesday-night film screenings. Tues–Sat noon–7pm.

Granclement Av Central, at C 4; map p.532. Head here when you're feeling indulgent; US$2.75 may seem pricey for a scoop of ice cream, but this French-style artisanal ice cream, served in a waffle cone, is to die for, from creamy rich chocolate concoctions to mouthwatering sorbets. Daily noon–8.30pm.

Super Gourmet Av A, at C 6 ☎ 212 3487, ⓦ supergourmetcascoviejo.com; map p.532. A café and deli serving tasty baguette sandwiches (US$6), excellent daily specials (US$7), and the best coffees in the old town. At the time of writing was experimenting with late opening. Mon–Sat 8am–9pm, Sun 10am–4pm.

CALIDONIA AND LA EXPOSICIÓN

Café Boulevard Balboa Av Balboa, at C 30 Este; map pp.530–531. The spartan 1970s interior is enlivened by a smart lunchtime crowd of local politicians and office workers. Although specializing in toasted sandwiches (US$5–8), the lengthy menu also includes filling Panamanian dishes (from US$6), and a superior 3-course *menú del día* for US$8. Mon–Sat 6.30am–1am.

Mercado Público Av B, at Av Balboa; map pp.530–531. Seek out the food court, where you can choose from a dozen *fondas* serving hot, heaped platefuls of noodles or rice with bits of meat, seafood and veg for under US$4. Mon–Sat 6am–3pm.

Restaurante de Mariscos Av Balboa, above the Mercado de Mariscos ☎ 212 3898; map pp.530–531. Pick a fresh seafood dish from their own menu, or buy something from the stalls downstairs and get them to cook it for you, served with rice or *patacones*. Daily 11am–6pm.

El Rincón Tableño Av Cuba at C 31; map pp.530–531. One of the city's ubiquitous cafeteria-style restaurants, serving *comida típica* with relish and at economical prices (under US$6). Try the *sancocho*, Panama's favourite meat-and-veg soup. Daily 6am–4pm.

BELLA VISTA AND EL CANGREJO

Athens Pizza C 57 Este, off Vía España, opposite *Napoli's* ☎ 223 1464; map pp.530–531. Tasty, filling meals from around US$7. The Greek dishes, including salads (US$8), are abundant and the pizza is great comfort food. Wed–Mon 11am until late.

Caffè Pomodoro C 49B Oeste in *ApartHotel Las Vegas*; map pp.530–531. Extremely popular Italian restaurant, with outdoor seating in an enclosed tropical garden. One of several venues owned by local celebrated chef Willy Diggelmann, with a menu of antipasti, salads, pastas and pizzas from US$6. Daily 7am–midnight.

Churrería Manolo Vía Argentina 12; map pp.530–531. Café specializing in sweet, cigar-shaped *churro* pastries for around a dollar, as well as serving coffees, *emparedados* and more substantial mains (US$8–11). Daily 7am–1am.

Jimmy's C Manuel Icaza, off Vía España; map pp.530–531. Enjoy the comfy seating while you peruse the wide-ranging, affordable menu of Panamanian and Greek dishes – meat and fish mains from US$6, or *sancocho* for under US$5. Daily specials and light bites also available. Mon–Sat 7am–11pm.

The Loving Hut C Manuel Espinosa Batista, Edif Cali ☎ 240 5621, ⓦ lovinghut.com/pa; map pp.530–531. What this no-nonsense vegan cafeteria lacks in charm it makes up for in value – provided you catch the cafeteria fare when it's fresh or order à la carte. You can "pick and mix" a healthy plateful for under US$5. Mon–Sat 10.30am–8pm.

★**New York Bagel Café** Cabeza de Einstein, C Felipe Motta at Vía Argentina; map pp.530–531. The exposed brick walls and large open kitchen lend a touch of the Big Apple to this popular hangout for travellers, expats and Panamanians. *NY* serves a wide variety of home-made bagels with house cream-cheese (from US$3), huge breakfasts and burgers, fruit smoothies, good coffee and more. Mon–Fri 7am–8pm, Sat 8am–8pm, Sun 8am–3pm.

Niko's Just off Vía España, opposite *Plaza Regency*; map pp.530–531. Busy 24hr cafeteria with branches all over the city (notably in the bus terminal) serving a wide choice of Panamanian and international fast food. Much of the large menu, from grilled meat and fish to sandwiches,

pizza and strong coffee, can be tasted for under US$6. Takeaway available.

Rincón Habanero Vía Argentina, opposite *El Trapiche* ☎ 202 0872; map pp.530–531. Great little tucked-away Cuban-owned restaurant with images and sounds of old-time Havana on the walls and plasma TV. Plantain, beans and rice all feature heavily on the modestly priced menu (mains from US$10), and the mojitos are a must. Mon–Sat noon–10.30pm.

DRINKING AND NIGHTLIFE

Panama City is a 24hr metropolis, and its residents like nothing better than to drink and dance into the early hours. At one end of the great range of places to go are the cantinas and bars around Av Central: hard-drinking dives where women are scarce. Most of the upmarket places affordable to budget travellers are found around El Cangrejo – around C Uruguay in particular – and Casco Viejo, though the colonial centre also has some less expensive, more bohemian spots. Once in a particular neighbourhood, it's easy and relatively safe to walk between venues at night though you should go out in a group; and note that every few months there's the occasional drug-related shoot-out, when it's possible to be caught in the crossfire. Most clubs are closed on Mondays and Tuesdays and don't get going until around midnight. Cover charges, mostly levied on weekends and for live acts, tend to be high, but often include several free drinks.

CASCO VIEJO

★**Mojitos (sin Mojitos)** Plaza Herrera; map p.532. This small, intimate cellar-like bar, buzzing with expats, locals and travellers, is a must for a night out in Casco Viejo, offering cheap drinks (though no Mojitos!) and tasty home-made meat and veggie burgers (US$6). Tues–Sat 6pm until late.

Onplog C 11, at Av Eloy Alfaro ⓦ facebook.com/onplog; map p.532. Funky Bohemian cultural space owned by Panamanian musician Cienfue, aimed at encouraging and promoting new artists, with rock featuring heavily. The distinctive decor includes umbrellas hanging from the ceiling and a host of recycled materials. US$5 cover for events. Tues–Sat 7pm until late.

Relic Luna's Castle, C 9A Este between Avs B & Alfaro ☎ 262 1540, ⓦ lunascastlehostel.com; map p.532. Rather gloomy crypt-style interior and dark courtyard, ventilated by noisy giant fans. The place heaves until the wee hours, fuelled by cheap booze, pulling in a healthy mix of locals and travellers, especially once the DJ hits the decks. Mon–Sat from 8pm.

Villa Agustina Av A, between Plaza Herrera & C 8; map p.532. Trendy outdoor party venue set in a painted and plant-filled courtyard illuminated by pretty lights. It's a hot spot in the dry summer months – less so in the rainy season – popular with backpackers and locals, with cheap booze and occasional big-name DJ events blasting out *música varieda*, heavily laced with *electrónica*. Cover charge for events. Thurs–Sun 6pm until late.

BELLA VISTA AND EL CANGREJO

Habibi's Off C Uruguay; map pp.530–531. A great corner terrace right in the thick of things, *Habibi's* has seemingly limitless indoor and outdoor seating perfect for enjoying hookahs, cocktails (from US$6) and pricey Lebanese snacks. Daily 11am until late.

Istmo Brew Pub Av Eusebio A. Morales; map pp.530–531. If you're craving something other than the standard local *cerveza*, try the half open-air, half covered *Istmo* – all the beer is brewed on site (from US$4) in beautiful copper kegs, plus there's affordable pub grub on offer. The pool table and televised football matches are further pluses. Daily 4.30pm until late.

La Rana Dorada Vía Argentina, at Einstein's Head; map pp.530–531. Brasserie-bar popular with young expats and wealthy Panamanians, serving beer, cocktails (from US$4) and food (from US$5). The home-brewed beer and the trendy location has the crowds spilling out onto the street. Its equally popular sibling bar is in Casco Viejo (see map p.532). Daily noon until late.

S6is C Uruguay between C 48 & C 49 ☎ 264 5237; map pp.530–531. A mainstay of the party scene, popular with various age groups, this small cocktail lounge with DJ can get packed at weekends. It's pronounced "seis". Thurs–Sat 8pm–4am.

OTHER AREAS

Icon Club Av Juan Pablo II, at Tumba Muerto ☎ 6230 0378; map pp.530–531. The city's biggest gay club, featuring laser lights, foam parties, dancing boys and drag acts. Cover charge for events (up to US$10). Thurs–Sun 9pm–3am.

ENTERTAINMENT

Most theatre productions are in Spanish, and can be found advertised outside theatre buildings and in *La Prensa*. Rock concerts and the like happen at the convention centres of ATLAPA (🌐atlapa.gob.pa) and Figali Convention Center (🌐figaliconventioncenter.com). Check the papers, as well as 🌐quehacerhoypanama.com, 🌐thepanamanews.com and 🌐prensa.com, for entertainment listings, including live music and theatre.

Cinema There are many cinemas showing current, mainly subtitled, Hollywood blockbusters; check 🌐cinespanama .com for schedules. Try Cinemark, in the Albrook Mall, across from the bus terminal, and in Multicentro on Av Balboa, near Punta Paitilla.

Teatro Nacional Av B, Plaza Bolívar, Casco Viejo ☎ 262 3525. Opera and ballet productions.

SHOPPING

There are several souvenir shops lining Vía Veneto in El Cangrejo, and a handful of shops catering to tourists clustered along C 1 in Casco Viejo – the best is the Galería de Arte Indigena. Av Central, the pedestrian zone running between Plaza Cinco de Mayo and Casco Viejo, is the place to go for low prices on any type of goods.

Crafts Mercado de Buhonerías y Artesanías (Mon–Sat 9am–6pm) is on Plaza Cinco de Mayo behind the old railway building, while the Centro de Artesanías International on the Amador Causeway, next to the Figali Convention Centre (Mon–Sat 9am–6pm, Sun 10am–5pm), has a good selection from Panama and other Latin American countries. There's also a good selection at Panamá Viejo (see p.540).

Exedra Books Vía Brazil, at Vía España. Large, modern bookshop with café and free wi-fi. Mon–Fri 11am–7pm, Sat 10am–6pm.

Gran Morrison Vía España, El Cangrejo. English-language books on Panama, with a souvenir section. Daily 9am–6pm.

Malls Albrook Mall across from the Albrook bus terminal; MultiPlaza Mall, at Vía Israel & C 50; Multicentro on Av Balboa, at Plaza Paitilla.

DIRECTORY

Banks and exchange The Banco Nacional de Panamá and Banistmo – each with several outlets across the city, including on Vía España in El Cangrejo – allow cash withdrawals on credit cards; most banks also have 24hr ATMs. Foreign currency is more difficult to change – foreign banks will generally change their own currency, and there is a licensed exchange house, Panacambios (Mon–Fri 8am–4pm; ☎ 223 1800), in the Plaza Regency Building on Vía España, opposite the Rey supermarket.

Car rental Most major rental companies have desks at the airport and some have offices along Vía España.

Embassies Australia – seek advice from Canadian embassy; Canada, C 53E, Torres de las Américas, Tower A, 11th floor, Punta Pacífica (☎ 294 2500); Costa Rica, Av Samuel Lewis, Edif. Omega, 3rd floor (☎ 264 2980); Ireland, Torre Delta, 14th floor, Vía España (☎ 264 6633); UK, MMG Tower, C 53, Marbella (☎ 269 0866); US, Av Demetrio Basilio Lakas, Clayton (☎ 207 7000).

Health Hospitals include Hospital Nacional, Av Cuba, C 38/39 (☎ 207 8100); Centro Médico Paitilla, C 53 & Av Balboa (☎ 265 8800); and Hospital Punta Pacífica, Blvd Pacífica & Vía Punta Darién (☎ 204 8000). Pharmacies are found all over the city and often have a big green sign with a cross; Farmacia Arrocha is popular – the largest branch is on Vía España in front of *El Panamá* hotel, and there are others on Vía Argentina and in Albrook Mall. City-wide branches of El Rey supermarket (24hr) and Super 99 often have 24hr pharmacies.

7

Immigration M*igración* is in Tumba Muerto outside the city centre (Mon–Fri 8.30am–3.30pm; ☎507 1800, Ⓦmigracion.gob.pa); you won't need to go there unless you have overstayed your visa or want to change status.

Internet There are many internet cafés throughout the city, especially in El Cangrejo around Vía Veneto, C 49B Oeste, a block up from Vía España (around US$1/hr).

Police Emergencies ☎104; tourist police ☎269 9261.

Post office The most central post office is on Av Central at C 34, opposite the Don Bosco basilica; there's another in El Cangrejo in the Plaza de la Concordia shopping centre on Vía España (both Mon–Fri 7am–6pm, Sat 7am–3pm).

Telephones Public phone booths throughout the city take phonecards; some take coins. Most internet cafés offer cheap international calls for about US$0.10/min.

AROUND PANAMA CITY

Two contrasting attractions provide welcome escapes from the frenetic pace of the capital: to the east, a short bus ride away, lie the ruins of **Panamá Viejo**, once the premier colonial city on the isthmus; to the southwest, and an hour by boat, tropical **Isla Taboga** provides a peaceful setting for some gentle hiking and beach-lounging.

Panamá Viejo

On the coast about 8km northeast of the city centre stand the ruins of **PANAMÁ VIEJO**, the original colonial city founded by Pedro Arias de Ávila in 1519. Abandoned in 1671 after being sacked by Henry Morgan and his band of pirates, many of its buildings were later dismantled to provide stones for the construction of Casco Viejo, and in recent decades much of the site has been built over as the modern city has spread eastward. Despite this encroachment, a surprising number of the original buildings still stand.

The best place to start a visit is the **museum** (Tues–Sun 9am–5pm; US$3, US$6 with entrance to ruins; ☎224 2155, Ⓦpanamaviejo.org) on Vía Cincentenario near the ruins, where exhibits explain the changes that have taken place since this was a tiny village around 500 BC. The major draw here is the three-storey square stone tower of the cathedral, built between 1619 and 1629. It has a modern stairway with a lookout at the top and is flanked by the square **cabildo** (town hall) to the right and the bishop's house to the left. Nearby, and free to the public, is the site of La Merced, the church and monastery where Francisco Pizarro took communion before embarking on the conquest of Peru in 1531. La Merced was once considered Panamá City's most beautiful church, and survived Morgan's burning of the city by his use of it as a headquarters.

To **get to** Panamá Viejo, either take a taxi (US$7–8) or catch any bus marked "Panamá Viejo" or "Vía Cincentenario" from along the Cinta Costera or just off Plaza Cinco de Mayo.

Isla Taboga

Some 20km off the coast and about an hour away by boat, tiny **ISLA TABOGA** is one of the most popular retreats for Panama City residents, who come here to enjoy the island's clear waters, peaceful atmosphere and verdant beauty. Known as the "Island of Flowers" for the innumerable fragrant blooms that decorate its village and forested slopes, Taboga gets very busy at weekends, particularly during the summer, but is usually quiet during the week.

Taboga's one **fishing village** is very picturesque, with narrow streets, whitewashed houses and dozens of gardens filled with bougainvillea and hibiscus. Most visitors head straight for a section of **beach**, either right in front of the village or in front of the defunct *Hotel Taboga*, to the right of the pier as you disembark. The water is calmer here and the view of Panama City is magnificent, though the rubbish that frequently washes up on the beach is unsightly.

Behind the village, forested slopes rise to the 300m peak of **Cerro Vigía**, where a viewing platform on top of an old US military bunker offers spectacular 360-degree views. It's about an hour's climb through the forest to the *mirador* – follow the path some 100m up behind the church until you find a sign marked "Sendero de los Tres Cruces", beyond which the trail is easy to follow. It's a great area for spotting poison dart frogs and tarantulas, especially after some rain. The other side of the island is home to

---

ISLAS PERLAS

While no longer exclusively the playground of the rich and famous, the sugary beaches of the Islas Perlas (Pearl Islands) – so named after their once prolific black-lipped pearl oysters – are nevertheless still generally considered to be out of reach of most budget travellers. But the relatively new ferry services to islas Contadora and Saboga, which both boast some great stretches of sand, often run promotional specials, making them more affordable and worth considering for even a day-trip.

Sea Las Perlas (ⓦ sealasperlas.com) operates daily departures from the Balboa Yacht Club on the causeway (to Contadora: 7.30am, returning at 3.30pm; 1hr 40min each way; US$90 return). Ferry Las Perlas (ⓦ ferrylasperlas.com) departs from the *Trump Ocean Club* in Punta Pacífica, providing a faster and slightly pricier service to both Contadora and Saboga, and has great seasonal day-specials, sometimes including a meal and beach umbrella for under US$100.

On both islands a few local restaurants dish up cheap *comida corriente*, though the only budget accommodation to be had is in Puerto Nuevo, the main village on Saboga, where you'll get a warm welcome at Sra Mare's (☎6641 0452), who rents out simple rooms in her home for US$25.

7

one of the largest brown pelican breeding colonies in the world and, together with the neighbouring island of Urabá, forms a protected wildlife refuge.

ARRIVAL AND DEPARTURE

By boat Daily departures on the *Calypso Queen* passenger ferry (US$14 return; ☎314 1730) leave for Isla Taboga from next to the Punta Culebra Nature Center on Isla Naos on the Amador Causeway (8.30am, returning 4.30pm), with extra ferries at 10.30am and 4pm at weekends and on public holidays and at 3pm on Fridays.
Money Make sure you take sufficient cash with you as there is no ATM on Taboga.

ACCOMMODATION AND EATING

Though you can stay on Taboga (see ⓦtaboga .panamanow.com), the island is easily explored in a day.
Restaurante Mundi By the jetty. Comprising a few tables on a small deck over the water, this informal restaurant serves up tasty seafood dishes with rice or *patacones* (from US$8), even delivering to the beach if required. Daily 7am–9pm.

The Panama Canal and Colón Province

Stretching 80km from Panama City in the south to Colón in the north, the **Panama Canal** is a work of mesmerizing engineering brilliance. One of the largest

and most ambitious human endeavours, the waterway allows massive vessels – which otherwise would have to travel all the way south around Cape Horn – to traverse the isthmus in less than one day. East of the canal spreads the rainforest of **Parque Nacional Soberanía**, the greatest possible contrast to its mechanical might. Delve into the park's humming, humid atmosphere on one of its many accessible pathways, and you'll discover unparalleled biodiversity. **Colón**, at the Atlantic entrance to the canal, and only a boat or train or bus ride away from Panama City, seems like a different world from the capital – a brief tour of the poverty-stricken city from the safety of a taxi leaves you in no doubt about the canal's socioeconomic importance, and the depth of Panama's social inequalities. Some 45km northeast of Colón lies another port – **Portobelo** – whose glory days are even more distant. Its riches once proved irresistible to such pirates as Sir Francis Drake and Henry Morgan, and its once-mighty fortifications are now atmospheric ruins.

THE PANAMA CANAL AND THE CANAL ZONE

The **PANAMA CANAL** really is amazing, both physically and in concept. The basis of the country's modern economy, it's also the key to much of its history: were it not for the US government's determination to

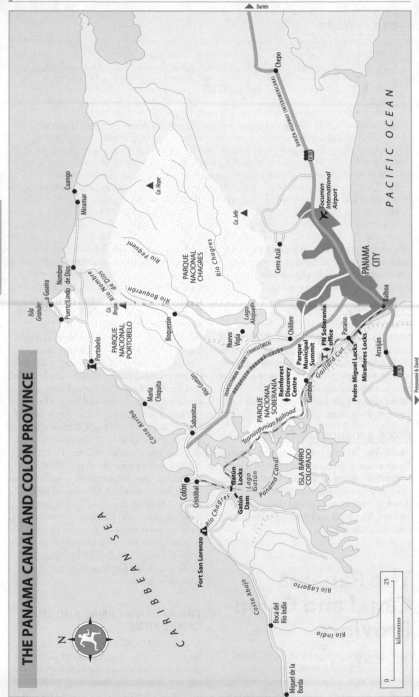

THE PANAMA CANAL AND COLÓN PROVINCE

THE PANAMA CANAL AND COLÓN PROVINCE **PANAMA** | 543

build the waterway, Panama might never have come into existence as an independent republic. Construction on the project began in the late nineteenth century, initiated by the French, but their efforts were abandoned in 1893, having taken the lives of nearly 22,000 workers through disease. The US took up the construction just over ten years later, aided by more powerful machinery than the French had been using, and improved understanding of malaria, yellow fever and the engineering that was necessary. The job was finally finished in 1914, the isthmus having been breached by the 77km-long canal, with vessels raised from and lowered to sea level by three sets of locks totalling 5km in length.

From 1903 to 1977, the strip of land that extends 8km on either side of the canal was de facto US territory, an area known as the **Canal Zone**. After more than ninety years the waterway was finally handed over to Panamanian jurisdiction at midnight on December 31, 1999, to be managed thereafter by the Autoridad del Canal de Panamá (ACP). In 2006 a proposal for a US$5.25 billion expansion of the canal was approved first by President Torrijos and then by public referendum. The ACP claims that the expansion will directly benefit Panama's people, though critics contend that the country will be crippled by debt – the project will be paid for by increased tolls, supplemented by US$2.3 billion in loans – and that only the elite of society will benefit. Due to be completed by the end of 2015, the project has been plagued with strikes and delays over spiralling costs – now estimated at over US$7billion, compounded by concerns over a rival Chinese-funded canal to be constructed through Nicaragua.

GETTING TO AND AROUND THE PANAMA CANAL AND CANAL ZONE

By boat The most interesting way to explore the canal and its surroundings is by boat, though large commercial vessels are charged around US$126,000 to make the transit, you can pay a great deal less. Panama Canal Tours (☎ 226 8917, ⌨ pmatours.net) and Canal & Bay Tours (☎ 209 2009, ⌨ canalandbaytours.com), both in Panama City, offer half-day partial transits (generally Thurs–Sat in high season, Fri &

Sat the rest of the year) of the canal through Miraflores and Pedro Miguel locks, into the Gaillard Cut, and finishing in Gamboa (US$150). These tours are well worth the outlay, and include excellent bilingual commentary and a full lunch. Full transit, including Lago Gatún and Gatún Locks, is usually offered once a month (US$195). A much more affordable option, although unreliable, is to get taken on as a linehandler aboard one of the private yachts that transit the canal. Law requires four linehandlers on each boat. It's a straightforward role, but it carries genuine responsibility. You will not be paid, unless experienced, although food and drink are usually supplied. Your best chance of getting linehandling work is to register with ⌨ panlinehandler.com.

By bus Gamboa-bound SACA buses – all chicken buses – from Panama depart from the far end of the main bus terminal and take the road running 26km along the canal, past the Miraflores and Pedro Miguel locks (20min to either), to the town of Gamboa near Lago Gatún (50min). Buses pass the Parque Nacional Soberanía office (see p.545) and the entrances to the Parque Municipal Summit, which houses a small zoo in lovely grounds (see p.545). Buses to the Miraflores locks are more plentiful, as you can also catch the Metrobus (departing every hour, on the hour) to Miraflores, or to Clayton, from the front of the terminal. Colón is served by even more frequent buses from Panama City (see p.535).

By taxi Taxis in Panama City can take you to Miraflores for around US$10–15. The Gatún Locks, on the Caribbean side, can be visited via Colón (see p.546).

By train One of Central America's only passenger trains, the Panama Canal Railway (7.15am from Corozal – arrive at the terminal 30min in advance to secure a ticket; 5.15pm from Colón; US$25 one way; ☎ 317 6070, ⌨ panarail.com) runs along the east side of the canal. Though the line is primarily for moving freight, a commuter passenger train (Mon–Fri) makes the 1hr journey from Panama City to Colón and back. An observation carriage gives widescreen views and there are open-sided sections between carriages throughout the train. A taxi to the train station at Corozal, 2km north of Albrook bus terminal (see p.535), costs US$5–6, or you could take a bus to the terminal and a shorter taxi ride from there.

WHAT TO SEE AND DO

A day-trip from Panama City could see you scanning the rainforest canopy for harpy eagles from the top of a former radar station, taking in the engineering masterpiece of the **Miraflores Locks**, or visiting an Indigenous Emberá community in **Parque Nacional Chagres**. If you're in the mood for hiking, try out the celebrated routes of **Camino de Cruces** and the Pipeline Road in **Parque Nacional Soberanía**. A cool and comfortable

7

CANAL GEOGRAPHY

From the Bahía de Panamá on the country's Pacific coast, the canal runs at sea level approximately 6km inland to the **Miraflores Locks**, where ships are raised some 16.5m to Lago de Miraflores. About 2km further on, ships are raised another 10m to the canal's maximum elevation of 26.5m above sea level, after which they enter the **Gaillard Cut**. This 14km slice through the shifting shale of the continental divide was the deepest and most difficult section of the canal's construction and was plagued by devastating landslides and loss of life.

The canal channel continues for 38km across the broad expanse of **Lago Gatún**, once the largest artificial lake in the world. Covering 420 square kilometres, it is tranquil and stunningly beautiful; until you see an ocean-going ship appear from behind one of the densely forested headlands, it's difficult to believe that this is part of one of the busiest waterways in the world. At the lake's far end ships are brought back down to sea level in three stages by the **Gatún Locks**, after which they run 3km through a narrow cut into the calm Caribbean waters of Bahía Limón.

early-morning train ride on the **Panama Canal Railway** to Colón (see p.546) gives wonderful panoramic views of the canal and the rainforest, and from the city it's a hot bus-ride northeast along the coast to the colonial ruins of **Portobelo**.

Miraflores Locks

Heading north out of Panama City along the canal, the first sight of note is the **Miraflores Locks**. The first lock gates here are the tallest in the whole canal system. Even so, they open in just two minutes, guiding ships through by electric locomotives known as mules. The **visitor complex** (daily 9am–5pm; US$15; ☎276 8325, ⓦpancanal.com) is a ten-minute walk from the point on the main road where any Gamboa- or Paraíso-bound **bus** from Panama City can drop you off (see p.535) – just ask the driver. The best time to see ships passing through is 8am to 11am, when they come up from the Pacific side, and after 3pm, when they complete their transit from the Atlantic side. Crowds build in high season, so go early or head for the much quieter Gatún Locks (see p.547). There is an overpriced café here, as well as an expensive restaurant and a souvenir shop.

Parque Municipal Summit

At a fork in the road 9km beyond the Miraflores Locks is the office for Parque Nacional Soberanía (see opposite). The left fork, heading towards Gamboa, brings you to **Parque Municipal Summit** (daily 9am–3pm; US$5; ☎232 4850). Any Gamboa-bound **bus** from Panama

City (see p.535) can drop you off at the entrance.

Established by the US in 1923, these botanical gardens house more than fifteen thousand plant species spread throughout the landscaped grounds, as well as a popular zoo, which more recently has been populated by rescue animals. Star attractions include a tapir and a jaguar, and a harpy eagle in new but rather small enclosures. Avoid weekends and holiday periods when the place is crammed with picnicking families, often playing loud music.

Gamboa

Some 8km north of the botanical gardens lies the curious town of **GAMBOA**, which became the centre for the canal's dredging in the 1930s. With its wooden buildings and derelict baseball diamond, it feels like an abandoned, small American town. The Smithsonian Tropical Research Institute has a small dock, 1km beyond Gamboa's central park, which is the jumping-off point for trips to Isla Barro Colorado (BCI), the principal site for their research (see opposite). Just before the Smithsonian dock, a road signposted off to the right leads to the entrance to **Pipeline Road** in Parque Nacional Soberanía (see opposite).

ARRIVAL AND INFORMATION

By bus Buses run from Panama City to Gamboa (Mon–Fri 9 daily, 4.45am–9pm, Sat & Sun 6am–9pm; 50min), departing from the far end of the Albrook bus terminal.
Bank There's an ATM by the entrance to the dredging division, in Gamboa's central park, by the bus stop.

ACCOMMODATION AND EATING

Mateo's Bed & Breakfast C Humberto Zárate 131A ☎ 6690 9664, ⊚ gamboabedandbreakfast.com. You'll get a warm welcome in these simple fan-ventilated wooden cabins with large windows and two single beds (cold water only) – though ask if possible to stay in the rooms in the canal-era house over the road. Surrounded by tropical vegetation and a well-tended garden, there is plenty of space to indulge in armchair or hammock birdwatching. Good value, with breakfast included. Use of kitchen or other meals on request. US$40

Food A small grocery shop lies just off the central park, where informal food stalls at lunchtime feed the dredging division workers. Daily 8am–7pm.

Parque Nacional Soberanía

Stretching along the eastern flank of the canal, the 220-square-kilometre **PARQUE NACIONAL SOBERANÍA** (daily 6am–6pm) provides essential protection for the rainforest-covered watershed that is vital for the canal's continued operation. Just thirty minutes from Panama City by road, Soberanía is the most easily accessible national park in Panama and is popular with both locals and visitors. Most spend just a few hours exploring one of the trails, which are mostly well marked and pass over rugged terrain cloaked in pristine rainforest, offering reasonable odds of seeing monkeys and innumerable birds as well as smaller mammals such as sloths and agoutis.

You can collect **trail** information and pay the entrance fee at the **park office** (Mon–Fri 7am–4pm; ☎ 232 4192; US$5), where the road to Gamboa branches off the main road from Panama City. Indicate to the bus driver that you want to go to the park office. If you ring in advance you may be able to engage the services of a park warden as a guide (around US$40–50/day for two people for the shorter trails; U$70–80 for the Pipeline Road).

All the trails have something to recommend them, but a few stand out. The 24km **Pipeline Road** (Camino del Oleoducto), accessed from Gamboa, is world famous for its birding opportunities; you can also visit the excellent, but costly, nearby Rainforest Discovery Center (US$30 6–10am, US$20 10am–4pm; ⊚ pipelineroad.org), whose highlight is a canopy observation tower. **Plantation Road** (Sendero de la Plantación), which begins at a right-hand turn-off 1.5km past the Parque Municipal Summit (see opposite) – tell the bus driver where you want to get off – follows a stream and offers great birdwatching. It runs some 4km to an intersection with the 10km **Camino de Cruces**, the only trail for which you would need a guide. The Camino is a remnant of the cobbled track the Spanish colonists used to transport their goods and treasures to Portobelo on the Caribbean coast.

Isla Barro Colorado

As the waters of Lago Gatún began to rise after the damming of the Chagres in 1913, much of the wildlife in the surrounding forest was forced to take refuge on points of high ground, which eventually became islands. One of these, **ISLA BARRO COLORADO** (BCI), administered by the Smithsonian Tropical Research Institute, is among the most intensively studied areas of tropical rainforest in the world. Though the primary aims of the reserve are conservation and research, you can arrange visits through the STRI (one tour daily Tues, Wed & Fri–Sun; US$80, students US$50; ☎ 212 8951, ⊚ stri.org) – contact them well in advance. The tour lasts between four and six hours and most guides speak English (double-check when booking). The cost covers the boat from Gamboa pier, the tour and lunch on the island.

Parque Nacional Chagres

East of the older highway that connects Panama City with Colón – the Transístmica – lies **Parque Nacional Chagres**, 1290 square kilometres of mountainous rainforest comprising four different life zones that are home to more than three hundred bird species and several Embera communities displaced by the flooding of Lago Bayano, further east. Day-trips to the park (see p.546) include transport – bus from Panama City – followed by a glorious trip by motorized dugout up the **Río Chagres**, a rainforest walk, a traditional meal, and the opportunity to buy handicrafts directly from producers. Note that sometimes these Embera villages can be overrun with cruise ship groups (Dec–April); you'll find fewer visitors in the Embera communities of the **Darién** (see box, p.554).

ARRIVAL AND DEPARTURE

Tours Parque Nacional Chagres is tricky to get to independently but the Embera–Drua community is one of several villages that organizes tours (ⓦtrail2.com /embera; US$40–45 for a day-trip, leaving from Lago Alajuela, with a minimum of four people; often cheaper with larger groups). Alternatively, go with a Panama City tour operator, such as Embera Tours (see box, p.535).

COLÓN

Officially founded by the Americans in 1852, as the Atlantic terminus of the Panama Railroad, **COLÓN**, at the Atlantic entrance to the Panama Canal, is all rubble and attitude. The city is dangerously poor, with a bad record of violent crime, set in a crumbling colonial shell that begs for renovation, which the current government has finally pledged to undertake. Colón's fortunes have fluctuated with those of the railway, and later the canal. Despite its status as Panama's main port, not to mention the financial success of both the canal and the Free Zone (established in 1949), very little of the money generated stays here, and many people who work in these areas live in Panama City. In the face of extreme poverty and unemployment levels, the crime rate – particularly **drug-related crime** – has rocketed.

For many, Colón's edginess will not appeal in the slightest, and a visit will only be a necessary evil in order to visit the nearby **Gatún Locks**, **Fort San Lorenzo** or the **Costa Arriba**. Many people come solely to shop at the **Colón Free Zone** – a walled enclave where goods from all over the world can be bought at very low prices – and assiduously avoid the rest of the city. However, the combination of a luxurious rail trip from Panama City followed by a taxi tour of this unique and decaying place can be fascinating, giving powerful insights into what the canal and the railroad have meant physically and economically to the country.

WHAT TO SEE AND DO

The best and safest way to explore Colón is by taxi (see box opposite), taking in the main streets, the historic *New Washington Hotel* and the adjacent dark-stone Episcopalian **Christ Church by the Sea**, the first Protestant church in Central America, built in the mid-1860s for the railroad workers. You get great views of ships waiting to enter the canal from the seafront.

The southeast corner of Colón is occupied by the **Zona Libre**, or Free Zone (ⓦcolonfreezone.com). Covering more than a square kilometre, this is the second-largest duty-free zone in the world after Hong Kong, with an annual turnover of more than US$10 billion. Colón's residents are not allowed in unless they work here, but you and your wallet are free to enter if you present your passport at the gate, though the place holds minimal interest for the casual shopper.

Near the Free Zone an enclave known as **Colón 2000**, which comprises a handful of souvenir shops and restaurants, has been established in the hopes of luring passengers from the many cruise ships that pass through the canal.

FERRY SERVICE TO COLOMBIA

A new luxury passenger and car ferry service, Ferry Xpress (ⓣ380 0909, ⓦferryxpress.com), operating between Colón and Cartagena, Colombia, is offering a new, more comfortable way to bridge the infamous Darién Gap. As it only started at the end of 2014 it was, at the time of writing, having a few teething problems. Car ferry crossings had been suspended and only passengers and motorbikes were being transported, so try to check this before you go. The cost for a passenger to bag a seat for the 18-hour crossing is US$100; cabins inevitably cost more. Since the onboard food is not cheap, budget travellers should take supplies for the journey. Departures from the cruise ship terminal, Colón 2000, are at 7pm on Mondays and Wednesdays; departures from Cartagena are at the same time on Tuesdays and Thursdays.

SAFETY IN COLÓN

Colón's reputation throughout the rest of the country for **violent crime** is not undeserved, and if you come here you should exercise extreme caution – mugging, even on the main streets in broad daylight, does happen. Don't carry anything that may attract attention or that you can't afford to lose, try to stay in sight of the police on the main streets and take **taxis** rather than walk. Many drivers will give tours of the city (about US$15/hr); consider hiring one if you want to explore. Asking for Pablo (who speaks English and Spanish) at the *Hotel Internacional* (see below) is a good option.

ARRIVAL AND INFORMATION

By boat Yachts transiting the canal dock at the Shelter Bay Marina (ⓦ shelterbaymarina.com) in the former Fort Sherman, west of Colón, on the road to Fort San Lorenzo. Ferry Xpress, the new passenger and car service to Cartagena, Colombia (see opposite), departs from Colón 2000.

By bus The bus terminal is on the corner of Av del Frente & C 13.
Destinations Gatún Locks (every 20min until 5pm; 20min); La Guaira for Isla Grande (6 daily; 2hr–2hr 30min); Miramar (6 daily; 3hr); Nombre de Dios (6 daily; 2hr–2hr 30min); Panama City (daily every 20–30min, 4am–10pm; 1hr 30min–2hr); Portobelo (daily every 30min until 9pm; 1hr 30min).

Tourist information The ATP office in Colón 2000 (Mon–Fri 8.30am–3.30pm; ☎ 475 2300) has little useful information.

Taxis Most trips in the city will cost US$2.

ACCOMMODATION

If you are going to stay overnight, it's worth splashing out on a more expensive hotel with armed security and a restaurant so you won't have to go out after dark.

Hotel Internacional Av Bolívar & C 12 ☎ 447 0111. A good deal in one of the safest streets in the city, within a stone's throw of the bus station. Rooms are basic but clean and comfortable with a/c, cable TV and wi-fi. There are also a couple of PCs, a sporadically open rooftop bar and a reasonable restaurant (mains US$7–8; closed Sun). **US$40**

Hotel Meryland C 7, opposite Parque Sucre ☎ 441 7055, ⓦ hotelmeryland.com. Little atmospheric, but it's tucked away in a leafy and relatively safe patch of the city and is a cut above all other options. Smartly tiled, spacious and professionally staffed, with en-suite, a/c rooms and large, firm beds. The restaurant serves filling soups and a good selection of mains (from US$8). **US$60**

EATING AND DRINKING

Arrecifes C 3 Paseo Gorgas, behind Colón 2000 ☎ 441 9308. Nice terrace overlooking the sea slightly away from the cruise-ship crowds, and with air-conditioned tables too. Offers a superior *menú del día* for US$7 and plenty of seafood dishes. Mon–Sat 11.30am–10pm, Sun 11.30am–7pm.

★ **Nuevo Dos Mares** C 5, between Av Central & Arosemena ☎ 445 4558. Behind an unpromising frontage, this place dishes up excellent Caribbean cuisine, with a wide range of tasty fish and seafood dishes (from US$7), served with coconut rice, fried *yuca* or *patacones*. Make sure you take a taxi there and organize a pick-up time. Mon–Sat noon–7.30pm.

DIRECTORY

Banks The safest ATM is inside the 24hr Super 99 in Colón 2000.

Car rental Renting a car for the day is a good idea if you want to visit the locks and San Lorenzo. You'll find Budget, Avis and Hertz in Colón 2000.

Hospital Hospital Manuel Amador Guerrero (☎ 441 5060), between C 10 & 11 at Paseo Gorgas, by Colón 2000.

Pharmacy In the Super 99 supermarkets, on Av Bolívar or in Colón 2000.

AROUND COLÓN

If you don't fancy a taxi tour of Colón, get straight onto a bus to the mighty **Gatún Locks** or splash out on a taxi to the beautiful and atmospheric **Fort San Lorenzo**.

Gatún Locks

From Colón, a road runs 10km southwest to the **Gatún Locks** (daily 8am–3.45pm; US$5), where ships transit between Lago Gatún and Bahía Limón. The nearly 2km-long locks, which raise and lower ships the 26.5m between the lake and sea level in three stages, are among the canal's most monumental engineering features. The **observation platform** at the visitors centre is so close to the canal that you could speak quite easily to anyone on the deck of the ships – your best chance of having a chat is between 8am and 11am, and after 3pm. The locks can also be visited as part of a tour (see opposite).

ARRIVAL AND INFORMATION

By bus Buses bound for the Costa Abajo from the Colón terminal will drop you just before the traffic lights at the swing bridge across the canal, by a road branching off to the left.

7

By taxi A taxi from Colón costs about US$12 each way, plus more for wait time.

Tourist information The visitors centre, which also has an ATM and gift shop, is a 1km walk down the side road from the point at which the bus stops.

Fort San Lorenzo

With a spectacular setting on a promontory above the Caribbean and overlooking the mouth of the Río Chagres, **Fort San Lorenzo** (8.30am–4.30pm; US$5) is the most impressive Spanish fortification still standing in Panama. Until the construction of the railway, the Chagres was the main cargo route across the isthmus to Panama City, and thus of enormous strategic importance to Spain. The first fortifications to protect the entrance to the river were built here in 1595, but the fort was taken by Francis Drake in 1596 and, though heavily reinforced, fell again to Henry Morgan's pirates in December 1670. Morgan then proceeded up the Chagres and across the isthmus to ransack Panama City. The fortifications that remain today were built in the mid-eighteenth century. The site as a whole is imposing, with a moat surrounding stout stone walls and great cannons looking out from the embrasures, all of it kept in isolation by the dense rainforest all around.

ARRIVAL AND INFORMATION

By car or taxi The fort can only be reached by car or taxi. With wait time, and dropping in at the locks on the way, it is a US$50–60 return trip from Colón, 1hr each way, passing through rainforest and the former US training base of Fort Sherman, which until 1999 was home to the 17,000-acre US Army Jungle Warfare Training Center and is now the location of the *Shelter Bay Marina*

If you plan to visit Portobelo or points further east, be aware that the new **ATM** in Portobelo is often broken or out of money, especially on busy holiday weekends. It's wise to take money out in Colón (see p.546) or in the supermarket at Sabanitas – where there's also an ATM – before making your way along the coast.

(ⓦshelterbaymarina.com). You might also consider renting a car for the day from Colón. Note that if a vessel is passing through Gatún Locks, you may be stuck on either side for around 45min.

Food The *Shelter Bay Marina* is a good place to stop off for a bite to eat (daily 7.30am–9.30pm).

PORTOBELO

The **Costa Arriba**, stretching northeast of Colón, features lovely beaches, excellent diving and snorkelling, and the historic towns of Nombre de Dios and **PORTOBELO** ("beautiful harbour"). Though Portobelo today has a somewhat stagnant atmosphere, the remnants and ruins of its former glories retain an evocative power. More powerful still – at least to the thousands of pilgrims who come to gaze on it – is the agonized face of the small **Black Christ** statue in the Iglesia de San Felipe (see oppsie).

Every two years in early March, Portobelo hosts the hugely enjoyable Afro-colonial **Festival de Congos y Diablos** (ⓦdiablosycongos.org), with smaller celebrations over the weekends leading up to it. Originating from *cimarrones* – outlawed bands of escaped slaves (see box, p.554) – in the sixteenth century, these colourful explosions of drumming, dancing, devil costumes and satirical

PORTOBELO HISTORY

After the town of Nombre de Dios was destroyed by Francis Drake in 1597, Portobelo was founded to replace it as the Atlantic terminus of the **Camino Real** – the route across the isthmus along which the Spanish hauled their plundered treasures. Portobelo's setting on a deep-water bay was supposed to make it easier to defend from the ravages of pirates, and for 150 years it played host to the famous **ferias**, grand trading events held when the Spanish treasure fleet came to collect the riches that arrived on mule trains from Panama City. Unsurprisingly, the pirates who scoured the Spanish Main – most famously Henry Morgan – could not resist the wealth concentrated in the royal warehouses here. Eventually the Spanish decided enough was enough: the treasure fleet was rerouted around Cape Horn and Portobelo's star began to fade.

THE BLACK CHRIST OF PORTOBELO

Without question the most revered religious figure in Panama is the **Black Christ** or *Cristo Negro* in Portobelo, which draws tens of thousands of pilgrims to the town every October. A small effigy carved from black cocobolo wood with an anguished face and eyes raised to heaven, the Black Christ is reputed to possess miraculous powers. The origins of the icon still remain something of a mystery. Some say that it was found floating in the sea during a cholera epidemic, which ended after the Christ was brought into the town; others maintain it was on a ship bound for Colombia that stopped at Portobelo for supplies and was repeatedly prevented from leaving the bay by bad weather, sailing successfully only when the statue was left ashore. Every year on October 21 up to fifty thousand devotees, known as Nazareños and dressed in purple robes, come to Portobelo – a number walking or crawling the last few kilometres – for a huge procession that is followed by festivities throughout the night.

play-acting were originally aimed at mocking their former colonial rulers.

WHAT TO SEE AND DO

Most of Portobelo is pretty down-at-heel. Other than the highly revered **Cristo Negro**, which fills the town every October (see box above), the **ruins** are the main attraction. Walking into Portobelo along the road from Colón brings you to the well-preserved **Santiago Battery**, which still features fourteen rusting but menacing cannons. The road then leads to the main tree-shaded **plaza**.

Casa Real de la Aduana

Just off the main plaza stands the impressive **Casa Real de la Aduana** (daily 8am–4pm; US$5), the royal customs house, which has been restored with Spanish help and now houses a small, rather overpriced museum outlining the history of the town. It was the largest civil building in colonial Panama and stored the Camino Real treasure awaiting transport to Spain.

Iglesia de San Felipe

On the square, 100m along the main road, beyond the Casa Real de la Aduana, the large, white **Iglesia de San Felipe** (daily 8am–6pm) houses Panama's most revered religious icon, the *Cristo Negro*, or Black Christ (see box above). Tucked away behind the church, a small museum (under restoration at the time of writing) exhibits an intriguing display of some of the opulent claret and purple robes donated each year to the Black Christ. Outside the church is the tiny **Mercado**

San Felipe, a small cluster of stalls selling religious (often quite kitsch) paraphernalia, most of which depicts the image of *El Cristo*, and a variety of Panamanian *artesanía*.

San Geronimo Battery

Looking out onto the bay behind the Church of San Felipe are the town's most impressive ruins, those of the **San Geronimo Battery** – creep to its outermost edge and peep out through the arrow slats

ARRIVAL AND INFORMATION

By bus Buses for Portobelo leave from Colón; if you're coming from Panama City and want to avoid Colón, change at the El Rey supermarket in Sabanitas, 14km before Colón. Buses from Colón arrive near the Church of San Felipe in the centre of town, within a few minutes' walk of the main sights and accommodation. Through-buses pick up and drop off on the main road opposite the park.

Destinations Colón (every 30min until 6pm; 1hr 30min); La Guaira (6 daily; 30min–1hr); Nombre de Dios (6 daily; 30min–1hr).

Money There is a new ATM opposite the Panadería Nazareño, but see p.550.

Tour operators The hotel *Coco Plum* (see below) can organize diving. Otherwise, Scuba Panamá, in Panama City (☎261 3841, ⌨scubapanama.com), has its dive centre on the road into Portobelo from Colón, which also has reasonable accommodation open to non-divers. *Captain Jack's* (see p.550) can arrange passage by yacht to Colombia.

Tourist information There's a large ATP office (Mon–Fri 9.30am–5.30pm; ☎448 2200) on the main street, opposite the Mayor's office.

ACCOMMODATION AND EATING

Las Anclas *Coco Plum*, on the road into Portobelo ☎448 2102. The most charming restaurant in the area specializes in fish (US$9–13) – try the mixed seafood in coconut milk

(US$11) – with alternatives including burgers. Also offers breakfast (from US$4). Daily 8am–8pm, until 9pm at weekends.

Captain Jack's 200m up the hill from the main road in the town centre ☎ 448 2009, ⓦ hostelportobelo.com. Rather cramped place with four dank fan-ventilated dorms with good mattresses, usually packed with travellers arriving from, or waiting for, a boat to Colombia. It also hosts a surprisingly pricey, though good, restaurant. Tuck into Thai chicken curry, pasta or seafood mains (from US$12) on the breezy veranda, which offers nice views of the church and bay. Breakfasts (from US$4.50) are more affordable. Restaurant Wed–Mon 11am–11pm. Dorms US$13

Ofiuras Hostal On the road into Portobelo ☎ 448 2400. A small family-run business set on the water's edge, with a handful of clean, simple rooms with fans and cable TV (US$10 extra for a/c); the friendly owners also run local boat tours. US$30

★Panadería Nazareño On the main street. This bargain bakery sells juices for a couple of dollars, tasty sandwiches from US$3 and a delicious variety of fresh bread. Tues–Sun 7am–9pm.

AROUND PORTOBELO

Isla Grande is a well-established getaway for Panamanians and tourists alike, while a more adventurous trip may explore the little-visited, windswept **beaches** further east.

Parque Nacional Portobelo
The **PARQUE NACIONAL PORTOBELO** encompasses the town and surrounding coast, although the area receives little protection or responsible management and you don't need permission from ANAM to enter. It does have good **beaches** and some of the best diving and snorkelling on the Caribbean coast, including coral reefs, shipwrecks and, somewhere in front of Isla de Drake, the as-yet-undiscovered grave of Francis Drake, buried at sea in a lead coffin after he died of dysentery in 1596. Most of this area can only be reached by sea; you can either hire a boatman – in Portobelo, Isla Grande or **Puerto Lindo**, a fishing village 14km northeast of Portobelo – or join an excursion; PADI-certified dive trips take place within the park (see p.549).

ACCOMMODATION AND EATING

There are a couple of decent budget lodgings in the fishing hamlet of Puerto Lindo, 14km northeast of Portobelo; you can get there on the La Guaira-bound bus from Colón (6 daily; 1hr 40min) via Portobelo, so it's within striking distance of both.

Casa X Water's edge by the yacht club, Puerto Lindo. A handful of plastic tables by the bay, where you can enjoy fresh, inexpensive seafood dishes with salad, *patacones* or rice (US$8), and wash them down with a glass of wine. Daily noon–8pm.

Hostel Wunderbar At the western entrance to Puerto Lindo ☎ 448 2426 or ☎ 6626 8455, ⓦ hostelwunderbar .com. In a nice, lush setting, this former backpackers' hostel now only offers a handful of small en-suite doubles with a/c (some with TV) of varying prices in a modern building. There's a kitchen, and a basic grocery, restaurant and bar nearby. Water outages can be a problem. US$35

INTO COLOMBIA BY BOAT

One of the most popular and adventurous ways to get to and from **Colombia** is by private yacht or catamaran, either to Cartagena, from Portobelo or Puerto Lindo, or to Sapzurro, just over the Colombian border from Puerto Obaldía (see p.562). Prices range from US$450–600 (generally including all meals and water), with boats varying in comfort, size and number of passengers. Taking the Cartagena route, the boat spends three days in the Guna Yala Archipelago, before taking on the rougher open water to Cartagena. The newer Sapzurro route is usually cheaper, avoids the rougher open seas and spends more of the journey island-hopping in Guna Yala. Note that there are fewer departures between December and February/March as the seas are particularly rough and dangerous, and some captains avoid sailing during this period. **Hostels** in Panama City (see p.536) usually have up-to-date information on boat departures. You are strongly advised to get a sense of a captain's reputation before signing on – there are nightmare tales of drunken captains, vastly overcrowded boats, poor seamanship and, worst of all, drug-running. Hostels should be able to advise you, but view their advice critically – they often get commission on sailings – and make sure you also consult other travellers who have made the journey. There is also now a new passenger and car ferry service from Colón to Cartagena (see box, p.562).

El Perezoso 2–3km before Puerto Lindo, on the right ☎ 6962 6060, ⍟ perezosopanama.com. The open sided garden restaurant of this Italian-run establishment, with an Italian and Panamanian menu, is a delight, as is the food. Best to get in touch if you're intending to dine, since it closes early if business is slack. There are also two extremely rustic wooden A-frame cabins (for 4–6 people) with fans and mosquito nets, which are rather run down but inexpensive. Camping/person <u>US$5</u>, cabins <u>US$30</u>

Isla Grande

Some 12km northeast along the coast from Portobelo, a side road branches off left and runs a few kilometres to the tiny village of **La Guaira**. Here *lanchas* provide transport to **ISLA GRANDE**, a short 300m hop from the mainland. A hugely popular weekend resort for residents of Colón and Panama City, topped by a rickety 200-year-old **lighthouse**, the island has become rather spoilt by unchecked development and the gradually receding beach, but it's a pleasant enough day-trip if you're killing time in Portobelo or Puerto Lindo waiting for a boat to Colombia.

Isla Grande fills up at weekends, and peaks during national holidays; during the week it is so quiet you can struggle to find a place open to serve you food. The only real sand **beach**, known as "La Punta", is around the island to the southwest, and you'll need to pay US$4 to use most of it (entry gives you access to *Hotel Isla Grande's* showers and lounge chairs). Around to the east by *Sister Moon* you'll find a reef break that's good for **surfing**. There's also some **snorkelling** round the northern part of the island by the now defunct *Bananas Village Resort*.

ARRIVAL AND DEPARTURE

By bus and boat *lanchas* (US$3) shuttle over to Isla Grande from La Guaira, which is served by infrequent and unreliable buses from Colón, via Portobelo (6 daily from Portobelo, last returning around 1pm, 4pm on Sun; 1hr 40min).

EATING

El Bucanero Close to La Punta. Relaxed beach bar-restaurant, where you can sit with your toes in the sand at a couple of tables with umbrellas, or under a makeshift awning, or up at the bar. Fairly inexpensive seafood dishes (US$8–9) are served. Daily 11am–8pm or 9pm.

Darién

The sparsely populated 17,000 square kilometres that make up **Darién** are one of the last great, untamed **wildernesses** in America. The beginning of an immense forest that continues almost unbroken across the border into the Chocó region of Colombia and down the Pacific coast to Ecuador, this was the first region on the American mainland to be settled by the Spanish. Although they extracted great wealth from **gold mines** deep in the forest at Cana, they were never able to establish effective control over the region, hampered by the almost impassable terrain, the fierce resistance put up by its inhabitants and European pirates and bands of *cimarrones* (see box, p.554).

The **Interamericana** is the only road that takes the plunge and enters the region, but it goes no further than the small town of **Yaviza**, 276km southeast of Panama City. Along the border with Colombia, the **Parque Nacional Darién**, the largest and most important protected area in Panama, safeguards vast swathes of forest that support one of the most pristine and biologically diverse ecosystems in the world, as well as a large indigenous population.

Until quite recently, the combination of drug trafficking and the decades-long Colombian civil war spilling over into Panama has made the border area utterly treacherous. The Marxist guerrillas of the Colombian Revolutionary Armed Forces (FARC) have long maintained bases close to the border in Darién, but right-wing paramilitary groups backed by powerful landowners and drug traffickers have taken to pursuing them, terrorizing isolated Panamanian communities they accuse of harbouring the guerrillas. Given the **security concerns** affecting the border area, including parts of the national park and the Comarca Emberá–Wounaan Cémaco (see box, p.554), a visit to southwestern Darién is the safest way to experience the ecology and culture of the region independently. The two most **popular routes** into the area are via Yaviza

7

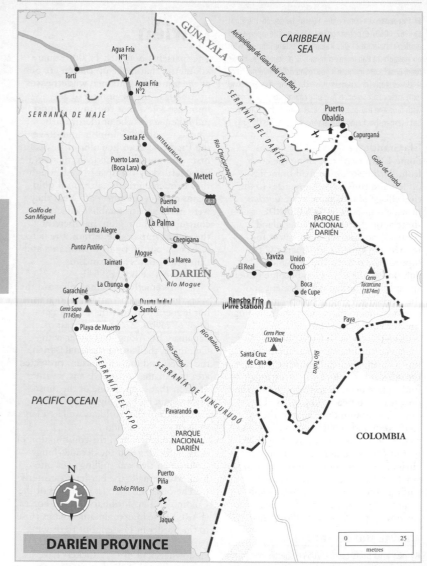

DARIÉN PROVINCE

and **El Real** to the national park's ranger station at Rancho Frío (also called Pirre Station), or via La Palma to the various Embera communities, such as the twin Embera/Afro-Darienite settlement of **Puerto Indio/Sambú** up the Río Sambú, or the community of Mogue. Once in Darién, you can ask for news of recent incidents or developments.

ARRIVAL AND DEPARTURE

TOURS
Most people who travel to Darién go with a tour. A couple of operators in Panama City (see box, p.535) run affordable trips and can help arrange travel in the region.

INDEPENDENT TRAVEL
Travelling independently is feasible, though in recent years travel restrictions have been increased. Going it alone does

require some knowledge of Spanish and a certain leap of faith – you can't plan every last detail before you leave but the very fact that it is not a simple undertaking is what makes it so special. More of your money will go to the host indigenous populations if you travel independently and organize your stay and excursions with villages once there.

Red tape Recent restrictions on travel for foreigners in Darién mean that you now need to get permission from SENAFRONT (Freephone within Panama ☎ 800 2762, ⊕ senafront.com) – the national frontier police – in Panama City a couple of weeks in advance. This tedious process involves detailing exactly when and where you want to visit, preferably in Spanish. The SENAFRONT office (Mon–Fri 8.30am–3.30pm) is in Corozal, just across the road from the train station (see map, p.528). They will tell you who to address the letter to and dictate if necessary. If you are lucky, the permit (free) will be granted within a day, but it may take up to three days.

By plane Air Panama (☎ 316 9000, ⊕ airpanama.com) offers flights to Darién, to Bahía Piña and Jaqué in the far south of the region as well as to Sambú and Garachiné, both of which lie near the Gulf of San Miguel and are good starting points for boat-based exploration of the more accessible – and safer – parts of Darién.

By bus Buses run from Panama City to Metetí and Yaviza (see p.554).

GETTING AROUND

By boat Once you've arrived in Darién, boats are the best, and sometimes the only, way to get around. Locals use *piraguas* – motorized dugout canoes – as well as slightly more modern *lanchas*. Fuel prices have risen steadily over the last few years, so in order to keep costs down you will need to be prepared to hang around, sometimes for a couple of days, to take one of the scheduled departures that is already heading in the direction you want to go

(trading, fishing or community boats) – you are effectively hitching a ride, rather than chartering a boat and crew. A ride from La Palma to Sambú could be as little as US$20/person if you travel this way, compared to upwards of US$150/boat if you have to hire someone's services. Before hopping aboard a boat, especially when chartering a vessel for an excursion, check its seaworthiness, including the engine size and the availability of life-jackets, as the Gulf of San Miguel can be rough.

THE DARIÉN HIGHWAY

East of Panama City the **DARIÉN HIGHWAY** (the Interamericana) is now paved all the way to Yaviza, though lack of maintenance and heavy rainfall at certain times of year mean that you're bound to experience some bumpy patches along the way. Just before the large reservoir that is Lago Bayano, the highway passes through the quiet village of El Llano, where a side road leads up towards **Guna Yala** (see p.558). From the lake the highway rolls on for 196km through a desolate, deforested landscape, passing Embera-Wounaan hamlets, with their characteristic open-walled houses raised on stilts, and half-hearted roadside settlements. The highway ends on the banks of the Río Chucunaque at **Yaviza**, the start of the Darién Gap, though most buses only go as far as **Metetí** (see below).

Metetí and Puerto Quimba

Some 50km before the highway ends in jungle it passes through **METETÍ**, an

---

KITTING YOURSELF OUT IN DARIÉN

Whether you visit Darién with a tour operator or on your own, you should pack wisely.

Clothing You will need trousers and long-sleeved shirts, partly to keep the huge variety of insect life at bay, but also because it can get quite cool during the night. Do not take or wear anything that resembles army fatigues or has a camouflage pattern.

Equipment You'll be able to pick up basic provisions (including bottled water), but it is advisable to pack a small supply of food even so, plus a ration of bottled water, and water-purifying tablets. Whether in a village or in the park you will need a sheet sleeping bag, a mosquito net and a torch. Bring a cover for your pack for boat travel and damp conditions and pack some toilet paper. Binoculars will greatly enhance your chance of appreciating the area's abundant birdlife.

Medication You should start taking antimalaria medication well before you arrive. Note that chloroquine is not sufficient in Darién – check the exact requirements with your doctor before your trip. Also ensure you have insect repellent and antihistamine cream, to sooth your bites.

Money There are only two banks in the region, both with ATMs: at Metetí and La Palma. It's a good idea to bring a large stash of small denomination bills.

7

THE PEOPLE OF DARIÉN

Darién's **population** is made up of three main groups: black, indigenous and colonist.

Other than a few Guna communities, the **indigenous** population of Darién is composed of two closely related but distinct peoples, the **Wounaan** and the more numerous **Embera**, both originally seminomadic South American rainforest societies. Recognizable by the black geometric designs with which they traditionally decorate their bodies, the Embera-Wounaan, as they are collectively known, have been migrating across the border from Colombia for the past two centuries. Only since the 1960s have they begun to settle in permanent villages and establish official recognition of their territorial rights in the form of a *comarca*, divided into two districts: the **Comarca Emberá–Wounaan Cémaco**, in the north, and the **Comarca Emberá–Wounaan Sambú**, in the southwest.

The **black people** of Darién, descended from *cimarrones* and released slaves, are known as **Darienitas** or **libres** (the free) and are culturally distinct from the black Afro-Antillano populations of Colón and Panama City (see p.533).

The **colonists** (*colonos*), meanwhile, are the most recent arrivals, poor mestizo peasants forced to look for new land to cultivate after having degraded their own lands in the central Panamanian provinces of the Azuero Peninsula through overgrazing cattle. Many colonists still wear their distinctive straw sombreros as a badge of identity and maintain the folk traditions of the regions they abandoned. The construction and subsequent improvement of the Darién Highway has facilitated the colonists' access to new land, which has inevitably brought them into conflict with the indigenous populations, as some make illegal encroachments into indigenous territory.

---

increasingly important commercial centre that leads on to Yaviza or southwest to the jumping-off point for most Darién exploration, at **PUERTO QUIMBA**.

ARRIVAL AND INFORMATION

By bus For most buses, including those from Panama City (4am–4.40pm, roughly every 40min; 5–7hr), Metetí's miniature Terminal de Transporte de Darién (1.5km down the road to Puerto Quimba) is the end of the road. The *chiva* (5am–5pm; every 30min; 30min) that shuttles back and forth between Metetí and Puerto Quimba also leaves from this terminal. Minibuses also run regularly to and from Yaviza (5.30am–5pm; every 30min; 1hr30min). The last bus back to Panama City leaves at 5pm.

By water taxi Water taxis (5am–5pm; every 30–40min; 30min; US$4) to La Palma depart from Puerto Quimba's dock area, comprising a car park, a pier, a police hut (where you have to present your passport and SENAFRONT letter) and a bar-restaurant.

Banks Metetí is one of the last stops for cash before entering the jungle, with a branch of the Banco Nacional and a 24hr ATM on the Interamericana 2km before the junction.

ACCOMMODATION AND EATING

If you miss your onward connection you can stay at one of the basic hotels in Metetí – note that, like the rest of the town, they suffer from frequent water outages.

Crown Darién 500m before the bus station on the Puerto Quimba road ☎ 6763 9084, ✉ crowndarien14@gmail.com. This small, new, gleaming hotel gets top billing, with

thirteen en-suite rooms – some with balcony – offering tepid showers but enhanced by a/c and cable TV. The on-site bar-restaurant dishes up a few basic numbers. ⎯US$23⎯

Restaurante Bellagio Signposted off the Puerto Quimba road to the right before the bus station ☎ 6521 8753. The best place to eat in town, and in air-conditioned comfort. Dishes, including rabbit and peccary, are roasted or grilled, a rare pleasure in Darién, where most food is fried (mains from US$6). Daily 11am–10pm.

Yaviza

Edgy, run-down **YAVIZA** marks the end of the Interamericana and the beginning of the Darién Gap. It is also the gateway into the **Parque Nacional Darién** (see p.555). You are required to check in with the police in Yaviza before moving on.

ARRIVAL AND INFORMATION

By bus There are few direct buses from Panama City to Yaviza – currently only the 6.20am departure and the more expensive midnight express bus are guaranteed to run to the end of the road; most stop at Metetí (see above), where you will switch to a smaller bus unless the majority of passengers are bound for Yaviza. The last bus out of Yaviza to Metetí departs at 5pm.

ANAM Darién National Park office (Mon–Fri 8.30am–3.30pm; ☎ 299 4495). After you have been to the SENAFRONT office next door, which can advise you on the security situation, you'll need to check in here before proceeding to the park itself. Both offices lie down the cement path at right angles to the wharf. Given the ANAM office opening hours, avoid arriving at the weekend. If you have not already arranged a guide and transport into the park, you will need to do that here too (see opposite).

Getting to Parque Nacional Darién To get to the park from Yaviza, head down to the wharf in the morning, when there are likely to be lots of motorized dugout canoes (*piraguas*) trading goods. Provided transport is headed downriver, you can usually get an inexpensive ride to El Real (around US$5–7/person; US$80 to charter a whole boat), a settlement some 15km down the Río Chucunaque (then a couple of kilometres up the Río Tuira), which is the access point to the park.

ACCOMMODATION AND EATING

Hotel Yadarien 50m along the main cement path from the wharf ☎ 6383 3473. If you have to stay the night, this basic place, with twenty en-suite rooms (with fan; a/c US$5 more) and beds in varying states of repair, is your best bet. US$15

Restaurante Oderay 40m along the cement path from the wharf. This reasonable eating option dishes up a decent plate of fried chicken or fish (and has a good toilet). Daily 7am–7pm.

PARQUE NACIONAL DARIÉN

Covering almost 5800 square kilometres of pristine rainforest along the border with Colombia, **PARQUE NACIONAL DARIÉN** is possibly the most biologically diverse region on earth – more than five hundred bird species have been reported here. Inhabited by scattered indigenous communities, the park contains the largest expanse of forest in Central America that has not been affected by logging and provides a home for countless rare and endangered species,

including jaguars, harpy eagles and several types of macaw. From the ranger station at Rancho Frío – currently the only place to stay within the park – there are several trails, including a challenging overnight hike up Cerro Pirre (1200m).

ARRIVAL AND INFORMATION

Permission To enter the park you have to seek permission from SENAFRONT in Panama City (see p.553) as well as from the ANAM Darién National Park office in Yaviza (see p.554), where you pay the park entry (US$5) and other fees. Note that most of the rangers speak only Spanish.

Transport Ask the park office to help you arrange transport to Rancho Frío, accessed via the ANAM office in El Real; transport will cost US$35 from El Real.

Guides It is mandatory to have a guide in the park. The park office in Yaviza can arrange for a warden (*guardaparque*) to guide you (US$25/day) – they may try to encourage you to go with a more expensive, independent guide, but insist politely. Ensure you have the necessary food and other supplies (see p.553), which are best acquired in Yaviza, including food for the guide.

ACCOMMODATION

The Ranger Station Rancho Frío (no phone; contact through the ANAM office in Yaviza or El Real). Currently the park's only accommodation option, the ranger station has a dormitory but there is no bedding provided. Use of kitchen (without a fridge) permitted. US$15

LA PALMA

LA PALMA's spectacular setting, overlooking the broad mouth of the Río Tuira, surrounded by densely forested mountains and with ruined colonial forts for neighbours, makes it a worthy capital

---

INTO COLOMBIA: THE DARIÉN GAP

The **Darién Gap** is a band of dense and entirely untamed rainforest, 100km or so in length, that keeps the northern strand of the Interamericana (Panamerican Highway) from joining up with the southern strand. Crossing the Gap was, for many years, one of the most celebrated adventures in Latin America. However, for some time its undertaking has been **banned** by the Panamanian authorities while travellers who have ignored this ruling have disappeared or been killed attempting the trip. It's also worth remembering that there is a **war** raging across the border in Colombia.

Currently the Panamanian authorities do not allow civilians to travel east of Boca de Cupé. The two ways to travel to Colombia are via Guna Yala (see p.562) and along the Caribbean coast (see p.550), or along the Pacific coast, by catching a ride in one of the commercial boats that leaves Panama City or La Palma for Jaqué, and then from there to Colombia. This latter route is not recommended as boats are very infrequent, and will be extremely basic, may lack sufficient life-jackets, or may not be robust enough for the sea when rough.

7

of Darién Province, however small. Brightly painted houses are cake-layered down a steep slope to the waterfront and the town's only **street**, a narrow strip of concrete. The rubbish that clings to the pilings by the water's edge makes the place less scenic than it might be, and there's not a whole lot to do other than soak in the views and watch a game of frenetic five-a-side soccer or basketball at the community sports stadium (on the main street) before moving on.

The main reason to visit La Palma is to organize onward travel to **indigenous communities**, either in the Sambú area, or up slightly more accessible tidal rivers, such as Mogue and La Marea. Afro-Darienite communities such as Punta Alegre are also possible day-trip destinations.

ARRIVAL AND INFORMATION

By boat Boats and water taxis from Puerto Quimba (6am–4.30pm) every 30–45min; 30min; US$4) arrive at the passenger dock below the main street, opposite minimercado La Virgen del Carmen. Return boats to Puerto Quimba are met by the *chiva* back up to Metetí (see p.553). Get to the dock at least 30min before the first or last boat leaves. The last water-taxi back from La Palma leaves at 4.30pm. For boats to Embera and other communities, see below.

Bank Banco Nacional (Mon–Fri 8am–3pm), at the far end of town (take a right from the water-taxi dock), has a 24hr ATM.

Hospital There is a small hospital (☎ 299 6219) behind the main street, to the left of the passenger dock.

ACCOMMODATION AND EATING

Accommodation is extremely basic in La Palma, and there is little culinary joy to be had. Most places keep irregular hours and often close very early.

Hospedaje Tuira Main street ☎ 299 6490. This waterfront building has very basic rooms, with a fan and worn mattresses. A/c costs US$10 more. US$15

★**Hotel Biaquirú Bagará** Main street ☎ 299 6224. This family-run place above a general store is simple but handsome. En-suite rooms with a/c are wood-panelled with bamboo ceilings, and the huge upstairs terrace offers hammocks and breezy sea views. US$25

Maribel's Diagonally opposite the water-taxi dock on the main street. Squeeze into this small hole-in-the-wall café to tuck into fresh fish with coconut rice or *patacones* for around US$4. Daily 7am–7pm.

AROUND LA PALMA

Exploring La Palma's **surroundings** in the **Golfo de San Miguel** and beyond requires a bit of preparation and can be accomplished in several ways.

ARRIVAL AND GETTING AROUND

Information on boat transport Ask at the booth opposite the water-taxi dock for information on boats headed for villages in the surrounding area or at the casa de campesino, located at the far left end of the main street from the water-taxi dock, which is the rest house and general waiting area for visiting villagers. Boats to Sambú/ Puerto Indio (US$20) usually travel Mon, Wed & Fri. Boats to and from other villages that welcome tourists, such as Mogue and La Marea, are more likely on weekdays, with departures depending on the tides.

By cargo boat Sometimes a cargo boat delivering and collecting goods in Darién's villages will be heading in a convenient direction, in which case you may be able to jump aboard for a fee of US$10–20.

By fishing boat Hitching rides with fishermen is the cheapest way to visit nearby communities, beaches and islands – just be sure to check out the condition of the boat beforehand and arrange your pick-up before disembarking.

ARTESANÍA AND SEAFOOD: RICHES OF DARIÉN

Darién's **Golfo de San Miguel**, where the flow of jungle rivers meets the abundant Pacific Ocean, is a nutrient-rich, predator-safe environment in which **seafood** flourishes. Calamari, giant shrimp, sea bass, snapper, black conch, oysters and lobsters are only a few of the marine treats you'll find in many a fisherman's catch – though sadly they don't often make it into the region's restaurants.

The other speciality of the region is the *artesanía* made by the Wounaan and Embera communities: weavings of delicately intricate baskets, plates and masks are made with dyed and natural grasses to create stunning works of art; incredibly intricate carvings are also fashioned out of tagua (vegetable ivory) or cocobolo wood. You can visit indigenous communities, meet the artists and directly support the communities by buying local pieces. Many of the finer items, often sold to exclusive shops in Panama City, where the prices are hiked, take several months to create.

Punta Alegre

You may be able to find a boat from La Palma headed towards the Afro-Darienite fishing village of **PUNTA ALEGRE**, otherwise you'll need to charter a private boat. The trip takes you 17km southeast of La Palma, a fantastic hour or two across the Gulf of San Miguel, passing forested islands and a wild coastline fringed with mangroves and deserted beaches. Once in the village, there's not much to do other than visiting the shell-strewn, jungle-fringed beaches.

Mogue and La Marea

The Embera communities of **Mogue** and the less visited **La Marea** lie in opposing directions from La Palma (see map, p.552), but both offer opportunities to stay in traditional stilted thatched accommodation – in a tourist-allocated place in Mogue and as a homestay in La Marea – and experience the evolving mix of traditional and modernizing village life. In both, possible activities include visiting a harpy eagle nest, hiking, birdwatching, fishing, body painting and learning about and purchasing *artesanía* (see box opposite) – at far cheaper rates than you'll encounter in Panama City. Mogue in particular is renowned for its masks; it also has more developed facilities.

ARRIVAL AND INFORMATION

By boat Community boats from La Palma to either Mogue or La Marea are not scheduled. Contact the respective tourism coordinator for information on river transport, or just turn up in La Palma, make enquiries and be prepared to wait (see opposite).

Tourism coordinators For La Marea contact Turiano ☎ 6742 3615; for Mogue contact Alberto Rito ☎ 6653 3379. Bear in mind that they are without mobile phone coverage much of the time.

Accommodation and eating You'll need to budget for around US$35–40/person/day to cover board and lodging and your tourism coordinator fees. Diet is very limited in both places so stocking up on fresh fish or chicken at La Palma for your allocated cook to prepare is a wise move.

Costs Bank on paying between US$10–20 for each activity or guiding services.

SAMBÚ

The small riverine town of **SAMBÚ**, the most developed settlement for many

kilometres around in this part of the jungle, is the best place to base yourself for affordable exploration in Darién. Although there's little to do in the town itself, a day spent among the locals lends valuable insight into the simple and tough livelihoods of those inhabiting this culturally diverse and isolated community. Moreover, the boat trip up the sinuous Río Sambú is a thrill in itself.

WHAT TO SEE AND DO

Exploring the area around Sambú is most rewarding if you are flexible about where you want to go. Activities range from day-trips **hiking** in the surrounding rainforest, or **fishing** and **birdwatching** on the river, to overnight stays in Embera communities such as **Villa Queresia** – or, when water levels are high enough, remote **Pavarando**, a village marking the last navigable point of the Río Sambú. Your accommodation may be able to fix you up with a guide, and you can organize a guide via the tourism committee in Puerto Indio (see below) if you want to explore the *comarca* itself.

Puerto Indio

A rickety suspension bridge on the edge of the town leads to **PUERTO INDIO**, the administrative centre of the **Comarca Emberá–Wounaan Sambú**. This indigenous territory resides under its own legal jurisdiction, separate from Panamanian law. Locals are deeply protective of their culture and serious about the formalities of receiving visitors. Upon crossing the bridge, the architecture visibly shifts from Sambú's concrete constructions to traditional stilted huts with single-log ladders, though the centre of social life in the late afternoon centres on the basketball court. Visitors should report to the *Cacique Regional* Tino Quintana (regional chief), or a senior member of the tourism committee, in order to pay the US$10 entry fee. The tourism committee can organize tours of Puerto Indio, rainforest hikes – including a visit to a harpy eagle nest – and overnight trips to Villa Queresia and more remote communities.

ARRIVAL AND INFORMATION

By boat The community boats from La Palma to Sambú (Mon, Wed & Fri; 2hr 30min; US$20) leaves the passenger dock some time in the morning, depending on the tide.

By plane Air Panama (⚬airpanama.com) flights arrive from, and depart for, Panama City twice a week (Wed & Sat; 1hr) at the airstrip right by the town.

Registration All tourists arriving in Sambú must register with the frontier police, at the airstrip.

Health There is a health centre across the airstrip, opposite the police station.

Phone The community payphone (☎ 333 2512) is at the end of the airstrip.

ACCOMMODATION AND EATING

Benedicta's Behind a shop close to the airstrip. Sturdy cane building where good breakfasts and filling lunches of *comida típica* are prepared, for around US$4. Evening meals are a case of what's left over. Daily 7am–8pm.

Hotel & Restaurante Mi Sueño At the end of the airstrip. Eleven simple, fan-ventilated wooden rooms with thin mattresses and shared showers, plus a communal balcony overlooking the airstrip. The occasionally functioning restaurant offers cheap meals. <u>US$12</u>

Villa Fiesta At the end of the airstrip ☎ 6687 2271. Fairly comfortable good-value option, offering three en-suite rooms with a/c, which can accommodate 2–4 guests, with firm mattresses and a mini-fridge. <u>US$25</u>

Guna Yala

Stretching nearly 400km, **Guna Yala** – the autonomous *comarca* (territory) of the Guna people – takes in the narrow band of mainland Panama north of the Serranía de San Blas and the sweep of nearly four hundred tropical islands that is the **Guna Yala Archipelago** (often referred to as San Blas or Kuna Yala). Only about forty of the minute islands are inhabited; some strain to contain towns, while others are little more than sandbanks that a lone family has made their home. The administrative capital, **El Porvenir**, lies on a small, narrow island off the tip of the peninsula at the far western end of the *comarca*.

Changes in recent years, including a direct road from Panama City and mobile phone reception for many of the islands, have opened up **travel** in the region, while increasing pressure on the environment and on traditional cultural values.

The Guna gradually made their way here over the centuries, migrating first from Colombia to the Darién region sometime in the sixteenth century. Abandoning that area after years of struggles with the Spanish and the Embera, they settled afresh along the coast and on the islands in the nineteenth century, but it took what they call "the Tule Revolution" in 1925 to have the territory recognized as theirs alone. To this day, no non-Guna may live in the *comarca*; it's a privilege just to enter it and an even greater one to hop among the islands, soaking up their beauty, and to spend the night in the community, perhaps sleeping in the same room as a Guna family. Learning a little about their cultural heritage and observing the fascinating ins and outs of island life are excellent reasons to come here – even if you can't stand idyllic beaches.

WHAT TO SEE AND DO

You're most likely to base yourself on one of the tiny uninhabited islands in western Guna Yala – all of which are palm-topped and encircled by thin white-sand beaches. Accommodation options on each one offer day-trips, usually for a fee, to other picturesque, uninhabited islands. Good bets include the tiny **Isla Perro** (Achutupo – Dog Island; US$2); a cargo ship was wrecked in the shallows here in the 1940s, making for great snorkelling, but it should be avoided if possible at weekends during high season as every speck of sand is likely to be covered by hordes of day-trippers from Panama City. Snorkels can be rented on the beach (US$3). **Isla de las Estrellas**, its shallows dotted with its namesake starfish, is also popular.

The **Cayos Holandéses**, however, are generally considered to offer the most spectacular underwater scenery. Protected by an outer reef, they offer natural swimming pools showcasing an array of sponges and corals that attract rays, reef sharks and a plethora of rainbow-coloured fish. At the outer limit of the *comarca*, 30km from shore, they are inaccessible when the seas are rough (especially Dec–Feb) and the extra fuel needed to reach the cayes means a day-trip here usually carries a hefty supplement.

GUNA CULTURE

Guna society is regulated by a system of highly participative **democracy**: every community has a *casa de congreso* where the *onmakket*, or congress, meets regularly. Each community also elects a *sahila*, usually a respected elder, who attends the Guna General Congress twice a year. The General Congress is the supreme political authority in Guna Yala, and in turn appoints three *caciques* to represent the Guna in the national government.

Colonial missionaries struggled in vain to Christianize the Guna, who cling to their own **religious beliefs**, based above all on the sanctity of Nan Dummad, the Great Mother, and on respect for the environment they inhabit. Though Guna men wear standard Western clothes, **Guna women** wear gold rings in their ears and noses and blue vertical lines painted on their foreheads; they don headscarves and bright bolts of trade cloth round their waists, their forearms and calves are bound in coloured beads and their blouses are sewn with beautiful reverse-appliqué designs known as **molas**.

Given that no non-Guna is permitted to own property on the islands and that **tourism** is a prickly issue, your status as an outsider is symbolic and your behaviour will probably be scrutinized. Cover up on the inhabited islands and cut out public displays of affection. You must ask permission from the **saila** (chief) to visit inhabited islands in the less touristy central and eastern islands of the *comarca* – ask the advice of people you meet to find a contact – and to take photographs, which are banned on some islands, as is alcohol.

In 2011 the general congress passed a law to standardize the Guna alphabet, removing the letters "p", "t" and "k". Thus the area previously known as Kuna Yala is now called Guna Yala, though the pronunciation remains the same.

7

Other excursions are sometimes made to an inhabited island, or to the mainland to visit a **Guna cemetery** or to go for a walk through the rainforest to a **waterfall**.

All of the islands are privately "owned" by the Guna, and when your hotel drops you off for an afternoon of sun-drenched laziness you will be approached for your payment of a visitor tax, usually US$2–5 – check with your guide beforehand, as it may be included in the price of the trip. When going on an excursion, be sure to bring **water** and something to do, whether it's a book, a pack of cards or snorkelling gear (though some islands do have snorkelling gear for rent).

Carti

Carti refers to a group of islands and an area on the mainland at the western end of Guna Yala. **Carti Sugdub** (Sugdub is also frequently used) is the most populated island in western Guna Yala, with a health centre, school, library and a couple of small restaurants.

The island is crowded, with little to do aside from visit the small, interesting **museum** (US$5; US$3 if you go with a Guna guide). Fascinatingly cluttered, it's covered floor-to-ceiling with drawings and paintings in various styles – some by children – representing different aspects of Guna culture, myth and history. If you're lucky enough to be visiting in the days leading up to the anniversary of the 1925 Guna revolution on February 25, you can catch dramatizations of the clashes that took place between the Guna and the Panamanian authorities, for which a number of the islanders dress, disconcertingly, as police officers.

Swimming is not an option on Carti Sugdub, as much of the waste ends up in the surrounding waters.

Icodub

Also known as Isla Aguja (or Needle Island), **Icodub** is topped with dreamy coconut palms and fronted by a lovely beach with a beach volleyball court. Prices are slightly higher here than on many of the other western islands, as facilities are slightly more developed. You should avoid weekends in the dry season and holiday periods, however, when the island is inundated with visitors from Panama City. Day-trippers to the island are charged US$5.

Isla Iguana

Providing a simple castaway experience, slender **Isla Iguana** (or Aridub) is fairly

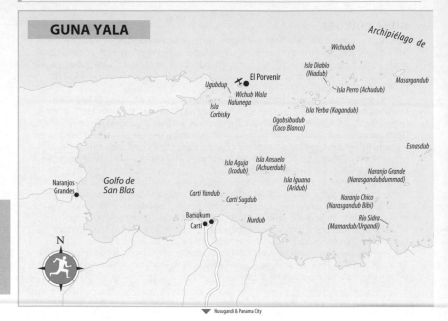

GUNA YALA

Archipiélago de

Wichudub

Isla Diablo (Niadub)

El Porvenir

Ugubdup

Wichub Wala

Nalunega

Isla Corbisky

Masargandub

Isla Perro (Achudub)

Isla Yerba (Kagandub)

Ogobsibudub (Coco Blanco)

Esnasdub

Isla Aguja (Icodub)

Isla Ansuelo (Achuerdub)

Naranjos Grandes

Golfo de San Blas

Carti Yandup

Carti Sugdub

Isla Iguana (Aridub)

Barsukum

Carti

Nurdub

Naranjo Grande (Narasgandubdummad)

Naranjo Chico (Narasgandub Bibi)

Río Sidra (Mamardub/Urgandi)

N

Nusugandi & Panama City

---

undeveloped and quiet, with a palm-shaded beach and volleyball court.

Senidup

Offering some of the cheapest and most popular lodging in Guna Yala, postage-stamp-sized **Senidup** can be circumnavigated in a matter of minutes – at a leisurely amble along a pristine beach. It is divided into two lots of accommodation, either side of a chainlink fence.

Naranjo Chico

Narasgandub Bibi, or **Naranjo Chico**, which both translate as "Little Orange Island", is a backpacker favourite, with several options for bedding down, a spread of lush vegetation sprinkled with hibiscus flowers, and a lovely swathe of a coconut-palm-fringed beach, though the island's recent increase in popularity is beginning to take its toll.

ARRIVAL AND INFORMATION

The easiest way to experience the Guna Yala Archipelago is to book a package deal to an island in western Guna Yala through one of the Panama City hostels (see p.536). It is possible to visit independently, for around the same price.

Entry fee All visitors, including non-Guna Panamanians, have to pay an entry fee to the *comarca* (US$20 for foreigners), collected at the entry point to the *comarca*; this fee is not usually included in any package, though it's worth checking.

Supplies The prices given here for accommodation, and those quoted for tours, are per person per night, and include three basic meals. Meal portions are often quite small in the really budget places, so it's a good idea to bring extra snacks, and large containers of water with you, as water is not drinkable in Guna Yala – be sure to take the empty containers back out with you. When travelling by road, whether travelling independently or on a package deal, you will usually stop off at a supermarket en route, where you can stock up on supplies.

Electricity Bring a torch, as electricity, if there is any, is usually switched off at around 9 or 10pm.

INDEPENDENT TRAVEL

By plane Air Panama (☎316 9000, ⍟airpanama.com) provides daily flights from Albrook airport in Panama City from around US$75 one way. In the archipelago, the principal airstrip for visitors is on El Porvenir. Other destinations include Achutupo, Corazón de Jesús, Mulatupo, Playón Chico (30min–1hr 15min) and Puerto Obaldía (see p.562). Flights theoretically leave around 6am and island hop but are frequently delayed or cancelled, and there are sometimes flights not listed on the website, so phone in advance. To book a return flight when in the archipelago, you can ring Air Panama and reserve on a

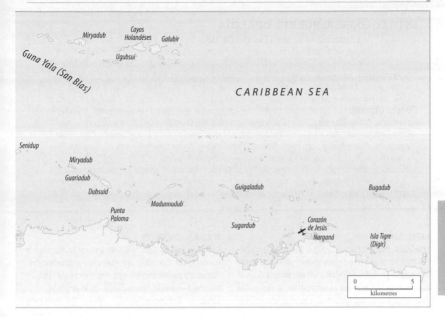

7

credit card, which is swiped on arrival in Panama City. Luggage exceeding 12kg incurs a surcharge of one percent of the published fare.

By 4WD You can book transport for US$30 each way (the standard price) by calling Guna Yala transport in Panama City (☎ 225 4900 or ☎ 225 2387) to arrange a pick-up at your lodgings.

Accommodation Most lodgings accept independent bookings and will pick you up from the jetty at the old Carti airstrip, or at Barsukum river dock (where you'll pay a US$2 "river tax"). With more expensive lodging there's no charge for this ride – just confirm in advance; otherwise you'll pay US$20–30 return from the dock to your island lodging depending on where you're staying. All the accommodation we have listed below can also be booked through the Panama City hostels (see p.536).

TOURS

Budget tours Budget tours to the region usually comprise transport from Panama City by 4WD to the Carti or neighbouring Barsukum dock (3hr), pick up from here by the owners of the accommodation you have been booked into, and transport by boat to the designated island, though sometimes that's extra. A night's stay as part of a package costs from US$25–35 in a dorm at the budget end of the scale, which includes three basic set meals. Most lodgings also offer excursions to other islands (from US$5–30, depending on demand, distance to the island and the quality of the boat).

ACCOMMODATION AND EATING

CARTI SUGDUB

Hospedajes There are several *hospedajes* in Carti Sugdub, but given the wealth of uncrowded *islitas* nearby – where you can loll on empty beaches and snorkel in crystalline waters – you are unlikely to find a reason to spend the night.

Restaurants Carti Sugdub has a handful of restaurants that serve up fried chicken, rice, salad and lentils for around US$4.

ICODUB

Cabañas Icodub ☎ 6660 7908. Accommodation is in tents – mattress, pillow and sheets provided – or in a handful of cane or wooden cabañas, some of them en suite, with use of hammocks and deckchairs for an additional few dollars. You get a proper tiled toilet/shower block here, and a tiled restaurant – seafood, pork and chicken are usually on the dinner buffet menu, but you have to pay extra for lobster or *langostinos*. You can also pitch your own tent here (US$16/person – meals not included). Tents/person US$40, cabañas: shared bathroom US$50, cabañas: en suite US$60

ISLA IGUANA

Cabañas Iguana ☎ 6807 2764 or ☎ 6151 7379. A clutch of cane-and-thatch huts, and a small bar-restaurant on a raised wooden deck, serving tasty seafood. Dorms US$35, cabañas US$50

7

INTO COLOMBIA: PUERTO OBALDÍA

You can enter **Colombia** by boat via **Puerto Obaldía**, a remote border outpost at the far southeastern edge of Guna Yala, served by light aircraft from Panama City. Air Panama flies three times a week (Tues, Sat & Sun; 1hr; US$94); seats go quickly so book in advance. After going through customs and providing the Colombian consulate with proof of onward travel, you can take a **boat** (about US$10) to Capurganá, a small fishing village and holiday resort on the Colombian coast, where DAS (🖰 das.gov.co) will stamp your passport. You can also reach **Puerto Obaldía** or Capurganá by using the occasional speedboat service from Carti offered by Andutu in Panama City (Av Justo Arosemena & C 34; ☎ 6060 9104, 🖰 andutu.com). The 7hr journey costs US$125, or US$165 including taxes and land transfer from Panama City. From Capurganá, ADA (🖰 ada-aero.com) flies to Medellín and other destinations in Colombia. There are also boats from Capurganá across the Gulf of Urabá to Turbo (US$30). From Turbo you can catch one of the regular light aircraft flights to Medellín and Cartagena, or continue your journey by bus. There are places to change money around the border, but they charge hefty commission, so it is best to change only a small amount; Turbo is the first place with an ATM.

SENIDUP

Franklin's Place (officially *Cabañas Dubesenika*) ☎ 299 690 2863. Party spot with eighteen tightly packed cane huts with sand floors, a dirt-volleyball court and dreamy views of a palm-framed Caribbean. Guests share a communal shower/toilet area, and luxuries such as juice, snacks, beer and cigarettes can be bought at the main "office". Rates include (basic and sometimes small) meals. Because of the larger numbers, island-hopping boat trips and fishing excursions are cheap. Dorms US$26, cabañas US$35

★TREAT YOURSELF

If you're interested in Guna culture, and want to escape the backpacker scene, you can't do better than a stay on **Isla Tigre** (or Digir), one of the most traditional communities, which still practises many communal activities.

The Guna dance originated here, and the island attracts dance troupes from all over the *comarca* in the annual **Feria de Isla Tigre** in mid-October. A slender, elongated island, it is partitioned into two: the village proper with a wide, sandy main street, and the grassy tourism-designated area, which contains a handful of simple cane cabañas (dorms US$10, en-suite double US$30), a sliver of beach, a rancho hung with hammocks, and an excellent bar-restaurant offering some of the best food in the *comarca*; the bar is also a good place to meet some of the (male) villagers. The best way to get here is to fly to Corazón de Jesús (US$136 return), from where it's a 30min boat ride to the island (US$5 in *colectivo*). To reserve, ring ☎ 6099 2738, or just turn up.

NARANJO CHICO

Cabañas Ina (☎ 6035 7692). Backpacker favourite with the best strip of beach, a volleyball court and hammocks. Visitors are packed into ten-bed dorms and cane cabañas housing 2–4 people. Dorms US$25, cabañas US$50

Cabañas Robinson (☎ 6721 9885). The engaging Arnulfo Robinson runs what are probably the cheapest cane huts in the whole of western Guna Yala – so don't expect much, though they are enlivened by the odd flowerbed. Shared makeshift shower and bathroom and rock-bottom-priced excursions too. Dorms US$20, cabañas US$25

Central Panama and the Península de Azuero

Central Panama is a strikingly diverse region. Heading west from Panama City the **Interamericana** runs along a narrow plain squeezed between the Pacific and the slopes of the Cordillera Central. Your bus will barely have hit top speed before you can hop off and spend some time sprawled on one of the abundant **beaches** just south of the Interamericana. Though they're fine for a weekend escape from Panama City, they don't compare with the offerings on some of the Islas Perlas, or the islands of the Golfo de Chiriquí, Bocas del Toro or Guna Yala. It is, however, worth heading north off the Interamericana to spend a night in the relative cool of **El Valle**, a popular retreat for the capital's elite, before venturing further into spectacular mountain scenery round the village of **El Copé** and the **Parque Nacional Omar Torrijos**.

At the border of Coclé Province, 193km from Panama City, the road forks at **Divisa**: the Interamericana continues west to Santiago, the capital of Veraguas Province, but consider turning south down the Carretera Nacional into the **Península de Azuero**, which hosts some of the country's most vibrant festivals in the colonial towns of Guararé and Las Tablas, contains some splendid surfing beaches, and has two fascinating islands – Isla Iguana and Isla Cañas – to explore.

EL VALLE

About 100km west of Panama City, a twisty road climbs up into the cordillera to **EL VALLE**, a small village in a fertile valley that was once the crater of a volcano. At 600m above sea level, El Valle is comparatively cool, and the surrounding countryside is good for walking or horseriding. Renowned for its flowers – particularly orchids – the area is a favourite getaway for wealthy Panama City residents at weekends, when the place is awash with 4WDs and golf carts.

WHAT TO SEE AND DO

Most of the village's amenities can be found on **Avenida Central** (also called Avenida Principal), along with signposts pointing the way to local attractions, mostly located on the outskirts of the village. In the centre, the modest daily market draws the biggest crowds, especially on Sundays, when locals sell fruit, flowers and crafts. A small **museum** (Sat & Sun 10am–2pm, but ask for David across the road at other times; US$0.75), run by nuns, houses exhibits on local history and folklore and stands next to the church of San José. Beyond the church by the Río Anton, a side road leads to the enjoyably quirky **thermal baths** (daily 8am–5pm; US$3), or *pozos termales*, reputed to have medicinal powers – they

are best avoided on summer weekends and during holidays. Meanwhile, to see wonderful specimens of the orchids that grow around here, explore the **APROVACA Orchid Nursery**, signposted off to the left from the main road as you enter town (daily 9am–4pm; US$2). There's also a pretty, if vastly overpriced, butterfly house (daily 9am–4pm in high season; otherwise closed Tues and in Oct; US$5) and a rather cramped serpentarium (open daily – hours irregular; US$3). Horseriding is also an option – enquire at the kiosk before *Hotel Campestre*, in Calle El Hato.

El Chorro Macho

One of the most worthwhile sights in the vicinity of El Valle, **El Chorro Macho** is a 35m waterfall in a private reserve (daily 8am–5pm; US$4), with **ziplines** (8am–3.30pm; US$54) fitted around it. However, with just five ziplines, one of which crosses the waterfall, it's only worth a trip if you aren't heading for Boquete, which boasts the country's best canopy adventure. To get here, take a local bus headed for La Mesa from Avenida Central, or walk (30min along the main road round to the right at the western end of town).

El Nispero zoo and plant nursery

Head 1km up a signposted side road off Avenida Central to visit the **El Nispero zoo and plant nursery** (daily 7am–5pm; US$5). It's a great spot to view the many orchids that grow here – as well as Panama's endangered golden frog, housed in a new amphibian centre – but the animals generally aren't the happiest-looking creatures.

Hiking trails

Innumerable trails climb up into the **cloudforests** of the surrounding mountains. Best known is the trail that peaks at **La India Dormida**, a mountain ridge looming west of the valley, whose silhouette quite strikingly resembles a woman lying on her back. The passage to the **Piedra Pintada** (US$3 community fee), an ancient rock with petroglyphs, is somewhat less visited, with a series of waterfalls to cool you

7

down on the way. **Cerro Gaital**, which dominates the town and is often swathed in mist, is an even greater challenge, but doable without a guide.

ARRIVAL AND INFORMATION

By bus Buses pull in at the covered market on Av Central. There are direct buses from Panama City (7.30am–6.30pm; every 30min; 2hr 30min); the last bus back to the capital leaves from the market at 4pm. Coming into El Valle from the west, get off at "*la entrada*" at Las Uvas and catch a bus up to El Valle; heading back west, catch a Panama City or San Carlos bus (every 20min) to the junction with the Interamericana (40min), where you can flag down a bus heading west. There is also an irregular bus service from Penonomé (8 buses daily, last return bus from El Valle at 3.15pm; 1hr 20min).

Tourist information The small, helpful ATP office (daily 8.30am–3.30pm) is in a kiosk next to the market; they can provide you with a map and will ring for accommodation, but your hostel owner will probably have as much knowledge about tourist activities in the area. Also check ⓦel-valle-panama.com.

Bike rental *Don Pepe's*, by the market, and a few other places rent bicycles (US$2/hr, US$15/day).

Banks Banco Nacional has an ATM on Av Principal, near the turn-off for El Nispero; there's also an ATM in the supermarket.

Internet There are a couple of internet cafés on Av Central, both charging US$1/hr.

ACCOMMODATION

Accommodation prices in El Valle reflect its popularity among wealthy Panamanians, who flock here for Carnaval, public holidays and weekends, when prices are often higher. That said, there are a couple of newly open options catering to travellers on a tighter budget; most accept cash only.

APROVACA Orchid Nursery Signposted left off Av Central, on the way into town ☎ 983 6472. A quiet place to stay, though it is looking a little careworn. Bag a bunk in a six-bed dorm with interior bathroom or in one of their two en-suite rooms. There's a small kitchen, patio area and laundry facilities. Rates include wi-fi and entry to the orchid nursery. Dorms US$12, doubles US$25

★**Cabañas Potosí** 150m past the church, take the road to the right, then the fork to the left and continue for 1.5km ☎ 983 6181, ⓦ elvallepotosi.com. Comfortable, good-looking rooms in smart concrete cabañas with plenty of birdlife in the garden. Also offers camping across the road (bring your own tent, or pay an extra US$10 for an equipped tent) with bathroom and kitchen facilities. Camping/person US$5, doubles US$59

La Casita de Don Daniel At the foot of La India Dormida ☎ 6615 5511, ✉ lacasitadedondaniel@hotmail.com. Friendly, family environment with three inexpensive

double rooms and a riverside campsite, where you can rent a tent (US$20) or pitch your own, with use of bathrooms and communal kitchen. Local crafts are sold on site, while the weekends offer live music and snacks. Best to contact in advance as not always open. Camping/tent US$10, doubles US$40

Windmill Hostel 60m off Av Central ☎ 6344 1199, ⓦ windmillhostel.com. Run by long-standing US residents of El Valle, this place may lack the hostel vibe but offers great value with comfortable, if dark, private rooms and dorms with plenty of amenities – well-equipped kitchen, several shared bathrooms, swimming pool, hammock-strung rancho, table tennis, bike hire, etc. Book in advance as it's often full. Dorms US$15, doubles US$30

EATING

Buon Appetito Off Av Central before the Cano bakery ☎ 6401 6301. Top-notch, authentic Italian restaurant serving scrumptious crispy pizzas (from US$6) and home-made pasta favourites. Very popular, so you'll need to book. Thurs 6–9pm, Fri & Sat noon–9pm, Sun noon–8pm.

Carlito's Av Central close to the market. At weekends this popular chain's patio restaurant is the liveliest spot on the street, plying non-greasy Argentinian *empanadas* and average pizzas and burgers (from US$9) as well as a few pricier fish and meat dishes. Daily 11am–8pm.

Panadería y Dulcería Cano Av Central. Just the place to stock up on sticky buns, cakes and bread to keep you going on a hike. Daily 7.30am–8pm.

Restaurante Massiel Av Central. Friendly, efficient place serving *comida típica* and fast food – chicken with rice is US$6 and hamburger combos go for much the same. Also good for breakfast. Daily 5.30am–4pm or 5pm.

PENONOMÉ AND AROUND

Founded in 1581 as a *reducción de Indios* – a place where conquered indigenous groups were forcibly resettled so as to be available for labour service – and briefly the capital of the isthmus after the destruction of Panamá Viejo, **PENONOMÉ** was named after Nomé, a local chieftain cruelly betrayed and executed here by the Spaniards after years of successful resistance. Now the capital of Coclé Province, Penonomé doesn't have much to see apart from the pretty stained-glass window in the main church and a small museum, though it makes a good enough base for exploring the surrounding area, and if you're in the area during Carnaval, make sure you catch Penonomé's unique **aquatic parade**.

Chiguirí Arriba

Of the potential destinations in the mountains, **Chiguirí Arriba**, 29km to the northeast, makes an easy day-trip from Penonomé. There are plenty of good hiking trails, spectacular views, plump red chickens running about and Cascada Tavida, a 30m waterfall nearby (US$5).

ARRIVAL AND DEPARTURE

PENONOMÉ

By bus In addition to direct buses from Panama City to Penonomé (4.50am–10.45pm; every 20 min; 2hr), buses from the capital bound for Chitré (hourly; 1hr 30min), Las Tablas (hourly; 2hr) and Santiago (every 30min; 1hr 30min) pick up and drop off in Penonomé at the Interamericana opposite the *Hotel Dos Continentes* at the junction with Av Arosemena (Vía Central). Buses from Penonomé for Panama City leave every 15min (2hr) south of the Interamericana at that junction.

By minibus From the market area, *chivas* and *busitos* (minibuses) head off into the mountains, aiming for Chiguirí Arriba (6am–6.30pm; every 15min; 1hr) and El Copé (6am–9pm; every 20min; 1hr), as well as buses to El Valle (6am–5.30pm; 10 daily at irregular intervals; 1hr 20min).

ACCOMMODATION AND EATING

PENONOMÉ

Hotel Dos Continentes Av Arosemena (Vía Central), at Interamericana, opposite the bus terminal ☎ 997 9325, ⓦ hoteldoscontinentes.net. Large, sprawling place offering unironically retro en-suite rooms, with a/c, sleeping up to four. The very popular restaurant serves good food: try the shrimp omelette and *patacones* (US$6) and steak and fish dishes (from US$7). They also serve *bollo* – plantain mashed and then compacted into chunks (tastier than it sounds). Rooms are more expensive at weekends. U̲S̲$̲4̲4̲
Panadería y Pizzería El Paísa Vía Central, just before the church. Busy bakery with a large selection of bread, pastries and sandwiches (US$2–4), with an adjoining pizza joint, plus outdoor seating where you can soak up the town's atmosphere. Bakery daily 6am–10pm; pizzeria daily 1–10pm, closed Mon.

PARQUE NACIONAL OMAR TORRIJOS

Straddling the continental divide just over 30km northwest of Penonomé is the little-visited but spectacular **Parque Nacional Omar Torrijos** (often called "El Copé" after the nearby village of the same name; US$5), named after Panama's flamboyant populist leader whose plane mysteriously crashed into one of the park's highest peaks. Scenery ranges from mist-shrouded cloudforest to abundant subtropical vegetation, offering excellent opportunities for birdwatching and hiking, and the park is chock-full of wildlife.

ARRIVAL AND INFORMATION

By bus and minibus To get here, take a bus from Penonomé to El Copé, where you can connect with a sporadic local minibus to the village of Barrigón. From here you'll need to hike the remaining 4km up to the park entrance, or hire a 4WD pick-up (around US$6).
Guides and tours To make the most of the area, and to enjoy the services of a guide, it's a good idea to stay in the park or nearby, either in Barrigón or in the small community of La Rica, which, a day's trek over the continental divide, enjoys a verdant setting laced with waterfalls; contact the Navas family (see below).

ACCOMMODATION

ANAM refugio Park entrance. A refuge offering bunks, kitchen and camping space – bring your own food and sleeping bag and wrap up warm. Camping/person U̲S̲$̲5̲, dorms U̲S̲$̲1̲5̲
🔺 **Navas family** Barrigón ☎ 902 8130. The welcoming and experienced Navas family offer simple rooms in their home, excellent guiding services and tasty home-cooking. Per person, including meals and guide U̲S̲$̲3̲5̲

CHITRÉ

The capital of Herrera Province and the largest town on the Azuero Peninsula, **CHITRÉ** is a slow-paced market centre studded with colourful discount stores. Other than the market and a museum, there's not much to see here, but the town is the peninsula's main transport hub and a good base for exploration.

WHAT TO SEE AND DO

Chitré centres on the bandstand, trees and benches of **Parque Unión**. The square is flanked on one side by the gleaming white **Catedral San Juan Bautista**, with its impressive, vaulted wooden roof and extensive gilded wooden panelling.

Museo de Herrera

Chitré cathedral faces down Avenida Herrera – walk down a block and turn left onto Calle Manuel Correa and you'll reach the **Museo de Herrera** (Tues–Sat

7

8am–noon & 1–4pm, Sun 8am–noon; US$1), three blocks away. This is probably the best museum outside Panama City, set in an elegant colonial mansion, exhibiting a collection of pre-Columbian pottery from the surrounding area with a good display on local folklore and customs, featuring traditional masks, costumes and musical instruments.

ARRIVAL AND INFORMATION

By bus Buses to and from Panama City and other destinations pull in at the terminal on the southern outskirts of town, 1km (or a 15min walk) from the centre. Local buses run to the centre from the bus terminal; buses returning to the bus terminal can be boarded at the main square, or outside the museum.

Destinations Las Tablas (every 15min; 45min); Panama City (hourly; 4hr); Santiago (every 30min; 1hr 20min).

Tourist information There's a CEFATI office in the Parque Industrial La Arena, on the road into town (☎ 974 4532).

ACCOMMODATION

Don't expect to find anywhere to stay during Santa Librada or Carnaval (see box below).

Hotel Rex Opposite Parque Unión ☎ 996 2391. The fanciest spot in central Chitré, overlooking the park but with faded furnishings. A/c rooms come with breakfast in the on-site restaurant. US$45

Hotel Santa Rita C Correa & Av Herrera, north of the cathedral ☎ 996 4610. Run by the same family for over a hundred years, this friendly, central hotel has lost its period charm but its clean, though rather dark, crumbling fan-ventilated rooms are excellent value (a/c is US$5 more). You may want to test out a few rooms, as some of the mattresses aren't up to much. US$23

Miami Mike's Av Herrera at C Correa, north of the cathedral ☎ 910 0628, ⓦ miamimikeshostel.com. The only real hostel in town, with a massive roof terrace, cheerfully painted themed rooms and an affable American owner, who's happy to provide you with travel info. Also a communal kitchen, living room, wi-fi and lockers – but cleanliness is not high on the agenda. Dorms US$10, doubles US$30

EATING

Panadería Chiquita Av Herrera. Large open-fronted café; a popular spot to grab a sticky bun or *empanada* with a Styrofoam cup of coffee or *chicha*, all for under US$1.50. Daily 5am–10pm.

★ **Pizzería Ebeneezer** A couple of blocks southwest of the church. Appealing place with indoor and patio seating serving inexpensive pizzas from US$5, alongside tacos, burritos and the odd Greek dish. No alcohol. Mon–Sat 11.30am–10pm, Sun 4–10pm.

Restaurante El Aire Libre Av Obaldía, Parque Unión on the corner opposite the church. Small restaurant, often overflowing at lunchtime, serving a tasty *menú del día* for just over US$3 and other dishes for US$3–4. Daily 6am–9pm.

FESTIVALS IN THE PENÍNSULA DE AZUERO

Jutting out into the Pacific Ocean, the **Península de Azuero** was one of the first regions of Panama to be settled by Spanish colonists. The towns and villages you come across – the main recommended bases include Chitré, Las Tablas and Pedasí – in this dry, scrubby landscape hum with their colonial heritage, visually manifested in the traditional handicrafts and folk costumes of the region, but the real giveaway is the gusto with which the people throw themselves into their **religious fiestas**. Usually honouring a particular patron saint, many of these date back almost unchanged to the days of the early settlers. Religious processions are accompanied by traditional music, fireworks and costumed folk dances, which are as pagan as they are Catholic. As the night wears on the *seco* tends to flow and DJs take over. Listed below are just a few of the major events; every village and hamlet has its own fiesta, and there's almost always one going on somewhere.

Jan 6 Fiesta de Los Reyes and Encuentro del Canajagua, Macaracas.

Jan 19–22 Fiesta de San Sebastián, Ocú.

Feb (date varies) Carnaval in Las Tablas (and everywhere else in the country).

March/April (date varies) Semana Santa, celebrated most colourfully in La Villa de Los Santos, Pesé and Guararé.

Late April Feria International del Azuero, La Villa de Los Santos.

May/June (date varies) Corpus Christi, La Villa de Los Santos.

June 24 Patronales de San Juan, Chitré.

July 20–22 Patronales de La Santa Librada and Festival de La Pollera, Las Tablas.

Aug (second week) Festival del Manito, Ocú.

Late Sept Festival de la Mejorana, Guararé.

Nov 10 The "First Cry of Independence", La Villa de Los Santos.

LAS TABLAS

LAS TABLAS, south along the peninsula's coast from Chitré, was founded in the seventeenth century by refugees fleeing by sea from Panamá Viejo after Henry Morgan and his band of pirates sacked it. The settlers dismantled their ships to build the first houses, hence the town's name, which means "the planks".

Though you wouldn't believe it if you turned up at any other time of year, this quiet, colonial market town hosts the wildest **Carnaval** celebrations in Panama. For five days in February the place is overwhelmed by visitors from all over the country, who come here to join in the festivities. The town divides into two halves – **Calle Arriba** and **Calle Abajo** – to fight a pitched battle with water, paint and soot on streets awash with *seco*, Panama's vicious firewater. Less raucous but just as colourful is the fiesta of **Santa Librada** in July, which includes the **Festival de la Pollera**, celebrating the peninsula's embroidered, colonial-style dresses. Produced in the surrounding villages, they are something of a national symbol.

WHAT TO SEE AND DO

In addition to its few sights, Las Tablas is also a choice spot to experience the extremely festive atmosphere of a **baseball** match (Jan–May) at the Estadio Olmedo Solé.

Iglesia de Santa Librada

On the main square, known as **Parque Porras**, the **Iglesia de Santa Librada** is the most popular sight in Las Tablas. The church has a magnificent golden altar illuminating an otherwise dull interior, with a figurine of the patron saint, set in the facade's apex, overlooking the square.

Museo Belisario Porras

In a lovely colonial building diagonally across the square from the church, the tiny **Museo Belisario Porras** (Tues–Sat 9.30am–4pm, Sun 8am–noon; US$1) houses an array of belongings and articles pertaining to Panama's most revered president, who was born here in 1856. An enthusiastic guide will proudly explain (in Spanish only) the considerable achievements of the great man and the significance of items on display, including presidential correspondence and several splendid outfits worn by Porras – a lovingly assembled collection, best suited to history buffs.

ARRIVAL AND DEPARTURE

By bus Buses from Panama City arrive at and leave from the bus terminal on Av Laureano López, near the Shell station, a few blocks from the main square (hourly 6am–7pm; 4hr 30min). Buses from Chitré (6am–9pm; every 10min; 45min) drop off at Parque Porras, then pull up on Av Porras a few blocks beyond the square, outside a supermarket, behind the minibuses that run to Pedasí (6am–6.45pm; every 45min; 45min). Return buses to Chitré can be flagged down on C Espino, which runs parallel to Av Porras. The daily bus to Playa Venao (1–2pm; 1hr 30min) leaves half a block north of the plaza round the corner from Pharmacy Miriam. To head west from Las Tablas, take a Panama City bus and get off at Divisa. Cross over the highway to catch westbound buses for either Santiago (30min), roughly the halfway point between Panama City and David, or David itself. Alternatively, take a bus to Chitré, where you can get a direct connection to Santiago.

ACCOMMODATION

If you want to come for Carnaval, you'll have to book several months in advance, though people do rent out rooms in their houses to make up for the shortfall in accommodation, and you could always join the hordes that sleep in the park.

Hotel Piamonte Av Porras ☎ 923 1903. Rooms vary in quality, so ask to see a few; the smaller, cheaper rooms in the annexe over the road – without hot water or wi-fi – offer better value. There's also a restaurant. US$40

Hotel Sol del Pacífico C Cano ☎ 994 1280. The best value in town, offering simple en-suite rooms with double bed and a/c plus cable TV, or pricier ones with three beds (US$55) and mini-fridge; also now with some larger, fancier, and more expensive rooms on the ground floor. US$30

EATING AND DRINKING

Bamboo Parque Porras ☎ 923 1910. Bar-restaurant offering cheap drinks and Panamanian pub grub (steak or pork chops and chips), on an upstairs balcony, with atmospheric views of the park and town below. DJs and live music, especially on Fri. Wed–Sun from 4pm.

★**Restaurante El Caserón** C Agustín Bautista. The fancy joint in town, with lots of wood and cheery red tablecloths, charging surprisingly modest prices. Their mixed meat grills (US$7–9), the house speciality, are highly recommended. Daily 7am–11pm.

7

DIRECTORY

Banks Av Porras is awash with banks and ATMs.

Pharmacy There are two on Parque Porras.

Post office C Francisco González, three blocks north of the square on a road parallel to Av López (Mon–Fri 7am–5pm, Sat 7am–1pm).

PEDASÍ

It's 42km south through cattle country from Las Tablas to **PEDASÍ**, a friendly, quiet little village that is fast becoming a surf destination, best known as a jumping-off point for Isla Iguana, Isla Cañas and a wealth of beaches in the surrounding area.

WHAT TO SEE AND DO

Other than having a quick peek at the unlikely chandeliers in the **church** on the town square, activities in Pedasí involve day-trips to the **islands and the nearby surf breaks** (see opposite).

Playa El Arenal

Playa El Arenal, a very long, very empty and very flat beach, is just a thirty-minute walk from town (US$3 by taxi).

ARRIVAL AND DEPARTURE

By bus Buses pull up on the main street that runs through the town in front of *The Bakery*. Buses for La Tablas (6am–6pm; every 45min; 45min) leave from beside the supermarket. The three daily services for Cañas village (7am, noon & 2–2.30pm, but often leaves early or late; 1hr) pass Playa Venao; two depart from the main street and the last bus passes through en route from Las Tablas (see p.535). Bus timetables are subject to change, so check locally.

By taxi Taxis hang out beside the supermarket, charging the following rates: Playa Arenal US$3; Playa de los Destiladores US$7; Playa Venao US$24; Isla Cañas US$30.

INFORMATION AND TOURS

Tourist information The ATP office (Mon–Fri 8.30am–3.30pm) is on the second left as you enter the village from the north.

Tours Dive 'N' Fish, a certified dive shop and tour operator based in Pedasí Sports Club (ⓦ pedasisportsclub.com), and Pedasí Tours (ⓦ pedasitours.com) both organize snorkelling tours to Isla Iguana, horseriding in the hills, and seasonal (June–Oct) whale-watching trips or nocturnal trips to Isla de Cañas for turtle-watching (see p.570) – most for US$50–100/person. Shokogi, an Israeli-run outfit, offers trips in the area as well as kitesurfing and SUP lessons and

rentals (ⓣ 6921 1532, ⓦ surfpedasi.com). Most lodgings can rustle up a boat for you to visit Isla Iguana.

Banks Banco Nacional and Caja de Ahorros, both on the main street, have ATMs.

ACCOMMODATION

★**Dim's Hostal** Main street ⓣ 995 2303. This long-established option has pretty, cosy en-suite rooms with dainty curtains and comfortable beds. There's a hammock-slung patio in the lush garden out back with a large, palm-thatched roof anchored to the trunk of a vast mango tree – a nice place for a beer and a snooze. Prices include buffet breakfast, a/c, wi-fi and TV. <u>US$52</u>

Residencial Moscoso Main street ⓣ 995 2203. Well acquainted with backpackers, the *Moscoso* is rudimentary but clean and inexpensive – the reception is in the owner's living room. Rooms (fan-ventilated; a/c US$10 more) have shared or private bathroom. <u>US$20</u>

EATING

PEDASÍ

Bienvenidush C Agustín Moscoso. Small deli-cum-wine bar serving healthy light bites; freshly prepared wraps, hummus, shawarma and the like (from US$5), enjoyed with a glass of wine. Daily 11am–4pm & 7–10pm; closed Tues.

Dulcería Yely Main street, diagonally opposite *Residencial Moscoso*. Legendary cake shop with a cabinet full of stodgy sponges and crispy pastry *empanadas* (from around US$2), to be enjoyed with a cup of *chicha* or a shot of coffee. Daily 6am–9pm.

★**Pasta y Vino** Road to Playa El Toro, three blocks from the plaza ⓣ 6695 2689. Authentic Italian home-cooking in the owners' house – so with only a handful of tables (book ahead) – and a small, though changing, menu of lovingly prepared, inexpensive food. Tues–Sun 6–10pm.

Restaurante El Ejecutivo C Las Tablas, across from the square. The cheap choice, with *típica* breakfasts for US$4 and heaped greasy dishes of beef, chicken, pork or fish with rice or *patacones* and a small salad from US$6. Mon & Wed–Sun 8am–10pm, Tues 5–10pm.

PLAYA EL ARENAL

Coco's The beach. Owned by a local co-operative and serving delicious fried fish (US$4 with *patacones*), fresh from the fishermen's nets, at rock-bottom prices – an experience enhanced by the view, the beer and the sense of calm. No fixed hours.

AROUND PEDASÍ

Pedasí is a great base from which to explore the area's fascinating marine attractions. You can set off in search of whales, iguanas and sea turtles, safe in the knowledge that you can come back and lay your head somewhere cosy.

Isla Iguana

Some 7km off the coast of Pedasí lies **Isla Iguana** (US$10), an uninhabited wildlife reserve managed by the state and surrounded by the most extensive **coral reefs** in the Bahía de Panamá, making it one of the best sites for **snorkelling** and **diving** in the country. The island has white-sand beaches, crystalline waters and a vast colony of magnificent frigate birds, and between June and December you may see **whales**. Despite the island's name, iguanas have become scarce due to the locals' fondness for their meat – though since the island was declared a national park, their numbers have been increasing.

ARRIVAL AND DEPARTURE

By boat You can hire a boat to bring you to the island from Playa El Arenal (see opposite). Fishermen charge about US$70 for a return trip (20–30min each way); at weekends you may find other visitors to share the cost. Alternatively, book a trip with one of the tour operators (see opposite). Avoid summer weekends and holiday periods, though, when the place is overrun with visitors, and remember to arrange a pick-up time with your boatman.

ACCOMMODATION AND EATING

Camping You can camp on the island but you'll need to be self-sufficient and note that, other than toilets, there are no facilities. Per person US$10
Food Take all the food and drink you need.

Playa Venao

Surfers' beach **Playa Venao** lies thirty minutes by car (45min by bus) from Pedasí. The beautiful bay is undergoing rapid development – not all of it good – but the waves are still beguiling and there are still plenty of places to swing in a hammock and watch the pelicans glide past.

ACCOMMODATION AND EATING

All the listings below have self-catering options, for which you should stock up in Las Tablas or Pedasí on the way.
La Choza 200m from the beach break; contact *Hotel El Sitio* ☎832 1010, ✉lachozapv@gmail.com. Dorm beds and compact, comfortable fan-ventilated rooms (US$10 more for a/c), plus a breezy balcony and intimate garden-*rancho* kitchen facilities. Dorms US$13, doubles US$35

★ **Hostel Eco-Venao** On a bluff across the road at the west end of the beach ☎832 5030, ⓦecovenao.com. Harmonize with your surroundings and support sustainable ecological development of the area with a stay here. The property encompasses a large patch of reforested mountainside and offers great views. Accommodation ranges from an eco-campsite and a dorm to private rooms and cabañas. The attractive on-site bar-restaurant serves superb food (mains from US$9); alternatively, use the communal kitchen. Four-night minimum stay and prices hiked 30 percent for holiday periods. Camping/person US$7, dorms US$12, doubles US$39, cabañas US$55
Selina Hostel East end of the beach ☎202 5919, ⓦselinahostels.com. Rather disorganized party place comprising two opposing rows of brightly painted cabins offering various dorm combinations (with a/c and bathroom) plus a few seriously overpriced en-suite doubles. The bar-restaurant pumps out music and serves cheap comfort food, plus there's a pool table and occasional DJ operating out of a thatched VW van. Offers rental and classes for surfing, kitesurfing and SUP. Dorms US$12, doubles US$126
★ **Venao Cove** West end of the beach ☎6427 2129, ⓦplaya-venao-panama.com. Wonderfully relaxing spot even for non-surfers, down at the quiet end of the beach. Fan-ventilated dorms with medium fluffier four private rooms and shared bathrooms in a brightly painted hostel surrounded by trees. Shared kitchen and an honesty bar plus bags of hammock room outdoors for lazing about. Camping/person US$5, dorms US$12, doubles US$45

Isla Cañas

Archeological evidence suggests that people have been coming to the area now designated as the **ISLA CAÑAS WILDLIFE RESERVE** to hunt turtles and harvest their eggs for many centuries, although the island was only settled in the 1960s. Since 1988, the hunting of turtles here has been prohibited and a co-operative has been established to control the harvest. Members watch over the beaches at night and collect the eggs as soon as they are laid, keeping eighty percent for sale and consumption, and moving the rest to a nursery where the turtles can hatch and return to the sea in safety.

A night-time **turtle walk**, at least half an hour in each direction along the beach and led by a trained guide, will set you back about US$15 per small group. Torch use is stringently rationed as the turtles are frightened by the piercing beams. The long, near-silent walk along

7

THE ISLA CAÑAS ARRIBADA

Isla Cañas has one of the few beaches in the world that sees the phenomenon known as the **arribada**, when thousands of female sea turtles simultaneously come ashore to lay their eggs. It's still not entirely understood what triggers this mass exodus from the sea at one particular moment, though smaller numbers emerge at other times, too, within a roughly ten-day period on either side of a full moon (when tides are highest, allowing the turtles to lay their eggs further up the beach).

Whether or not your visit coincides with an *arribada* (usually Aug–Nov), if you come between May and January you'll almost certainly see Olive Ridley or green turtles – with a small chance of spotting loggerhead and hawksbill – laying their eggs at night. From December to March there's also a chance of seeing leviathan-like leatherbacks, which can weigh over 800kg.

soft sand, the lapping water and the incredible number of stars may just lull you to sleep on your feet.

The functional but unmemorable **main village** on Isla Cañas is prepared for visitors – as are the mosquitoes and sandflies.

ARRIVAL AND INFORMATION

By bus Two daily buses from Pedasí (7am, noon; 1hr) go to Cañas village; you could also flag down the 1–2pm bus from Las Tablas, which passes along the main street of Pedasí (1.30–2.30pm). Returning from Cañas village, three daily buses run to Pedasí (7am, which continues to Las Tablas, 9am, 3pm).

By taxi You could take a taxi from Pedasí for around US$35. There are no taxis in Cañas village.

By boat For a couple of extra dollars, buses to Cañas village may take you to the "dock" – essentially the point where the road ends and the mangrove swamp begins, and which is the jumping-off point for the island. Arrange to have a boat waiting.

INFORMATION AND TOURS

Tours Isla Cañas Tours (☎6718 0032, ⓦfacebook.com /infoictours) is the village tourism co-operative. They do all-inclusive packages to the island, and can also give information on getting there yourself. You can contact their president, Daniel Pérez, directly on that number (in Spanish), or via the tourist office in Pedasí (see p.568); emails are answered promptly. In addition to the tour

operators based in Pedasí, several lodgings in the village organize excursions, as does the ATP office (see p.568). Fernando Dominguez (☎6716 4095) is a reliable local guide with a couple of boats, who can take you to explore the mangroves and nearby river estuary on the lookout for crocodiles, or just for a spot of artisanal fishing.

ACCOMMODATION AND EATING

The village co-operative (Isla Cañas Tours; see above) has very rudimentary cabins with fans (a/c US$10 extra). Alternatively you can pitch a tent or stay with a family. There are also a couple of small, inexpensive restaurants. Camping/person <u>US$5</u>, cabins <u>US$20</u>,

Veraguas Province

Although many travellers only see Veraguas while en route between David and Panama City, there are a growing number of reasons to stop here, from the stunning marine life in **Parque Nacional Coiba** and the glorious mountains of **Santa Fé** to the pounding surf of **Santa Catalina**. Travel in the area is relatively simple as most destinations are accessed from the Interamericana, with the majority of attractions within easy reach of the provincial capital **Santiago**.

SANTIAGO

The halfway point between Panama City and David, **SANTIAGO** has few sights apart from its main square, which hosts the pretty **Catedral Santiago Apóstol** and a modest one-room archeological **museum** (Tues–Sat 9am–4pm; free), but if you're headed for Santa Fé or Santa Catalina you may have to stop over if you miss the last bus.

ARRIVAL AND DEPARTURE

By bus Buses between Panama City and David stop at *Restaurante Los Tucanes* or Centro Piramidal, both roadside pit stops on the Interamericana in Santiago, with bathrooms, a café and a pharmacy. You can sometimes get a seat on these buses but rarely at weekends or during holiday periods. A new, direct (though less comfortable) Coaster service to David now departs from the bus terminal (6am–7pm; every

45min; 3hr), where you can also catch a bus for Santa Fé (5am–7pm; every 30min; 1hr–1hr 30min) and Soná (6am–7pm; every 20min; 1hr); there you can connect with the Santa Catalina-bound bus (see p.535).

ACCOMMODATION

Residencial Camino del Sol Across from the bus station ☎ 993 0371. These lodgings may not be very inspiring, but they're clean, functional and cheap, with wi-fi. US$33

SANTA FÉ

The laidback mountain village of **SANTA FÉ** has become popular as a retreat from the "backpacker trail" – which ironically has put it firmly on the must-do list. Like El Valle, the village enjoys lush hillsides and a cool microclimate, but the scenery is far more impressive and, unlike El Valle, Santa Fé is a genuine thriving village – rather than a weekend playground for Panama City's elite. It is famous for its **co-operatives**, which were founded in the late 1960s by a young Colombian priest named Héctor Gallego, who wanted to help local farmers get a fair price for their goods. For reasons that are unclear, he was persecuted and eventually murdered by General Noriega's henchmen but his presence lives on here: a statue of him marks the village entrance and a foundation in his name continues to help local farmers.

There's a wealth of **outdoor activities** here, including hiking, tubing, horseriding and waterfall trips; to organize these, contact staff at *La Qhia* (see below), who can provide trail maps or put you in touch with a local guide.

ARRIVAL AND INFORMATION

By bus Buses arrive from Santiago and leave from the bus station in Santa Fé, 100m down from *Hostal La Qhia* at the top end of the village (5am–7pm; every 30min; 1hr–1hr 30min).

Information and tours 100m up the road from *Hostal La Qhia*, the Fundación Héctor Gallego offers internet access (US$1/hr) and can fix up a tour of the coffee co-operative (in Spanish) or organize a birding or hiking guide.

ACCOMMODATION AND EATING

★**Anachoreo** Left after the bus station and first right down a dirt road ☎ 6911 4848. The rather unatmospheric, cavernous dining room is more than compensated for by the delicious Cambodian cuisine – stir-fried vegetables, ginger chicken and fish amok (all about US$10) using fresh green vegetables and herbs from the garden. All dishes come with steamed rice. Reservations advisable. Wed–Sun 6–8pm.

Fonda Hermanos Pineda Just off main road; Gloria open later than most, this is a popular spot for a beer as well as inexpensive chicken and rice. Daily 7am–8pm.

★**Hostal La Qhia** 100m up from the bus station ☎ 954 0903, ⓦ panamamountainhouse.com. Dorms and private rooms (most with shared bathroom) come with use of a small, semi-open kitchen and a large, hammock-strewn *rancho*, where you can take in the views of surrounding hills even if you don't want to hike them. Dorms US$12, doubles US$39

7

SANTA CATALINA ACTIVITIES

In addition to those listed below, other activities in Santa Catalina include horseriding, yoga and massage – ask at *Buena Vida* (see p.573) – and birdwatching or hiking – contact Javier (ⓦ birdcoiba.com).

Diving Trips to Coiba, for experienced divers, and to nearby dive sites can be arranged through several scuba operators: Scuba Coiba (ⓦ scubacoiba.com) and Coiba Dive Center (ⓦ coibadivecenter.com), the two most experienced outfits, offer local two-tank dives from around US$65, and around US$115 for Coiba, not including park fees.

Kayaking Kayaks can be rented from Rolo's (US$15) or Fluid Adventures (US$35; ⓦ fluidadventurespanama.com), which also offers highly recommended kayaking tours, from a day-trip to Isla Santa Catalina (US$60/person) to more expensive multiday adventures paddling and camping on Coiba.

Surfing Boards can be rented (from US$10–15/day) at most camps (see p.572) with good weekly rentals from Surf and Shake (ⓦ surfandshake.com) on the beach road. Lessons (usually 1hr 30min–2hr) range from US$20 to US$35 and may include use of the board for the rest of the day. SUP is also possible, either rental or tours: contact Amparo Salazar (☎ 6911 0960, ✉ ampysg@gmail.com).

SANTA CATALINA AND AROUND

Boasting world-class surf and beautiful beaches, **SANTA CATALINA** is considered by many to have the most impressive waves in Panama. Catalina's popularity has skyrocketed in the last decade, through **surf tourism** and as the jumping-off point for **Isla Coiba**, which offers similarly world-class diving, but the distance from major cities and airports has left this small fishing village fairly well preserved.

WHAT TO SEE AND DO

The village and most of its businesses – mainly owned by expats – are based around the **main street**, the road from Soná, which ends where the concrete meets Santa Catalina **beach**. It is an unimpressive pebble-strewn strip, where the fishermen pull up their boats and unload their catch, and where boats leave for **Coiba**. Most of the accommodation and restaurants are located off what is often called the **beach road**, which deviates left at the public phone boxes, ending 2km later in the swathe of sand that is **Playa del Estero**. This is a far nicer beach, where most of the **surf** classes take place. If you can't afford to go to Coiba, you'll find plenty of decent snorkelling and nice white sands at the nearby islands of **Santa Catalina** and **Cébaco**.

Parque Nacional Coiba

Blessed with a striking abundance of marine biodiversity, the group of 38 islands that make up **Parque Nacional Coiba** (including the namesake) has become one of Panama's most popular national parks, although strict conservation laws and limited access mean that tourism here is still relatively underdeveloped. For independent travellers, Santa Catalina is the closest destination from which you can access the park, on **tours** run by locals (see below) though it's hard to achieve if you're on a tight budget. To really have a chance of spotting wildlife, you should arrange to stay overnight (see below), so that you can get into the forest at first light. So far, the only accommodation is on **Isla Coiba** – a former penal colony, and the park's largest island.

ARRIVAL AND DEPARTURE

By bus Santa Catalina is best accessed from Santiago's main terminal. Take a bus to Soná (6am–7pm; every 20min; 1hr), where you get aboard an onward bus to Santa Catalina (5.30am, 8.40am, 11.20am, 1.35pm, 2.40pm & 4.45pm; 1hr 30min). Return buses to Soná leave Santa Catalina at 6.15am, 7am, 8am, 10.20am, 1.15pm & 3.30pm. Frequent buses run from Soná to Santiago (6am–7.40pm; every 20min; 1hr); eight of these travel on to Panama City (5hr).

By taxi Taxis from Soná cost US$35–40, and hang around the bus station to catch travellers who can't be bothered to wait for the bus, or who have missed the last one.

INFORMATION AND TOURS

Tourist information There's no tourist office but there are two good village websites: ⓦ visitsantacatalina.com and ⓦ santacatalinabeach.com.

Coiba tours Various fishermen advertise outside their houses about tours to Coiba. Rates are fairly standard but the service is not – ask for advice. A day-trip will cost US$60/person (minimum of 6 people), not including park fee (US$20/person) or food – *Buena Vida* can do you a packed lunch. It is also possible to stay on Coiba (see opposite).

Money Note that there is no ATM in Santa Catalina, and that the one in Soná often runs out of cash during busy periods.

Internet Several hostels and restaurants in Santa Catalina offer slow wi-fi.

ACCOMMODATION

SANTA CATALINA

A large number of surf camps and budget hostels have kept prices low and availability likely although advance bookings are necessary in holiday periods. Most only offer cold- or tepid-water showers and expect power and water outages.

Brisa Mar Near the beach on the main road ☎ 6500 1450, ⓦ brisamarpanama.com. Six basic en-suite rooms above the *Dive Stop* bar, surprisingly well insulated against the music. Rooms are very clean, spacious and light, with good mattresses, fans or a/c (US$10 extra) and well-screened windows. US$30

Cabañas Las Palmeras Off the beach road. Panamanian-owned, comprising a handful of compact, en-suite cabins with a/c and private porch offering partial sea views (US$10 more Fri & Sat), plus small dorms of 3–4 beds of varying prices depending on ventilation and bathroom. Small *rancho* with hammocks overlooking the ocean, and horseriding can be organized. Camping/person US$6, dorms US$10, cabins US$40

★ **Oasis Surf Camp** Playa del Estero, at the back of the beach ☎ 6588 7077, ⓦ oasissurfcamp.com. Best beachside location offering clean, cheerfully painted bungalows with fan or a/c (US$10 more) and private porches right on the beach, beneath shady trees. Also has a decent restaurant (mains from US$6). Camping is possible in their tents, with mattresses supplied (US$13/person), or in your own. Camping/person US$8, bungalows US$40

Rancho Estero Beach road just before Playa Estero ☎ 6415 6595, ⍟ ranchoestero.com. A handful of simple cane-and-thatch cabañas with shared bathrooms sprinkled on a shady grass bank on a bluff, affording nice sea views. A decent shared kitchen and relaxing deck and bar make this a good-value choice. US$20

★ **Rolo's** Just before Santa Catalina beach ☎ 6494 3916, ⍟ rolocabins.net. Spotless cabins with decent pine furniture, fridge and a/c, complete with balconies and hammocks, as well as dorms (for 2–3 people) with shared kitchen. Also available are neat, clean en-suite rooms with decent mattresses, pine furniture and a/c in a house (La Sirena) next to *Pizzería Jamming*. Boat trips, surf lessons and board and kayak rentals can be arranged. Dorms US$10, doubles US$40

Santa Catalina Surf Point Beach road just before Playa del Estero ☎ 6923 6695, ⍟ santacatalinasurfpoint.com. Friendly, family-run hostel set around a small garden on a bluff overlooking the beach. There are a handful of basic private rooms (with shared or private bathroom) and two dorms – one with a/c for US$3 more. Also a couple of tents with mattresses for rent, with just about space to squeeze in your own. Good bar-restaurant on site, too. Camping/person US$5, dorms US$12, doubles US$50

PARQUE NACIONAL COIBA

ANAM ranger station Isla Coiba ☎ 998 0615. The only accommodation in the national park, offering basic shared cabins with a/c (6–11pm), provided the generator is working. ANAM charges US$15 for the use of the kitchen, and you need to take supplies from Santa Catalina and budget to feed your boatman/guide. Camping/person US$15, dorms US$20

EATING AND DRINKING

Buena Vida *Buena Vida* hotel, on the road into the village. Pleasant terrace café enlivened by original mosaics and wrought-ironwork created by the artistic owners. Open for healthy breakfasts – vast fruit platters or a "Greek scramble" (US$6–7) – and lunches, which include interesting salads (US$6–8). Daily 6am–2pm.

★ **Jammin'** Off the beach road. The surfers' social hub in a pleasant garden setting, dishing out excellent thin-crust pizzas baked in a wood-fired oven (from US$6), washed down with an ice-cold beer accompanied by a steady dose of reggae. Fri–Sun from 6.30pm.

Mama Inés At Santa Catalina Surf Point on the beach road just before Playa del Estero. Perched on a bluff with a great sea view, this is an ideal location for an inexpensive lunch (tacos, burgers, pasta) or a relaxing drink. Daily 8–10am, noon–3pm & 7–10pm.

El Pacífico Down by Santa Catalina beach, below *Rolo's*. With a partial view of the beach, this is a pleasant spot for a Panamanian breakfast: you can get fluffy eggs or juicy beefsteak with *hojaldres* for US$3–4, and modestly priced mains from US$5 later in the day, served with beans and rice or chips and salad. Daily 7am–10pm.

Los Pibes Off the beach road. Pleasant Argentinian-run open-air bar-restaurant (with TV and pool table) dishing up *empanadas*, home-made burgers, fish and other meats chargrilled to perfection and complemented by fresh salads. Mains from US$7. Daily 6.30–9.30pm; usually closed Wed.

Surfer's Paradise Off the beach road 1.5km from the junction. Boasting Santa Catalina's best viewpoint, from a cliff overlooking the sea, this is the spot to enjoy a sundowner. The amiable owner, Italo, also does an occasional all-you-can-eat Brazilian BBQ, usually on Saturdays in high season, a must for hardcore carnivores. Daily 8am until late.

Chiriquí Province

West of the Península de Azuero lies the rich agricultural province of **Chiriquí**. Here you'll find **David**, Panama's second city and a crossroads for travellers heading through Central America. North of David, you can escape the flat heat of the city and take refuge up in the cool of the **Chiriquí Highlands**, a beautiful region of cloudforests, fertile valleys and impressive mountain scenery. The varied landscapes all share the same basic characteristics of head-clearing air, cold nights and a deep, relentless green. National parks here – including **Volcán Barú** and **La Amistad** – are well protected, offering wonderful natural encounters and endless hiking opportunities. The substantial town of **Boquete** has many attractions of its own – particularly coffee- and flower-related – but it's also a great base for activities, from rafting to hot-spring soaks. In contrast, the lowlands of the **Golfo de Chiriquí** hold other pleasures: from the laidback beach scene at **Las Lajas**, a broad belt of sand midway between Santiago and David, to **Isla Boca Brava**, further west, which affords access to islands with white-sand beaches and bird-rich mangroves. Western Panama is also home to the country's most numerous indigenous group, the Ngäbe, whose women are instantly recognizable by their traditional, brightly coloured, long cotton dresses.

DAVID

Three Spanish settlements were founded in this area in 1602; **DAVID** was the only one to survive repeated attacks from indigenous groups. It developed slowly as a marginal outpost of the Spanish Empire, but in 1732 it was overrun and destroyed by British-backed Miskito groups raiding from Nicaragua. As settlement of Chiriquí increased in the nineteenth century, David began to thrive once again. Today, despite being a busy commercial city – the second largest in the country after Panama City – it retains a sedate, if hot and dusty, provincial atmosphere. While it is not so much a destination in itself, plenty of travellers stop here en route to or from Panama City, Costa Rica, Boquete or Bocas del Toro, and find they enjoy the visit. At Carnaval, of course, things spice up considerably, and David also has a festival all of its own: the **Feria de San José** thunders its way through ten raucous days every March.

WHAT TO SEE AND DO

David centres on **Parque Cervantes**, a fine, tree-shaded place to people-watch with a cup of freshly squeezed sugar-cane juice (*caña*) perked up with tropical lemon, or a dose of coconut water (*agua de pipa*). Five blocks southeast of the park stands the city's ancient bell tower, and the **cathedral** – worth a peek inside to take in the garish modern murals.

ARRIVAL AND DEPARTURE

By plane The airport is about 5km out of the city; taxis cost US$4–5. Air Panama (☎316 9000, ⍵airpanama .com) has daily flights between David and Panama City (4 daily; 1hr) and three flights a week to San José, Costa Rica (Mon, Wed & Fri; 1hr). Copa Airlines now also operates return services (two daily; 1hr) from David to Tocumen International Airport, Panama City, to connect with their international flights.

By bus Buses from Panama City, Almirante, Boquete, Cerro Punta and Paso Canoas, as well as Tracopa international buses from San José, pull in at, and leave from, the terminal on Paseo Estudiante.

Destinations Almirante (take Changuinola-bound buses and ask to be let off at the entrance to Almirante); Boquete (6.30am–10.15pm; every 20min; 45min); Cerro Punta (5am–8pm; every 15min; 2hr); Changuinola (5am–7pm; every 25min; 4hr 30min); Las Lajas (4 daily; 1hr 30min); Panama City (6.30am–8.15pm; roughly hourly; 7hr; express 10.45pm & midnight; 6hr); Paso Canoas (4.30am–9.30pm; every 10min; 1hr 20min); Santiago (5.20am–7.20pm; every 45min; 3hr), from across the road from the main bus terminal.

INFORMATION

Tourist information The ATP office (Mon–Fri 9am–4pm; ☎775 4120), between C 5 & C 6, is friendly, but you'll get more useful information at the hostels.

ACCOMMODATION

★**Bambú Hostel** C de la Virgencita, Urbanisación San Mateo Abajo ☎730 2961, ⍵bambuhostel.com. Southwest of the centre, a 5min taxi ride from the bus station, the funky *Bambú* is owned by two fun-loving musicians. There is a variety of dorm and private accommodation options, including a wooden jungle house in the large garden, which contains fruit trees, a swimming pool and a bar. There's also a shared kitchen, laundry room, free wi-fi and lots of extras. Dorms US$11, doubles US$35

Hostal Chambres en Ville Diagonally across from La Universidad Latina ☎775 7428 or ☎6404 0203, ⍵chambresenville.info. A good choice for couples and mature travellers, with cosy en-suite private rooms that are a little dark, but brightened up with colourful murals. The large open-air kitchen leads to a fruit-filled garden, complete with hammocks and a decent-size swimming pool – though the caged toucan might upset some visitors. French spoken. US$35

★**Hostel El Morpho** Behind Mall Terronal, just north of C T Norte ☎730 1816. Palatial bathrooms and purring a/c in the two dorms and three privates (which also enjoy flat-screen cable TV), masses of space both inside and in the garden, a spotless, well-equipped kitchen and table tennis feature in this rather unlikely, quiet hostel located in an upmarket suburb a stone's throw from the city's smartest mall and the Boquete bus stop. Breakfast included. Dorms US$15, doubles US$36.

Hotel Toledo Av 1 Este between calles D & E Norte ☎774 6732. Friendly, good-value hotel offering spotless en-suite rooms – all with hot water, a/c and cable TV – a stone's throw from the bus terminal. US$39

The Purple House Hostel C Sur, at Av 6 Oeste ☎774 4059, ⍵purplehousehostel.com. David's original hostel, obsessively decorated in shades of lavender. The small dorms and private rooms are clean (with or without a/c) and well kept, with internet, wi-fi and coffee on the house

– though hot water showers and a/c are extra – plus there's a small garden with cooling sprinkler and plenty of information available to browse. Dorms <u>US$10</u>, doubles <u>US$29</u>

EATING

Boca Chica C A Sur between avenidas 4 & 5 Este. The pleasant fan-ventilated patio is a prime spot to tuck into some tasty, good-value food, including filet mignon for under US$10, washed down with cheap beer. Daily 11.30am–10pm.

Mercado Municipal de San Mateo C F Sur, at Av 4 Oeste. New home for the former street stalls of the evening Mercado de Fritura (open from around 6pm), frying tasty bits and pieces (such as *hojaldres*, or pan-fried bread, stuffed *yuca*, beef and pork) until the early hours. There are also stalls selling platefuls of noodle- or rice-heavy dishes for a couple of dollars throughout the day. From 6am.

MultiCafé No 2 Next to *Hotel Castilla*. Huge and deservedly popular canteen serving tasty international standards such as lasagne, a range of Mexican-influenced dishes and Panamanian staples for a few dollars. The queues for Sunday breakfast are legendary. Mon–Sat 7am–8pm, Sun 7am–3pm.

Restaurante La Típica C F Sur, at Av 3 Este. Bright, clean cafeteria-style restaurant, tucked behind a hedge, serving vast portions of *comida típica* and Chinese dishes from US$4. Daily 24hr.

DRINKING AND NIGHTLIFE

The nightlife scene is constantly changing so ask around on arrival, or just listen for music playing. Wednesdays are generally Ladies' Nights, with free or cheap entry and drinks promotions for women. There are no established gay clubs in the city.

Opium Next to the Crown Casino, opposite Super 99 supermarket on C F Sur. This place, largely playing electrónica, is currently in favour with David's in-crowd. It doesn't usually get going until around 11pm. Men need to dress smartly. Entry around US$5.

Top Place C F Sur, opposite Super 99 supermarket; C Central, at Av Cincuentenario; Av Obaldía, near the bus terminal. Good spots for a beer and a game of pool, although solo women might be overwhelmed by all the testosterone.

INTO COSTA RICA: PASO CANOAS

You can cross the border into **Costa Rica** at the Paso Canoas crossing, 56km west of David along the Interamericana. After passing through *migración* (7am–11pm) and customs (a formality unless you have anything to declare), you simply walk across the border, though queues for both can be long if international buses are passing through. The banks in David can be reluctant to change dollars to colones so it's best to change them at the border. There are banks (Banco Nacional de Panamá and Banco Nacional de Costa Rica) on both sides of the border that will usually change currency, as well as individual moneychangers.

DIRECTORY

Cinema The screens at the *Gran Hotel Nacional* (C Central) and in the Chiriquí Mall show Hollywood's latest, usually in English with Spanish subtitles.

Consulate Costa Rica, Torre del Banco Universal, C B Norte, at Av 1 Este (Mon–Fri 9am–1pm; ☎ 774 1923).

Banks Banco Nacional (Mon–Fri 8am–3pm, Sat 9am–noon), Parque Cervantes; Banistmo (Mon–Fri 8am–3.30pm, Sat 9am–noon), a block away from Parque Cervantes on C C Norte. Both have 24hr ATMs.

Health There are two well-regarded private hospitals: Hospital Chiriquí, C A Sur, at Av 4 Oeste, and Mae Lewis Hospital, which is on the Interamericana. Both Super 99 and Romero supermarkets, on C F Sur, have a 24hr pharmacy; Farmacia Revilla (Mon 7am–11pm, Sun 8am–10pm) is on Parque Cervantes.

Immigration Migracíon, C C Sur, between Av Central and Av 1 Este (Mon–Fri 8.30am–3.30pm; ☎ 775 4515).

Internet There are plenty of internet cafés, including a 24hr one opposite Super 99 on C F Sur and Planet Internet just off Parque Cervantes (daily 8am–11pm).

Laundry C Central, at Av 6 Este (daily 8am–6pm); Lavandería Lux, C F Sur, at Av 3 Oeste (Mon–Sat 7am–8pm, Sun 9am–1pm).

Post office A block from Parque Cervantes on C C Norte (Mon–Fri 7am–5pm, Sat 8am–3pm).

ISLA BOCA BRAVA

The attractive Pacific island of **ISLA BOCA BRAVA** has two **beaches** – both quite plain – and its patch of rainforest is crisscrossed by paths that are nice to ramble around while you seek out howler monkeys, armadillos and the like. The island's small size ensures that you're not in any danger of getting lost. You can also arrange a **snorkelling** trip to nearby islands with white-sand beaches (US$135/boat for up to 6 people), or rent a double kayak for US$35 for half a day from *Hotel Boca Brava*.

ARRIVAL AND INFORMATION

By bus and boat Take a David-bound bus from Panama City (hourly 6am–8.30pm; 7hr) or from Santiago (every 45min, 6am–7pm; 3hr), alighting at the turn-off (*"el cruce"*) from the Interamericana for Horconcitos, 36km east of David. From David you can take a bus bound for Las Lajas, Tolé or San Félix, alighting at the same junction. There you may be able to connect with the intermittent local bus service to Boca Chica (no fixed timetable). There are also hourly buses (45min) from David to the village of Horconcitos. During the day in high season taxis are also often waiting at the junction to take you the 14km down to the village of Boca Chica (20min; US$15), where water taxis will transport you to the island (US$3/person). Whether arriving by bus or taxi, you'll be dropped at the dock, where there is a bar-restaurant and hotel.

Banks With no ATM in the village, you'll need to bring cash with you.

ACCOMMODATION AND EATING

There are a couple of more informal campsites a 10min walk away that operate in high season, a good option if the hotel is full or the prices seem too high there.

Hotel y Restaurante Boca Brava ☎ 851 0017, ⓦ hotelbocabrava.com. While not the backpacker magnet it used to be – with dorms and hammocks being phased out – it is still an affordable and idyllic spot to chill for a few days. You can book a simple fan-ventilated tiled room with shared bathroom facilities, paying more for private bathrooms, a/c and better views. Outside peak season (Dec–April) prices are lower. Best of all there's a great, breezy restaurant, offering fabulous views and decent, moderately priced food: mains from US$8, though it's worth splurging on the supremely fresh seafood straight from the net. US$50

PLAYA LAS LAJAS

The impressive 12km band of soft tan sand that is **PLAYA LAS LAJAS** lies 124km west of Santiago and 81km east of David. At weekends and during holiday periods it attracts hordes of city-dwellers desperate to escape the heat, who fill up the handful of hotels and cabañas or camp under thatched shelters lining the back of the beach. At other times, the place is deliciously deserted. There's nothing to do but play in the waves, watch the formations of pelicans and chill out. It's perfect for wild beach camping, and there are a couple of local restaurants. A **dive centre** offers dive trips to Coiba and Islas Secas (ⓦlaslajasbeachdivers .com) plus a variety of **snorkelling** trips from US$35 per person.

ARRIVAL AND INFORMATION

By bus and taxi Westbound buses to David can drop you at the Las Lajas crossroads ("*el cruce*"), a major pit stop for drivers on a long haul, with a large supermarket. Here taxis hang around during daylight hours to take you to Playa Las Lajas, 7km away, beyond Las Lajas village (US$8). From David there are four daily buses to Las Lajas village (11.45am, 12.45pm, 3pm and 5.20pm; 1hr 30min), though you'll have to pay for a taxi from the village (US$6).
Banks There is no ATM in Las Lajas.

ACCOMMODATION AND EATING

Hospedaje Ecológico Nahual At the beach T-junction ☎6620 6431, ⓦnahualpanama.com. Two minutes from the sand, rustic cane-and-bamboo lodgings set in a luxuriant garden (so plenty of bugs) following strict eco-friendly principles – biodegradable products only, which may not be for everyone. Dorms and triples share showers and there are shared kitchen facilities. Healthy vegan meals served for US$5. Dorms US$10, doubles US$40
Naturalmente Boutique Bungalows ☎727 0656, ⓦnaturalmentepanama.com. A gem of a place on the outskirts of the village (a short taxi ride from the beach), comprising four airy, fan-ventilated thatched cabañas, one of which hosts a three-bed dorm. The fresh produce from the garden (which has a small pool to cool off in) goes into the restaurant's well-prepared Mediterranean cuisine, in which pizzas feature strongly. Rates include a superior breakfast, and there are substantial reductions in low season. Dorms US$20, doubles US$65

BOQUETE

BOQUETE is set in the tranquil Caldera Valley, 1000m above sea level. Some 37km north of David, it is the biggest town in the **Chiriquí Highlands**, and sits smack in the middle of Panama's two coasts. The road to Boquete ends in the highlands, so those wishing to travel on

to Bocas del Toro from here must go back to David before catching a bus onwards. The slopes surrounding the town are dotted with coffee plantations, flower gardens and orange groves, and rise to rugged peaks that are often obscured by thick clouds. When those clouds clear, however – most often in the morning – you can see the imperious peak of **Volcán Barú**, which dominates the town to the northwest. Foreign investment targeting retirees from the US has flooded the area in recent years, seeing the construction of all-inclusive luxury condos and the clearing of cloudforest to make way for golf courses and retirement homes, causing various tensions within the community. For all that, Boquete remains an attractive destination offering a host of activities.

WHAT TO SEE AND DO

The main attraction of Boquete is the opportunities it affords for exploring the surrounding **countryside**. As well as the climb to the summit of the volcano (see p.580) – a strenuous day's hike – there are plenty of less demanding walks you can make along the narrow country lanes.

One of these walks, heading out of Boquete to the north towards the hamlet of Alto Lino, takes you past the **Café Ruiz factory**, a ten-minute stroll from town. Full tours (Mon–Sat 9am; 3hr; US$30; ☎720 1000, ⓦcaferuiz-boquete.com) explore every step of the coffee-making process; there's also a 45-minute option (8am; US$9) that limits the visit to the roasting plant.

Los Pozos de Caldera

At **Los Pozos de Caldera** (no official hours; US$2 paid to caretaker), the hot springs just outside the nearby town of Caldera, you can alternate between dips in scalding hot water and pulse-quickening splashes in the very cold river.

Guides and tour operators bring groups here (on trips that can be combined with horseriding or an ATV ride) from around US$35 per person, but if there's a group of you, it's probably cheaper to hire a taxi from Boquete (US$35 including wait time). Alternatively, take one of the

7

7

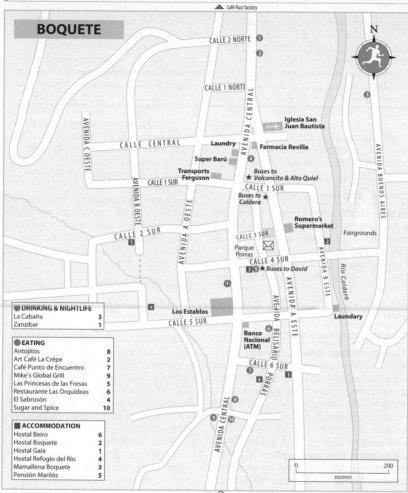

▲ Café Ruiz factory

BOQUETE

N

CALLE 2 NORTE ❶
❷

CALLE 1 NORTE
❸

Iglesia San
Juan Bautista

AVENIDA C OESTE

CALLE CENTRAL   Laundry   Farmacia Revilla

AVENIDA CENTRAL

Super Barú ❹

Transports
Ferguson   Buses to
★ Volcancito & Alto Quiel

CALLE 1 SUR   CALLE 1 SUR

Buses to ★
Caldera

AVENIDA BUENOS AIRES

AVENIDA B OESTE

AVENIDA A OESTE

Romero's
Supermarket

Fairgrounds

CALLE 2 SUR   CALLE 3 SUR

Parque
Porras ✉

AVENIDA B ESTE

Río Caldera

❶

CALLE 4 SUR

❸ ❺ ★ Buses to David

@

AVENIDA A ESTE

DRINKING & NIGHTLIFE
La Cabaña	3
Zanzibar	1

❹   Los Establos

CALLE 5 SUR   Laundary

EATING
Antojitos	8
Art Café La Crêpe	2
Café Punto de Encuentro	7
Mike's Global Grill	9
Las Princesas de las Fresas	5
Restaurante Las Orquídeas	6
El Sabrosón	4
Sugar and Spice	10

Banco
Nacional
(ATM) ❻

AVENIDA BELISARIO PORRAS

CALLE 6 SUR

❼
❻ ❺

ACCOMMODATION
Hostal Beiro	6
Hostal Boquete	2
Hostal Gaia	1
Hostal Refugio del Río	4
Mamallena Boquete	3
Pensión Marilós	5

❽

❾ ❿

AVENIDA CENTRAL

0	200
metres	

▼ ⓘ , David, Los Pozos de Caldera & Spanish by the River

infrequent buses from Boquete to Caldera (7am, 10.45am, 1.15pm; last bus back 4pm; 1hr); the springs are about a 45-minute walk south of town. Note that the 7am bus leaves from outside the fire station, not from the usual place. Ask for directions once in Caldera.

Watersports

More than 35 rivers in Chiriquí Province are used for **kayaking** and **rafting**, including the Río Caldera, Río Gariché, Río Chiriquí and Río Chiriquí Viejo – offering the greatest adrenaline rush – with whitewater of every classification.

Tour operators in town (see box opposite) can arrange day-trips and courses for all experience levels, for around US$65.

ARRIVAL AND INFORMATION

By bus Buses from David arrive at, and depart from, the main square, Parque Porras (6.30am–10.15pm; every 20min; last bus to David 7.45pm; 50min). Minibuses head up to the surrounding hamlets from the streets above this same square – taking one of these and then walking back to town is a good way to see the nearby countryside.

Tourist office The poorly located tourist office, on the road to David, is due to be relocated to the town centre but in the meantime is not worth the hike. The hostels and tour operators can provide plenty of info, though they may

BOQUETE TOURS AND ACTIVITIES

There's a wealth of nature-themed trips and tours to keep you occupied in Boquete; the operators listed below offer some of the most economical and interesting packages in town.

Boquete Mountain Safari Tours Av Central, south of the main square ☎730 9353 or ☎6627 8829, ⓦ boquetesafari.com. Trips to the Pozos de Caldera – on an ATV if you fancy – as well as horseback or coffee-tasting tours and cloudforest visits, US$35–100/person.

Boquete Outdoor Adventures In the Los Establos complex, Av Central, at C 5 Sur ☎720 2284, ⓦ boqueteoutdoadventures.com. The founder of this outfit has been running whitewater kayak and rafting trips since 1997.

Boquete Tree Trek At the Los Establos complex, Av Central, at C 5 Sur ☎720 1635, ⓦ boquetetreetrek.com.

A twelve-line 4hr zipline tour (pick-ups Mon–Sat 8am & 1pm) across the canopy above Boquete (US$65, including transport).

Franklin's Horseback Riding ☎6588 5054, ⓦ boquetehorseback.com. Extremely popular, well-run outings across the rolling hills by Caldera for riders of all experience (US$35/person; 3hr).

Panama Rock Climbing ☎6764 7918, ⓔ panamarockclimbing.blogspot.com, ⓔ boquete climbing@yahoo.com. Run by the personable, US-certified, bilingual local guide César Meléndez (US$45/person; 3hr).

7

push you towards particular tours and services. Research all options thoroughly.

ACCOMMODATION

Some accommodation prices increase during festivals and holidays, so check in advance.

Hostal Beiro Av Porras ☎6478 4015. Friendly local landlady offering four compact, clean en-suite rooms in an annexe, which share a small patio with a hammock and rocking chair. It's a good budget choice if you want to avoid the hostel scene. US$30

Hostal Boquete Av B Este, on the riverfront, just left of the bridge ☎720 2573, ⓦ hostal-boquete.com. Nine compact en-suite rooms, some with balcony, aimed at the Panamanian market – hence the DSTV in each room. There's a shared kitchen and a great communal deck overlooking the river. US$30

Hostal Gaia ☎720 1952, ⓦ hostalgaia.com. Away from the party scene, this tidy, friendly hostel was recently renovated and has relocated to a quiet backstreet. It hosts a mixed clientele in its two dorms (each with its own bathroom) and three private doubles. Has a clean kitchen and lounge area with TV and a small outdoor terrace with hammock. Dorms US$11, double US$44

★**Hostal Refugio del Río** Av B Oeste ☎720 2088, ⓦ refugiodelrio.com. Handsome place by a stream, where even the dorm bedding, seemingly of crushed velvet, exceeds expectations. Choose from dorm beds, en-suite rooms, wooden cabañas overlooking the stream and tents of various sizes (with mattresses and bedding) pitched in the garden. There's also internet, a kitchen, a lovely gazebo with barbecue pit, and a jacuzzi. Camping/person US$13, Dorms US$13, doubles US$36

Mamallena Boquete Parque Porras ☎720 1260, ⓦ mamallenaboquete.com. The Boquete branch of *Mamallena* caters to a backpacker crowd, with tidy, small

dorms and private rooms in a lovely converted wooden house in the most central location possible. Rates include pancake breakfast. Lots of inexpensive tours, bike rental (US$15/day) and transfer to Bocas (US$25) also offered. Dorms US$14, doubles US$30

★**Pensión Marilós** Av A Este at C 6 Sur ☎720 1380, ⓔ marilos66@hotmail.com. Homely environment where you can share the pleasant lounge-dining area with your hosts – plus Ricky the talking parrot – and use the kitchen. Rooms with private or shared bathroom are airy, and the beds snug. The owner speaks English. US$20

EATING

Despite being a touristy place, kitchens close early in Boquete, especially before or after a major festival or if there aren't many customers around. Don't get caught out.

Antojitos Av Central. Pleasant and cheerfully decorated open-sided covered patio serving inexpensive (from US$8) Tex-Mex favourites: enchiladas, quesadillas, chilli con carne and plenty of veggie options. Daily noon–8.30pm.

Café Punto de Encuentro C 6 Sur, off Av Central ☎720 2123. This pleasant terrace overlooking a garden is a popular spot for brunch, attracting Panamanians and foreigners alike, who can feast on a varied menu of eggs with great crispy bacon, French toast, tortillas, pancakes or waffles (most around US$5). Service can be slow when it's busy. Daily 7am–noon.

★**Mike's Global Grill** C 7 Sur, at Av Central. Outdoor seating overlooks a stream while indoors is more like a US sports bar, but with a friendly vibe. The menu is international, eclectic, affordable (many mains US$7–10) and delicious, ranging from burgers to *pad Thai*, falafel to Chinese stir-fry, plus great breakfasts and free wi-fi. Tues taco night, Wed quiz night, Thurs open mike & Fri fried chicken. Daily 8am–10pm (kitchen until 8.30pm).

Las Princesas de las Fresas Corner of Parque Porras, C 4

7

BOQUETE FESTIVALS

January's **Festival de las Flores y del Café** (⦾feriadeboquete.com) sees Boquete's otherwise tasteful and discreet appreciation of coffee and flowers give way to lusty, noisy rejoicing. Throughout the ten-day celebrations, which coincide with the coffee harvest, the local fairgrounds explode with flower fireworks – you'll never see so many orchids – and the locals plant their own gardens accordingly. Stalls spring up selling food, handicrafts and coffee to the thousands of visitors wandering around, followed everywhere by loud, live music. In the evenings the rum is cracked open and people dance around the fairgrounds until dawn. Book accommodation well in advance and avoid the fairground area if you want to get any sleep.

The fairgrounds bloom again in April for the **orchid festival**, while the annual **jazz and blues festival** in March is also a big crowd-puller (⦾boquetejazzandbluesfestival.com).

Sur, at Av Belisario Porras. Small kiosk serving local strawberries every which way – plain with yoghurt, as ice-cream, or lathered in melted chocolate – all for US$1–3. Daily 9.30am–6pm.

★ **Restaurante Las Orquídeas** Av Belisario Porras, at C 5 Sur. Small, friendly, family-run restaurant in a quiet spot with a few patio tables. Tasty, nicely presented *menú del día* for under US$4. Fresh juices and *batidos* too. Mon–Sat 7.30am–6.30pm, Sun 7am–4pm.

El Sabrosón Av Central, between C Central & C 1 Sur. Plain and airy canteen with good Panamanian food and fish cooked to order. Rice, beans, salad and something meaty from around US$4. Daily 7am–3.30pm.

Sugar and Spice Av Central, at C 7 Sur. This international bakery and café is a major expat meeting place, serving decent breakfasts (US$4–5) and salads and sandwiches using their posh breads, such as sourdough, nine-grain and rye. The host of sweet snacks includes a mouthwatering array of muffins. Mon, Tues & Thurs–Sun 8am–6pm, Sat 8am–4pm.

DRINKING AND NIGHTLIFE

La Cabaña Over the bridge and 200m north of the fairground. Try out the dark recesses of the town's main dance venue, complete with flashing lights, plasma screens and *música varieda*. Fri & Sat 9pm until late.

Zanzibar Av Central, at C 2 Norte. African-flavoured bar covered in animal prints and themed artwork, where

---

★ **TREAT YOURSELF**

Art Café La Crêpe Av Central, at C 2 Norte ☎720 1821 or ☎6769 6090. A wee gem, with brightly painted walls covered in Art Deco posters, offering superb French cuisine. Enjoy one of its savoury namesakes (US$9) or trout with almonds (US$17) for your main; desserts include more crêpes and a delicious *crème brûlée*. Reservations are recommended for dinner, especially at weekends. Tues–Sun 12.30–8.30pm.

---

partying travellers and locals come for cocktails (from US$5) and hookahs (US$10). Open late at weekends, when the place gets packed. Happy hour 6–7pm (if open), DJ on Fri & Sat. Wed–Sat 6/7pm until late.

DIRECTORY

Banks There are several banks with ATMs, including Banco Nacional (Mon–Fri 8am–3pm, Sat 9am–noon) on Av Central, and an ATM in the Los Establos complex.

Health 24hr pharmacy in Romero's supermarket behind the main square. Farmacia Revilla on Av Central, at C Central (Mon–Sat 7am–9pm, Sun 10am–5pm).

Internet Hastor Computers Internet Café (Mon–Sat 8.30am–9pm, Sun 10am–5pm; US$1/hr) is on the second floor of the building opposite *Pizza La Volcánica* on Av Central. Also has cabins for international calls.

Language schools Boquete is a popular spot to learn Spanish (approx. US$225–250/week for small-group lessons), with two good schools: Habla Ya (⦾hablaya panama.com), in the Los Establos complex, comes highly recommended and is most central while Boquete Spanish by the River (⦾spanishlocations.com) is slightly out of town.

Post office On the main square (Mon–Fri 8am–4pm, Sat 8am–12.30pm).

PARQUE NACIONAL VOLCÁN BARÚ

Covering an area of 140 square kilometres, **PARQUE NACIONAL VOLCÁN BARÚ** runs between Boquete across the northern flank of Volcán Barú, Panama's highest peak, and Cerro Punta, Panama's highest major settlement (see p.582).

Sendero Los Quetzales

Hiking the well-known **Sendero Los Quetzales** between Boquete and Cerro Punta (10km; 4–6hr at a moderate pace with stops) can be done in both directions. The trail, which allows you to travel between the Highlands' two principal settlements through stunning scenery, is immensely satisfying, especially as it avoids a lengthy bus journey up the mountain from David and down again. There are **trailheads** at El Respingo, near Cerro Punta, and Alto Chiquero, near Boquete.

Starting from Cerro Punta you get more downhill walking, though this is much more difficult and slippery after rain. From Boquete there is more uphill, though only the last section is very steep – and it is easier to climb than descend after rain. In this direction, you also get into the forest earlier and are therefore more likely to see quetzals.

A **guide** is highly recommended, and you shouldn't attempt the hike after very heavy rain since the river you have to ford will likely be impassable.

ARRIVAL AND DEPARTURE

By taxi If hiking independently, you will need to take a taxi to your start point: around US$10 to the trailhead at the El Respingo ranger station from Cerro Punta or US$6 from Guadalupe; around US$10 from Boquete to the Alto Chiquero ranger station. Whichever direction you walk, you can arrange for pick-ups at the other end in advance. Park entry fees (US$5) are payable at either ranger station.

Guides and tours If you come on a tour, the guides or tour operators can arrange transport – which may be included in the price – to and from the trailheads.

ACCOMMODATION

Camping You can camp at both the trailhead refuges (see below). There's also a spot midway along the trail, though it has no facilities. US$5

Refugios El Respingo and Alto Chiquero. Each ranger station has a *refugio* with bunk beds, kitchen facilities and water. To avoid having to carry your pack, get Transportes Ferguson in either Volcán (on the main street) or Boquete (just off the main street) to transport it by road to your next lodging for US$10. US$15

Volcán Barú

Volcán Barú is Panama's tallest mountain (3475m) and an extinct volcano that dares all visitors to take it on. From the park entrance (US$5), south of Boquete, a 13.5km-long boulder-strewn road, passable only with a customized 4WD, winds up to the cloud-shrouded peak. It's a steep and strenuous four- to eight-hour hike, and much the same back to Boquete.

From the top, the cloud cover breaks every so often to reveal the sight of at least one of the oceans. Your best chance of catching the breathtaking view of both the Pacific and Atlantic is to climb in the dry season (late Dec–April), in the dark (torch needed), setting off around midnight or 1am, to arrive at the summit at dawn. Although the trail is for the most part clear and not technical, a guide is strongly recommended (see box below).

ARRIVAL AND ACTIVITIES

By taxi If you'd prefer to climb alone rather than with a guide, you will need to take a minibus or a 4WD taxi (US$8 during the day, up to US$15 at night) from Boquete. This will bring you 6km to the end of the paved road and the park office (US$5 entry, payable on exit if you climb at night). You will also need plenty of food and water. *Mamallena* operates a night shuttle minibus for US$5.

7

SAFETY IN THE MOUNTAINS

Even with experience and the right gear, climbing Volcán Barú is physically demanding; without either it can be unpleasant, and without an **experienced guide** it can be downright dangerous for less hardened hikers if weather conditions worsen during the climb; this is especially true at night. You need a guide with a **first-aid kit** and the means to deal with hypothermia, again particularly if you attempt the night ascent. Don't be coaxed by the "there's-a-path" brigade of fellow travellers who have already been up alone without a hitch; while they may not have had any problems, every trip is different and there is always a risk when the clouds close in: every so often ill-prepared hikers going it alone (or with an inexperienced and/or unqualified guide) get **hypothermia** or get lost, sometimes for several days.

Make sure you have warm clothing for the top; it can be bitterly cold, and dress in layers – don't wear jeans as they're heavy and uncomfortable in rain, and don't dry well. Take sufficient food and water, waterproof clothing and sturdy trainers/hiking boots, and ensure your daysack is lined with a plastic bag to keep everything dry inside. You'll need a headlamp or torch if climbing at night.

7

Tours and guides Tours can be arranged through several operators or you can hire an independent guide; by far the most reliable and experienced mountain guide is Feliciano González (approx US$65/person for two people, less for three or more, including park entry; ☎ 6624 9940, ✉ felicianogonzalez255@hotmail.com). Jason Lara (☎ 6718 6279, ✉ jthunder12@hotmail.com) is also a renowned bilingual birding and hiking guide. Some hostels supply guides, but prioritize quality over price (see p.581).

ACCOMMODATION

There is an area close to the summit where you can set up your tent, but it has no facilities. Alternatively, you may be able to sleep at the police station up there, or keep warm if you get there before sunrise, though it depends who's on duty. Camping/person US$5

CERRO PUNTA AND AROUND

Almost 2000m above sea level in a bowl-shaped valley surrounded by densely forested mountains, **CERRO PUNTA** is the highest village in Panama. Its fertile soil produces around eighty percent of all the vegetables consumed in Panama – there are little patches of cultivated land everywhere you look – although this agricultural boom has not done the surrounding forests any good. The town's altitude gives it a crisp atmosphere, and the taste of the food and the smell of the orchids seem all the better for it.

WHAT TO SEE AND DO

Everything in tiny Cerro Punta is spread out along the main road from David and a side road leading towards **Parque Internacional La Amistad** (see below). The scenery, together with the fresh mountain air, makes Cerro Punta – and nearby Guadalupe (see below) – a perfect base for **hiking**; the pristine cloudforests of the national parks of Amistad and Volcán Barú are both within easy reach, and are two of the best places in Central America to catch a glimpse of the elusive **quetzal**, early in the morning in the dry season (Jan–April).

Guadalupe

Local buses run from the centre of Cerro Punta to the even smaller nearby hamlet of **GUADALUPE**, famous for its orchids,

neat little gardens and its jam – made from local strawberries. Buy some at one of the roadside stalls, or tuck into a bowl of strawberries with *natilla* – a local cream concoction.

ARRIVAL AND DEPARTURE

By bus Services to and from David (from David 5am–8pm; every 15min; from Guadalupe/Cerro Punta every 15min 5am–7pm; 2hr) stop on the main road in Cerro Punta, which runs through the village, before going on a short loop of even smaller communities, including Guadalupe.

ACCOMMODATION AND EATING

Hotel Cerro Punta Main street, Cerro Punta ☎ 771 2020. Chalet-style lodging whose simple rooms have pretty curtains. The windows, however, don't face the mountains, unlike at the hotel's excellent restaurant where you can gaze at the view as you eat carefully prepared meals – a plateful of grilled fish with chips and broccoli salad (US$10) is worth every cent. Restaurant daily 8am–8pm. US$31

★**Hotel Los Quetzales Ecolodge & Spa** Guadalupe ☎ 771 2182, ⊛ losquetzales.com. This hotel accommodates backpackers, honeymooners, Panamanian families and expats, and makes it look easy. Budget travellers will find only the dorms affordable – chunky wood, quality bedding, bedside lights and really hot showers – though there are also plush rooms, suites and cloudforest cabins on offer, whose prices include a guided hike. All guests have access to the comfy lounge and games room, full of books and sofas, warmed by a log fire, and with table tennis. Activities include spa treatments, cycling, horseriding, and walks through the surrounding cloudforest. The excellent restaurant serves delicious soups with home-made bread (US$4), and pizza and pasta for around US$8, but it's worth splurging on one of their pricier mains, accompanied by more vegetables than you are likely to see in a month elsewhere in Panama. Restaurant daily 7am–8pm. Camping/tent US$22, dorms US$20, doubles US$94

PILA restaurant At the entrance to Parque Internacional La Amistad. Run by a local women's co-operative, the restaurant serves *comida corriente* (US$3 for breakfast, US$5 for lunch) such as *arroz de guandú* (rice and beans) with chicken, pork or beef, which you can enjoy on a wooden balcony. Daily 8am–5pm.

PARQUE INTERNACIONAL LA AMISTAD

PARQUE INTERNACIONAL LA AMISTAD covers four thousand square kilometres of rugged, forested mountains teeming with wildlife (including five cat species), on either side of the border with Costa Rica. Although most of Panama's share technically falls in Bocas del Toro, the sliver that is in Chiriquí is best prepared for visitors, with three well-marked **trails**, including a 4km return trip to a 55m waterfall.

ARRIVAL AND INFORMATION

By taxi The park entrance is at Las Nubes. Bus services to Las Nubes are sporadic and unreliable, so you'll probably have to get a taxi (US$6–8) from Cerro Punta or Guadalupe, or hitch.

Entry fee The US$5 entry fee is payable at the park office, a few hundred metres beyond the entrance.

ACCOMMODATION

Camping A few hundred metres beyond the entrance. You can camp in the clearing by the park office. Per person US$5

Refuglo Park office, a few hundred metres beyond the entrance. Bring your own food, warm clothes and, ideally, a sleeping bag, as it gets cold at night – they have some extra bedding, though. US$15

Bocas del Toro

Isolated on the Costa Rican border between the Caribbean and the forested slopes of the Cordillera Talamanca, **Bocas del Toro** ("mouths of the bull") is one of the most beautiful areas in Panama. It's also one of the most remote – the

mainland portion of the province is connected to the rest of Panama by a single road, and the island chain offshore requires a ferry ride to reach.

Despite recent rapid development (see box below), the archipelago remains home to an **ecosystem** so complex and well preserved that it has been described by biologists as "the Galápagos of the twenty-first century". This, and the equally unusual diversity of the human population – Ngäbe, Buglé, Naso and Bribrí populate the mainland, while the islands are dominated by the descendants of **West Indian** migrants who still speak Guari-Guari, an English patois embellished with Spanish and Ngäbere – make Bocas a fascinating area to visit.

ALMIRANTE

From the village of Chiriquí, 14km east of David on the Interamericana, a spectacular road crosses the continental divide, passes over the Fortuna hydroelectric dam, through the pristine forests that protect its watershed and the small town of **Chiriquí Grande**, then, 50km on, into **ALMIRANTE**. This ramshackle port town of rusting tin-roofed houses, propped up on stilts over the calm waters of the Caribbean, is the place to catch a water taxi to the Bocas del Toro archipelago.

7

BOCAS DEL TORO HISTORY

Christopher Columbus first explored the coast of Bocas del Toro in 1502 in the search for a route to Asia; later, during the colonial era, European pirates often sheltered in the calm waters of the archipelago. By the nineteenth century, English ships from Jamaica were visiting the coast frequently, but it wasn't until 1826 that West Indian immigrants founded the town of Bocas del Toro, still the province's largest settlement.

The arrival of the United Fruit **banana plantations** in the late 1800s gave the islands a measure of prosperity; by 1895 bananas from Bocas accounted for more than half of Panama's export earnings, and Bocas Town boasted five foreign consulates and three English-language newspapers. Early in the twentieth century, however, banana crops were repeatedly devastated by disease, causing the archipelago's economy to suffer.

In recent years, **tourism** and real estate speculation have come to the economic forefront in Bocas. Foreign investors have bought huge portions of the archipelago in order to develop luxury resorts and holiday homes. While this boom has enhanced the region's wealth, generating employment and income for locals, much concern still exists over how economically and environmentally sustainable it really is.

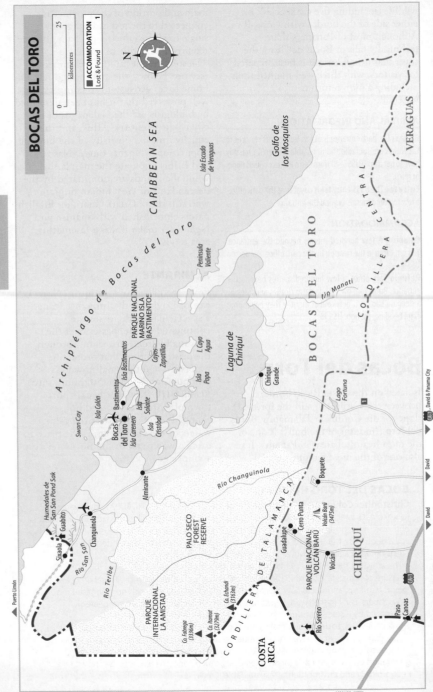

BOCAS DEL TORO

N

ACCOMMODATION
Lost & Found 1

0 — 25 kilometres

CARIBBEAN SEA

VERAGUAS

Isla Escudo de Veraguas

Golfo de los Mosquitos

Peninsula Valiente

CORDILLERA CENTRAL

BOCAS DEL TORO

Rio Manati

Archipiélago de Bocas del Toro

PARQUE NACIONAL MARINO ISLA BASTIMENTO

Isla Bastimentos

Cayos Zapatillas

I. Cayo Agua

Laguna de Chiriquí

Isla Popa

Chiriquí Grande

Swan Cay

Isla Colón

Bastimentos

Isla Solarte

Bocas del Toro

Isla Carenero

Isla Cristóbal

Lago Fortuna

David & Panama City

Humedales de San San Pond Sak

Almirante

Rio Changuinola

David

Guabito

Changuinola

Rio San San

PALO SECO FOREST RESERVE

Boquete

Sixaola

Rio Teribe

Puerto Limón

Rio Changuinola

CORDILLERA DE TALAMANCA

Guadalupe

Cerro Punta

Volcán Barú (3475m)

PARQUE NACIONAL VOLCÁN BARÚ

Volcán

PARQUE INTERNACIONAL LA AMISTAD

Ca. Fabrega (3336m)

Ca. Itamut (3279m)

Ca. Echandi (3163m)

CHIRIQUÍ

David

COSTA RICA

Rio Sereno

Paso Canoas

San José

7

ARRIVAL AND DEPARTURE

By bus Long-distance buses to and from Panama City and Changuinola (see box, p.586), and David and Changuinola (5am–7pm; every 25min; 4hr 30min), drop off and pick up passengers at "La Y" on the main coastal road, from where it's a 5min taxi ride or about a 15min walk to the dock. Local buses shuttle to and from Changuinola (6am–10pm; every 20min; 30min), and head for the bus terminal in town, but ask to get off before then at the "*parada de las lanchas*".

By water taxi to Bocas Two water-taxi companies, Taxi 25 & Bocas Marine Tours, run the same service for the same price (6am–6pm; every 30min; 30min; US$4).

By car ferry to Bocas There's a slow and unreliable car ferry to Bocas from the car ferry dock (Tues–Sun 8am; 1hr; motorbikes US$10; bicycles US$3).

CHANGUINOLA

Some 16km from the border and 29km west of Almirante through seemingly endless banana plantations, **CHANGUINOLA** is a typically hot and uninteresting banana town where almost everyone works for the Bocas Fruit Company ("the Company", successor to United Fruit and Chiquita). Only travellers heading to or from the Costa Rica border come here, though the charming **San San Pond Sak Wetlands** are reason enough to linger for a night.

Humedales de San San Pond Sak

Just 7km north of Changuinola lie the wildlife-rich **Humedales de San San Pond Sak** (San San Pond Sak Wetlands). An early morning boat trip downriver to the lagoon offers excellent birdwatching – parrots, hawks and herons abound – as well as the chance to see sloths and snakes. Even more enticing is the opportunity to catch sight of the elusive

West Indian manatee, or sea cow. This involves a potentially lengthy stakeout on a viewing platform while being eaten alive by sandflies, but the sight of this shy and extraordinary-looking beast chomping away at banana leaves is well worth the wait. To arrange an early morning boat trip to see the manatees (around US$65/person plus US$5 park fee), contact AAMVECONA (☏6679 7238, ✉info@aamvecona.com), or ask at the ANAM office in Changuinola (two blocks from the main street).

ARRIVAL AND DEPARTURE

By bus Most buses arrive at and depart from the main bus terminal on the main street in the town centre, though buses for David and Panama City leave from the Terminal Urracá (see box, p.586).

Destinations Almirante (6am–10pm; every 20min; 30min); David (5am–7pm; every 25min; 4hr 30min); Guabito (5.30am–7pm; every 20min; 30min); Panama City (see box, p.586); San José, Costa Rica (daily, 10am; 8hr).

ACCOMMODATION AND EATING

Golden Sahara Main street, 100m north of Terminal Urracá ☏758 7478. Your best bet should you need to spend the night here – not an enviable prospect – with decent, inexpensive rooms. US$32

Restaurante La Fortuna Main street, 100m north of Terminal Urracá, next door to *Golden Sahara*. Good Chinese food in a handy location (with a/c) adjoining the town's best accommodation option. Daily 11.30am–10pm.

BOCAS TOWN

On the southeastern tip of Isla Colón, the provincial capital of Bocas del Toro, otherwise known as **BOCAS TOWN**, is the easiest base from which to explore the islands, beaches and reefs of the

7

LOST AND FOUND: A HOSTEL WITH A DIFFERENCE

The Lost and Found On the road between David and Changuinola ☏6432 8182, ⓦlostandfoundlodge.com. A wonderful ecofriendly lodge set-up high in the cloudforest on the boundary of the La Fortuna reserve. Guests hang out on the deck, where meals are taken – the coffee you drink at breakfast is processed from berries growing a few metres away – and the observation platform sees nightly visits from local animals. Chilly weather is countered with fleece blankets, luxurious hot-water showers with serene forest views, and beer-and-foosball sessions in the bar. Wild, mostly unmarked trails offer potential wildlife encounters and can be explored at your leisure, or on one of the lodge's many tours (most US$25–40/person). Pick-ups from David, Boquete and Almirante can be arranged; the website details how to get here by public transport. Reductions for stays of several nights. Dorms US$14, double US$33

7

TRAVEL BETWEEN BOCAS DEL TORO AND PANAMA CITY

The overnight **bus route** from Changuinola to Almirante and Panama City is served by one company, TRANCEIBOSA (☎ 303 6326 in Panama City; ☎ 758 8455 in Changuinola; ☎ 758 3278 in Almirante; ☎ 757 9493 in Bocas, at the Taxi 25 dock), whose main office is in the Terminal Urracá in Changuinola, 200m north of the main bus terminal. Buses from Changuinola (daily 7.30am & 6pm; 45min; US$27.80) stop at "La Y" in Almirante. Buy tickets as early as possible. Note that the a/c on these long-distance buses is usually glacial, so wrap up warmly.

---

archipelago. The town, connected to the rest of the island by a narrow causeway, is busy and bustling, especially during the high season (Dec–April), when it explodes with tourists and backpackers. Rickety wooden buildings painted in cheerful colours and a friendly and laidback, mostly English-speaking population welcome you to the island's casual mêlée. The palm-fringed Caribbean beaches, decent waves, and a buzzing young nightlife have made these islands a must-see for partying backpackers.

WHAT TO SEE AND DO

Bocas Town offers a variety of aquatic activities, and an increasing number of operators (see box, p.589) are offering land-based activities such as cycling, horseriding, yoga and learning Spanish.

Surfing

Surfing is the most popular activity in the area, with an abundance of spots for both beginners and experts, with various surf schools (see box, p.591) offering **lessons**, as well as board rental.

Boat tours

Endless possibilities exist for **boat excursions**. The three most common trips, sold by most tour operators for the same price (around US$20–25/person), take in a combination of **wildlife viewing** – such as seeking out the shy bottlenose dolphins in Dolphin Bay, or viewing hundreds of seabirds wheeling round Swan Caye – **snorkelling**, especially among the rainbow-coloured coral of Cayo Crawl, a beach or two, often including Cayos Zapatillas, and a lunch stop (not included in the price). Other trips take you into the islands' rainforests, or even over to the mainland to visit

Ngäbe communities, where you'll get much more from a homestay than a brief day-visit. Relaxing on a **catamaran cruise** is another popular way to experience the archipelago (see box, p.589). If the tour enters the Bastimentos marine park, expect to pay an extra US$10. Red Frog beach on Isla Bastimentos also demands a US$3 entry. **Diving** is big in Bocas, too; aficionados consider Escudo de Veraguas to be one of the best diving spots in the Caribbean.

When booking a tour or diving excursion, be aware that bad weather may result in a change of itinerary or even cancellation, and that beyond the main islands, the sea can get very rough.

ARRIVAL AND DEPARTURE

By plane Bocas airport is just four blocks from the main street. Air Panama (☎ 757 9841, ⓦ airpanama.com) offers flights from and to Panama City (2–3 daily; 1hr) while Air Nature (☎ 757 9963, ⓦ natureair.com) connects with San José, Costa Rica (5 weekly; 1hr).

By bus The island's only bus service runs from the Parque Bolívar in Bocas Town to Bocas del Drago, 17km away on the northwestern tip of Isla Colón (7am–5pm; hourly; 30min). Extra private minibuses run for the same cost in high season.

By water taxi Two companies, Taxi 25 and Bocas Marine Tours, run water taxis between adjacent docks in Almirante and their own jetties in Bocas Town (both 6am–6pm; every 30min; US$6).

By shuttle Both Caribe Shuttle (ⓦ caribeshuttle.com) and Hola Panama Travel (ⓦ holapanamatravel.com) run daily shuttles (US$32, including the water taxi) to Puerto Viejo and to San José (US$75) in Costa Rica (see p.139), and to and from Boquete (US$30; see p.577).

By car ferry The lethargic car ferry from Almirante (Tues–Sun 8am; 1hr; bikes US$3, motorbikes US$10) pulls in at the southern end of the main street, returning to Almirante at 4pm.

By taxi Taxis charge around US$15 to go to Boca del Drago, or to head up the dirt road to Playa Bluff, for which you'll need a 4WD.

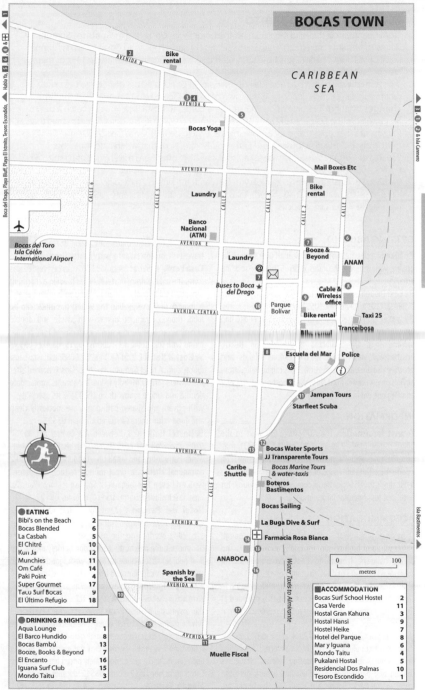

BOCAS TOWN

CARIBBEAN SEA

AVENIDA H

Bike rental

AVENIDA G

Bocas Yoga

Mail Boxes Etc

AVENIDA F

Bike rental

Laundry

Banco Nacional (ATM)

AVENIDA E

Bocas del Toro Isla Colón International Airport

Laundry

Booze & Beyond

ANAM

Buses to Boca del Drago

Cable & Wireless office

Taxi 25

Parque Bolívar

AVENIDA CENTRAL

Bike rental

Tranceibosa

Escuela del Mar

Police

AVENIDA D

Jampan Tours

Starfleet Scuba

AVENIDA C

Bocas Water Sports

JJ Transparente Tours

Caribe Shuttle

Bocas Marine Tours & water-taxis

Boteros Bastimentos

Bocas Sailing

AVENIDA B

La Buga Dive & Surf

Farmacia Rosa Bianca

Om Café

ANABOCA

Spanish by the Sea

AVENIDA A

Water Taxis to Almirante

AVENIDA SUR

Muelle Fiscal

0   100
metres

Isla Bastimentos

N

EATING

Bibi's on the Beach	2
Bocas Blended	6
La Casbah	5
El Chitré	10
Kun Ja	12
Munchies	11
Om Café	14
Paki Point	4
Super Gourmet	17
Taco Surf Bocas	9
El Último Refugio	18

DRINKING & NIGHTLIFE

Aqua Lounge	1
El Barco Hundido	8
Bocas Bambú	13
Booze, Books & Beyond	7
El Encanto	16
Iguana Surf Club	15
Mondo Taitu	3

ACCOMMODATION

Bocas Surf School Hostel	2
Casa Verde	11
Hostal Gran Kahuna	3
Hostal Hansi	9
Hostel Heike	7
Hotel del Parque	8
Mar y Iguana	6
Mondo Taitu	4
Pukalani Hostal	5
Residencial Dos Palmas	10
Tesoro Escondido	1

Habla Ya,

Boca del Drago, Playa Bluff, Playa El Istmito, Tesoro Escondido,

& Isla Carenero

Almirante

7

7

INTO COSTA RICA: GUABITO

From Changuinola the road runs 16km to the border with Costa Rica at **Guabito–Sixaola**, where there's little more than a few shops selling consumer goods to Costa Rican day-trippers. Local buses from Changuinola bus station can take you to Guabito (see box, p.143), or there are *colectivos* and taxis (US$8).

It's a short walk from *migración* (daily 8am–6pm) in Guabito across a bridge to Costa Rica, where you can change currency in the town of Sixaola (see box, p.143). Note that the **time changes** (shifting 1hr back) when you cross the border to Costa Rica. You can catch a bus to San José from the border (daily 8am, 10am & 3pm; 6hr) or, if you just don't want to leave that Caribbean vibe behind, stop for a while in Puerto Viejo de Talamanca (see p.139) in northeastern Costa Rica (buses 6am–5pm; hourly; 4hr). Note that when entering either Panama or Costa Rica, you may be asked to show proof of onward travel (such as a return air ticket). If you can't, you may be made to buy a US$13 return bus ticket.

Arriving in Guabito from Costa Rica, you can catch the bus to Changuinola until 7pm, or take a taxi (US$10 private; US$1.50 shared). Taxis also run directly to Almirante (US$25), where you can catch a water taxi to Bocas.

GETTING AROUND

By bike Bicycles are available for rent all over town; bike quality varies, as do the rates (US6–$10/day), so shop around.

By taxi Though everything in town is within easy walking distance, taxis are available (US$1/person).

By water taxi To get around the islands, you need to hop in and out of water taxis. As well as the scheduled transfers to and from the mainland and Red Frog Beach, unscheduled water taxis to the various islands and beaches also dock at these jetties. Boats can be hailed from anywhere on the seafront. Just stand at the end of a pier and flag one down.

INFORMATION

Tourist information The ATP office, C 1 next to the police station (daily 9.30am–5.30pm; ☎757 9642), may be able to provide a map but is otherwise short on information. Detailed maps of the area are available from most shops for US$4; ⓦ bocas.com is a good resource for hotel and tour operator information.

ACCOMMODATION

There's a good range of accommodation in Bocas, though places fill up in high season, especially at weekends and during holidays. It pays to book accommodation in advance where you can, though many hostels don't accept reservations: in which case try to arrive by mid-morning to ensure you get a bed. Hot water is not usually provided at the budget lodgings and the area suffers periodically from water shortages.

★ **Bocas Surf School Hostel** Av H, at C 6 ☎6852 5291, ⓦ bocassurfschool.com. Lovely converted wooden Bocatoreño house accommodating eleven travellers sharing two bathrooms, a kitchen and a deck over the water at the back. Rooms are small but the bunks are ample with decent mattresses. Great for budget solo travellers who don't want a party hostel. Dorms US$20

Casa Verde Av Sur, at C 4 ☎6633 8050, ⓦ casaverdebocas .com. The only seafront hostel in Bocas Town in a charming converted traditional wooden building with great bar and hammock deck overlooking the water; the music can be loud, though. Cramped dorms with single and double bunks, a/c and mini-fridges plus a handful of tired private rooms with shared showers. Dorms US$15, doubles US$37

★ **Hostal Hansi** C 2, at Av D ☎757 9085, ⓦ hostalhansi .bocas.com. A tight German-run ship, *Hansi* is named after the owners' former friendly feline. The simple, immaculate double and single rooms (from US$13) – its speciality – with private and shared bathrooms, are spotlessly clean and good value. There's a shared kitchen. US$25

★ **Hostel Heike** C 3, between Avs Central & E ☎757 9708, ⓦ hostelheike.com. Dorms with shared clean, hot-water bathrooms, and small private rooms. There's also a communal kitchen, a great rooftop terrace, computers, wi-fi and even free beginners' Spanish lessons. Pancake breakfast included. Dorms US$10, doubles US$22

Hotel del Parque C 2, at Av Central ☎757 9008, ⓦ hdelparque.webs.com. This warm, family-run place has a balcony overlooking the main square and a quieter hammock-hung one at the back. Cool, homely rooms (for 1–4 people) that include cable TV, wi-fi, good hot-water showers and a/c (or fan) and use of a small kitchen. US$50

Mar y Iguana Feria del Mar ☎6047 2413, ⓦ mareiguanahostel.com. A stone's throw from the beach, this cosy hostel north of Bocas Town comprises seven small private rooms (with shared or en-suite bathroom) and one dorm, all with a/c, set around a small garden – where there's room for a few tents – with a two-tier *rancho* for reading and relaxing and a good, moderately priced bar-restaurant. Camping/person US$7, dorms US$12, doubles US$35

Mondo Taitu Av G, between C 4 & C 5 ☎757 9425,

TOUR OPERATORS IN BOCAS TOWN

There are many tour operators in town – below is just a small selection. Tours cost US$20–30, depending on the distance to destinations and gear rental. Check whether costs include park fees.

ANABOCA C 3, between Avs A & B ☎ 6843 7244 or ☎ 6671 5794, ⓦ anaboca.org. Set up to support the STC (Sea Turtle Conservancy), this community-led organization runs turtle-watching tours on Playa Bluff during the nesting season (April–Sept; US$15).

Bluff Beach Retreat ☎ 6677 8867, ⓦ bluffbeach retreat.com. Offers highly praised 2- to 3-hour horseriding excursions along Bluff Beach Road for US$45.

Bocas Sailing C 3, between Avs B & C ☎ 757 9710, ⓦ bocassailing.com. Spend a glorious day gliding around the islands on a catamaran and slipping into the water to snorkel for US$48. Picnic lunch included.

Bocas Water Sports C 3, at Av C ☎ 757 9541, ⓦ bocaswatersports.com. Professional and well-established US-run outfit offering diving, kayaking

and snorkelling outings as well as equipment rental.

Boteros Bocatoreños C 3, at Av A ☎ 757 9760. An association of local boatmen formed to try and compete against some of the slicker foreign tour operators, offering the usual excursions, often at slightly lower prices, and with bags of local tales to tell – but be sure they don't hassle the dolphins.

La Buga Dive & Surf C 3, at Av B ☎ 757 9534, ⓦ labugapanama.com. Friendly and fun PADI-certified outfit and surf school. Also rents out SUPs and kayaks.

Starfleet C 1, at Av D ☎ 757 9630, ⓦ starfleetscuba .com. Canadian company with a friendly, professional team focusing on diving excursions and full PADI open-water diving courses (about US$225). Starfleet also offers the only spa in Bocas Town (high season).

7

ⓦ mondotaitu.com. The cheap booze still flows and the parties still throb through the night, but this pioneering surfer hostel/party bar is showing its age. Cramped rooms and dorms (with fan or, for a couple of dollars extra, a/c) share hot water bathrooms, plus there's a communal kitchen and a legendary, tiny cocktail bar plus lots of extras. Dorms U̲S̲$̲1̲1̲, doubles U̲S̲$̲2̲8̲

Pukalani Hostal 3km north of Bocas Town, close to Playa Paunch ☎ 6949 6465, ⓦ pukalanihostalpanama .com. With unexceptional private rooms and four dorms, this hotel/hostel offers the only cheap lodging on the beach – though you'll find little in the way of sand. There's a nice open bar-lounge area, a pool and *rancho* over the water which houses a bar and pool table. The bar-restaurant serves breakfast (included for private rooms) and US-style comfort food, plus there are free kayaks, cheap bike rental and a free shuttle service into town three times a day. Dorms U̲S̲$̲1̲5̲, doubles U̲S̲$̲6̲6̲

Residencial Dos Palmas Av Sur, between C 5 & Av A ☎ 757 9906. Bocatoreño-owned establishment offering a handful of well-kept, compact rooms each with fan, small private bathroom and electric hot water shower, at the quieter southern tip of town. There's also a reading deck over the water. Very good value. U̲S̲$̲2̲8̲

EATING

Bocas has an excellent range of restaurants, with several international options, though consistency is an issue and prices have soared in the last few years. Luckily cheap, good-quality street food is on the increase – seek out the falafel van. Lobster, conch, octopus and other locally caught specialities taste particularly delicious in local coconut milk and Caribbean spice preparations, though

you should not be offered them during the closed season (March–June). Tap water is not drinkable, so don't expect free iced water. Opening hours can be erratic. A large range of groceries is available at the many supermarkets, though prices are higher than on the mainland.

★**Bocas Blended** C 1, at Av E. Unmistakeable sky-blue converted bus dishing up tasty breakfasts and delectable salads and wraps filled with fresh ingredients at modest prices (US$5–7), as well as smoothies and juices. You can take away or "eat in", and take advantage of "wrappy hour" (4–5pm) and excellent-value lunch combos. The best table in the house is on the bus roof, where your food is served via a dumb waiter. Unforgettable. Mon–Sat 8am–5pm.

La Casbah Av H, at C 4 ☎ 6477 4727. Cosy restaurant with indoor and outdoor seating serving nicely presented Mediterranean cuisine, though only the salads and starters are affordable for those on a tight budget; try the "La Casbah" salad of feta cheese, organic greens and grilled Mediterranean veg for around US$10. Tues–Sat 6–10pm.

El Chitré C 3, at Av Central. Locals trust this small cafeteria-style restaurant and so should you. *Comida típica* (from around US$3 for breakfast, US$4.50 for lunch or dinner) is eaten on a small patio. Daily 6am–9pm.

Kun Ja C 3, at Av C. This Chinese restaurant, with indoor and waterfront seating, is one of the friendliest budget spots in town. It serves large portions of tasty meat and seafood dishes with fried rice, chow mein or chop suey (US$6). Takeaway available. Mon & Wed–Sun noon–11pm.

Munchies C 1, at Av D. Small wooden kiosk set back from the road serving up Bocas' best burgers (fish, chicken, veggie or beef) for under US$8 with fries an additional US$2, to be washed down with a chilled beer. Daily 6pm–late.

★Om Café C 3, between Avs A & B. The Canadian-Indian owner draws from traditional family recipes, dishing up excellent curries with rice, naan and home-made chutney (from US$9). Mon, Tues & Fri–Sun 8am–4pm & 6–10pm.

Paki Point At Playa Paunch, 3km up the coast from Bocas Town. Bang on the beach, this is a top spot to watch the surfers ride the waves as you tuck into the catch of the day, bite into a jalapeño burger or sip a cocktail. Chill to the hypnotic house beat while dozing on a beanbag or sprawling on a sun lounger, and let the day slip by. Mains from US$9. Daily 10.30am–7pm or 8pm.

Super Gourmet Av A, between C 3 & C 4. A posh grocery store with a decent deli counter making substantial, satisfying deli sandwiches in baguettes (US$5.50–8), plus filling bean salads and the like. A good option for vegetarians. Mon–Sat 9am–7pm.

★Taco Surf Bocas C 2 at Mono Loco Surf School. Tasty, inexpensive burritos, nachos and tacos – try the fish ones with a dose of hot sauce – plus beans, rice or fries on the side, for under US$10. The house lemonades and margaritas just seal the deal. Mon, Tues & Fri–Sun noon–8pm.

DRINKING AND NIGHTLIFE

Several restaurants double as music and drinking venues in the evening, plus there are a few good bars where you can relax with a cold Balboa Ice or cocktail.

El Barco Hundido C 1, beside the Cable & Wireless office. Locally known as the "Wreck Deck", this spot used to be the most popular hangout for locals, tourists and surfers, who came here to drink cold beer (US$2) until the early hours. Though no longer the hottest joint in town, it's still a top spot, with regular DJs playing a mix of modern r'n'b, '80s pop and the ubiquitous Bob Marley. Plus it stays open later than anywhere else. Daily 7pm until late.

Bocas Bambú C 3, at Av C. A humming spot with a striking canvas of vast tent-awnings supported by thick bamboo poles, a large video screen showing surfing and pop videos, and probably the longest bar in Panama. Plus affordable daily meal specials (US$8–9), nightly

---

> ## ★ TREAT YOURSELF
>
> **El Último Refugio** Av Sur at C 5 ☎6726 9851, ⓦultimorefugio.com. The only restaurant in town where you can watch the sun set over the mainland from the water's edge, best enjoyed while sipping one of their signature cocktails. Run by an experienced US duo, this spot offers a daily changing menu of creative, succulent mains (from around US$13), with seafood the speciality, and delicious desserts as well as occasional live music. You'll need to reserve a table. Mon–Fri 6–10pm.

---

flame-throwing, reggae DJ 8pm every Sat and occasional live acts. Daily 6.30–11pm.

Booze, Books & Beyond Av E, at C 2. Sells a good selection of secondhand books in English (US$5–10), and will buy used books. Also a popular expat bar selling cheap beer, with additional entertainments in the form of a pool table, a tattoo parlour and a giant game of Jenga. Often hosts live music. Mon–Sat 10am until late.

El Encanto C 3, between Avs A & B. At the southern tip of the street, come here for a local experience, with cheap drinks, a dark deck enlivened by fairy lights, monster speakers and dancing to a DJ at weekends. Also occasional live music. Daily 6pm until late.

★Iguana Surf Club C 1, between Avs A & B ☎757 9812. Refurbished and back in action, with an all-female bar staff, this is currently the hottest spot in town, pulling in a young crowd with a mix of pop, hip-hop and house, plus heavy doses of reggae and rock. There are live bands and DJs at weekends and great cocktails to linger over on the waterside deck. Decent pizzas (from US$9) sold at the adjacent *La Italiana PizzaBar* help line the stomach before the serious partying begins. Ladies' nights Mon & Thurs. Daily 9pm– late.

Mondo Taitu Av G, between C 4 & C 5. With all kinds of cheap, creative cocktails and drink specials, there's a frat-house-style theme party here many nights. The actual bar is so small the action soon spills out into the street. Daily 7pm until late.

DIRECTORY

Bank Banco Nacional, C 4 (Mon–Fri 8am–3pm, Sat 9am–noon), has a 24hr ATM.

Health The island's one hospital, Av G, at C 10 (☎757 9201), has 24hr emergency services. Rosa Blanca Pharmacy is on C 3 near Av B.

Internet Galaxy Internet, C 2 (10am–8pm; US$1.50/hr). Also offers international calls.

Language schools Spanish by the Sea, Av A, at C 4 (☎757 9518, ⓦspanishbythesea.com), and Habla Ya, Av G, at C 9 (☎757 7352, ⓦhablayapanama.com), have good reputations (weekly rates for small group classes around US$225–250).

Laundry Between Av E & F (US$4–5/bag).

Post office The post office is north of Parque Bolívar, at C 3 (Mon–Fri 8am–4pm, Sat 8am–noon). There's also Mail Boxes Etc., Av F (Mon–Fri 8am–5pm, Sat 8.30am–noon).

AROUND BOCAS TOWN

The islands, cayes and mainland waterways surrounding Bocas Town offer wide-ranging opportunities for relaxing on pristine beaches, visiting Ngäbe villages and diving near unspoilt coral reefs. A quick bus or taxi ride away are

Tesoro Escondido ☎ 6782 0512, ⓦ bocastesoroescondido.com. A great escape from the party atmosphere in town, this genuine eco-hotel is set near Playa Bluff, on land which slopes from the bluff to the beach. It offers excellent views and a choice of lodgings including airy rooms and charming cottages, with reductions for long-term stays. All accommodation has kitchen access, though there's a great restaurant if you can't be bothered to cook. Doubles **US$35**, cottages **US$65**

the beaches of the rest of **Isla Colón**, while nearby islas Carenero and Bastimentos are favoured by visiting surfers. Most visitors make a point of exploring the **Parque Nacional Marino Isla Bastimentos**, a renowned marine park that stretches across a series of islands in the archipelago.

Playa Bluff

Some twenty minutes from Bocas Town by taxi, **PLAYA BLUFF** sees some of the heaviest action at the height of the Bocas surf season. It's also a good place to observe nesting **sea turtles** (May–Sept); contact the ANABOCA office, next to ANAM (ⓦ anaboca.org), to organize a visit. There are several places to stay and eat here, and the distance from town results in a more tranquil pace that is often preferred by couples and more mature travellers.

As taxis are expensive and car rental is not possible, the easiest way to get

around Playa Bluff is to rent a bicycle in Bocas Town (see p.588).

Boca del Drago

A popular excursion – by boat, bike or bus – leads 15km across the island to **Boca del Drago**, on the northwest tip. The main draw is nearby **Playa Estrella** (Starfish Beach), which has precious little sand but its translucent shallows are filled with dwindling numbers of its namesake, which you should be careful not to touch so as not to harm them. Avoid the weekend crowds if possible.

ARRIVAL AND DEPARTURE

By bus A local bus shuttles back and forth from the park in Bocas Town to Boca del Drago (7am–5pm; hourly; 30min).

EATING

Yarisnori Playa Estrella ☎ 6613 1934. Round off the visit with a tasty and leisurely seafood lunch (around US$10) here or at one of the other informal restaurants on the beach. Daily 9am–6pm.

Isla Carenero

Just 200m across the water from Bocas Town, tiny **Isla Carenero** is beginning to receive more visitors thanks to hostel and adult playground *Aqua Lounge* (see p.592), and the most accessible and consistent surf break in the archipelago at Punta Carenero. On the westward side of the island, a narrow concrete path goes as far as the small marina; the island is rather dingy here, and wooden houses on stilts stand over the partially waterlogged and heavily littered ground. Quieter than Bocas Town, the island has its charms, but these may be outweighed by the hefty

7

In the past few years, Bocas has garnered a lot of attention as an international **surfing** destination. The best waves hit between December and March, and there are many excellent and varied surfing spots in the area. Although none is within walking distance of Bocas, the town remains the best base for catching taxis or water taxis to your wave of choice.

The main hotspots include **Carenero**, off the northeastern tip of Isla Carenero; **Dumpers**, **Paunch** and **Bluff**, on the eastern side of Isla Colón; **Red Frog Beach**, on Bastimentos; and **Silverbacks**, between Bastimentos and Carenero. Most break over reef, some of which is fire coral, so wear booties or be careful.

You can **rent surfboards** for US$10–20 per day, but prices vary with size, quality and availability. Rental places include Escuela del Mar (see p.592), Bocas Surf School and hostels such as *Gran Kahuna*, *Heike* and *Mondo Taitu* (see p.592).

populations of sandflies and mosquitoes that plague beachgoers.

Bibi's restaurant (see below) houses the Escuela del Mar (☏757 9137 or ☏6785 7984), offering **snorkel and kayak rental**, surfboard and SUP (Stand Up Paddle board) rentals and lessons, as well as surfboard repairs. The surf school also has an office in Bocas Town on C 1 across from the tourist office.

ARRIVAL AND DEPARTURE

By water taxi To get to the island, catch a water-taxi (US$1) from the northern end of Bocas Town.

ACCOMMODATION AND EATING

Bibi's on the Beach Great seafood (from US$9) at this place looking out over the water at a popular beginners' surf spot; the large balcony provides the perfect refuge from the pestering insects on shore. Happy hour (4–7pm) is a must. Mon & Wed–Sun 8am–9pm.

★**Hostal Gran Kahuna** C 3, at Av B ☏757 9038, ⊛grankahunabocas.com. A solid budget option right on the beach attempting green practices, consisting of dorms (single and double bunks) with lockers and surfboard storage space, and private en-suite rooms. A/c and good mattresses in both. Nice garden and social area to chill in, with comfy sofas and hammocks facing the sea. Also a moderately priced bar-restaurant. Dorms US$14, doubles US$55

DRINKING AND NIGHTLIFE

★**Aqua Lounge** Isla Carenero ⊛bocasaqualounge.info. *Aqua Lounge* really gets going on ladies' nights (Wed & Sat), with free drinks until midnight for women, a big, starlit dancefloor and a water trampoline and diving board on which to cool your heels. This Peter Pan playground hosts legendary parties, where the sandflies and mosquitoes are the only unwanted guests – come prepared with plenty of repellent. Occasional live bands. A place to party rather than to stay. Bar daily 2–10pm, much later on Wed & Sat. Dorms US$12, doubles US$28

Isla Bastimentos

Outside the national marine park on the western tip of **Isla Bastimentos**, the small Afro-Antillano fishing community of Old Bank, or **BASTIMENTOS**, is not really set up for mass tourism, though there are several budget lodgings and places to eat. Be sure to bring cash, though, as there's no bank or ATM on the island.

An undulating concrete path acts as the community's main thoroughfare, snaking its way between the coastline and a steep, green hillside dotted with wooden stilt houses. A jungle path, occasionally impassable after heavy rains, leads to several pristine **beaches** twenty minutes away on the other side of the island. Periodically there have been muggings on this trail, so enquire about the current situation before setting out.

The future of this spectacular island remains shaky, as locals and environmental enthusiasts continue to fight with potential developers – building projects, unless very carefully planned and executed, will almost certainly cause irreparable damage to the fragile ecosystem.

ARRIVAL AND DEPARTURE

By boat Frequent boats run to and from the Bastimentos water-taxi terminal at the southern end of Bocas Town (US$3), and arrive at the main dock; Jampan tours also runs regular water-taxis to the dock at Red Frog Beach (US$4 single, US$7 return) on a fixed timetable. It's then a 10min walk on a sandy path across (US$3) to the beach

ACCOMMODATION AND EATING

Alvin's and Kecha's Left of the main dock. After passing through an unpromising darkened room you emerge in a cheery restaurant over the water. Enjoy tasty, simple home-cooking, ranging from ubiquitous Panamanian staples such as fried chicken, rice and beans to more Caribbean-style seafood dishes accompanied by coconut rice, *patacones* or fried *yuca*. Mains from US$7. Daily 8am–9pm.

★**Beverly's Hill** Left from the main dock ☏757 9923, ⊜beverleyshill@gmail.com, ⊛beverlyshill.blogspot.com. A gem on the hillside, with charming rustic cabaña rooms (with kitchenette and shared or private bathroom) set in a lush tropical garden that's home to the elusive red frog, and brimming with birdlife. If you can afford it, splash out on the suite at the top (US$70) for stunning Caribbean views. US$30

★**Hostal Bastimentos** Set back from the main path, on the hillside ☏757 9053, ⊛hostalbastimentos.com. A sprawling maze of a backpackers' hostel affording a choice of accommodation, from fan-ventilated dorms to posh bedrooms with a/c and hot water. There's a communal kitchen, a garden *rancho* hung with hammocks, and a mellow vibe. Dorms US$7.50, doubles US$20

Hostal El Jaguar Off the main path, on the seafront, right of the main dock ☏757 9383, ⊛hostaleljaguar .bocas.com. This hammock-strewn spot over the water is clean, comfortable and run by the Archibalds, one of the best-known families on the island. Fan-ventilated rooms are cheap and cheerful, and tours or kayak rental are available. US$22

★**Palmar Tent Lodge** Red Frog Beach ☎ 6880 8640, ⓦ palmartentlodge.com. Simple private safari tents and tent-cabin dorms (two-night min stay for all) set in rainforest at the back of the beach with solar-powered fans, lamps and showers plus an array of amenities and services. Camping/person (own tent) US$10, dorms US$15, doubles in safari tents US$55

Roots 200m right of the main dock under a mop of thatch ☎ 6473 5111. The most popular watering hole in town – beer goes for US$1. *Roots* also serves dynamite Caribbean dishes of fresh seafood and coconut rice for US$9–10. Daily 12.30–9pm.

Tío Tom's Just left of the main dock ☎ 757 9831, ⓦ tiotomsguesthouse.com. A thatched wooden inn, built over water, with six simple, fan-ventilated en-suite rooms – a bungalow is also available. Food, including great German breakfasts, is modestly priced – unlike the rooms – and served on the small deck. Good tour rates plus kayak and snorkel equipment rental. US$38

Parque Nacional Marino Isla Bastimentos

Most visitors to Bocas come to explore the pristine beauty of **PARQUE NACIONAL MARINO ISLA BASTIMENTOS**, a 130 square kilometre reserve encompassing several virtually undisturbed ecosystems that include rainforest, mangrove and coral reef supporting an immense diversity of marine life, including dolphins, sea turtles and a kaleidoscopic variety of fish.

Some of the best **beaches** in the archipelago are also in the park, on the eastern side of the island facing the open sea. Due to their powerful surf and currents, swimming here is dangerous, but they are huge, uncrowded and undeveloped. The most popular is **Red Frog Beach**, an idyllic stretch of sand that takes its name from the tiny bright-red strawberry poison-dart frogs (don't touch!) that inhabit the forest behind the beach.

Much further east, the 6km stretch of **Playa Larga** is an important nesting site for **sea turtles** (May–Sept).

Southeast of Isla Bastimentos, but still within the park, are the **Cayos Zapatillas**. Two dreamy, coral-fringed islands, the Zapatillas are excellent for snorkelling, but you must pay the park admission fee (US$10) at the ANAM station on the southern island. Camping is possible on the northern island (see below).

ARRIVAL AND DEPARTURE

By tour The easiest way to visit the marine park is with a tour operator (see p.589). A large number of agencies offer day-trips to beaches and snorkelling spots in and around the park, typically costing US$20–30/person (not including the park fee, which is not always collected) and including a lunch stop at an over-the-water restaurant (US$6–10). The most popular tour often includes free cold drinks and snorkelling equipment.

By boat Alternatively, you can hire a boat in Bocas Town or Bastimentos: with a group of four or more people this could be cheaper than an agency tour and lets you decide exactly where you want to go.

ACCOMMODATION

Cayos Zapatillas camping Contact ANAM in Bocas Town (ⓦ anam.gob.pa). Camping is possible, with permission, on the pretty northern island, which has toilet and limited water (from collected rainwater) facilities. Per person US$10

7

COMMUNITY-BASED TOURISM

Bocas is not all about surfing, sand and partying. An increasing number of visitors are being drawn to the community-based tourism being offered by some of the archipelago's and mainland's Ngäbe communities as well as the small Naso kingdom up the Río Teribe, on the boundary of the Amistad International Park (see p.582). To get the most out of the experience, consider a village homestay. A standout highlight is the chocolate tour of the cocoa farm in the Ngäbe village of Río Oeste Arriba (US$30), which as well as being highly informative includes plenty of chocolate tasting; it's a 15min bus ride from Almirante up a scenic valley. Contact Samuel, who speaks good English (☎ 6411 5670, ⓦ oreba.bocasdeltoro.org). The community gets more of the money if you contact them directly, though you can organize the tour through operators in Bocas.

The Bocas community tourism website (ⓦ redtucombo.bocasdeltoro.org) and the Bocas Sustainable Tourism Alliance (ⓦ discoverbocasdeltoro.com) give contact details and information on the activities each village offers.

Spanish

There are more than thirty languages spoken across the Central American isthmus. Fortunately for the traveller, just two dominate – Spanish, of course, but also English, spoken primarily in Belize and the Bay Islands of Honduras.

Luckily, too, **Spanish**, as spoken across Latin America, is one of the easier languages there is to learn and even the most faltering of attempts to speak it is greatly appreciated. Taking the trouble to get to know at least the basics will both make your travels considerably easier and reap countless rewards in terms of reception, appreciation and understanding of people and places.

Overall, Latin American Spanish is clearer and slower than that of Spain – gone are the lisps and bewilderingly rapid, slurred, soft consonants of the old country. There are, however, quite strong variations in accent across Central America: Guatemalan Spanish has the reputation of being clear, precise and eminently understandable even to the worst of linguists, while the language as spoken in Honduras – thick and fast – can initially bewilder even those who believed themselves to be reasonably fluent. Nicaraguans in particular take great pleasure in fooling around with language, creating new words, pronouncing certain letters differently and employing different grammar. There are enough *Nicaraguanismos* – words and sayings particular to Nicaragua – to fill a dictionary. As far as pronunciation goes, the "d" is often dropped from word endings and the "v" and "b" sounds are fairly interchangeable.

Pronunciation

For the most part, the rules of **pronunciation** are straightforward and strictly observed. Unless there's an accent, words ending in d, l, r and z are **stressed** on the last syllable, all others on the second last. All **vowels** are pure and short.

A somewhere between the "A" sound of back and that of father.

E as in get.

I as in police.

O as in hot.

U as in rule.

C is soft before E and I, otherwise hard; cerca is pronounced "serka".

ENGLISH AND CREOLE

The language you'll hear widely spoken in **Belize** may sound familiar from a distance and, if you listen to a few words, you may think that its meaning is clear. Listen a little harder, however, and you'll realize that complete comprehension is just out of reach. What you're hearing is, in fact, **Kriol**, a beautifully warm and relaxed language, spoken in various forms (as Creole) along the Caribbean coast from Belize down to Panama. This pidgin language is loosely based on English – mixed with elements of West African languages, indigenous Miskito, and some Spanish – and is similar to Jamaican Creole, or Patois. Written Kriol, which you'll come across in Belizean newspapers, is a little easier to get to grips with. There's an active movement in Belize to formalize the language, which led to the publication of the *Kriol-Inglish Dikshineri* in 2007. Luckily, almost anyone who can speak Creole can also speak English.

In the Bay Islands of **Honduras** things are much simpler. English is English rather than Creole, and immediately understandable, albeit spoken with a unique, broad accent. Influenced by Caribbean, English and Scots migrants over the years, local inflexions turn even the most commonplace of remarks into an attractive statement. English, however, is slowly being supplanted by Spanish as the language heard on the street, as growing numbers of mainlanders make the islands their home.

G works the same way – a guttural "H" sound (like the ch in loch) before E or I, a hard G elsewhere; gigante is pronounced "higante".

H is always silent.

J is the same sound as a guttural G; jamón is pronounced "hamon".

LL sounds like an English Y; tortilla is pronounced torteeya.

N is as in English, unless there is a tilde (accent) over it, when it becomes like the N in "onion"; mañana is pronounced "manyana".

QU is pronounced like an English K.

R is rolled, **RR** doubly so.

V sounds like a cross with B, vino becoming beano.

X is slightly softer than in English, sometimes almost like SH, so that Xela becomes "sheyla"; between vowels in place names it has an H sound – México is pronounced "May-hee-ko".

Z is the same as a soft C; cerveza is pronounced "servesa".

Formal and informal address

For English-speakers one of the most difficult things to get to grips with is the distinction between formal and informal address – when to use it and to whom, and how to avoid causing offence. Generally speaking, the third-person "**usted**" indicates respect and/or a non-familiar relationship and is used in business, for people you don't know and for those older than you. Second-person "**tú**" is for children, friends and contemporaries in less formal settings. (Remember also that in Latin America the second-person **plural** – "vosotros" – is never used, so "you" plural will always be "ustedes".) In day-to-day exchanges, genuine mistakes on the part of an obviously non-native speaker will be well received and corrected with good humour.

One idiosyncrasy is the widespread use of "**vos**" in Central America. Now archaic in Spain, it is frequently used in place of *tú*, as an intimate form of address between friends of the same age. In most tenses, conjugation is exactly the same as for *tú*. In the present indicative, however, the last syllable is stressed with an accent (*tú comes/vos comés*); in "-ir" verbs in this tense, the final "i" is kept instead of changing to an "e" (*tú escribes/vos escribís*). In commands, the "vos" form drops the final "r" of the infinitive, replacing it with an accented vowel (*tú come/vos comé*). Take your lead from those around you – if you are addressed in the "vos" form it is a sign of friendship and should be reciprocated; on the other hand it is sometimes seen as patronizing to use it with someone you don't know well.

Nicknames and turns of speech

Nicknames are very common in Central America, used in both speech and writing and for any situation from addressing a casual acquaintance to referring to political candidates. Often they centre on obvious physical characteristics – *flaco/a* (thin), *gordo/a* (fat), *rubio/a* (blond).

Often, these nicknames will be further softened by **diminution** – the addition of the suffix *-ito* or *-ita* at the end of nouns and adjectives, a trend used sometimes with a passion in everyday speech. You are quite likely to hear someone talk about their *hermanito* for example, which translates as "little brother" regardless of respective ages, while *mi hijita* ("my little daughter") can as easily mean a grown woman as a child.

Also very common are **endearments**, used lightly in brief encounters and to soothe transactions. Heard in virtually every country are *(mi) amor* – used in much the same way as "love" in England and also between friends – as is *jóven* or *jovencito/a*, young one. More specific to each country (often but not always between men) are terms used to make casual questions or remarks less intrusive. *Papa* (literally "father") is used daily in Honduras, for example as in "*¿Qué hora tiene, papa?*" (What time is it?), while the Nicaraguans use *primo* (cousin). Panamanians address one another as *joven* (youth), regardless of age, and refer to friends as "*mis panas*" (my "panas", or Panamanians). In Nicaragua light-skinned or fair-haired visitors will be referred to or addressed as *chele/a*; the syllables of *leche* (milk) in reverse.

Politesse

Verbal courtesy is an integral part of speech in Spanish and one that – once you're accustomed to the pace and flow of life in Central America – should become instinctive. Saying *buenos días/buenas tardes* and waiting for the appropriate response is usual when asking for something at a shop or ticket office for example, as is adding *señor* or *señora* (in this instance similar to the US "sir" or "ma'am"). The "you're welcome" response is more likely to be *para servirle* (literally "here to serve you") rather than the casual *de nada* ("you're welcome"). The *tss tss* sound is commonly employed to attract attention, particularly in restaurants. In this very polite culture shouting is frowned upon.

On meeting or being introduced to someone, Central Americans will say *con mucho gusto*, "it's a pleasure", and you should do the same. On departure you will more often than not be told *¡que le vaya bien!* ("may all go well"), a simple phrase that nonetheless invariably sounds sincere and rounds off transactions nicely. In rural areas, especially, it is usual to leave even complete strangers met on the path with *!Adiós, que le vaya bien!* Note that the Castilian term **coger** (to take/grab) has a very different meaning in Central and South America; here this refers to the act of sex, while the verb **tomar** is used for take/grab. Make sure you therefore say "*tomar un autobus*" (get the bus), instead of the Castilian "*coger un autobus*"!

WORDS AND PHRASES

BASIC WORDS

a lot	mucho
afternoon	tarde
and	y
bad	mal(o)/a
big	gran(de)
boy	chico
closed	cerrado/a
cold	frío/a
day	día
entrance	entrada
exit	salida
girl	chica
good	bien/buen(o)/a
he	él
her	ella
here	aquí
his	suyo
hot	calor/caliente
how much	cuánto
if	si
information	información
later	más tarde/después
less	menos
ma'am/missus	señora
man	señor/hombre
miss	señorita
more	más
morning	mañana
night	noche
no	no
now	ahora
open	abierto/a
or	o

please	por favor
she	ella
sir/mister	señor
small	pequeño/a
thank you	gracias
that	eso/a
their	suyo/de ellos
there	allí
they	ellos
this	este/a
today	hoy
tomorrow	mañana
what	qué
when	cuándo
where	dónde
with	con
without	sin
woman	mujer/hembra
yes	sí
yesterday	ayer

BASIC PHRASES

Hello	¡Hola!
Goodbye	Adiós
See you later	Hasta luego
Good morning	Buenos días
Good afternoon	Buenas tardes
Goodnight	Buenas noches
Sorry	Lo siento/Discúlpame
Excuse me	Con permiso/Perdón
How are you?	¿Cómo está (usted)?/ ¿Qué tal?
Nice to meet you	Mucho gusto
Not at all/You're welcome	De nada

I (don't) understand	(No) Entiendo
Do you speak English?	¿Habla (usted) inglés?
I (don't) speak Spanish	(No) Hablo español
What?/How?	¿Cómo?
Could you ..., please?	¿Podría ... por favor?
... repeat that	... repetirlo
... speak slowly	... hablar más despacio
... write that down	... escribirlo
My name is ...	Me llamo ...
What's your name?	¿Cómo se llama usted?
I'm from	Soy de ...
... America	... Estados Unidos
... Australia	... Australia
... Canada	... Canadá
... England	... Inglaterra
... Ireland	... Irlanda
... New Zealand	... Nueva Zelanda
... Scotland	... Escocia
... South Africa	... Sudáfrica
... Wales	... Gales
Where are you from?	De dónde es usted?
How old are you?	¿Cuántos años tiene? (usted)
I am ... years old	Tengo ... años
I don't know	No sé
Do you know ...?	¿Sabe ...?
I want	Quiero
I'd like ...	Quisiera ... por favor
What's that?	¿Qué es eso?
What is this called in Spanish?	¿Cómo se llama este en español?
There is (is there)?	Hay (?)
Do you have ...?	¿Tiene ...?
What time is it?	¿Qué hora es?
May I take a photograph?	¿Puedo sacar una foto?

BASIC NEEDS, SERVICES AND PLACES

ATM	cajero automático
bank	banco
bathroom/toilet	baño/sanitario
beach	playa
bookstore	librería
border crossing	frontera
cheap hotel	un hotel barato
church	iglesia
embassy	embajada
highway	carretera
immigration office	Migración
internet café	cibercafé
lake	lago
laundry	lavandería
library	biblioteca
main street	calle principál
map	mapa
market	mercado
museum	museo
national park	parque nacional
pharmacy	farmacia
(main) post office	correo (central)
restaurant	restaurante
supermarket	supermercado
telephone office	cabina de teléfono
telephones	teléfonos
tourist office	oficina de turismo

NUMBERS

1	un/uno/una
2	dos
3	tres
4	cuatro
5	cinco
6	seis
7	siete
8	ocho
9	nueve
10	diez
11	once
12	doce
13	trece
14	catorce
15	quince
16	dieciséis
17	diecisiete
18	dieciocho
19	diecinueve
20	veinte
21	veintiuno
22	veintidos
30	treinta
40	cuarenta
50	cincuenta
60	sesenta
70	setenta
80	ochenta
90	noventa
100	cien
101	ciento uno
200	doscientos
201	doscientosuno
500	quinientos
1000	mil
1999	mil novecientos noventa y nueve
2000	dos mil
100,000	cien mil
1,000,000	un millón
first	primero/a
second	segundo/a

third	tercero/a
fourth	cuarto/a
fifth	quinto/a
tenth	décimo/a

MONTHS

January	enero
February	febrero
March	marzo
April	abril
May	mayo
June	junio
July	julio
August	agosto
September	septiembre
October	octubre
November	noviembre
December	diciembre

DAYS (DÍAS)

Monday	lunes
Tuesday	martes
Wednesday	miércoles
Thursday	jueves
Friday	viernes
Saturday	sábado
Sunday	domingo

COLOURS

black	negro/a
blue	azul
brown	marrón/café
green	verde
grey	gris
indigo	índigo/a
orange	naranja
red	rojo/a
violet/purple	violeta
white	blanco/a
yellow	amarillo/a

TRANSPORT

bus	autobús/camión
bus station	estación de autobuses
bus stop	parada de autobús
boat	barco/lancha
ferry	transbordador
dock/pier	muelle
airplane	avión
airport	aeropuerto
car	carro
4WD	tracción integral
taxi	taxi
truck	camión

pick-up	camioneta
hitchhike	hacer autostop
	(to hitchhike)
	or pedir un ride
	(to ask for a ride)
train	tren
train station	estación de trenes
bicycle	bicicleta (abb. bici)
motorcycle	moto
ticket	boleto
ticket office	taquilla/ boletería
I'd like a ticket to …	(Necesito) un boleto
	para …
How much is a …	¿Cuanto cuesta un …
ticket from…to…?	boleto de …a…?
… first-class	… primera clase
… second-class	… segunda clase
… one-way	… sólo ida
… return/round-trip	… ida y vuelta
I would like to rent a …	Me gustaría alquilar un/
	una …
Where does … to	¿De dónde
… leave from?	sale …para …?
What time does the…	¿A qué hora sale …
leave for …?	para …?
What time does the …	¿A qué hora llega …
arrive in …?	en …?

DIRECTIONS

Where is …?	¿Dónde está …?
How do I get to …?	¿Como llego a …?
I'm looking for …	Estoy buscando …
Is this the way to …?	¿Es esta la carretera
	hacia …?
I'm lost	Estoy perdido/a
Is it far?	¿Está lejos?
left	izquierda
right	derecha
straight ahead	derecho/recto
north	norte
south	sur
east	este
west	oeste
street	calle
avenue	avenida
block	cuadra

MONEY (DINERO)

How much is it?	¿Cuánto es/cuesta?
It's too expensive	Es demasiado caro
Do you have anything	¿No tiene algo más
cheaper?	barato?
Do you accept …?	Aceptan …?
… credit cards	… tarjetas de crédito

... travellers' cheques	... cheques de viajero
... US dollars	... dólares americanos
I would like to change some dollars	Me gustaría cambiar unos dólares
Can you change dollars?	¿Se puede cambiar dólares?
What is the exchange rate?	¿Cuál es el tipo de cambio?

SHOPPING

I would like to buy ...	Me gustaría comprar ...
... a bag	... una bolsa
... a book	... un libro
... clothes	... ropas
... film	... una película
... a hammock	... una hamaca
... a hat	... un sombrero
... a jacket	... una chaqueta
... a mobile phone	... un celular
... a painting	... una cuadra
... a shirt	... una camisa
... shoes	... unos zapatos
... a skirt	... una falda
... a sleeping bag	... un saco de dormir
... socks	... unos calcetines
... a tent	... una carpa
... trousers	... pantalones
... underwear	... ropa interior
I'm just looking	Estoy mirando
Could I look at it/that?	¿Puedo ver eso/aquello?
Please give me ...	Por favor deme ...
... one like that	... uno así

ACCOMMODATION

Is there a ... nearby?	¿Hay ... aquí cerca?
... guesthouse	... una casa de huéspedes
... hotel	... un hotel
... hostel	... un hostal
... campsite	... un camping
Do you have ...?	¿Tiene ...?
... a room	... un cuarto
... with two beds	... con dos camas
... a double bed	... con cama matrimonial
... a dorm room	... dormitorio compartido
... a tent	... una carpa
... a cabin	... una cabina
It's for	Es para
... one person	... una persona
... two people	... dos personas
... for one night	... una noche
... one week	... una semana
Does it have ...	¿Tiene ...?

... a shared bath	... baño compartido
... a private bath	... baño privado
... hot water	... agua caliente
... air conditioning	... aire acondicionado
Can one ...?	¿Se puede ...?
... camp (near) here	...acampar aquí (cerca)
... sling a hammock here?	... poner una hamaca aquí
... swim here?	... nadar aquí
How much is it ...?	¿Cuánto es/cuesta ...?
... per night	... por noche
... per person	... por persona
... per room	... por cuarto
Does the price include breakfast?	¿El precio incluye el desayuno?
May I see a room?	¿Puedo ver un cuarto?
May I see another room?	¿Puedo ver otro cuarto?
Yes, it's fine	Sí, está bien
I'd like to reserve a ...	Me gustaría reservar un/una ...

HEALTH AND SAFETY

I'm ill	Estoy enfermo/a
He/she is ill	Él/Ella está enfermo/a
I'm allergic to ...	Soy alérgico a ...
He/she is allergic to ...	Él/Ella es alérgica a ...
I need to see a doctor	Tengo que ver un doctor
He/she needs to see a doctor	Él/ella tiene que ver un doctor
I need to go to ...	Tengo que ir ...
... the hospital	... al hospital
... a health clinic	... a una clínica
... a pharmacy	... a una farmacia
He/she needs to go to ...	Él/ella tiene que ir a ...
I have a ...	Me duele ...
... headache	... la cabeza
... stomachache	... el estómago
I have a fever	Tengo fiebre
I have hurt my ...	Me hice daño ...
... arm	... al brazo
... back	... a la espalda
... foot	... al pie
... head	... a la cabeza
... hand	... a la mano
... knee	... a la rodilla
... leg	... a la pierna
... neck	... al cuello
He/she has hurt	Él/ella se hizo daño ...
I was bitten/ scratched/stung by ...	Me mordió/arañó/picó
... a dog	... un perro
... a cat	... un gato
... a snake	... una serpiente

… a mosquito	… un mosquito	tourist police	policía turística
… a spider	… una araña	ambulance	ambulancia
… a jellyfish	… una medusa	fire brigade	bomberos
He/she was bitten/ scratched by …	Le mordío/arañó/picó un/una …	Red Cross	Cruz Roja
I am dehydrated	Estoy deshidratado/a	Help!	¡Ayuda!
medicine	medicina	Fire!	¡Fuego!
dose/dosage	dosis	Go away!	¡Váyase!
sunscreen/sunblock	crema solar/filtro solar	Leave me alone!	¡Déjeme en paz!
bug repellent	repelente para insectos	I've been robbed	Me han robado
antibiotics	antibióticos	He/she has been robbed	Le han robado
It's an emergency	Es una emergencia	I need to fill out an insurance report	Tengo que rellenar una reclamación de seguro
police	policía	I need help	Necesito ayuda
policeman	un policía	Please can you help me?	¿Me podría ayudar por favor?
police station	comisaría		

A SPANISH MENU READER

While dishes vary by country and region, these words and terms will help negotiate most menus.

BASIC DINING VOCABULARY

almuerzo	lunch	azúcar	sugar
carta (la)	menu	chile	chilli
cena	dinner	galletas	biscuits
cocina	kitchen	hielo	ice
comida corriente	cheap set menu, usually served at lunch time	huevos	eggs
		mantequilla	butter
		mermelada	jam
comida típica	typical cuisine	miel	honey
cuchara	spoon	mixto	mixed seafood/ meats/salad
cuchillo	knife	mostaza	mustard
desayuno	breakfast	pan (integral)	bread (wholemeal)
merienda	afternoon tea	pan de coco	coconut bread
mesa	table	pimienta	pepper
plato	plate	queso	cheese
plato del día	dish of the day	sal	salt
plato fuerte	main course	salsa de tomate	tomato sauce
plato vegetariano	vegetarian dish		
servilleta	napkin	**FRUTAS (FRUIT)**	
silla	chair	banano	banana
taza	mug/cup	cereza	cherry
tenedor	fork	ciruela	plum
vaso	glass	coco	coconut
La cuenta, por favor	The bill, please	durazno	peach
¿Contiene ?	Does this contain …? (for food allergies, vegetarians, etc)	fresa	strawberry
		guayaba	guava
		higo	fig
Soy vegetariano/a	I'm a vegetarian	lima	lime
No como carne	I don't eat meat	limón	lemon
		manzana	apple
STAPLES		maracuyá	passion fruit
aceite	oil	melón	melon
ajillo	garlic butter	mora	blackberry
ajo	garlic	naranja	orange
arroz	rice	papaya	papaya

pera	pear	jamón	ham
piña	pineapple	lechón	roasted pig
pithaya	dragon fruit	lomo	steak
plátano	plantain	pato	duck
sandía	watermelon	pavo	turkey
tamarindo	tamarind	pollo	chicken
tomate	tomato	res	beef
toronja	grapefruit	ternera	veal
uva	grapes	tocino	bacon
		venado	venison

LEGUMBRES/VERDURAS (VEGETABLES)

aguacate	avocado
alcachofa	artichoke
apio	celery
arvejas	peas
berenjena	aubergine/eggplant
brécol	broccoli
calabaza	pumpkin
calabazín	courgette/zucchini
cebolla	onion
champiñón/hongo	mushroom
coliflor	cauliflower
curtida	pickled cabbage, beetroot and carrots
ensalada	salad
espinaca	spinach
frijoles	beans
frijoles volteados	refried beans
gallo pinto	mixed rice and beans
lechuga	lettuce
lentejas	lentils
maíz	sweetcorn/maize
menestra	bean/lentil stew
palmito	palm heart
papa	potato
papas fritas	French fries
pepinillo	gherkin
pepino	cucumber
tomate	tomato
zanahoria	carrot

CARNE (MEAT) AND AVES (POULTRY)

bistec	steak
búfalo	buffalo
carne	beef
carne de chancho	pork
cerdo	pork
chicharrones	pork scratchings, crackling
chuleta	pork chop
conejo	rabbit
cordero	lamb
filete	steak
gallina	hen

MENUDOS (OFFAL)

chunchules	intestines
corazón	heart
guatita	tripe
hígado	liver
lengua	tongue
patas	trotters

MARISCOS (SEAFOOD) AND PESCADO (FISH)

almejas	clams
anchoa	anchovy
atún	tuna
bacalao	cod
calamares	squid
camarón	shrimp
cangrejo	crab
ceviche	raw seafood marinated in lime juice with onions
corvina	sea bass
erizo	sea urchin
gambas	prawns
langosta	lobster/crayfish
langostino	king prawn
lenguado	sole
mejillónes	mussels
ostión	oyster
pargo rojo/blanco	red/white snapper
pulpo	octopus
trucha	trout

SOPAS (SOUPS)

caldo	broth
caldo de gallina	chicken broth
crema de espárragos	cream of asparagus
sopa de caracol	spicy conch stew
sopa de frijoles	bean soup
sopa del día	soup of the day
tapado	a seafood soup, served on the Caribbean coast of several countries in the isthmus

BOCADOS (SNACKS)

bocadillo	little snack
casado	meal of rice, beans, salad and meat or fish (phrase mainly seen in Costa Rica, translating to "married")
chuchito	corn-dough parcels made with beans and eggs (sometimes also pork), popular in Guatemala and El Salvador
empanada	cheese/meat pastry
hamburguesa	hamburger
nacatamales	Nicaraguan corn-dough parcels filled with vegetables, pork, beef or chicken
patacones	fried green plantains
pupusa	small, thick Salvadorian tortilla filled with cheese, beans or pork and topped with salad
salchichas	sausages
tamale	ground maize with meat/ cheese wrapped in leaf
tortilla	toasted maize pancake
tortilla de huevos	omelette
tostada	toasted (usually tortilla)

POSTRES (DESSERTS)

ensalada de frutas	fruit salad
flan	crème caramel
helado	ice cream
pastel	cake
piñonate	candied papaya
torta	tart
tres leches	cake made with three varieties of milk

BEBIDAS (DRINKS)

agua (mineral)	mineral water
... con gas	... sparkling
... sin gas	... still
... con/sin hielo	... with/without ice
... con limón	... with lemon
aguardiente	raw alcohol made from sugar cane
balde	bucket of beers on ice
café	coffee
café con leche	milk with a little coffee
cerveza	beer
gaseosa	fizzy drink
horchata	milky, cereal-based drink sweetened with cinnamon
jugo	juice
leche	milk
licuado	fresh fruit milkshake
limonada	fresh lemonade
raspados	ice shavings with sweet topping
refresco	generic term for a cold drink
ron	rum
licor	spirits
té	tea
té aromática	herbal tea
... hierba luisa	... lemon verbena
... manzanilla	... camomile
... menta	... mint
vino blanco	white wine
vino tinto	red wine

COOKING TERMS

a la parrilla	barbecued
a la plancha	grilled
ahumado	smoked
al ajillo	in garlic sauce
al horno	oven-baked
al vapor	steamed
apanado	breaded
asado	roast
asado al palo	spit roast
crudo	raw
duro	hard boiled
encebollado	cooked with onions
frito	fried
picante	hot, spicy
puré	mashed
revuelto	scrambled
saltado	sautéed
secado	dried

GLOSSARY

aguacero downpour
ahorita right now (any time within the coming hour)
alcalde mayor
aldea village
algodón cotton

almohada pillow
artesanía arts and crafts
bahía bay
balneario resort or spa
barranca steep-sided ravine

barrio neighbourhood, or area within a town or city; suburb

biotopo protected area of national ecological importance, usually with limited tourist access

bomba pump at a petrol station

caballo horse

cabaña literally a cabin, but can mean anything from a palm-thatched beach hut to a room; usually applies to tourist accommodation

cabina cubicle/booth/cabin

cacique chief (originally a colonial term, now used for elected leaders/figureheads of indigenous *comarcas* in Panama)

cafetería café

calzada road/carriageway

cama bed

camioneta small truck or van (in Guatemala, a chicken bus)

campesino peasant/farmer

campo countryside

cantina local, hard-drinking bar, usually men-only

carro car, equivalent of the Castilian *coche*

casa de cambio currency exchange bureau

cascada waterfall

caseta telefónica phone booth

ㅁㅁㅅㅁㅁ ㅁㅁㅁ ㅁㅁㅁ

cepillo de dientes toothbrush

chabola shack

chapín slang term for someone from Guatemala

chicle chewing gum

chorreador sack-and-metal coffee-filter contraption, still widely used

Churrigueresque highly elaborate, decorative form of Baroque architecture (usually found in churches)

cigarrillo cigarette

ciudad city

Clásico period during which ancient Maya civilization was at its height, usually given as 300–900 AD

colchón mattress

colectivo shared taxi/minibus, usually following fixed route (can also be applied to a boat – *lancho colectivo*)

colina hill (also *el cerro*)

colonia city suburb or neighbourhood, often seen in addresses as "Col"

comedor basic restaurant, usually with just one or two things on the menu, always the cheapest place to eat; literally "dining room"

conquistador "one who conquers": member of early Spanish expeditions to the Americas in the sixteenth century

convento convent or monastery

cordillera mountain range

correo aéreo air mail

corriente second-class bus

cuadra street block

cuevas caves

descompuesto out of order

Dios God

discoteca club/disco

Don/Doña courtesy titles (sir/madam), mostly used in letters, for professional people or for a boss

dolor pain/ache

edificio building

efectivo cash

ejido communal farmland

encendedor lighter (for cigarettes)

encomienda package/parcel

entrada entry/entry fee

estatua statue

extranjero foreigner

fecha date

feria fair (market); also a town fête

fiesta party

finca ranch, farm or plantation

fósforos matches

gambas buttresses; the giant above-ground roots that some rainforest trees put out

gasolina petrol

gasolinera petrol station

golfo gulf

gringo/gringa specifically American, but used widely for any white-skinned foreigner; not necessarily a term of abuse, it does nonetheless have a slightly Pejorative connotation

gruta cave

guaca pre-Columbian burial ground or tomb

hacienda big farm, ranch or estate, or big house on it

henequén fibre from the agave (sisal) plant, used to make rope

hospedaje very basic *pensión* or small hotel

huipil Maya woman's traditional dress or blouse, usually woven or embroidered

huracán hurricane

I.V.A. sales tax

indígena an indigenous person; preferred term among indigenous groups, rather than the more racially offensive *indio*

invierno winter (May–Oct)

isla island

jardín garden

juego de pelota ball game/ball court

ladino a vague term – applied to people it means Spanish-influenced as opposed to indigenous, and at its most specific defines someone of mixed Spanish and indigenous blood; it's more commonly used simply to describe a person of "Western" culture, or one who dresses in "Western" style, be they of indigenous or mixed blood

lanterna torch

lavabo sink

litera bunk bed

llave key

malecón seafront promenade

mar sea

mestizo person of mixed indigenous and Spanish blood, though like the term *ladino* it has more cultural than racial significance

metate Pre-Columbian stone table used for grinding corn

milpa maize field, usually cleared by slash-and-burn farming

mirador lookout point

mochila backpack

mochilero backpacker

moneda coins

montar a caballo to go horseriding

neotrópicos "neotropics": tropics of the New World

noreste northeast; often seen in addresses as "NE"

noroeste northwest; often seen in addresses as "NO"

nublado cloudy

occidente west

oriente east; often seen in addresses as "Ote"

otoño autumn

paisaje landscape

palacio mansion, but not necessarily royal

palacio de gobierno headquarters of state/federal authorities

palacio municipal headquarters of local government

palapa palm thatch (used to describe any thatched/ palm-roofed hut)

panadería bakery

parque park

paseo a broad avenue; also a walk, especially the traditional evening walk around the plaza

pasta de dientes toothpaste

pelota ball, or ball court

peón farm labourer, usually landless

personaje someone of importance, a VIP, although usually used pejoratively to indicate someone who is putting on airs

piscina swimming pool

planta baja ground floor – abbreviated PB in elevators

Plateresque elaborately decorative Renaissance architectural style

plaza square

poniente west; often seen in addresses as "Pte"

Postclásico period between the decline of Maya civilization and the arrival of the Spanish, 900–1530 AD

Preclásico archeological era preceding the blooming of Maya civilization, usually given as 1500 BC–300 AD

primavera spring

propina tip

pueblo town/village

puente bridge

puerta door

pulpería general store or corner store; also sometimes serves cooked food and drinks

quetzal quetzal (bird), and also the currency of Guatemala

rancho palm-thatched roof; can also mean a small-holding

recibo receipt

redondel de toros bullring, used for local rodeos

río river

ruinas ruins

sábana sheet

sacbé Maya road, or ceremonial causeway

saco de dormir sleeping bag

santo saint

seda silk

sendero path

sierra mountain range

sincretismo syncretism, the attempted amalgamation of different religions, cultures or schools of thought; mainly applied to religion and in Central America usually refers to the merging of Maya and Catholic beliefs

soda Costa Rican cafeteria or diner; in the rest of Central America it's usually called a *comedor*

sol sun

sótano basement

stele freestanding carved monument; most are of Maya origin

sudeste southeast (also *sureste*) ; often seen in addresses as "SE"

sudoeste southwest (also *suroeste*) ; often seen in addresses as "SO"

temblor tremor

temporada season: *la temporada de lluvia* is the rainy season

terremoto earthquake

terreno land; small farm

tiempo weather (can also mean time)

tienda shop

tierra land/earth

típico/típica literally "typical"; used to describe anything pertaining to a specific culture, from food to dress to art

traje traditional costume (also means suit)

vaquero cowboy

vela candle/sail (of a boat); also means "wake" or funeral gathering in Nicaragua

ventana window

verano summer (Nov–April)

vista view

volcán volcano

Small print and index

A ROUGH GUIDE TO ROUGH GUIDES

Published in 1982, the first Rough Guide – to Greece – was a student scheme that became a publishing phenomenon. Mark Ellingham, a recent graduate in English from Bristol University, had been travelling in Greece the previous summer and couldn't find the right guidebook. With a small group of friends he wrote his own guide, combining a highly contemporary, journalistic style with a thoroughly practical approach to travellers' needs.

The immediate success of the book spawned a series that rapidly covered dozens of destinations. And, in addition to impecunious backpackers, Rough Guides soon acquired a much broader readership that relished the guides' wit and inquisitiveness as much as their enthusiastic, critical approach and value-for-money ethos.

These days, Rough Guides include recommendations from budget to luxury and cover more than 120 destinations around the globe, as well as producing an ever-growing range of ebooks.

Visit **roughguides.com** to find all our latest books, read articles, get inspired and share travel tips with the Rough Guides community.

Rough Guide credits

Editors: Rebecca Hallett, Greg Ward
Layout: Anita Singh
Cartography: Lokamata Sahu
Picture editor: Aude Vauconsant
Proofreader: Diane Margolis
Managing editor: Andy Turner
Assistant editor: Sharon Sonam
Production: Jimmy Lao

Cover design: Michelle Bhatia, Chloe Stickland, Anita Singh
Editorial assistant: Freya Godfrey
Senior pre-press designer: Dan May
Programme manager: Gareth Lowe
Publisher: Keith Drew
Publishing director: Georgina Dee

Publishing information

This fourth edition published November 2015 by
Rough Guides Ltd,
80 Strand, London WC2R 0RL
11, Community Centre, Panchsheel Park,
New Delhi 110017, India
Distributed by Penguin Random House
Penguin Books Ltd,
80 Strand, London WC2R 0RL
Penguin Group (USA)
345 Hudson Street, NY 10014, USA
Penguin Group (Australia)
250 Camberwell Road, Camberwell,
Victoria 3124, Australia
Penguin Group (NZ)
67 Apollo Drive, Mairangi Bay, Auckland 1310,
New Zealand
Penguin Group (South Africa)
Block D, Rosebank Office Park, 181 Jan Smuts Avenue,
Parktown North, Gauteng, South Africa 2193
Rough Guides is represented in Canada by Tourmaline
Editions Inc. 662 King Street West, Suite 304, Toronto,
Ontario M5V 1M7
Printed in Singapore by Toppan Security Printing Pte. Ltd.

616pp includes index
A catalogue record for this book is available from the
British Library
ISBN: 978-0-24118-231-4
The publishers and authors have done their best to ensure
the accuracy and currency of all the information in **The
Rough Guide to Central America on a Budget**, however,
they can accept no responsibility for any loss, injury, or
inconvenience sustained by any traveller as a result of
information or advice contained in the guide.
1 3 5 7 9 8 6 4 2

Help us update

We've gone to a lot of effort to ensure that the fourth
edition of **The Rough Guide to Central America on
a Budget** is accurate and up-to-date. However, things
change – places get "discovered", opening hours are
notoriously fickle, restaurants and rooms raise prices
or lower standards. If you feel we've got it wrong or
left something out, we'd like to know, and if you can
remember the address, the price, the hours, the phone
number, so much the better.

Please send your comments with the subject line
"**Rough Guide Central America on a Budget update**" to
✉ mail@uk.roughguides.com. We'll credit all contributions
and send a copy of the next edition (or any other Rough
Guide if you prefer) for the very best emails.

Find more travel information, connect with fellow
travellers and plan your trip on ⓦ roughguides.com.

Acknowledgements

Dawn Ann Curtis: Thanks to the team at Rough Guides for their continued trust and support. To all those who helped me on the road, particularly Leasa, Vicente and Bradley in San Juan del Sur and *Guardabarranco Hostel* in Leon. Sobre todo gracias a mis amigos y familiares en San Isidro – soy vaga, pero siempre regreso a casa.

Sara Humphreys: Thanks to Raffa Calvo for company in the Darién, and for a rapid recce of the Costa Arriba; also to Italo for a memorable excursion to Puerto Mutis, and to Michelle in Santa Catalina for a news update.

Shakfik Meghji: Many thanks to all the Ticos and travellers who helped me out with my research. A special muchas gracias must go to: Andy Turner, Rebecca Hallett, Mani Ramaswamy, Keith Drew, and Rachel Dixon at Rough Guides; Greg Ward; Steven Horak; Glenn and Teri Jampol; Natalie Ewing; Keith Flanaghan; Jayne Lloyd-Jones; Dana Cohen; Jean, Nizar and Nina Meghji; and Sioned Jones.

AnneLise Sorensen: In Belize, thanks to all who welcomed me in and shared information, advice, stories, lively evenings and chilled Belikin and cashew wine. Thank you to the Belize Tourism Board (BTB); the wonderfully inviting Kelly and Mukul at *Blue Water Grill*; the supremely knowledgeable Lascelle Tillett at S&L Travel and Tours; the inspiring Rowan Garel and his mother Milagro; Douglas Thompson and his team at the beautiful *Black Orchid Resort*; Erin De Santiago, for giving me the scoop on San Pedro; Villa Boscardi; Mayan Princess; and *Tropical Paradise*. A big thank you to my co-authors and top-notch editorial team – Andy Turner, Rebecca Hallett and Emma Gibbs. And, gracias to all my friends, family and guapo for their cheery emails and support. Cheers!

Iain Stewart: Many thanks to Lorena and Henk, José and Carmen, Deedle and Dave, Tom in Xela, Don David, Matt for the house in Lanquin and Annie Vanderboom for help in Monterrico.

Greg Ward: Thanks to Kirsten Long, Saint Malo and everyone in Belize who helped along the way.

Readers' updates

Thanks to all the readers who have taken the time to write in with comments and suggestions (and apologies if we've inadvertently omitted or misspelt anyone's name):

Marieke and Jacco, Jane Atkinson, Robert Beins, Ernest Chan, Fernando Cojulun, Chris Collington, Rigoberto Pablo Cruz, Carole Devine, Holly Dudley, George Fowler, Joe and Ana Frankie, Meraid Griffin, Frits Kleinen Hammans, Marian Hawkes, Allison Hawks, Nicholas Henman, David Halloway, Mathias Kamph, Alex Larsen, André Lemm, Jodie Madigan, Adam Mason, Griff Mercer, Andrew Moody, Aaldrik Mulder, Jos. Mulligano, Rosalie Novara, Ramon Peneleu, Paola Pireddu, Kim Puccetti, Alberto Rivera, Thomas Schroeder, Micah Smith, Marcin Stanek, Erick Tichonuk, Tara Tiedemann, Russell Vinegar, Thea Winning, Parina Wissing, Martin Wronna.

Index

Maps are marked in grey

Map symbols

The symbols below are used on maps throughout the book

Main road	Internet access	Precolumbian ruin	Waterfall
Minor road	Post office	Place of interest	Volcano
Motorway	Information centre	Gardens/fountains	Oasis/palm tree
Pedestrianised road	Telephone office	Mountain refuge/lodge	Lighthouse
Steps	Hospital	Ranger station	Immigration/border crossing
Unpaved road	Pharmacy	Ruin	Reef
Railway	Toilet	Castle	Gorge
Path	Parking	Fortress	Bridge
Wall	Embassy/consulate	Arch	Building
Ferry	Fuel/gas station	Gate	Market
International airport	Campsite	Viewpoint	Church
Domestic airport	Statue	Mountain range	Stadium
Transport stop	Museum	Mountain peak	Park/national park
Boat	Monument	Cave	Christian cemetery
Metro/subway	Archeological site	Marsh/swamp	Beach

Listings key

- Accommodation
- Eating/drinking/nightlife
- Shop

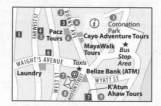